D0984758

The Letters of SYLVIA PLATH

VOLUME II

1956–1963

By Sylvia Plath

poetry
ariel
the colossus
crossing the water
winter trees
collected poems
(edited by Ted Hughes)
selected poems
(edited by Ted Hughes)
ariel: the restored edition
(Foreword by Frieda Hughes)
poems
(chosen by Carol Ann Duffy)

fiction
the bell jar
johnny panic and the bible of dreams

non-fiction
the letters of sylvia plath
Volume 1: 1940–1956
(edited by Peter K. Steinberg & Karen V. Kukil)
letters home: correspondence 1950–1963
(edited by Aurelia Schober Plath)
the journals of sylvia plath
(edited by Karen V. Kukil)
sylvia plath: drawings
(edited by Frieda Hughes)

for children
the bed book
(illustrated by Quentin Blake)
the it-doesn't-matter suit
(illustrated by Rotraut Susanne Berner)
collected children's stories
(illustrated by David Roberts)

The Letters of

SYLVIA PLATH

VOLUME II

1956–1963

EDITED BY

PETER K. STEINBERG AND

KAREN V. KUKIL

HARPER
An Imprint of HarperCollins*Publishers*

HarperCollins books may be purchased for educational, business, or sales promotional use. For information, please email the Special Markets Department at SPsales@harpercollins.com.

Originally published in the United Kingdom in 2018 by Faber & Faber Ltd.

FIRST U.S. EDITION

Library of Congress Cataloging-in-Publication Data has been applied for.

ISBN 978-0-06-274058-8

18 19 20 21 22 LSC 10 9 8 7 6 5 4 3 2 1

CONTENTS

ACKNOWLEDGEMENTS

A remarkable collaboration produced this edition of *The Letters of Sylvia Plath*. We have many people to thank. Editing Sylvia Plath's letters began as an academic interterm course taught at Smith College by Karen V. Kukil for the Archives Concentration Program. Students in Editing Sylvia Plath's Correspondence learned the art of exact and accurate transcription, proofreading, and emendation based upon primary resources. A few years before the class began, Rebecca Rosenthal, class of 2007, processed the correspondence in the Sylvia Plath Collection held by the Mortimer Rare Book Room at Smith College. From January 2009 to January 2013, students in Kukil's interterm classes transcribed all the letters at Smith College. In January 2012 Plath scholar Peter K. Steinberg co-taught the course and then proceeded to locate, transcribe, and annotate all the extant Sylvia Plath letters in other collections. This edition of Sylvia Plath's letters is the product of our partnership with many students at Smith College, including Robin Whitham Acker '12; Sylvia L. Altreuter '12; Taylor A. Barrett '15; Taylor M. Bayer '12; Rachel E. Brenner '14; Ingrid Brioso-Rieumont '15; Virginia Choi '11; Melanie S. Colvin '13; Emily Cook '11; Ellen Cormier '11; Kristen L. De Lancey '15; Caroline F. T. Doenmez '09; Amanda P. Ferrara '13; Hope C. Fried '14; Alexandra Ghiz '12; Noa R. Gutterman '14; Kristen F. Haseney '04; Catherine Hatas '13; Victoria K. Henry '13; Cheryl R. Holmes '11; Katherine M. Horning '13; Angelica Huertas '10; Eve N. Hunter '12; Salma Hussain '14; Esra Karamehmet '12; Jinjin Lu '13; Emerson M. Lynch '15; Taylor A. Marks '15; Grace K. Martin '13; Katherine A. Nelson '12; Rebecca L. O'Leary '13; Lois Jenkins Peters '09; Emma Ramsay '12; Anne M. Re '13; Maris E. Schwarz '15; Chelsea A. Seamon '13; Joyce P. Shalaby '13; Jihyun J. Shim '14; Naomi Sinnathamby '14; Gabrielle E. Termuehlen '16; Dior Vargas '09; Alexandra B. von Mering '14; Drew L. Wagner '11; Genevieve C. Ward- Wernet '13; Erin M. Whelchel '09; Kaidi Williams '11; and Alison R. Winger '14. Professor Adrianne Andrews and other faculty members at Smith College also participated in the project.

A number of family, friends, and professional contacts of Sylvia Plath provided information reflected in the footnotes. In addition to Frieda Hughes, we would like to thank Warren Plath and his daughters Susan

Plath Winston and Jennifer Plath. We also appreciate the information received from Jane Baltzell-Kopp, Joan Cantor Barnes, Sarah Christie Bellwood, James B. Biery, Susan O'Neill-Roe Booth, Janet Burroway, Jonathan Christie, Susan Stetson Clarke, David Compton, Liadin Cooke, Blair Cruickshank, Ann Davidow-Goodman Hayes, Dena Dincauze, Jacquie Dincauze, Ruth Fainlight, Aidan Foster, Marian Foster, Johannes B. Frankfort, Nicholas Frankfort, Michael Frayn, Cary Plumer Frye, Charles S. Gardner, Ruth P. Geissler, Leo A. Goodman, Carol Hughes, Daniel Huws, Judy Kahrl, David N. Keightley, Elinor Friedman Klein, Lynne Lawner, Philip E. McCurdy, James McNeely, Eugene L. Mark, Doug Miller, Marcia Momtchiloff, Jane Nalieri, Kenneth Neville-Davies, Dr Richard Newell, Dr Perry Norton, Dr Richard A. Norton, Judith Raymo, Simon Sidamon-Eristoff, Elizabeth and William Sigmund, Robert Truslow, Louise Giesey White, Rosemary Wilson, J. Melvin Woody, and Nicolette Zeeman.

Professor Linda Wagner-Martin first articulated the need for a full edition of Sylvia Plath's letters during her plenary lecture at the Sylvia Plath 75th Year Symposium at Oxford University in 2007. A number of other scholars later contributed their insights and expertise as well. We would particularly like to thank professors Lynda K. Bundtzen (Williams College), Anita Helle (Oregon State University), Dianne Hunter (Trinity College), and Susan Van Dyne (Smith College) for their guidance. In addition, we would like to thank Dr Amanda Golden (New York Institute of Technology) for sharing her expansive knowledge of Plath's and Hughes's pedagogy, marginalia, poetry, and literary influence. Dr Gail Crowther provided invaluable research and information, as well as immeasurable support during the project. Gail was a vital contributor in building the notes to add context to Plath's activities. Gail located the two late letters to Gilbert and Marian Foster, which in addition to being fascinating documents add a new dimension to Plath's late interpersonal relationships. Her friendship, advice, and expertise helped to make this book possible. Likewise, without the dedication, passion, and camaraderie of David Trinidad, this book would be a shell of itself. David compiled an initial list of known letters, believed in the project since its inception, shared tireless thoughts with us in Plath-like 'bull sessions', located letters, and provided information for the notes. The amount of credit Golden, Crowther, and Trinidad deserve is unquantifiable.

The archivists, librarians, and curators responsible for photocopies and scans of Plath's letters, as well as for research assistance, who must be thanked for their tireless and important work are: Christine Barber and Peter Nelson at Amherst College; Elizabeth Maisey at Assumption College; Louise North at the BBC Written Archives Centre; Andrew Gough and Helen Melody at the British Library; James Maynard at the University of Buffalo; Jacqueline Cox, Patricia McGuire, and Anne Thomson at the University of Cambridge; Rochelle Rubinstein at the Central Zionist Archives; Christine Colburn and Barbara Gilbert at the University of Chicago; James Merrick at Colby College; Tara C. Craig and Brigette C. Kamsler at Columbia University; Rebecca Parmer at Connecticut College; Allyson Glazier, Barbara L. Krieger, and Morgan R. Swan at Dartmouth College; Emily Erwin Jones at Delta State University; Claudia Frazer at Drake University; Seamus Helferty at University College, Dublin; Sara J. Logue and Kathy Shoemaker at Emory University; Robert Brown, archivist at Faber & Faber; Dr Caroline Oates, Folklore Society Librarian, Allison Haack at Grinnell College; the reference staff at Harvard University; Cara Bertram and Anna Chen at the University of Illinois at Urbana-Champaign; Zachary T. Downy, David Kim Frasier, Sarah McElroy Mitchell, Cherry Dunham Williams, and the staff of the Lilly Library, Indiana University at Bloomington; Karen Cook at the University of Kansas; Alexander Koch at Kenyon College; Fran Baker at University of Manchester; Anne L. Moore and Caroline White at the University of Massachusetts at Amherst; Renu Barrett at McMaster University; Katie Wood at the University of Melbourne; James Moske at the Metropolitan Museum of Art; Erin George at the University of Minnesota; Melina Baron-Deutsch and Deborah Richards at Mount Holyoke College; Michelle Harvey at The Museum of Modern Art, New York; Lyndsi Barnes, Isaac Gewirtz, Tal Nadan, Lee Spilberg, Weatherly Stephan, and Kyle R. Triplett at the New York Public Library; Connor Gaudet at New York University; Brooke Guthrie at the University of North Carolina at Chapel Hill; Susan Liberator and Lindy M. Smith at Ohio State University; Sylvie Merian and Maria Isabel Molestina-Kurlat at Pierpont Morgan Library; James Booth at the Philip Larkin Society; AnnaLee Pauls and Gabriel Swift at Princeton University; Ellen Shea at the Radcliffe Institute; Natalie Ford and Jean Rose at the Random House Group Archive & Library; Laura Buchholz at Reed College; Jenifer Monger at Rensselaer Polytechnic Institute; Blair A. Benson at the University of Rochester; Matthew Reynolds at Sewanee: The University of the South; Jason Wood at Simmons College; Kevin Auer, Jean Cannon, Susan C. Floyd, Kurt Johnson, Jordan P. Mitchell, Marian Oman, Emily Roehl, Richard B. Watson, and Richard Workman at the University of Texas at Austin; Milissa Burkart and Kristina Rosenthal at the University of Tulsa;

Amanda Leinberger at the United Nations Archives; Lisa Jonsson and Lotta Sundberg at Uppsala University; Molly Dohrmann and Teresa Gray at Vanderbilt University; Victoria Platt at the Archive of Art and Design, Victoria and Albert Museum Archives; Sarah Schnuriger at Washington University, St Louis; Chery Kinnick and Carla Rickerson at the University of Washington; Sue Hamilos at the Wellesley Free Library; Kathleen Fahey at the Wellesley Historical Society; Linda L. Hall at Williams College; and Heather Abbott, Jessica Becker, Michael Frost, Nancy F. Lyon, and William Massa at Yale University. Smith College colleagues and former colleagues who deserve special thanks include Martin Antonetti, Barbara Blumenthal, Mary Irwin and her student assistant Erinn Summers '16, Dr Meg Meiman, Christina Ryan, and Nanci Young.

The following array of scholars and friends have also provided assistance that in various ways greatly benefited this book: Anna Arays, Sir Jonathan Bate, Carol Bere, Laura Joy Broom, Sarah Funke Butler, Ruby Butler-Weeks, Jessica Butterworth, Heather Clark, Rosemary Clark; Vanessa Cook, Diane Demko, Suzanne Demko, Joseph J. Feeney, SJ, Gunnar Fernlund, Amanda Ferrara, Pamela Fox, Susan France, Gwen Fries, Peter Fydler, Andre Gailani, Mackenzie Garrity, Sarah George-Waterfield, Sara Georgini, Jonathan Glover, Julie Goodspeed-Chadwick, Julia Gordon-Bramer, Alix de Gramont, Nicholas M. Hasenfus, Kelly Holbert, Eric Homberger, Richard Honan, John Hopkins, Shaun Kelly, An Kieu, Jocelyne Kolb, Barbara F. Kozash, Arthur Languirand, Paul Lannon, Richard Larschan, Jane Lawrence, Carol Lewis, Amy S. Li, Maria R. Lichtmann, Annika J. Lindskog, Kim Maddever, Ieuan Mahony, Ann Safford Mandel, Sherry Marker, Laura Anderson Martino, Lisa Matchett, Gesa Matthies, Aubrey Menarndt, Mark Morford, Catherine Morgan, Abby Norman, Maeve O'Brien, Kevin O'Donnell, Laura de la Paz Rico, Cornelia Pearsall, Hannah Piercy, Dipti Ramnarain, Neil Roberts, Carl Rollyson, Harriet Rosenstein, Judith A. Salinas, Angelyn Singer, Ann Skea, Tristine Skyler, Nick Smart, Benjamin M. Stern, Jeffrey Summers, Angélique Thomine, Angeline Wang, Louise Watson, Reverend Nick Weldon, Ian Widdicks, Dianne Wieland, Lydia K. Wilkins, Andrew Wilson, Elizabeth Winder, and Mark Wormald.

For permission to quote from published material, we gratefully acknowledge Carcanet Press Ltd.

Our gratitude must extend to those at Faber & Faber who were instrumental in parts of this project, including Erica Brown, Emma Cheshire, Pauline Collingridge, Matthew Hollis, Hamish Ironside, Lavinia Singer, Camilla Smallwood, Donald Sommerville, and Martha Sprackland. The commitment of Matthew Hollis and his team at Faber & Faber to publish a complete edition of Sylvia Plath's letters is greatly appreciated. We also thank Terry Karten and her colleagues at HarperCollins: Milan Bozic, Laura Brown, Lily Lopate, and Jennifer Murphy.

Personally, Karen is grateful to Sylvia Plath's friends who recognized her talent, preserved her letters, and donated them to Smith College where they are cherished. Generous support from President Kathleen McCartney, Provost Katherine Rowe, Dean of Libraries Susan Fliss, former President Ruth Simmons and alumnae, including Rachael Bartels, also added select letters to the collection. Karen also thanks Beth Myers, director of special collections, and Christopher Loring, former director of libraries, who extended all the resources of the Smith College Libraries for the duration of this independent project. In addition to former curator and mentor Ruth Mortimer, who collected the papers of Sylvia Plath for Smith College with the support of former President Jill Ker Conway, Karen would like to recognize her first professional mentor, Wilmarth S. Lewis, who edited the *Yale Edition of Horace Walpole's Correspondence* and taught her the exacting art of editing letters. Karen is particularly indebted to her brilliant coeditor, Peter K. Steinberg, who completed the lion's share of work on this edition with superior erudition and dedication. Most profoundly, Karen wishes to thank her extended Valuckas and Kukil families, especially her husband, Bohdan Kukil, for his humour and unwavering love and support during this intense editing project.

Peter would like to thank his wife Courtney for her love, extraordinary patience, and support for the duration of this project. The love and understanding of the families Steinberg, Levine, Little, and Plocinski at home and during vacations over the last five years must be recognized. Peter would not have pursued his interest in Sylvia Plath were it not for the initial encouragement from Andrea Holland and Jamie Wasserman. Since meeting Karen V. Kukil in 1998, she has always been a mentor and inspiration, helping both personally and professionally. Peter would like to thank Karen for her complete belief and trust in him, which made his contribution to this project possible.

ILLUSTRATIONS

24. Redactions and annotations by Aurelia Plath on page 2 of Sylvia Plath to Aurelia Plath, 23 September 1962.
25. Sylvia Plath's Letts Royal Office Tablet Diary, 21–27 October 1962.
26. Redactions and annotations by Aurelia Plath on page 1 of Sylvia Plath to Aurelia Plath, 22 November 1962.
27. Redactions and annotations by Aurelia Plath on page 2 of Sylvia Plath to Aurelia Plath, 22 November 1962.
28. Sylvia Plath's Letts Royal Office Tablet Diary, 16–22 December 1962.
29. Sylvia Plath with Nicholas Hughes, Court Green.
30. Vandalism (removal of SP's signature) from Sylvia Plath to Aurelia Plath, 4 February 1963.
31. Sylvia Plath to Ruth Beuscher, 4 February 1963, Page 1.
32. Sylvia Plath to Ruth Beuscher, 4 February 1963, Page 2.

FOREWORD

This second volume of letters continues my mother's documentation of her life and captures a flavour of her many friendships and relationships – including her relationship with my father through fourteen letters to her psychiatrist, Dr Ruth Beuscher, letters that I never thought would be included in this book. It is these letters I want to write about.

Until the end of 2016 I didn't know these letters existed, so their inclusion wasn't in question. And when I did find out about them, it transpired that, in my foreseeable future, their content might not be made available to me. It seemed it could be years – if ever – before I knew what revelations they might contain.

There was something deeply saddening about this; I felt excluded from my own mother's personal feelings, feelings that other people – strangers – had already pored over. And the lack of any information about the content of those letters persuaded me to fear the worst; I imagined the terrors and anguish my mother could well have expressed in those letters in a bloody sort of way – heightened emotions and tortured thoughts all spilling out to a woman who was, to all intents and purposes, supposed to be a locked box, a professional confidante, and the trusted recipient of my mother's self-exposure at a time in her life when her world as she knew it was disintegrating. In truth, neither I nor anyone else should ever have known those letters between a patient and her psychiatrist existed. Perhaps to preserve the doctor–patient dynamic, my mother always addressed Ruth Beuscher as Dr Beuscher, but had my mother's suicide and subsequent fame somehow made patient confidentiality irrelevant?

Then, to my dismay, some of the contents of those letters were part-exposed on the international stage of the internet when they were put up for sale by a book dealer in the USA in March 2017. The dealer was acting for a client who'd had the letters in their possession for several years. The client had once worked on an unrealised biography of my mother in the 1970s and had communicated with Dr Beuscher. Beuscher had allowed the biographer to see, read and touch those letters as I could not – I imagine to better access the reality of my mother at her most vulnerable.

In preparing to sell the letters, the dealer pasted photographs of them on his website and large parts were clearly legible, irrespective of the law of copyright, and with no regard to the sensitive nature of the content – least of all the fact that the letters were between a client and her psychiatrist.

And so began a sort of rollercoaster hell; newspaper articles appeared about the letters, and quotes were bandied about, but only the most contentious, heart-rending quotes would do. One newspaper emailed me questions out of the blue – questions I couldn't possibly answer – based on the quotes below, which I'd never seen until then:

> *22 September 1962:* 'Ted beat me up physically a couple of days before my miscarriage: the baby I lost was due to be born on his birthday.'
> *9 October 1962:* Plath wrote that Hughes 'seems to want to kill me'.
> *21 October 1962:* Plath claimed that Hughes 'told me openly he wished me dead'.
> *4 February 1963:* 'What appals me is the return of my madness, my paralysis, my fear.'

In my mind, the letters were written by my distraught mother in the throes of real emotional pain; her side of the argument was the only side, and that was the side that everyone was sure to take. There would be no balancing argument; the quote that rendered my father a wife-beater had already been seized upon. He might be no angel, but where was the perspective? What else was said? Having no idea what was in those letters, other people were now writing my worst fears into them. Loving both my parents I was – I am – acutely aware of their humanity and fallibility, but these elements could be easily disregarded by others who had their own ideas and wanted to shape their own arguments.

The posting on the book dealer's website was suddenly taken down, whether for copyright reasons or not I didn't know, and, although I was grateful for the respite, much had escaped that caused me grief, albeit not enough to make sense of, so I dreaded the rest.

The months passed and Smith College, my mother's college, eventually came into possession of the letters. They contacted me to discuss how students and academics might access them – at this point, publication was as far from my mind as Saturn. Conscious that the material was supposed to have been confidential in the first place, I asked to read them before we discussed this, and was sent scans: at last, my fears were going to be addressed.

It was a Sunday morning when I took the letters to bed to work my way through them – it seemed a more comforting environment; at this point, before transcription, I was struggling to read enlargements of the scans, having darkened the type on the photocopier in an attempt to make the words more legible – the letters were faded and worn with age.

I simply wept over the contents.

Those fourteen letters were snapshots of my parents' passionate relationship and subsequent marriage; the finding of a city home, the birth of children, their move to the country and the adoption of what would be an unsustainable idyll, followed by my mother's suspicion of my father's affair, the confirmation of that suspicion, her decision to separate, the strengthening of that resolution, the apparent realisation that they had been living in what I think of as a hermetically sealed bubble in which they ran out of oxygen, then the decision (following Ruth Beuscher's written advice) that divorce was the best option, and finally, the letter I feared most, the letter in which my mother's madness returns just before she kills herself.

My journey began with the first of the letters, dated 18 February 1960, almost exactly three years before my mother died. In it, she describes how she and my father found their new home, the tiny flat at 3 Chalcot Square, Primrose Hill, in London. She was pregnant with me, had just received an acceptance from Heinemann for her first book of poems, *The Colossus*, and was overjoyed to be in London: 'I can't think of anywhere else in the world I'd rather live . . .'

This letter, I thought with some relief, was wonderfully positive and full of hope. It was followed by one written on 2 April, announcing my home birth the day before in the kind of detail no child really wants to know from a parent; my mother had written about everything from the Indian midwife on a bicycle, to the length of her contractions, the details of dilation, and my appearance upon arrival. The publication of my father's book *Lupercal*, and my mother's book *The Colossus*, were also almost upon them – additional births.

The picture of my parents in my mind solidified; it was mutually supportive and intensely close, they were working together for common goals and I could see the hulk of my father writing away in the 'windowless hall', my mother holding me as she slipped him cups of tea. I've visited the flat in Chalcot Square only once, when an English Heritage Blue Plaque was put on it in 2000 and my late brother, Nicholas, and I unveiled it together: it is so tiny that when I stepped into the hallway it was one pace past the bathroom, two paces into the kitchen, turn right and one pace into the tiny living room, one pace across the living room, turn right and one pace into the bedroom, which was so small it wasn't possible to swing a gerbil. I changed my clothes for the unveiling in the bedroom I was born in.

In the third letter, dated 7 November 1960, describing scenes of domesticity and industry, my mother explained how they were together so much that it was good they now had to explore London separately, my father being 'an angel about my excursions, feeds Frieda lunch and so on'. So far, so good, I thought, dreading the impending dissolution of my family as I continued to read . . .

The fourth letter was misdated as 4 January 1960, when it should read '4 January 1961': I am still a baby. It concerns 'an old and ugly problem . . . namely Ted's sister'. In this long letter my mother describes my Aunt Olwyn's behaviour towards her over Christmas in 1960 – behaviour that can only be described as abusive. She writes: 'my presence is intolerable to her' and correctly surmises that Olwyn disliked all the 'other' women in my father's life, being irrationally possessive of him. So I had not been the only recipient of my aunt's excoriating remarks and furious verbal attacks over the years; my mother had suffered them too. It was strangely comforting reading my own experiences through my mother's words; her description of my aunt was disturbingly familiar to me.

In the fifth letter dated 27 March 1962 she writes about the discovery of the house in which my brother was born on 17 January earlier that year, and where he and I were (mainly) to live until we finally left home – Court Green in North Tawton, Devon. The rooms were 'huge' my mother wrote, then going on to describe my brother's character: while I was 'lively, hectic, & a comic' he was 'dark, quiet, smily', and there was a 'very nice ruddy Devon woman in 3 mornings a week . . . to do all the work I hate ---ironing, floor-scrubbing'. Life was full of promise, it seemed, and all my parents had to do was survive what some would find a stifling proximity as they both lived and worked at home, now with two babies.

In this letter there is also the mention of her miscarriage: 'I had lost the baby that was supposed to be born on Ted's birthday this summer at 4 months, which would have been more traumatic than it was if I hadn't had Frieda to console and reassure me. No apparent reason to miscarry, but I had my appendix out 3 weeks after, so tend to relate the two.' I was hugely relieved; there was no mention of ill-treatment by my father as quoted in the newspapers, only an appendectomy . . . surely my mother would have mentioned something to Beuscher at this point if my father had been abusive?

But by the sixth letter, dated 11 July 1962, the cracks were beginning to show; my mother had noticed a change in my father's behaviour, as if he had found a new lease of life sparked by people and situations she did not know about and could only guess at: the woman who took over the lease on Chalcot Square kept phoning my father 'seeming almost speechless when she got me'. Now there was anguish, paranoia and suspicion. My mother frantically analysed the permutations of my father's apparent new interest, fearing that, if he left her, she would not find another like him. Her own mother was staying for six weeks, and my father was away in London; how would she keep up the appearance that all was well? She was, however, certain that she didn't want a divorce: she would like to 'kill this bloody girl to whom my misery is just sauce'.

By the seventh letter, dated 20 July 1962 my mother is begging Beuscher to charge her some money: she is, after all, a client writing to her therapist. She is also, it seems, feeling more open-minded and less reactionary: 'I remember you almost made me hysterical when you asked me, or suggested, that Ted might want to go off on his own . . . How could a true-love ever want to leave his truly-beloved for one second? We would experience Everything together.' It is hard to imagine that anyone looking into my parents' relationship from the outside wouldn't think it so claustrophobic that something must give, if they didn't each develop a life outside the marriage.

She admits: 'I think obviously both of us must have been pretty weird to live as we have done for so long.' Her feelings towards her father, Otto Plath, she confessed, would further complicate their relationship – as, she surmised, would my father's feelings for his mother and sister. She called my father's love-interest, Assia Wevill, 'this Weavy Asshole'; flashes of defiance and imaginings of what might be going on in Wevill's head fill the pages. My father was drifting away, he no longer did 'any man's work about the place'. My mother wrote too, about sex; in a plain, matter-of-fact kind of way I was given a brief history of her sexual education. She sounded stronger too: 'I don't think I'm a suicidal type any more . . .' I could only wish that had been the truth.

In her eighth letter, written on 30 July 1962, my mother's possessiveness over my father drove her to write: 'What can I do to stop him seeing me as a puritanical warden?'. She compared him to the hawk in his favourite poem that kills where it pleases and wrote: 'I realise now he considered I might kill myself over this . . . and what he did was worth it to him.' I consoled myself that these were her words in elaboration of some other truth, not his, because as we work ourselves out through adversity we conjecture and suppose and imagine and can drive ourselves into the floorboards like a nail in this way. She added: 'And he does genuinely love us. He says now he dimly thought this would either kill me or make me, and I think it might make me. And him too.' Being broken apart, it seemed, might create as much energy and art-flow as getting together had – after all, it was all born of their heightened emotional states.

By letter nine, dated 4 September 1962, and suffering what seems to be never-ending influenza, my mother was more resolute about a separation; she was impatient, angry at her illness, and determined to forge ahead despite my father's prospective absence from her life.

Her dependence on advice from Dr Beuscher is emphasised in the tenth letter, dated 22 September 1962: 'I am really asking your help as a woman, the wisest woman emotionally and intellectually, that I know.' A childhood memory is the basis of my belief that my mother asked my father to leave, but in her letter to Beuscher she wrote: 'Ted "got courage" and left me.'

Undoubtedly, my father would have made it easy for my mother to ask him to leave, through his behaviour, his affair, and his deceit. Then here was my mother, writing how for weeks she had been on a liquid diet, apparently highly strung, volatile, paranoid and accusatory; was it a result of the disintegrating marriage? A sick person can rule through their sickness as, in one letter, my mother believed my father imagined she *was* doing. They were two people negotiating the difficulties of what had become a stifling partnership in which feelings of ownership appeared to be a contributory factor, certainly on my mother's side. My father may have reacted to a perceived lack of freedom and had his affair, but culpability lay with both of them. There was nothing new or groundbreaking in this; it was simply a case of two people having lived so closely that they imploded, tearing one another apart in the emotionally messy way that thousands of other couples do.

But these were my parents, which made their situation all the more harrowing for me. They were also writers, who focused and directed their experiences through words; individuals whose emotions were the driving force behind their creativity. If feeling nothing produced nothing, then they felt everything.

As a result, in reading my mother's letters I felt to be taking part in a breath-taking – albeit one-sided – race through the evolution and collapse of a powerful love affair. It seemed to me that the spark of my parents' first meeting ignited a fire, which then burned so brightly in the microcosmic universe they constructed for themselves that they ran out of oxygen. Suddenly, the outside world with all its temptations and the influences of others could not be held at bay, because these two people were no longer on the same side, supporting and loving each other. My mother now found my father 'ugly', his apparent preoccupation with Assia Wevill tearing at her like a hungry dog.

It was in this letter that my mother again wrote about her miscarriage – the miscarriage of the baby that was to have been born on my father's birthday as already mentioned in her 27 March 1962 letter, in which she linked the miscarriage to her subsequent appendectomy. Only this time she wrote: 'Ted beat me up physically a couple of days before my miscarriage: the baby I lost was due to be born on his birthday.' This was the phrase that newspapers had seized upon in 2017, when several of the letters were, for a short time, visible on the internet. It was intensely painful to read this; in all my life with my father I had never seen this side of him.

What, I asked myself, would qualify as a physical beating? A push? A shove? A swipe? This assault had not warranted a mention in that earlier letter when my mother had written there was 'No apparent reason to miscarry.' But of course, now that the relationship was disintegrating, what woman would want to paint her exiting husband in anything other than the darkest colours? I almost laughed when I read what came next; it confirmed that context is not only important, it is *vital*, and it confirmed in my mind that my father was not the wife-beater that some would wish to imagine he was. My mother had written:

> I thought this an aberration, & felt I had given him some cause, I had torn up some of his papers in half, so they could be taped together, not lost, in a fury that he made me a couple of hours late to work at one of the several jobs I've had to eke out our income when things got tight-----

I'd hazard a guess that the stickability of the two halves of my father's papers would not have been uppermost in my mother's mind as she tore into them. In 1962 manuscripts could not be photocopied or scanned or reprinted from a conveniently backed-up hard-drive – there was no facility for that. If work was torn up, it was torn up, and all the sticky tape in the world would not save the writer from having to retype the whole thing – pages and pages . . .

To my mind, it seemed an excessive punishment for my father's crime, although I imagine my father's infidelity would surely have been tied to it. My mother had hit out at the thing they both knew was most precious – typescripts of their own work.

Money, my mother wrote, was also a problem, adding, however, that although my father wanted to live his own life he would 'send us 2/3 of what he earns'.

In the eleventh letter, dated 29 September 1962, my mother writes that she thinks she is dying; she hadn't seen my father for two weeks and had found the love-poems my father had written about Assia. Worse still, she found herself describing them as '. . . fine poems. Absolute impassioned love poems . . .' Even in the face of betrayal, the writer in her could not ignore the veracity of the work. She was lost in the face of the evidence that my father loved elsewhere. And she was frantic about money: although previously writing that my father wanted to give her the majority of his earnings she had discovered that, legally, she was entitled to only one-third. The detail she goes into describes the spiral of her mindset as it coils in upon itself.

On 26 September 1962 Ruth Beuscher had written advising divorce, if my mother truly disliked my father as she professed, but also, in a previous letter (see appropriate footnotes with the letters), had advised my mother: 'Do not imagine that your whole being hangs on this one man . . .' Nevertheless, my mother appeared to have done so, and was feeding her thoughts of my father and his wanton new love, giving strength to the most torturous imagery.

In her twelfth letter, dated 9 October 1962, my mother wrote of situations resolving; my father was moving out: 'he seems to want to kill me, as he kills all he does not want.' But this was metaphorical, not actual. He was giving her the house and the car and £1,000 a year, but this was not enough; she wanted more. She painted one scenario after another, and in all of them she was the martyr – but I don't know if there is a woman alive who, in the same situation, wouldn't feel that way.

She wondered if once the 'kicking, killing passion is past, & he is free' he may not be 'such a bastard'. She admitted: 'Our marriage had to go, okay.' But she was also talking of future plans, and how and where she wanted to live – in London, with the Devon house as a holiday home. She wrote how she is 'in my good minutes, excited about my new life'.

By the time my mother wrote her thirteenth letter to Beuscher, on 21 October 1962, she seemed to be taking a more objective view of her marriage to my father and its dissolution; she couldn't wait to get divorced. She admitted that she had been treating him more and more like a father than a husband, 'hating myself for it.' After dropping him off at Exeter Station for the last time, she returned home not to misery but to ecstasy: 'My life, my sense of identity, seemed to be flying back to me from all quarters, buried hidden places. I knew what I wanted to do, pretty much who I was, where I wanted to go, who I wanted to see . . . I was my own woman.'

Although still taking sleeping pills, my mother was now writing ferociously every morning when she woke in the early hours. Her emotions were mustered, and she was more in control. She was writing a poem a day: poems that would become *Ariel*, the poetry collection that, under the auspices of my father, made her name.

Her letter stated: 'He told me openly he wished me dead . . .' Something my father apparently said, but in what way? And what was the context? She went on to list the terrible things he'd told her, and I had to remind myself that there were two sides to this: exaggeration and hyperbole had been employed here regularly in any case, and these were two people fighting over their ending. What did she say to him? My mother would not have been without comment. So, there I was, sitting in bed, re-living the one-sided end of my parents' marriage through my mother's words – although it could have been any marriage, as messy and cruel as endings are. If there is no passion in the beginning, then there would be little to burn off at the end: where there is great passion, as in my parents' case, surely there must be great pain, great argument, great rage, and great sorrow before there is great clarity?

My mother now seemed to question her previous devotion to the very domesticity that she had initially embraced: 'I am ravenous for study, experience, travel.' She was craving life, but wanted it made easy with more money. She also wrote that she didn't think she could be with any one man for too long, as she liked being alone too much – being her 'own boss'. She was already thinking beyond my father, who appeared to be rapidly sinking into the background of this new and exciting life – no more than an inconvenient anchor to something old, tired, and out of date: 'It is as if this divorce were the key to free all my repressed energy, which is fierce from six years of boiling in a vacuum.' In this, she might also have been describing how my father felt. She was freer, too, to admit the increased intensity of her dislike for her mother, her 'cravenness. Her wincing fear, her martyr's smile.'

I had got this far and found the evolution of my parents' relationship neatly encapsulated; these letters to Dr Beuscher were an extraordinary summary of their lives together. Now I had to brace myself to read my mother's last letter, which was written on 4 February 1963 and sent from 23 Fitzroy Road, the flat in London into which she'd moved with my brother and me only a few weeks earlier. Seven days later she took her own life.

She had read the psychologist, Erich Fromm, as a result of Dr Beuscher's encouragement, and thought that she had been guilty of 'Idolatrous love'. She had lost herself in my father, she wrote, instead of finding herself as she once imagined she had. There was some compassion and understanding: 'I had a beautiful, virile, brilliant man & he still is, whatever immaturities there may be in his throwing over everything in such a violent way. He has said he is sorry for the lying, and shows concern that we get on on our own.' I was moved by this admission, in my mind it was a counterbalance for all the fury that had gone before.

But then: 'What appals me is the return of my madness, my paralysis, my fear & vision of the worst – cowardly withdrawal, a mental hospital, lobotomies.' She feared this might be accentuated by seeing my father once a week when he came to visit me (she doesn't mention my brother), because she could imagine what good friends they could be 'if I could manage to grow up too'. Her feelings confuse her; she tries to follow Fromm's advice for concentration, patience and faith, but keeps 'slipping into this pit of panic and deepfreeze . . .' She wants to 'die and be done with it'; it is becoming too difficult to keep going, and her self-admitted defeatist thoughts are allowed free rein. She feels a 'lack of center, of mature identity . . .' and in the end she writes 'I am incapable of being myself and loving myself . . .' and that she must take Nick and me out for tea, because we are crying.

As miserable as I might feel in reading a first-hand account of the collapse of a relationship that should have seen my brother and me into adulthood, I was struck by the sensation of standing in the room with my mother; I could almost smell her. And I knew what our house and furniture looked like – I even remembered the visit from my grandmother that summer in 1962, because it changed my life (another story) in the most dramatic way.

Smith College would soon be calling me to see how I felt the letters should be handled for scholars to study; there would be no undoing the knowledge that this correspondence existed. Raw, honest, happy, exuberant, tragic and angry, these letters would sit in a library and be pored over by more strangers – the sensationalist phrases that had already leaked into the public domain would remain without context or explanation, warped and distorted by the views and impositions of other people's agendas and theses.

This scenario, where the letters – with their private patient–psychiatrist contents – were buried, left me feeling suffocated. It would render them dumb. While my father does not come out of these letters as a saint, neither does my mother; in my view, they are both flawed and impassioned human beings and I love them more for this. They both suffered, they both made mistakes, they were going through the same kind of hell that literally thousands of other couples go through every day, and, in fact, the letters are profoundly illuminating in this respect.

Yet, in the beginning, there was great goodness and generosity, and the kind of love that some of us never find in our lifetimes. In fact, my mother's overwhelming love for my father is expressed in every line of the sixteen letters she wrote to him in 1956 (see Volume I of these *Letters*) during a short period of separation. There was nothing they would not do for one another; they existed to be together, and their mutual work ethic bound them all the more tightly.

It struck me sharply that, if this book were to be published without my mother's letters to Dr Beuscher, I would forever feel that it was unfinished. So, I decided to let people make up their own minds and, hopefully, find the kind of understanding that my mother was working towards near the end, despite the return of the 'madness' that took her anyway.

I telephoned Faber. There was just time.

Frieda Hughes
2018

PREFACE

This complete and unabridged edition of Sylvia Plath's letters, prepared in two volumes, finally allows the author to fully narrate her own autobiography through correspondence with a combination of family, friends, and professional contacts. Plath's epistolary style is as vivid, powerful, and complex as her poetry, prose and journal writing. While her journal entries were frequently exercises in composition, her letters often dig out the caves behind each character and situation in her life. Plath kept the interests of her addressees in mind as she crafted her letters. As a result, her voice is as varied as the more than 1,400 letters in these volumes to her more than 140 correspondents.

Plath's first letters to her parents were written in pencil in a cursive script. She often illustrated her early letters with drawings and flourishes in colour. Later letters were either written in black ink or typed on a variety of coloured papers, greeting cards and memorandum sheets.

Most of the original letters are held by the Lilly Library, Indiana University, Bloomington, Indiana, and the William Allan Neilson Library, Smith College, Northampton, Massachusetts. Additional letters are dispersed among more than forty libraries and archives. Some letters are still in private collections.

Sylvia Plath was extremely well read and curious about all aspects of culture in the mid-twentieth century. As a result, the topics of her letters were wide-ranging, from the atomic bomb to W. B. Yeats. All phases of her development are documented in her correspondence. The most intimate details of her daily life were candidly described in letters to her mother from 1940 to 1963. (This correspondence, originally published in an abridged form by Aurelia Schober Plath as *Letters Home*, appears here in a complete transcription for the first time.) Plath wrote about early hobbies, such as stamp collecting, to one of her childhood friends, Margot Loungway Drekmeier. During high school, she explained the intricacies of American popular culture to a German pen pal, Hans-Joachim Neupert. There were many men in Plath's life. To an early boyfriend, Philip McCurdy, she wrote about friendship as their romance waned. Later to some of her former Smith College roommates, such as Marcia Brown Plumer Stern, she wrote about her travels in Europe, marital relationships, motherhood, and domestic crafts. There are sixteen letters written to Ted Hughes shortly after their marriage and honeymoon, while fourteen later letters to her psychiatrist Dr Ruth Beuscher chart the disintegration of that marriage in harrowing detail. Her discussion of her own and Hughes's poetry documents their extraordinary creative partnership. Plath's business-related letters show a different side. Readers familiar with her journals will know she long sought publication in the *New Yorker*. Plath's correspondence with several editors of the *New Yorker* demonstrates her efforts to satisfy concerns they had about lines, imagery, punctuation, and titles. Her submissions were not always accepted, but what arises is a healthy working relationship that routinely brought her poetry to publication. In addition to her literary development, the genesis of many poems, short stories, and novels is fully revealed in her letters. Her primary focus was always on her poetry, thrusting up from her 'psychic ground root'.

Some memorable incidents from Plath's life were recounted and enhanced multiple times in her letters and often found their way into her prose and poetry. She was so conscious of her audience that even when her experiences were repeated there were subtle variations of emphasis aimed to achieve a maximum response or reaction.

When Plath's *Letters Home* was published in the United States in 1975 (and in the United Kingdom the following year), the edition was highly selected with unmarked editorial omissions, changes to Plath's words, and incorrect dates assigned to some letters. Only 383 of 856 letters to her mother and family were partially published in *Letters Home*. By contrast, the goal of this edition of Plath's letters is to present a complete and historically accurate text of all the known, existing letters to a full range of her correspondents. The transcriptions of the letters are as faithful to the author's originals as possible. Plath's final revisions are preserved and her substantive deletions and corrections are discussed in the footnotes. Plath's spelling, capitalization, punctuation, and grammar, as well as her errors, have been carefully transcribed and are presented without editorial comment. Original layout and page breaks, however, are not duplicated. Incredibly frugal and conscientious of the limited space available to her, Plath wrote and typed to the very edges of her paper. This was especially the case when she wrote from England on blue aerogrammes. Occasionally, punctuation marks are not present in the original letters, but are implied by the start of a new sentence or paragraph. As a result, when Plath's intention was clear, punctuation has been added to the letter without editorial comment.

Dates for undated letters were assigned from postmarks and/or internal and external evidence and are identified with a *circa* date (for example, to Ann Davidow-Goodman, *c.* Friday 12 January 1951). In some instances where dating a letter exactly proved difficult or uncertain, we have offered either a range of days or simply the month (for example, to *Mademoiselle*, *c.* February 1955). Locations of the original manuscripts are also included in the header for each letter. Scans of drawings included in letters by Plath and photographs of her life are gathered together in the plates. Enclosures of early poems have been transcribed and included with the appropriate letter. Many of these photos and poems have never been published.

Comprehensive factual and supporting footnotes are provided. These annotations aim to bring context to Plath's life; her experiences, her publication history and that of Ted Hughes, cultural events, and her education and interests. Significant places, family, friends and professional contacts are identified at their first mention. Where possible, the footnotes supply referential information about the letters to which Plath was responding, as well as the locations for books from her personal library and papers written for her university courses. We made use of Plath's early diaries, adult journals, scrapbooks, and personal calendars to offer additional biographical information in order to supply, for instance, dates of production for her creative writing.

An extensive index completes the publication and serves as an additional reference guide. The adult names of Plath's female friends and acquaintances are used, but the index also includes cross references to their birth names and other married names.

As we read, edited, and annotated the letters initially available to us, we kept a running list of all the other letters Plath mentioned writing, which number more than 700. Some letters were destroyed, lost or not retained, such as those to Eddie Cohen and to boyfriends Richard Sassoon and Richard Norton. Other letters are presumed to remain in private hands, such as a postcard sent from McLean Hospital in December 1953, which was offered for sale at Sotheby's in 1982. Plath wrote letters and notes to many other acquaintances, Smith classmates, publishers, teachers, and mentors, as well as to family friends. We attempted to contact many of these recipients; a majority of these requests went unanswered. Those who did respond yielded some positive results. After this edition of *The Letters of Sylvia Plath* is published, additional letters that are discovered may be gathered for subsequent publication.

Peter K. Steinberg and *Karen V. Kukil*
2018

INTRODUCTION

Over the past five years, we have scoured the archives of Sylvia Plath's family, friends, and professional contacts assembling as many letters as possible so that Plath may tell her own story in her own words at her own pace. While Sylvia Plath's letters in Volume I (1940–1956) reveal her full-throttled embrace of life and the extraordinary talents, ambition, love, and dreams that she brought to the beginning of her marriage to Ted Hughes, Volume II (1956–1963) provides a detailed portrait of their marriage and continues the saga of Plath's life to its tragic conclusion. There are 575 letters to 108 recipients in Volume II, written between 1956 and 1963. They begin on 28 October 1956, the day after Plath's twenty-fourth birthday on which Hughes gives her 'a lovely Tarot pack of cards', and end on 4 February 1963, a week before Plath's death at the age of thirty.

Plath's voluminous letters to her mother form the backbone of the narrative. There are 230 letters to Aurelia Plath in this volume, chronicling Plath's last year at the University of Cambridge as a married woman (1956–7), vacationing with Hughes at Cape Cod (summer 1957), teaching at Smith College and living together in Northampton, Massachusetts (August 1957–August 1958), pooling their savings to live in Boston and write full-time (September 1958–June 1959), travelling across North America to California (summer 1959), residing at Yaddo in Saratoga Springs, New York (autumn 1959), and finally settling in England (December 1959–February 1963). Only bits and pieces of these letters were published in 1975 by Aurelia Plath in *Letters Home* whereas every extant readable word Plath sent to her mother has been included in this edition of *The Letters of Sylvia Plath*. Plath's almost weekly letters to her mother are generally upbeat and focused on practical matters since Plath knew that her mother had difficulty handling her darker moods. Plath was much more honest with her brother, Warren. When he is in Germany on a Fulbright fellowship in 1957, Plath admits she is in a 'black mood' because her 'ideal of being a good teacher, writing a book on the side, and being an entertaining homemaker, cook & wife is rapidly evaporating' (5 November 1957). After teaching for a year at Smith College she decides that an academic career 'is Death to writing' and devotes herself to creative writing for the rest of her life (28 November 1957).

There are twenty-six previously unpublished letters to Hughes's parents in Yorkshire. Plath often writes in British style. She is clearly trying to impress her new in-laws by showcasing the literary accomplishments of her husband as well as herself. Many letters are written jointly, but Ted Hughes's contributions are not transcribed in this edition at the request of his copyright holder, although paraphrases are occasionally included in footnotes. Plath is particularly thrilled when she and Hughes are published together for the first time in *Granta* (5 May 1957). 'Isn't it poetic justice', she later tells her in-laws who knew their son was considered a wild ruffian at Cambridge, 'that Ted's former teachers & lecturers are being paid to review his work!' (5 November 1957). Plath is proud of her role in launching Hughes's career when she writes to her sister-in-law, Olwyn Hughes, on 9 February 1958: 'How does it feel to have a great and burgeoning poet for a brother?' Plath is also quick to tell the family when she sells her own 'two longest poems to The New Yorker' (30 June 1958) or when Hughes wins honours like the Guinness Poetry Award for 'The Thought-Fox' (18 September 1958), the Somerset Maugham Award for the *Hawk in the Rain* (24 March 1960), and the Hawthornden Prize for *Lupercal* (27 March 1961). She tells Gerald Hughes in Australia that his younger brother 'is appearing, it seems, in print every week in England' (13 August 1958). The letters provide detailed information about Ted Hughes's early publications in addition to her own. When their 'rosebud' of a daughter is born, Plath tells Olwyn that 'Ted's hypnosis, I am sure, made this unusual first labor possible' (2 April 1960). She also regales Olwyn with some of the literary invitations they receive, such as 'cocktails with Auden at Fabers' (16 May 1960), and is pleased with a 'spate of rave reviews' of her own poetry in the *Observer*, the *New Statesman*, and over the BBC (1 January 1961). But Olwyn, who according to Ted is jealous of Sylvia, calls Plath a 'nasty bitch' one Christmas in Yorkshire causing a permanent rift in the family. Plath tells her mother: 'Olwyn made such a painful scene this year that I can never stay under the same roof with her again' (1 January 1961).

Some of Plath's close classmates from Smith College, including Marcia Brown Stern and Ann Davidow-Goodman, receive very candid letters about the new stages in Plath's adult life, from marriage and motherhood to Plath's heartbreak over her husband's infidelity and her plans for divorce. During Plath's last semester as 'the only married undergraduate, woman in Cambridge', she is able to keep house and complete all her academic requirements at the same time – to 'cook and cogitate' as she tells Marcia on 15 December 1956. As a supplement to her exams, she even plans to turn in 'a book of poems'. Occasionally, Plath is filled with confidence about 'being a triple-threat woman: wife, writer & teacher (to be swapped later for motherhood, I hope)' (9 April 1957). Plath tells Marcia that she plans to have Frieda Rebecca Hughes at home in London with the help of a midwife: '[I] am taking this chance to have the baby perfectly free after paying to make sure of conceiving it!' (8 February 1960). Hughes adores Frieda and is continually marvelling 'how beautiful she is' (11 May 1960). 'Her eyes are so blue they send out sparks' (21 May 1960). Plath admits to fellow American poet Lynne Lawner, that 'the whole experience of birth and baby seem much deeper, much closer to the bone, than love and marriage' (30 September 1960).

Plath's focus, drive, and ambition for the success of her writing and that of Hughes are astounding in this second volume of letters. For any novice writer, these letters provide a stunning blueprint of the talent and dedication required to succeed. Plath types Hughes's poetry and her own and submits their work to magazines, keeping '20 manuscripts out continually from both of us' (7 March 1957). Serving as Hughes's secretary and American literary agent, she arranges his book manuscripts and submits them to literary contests, such as 'a first-book-of-poems contest run by Harper's publishing company', which Hughes later wins (21 November 1956). *The Hawk in the Rain* launches his career and is dedicated to Plath. When Plath met Hughes, she guaranteed him '15 poems sold in a year if he let me be his agent'. On the day that Faber & Faber accepts Hughes's poetry book for publication in Britain, Plath brags to her mother that true to her promise: 'Ted has sold 14 poems, a broadcast poem & a book to two countries' in the past year (10 May 1957). *Hawk in the Rain* wins the Poetry Society choice for autumn 1957, which guarantees, as Plath tells Lynne Lawner, 'a sale of 800 copies, close to miraculous in England' (1 July 1957). But in order for their poetry to earn as much money as possible, Plath realizes that Hughes's next book, *Lupercal,* 'will be made up only after all the poems in it are already sold to magazines' (19 March 1957). Plath tells her brother that 'Ted has the makings of a great poet', and he also has the loyal support of Marianne Moore and T. S. Eliot (11 June 1958). Throughout her life, no matter the circumstance, Plath never wavers in her assessment of Hughes as a genius of a writer. However, part of the couple's success as poets is their influence on each other. Plath tells Warren: 'we are extremely critical of each other, & won't let poems pass' before each word, image, and rhythm is examined (25 June 1958). As Hughes becomes more famous, Plath's creative writing time is occupied in answering his 'voluminous correspondence' (21 May

1960). She tells her mother on 22 April 1961: 'It is so marvelous having married Ted with no money & nothing in print & then having all my best intuitions prove true!'

Plath's publishing success is more gradual and her evolving philosophy of writing is clearly articulated in her letters. Her first poetry book is not published until 1960. She submits her poetry manuscript under three different titles to the Yale Series of Younger Poets contest without success. She finally starts weeding out her early poems as 'too romantic, sentimental & frivolous & immature' and tells her brother on 11 June 1958, 'my main difficulty has been overcoming a clever, too brittle & glossy feminine tone, & I am gradually getting to speak "straight out" and of real experience, not just metaphorical conceits'. She becomes attracted to more 'ugly' topics and tells Ann Davidow-Goodman that she slowly writes poems about 'cadavers, suicides, Electra complexes' (12 June 1959). Plath explores all kinds of publishing options for *The Colossus* (the seventh title for her book), including the World Publishing Company, before Heinemann in London (18 February 1960) and Knopf in New York (1 May 1961) accept her revised manuscript. Marianne Moore is critical of *The Colossus*. Plath responds to Judith Jones at Knopf: 'I am sorry Miss Moore eschews the dark side of life to the extent that she feels neither good nor enjoyable poetry can be made out of it' (5 September 1962). Other poets are more supportive. Behind the scenes, W. S. Merwin arranges for Plath to receive a 'first reading' contract from the *New Yorker* (26 February 1961) and loans Plath his study in London where she eventually writes *The Bell Jar*, 'a novel about a college girl building up for and going through a nervous breakdown' (17 April 1961). Plath's poem 'Insomniac' wins the 1961 Guinness Poetry Award and first prize at the 1961 Cheltenham Festival of Art and Literature. Plath is asked to be a judge for subsequent Guinness and Cheltenham contests and champions upcoming American writers throughout her career.

The poetry of Plath and Hughes is different, and in some cases disturbing, compared to the 'new movement poetry' popular at the time. Even Plath's early poems, such as 'Spinster', which appears in the new Oxford–Cambridge magazine *Gemini*, is reviewed as 'sharp-edged' (18 March 1957). But it takes dogged determination in the early days of their writing careers to be published: 'We still get on an average two rejections apiece to every acceptance' (13 April 1957). The *New Yorker* rejects Hughes's signature poem, 'The Thought-Fox' a year before they accept it and finally, after ten years of rejections, Plath wins her own first coveted acceptance by the magazine in June 1958. Even on their cross-America camping trip during the summer of 1959, Plath asks her mother to 'make a chart of all poems accepted' and send a carbon of it to Frieda Heinrichs, Plath's aunt, who lives at their ultimate destination in California (12 July 1959). 'You need to develop a little of our callousness and brazenness', she continues, 'to be a proper sender-out of mss' (2 August 1959). Once the quality of their poetry is recognized they are quickly anthologized. Oscar Williams includes Hughes in the 1958 revised edition of the *Pocket Book of Modern Verse*, which begins with Walt Whitman and ends with Hughes. Williams also introduces Plath and Hughes to all the publishers in New York City, including the editor of the *Hudson Review*, who later publishes their poetry. They both have poems included in the annual British PEN and Borestone anthologies (11 June 1958). Because Plath lives in England and is married to an Englishman, she is even included in the *Penguin Book of Contemporary Verse 1918–60*, an anthology of modern British poetry (1 January 1961), as well as the following year in *New Poets of England and America: Second Selection* (31 January 1962).

Plath is in charge of the couple's finances, always looking ahead for ways to supplement their income, and becomes 'extremely interested in money-managing' in the process (9 July 1958). While she is still a student at Cambridge, Plath sends queries to some of her Smith College contacts, such as Professor Robert Gorham Davis, about future teaching vacancies. Her former English professor, Mary Ellen Chase, becomes one of her most ardent advocates and Plath is later offered a job as 'freshman English instructor at Smith' (9 April 1957) and Hughes is offered a 'full-time instructorship at the University of Massachusetts in English' (6 January 1958). In 1959 Hughes is awarded a Guggenheim fellowship and Plath also secures artistic residencies for both of them at Yaddo in the fall. When they live in London, Plath sends cheques from American publishers to her mother to deposit in their account at the Boston Five Cents Savings Bank where they receive 3½% interest instead of 2% offered in Britain (16 January 1960). Dr Horder, Plath's favourite physician in England, gives her a letter of introduction to view a house at 4 Chalcot Crescent where she wants to live: 'I do so want at least four children & am head over heels in love with London' (28 November 1960). After five years they are able to buy a house in the country on their savings. Almost any goal Plath articulates in her letters later comes to fruition.

It is possible to witness the specific experiences of Plath and Hughes described in letters that later result in poems. While they are living in Cambridge, Plath visits her bust, sculpted by Smith classmate Mary Derr Knox, that now resides in one of the trees on Grantchester Meadows and writes 'The Lady and the Earthenware Head' (3 February 1957). In April 1957 she walks with Hughes at dawn to Grantchester and stands on a stile to recite 'in a resonant voice' all she can remember from the *Canterbury Tales* to twenty cows (8 April 1957). Many years later Hughes publishes the poem 'Chaucer' about this incident in the *New Yorker* and in his book *Birthday Letters*. A cornered groundhog on Mount Holyoke in Hadley, Massachusetts, inspires Plath's poem 'Incommunicado' (5 July 1958). A walk with Aurelia, Warren, and Ted around Beacon Hill inspires 'A Winter Tale' (13 October 1959). The birth of Frieda is chronicled in 'Morning Song' (15 April 1960). 'Tulips', which is commissioned for the summer poetry festival at the Mermaid Theatre in London and later published in the *New Yorker*, is written after Plath's 'latest bout in hospital' for an appendectomy following her miscarriage three weeks earlier (13 April 1961). Plath's radio play *Three Women* is also partially based on this hospital experience as well as two poems published in George MacBeth's *Penguin Book of Sick Verse* (1963).

In addition to poetry, Plath and Hughes try other kinds of writing to earn money. Plath sends short stories, such as 'The Perfect Place', to British women's magazines, essays with original drawings to the *Christian Science Monitor*, and, early in her career, toils daily on the rough draft of her first novel *Hill of Leopards* (later entitled *Falcon Yard*), which is never published (7 May 1957). She later reviews children's picture books for the *New Statesman* because of her interest in the art of illustration. Hughes initially writes short stories for children published in *Jack and Jill* (6 January 1958) and *Meet My Folks!* – 'a book of humorous poems about relatives' that T. S. Eliot accepts for Faber & Faber with a few suggested revisions (December 1958). Plath also writes a children's book (*The Bed Book*) and tells Ann Davidow-Goodman that she wishes Maurice Sendak would do the illustrations (12 June 1959). During their ten-week stay at Yaddo, Plath writes another children's book (*The It-Doesn't-Matter Suit*) while Hughes writes a play (*The House of Taurus*), 'based on the Euripides play The Bacchae' (7 October 1959), followed by *The House of Aries* (9 July 1960), a libretto of an opera based upon *The Tibetan Book of the Dead* (19 July 1960), and *The Calm*, 'a sort of dark opposite to Shakespeare's Tempest' (26 February 1961). Hughes eventually garners success with his adult short stories, such as 'The Rain Horse' published in *Harper's*, which Plath thinks is a real masterpiece 'better than DH Lawrence's descriptive stories' (8 October 1959). Some of Plath's psychological short stories, such as 'The Daughters of Blossom Street', are accepted by the *London Magazine* (12 November 1959). On 26 December 1959 Hughes even makes fair copies of his two poetry book manuscripts to sell and is offered £160 (about $450). Plath later sells 130 pages of her early poetry manuscripts for £100 ($280) to the same bookseller in London 'who is buying stuff for the University of Indiana' (20 November 1961).

Recording programmes for the BBC is their most lucrative venture besides publishing. In April 1957, after Hughes broadcasts his poems over the BBC Third Programme, Plath writes directly to D. S. Carne-Ross to try out for the 'Poet's Voice' herself. However, her first extant poetry recordings are for the Library of Congress with Lee Anderson on 18 April 1958 and on two occasions at Steven Fassett's studios on Beacon Hill for Harvard (13 June 1958 and 22 February 1959). Once the BBC is willing to record her 'odd accent', Plath suggests a programme about young American women poets (24 October 1960). In addition to recording their poetry and Hughes's verse plays and partial translations of the *Odyssey*, they are also interviewed for *Two of a Kind* and other programmes. Plath confides to Marvin Kane that she is excited about participating in *What Made You Stay?* and 'being on a program all to myself' (15 July 1962).

Literary influences are legion in Plath's correspondence. She reads Virginia Woolf's novels, for example, and tells her mother that she finds 'them excellent stimulation for my own writing' (21 July 1957). She and Hughes read *The Sea Around Us* by Rachel Carson. Plath tells her mother: 'I am going back to the ocean as my poetic heritage' (5 July 1958) and later writes a series of poems about the sea surrounding Winthrop, Massachusetts, and a BBC script on the influence of this childhood setting on her writing. She tells Lynne Lawner that she admires Robert Lowell 'immensely as a poet' and audits his poetry course at Boston University (11 March 1959). Plath also likes poems by her Boston University classmate Anne Sexton, which she includes in her 1961 supplement to the *Critical Quarterly* entitled *American Poetry Now*. Sexton's second book, *All My Pretty Ones*, particularly inspires Plath's late poetry because it is, as she says: 'One of the rare original things in this world' (21 August 1962). Near the end of her life, Plath advises Catholic priest-poet Father Michael Carey to 'study the assonances & consonances in Emily Dickinson (beloved of me) for a subtlety far beyond exact rhyme' (21 November 1962).

Plath and Hughes were equally strong-willed individuals. There are many warning signs in the early days of their marriage that all is not harmonious. Plath tells her mother that she and Hughes 'sometimes have violent disagreements' (9 January 1957) and later realizes that 'one must never push him' (26 March 1957). Carving out sacrosanct time to write is the main challenge of their marriage. Plath tells her mother: 'Both of us feel literally sick when we're not writing'. Plath is determined to make her marriage successful. She tells her mother: 'I am one of those women whose marriage is the central experience of life, much more crucial than a religion or career' (7 May 1957). Plath thinks they are 'both ideally suited temperamentally, with the same kind of life-rhythm, needing much sleep, solitude & living simply' (17 June 1957). But the following year Plath confides to her brother: 'we have rousing battles every so often in which I come out with sprained thumbs & Ted with missing earlobes' (11 June 1958). Plath admits to Gerald Hughes that if Ted has any faults it is 'the occasional black Moods' (24 May 1959). When outfitting their new unfurnished flat at 3 Chalcot Square in London takes two months of their time, Plath admits to her mother that Ted 'gets almost nervously sick when he hasn't written for a long time, & really needs careful handling' (24 March 1960).

Plath is formidable herself and can be devastatingly cynical in her correspondence. She thinks her upstairs neighbour in Cambridge, 'the one & only son of Siegfried Sassoon is partly inhuman' because he 'runs a ham radio', and describes Marianne Moore as filled with 'old-maid blood' because she wants to omit Hughes's poems with sexual imagery from *The Hawk in the Rain* (15 March 1957). Plath finds many British women insufferable. They are all 'shy, gauche and desperately awkward socially, or if social, dizzy butterflies' (22 October 1957). She thinks the faculty members at the University of Massachusetts are 'pedantic and cranky' (20 January 1958). Theodore Roethke's wife is 'about as nice as nails' (2 February 1961). And she tells her mother with disgust that recipes in British women's magazines 'are for things like Lard & Stale Bread Pie, garnished with Cold Pigs Feet' (7 December 1961).

Plath is multitalented and exceedingly industrious, often taking part-time jobs so that Hughes can write full-time. She continues to study foreign languages throughout her marriage. She renews her German by reading Grimm's fairytales and 'trying to review one grammar lesson a day' (5 July 1958). She also learns practical skills, such as stenotype, that help her secure part-time jobs to pay for groceries. When the couple live in Boston, Plath works as a secretary at the Massachusetts General Hospital and later for the chairman of the department of Sanskrit and Indian studies at Harvard. In preparation for possibly visiting Italy on Hughes's Maugham award, Plath begins lessons in Italian at the Berlitz School. Plath also takes a part-time job in London at the *Bookseller* as a copy-editor and layout artist to earn money over their 'bare time between grants' (27 January 1961). Plath is a pacifist and interested in world events. She asks her mother for a subscription to the *Nation* in order 'to keep up with American liberal politics' (25 February 1960). Plath's first outing with her daughter is attending a 'Ban the Bomb' march in Trafalgar Square. She hopes her mother will not vote for Richard Nixon, 'a Macchiavelli of the worst order' (21 April 1960). Plath also worries about 'the repulsive shelter craze' in America (7 December 1961). When Plath and Hughes live in the country, they buy a radio so that Plath can continue her language lessons in French, Italian, and German, and hear Hughes's new BBC play *The Wound* (31 January 1962).

Cultural experiences are also very important to Plath. She tells her high school teacher Wilbury Crockett that she and Hughes 'glut ourselves on the cheap play tickets, foreign films, galleries and all the best fare' in London (17 December 1960). Other activities that Plath enjoys include cooking, rug braiding, and sewing (26 February 1959). She tells Olwyn: 'Ted reads me Shakespeare while I work' (25 May 1959). She also loves clothes even though she cannot afford the latest fashions. In the country, Plath takes riding lessons, enjoys fishing, keeps bees, and grows flowers, particularly poppies, cornflowers, and nasturtiums. In London, Plath and Hughes watch Ingmar Bergman films, Lawrence Olivier in Ionesco's play *Rhinoceros,* Brecht's *Galileo,* and *The Duchess of Malfi* starring Peggy Ashcroft. Dinner at T. S. Eliot's house, described as 'one of those holy evenings', is particularly fascinating: 'Talk was intimate gossip about Stravinsky, Auden, Virginia Woolf, D. H. Lawrence' (5 May 1960). Dinner and conversation at Natasha and Stephen Spender's house with Rosamond Lehmann also turns to stories 'about Virginia (Woolf)' (26 October 1960). Stephen Spender even gives Plath a press ticket to attend the last day of the *Lady Chatterley* obscenity trial on her twenty-eighth birthday. American friends Leo and Ann Davidow-Goodman drive the Hughes family to Stonehenge and Vita Sackville-West's Knole. Once they buy their own car, Plath and Hughes even visit remote towns in France. They regularly attend museum shows, such as the Picasso exhibition in London (13 September 1960), as well as visiting the small local galleries in Primrose Hill and Camden Town. Plath later tells Gerald Hughes that art is her 'alternate love to writing' (19 August 1961). At a party, Theodore Roethke offers Hughes a teaching post at Washington State University, which Plath looks forward to in a couple of years after they buy a house in England that they can rent out while they are away (2 February 1961).

'Ted is in seventh heaven' when 'Sir Arundell agreed on the price of 3,600 pounds' for Court Green in North Tawton, Devonshire (7 August

1961). Plath follows him into the country with Frieda even though she is 'much more of a city-dweller than Ted' and eventually hopes they can 'be in London half a year and there half a year' (28 September 1960). Plath tells her mother that the 'move away from my marvelous midwives, doctors, friends, butcher & baker and parks and plays and all I enjoy so much is unbearable' (14 April 1961). But Plath realizes Court Green is important to Hughes and writes to her mother after they move: 'I never have known such satisfaction just seeing him revel in this place and leading at last exactly the life he wants' (15 September 1961). Once again, Plath takes care of all the practical details in their daily life, such as hiring plumbers to lay the pipes for their Bendix washing machine, after which Plath tells her mother that she has 'no worries about managing the new baby now' (22 October 1961). 'A house this old', she tells Gerald and Joan Hughes, 'needs one five-year plan, then another' (6 December 1961). She even wins a $2,000 Saxton grant for prose writing on which they live for their entire time together at Court Green. Planning ahead, Plath has already written *The Bell Jar*, tied up into four parcels, for the Saxton's required quarterly submissions. She sells 'The Moon and the Yew Tree' and other poems to the *New Yorker* to begin rebuilding their Boston Five Cents Savings Bank account after they deplete it to purchase Court Green. 'Ted & I had nothing when we got married, & no prospects', she tells her mother. 'And in 5 years all our most far-fetched dreams have come true' (12 January 1962).

The remaining letters in this volume chronicle the events that lead to the dissolution of the marriage, Plath's valiant struggle to survive with her two children, and her eventual descent into depression and suicide. Discovering the unpleasant truth and background reasons for events often requires comparing descriptions of the same incident in a series of letters. Nicholas Farrar Hughes, for example, is born on 17 January 1962 and Plath writes ecstatic letters to her family and friends. However, to mutual friend Helga Huws, who knows Ted very well, she writes: 'I am delighted with our Nicholas [but] Ted is cooler. I think he secretly desires a harem of adoring daughters' (29 March 1962). She tells close friend Ruth Fainlight (wife of Alan Sillitoe), also the mother of a new son, that 'Ted never touches him, nor has since he was born' (8 September 1962). During the lingering bone-chilling winter in Devon, Plath suffers from a series of milk fevers and chilblains and she and Hughes hardly see each other 'over the mountains of diapers & demands of babies' (2 February 1962). Plath complains to Marcia Stern that Hughes finally paints the floorboards of their fifteen-room house 'after much procrastination', even though laying their turkey red and forest green carpets is a top priority (7 December 1961). Plath tells Smith-friend Clarissa Roche: 'We are so stuck, with this new infant, and very broke with piles of necessary house repairs, plus investment in what Ted hopes will be a sort of lucrative garden' (11 March 1962). Hughes plants the vegetable gardens on their 2½ acres while Plath does all the weeding, but the delicate plants suffer in the summer drought. Nothing materializes in the way they envision it, except for their hillside of daffodils, which bloom 'in their heavenly startling way, like stars' (27 March 1962). In the spring they entertain a string of visits from friends and family. Ruth Fainlight and Alan Sillitoe are no strain, whereas David and Assia Wevill, according to Plath, need to be formally 'entertained' (7 June 1962). Before the visit, Plath characterizes Assia Wevill, the wife of Canadian poet David Wevill, as 'very attractive' and 'intelligent' (14 May 1962). After the Wevills' visit, Hughes begins spending more time in London. When Aurelia Plath arrives for a six-week stay, Plath hopes to get back to her study: 'my poultice, my balm, my absinthe' (18 June 1962). But, in front of her mother, Plath discovers to her horror that Hughes is having an affair with Assia Wevill, which destroys her health, concentration, and the idyll of her marriage. For healing she turns to the sea and makes arrangements to visit poet Richard Murphy in Ireland with Hughes: 'I desperately need a boat and the sea and <u>no squalling babies</u>' (21 July 1962).

When Plath returns to Court Green alone, she completes her book manuscript of *Ariel* over the autumn, writing as many as two startling poems every morning. She tells Richard Murphy: 'I get up at 4 a.m. when I wake, & it is black, & write till the babes wake. It is like writing in a train tunnel, or God's intestine' (7 October 1962). The poems help her process her intense emotions following Hughes's cruel desertion on their trip to Ireland (to join Wevill for a secret holiday in Spain) and the subsequent breakup of their marriage. She tells Ruth Fainlight: 'the muse has come to live, now Ted is gone, and my God! what a sweeter companion'; she is 'producing free stuff I had locked in me for years' (22 October 1962). She tells her 'literary godmother' Olive Higgins Prouty: 'I have never been so happy anywhere in my life as writing at my huge desk in the blue dawns, all to myself, secret and quiet' (25 October 1962). When her mother suggests that she write happier poems, Plath responds: 'What the person out of Belsen---physical or psychological---wants is nobody saying the birdies still go tweet-tweet but the full knowledge that somebody else has been there & knows the <u>worst</u>, just what it is like' (21 October 1962). Many of Plath's observations in her letters from this period, such as her 'enforced purdah in the West Country' (26 October 1962) or a cut thumb, are recycled in her poetry. Plath tells Prouty that she feels like she is 'writing in the blitz, bombs exploding all round' (2 November 1962). Plath dedicates her '2nd book of poems (almost done) to Frieda & Nicholas' (7 November 1962). Later, in London, when the poetry editor at the *Observer,* Al Alvarez, reads some of Plath's poems for *Ariel*, he takes two on the spot ('Poppies in October' and 'Ariel', both written on her thirtieth birthday), and tells Plath her book 'should win the Pulitzer Prize' (14 December 1962). The next day, Plath submits a selection of her new poems, with commentary, to the BBC for a future broadcast. She tells Ruth Fainlight that she plans to sell the *Ariel* poems 'one by one' for much-needed income and then try to get the book published in London and New York (26 December 1962).

Plath contemplates wintering with the children in Spain or Ireland, but follows Prouty's advice 'to strike London now' and goes up to look for a flat (2 November 1962). She takes out a five-year lease on a two-floor maisonette at 23 Fitzroy Road, the childhood home of W. B. Yeats, and tells Prouty: 'I certainly think it would be symbolic for me to live in the house of a great poet I love' (20 November 1962). Once she is able to secure an au pair, Plath plans to finish her second novel ('Doubletake') a semi-autobiographical work set in Devon 'about a wife whose husband turns out to be a deserter and philanderer' (20 November 1962). She plans to dedicate this novel to Prouty.

Plath's letters are filled with fury and vitriol against Hughes while she pursues legal action and closes up Court Green to move to London. To justify a divorce on the basis of desertion, she tells her mother, 'a father who is a liar and an adulterer and utterly selfish and irresponsible is worse than the absence of a father' (27 August 1962), but Frieda misses him and 'lies on the floor all day & sucks her thumb & looks miserable' (29 September 1962). Plath tells her friend Kathy Kane that amputating Hughes from their life like a gangrenous limb is horrible, but 'the only thing to do to survive' (21 September 1962). She tells her mother: 'Ted has spent all our savings to the tune of $100 a week & hasn't worked for 4 months' (23 September 1962); 'He is a vampire on my life, killing and destroying all' (26 September 1962); 'He has behaved like a bastard, a boor, a crook, & what has hurt most is his cowardice---evidently for years he has wanted to leave us & deceived us about his feelings' (12 October 1962). None of these passages was included in *Letters Home*. To Aurelia's request for Sylvia to return home, Plath retorts: 'America is out. Also, as you can see, I haven't the strength to see you for some time. The horror of what you saw & what I saw you see last summer is between us & I cannot face you again until I have a new life' (9 October 1962). Plath tells her brother that Ted is 'just reverting to type' (12 October 1962); 'he can't understand why I don't kill myself' (18 October 1962); and she resents having to 'cope with the endless practical ruins that ass left behind him' (25 October 1962). She tells Prouty on 18 October 1962 that he has 'been secretly planning to desert us all along, withdrawing money from our joint account unknown to me, getting a London flat and mailing address, and leaving us with no access to him at all, and no explanation'. Plath is also hurt that the Hughes family – 'the meanest, most materialistic of the English working class' – support him and not her and the children. With disdain, she calls Hughes a gigolo, 'vain & despicable' as he dates various women, including Susan Alliston Moore, who works at Faber & Faber and is the ex-wife of Warren's roommate from Harvard (22 November 1962).

Plath's evolving and crumbling marriage is documented in intimate detail in fourteen letters written between 18 February 1960 and 4 February 1963 to Dr Ruth Beuscher, Plath's former Boston-area therapist, as described in Frieda Hughes's Foreword for this volume. Because Plath trusts and respects Dr Beuscher, whom she calls her spiritual midwife, she can be utterly candid. As a result, these letters are very difficult to read. Plath equates her gradual knowledge of Hughes's lies and infidelities to 'the old shock treatments' she used to fear so at McLean Hospital (20 July 1962). With Beuscher's encouragement, Plath finally begins divorce proceedings after she reads Hughes's 'impassioned love poems' to Assia Wevill and realizes their marriage is over – 'the knowledge that I am ugly and hateful to him now kills me' (29 September 1962).

During the stress of Hughes's desertion, Plath suffers from high fevers, loses twenty pounds in weight, takes up smoking, and becomes addicted to sleeping pills. She tells Marcia Brown Stern that she is 'utterly flattened by having to be a business woman, farmer', as well as 'mother, writer & all-round desperado' (2 January 1963). Even though ill health continues to plague Plath, she does not lose her sense of humour in her correspondence. To London friend Eric White, she writes: 'I am just through a week of influenza & about as strong as a dead codfish' (3 September 1962). She tell Elizabeth Sigmund that she looks forward to reading David Compton's latest book all about murder – 'just the thing to cheer me up' (8 September 1962). When her Saxton grant runs dry, Plath continues to send her unpublished poems to Al Alvarez and other editors. To counteract Hughes's characterization of her as a 'hag' compared to all the beautiful, stylish models he dates, she is determined to begin her life over 'from the skin out'. She has her hair cut in a modern 'fringe' and buys a 'gorgeous camel-colored suit' with a gift cheque from Prouty (20 November 1962). Desperate to try anything to improve her morale, she even pays attention to 'directions of the Taroc pack' (25 October 1962). She paints the living room of her new flat in London midnight blue with accents of lilac and apple green, as she tells her mother, because 'Ted never liked blue, & I am a really blue-period person now' (21 December 1962).

Once the upheaval of her move is over, Plath begins to reminisce about the good times in her marriage and feels the finality and loneliness acutely, although on some level Plath realizes she is 'mourning a dead man' (29 September 1962). She agrees with mutual friend Daniel Huws that part of Hughes's brutal behaviour is probably due to his guilt. She tells Prouty that Frieda in her innocence and heartbreak over her father's absence holds a mirror up to Plath that reflects her 'own sense of loss' (22 January 1963). The last few weeks of Plath's life are affected by the extreme winter weather of the time and her family's acute sickness. Dr Horder orders Plath 'a private day-nurse for 10 days' when she and the children suffer 'scalding fevers' from the flu. Plath tells Paul and Clarissa Roche that, as a result, she 'began having blackouts' and thought she was dying (9 January 1963). She tells Marcia Brown Stern on 4 February 1963 that 'Everything has blown & bubbled & warped & split---accentuated by the light & heat suddenly going off for hours at unannounced intervals, frozen pipes, people getting drinking water in buckets & such stuff---that I am in limbo between the old world & the very uncertain & rather grim new.' On the same day she tells Father Michael Carey that she writes at present 'in blood, or at least with it'. In her last letter to Beuscher, posted on 8 February 1963, Plath writes of the return of 'my madness, my paralysis, my fear & vision of the worst---cowardly withdrawal, a mental hospital, lobotomies' and of 'wanting to give up'. Without psychological support or a devoted husband by her side, Plath cannot love herself enough to face the extraordinary demands of her current situation. She commits suicide on 11 February 1963 despite her earlier mantra: 'I am stubborn. I am a fighter' (9 October 1962). But the resistance that Plath could not muster for her own survival would be poured into her powerful poetry drafts, which she left on her desk in her bee-coloured bedroom for the ultimate benefit of her beloved children, Frieda and Nicholas Hughes.

Karen V. Kukil and *Peter K. Steinberg*
2018

CHRONOLOGY

1932

27 October	Sylvia Plath born in Boston, Massachusetts, to Otto Emil and Aurelia Schober Plath; the family lives at 24 Prince Street, Jamaica Plain, a neighbourhood in Boston.

1935

27 April	Warren Joseph Plath born.

1936

Autumn	The Plaths move to 92 Johnson Avenue in Winthrop, Massachusetts.

1937

September	Enrols in the Sunshine School, Winthrop.

1938

September	Enters Annie F. Warren Grammar School, Winthrop.

1940

February	Writes first letters to her parents.
September	Enters E. B. Newton School, Winthrop.
October	Otto Plath admitted to the New England Deaconess Hospital, Boston; his left, gangrenous leg amputated.
5 November	Otto Plath dies from an embolus in his lung.

1941

10 August	'Poem' appears in the *Boston Herald*; her first publication.

1942

October	Moves with her mother, brother, and grandparents, Frank and Aurelia Schober, to 26 Elmwood Road, Wellesley, Massachusetts. Enters the Marshall Perrin Grammar School.

1943/4

Summers — Attends Camp Weetamoe in Center Ossipee, New Hampshire.

1944

January — Begins writing in a journal.

September — Enters Alice L. Phillips Junior High School, publishes in school paper.

1945/6

Summers — Attends Camp Helen Storrow in Plymouth, Massachusetts.

1947/8

Summers — Attends Vineyard Sailing Camp at Oak Bluffs, Martha's Vineyard.

September — Enters Gamaliel Bradford Senior High School, Wellesley.

1948

June — Named co-editor of school newspaper, *The Bradford*.

1949

March — Publishes poem 'Sea Symphony' in *Student Life*.

Summer — Attends Unitarian conference at Star Island, New Hampshire.

1950

March — Publishes article 'Youth's Plea for World Peace' in the *Christian Science Monitor*.

May — Accepted into Class of 1954 at Smith College, Northampton, Massachusetts. Receives Olive Higgins Prouty scholarship.

Summer — Works at Lookout Farm with Warren Plath in Natick, Massachusetts.

August — Publishes short story 'And Summer Will Not Come Again' in *Seventeen*.

Autumn — Enters Smith College, resides at Haven House. Meets Prouty.

1951

February	Begins dating Richard 'Dick' Norton, a senior at Yale University and Wellesley resident.
March	Attends Yale Junior Prom with Norton. Meets Eddie Cohen.
Summer	Works as nanny for Mayo family in Swampscott, Massachusetts. Her friend Marcia Brown nannies nearby.
Autumn	Writes articles for local newspapers as Press Board correspondent for Smith College.

1952

Summer	Waitresses at the Belmont Hotel in West Harwich, Massachusetts. 'Sunday at the Mintons'' wins *Mademoiselle* short fiction contest. Works as nanny for the Cantor family in Chatham, Massachusetts.
September	Moves to Lawrence House, a cooperative house, at Smith College.
Autumn	Continues writing for Press Board. Dick Norton treated for exposure to tuberculosis in New York.
November	Meets Yale student Myron Lotz; relationship with Norton strained.
December	Visits Norton at Ray Brook, New York; breaks leg in skiing accident.

1953

February	Dates Lotz and Gordon Lameyer, a senior at Amherst College. Writes villanelle 'Mad Girl's Love Song'.
April–May	*Harper's* accepts three poems; wins Guest Editor competition at *Mademoiselle* in New York City.
June	Lives at Barbizon Hotel in New York; works at *Mademoiselle*.
July–August	Treated for insomnia and exhaustion; counselled by psychiatrist; given poorly administered outpatient electro-convulsive shock treatments.
24–26 August	Attempts suicide in the basement of her house by taking an overdose of sleeping pills. When found, admitted to Newton-Wellesley Hospital.
September	Transfers first to Massachusetts General Hospital, Boston, then to McLean Hospital, Belmont, Massachusetts. Begins treatment with Dr Ruth Beuscher.

1954

January	Re-enters Smith College; repeats second semester of her junior year.
April	Meets Richard Sassoon, a Yale student.
Summer	Attends Harvard Summer School and lives in Cambridge, Massachusetts.
Autumn	Senior year at Smith College on full scholarship; writes thesis on Dostoevsky.

1955

February	Accepted by Newnham College, University of Cambridge.
April	Competes in Glascock Poetry Contest, Mount Holyoke College, Hadley, Massachusetts.
May	Wins Fulbright scholarship to University of Cambridge.
6 June	Graduates Smith College, *summa cum laude*.
September	Sails on the *Queen Elizabeth* to UK.
October	Begins courses at Newnham College.
Winter	Travels to Paris and the south of France with Sassoon.

1956

25 February	Attends party at Falcon Yard, meets Edward 'Ted' James Hughes.
March–April	Travels through France, Germany, and Italy with Gordon Lameyer.
16 June	Marries Ted Hughes at St George-the-Martyr, Queen Square, London.
Summer	Honeymoons in Alicante and Benidorm; meets Warren Plath in Paris; lives at the Hughes home, The Beacon, in Heptonstall, Yorkshire.
Autumn	Begins second year at Newnham College; keeps marriage a secret.
December	Moves to 55 Eltisley Avenue, Cambridge, UK.

1957

23 February	Hughes's poetry collection *The Hawk in the Rain* wins *Harper's* poetry prize.
12 March	Smith College offers Plath teaching position on English faculty.

June	Finishes programme at Newnham and earns her second B.A. in English from University of Cambridge; sails on *Queen Elizabeth* to New York.
Summer	Vacations in Eastham, Massachusetts.
September	Moves to 337 Elm Street, Northampton, Massachusetts; begins teaching at Smith College.

1958

June	Leaves position at Smith College. Records poems for Woodberry Poetry Room, Harvard. Receives first *New Yorker* acceptances for 'Mussel Hunter at Rock Harbor' and 'Nocturne' ['Hardcastle Crags'].
9 August	'Mussel Hunter at Rock Harbor' appears in *The New Yorker*.
September	Moves to 9 Willow Street, Beacon Hill, Boston.
10 December	Resumes seeing Dr Beuscher, records details in her journals.

1959

February	Records more poems for Woodberry Poetry Room. Attends Robert Lowell's poetry course at Boston University, meets Anne Sexton.
8 March	Visits father's grave in Winthrop.
July–August	Travels across North America; becomes pregnant.
Autumn	Spends two months at the writer's colony Yaddo, Saratoga Springs, New York. Has creative writing breakthrough.
December	Sails on the *United States* to UK.

1960

January	Rents flat at 3 Chalcot Square, Primrose Hill, London.
10 February	Signs contract with Heinemann in London to publish her first collection of poetry, *The Colossus and Other Poems*.
1 April	Daughter, Frieda Rebecca Hughes born.
31 October	*The Colossus* published in Britain.

1961

February	Suffers a miscarriage.
March	Has an appendectomy.

Spring	Begins writing *The Bell Jar*.
June	Records poems for BBC series *The Living Poet*. Aurelia Plath visits England from mid-June to early August.
July	Travels to France; reads 'Tulips' at the Poetry at the Mermaid festival in London.
August	Purchases Court Green in North Tawton, Devonshire; sublets London flat to David and Assia Wevill.
1 September	Moves to Court Green.

1962

17 January	Son, Nicholas Farrar Hughes born.
May	Visits from Ruth Fainlight and Alan Sillitoe, as well as the Wevills.
Summer	Assia Wevill and Hughes begin an affair. Aurelia Plath visits Court Green.
September	Visits Irish poet Richard Murphy in Cleggan, Ireland; Hughes abruptly leaves.
October	Writes twenty-five poems; records 'Berck-Plage' for BBC and fifteen poems for British Council/Woodberry Poetry Room.
November	Rents flat at 23 Fitzroy Road, London, formerly a residence of W. B. Yeats.
10 December	Moves with Frieda and Nicholas into Fitzroy Road flat.

1963

January	Dubbed the 'Big Freeze of 1963', London experiences its coldest winter of the century.
10 January	Records review of Donald Hall's *Contemporary American Poetry* for BBC.
14 January	Heinemann publishes *The Bell Jar* under the pseudonym Victoria Lucas.
4 February	Writes last known letters.
4–5 February	Writes last known poems.
7–10 February	Stays with Jillian and Gerry Becker at nearby 5 Mountfort Crescent, Islington.
11 February	Protects children then commits suicide by gas poisoning.
18 February	Laid to rest in Heptonstall.

ABBREVIATIONS AND SYMBOLS

AL	autograph letter (unsigned)
ALS	autograph letter signed
ASP	Aurelia Schober Plath
FH	Frieda Hughes
Lilly Library	Lilly Library, Indiana University at Bloomington
SP	Sylvia Plath
TH	Ted Hughes
TL	typed letter (unsigned)
TLS	typed letter signed
< >	editorial intervention – where ( ) and [ ] are printed in letters these are as used by SP

THE LETTERS
1956–1963

1956

TO *Aurelia Schober Plath*[1]

Sunday 28 October 1956 TLS (aerogramme), Indiana University

sunday, october 28

Dearest mother . . .

What a lovely birthday I had! Your wonderful warm plaid brown jacket came which I shall delight wearing belted around the house over sweaters. Also Warren's[2] hysterically funny card arrived Exactly On The Day; how I loved hearing from him. Dotty[3] sent $5 and Mrs. Freeman[4] an embroidered handkerchief (which I shall give to some little girl when I'm matronly enough). Do thank them both warmly and say I'll write as soon as I can. Why don't I send you a list of the people to whom to send engraved invitations announcing our wedding on Dec. 16th, or whatever you think best. I think our engagement should appear in the Townsman first, though. I've told my dear Dr. Krook[5] who is very reassuring and says she'll find out the best way for me to approach the Newnham officials this week; I'm also making an appointment with the Fulbright officials this week. It will no doubt be arduous to get all the proper sanctions and consents but I have no doubt that they will be given.

Ted[6] came up to Cambridge after his recordings at the BBC Thursday and has been here since; I wish you could see his pay rates! It is probably the most lucrative free-lance work there is; he gets paid again each time

1–Aurelia Schober Plath (1906–94); associate professor, College of Practical Arts and Letters, Boston University, 1942–71; SP's mother.

2–Warren Joseph Plath (1935–); educated at Phillips Exeter Academy, Exeter, New Hampshire; A.B. 1957, Harvard College; Fulbright student at the University of Bonn, 1957–8; Ph.D. 1964, Harvard University; SP's brother.

3–Dorothy Schober Benotti (1911–81); SP's aunt; married Joseph Benotti (1911–96) on 19 April 1941; SP served as flower girl. They lived at 49 Silver Hill Road, Weston, Mass.

4–Marion Saunders Freeman (1908–98), lived at 8 Somerset Terrace, Winthrop, Mass. The Freemans were neighbours of the Plath family.

5–Dorothea Greenberg Krook-Gilead (1920–89); research fellow at Newnham College, Cambridge, and assistant lecturer in English, 1954–8; SP's supervisor.

6–English poet Edward James ('Ted') Hughes (1930–98); B.A. 1954, archaeology and anthropology, Pembroke College, Cambridge; SP's husband, 1956–63.

they re-broadcast: they recorded much of Yeats[1] and one of his own poems;[2] they liked his recording of Yeats so much they are asking him back this Thursday to do some more! And these two days should amount to well over $150! I am so very proud. He is now trying to get a job teaching evenings at the American airbases which is also enormously lucrative and will see if he can also enter the program at Cambridge to get a teaching diploma in one year, even though he has missed the first term. In two or three weeks we should be certain of all these hanging question-marks.

We are looking for an apartment in Cambridge or, better still, Granchester. I hope to move out of here the day term ends: Dec. 7th. Ted is so magnificent; he wants me to get a First, the highest exam mark, and when we are finally together with all this red-tape over, in 6 weeks, I shall be able to study as I never have before. Also write. I have done so many good poems lately[3] and will send a mss. of 48 (11 more to be written) to the Yale Series of Younger Poets contest in February; Ted is amazingly struck by my "book" (all the poems I have together, very few "old" ones ---only those which have previously been published, in fact) and claims that it will be a best-seller because it is all song, but also logic in music; or something. We shall see. We celebrated my birthday yesterday: he gave me a lovely Tarot pack of cards and a dear rhyme with it, so after the obligations of this term are over your daughter shall start her way on the road to becoming a seeress & will also learn how to do horoscopes, a very difficult art which means reviving my elementary math.

A very strange thing: three times now, I have had extremely vivid dreams: about Mrs. Cantor,[4] and Warren; the third wasn't a dream, but a peculiar compulsion to tell Ted one evening why I hated my month in New York at Mlle so much; the very next morning: a letter from Mrs. Cantor, Warren's birthday card (whose message was intricately related to the dream!) and a questionnaire from Mlle asking me to describe my reaction to New York;

1–Irish poet W. B. Yeats (1865–1939).
2–Ted Hughes, 'The Martyrdom of Bishop Farrar', *The Poet's Voice* (14 April 1957); re-broadcast, *Recent Verse* (16 April 1957).
3–According to SP's calendar, she wrote 'Sunset after Squall' on 24 October 1956, 'On the Plethora of Dryads' during 24–6 October 1956, and a draft of 'Vanity Fair' on 28 October 1956.
4–Margaret Kiefer Cantor (1910–2003); married to M. Michael Cantor (1906–2003). During the summer of 1952, SP was a mother's helper at the Cantors' summer home on Bay Road, Chatham, Mass., where she took care of their children: Joan (1939–), Susana (1947–), and William Michael (1949–). The Cantors lived at 276 Dorset Road, Waban, Mass.

all my horoscope points to my psychic, occult powers, & certainly if I give them play, I should at least, with my growing "woman's intuition" be able to join Ted in becoming a practising astrologist. The latest is the Ouija board we made; listen to this: we made a simple board by cutting out letters of the alphabet and arranging them in a circle on my coffee table, with a "yes" and "no" at opposite points, and put our fingers on a wine glass; we got the strangest answers, and worked & worked; all the heat went out of my arm---it must take terrific heat energy to move the glass from letter to letter; we got the most unusual spirits---named Keva (very infantile, who swore a good deal; said she lived "in core of Nerve",[1] both our nerves & belonged to both of us), then Pan, who told us there was a life after death, that he lived in "God-head" and claimed "Iv world enough". The best was Jumbo. I'm telling you this so that If it happens, you will witness it was foretold. We asked Jumbo if he could tell the future & which of our manuscripts would be accepted. Well! He said, or rather, spelled out "Multiply", which we interpreted to mean several; then we asked particulars; I'm telling you, because if it doesn't come true, we can just toss if off: he said the first ms. accepted would be a story, spelled out "New Yorker", said the acceptance would come this Tuesday! Before any others. Well, we had 3 batches of poems sent out long before my New Yorker story ("Remember the Stick Man") and it seemed strange that the story should come back first. Then Jumbo spelled the name of the poem of Ted's the London Magazine would accept: "The Martyrdom of Bishop Farrar"; said Poetry would accept 4 of his: "Law in the Country of Cats", "The Man Seeking Experience," "The Man Going Away", "Six Young Men", and that the Atlantic would accept Ted's "Whenever I am got under my gravestone"[2] & "Casualty". Now even if these spirits live "in core of nerve"---our nerve, they plumb our subconscious depths & powers of clairvoyance, which is of value: I have prayed no envelopes come back before Tuesday---we did this Thursday night: only one more day to go; we wait in curiosity & awe; neither of us would predict a NY story acceptance – but IF it should come, think how likely it would be for the rest to be true! Then we'd teach Jumbo to forecast the football pools & win a fortune!

Cross your fingers
xxx
SYLVIA

1–See Sylvia Plath, 'Dialogue Over a Ouija Board'. See also TH to Lucas Myers, 16 November 1956; held by Emory University.
2–Ted Hughes, 'Soliloquy'.

<on the return address side of letter>
ps – am wearing your lovely warm plaid jacket over sweater & skirt – love sleeves & pockets – if it's not asking for too much, could you send me either or both red & black ballet shoes – a year of continuous wear has worn mine out & they simply dont make them here – pappagallo – 7B or some such

TO *Aurelia Schober Plath*

Thursday 1 November 1956 TLS (aerogramme), Indiana University

Thursday: November 1, 1956

Dearest mother . . .

Well! Between my private crisis and the huge crisis aroused by Britain's incredible and insane bombing of Egypt, the universe is in a state of chaos! You have no idea what a shock this bombing caused us here---the Manchester Guardian, my favorite British paper, called this armed aggression by Britain "a disaster"[1] and I cannot understand what Eden[2] hopes to gain by it other than such a loss of face, aid and support among Britain's colonies, allies, and, of course, growing enemies as can never be remedied. The crass materialistic motives of this attack on the Suez are so apparent as to give Russia food for propaganda for years to come; I shall be eager to hear Cambridge student opinion about this---letters of horror have deluged 10 Downing Street from all over Britain; the eloquence of Gaitskell[3] in the Opposition is heartening.[4] To think I literally rubbed elbows with Eden at that Claridge reception![5] The British arrogance---that old smug commercial colonialism---alive still among the Tories, seems inexcusable to me; I think the British policy in Cyprus has been questionable enough. This is the last. All the newspapers look to American foreign policy in a way which makes me hope fervently that Washington lives up to the UN and not its old loyalty to Britain. What joy there must be in Moscow at this flagrant nationalism and capitalism! This aggression

1–Probably 'A Disaster', *Manchester Guardian* (1 November 1956): 8.
2–British Conservative Party politician (Robert) Anthony Eden (1897–1977); Prime Minister 1955–7.
3–English politician and leader of the Labour Party Hugh Gaitskell (1906–63).
4–Probably 'Mr. Gaitskell "Extraordinary Omission"', *Manchester Guardian* (1 November 1956): 2.
5–See *Letters of Sylvia Plath*, Vol. 1, 1176–7.

by force, which has always been the cry of the Western Allies against totalitarians. The invasion of Egypt by Israel, followed by this bombing, stinks to high heaven. Even Budapest has been thrust to the back page by this; the Russians are leaving. What a world! I remember that Persian diplomat who interviewed me about the job teaching in Africa[1] saying that the western powers were like children in their ignorance about the immense force and manpower on tap in Arabia and Africa. The editorial in the Manchester Guardian was superb: this attack is a disaster from every angle: moral, military, political! Britain is dead; the literary and critical sterility and amorality which I long to take Ted away from is permeating everything. God Bless America. How I long to come home!

Now, for the private crisis. What a week! The Ouija board was "misinterpreted" about the New Yorker which remains adamant as ever. I am really emotionally exhausted by the rapid practical developments in my own state: I went to London yesterday to make my announcement of marriage to the Fulbright.[2] As I expected, they raised no question of continuing my grant; I did not expect, however, the royal welcome I got! Congratulations from the handsome young American head who told me my work, both social and scholastic, in Cambridge was so fine they wished they could publicize it (!) and much more in the same vein; one of their main qualifications of the grant, I discovered, is that you <u>take back</u> your cultural experience to America, and they were enchanted at my suggestion that I was taking back double, in the form of Ted as a teacher & writer. We had a rather gruelling day in London, me being very tired & feeling the usual blueness the day before my period; Ted being tense about his own prospects & ours. By a stroke of luck, we were accepted as tenants for a flat just 5 minutes away from Whitstead[3] nearer Granchester & the country, but still convenient to here. To my chastened eyes, it looks beautiful; we share bathroom with a Canadian couple upstairs & have the whole first floor: living room, bedroom, large sort of dining room, antique but sturdy gas stove & pantry; I met the landlady today who, pleasantly lives in another town; she assured me we could paint the walls (now a ghastly yellow) as long as we didn't have them purple or orange. Well, no doubt she'd be only too happy for free improvements; but what a change in my attitude. Nothing I'd rather do than paint it all a lovely blue-

1–See *Letters of Sylvia Plath*, Vol. 1, 889.

2–According to SP's calendar, she met Dr William L. Gaines.

3–Whitstead Hall, 4 Barton Road, Cambridge, was the residence for foreign students attending Newnham College, Cambridge University; SP lived there from October 1955 through early December 1956.

gray! Ted and I will really feel we "make" a home, then. The rent is £4 a week plus expenses for gas, light, phone and coal. We'll keep the place extravagantly warm! It even has two apple trees in the ragged little back yard, & a bay tree; it's got pots & pans, old kitchen silver, & a few old sheets for the double bed. I'll make it like an ad out of house and garden with ted's help. He is in London today, doing a second reading of Yeats for the BBC. He is trying simultaneously for a job teaching two nights a week at the American Air Base program (very very lucrative, if possible) as well as combining it with getting a teaching diploma from Cambridge: if only both worked out! The hardest part, seeing my tutor at Newnham,[1] came this afternoon. When I realize what ease I'd have had in arranging this, I'd never have contemplated keeping my wedding secret here; the secret part was hardest to explain. My tutor, whom I dreaded approaching, was heavenly; she scolded, of course, for not coming to her in the first place, and the one problem now is getting another affiliated student to come to Whitstead for the next 2 terms, but I think that will work out; she's invited Ted & me to sherry Sunday. I'm not going to tell anyone else until I actually move on December 7th, the end of the term; Ted will start living in our new home tonight, & we'll fix it up gradually. It would simplify matters if you'd announce it about December 7. That would give me time to write friends & coincide with my moving & informing people here whom I don't want on my neck now. We will fight a good life out of this: now, of course, is the hardest time. Only 5 weeks! Until we're officially living together in our own apartment. Have tentatively reserved places for us on the Queen Elizabeth leaving here June 20 & getting us to NYC on June 25th or so! Cross your fingers that reservations go through. When I write Mrs. Prouty[2] & ME Chase,[3] shall I tell them when I was married – or just say I am? It will leak out anyhow – the date – I mean.

xx

Sivvy

<on bottom of page 2 of letter>

PS Who are you & Warren voting for this week??? I suppose your silence means Eisenhower![4]

1 – Irene Victoria Morris (1913–2007); lecturer in German, Newnham College, Cambridge, 1947–66; SP's tutor while on Fulbright at the University of Cambridge.

2 – American novelist Olive Higgins Prouty (1882–1974). SP received the Olive Higgins Prouty Scholarship as a student at Smith College. Corresponded with SP 1950–63.

3 – American writer Mary Ellen Chase (1887–1973); professor of English, Smith College, 1926–55; SP completed English 11 (Freshman English), directed by Chase, 1950–1; SP's colleague 1957–8; Chase lived at 54 Prospect St, Northampton, Mass.

4 – Dwight D. Eisenhower (1890–1969), 34th president of the United States (1953–61).

TO *Aurelia Schober Plath*

Tuesday 6 November 1956 TLS (aerogramme), Indiana University

November 6: Tuesday

Dearest mother . . .

Received your letter today---I look so forward to them. About the wedding announcements first: yes, it would so simplify matters for me to have you engrave them---all the people I'd like to have know, but couldn't spare time to write to separately could thus be informed. Our home address will be: 55 Eltisley Avenue, Cambridge; Ted's living there now.

I am so emotionally exhausted after this week, and the Hungarian and Suez affairs have depressed me terribly; after reading the typed last words from Hungary[1] yesterday before the Russians took over I was almost physically sick. Dear Ted took me for a walk in the still, empty Clare gardens by the Cam, with the late gold and green and the dewy freshness of Eden, with birds singing as they must have for centuries; we were both stunned and sick; the whole world, except us, we felt was utterly mad, raving mad. How Britain's crazy hope for quick success (after which most nations would be too lazy to do anything about it) covers the real cry of the Hungarians is disgusting; it makes the west have no appeal against Russia in the hungarian case; Eden is, in effect, helping murder the Hungarians. There have been riots in London;[2] even though a lot of commercially-interested Tories uphold Eden, Oxford and Cambridge are sending delegations & petitions against him; the horror is, that with time and enough propaganda yelling about Americas danger of becoming a bedfellow with Russia, America will no doubt support Eden too. A prospect which will make it insupportable for me; if only we would act as the Suez situation demands & stop Britain & France, who are agressors; it is all, Ted says, churned up by the oppositions of the planets. So, it seems is our own private life. We will come to work in America and then want to find some corner of the world where it is not strategic, some island or other, if we can get money enough, and go there & try to live a creative honest life; if every soldier refused to take arms & did this, there would be no wars; but no one has the courage to be the first to live according to christ & socrates, because in a world of opportunists

1–Possibly Peter Howard, 'The Last Minutes of Freedom', *Manchester Guardian* (5 November 1956): 1.

2–Probably 'Wild Scenes at Whitehall', *Manchester Guardian* (5 November 1956): 1.

they would be martyred. Well, both of us are deeply sick; the creative forces of nature are the only forces which give me any peace now; and we want to become part of them; no war, after these mad incidents, has any meaning for us. All I think of are the mothers & children in russia, in egypt, and know they don't want men killed, & we refuse to fight & kill. I wish Warren would be a conscientious objector; it is wrong to kill; all the rationalizations of defense & making peace by killing & maiming for decades are crazy. I hope Eisenhower gets in and keeps up whatever policy he has against the British; rumors go that Stevenson[1] would support the British; they are all crazy.

Anyhow, in addition to this, my week has been spent in appearing before every necessary official at Fulbright & Newnham, which has involved tutor, director of studies,[2] college principal,[3] etc. With each one, I had to begin all over; naturally the secret part was hardest to explain. They fired questions at me ranging from wouldn't cooking take time & why didn't I wait a year but in the end every one said it seemed to be a good thing in my case (I felt like some lawyer defending my marriage) & the official council will give me their official decision about me continuing my studies this Saturday: I don't think there will be any trouble; I put up with scolding day after day, thinking: only 5 weeks, & I move into the apartment with Ted.

The next 5 weeks will be hardest; Ted has his applications in for a job at the American air bases (very lucrative teaching evenings), the teaching diploma course here (for which he is probably much too late) & part-time teaching at one of the language schools; we both feel tense, with his having to wait a few weeks, no doubt, till these things work through, & all our beginning expenses with the apartment which, with my present studies, I can't begin to work at (we're going to paint it, buy a 2nd hand couch & a few odd things like curtains, pillow covers) until the first week in December; there isn't a comfortable thing to sit or study on yet (we saw a nice old couch the other day--faded, patterned in blue-gray & white: our living room will, I think, have pale blue-gray walls and bright red & white accents in curtains, pillows, etc.) So I study here. I have got a grocery to

1–American politician and presidential candidate Adlai Ewing Stevenson II (1900–65). Probably his 'Text of Stevenson Speech of Welcome to Convention', *New York Times*, 22 July 1952, 12.

2–Kathleen Marguerite Passmore Burton (1921–); lecturer in English, Newnham College, Cambridge, 1949–60; director of studies in English, 1952–60; SP's director of studies and supervisor under whom she studied Tragedy and Practical Criticism.

3–Ruth Louisa Cohen (1906–91); Principal of Newnham College, Cambridge, 1954–72.

deliver weekly. All the nagging little things, which I would love to do in vacation, come, of course, now: electric companies, deliveries, bank changing of name & getting new account, etc. But I'll try to be stoic. We bore two depressing rejections: of Ted's poems from London magazine – & my story from the New Yorker (a Smith girl secretary there---they're everywhere---who admired my work, told me they accept stories only from a very narrow clique of writers usually; better to send poems, which I did). BUT: one very bright note: this morning Ted got another poem "The Drowned Woman"[1] bought by poetry (Chicago) & ONE BOUGHT BY THE ATLANTIC, "The Hawk In the Storm"![2] I am so very proud. We want to send dollar checks to deposit in my American account so no exchange tax will be taken off: can ted write "Deposit to the account of Sylvia Plath" & sign on the back & mail to you??? I love you; don't worry about us; Ted & I are together & after Dec. 7 will be living together in our first "social" quarters. He is wonderful & we'll face everything that comes with as much courage as we can.

much much love to you & Warren
your own Sivvy

TO *Edith & William Hughes*[3]

Monday 12 November 1956 — ALS with envelope, Family owned

Monday
November 12

Dear Ted's mother & dad . . .

Hello there! I did want to write and tell you how things are going myself – whatever Ted told you over the phone, I'm sure he didn't brag enough about the two poems he got accepted this week, one by the Atlantic Monthly (the magazine that accepted my poem while I was at the Beacon – remember the blood-curdling yell I let out?) – well, it's a fine magazine, with all the reputation the London magazine has here, and more; it's put out by the same press where I sent Ted's wonderful children's animal

1–See Henry Rago to TH, 2 November 1956; held by Emory University. Ted Hughes, 'The Drowned Woman', *Poetry* 89 (February 1957): 296–7.

2–See Phoebe Lou Adams to TH, 2 November 1956; held by Emory University. Ted Hughes, 'The Hawk in the Storm', *Atlantic Monthly* 199 (February 1957): 53; later revised and retitled 'The Hawk in the Rain'.

3–Edith Farrar Hughes (1898–1969) and William Henry Hughes (1894–1981); SP's mother- and father-in-law; lived at the Beacon, Heptonstall Slack, Yorkshire.

fables[1] which they should be reading now. Also, Poetry (Chicago) bought a 2nd poem from him & the editor[2] obviously likes Ted's work. And the Nation bought the poem "Wind"[3] which is a terrific one.

So I am very proud; we sent another great batch of 30 poems out to various places[4] this week. The Christian Science Monitor, the international newspaper, bought my article on Spain & all 4 pen & ink drawings;[5] in spite of regular rejections from the posh distainful New Yorker, we manage.

As for me, it seems all the wrath of heaven descended this week – I've spent a gruelling time telling Fulbright people & countless grave Newnham Victorians about my marriage & convincing them I could still think while cooking for Ted. The Fulbright people were lovely, treated me like Grace Kelly having just been married to a Dark Foreign Prince – my grant will continue till June, praise be! Newnham was much tougher – I felt like an orator on the creative virtues of marriage before a jury of intellectual nuns. But I won – the Council decided this week I could go on for my degree.

In the midst of these grimly-gained miracles, plain sick grief over the rebel Hungarians & rage at Eden, a violent sneeze somehow disabled me – vague murmurs over x-rays of my offending spine in the casualty ward & orders to stay in bed a week; and, just as my back felt better, a nasty cold. I growl, I take bitter medecines; all shall pass in a week, & I really feel blissful I can continue on my Fulbright studying at prim Newnham as Mrs. Sylvia Hughes.

You should see the flat we have got, by sheer luck, at this unpromising time of year! – I move in on Dec. 7, the minute term ends. We have livingroom, bedroom, kitchen & pantry – lots of dishes, pots, & an iron & linen there already – & share bath with queer couple of chemists upstairs. 55 Eltisley Avenue, our address will be. It needs paint badly & new curtains & slipcovers, which we hope to finish fixing before I move

1 – According to SP's calendar, she mailed 'How the Donkey Became' to the Atlantic Monthly Press on 23 October 1956.

2 – American poet and editor Henry W. Rago (1915–69).

3 – Ted Hughes, 'Wind', *The Nation*, 10 November 1956, 408.

4 – According to SP's calendar, she sent TH's poems to *Harper's*, *Kenyon Review*, *Nimbus*, *Paris Review*, and *Virginia Quarterly* on 6 November 1956.

5 – Sylvia Plath, 'Sketchbook of a Spanish Summer', *Christian Science Monitor*, 5 November 1956, 15, with drawings captioned 'Sardine boats and lights patterned the beach during daylight hours' and 'At sunup, the banana stand at the peasant market in Benidorm opened for business'; and 6 November 1956, 19, with drawings captioned 'Palms and pueblos on the sea cliffs at Benidorm, Spain' and 'Arched stairway to Castillo, in Benidorm'.

in with my million books. We had our first "dinner" in the gas oven this last weekend – roast beef, mashed potatoes, peas, raspberries & cream. Such elegance! I can't wait to get out of Whitstead, nice as it is, & have, for once, a place & kitchen of my own!

Well, that's about all the news for now. Please say hello to Olwyn[1] for me & tell her I hope I'll be breathing & walking properly when she comes down – she could taxi to Whitstead or 55 Eltisley Road, where Ted is staying & we would celebrate with a royal dinner, etc. I do hope to meet her before she returns to Paris –

Meanwhile – much love to you both –

Sylvia

TO *Aurelia Schober Plath*

Tuesday 13 November 1956 TLS (aerogramme), Indiana University

Tuesday morning: Nov. 13

Dearest mother . . .

It was so lovely to get your sunny letter; first of all, congratulate Warren a million time for being Phi Bete; I'm so proud. I am rather blue today, all the meanness of fate falling on me over the weekend in the form of a nasty sinus cold, a very painful "slipped disc" in my back which, since saturday, has gotten better so rapidly that ted & I think it must have been only a muscle or something (we had it x-rayed) but it was an unpleasant shock---I sneezed violently saturday just as we were setting out to cover poppy day festivities here,[2] & fell to the floor in violent crippling pain; rest has improved it much, though: also, two rejections of poems and stories from the distainful New Yorker. If people only knew the miseries one goes through & the discouragements they would realize how much balances out the small successes. The Monitor sent me no letter accepting my drawings & article, only a check, which I find strange; I didn't even know they'd come out until you wrote me, and am eager to see them. Ted & I tried a new ouija character "G. A." last night who claimed to be able to predict the football pools (a fortune of £75,000 is given away each week to the winner!) I hope this one is more responsible than Jumbo.

I must say I am eager to get to America and Ted & I can certainly do with a few parties & presents---the next two months will be very hard,

1 – Olwyn Marguerite Hughes (1928–2016); SP's sister-in-law.
2 – Sylvia Plath, 'Poppy Day at Cambridge'; held by Lilly Library.

having to pay bills at both Newnham & the 55 Eltisley Avenue place. Ted has not as yet got a job---he probably can get teaching jobs In January, the start of the new term, but it is very difficult now; he may have to take a laboring job for these first months to cover coal, electricity, gas & food bills.

We have bought a huge rather soiled but comfortable second-hand sofa for our livingroom for £9. 10s. which we'll sell again next spring, and a can of paint for the dirty yellow walls; how I long to get away from the dirt here; everything is so old and dirty; soot of centuries worked into every pore. But I managed to turn out, by utter luck, a delicious roast beef dinner in our strange gas oven, our first dinner there: rare (!) roast beef, buttery mashed potatoes, peas, raspberries & cream; I'll be glad to move there on Dec. 7 (that's Friday; is that our official wedding date, not Saturday?) & forgo this split existence.

This Saturday, by the way, the official council at Newnham met & decided I could go on working here; they had told me not to worry, but the ingrained English maxim that a woman cannot cook and think at the same time had me dubious enough. So my Fulbright continues, & I continue. The difficult person will be Mary Ellen Chase. I'm writing her soon, & will say I'm married, but when she comes over here this winter, she'll find from Newnham I was married in June. Better not send out engraved invitations. Do make a newspaper announcement, though.[1] And tell everybody in Xmas letters, as I will do.

I'd love vitamins; I'm convinced everything the British sell is without any nourishment whatsoever. And could you send more 3cent stamps? I'm almost out. Very very slowly Ted is getting noticed here---his poems; the stupid magazines still haven't printed any, but critic G. S. Fraser[2] wishes he'd had some for his recent anthology of young poets & wishes to see more; he also got a letter, after a friend read aloud some of his poems in a London poetry circle, which rather shocked me. A young Australian,[3] on hearing Ted's poem "The Martyrdom of Bishop Farrar" read (the one the BBC recorded) wrote to ask if Ted felt strongly enough about martyrs to

1–'Sylvia Plath Wed in England to Mr. Hughes', *The Townsman* (20 December 1956): 5.

2–G. S. (George Sutherland) Fraser, *Poetry Now: An Anthology* (London: Faber & Faber, 1956).

3–Roy MacGregor-Hastie to TH, 8 November 1956; held by Lilly Library. In the letter, MacGregor-Hastie writes he heard the poem read by Peter Redgrove at the home of G. S. Fraser.

join him in Baron Hudja's guerilla forces in the mountains of Hungary;[1] thank God Ted would rather make a creative life here than sacrifice himself there; I am sure a hidden death-wish and desire to fight for a noble Cause motivates the young men who go there; it is tragic enough.

Tell anyone-who-wants-to-send-me-gifts of a bulky or house-furnishing nature to send them to 26-Elmwood. Personal gifts might come here, if any, like clothes. But I want to have some nice things waiting when I come home; I've given up all the ceremony & presents belonging to a new bride, and would like to feel we'd have it easy for once in the near future in America. I am sick of battling the cold and the dirt away from all my friends. America looks to me like the promised land; as long as we can stay out of the appalling competitive, comercial race I'll be happy; I'd like New England teaching & writing years & leisurely Cape summers. Do tell Mrs. Prouty Ted has got a poem in the Atlantic too. I love that woman so, & look so forward to bringing Ted to meet her.

If I sound a little morose, it is only this sinus cold which I have to wait out, which makes me more sensitive to rejections. Ted brings food to cook here, like a darling, and is loving and considerate in every way. I cant believe it is only seven months till I come home! I feel like Rip Van Winkle. Can't wait till this vacation when I can write in peace & catch up on all my reading. Give my love to everybody . . . and write a lot . . .

Love from

Sivvy

PS. Why don't you call on Sunday Dec. 9th? We'll be in our new house then & would love to hear your voices there, to bless it. Tell dear Betty & Duane[2] what a lovely idea it is! Our 55 ETISley Ave. number: TEL: CAMBRIDGE 54589.

1–MacGregor-Hastie wrote 'Baron Hajdu is organising an armed expedition to assist the guerillas in the mountains there; I would be delighted to put you in touch with him and see you at arms.'

2–Elizabeth ('Betty') Cannon Aldrich. Wife of C. Duane Aldrich, who lived across the street from the Plaths at 23 Elmwood Road, Wellesley. The Aldriches had nine children: Duane, Peter, Stephen, John, Mark, Elizabeth ('Libby'), Ann, Amy, and Sarah.

TO *Edward Weeks*[1]

Tuesday 13 November 1956 TLS (photocopy), Yale University

Whitstead
4 Barton Road
Cambridge, England
November 13, 1956

Editor Edward Weeks
THE ATLANTIC MONTHLY
8 Arlington Street
Boston 16, Massachusetts
U.S.A.

Dear Editor Weeks,

I am enclosing three stories among which I hope you may find something suitable for publication in the Atlantic--"That Widow Mangada",[2] "The Black Bull",[3] and "Afternoon in Hardcastle Crags."[4] I've had stories published previously in Seventeen and Mademoiselle magazines.

Thanking you for your time and consideration, I am

Sincerely yours,
Sylvia Plath

TO *Aurelia Schober Plath*

Wednesday 21 November 1956 TLS (aerogramme), Indiana University

Wednesday: November 21

Dearest mother . . .

How I look forward to your letters; your calm voice and kind advice really heartens me. I am, comparitively, feeling magnificent this week, although grimly plodding through an incredible mountain of reading---

1–American author and editor Edward Weeks (1898–1989); editor of *Atlantic Monthly*, 1938–66.

2–According to SP's calendar, she worked on 'That Widow Mangada' during 3–9 August 1956.

3–According to SP's calendar, she finished typing 'The Black Bull' on 2 August 1956. An incomplete typescript (pp. 9, 11–12) of the story is held by Emory University.

4–According to SP's calendar, she wrote 'Afternoon in Hardcastle Crags' during 7–10 September 1956. Typescript p. 5 held by Emory University; typescript p. 6 held by University of Victoria. Hardcastle Crags is a wooded valley in the Pennines just above Heptonstall.

Hume, JSMill Chaucer & all the medieval poets (it appears) for Moralist papers[1] & a great Chaucer paper[2] by the Dec. 7th end of term. My cold is gone (poor Ted caught it, & I went over to tend him & cook last weekend) & my back seems fine. The next 2½ weeks I am prepared to trudge through all the academic obligations that have piled up in this term of interviews re marriage, & colds. On Dec. 7th a new life will begin, looking like utter heaven compared to this split one; I study here at Whitstead, rather than the new flat, because there I'm too distracted by wanting to paint the floor & the kitchen & make a big bookcase out of wood & bricks: we're postponing this till vacation. Oddly enough, under all this pressure, I've written several very good poems[3] & the more I write, the better. Yesterday I devoted to typing Ted's first book of poems (which makes the one we sent off last spring look like juvenalia): 40 magnificent poems, 51 pages (6 poems out of that already accepted 2 each by Poetry[4] & The Nation;[5] 1 Atlantic, 1 BBC). We're submitting it for a November deadline for a first-book-of-poems contest run by Harper's publishing company; Marianne Moore,[6] Stephen Spender[7] & WH Auden[8] will judge. I don't see how they can help but accept this it's the most rich, powerful work since Yeats & Dylan Thomas.[9] My own book of poems (now titled "Two Lovers & A Beachcomber") grows well & I should have 50 good poems by the time I submit it to the Yale Series of Younger Poets in February.

1–Sylvia Plath, 'The Utilitarianism of Bentham and Mill: Some Comparisons and Contrasts', 27 November 1956; held by Lilly Library.
2–Sylvia Plath, 'Chaucer: The Most Versatile of Fourteenth Century English Poets', 7 December 1956; held by Lilly Library.
3–According to SP's calendar, she re-wrote 'Black Rook in Rainy Weather' and wrote 'Soliloquy of the Solipsist' and 'April Rhapsodies' on 18 November 1956, and wrote 'Letter to a Purist', 'On the Extra', and 'Ode to an Onion' on 19 November 1956, and poems titled 'Item' and 'Megrims' on 21 November 1956. An incomplete copy of the otherwise lost poem 'Megrims' was identified by Peter K. Steinberg in March 2015 on a piece of carbon paper. Clearly readable are the first four lines and last seven lines. An additional lost poem of 22 lines, 'To a Refractory Santa Claus', is captured on the carbon paper. Other traces present on the carbon paper are notes from SP's Government 11 course completed in 1951–2, SP's poems 'The Shrike' (written 3 July 1956) and 'Natural History' (written 23 November 1956), and the table of contents and acknowledgements for TH's book *The Hawk in the Rain*, which SP typed on 23 November 1956. The carbon paper held by Lilly Library.
4–Ted Hughes, 'Bawdry Embraced', *Poetry* 88 (August 1956), 295–7.
5–Ted Hughes, 'The Hag', *The Nation*, 18 August 1956, 144.
6–American poet Marianne Moore (1887–1972).
7–English poet Sir Stephen Harold Spender (1909–95).
8–English-born poet Wystan Hugh Auden (1907–73); William Allan Neilson Research Professor, Smith College, 1953.
9–Welsh poet Dylan Thomas (1914–53).

Item: Do write "married recently" in our marriage announcement & say after Dec. 7 "the couple will be at home at 55 Eltisley Avenue, Cambridge, England." I'd rather not even have a politic untruth in print about the date. I received today the most beautiful nightgown from Mrs. Cantor I just cried out with joy---all frothy and pinky and lace, like a rosy snowflake at this bleak time. Give her my most enthusiastic thanks. Tell all these good people I'll write them in a Christmas letter after Dec. 7 but just can't manage a line even right now.

Good news: Ted has, by the same miracle that got us a flat the day we wanted it at an impossible time of year, got a job starting this very Monday! He is too late for getting a Cambridge teaching diploma, and, as the work & people are very stuffy in that program, I'm just as glad. He'll be teaching from now till June at a day-school in Cambridge[1] for teen-age boys; not smart, but very dumb. He will officially be teaching English, but also helping in athletics & drama productions & everything in general; the master told him a touching story about how these boys, ignorant, marking time till they get trade jobs, can be "shocked" into awareness that might make life a little richer for them: once the master was talking about "treasure", & took out the things in his pocket, among them a colored pebble he'd picked up on a beach; that was, he said, treasure: he could, by looking at the pebble, recall the sun, the sea, the whole day. He told the boys to bring a "treasure" to class the next day; among them, one boy brought a fossil. The master sent him over to the nature lab to learn about it & in no time the boy had taught himself to read (some can't even do that!) & soon had the best fossil collection in Cambridge.

The master said Ted can use any methods he wants in teaching, no matter how unconventional; the main thing is energy & enthusiasm: the boys will like what he likes. Ted is very happy about this as it has been a difficult time for both of us with no money coming in & the double expenses of Newnham & the new flat this December; too, the job is just what he'll be terrific at. We'll manage all right, now, I'm sure of it; as soon as he starts drawing a regular salary, the acceptances will begin coming in! (The ship fare for him is about £70, & the visa expenses £9). Thanks for the money; & we'll have a good picture taken this vacation, you may be sure!

We'll expect your call eagerly at 8 pm our time on December 9th Sunday. How exciting it will be; do try to have Warren there!

Your dinners sound incredibly delectable; how happy I will be at 55

1–TH taught at the Coleridge Secondary Modern School on Radegund Road, Cambridge.

Eltisley to start something more ambitious than this quick frying of steak or pork with peas. We shall eat in style. Olwyn, Ted's sister, stopped by this weekend on her way from a stay at home to her job in Paris; she is 28, and very startlingly beautiful with amber-gold hair & eyes; I cooked a big roast beef dinner with red wine & strawberries & cream. She reminds me of a changeling, somehow, who will never get old; she is however, quite selfish, & squanders money on herself continually, in extravagances of clothes & cigarettes, while she still owes Ted £50. But in spite of this, I do like her. Do send me some recipes as soon as you can for apple cake, tollhouse & oatmeal cookies, fish & corn chowder; I'd love some Flako piecrust mix, corn muffin mix & chocolate bits for cookies; I am dying to bake for Ted. Keep writing me morale-building letters up till Dec. 7th! I'll need them.

Much much love to you & Warrie---
your own sivvy

<on the return address side of letter>

PS: Urgent: Can I send Ted's dollar checks from the Nation, Atlantic Monthly, etc. to you to deposit to my account in Wellesley if he signs them: "Deposit to the account of Sylvia Plath" & signs them? We want to build up a dollar fund to greet us on our return!

TO *Aurelia Schober Plath*

Thursday 29 November 1956 TLS (aerogramme), Indiana University

Thursday morning, Nov. 29

Dearest mother . . .

I have no idea how long its been since I last wrote home, but I hope you'll understand that work has piled up enormously and that maybe you'll tell people they'll hear from me after Dec. 7th when we're settled in our new house---do thank Mrs. Cantor for the beautiful nightgown! It seems I'm always making requests---could you please send back our original marriage license as soon as you can---we have to have it, along with hundreds of other triplicated documents to turn in for Ted's visa---the most complicated form I've seen yet. Also, I'd appreciate it so much if you'd also put my wedding announcement in the NYTimes---all my old friends read that, and no other paper, so I'd like to have it there, since I'm not sending out invitations. News that I am already married will no doubt leak out anyway, so I'm glad you're putting "recently." Dick

Baugham[1]---I don't know if you remember him, but he was a few years behind me, at the Unitarian church, Amherst, med. school, etc., & is now over here---came up to see Ted & me & said he'd just read the Townsman announcement of my engagement[2] & here I was married. That sort of thing. I dont think it really matters too much, though.

I am going through a very trying time just now which is why I haven't written---from those gruelling two weeks of interviews about my marriage and being down with a sinus cold & slipped disk, work has piled up so hugely that it seems I have to read all of medieval poetry & write a long paper, plus do my weekly philosophy essays all before December 7th. There have been times where I've felt terribly tired---if I can just plod to that glorious day, my whole life will come together & I can work through my blessed 5 weeks vacation at leisure---(but right now it seems as if I'll never be free of this weight of back-work). All demands have come at the same time---I have to prohibit myself from going over to our flat on <u>55 Eltisley Avenue</u> because I want so much to fix up the hideous kitchen, which we will paint all light blue & fix the scabrous ceiling. I have not been able to resist doing work on the living room with dear Ted: I wish you could see it! It has dark brown woodwork, & Ted painted the walls a heavenly shade of light blue; he painted the floors black (which I scrubbed) & we bought four beautiful 6 foot 6 boards and Ted sawed them to fit our homemade "built-in" bookcase---I painted 40 firebricks to hold up the bookcase light blue to match the wall, and we are both awed by the beauty of our room now, with my Braque over the mantel, & our big comfortable 2nd hand sofa, & the color-combination is dark brown, light blue with cheerful bright yellow accents on pillows & lampshades. You see my dilemma---I'm just dying to fix up the house & take care of my wonderful Ted, who has been going to his job all week, but I must fight my homemaking instinct & work for another gruelling week without stop. Then I will get a van to move my heavy stuff Friday, and we will go out to Miller's for a luxurious celebrating dinner with white wine & smoked salmon & partridge and at last begin our life together which we have been fighting for for so long. We looked back on the last six months as a kind of marathon---really no rest & peace in our own place except for a few weeks in Spain, which was complicated by worry about money, jobs, separation, etc. I feel we have had every disadvantage at the start---

1–Richard DeWeese Baughman (1934–); B.A. 1955, Amherst College; M.D. 1960, Harvard University.

2–'Sylvia Plath Is Betrothed to Mr. Hughes', *The Townsman* (8 November 1956): 4.

no money coming in, no jobs, and a large load of uncertainty; I think we deserve every bit of good fortune we get from now on---we work so hard all the time; but just being with Ted is a blessed relaxation & peace for me, no matter what I'm doing.

I am so proud of Ted. He has just walked into this job and the boys evidently are just fascinated by him; he says he terrifies them, and then is nice, & with his natural sense of the dramatic, can interest them & have them eating out of his hand; he brings home their compositions & exams to correct & reads them aloud to me---I get such a touching picture of those individual simple little minds. Ted says they loved some ballads by WH Auden he read them, yelled for him to do them over, & then he told them to write 8 lines of a story-ballad; they did, & very enthusiastically ---and these are all candidates for juvenile delinquents. Ted teaches math, social studies, english, dramatics, art & just everything---on a very simple level, of course, but thus even more demanding for a brilliant intellect like his; he seems very happy about the job, & will get paid over vacation etc. You should see him---he gets books on Russian history, on the Jews, on the Nazis out of the library---the boys are very interested in these topics, & Ted can just absorb knowledge in no time. I am convinced he is a genius. We have such lovely hours together; I just long to be over in our own house, cooking & keeping it in order for him & packing delicious lunches for him. We read, discuss poems we discover, talk, analyze---we continually fascinate each other. It is heaven to have someone like Ted who is so kind, & honest, & brilliant & always stimulating me to study, think, draw & write--he is better than any teacher, even fills somehow that huge sad hole I felt having no father--I feel every day how wonderful he is and love him more and more. My whole life has suddenly a purpose; I really am convinced he is the only person in the world I could ever love; my demands are so high---for health, brilliance, creativity, faithfulness ---all those qualities that seldom, if ever, go together & he has all & much more. We look so forward to hearing from you on Dec. 9th at 8 pm our time.

Much, much love – your own

sivvy

<on the return address side of letter>

PS: am sending / $32. of checks under separate cover.

TO *Aurelia Schober Plath*

Thursday 29 November 1956[1] TLS, Indiana University

Thursday, also

Dearest mother . . .

Enclosed please find $32 in the form of three checks to deposit to my account, which I'll change to a joint account when we come over. I just sent off Ted's book of poems to the contest this week, to be judged by WH Auden, Stephen Spender & Marianne Moore---all of whom, ironically, I've met at one time or another. If they don't pick Ted's book to be published they are all crazy. It is 51 pages of vital, disciplined, brilliant, rich poetry.

I was most moved by your account of Steve Clark,[2] & couldn't resist putting a letter in with this about him. I suddenly "felt myself into" his state where he must feel, as I felt, only a little over three years ago, that there is no way out for him scholastically. I wish you could somehow concentrate on him--have him over alone for a weekend, get him to talk, break down whatever sick reserve & terror he has & even get him to let go and cry. If you think you can, use me as an example. I'm sure he thinks that even though I went to a mental hospital, I never had any trouble about marks. Well, tell him I went through 6 months where I literally couldn't read, felt I couldn't take courses at Smith, even the regular program, because of my badly planned course-program, and felt I wouldn't be admitted to a place like B.U. because, paradoxically, they demanded more set subject requirements, which I just didn't have. Tell him I went back without a scholarship for my half year. I know only too well how it is to have nothing anybody says help. I would have felt almost better if people had not tried to be optimistic when I honestly believed there was no hope of studying & thinking; I am sure he is not that badly off. Find out what his marks are. Is he in danger of failing? If not, tell him that (even in our competitive American society) while marks may get scholarships, people are judged by very different standards in life; if he tries to enjoy his studies (I assume he is now taking some courses he likes), he will be enriched throughout life; try to give him a life-perspective: to walk out in nature maybe & show him the trees are the same through all the sorrowful people who have passed under them, that the stars remain, and that, as you once wrote me, he must not let fear of marks blind him

1–Date supplied from internal evidence.

2–Probably Stevens Hall Clarke; B.A. 1958, Harvard; LL.B. 1966, Columbia. Clarke was a guest of the Plaths for Thanksgiving, 1954.

to the one real requirement of life: an openness to what is lovely, among all the rest that isn't. Get him to go easy on himself; show him that people will love & respect him without ever asking what marks he has gotten. I remember I was terrified that if I wasn't successful writing that no one would find me interesting or valuable.

Get him to see that he must like his work for itself first; let him work, but tell him to force himself, every time he does a paper or exam, to think: whatever mark I may get, I liked this, and that; I have discovered such and such; I am that much richer whatever the examiners may think. Marks have no doubt become the black juggernaut of his life; do not try to be over-optimistic, because that will only make him lose trust in you. Take him aside, agree with him about the problem; even if it is dark. Start from the bottom; if he is not failing, tell him how good that is. If he likes any subject, tell him how important that is. If he gets despairing or frantic & thinks he can't work or think, give him some ritual phrase to repeat sternly to himself: let him be gentle in his demands; tell himself he has as much right to work and be at Harvard as anyone. If he is worried about money, tell him a job on the Cape can help earn much. If he can manage it, tell him to work part-time, and study over the summer at more leisure. Tell him he can always re-apply for scholarship; that personality & character-references matter as much as marks. Even if he goes to a med school with lower reputation, He can be a fine doctor. I know med-student bar-tenders on the cape who earn up to $1000 a summer.

Above all, don't try to be rosy; start from what he thinks is the situation, no matter how black; show him how much worse it could be; use me as an example---I thought no university would ever accept someone who couldn't read, who hadn't had the requisite courses; I thought my life was ruined because no one would employ a girl without a university degree. Now, if he is not failing, surely he will get a degree. That is of first importance.

Tell him, if you think it will help, that you wrote me he was concerned about marks, and that I only want to share some of my own experience with him; that I thought and fully believed for almost a year that that my case was utterly hopeless; tell him (if he says---oh, she has a Fulbright & always got good marks) that I had to go back without a scholarship to Smith & took only 3 courses, because I was afraid I couldn't even read for them. He surely must be better off than I was! Do ask him out alone & talk straight out with him. It is better he should break down & cry, if he has to. I think psychiatrists are often too busy to devote the right sort of care to this; they so seldom have time to get in deep & blither about father & mother relationships when some common sense stern advice about practical things & simple human intuition can accomplish much. I am sure you could help Steve, and I only wish I was there to take over for a time. Don't let him go around trying to cover what he thinks is a black pit of failure in himself; get him to talk it out, to say how black it is; agree where it seems close to true (marks are very important to scholarships etc. don't minimize this). He will trust you if you treat his problems as real ones. The thing to do, if possible, is to make him understand that his love of his work is what matters to him, no matter what the examiners say. If he can have joy in his work, instead of having it go bitter because he is manipulating it for marks & not getting them, that will be good. Let him go slowly, step by step. First to like his work for itself no matter how many relapses he has to fearing bad marks. When he dies, his marks will not be written on his gravestone; if he has loved a book, been kind to someone, enjoyed a certain color in the sea; that is the thing that will show whether he has lived.

He probably feels something like a hypocrite, as I did---that he is not worth the money & faith his parents have put in him, and that more & more this will be revealed (by things like losing his scholarship). Show him how much chance he still has---is he a sophomore or junior? Help advise his summer plans. But don't be rosy; be tough & practical; get him to be happy with a minimum---what he now has; show him the various ways he can work himself up from there. Do invite him over. And tell me more details about him. I wish you would sort of give him as much time & energy as you can through this time – adopt him for my sake & (like the Cantors did) have him over, show you love him & demand nothing of him but the least he can give.

xx
Sivvy

TO *Aurelia Schober Plath*

Tuesday 4 December 1956 — TLS (aerogramme), Indiana University

Tuesday, December 4,

Dearest mother . . .

What a miraculous creature you are! As if it weren't enough to drive a car, jaunt about Europe in the summer, you now are conquering TV! I am so proud; you will do much better before the camera than ever I would have done, with your poise & ease from teaching. I am overjoyed that dear Mr. Crockett[1] is getting public tribute. It is rare people like him who influence, very deeply, the whole course and spirit of people's lives. I shall write a few inadequate lines towards the end of this. I feel very humble; he is really saintlike.

You were darling to send the recipes and the stamps. I only hope the packages won't take all your energy & money! Ted & I are just gritting our teeth until this week is over; I have a paper to write this morning,[2] then another cram of reading & paper to write thursday; Friday I'll call a moving van. Saturday night we're going for a celebrating dinner to Miller's for duck (where we went with dear Betty & Duane that time). We'll be home all Sunday, eager to hear from you at 8. I just got my SAILING DATE confirmed! We leave England on the Queen Elizabeth June 20th, the day my Fulbright ends! So we should be in NYC about June 25th. I never thought I would be so overjoyed about anything; to see the blessed Statue of Liberty & the lovely rock-crystal towers of Manhattan side by side with Ted is my favorite dream now. The fare is phenomenal---£72 for Ted; we'll try to pay the £15 deposit this month; but it will be a long haul; the visa costs £9, and our year was really knocked by the £22 dentist bill & the £ 46 tailor's bill for Ted---both necessities in their own way. However, we still have about $100 due for our poems, so we'll cash it here. Ted will be earning a regular salary now each week & my Fulbright, after January, will be free to use for our rent & food expenses.

Of course, while I am cramming this week, I am distracted by dozens of practical thoughts and plans. I really think it would be inadvisable, after all, to spend my first year teaching at Smith, even if they did ask me back; I have written Mary Ellen Chase. It would be rather like taking your first job working for pay from your mother---a rather uneasy ambivalence, wondering how much praise or criticism came out of love, how much out of impersonal standards of work. I'd much rather prove myself and get confidence at a place which wasn't already so biased in my favor---this month I'll apply for Ted to teach creative writing at Harvard (the one place in that faculty where they don't require PhDs,) and see if I can get a position at Radcliffe, Tufts, or some such; it would be a heavenly dream to live in the other Cambridge, so close to home. CROSS your fingers!

1–Wilbury A. Crockett (1913–94); SP's English teacher at Wellesley High School (formerly Gamaliel Bradford Senior High School), 1947–50; lived at 82 Forest Street, Wellesley, Mass., with his wife Vera M. Crockett, and their children Deborah L. and Stephen Crockett.
2–Sylvia Plath, 'Literature Versus Dogma', 4 December 1956; held by Lilly Library.

Ted has just had another poem accepted by the Nation for publication sometime before Xmas (it is called "Roarers In a Ring",[1] set in a pub on the moors on Xmas eve): this is the 3rd they've bought from him! I'm so proud. Also, and keep this under your hat, the woman at the Atlantic Monthly Press children's dept.[2] was very interested in his animal fables & said that although, as they stand, they need to be specifically simplified for children, she would be delighted if Ted were willing to try to rewrite them; she sent a fine letter[3] with suggestions (we'll have to use the Aldrich children to test stories until we have our own). So Ted is re-writing them this vacation. We are hoping a published book will be the result, if she likes the re-write. We now have 20 manuscripts out between us! I can't wait till vacation to enjoy, for the first time, our own home!

Turn over for some words on Mr. Crockett – very inadequate – but sincerely meant – do add or subtract, as you think best.

"I only regret that I am not able to be with you today in person to give tribute to Mr. Crockett. Yet it is actually due to Mr. Crockett that I am over here in Cambridge (England) at all, for it was he who first described the beauties of this university town to me and said "You must study there."[4] How many of us, I wonder, can in a similar way trace back our choice of college or career, our search after "the best that has been thought and said",[5] and even the very principles of integrity that guide us, to our experience in Mr. Crockett's classes---an experience of inquiry and discovery not confined within classroom walls, but reaching deeply into our minds and hearts; an experience outlasting the limits of any school year and lighting us through the rest of our lives. Lovingly, and relentlessly, be<u>cau</u>se lovingly, Mr. Crockett demanded the best of us. And if we discovered abilities and interests we never knew we had, it is he who awakened us to them. If we made dreams become realities, it is because of his daily encouragement and unceasing inspiration. His rare wisdom and insight cannot be calculated with tape-measurers; his

1–See Robert Hatch to TH, 27 November 1956; held by Emory University. Ted Hughes, 'Roarers In a Ring', *The Nation* (22 December 1956): 543.

2–American author Emilie Warren McLeod (1926–82); children's book editor at the Atlantic Monthly Press, 1956–76, associate director, 1976–82.

3–Emilie McLeod to Ted Hughes, 28 November 1956; held by Lilly Library.

4–See *The Journals of Sylvia Plath* (London: Faber, 2000), 147–8. According to SP's calendar, she visited Wilbury Crockett on Saturday, 20 September 1952.

5–Matthew Arnold, *Culture and Anarchy: An Essay in Political and Social Criticism* (London: Smith, Elder & Co., 1869); SP quotes from the preface: '. . . culture being a pursuit of our total perfection by means of getting to know, on all the matters which most concern us, the best which has been thought and said in the world . . .' (viii).

generous kindness and concern for his pupils cannot be weighed by our inadequate words. Suffice it to say that again and again through the years, whether in thought or in person, we all come back to him. And we come back with the warmest admiration, gratitude, and love. I feel that I can speak for all of us who have ever sat, discussing and debating, about Mr. Crockett's round-table when I say that Mr. Crockett is far more than the Teacher of the Year: he is the teacher of a lifetime."

You must report to me how all goes: what is said, etc. I can't wait to have Ted meet Mr. Crockett. I will write all these good people Christmas letters this next week. Good luck.

Much love,
Sivvy

PS – The quote about the "best thought & said" is Matthew Arnolds's[1] definition of culture.

TO *Aurelia Schober Plath*

Monday 10 December 1956 — TLS (aerogramme), Indiana University

Monday morning
December 10, 1956

Dearest mother . . .

It was so incredible to hear your voice last night---filling our little hallway; I felt very homesick afterwards, though. I do hope we can all see a great deal of each other this next summer; I look so forward to coming home now; our house, our yard, the cape---all looks like a dream of eden to me from here; I will certainly appreciate every little thing from central heating to hygenic kitchens with a new and chastened eye! Warren's voice was so low over the phone it was very hard to make out what he was saying. Do thank the Aldriches for making it possible to call. I miss you & Warren so much. I don't know what I'd do without Ted; he is so thoughtful and loving that it is simply amazing. I saw him off this morning for the first time to work (he goes on my bike, it's about a 20 minute trip) after a good breakfast of fried eggs, bread & butter, cold roast beef & coffee. He is such a wonderful person, I can hardly bear to have him away for the whole day. Those boys must just adore him; he has got them enthusiastically writing little ballads like WH Auden's, reads

1–British poet Matthew Arnold (1822–88).

them Robert Frost,[1] and tells them about the history of Russia, of the Jews, America, bull fights---everything. He is staying after school tonight to start rehearsals for some little miracle plays they are putting on. It is so lucky he got such a good job this queer time of year, which means he'll get paid a good bit before Christmas, to help with our many bills. Do tell everyone I'm writing Christmas letters this week---dear Mrs. Freeman sent a check for $10 and Dot, Joe & Grampy[2] $20. It all helps so much, & I will write them very soon.

I have to finish writing my Chaucer paper today; we both really were exhausted after this last week---I spent all Friday packing at Whitstead, helping load things on the van, and cleaning house and unpacking here. The living room is lovely now, with the light blue walls, big rather dirty blue patterned sofa (very comfortable) facing the coal fireplace, Braque still life over the dark brown wood mantel, brown & yellow blanket over the cot[3] under the three windows in front, one nice carved wood cabinet with books & bowl of fruit under mirror, and huge 5 shelved bookcase (shelves <u>6</u> feet 6 inches long!) we built with fire bricks, also painted to match walls. Yellow pillows, tablecloth & lampshades make it very sunny. We do our eating & writing in here. The little scruffy kitchen is next on the list to clean up; I hope to scrape off the dirty paint & paint it all light blue next weekend & put in gay red & white checked oilcloth over things. I will have a fine chance to catch up on reading this vacation, and to write, so don't worry. Ted is so helpful about my studying; he knows all the literature in English there is, and will help me so much on learning how to date things. I am so happy with our little flat; your cooking things came in so handy---especially the copper scrubbers & rubber scrapers & blessed carrot scraper. I use them all the time; Ted is so happy with his brief case. By the way, do tell me if you included a hairbrush in his shaving kit (that is what you are sending, isn't it?) If not, I want to get him one. The poor dear needs so much---if ever you want to send shirts, his neck size is 16½ & size large. I'm getting him little things for Christmas, & waiting till January sales for big things, like a wool bathrobe. Today I'll go out & get cookie sheets. It is cold enough in the pantry to be an icebox, but I have no regulator on the oven heat, so I never know how hot it is. I'll be eager to try my first baking & see how intuition works.

1–American poet Robert Frost (1874–1963).

2–Frank Schober (1880–1965); maître d'hôtel at Brookline Country Club; SP's maternal grandfather.

3–SP uses 'cot' here probably to mean a plain, narrow collapsable (movable) bed.

You can imagine how wonderful it is to stay in Cambridge after all our summer travels. Even in this cold gray weather, the peace of not packing & living & eating out is so nice. I'll really rest now, and work steadily. Unless we get a book or a big story accepted, we most likely will hardly be able to save anything toward next summer, because Ted's ship fare bulks so big now. I am going to try writing for the women's magazines this vacation again. I never really worked constantly at it, and I got nice letters from every editor I sent to. Once I could establish that as an income, we'd be fine, what with two teaching salaries coming in. We have sent you off an Xmas present but it may come late; we'll send Warren a little something, too, but it will be late. We have been so harried up to now we haven't been able to do anything but work & eat. For the first time in 6 months our lives are coming together in a kind of calm; we have really fought for this through some grim times---only a month ago, Ted was trudging about looking for a job, I did'nt know if Newnham would keep me on, & we weren't sure of a flat. Now that is all set and after we pay these bills, we'll be more at ease. I only hope you rest now over the vacation and are plump and healthy when we come home in June. We'll want to stay in the house at least a week or two before going down to the Cape. I will get Ted's visa and all the hundreds of triplicate documents off by the end of this month, along with applications for teaching positions. When we get jobs, we can see about an apartment before we go to the Cape for the summer. I got a dear letter from Frank and Louise,[1] all about their amazing new house; it sounds like a palace. After a year, perhaps two, teaching & saving money in America, Ted & I dream of spending a whole year in sunny Italy writing; by then, maybe one of us will have a writing grant. Do write us often. We do so love to hear from you. Ted is the most wonderful man that ever lived – far above any dreams I ever had!

much much love,
Sivvy

1–Louise Bowman Schober (1920–2002); married SP's uncle Frank Richard Schober (1919–2009) on 27 June 1942; SP was flower girl at the wedding.

TO *Edith & William Hughes*

Monday 10 December 1956[1] ALS, Family owned

55 Eltisley Avenue
Cambridge
Monday morning

Dear Ted's mother & dad –

I've just seen Ted off after a good breakfast of fried eggs, cold roast beef, bread & butter and coffee, and finished picking up the house. It is so wonderful to be here at last after this hectic month! I moved in Friday & got a big British railways van to move all my heavy things for a few shillings. I'm so glad everything is at last settled until this June – our nice flat, Ted's fine job, & my grant & study at Newnham. I am so proud of Ted & his job – those little boys must just love him; he has got them writing little ballads, & acting little plays; he teaches them everything from maths, to history of Russia & about bull fights – speaking of bull fights, Ted wanted me to ask you to please send this little pamphlet on bulls he left in his room – he says he thinks it's over the mantel in his room – it has a picture of a bullfighter on it. The boys want to build a bull-ring out of cardboard! I'm sure having Ted as a teacher will be something they'll remember all their lives – he's so handsome & strong, too – not like most teachers; they really admire him!

I am finishing my last paper for this term now & will be glad to study & write in my own time this next month. Ted is writing another good story & more poems. Did he tell you the editor of the publishing company liked his animal fables very much & asked him to revise them some more for children (parts of them were a bit too bloodthirsty) – & we hope after he revises them they will be pleased enough to buy it & publish it – it looks promising & the editor send a lovely helpful letter. Keep your fingers crossed! We look so forward to coming up to be with you over Christmas!

Much love to you both –
Sylvia

1 – Date supplied from internal evidence.

TO *Marion Freeman*

c. Wednesday 12 December 1956[1] ALS in greeting card,[2]
Smith College

<printed greeting>

WITH ALL GOOD WISHES FOR CHRISTMAS / AND THE NEW YEAR / *from*

<signed>

sylvia

Dearest aunt marion . . .

How Ted & I loved your beautiful letter which described with such lovely colors the airport & scenes of my childhood home (it made me see it all so vividly again, & be a bit homesick). And then your generous wedding gift! You may imagine, it is rather difficult to start housekeeping from scratch – (luckily our flat is furnished) so I'll have to wait with most things till we come home next June – but Ted & I did go out & buy one of our favorite Braque reproductions – a still life, & had it framed to have over our mantel – I'm sure you would like it – all muted shades of rich browns, yellows & greens – it hangs in a place-of-honor above our mantel. I can't wait to bring Ted home in June! We are so happy in our little flat, which we painted & decorated, building in a huge 6-foot bookcase and all. Ted is the dearest, kindest, handsomest husband ever. He is looking so forward to meeting you – I've told him so much about my home & friends. He's teaching English here now at a boy's school & writing a book of children's animal stories – maybe Ruth's baby[3] will be old enough to appreciate them when we come home –

Love from us both & warmest thanks for your dear card & gift –

sylvia

1–Date supplied from internal evidence.

2–Christmas card produced by K. J. Bredon.

3–Ruth Prescott Geissler (1933–); B.A. 1955, University of Massachusetts at Amherst; SP's childhood friend from Winthrop, Mass.; married Arthur Geissler, Jr (1932–2013); degree in Business Administration 1954, University of Massachusetts at Amherst; SP was maid of honour at their wedding on 11 June 1955. Ruth and Arthur Geissler had four children: Susan (1956–); Joan (1957–); William (1958–); and David (1960–).

TO *Peter Davison*[1]

c. Wednesday 12 December 1956[2] ALS in greeting card[3] (photocopy), Yale University

<printed greeting>
WITH ALL GOOD WISH FOR CHRISTMAS / AND THE NEW YEAR / *from*
<signed>
sylvia

Dear Peter . . .

After a hectic term of papers & protocol Ted & I are now married & living in our own flat – writing furiously & applying for teaching jobs together – (Ted's now teaching English & drama at a Cambridge boys school). Ann Hopkins[4] mentioned some jobs open for intermediate writing courses at Harvard for which Howard Mumford Jones[5] is judging. So Ted wrote him credentials on off chance. We sail for home on June 20 & hope to write solidly all summer before starting jobs where & whenever –

Best Christmas wishes from us both –

Sylvia

TO *Elinor Friedman Klein*[6]

Saturday 15 December 1956 TLS in greeting card,[7] Smith College

<printed greeting>
WITH ALL GOOD WISHES FOR CHRISTMAS / AND THE NEW YEAR / *from*
<signed>
sylvia

1–Peter Hubert Davison (1928–2004), American poet, assistant editor at Harcourt, Brace & Co., 1953–5; assistant to the director at Harvard University Press, 1955–6; editor at the Atlantic Monthly Press, 1956–85; dated SP in 1955. Davison married SP's Smith housemate Jane Truslow in 1959; father of Edward Angus and Lesley Truslow.

2–Date supplied from internal evidence.

3–Christmas card produced by K. J. Bredon.

4–Ann Hopkins; resident of Cambridge, Mass.; summer resident of Martha's Vineyard; friend of Peter Davison and SP.

5–American intellectual historian Howard Mumford Jones (1892–1980).

6–Elinor Linda Friedman Klein (1934–); B.A. 1956, Smith College; SP's friend.

7–Christmas card produced by K. J. Bredon.

<drawing of a woman's head and three stars>

Dearest Elly . . .

Forgive this delinquent. But it has taken me all this time to get through papers, protocol etc. & at last am married, with Fulbright, still at Newnham,& living in this first floor flat we scrubbed, painted & just finished building in a 6foot6 huge bookcase. We loved the Paddy Chayefsky book;[1] if Ted ever gets a TV play accepted it will be you sent inspiration. Life was very grim this term– us not knowing about if I could stay on, keep grant, get flat, or Ted find job. After interviews & much rain, one flat fell open, one job teaching English & drama to semi-cretin boys opened the day Ted applied. We work, we thrive. Ted keeps getting poems accepted by the Nation (3 so far), Poetry, & one to the Atlantic Mo. I told poetry mag to let you know when my 6 come out this winter;[2] look up somewhere & see if you like. Ted's revising the children's fables (the Atlantic Press liked, but wants much revision & waits till it's done for verdict). No prose bought yet. Blood, sweat. Please write us. How you are. O 17. Such salad days. What is playing on Broadway? Etc.

With love & merry Christmas from us both . . .

sylvia

TO *Marcia B. Stern*[3]

Saturday 15 December 1956 TLS in greeting card,[4] Smith College

<printed greeting>

With all Good Wishes / for Christmas / and the Coming Year

<signed>

much love, / sylvia → / (inside)

1–Paddy Chayefsky, *Television Plays* (New York: Simon & Schuster, 1955); SP's copy held by Lilly Library.

2–Sylvia Plath, 'Two Sisters of Persephone', 'Metamorphosis', 'Wreath for a Bridal', 'Strumpet Song', 'Dream with Clam-Diggers', and 'Epitaph for Fire and Flower', *Poetry* 89 (January 1957), 231–7.

3–Early education specialist Marcia Brown Stern (1932–2012); B.A. 1954, sociology, Smith College; M.A., early childhood education, Lesley University; SP's friend and roommate at Haven House during her sophomore year. Only child of Archibald L. and Carol Taylor Brown. Marcia Brown married Davenport Plumer III in 1954 (divorced 1969) and later married Ernest Stern in 1971. Corresponded with SP, 1951–63.

4–On Gaberbocchus Christmas card designed by Franciszka Themerson.

Saturday, December 15, '56

Dearest Marty. . .

At last, at last! Believe it or not, I have been mentally writing you letter after letter all this past hectic term, but had to wait till this week & all papers, protocol and sundries were over. Your fine letter and the wonderful color shot came this morning & was like eating a Christmas plum-cake. My wanderlust (which I thought was inexhaustible) came to an end with a rapid bang after this summer of lugging pack on back to London, Paris, all through Madrid (bull-fights, roast pig) to an incredible lovely little Spanish resort fishing village a couple of hours down from Valencia where from the huge white house I lived in (with its own fig tree & grape arbor) I could see a minute corner of the blazing Mediterranean for the 5 weeks I lived, swam wrote & sunned there. I'm enclosing[1] a bad article with some drawings I did of the place; I've started drawing again, these queer blocky little sketches & it is a good feeling.

How I got through one paragraph without telling you my enormous news shows how disciplined I've become! I am, wonder of wonders, married! I have been so frantic with work, official interviews & moving out of Whitstead into the new apartment I haven't had a chance to write a soul except mother. His name is Ted (Edward James) Hughes and he is the most magnificent man ever. I can't wait for you to meet him. We're coming home at the end of next June (he's a roaring hulking Yorkshireman & this will be his first time in America; we're both crossing our fingers that we can get teaching jobs together in New England). I can't really describe how all this happened---I simply couldn't imagine myself married, at least not to anybody I'd ever met. And then one blustery Saturday night last winter I walked into this wild literary party given for a new magazine---I'd read it, & was awestruck and admiring of one poet's poems. I met all the other writers---little scrawny midgets, & saw this great looming ferocious man across the room. "Who's he?" said I. Well, he is now my husband. Ironically, he'd read some of my poems before meeting me, & there was a sudden sound of hurricanes in my ears & I just knew. I went off on a horrid mad spring vacation---sketching in Paris, going to Rome with Gordon,[2] and Venice, & breaking off with everybody I knew.

1–The article and drawings are no longer with the letter.

2–Gordon Ames Lameyer (1930–91); B.A. 1953, Amherst College; dated SP 1953–5; travelled with SP in Europe, April 1956. Gordon Lameyer was encouraged to date SP by his mother Helen Ames Lameyer (1894–1980); B.A. 1918, Smith College. Lameyer's father, Paul Lameyer (1885–1960), was an artist; during World War II he was interned by the FBI at a camp for German-born US citizens.

I flew back from Rome to London on a black Friday the 13th in April, & we haven't been apart a day since. I found Ted living in a condemned London slum (where Dylan Thomas used to stay) & working as a reader for J. Arthur Rank, saving money to go to Australia. He was very simply the only man I've ever met whom I never could boss; he'd bash my head in. We had the most incredible spring in Cambridge---Ted is a crack shot & fisherman, discus thrower & can read horoscopes like a professional; he shoots rabbits & I stew them. Oh he is a lovely one. Both of us write like fury & are each others best critics. He started me writing & drawing again after a bad winter & I am his secretary & his American agent. He's got enthusiastic acceptances of his poems (3) from the Nation, Poetry (Chicago) and we've both got a poem each accepted by the Atlantic Monthly; I'm getting 6, miracle of miracles published in Poetry magazine this January I think, so take a look & see if you like. We both will have books of poems, about 50 apiece, ready to try for publishing this year & Ted is revising a book of children's animal fables the Atlantic Press is nicely interested in---it is all much work & more typing & huge postage, but we have our fingers crossed. It has been a grim, bleak semester---there was a time of Ted & mẹ trudging desolately around in the rain not knowing if the Fulbright would keep on, or Victorian Newnham college keep me, after marriage, & hunting for a flat & job for Ted at this unlikely time of year; no money either & many bills. Well, it all ended with blessings: I'm the only married undergraduate, woman, in Cambridge (they don't think you can cook & cogitate at the same time, generally) on my lovely grant, & we found a cheap flat right on the edge of the Granchester meadows, with river & cows & a job opened for Ted teaching English & drama to a secondary modern boys school of near cretins---about 13 to 14 years (many borderline juvenile delinquents) & he is great at it---terrifies them into admiration, has them writing Audenesque ballads, reading Russian history, building bullrings in cardboard, etc. He & Mike[1] should have a lot of notes to compare!

Anyway, we got this old flat for about $11 per week because the old couple kept falling on their heads, poor things, and had to go to a home. It was an ungodly mess, filthy dirty (England's history is literally written in dust) & painted the yellow shade of spoiled pears. Well, we scrubbed, while I was writing my last term papers, painted the livingroom (nice

1–Davenport Plumer III ('Mike'; 1932–); B.A. 1955, Dartmouth College; married SP's friend Marcia Brown on 15 June 1954 in Dartmouth, New Hampshire; SP served as bridesmaid; divorced 1969.

& big) pale blue, bought a huge comfortable 2nd hand dingy blue sofa, yellow lampshades & pillows, dark brown woodwork & furniture (it's all furnished, luckily; we have nothing to our name but a wood coffee table, travel rug & very sharp steak knife). We painted myriads of fire bricks to match the walls & got good pine boards & built a 5-shelved bookcase 6 & ½ feet long, on which our growing book collection is stocked---very fine, our one wealth---I've got a $100 book allowance this year & will use every bit. Your place sounds like heaven. If only you could imagine how grim England is in winter! I am actually continually cramped in a shivering lump by the coal fire in the livingroom to keep warm. We have to heat hot water by coal fire if we want it in 2 hours, & even then, my breath comes out in great white puffs & tinkles in icicles to the floor when I take my weekly ordeal bath. Nothing ever gets dry or clean; no iceboxes (one really doesn't need them) & everything falls apart in your hands---carpet sweepers, plumbing pipes, wiring. Oh God Bless America, land of the Cookiesheet, Central Heating & Frozen Orange Juice!

I can't wait to get home. Ted is staunchly British, but I am hoping that he will see the enormous difference in America & want to settle there eventually. England is no place to bring up children---bad teeth, lousy dentists, careless overworked Mds. It is, really, a dead country. Ted has been lucky earning free-lance money (fabulous rates, about $3 a minute!) reading Yeats for the BBc 3rd program & some of his own poetry; as a result of the latter, a terrific bloody powerful poem on the martyrdom of a bishop he got a serious invitation to join some unpronounceable Baron's geurilla forces fighting in the mountains in Hungary. Thank God he is going to keep on writing; he served two years in the RAf, so that's over. He is incredibly exactly the sort of person I've always needed but never thought could exist all in one frame---a big, 6 foot 2 strong brute with dark hair, in great unwieldy amounts, & green-blue-brown eyes, depending on weather, & sings ballads, knows all Shakespeare by heart; we read aloud, hike, write & you know all about how magnificent it is to have someone, one someone who speaks the perfectly same language & learns all the time with you so each day there is more & more to share & look at & love. Well it is great & beautiful. We will always no doubt be very poor, but we had a Mediterranean summer on just nothing, vomiting back across the choppy channel without a shilling to stay with Ted's dear parents in the Yorkshire moors, hiking to Wuthering Heights & eating rabbits, wild rabbits. It can sound idyllic, because the important part is, but materially I am a shivering housefrau waging a day to day battle against cold & dirt. O how I long to be home & walk from room to room without mufflers, snowboots & mittens, to bake cookies (my little oven has no regulator) & use frozen foods. I must say, I have lived in the most unlikely dumps & on so little it often stuns me. I would love it if you would give me a brief refresher course when I get home next June about prices, how to make economies and so on and so on. The cost of living there will probably turn me blue at first!

Ideally, ideally, we'd like to live in your Cambridge & work teaching in Cambridge or Boston, but God knows. I'm not so worried about my getting a job, because I've got American credentials, but Ted might be harder, because he only had 2 years of English at Cambridge (gets an automatic MA this year) and took Archaology & Anthropology his last year; he wants to teach college-age people, because the free hours for writing are better. We'll see. It would be so wonderful if we could live in Cambridge, too. I am unbelievably hungry for home & news of everyone. I'm so happy about Carol[1] & your mother. My mother had a hard time last winter & spring with my dear grammy[2] dying very slowly and terribly & bravely of cancer. My grandfather is just lost without her, & my marriage is the main thing that keeps mother going alone in the little house; but she is a new woman! I feel I have suddenly found a mother. A friend left her a small sum in a will, & she came to Europe for the first time last summer---I showed her London & Cambridge & tried to get her rested after the ordeal of grammy's funeral; Ted & I took her to Paris (she loves Ted dearly, it is wonderful) & she was like a young girl---taking pictures, drinking wine, etc. She then left us to go to Austria & pay a pilgrimage to all grammy's relatives there & see the places where grammy lived when she was little. Mummy is suddenly become flexible & getting healthily self-concerned---entertaining, driving to work. I am so proud. Funny, how one ends up wanting to re-educate one's parents. I was concerned so much at one time, & now she is making a life at the age of 50. I'll be glad when Ted & I are in America, sharing some of our active life with her. Warren met Ted, too, in Paris (Warrie got an Experiment fellowship to Austria for the summer, & in his senior year at Harvard is president of the German club & almost, I gather, bi-lingual---his subject is fascinating, but incomprehensible to me---linguistics, with a combination of math & psychology---a really new field, & rare combination; most language majors can't add a sum & vice versa). Warren & Ted get along

1–Carol Pierson Ryser (1932–2012); B.A. 1954, sociology, Smith College; SP's friend and housemate at Haven House.

2–Aurelia Greenwood Schober (1887–1956); SP's maternal grandmother.

fine too. I am convinced Ted is the only man in the world I could ever speak to with my whole self or love and day by day it gets better & richer. We work, & are generally by ourselves writing when we're not studying, me, or teaching, he. He thought your picture was great & we're both very eager to see you & Mike. Where will you be next summer?

Do write soon again. I love hearing from you, about you, & the little items of news about the people we know. Two years is a long time away; Ted & I plan to work hard in America a year or two, go back to Italy or Spain a year to write concentratedly, & probably then start an enormous family. You know, once you're over here, the world looks so small! Cambridge boys went to Budapest during the riots; African trips, Israeli trips, etc. during the summer. Cambridge is full of foreigners--Scandinavians, Indians, Negroes of all sorts: the debates raging here since the ghastly bombing of Egypt by A. Eden were furious; we have our own Communist cell in Cambridge---most members breaking up over the hungarian crisis.

Well, we'll be arriving in blessed NYC around the 25th of June, staying in Wellesley a couple of weeks---I want Ted to meet relatives & friends ---we had a perfectly quiet private London wedding (I was going to try & wait till this June & home, but gave up the ceremony & circumstance because it seemed absurd to postpone our forces working together for such a crucial half-year of our lives). Ted is just 26, & I am convinced will be the best poet since Yeats & Dylan Thomas. Eventually. He has got raging power & violence combined with amazing discipline & a great sense of humor. Oh my. If I sound slightly ecstatic it is only because for 6 months I've nudged & heaved through about every material problem there could be---money, inlaws, uncertainty, English dirt, and now, at last, we are in our own place, with our own grubby stove, & are very happy; peace, peace. I hope we get jobs in Massachusetts. It would be heavenly to be near you. I miss woman-talk. The English women are pathetic. Either blue-stocking cows or butterflies with frivolous hectic accents. My greatest woman friend is my philosophy instructor---a blazing brilliant South African jewish woman, incandescent with brilliance and creative and lovely. She gives me an extra hour each week & has been my salvation among the grotesque female dons at Newnham.

If you have waded through all this you are amazing. Do write back soon. I can't wait till June. Ted sends Christmas greetings & says hello too.

Much love to you both –
sylvia

TO *Robert Gorham Davis*[1]

Monday 17 December 1956[2] TLS (aerogramme), Smith College Archives

55 Eltisley Avenue
Cambridge, England

Dear Mr. Davis,

Greetings from Cambridge. As I write, the British winds are turning my fingers blue and in spite of a blazing coal fire, my breath hangs in white puffs on the frigid air.[3] I'm at present studying for my final exams at Newnham College this coming June, when my two-year Fulbright grant is up. After many months spent in Paris, Spain and Italy, my wanderlust is, temporarily at least, cured, and I am most eager to return home.

I'll be coming back to Wellesley at the end of June, 1957, with my husband, who is a young British poet (at present teaching English at a secondary modern boys' school here). Both of us hope to apply for teaching positions close together, and I wondered if there might be a vacancy in the English 11 staff for the year 1957-8; if so, I would be interested in applying. Writing goes well---the Atlantic has just bought a long poem,[4] and a batch of six will be appearing in Poetry (Chicago) this January. My husband, Ted, is my best critic, very demanding, stimulating, but kind and most encouraging, too. Both of us are preparing books of about 50 poems each to send around to publishers this winter, and Ted is doing well in America, publishing in the Atlantic, the Nation, Poetry, and other magazines, and reading poetry free-lance for the BBC over here.

Do let me know if you think there would be a possibility of my applying to teach on the English 11 staff next year. Warmest Christmas wishes to you and your wife . . .

Sincerely,
Sylvia Plath Hughes

1–Robert Gorham Davis (1908–98); English professor, Smith College, 1943–58. Davis taught studies in style and form (English 247), a creative writing course completed by SP, 1952–3. SP also served on Honor Board with Davis, 1952–3. Married to the writer Hope Hale Davis (1903–2004).

2–Date supplied from postmark.

3–Cf. SP's poem 'To A Refractory Santa Claus', which features similar imagery: 'Where teeth / Don't chatter, where breath / Never puts on the white disguise / Of freezer air.'

4–Sylvia Plath, 'Pursuit', *Atlantic Monthly*, January 1957, 65.

TO *Aurelia Schober Plath*

Thursday 20 December 1956 TLS in greeting card,[1]
Indiana University

<printed greeting>
With all Good Wishes / for Christmas / and the Coming Year
<signed>
much love – / sylvia and Ted / (see inside →)

December 20, 1956

Dearest mother . . .

Well, here are enclosed a few of the best of the grisly proofs;[2] Ted and I really don't like them, considering ourselves much more beautiful---these are more like passport shots without imagination or sensitive lighting; in fact Ted hates them all. But I am sending them on to you until we have something better done, which we will do soon---this lady[3] was an expensive crook. Tell me which one or two numbers, if any, you want made up---it's part of the sitting price, four pictures, so you might as well have something while waiting for the rest if we can get a good one. If you want one with hands, I should think we could have the knotted monstrosities cut off & the picture shortened to head & shoulders. *Choose four different ones, if you want that many; keep the proofs till we find out if we have to have them back.

We've already gotten two of your packages---a big one which is faithfully unopened, & the small one of cookies which, when Ted saw the label, couldn't be kept till Christmas. The lovely little angel hangs up over our livingroom mirror & we christened the wonderful steak knives that very night. I do hope that we will get some presents on our arrival home; I shudder to think of items like pots & pans, sheets, towels, blankets & silver ware. We bought ourselves a huge cutting knife for bread & meat and a great Shorter Oxford Dictionary[4] which is now our favorite book---for our own Christmas presents.

I'm enclosing a check from dear Mrs. Prouty for $25 as an Xmas present to deposit in my account. Did you tell her I'm married & all? I just wrote

1–On Gaberbocchus Christmas card designed by Franciszka Themerson.

2–The photographs are no longer with the letter.

3–Lettice Ramsey (1898–1985). SP and TH had at least thirteen photographs taken by the firm Ramsey & Muspratt. Ramsey maintained her studio in Cambridge; Helen Muspratt (1905–2001) was based in Oxford.

4–SP and TH's *Oxford Shorter Dictionary* (Oxford, Clarendon Press, 1955), appeared at auction via Bonhams on 21 March 2018.

her a long Christmas letter, and am finishing the last of those today. How did the TV program go? It is this coming Saturday, isn't it? Or was. Ted & I are sending you, or have sent, a Christmas present which we hope will vividly remind you of some of the things you saw this summer; and a silly trifle to amuse Warren in another package. They may be late, but our thoughts are there.

The Rice's[1] sent us the strangest Christmas card! Did you get one like it? Bilious green with oriental waves & an ominous rhyme of sorts full of mixed metaphors! Well, no doubt they have the best intentions!

It is wonderful for both of us to be on vacation at last; we are just relaxing after the rigors of this past term. Ted is going for an interview in London in the first week in January about a job teaching two nights a week at an American Army Air Base near here which would double his salary. I hope it works out. We sure need the money. It should help his applications to teach in America too. We are hoping to get our grim scabrous hole-of-calcutta kitchen painted this week too; I won't shudder aesthetically every time I enter it then, even if it's frigid. Oh, how I secretly hope that Ted finds America the wonderland I feel it is and wants eventually to settle there---we'd both like a year writing in sunny Italy after one or two teaching, but I would never want to live in England or bring up children here; it is a dead, corrupt country. How I long to get home!

We have gone out twice this week---once to a nice sherry part given by Wendy Christie,[2] a very sweet mother of two children[3] who listens in at my moralist supervisions; her husband[4] died while they were here & she is South African, but staying on because of the good schools; Ted met several old dons of his from Pembroke who were evidently surprised at his change in circumstances---he was considered a wild ruffian in those old days, I guess. Tuesday night we went again to Wendy's for the most delectable dinner imaginable with my dear lovely Dr. Krook, whom Ted met for the first time---just the 4 of us. We ate, drank wine, sherry, tea & coffee, feasted on chicken, rice & nut casserole, feathery breads, chocolate mousse & talked till 3 am. Then Wendy drove us all home in a dense wet blue moon-fog. Our manuscripts all hang fire. Best love to you & dear

1–Unitarian Universalist minister William Brooks Rice (1905–70) and his wife Elizabeth Lindsey Rice.

2–Margaret Wendy (Campbell) Christie (1921–2009); friend of Dorothea Krook and SP from Cambridge. Christie lived at 8 Harvey Street, Cambridge.

3–Sarah Christie Bellwood and Jonathan Christie.

4–Stuart Murray Heys Christie (1917–54); married on 31 July 1943 in Johannesburg, South Africa.

Warrie & grampy this Christmas. Next Christmas, joy of joys, Ted & I will be with you at last to celebrate. How I love your newsy letters---they're good as plum-cakes! Take good care of yourself. I want to come home to a fat, rosy mummy!

Love,
Sivvy

The cookies are delectable! What's your recipe for oatmeal & raisin cookies?

TO *Warren Plath*

Thursday 20 December 1956 TLS (photocopy), Indiana University

December 20th

Dearest Warren . . .

Best (and probably belated) Christmas wishes. I really felt how much I miss you when I heard the the thunder and crackle of your voice over the phone on the 9th---about all we could manage to hear of you; you seemed to be murmuring something about "up the street" & we are still dying of curiosity to know what it was. Ted & I sent you a trifle to cheer exam period, but it will now no doubt arrive next month sometime.

I was so proud of the announcements[1] of your Phi Beta Kappa award. It simply means much more convenience in writing for applications---you just need to mention that & fine records are assumed. Let us know the minute you hear about your fellowship results. I know the Fulbright prefers people who have not been abroad before, so don't think it's anything but that if it doesn't work out; with your record, I don't see how they can refuse you!

We'll also be so interested to hear about your summer plans---ideally, Ted & I would like to spend the months of July & August on the Cape, but as mother says, it is so expensive it is prohibitive. If we could get in the Spaulding's[2] place, we'd have to have a car or two bikes. Unless we sell Ted's book of children's fables (which is a real possibility if the Atlantic Monthly Press likes the re-write he is working on this vacation) or I sell a

1–'Warren J. Plath, Harvard Senior, A Phi Beta Kappa', *The Townsman* (29 November 1956): 3.

2–Myrtle and Lester Spaulding; proprietors of Hidden Acres, a cottage colony on McKoy Road in Eastham, Mass. SP and TH stayed in one of the Spauldings' cabins during the summer of 1957.

story to a Woman's magazine, we'd have to make other plans. I'd like to stay at home for a couple of weeks maybe, but no more than that. We're so used to living independently now, it's a strain not being ourselves---our program is so rigorous & depends on our own idiosyncrasies. Perhaps, if we both by then have got teaching jobs---ideally, again, Ted teaching creative writing at Harvard (he's applying on the off-chance---they don't require Phds for that) & me somewhere like Tufts, or maybe even Smith-Amherst---lord knows now---we could move into our new house, wherever it is, & get settled there. I'll be so relieved when that's worked out.

Our front room is really comfortable now---it is big with 3 windows, a cot, comfortable couch, large working table, small bookcase & fruit stand & our monumental homemade bookcase which covers half of one wall; all dark brown woods, light blue walls & sunshiny yellow pillows, lampshades, etc. Even the coal fire won't warm the whole room, though, on coldest days & nights, so I keep on the movable electric fire by my blue toes & fingers while I work. The kitchen, a little dank cell smelling suspiciously of mushrooms (which no doubt sprout in the pots overnight) is a hole-in-the-wall full of drafty doors to the hall, pantry, coal-shed & outside backyard; it is always freezing, except when I cook a roast dinner, & then the steam warms it a bit. If we scrub it and paint walls & ceiling a light airy blue & I cover surfaces with red & white checked oil-cloth I should at least enjoy working in it; we hope to get it done before Christmas. I sometimes feel like taking a hatchet & going out like the old foolish knights to slay the Cold. I picture a transparent bluish villainous character with a blowtorch of ice, a north windy voice & numerous instruments of contracting torture. When you walk from room to room without wincing & chattering at home, count your blessings! But it is amazing what the human frame can weather. I wear several sweaters, wool socks & slippers & slacks continually. Funny, how one discounts America's material conveniences when living in the midst of them with a lordly intellectual air---oh, I'm above such things! I know I did. But here it wastes so much energy just coping with Cold and Dirt. Dust is older & thicker than British history. Poor Ted gets such sneezing fits in the morning---like yours---I'm sure it's an allergy of some sort. But in spite of these rough conditions, we work hard & thrive. My whole life has a purpose now, and even when I'm tired or going through a barren spell writing, I can have the pleasure & comfort of sharing Ted's kindness & work. We are growing more and more curious about the 20 manuscripts we have out---they seem out much longer than usual & suspense is mounting. At last I have found someone else who is pathologically avid to hear the gate-latch click & who recognizes the mailman's steps a mile off! Wish us luck. We are looking so forward to sailing June 20th & I hope the 4 of us can be close together most of the summer.

Do write! We long to hear from you!

Much love –

Sivvy

1957

TO *Aurelia Schober Plath*

Wednesday 2 January 1957 TLS (aerogramme), Indiana University

<SP wrote 'No. 1' and 'No. 2' on the address side of these letters; the postmark is present on No. 1, indicating the second letter was enclosed.>

January 2, 1957
Wednesday

Dearest darling mother . . .

Happy New Year! I hope the reason we haven't heard from you since Christmas isn't the same as ours for not writing---Ted and I both caught miserable winter colds on the long gruelling trip back here from Yorkshire ---a nasty series of short train trips, two hour waits in unheated stations, and stiff sitting. First he came down, then me, and I just stopped the wet sneezy excruciating stage this morning and am now convalescing & feeling much much better; Ted went to get me a nosedrop prescription yesterday ---all the care one finds here is a prescription for weak useless drops, an inhaling fluid Sue Weller[1] (who is staying at Cambridge a week or two) says they prescribed in 1890, less help, & the suggestion to come back in a week if not feeling better. Ha. Sue & I reminisced yesterday about dear Smith infirmary[2] with their three-pill quick cure, which immediately dries the nose-tissues, cuts pain & twitching, and gives a buoyant surge out of depression. Well, enough griping; the next three months are the grimmest, but at least I have the house all fixed up & the heating relatively good; heat & food are the two things I refuse to economize on. Now, I have got my Anglo-phobia out, for the brighter side:

First: if only you could have seen Ted & me opening our presents! It is, we feel, as if you had been secretly listening to all our out-loud wishes

1–Susan Weller Burch (1933–90); B.A. 1956, economics, Smith College; B.A. 1958, philosophy, politics, and economics, Somerville College, Oxford; SP's housemate at Lawrence House.

2–The Elizabeth Mason Infirmary, 69 Paradise Road, Northampton, Mass.

this past month & filled them to the letter! I was debating whether to write you about a warm nightgown (you can imagine what the atrocities are like here!) & I can hardly bear to get out of the warm silky lovely aqua robe which matches our walls---I swish around in the luxurious full-length skirts feeling very grand. I think the package with all the many presents was our very favorite! I have been dancing around the house, using the polishing-duster, the dish cloths, the oven regulator thermometer (a blessing especially for baking) & the marvelous meat-thermometer, which did a shoulder of lamb perfectly over the weekend ---Sue came Sunday, is staying in a rooming house nearby & studying; she is engaged to be married to a nice boy Whitney Bolton,[1] a Princeton Phd & former Fulbright, Ted's age (but very nervous & rather weak in health) who is finishing his navy stint now; I am so glad, for it makes it easier to talk to Sue; his mother[2] is one of the associate editors at Doubleday, his father[3] a well-known New York play critic, his step-mother[4] a Broadway actress; and with all this, Sue's stupid family won't approve or come to a wedding because he is half Jewish! Well. I am so happy about Ted's just fitting into our family so naturally. Ted is overjoyed about the shaving set; I myself have never seen anything so beautiful---& the sumptuous monograms. He just threw away all his old things & is using it daily. The darling one has just never had anything nice; I got him some beautiful brown felt wool-lined slippers, a fountain-pen, socks,& ourselves some books & two giant pottery coffee mugs good for soup etc. He gave me a lovely scented powder & the most gorgeous big black mohair shawl-stole which feels warm as feathery-fur. We went up to Yorkshire the day before Christmas, bringing a duck & some sweets & scarves for Ted's parents; Ted's mother had a heart-attack a month ago because of high blood pressure due to overweight, but looked fine. Ted & I cooked the Christmas dinner---my first roast duck, which I stuffed with mashed potatoes '& onion & basted with orange juice; very good. Dear thoughtful Ira Scott[5] sent us a huge SS Pierce[6] box of delicacies---I was delighted: maple sugar (which Ted had never tasted & made me homesick it was so delicious), jams, pickled peaches & sweet

1–W. F. (Whitney French) Bolton (1930–); B.A. 1951, Bard College; Ph.D. 1954, Princeton University. Bolton and Weller married on 18 August 1957.
2–Bolton's biological mother was Frances Schiff Bolton.
3–Whitney Bolton (1900–69).
4–American actress Nancy Coleman (1912–2000).
5–Ira O. Scott, Jr (1918–2002), American; instructor at Harvard University, 1953–5; dated SP, summer 1954.
6–S. S. Pierce was a grocery store in Boston and Brookline, Mass.

watermelon pickle, cheese crackers, & even a tin of crepe suzettes! I felt like a refugee marvelling over a Care package. Both Dot & grampy sent $10 each (do thank them so---I'll write a note soon), Mrs. Prouty the $25 check I sent you to deposit; dear Aunt Helen[1] $2. I'll write them all, but do thank them if you see them. How did the TV program go? I hope you got our card in time, & Warren. Have our presents to each of you come yet? Let us know if you like any of the pictures. I spent the whole week before Christmas shopping & writing about 25 Christmas letters. Whew. Now, after this cold, I hope to have no hindrance for the next two weeks of intense writing & study before term begins. I am gradually coming to cope with practical business without too much effort---a grocer delivers stock supplies once a week; we have our own butcher (only regular customers get the good cuts), milk is delivered every day, & I have just started to use a laundry service for sheets & Ted's shirts; it's a 3-mile round-trip bike ride to the one town Bendix laundromat in town & nothing dries in our kitchen & ironing takes too much time with my academic schedule; so it will be a load off my work---I still take all little things, towels, socks, underwear etc. to the laundromat. I just discovered that the British currency is simply not exchangeable into dollars---it is almost a dictatorial prohibition for Britishers to travel to the USA---we're going to find out how much Ted is allowed to bring over. But with all our big bills---visa (£9), ship-fare (£72), packing costs, etc., we shouldn't have to worry about anything left over in pounds; however, we don't want to lose any precious dollars by changing them in ££ here & so will send all checks post haste to you to deposit. How much have I in my little bank account now? I've written letters to (continued next letter→)

xx

Sivvy

(continued)

Hello again!

As I was saying, I've written letters to ask if there would be a chance for us to apply for a position teaching freshman English next year---I've written for Ted to Harvard & Amherst (& I think may also try Brandeis & Tufts) & for myself to Smith, Radcliffe, Jackson[2] & Brandeis. I do hope something works out; I realize what competition one is in for Phd candidates with teaching experience are increasing yearly; will you

1–Possibly Helen M. Corcoran, whose address appears in SP's 1955 calendar. Corcoran lived at 52 Weld Hill Street, in the Forest Hills district of Boston.

2–The Jackson College for Women was established in 1910 and affiliated with Tufts University; it integrated with the College of Arts and Sciences at Tufts in 1980.

suggest any other places in Massachusetts? If Ted could be considered for the Harvard job teaching creative writing, I wouldn't care where I taught thereabout! The first year is more or less expendable; I'll consider us lucky if we get anything together!

Just before Christmas, Ted & I banded forces for two days to attack the kitchen, which made me shudder each time I walked into it, it was so filthy dirty; we heated tons of hot water, gingerly threw all the filthy dishes & useless trash from the pantry (discovering, o horror, countless spiders) & scrubbed ceiling (where plaster flaked like leprousy), walls, cold stone floors (no basements, so you can imagine how cold!) & got the years accumulation of dirt silted in corners out with a knife. We painted ceiling & walls a lovely light blue, & I got red & white checked oilcloth for all the shelves; with my pots & marvelous new utensils from you hanging up it all looks beautifully hygenic now; we are seeing about a paraffin heater to keep going in it all day.

Now for something very important: we're getting to work on Ted's visa form, which is a terrible nuisance because all documents have to be original with two duplicates, so we have to write off for all of them.. The thing is, will you please be Ted's sponsor? It involves a good deal of red-tape, but I'll copy it all here.

He has neither personal funds nor yet an assured job to prove he won't be a "charge" on America, so the only alternative is to have an American sponsor. Here are the items to be included, everything IN DUPLICATE:

Affidavits of Support: "There is no prescribed form for an affidavit of support other than that it be a statement (IN DUPLICATE) sworn to before a notary public. However, in order to assist the sponsor, there is suggested below the information he may wish to include in his affidavit. Each item should be FULLY covered, using complete sentences.

1. Sponsor's full name and address, place and date of birth, present marital and citizenship status and number of dependents.

2. Applicant's name and address. (Ted's)

3. Sponsor's statement guaranteeing the applicant's support, should the need arise, until the applicant becomes an American citizen or permanently departs from the United States, whichever is sooner, & giving the reason why he is willing to undertake such obligation (relationship, friendship, etc.)

4. Information concerning the sponsor's occupation & salary, & value of real estate, bank deposits, bonds, insurance policies & other assets such as car, furniture, etc.

5. If the sponsor is planning to marry the applicant he should state that the is legally free to marry. (Not applicable!)

Also: EVIDENCE OF SPONSOR'S FINANCIAL RESOURCES Important: The sponsor, in addition to the affidavit, should furnish evidence of the value of his assets as proof that he is financially able to support the applicant if the need arises. Such evidence should be in DUPLICATE & should preferably be of the types described below:

Types of Assets: prefered evidence, in DUPLICATE:

1) Income: Certified copy of latest income tax return, or employer's statement indicating salary and length and permanency of employment

2) Bank deposits, stock & bonds: Bank official's or stock broker's statement indicating bank balance and when account opened & present market value of any bonds or stocks.

3). Real estate: Real estate agent's statement indicating value of equity in real estate.

4). Insurance: Insurance agent's statement indicating policies cash surrender value.

Whew! That's that! We realize it's a terrible bother, but would appreciate it so if you would help us out on it as soon as possible. Remember to write Ted's name fully as EDWARD JAMES HUGHES the whole time. (He is not a junior; his parents are The William Hughes).

Actually, I am most happy at last, settled down, in spite of my eagerness to be back in my beloved New England; how lucky I am to be married to such a kind, handsome wonderful person, though; I don't know what I would have done through this 2nd year alone! We share our thoughts continually on our most intense interests, all we read, write & think; how much closer we must be than couples where the man has a business job he wants to forget when he comes home, or one the woman understands nothing about! Ted is so appreciative about my cooking it makes kitchen work a joy; we have steak fish-in-milk; rich vegetable stews; marvellous Italian spaghetti with meat-sauce; pork & sweet breads, fruit all the time heaped on the sideboard (we take your super-vitamins religiously). But I can't wait to make him cakes, feathery pies, broiled chicken, parfaits etc etc. Do write; I hope you are well after the strain of Christmas preparations; take good care of yourself; we look so forward to coming home.

much love –
your own
Sivvy

TO *Aurelia Schober Plath*

Wednesday 9 January 1957 TLS (aerogramme), Indiana University

Wednesday night
January 9, 1957

Dearest darling mother . . .

It was so wonderful to get your rich, newsy letter yesterday, the same day your cable came. I look so forward to hearing from you, and read the letters aloud to Ted, & over & over to myself, that I am very sensitive to "expecting" them, and couldn't understand why I hadn't heard a word for such a long period over a time where it seemed to me you would have much news. I saw from the postmark of your letter---Jan. 1,---that it took the unprecedented time of a week by airmail, where it's usually only 4 days. Anyway, I was so happy to hear all about your wonderful festivities that I forgot my previous concern.

One thing you didn't mention, though---the TV program. Did it come off all right? I am also dying with eagerness to get my copy of the Atlantic Monthly. I didn't know my poem had come out till I got your letter, and after my sharing my wish to get into the Atlantic with Nat LaMar[1] last year at Cambridge, I am overjoyed to be in the same issue with his story:[2] the first page of which I read last year in the process---I also saw him the day it was accepted. My 6 poems in Poetry (Chicago) should also come out this month, so look them up. The magazines will undoubtedly be sending me copies regular mail, so don't you bother. I am so impatient with this overseas mail delay, I'll be overjoyed to get back home & be in the thick of things again.

As I write, the livingroom is lovely and warm with the coal fire, which I've kept going all day. Teddy is sitting nearby reading American history, after a delicious dinner of cheese, tuna and macaroni casserole, red wine, pineapple & heavy cream. It has been a very happy day--Ted got his first acceptance from a British magazine, Nimbus, this morning, of one or two poems[3]---they haven't selected the exact titles yet. It has a very impressive format, like the Atlantic, but, the editor says, was on the brink of failing. Naturally we hope & pray it sticks together long enough for

1–Nathaniel D. LaMar, Jr (1933–), American; A.B. 1955, Harvard College; research student on a Henry Fellowship at Pembroke College, Cambridge, 1955–6; dated SP, 1955–6.

2–Nathaniel LaMar, 'Miss Carlo', *Atlantic Monthly*, January 1957, 61–4.

3–There are no publications of TH's poems in *Nimbus* listed in his bibliography. No Hughes poems were found in the issues consulted by the editors.

Ted's poems to come out. But the very interested acceptance gave us both a gay mood. We work really hard, and the British magazines have hitherto ignored us both continually. However, the planets point to a magnificently successful year for us both, & we will work to make it come true. Ted has me memorizing a poem a day, which is very good for me,[1] and we are working out a schedule of going to bed at 10, getting up at 6, and writing two hours steadily before Ted bikes off to work (he started teaching his little thieves again this Monday). This way we accomplish much, and Ted feels his job isn't taking all his writing time. We are both "early morning" people, & need about the same amount of sleep. Term starts for me next week, so I am cramming reading for it. I didn't have a chance to write all last term, so am working on two love stories for the women's magazines: one set, I hope originally, in a laundromat;[2] the other a college girl story about someone like Nancy Hunter.[3] I will slave & slave until I break into those slicks. My sense of humor should be good for something. This next week I hope to type the revision of Ted's childrens fables & the poems I will send off to the Yale Series of Younger Poets. Sue Weller has been in Cambridge a week, just left today, so I have been feeding her cheese omelets, roast beefs, sherry, etc., trying to cheer her up---she is very lugubrious, rather depressive anyway, but especially so about her boyfriend's being in duty in the navy this year & having to postpome their intended marriage indefinitely. I feel so happy, I was almost feeling guilty talking to her. Ted & I sometimes have violent disagreements, to be sure, but we are so very joyous together & have such identical aims and expectations of our lives, that we never have conflict over any serious issues. I really don't know how I existed before I met Ted. I can't imagine spending a day without him---he is so kind and loving and appreciative of my cooking that I delight in trying new things for him. He is also very strictly disciplining about my study and work. It couldn't be better. I'm so glad you like the art book. What fun we'll having coming home to our little house & listening to the records & looking at pictures, & cooking delectable meals. Except for a week or two being very social, Ted & I really must hibernate for the rest of the summer, writing furiously & preparing our teaching courses---if we have jobs! Which brings me to another favor to ask you. I have written to Jackson (of Tufts), Brandeis,

1–According to SP's calendar, on 9 January she memorised 'The Equilibrists' by John Crowe Ransom.

2–Sylvia Plath, 'The Laundromat Affair'; an incomplete copy held by Emory University.

3–Nancy Hunter Steiner (1933–2006); B.A. 1955, history, Smith College; SP's friend and roommate at Lawrence House, 1954–5.

Smith & Radcliffe for myself; no answers yet, except a letter from this Herschel Baker,[1] Chairman of the Eng. Dept. at Harvard (I sent the letter to Radcliffe) saying "this department teaches only advanced courses" & so there will be no jobs available for freshman English. Now there must be a freshman English program at Radcliffe (maybe there isn't, on 2nd thought, but that seems strange). Could you find out if there is, & if so, the name & address of whom I should write to?? Also, see if you can find out about "opinions" of Brandeis & Jackson. Waltham & Medford I suppose would mean commuting, if we lived in Cambridge. Is there anywhere else you'd suggest applying? I will really be glad when we get this settled. Of course we can always be bartender & waitress if worst comes to worst, but I hope it won't. Hope you can get Ted's visa duplicate affadavits of support without too much annoyance on your part. Ted joins me in sending much love---to you, Warren & dear Grampy---

love,
Sivvy

TO *Aurelia Schober Plath*

Monday 14 January 1957 — TLS with envelope, Indiana University

Monday noon
January 14, 1957

Dearest mother . . .

It has been so wonderful to get your long, newsy letters---I realize how much I miss being in the center of things at home by the way I eat up every speck of news: if Libby Aldrich tied a red ribbon in her hair, for example, I should be fascinated to hear about it! It sounds so strange to hear you talk about blizzards. Imagine, we haven't had a flake of snow yet! Just rain and freezing clear blue weather---our worst season of sleet is just coming up---February & howling March. We are buying a paraffin portable heater from the people upstairs when they go this next week for about £4, so at last my deep-freeze of a kitchen should be pleasant---I'll keep the heater going all day.

Both Ted and I are very excited about the Royal Standard you bought, and overjoyed. We need a heavy big machine so badly---we type all day.

1–Higginson Professor Emeritus of English literature at Harvard University Herschel Clay Baker (1914–90).

Now could you tell me roughly from what price to what price I could ask for my Smith Corona? I thought we'd advertise for it through private sale as we could probably ask much more than to a typewriter-buying firm. Do let me know.

We'll take the proofs down to have 4 developed this week. I hope you are able to send us all the visa statements without too much trouble and annoyance. It is such a bother, but we have all the other documents here now, and would like to get the mammoth batch off by the end of the month if possible.

I'm enclosing a check for $75 for my six poems in Poetry this month ---neither of my magazines have come, and as these are the first poems I've had published for over a year and a half, I am very eager to see how they look.

Term begins officially tomorrow, and classes Thursday, so I must cram down a few books before then. Wrote two longer, more ambitious poems of about 50 lines each[1] this weekend and feel much better having broken my dry spell of this fall term, which was due to my disturbing practical concerns. Now, I am so happy in our cheerful front room & cooking in my little light blue kitchen, I really feel deeply peaceful at the center. Ted is an angel, and understands me so well & is so dear about my writing that I keep pinching myself to be sure it is all true---we have everything---health, books, talent & ambition & love---all but money, and I hope we get a little more of that to make things less hand-to-mouth. I am convinced Ted is the one person in the world I could ever have married; it is simply impossible to describe how strong, and kind of fun-loving and brilliant he is.

Your papering & painting about the house sounds magnificent: I can't wait to see it all: our house seems the most beautiful palace to me now. I hope, by the way, that you are still taking me off your income tax--- I believe you can do so by simply saying I'm at a university.

Warren wrote the dearest letter---about how he'd been to talk to the head of the Harvard English dept. They seem to run a closed shop, with Phd. candidates teaching sections, but I got a letter suggesting I write to this Prof. Bate[2] in spring, although they said any vacancies were extremely unlikely. About the Michigan prospect---I simply don't know how I could stand being away from home and friends again, in that cold climate, too---they say it's worse than England. Should I bother to write

1–Probably Sylvia Plath, 'The Snowman on the Moor' and 'Sow'.
2–A. Kingsley Porter University Professor Emeritus at Harvard University Walter Jackson Bate (1918–99).

if I really don't want to go there? One of us should get a teaching job in New England, and the other can always do some different kind of work if absolutely necessary. Cambridge looks like the best center---there are so many colleges around. I probably said before I have applied for myself at Jackson & Brandeis & Radcliffe & Smith---but the last two seem highly dubious: Radcliffe with no openings, & my not really wanting to go back to Smith for my first year until I've proved myself elsewhere---the situation would be too emotionally complicated. If Ted got a job at Amherst, I would consider it in a more favorable light, however. I haven't heard from Mr. Kazin[1] yet about answering my Xmas note asking for the name & address of the head of the Eng. Dept. to write to Amherst there. Could you find it out for me---? It would no doubt be better & quicker than depending on a busy man like Mr. K. Also, should I write to Tufts & Brandeis for Ted also? Could we commute there from Cambridge? Commuting is the problem---I believe those colleges are in Waltham & Medford respectively. I think of you as in the heart of Boston teaching world & maybe you could help by sending just one or two names of heads of departments of any places I haven't thought of---Warren said something about the boys' prep school, Brown & Nichols[2]---maybe you could write me the name & addresses of whatever boys' prep schools are in or very near Cambridge.

On second thought, should I apply for the teaching job in Michigan for both of us? Can't one always refuse? Of course, I don't know the protocol of accepting & refusing, or deadlines for applying either. Another place that occurred to me is the Univ. of Connecticut---isn't that better than most state universities. I don't want to be stuck with mere grammar---I don't mind themes at all, but a place like Mass. State I'd abhor. Ideally, if we could get a job on the East Coast this coming year, we could apply for jobs at one of the great Californian universities the next year & take a tour of the States in the summer, which I've always wanted to do, & with Ted & both of us sharing the new sights it would be marvelous. But I am already so homesick that I don't know how I could teach so far away from home as the U. of Michigan this year! I want to be able to come home for Thanksgiving, Christmas & Easter. We'll be travelling around the world enough, later on, hoping after two years of teaching to have a year writing in Italy, if one of us could get a writing grant.

1–Alfred Kazin (1915–98); William Allan Neilson Research Professor, Smith College, 1954–5. Kazin taught short story writing (English 347) and the twentieth-century novel (English 417), completed by SP 1954–5.
2–Now Buckingham, Browne & Nichols, a day school in Cambridge, Mass.

Anyway, let me know any advice or information you manage to unearth. Ted's teaching experience this year should help him if he applied to a boys' prep school, & we hope he may get a job teaching two nights a week at an American army base near here---it's said to be very lucrative. Well, I must be off to shop. My best love to you, and Ted sends his, too.

Love,
Sivvy

TO *Aurelia Schober Plath*

Saturday 19 January 1957 — TLS (aerogramme), Indiana University

Saturday afternoon
January 19, 1957

Dearest mother . . .

Your lovely plump pink letter came this morning & I read it aloud to Ted over coffee. We both enjoy every word you write so much. I don't know how you manage all you are doing---teaching, home-making, studying,---and am so grateful you will take on the additional bother about those verified forms. I took the proofs to be made up last week, but it will probably take 3 weeks to get them sent off. Don't worry, by the way, about the paraffin heater: we only use it in the kitchen, and it stands in the middle of the stone floor like a little flaming island on the polar cap. Ted supervises our using it, so it's perfectly safe. I am so glad Ted is such a practical man-about-the-house---much like Frank: he twists a wire here, a knob there, and we have a victrola working, a bed-lamp for reading, like magic.

I really feel much livelier & healthier since I've been taking those Supercap pills! We'd welcome more, with the coryza (what are they, by the way?---like anti-histamine? better tell us the directions) because I can "feel a cold coming on" but have nothing to fight it with here. The British "Excellent Remedy For Colds & Influenza" is so much chalk powder: I took them by the dozen & almost perished with mean twitchy sneezes & sleepless days. Ted & I really hope to avoid more colds---they're so undermining, and now the bad months are coming February & March. You take good care, though. Don't risk anything of your health, no matter what. And don't shovel snow. I am aghast at your accounts of the blizzards---we still haven't had a flake---only blue frosts. I am so glad you're playing the piano[1]---it's such a peaceful, releasing act, isn't it?

Why don't you take lessons this summer---just for your own pleasure. There's such a feeling of accomplishment when one masters a new piece. We're fascinated to hear about food prices in America---I have absolutely No Idea about living costs. Also, please give me some ideas of your salary, & what salaries for beginning teachers are like. /3 thousand? 7 thousand? What? Our rent for the flat is only $12 a week: what are rates in America? I have a few straw mats in the kitchen which make it bearable to stand on. Ted loves casseroles, so I make them to alternate with our steak and roast beef days: shrimp, peas & rice, or corn, tomatoes & eggs. My Joy of Cooking[2] is a blessing & so is the oven thermometer, measuring cups, spoons, etc. I use them joyously every day. Chicken is out because it is a luxury here---you should see the scrawny, bony "boiling" chickens that appear in butchers windows---how I miss our lovely delicate toasty golden-brown fryers!

About teaching jobs: I don't have the Lovejoy catalogue[3] here with me, so am utterly at a loss for names & addresses of universities. It was such a relief to hear in your letter more names than I'd thought of---but please, do try to look up the Chairman of the English Dept., the college address, for me, & send them off. Do investigate about B.U. (but dont try to use pull), Simmons, Mt. Holyoke, & especially Haverford & Swarthmore ---names & addresses of these (I'd forgotten all about Pennsylvania!) I'll write for both Ted & myself in one letter, for jobs for either or both of us ---they may want a man, or they may prefer an American graduate. In any case, if you could look up the address info in the B.U. libe or somewhere, & send them, I'll get letters off right away. I haven't heard from Smith, but Mary Ellen Chase had just arrived in Cambridge, so she'll be able to enlighten me about chances there---actually, I'd much rather avoid the emotional ambivalence about joining the Smith faculty my first year teaching & be at a place where I'm new & in a simple business position. Do let me know the names & addresses of the places I've mentioned, & any more you can think of. I've already heard negatively from Brandeis & Radcliffe doesn't hire outside their Phd candidates, although they suggested I write Prof. Bate this spring. What you must understand is that

1–The Plaths had an upright piano, manufactured by Roberts & Co. of Boston, in their living room.

2–American cookbook author Irma von Starkloff Rombauer (1877–1962), her *The Joy of Cooking* (New York: The Bobbs-Merrill Company, 1953). SP's copy, with numerous annotations, appeared at auction via Bonhams on 21 March 2018.

3–Clarence E. Lovejoy edited *Lovejoy's Career and Vocational School Guide* published by Simon & Schuster.

Ted does not want to be a university professor for a career. He wants to write, now & for the rest of his life. And in marrying a writer, I accept his life. For teaching, it is plainly necessary to have a Phd. at university level, unless you're rare, like Alfred Kazin & have written a mountain of critical work. Ted has no desire to do any more academic work---although he has the most brilliant mind I know, & gave me a rich, vivid picture of literary history from Chaucer's day to this, he'll only teach if they'll take him on his publishing & Cantab. M.A. So the American dream of a secure sinecure writing on campus seems out for our future life. I find it best not to argue---Ted is so understanding about my need to get a self-respecting teaching job in America & "give out" & eager to teach anywhere he can himself for a year or two. He wants to go to Italy for a year then, & teach English in Europe in the language schools. Writing comes first with both of us, and although Wilbur[1] & some large amounts of other writers find their plums in the academic world, Ted just doesn't want to spend years getting necessary degree qualifications when he should be writing hardest. And my faith in him & the way we two want to live understands this. He may change his mind if he likes America enough---but I'll wait & see. I know Ted's mind is magnificent, not hair-splitting or suavely politic---but employers may find Phd's more convincing. Whatever we do we're together – & that & writing makes our joy. Don't want to be far off in Michigan – do write Chairmen's names & univ. addresses.

much love –

Sivvy

<on the return address side of letter>

PS: Double-bed size sheets; white, aqua & perhaps big white & black diamonded towels like Cantor's.

TO *Aurelia Schober Plath*

Monday 28 January 1957 TLS (aerogramme), Indiana University

Monday morning
January 28, 1957

Dearest mother . . .

It is just after 8:30 . . . Ted's biked off for work, and I am preparing for a day of intense Chaucer reading. At 11 I have coffee with Mary Ellen

1–American poet Richard Wilbur (1921–2017).

Chase---the first chance I'll have had to talk with her since her arrival about two weeks ago, and I hope to get a reliable picture of teaching prospects, at least in New England. From the reception of the few letters I've sent off---to Radcliffe, Tufts, & Brandeis, I don't believe America needs any teachers at all; they all "have no positions" open next year & will keep letters on active file, which no doubt means as penwipers or something equivalent. I am so eager to have you write me the addresses of places like Swarthmore & other places in Pennsylvania & Connecticut ---my hands are tied until I get a list from you, and I feel so cut off from everything---unable to arrange interviews, etc. I would rather be an office typist in New England than teach in Michigan. I just want to be in New England for a year---otherwise, we might as well apply for jobs teaching with the Univ. of Maryland program at army bases overseas. Please send me the address of Holyoke, etc. Should I bother applying at Wellesley? They have Wilbur & Philip Booth[1] as poets already. Ted will have teaching experience & a matured MA from Cambridge, & me only two Ba's and no teaching experience, and a few scattered published poems, so, brilliant and rare as we are, how can we hope to compete either with the regulation Phd-experienced people or the 10-books-of-poetry-published people??? Heaven knows. Also, when do faculties decide their final lists of teachers? Surely not 8 months ahead? I feel it would be a very great strain for me trying to teach at Smith even if the miracle happened and they wanted to employ me, which they probably wouldn't consider unless I got a First degree here or something. Well, I'll talk all that over with Miss Chase. Also, what's this I hear about "nepotism"---the habit of not employing relatives (eg, husbands & wives) on the same university staff? I don't know whether I should apply for Ted & me in the same letter or in two separate letters. Please, rush the names of those other colleges in Penn, & Conn. so I can at least feel I've written as many places as possible. These jobs refusals plus a pile of rejections (of really fine poems, too) are enough to make me think the teaching profession is run by slick closed-shop businessmen and the literary magazines by jealous scared over-cerebral fashion-conscious idiots. Our problem is that we are primarily writers (and very far from being established or earning) and only secondarily academic (and not desiring the sure fire cure of Phd & postponing life ad infinitum or being "household" poets). It is only too easy for me to convince myself that I haven't read anything and don't know anything; I'd like to have at least one year of teaching to get rid of

1–American poet Philip Booth (1925–2007).

this strange need I have to prove I can support myself by doing something I like, or, relatively, prefer about other jobs. I'm sick, for now, anyway, of living on grants & being a perpetual student. I'll put in a concentrated effort this spring on stories for the women's magazines; that would be a break, & I've never worked at it---when you think of the years it takes to make a doctor, expecting success posthaste in writing "or I'll give it up" is ridiculous. Both Ted & I depend on writing & could never give it up, even if we never published another line all our lives. Ted is so magnificent & understanding about my writing & study & needs & I too feel so close to him, it is a blessing. I can't conceive how I ever lived without him; no wonder I was dissatisfied with men: there isn't a brain I know that can match his, and all the intelligent or so-called brilliant men from the best east colleges are either narrow old-maids or sick malicious ninnies. Ted has such a huge, uncompromising generosity and large scope & stern discipline it can hardly be contained in the safe narrow molds---marking time at a job so ten years later you'll be an associate instead of an assistant. And I am so gloriously glad to find a rugged kind magnificent man, who has no scrap of false vanity or tendency to toady to inferior strategic officials that I am only too willing to accept the attendant temporary uncertainties. Only I feel that in America, of all countries, there should be a place for us both. Our rejections make, by contrast, people like Editor Weeks, the editor of Poetry & the Nation,[1] seem like large worthy guardian angels. Writing is first for us both. I'm typing Ted's revised fables & my 40 poems these next two weekends, then working on women's stories & he on a play. Maybe after a year or 2 in America we'll get a job with the U. of Maryland overseas---we just talked to a couple who've been transferred from Germany to England & the schedule is perfect for writing---four 3-hour evening classes a week! Concentrated, but that's all to the good. What, by the way, are beginning teacher salaries like? 2 thousand? 5 thousand? I have no idea. Your wonderful package of food-mixes arrive this Sat. by the way, & I was happier than with anything so far: within half an hour I have a hot lunch of corn-muffins & pea soup ready, & am dying to try the cake mixes. Ted would be so happy to have a job that's more than policing & discipline; we're lucky he has anything, & it will give another vacation, but it does tire him. We love all the things you've sent: the roast thermometer does meat perfectly ---I'd never know what was "done" in my crazy oven! Had shoulder of

1 – The poetry editor for *The Nation* at this time was American poet and critic M. L. (Macha Louis) Rosenthal (1917–96).

lamb yesterday, breaded plaice with mushroom & parsley sauce before. Vitamins are a great help.

Do write soon – much love to you & dear Warren –

Sivvy

TO *Aurelia Schober Plath*

Tuesday 29 January 1957 TLS (aerogramme), Indiana University

Tuesday morning
January 29, 1957

Dearest mother . . .

It is just about 9.30, and I am waiting for the butcher delivery before biking off to the University library to study. Your two letters came this morning, & thank you for the addresses (the grocery box & vitamins have come). I was terribly distressed to hear about your large devastating bout with the dentist & the coming work: why didn't you know about it sooner---you mentioned you had that other dentist while Dr. Gilmore[1] was ill---was he worse or better? And why should you have infections? I only hope they will give you the proper anesthetics---insist on that, and that it will not be painful. You <u>must</u> look at it as an investment to your own peace of mind & safe future. We all love you so & Ted & I are concerned only that you get completely fixed up. Don't regard your teeth as an indication of age, as if less teeth put you in another age group! Just imagine: when Ted's mother was a blooming young girl working in the wool mills, she overhead someone saying: "If Edith only had straight teeth, she'd be the prettiest girl in the factory." Well, Edith went right to the dentist, had all her teeth extracted, and a set of straight, artificial teeth put in! From what you say, you won't have to have everything extracted: but do what's best. I can sympathize so keenly: if you'd had your braces put in in this day and age, you no doubt wouldn't have this trouble. But you must grit your teeth (on the dentist's fingers, if necessary) & go through with the ordeal. You will feel so much better when it is done. Keep me posted. Plan little treats for yourself after each time---a play, or reading a new book---the way you did for Warren & me when we were little. Ted is so understanding & concerned, too; he says the dentist that saved his mouth last spring told him for a "perfect job" he'd have to make a bridge

1–Dr George Gilmore.

to fill Ted's 3 noticeable cavities where teeth are missing, & that the price was a few hundred pounds for such work; as it is, he knocked £5 or £6 off Ted's bill & saved 3 teeth no British dentist would have saved. So you are in the best hands, in America. I'm taking Ted at the end of the term to London & having both our teeth seen to by this man; the expense now will save it later. We will be home in less than 5 months, & see that you have some fun with us to make up for this ordeal; I only wish I were home now, to make things easier: lay off entertaining while you go through your extractions & don't expect to feel in top form---I know how groggy gas made me when I had my 4 teeth out. And be glad you had Europe! If Ted & I get to Italy in a couple of years, we will expect you to come & visit us, so don't consider it your last fling by any means.

My coffee session with Miss Chase yesterday took several black loads off my mind. First, about my worries over competing with people who have doctorates: "You & Ted would be crazy to get doctorates!" were her very words. She said they figured grad school grind in America would kill me, so "they sent me to Cambridge." I gather "they" feel some control over my life which explains Miss Chase's shock when I told her about my coming marriage last spring. They hadn't allowed for love, evidently, and no doubt didn't want to waste their efforts. Well, she said I shouldn't ever think of getting a doctorate: I wasn't going to be a scholar or academic; nor Ted either. Also, wifes & husbands are often hired on the same faculty. They would rather have me have poems & essays published in the Atlantic than a Phd. The indefatigable Miss Chase is finishing a new novel "The Edge of Darkness"[1] about---guess what: life in a Maine fishing village. Well, she claims to have no illusions about being a good novelist, modestly mentioned she could count on at least 75,000 in sales, judging from her White Gate which evidently sold like hotcakes---her two former novels were London Book-of-the-Month club selections, so she covers dear Mrs. Prouty's field. She'd evidently interviewed my tutor & director of studies & instructors here (no doubt to see if marriage & studies went together) & told me not to apply anywhere now until she's written the head of the dept. at Smith---Mr. RG Davis. My main rival, I gather is the other American girl here, Jane Baltzell[2] from Pembroke, a very good-

1–Mary Ellen Chase, *The Edge of Darkness* (New York: W. W. Norton, 1957).

2–Jane Baltzell Kopp (1935–), born in El Paso, Texas; B.A. 1955, Brown University; B.A. 1957, Newnham College, Cambridge; Ph.D. 1965, University of California Berkeley; associate professor of English, University of New Mexico, 1964–70, 1975–81; married American poet Karl C. Kopp, 1969. Jane Baltzell read English on a Marshall Scholarship at Cambridge and was SP's housemate at Whitstead, 1955–6. The Kopps were ordained

looking blonde who has made a fine impression on the British faculty. But Jane is undecided about whether she'll marry an old flame in Japan, so I don't know how it will work out. There will be A Place at Smith next year (a highly-recommended but "dull" Radcliffe-Harvard girl[1] is being dismissed--so much for Radcliffe) & of course the faculty would be concerned, as I am, ironically, about my being "too close" (Jane, you see, would be new to Smith). But my attitude about teaching there has changed. The freshman English program is ideal---only 3 sections, 9 teaching hours a week, and arranged to cover only 3 or 4 consecutive days! Beginners salaries are only about $3,000. But I could write & it would be a terrific chance. They even said, Miss Chase did, that If they offered me an appointment (still dubious, so don't mention it) Ted might very well get one the next year. This year will be hard for him as several interviews are necessary anywhere for a "foreigner." But she suggested various boys prep schools. If Smith falls through, I'm relatively sure she will help us get jobs elsewhere, & her word wields tremendous influence. Forget Babson. BU, et. They want <u>women</u> at Smith, amazingly enough; the faculty is over balanced with men. I want to dazzle the British here with my exams---my only real way of matching them---they ignore writing altogether but still I'm turning in a book of poems as a supplement to my exams.[2] Wish us luck & look in[3] this summer over dentists & all

xxx
Sivvy

TO *Aurelia Schober Plath*

c. Sunday 3 February 1957[4] TLS, Indiana University

55 Eltisley Avenue
Cambridge, England

Dearest mother . . .

So happy to hear you liked our poems---we've garnered a huge batch of rejections this month---many "letters from the editor", but nonetheless

and taught in Advaita Vedanta (an ancient spiritual psychological/philosophical tradition of India).

1–Probably Betty Isobelle Bandeen (1929–2006); M.A. 1950, Ph.D. 1958, Radcliffe College.

2–SP's manuscript of 'Two Lovers and Beachcomber' was submitted as part of her English tripos, II. It was found in early 1969 in the English Faculty Library. A fair copy is held in the Add MS 88589, Alvarez papers, British Library.

3–It is unclear what this word is.

4–Date supplied by ASP.

causing chagrin, so it's pleasant to see even the revival of old things. Get a copy of the February Poetry: Ted has a poem in it! Isn't it strange the way the Atlantic & Poetry both printed me in January & Ted in February. We look forward to the day we both publish in the same magazine. I'm enclosing Ted's check for $14 for the "Drowned Woman" to be deposited in my account, which we'll change to a dual account when I come home.

I'm also enclosing two pictures[1] of Teddy taken on the morning of his graduation from Cambridge---we had them enlarged from a group photo, so they're a little blurry but make him look almost handsome as he really is.

We got the affadavits & thank you a thousand times. I can understand by reading the many various letterheads & signatures just how much time & effort it all must have cost you, but it should bring you home a handsome brilliant wonderful strong son-in-law. I love Teddy more & more each day & just can't imagine how I ever lived without him. Our lives fit together perfectly. He is so helpful and understanding about my studies & has made a huge chart of the English writers & their dates (dating & knowing styles is necessary here and I had nothing of that unfortunately at home) and stuck it up all over one wall of the bedroom where I can learn it.

One more request---I do hate to always be asking things. But we need more / 3cent stamps. It will pay off in the long run, I hope---your 3 cent stamps have got us in the Atlantic, the Nation & Poetry so far. Maybe more before we come home. I had a recent story of mine "The Wishing-Box" published in Granta here this week,[2] very nicely set up---I'll send you a copy when the pictures of Ted & me come back & I send them. I'm also having two rather good poems coming out in March in the new first issue of the Oxford-Cambridge magazine Gemini[3] which has another story of mine scheduled for the May issue[4] and has asked me to review a book of poems[5] by a Classics don at Oxford. I was rather amazed, but will try to do my best.

My Chaucer supervisor is lovely---the 2nd young woman I've really liked at Cambridge:[6] she looks very much like Betty Aldrich, very small & pretty

1–The photographs are no longer with the letter.

2–Sylvia Plath, 'The Wishing Box', *Granta* 61 (26 January 1956): 3–5.

3–Sylvia Plath, 'Spinster' and 'Vanity Fair', *Gemini* 1 (Spring 1957): 6–8.

4–Sylvia Plath, 'All the Dead Dears', *Gemini* 2 (Summer 1957): 53–9.

5–Sylvia Plath, review of C. A. Trypanis, *Stones of Troy*, *Gemini* 2 (Summer 1957): 98–103. C. A. (Constantine Athanasius) Trypanis (1909–93) was a Greek classicist.

6–Middle English scholar and university professor Elizabeth Zeeman (later Salter, 1925–80). According to SP's calendar, the Zeemans lived at 7 Grange Road.

with vital blue eyes---married to a math prof[1] here & just had a baby,[2] and is also a university lecturer---quite versatile & rare for Cambridge. She's invited Ted & me to cocktails next week---with a bunch of other students.

In spite of my grim feeling I must read all of English literature in the next 4 months, Ted keeps me calm & stoically working & in spite of the rejections, I am very happy and alive and writing better poems---a big one about a Sow, about 45 lines & one about "The Lady and the Earthenware Head" which has the best verse I've ever written. Hope I can find a good berth for them somewhere.

It is often infuriating to read the trash published by the Old Guard, the flat, clever, colorless poets here (in America there is, with much bad, much color, life & vigor). I have my fingers crossed that Ted will come to associate America with the growing acceptance and publishing of his writings. England is so stuffy, cliquey and plain bad bad.

Please keep me posted about the work on your teeth: will it be done by the time we come home? Be sure to have a thorough complete job, no matter what the cost. Demand best care. We love you so & will be wishing you to get through this quickly and painlessly as possible. Much much love from us both. Let us know as soon as anything comes through about dearest Warrie. . . .

your own
sivvy

TO *Aurelia Schober Plath*

Friday 8 February 1957 — TLS (aerogramme), Indiana University

<SP wrote 'No. 1' on address side of letter>

Friday morning
February 8, 1957

Dearest mother . . .

It is just 10:30 and I am fresh from a morning walk through the meadows to Granchester. The sun is flooding into our livingroom, the birds chirruping, and all is wet, melted, and spring smelling. We still have had no snow here! I wish I could describe the beautiful walk--- I set off after Ted left & I had cleaned up the house, and met not a soul.

1–Mathematician and university professor Sir Erik Christopher Zeeman (1925–2016). The Zeemans divorced *c.* 1959–60.

2–Middle English scholar and university professor Nicolette Zeeman (1956–).

I tramped over a mud-puddled path, through a creaky crooked wooden stile, and strode along---meadows shining bright silver-wet in the sun, and the sky a seethe of grey clouds and egg-shell blue patches, the dark bare trees along the river framing brilliant green meadows. On my right was a knotty, gnarled hawthorn hedge, red haws bright; and behind the hedge, the allotment gardens of cabbages and onions rose to the horizon, giving way to bare plowed fields. I found a squirrel tree---I saw a bushy-tailed grey squirrel clamber up and vanish in a little hole; I started flocks of great hook-beak black rooks wheeling, and watched a glistening slim pinkish-purple worm stretch and contract its translucent coils into the grass. There was a sudden flurry of rain, and then the sun shed a silver light over everything and I caught a passing rainbow in a pastel arc over the tiny town of Cambridge, where the spires of King's chapel looked like glistening pink sugar spikes on a little cake. I kept smelling the damp sodden meadows and the wet hay and horses, and filling my eyes with the sweeps of meadow rises and tree clumps. What a lovely walk to have at the end of the street! I felt myself building up a core of peace inside and was glad to be alone, taking it all in. I went to visit my head, too. Remember the model head MB Derr[1] made of me? Well, it's been knocking about, & I didn't have the heart to throw it away, because I'de developed a strange fondness for the old thing with passing years. So Ted suggested we walk out into the meadows and climb up into a tree & ensconce it there, so it could look over the cow pastures and river. I returned there for the first time today, and there it was, high up on a branch-platform in a gnarled willow, gazing out over the lovely green meadows with the peace that passes understanding. I like to think of leaving my head here, as it were. Ted was right: every time I think of it now, I feel leaves and ivy twining around it, like a monument a rest in the midst of nature. I even wrote a rather longish poem about it (only ending differently) which I'll type out in an adjoining letter & send you.

Somebody at last has decided to take the flat upstairs. We really put ourselves out, as the landlady lives in another town, to show people the flat in the evenings & I'd gotten fed up trying to excuse its barren discomforts to people who complained to me, so Monday when another couple called up to see it, I said to myself it was the last one I'd show around. Where we have to share the bathroom upstairs, I hoped it wouldn't be some mad, suspicious assassin-type couple, like some that came. Well it was a rather sickly looking pair---the boy still in University studying natural sciences & a rather stupid pallid thick-ankled Scots-girl wife who had left highschool

1–Mary Bailey Derr Knox (1932–), B.A. 1954, art, Smith College.

to get married. Ironically enough the boy's name was George Sassoon.[1] "Any relation to Siegfried Sassoon?"[2] I asked idly. It turned out that the boy was his son. And a pale, sick looking runt of a wealthy stock he is, too. They move in sometime next week.

Ted is so much happier about his teaching. I have never seen such a change. He doesn't come home utterly exhausted the way he used to, and proudly tells me how he's learned to make his discipline work, & how his psychology of treating them works out. He has become interested in one or two of the boys & given them extra reading etc. I feel he is mastering his work now, not letting it sap all his energy & letting the boys run all over him. They must really admire him, he is such a strong fascinating person, compared to the other sissy teachers they get. He told me how he had them shut their eyes & imagine a story he told them---very active & vivid---& when the bell to end school rang, they all groaned & wanted him to finish the story. So I am glad that he is literally making the best of a very hard job.

Good news about the visa came today---due to our combined efforts & your wonderful slew of forms, they approved Ted's application & (although he hasn't got the actual visa yet) he will get it on reporting to London for a medical exam sometime in April. So that is one more albatross gone.

I do wish we could win the pools. Pan (our ouija imp) has been getting better & better about it & tells us more & more accurately. Last week we got 20 points out of a possible 24 (which would be a fortune of £75,000, given out every week). We keep telling Pan we want it so we can have leisure to write & have lots of children, both. Pan is very understanding & really works at it: one evening a week we perform our ritual of sitting by the fire, drinking port, & asking Pan, one by one, the 55 game results: he only has to say whether the teams will tie or not. If we won, we could deposit the money & live off the interest---write when & wherever we wanted & not get desperate about jobs. I feel I could write a good novel if I had a year off---I need time & space. Oh well, it's a nice dream. Wish us luck, anyhow

xxx
sivvy

1–George Thornycroft Sassoon (1936–2006), British; B.A. 1958, natural sciences, King's College, Cambridge; son of Siegfried Sassoon and distant cousin of SP's former boyfriend Richard Sassoon. In 1957, George Sassoon and his wife Stephanie Munro Sassoon (1938–) lived above SP and TH at 55 Eltisley Avenue.

2–English poet Siegfried Sassoon (1886–1967).

TO *Aurelia Schober Plath*

Friday 8 February 1957[1] TLS (aerogramme), Indiana University

<SP wrote 'No. 2' on address side of letter>

Friday morning
later

Dear mother . . .

Here is a copy of the poem I said I'd send. It is called The Lady & the Earthenware Head.

Fired in sanguine clay, the model head
Fit nowhere: thumbed out as a classroom exercise
By a casual friend, it stood
Obtrusive on the long bookshelf, stolidly propping
Thick volumes of prose---
Far too unlovely a conversation piece,
Her visitor claimed, for keeping.

And how unlike! In distaste he pointed at it:
Brickdust-complected, eyes under a dense lid
Half-blind, that derisive pout---
Rude image indeed, to ape with such sly treason
Her dear face: best rid
Hearthstone at once of the outrageous head.
With goodwill she heard his reason,

But she---whether from habit grown over-fond
Of the dented cariacature, or fearing some truth
In old wives' tales of a bond
Knitting to each original its coarse copy
(Woe if enemies, in wrath,
Take to sticking pins through wax!)---felt loath
To junk it. Scared, unhappy,

She watched the grim head swell mammoth, demanding a home
Suited to its high station: from a spectral dais
It menaced her in a dream---
Cousin perhaps to that vast stellar head

1 – Date supplied from postmark.

Housed in stark heavens, whose laws
Ordained now bland, now barbarous influences
Upon her purse, her bed.

No place, it seemed, for the effigy to fare
Free from annoy: if dump-discarded, rough boys
Spying a pate to spare
Glowering sullen and pompous from an ash-heap
Might well seize this prize
And maltreat the hostage head in shocking wise
Afflicting the owner's sleep---

At the mere thought her head ached. A murky tarn
She considered then, thick-silted, with weeds obscured,
To serve her exacting turn:
But out of the watery aspic, laurelled by fins
The simulacrum leered,
Lewdly beckoning. Her courage wavered:
She blenched, as one who drowns,

And resolved more ceremoniously to lodge
The mimic-head---in a crotched willow tree, green-
Vaulted by foliage:
Let bell-tongued birds descant in blackest feather
On the rendering, grain by grain,
Of that uncouth shaped to simple sod again
Through drear and dulcet weather.

Yet, shrined on her shelf, the grisly visage endured,
Despite her wrung hands, her tears, her praying: Vanish!
Steadfast and evil-starred,
It ogled through rock-fault, wind-flaw and fisted wave---
An antique hag-head, too tough for knife to finish,
Refusing to diminish
By one jot its basilisk-look of love.

And that's that. Excuse the rather patched appearance occasioned by run-on lines!

xx
Sivvy

TO *Aurelia Schober Plath*

Saturday 16 February 1957 — TLS (aerogramme), Indiana University

Saturday, Feb. 16, 1957

Dearest mother . . .

It is a lovely sunny clear frosty morning, which probably means it will pour buckets before afternoon. I so appreciated the 3cent stamps: they came just in the nick of time. Ted & I sent off two big manuscripts this week, which meant a lot of typing: Ted's 2nd draft of his children's animal fables, much improved with 3 newly-written ones substituted for 3 less successful ones---we have our fingers crossed that the Atlantic Press lady will be pleased about them & perhaps now think of publishing them: one thing, I am now sure they are salable, which neither of us could tell before we had an official outside opinion. I am also sending my present batch of poems to the Yale Series Of Younger Poets' Contest today---a double-spaced book of about 55 pages of poetry (63 including contents, acknowledgements, etc.). Ted's fables run to 48 pages. I have really been ripping through the corrasable bond![1]

No new publishing news; a few rejections, & all else hangs fire. Somehow my projects always come to a discouraging standstill in mid-winter, but they usually flower in spring. Dear Dr. Krook has insisted on us borrowing her lovely Fyrside kerosene heater for the rest of the year as she has moved into a flat with central heating---I wouldn't borrow it till she insisted. It means we can sell the old one we bought now while there is still a demand, cease using the filthy coal altogether (which had to be stoked every hour or so & was either too hot or too cold) & this heater can be regulated & is really lovely and even-temperatured warm.

Ted & I went to Mrs. Zeeman's cocktail party & found it a dreadful bore---the gauche awkward students standing in stiff awkward little groups & only getting verbose when they'd drunk enough---and although the Zeemans were nice enough, they seemed so "easy", so accessible. It must be a kind of tyranny to have to invite people to parties who are dull. Wendie Christie's parties are much more fun--she is a perfect hostess: a friend of Dr. Krook's, I may have mentioned, whose husband died tragically while she was over here, leaving her with two children. She loved her husband very dearly, & is very courageous. She sits in on my supervisions & tonight I am going over to her house while she teaches

1–A brand of erasable typing paper.

me how to make one of her famous stews, & Ted will come over later & help eat it.

We will probably postpone London, dentist, etc until my vacation & have Ted's physical for his visa then, as they suggested: I am so relieved he is approved (probably being married to an American has a lot to do with it). I only hope subtly I can make him fall in love with America: show him that the "pressure" & public-affairs are non-existent, almost, if one leads one's own life: show him the Cape & give him lots of time to write. Much as I would like to live at home all summer, I am afraid it would really curtail our work: I know that there will probably be a whirl of dinners & meeting people for a week or two---and look very forward to it. But Ted & I treasure our complete privacy & I feel it might be awkward to be in such a small neighborhood & not want to socialize at all after the first meeting. If we don't write furiously all summer, we'll not feel willing to accept the demanding responsibility of a first job. I do wish we could work out the cape: if only we could sort of be caretakers in a rich person's cottage on the cape---ted mowing lawns & me helping cook or something---but of course the danger there is of indefinite demands & encroachments. I still hope, that if Ted or I get any advances of money for books or writing that we can get a Cape cottage. I am very bad at having people saying: "Shh, they're writing." Writing is a strictly anti-social job, & we need to be away from phones & friends when we do it. Did you send Mrs. Prouty a Poetry with my poems? I hope not, because I'm going to send her one with a letter, & I think she prefers having me send things, because it means I've thought about her.

I have a rather jaundiced eye about Mary Ellen Chase. I feel she is just playing me off against this other girl, Jane Baltzell, who, as I said, would really be better at Smith as she is fresh & knows nobody there. If Jane decides she won't get married to this guy in Japan, she would choose to teach there. Meanwhile, I send out no letters; and you send me no names & addresses: of Swarthmore, U. of Conn., Amherst, etc. I need them. I'll want to write right away after letting Miss Chase have her play about. And I am helpless away from University catalogues: please send me the names of the heads of Eng. Depts. too. I really don't want to be a waitress. Miss Chase's peculiar dismissal of men in a woman's life is manifest in her statement that Ted could get a job in Conn. if I taught in Mass. & we could "see each other on weekends." That is not the kind of woman I want to fix up our jobs. If she doesn't come through with one for me, so Ted can get something close by, well, too bad for the teaching profession. What is Warren doing this summer? I made a terrific lemon-meringue pie last night, my first, & the Flako crust is wonderful & it looks like a dream---with the oven thermometer I no longer scorch things & am very pleased. Hope to learn a whole lot of our old home-recipes when I come home in June. Do write & send addresses. If they send my poetry Mss. back to Wellesley (I addressed the return envelope to 26 Elmwood) be sure & let me know right away –

xxx
Sivvy

TO *Aurelia Schober Plath*

Sunday 24 February 1957

TLS with envelope,
Indiana University

Sunday afternoon
February 24, 1957

Dearest mother . . .

Hello, Hello! I realized only after I had put the call through that it must not yet be 6 a.m. in the hamlet of Wellesley, but I thought you wouldn't mind being wakened up by such good news---and I simply couldn't keep it another minute. They had secretly changed your phone number, so there was much delay & waiting, but finally you were roused & discovered.

We walked around in a trance all yesterday. Ted & I felt grumpy Saturday morning after a week of three letters-from-editors rejecting Ted's poems for spurious reasons. They talk about having "room" for poetry as if they only had visas for a special secret aristocracy, & the visas were all taken: they are So Sorry. Well, the idiots should Make Room for fine poetry. & that's Ted's.

The big judges---W. H. Auden, Stephen Spender, & Marianne Moore (all of whom I've met, interestingly enough)---are big enough to be safe to recognize new poetic genius & not be scared of it as small jealous poets & frightened poetry editors are.

The telegram[1] came at about 10:30 yesterday morning. We gawped at it. At first we both thought that Ted's poem at the Atlantic had got some piddling prize. Then light dawned, and we both jumped about, yelling & roaring like mad seals. The telegram was from New York & said: Our congratulations that "Hawk In The Rain" judged winning volume Poetry Center First Publication. Award letter will follow!! Well, we await the letter in a fury of excitement to know details.

1 – See John Bleibtrau to TH, 22 February 1957; held by Emory University.

No money prize is offered---just publication---by Harper's, I believe. But under the auspices of these three fine judges---the 3 best living & practicing poets in the world today, I'm sure Ted's book will be a best seller!

We are dying to know when & how it will be published. I have written both to Mary Ellen Chase & Olive Higgins Prouty telling them the good news.

You know, it is, to the day, the anniversary of that fatal party where I met Ted! And I'd read his poems before & had a vision of how much I could do for him & with him! Genius will out. We are not letting it go to our heads but working twice as hard. I only hope he gets his book of children's fables accepted somewhere. He has got a terrific idea for another children's book, & we could demand a really good illustrator if this one were a published success: the 2nd one is about his demon-fairy, Snatchcraftington, taking a little boy, or boy and girl, on 26 adventures through the lands of each letter of the alphabet: from the Land of A to the Land of Z.

I am more happy than if it was my book published! I have worked so closely on these poems of Ted's and typed them so many countless times through revision after revision that I feel ecstatic about it all. I am so happy his book is accepted first. It will make it so much easier for me when mine is accepted---if not by this Yale Series, then by some other place. I can rejoice then, much more, knowing Ted is ahead of me. There is no question of rivalry, but only mutual joy & a sense of us doubling our prize-winning & creative output.

You know how breathlessly I always waited for mail & prize telegrams. Well, imagine how marvelous it is to have Ted grown equally sensitive to the mailman's miraculous potential footstep & wait as eagerly as I!

A whole pot of milk burned black out on the stove yesterday while we called you & danced about. We had to air the house---it was burnt down to a black crisp, the milk, I mean---and throw the pot away!

Then both of us wandered around town in the rain, shining with joy. We ate lunch at a lovely English bar, salad, bread & cheese, & ale, bought an armful of books, had tea opposite King's, and a delicious supper of soups, stuffed tomatoes, turkey, lemon mousse & Chablis (a habit the dear Aldriches started with us last spring, which we don't want to break) at a new posh restaurant. We didn't have enough money for snails & venison, but are going back to eat them if I win any poetry money soon.

Do tell Betty that, lacking children of our own at present, we need to borrow some of hers so Ted can tell them fairy-stories & see what parts interest them & what sort of adventures they like.

We don't care really, what reviews the book gets, as long as it's bought & read. It's magnificent---far superior to Richard Wilbur, who never treats the powerful central emotions & incidents of life. Wilbur writes with elegance, wit and grace, about autumn, falling icicles, potatoes, deaths of toads, ocean scenes, garden parties, & similes for ladies smiles. Ted writes with color, splendour & vigorous music about love, birth, war, death, animals, hags & vampires, martyrdom--- and sophisticated intellectual problems, too. His book can't be typed: it has rugged violent war poems like "Bayonet Charge" & "Griefs for Dead Soldiers", delicate, exquisite nature poems about "October Dawn", & "Horses", powerful animal poems about Macaws, Jaguars, & the lovely Hawk one which appeared in the Atlantic & is the title poem of the book. He combines intellect & grace of complex form, with lyrical music, male vigor & vitality, & moral committment & love & awe of the world.

O, he has everything.

And I am so happy with him. This year is hard for both of us. I should not have 3 jobs---writing, cooking & housekeeping, & studying for tough exams. I would like, after a year, maybe two, of teaching to satisfy my self-respect, to give up work & combine writing & being a wife & mother. But have children only after I have a poetry book & a novel published, so my children fit into my work routine & don't overthrow mine with theirs. We are such late-maturers---beginning our true lives at the average age of 25, that we don't want children for at least several years yet. Until we're well-off enough financially to afford a housekeeper like Mrs. Moore,[1] so I won't be torn between domestic chores & my writing fulfillment, which is my deepest health---being articulate in print. We plan to stay in America probably two years, then apply for writing fellowships, both of us---Saxton & Guggenheim, & live for a year or two writing solidly in Italy, in a villa near Rome. And then, if there are children, perhaps you would come over in the summer, like Mrs. Wilbur did, to live next-door, & help babysit now and then!

As Doctor Krook---who is Doris to me now, the dear woman---said so sweetly yesterday at my fine supervision on D. H. Lawrence:[2] it seems to be nothing but delightful choices & prospects for us two!

You see how honest talent & faith work out! Neither Ted nor I married for money, social position, or family heritage. Just love, & worshipping

1–American novelist and story writer Sarah-Elizabeth Rodger Moore (1909–85); B.A. 1931, Barnard College. Married Clement Sulivane Henry, Jr, 6 April 1933; divorced 1942. Married chemistry researcher Leonard Patrick Moore (1908–83) on 5 May 1945.
2–English writer D. H. Lawrence (1885–1930).

the gifts in each other & wanting to spend our lives fulfilling them in each other. & now we will have money, social position, & belong to the aristocracy of practicing artists, with our families, too!

Ted is particularly happy for the "social status" this news will give his dear parents for the rest of their days in Hebden Bridge. He says it will mean an increased income of several pounds a week for his father, who runs a tobacconist's shop---curious, awed townspeople coming to hear the story first hand about how "Willy Hughes' boy made good." Writing is looked down upon as "arty"---until it brings publication & Money. Well, the money doesn't matter to us. We both said we'd rather have this happen than win the Pools---the pools are a mere freak of luck, available to anybody. But this success radiates from the inside out, & is something unique.

I'm enclosing a check from the Nation for Ted's winter poem which I'd forgotten about.. Do deposit it to our account. I'd appreciate it so much if you would consider going ahead with plans for a cottage on the Cape for the summer. It would be such a bother for me to challenge another unfamiliar community in the Maine or NH woods somewhere. I long to go somewhere I know the shops & the routine, & to write in the sun & sand by the sea. It is part of my long-range project of making Ted love America. The money will come. I am sure of it. What about us taking a little cottage in Mrs. What's-her-name's[1] woods---it seems so quiet there ---none of the horrid gaudy commercialism. & if we could get bikes. Well, I suppose the market in Orleans is too far away for bikes. Do those grocers deliver?

We could only want it for 2 months, July & August, maybe through Labor Day. But we could go back to Wellesley in early September. Or maybe to wherever we'll be working, to settle.

If we were on the Cape, you could come down on weekends. If we had a spare room, you or Warren could come stay with us weekends, you see. It would be so wonderful. And those kitchens were so dear & well furnished. I could bake blueberry muffins! We can't stay in Wellesley, I know ahead of time, because we'd be so put upon having to refuse invitations & being by the phone. We want none of that. We want to be antisocial & write & sun for two months. And of course if we are to teach, there will be the strain of preparing lectures etc.

Perhaps if you mentioned that two writers wanted peace & quiet for the summer, Mrs. ? would lower her rent a little? Don't we have enough

1–Myrtle Spaulding.

for a month's rent already??? In our little bank. Then there's only another month's rent to earn, & food. We'd live very simply.

Do let me know about Warren's choice of a job. I am so eager to know which among his lovely lucrative possibilities he chooses!

Do think about all this, & let us know what you think. Wellesley, except for about 10 days, is out. It's too polite & social & over-civilized for us rough island writers. & only the Cape could offer health & beauty with peace to write away from phones, etc.

Write soon. Treat yourself after the dentist, now!

xx

Sivvy

<on verso of envelope>

ps. – wish we could see john ciardi's articles[1] & all about them – am very interested & have sent off poems from both ted & me – could you possibly clip them from somewhere & send them?

----

what is the name of head of Amherst's eng. dept?

----

why is apple pie full of watery sugary fluid?

----

what's your recipe for our lovely bland homemade mayonnaise???

xxx

Sivvy

1–American poet and translator John Ciardi (1916–86). Ciardi published a number of articles in the *Saturday Review* including 'What Every Writer Must Learn' (15 December 1956): 7–8, 37–9; 'Verse to Remember' (22 December 1956): 15; 'A Close Look at the Unicorn' (12 January 1957): 54–7; 'The Reviewer's Duty to Damn: A Letter to an Avalanche' (16 February 1957): 24–5.

TO *Smith Vocational Office*

Sunday 24 February 1957 — TLS on Vocational Office postcard, Smith College Archives

Feb. 24, 1957

I should be very interested in a position teaching freshman English on college level in or near New England this coming year---if possible a co-ed college, or near a boy's prep school or college where my husband could also teach English. (He's a teacher and published poet).

Sylvia Plath Hughes

55 Eltisley Ave.
Cambridge, ENG

TO *John Lehmann*[1]

Tuesday 26 February 1957 — TLS, University of Texas at Austin

55 Eltisley Avenue
Cambridge
February 26, 1957

Mr. John Lehmann
Editor
THE LONDON MAGAZINE
31 Egerton Crescent
London S.W.3

Dear Mr. Lehmann:

I am sending along several poems[2] among which I hope you may find something suitable for publication in The London Magazine.

Within the last few years my poems have appeared in The Atlantic Monthly, Harper's, Mademoiselle, The Nation, Poetry (Chicago) and other magazines.

Thanking you for your time and consideration, I am

Very truly yours,
Sylvia Plath

1–English poet and editor Rudolf John Frederick Lehmann (1907–87).
2–Notes on SP's letter in unknown hands comment on 'Spinster' and 'Black Rook in Rainy Weather' only.

TO *Edith & William Hughes*

Wednesday 27 February 1957[1] ALS, Family owned

Wednesday morning

Dear Ted's mother & dad!

Isn't he wonderful! You know, the telegram came Saturday, exactly a year after our first meeting at the St. Botolph's party[2] celebrating Ted's poems & I knew then – having read his poems even before I met him – in a kind of intuitive vision I saw he could be a great poet – like Yeats, or Dylan Thomas & probably better. On our wedding day, last June, Ted's first poem was accepted by Poetry – and now, hundreds of typed pages later, his first BOOK! I knew it would come – but hardly dared hope for it so soon.

We await the award letter, with its details (we still don't know when the book will be published). The contest was put on in all England & America by Harper's publishing company – an enormous posh company with offices in New York & London.

The judges were not mealy-mouthed little poets (who I honestly believe are scared to publish Ted's work for fear his brilliance will eclipse their own piddling poems) – nor un-poet editors – but the 3 greatest living poets today! You know, it is very strange, but a good omen, I think, that I have met all 3 judges personally: WH Auden lived & lectured at Smith College (my old Alma Mater) in 1953 & I met him then. Marianne Moore (the most famous American poetess) judged my poems which won at a little contest in America just before I sailed for England (& autographed a book of hers I still have)[3] & I met Spender at a tea-party at Cambridge last year – all brilliant people, big enough to recognize genius when they see it – & the genius is Ted!

Just picture the scene Saturday morning: we were doing usual things – Ted tying his tie, me heating milk for coffee – when the telegram came. We read it, & stared. And read it again. And again.

Then, at last, the meaning of the news sank in & we began to jump up & down, roaring & skipping like Donkey in Ted's animal fables, letting out little yips of joy and excitement. All this while, the little telegraph boy stood on the doorstep gaping at us–goggle-eyed–I don't think he knew

1–Date supplied from internal evidence.

2–SP and TH met on 25 February 1956 at a launch party for a journal called *Saint Botolph's Review* at Falcon Yard, Cambridge.

3–Marianne Moore, *Collected Poems* (New York: The Macmillan Company, 1953); SP's signed and inscribed copy held by Smith College.

whether our hometown had perished in a flood or if we'd just won the pools!

Immediately, then, we called you up in Hebden Bridge & afterwards, I felt I had to call mother up in America, & tell her the wonderful news – so I did. I forgot it was 5 hours earlier there, so woke her up at about 6, a.m. in the dawn hours. But she was so happy for Ted & me she just burst into tears of joy over the 'phone. And all this time, the milk was boiling merrily to a black crisp on the stove! It was just a cinder when we went out into the kitchen, smoking the house so we tossed out the pot & all & waltzed about.

The prestige & reputation of this – I imagine the book will be published both in England and America – makes up for the fact that poetry books don't generally earn money. But of course, under the auspices of these grand judges, it may turn into a best seller – we'll notify the papers.

You should see what an impressive book it is! It is called "The Hawk In the Rain", after the title of the first poem which was published in the Atlantic Monthly this February. I typed it all up on special paper in November & it is over 50 pages long – very fine – most first poetry books are about only 30 pages.

We hope to get as many of the poems as possible published in magazines before the book comes out. You'll see it reviewed in all the papers! Just wait!

I am so proud of Teddy & hope some day both of us can give up teaching & studying & devote all our time to our writing. We'll be seeing you a few days over Easter probably – give our love to Walt,[1] Vic[2] & Hilda[3] (thank Hilda for her sweet letter – we'll write soon) & lots of love to you both –

SYLVIA

1–TH's uncle Walter Farrar (1893–1976); married to Alice Horfsall Thomas Farrar (1896–1968). Their children were Barbara Farrar (1928–91), Edwin T. Farrar (1931–52), and James M. Farrar (1932–43).

2–TH's cousin Victoria Farrar Watling (1938–).

3–TH's aunt Hilda Annie Farrar (1908–2003); sister of TH's mother Edith Hughes.

TO *Warren Plath*

Thursday 28 February 1957 TLS (aerogramme, photocopy), Indiana University

Thursday morning
February 28, 1957

Dearest Warren . . .

By now you must have heard the wonderful news. Ted & I still wait eagerly for the letter---with all its details---to follow up the telegram notifying us about the "Hawk In The Rain" winning Harper's first publication prize. We have the telegram stuck up on our mirror, or we'd think we dreamed it! What a wonderful family we are! Some day we must all get together---Ted's brother Gerald & his wife in Australia,[1] his sister Olwyn in Paris, & Ted, you & me. I really feel there are few people like us in the world: both tall, strong, healthy, & all with special talents, & creative lives.

Mother's letter about your job offers just astounded Ted & me! We are both so proud. You are obviously destined to be the wealthy one---I never heard of such juicy salaries, & offering to pay graduate school fees, too! I believe you must walk quietly with yourself & think first how you want to develop your gifts & fine combined major, & then you will have the miraculous chance to choose & do just what you want! And how many people in the world today can "earn their living" by living, the way they want most to live! If your work is your "living", everything else follows. I only hope you can get one of those "valuable for science" positions which will make you exempt from the draft. I don't like that big 5-year plan with weekly nights, of training. The countries can't afford to knock off their scientists---oh, poets they can well spare---so many promising young poets lost their lives in the last days of the 1st world war. But now you are experiencing the wonder of being The Scientist in an age where the Scientist is at a premium & can call his own tunes. Bang, Crash! We are really excited about seeing you---less than four months, now! And so proud to have a scientist in the family. We may be famous writers someday,---Ted surely has made a fine beginning---but you see poems just aren't as negotiable for as cash as test-tube results!

1–Gerald Hughes (1920–2016), TH's brother, married to Joan (Whelan), 1950; father of Ashley (1954–) and Brendon (1956–).

I notice with horror that three huge magazines have failed the last year: all potential markets, alas, for me: the American,[1] Collier's[2] & Woman's Home Companion![3] Didn't Mrs. Moore write for the American?[4] Where will she turn her allegiance. Ask Clem[5] if she is writing on that novel she mentionned when we were last there. I admire her so much & hope she can meet Ted sometime.

This letter is really for you: in answer to your fine one, so share the news with mummy. Our letters crossed, both talking about the chances of Ted & me taking grammy's place at the Spaulding's for the summer. I just got mummys letter today. I can't think of any place I'd rather be ---except of course, at Cantor's in Chatham, right on the beach. But we would really rather write privately in those little woods & I'd know how spic & span & well-stocked the kitchens are---and after living in near squalor here, it would be heaven. Tell mother we'd like to plan 8 weeks, not just 6---we know the money will come from somewhere & both of us should earn something from writing by then. Tell her to talk Mrs. Spaulding into some good arrangement---be indefinite at first---we're young writers, poor, etc. Then: 8 weeks from Sat. July 6 to Sat. August 31st---perhaps 7 weeks, if we cut back to August 24th---but we'll want to get to work earlier in July---the 6th & that still gives about 11 days home.

The best thing about this arrangement is that you could drive mother down & stay with us every, or at least every other weekend! It is would be so economical that way! I don't like to think of mother driving herself, & we'd love to see you every weekend & see summer theater, Provincetown, go deep-sea fishing, etc. My second campaign is to make Ted love America, which only experience can do: writing for him is 1st: So---plenty of time to write during the week. We'd like the quietest, most shaded, secluded cabin---I feel sentimental about grammy's & would like that most. Then mother could sleep in Grammy's room & you on the porch. How heavenly it would be. After this stoic year---me having to sacrifice too much time to studies for exams, Ted exhausting himself over his juvenile delinquents, we'll need utter Rest to write. & also prepare for our teaching jobs in fall---whatever they may be. So: the Cape. The cost will be repaid tenfold by what we produce & the rest & vigor it

1–*The American Magazine* was a monthly magazine that published until August 1956.
2–*Collier's* was a weekly magazine that published until 4 January 1957.
3–*Woman's Home Companion* was a monthly magazine that published until January 1957.
4–Sarah-Elizabeth Rodger Moore published nearly two dozen stories in *The American*.
5–Clement Moore Henry (1937–); Warren Plath's roommate at Phillips Exeter Academy; A.B. 1957, Ph.D. 1963, Harvard University; M.B.A. 1981, University of Michigan.

gives us to face our jobs. & how rich for mother to have you, me & ted for 2 whole months. Let me know the minute you hear about your plans for Germany. I'm so glad we plan to be in New England till you come back. I don't ever want mother left all alone---we'll spend Thanksgiving, Xmas & Easter vacations with her, of course. I am so ecstatic about Ted's book! It is the 1st of many---I always wanted a man to look up to---and now, you will understand, how much easier it will be for me when one of mine gets accepted---having him there 1st. Oh, some day, we dream, we'll get writing fellowships to Italy---to Rome, in about two years & having nothing to do but write. Our fondest dreams. Now, mother must be starting her teeth operations now---very gruelling & a sore point with her, as with any woman. You can help & relieve me if you give her a treat after the worst times---buy her play tickets, or concert tickets---take her for a driving jaunt to dinner at a country inn instead of making her cook ---build up her morale all during it.

Oh, I just live till June 25th! Do write –

xxx

Sivvy

<on the return address side of letter>

p.s. – Thank mummy for all the university addresses –

xxx

s.

TO *Michael Frayn*[1]

Saturday 2 March 1957 TLS, Michael Frayn

55 Eltisley Avenue
March 2, 1957

Dear Michael . . .

Thank you very much for your letter. I thought your comments on the two stories – "Invisible Man" & "Wishing Box" quite just – although I am still regrettably fond of the first – I suppose the elaborate style and whimsy is a kind of safeguard against the impact of the actually ghastly naked situation – which in both cases is a complete annihilation of the creative identity. But perhaps I'll be able to write that straight out, bang crash, someday, without getting fancy & hedging.

1–Michael Frayn (1933–), British playwright; B.A. 1957, modern languages (French and Russian) and moral sciences, Emmanuel College, Cambridge; guest editor of *Granta*, Summer 1957.

I think it would be fine if you were willing to come look at some poems, etc. over here – and I can guarantee great mugs of coffee. Do plan to come when you won't be in a fearful rush so we can talk over some of the things. How about either this Friday, March 8, at around 10:30 am – or, if you have classes, Monday, March 11, at the same time. In fact, name your time either of these two mornings & drop me a line saying which is best.

I hope you can discover the flat all right – Eltisley Ave. is right on the way to sludgy Granchester Meadows; the house, on the right, looks nightmarishly exactly like all the rest, except that is has a small, tortuously withered tree by the front hedge –

Looking forward to seeing you –
Sylvia

TO *Aurelia Schober Plath*

Thursday 7 March 1957

TLS (aerogramme),
Indiana University

Thursday, March 7, 1957

Dearest mother . . .

Well, each day I have said: "If I just wait one more day with a letter, then the letter from the Poetry Center will have come, & I can quote it to mother." Almost 2 weeks have passed & no letter yet. I suppose it will be a detailed thing, with all sorts of practical matters in it about publication date, etc. but we live in a kind of suspension, under the bright light of the telegram which is stuck in a place of honor over our livingroom mirror next to the dear wood-shaving angel you sent at Christmas, which we believe brings us luck. I'll let you know as soon a I do about the news.

The most blissful thing is your two letters about the Spaulding's cape cottage. You don't know the change that's come over Ted & me, just dreaming of it. For us, it's the most magnificent present in the world: a Time and a Place to Write! And the Cape is my favorite place in the world. Just the <u>vision</u> of that little spic-and-span kitchen with the icebox & stove & the sun streaming in, sustains me through the grim plodding of studying masses for exams. And to have a place I <u>know</u> will be such a rest. It is really exhausting to "discover" a new town---shops, quiet nooks, etc. And I think the 7 weeks on the Cape will be the best start on my secret campaign to make Ted fall in love with America---he is getting really excited & glad about it now, and I, vicariously, am more than doubly glad to go back and open up its treasure chests to him. He loves to fish, so maybe you & I can accompany him & Warren deep-sea fishing some weekend. We'd love a party on June 29th & should be marvelously rested from the boat trip. My exams finish about June 1st, so I'll have leisure to pack while Ted goes on teaching right up to sailing date.

By dint of much typing, I manage to keep 20 manuscripts out continuously from both of us. There was a dead lull for a week after the telegram: Ted & I both had miserable colds last weekend, he having to miss a day of school & me a day of class: the Corizin pills just covered his cold & kept him from the miserable sneezy stage, but when I came down with my cold, as I do, immediately after nursing him through his, there were none left, so I gritted on doping myself with Empirin. We'd really appreciate another little bottle of those anti-cold pills if you wouldn't mind sending them. We have plenty of vitamins to last us till we get home.

Amusingly, after Ted & me saying: "Well, the answers to our mss have to come someday" & envisioning the Post Office hiring a truck to bring us the accumulation of tardy mail, I opened the door this week & saw the postman a picture more complete than my wild dreams: there he stood, laden with an armful of packets & envelopes---about 10 or 12 in all. Your marvelous letters about the Cape among them. Along with the routine rejections, Ted got 2 poems accepted by Accent[1] & me one accepted by The Antioch Review[2]---both small academic reviews, nothing like the Atlantic, but more readers, & a new name for each of us on our acknowledgements list.

Miraculously, with the publication of a sumptuous new Cambridge-Oxford magazine (which contained 2 of my poems right after an article by Stephen Spender[3] – on request from the editor), our fame has spread around Cambridge, among the students. Editors of Granta, the Cambridge "New Yorker", have humbly asked both Ted & me for stuff. I came home after my classes late yesterday afternoon & found a very sweet boy talking to Ted---editor for one of the spring issues:[4] I made coffee & gave them a piece of orange chiffon pie & we had a good talk. Ted is much more modest than I about his work, so I act as his agent. The next issue of Gemini (the new magazine) in May will carry 3 poems by Ted,[5] & a story and book-review by me. & I think Granta may well

1–See Daniel Curley to TH, 2 March 1957; held by Emory University. Ted Hughes, 'The Little Boys and the Seasons' and 'Billet-Doux', *Accent* 17 (Spring 1957): 82–3.
2–Sylvia Plath, 'Black Rook in Rainy Weather', *The Antioch Review* 17 (June 1957): 232–3.
3–Stephen Spender, 'Oxford and Cambridge Poetry', *Gemini* 1 (Spring 1957): 3–5.
4–Possibly Nicholas Monck (1935–2013), guest editor of the 18 May 1957 issue of *Granta*.
5–Ted Hughes, 'Famous Poet', 'Wind', and 'Macaw and Little Miss', *Gemini* 2 (Summer 1957): 3–4, 15.

produce us both:[1] we do love to appear together. & at Cambridge, the undergraduate magazines are read in London by the editors---there are so few university writers---whereas in America, undergrad publications are legion & ignored by higher-ups. I've convinced Ted that his book will sell better if people get to read & hear & like his poems first---he is difficult & strong & overpowering & needs to be read much. So he should publish everywhere he can. I have another little editor coming tomorrow---really a nice fellow, very brilliant, who went to Moscow this year on a student-visit, who translates Russian short stories, etc. Shall try another apful Kuchen. I love giving hospitality to intelligent people. I am so happy we'll be staying with you till July 13th. I want you to give me a constant cooking course---so I can see & make all our family recipes---strawberry chiffon pie, roast ham, chicken, etc. Ted is a most appreciative & heart-warming consumer of everything I make.

Yesterday---as a kind of "omen", we each got a very nice impressive formal printed announcement of the safe arrival of our manuscripts at our respective publishers---Ted's book "How the Whale Became & Other Stories" at the Atlantic Press & my poem book "Two Lovers & A Beachcomber" at the Yale Univ. Press.[2] O, bless those books for us. How wonderful it would be if they both got accepted---then Ted could write on a play & a second children's book this summer & I concentrate on short stories & my novel! Had a lovely dinner with M. E. Chase at the Garden House[3] Sunday---Ted shone, & this book news has really made her sure she can "stake her reputation" on us: she's an amazing woman---also, had dinner at an English dream cottage---all modernized, but with old brick fire places, wood beams, white plaster – a sundeck, all glassed in, which had Ted & me groaning with envy – a rather plodding American couple, too – we felt we should have it!

xx
S.

1–Sylvia Plath, 'Mad Girl's Love Song' and 'Soliloquy of the Solipsist', *Granta* 61 (4 May 1957): 19; Ted Hughes, 'Bartholomew Pygge Esq.', *Granta* 61 (4 May 1957): 23–5.
2–See J. Lebowitz to SP, 21 February 1957; see SP's publications scrapbook held by Lilly Library.
3–The Garden House Hotel was at Little Saint Mary's Lane, Cambridge.

TO *E. Lucas Myers*[1]

Thursday 7 March 1957 ALS,[2] Emory University

Thursday
March 7th

Dear Luke . . .

I couldn't let Ted's letter fly off without talking some, too. It was great hearing from you & we both miss you very much. We sail from here to god-bless-America on June 20th, & both of us would be so glad if you happened to come up to Cambridge earlier than August – we've got a spare bed & I'm learning to cook all sorts of good things like "gaston beef stews" & "Orange chiffon pies", as my cookbook calls them – so, I'm through my exams June 1st & we'd love to have you come visit us . . .

Ted & I are gritting our teeth through these next 4 months – his teaching is the most demanding job – the kids respect him terrifically – a great change, he must be, from the foppish English schoolmasters – & you would be amazed to see how their writing has changed since he started bringing their papers home – vivid & often startlingly funny. But both of us were made to be wealthy, endowed writers with no need to work – more than an hour or two a day, at least. I find myself rebelling against writing midnight supervision papers instead of on a novel – it's as if both of us had to go through a kind of purgatorio before being blessed by the Green Lady at the Golden Door.[3] I am regarded as a Phenomenon by the virginal victorians at Newnham – "Think & cook at the same time?" They titter incredulously. I am rather oppressed by my colossal ignorance of traditional lit. – I ignored everything except poets & novelists who were of use to my writing & now it looks as if I have to swallow all of English lit. before the end of May – but my philosophy prof – Doris Krook – is brilliant & terrific – Ted & I have sat up after gourmet dinners arguing with her till 3 & 4 a.m. & Ted & I keep each other sane. But both of us yearn for Italy, a villa, <u>sun</u> & whole long days to write & <u>live</u> & read. His teaching & my studying eats up too much energy. Damn money anyhow.

BUT – The world isn't such an idiotic closed shop as we thought – wait till Ted's book hits the stands! We can't believe it, but the Big Poets

1–Elvis Lucas Myers (1930–), American; B.A. 1953, University of the South; B.A. 1956, archaeology and anthropology, Downing College, Cambridge; friend of TH and contributor to *Saint Botolph's Review*.

2–SP's letter is at the end of a letter begun by TH, which has not been transcribed.

3–Probably a reference to the Statue of Liberty in New York and a plaque inscription which concludes 'I lift my lamp beside the golden door!' The inscription is commemorated in the poem 'New Colossus' by Emma Lazarus.

seem more open to genius than the scared small poets & neurotic cliquey editors. It is a book – "The Hawk in the Rain" at which to stare awestruck, read in wild reverence, & built a great rock altar for in the middle of wild islands. By constant typing, I manage to keep 20 manuscripts – poems & stories – from both of us always out at editors. Ted has a book he wrote this summer in Spain & here – children's fables: "How the Whale Became & Other Stories" under consideration at the Atlantic Monthly Press for which cross your fingers – & I've sent about 40 poems to the Yale Series of Younger Poets, from which I don't hope much.

Now please, please send us whatever you've written & write. Let me be a kind of secretary: I really can claim professional status now & I'd be glad to type them up & send them around – also to type your book, whenever you get together your poems. I was reading through my diaries of last year & came to the part I wrote after I read the 1st issue of Botolph's – before I'd even met or seen you or Ted. I was stunned & awed then by both of you & wrote a whole paragraph beginning: "And I have learned something from E. Lucas Myers' poems although he does not know me & will never know I've learned it . . ."[1] & proceeded to say in detail why I felt you were the fine poet you are. I had one of my blinding flashes of intuition about you & Ted then – that you both were destined to be poets & the preview of your own book broke in on my mind like lightning – Do send us stuff as you write it. & Write. How I envy you Italy – are you teaching? How? Where? What? After one year – maybe two, in America, working & writing, Ted & I want to get Guggenheims or something & come to Italy & write – so you're two years ahead of us.

Do think seriously about visiting us in June – & do write – poems & to us –

Sylvia

1–Sylvia Plath, journal entry dated 25 February 1956. SP slightly misquotes her journal, which reads, 'And I have learned something from E. Lucas Meyers although he does not know me and will never know I've learned it.' See Karen V. Kukil (ed.), *The Journals of Sylvia Plath* (London: Faber & Faber, 2000): 207.

TO *Aurelia Schober Plath*

Tuesday 12 March 1957 TLS (aerogramme), Indiana University

Tuesday: March 12, 1957

Dearest mother!

It is with the maximum of self-control that I don't at this moment rush to call you up again over the phone and rouse you at what must be 4 a.m.! Hold on to your hat for some wonderful news:

I have just been offered a teaching job for next year!

AT SMITH!

I got the nicest little letter[1] from blessed R. G. Davis this morning (I know dear blessed Miss Chase is responsible for this---and for my knowing so early). The salary sounds very fine to me: $4200!!!. He writes:

"I am happy to announce that I have been authorized by President Wright[2] and the appointments committee of the Department of English to offer you a one-year term as instructor at a salary of $4200. Such terms are renewable. I naturally hope that you will accept. Could you let me know as soon as possible? This will be for the teaching of three sections of freshman English. I shall be glad to answer any questions."

Well! You can imagine how much indefinite vague concern this sets at rest! I am just walking on air. Ted is so happy for me & is really excited. He will help me in every way. We are writing Amherst for him, & if there is nothing there, will try surrounding boys' schools. But with my good salary, I'd rather have him working part-time at a radio station or on a newspaper than have a killing program like he has this year.

As I see it, this means 9 hours of teaching a week (3 classes of 3 hours each) and only 4 teaching days a week! I know they are the last stronghold of liberalism at Smith---Harvard, et al. are producing Phd businessmen. Did you see in the Alumni Quarterly[3] where Pres. Wright stood up against the project to lengthen PhD term of work & advised against the absurd requirement to have the PhD thesis "add to the sum of knowledge" (as it made people spend years on ridiculous worthless subjects). He said these requirements might be all right for the "plodder", the routine stodgy type,

1–Robert Gorham Davis to SP, undated; held by Lilly Library. Copy held by Smith College Archives.

2–Benjamin Fletcher Wright (1900–76); president of Smith College, 1949–59; lived at 8 Paradise Road, Northampton, Mass.

3–'Faculty Headlines', *Smith Alumnae Quarterly* (February 1957): 100. The article is slightly misquoted, it reads 'add to our sum of knowledge' and where SP writes 'plodder', the article says 'capable routiners'.

but would discourage brilliant young potential teachers with a creative gift. Imagine what pride I'll feel working under a President with such fine ideas!

I'm writing dear Mrs. Prouty at the same time, so you can share the news with her, feeling I've already told her first hand---wait a day or two to allow for mails.

Guess who'll be eating Thanksgiving dinner & Christmas dinner with you in Wellesley next year! Us! Ponky & Poo! What fun we'll have!

I know just what you mean about "winter doldrums". I've started taking thyroid again & feel much better---it got so I couldn't work after 2 pm, I felt so sleepy & uncaringly exhausted. But I feel suddenly as if I see light behind the grim advancing hydra of exams: beautiful light: writing furiously on the Cape, teaching & writing furiously at Smith---in the lovely pioneer Valley, among the people I admire most in the world! What an introduction for Ted. We <u>still</u> wait for the letter about his book, but I imagine it will come out next fall---and then, what fine publicity it will have, in the center of these poetry-conscious university communities! So light your way through this gruelling run-down month with vision of a summer & academic year within driving distance of us!

I was thrilled by your descriptions of the program by Anga Enters:[1] wish Ted & I could have shared it! I am also agape perpetually at Warren's chances: how wonderful to feel he'll be "doing a favor" to any one he accepts! I am so proud of him, & have written him saying so. Which, of all these summer plums, is he picking???

Naturally, I'm humble & a little awed by this teaching job. I'll want advice from you & courage this summer: I want to make them work devilishly hard & love every minute of it. I can't think of anything I'd rather do than teach at Smith. I <u>know</u> it: of course, not the "higher up" ins & outs of the department, but what they do: I remember the dull fat teacher <u>I</u> had for Freshman English[2] & will do my best to fascinate the little girls & keep them gaping at dangling carrots. I am thinking of having a suit or two tailor-made here: I'll throw away my kneesocks for good & be a grown woman! How wonderful not to be always receiving! If I'd been offered a writing fellowship I'd have turned it down: I feel a deep need to develop my self-respect by teaching: by "giving out" & Ted understands this so well.

1–Angna Enters (1897–1989) was a dancer, writer, mime, and painter. Enters performed 'The Queen of Mime' on Thursday 7 March 1957 at the Dana Hall School, Wellesley, Mass.
2–Albert Pierpont Madeira (1911–64) and Beatrice vom Baur Madeira. Madeira was instructor in English, Smith College, 1948–51; taught SP's section of English 11, 1950–1.

My joy in Ted increases every day. I've been bogged down on the 2nd of two stories I'm working on for the Ladies' Home J. market (this last one based on the character of Nancy Hunter & called "The Fabulous Roommate").[1] Well, he took me on a long evening walk, listened to me talk the whole plot out, showed me what I'd vaguely felt I should change about the end. Last night he read all 30 pages of it, word for word, unerringly pointing out awkwardness here or an unnecessary paragraph there: he is proud of the story, thinks it's exciting & valid as a character study (not an "art" story), but the sort of thing that takes up where I left off in 17. I think Mrs. Prouty would like it: I send the 2 stories off this weekend. Last week of term. How I long for F.T.G!!

Love to you & dear Warren
your happy
Sivvy

TO *Robert Gorham Davis*

Wednesday 13 March 1957 — TLS (aerogramme), Smith College Archives

55 Eltisley Avenue
Cambridge, England
March 13, 1957

Mr. Robert G. Davis
Department of English
Smith College
Northampton, Massachusetts
U.S.A.

Dear Mr. Davis:

I feel both delighted and honored to accept the position of freshman English instructor at Smith for the coming year.

My husband and I will be returning to America at the end of June, so it might be advisable for us to make a trip to Northampton then to find out about housing for September. Perhaps, if you were available, I could see you at that time.

1–SP's 'The Fabulous Roommate' and 'The Laundromat Affair'. Emory University holds an incomplete copy of 'The Laundromat Affair' (pp. 1, 3, 4, 5, 7, and 9). According to SP's calendar, she got the idea for 'The Fabulous Roommate' on 10 August 1956.

I suppose the freshman English program has altered considerably since I was a freshman, seven years ago. In any case, I'd very much appreciate having a list of the novels, stories and poems from which we select our course material. I'd like to read through whatever is relevant and begin preparing myself for classes during the summer. The minor, practical questions can wait until I see you in Northampton.

As you may imagine, I find the prospect of teaching at Smith most challenging and stimulating, and am looking very forward to the next year.

With best wishes,
Sylvia Plath Hughes

TO *Edith & William Hughes*

c. Friday 15 March 1957[1] ALS,[2] Emory University

Hello there!

I thought I say hello before Ted mailed this, seeing there's a corner of room.

Isn't the letter from the Poetry Center nice?[3] And just imagine how wonderful it will be for Ted to have a party given for him in New York this summer. We'll tell you all about it – I'm sure lots of writers & artists will be present & it will be a good way for him to meet fascinating people. –

I am very relieved & happy that I have gotten a fine job teaching at my beloved Smith College – there are lots of dear, brilliant people on the English faculty & I'm sure when they meet Ted they'll want him to teach there too – next year, if not this. It's the biggest women's college in the world – with 2,500 women, so I feel very honored.

Mummy says you've written her the loveliest letters – she's so lonesome at home, now grammy's gone, that it means very much to hear from you –

Love to you both –
Sylvia

1 – Date supplied from internal evidence.
2 – SP's letter is at the end of a letter begun by TH, which has not been transcribed.
3 – John Bleibtreu to TH, 11 March 1957; held by Emory University.

TO *Aurelia Schober Plath*

Friday 15 March 1957 TLS, Indiana University

Friday morning: March 15

Dearest darling mother . . .

It is about 10, and I am slightly groggy with sitting up last night to type my last paper of the term.[1] I have two supervisions today---the last day of term, praise be, and shall grit my teeth and endure. I feel if I had one more minute of pressure I should explode. Actually, I feel I should be doing much more than I do, but small things come up---the young couple upstairs has a ham radio set & Ted & I have spent some time & energy going on a campaign to make them see how their perpetual shrieking jabbers & midnight phonecalls lasting half an hour were impossible if they wanted to stay on, since I study here in the day & we turn in early. The boy---the one & only son of Seigfried Sassoon, is partly inhuman (as I believe everyone must be who runs a ham radio) & sickly, with sinus & going deaf & barely getting the lowest pass at Cambridge because his father never finished & wanted him to. The girl has "1500 years of pure Scots blood" in her pale blue veins, about which I'm afraid I was rather skeptical---as to its glorification of her, at any rate. They are smug, babyish, with an "income" & will never have to work. How I despise the dead ideas, the dead blood, the dead dead aristocratic inbreds. England is dying so fast it is unbelievable: but I gather, from reading Blake[2] & D. H. Lawrence, the deadness has been growing for a long time. Everything is frozen, stratified. The "social security" system is a laugh: doctors are striking to get off it & charging $3 for any visit now---even a nosedrop prescription. & tales of operations & mistakes are gory & numerous. I can't wait to get Ted out, & he can't wait to go.

Well: enough moralizing. I'm enclosing a carbon[3] of the letter Ted got from the Poetry Center yesterday---on very impressive stationary with a list running from top to bottom of lecturers & readers they'd sponsored: from Auden to Thomas Mann[4] to William Carlos Williams.[5]

As you can see, the decision was unanimous, but the old-maid blood in Marianne Moore is showing. The 3 poems she asked to have omitted were all rich with sexual imagery. Ted & I talked this over---I think the

1–Sylvia Plath, '"Damn Braces. Bless Relaxes". Blake and Lawrence: A Brief Comparison and Contrast', 14 March 1957; held by Lilly Library.

2–English poet, painter, and printmaker William Blake (1757–1827).

3–The carbon is no longer with the letter.

4–German writer Thomas Mann (1875–1955).

5–American poet William Carlos Williams (1883–1963).

other two men judges will down-vote her---& both felt that the "Little Boys & The Seasons" was a juvenile, awkward poem, his first, & would make it a better book if left out. The other two---"Bawdry Embraced" & "The Drowned Woman" (both printed in Poetry, Chicago), are finely, tightly written poems: the former, as Ted wrote in his eloquent defense of it, spoken by "Falstaff, age 25", & celebrating the vigor & faith of physical love in the face of promiscuity & prurient puritanism, the 2nd, presenting the pathetic sterile figure of the whore against a natural, innocent background of children & nature. Both are vigorous, vehement ---good in form, and highly moral in content. We feel, strongly, that to cut these two out would be to silence a large part of Ted's voice: which is raised against the snide, sneaking, coy weekend-review poets whose sex is in their head, & the prissy abstract poets who don't dare to talk about love in anything but mile-distant abstractions. It is Dylan Thomas, but with a faith & deep religious morality which is also Lawrence (both misunderstood by many blind people). Anyhow, it will be interesting to see how this works out.

Ironically enough, I opened Marianne Moore's book of critical essays to see if she ever treated poets who wrote about sex directly & honestly, and the page fell open to this letter from D. H. Lawrence to Miss Moore when she edited the Dial: "I knew some of the poems would offend you. But then some part of life must offend you too, and even beauty has its thorns and its nettle-stings and its poppy-poison. Nothing is without offense & nothing should be: if it is part of life, & not merely abstraction."[1]

Naturally, Ted & I agree with Lawrence. I think he puts his finger on her blind spot most eloquently.

I hope you are properly joyous about my appointment to teach at Smith: I am & so is Ted. I got a lovely letter from my dear professor Alfred Young Fisher[2] (my poetry instructor last year) welcoming me back, saying since both Smith & I are "good", the arrangement should be a pleasure & profit to both. I'll want to take a carton of books down to the cape with me & get my ideas for the first term underway. Miss Chase has promised to look around for an apartment when she gets back, & perhaps Ted & I can drive up in early July & get my questions answered before I go to the blessed Cape.

1–Marianne Moore, '*The Dial*: A Retrospect', *Predelictions* (New York: Viking Press, 1955): 107–8. SP's copy held by Smith College.

2–Alfred Young Fisher (1902–70); English professor, Smith College, 1937–67; SP's colleague, 1957–8. SP completed a special study in poetry writing with Fisher, 1954–5. Alfred Young Fisher to SP, 10 March 1957; held by Lilly Library.

Won't it be nice if he can do a recording when he arrives for the radio, as they suggest? And how much fun to have our first New York publisher's party, which they'll surely give as we're coming, & which will no doubt be full of editors & other artists!

I got an interesting & rather pleasant letter from a London literary agency with offices in New York saying they'd read my poems in Gemini (the new Oxford-Cambridge magazine) with admiration & would be interested in handling any stories or novels I wrote & would I care to come to lunch in London to talk this over. Ted & I may stop in---we keep planning this London trip to cover all our business---for the lunch & to learn answers to a lot of our questions about copyrights, etc., but since the agent in America is the mother[1] of that lifeguard[2] on the Cape whom I met just before I left, & since I don't like her, I won't bother with agents till we get home & I get advice from friends like Peter Davison.

Tomorrow I'll feel wider awake & relaxed in the beginning of vacation: what bliss to study at random, of a choice of 100 & more books, not to turn out any more blithery papers! I'll really enjoy correcting themes, I think, for a change!

Take care, this gruelling month, it's the hardest of the year: spring is so near, & yet winter is still with us. My best love to you & Warren. I can't wait to run up my beloved Nauset beach in the sun.

Love,
Sivvy

TO *Aurelia Schober Plath*

Monday 18 March 1957 TLS (aerogramme), Indiana University

<SP wrote 'No. 1' on address side of letter>

Monday, March 18, 1957

Dearest mother . . .

I eagerly await to hear your reactions about my position teaching freshman English at Smith. Mary Ellen Chase wrote a lovely letter[3] when I told her the news & says she will begin looking for an apartment for us

1–Before SP left for England, she met the editor and literary agent Constance Smith Whitman (1905–93). Smith was employed for a time with Harold Ober Associates before beginning her own agency, Constance Smith Associates, in the 1950s.

2–According to SP's calendar, this was Anthony Whitman.

3–Mary Ellen Chase to SP, 15 March 1957; held by Lilly Library.

when she gets back next month. Naturally Ted & I will no doubt want to pick out a place of our own in June, but I appreciate her thought. Dear Mr. Fisher, as I perhaps said, wrote a lovely welcoming letter too. I will really feel I'm doing the utmost I can to "serve" both my Smith benefactors and the Fulbright people.

I am slightly punch-drunk with fatigue. We stayed up late last night while I finished my last term chore: the book review of The Stones of Troy by Trypanis, the Oxford don. It was a difficult job, as I felt most of the poems were weak, & fought hard to be positive & quote a lot in my 7-page review. But also graphically showed in detail why I felt such worn adjective-noun combinations as "haunted gardens","golden toys", "jasmine throat", "dusty grey","ivory chariots" etc.[1] did little to re-awaken the vigor of the greek myths or transform the greek legends vitally in the context of modern poems. Honestly, when I pick up The two British monthlies: Encounter & The London Magazine, I shudder & grit my teeth at the cheap, flat "new movement poetry", which never commits itself, but talks about and about: the meanings are dull, often superficial "top-of-the-head" philosophizing, and there is no music, no sense picturing. It is hogwash; not even that good. Both Ted & I are alone, really alone, I feel among young modern poets (with the exception, obviously, of Wilbur---who doesn't dare or care to treat the great subjects of life: love, death, war, etc.

Karl Shapiro,[2] Elizabeth Bishop[3] & a few others. All the other poets we admire are in the older generation: Thomas, Yeats, Eliot,[4] W. C. Williams, Stevens,[5] etc. We want logic, but not without blood feeling; music without vague emotion. I can't wait to see Ted's impact on the world of poetry. The British lights, like GSFraser, who pretend to nurture every tremulous poetic voice will blush at ignoring & rejecting Ted within the year. They think they can ignore us in their magazines, because we are too disturbing. In a year, the whole picture will be changed. Ted's book will put their eyes out. (He has, by the way, written an admirable letter to the Poetry Center, justifying 2 of his poems which Miss Moore objected to: a fine letter). We wait to hear from Harper's Brothers themselves. About money. And so on.

1–SP quotes from the following poems in Trypanis' *Stones of Troy*: 'Venetian Mirrors', 'Tutankhamun', 'Necrophilia', 'Venetian Mirrors', and 'The Games': 36, 34, 24, 36, and 25.
2–American poet and editor Karl Shapiro (1913–2000).
3–American poet Elizabeth Bishop (1911–79).
4–American poet, writer, critic, and publisher Thomas Stearns Eliot (1888–1965).
5–American poet Wallace Stevens (1879–1955).

Both of us are really beat this week. Me with the end of term, Ted with his school play which he has been rehearsing single-handed---he even had to make up a 3rd play himself. This has involved an hour or two after school every night for a month: the 3 nights of performance are this week. Praise be. Then all will be lovely. It has been like spring here: daffodils, forsythia, mild green days.

Another rather surprising piece of news---dear Wendy Christie (that nice widow-friend of Dr. Krook's) burst in yesterday waving a London Sunday Times. To my amazement, Harold Hobson,[1] well-known theater critic, in his weekly column, devoted several lines to a very favorable review[2] of "Spinster", one of my 2 poems in the new Oxford-Cambridge Gemini! I was astounded & overjoyed: tried to get copies today, but couldn't, so I quote (look it up if you can: it's really a terrific honor---a poem reviewed in a theater column!) Mr. Hobson starts the top of his 3rd column review of As You Like It (a Cambridge undergrad production) with the following words:

"The young ladies of Cambridge, it appears, know all about love. On my way from Liverpool Street I read in the new university magazine "Gemini", a poem "Spinster", by Sylvia Plath, twelve times, no less. Here, sharp-edged, memorable, precise, is a statement of the refusal of love, a firm, alarmed withdrawal of the skirts from the dangerous dews." Then he goes on to praise Rosalind. Isn't that nice, though? Ted & I agreed the greatest joy a poet has is writing something a perfect stranger can want to read "twelve times"! Do share this with dear Mrs. Prouty. In the London Sunday Times! I still have to pinch myself.

I have just typed & sent off two stories to the Ladies' Home Journal: about 43 pages in all: "The Laundromat Affair" and "The Fabulous Roommate": wish me luck. I really don't think I've done too badly for writing during a full term, but feel, of course, that I've done nothing. I'll be so glad when exams are over. How I dream of this summer! It sustains me through these weary days. I still manage to keep 20 manuscripts between us out. Thanks for the cold pills by the way: hope they'll be a good charm & ward off any symptoms.

I plan to sell my bike: transportation home would cost more than it's worth & it's gotten pretty rusty. I'll either rent, borrow or buy a 2nd hand one for the Cape so Ted & I can bike to Nauset Beach. Will advertise for my other typewriter trying to sell it at the beginning of next term. My

1–English drama critic and author Harold Hobson (1904–92).

2–Harold Hobson, 'A Good Home', *The Sunday Times* (17 March 1957): 19.

watch bracelet, by the way, has deteriorated inside. Should I fix it or turn it in & buy another? I don't want to pay repairs if it will just fall apart again. Well, to try to make a rhubarb pie before Ted gets back, I'm off . . .

Much love to you & Warren –

Sivvy

TO *Aurelia Schober Plath*

Tuesday 19 March 1957 — TLS (aerogramme), Indiana University

<SP wrote 'No. 2' on address side of letter>

Tuesday: March 19, 1957

Dearest mother . . .

Such a nice mail today, and I feel so much brighter after a good night's sleep that I thought I'd write a follow-up to my last letter written yesterday. I'm so glad you too are rejoicing about the Smith job. I will no doubt be scared blue the first few days, but from the keen way I enjoyed managing those round-table discussions on poetry at the English festival in New York state,[1] I'm sure I'll love my work. The schedule is surely the freest anywhere, the girls intelligent & willing (at least the larger proportion) & since they're not lectures but discussion courses (every girl has to do an 8-page theme every 2 weeks) I should learn a lot & where Ted & I are "young poets" & writers, with strong integrity & critical views, I should have pride enough to feel that my viewpoint, growing as it is every day, may help them gain new insights at their stage of development---after all, they are 7 years behind me!

The big brown envelope came from Harper's today.[2] Very exciting. A huge blue contract to sign with hundreds of little bylaws. Ted gets the chance to negotiate with a British publisher himself, so I think we'll write to Faber & Faber, TS Eliot's place. They should, I hope, jump at the chance. As I said before, the book is scheduled for publication in mid-August. We are going to have a decent picture taken of Ted Saturday. The Harper's letter began:

1 – See *Letters of Sylvia Plath*, Vol. 1, 924–6.

2 – Elizabeth Lawrence to TH, 15 March 1957; held by Emory University.

"You know from Mr. Bleibtreu[1] of the Poetry Center how warmly we at Harpers concur in the decision of the judges for the Publication Award. The Hawk in the Rain, quite apart from its success in the contest, is a collection we are delighted to have on our list."

I am going to buy a huge scrapbook[2] when I come home & paste up all Ted's acceptances & important letters (they have only dinky scrapbooks here). These are things our grandchildren should treasure!

Also, in the same mail, a nice letter for Ted from Henry Rago, editor of Poetry (Chicago), accepting 4 long poems.[3] We ran to count up the lines (mercenary creatures that we are) and figured the check should amount to $64. Quite nice. Imagine, the royalties on the book will be only 15% of 43% of the retail price (the 43% is the wholesale price!) On a $3 book this means the measly sum of about 10 cents a copy! To make the paltry sum of $100 you'd have to sell 1000 books. I hope the reviewers make it a best seller! They should! You see, selling the poems to magazines earns far far more. Poetry prizes, too. So the next book, we think, will be made up only after all the poems in it are already sold to magazines. I must find out about copyright laws. I think we both must get agents in New York, now. Especially if I sell anything to the women's magazines.

I would like very much for you to arrange a session at Dr. Gulbrandson's[4] with both Ted & me as soon as possible when we come home (so if we need to make several trips we can do it before we go to the Cape). I know I must have a cavity, but don't want the expense in £££ now in England, as we are still desperately trying to save £60 for Ted's ship fare. We have just this month caught up with our bills, our beginning of the year extra-expenses were staggering---Ted's tailor, dentist, visa fee, ship deposit & my £60 for the first term at Newnham. I feel we've done well to pay our bills. Now at last we can get ahead and save something! I accompany Ted to his play tonight & tomorrow---the first time I'll have been at his school. We are so glad it is getting over with; Ted has been so deadly exhausted, I am insisting he gives up teaching on June 1, the day I finish my exams & we will both take a rest-trip to Yorkshire to bid goodbye to his parents, & then perhaps visit Scotland. I have seen next to nothing

1–John Bleibtreu was Chairman of the Poetry Center of the Young Men's and Young Women's Hebrew Association (YM-YWHA), which is now usually called the 92nd Street Y, located at 1395 Lexington Avenue, New York.

2–SP's scrapbook of TH clippings held by Emory University.

3–See Henry Rago to TH, 15 March 1957; held by Emory University. Ted Hughes, 'The Casualty', 'The Ancient Heroes and the Pilot' ['The Ancient Heroes and the Bomber Pilot'], 'The Jaguar', and 'The Martyrdom of Bishop Farrar', *Poetry* 90 (August 1957): 279–83.

4–Dr Melvin H. Gulbrandsen (1920–91).

of England's natural beauty & feel I should, I am so prejudiced against it in everything else: politics, class-system, medical system, fawning literary cliques, mean-minded critics (the irate, nasty person-to-person letters the most respected critics---GS Fraser, Louis MacNeice,[1] Spender, Leavis,[2] et al throw back at each other in the weekly papers are shockingly mean & narrow). Of course, for official purposes, I have found England heavenly (and, for myself, I have): the one place in the world that offered me the husband of my whole life & love & work. Ted & I are so happy together. Our love seems deeper & richer every day: I feel more in love with him now than I ever did before we were married. And this marvelous chance of both of us beginning from scratch & working up together has been magnificent.

I am fascinated to hear about Warren's prospects. Let me know the minute you hear of his deciding anything. I do hope he gets a fellowship to go abroad. I am amazed and overcome at his offers: what a life he has ahead of him! He'll be building Connecticut Valley mansions like Clem Moore's father!

My best baking product is apful kuchen: I have got it as close to grammy's as possible & feel so nostalgic whenever I make it. What fun we'll have cooking for Ted & Warren! We must experiment lots & you show me all sorts of things. Remember: give yourself treats after every dentist session! It seems scarcely possible that we sail for America in only THREE MONTHS from tomorrow!

Lots of Love,

Sivvy

<on the return address side of letter>

PS: I know it's wicked to ask you to send anything more, but I'm down to my last Flako pie crust mix & would be unendingly grateful if you could sometime manage to send off a couple of boxes: I make about a pie a week---usually open meringue to save the crust. It is the only thing that keeps in this damp weather. All else goes soggy. (Also love minute rice).

xxx

s.

1–Irish poet and playwright Louis MacNeice (1907–63).

2–Frank Raymond Leavis (1895–1978); lecturer, Downing College, Cambridge University.

TO *Aurelia Schober Plath*

Tuesday 26 March 1957 — TLS (aerogramme), Indiana University

Tuesday noon, March 26

Dearest mother . . .

This must be a gruelling time of year for everybody. Ted and I both were exhausted and blackly depressed this weekend as an aftermath of little sleep & a term's accumulation of fatigue and last-minute slaving by both of us, Ted on his play, me on my papers & articles. Sunday loomed blacker than pitch, & it seemed an intolerable effort to move to go to bed. We took a long night walk & felt much freer & with early bed this week, & me "free" from the paper-producing routine, & Ted's play over, we improve rapidly. Both of us haven't written anything to please ourselves for months, it seems, but now, suddenly with the clearing spring air, we feel much more optimistic. But so much still hangs fire---15 manuscripts of poems & stories & our two books: my poems & Ted's animal fables.

Ted's play enchanted me. I haven't laughed so hard or enjoyed myself so much at a play since I've been here. The children, in gay little Elizabethan costumes, looked simply edible & the little boys dressed as girls made the most adorable figures. They did two short plays---about a roast-meat seller & a play about Jove & the weather: every character was perfect, not a line missed & they obviously loved doing it. They looked so scrubbed & their little cockney voices were so husky. They sang songs & did dances in the interval. I wish you could have seen it: Ted was amazed, himself, and very pleased. The audience really brought out the best in them. I was astonished at the maturity & mastery they showed. What a sad thing, such grim futures facing them. I never want Ted to have to undergo a year of strain like this again. I don't care if he only gets a part time free-lance job this next year, I want him to write above all. Both of us feel literally sick when we're not writing. My Smith teaching is something I need as much as writing time: it's the best thing for me, psychologically, to feel I'm not a perpetual student. I want to work: to earn a salary, not live off a grant: I want to remember how young & unread 17-year old girls still are. I want, above all, to make them love their work & shock & stir them into new awarenesses. Which will teach me immeasurably much & also give me a sense of joyous pride: the more I put off teaching, the more I feel "I'll never know enough." Well, I never will, but I can & should be able to do a good job teaching freshman.

Must read novels this summer: George Eliot,[1] etc. Ted & I have read scarcely any novels. How we both look toward this summer! It hasn't been an easy year for either of us.

Ted was very impressed about the news of Wilbur's astounding fortunes.[2] When I think that Wilbur was publishing his first book of poems at Ted's age, ten years ago, I don't feel we are so retarded. I am secretly hoping Ted will get a good college teaching job---maybe at Amherst, the 2nd year (if I'm asked back to Smith) & will discover how unique the chance is for American poets & even though we travel abroad, want to come back. There is not a question of our living in England: both of us are eager to get out (although I am terribly fond of Cambridge). It's Europe x America. Ted is so eager to go: he feels the opportunity there more & more, I think. And if I manage this year right---giving him time, leisure & peace to write (the Cape is perfect: your most significant present!) maybe he'll want to center his life there. But one must never push him: he'll come round of his own accord. Maybe he can be a part-time reader of exams in the large lecture courses at Smith. Or work on a radio station. We'll see. I'm sorry about there being no openings at Amherst, but not worried, now I have a good job.

Ted had a talk with the radio-ham upstairs and all is well: they shut up, make fewer phone calls & were pathetically eager to please: the girl, especially: she isn't very healthy, had a miscarriage a year ago & has nothing to do but want a baby: he is going slowly deaf & is continually sick with sinus. God, how healthy & productive Ted & I feel in comparison: crude, peasant-born stock in comparison to the Persian-Jew Scotch-chieftain combination upstairs, & joyous. My scorn for their pampered, paid life (they'll never have to work) has dwindled to a kind of tolerant pity. I grind daily on the rough draft of my "novel": I only know that it will cover 9 months & be a soul-search, American-girl-in-Cambridge, European vacations etc. If I do my daily stint, mere un-rewritten blatting it out, I should have about 300 single-spaced pages by the time we sail for home: a ragged, rough hunk to work from this summer. Once I see what happens myself, I'll start careful rewriting: probably chuck this & rewrite the whole mess. Hope tentatively to have it ready to be looked at by Peter Davison in the fall, rewritten through the spring of next year. I get

1–Pen name of British writer Mary Ann Evans (1819–80).

2–Richard Wilbur won the National Book Award for his *Things of This World* (New York: Harcourt, Brace, 1956) which included a $1,000 cash prize.

courage by reading Virginia Woolf's "Writer's Diary":[1] I feel very akin to her, although my book reads more like a slick best-seller than anything. Her moods & neuroses are amazing. You must read this diary. Most illuminating. Have just sent off the colossal sum of £56. 10s to pay the rest of Ted's shipfare. We'll live on a shoestring till next month, but the albatross is off. After much inner debate, we're leaving out those two controversial poems. Both of us feel better. I only hope you take it easy on typing Warren's thesis:[2] I am sorry he didn't get a Cambridge typist: he should have, like I did for mine:[3] it is too easy to put it on you. We thought of getting a typist for redoing our two poem books of Ted's (one copy for my Eng. dept. here, one extra for Harper's & a carbon to farm out to some Eng. publishing firm here) – but it wasn't worth it, so I set to work again today! It borders on drudgery now but does save money –

xxx
sivvy

TO *Aurelia Schober Plath*

Monday 1 April 1957 — TLS (aerogramme), Indiana University

Monday Morning
April Fool's Day

Dearest mother . . .

A gray raw day, after a balmy sunlit March, welcomes in your month. Ted & I have started our 6 am rising schedule again, after time out for a week's recuperation from our school-work, so I am renewing myself in mid-morning with coffee, and a piece of the best cake I've ever made: caramel cake, with caramel frosting. I really need a candy-thermometer when I come home: the directions said boil sugar & milk till 238 degrees or the "soft ball stage": in my innocence I thought this might be immediately, and after hours of burning my tongue (I can't help tasting things) & using up half the stuff by trying to make soft balls, it seemed done: thick as molassas & very good. Is it supposed to take ages to boil to the right consistency?

1–English writer Virginia Woolf (1882–1941). Virginia Woolf, *A Writer's Diary* (London: Hogarth Press, 1954); SP's copy held by Emory University.
2–Warren J. Plath, 'The Relative Frequency of English Consonantal Patterns', thesis (A.B., Honors), Harvard University, 1957.
3–See *Letters of Sylvia Plath*, Vol. 1, 854.

Ted & I improve. His vacation begins in two weeks, just as mine ends, & we have two days of appointments for his medical exams & visa interview in London on April 17th & 18th, so we'll look about for a stainless-steel pattern then & maybe see that agent who offered me a free lunch[1] & some information: I won't sign up, as I hate the New York agent for their firm: that woman I met before I left.

Good news for me today (Ted predicted last night that this was a fine day for Scorpios). Poetry (Chicago) has just bought 4 of my longest poems![2] After buying 4 of Ted's last week! We're crossing our fingers that we may at last come out in the same issue. We won't get our checks for months, till they're published, but with the $62 for Ted's and $89 (!) for mine, we should be better off in our bank-account, at least!

I am very pleased with the ones they took: "Sow", the long one about the gigantic pig; "The Snowman On The Moor", a 50 line one about a man & woman fighting in the winter & she running out onto the moors & having a vision (two of my best poems, I think) and dear silly "Ella Mason & Her 11 Cats"[3] and a philosophical one: "On the Difficulty of Conjuring Up A Dryad" about the death of the imagination. They bought "Bishop Farrar" & others of Ted's best, too. Very fine. Of the 5 batches we've sent them between us, we've had acceptances every time. Now, of my book of 42 poems, I'll have had 20 published, 10 of these in blessed Poetry.

Ted got a letter from a literary friend in London today saying that GS Fraser (one of the leading London critics) is cursing himself for not being the one to "discover" Ted, put him in his young poets anthology, etc. Well, a toady of his rejected Ted's poems when the Great Man had a cold, and evidently threw out a personal letter from Ted with them. But we are both rather chuckling at the amazingly strategic way things are working out: Ted's leaving just as London realizes (too late) that they've been ignoring a genius & their only true living poet (young) is perfect. Also arriving in America just as his book comes out. In Cambridge, at least, magazines no longer dare to come out without the editors asking us for things! Hope it gets that way in professional circles, too.

I have at last got both our poetry manuscripts retyped: the charges of agencys were ridiculous $1 for 1000 words! It was foolish to pay such a price. So I did it in about 3 days of dogged work. Am distressed

1 – 'offered me ~~lunch for~~ a free lunch' appears in the original.

2 – Sylvia Plath, 'The Snowman on the Moor', 'Sow', 'Ella Mason and Her Eleven Cats', and 'On the Difficulty of Conjuring Up a Dryad', *Poetry* 90 (July 1957): 229–36.

3 – Ella Mason was a neighbour of the Freemans at 7 Somerset Terrace, Winthrop, Mass.

Warren's thesis is your job. This summer, I am going to see to it you have a complete rest & nothing but fun. You must be our agent & clip every review of Ted's book that comes out: I'll make a scrapbook.

Our radio ham upstairs got Stoughton, Mass. yesterday & is trying to get a ham in Wellesley for me: the usual thing is: you go to the ham's station if he lives near-by, & talk through the microphone to me at this ham's station: so don't be surprised if we get through. It would be fun not to pay for a change. I also have ideas for a SatEvePost type story about a ham & a girlfriend, calling it "The YL And The Ham" tentatively & the boy has promised to OK the technical stuff when I get it finished. Both Ted & I keep each other going with dreams of this summer: we both need leisure & sun so much & will write and write, without worry of money for once, me with my job waiting, etc. Since I know the campus & town of Hamp so well, the strain of teaching at first should be really the only problem. We had a good supper at Wendy Christie's Saturday night: Dr. Krook & her lovely young sister Anita[1] were there & we had a fine time. Ted & I are trying to sell the book to an English company (Harper's gave us the rights to do that) & it is now at the one of our first choice, Faber & Faber, the place where TS Eliot works. I do hope they accept it, it will make things so much easier. Ted finally has got one handsome picture: his face did it, not the photographer, who was an idiot. Do ask Mrs. Cantor if she will take a series of her wonderful shots of us together. She is such a professional & so artistic. I want to start a scrapbook. Our life together.[2] We are very happy, in spite of work & often weariness. Wilbur's success has impressed Ted very much & he is even willing "to think about" changing his citizenship (I mentioned the huge grants: Guggenheims, Saxtons, etc.) available to American citizens: he is looking very forward to coming, & I think the Cape summer will really persuade him: I'll just let him write & do what he wants & he'll love it. I hope you & dear Warren are weathering this tense time: are you almost done with the dentist???

Give yourself treats, remember – we're counting the days until June 20th!!

xx
Sivvy

1–Anita Krook Jackson.

2–The Ted Hughes papers at Emory include many photographs, some loose and some pasted into a scrapbook, with annotations made by SP.

<on the return address side of letter>

PS: believe it or not, we're almost out of 3¢ stamps again! Would you mind sending one more sheet – promise it's the last we'll need –

xxx
Sivvy

TO *Poetry Editor*, Accent

c. Monday 1 April 1957[1] TLS, University of Illinois, Urbana-Champaign

55 Eltisley Avenue
Cambridge, England

Poetry Editor[2]
ACCENT
Box 102, University Station
Urbana, Illinois
U.S.A.

Dear Sir:

I am enclosing several poems[3] among which I hope you may find something suitable for publication in ACCENT.

Poems of mine have been published previously in The Antioch Review, The Atlantic Monthly, Harper's, The Nation, Lyric, Mademoiselle, Poetry (Chicago) and other magazines.

Thanking you for your time and consideration, I am

Sincerely yours,
Sylvia Plath

1–Date suggested by a reader's report form dated 5 April 1957.

2–In SP's address book she has written Daniel Curley in her entry for *Accent*. Daniel Curley (1918–88).

3–A note written in an unidentified hand in the *Accent* records indicates that 'Recantation' and 'Tinker Jack and the Tidy Wives' were accepted on 23 April 1957. The other poems submitted are unknown at this time. 'Recantation' and 'Tinker Jack and the Tidy Wives', *Accent* 17 (Autumn 1957): 247–8.

TO *Aurelia Schober Plath*

Monday 8 April 1957 — TLS (aerogramme), Indiana University

Monday am: April 8, 1957

Dearest mother . . .

It was so lovely to get your last letter with the $25 check from Borestone: my meeting that Gertrude Claytor[1] at the poetry reading at Holyoke in spring 1955[2] has netted me $125 so far---that Lyric young poets prize last year, & now this. What a shocking letter! All those misprints & grammar flaws! and this man is the head of those administering $3000 per year to poets. The most money anyone gives: and such people dole it out. Ironically, I was much encouraged by this prize, but for an inverse reason. I dug up the poem, "April Aubade", which I wrote in the spring of my senior year, and gaped: it seemed simply terrible to me now, coy, feminine, iambic pentameter sonnet, and it will be published between hard covers in their Borestone Annual book[3] brought out by the Stanford U. Press! I blushed, and then thought: it shows how incredibly far I've come in two years! Ironically too, I think I'm far too good now to win a Borestone prize! Ted & I chuckled over the whole thing. I think I'll cash the check here: I want very badly to have at least one suit made for me for teaching (I have hardly anything suitable) before I leave England & Ted & I went Saturday & picked out a lovely black tweed with a kind of a pale white herringbone pattern, almost invisible. I feel I need a basic stylish suit which I can vary infinitely for day & cocktail use & this should be fine. If we can get some green corduroy from Ted's uncle, I'll have a green casual one made too: I'd never find just what I wanted in America, & here, for lots less, can have made up exactly what I want from my chosen material. I am very happy Poetry (Chicago) is publishing 4 each of Ted's & my best poems. Much else out, no news. But I feel lots more good will come. Am at last coming out of a "ghastly stretch of sterility" put upon me by writing countless essays last term, taking all my writing energy. After writing one or two painful bad poems, I just yesterday finished one of my best, about 56 lines called "All The Dead Dears". I so appreciated

1–Gertrude Boatwright Claytor (1890?–1973).

2–See *Letters of Sylvia Plath*, Vol. 1, 907–9.

3–Sylvia Plath, 'Aubade' ['April Aubade'] and 'Two Lovers and a Beachcomber by the Real Sea', *Best Poems of 1955* (Stanford, Calif.: Stanford University Press, 1957): 111–12; SP's copy held by Lilly Library.

your apropos quotes from Auden & Cronin:[1] they help so much: just to know it is normal to have cycles of feeling barren as hell sustains one. I am now growing more & more accustomed to it: but both Ted & I realize the fatality is to stop writing: we would go on, daily, writing a few pages of drivel, until the juice came back, rather than stop, because the inertia built up is terrible to conquer. So, for our "health" we write at least two hours a day. I am plodding daily on my "novel" & have about 80 single-spaced pages ground out (actually 160 ms. pages): my aim is 300 single-spaced pages by the time I come home. Then the blessed summer to ram it into shape. I must say, I have the most peculiar feeling about my Book. I am grinding out a lot of tripe, having never written a novel, & as Ted says, won't know what I'm saying till I've written the first draft: but it's a place to put everything in: a kind of repository for my thoughts & feelings & freeing them, with this wonderful fluency: I have a feeling in flashes that I can make it a best-seller. But only with at least a year's work: I'd love to dedicate it to Mrs. Prouty & hope I can get her to approve, when it's done: she wrote me the loveliest letter[2] about my poems: and asked what she could give me for a wedding present: perhaps you could tell her: I don't know. We don't want furniture, as we'll no doubt have to live in semi-furnished apts. for a while: but will choose our stainless steel pattern in London next week when we go down for Ted's visa exams & interview: I'll let you know: also I'd love pottery dishes (rough & rugged), pans & innumerable pots, salad bowls, sheets, blankets, kitchen gadgets, rough table linen: I like modern handweaves: aqua, red, brown, black, white, etc.

Will send along a guest list in a day or so. Had a delectable Saturday night dinner again with Wendy Christie & met a charming South African couple with 3 children (2, 4, 8): he's teaching this coming year on an exchange grant at BU in the Economics dept. The wife is a lovely blonde, & the husband a courageous, interesting man, with one arm shot off in the war (he'd wanted to be a research chemist & had to change his whole career). I gave them our address & the name of the Nortons[3] & hope we can have them over in early fall when they come: they really are delightful. Got up at 4:30 am. this day, with Ted & went for a long walk to Granchester before settling down to writing. I never want to miss another sunrise. First the luminous blue light, with big stars hanging; then

1–Probably Scottish novelist and physician A. J. Cronin (1896–1981).

2–Olive Higgins Prouty to SP, 29 March 1957; held by Lilly Library.

3–William Bunnell Norton (1905–90) and Mildred Smith Norton (1905–2001). The Nortons lived at 47 Cypress Road, Wellesley Hills, Mass., and were friends of ASP.

pinkness, spreading, translucent & the birds beginning to burble & twit from every bramble bush: owls flying home, & we saw over 15 rabbits feeding. I felt a peace & joy, being all alone in the most beautiful world with animals & birds: little shrews twitted from the tall grass, & we saw two lovely brown furred water-rats (remember the Wind in the Willows) feeding on the bank, then skipping in to the water & swimming. You'd laugh (I'm going to put this scene into my novel): we began mooing at a pasture of cows & they all looked up & as if hypnotized, began to follow us in a crowd of about twenty, across the pasture, to a wooden stile, staring, fascinated. I stood on the stile, & in a resonant voice, recited all I knew of Chaucer's Canterbury Tales for about 20 minutes: I never had such an intelligent, fascinated audience: you should have seen their expressions, as they came flocking up around me: I'm sure they loved it! I think I'll practice my Smith teaching lessons on them: they're so receptive. Well, must be off to shop & laundry now. Am ripping through French translations of Baudelaire[1] & Stendhal[2] & feeling virtuous. What news of dear Warrie?

Love to you both,
sivvy

TO *Elinor Friedman Klein*

Tuesday 9 April 1957 TLS (aerogramme), Smith College

Tuesday: April 9

Dear Dear Elly . . .

It seems all I do these days is sit in bramble patches like Eyore, imagining the lovely decks of the Queen Elizabeth & the shiny little cottage at Hidden Acres with <a>[3] shiny little icebox & shiny little stove <w>here my blessed mother has got Ted & me <s>towed away for 7 weeks on the Cape: because <w>e didn't have a white wedding, with giant <o>rgans. I feel all itch to get home & Ted <i>s, thank god, dying to leave England & come along. We dock at Pier 92 on June 25th. We are gritting our teeth, me studying for these monolith behemoth exams covering 2000 years of tragedy, morality, etc. etc. in 5 days of 6 hours a day writing. I tried to get

1–French poet Charles Baudelaire (1821–67).
2–French writer Marie-Henri Beyle, known by his pen name Stendhal (1783–1842).
3–Six lines of text in the first column of SP's letter was damaged, probably when the letter was opened. The text appearing in < > is supplied by the editors based on the remaining evidence.

leave to hire a stenographer, being as my pen-hand is as useful to me now as the vermiform appendix. But no.

The main difference, when you will see us (apart from my hair being 2 inches longer) is that Ted is very famous. Only a select few know how famous. It is like this.

We received a telegram (or rather Ted did, I am vicarious) recently to the effect that Ted's first book of poems "The Hawk In The Rain" has won the Anglo-American contest sponsored by the New York City Poetry Society & judged (hold your hat) by W. H. Auden, Stephen Spender, & Marianne Moore: Harper's is publishing the book this August & the Poetry Center man (who sounds lovely---he just had a baby boy, or his wife did) says everyone who's read the book is "raving", hopes success won't spoil Rock Hunter,[1] etc. Our First Publishing Party. The fusty headed British editors are just waking up to the fact that their only hope, the Light of future British poetry, is sailing away to greener pastures, if that is metaphorically possible.

And me: I am peculiarly happy with a job teaching freshman English at yes, Smith. I'll have plenty of time to write & must admit that I'm really excited at the prospect: near Nyc, Boston, publishers, editors & I do love the English faculty. Ted will try to get a part-time job when we arrive, because People like interviews.

He is very ready to shake hands with Russ Morrow,[2] I think.

Some wealthy backer of Time & Life is flying a chartered planeful of debutantes over here for May Balls in June: could you stow away?

All the knots we were in last August, with the absurd & inhuman prospect of me living incognito at Newnham have melted. I am home. At home. Eating peanuts & making my own good coffee au creme. Pot au feu.

I wish you would be an actress. Full time. Saw a picture of actress in Camino Real which just opened in London[3] & wanted it to be you. you have Got It. I wish you would be one. Is it true, how lovely, charming, that one Jody B.[4] is engaged by Columbia pictures.

1–A reference to George Axelrod's play *Will Success Spoil Rock Hunter?* (1955) starring Jayne Mansfield, Walter Matthau, and Orson Bean. Made into a 1957 film.
2–Thomas Russell Moro (1932–2008); B.A. 1953, Amherst College.
3–Tennessee WIlliams's *Camino Real* opened at the Phoenix Theatre, London, on 8 April 1957. A photograph of stars Diana Wynyard and Harry Andrews was printed in 'Phoenix Theatre', *The Times*, 9 April 1957: 3.
4–Joanna Barnes (1934–); B.A. 1956, English, Smith College. Barnes has appeared in numerous television shows and films.

Poetry Chicago has just accepted 4 very long poems from each of us to come out abóut June or July: they're very symmetrical: one for you, one for you, and one for Peter Geekie.[1]

Mother is throwing a little backyard reception Saturday afternoon, June 29th & you will be formally invited but both of us want very much for you to come. Please do. We want to see you soon, so write anyway until we can.

Much love from us both . . .
sylvia

TO *Marcia B. Stern*

Tuesday 9 April 1957 TLS (aerogramme), Smith College

tuesday morning: april 9

dearest marty . . .

I was so happy to get your letter. although I've supposedly been on vacation for 3 weeks it's taken me this long to unwind from the last flurry of academic essays I ever hope to do & wind up for the coming seige of exams covering 2000years of tragedy, moralists, etc. ted & I dream & dream of the little cottage in the pine woods which mother has reserved for us for 7 weeks near orleans on the blessed cape (because of us not having white wedding, giant organs, etc.) we both have been gritting our teeth this year, most of our time taken up by jobs neither of us wish to repeat again: me studying (which eats up energy I want to use for writing) & ted "teaching" a gang of 40 teddy-boys, teen-age, who carry chains & razors to school & can't remember their multiplication tables for 2 days running: a most moving, tragic & in many ways rewarding experience, but taking much too much out of ted, who finds the continual need to maintain physical & emotional discipline taxing (the cane is still used here!) I saw the boys in a series of little elizabethan plays ted produced & my heart bled for them: adorable, clever, huggable darlings they seemed & the deadly jobs that await them & their family backgrounds etc. is terrifying. you must know all about this: your work is, to me, an ideal of service & vital giving out that many people dream of but can't do. I long to hear so much about your work: in person. I identify so stupidly with unfortunate people that I can't give them practical help, but can only

1 – Probably Peter Davison; the *Atlantic Monthly* published poems by SP and TH in back-to-back issues in January and February 1957.

write about them: which is a creation in its way, but nothing so immediate & vivid as your work. I feel I've been a private sec. these last months: typing continually, endless letters & manuscripts---well over 1000 pages. ted's & mine.

our best news is, we think, very exciting. ted just got a telegram last month saying his first book of poems, "the hawk in the rain", won the recent anglo-american contest sponsored by the NYC poetry center & judged by w. h. auden, stephen spender, & marianne moore (no less!) harper & brothers will publish the book this august & already the very delightful poetry center man writes that everyone who has read the book is "raving" about it, even the "callous people at harper's", who are concerned that success might spoil rock hunter, etc. every now & then, this news re-takes us with a flood of joy: the First Book. we are really dying to see how the book's received & learning all about the fascinating details of publishing. literature in england is dead, killed by the academics, & the editors are just waking up to the fact that their one hope (excuse the eulogies, but I can't help it) is sailing for greener pastures, if that is metaphorically possible. I've told ted so much about you & mike, & we're both hoping to see you very very soon after we get home on june 25th. mother is throwing a little backyard reception on sat. pm june 29th & please you & mike both come.

after a grim winter of worrying about jobs for us which would give us money, congenial work & lots of time to write, I've just been given, miraculously & rather terrifyingly for me, a position as freshman english instructor at smith. 9 teaching hours a week, I think. I'll be scared to death the first day, but am really excited about it: if I had a million dollar fellowship to write in italy next year, I would refuse it: I've gotten sick of living on great grants & feel very much that need, which you mentioned in your letter, of "giving out" in some kind of work: my way, apart from writing, I know is teaching. I'll probably learn a hell of a lot more from them than they from me, but 7 years age & reading difference between me & my pupils is enough to give me courage.

ironically, one of the most practical reasons for my longing to be back in america is what I formerly scorned: iceboxes, wash machines, hot water, stoves that do more than burn the top & leave the bottom soggy. I know now that if I want to keep on being a triple-threat woman: wife, writer & teacher (to be swapped later for motherhood, I hope) I can't be a drudge, the way housewives are forced to be here. my whole range of cooking is very limited by the fact I have no icebox & my stove doesn't cook deep things & the heat will be one minute 200, the next 500. and it is impossible to get these old furnished apts. anywhere near clean: walking on the rug sends up clouds of desert dust, even after furious beating, & so on. coal stoves silt everything up, & medical care is so bad, not to mention dental care, that everybody by the age of 20 has several front teeth out (it's such a bother to fill them) or rotted away. no promising jobs, starvation wages. ah, me. I am become an american jingo.

so much I want to talk to you about. long & long. we're so glad you'll be nearby. I love to hear news about people. especially like carol p. I hear anthony eden is perishing in boston.[1] I quote from one of ted's pupil's themes on the subject: what would you do if you could: "I would then walk in a sweet shop & eat 10 lb. sweets. I would walk into a cigaret shop & smoke about 50 cigarets. Then I would go to Hallens a take a thousand c.c. scrambeler round the town at 90 mh and crash into a jewelers shop and put all gold watches on my arms. I would then rob a bank & buy myself a gold plated suit & shoes made out of unranium . . . Then I would tie A. Eden to a barbed wire fence then I would cut Him to ribbens with a razor . . . I would then go to bed with a dead chicken and eat it." Hail, Britannia! To laugh or cry?

Do write. We'll see you soon & send love . . .

Sylvia

TO *Aurelia Schober Plath*

Saturday 13 April 1957 TLS, Indiana University

Saturday morning
April 13, 1957

Dearest darling adorable mother . . .

It has been so lovely to get your happy letters this week: so glad Warren's thesis is done & am sure it is brilliant, although far over both our heads! Has he heard from any of his fellowship applications yet? It has been frigid cold here this past week with an icy pushing wind from the steppes of Siberia, so strong I had to walk to town, unable to bike against it.

We have had a rather taxing week, but with a nice climax today. Ted & I got four rejections between us on Tuesday (two each: our literary life is very symmetrical). Ted's book of children's fables (alas) which they ultimately decided was "too sophisticated" (I'm going to keep on trying the big companies like Macmillan: small ones don't take risks: if

1 – Eden was hospitalized in Boston, for a gall bladder condition. See 'Another Operation for Sir Anthony?', *Manchester Guardian* (9 April 1957): 11.

the "Hobbit" wasn't "sophisticated", what is?), some of Ted's poems from the SatRevLit (Ciardi is making a big mistake in rejecting us: he's "overstocked": I bet: with his own poems); some of my poems from the Paris Review, with a very nice letter asking me to send more & two stories from the posh Sewanee Review with a rather amazing letter from the editor[1] to the effect that my stories showed a "spectacular talent", which from a conservative editor is rather encouraging. Well, we weathered this news, with typing & retyping sessions sending 5 or 6 more mss. out, & this morning got our reward, again, in a twin package, from guess where, John Lehmann at the London Magazine! Our first real professional "British" acceptance, & it is the Atlantic Monthly of England! They accepted two of my poems: "Spinster" (the one favorably reviewed in the Sunday Times) & "Black Rook In Rainy Weather" (about to be published also in The Antioch Review). They accepted a longish one of Ted's, "Famous Poet"[2] & obviously felt they could not resist the pressure of such about-to-be-world-celebrated poets. At last! The halls of British conservatism have recognized us. Of my two, the impeccable Mr. Lehmann wrote: "Your outstanding gift seems to me a sharply focussed truth of feeling and observation, at its most effective in Spinster and Black Rook."[3] We aren't really bragging, but only childlikely happy our sweating & work-of-our-life is recognized. We still get on an average two rejections apiece to every acceptance, but no editors now dare to reject us without personal letters. Which is pleasant. Both of us feel that money grants & reputation (in particular, with British women poets, but also men) are going to undeserving & pernicious writers. Ted's book has catapulted him over the heads of the poet-making editors here & they are, amusingly, almost forced to acknowledge him to keep up their own reputations! The joy is, in these rejections, of people saying we have a gift: that's all we need to know, although we do know it deep in ourselves. All that a gift demands to be recognized is constant deep thinking & sweating continuous work: no public literary-lion life for us: although, on the occasion of a book-publishing we will modestly appear, gaunt-cheeked & prophet-eyed, to partake of free champagne and caviare!

1–Monroe Spears to SP, 28 March 1957; held by The University of the South. The letter reads, in part, 'Both of them seem to me, frankly, to rely a little too much on the gimmick. But I think they show a spectacular talent, and I hope that you will let me see your future work.'

2–See John Lehmann to TH, 12 April 1957; held by Emory University. Ted Hughes, 'Famous Poet', *London Magazine* 4 (September 1957): 23.

3–See John Lehmann to SP, 12 April 1957; (photocopy) held by Smith College. Sylvia Plath, 'Spinster' and 'Black Rook in Rainy Weather', *London Magazine* 5 (June 1958): 46–8.

I want to get a sumptuous scrapbook at home for Ted's clippings & mine: also one for pics of us & for our children. Roughly we plan two years in America: then, both applying for writing fellowships: Guggenheims, Saxtons, etc. for a year in Italy (hoping you can visit us in the summer, free from any expenses incurred by your to-be-wealthy children) & then hundreds of children. Both of us feel very late maturers, only beginning our true lives now & need to devote the next two or three years to establishing the depths of our talent, & then having children, but not until they can't undermine our work. Our own personalities are still squeaking new & wonderful to us.

I'm enclosing one of the pictures[1] we are sending off of Ted for publicity purposes: already, this Paul Roche,[2] some young Eng. Poet (of whom we've never heard) has offered us his house to rent for the summer in Northampton, but I can't think of any place I'd rather stay less: that hot inland city! I dream of our Cape cottage. Blueberry muffins & fried chicken. We must have a lobster barbecue someday, with the Cantors, etc. Ted would love to go deep-sea fishing. Could we visit Frank & Louise a day or two in Pa. before we go to the Cape? We'd love to. Do ask them. & they could show Ted & me around. Nothing planned, just a simple visit. Ted would love the tough little boys. What fun we'll have, clipping Ted's reviews! I'm sure he'll get a job at Amherst the 2nd year, if only I'm good enough to get my appointment renewed at Smith! We are going to catapult to fame, I predict. Simply because it means so little to us, & our writing & being Heard & Read is everything.

Here are some (all I can think of) of the people to invite to our June 29th party (what'll we do if it rains? Have it at Aldriches? Do ask them.

All the Aldriches, Dot & Joe Benottis,(Miss Corcoran), the two Crocketts, all the Cantors, Peter Davison (43 Bowdoin Street, Cambridge), Mrs. Freeman, Dave,[3] Ruth & Art Geissler, Elinor Linda Friedman (Elly: 704 Laurel Street, Longmeadow, Mass: please forward to NYC); Mr. & Mrs. Dean Hildebrandt,[4] c/o 40 Columbia Place, Mt. Vernon, NY); Mrs.

1–The photograph is no longer with the letter.

2–Donald Robert Paul Roche (1928–2007); instructor of English, Smith College, 1956–8; SP's colleague, 1957–8; married to Clarissa Tanner Roche (1931–2004); divorced 1983. Mother of Pandora, Martin, Vanessa, and Cordelia. Paul Roche was hired as an instructor at Smith College through the connections of Clarissa Roche's aunt Virginia Traphagen (1904–68); B.A. 1926, Smith College.

3–David C. Freeman (1932–2007), Ruth Geissler's brother.

4–Dorrit Licht Hildebrandt Colf (1934–); B.A. 1955, music, Smith College; SP's friend. SP attended Licht's wedding at the First Presbyterian Church, Mount Vernon, New York, to Frederick Dean Hildebrandt (1933–2010) on 26 March 1955 (divorced); married Howard D. Colf on 14 June 1965.

Lameyer & Gordon???;[1] Pat O'Neil,[2] 19 Kipling Road, Wellesley; Mrs. Prouty; Marcia & Mike Plumer, 74 Buckingham St., Cambridge; Frank & Louise; Alison Smith[3] (Apt. 9d, 1165 Park Ave., NYC). Maybe Louise & Eddie White[4] if you know their addresses. & then the neighbors, McGowans,[5] Pullings,[6] Cruikshanks[7] et. al. Mrs. Prouty will probably rather see us in quiet at her place, & the Lameyers it might be very tactful to leave out. So do what you want with the list. What are you having to drink? Sherry? It always helps. Let me know roughly who you'll be having.

Am so glad you've gained weight. See that you keep it up so I'll have a plump mother to hug when I come home!

I am, by the way sending a little something for your birthday to be put in our dining room, which probably won't arrive for weeks. Do let me know the condition its in!

Bye for now, much love to you & Warrie,

sivvy

TO *Aurelia Schober Plath*

Saturday 20 April 1957 — TLS (aerogramme), Indiana University

Saturday pm
April 20, 1957

Dearest mother,

Well, we are two days back from London already & just recovering from the tension, soot, noise, blare & general exhausting mess of that

1–In the letter, Gordon's name is struck through in an unknown hand.

2–Patricia O'Neil Pratson (1932–); B.A. 1954, English, Smith College; SP's friend from Wellesley.

3–Alison Vera Smith (1933–97); SP's friend and Smith classmate from New York City. In June 1952, Alison Smith withdrew from Smith College to attend Johns Hopkins University.

4–Louise Giesey White (1932–); B.A. 1954, government, Smith College. Resident of Hopkins B House. Classmate of SP in high school in Wellesley, class of 1950. Edward Allen White (1932–); schoolmate of SP's in Wellesley, class of 1949. Giesey and White married on 25 June 1954.

5–Either Ruth C. McGowan and Robert G. McGowan, who lived at 4 Ingersoll Road, Wellesley, or Edith A. McGowan and Robert McGowan of 27 Elmwood Road, Wellesley.

6–Grace E. Pulling and Richard A. Pulling, who lived at 19 Pine Plain Road, Wellesley; parents of David and Lynda.

7–Dorinda Pell Cruickshank and William H. Cruickshank lived next door to the Plath family at 24 Elmwood Road, Wellesley, with their four children: Dorinda, Pell, Blair, and Cara.

city. Ted has, praise be, got his visa at last, at an expense of over $30 and two days of tests, waiting about, interviews, & more waiting about at the American embassy.

Neither of us slept on Tuesday night, before we went down, out of sheer nervousness that some quirk of fate might put a hitch in our so-optimistic plans. Ted has a friend whom we just met before we left who has a magnificent job waiting for him at MIT but whose visa was refused because he didn't report a $25 camera in customs & was honest enough to admit it. The case went to Washington & was rejected, so he wastes his time working in a Guiness brewery, with this job still open: England hasn't got the equipment for his talent. We stayed overnight with one of Ted's Yorkshire friends: a genial, young one-armed commercial artist who, hearing of our plans, says he hopes to go to America also: the business firms in London are so stodgy & conservative that there is little, if any, opportunity for an original mind. Ted had blood tests, X-rays etc. & was pronounced in excellent health. The Vice-consul welcomed him as a teacher. We went to the portrait gallery, lay out in the sun in Hyde park, ate again at Schmidt's[1] (remember, the German place where we three shared our "wedding breakfast"), saw a magnificent movie, "The Lost Continent",[2] in technicolor about the natives of Bali, Borneo, etc. So fine, we were all horrified to come out into the mechanical grating life of London. Ted & I long for the moors & the ocean.

We spent a fascinating hour browsing about in Liberty's over rugs, etc. We both picked up Facette stainless steel & do like it very very much so will you please announce generally to anyone who wants to know that's our pattern. I love brown, black & white for luncheon colors (saw a very effective set of napkins & mats of linen in these colors: plain or patterned): with either turquoise, aqua or forest green as a "color": whatever's easiest to get, but I do like a good strong aqua.

By now you must have got our letters about our acceptances in the London Magazine: the radio-ham got the numbers reversed: 2 poems for me, 1 for Ted. Also, Ted's poem "Bishop Farrar" was broadcast twice this week over the BBC 3rd program "The Poet's Voice", Sunday & Tuesday. The last of a group of poets reading their own poems: Ted's was far & away the finest, & we got letters from friends about the broadcast Sunday, so were able to get the radio-ham upstairs to tune us in on it

1–Schmidt's, a German restaurant, at 33–43 Charlotte Street, London, according to SP's address book.

2–*The Lost Continent* (1951) played at the Academy Cinema, Oxford Street, London.

Tuesday. Ted's just got a note from Chris Levenson,[1] a Cambridge poet whom neither of us like, but who serves to offer literary gossip: he & a boy from Oxford[2] have been asked to do an anthology of about 8 young British poets who have been ignored by the recent cliquey anthologies & would like about 10 of Ted's poems for it: we'll have to wait & see what Ted's British publisher (if we get one) will say, but it would be very good publicity.

Perfectly happy to have Elly meet us at the ship: we sail in exactly 2 months from today!!! I can at last see the light of my homecoming ahead: this house has been getting on my nerves, it is so dirty & gloomy, all except the front room: in an access of spring cleaning I just threw all her filthy old rugs under the stairs with the rest of her filthy old junk & Ted is varnishing the bare floors: much more sanitary. Beating only elicits more dust out of an infinite supply in the rug's antique fabric. We got 2 rejections apiece this week & with the fatigue of tension from the visa trip, we're a bit gloomy: my exams loom very near: the week of May 28th: 6 hours of solid writing a day!

Can I ask for a tentative recipe for our home coming dinner, seeing you're not going to be meeting us at the dock? O, they all sound so good, I can't choose: but maybe broiled chicken, bread-crumbed tomatoes & tossed salad with crispy potatoes? With a jarful of cookies: tollhouse, molasses, or oatmeal, & specially (it's strawberry season, isn't it?) that heavenly strawberry chiffon pie you make so angelically? You have no idea how your menus make me homesick: Grammy's fish soup is Ted's favorite dish & we have it about once a week. I have to stick to pies or 2-layer cakes: date-nut bars, gingerbread, etc. just stay soggy in the middle no matter what I do as the oven heat rises from back to front. It's infuriating. Your piecrust mixes have been a godsend: I'm on my last one this week. Made a coconut cream pie, which Ted likes. In the 2½ weeks we'll be home, you must give me a capsule cooking course & we'll feast Ted & Warren daily!

Ted walks me to the Univ. Library at noon, where we have a delicious cheap lunch, & I go to study from 1 to 6:30 while he writes at home & calls for me. It is the only way I can work as at home butcher, baker, mailman etc. are continuous interruptions. Ted is so marvelously understanding about everything. We get along just perfectly & are only

1–Christopher Rene Levenson (1934–), British; B.A. 1957, English and modern languages, Downing College, Cambridge; dated SP, 1955–6. Levenson was an editor of the Cambridge magazine *Delta*.

2–Indian writer and poet Dom Moraes (1938–2004).

longing to get out of England to America. We'll go up to the moors for a week's recuperation after exams & Ted's teaching finish on June 1st. Much love to you & Warrie. How's dear Grampy? Let's have one great lobster & corn-on-the-cob feast on the Cape some weekend in August. What fun!

Much love from us,
sivvy

TO *D. S. Carne-Ross*[1]

Sunday 21 April 1957 TLS, BBC Written Archives Centre

55 Eltisley Avenue
Cambridge
April 21, 1957

Mr. D. S. Carne-Ross
Talks Department
THE BRITISH BROADCASTING CORPORATION
Broadcasting House
London, W.1

Dear Mr Carne-Ross:

I should be interested to know whether there would be any possibility at this time of my coming to London to try out for a reading of my own poems over the "Poets Voice."

I am enclosing four recent poems for your perusal, two of which---"Spinster" and "Black Rook In Rainy Weather"---have been accepted for publication by The London Magazine; the former poem was also reviewed by Harold Hobson in the Theater section of the Sunday Times.

Apart from publishing regularly in the Cambridge and Oxford publications (Gemini, Granta, Chequer, Delta, Isis, etc.) I have also had work appear in The Antioch Review, The Atlantic Monthly, Harper's, Lyric, Mademoiselle, The Nation, The New Orleans Poetry Journal, Poetry (Chicago) and other magazines.

I am enclosing a stamped self-addressed envelope for your convenience.

Hoping to hear from you in the near future, I am

Sincerely yours,
Sylvia Plath

1–BBC producer in the Talks Department, D. S. Carne-Ross (1921–2010).

TO *Aurelia Schober Plath*

c. Tuesday 23 April 1957[1] TL (copy), printed from *Letters Home*

<drawing of a calendar showing date of 'April 26' adorned with a tulip, daisies, and a daffodil>
<drawing of SP and TH in profile>
<drawing of ASP hiking in the Alps above which is a wedding ring>
<drawing of ASP sitting at a café table with a fountain and the Eiffel Tower in background>
<drawing of ASP driving a car in Massachusetts toward Big Ben>
<drawings of stars, a crescent moon, musical notes, and birds over entire card>

HAPPY BIRTHDAY TO YOU!
There was an invincible mother
(I defy you to show me another!)
Who in some magic way
Grew younger each day
And never found birthdays a bother.

Her feats are too great to be reckoned:
One summer the continent beckoned:
She mastered a car,
Said: "Big Ben's not so far!"
And whiz! she was there in a second.

Gay Paree and much vin did not wearia;
She thought Rembrandt's exhibit[2] superia;
From bottom to top
Of the Alps she did hop---
Next year she'll be conquering Siberia!

At the green age of fifty-one, this is
A health to our venturesome missis!
May her next fifty springs

1–Date supplied from internal evidence.
2–ASP may have visited the Rembrandt House Museum when she was in Amsterdam in July 1956.

Bring new joys and jauntings!
From S & T here is love, hugs and kisses!

TO *Warren Plath*

Tuesday 23 April 1957 TLS (photocopy), Indiana University

Tuesday, April 23rd

Dearest Warren,

It was so good to get your letter: we love hearing from you, and your job with Melpar[1] this summer sounds extraordinary. I'm sure you'll walk through life picking your jobs & salaries like plums. To both of us unscientific cloud-headed poets you sound like the coming Einstein,[2] and your major most versatile & reassuringly human, with its psychological side. We long to have you explain at length about your work & look forward to our two and a half weeks at 26 Elmwood (maybe we could drive to Ipswich now and then) & hope to initiate Ted to American cooking & picnics.

Just now the weather is heavenly: mild, sunny & the evenings we spend walking out in Granchester Meadows watching water-rats & rabbits.[3] Once a little water-rat (looking much like Max, who, I gather, is a hamster) swam right up to our feet, chewed off a huge reed, and swam off dragging it to a little hole. We heard a lot of munching, then replete silence. Walking in the country does wonders to calm us: Ted has just finished his first week of 3 weeks vacation & gotten his visa in London, praise be. We were really anxious about it, & I was running through my various acting schemes suitable for any snags we ran into.

My exams are well piled together in the week of May 28th which is uncomfortably close, & I must work like a slow dog till then. I have to go to the University libe which is the one place I can concentrate: living in a two-family house, which is linked by their having to go by or through our rooms to go out, is a bother. Especially since we despise the Sassoon couple upstairs. They live like pigs, dropping cigarette butts, as it were, into nearby human eyesockets, & are so wealthy they will never have to do anything but destroy old ladies TV programs by their radio waves: on

1 – An American government contractor with plants located in Alexandria, Virginia, and Cambridge, Mass.

2 – German-born theoretical physicist Albert Einstein (1879–1955).

3 – See SP's 'Watching the Water-Voles'; held by the Lilly Library.

top of all this, the stupid boy, who is being forced by his father Siegfried, to go to Cambridge, is "hoping" to fail his exams. A rather infuriating couple: the girl openly admits "I am a perfect little cabbage. I don't want to do anything but raise cabbages." They are unbelievable & don't deserve to live.

We both are dreaming of June 1st, when Ted's job & my exams are over. Then, to the moors, to the sea, & home. Are you already working at Melpar when we get to NYC the 25th? I suppose they want to snap you up.

Do see that mother takes it easy & doesn't tire herself fixing up the house for us. Teddy is so eager about coming that I can't wait to see everything through his eyes. I look most forward to the family cookout at Joe's: be sure to tell him that: Ted has never been to a proper cookout before. And I hope some weekend when you come to visit us at the Cape, the three of us can go deepsea fishing on one of those boats. Ted loves to fish.

What have you heard about your German applications? Did you apply for the Fulbright (I think you said you did) or get a kind of preliminary acceptance this winter? They usually like to give them to people who have never been abroad before & since they distribute them regionally, competition from the East coast colleges is very high. It would be a terrific experience for you though & you could travel about Europe in your vacations.

We plan, roughly, to spend two years in America (Ted is even thinking, just thinking, of changing his citizenship for the simple purpose of becoming eligible for all the writing awards America offers) and then both of us hope to get writing grants to Italy for a whole year.

This note brings you birthday wishes from both of us. I am never sure even of my own, but I think it must be about your 22nd. But anyway, we are both delighted that the first day occurred.

much love to you & do write when you can,

sivvy

TO *Aurelia Schober Plath*

Friday 26 April 1957 — ALS with envelope,[1] Indiana University

A very happy birthday for you and your pale blue diningroom

With love –
Sivvy & Ted

TO *Aurelia Schober Plath*

Sunday 28 April 1957 — TLS (aerogramme), Indiana University

Sunday afternoon, April 28

Dearest mother . . .

Well, you and Warren have just completed your birthdays & I hope my little cards arrived in time & that my small blue gift to you came.

In four weeks my exams begin: I am living at the university library from morning to night, which is the only place I feel complete peace & immunity from domestic bothers, tradesmen, passers-by, etc. I am enjoying my work, really, steadily reading tragedy now, the Greeks, then on through 2000 years up to Eliot, concentrating on several major figures: Corneille,[2] Racine,[3] Ibsen,[4] Strindberg,[5] Webster,[6] Marlowe,[7] Tourneur,[8] Yeats, Eliot: there are so many. This tragedy paper (only a 3 hour exam for all that) is a fine help on my reading: I'd never read any of the plays before, really. This summer I must devour crucial novels: Ted & I have read hardly any prose!

We have decided to leave this house for good on June 5th and spend our last two weeks before sailing in Yorkshire with Ted's parents without returning to Cambridge as we had planned to cover the May balls. We'll pack & get our stuff crated in the few days after we finish work & be off for the therapeutic Wuthering Heights country, when I hope to begin writing again: I feel seething when I'm not writing daily & am forced now

1 – On a notecard of 'The Designer Craftsmen', 10 King's Parade, Cambridge.
2 – French tragedian Pierre Corneille (1606–84).
3 – French dramatist Jean Racine (1639–99).
4 – Norwegian playwright Henrik Ibsen (1828–1906).
5 – Swedish playwright August Strindberg (1849–1912).
6 – English Jacobean playwright John Webster (*c.* 1580–*c.* 1634).
7 – English playwright Christopher Marlowe (*c.* 1564–93).
8 – English dramatist Cyril Tourneur (d. 1626).

to give it up for these next 5 weeks. But my novel becomes more & more exciting to me & I hope to work on it all summer. We are already sending our manuscripts with the Wellesley address on return envelopes, so open anything that looks official to either of us & communicate the contents.

Your package of blessed food came this week in the nick of time, just as my most difficult period begins: what a relief: the soups & rice & piecrusts will save me precious time & cut marketing to a minimum. Ted is so understanding & helpful: dries dishes with me, hypnotizes me into relaxing deeply, walks in the country, bolsters my morale & is generally just the dearest person imagineable. What fun we'll all have this summer! These exams serve to put the lid on my pressure-cooker & I can feel stories, poems & novel just bursting to come out the minute I'm free: I know I have the talent, as Ted knows he has it: both of us are dedicated to deepening our imaginations & work, work, work. We are our own best safeguards against fame going to the head or outside distractions.

Ted's visa seems to be for residence, with all that implies. I think he might be willing even to change citizenship, although I will not try to persuade him, because America is uniquely the country which gives its poets a kind of "patronage" at the universities. You should have seen him eat up that chocolate pudding you sent! He is so delighted by the simplest good food, that I really adore cooking for him. He has just written one of his best poems today (after a long dry spell) on the recent auto death of Roy Campbell[1] & is generally happy: one more week of vacation for him, & then only 4 more weeks of the wicked teaching. 4 weeks of solid study for me & one of exams: then we are free for a more creative happier life in a wonderful country. How I long to be at home with you & Warrie & Ted, cooking good meals & learning so much about cooking & sewing (mending) etc. from you & doing laundry in our own machine to hang out in our own lovely sunny green yard. And to write. We plan, after 2 years, definitely to get writing fellowships to Rome. I hope you'll brave the seas on a bigger ship then & spend at least the summer with us in a nearby villa!

Ted enjoys your letters so much & says he is so happy I have such a lovely mother! I do think his parents are dear & we both have in common coming from good solid stock where the sole endowments are talent & intelligence & health: name & money we'll make ourselves, step by step, together.

1–South African poet Roy Campbell (1901–57) died in a car accident in Portugal; the poem may not be extant.

Already I've mentally packed my trunk a hundred times, sailed to NYC, taken the train, eaten dinner at home & begun living on the Cape! I really live in that future now, & long to get out of this dark, gloomy house, where the livingroom is the only living-room. Both Ted & I feel our best life beginning now & are so very happy together, more so each day. I couldn't have dreamed up a more perfectly wonderful husband than he if I'd tried every minute of my life. Nothing I ever vaguely imagined could equal his simple dearness in every respect & perfect intellectual, creative & emotional understanding! And how many poets does one find who are healthy, brilliant, articulate, handsome & intransigeantly faithful to the purpose & ideal without being vain or seeking public adulation? I'm sure the adulation will come, for both of us, in its way, but our work & love for each other's potential stands above all.

Here I am, already planning: we'll telephone you from NYc as soon as we get through customs & tell you what train to meet at Route 128:[1] the best place, I think. All my woolens, by the way, must go to the cleaners: cashmeres & all: two years of wear, & they must be renewed. Do tell me how much we have in bank & checking account (I've just drawn $8 from the latter to get the copyright for 2 poems).[2] We should be getting $150 more from Poetry mag. for the 4 poems each they recently bought. Do write as much as you can--even with your exam correcting – I look so forward to your letters & so does Ted. Love to Warren & congratulations on the Harvard scholarship.

xxx your own
Sivvy

1–A suburban, regional and commuter rail station in Westwood, Mass. In chapter 10 of SP's *The Bell Jar*, Esther Greenwood alights at 'ROOT WAN TWENNY ATE!' where 'the motherly breath of the suburbs enfolded' her (Heinemann [1963]: 119).
2–See letters from Donald Snyder of the *Atlantic Monthly* to SP and to TH, 13 February 1957; held by the Lilly Library.

TO *Gerald & Joan Hughes*

c. Wednesday 1 May 1957[1] TLS,[2] Indiana University

Dear Gerald & Joan,

Hello:

You won't be able to distinguish the typescript, or perhaps even the tone of voice, but this is Sylvia speaking. Ted kindly left me some of this green space & so I'm taking it up. Perhaps he's already told you about the acceptance of his poem (called "Famous Poet"---which he'll be before summer's out) in the London Magazine: we both got poems accepted by this holy pamphlet the same day: our luck seems to run in the same stream; all I need now is to get my book accepted: I'm still waiting to hear word of it, but probably won't till we get home to America.

I am living, these next 4 weeks, with nose worn to the nub on the academic grindstone. I really love the stuff I'm reading: tragedies, modern plays, French novels & plays & poems, etc., etc., but the pressure of crystallizing all my immortal knowledge in six 3-hour exams tends to zap some of the fun. Also, I dread sudden paralysis of my right hand which may well rebel at writing with a pen after so many years of pampering on the typewriter keys, I live in the future, thinking of the two weeks we'll spend at The Beacon wandering the moors & gazing blissfully at the moor sheep, etc., before sailing. We'll both deserve a total rest: after my exam grind & Ted's last 4 weeks knocking in the bullet-heads of those devils.

I loved the pictures of you both, & Ashley. By the time we get to see him he will no doubt have dozens of pale, tear-stained, adoring women languishing in his wake: he is a handsome fellow, all right. I'm really convinced that in case of any such horror as H-bomb warfare, our two families: you both, Ted, me, Olwyn, my brother Warren & appropriate mates, could re-people the world to its own advantage. O for an island. We want to get wealthy & buy one someday.

I am dying to show Ted Cape Cod (where mother has got us a little cottage for a summer of writing, swimming, sailing, etc.): scrub pines, lakes, sand cliffs & tons of icy green-blue Atlantic ocean pounding 20 miles of almost deserted shoreline: have spent my happiest days burnt darker than an Indian by the hot sun, racing the gulls & terns in and out of the breakers & daring the waves to smash me. They do, more often than not, & can send a reckless swimmer up on the shore in a shower

1–Date supplied from internal evidence.

2–SP's letter is at the end of a letter begun by TH, which has not been transcribed.

of sand, pebbles & stones, sputtering & wind knocked out of him. Also hope we can explore the rest of my country too, which I've never seen: New Orleans, Grand Canyon, west coast, etc.

Do keep writing to us often & send pictures: until we can actually meet that will have to do. We'll send some pictures taken in America as soon as we get some.

Well, will sign off for now, & walk out with Ted for a bit to clear my head of Greek tales of incest & blood revenge.

Love to you both, & also the boys,
sylvia

TO *Edith & William Hughes*

c. Sunday 5 May 1957[1] ALS, Family owned

Sunday afternoon

Dear Ted's mother & dad –

I am still here in the kitchen watching my Yorkshire pudding bake in the oven to go along with our Sunday roast and looking so forward to our coming up to stay in Yorkshire around June 5th until we sail the 19th. Ted starts work again tomorrow after a 3-weeks vacation & he has been writing some more very good poems. I'll be up to my eyes in work until exams are over on June 3rd – am now studying at the library from 9:30 to 6:30 pm everyday & it seems I have to read every play & every bit of philosophy written in the last two thousand years! Fortunately I love my work, which makes this routine bearable & Ted takes me for lovely walks along the river in Granchester Meadows to look for water-rats & owls when my eyes get tired of reading print. At least our work will all be over in a month's time & the new life will begin – I can't wait to start writing again –

You have no idea how forward I look to living at the Beacon again. I catch myself daydreaming about the moors, with the mad-eyed moor sheep, & then the wonderful view from your livingroom windows over the green fields which always makes me think of living on top of the world – and I can't wait to come back up there with Ted for a restful two weeks with you both: your dear house has come to be "my home away from home" and I really miss it.

1 – Date supplied from internal evidence.

We plan to stay here only a few days after my exams to go through the huge job of packing my trunk, suitcases & our 300 to 400 books & paying bills etc. so we can come right to your place & stay till the day before we sail. We both have really worked hard this year & will feel we deserve a summer devoted to writing – you wait, we'll produce a book each. Ted's fable on the Pygge came out this week in the same issue of Granta as two of my poems – & our names were on the poster together: our first publication together – we'll send up a copy – another magazine comes out next week, too, with poems by Ted & a story by me –

much love to you –
Sylvia

TO *Aurelia Schober Plath*

Tuesday 7 May 1957

TLS (aerogramme),
Indiana University

Tuesday morning
May 7th

Dearest darling mother!

How happy your letter made us this morning with the wonderful news of Warrie's Fulbright! I'm writing him a note this morning too before I go biking off for my routine day from 10 to 6 at the University library devouring tragedies. I ran to my map of Europe & underlined Bonn in red, and immediately began thinking of all the wonderful chances Warren will have to live with something of a "splurge" for a change. I hope he travels ---Paris looks so near, direct by rail, and so is Italy & the Mediterranean! I can help him a bit, I think, in telling him what the Fulbright reports like to hear (the director in London told me I'm a model grantee) and also giving him simple hints about the money-spending & importance about a wide cultural background-sharing, which is more important (in their huge end-of-the-year triplicate form which I'm just filling out) than academic work which must, of course, be very good too! I really want to see Warrie 'have the chance to enjoy life and the Fulbright allowances are good enough to let him take girls out etc. with "special" treats like operas & things, & he should meet lots of fascinating women & develop endless self-confidence. Elly thinks he is just marvelously handsome and dear.

It is one of those clear rare champagne-aired mornings which make me feel like a sinner against creation when I go into the huge factory-stacked library not to glimpse the sun again before it sets, but my dreams of the moors & the Cape sustain me. I will not feel at all "guilty" in indulging in sun & sea there. You know, I think that through our years of family scraping to get money for scholarships etc. we three developed an almost Puritan sense that being "lazy" and spending money on "luxuries" like meals out, or theater or travel was slightly wicked! And I think all three of us are being given the rare chance of changing into people who can experience the joys of new adventures and experiences. You are the lesson to us all: I really think you have grown, in the past year, at least 25 years younger: in the sense that you are so wonderfully open to experience! So few women manage this. Ted & I look forward to having such fun with you this summer & next year, simply picnicking on Nauset beach, & swimming & talking & taking long walks. We live very simply by nature, in our favorite old clothes & with our cheap red wine for dinner & (this year at least) no theater, movies or extras. But every now & then we believe in going out to dinner, or dressing up, like we did this last Saturday night & going to a party. The editor of Gemini[1] gave a cocktail party to all The Literati of Cambridge, & Ted & I had never met him, so went: I in that lovely pink knit dress I wore for my wedding, & new white heels (what a blessing to wear heels with Ted & still be "little") and a silver head-band he'd bought me for a surprise for a time when I was depressed about exams. A most enlightening affair. The change in attitude from my last social appearances last year was a pleasant shock: I was simply chuckling inside: all the writers & editors flocked around, every remark I made was repeated as ultimate in wit, and both Ted & I left practically stifled with laughter: we are simply the literary paragons of Cambridge & our year's absence from social affairs plus the fact that we publish in every magazine that comes out, has done amazing things to our reputations. It was fun to get an objective look at the world: we work so hard & are so demanding of ourselves that if we take a breath or sleep late one morning a week we feel Lazy. And compared to most humans, ironically, we are madly productive genii!

I sold my beloved old Smith-Corona last week for £15. 15s---about $44. We put two adds in the paper[2] & only one couple came & bought

1–English satirist and writer William Donaldson (1935–2005) and British playwright Julian Mitchell (1935–). At the time, Donaldson was at Cambridge and Mitchell at Oxford.

2–The two adverts read: 'SMITH-CORONA Portable typewriter, good condition. 15 gns. – 55, Eltisley Avenue, after 7p.m.', *Cambridge Daily News* (27 April 1957): 15, and 'SMITH Corona Portable, good condition, 15 guineas. 55, Eltisley Avenue, after 7p.m.', *Varsity*, (4 May 1957): 4. Seven items below the *Varsity* advertisement was a notice for the current *Granta* issue listing both SP and TH among the contributions. SP most likely had a Smith-

it: very lucky for us. Granta came out this week with 2 poems by me & a fable "Bartholomew Pygge Esq" by Ted: our first appearance in the same mag. together: the poster had our names in the list in big black letters: I'm going to try to steal one. It is so symbolic of our life & work together. Got your packet of food, as I may have said, just in time for my exam-grind: so invaluable. What fun we'll have making up boxes of goodies for Warrie! When Ted & I go to Italy for a year, we'll expect you to come for the summer & take an adjoining villa! Next week the 2nd Gemini comes out with 3 poems by Ted & a story & book-review by me: we'll send you a copy. We've decided to leave Cambridge June 5th, giving only a couple of days for the colossal job of packing & then spend the rest of the 2 weeks on the moors with Ted's parents before we sail: one of our happiest thoughts is that our beloved parents can share in all our good fortune & happiness. Ted is the most understanding dear about my work: when he sees I'm very tired from studying he insists on doing the dishes or making morning coffee or some little thoughtful thing which makes me feel like the queen. I really feel I am one of those women whose marriage is the central experience of life, much more crucial than a religion or career or anything: and I have found the only perfect husband for me & so can write & work & do all the rest from a solid happy center. We look so forward to leaving this gloomy dusty house: each time I go past the landlady's filthy junk under the stair, or beat endless dust out of blankets etc., or battle the oven, I think: only one month more, then home! every step from here will be one better for us. Can't wait to write on my novel this summer. I really feel I am going to do a fine one! All my love to you & our wonderful Warren. After all these years of work, sickness & death & bearing others sufferings, you must enjoy every minute of life with Warrie, me & Ted

xxx
Sivvy

Corona Silent model which is visible in a photograph of her desk in Lawrence House, Smith College, taken in *c.* April 1955; see Smith College scrapbook, p. 71; held by Lilly Library.

TO *Warren Plath*

Tuesday 7 May 1957[1] TLS (aerogramme, photocopy), Indiana University

Tuesday morning

Dearest Warren!

Congratulations! Mother's letter came this morning with the marvelous news of your Fulbright grant! O, how wonderful it is for me to re-live my own excitement & picture the terrific experiences which you will have! I'll be so interested to see how they run the program in Europe & Bonn looks like a fine location: rail to Paris, & so near (compared to Cambridge) Italy & the mediterranean. You will surely have long vacations, like I did, in which to travel to your heart's content. Paris, Rome, etc. Is it a one-year program, & what will you be studying. I feel I'm handing the Fulbright torch to you & think it's the best thing you could have! I feel I have found not only an exquisite little town in Cambridge, but also journeyed to find myself & certainly came through trials & triumphs to get there. Something, paradoxically, which I had to go away from America to do. Ted read mother's letter with me & just beamed. Do count on our seeing you off from New York! & try to take a minute to write us a line about your program of study, etc. How many others will be in Bonn on the program?

I am now in the tensest time of exam study, from morning to night & there <u>still</u> isn't enough time: and it is the most beautiful season of the year here, which I must forgo. But I live in dreams of the cape & our summer. You must drive down with mother every weekend to stay with us: as I remember there's an extra bedroom with twin beds & a cot on the porch. That way we'll get double our worth for the rent. I'll be reading madly in preparation for my courses at Smith & writing on my novel, tentatively to be called "Hill of Leopards" about an American girl finding her soul in a year (or, rather, 9 Fulbright months) at Cambridge & on the continent. it will be very controversial as I intend to expose a lot of people & places. And start my new gospel, which is as old as native rituals, about the positive acceptance of conflict, uncertainty, & pain as the soil for true knowledge and life. How I long to begin it! Ted & I want to devote our lives to writing & travel & raising a family of at least 4. He admires you very much & hopes you can take us both fishing on one of those ships on the cape some time. Ted loves to fish & is so marvelously restful to be

1–Date supplied from postmark.

with. How heavenly it will be. I can't wait to get out of this dusty dirty gloomy coal-bin of a house (except for the front room in which I am now writing) to go to the moors, then the Atlantic, then home, then the Cape. Smith scares me, but only in a healthy way. I will gain the much-needed sense of "giving" and (for once) supporting myself, which I could not live without. I will work to really interest my students (I imagine I'll have close to 100 in all!) and feel it will be a perfect way to "share" my Fulbright experience & learning, as well as by writing. Isn't it a relief to know you've got the Fulbright just as you begin taking exams? I remember my announcement came on the day of my first final exams at Smith[1] & I gained the confidence of knowing the exams weren't deciding my future, & so did well on them. Mother says you've put up the screens & doctored the lawn. My little white house shines in my head like a small sun. You, too, I think, will know what it means, when you've been away a year. We must always keep 26 Elmwood road in our family, no matter what! You must think of your Fulbright year as life & experience as much as study, spend all your allowance & travel much. The allowance is very liberal, I think, & I'll be so interested to know how yours runs.

We've just heard that Macmillan Co. has received the manuscript of Ted's animal fables & hope that a larger firm might be more adventurous than the tiny children's department at the Atlantic Monthly Press who finally rejected it. We have no more news of acceptances since our London magazine one, but this very nice ex-Cambridge grad in London who works for an agency (I haven't signed up or anything, because their american agent is that horrid New York gin-drinking painted lady, once a fiction editor at McCall's whom I met at the Cape just before I left, mother of that imbecile life-guard) says my story "The Smoky Blue Piano"[2] (which I sent to every magazine in America) is "quite excellent" & they will send it about here for me: I changed the background to London, cosmopolitan as I am getting to be. I hope to break into the woman's slicks this summer. I just haven't had the time to rewrite. The Ladies' Home Journal liked my laundromat story (two people meet at a laundromat via a very funny 13-year old girl quiz-kid type & fall in love finally) and said they'd look at it again if I rewrote the ending: no promises. Well, I sent it to Good Housekeeping & when it comes back will rewrite it: I think I should sell

1–See *Letters of Sylvia Plath*, Vol. 1, 928. According to SP's calendar, she received the reward on 20 May 1955.

2–Smith College holds a typescript of 'The Smoky Blue Piano' with a 55 Eltisley Avenue, Cambridge address. Additional typescript copies are held by the Rose Library at Emory and the Lilly Library.

it somewhere, the setting is quite "original": their motto is: LOVE LOVE LOVE: but not, please, in the same old setting: Love in jet-planes, Love on water-skis, Love in Sumner Tunnel[1] (traffic jam, etc.) but never Love plain. So I put mustard, pepper & curry powder on it. O the sun is so lovely, & I must bury my bleared eyes in 2000 years of Tragedy. My life is just balancing till the end of the month. Then, whoopee! novels, stories, poems. I can feel them battering to get out. DO WRITE. We both send love & congratulations & an invisible rabbit's foot for your exams.

Love,
Sivvy

TO *Henry Rago*

Tuesday 7 May 1957 — TLS (aerogramme), University of Chicago

55 Eltisley Avenue
Cambridge, England
May 7, 1957

Dear Mr. Rago:

I was very pleased to hear you'd accepted my four poems for publication in Poetry and am just now jotting down the few relevant items that might be appropriate for your Notes on Contributors column.

Since last writing you, I've had poems accepted for the first time by Accent, The Antioch Review and the London Magazine. After my tripos exams in English lit. this month, I'll proceed home with my British husband to write on the Cape all summer and then to Northampton, Mass., where I begin teaching freshman English at Smith College this fall.

My address after June 5th, by the way, will be:

26 Elmwood Road
Wellesley, Massachusetts

With all good wishes,
Sincerely yours,
Sylvia Plath

1–A tunnel under Boston Harbor which connects East Boston to Boston. At the time of this letter, traffic travelled both ways in the tunnel.

TO *Aurelia Schober Plath*

Friday 10 May 1957 TLS (aerogramme), Indiana University

Friday am, May 10

Dearest mother . . .

Couldn't resist sitting down & writing some more good news about my wonderful Ted which came this morning before burying myself in the library for the day. FABER & FABER, The British publishing house, has just written to accept Ted's poetry book for publication in England! Not only that, Mr. T. S. Eliot (who is on their staff) read the book & the publisher writes:

"Mr. Eliot has asked me to tell you how much he personally enjoyed the poems and to pass on to you his congratulations on them."[1]

We were concerned about getting a British publisher as this was left up to us by Harper's & Faber & Faber was the 1st we sent the book to (after my re-typing the whole thing) & it publishes people like WH Auden, Spender, Marianne Moore &, yes, Richard Wilbur (Ted & I have just bought his collected volume[2] which came out here this spring). The only snag now is whether Harper's will be willing to wait a month till September with publication as Faber wants to submit the book for British Poetry Book Society choice & it has to come out here first for that: the book would thus be guaranteed a sale of 800 copies plus very wide publicity. Otherwise, Faber wouldn't be able to publish it till next spring. I do hope Harper's sees the light & waits that extra month. Ted gets 15% royalties from them, 10% from Faber: so little but I suppose the publishers publish poetry as a favor & make most poets pay their own printing costs. But with TS Eliot added to the list of notables endorsing Ted, I don't see how he can lose! I am so proud.

I want to buy a super scrapbook for Ted & paste up his letters & poems for him & our posterity. I am living in my head already at home. Eating cookies, eating breakfast with you & Warren on our little greened-in porch, driving for a picnic at Ipswich. O how lovely it will be to immerse myself in Family. You & Warren must drive down to the Cape every weekend to stay with us. There are plenty of beds & what fun we'll have. I dont want to miss a minute with you two: Ted & I will work all week

1–Charles Monteith to TH, 9 May 1957; held by Emory University.

2–Richard Wilbur, *Poems: 1943–1956* (London: Faber & Faber, 1957). SP's copy is held by Smith College.

& take part of the weekend off to go to the beach with you. Warren can drive, because I wouldn't want you driving down & back alone. Ted & I will write enough I'm sure to pay for our summer. Also, we'll be bringing from 1 to 2 hundred dollars home as we are saving like fury, now that the ship fare is off our necks.

Smaller items: I got two poems accepted this week by ACCENT, an avant-garde literary quarterly that accepted two of Ted's poems only about a month ago. And Ted got one poem (not in this book, but beginning his 2nd) accepted by the New Statesman & Nation,[1] a weekly like the Nation in America, very good & left labor, to which we subscribe. He has already a folder labeled: "2nd book" which has about 5 or 10 good poems in it already. Do tell our mailman you're going to start getting letters addressed to Hughes. We're putting our return envelopes in with the Wellesley address now. Since last June Ted has sold 14 poems, a broadcast poem & a book to two countries: I guaranteed 15 poems sold in a year if he let me be his agent when I first met him & he's written his best since we've been working together. Even as I have: I've had 16 sales since August (just twice as many as I'd sold in the 5 years before meeting Ted) and many of these, like Ella Mason & her 11 Cats,[2] were assignments Ted gave me last spring! If only I can get my book accepted in the next few months it will be perfect.

My two main ambitions this summer (apart from preparing my course at Smith & writing poems, naturally) are my novel[3] & breaking into the women's slicks finally: I feel years older than I was the summer I left & my stories which I wrote this year, particularly the one set in a laundromat, are really much much improved. If I devote my whole self & intelligence to it, I know I can make it & 5 stories would be a year's salary. Ted wants to make children's books his other field. Also, my novel is The Thing & I want to get the whole damn thing written this summer & get Peter Davison to look at it, suggest re-writing, & then submit it to one of the novel contests. Novels are a cinch to get published compared to poetry. We are so devoted to work & only long for this month to be over to get into it. I am planning to try an article on Cambridge for Harper's & a story on Cambridge for the Atlantic: both editors said they would be interested in seeing my results as such. The doors are open: one only has to slave & work & live for the art of writing as well as living with the utmost integrity & emotional sympathy.

1–Ted Hughes, 'Letter', *New Statesman* (28 September 1957): 387.

2–According to SP's calendar, she wrote 'Ella Mason and Her Eleven Cats' on 2 June 1956.

3–'~~is~~ are my novel' appears in the original.

Do you think Mrs. Moore might come on the 29th if you asked her? I do admire her so & thought she might be up that way for Clem.

I glow with pride every time I think of Warren's Fulbright. I should think it would sustain him through exams. Mine begin in two weeks from this Monday & I won't know my schedule till next week: even that will be a relief, in planning my work. Do take care & don't do any work for us: let us fix up the garden etc. we'll be rested from the moors. What fun to have you in Italy with us in two years. You must plan on at least a summer there: all the art & sun. Maybe we'll have a grandchild for you by then, even, if we can afford it & have our writing well advanced.

much love,

Sivvy

Do write as often as you can: Ted & I love to get your letters!

S.

TO *Aurelia Schober Plath*

Sunday 12 May 1957 TLS, Indiana University

Sunday afternoon
May 12, 1957

Dear mother . . .

I'm enclosing a little assortment of the Cambridge magazines. Gemini is rather impressive with its 100 pages & guest contributors & the Granta art & layout is exceptional, I think.

You'll find two of my poems in the 1st Gemini: "Spinster" is the one accepted by the London Magazine & reviewed in the Sunday Times. The 2nd Gemini includes a rather tedious ghost-story by me & a book-review of some Oxford dons poems plus three fine poems by Ted: "Wind" appeared in the Nation, & the "Famous Poet" is accepted also by the London mag. Granta has one old, one new poem by me & an old fable of Ted's: nowhere near as good as his new ones.

In two weeks exams begin; then in 3 weeks they're over. We are eating well. I am just dying to come to America. & write. We are so happy Ted's book is accepted by Faber & Faber & that T. S. Eliot likes it! I have been living on that news while studying all week. It seems the greatest living poets think Ted is wonderful & under these auspices, his book might even make a little money!

xxx

sivvy

TO *Lynne Lawner*[1]

Thursday 16 May 1957 — Printed from *Antaeus* 28, Winter 1978

Thursday, May 16, 1957

Dear Lynne,

Your letter caught me just as I biked home for lunch between my daily intellectual safaris at the Univ. Libe where I am crystallizing my opinions on 2000 years of tragic drama (that started to be trauma) and 2000 years of moral philosophy from Socrates to DH Lawrence not to mention French, Med. English and all sorts of other lovely things. Exams start in 10 days & the prospect of writing solidly from 9 am to 4:30 pm with an hour off for lunch for 3 days strikes me as preposterous yet, after my halcyon days typing exams at Smith: I should be practising penmanship even now, because my pen-hand is as functionless as the vermiform appendix.

It was good hearing from you: so good, in fact, that I consider it a treat to sit down & write a letter before biking back to my purgatory. Which I actually like, in its own way: poems & stories seethe to be written when I have to discipline writing for a month like this & again I say: Wait Till This Summer.

Speaking of which, I hope I can see you before you go to Cambridge & hundreds of congratulations on the Henry. You must know the novelist Nat LaMar from Harvard (mustn't you? I am so sure everyone must know everyone, because all the loose ends get tied up eventually & you find that the two friends of yours you are introducing for the first time to each other have been married for seven years) – he had a Henry to Cambridge last year & I hear he has finished the first draft of his first novel via the old international grape-vine. Do let me know what you hear of him & if you see him say I hope Ted & I might see him when we come home this summer.

Ted being my husband for almost a year now: a poet, like they say, but Yorkshire, not Welsh & unlike Dylan in much more than poetry. It would be too impossible to go into the vision clairvoyance etc. involved in our life & the amazing way it's worked out: suffice it to say I can't remember a time I wasn't married to him. He will daze them all: even Wilbur who (shh!) seems to avoid the really jolting experiences like birth, sex, war, etc. in favor of such elegantly modulated nature & philosophy pieces. However: we have got his anthology (published in Eng.) & admire him

1 – American poet and art scholar Lynne Lawner (1935–); B.A. 1957, Wellesley College.

immensely & long to meet him. Ted who has been hitherto ignored in England (poetically speaking) for various reasons of deadness, sterility & incredible intellectual corruption (cf. Lawrence on this) suddenly leapt over their heads & won the New York Poetry Center First Publication Prize for his first book which should be published this fall by Harper's: W. H. Auden, Stephen Spender & dear familiar Marianne Moore (who objected to 3 "bawdy" poems which weren't really) judged this Anglo-American affair. Faber & Faber has just accepted the book for publication here with the express personal congratulations & approval of Mr. T. S. Eliot. So we sail for America & should arrive in Wellesley around June 26th. Will be at 26 Elmwood Road until July 12th: is there a chance you could drop over? I'd much rather have a person-to-person talk of Cambridge than try to write about it. Never met Leavis or Daiches[1] personally but went to their lectures. Dr. Doris Krook is the most magnificent woman lecturer going whose pet love is Henry James[2] (she gives a fine series of lectures on him) & also philosophy. An Admirable woman. No blue-stocking don. The gospel of the redemptive power of love in a religious humanist framework. Get her for your supervision in something (James or phil.) supervision like "honors unit". Ask to go to Leavis' supervisions in criticism: you have to have a will, which the Br. girls don't have, to manage these plums. You will invariably feel like Isabel Archer in Gardencourt[3] before starting on the voyage to a soul through the various overcivilized corruptions of Europe. British men are very lovely to look at, but except for a rare few, scared of intelligent women who are pretty too: a fashionable lawyer expounded to me the system of double-morality which I think you probably have agreed with me on & vice versa in our Holyoke talk: there are very few men who can take a woman who is vital & creative plus intelligent. Such as one Oxford chap: happy to adore you as the eternal feminine over candles & partridge, but damned if he's going to discuss philosophy, religion, politics or anything else that matters: get to know Nicholas Monck, the Granta editor (about the only magazine). You'll become known as a poetess: I've had about a fourth of all the stuff I've written in 2 years published here & even reviewed in the London Sunday Times. Much is dead here (you'll probably take a much more laudatory view of writing in America) but it's a magnificent experience & it is possible to discover yourself in ways not really easy at home by giving yourself greater challenges. *Please* tell me

1 – Scottish literary historian and literary critic David Daiches (1912–2005).
2 – American writer Henry James (1843–1916).
3 – Henry James, *The Portrait of a Lady* (1881); Isabel Archer is a main character.

what you meant by *Best Poetry 1955*: is it the Borestone annual & if so I haven't seen it & what in heavens name have I got in it? I got a strange note about an antique sonnet I wrote at college, accepting it for some such, but do tell me. Have you a book ready yet? Loved your account of the Holyoke reading.[1] Saw Don Lemkuhl[2] arrive here last year with a peroxide blonde matron whom he claimed was his aunt, but didn't follow him up. Insist on *Whitstead* as the place for "digs": lovely old house for 10 girls, green garden, etc. In college is like a reformatory: flats generally dirty & grubby with shrew landladies. Do write very soon & describe Wilbur. He certainly has catapulted to fame. Is he staying at Wellesley? Also, news of you: poems, thoughts, etc.

best wishes –
Sylvia

PS: If you want to see about 6 poems written in Cambridge look up <u>Poetry</u> (Chicago): for January 1957.

TO *Aurelia Schober Plath*

Sunday 19 May 1957 TLS (aerogramme), Indiana University

Sunday noon: May 19th

Dearest mother . . .

I have the feeling I haven't written for quite a few days but have had no special news & been working doggedly at the library. Got your red-ink letter with the happy smiley face & just think! In a month from tomorrow we'll be sailing on our blessed way home! I can't imagine it, it seems such a dream. I was so interested to hear your views on Wilbur: his collected poems (which we've bought) were well reviewed here this week as "workmanship" but the reviewer said something which I believe: that Wilbur had nothing really centrally interesting to say about life.[3] He

1–Lawner participated in the Glascock poetry competition for a second time in 1957. Other poets included: Robert Ely Bagg, Terry Brook, Michael M. Fried, Constance Horton, and F. L. Seidel. Judges in 1957 were Anthony Hecht, Howard Nemerov, and Andrews Wanning.
2–Donald Lehmkuhl; B.A. 1955, Columbia University. In the *Best Poems of 1955*, Lawner won first prize for her poem 'Wedding Night of a Nun'; Lehmkuhl second prize for his poem 'Hart Crane'; and SP third prize for 'Aubade'.
3–G. S. Fraser, 'Parnassian Grades', *New Statesman* (18 May 1957): 649–50. Fraser writes, 'He does not seem to me to have anything centrally interesting to say about life, but he is a superb verse craftsman who makes most of his English contemporaries – those between thirty and forty – looks like fumbling amateurs . . . Mr. Wilbur's book should be bought and

is magnificent writing on potatoes, toads, similes for her smile & roman fountains & philosophical witticisms but he completely misses writing about war, birth, love, etc. I am sure Ted is potentially a much richer & powerful poet! Something about Wilbur smacks of milk & honey instead of blood.

Anyhow, Ted will win the Pulitzer[1] some day too. & we will get Saxtons & Guggenheims, just watch. I am delighted at the way Ted looks forward to America: more & more in every way. He just can't wait to get out of England. & neither can I. Glad you are happy about Faber & Faber. If only Harper's will approve their scheme to bring the book out here first, so the Poetry Society might select it! We would like very much to meet Wilbur & his wife[2] and I feel someday they'll want to meet us. Let us know right away if any rejected manuscripts come home to you, for we've sent some with that address. After June 4th our address will be care of Ted's folks. New England certainly seems to be the center of holocausts! That terrible fire[3] & just before I left the hurricane.[4] Maybe it's the stupid H-bombs. Hope the paint comes out all right: what a bother to have it done again! Don't work at home though. Just rest & rest. & remember we are counting on helping you fix up things for the party, so just wait till we get there. How lovely to have another man in the family, and such a man! This has, alas, been a very trying week for us: a stream of rejections & nothing very cheerful, just work, with exams beginning for me a week from tomorrow. I have a very heavy schedule, but it is over at noon on Friday May 31st which is the day Ted gets finished teaching. I Have two exams each on Monday & Tuesday which means I'll be writing from 9 am to 4:30 both days with an hour off for lunch. French & 3-hour essay Monday, Criticism & Moralists (the heaviest paper) Tuesday; then 2000 years of Tragedy Wednesday afternoon & a blessed holiday & Chaucer friday morning. Be wishing me luck. I'd actually rather have it hardest the first two days & taper off. But the mere feat of writing for a whole day is rather exhausting. The minute I stop exams I'll be doing the herculean labor of packing our 300 books & clothes etc. We are going to try to sell our beloved coffee table, the one bit of furniture I like, & our rusty bikes

---

read, both for sensuous pleasure, and as an example of what sheer workmanship in verse means.'

1–Richard Wilbur won the 1957 Pulitzer Prize for *Things of This World*.

2–Richard Wilbur was married to Mary Charlotte Hayes (Ward) Wilbur (1922–2007).

3–Due to drought conditions, severe forest fires broke out in Massachusetts and throughout New England.

4–See *Letters of Sylvia Plath*, Vol. 1, 946n, 952, 955–6.

& couch & get some money that way. It is amazing to me how we have paid all these huge bills for tailor, dentist, ship, visa, etc. Really colossal for our budget, but we have done it. The house rent at only $12 a week has helped.

Now Teddy has no summer clothes. Can Warren go or you & I go & get him a summer suit as soon as we get home? I don't know what the men wear, but Warren will. & he needs a bunch of white shirts & a winter coat. How strange, my whole wardrobe interest has shifted & I'm as excited at Ted's new purchases as mine: he literally had nothing but dungarees & a dress suit when we married & now at least has a fine charcoal grey wool suit & two casual jackets. We must get him fitted up in a nice wardrobe he likes, very subtly.

Ted & I just got the dearest letter imaginable from Do & Bill Cruikshank. Do tell them how we both loved hearing from them & it's only my exams & packing that prevent me writing back in person right away, but we'll make up for it when we see them in person. Tell Do especially that what she said about marriage is exactly true & she is a darling. By the way did you get your little pottery dish that I had sent off before your birthday? I don't want to pay the bill till I'm <u>sure</u> you got it intact (It was insured for breakage).

We have my driver's license here & will bring it with all our great official envelopes, visa, certificates etc. Ted is coming as an emigrant & we want to establish a homestead in America from which we can travel. Ted is sharinghis lovely little house on the moors with his sister for the rest of his life & we will want to travel about some always. We are both perishing to get writing in earnest again. One must really be anti-social for the bulk of the year to be a writer who also works & keeps house! But this summer should be heaven. In the first 2 or 3 years of our marriage we would like at least 2 books each accepted: one poetry book for each of us, a novel for me & a children's book for Ted. Just wait.

Went for a walk yesterday just after a rain & saw eight baby swans, five baby ducks & the most amazing assortment of brightly colored iridescent snails by the roadside: pink with black stripes, yellow, pale green, etc. quite astonishing. Do write as much as you can these next weeks to keep my morale up. We so love to hear from you. Love to Warren & dear grampy.

xxx
Sivvy

TO *Aurelia Schober Plath*

Friday 24 May 1957

TLS (aerogramme), Indiana University

May 24: Friday

Dearest mother . . .

How lovely it was to get your letter this cold gray morning: Ted & I read it aloud over breakfast & both of us send congratulations & much love to our new Associate Professor! Really, though, you have long deserved it, I should think. Does your salary improve much? I would appreciate it so much if you would have a long talk with us over finances in America because we have been living from hand to mouth literally with all our big expenses like shipfare, dentist, tailor etc. & at this point can't imagine how people afford their own furniture, linen, clothes, kitchen iceboxes etc. Not to mention children. We want to start saving in America & I suppose it would be advisable for Ted to take out life insurance & both of us to have blue-cross or something. We would like to set up housekeeping in America & travel from there: in other words, leave our furniture etc. there when we go to Italy, say & travel only with our books, clothes & kitchen essentials. Ted is daily getting more of an America-lover. I tell him there is much there to disagree with but one can live one's own life at one's own speed & writers are welcome & can live well, which is impossible here. We both couldn't bear living in England for myriad reasons & would never want to settle in Europe: just a year here & there. We'll need your advice about saving, rent, etc. Both of us want to rent a house in Northampton, no more of this apartment living. Neither of us can stand having other people walking through our rooms, phoning outside our livingroom & surrounding us on all sides: the extra rent would be worth the house psychologically. We want a study just for writing & studying: not the livingroom or the bedroom but a real writing-room. We can't wait to get out of this house with that stupid couple upstairs. I hate them coming through my kitchen when I'm cooking to empty garbage, or get coal out, etc.

Which brings me to say how happy I am that Aunt Marion[1] will be moving in with you next fall. Ted thinks it's a good idea too. Both of us forbid you to ever let strangers rent the house under any circumstances: it would be intolerable. Psychologically super-sensitive as we are in our family (Ted is too) we feel like outlaws in our own home if some stranger

1 – Marion Freeman. The Plaths used the term 'aunt' quite loosely.

is using things. Their presence is a constant nerve-racking abrasion. In one's home one shouldn't have to "prepare a face to meet the faces that one meets."[1] And having Aunt Marion come will be a fine thing. You both have shared so much of life & can be frank & not "company" but just good friends that you will have the advantage of sharing your thoughts & experiences & understand when you want to be alone etc. I think you should do it on a year's basis, depending on what happens when Warren comes back from Germany etc. He might want to live at home. Ted & I will naturally want to come down to be with you over Thanksgiving, Christmas & Easter at least & Marion will then of course want to be with her family so that will be fine. I am very happy about it & think you should enjoy each other immensely. How we envy you hearing Wilbur:[2] Ted & I will no doubt meet him sometime but he above all American poets is the one we'd like to ask hundreds of questions & get to know. Ted will be a real rival of his in a few years, I think! Perhaps I told you that in a review of Wilbur[3] here the critic said he was a superlative craftsman & workman & very elegant but had few if any "central truths about life." Which Ted does have.

We were stunned this week to get the proofs of Ted's book not from Harper's but from Faber & Faber,[4] one week after they'd accepted it! We've gone through & through it with a little but incomplete handbook page on proof-marks & put in endless commas & Ted has made some alterations: which I've limited: he would rewrite a poem to eternity & stop the presses: I don't mind retyping constantly but we realize we must be much more strict in checking the typed ms. we send. You need to review us on punctuation rules (have you a grammar book?) and ms. correcting. You must remember all this from daddy's[5] book & we need you as a 3rd impartial proof-reader. What fun it should be though! I don't count it as work at all: we'll be always having something to proofread I hope. By the

1–T. S. Eliot, 'The Love Song of J. Alfred Prufrock', *Complete Poems and Plays of T. S. Eliot* (New York: Harcourt Brace, 1952): 4; SP slightly misquotes: 'To prepare a face to meet the faces that you meet.'

2–It is possible ASP planned to hear Wilbur read at Brandeis University on 7 June 1957 as part of a 'Living Anthology' of poets honouring William Carlos Williams or a reading Wilbur gave at Wellesley College on 13 June 1957.

3–'of his Wilbur' appears in the original. SP did not cancel 'his', but did add 'Wilbur' by hand.

4–The corrected page proofs are held by Lilly Library.

5–Otto Emil Plath (1885–1940); German instructor and biology professor at Boston University, 1922–40; SP's father. Author of *Bumblebees and Their Ways* (New York: Macmillan, 1934).

way, Ted got an awfully nice surprise letter from Russell Lynes,[1] editor of Harper's magazine who was shown some of his poems, liked many very much & bought a short one "The Dove-Breeder"[2] for $25 to publish before the book is published (they have a long list of poems & won't have time to publish more than one before August). Isn't that fine! We'll have the check sent to 26 Elmwood. In a fit of excitement I added up the money we've earned since our wedding day last year when the first acceptance came: each of us have had 15 poems accepted apiece since then & each of us have had one poem accepted twice, both in America & England. Ted has earned $243 (much of it yet to come) with 4 poems not yet priced, so it will be more, & I have earned $231 (much to come) with 5 poems accepted that are not yet priced. So we figure that by our wedding day anniversary we will have earned between us $500 in poems & neither of us have been working at working but forced to teach & study. We can't wait till this summer! Me for my novel & stories & poems & Ted for his fables & children's books & poems. We heard dear shrewd funny lovable Robert Frost read[3] yesterday afternoon to a packed enthusiastic hall: he's getting an honorary degree from Cambridge this spring. Ted loved him & I feel the two of them have much in common. Well, I must gossip no longer but STUDY. I take exams at night in my dreams, alas, as well as next week. I'll do my best, but as Ted says, I have my education & the marks can't alter that.

We both send much love to you & Warren
In 32 days we'll be with you –

xxx
Sivvy

<on the return address side of letter>

ps – Has the pottery bowl I sent you insured early in April come yet?

1–American art historian, author, and editor of *Harper's Magazine*, Russell Lynes (1910–91). Russell Lynes to TH, 17 May 1959; held by Emory University.

2–Ted Hughes, 'The Dove Breeder', *Harper's* (August 1957): 65.

3–Robert Frost read at the Mill Lane Lecture Hall, Cambridge.

TO *Aurelia Schober Plath*

Wednesday 29 May 1957 | TLS (aerogramme), Indiana University

Wednesday am: May 29th

Dearest mother:

I am taking time early this sunny morning to limber up my stiff fingers in preparation for my Tragedy exam this afternoon and write you so you will know I'm still extant. Just. I have honestly never undergone such physical torture as writing furiously from 6 to 7 hours a day (for the last two days) with my unpracticed pen-hand: every night I come home and lie in a hot tub massaging it back to action. Ted says I'm a victim of evolution and have adapted to the higher stage of typing and am at disadvantage when forced to compete on a lower stage of handwriting! My exams Monday (another American girl & I went with knees shaking) were quite pleasant: French translation & notes fair & simple and the afternoon Essay topics varied and interesting, a marked change from papers of other years: I took "Stylization" and, I think, wrote a very clever essay ostensibly in praise of style in all its forms, as a religious devotee of style, defining it as that order, line, form & rhythm in everything from the sonnet to the whalebone corset which renders the unruly natural world of Becoming bearable: I made up a fable of God as the Supreme Stylizer & the fall, & an allegory of the history of man: a bloody pageant in search of the Ultimate Style of thought, ritual, etc. Bringing Yeats & Eliot in, etc. I wish I could have it back, but noone ever sees a paper again or knows what one gets on the separate papers. Anyway, I was elated Monday, but the exams yesterday were worse than anything I had imagined: Dating, that black terror of Americans who have no sense of the history of language, was compulsory, and it took half an hour simply to read the exam through. It seems so ridiculous to anaylize & compare the imagery thought, movement et. al of 3 poems in 10 minutes each, for there is no time to respond naturally & your opinion changes radically in that brief time. It was, aside from the dating & the impossible prose-passage analysis which I didn't even bother reading or chosing, fair. But to dash home a mile on the bike for homemade coffee (the acrid store-bought stuff began to make me sick) and back again without even time to wash my face, for the hardest paper of all and find the nastiest exam imagineable. The 27 questions (of which we always write 4) were either appallingly & uselessly general: "Where, among the authors you studied for this paper, do you find something like a 'philosophy of history' and how much interest do you think it has for the student of literature?" or appalling limited (and often unfairly). For example, for DH Lawrence I had read most of the novels & memorized passages on moral theory only to be forbidden to speak of his novels & requested to analyze his life development (a favorite word) from either his short stories or non-fiction and verse. I was so furious at this that I got back by writing on his fable "The Man Who Died" about Jesus under a question on fable & moral. I'm sure the examiners didn't think of this; all the questions bore no reference to the moral work of the writers, but were large general relations to politics, law, the "thought of the century", etc. A mean, vague, fly-catching mind behind it all. As one person said to me on going out: It took me an hour to find how I could fit what I knew into the questions. Well, I wrote on Hobbes',[1] Lawrence, Blake and Plato, with references to my reading which has certainly been wider than any of the other people's. It's disgusting to think that two years of work & excellent, articulate, thought-out papers should be judged on the basis of these exams and nothing else. I have been so wound up by the enormity of disgorging such amounts of knowledge morning and afternoon that I am just going to spend my time on the moors (after the colossal job of packing this weekend) lying in the sun, hiking & unwinding. I'll deserve it!

Your two letters came, monday & today and cheered me up immensely. Glad you liked the blue bowl & the magazines. Ted's book seems destined to good fortune: Harper's and Faber agreed to publish it simultaneously on Sept. 18th: a much better date than mid-August, when noone is about the bookstores & all are in Europe or at the beach. Now, it will come out just as college begins & be featured & not pushed back as old stuff in the dusty shelves! It will also be eligible for Poetry Book Society Choice here (which won't be decided till June) which would guarantee a sale of 800 copies to the Society, rare in England as a poetry sales chance. We are very happy about it: it's getting "special priority" at Faber: they don't even have time to add the 40th poem[2] which Ted sent to the Harper edition which will no doubt be the best production. Monday morning I also got a note from the Yale Press saying my book had been chosen among the finalists for the publication prize but Auden wouldn't have judged them till some time in the early summer. My heart sank as I remember his judgments on my early Smith poems but I do hope my book ("Two Lovers & A Beachcomber") shows change & would give anything to have it win: Auden would have

1–English philosopher Thomas Hobbes (1588–1679). SP had written 'Some Notes on Hobbes' *Leviathan*' on 8 November 1956; held by Lilly Library.

2–TH's poem 'Song'; both the Faber and Harper & Row editions of TH's *The Hawk in the Rain* contain forty poems, though the order differs.

to write a foreword to it then. At any rate, Ted & I were glad it came to encourage me through this week at least without worrying I'd get the book back every day. Ted has been a saint: making breakfast & heating water for a daily tub, meeting me at 4:30 after exams & last night (I was very exhausted & aching) served me with steak mushrooms & wine on a tray in bed, doing the dishes afterwards. He is just ideal & so encouraging & stands by through everything. I feel I can face everything life offers with him by my side. We'll have to get his suit in America: time there will be relaxed compared to our jobs here. I want Warren to go with him or at least you & me. No time to tailor a suit here. Do ask Dorinda & Bill & the Aldriches over before the 29th – we'd love them.

Wish me luck: 2 more to go –

xxx

Sivvy

<on the return address side of letter>

PS. Wednesday 6 pm – tragedy exam all over – very stimulating & fair to make up for yesterday's two horrors – only one to go Friday am: blessed Chaucer & a whole day (!) to study for it. Luck & love to Warren

xxx

Siv

TO *Aurelia Schober Plath*

Saturday 8 June 1957 TLS (aerogramme), Indiana University

Saturday noon, June 8

Dearest mother . . .

How lovely it was to get your letter here, at what I feel is the beginning of my new life. I am sitting comfortably ensconced in one of the great armchairs in the little livingroom with big picture windows overlooking a rainy landscape of green moortops and fields of cows: toasting my toes in front of the coal fire, browsing in James' short stories while Ted reads Chaucer nearby and his older sister, Olwyn, recovers by sleeping late from her trip up from Paris yesterday for a 10 day vacation. As for me, I am just beginning to feel reborn. We took the tiresome train trip up here Wednesday, and it took me till yesterday to get relaxed enough to sleep off my deep fatigue. I got up for coffee in the morning and went back to bed & slept all day, and am now gradually feeling a sort of "resonance" in myself, and not the desperate tenseness of the past month. The minute

I finished my exams Friday (a week ago) & Ted his job, we began the colossal job of packing (we had most of our books crated in one crate and in two small trunks of Ted's) and selling what we could of our things & settling with innumerable gas & electric meter men, baggage insurance, £ conversion to $, ad infinitum. We had not a moment of respite, and I felt as if a brand had been stamped on my head after exams (particularly the horrid moralist paper) which prevented me from absorbing anything, but only pessimistically rewriting the exams in my head. A very nasty young don took this opportune moment for making a devastating and absolutely destructive attack on one of my poems[1] by showing how "hollow" they were compared to---guess who---John Donne! Very typical of mean Cambridge criticism (all the other little "creative" writers[2] were similarly dismissed, but I was singled out for particularly vicious abuse) & this coming at a time of non-writing was especially trying.

Instead of bothering to stay around for the plethora of teas, dinners & sherries of lit. magazines & dons, we left the first day I could legally. I never parted from a house with more joy & feeling of good riddance: the deep-rooted filth of rugs, drawers (the landlady never cleaned out half of her parents' stuff) & floors showed nakedly when we took out our books. We felt a cleansing process packing out things & knowing that we wouldn't see them again for a month, but would go free to the moors. No more Sassoons upstairs or crowds of Granchester tea-trippers passing our front window & gabbling: just endless green moortops & cows & pigs. We walk for miles & meet not a soul: just larks & swallows & green green hills and valleys. I never would have sensed the complete rest & freedom from "preparing a face to meet the faces" that one meets if I'd hung around Cambridge. Ted's mother has fixed up our room &

1–'Cambridge Opinions', *Cambridge Review* 78 (28 May 1957): 585–6, 607, 609. The anonymous critique discussed SP's 'Epitaph for Fire and Flower', *Chequer* 11 (Winter 1956–7): 3. After quoting the first seven lines of the poem, the reviewer writes, 'What is persuasive here is the success with which Miss Plath has struck a rhetorical pose: the opening couplet has a vigour reminiscent of the seventeenth century, forceful enough to carry one over the following lines and conceal for the moment that "crack your skull", for example, is no more than tough verbiage. By the time the end of the stanza is reached, however, the hollowness behind the impressive-sounding gesture at the start has become clear and is only confirmed by the rest of the poem: Miss Plath simply dissipates the effect of her opening by dragging in one image after another, never giving space for them to carry any but the barest scrap of meaning. Donne, one feels, would have confined himself within the opportunities offered by the opening metaphor, would have concentrated his thought and produced a corresponding richness of meaning instead of the disconnected sparks of Miss Plath' (585–6).

2–Other writers discussed with SP were Robert Symmons, Kenneth Pitchford, and Christopher Levenson.

we read in bed & lounge about & by the time we come home should be rested & raring to write & work & happy to see people at home. Every step now is an advance: this has been in many ways the hardest drudging year of our lives: I can scarcely believe we've been married a year come June 16th! We counted days till now all through the long dingy winter & America looks like the promised land. Both of us are delighted to leave the mean mealy-mouthed literary world of England. The only person I shall miss is my dear moralist supervisor, Doris Krook, who is as close to a genius saint as I've ever met. Dear Wendy Christie, her widow-friend and a beautiful woman, had Ted & me to dinner with Dr. Krook our last night in Cambridge, all by ourselves for a last tribute to the shrine: Dr. Krook gave me a book of James' stories about writers[1] in parting & a hug: I feel she loves me almost as much as I do her, and my work teaching will, in a special sense, be devoutly dedicated to her own particular light, a small spark of which I hope to carry to my pupils at Smith.

I loved your story about dear Grampy: how I look forward to seeing him: the 2 lobsters remind me that a lobster dinner is one of Ted's special wishes & also corn on the cob. I do hope we have a barbecue of chicken at Joe's place: Ted & I would love that. I really want to learn cooking from you every minute I'm home. My chef d'oeuvres are few & simple compared to what I'll want to produce in America. The first day up here I made one of my good stews: full of onion, potatoes, carrots, meat, garlic, bouillon cubes, dash of tomato sauce, & either white wine or cider. Quite matches the French, in a modest way. Also did a little chocolate cake with orange frosting, but all I make is, I tell Ted, like the earthly flawed facsimiles of the Platonic ideal of Essences which one may attain in America! We have lived so spartanly this last month that we will, we hope, bring over $150 back to America which, although paltry by living standards there, is a lot to save with our huge expenses of ship, visa and transportation bills. By the way, both Ted & I gave our bank as the Newton-Wellesley savings bank (is that right?) and should have from $50 (me) to $100 (Ted) sent or transferred there by the time we come home by our own banks. Could you go down & tell them to expect it & open an account for Ted? I went for a fitting of my lovely suit which is heavenly: black otterburn tweed with a faint white stripe (which hardly shows) in a kind of herringbone: very warm, classically cut according to my own orders. Should get it sent up here: only $56! Would be at least 3 times that in America: liked it so

1–Henry James, *The Lesson of the Master and Other Stories* (London: J. Lehmann, 1948). SP's copy held by Smith College.

well I left a bolt of green corduroy, gift of Ted's aunt, to have one made up exactly like it for more daily wear (will cost about $30). When I come back in 2 years I'll have some more made in light tweeds: just what I want in style & material for reasonable prices. These two should be invaluable for teaching. Love to you & dear Warrie! Only 17 days! How incredible & wonderful it seems. We'll call from NYC right away!

xxx
Sivvy

TO *Aurelia Schober Plath*

Monday 17 June 1957 — TLS (aerogramme), Indiana University

Monday morning, June 17

Dearest mother . . .

Well, your daughter has been married a year and a day, as the fairy stories say, and hopes to be married a hundred more. I can't actually remember what it was like not being married to Ted: but, as our horoscopes read, when Leo & Scorpio marry, they feel they've known each other forever in a former life. We took yesterday off from relatives & spent it together on a shady hillside overlooking all the moors reminiscing about our wedding day & the tough times past & good times to come. I woke to see Ted lugging into the room a huge vase of pink roses; we packed chicken & steak & books and set off. The weather up here this past week has been exquisite: it is the one place in the world where I don't miss the sea: the air is like clear seawater: thirst-quenching & cool, and the view of spaces, unlike anything I've seen in my life: you would love it, there are magnificent walks to take. I have now got my seasonal sunburn & am rid of the first stings: I always get so carried away with the sun I simply can't expose myself coldly by 5 minute intervals. So will be protected by coat of tan on the ship & eager for Cape sea and sun. Teds book proofs from Harper's,[1] which we corrected up here, were elegant, so much more professional than Faber's, & their re-arranged order of the poems (which Faber is not following) infinitely better. I am thrilled that the book is dedicated to me! My first dedication! I am so proud of the poems; each time I read them I get shivers. Ted will leave even Wilbur far

1–The corrected page proofs are held by Lilly Library.

behind. I just got my first term syllabus for my English 11 course[1] this morning: fascinating. I can't wait to prove myself teaching: I am ashamed I haven't read half the novels on the list myself, but I'll get the ones we don't have & take them to the Cape this summer so I'll have read them all, & naturally pick the ones I am best in: marvellous choice is given us.

I still can't quite believe that in a week from tomorrow (!) we'll be sailing into Manhattan & having dinner with you & Warren! It seems incredible that we change so much country in so little time. Very happy about the dinner with Mrs. Prouty. Do try not to arrange anything with the "little" people, though. I hope those can be all taken care of on the 29th. We look specially forward to the barbecue at Dot's. I hope you & Ted & Warren & I can drive to Nahant with picnics now and then. Also, I will have to drive up to Northampton for a couple of days to see about a house, my teaching course & a job for Ted, so we must have a time free for that. We have been so busy seeing relatives here & just unwinding that we haven't been able to get to work writing, & so will not want any visitors on the Cape at all: except you & Warren now & then. Perhaps you better keep our Cape address secret & say we can be reached through you. We will need to be completely antisocial this summer & write without stop to make up for this year & prove to ourselves that it is possible to write in America. Ted will love the country if he feels he can write there. Naturally the two weeks we are at home we won't expect to work, because we will be glad to see people, but for every social month, we must spend 11 antisocial working ones. Ideally, when we are writing full-time, we can stop & fraternize in the evenings & for dinner, the way most people do, but while we have to have day-time jobs, we must write in our spare time & simply deny ourselves company. I want to get so well on in my novel that I can re-write it during the academic year & have it ready for publication in the spring. I think it will be called "Falcon Yard": after many trials & errors in titles, this came to me & Ted at the same minute: it is the name of the yard where we met & thus the central episode of the book. There is a good chance Ted may get a teaching job at Amherst the 2nd year in America & if I am only asked back to Smith, it would be perfect. Then we would both apply for fellowships to write for a year in Italy. Me, I hope, on my 2nd novel, by that time. By which time I shall be 27 with enough books & money behind us to start having our projected 3 or 4 children: it is very important for us to have them later in life, in the late 20s, because both

1–Daniel Aaron to SP, 11 June 1957; copy held by Smith College. English 11, *Freshman English*. From the course guide: 'Practice in expository and critical writing in connection with the study of selected literary forms' (76).

of us are slow late maturers & must get our writing personae established well before our personalities are challenged by new arrivals. Doesn't it all sound heavenly & exciting? Work, work, that is the secret, with someone you love more than anything. We are both ideally suited temperamentally, with the same kind of life-rhythm, needing much sleep, solitude & living simply but with a few good clothes, many books, & my one extravagance is good cooking materials: lots of fine meat, cream, butter, eggs, etc. Also travel, as much as possible. I would somehow like to "see America" in our 2nd summer: New Orleans, via the east coast, Mexico, California, the Grand Canyon. To discover it with Ted. Always, when asked about my country, I have to qualify, saying I'm a New Englander & my information is only regional. By the way, do approach the Newton-Wellesley savings bank & open an account for Ted & say money is being transferred for both of us. We'll need bikes on the Cape, I think, for the beach is too long to walk each day, isn't it (at Nauset). Warren's, & maybe I can borrow some girl's bike. We loved your anniversary card which arrived Saturday. Had a lovely tea out here with Ted's relatives & his amazing Dickensian-Falstaffian uncle (my favorite relative) who's a millionaire, gave us £50, which is a big help. By the way, we're having 3 trunks & a big crate of books (freight) arriving on the ship (dock 92) but can't arrange railway express to home from here. Can you call them & ask them to pick them up on the 20th? It would help immensely & we could then unpack before going to the Cape & send stuff to cleaners & get the books we need. We don't want to hang around NYC trying to find some office open. Will try to write from London. See you in a week!

xxx
Sivvy

TO *Aurelia Schober Plath*

Thursday 20 June 1957 — ALS (aerogramme), Indiana University

Thursday morning
June 20th!

Dearest mother –

At last! The big day is here! Ted & I are sitting in Waterloo Station on the Cunard boat-train to Northampton,[1] raring to be off. We officially set

1 – SP meant Southampton, from which city the letter was postmarked.

sail at 5 pm this afternoon, just a little after 6 hours from now. I can hardly believe it's true! What a time we have had! – managing visas, bus, boat & train tickets! We left the clear green moortops yesterday at 7 am. & took a delicious picnic down on a scenic bus ride, arriving in London last night. We rested up well & had breakfast in bed this morning, wandering about Trafalgar Square, saying goodbye. The weather has been heavenly. Ted has had £48 (or so) sent to the Newton-Wellesley Bank from Cambridge & £50 from Yorkshire. We should arrive with about $100 in cash & traveler's checks. I will be glad to get all our funds added up at last. I hope we'll have a good bit – we have about $200 to come, still, from poetry. Now the sun is in my eyes as we move slowly out of Waterloo into open air. Big Ben, to our right, says 10:45 a.m. I do hope our mail gets forwarded home all right – be sure to bring it all with you in the car to Route 128 when you pick us up Tuesday night (only 5 days from now)! We may not get in till late, what with our p.m. arrival in NYC, customs & train schedules, but we'll call you from Grand Central. We had a lovely last few days on the moors & very good time with Ted's parents, & aunt & uncle. Do write Mrs. Hughes often & describe our doings for she loves to hear from you & will miss Ted – I hope we can persuade dear Mrs. Cantor to take some color camera shots of us at home, She is better than a professional! I was just thrilled to hear of Warren's summa degree & all the ceremonies – what a wonderful brother I have! London was full of carts of ripe strawberries as we left – I couldn't get any in Yorkshire, so I hope we can make a strawberry chiffon pie at home. But don't run about working & baking before we come! I was concerned to hear about Warren's dumping his old stuff on you this last weekend – make him help with it, or let us do a good deal. Our deep Cambridge fatigue is all gone & we are healthy & fine.

Have you been able to get a railway express agency to pick up our 3 trunks & one box of books at the NYC piers? We'll just leave them there to be taken care of. I am already longing for your cookies & our iced lemon & grape drink (no iceboxes anywhere here), all is lukewarm in summer – We are coming with nothing to our name but a few knives & tea cups! I trust we'll get a house in Northampton early in July, & dig up a job for Ted. Coming home with Ted will be like discovering a new country & seeing it all through his eyes. But we want to relax & not rush about. What fun we'll have this summer, each one of us having some special thing to look forward to – Warren his Fulbright, Ted his book & me my excellent job! You must relax & rejoice with all three of us. Warren can use my trunk, or Ted's & benefit by our travel Experience! He must also take a supply of anticold medecine! I am counting the days. All from now on should be literally clear sailing!

We both send you, in advance, much love & More congratulations to Warren!

xxx
Sivvy & Ted

TO *Edith & William Hughes*

Thursday 20 June 1957[1] ALS on *RMS Queen Elizabeth* letterhead, Family owned

Dear Ted's mother & dad!

Here we are on the great ship at last after a steak lunch – we set sail in an hour or two – Customs let us go by without even taking a look at our smuggled drugs & diamonds. The chicken picnic yesterday was lovely & lasted us till London where we got a very nice hotel with bacon & egg breakfast in bed near the station. Will write more from America –

Best wishes to Walter & Hilda & love to you both –

Sylvia

TO *Edith & William Hughes*

Saturday 29 June 1957[2] ALS,[3] Emory University

& Sylvia

(P.S. Isn't he magnificent!!!)

1 – Date supplied from internal evidence.
2 – Date supplied from internal evidence.
3 – SP's signature and postscript are at the end of a letter begun by TH, which has not been transcribed. TH mentions receiving a telegram announcing *The Hawk in the Rain* as Poetry Society Book Choice, and discusses the wedding party hosted by ASP.

TO *Lynne Lawner*

Monday 1 July 1957 | Printed from *Antaeus* 28, Winter 1978

26 Elmwood Road
Wellesley, Massachusetts
July 1, 1957

Dear Lynne,

We seem destined to swap theaters of operation, characters included, on the principle of the near miss. Cambridge for Cambridge, Wellesley for Wellesley, and even Robert Bagg[1] hoisting trunks on the dock. Ted & I arrived last week, me very purged & ascetic from violent mal der mer after martinis on board the next to docking day, and Ted heroically shouldering suitcases, trunks, crates totaling, god save us, 1000 pounds of effects. Mainly books. We walked into the arms quite literally of tall dark Russ Moro who knew Ted at Cambridge, violent brilliant Ellie Friedman (Smith graduate & working on TV) whom I knew at Smith, & Ted & I knew in Yorkshire, and also one blond, butterscotch dipped, enigmatically-blue-eyed Robert Bagg whom neither of us knew but who knew Russ at Amherst, and, you. I felt, and still feel a bit, shook in a space-time continuum like an ice-cream soda in the electric blender. Two years. Everything seemed immensely sparkling & shiny & fast-paced & loud after my bucolic existence on the Backs and the Bronte moors. The customs man, fat, sweating & suspicious, made us hack open our crate of 500 books, at which I melted into salt sobs, envisioning my treasures scattered from Harlem to Battery Park. Highly encouraged, with a nose for drugs & diamonds, the vile man reached in, flourished "Lady Chatterley's Lover": "Whereja buy all these books?" Wondering fleetingly about the latest bans, I firmly told him I was going to be a college teacher & thus read a bit. "Yeah," he looks up & down, "you're too young to get a job like that." I wrinkle my face antiquely. He persists in opening it all, pocketbook & pockets. God shed his grace. We are here.

Business (it is late & I am verging on utter incoherence): Old Hall is "in" college: in one of the 4 red brick buildings making the 3-sided quad. The rooms are often quite nice, I think, the best overlooking the garden. Not quite as independent as Whitstead (a house for 10), more like dorm life. You'll get to know the English girls better than I did, but I feel you will find it much more fascinating to get to know the men, which you

1–Robert Bagg (1937–); B.A 1957, Amherst College.

will. For reference, a very nice moral sciences man (philosophy, to us), Nicholas Monck, of posh King's college, editor of Granta, the Cambridge New Yorker. Look him up & give him poems. He visited Ted & me a bit & seems uniquely unaffected, penetratingly thoughtful & dear. Don't know this Cook[1] person. But think she may be big-boned, blonde & young. I've glimpsed one like that: other alternatives: short, Chas. Addams-pallid, fungoid shape or shrunk withered & Robin-Goodfellow size. Ponder upon high table where the dons eat. Ours (Clough Hall) was a study in caricatures. And give my dearest love to Doris Krook (Mrs.), prof in philosophy & Henry James, who illumined my two years all by her own diamond-light.

Do you want a bike? Don't pay to cart one over as I did. I left mine at Whitstead to be sold, but said I'd give you first option. It's a 5-year-old English Raleigh, 3-speed, needs oiling but very reliable. Auction price or whatever I figure is either $18 or £6. 10. Let me know if you want it, & I'll write them & it will be waiting for you. Bike is a must for classes, late dates, etc. Also, left my old but good-condition black gown for you as a welcoming gift at Whitstead: it will make you feel like Poe's raven.[2] I put a paper with your name on it: demand it as your feudal inheritance from a former retainer. If you run across any reviews of Ted's book in the local Cambridge mags in September (October, rather), you might clip & send us. The Cambridge Review, if it notices, is sure to concoct an extra special venomous one. London telegram[3] just announces it won Poetry Society choice for autumn there: guaranteeing a sale of 800 copies, close to miraculous in England.

Please write soon –

Love,
Sylvia

1 – Possibly economist Pauline Lesley Cook; member of staff, Newnham College, Cambridge.

2 – American writer Edgar Allan Poe (1809–49); his poem 'The Raven'.

3 – See Charles Monteith to TH, 29 June 1957; held by Emory University. See also Eric Walter White to TH, 3 July 1957; held by Emory University.

TO *Elinor Friedman Klein*

Friday 12 July 1957 TLS, Smith College

26 Elmwood Road
Wellesley, Massachusetts
JULY 12

Dear Ellie . . .

On and on and on. Tomorrow we leave for the Cape at last and leave phones shopping loving neighbors infants cats dogs motor cars and all those ills suburbia is heir to. To write & read those hundred novels my freshmen will be dying to have expounded. We take our neccessities: typewriter & that enormous and magnificent American frying pan which we will be perching on the edge of and eating out of. You are the only person besides mother who knows our address, so keep it very secret, but if you can take a day off let us know & come by for long beach & talk (we have no car, only bikes, so must needs walk places): it is c/o Spaulding, Box 153 Eastham, just off the main turnpike, a left turn, after the little Eastham P.O. Natives should know.

People at the party said: Who Is That Striking/Vital/Fascinating and/or Electric Girl? It was you. You were wonderful to come, & I only wish you could have stayed. We hope you will keep your job a summer at least, because at the end there may be stories from the two of us. Got a nice letter from Editor Keightley.[1] Thank him for me, and at the end of the summer, if Auden doesn't like me, he may hear more from me.

I am simultaneously writing a note to your mother explaining the Monday Events. And why we didn't call to bother her. Ted & I walked into a providential situation. Got to hamp & Mrs. (Crook) Yates[2] & learned how dismal and horrid it is to get apartments in Hamp, not to mention houses. That very day, a woman in the 3rd floor flat next to her discovered she was enceinte or whatever & would have to move. We were sceptical, Elm Street, etc., just opposite high school. Took looks: very private, top floor, shiny kitchen, icebox, stove, small; tiny shiny bathroom; bigger bedroom, still shining, huge closets; small hall at top of stairs; big living room all furnished, painted & papered by hand, lots more closet room. All this, with the Elm Street traffic like a whisper, very cool in the sun-swelter. $85 per month, all utilities (except phone) included.

1–David N. Keightley (1932–); B.A. 1953, Amherst College; M.A. 1956, New York University; Ph.D. 1969, Columbia University; editor 1957–60, World Publishing Company, New York.

2–Catherine C. Yates; resident of 333 Elm Street, Northampton, Mass.; SP's neighbour.

It seemed steep at first, until we spent the rest of the day scouting about (the woman renting it[1] advised us to, to realize how nice her place was & be satisfied). We did. Ugh. Either $125 a month houses 8 miles out of town with all utilities to be paid, or hot horrid unfurnished Prospect St. apartments for $85 and Miss Corwin[2] & the retired dean of admission[3] etc. living overhead & underfoot & telling young couples not to leave their muddy shoes in the hall. College rentals, agencies, & newspaper tried with nothing but growing scorn. Mr. Bodden[4] in person advised us to grab the apt., as did blessed Dan Aaron[5] who is my boss & whom I really adore. We paid a downpayment on the apt. (337 Elm Street, Apt. 3, rear) & collapsed in Aaron's living room for gin & quinine among all his Leonard Baskin[6] books & engravings & Anya Vierick[7] who keeps running over (or Veirick? no) and being very hot and Russian and tense. I can't think of anyplace I'd rather live than Smith, oddly enough, now that I'm not in college: Aaron knows artists, Italians, editors & Ted likes him & we both felt we'd walked in on The Day, because houses are nonexistent & even the Great Nabobic people live in 3rd floor apts. generally with utilities not paid.

Ted just got two poems accepted by the posh intellectual, and at least fat Sewanee Review.[8] He is filling out myriad biographical forms. Do you like coffee with or without cream? Have you got any angles or friends on Vogue or Harper's Bazaar? How about a real dark Heathcliffe picture of Ted in "People Are Talking About"[9] with all his book prizes??? His

1–Constance Linko Whalen (1928–2011) and her husband, Northampton police sergeant James J. Whalen (1916–98), who lived in the house with their their three children: David, Lawrence, and Sara.
2–Virginia Corwin (1901–96), religion professor, Smith College, 1930–66.
3–Ruth W. Crawford (1892–1959); director of admissions, Smith College, 1932–56; lived at 69 Prospect Street, Northampton, Mass.
4–William Albert Bodden (1903–73), treasurer and controller, Smith College, 1946–65.
5–Daniel Aaron (1912–2016); English professor, Smith College, 1939–72; director of the freshman English course (English 11) taught by SP, 1957–8. Daniel Aaron lived at 85 Washington Avenue, Northampton, Mass.
6–American sculptor and graphic artist Leonard Baskin (1922–2000); founder of the Gehenna Press, 1942–2000; art professor, Smith College, 1953–74; SP's colleague, 1957–8; friend of TH and SP.
7–Anya de Markov Viereck (d. 1972), twice married and divorced to American poet Peter Robert Edwin Viereck (1916–2006), history professor, Mount Holyoke College, 1948–87.
8–Ted Hughes, 'The Good Life', 'Things Present', 'Witches', and 'Everyman's Odyssey', published as 'Four Poems', *Sewanee Review* 66 (Spring 1958): 256–8.
9–'People Are Talking About . . .' is a recurring feature of *Vogue*. T. S. Eliot was one of the writers featured on 15 September 1957 for his book *On Poetry and Poets* (New York: Farrar, Straus & Cudahy, 1957).

poetry center businessman wanted to do a movie (he has great ambitions for his own name) showing Ted's "mind & sensibility working" or "the workings of Ted's m & s" against the background of the Empire State. But Ted wants no personal circus, only poem readings & whatever magazine notes will help the book. Peace & Cape Cod.

Do write us. And if you can get off come for a day for beach & talk. We've still got shirt---what to do, send or wait to see you?

Love from us,
Sylvia

TO *Aurelia Schober Plath*

Sunday 14 July 1957[1] TLS, Indiana University

Dearest mother . . .

We are just now sending Warren off after a very filling Sunday dinner: menu: cold chicken, rice, corn niblets, bread, wine, two kinds of delicious cake, thanks to you, and a bowl of chocolate pudding I whipped up this morning. It is absolute heaven here: peace, quiet, and Space to put our things: no clamor of neighbors & odds & ends to do. We will take a siesta after Warren leaves & begin work tomorrow after catching up on sleep & buying a store of food provisions in Orleans. We look so forward to seeing you & Warren on the weekend of the 27th: could you bring our electric eggbeater (mixmaster), towels & facecloths (we have none of the latter), a good big nailnipper & our coffee mugs which we miss. If the borestone anthology comes to Hathaway (they should let me know by postcard(would you send it on or bring it too?[2] Let us know if you'll be coming Friday night the 26th & we'll be waiting eagerly.

Much love from both of us.
Sivvy

<on verso of letter>
To Mummy
26, Elmwood Road,
Wellesley, Mass.
July 8th .57

1–Date assigned from internal evidence; likely misdated by SP.
2–Hathaway House Bookshop, 103 Central Street, Wellesley, Mass.

TO *Aurelia Schober Plath*

Thursday 18 July 1957[1] TLS with envelope, Indiana University

Thursday evening

Dearest mother . . .

I have just finished the dishes and am sitting down to write the last few of my thank-you notes before turning to Virginia Woolf's next novel.[2] I miss hearing from you, except for that brief pink note & hope you will write us little things gossip and all. Now that I am home, and you are so near, I miss you more than I did in England, where I stoically knew you and Warren were far beyond easy commuting distance. We look forward to seeing you here a week from tomorrow: do let us know roughly what time. And don't bring a scrap of food, cooky or even a pinch of salt: I'll have fun cooking up a few little dishes for you for a change, in my own kitchen, so count on resting. I just tried out Mrs. Spaudling's oven this afternoon when we came back from swimming & made a beautiful little two-layer 8 inch cake, yellow with 3 egg-yolks, and tried out a maple syrup frosting with walnuts which Ted likes very much. The enormous frying pan Elly gave me works beautifully, but takes up a great deal of room: it makes heavenly fried eggs, hamburgs, griddle cakes: very flat & perfectly even heat, set right on the proper degree. I do like it enormously, enormous as it is, and will get more adventurous with it as I go on. Perhaps I'll leave the pressure cooker to learn on when you come: I am a bit more wary of it.

The weather here has been beautiful. Ted & I are just getting into a routine and the beginning writing is, as usual, awkward & painful. We will never get in this rusty state again, for writing is the prime condition of both our lives & our happiness: if that goes well, the sky can fall in. It is heavenly to write here: quiet, with no distractions or social duties. We try to get 4 hours of writing done by noon, bike to Nauset Light beach for the afternoon of swimming & running and readbooks in the evening. I shall only have to go shopping once a week, which is fine. We drove down with Mrs. Spaulding Monday & loaded up on myriad supplies & stores: $25 worth, rather staggering, but the first week is the most costly. We figure on $15 a week at most from now on, fingers crossed.

1–Date supplied from postmark.

2–SP's journal entry for this day mentions *Jacob's Room*; she also read *The Waves*; SP's copies of both books held by Smith College.

Mail has been rather dull: Ted's bank is, praise be, sending on his money: it should be about $270, so I'd appreciate it very much if you'd check with our bank on this & get a deposit slip.

Mrs. Prouty sent a lovely letter with a check for $150 (which staggered us both & will help relieve us wonderfully about the September bills). She didn't want it to be a "check in the bank" but to have us get something we loved: furniture, or such. I thought I'd write and tell her we're getting the pottery dinner set with it, as it is an exquisite one, and say we're going to buy our first furniture, a big writing desk, with the rest of it when we get to Northampton. Which we really are. Do you think that's all right?

I keep trying to think of what to tell you to bring: towels, facecloths, the electric mixer, & the one thing Mrs. S. doesn't seem to have: a grater, for carrots, cheese, etc. Also cookie sheets. That's it.

Also have Warren bring or send the key to his bike lock which he neglected to leave with us. I am a bit grumpy about not hearing from that poetry manuscript. By the time you get this it will probably have come back & you will have sent it down here. It would actually be a relief to stop wavering between hope & despair and learn its fate definitely. Do send it right on if it comes, And call up, of course, if it should be accepted.

We also could use pillowcases.

Both of us are getting deeply rested at last and losing the exhausting Cambridge scars. You could have done nothing more wonderful than giving us these seven weeks.

Will write more later. Love to Warren and you. Tell Dot we're enjoying her radio-clock.

Much love,
Sylvia

TO *Aurelia Schober Plath & Warren Plath*

Sunday 21 July 1957 TLS, Indiana University

Sunday evening
July 21, 1957

Dearest mother & Warren . . .

It was lovely getting the long letter yesterday. I am feeling very happy and complete now, because today, at last, at last, I began making progress writing a story[1] I'm really deeply fascinated by, with "real" characters, a

1–Probably Sylvia Plath, 'The Trouble-Making Mother'. See *Journals of Sylvia Plath*: 288.

good problem-plot and deft description. After bumbling about on the first 5 pages of it Friday, I really got back most of my old fluency, and have much richer thoughts & experience to work with. My mind (my creative mind) had been completely crammed by hour by hour exam-reading & endless practical details and concerns for the last 6 months. And within a week, I am in the middle of a story, with two more[1] acting themselves out in my head, and knowing that the more I write, the better, much better, I'll be. So my dull gloom and rusty fingers and head are all gone, and all the rest of life: meals, beach, reading, becomes utter delight.

Ted has some more wonderful news: good fortune really draws more good fortune like a magnet: imagine: the slick austere New Yorker has just accepted one of his poems, "The Thought Fox"[2] for publication in early september!!! We heard via the Harper grapevine (several of his letters have been mis-addressed to Easthampton!) that they'd shown the New Yorker his poems & we should be hearing from them. Ironically enough, a year ago, we sent the same poem to the New Yorker & it was rejected. What reputation does! In the same mail he got the proofs of two poems[3] & simultaneous acceptance, from the Spectator,[4] a witty London weekly. Sp we should have a steady income of small checks for the next few months: 15 of his poems are scheduled to come out in August & September, no less! He is writing on some Yorkshire tales now & has done a lovely bull-frog poem[5] and is looking tan, wonderfully rested, and enjoying my meals. We are really unfolding & getting into our stride. I suppose a week is very little time to get adjusted in, after a year of slavery, to freedom writing, but it's seemed an age to us & now we're happy as chipmunks, our cheeks chockful of ideas.

About next Friday, now. I ABSOLUTELY FORBID YOU TO BRING ANY CAKES, CHICKENS OR PREPARED FOOD. I am in my own little house now & want you & Warren to be our guests, which means I'll do the cooking. You might, however, bring the CORN which we'd love.

1–According to SP's journals, one of these was 'The Day of the Twenty-Four Cakes'. Another story referred to as 'the Eye-Beam story'. See *Journals of Sylvia Plath*: 288 and 292.
2–See Howard Moss to Frances Lindley, 17 July 1957; held by Emory University. Ted Hughes, 'The Thought-Fox', *New Yorker* (31 August 1957): 28.
3–See James Michie to TH, 15 July 1957; held by Emory University.
4–TH published four poems in *The Spectator* that summer: 'Meeting', *Spectator* 199 (19 July 1957): 111.; 'Parting' (later titled 'September'), *Spectator* 199 (2 August 1957): 166; 'Secretary', *Spectator* 199 (30 August 1957): 279; 'Two Wise Generals', *Spectator* 199 (6 September 1957): 311. Acceptance and solitication letters from Anthony Hartley held by Emory University.
5–Ted Hughes, 'Bullfrog'.

And perhaps show me how to use the pressure cooker. I have made your mayonnaise already & it is delicious & can do the cooking of most things before you come. Will you have had supper Friday? And roughly what time will you be arriving: 8ish, 10ish?

More things to bring:

The proofs of Ted's poetry book (Faber)
A roasting pan
Cookie sheets
Carrot grater (not scraper)
Large nail nipper (you can take it back then)
Towels & facecloths
Pillowcases
Mixmaster
Fishing tackle
Virginia Woolf's Writer's Diary (a white book)
A good grammar book

And I think that should be all. I do hope the weather is as good then as it has been this week. Today was our best: we found a fine sand bar halfway between Nauset Light Beach and Coast Guard beach which had clear level water & long rollers, wonderful for swimming, as the rest of the choppy sharply-dropping coast isnt. I hope to get two stories off to the Saturday Evening Post[1] by the time you come & begin on my novel after warming up. Have read 3 Virginia Woolf novels this week & find them excellent stimulation for my own writing. Bless you a thousand times for making this possible for us: perfect place for reestablishing our writing. Who knows, we may earn next summer here all by ourselves this summer if we work hard enough. Mrs. Spaulding is very dear & brought over a little quahog pie & blueberry muffins. Ted & I get along fine with them & she looks very forward to seeing you. And so do we! Do write more, we love to get your letters. My suits should be a black wool tweed & green corduroy, in separate boxes, one from Cambridge (green), one Yorkshire.

xxx Sivvy

1–According to SP's journal, she mailed 'The Trouble-Making Mother' to the *Saturday Evening Post* by 25 July. *Journals of Sylvia Plath*: 290.

TO *Marcia B. Stern*

Sunday, 21 July 1957[1] TLS, Smith College

c/o Spaulding
Box 153
Eastham, Massachusetts
Sunday night

Dear Marty . . .

Here I am with sandy toes and a peeling nose in our small gray cabin hidden in the pines, after promising myself to see you before going, and planning to be industrious about writing letters and things. Well, we drove up to Hamp the week after our lovely supper with you & Mike and were completely knocked out by our treking about there and our return to packing for the cape that we literally haven't come to till this minute, after a week of easy living, no phones, simple meals, and the painful process of getting writing again after nine months enforced rusty absence from the typewriter.

I wish I could see you, so the two of us could simply sit and talk and talk, and hope we can do this in early September before I go up to Hamp for the year---I'll be driving back & forth with Ted a bit to get all our paraphernalia up.

We had miraculous luck about getting a place to stay: after an inauspicious beginning, the lady at college hall being sick whom I was supposed to see, and Mrs. Yates, the capitalist rental agent being very practical, hard-headed & depressing (most every house & apartment gone by May, very expensive apts. unfurnished $85 a month without utilities, houses 10 miles out $125 a month without utilities, etc. etc.), she mentioned idly that a 3rd floor apartment had just come open that very weekend: nextdoor to her on Elm Street, just opposite the high school. A woman had providentially got pregnant & was having to move out. We looked: and I recognized it as our place immediately: furnished modernly, spic and span, freshly redecorated by our landlords (the man is a policeman no less), with refrigerator & stove in the tiny new kitchen (very tiny), a bathroom, bedroom, sort of stair-hallway half-room and large livingroom with enormous closets everywhere. It was amazingly cool, even on that most sultry day, being insulated and the Elm Street traffic was a mere whisper. You couldn't hear a word from the landlady's children on the first floor & the whole thing among the treetops was

1–Dated from internal evidence.

blissfully private. The price was $85, utilities included, which, a month ago, would have staggered me out of my eyes, but compared to the rest of Hamp prices, left me very calm. The young woman insisted that we look around at other places, just so we'd realize what a gem hers was. So we did: depressing in the extreme: agencies had nothing but houses with antiques out in the country at fabulous prices, apartments were stuffy, unfurnished, noisy, ugly, with retired Deans of Administration and Miss Corwin of the religious dept. etc. etc. above & below. The newspaper offerings were even worse: we got Mr. Bodden's advice (in person) and Dan Aaron's advice (also in person): they said jump at it, so we did, and flew back to come to practical terms. I do hope you & Mike will drive up sometime during the year when we are well settled & I accustomed to facing dungareed hordes & expounding the pragmatic syntax of William James:[1] in fact you must come. For dinner & much talk.

One of the finest things that happened while we were up there was our accidentally & luckily bearding Dan Aaron in his den where he was in khaki pants, straddling a typewriter, grinning crookedly the way he does & very reassuring about teaching. I've never known him, or had him for a course, which is good, as I don't have a student-professor relation with him. Ted & he got along famously & we went to his house for drinks, found he was a best friend of Leonard Baskin (that brilliant young engraver, painter & sculptor who teaches at Smith & has his own printing press), knew Ben Shahn,[2] and was deeply involved in the recent court case between Peter Viereck & his wife (I don't know if you heard, but at Holyoke Viereck had policemen surprise her in the house & drag her off to a mental hospital, with various professors from Smith chasing the policecar). Anyhow, Anya Viereck, very small, dark, Russian & extravagant, drifted in with a feather boa while we talked. The young faculty sounds like much fun, and I feel, whatever the problems that come up, we'll have a fine time there. Lots of writers & artists & so on.

Ted's book, even before printing, is drawing him more & more luck. We almost dropped yesterday to hear from Harper's that the New Yorker (after all these years of our banging at their door) had seen his poems & accepted one for publication in early September. He's now scheduled to

1–For English 11 (Freshman English), SP taught two chapters of William James, *Varieties of Religious Experience:* 'The Religion of Healthy-Mindedness' and 'The Sick Soul', which are heavily annotated in SP's Modern Library (1929) edition held by Smith College.

2–Lithuanian-born American artist, muralist, social activist, photographer, and teacher Ben Shahn (1898–1969). Leonard Baskin published drawings by Shahn in Wilfred Owen, *Thirteen Poems* (Northampton, Mass.: Gehenna Press, 1956).

have about 15 poems appearing in magazines between now & September, when the book comes out: in Harper's, The Nation,[1] The New Yorker, the Sewanee Review, The New Statesman & Nation, The Times Lit. Sup.,[2] The Spectator, The London Magazine, Encounter.[3] I knew this would happen from the minute I read his first poems, but it is blissful to have it come so soon. And he just sits, unshaved, his hair every which way, munching raw steaks & writing more. Very wonderful.

Both of us are having the time of our life here, as we are basically hermits, happiest in the same pair of dungarees day in day out if we are only turning out writing. We write all morning, bike a couple of miles to the beach for the afternoon, and read in the evening. I am, after a week of biting my nails over tripe and awkward sentences and such, at last fluently writing a short story, with another spinning itself in my head. I shall myself bang on the doors of the Saturday Evening Post and the beginnings of a novel, which I won't know about writing till I've written the first draft of it. The problem this year will be as ever, Time. At least I have the job I'd have chosen for myself: I need very badly to work: to feel I can, and can teach. The daily pragmatic feel of the thing. And I'll be teaching my favorite writers, who stimulate my own writing: Lawrence, Virginia Woolf, James Joyce,[4] Henry James, Dostoevski,[5] etc.[6] I will be blue with awe the first day, but look most forward to being in medias res.

Please do write, Marty. I'd love to hear from you on paper, until we can get together in September: what you think, puzzle or dream about & do. Let's have a good talk, some night or Saturday. Both Ted & I adore the magnificent teak tray and dear curved knife: it will be displayed as a work of art in the livingroom between hours of social use. Best to Mike,

Much love,
Sylvia

1–Ted Hughes, 'Incompatibilities', *The Nation* 185 (20 July 1957): 34.
2–Ted Hughes, 'The Hag', *Times Literary Supplement* (16 August 1957): xvii.
3–Ted Hughes, 'Thrushes', *Encounter* 10 (March 1958): 45.
4–Irish writer James Joyce (1882–1941).
5–Russian writer Fyodor Dostoyevsky (1821–81).
6–SP taught the following: by Lawrence: 'The Blind Man', 'The Princess', 'The Prussian Officer', and 'The Rocking-Horse Winner'; by Joyce: 'Araby', 'The Boarding House', 'Clay', 'The Dead', 'Grace', 'Ivy Day in the Committee Room', 'A Little Cloud', 'A Painful Case', *Portrait of the Artist as a Young Man*, and 'The Sisters'; by James: 'The Beast in the Jungle' and 'The Pupil'; and by Dostoyevsky: *Crime and Punishment*.

TO *Edith & William Hughes*

c. Monday 22 July 1957[1] TLS, Family owned

Monday morning

Dear Ted's mother & dad . . .

Just thought I'd snatch a minute to slip in this little note while Ted was writing the last of his business letters (it's like a real swift business office here this morning, me typing, Ted dictating, proofing, signing, etc.) I've never seen Ted looking so well: rested, tan and twice as handsome as ever. The sea air here, the privacy in the pine grove, the peace, the good food & shiny little cabin are working wonders on both of us. We'll be writing like fury the next six weeks, and it is heavenly not having to teach, or study, or pack and unpack trunks for a while.

Ted's book, I am sure, will be a best-seller here for poetry books! Magazines like the slick elegant New Yorker are clustering around buying a poem here, a poem there, to be ahead of the others & print one before the book comes out. Everyone who has met him, admires & likes him, and I'm sure that this year will establish him as the brightest young writer in America. I knew instinctively that this would happen the minute I met him and read his work: it only takes lots of typing & work, etc. and presto! he will be famous. We had a very happy time in Northampton, found a lovely spic and span furnished apartment and met my young, very nice supervisor at Smith, a fine fellow who knows all sorts of interesting artists, printers and editors, so we'll be living and working in the midst of a real cultural colony this year! Ted and I are thriving, but miss you both, and the lovely moors and curlews and great windy days.

Much love,
sylvia

TO *Aurelia Schober Plath*

c. Tuesday 30 July 1957[2] TLS, Indiana University

Tuesday afternoon

Dearest mother . . .

Just a note to say that we received your nice letter a short while ago and are so pleased that you had such a good time here with Warren: Ted and I loved every minute of your stay and it was great fun planning for it.

1–Date supplied from internal evidence.
2–Date supplied from internal evidence.

Ted's bank writes that they are just now getting around to sending his account over ("There was no Newton Wellesley Bank in existence") and other than that there is no real news. We had a rumbly thunderstorm with lots of heat lightning and some rain last night, but the sun is out now, and it is terribly still and sultry with the mercury up to 90. We haven't been to the beach these last two days, as I took the laundry down yesterday afternoon with Mrs. Spaulding (two of the dishtowels came back with the same dirt smudges which infuriated me: I'm sure they just run warm water over the stuff) and today I wanted to finish the first draft of a 15 page story[1] which was irking me: I had to get it down before beginning on something more intriguing. I am once more reading in the evenings: Faulkner[2] this week, whom I find very difficult, and must get used to. Could you possibly get the Viking Portable Faulkner on your discount and send it down soon? Or bring it when you come? I'll need it, and would like to read some of his short stories before starting to teach. I'll settle accounts with you when we come back at the end of August, as I think we'll need all the cash we have down here now.

Mrs. Spaulding sent over some delicious quahog fritter batter yesterday, so I fried it in mazola and Ted & I found it delectable.

This tropical climate makes me long for the nip of fall weather, even if it means my job upon me. I hope, roughly, that Ted & I can drive up to Northampton with you and Warren on Monday, Sept. 2nd and then you return home while we fix up the house till Friday, return to drive warren to NYC Sunday the 8th, and come back after Ted sees his publishing people etc. by Wednesday or so, stop a night in Wellesley, and head to Northampton in time for me to get in ten days rigorous work before classes begin.

Did you have Forster's <u>Howard's End</u>[3] on your list? Was that the one yet to come?

Let us know all your news. Life here is pretty much of a piece, a very nice piece, and we writing away. Remember to get a clip-board for Ted: a heavy board with a clip (five & ten?) to hold notepaper typing size. Maybe Warren could pick up a fishline to go with the rod, or something.

More later. Meanwhile, Ted joins me in sending much love,

sivvy

1–On 29 July 1957, SP was working on 'the cake-story', probably her 'The Day of the Twenty-Four Cakes'. No known copy is extant. See *Journals of Sylvia Plath*: 292.

2–American writer William Faulkner (1897–1962).

3–English writer E. M. Forster (1879–1970). E. M. Forster, *Howard's End* (New York: Vintage Books, 1954); SPs copy held by Lilly Library.

TO *Aurelia Schober Plath*

Sunday 4 August 1957 TLS, Indiana University

Sunday evening
August 4

Dearest mother. . . .

Ted & I are just drying off over hot onion soup after the wildest bike ride yet, about 12 miles or more round trip to Orleans in the drenching rain. Ted's left ear had been giving him trouble for the past week and although he claimed it was getting better, he winced whenever I touched it & today his face started to swell up with some sort of infection, so we made an appointment with the nearest doctor, in Orleans. We were going to ask the Spauldings to drive us over, but they told us they were going away to their daughters[1] for the day and so we didn't even tell them we were going to the doctors for fear they would feel worried about going off. It was only drizzling when we started out, but by the time we had biked against the wind along the back roads for a couple of miles the skies opened up and in spite of slicker & mac we were soaked to the skin by the time we arrived. The doctor said Ted had an abcess & put a kind of wick in his ear and gave him a shot of penicillin as his temperature was over 100. I was naturally very concerned as the bikeride back was like riding up against a mountain stream. The water in low places of the road was actually up to our knees, and thunder cracked over our heads while the rain almost blinded us. There was no sense waiting anywhere because the rain kept up till late evening. I put Ted right to bed after a hot shower and have been feeding him hot drinks. We are to go back again tomorrow morning, so I shall see if Mrs. Spaulding can drive us. I do hope he won't have to have his ear drained or anything.

We have both been a bit blue this week after your departure and a bunch of rejections and this strenuous biking in face of great odds. We were trying to economise on food this week, and now these doctor bills will probably make a big indentation in our budget. I am using the doctor as a gynocologist so you won't have to make an appointment with one at home for me. Luckily Ted got a check for $63 this week from the New Yorker for his poem,[2] the most he's ever gotten for a single poem yet, so this will help us. I'm sorry I forgot to give you the $10 for the paper and my Borestone Book, but will do so when we come home & I pay for the

1–The Spauldings had two daughters, Annabelle and Lesta.
2–See Howard Moss to TH, 30 July 1957; held by Emory University.

suit, shirt & belt of Ted's. Have you got the bill for that yet? Ted just got a letter from his stupid bank, as I perhaps wrote, & they said they are sending his money which should be about $270. The dentist bill was $68 which with my fall treatments will no doubt mount up to $100. I do hope Ted gets a good September check from his book: we'll need it. He has four published poems and seven others toward his second book[1] already, very good ones, too.

Tomorrow I hope to do a big marketing---we didn't buy anything this week but ate up what was in the icebox & I defrosted it, which I guess I should do every week as the ice was about 2 inches thick. Thanks for forwarding all our mail so promptly & for writing: we look so eagerly for your letters. Got a nice note from Peg Cantor who is coming down early this week: hope Ted is well enough to see her & go out. I have just written a letter to the Yale Press asking about my ms. Another company, the World Publishing Co. (an Amherst boy we met in NYC the night we landed is an editor at it) is interested in seeing a book of my poems after reading the July issue of Poetry---do you have it yet? I should be sent a copy. So I'll try them if Yale falls through.

Much love
Sivvy

TO *Aurelia Schober Plath*

Tuesday 6 August 1957[2] TLS, Indiana University

early tuesday morning

dearest mother . . .

just a note to go in with the copy of this bank statement: perhaps you could take down these signed slips (3 slips in all) with the bankbook and get the total entered. with the change of weather yesterday to clear and crisp our fortunes and moods changed too and we have been having a fine time. the held up mail yesterday brought us news of this welcome $258 addition to our account, a little check for $5 for a poem of mine which must have appeared in the Antioch Review recently and a little check for the English equivalent of over $8 for Ted's two poems in a July issue of the Spectator, and a nice letter asking him for more poems. I am at last writing my first poem for about 6 months, a more ambitious topic:

1–Ted Hughes, *Lupercal* (London: Faber & Faber, 1960).
2–Date supplied from internal evidence.

a short verse dialogue which is supposed to sound just like conversation but is written in strict 7 line stanzas rhyming ababcbc: it frees me from my writer's cramp and is at last a good subject: a dialogue over a ouija board, which is both dramatic & philosophical.[1] I really think I would like to write a verse play, now. If I practice enough on getting color into speech, I can write in quite elaborate rhymed and alliterative forms without sounding like self-conscious poetry, but rather like conversation. So I am much happier. I mailed my babysitter (or, rather, my mother's helper)[2] story to the Ladies' Home Journal yesterday along with a revised version of my laundromat story: both are very light & frothy as they say, with much funny dialogue, but the mother's helper story is richer in many ways than the earlier one. I am as yet most pleased, however, about the one I sent off to the SatEvePost just before you came which is the most dramatically tight story I've ever written, starting at the peak of a crisis in the morning, with very tightly-knit in flashbacks & four rich characters, even five, and a surprise end climax in the evening. I am really hoping to sell it somewhere as it is a central problem, but not a trite situation. I am now revolving ideas for a Harper's article (or, rather, article for Harper's) on student life at cambridge. I hope I can write about 10 witty vivid pages for it. I'd love to get an article in their magazine.

Called Mrs. Cantor at her friends last night as she wrote to, but could get no answer. Will try again this am. . . . Just did try: she'd given me the wrong phone number, which was bothersome. She proposed a picnic, and the afternoon, but since Ted & I didn't have any picnic-suitable food & didn't want to waste our time making one, I said we were going to Orleans for the morning, which is true, as Ted has another doctor's appointment, which I didn't mention: she's bringing another little boy along with Billy, so I felt very glad we didn't sign up for more time. Mrs. Spaulding has been so nice---always bringing over little jars of pickle the tenants leave, or blueberry muffins or fish or corn people give them: she drove us to the doctors again yesterday & Ted got another injection of penicillin: his temperature was down & he feels much better, so we celebrated with a delicious steak & asparagus supper & wine last night & I made a good chocolate cake with French icing. Will write more later,

Love to you & Warrie
xxx Sivvy

1–SP, 'Dialogue Over a Ouija Board'.
2–Sylvia Plath, 'Operation Valentine'.

TO *Aurelia Schober Plath*

c. August 1957[1] TLS, Indiana University

Dearest mother,

I'm taking you up on your wonderful offer to type out these poems for me. I'd dreamed of writing twenty more in 2 months to take the place of the folded ones in the back of this batch, with which I'm now unsatisfied, but since this isn't a book-publishing contest, I'll probably enclose them.

The ms. should be typed in triplicate---could you do it in regular type, not the little elite? I'd like all poems double-spaced, with my name, Sylvia Plath, in the upper right-hand corner of each page. Don't number the pages, as I can do that after I decide on the order. Also, ignore my red notations, underlines & magazine names.

I'll send you a copy of the title page, acknowledgment list etc. when I get the order arranged.

A million thanks,
love,
Sivvy

TO *Aurelia Schober Plath*

Thursday 5 September 1957 TLS with envelope, Indiana University

September 5, 1957
Thursday

Dearest mother . . .

Thanks so much for the letter. I wrote 3 thank-you notes to the people in question the minute I got here so that's off. Ted & I really love the apartment: everybody we meet asks in tones of amaze: how did you get it? It's impossible to get apartments here! So we feel wonderfully lucky: it's so light and airy. It is on a very busy intersection and we continually hear the screak of breaks. Yesterday we witnessed an accident from our window: a screak, and then the crackle of metal and tinkle of glass. A stupid gas station boy turned right into the driver's seat: of a car coming innocently along route 9, and one man cut his head against the windshield, but noone was hurt seriously. We'll probably witness worse before the year is out, and I am very very careful.

1–Date supplied from internal evidence.

The last few days have been full of business & things are at last quieting down. We've opened a bank checking account, and spent $18 for a very nice kitchen cabinet which I needed desperately to use as a kind of china closet & untensil drawer, with a formica top which I can use as a work area & place for my electric frying pan: the kitchen is now fine. The cabinet is waist height, with two shelves, the drawer, & a top. We really needed it. My pewter set is proudly displayed in the alcove on the stair landing on Marty's wood tray & looks gorgeous against the dark wood. You will be pleased to know Ted likes the pewter teaset & the stainless steel table ware best of anything we have. The dinner set is lovely too.

We definitely need the big black bookcase sent up. Do keep the shelves & screws very carefully till we come, and we will bring them up with our books & possibly the little writing desk for Ted. The landlady can't possibly object to the bookcase, and she would be horrified at our using bricks on the floor she has painted by hand which discards its paint on anything rough or rubbing. The bookcase will fit perfectly (I was amazed it is only 4 feet wide---I thought it was at least 6!) It will be less expensive in the long run than carting about 2 new bookcases which we'd have to buy, I think.

I managed to get the College Purchasing office to loan me an old desk for the year & won't buy one unless we get one by auction, cheap. So with my loaned desk (all my papers are helter-skelter) & the little one for Ted, we should be fitted out.

Ted's party, praise be, has been postponed till Sunday, October 20, which should be perfect for me, when I've the confidence of a few weeks of teaching behind me & can really enjoy it: they're timing it to coincide with the opening of the Poetry Center[1] for the year: just fine. Maybe a week or two after that you can come up here. For the weekend: if they're having anything nice on: eat here & room at some little Inn down the street.

I get homesick for Warren every time I use his lovely Faberware which I love: they pour fine, without spilling a drop, and clean beautifully. I miss him in advance, especially knowing he's still in America, & wish I could see him again. Give him my best love.

I have been rather disconcerted at the way our $300 is vanishing. We'll probably have to draw about $150 more out of our bank at home, leaving an even $100 in it, as I'll have another round of rent to pay Oct. 1 before my first salary check, and want to be ahead in bills, not behind: I mean,

1 – 'the opening ~~for~~ of the Poetry Center' appears in the original.

wanting to pay the Nov. 1 rent with my October check, & not the back rent: we have to pay promptly on the 1st of the month, & I don't think I get my check till the first week in Oct. The phone, which will be installed next Wed., will be very expensive: $4 for installation, and $4.68 a month, including tax, for local unlimited calls: a dial phone, which can even dial home or NYC. I hope we won't have to use it for long distance though, but it is a professional necessity for me, for my students & colleagues to get in touch. They took a $20 deposit which we don't get back till we leave, another dent. Paid remaining $45 sept. rent & 42.50 agents fee, plus dentist $68 and doctor's $18, not to mention $30 for food supplies and about $15 for the innumerable minor household needs: from orange squeezer to liquid soap to potholders. Now I am set, bills should decrease rapidly. I hope you don't mind my going over them, but I'm really the manager of the exchequer & it gives me a sense of accomplishment to discuss my managing with you, as you can suggest economies, etc. We'll see you Monday:

much much love,
Sivvy

TO *Aurelia Schober Plath*

Thursday 12 September 1957 TLS, Indiana University

Apt. 3 rear
337 Elm Street
Northampton
September 12, 1957

Dearest mother . . .

Just a note to say how nice it was to hear your voice last night, only a few seconds away via our dial phone: I simply dialed your code number(!) 617 and then your own, and there you were. The stupid phone boy connected our phone wrong, so we heard the rings of the other party but they came, chastened, and repaired it this morning, so all is fine.

I wondered if you could dig up the pad for this typewriter? I didn't take it to the Cape and don't know where it could be. We need it for quieting it as much as possible.

I'm enclosing a withdrawal order for our bank which I hope you won't mind signing and taking down when you next go. I needed another witness other than Ted or myself: we just want a check for $150 made out to me, to deposit in our checking account to cover the next month's rent

& our food. If you could also write down a few instructions about the car: like the grease change, the Oct. whatever-it-is we're supposed to get, I'd appreciate it so much.

We're moved in at last, and slept till after 10, exhausted from all the lugging of books & furniture downstairs, but the desk is in, & all fits perfectly.

The swelling on the back of my gum is really painful & I wish you would call up that damn dentist & ask his advice about which I should do: I want to try something myself before wasting more money on a doctor or dentist & it is his responsibility. He seems to have built the filling of my back left tooth too far back, or cut a flap of the gum, as it is puffy & swollen & I can't bite straight, or my upper tooth grazes it and have to hold my mouth askew, with my tongue between which is very annoying. The swelling hasn't gone down at all either.

Our Xmas vacation begins Friday Dec. 20, so perhaps you could make a dentist appointment for Ted & me on Sat. Dec. 21 or Monday the 24th[1] or the 26th. We will no doubt have to go back to Northampton & work soon after that to prepare for the 2nd term for which I haven't as yet got my syllabus & for which I'll have to do my work during this term.

I'm writing Mary Ellen Chase, hoping to see her sometime soon, for she will no doubt have good practical advice to give me.

I hope you are resting up and eating well. We are happy to be really settled in now, and the apartment is lovely. Tell the dentist my bite doesn't feel correct, as if the back filling were a lump in the way, or at least ask him what to do about the swollen flap of back skin, which is like this: <drawing of teeth and gum> & bleeds if I touch it. Sorry to bother you about it,

Much love,
Sivvy

1–24 December 1957 was a Tuesday.

TO *Aurelia Schober Plath*

Monday 23 September 1957 TLS, Indiana University

Apt. 3 rear
337 Elm Street
Northampton
Monday, September 23

Dearest mother . . .

Got your nice long letter today. Much appreciated the advice about deep breaths etc. I ricochet between chills & fever but am working on a rather devil-may-care attitude which seems to be best with me, as I am so over-conscientious I will never be anything less than conscientious at least. My first class is on Wednesday at 3 pm. My schedule is: a 3 o'clock on Wed, Thurs & Fri, and a 9 and 11 on Thurs, Fri & Sat. Thus, in effect, my 3 pm class will be a test for the next day's two morning classes & I can revise mistakes in between. I have 3 office hours & "by appointment" and am supposed to see all my 65 students for conferences as often as possible, which I see now will take much of my time, but I want to be very conscientious about this, too.

I share an office in the Library on the top floor with a very nice old 18th cen. lit. woman, Miss Hornbeak[1] (lovely name!) who seems most kind & helpful---I have never had her for anything, so it is pleasant, not too personal. I am very lucky to be in the library---right between the class buildings[2] I teach in: I have 3 different classrooms, so shouldn't have too much trouble placing what I've said to which classes. Did I tell you over the phone that Mr. Hill,[3] the acting chairman of the department, & his extremely kind wife[4] came over one evening last week. He stayed for coffee as she had a meeting of some sort, & the percolator made an excellent brew which I served with date nut bars. I had always avoided his course in the development of the British novel[5] (which as usual, I regret) as I thought he'd be dull, but I got along fine with him and really like him, which is convenient, & asked his advice about office hours, etc.

1–Katherine Gee Hornbeak (1897–1985); English professor, Smith College, 1930–62; SP's colleague, 1957–8. SP and Hornbeak shared an office (room 59) in the William Allan Neilson Library, Smith College.

2–The English department was located in Seelye Hall, room 511. It is possible SP taught in both Seelye Hall and Hatfield Hall, which are on either side of the Neilson Library.

3–SP's colleague Charles Jarvis Hill (1904–99); English professor, Smith College, 1932–66; acting chairman of the English department, fall 1957.

4–Ruth E. Hill.

5–English 314 'The Development of the English Novel. Daniel Defoe to D. H. Lawrence'.

This next week is full of meetings: oaths of allegiance, Department & faculty meetings, bouffet supper & president's reception next Wednesday. How I long to be busy! This brooding and isolation is something I must avoid. As soon as I am busy, with a hundred things to do, read, forms to fill out, I function very happily & efficiently. I am sure that once I get into a daily routine, I'll find that I don't have to spend all my time on class preparation & correcting papers, and it will be a relief to know we are discussing only 2 stories for tomorrow, say, instead of feeling, as I do now, the abstract simultaneous pressure of the term challenging me all at once. Ted is wonderful: so understanding & cooks me breakfast & cleans up the dishes. I hope I perhaps can see about his having driving lessons: he feels helpless, I think, not being able to drive the car & would like to do so. I can't take it on myself to teach him in traffic & don't want to wait until he gets friends enough with some other man, so shall see about driving schools: have you any advice about the kind of lessons to ask for?

I am trying at present to learn about our college library and reference catalogues and indexes as we have to teach the library and the forms of research papers to our students too, and I blundered along happily in my college days, practically ignorant of articles in magazines, or dictionaries of slang etc.

The head of the Hampshire bookshop, an ex-Smith woman,[1] very nice, sent Ted two little bottles of American champagne on his publication day, last wednesday, & Harper's sent a telegram.[2] We drank one bottle then, by candlelight & will drink the other (about a glass each) when I've finished my first week of teaching on Saturday.

My first day of class is very routine: I'll introduce myself, as you say, talk about the course & assign the terms books and the week's assignments, and ask them to write out a questionnaire I'll make up---about them, their interests, their reading, so I'll have a profile of each one to help me get to know them & to aid in filling out my own information: I'm free to tell them (and encouraged) to come around to my office just to "get acquainted", so will give my best to this, seat them alphabetically, etc. My 2nd class day I'll begin really teaching: the most difficult book of the course: 2 chapters from Will James. The classes are not lectures, but discussions, so I can only prepare the main points to cover & perhaps a little background material, & must learn what I can draw from them.

1–Possibly Marion E. Dodd (1883–1961); B.A. 1906, Smith College; co-founder of Hampshire Bookshop in 1916, served as the store's Chairman of the Board, 1951–7.
2–Elizabeth Lawrence to TH, 17 September 1957; held by Emory University.

I also want to learn how to explain grammar mistakes: I have an editorial eye & know something's wrong when I see it, but must learn the rules.

I was amused about Dotty & the hats. Don't let her go shopping with you. You should let me come: she has no sense of adventure, style, or flair. The feather hat sounded lovely & you can always carry a stylish umbrella if it rains. Buy a real special one. I feel accessories are more important than a new dress: I feel really special with a good bag, shoes & belt & don't mind wearing my basic dresses year in year out.

I noticed what you said about morale boosting was true, this Saturday. I desperately needed blouses, for I was afraid this hot tropical Indian summer weather would keep up & I would faint of heat in my sweaters. Do you or can you discover the crescent shoulder pads for my nylon short-sleeved blouse given me by Mrs. Prouty at home? Its a lovely blouse, but I can't wear it until I find these detachable white shoulder pads. In my drawers?

I bought a very nice opaque nylon blouse with a round neck & becoming short sleeves for $5.95 and another special washable pure silk in a lovely taupe, browny, blacky pattern with a bow tie, lovely & floppy, which will be ideal with black suit, jumper & for afternoon teas. I have very particular taste in blouses, but do like them. As these are washable they'll come in very handy.

Must run to my office now, where I plan to read all afternoon. Do call Wednesday eve at supper if you can get over to Aldriches. After six. I plan to spend the evenings home. We're scheduled to go to NYc Sunday oct. 20 for a reception & half hour reading for Ted. Much love. Bless me on Wed, Thurs, Fri. & Sat.

your own
Sivvy

TO *Lynne Lawner*

Tuesday 22 October 1957 Printed from *Antaeus* 28, Winter 1978

Apt. 3 rear
337 Elm Street
Northampton, Mass.
Tuesday, October 22, 1957

Dearest Lynne,

Courage! Your letters[1] have arrived, all, I think, and I only wish I could meet you in the atmosphere above the Atlantic for a vigorous heart-to-heart about Cambridge & Life in general. Looking back, from a birds-eye view, I pluck the idyllic strings of my past life there (so much happened, that if I concentrate on the nice events & people they seem to fill up most of the time & space), but your letters reminded me of much lousiness that I slogged, trudged and agonized through in my first year. You are not unusual: you are, as you say, freezing, sick, and uncertain. Well, so was I. Cambridge is worth this: there *is* a Cambridge that is aesthetically heaven (wait till spring, alas, & you'll see), intellectually rewarding & personally fruitful in human relations. However, you have to really fight through a lot of ice, sludge and sham to find it. I am sorry my former supervisor, Doris Krook, isn't there this year, for she was my academic savior. You, however, will have Daiches, and he should be a great help. Let's start at this thing topically. If I sound didactic, it's partly because I know, through much misery, whereof I speak, and partly because everything came out all right in the end, in spite of crises, muddles and run-ins with the Newnham authorities.

Your academic program first of all. You seem to have two choices & it isn't too late to change in October & "catch up" on the tripos. I forget the grant you have, or if you want to get a degree, or can bear at this point the idea of a 2nd year. However that may be, I strongly recommend your going to Miss Burton, explaining how upset, etc. you were on being away from home or something to that effect, and that you now see, as in a burst of clairvoyance, how very much of a good thing the tripos reading can be. If you are now feeling as ignorant, unread, unintellectual as I did (and still do: it's a perennial feeling), you would do well to discipline yourself: the tragedy reading is stiff but fascinating, you can go through the Greeks,

1–Lynne Lawner to SP, [13 October 1957] and 18 October 1957; held by Lilly Library. Lawner misdated her first letter as 26 October 1957; date here assigned from postmark.

Racine, Corneille, Ibsen (reading 20 plays), Strindberg, writing papers & really getting an extensive & thorough knowledge of drama. It is a Good Thing. Miss Bradbrook,[1] in spite of her reedy pipestem voice & queer grey Charles Addams head, gives good lectures on modern tragedy, from Racine to Eliot, & Northam[2] is good & entertaining on Ibsen. Practical Criticism supervisions will do you good too, although they terrified me & my other American cohort: we had absolutely no background in dating poetry or prose (and I'm still not much good at it), but buy the 3 or 4 centuries of Oxford books and start reading through them to get a sense of poetic development. Try Leavis's lectures. I don't know what other papers you'd like to read for: I did the moralists, which is too stiff for one year, French, which was fun, and Chaucer and the Scottish Chaucerians, who are delightful. But remember, I say this from the other end of having done them. I suffered, sometimes crammed, and got blear-eyed while in medias res. I do think it's most important for you to have a well and strongly structured academic program: you won't regret it & it will be a beginning at filling in those huge whistling gaps which I had, and still, of course, have, but which are less terrifying than they were. You can still keep up Daiches, and would be able to do the reading he advises, but would also be enriching yourself outside & feeling less blank. Start going to a certain number of lectures regularly, trying the ones I suggested maybe, and see if simple discipline helps a bit. If you are only planning to stay a year, you still can get a lot of directed reading done this way. Also, try to smooth things over with Burton, your tutor, and Miss Abbott.[3] Humble contrition, tearfilled eyes and honest endeavor (how Machiavellian are you?) always help. Admit you were wrong, confused, and sorry above all to have inconvenienced them in any way. It's better to have them on your side, as you never know when you will decide to stop and write a book, get married, or something needing legal support. I honestly feel you'll be happier with a normal tripos program: you have netted plums of varying flavors with Holloway[4] & Daiches, so start by getting interested in your work. Let me know what works out here: you really can have lots of fun reading for the tripos: tragedy and poetry especially.

1–University lecturer and Mistress of Girton College, Cambridge, Muriel Clara Bradbrook (1909–93).

2–Ibsen scholar and university lecturer in English at University of Cambridge John Richard Northam (1922–2004).

3–Christine Abbott, Newnham College Secretary.

4–Poet and professor John Holloway (1920–99); fellow and lecturer of Queens' College, Cambridge.

Whitstead can be grim, as can anyplace, depending on your mood. My first year was harder, I think, as breakfasts were stiff and awkward, except for another American, a Scots girl[1] & a vital South African[2] who joined me in a certain humorous view of the prim Britishers. If you find a decent British girl, let me know. I found them all insufferable, shy, gauche and desperately awkward socially, or if social, dizzy butterflies. The good American mixture of blood and brains, savoir faire and common sense seems non-existent in Britain. I missed a woman or girl friend more than anything: and finally substituted Doris Krook and her friend Wendie Christie, whom I'd like you to look up for me if you feel like it (I never look people up myself). Wendie is in her thirties, I guess, a dear, lovely South African (I thought they were all black at first, but they're not) widow whose husband died in Cambridge (she has never really got over it), who has 2 handsome children, is a wonderful cook & hostess. She has parties for the dons that are much fun & Ted & I ate and cocktailed with her a good deal in my second year. She lives, or did live (ask the phone operator) in 8 Harvey Street (bike up the Fen Causeway, cross left by the Royal Hotel & go down is it Lensfield Road to the big Catholic church, turn right on is it Hills Road? and then your first or 2nd left should be Harvey Street. Look it up on a map, which I don't have. Tell Wendie, if you will, that I haven't written because I've been in a black mood not because I've forgotten her. I will write her very soon, too. I remember her as one of my two favorite women in Cambridge – she balanced Doris Krook, who was a kind of female Plato, beautiful and Jewish & brilliant as a diamond and as dazzling.

Tell Wendie how you feel about things, if you happen to get along with her. She is very kind, and has this private sorrow of her own which must be really shattering. I know I found her dinners a delight for she knows the young and elderish dons & I was sick to death of young fops. Of course, even among the dons, there are even worse fops, but look at them with an observant Dickensian eye, if you can manage such so early. I couldn't.

Practical advice about the miserable cold. Wear stockings (nylon) & wool kneesocks over them. You will be Known for this, but warm & so what. Wear piles of sweaters. Get a hotwaterbottle & pre-warm your bed at night. Get 2 or 3 pounds of shillings at a time from the bank, secrete them in a drawer & put piles in the gas meter at a time and don't skimp.

1–Dr Isabel Murray Henderson (1933–); B.A. archaeology and anthropology 1957, Ph.D. 1962; Fellow of Newnham College, Cambridge.

2–Margaret Roberts (1933–2007); B.A. Rhodes University; B.A. Newnham College, Cambridge.

For colds, see your panel doctor (have you got one? try Dr. Bevan[1] at 2 or 3 Trinity Street), tell him you come down with hellish colds & try to get an advance supply of good nosedrops, some sort of antihistamine that will cut down the twitchings, and get also, for medicinal purposes, a bottle of good rum or brandy with which you will lace your hot milk at bedtime. Pamper yourself. Take all or none of this advice. Leave the Newnham infirmary alone, & if you come down with another cold, cut classes, supervisions – if possible go to the Silver Street butcher & get a good cut of steak, fry it over your gasfire or the kitchenette one, get frozen peas & lots of fruit, & try feeding yourself. I found Newnham food ghastly & sometimes rose actually gagged in the middle of the dinner meal and rushed out into the moonlit or raindrenched gardens to be alone away from the brittle British table babble. Or cooked at Whitstead for me & whatever man happened to be around.

The Granta crew et al are, just as you say, mainly pretentious babies. You may find one or two nice ones, honest artists, or something, but they are rare & you've got to wait & look & be patient. If I had known Ted would stalk onto my horizon on February 25th I would have been much happier, no doubt. He colors all Cambridge in retrospect, but I managed to live, however precariously, until then. I remember getting involved with the ADC my first term, playing for a couple of nights in a 9-night centenary performance the part of a cockney whore in yellow satin,[2] getting drastically ill, all chills and fever and no voice, and leaving to recuperate at Whitstead (a kindly Kingsman[3] brought an organ to my room & played me Bach in the afternoons, but that was luck) and finding they got on swimmingly without me after all.

Read "Lapis Lazuli" to yourself, and say how wise and noble you will be because of all this. Also try "Thou art indeed just, lord, . . ." and other Hopkins[4] sourdough poems. You can make it worth being there. But don't be fooled into thinking it's easy. It may be easy for the Mays,[5] but I

1–Possibly Dr Edward Vaughan Bevan (1907–88); his surgery was at 3 Trinity Street, Cambridge.

2–SP played Alice in *Bartholomew Fair* by Ben Jonson, ADC Theatre, Cambridge University, 24 November–3 December 1955.

3–Joseph Mallory Wober (1936–), British; B.A. 1957, natural sciences, King's College, Cambridge; dated SP, 1955–6. Wober lived at 7 Peas Hill, Cambridge.

4–English poet and priest Gerard Manley Hopkins (1844–89).

5–Probably May Collacott Targett (1931–); B.A. 1952, economics, Smith College; B.A. economics 1958, Newnham College, Cambridge. Targett took over SP's room in Whitstead when SP moved to 55 Eltisley Avenue in December 1956. See Rhoda Dorsey and Sophie Consagra, compilers, *Memories of Whitstead* (2007): 51.

doubt if you could care for that kind of life, or that kind of person, being her, I mean. Needless to say, this letter is a trade secret. Full of anti-British propaganda. There are fine ones. But they are rare.

You will probably feel more like going "out" when you're well & doing more in your studies. Then, let gentlemen take you to dinner, plays, concerts (go to Kings evensong & Christmas vespers: feed your senses and spirit) and enjoy them for what they give you in a very pragmatic way: you give them your brilliance, looks, company: that's more than they deserve. You stand every chance of meeting some really nice people: are you trying Europe in the winter & spring vacs? Do go with somebody. I remember a ghastly spring week freezing and outdoor-sketching in Paris[1] between travel-dates when I stopped going out after dark because I couldn't walk around a corner without being solicited by street-apes and French gentlemen in foreign cars and it wasn't at all romantic. Even if you're with a man you don't have anything more than a platonic relationship with, it's better, I think, than going alone. Unless, of course, you are fortunate in chance meetings.

I'd better grind to a close. Tell me if any of this helps. Try the tripos & keep the big men too. And see if you like Wendie: she isn't "intellectual" but is a kind, vital woman. You might well meet older people through her, and this could be a help.

I have myself been going through a black spell, after my 5th week of teaching 3 sections of freshman English at Smith, 65 papers to correct every other week, and a huge feeling, again, of ignorance among my old mentors & thirtyish Phd specialists. There is one young new British woman[2] here whom I hope to get to know who also feels "unacademic", whose husband is also a writer while she teaches, but even she has had years of experience in Helsinki. And she doesn't want to write herself. Which I do. So I have been exhausted, frustrated, etc. and find it very different to "teach" a story than to "know" it in my own head: we have to "teach" also, use of the library, which I managed never to learn about, but used with a kind of hit and run clairvoyance, and the technique of "research papers" etc. So I find myself slaving over correcting, private interviews, the next week's preparation, & feeling apart from the faculty of veterans and champing at the bit to do my own writing. I am, like you, "unacademic" and enjoy reading & studying, but not the kind of

1–See *Letters of Sylvia Plath*, Vol. 1, 1154–7.

2–SP's British colleague Joan Maxwell Bramwell (1923–); English professor, Smith College, 1957–92; married to British writer James Guy Bramwell.

grubbing one does for Phds. I also get very tired, & long to cook pineapple upsidedown cakes & write on a book of poems, but must put off such luxuries till June. Which is a large question mark. Ted's book has gotten some good reviews & he gave a reading at the NYC poetry center this Sunday which was a treat for both of us. One has to sacrifice much to be a good teacher: either skimp on housewifery or outside writing & even then, I don't have time to do more than prepare for my freshmen. One is, alas, human. Ergo, life is no blaze of success and lucky strikes. So imagine yourself teaching 70 Wellesley freshmen symbolism in Hawthorne[1] & the proper use of footnotes, count yourself in a potential heaven, have fun, and write me soon about everything.

With love,
Sylvia

TO *Aurelia Schober Plath*

c. 3 November 1957[2] TLS, Indiana University

Sunday afternoon

Dearest mother . . .

Enclosed, the letters from Warren which we enjoyed no end. I'll write him in a day or so.[3]

Ted wants to know if you'd like to order any more copies of his book through him, because he can get them at a discount and we don't want you to get them in the shops and waste money that way: if you want some for gifts, tell us how many & we'll order them.

Yesterday we drove through the beautiful countryside, into the mountains over to Holyoke hospital to visit David Keightley, an Amherst graduate, 1953 & friend of Russ Moro, that boy who gave us dinner the night we arrived in NYC. Ted had met Dave in Cambridge, & I'd just glimpsed him at Russ's dinner, so we didn't really know him, but he wrote us a touching letter asking if we'd sometime drop over: on a rainy day last August 26 he and Russ drove into a tree after a skid on a slippery hill, and while Russ, driving, only had some cuts & a broken nose, and is now in NYC, David, in the driver's seat, was badly knocked up and suffered a

1–American writer Nathaniel Hawthorne (1804–64). Plath taught the following stories by Hawthorne: 'The Birthmark', 'Ethan Brand', 'Goodman Brown', 'Lady Eleanore's Mantle', and 'Rappaccini's Daughter'.

2–Date supplied from internal evidence.

3–See SP to Warren Plath, 5 November 1957.

smashed thigh. So he has been in traction for over 7 weeks. Ted & I stayed all afternoon, talking to him & really getting acquainted: he is a charming, sensitive boy, one of the junior editors of the World Publishing Co, and he obviously wanted to talk to get his mind off his pain: a few remarks slipped out: he does feel Russ's carelessness to blame, & since Russ is just drifting about NYC & David has a job waiting, he feels it's ironic to be so isolated and he must be in real pain, as his muscles are atrophying from lack of exercise. I've never seen anyone in traction before, & it must be ghastly to lie & not turn over, with pins through your leg and hundreds of weights & pulleys night & day. We'll go again to visit him in 2 weeks ---I feel it takes his mind off his situation & forces him to think of other things: we brought him a box of candy, since we couldn't get flowers or think of anything else, as we didn't know him, but he doesn't have much appetite & I wish I could figure out something that would cheer him up. But I suppose our coming is enough.

I felt strangely rested, even though very tired, simply seeing someone outside the faculty and student community, who had a different kind of trouble, and to whom we could talk frankly. I wish we could get to know more people outside the faculty, and gradually develop an outside life: it is a rest to be away from my job, which I wasn't at all till yesterday afternoon, & I find it little relaxation to have evenings with the people in the department: the specter of my questions hovers always in the background & they don't want to talk shop any more than I do. But of course, I can't be really frank with them, or say how I begrudge not sitting and working at my real trade, writing, which would certainly improve rapidly if I gave it the nervous energy I squander on my classes.

By the way, we just opened our package of dishes from the Newton Potter's[1] and found one luncheon plate split in half. I won't pay the bill until I get a replacement of this plate. So would you help us by calling up, first asking why they didn't say they sent parcels collect (most other shops certainly don't charge postage for such a large order) and demand that they send along the proper plate: I could bring the pieces home in November, but am not going to spend more postage sending them now. It's a lunch plate, next size down from dinner. Let me know the result of your calling: their order was over a month & a half late.

Ted & I looked so longingly at the farms on the hilltops here: we would like a spreading house, with a couple of apple trees, fields, a cow, and

1–Newton Potters, 1021 Boylston Street, Newton Highlands, Mass. Purveyors of contemporary pottery, Swedish stainless flatware, and porcelains.

a vegetable garden, because we can't stand city living, and don't enjoy suburbs where neighbors children and radios impinge on the air. We are really country people, and there must be a sunny hilltop place we could buy sometime in the next 10 years. I like the hills in Hadley and Easthampton, on the other side of the river, very much.

I hope, as soon as my job ends this year, to apprentice myself to writing in earnest. Part-time dallying never got a beginner anywhere and now I don't even have time for that, and feel my talent rusting, and it is very painful to me. We love this apartment & will probably stay here all summer no matter what we are doing next year.

Much love,
Sivvy

TO *Warren Plath*

Tuesday 5 November 1957 — TLS (photocopy), Indiana University

Apt. 3 rear
337 Elm Street
Northampton, Mass.
Tuesday night, Nov. 5

Dearest Warren . . .

I have been very wicked not to write sooner and we loved your letters. But I've been in a black mood and haven't felt like writing anybody, because I haven't had anything particularly cheerful to share.

I've just now finished correcting a set of 66 papers on two Hawthorne stories I assigned and am faced with cramming for my preparation for this week's classes which begin for me tomorrow. This coming weekend will be the first where I haven't had a set of papers or exams to exhaust me and put me off preparing anything much for class, so I hope I can face my problems squarely and get some idea of what the hell I'm teaching. I keep feeling I <u>could</u> make up some good stuff out of my head to teach them about symbolism or style, but have so little time as yet, and am always deathly nervous. I must make up little brief 5 minute lectures on topics, for I am a hopeless extempore speaker. If I only <u>knew</u> my "subject" or was an expert, but I am struggling enough to review mere grammar & term paper forms, which bore me, alas. This week, too, I'm being "visited" by other professors which is enough to throw me into a cold twitch. I wish I were more conceited, it would be a big help.

Ted's reviews are really amusing: every reviewer praises him in some way, although one or two british ones are reluctant: they are really grotesque: each seizes one or two or three poems & raves about them, passes off one or two others---but each raves about different poems: some say he is all music but has nothing to say (a very stupid review) some say he is all profundity, but has slack lines of rhythm. They are all rather batty.

The dominant note, however, is real praise: every review, even if it includes other books (by Marianne Moore, among others) is headed with a phrase referring to Ted. The NY Times Review by Merwin[1] you've heard of: very good, with its own picture of a hawk.[2] We just got a clipping from the Baltimore Sun headed "Praise For A New Poet":[3] a marvelous vehement thing including the following: "The judges made a distinguished choice. Mr. Hughes's poetic gifts are unmistakable; his work is resolved and firmly controlled. His diction is always appropriate and occasionally perfect. His only fault---and it is a minor one---is that he tends to overpower the language---to burden his lines with excessive richness.[4] This shortcoming however is dwarfed by the author's rare ability to handle cosmic metaphors with accuracy and novelty . . ." & more specific praise. From the Fort-Worth Star-Telegram comes an article titled "Poetry Marked by Power, Sensibility"[5] which refers to Ted's book & not to the book of Howard Moss,[6] the New yorker editor, which is reviewed after it & coolly reviewed. They blither enthusiastically about Ted's versatile biography, and say: "Hughes's poetry has been published in the Atlantic, Poetry, The Nation, and Harper's indicative of the high quality of his verse. Strength, sensibility, a feeling for words and effects mark his poetry, which is rhythmical, though not always metrical, and which uses rime sparingly. (She talks as if it were paprika!) Under the accolade of Marianne Moore, W. H. Auden, and Stephen Spender, Ted Hughes is off to an enviable start as a poet."

1–American poet W. S. (William Stanley) Merwin (1927–). W. S. Merwin, 'Something of His Own to Say', *New York Times Book Review* (6 October 1957): 43.

2–Bluestone sculpture entitled *Hawk* by Norwegian-American sculptor Trygve Hammer (1878–1947).

3–Irving H. Bucher, 'Praise For A New Poet', *Baltimore Sun* (6 October 1957): FE6.

4–SP skips a sentence, giving no indication via ellipses: 'Too much brilliance can compromise a poem's unity of meaning'.

5–Artemesia Bryson, 'Poetry Marked by Power, Sensibility', *Fort Worth Star-Telegram* (6 October 1957): 4.

6–American poet Howard Moss (1922–87); his *A Swimmer in the Air* (New York: Charles Scribner's Sons, 1957). Moss was poetry editor of the *New Yorker,* 1950–87.

I'll send you more excerpts as they come in. We're really terrifically excited about all this. An excellent review came in the British monthly Encounter.[1] By a don at Cambridge![2] The man gives him almost two columns, quotes generously, & begins: "The most obvious thing to say about Ted Hughes is that he makes the impression of being a poet by nature and instinct. Not that this excludes at his present stage, several echoes, chiefly of Hopkins and Dylan Thomas. But the point is that a rich, even a turbulent life of feeling and observation seems to transfer itself immediately to his words, without diminution or impairment. Plenty of people have the feeling, a few have the words. The lucky ones, poetically speaking, are the very few in whom the passage between the two is open and untrammeled: (long quote)" The rest of the review is amazingly thoughtful and praising, especially for the weazel-eyed Cambridge critic who just wrote a smarmy-nasty book on D. H. Lawrence.[3]

The anonymous Times Literary Supplement[4] man who finds Ted's rhythm lacking (he just can't read) says: "Mr. Hughes has a great deal to say. "October Dawn", "Wind", or the "Two Wise Generals" are good enough, particularly in a first book, to excite one's enthusiasm, but to come upon such a poem as "Six Young Men" is thrilling and delighting, and there are other poems almost as greatly charged with humanity and compassion, and with a tenderness which never for an instant turns into sentimentality. There is a crisp and uncompromising intellectual content in the best of these poems."

This gives you an idea. Only one man[5] is "nasty" & says Ted gets his ideas out of Shakespeare[6] or "bits of Lawrence", & traces, falsely, echoes back to Marvell[7] & Chaucer[8] which doesn't mean anything, but just tried to show off his own Oxford knowledge. Even this man (in England)

1–Graham Hough, 'Landmarks and Turbulences', *Encounter* 9 (November 1957): 83–7.

2–English literary critic Graham Hough (1908–90).

3–Graham Hough, *The Dark Sun: A Study of D. H. Lawrence* (London: G. Duckworth, 1956).

4–[Patric Dickinson], 'Poems of Substance', *Times Literary Supplement* (18 October 1957): 626.

5–A. Alvarez, 'Tough Young Poet', *The Observer* (6 October 1957): 12. English poet, novelist, essayist, and critic Alfred Alvarez (1929–); poetry editor of *The Observer*, 1956–66.

6–Alvarez writes, 'It goes with a passion for Shakespeare's Coriolanus, from whom Mr. Hughes twice steals—once disastrously trying to rewrite the Bard himself' (12).

7–English poet Andrew Marvell (1621–78).

8–Alvarez writes, 'And often he seems to need other literature to give him his start: one poem plays variations on a theme by Marvell, two on bits of Lawrence's prose; whilst Robert Lowell prowls about' (12). There is no reference to Chaucer.

admits "Mr. Hughes's best poetry is original, powerful and difficult . . . his successes seem to me very impressive."[1]

As you may imagine, I feel very clairvoyant: I saw all this would happen: I also saw no critic would have my omniscient appreciation, but that all would rave about the poem or poems that fitted their view: war poems, or lyric poems, or rhymed poems, or nature poems. Edwin Muir in the New Statesman & Nation[2] said Ted's Jaguar poem is better than Rilke's panther poem![3] How's that! Did we tell you Ted has got 2 new poems accepted in the Sewanee Review?

I can't wait till June, if I live that long, to write again: for good, I hope.

I sometimes wonder if I can live out the grim looming aspect of this year without despairing. I miss not cooking & keeping up the house---Ted is an angel and makes my breakfast & lunch, but I only get a chance to make a desert on the Saturday afternoon after classes when I have one breath of freedom. I envision myself as writing in the morning & reading widely and being a writing-wife. I am simply not a career woman, and the sacrifice of energy and lifeblood I'm making for this job is all out of proportion to the good I'm doing in it. My ideal of being a good teacher, writing a book on the side, and being an entertaining homemaker, cook & wife is rapidly evaporating. I want to write first, and being kept apart from writing, from giving myself a chance to really devote myself to developing this "spectacular promise" that the literary editors write me about when they reject my stories, is really very hard.

Also, I don't like meeting only students and teachers. That is the life here, and it is, in a way, airless. Ted & I have been hashing this over & over. We need the stimulation of people, people from various jobs & backgrounds, for writing material. And I can't write about academics. We cast about for a place to live that wasn't New York and thought next year of living in Boston. Ted would get a job, not anything to do with a university, and I would write in the mornings & work part-time at odd jobs which would get me into meeting queer people and give me time to sketch and really work at writing. I would like to be anonymous for a while, not the returned and inadequate heroine of the Smith campus.

1–SP slightly misquotes Alvarez, whose review ends '. . . his successes seem to me to be impressive' (12).

2–Scottish poet Edwin Muir (1887–1959). Edwin Muir, 'Kinds of Poetry', *New Statesman* (28 September 1957): 391–2. In the last paragraph of the review Muir wrote, '*The Jaguar* is a better poem than Rilke's much admired *Panther*' (392).

3–Bohemian-Austrian poet Rainer Maria Rilke (1875–1926); his 'The Panther', written in 1902.

There is nothing worse than going back to a place where you were a success and being miserable. But I may feel better when I get more rested: at least, I am able to sleep now, and eat heartily on weekends. But this life is not the life for a writer: after I have written 20 stories and a book or two of poems, I might be able to keep up writing with work or a family, but I am needing to apprentice myself to my real trade which I hope to do next year.

I'm really wicked to run on about my problems like this, but it helps somehow to get them talked out. Every time you make a choice you have to sacrifice something, and I am sacrificing my energy, writing & versatile intellectual life for grubbing over 66 Hawthorne papers a week and trying to be articulate in front of a rough class of spoiled bitches. If I knew how to teach a short story, or a novel, or a poem I'd at least have that joy. But I'm making it up as I go along, through trial and error, mostly error. And our classes are going to be visited by Professors off and on from now on, so I shall probably be dismissed with a sigh of relief at the end of the year. The other young instructors are very nice: there's a young, vigorous Syrian Jew[1] with a psychoanalyst wife & a little boy: he's got a Phd from Yale and is writing a novel – (although he said he got no writing done his first 2 years here); there's a blond strange Englishman[2] who writes poems and animal fables and translates Sophocles for books & TV & has a degree in philosophy from Italy, and another girl, who is more or less in my situation except that she's getting her Phd soon. Sallie Sears[3] is quiet, rather retiring & nervous, and worse, unmarried. This is a very poor place for an unmarried woman, as it's full of young couples & babies. I am glad at least to know someone who gets tired & worn-out over her work: it's easier for the men, I think, because the Smith girls respect them more, and the older women have experience & a kind of authority & expertness which carries them through. It's Ted that really saves me. He is sorry I'm so enmeshed in this & wants me to write starting this June: being writers, not established, is difficult because you don't just want to take routine-jobs-with-no-future for money, but professional jobs take too much training & sacrifice to make writing possible. I'm glad you've seen Ted's reviews: he's got this good one in the November issue of Encounter,

1 – Stanley Sultan (1928–2013); instructor of English, Smith College, 1955–9; SP's colleague, 1957–8; married to Florence Lehman Sultan (d. 2013); divorced 1964. Father of James Lehman and Sonia Elizabeth.

2 – Paul Roche.

3 – Sallie Harris Sears (1932–); instructor of English, Smith College, 1957–61; SP's colleague, 1957–8.

a British monthly, and even the few nasties have been forced to admit that he's a "born poet": I'm pasting these clippings in Ted's scrapbook & in my next letter will quote some more.

Ted gave a good reading of his poems at the NY City Poetry Center to about 150 people on Sunday October 20th and the day and night there was a pleasant change: I feel, however, I'll be so happy not to come back to this grind of work after the year is over: every trip or movie is a kind of escape. How I long to write on my own again! When I'm describing Henry James use of metaphor to make emotional states vivid and concrete, I'm dying to be making up my own metaphors. When I hear a professor saying: "Yes, the wood is shady, but it's a <u>green</u> shade---connotations of sickness, death, etc.," I feel like throwing up my books & writing my own bad poems & bad stories and living outside the neat gray secondary air of the university. I don't like talking <u>about</u> D. H. Lawrence and about critics views of him. I like reading him selfishly, for an influence on my own life & my own writing.

Ted is working on a children's book & some poems, but I feel he'll do better when I'm through this and happy again. I can be a good writer & an intelligent wife without being a good teacher. But the ironic thing about teaching like this is that I don't have time to be intelligent in a fluid versatile way. I'm too nose-to-the-grindstone. The girls know I'm new at teaching & young & probably much more, & they take advantage of it, which they wouldn't if I were really good. Eh bien.

Do write me soon. I love to hear from you. So does Ted. Forgive this rather drear letter. Unlike mother, I am a writer, not a teacher, and must work at my trade in order to be worthy of the name. Ted has a 2nd poem coming out in the NYorker: about a "Bull Frog":[1] did mother tell you? Also, he's sold 1000 books of poetry in America! He got a royalty check for about $440 but must pay some crazy 30% tax on it: we're going to try to get legal advice about which country's taxes to pay. Car fine. We had brakes' repaired & lights fixed. Do write.

xx
Sivvy

1–Ted Hughes, 'Bullfrog', *New Yorker* (8 August 1959): 26.

TO *Edith & William Hughes*

Tuesday 5 November 1957 TLS, Emory University

Tuesday evening
November 5, 1957

Dear Ted's mother and dad,

I have been thinking of you so much, every day, and the heavenly time we had with you up on the moors last year, but have only just now gotten down to writing. I've been so tired with my new job demands that I hadn't even written my brother in Germany till today. I teach 4 days a week (on Wednesday to Friday), have lots of office hours to discuss papers & problems with my 66 students, and have had a great set of 66 papers or exams to correct every weekend so far, which really is work, as each paper takes about 15 or 20 minutes. This coming weekend, for the first time, I'll have no papers, so will have a chance to give my class preparation the time I need to do a good job. As I have to make up my course as I go along, I find it does take up most of my time and thought and energy, so I've just now gotten rested enough to get some perspective on it. I want you both to know how happy my lovely memories of The Beacon and our wonderful days, fall, winter and spring, with you both, have cheered me up as I make red marks for sentence mistakes or bad expression of ideas on the 50th or 60th paper. At this point my own sentences are rather rusty!

Ted did a wonderful job at his reading in NYC on the 20th! He looked handsome in his dark gray wool suit with the goldy-yellow Spanish tie I gave him for his birthday over a year ago, and I persuaded him to have a haircut (!) beforehand so he looked like a Yorkshire god. He read beautifully in a room of about 150 intent people who followed his reading in copies of his book which they had bought. They crowded up afterwards for autographs, and I lent Ted my shoulder for a writing desk. Has he told you he's sold 1000 copies of this book so far? He has been getting wonderful reviews in various newspapers here, which he'll quote to you: all praises.

You must buy the November issue of the magazine Encounter and clip out the wonderful review of Ted's book in it (along with about 4 others)[1] by Graham Hough, a don at Cambridge. Isn't it poetic justice that Ted's former teachers & lecturers are being paid to review his work! Now he's

1–Books by Robert Graves, Marianne Moore, Daniel Abse, and Thom Gunn were also reviewed.

teaching them something. Hough's review is very very favorable and quotes a good bit from Ted's poems, which I think is good. Do send us copies of any articles you run across in England.

I loved the earring for my birthday! They are beautiful, all mother-of-pearl shiny, and will go perfectly with my pink knit dress which I was married in! Ted is an angel, & helps with the dishes while I'm running to and from classes, and is working on a children's short story about a little boy's life on the moors. I told him he loved the moors so much he should try to write a children's story about them, instead of making up places, and he is evidently very happy doing it.

We hope to be living in Boston next year, me writing & being a housewife (I miss cooking deserts & things which I have time to do only over the weekend: made a very tasty lemon meringue pie this Sunday!) and Ted getting a job and writing. We both feel the academic life is probably not for us, because we see how completely it devours time & energy: a 9 to 5 job would be nowhere near as time-consuming. As it is, I work every day from about 8 a.m. till 10 at night, including weekends, at my teaching and homework. Did Ted tell you I just won a $100 prize[1] from Poetry magazine for the 10 poems of mine they published there this year? It is very encouraging, & I can't wait till June when I can start writing stories for the women's magazines which should be very profitable & fun.

Do give my best love to Hilda & Vicky and to Walter & Alice. I miss them & will try to write them soon.

Lots & lots of love to you both,
love,
sylvia

1–The Bess Hokin Prize, established in 1947. See Henry Rago to SP, 3 October 1957; held by Smith College.

TO *Warren Plath*

Thursday 28 November 1957 TLS[1] (photocopy), Indiana University

Thanksgiving Day, November 28, 1957
9 A.M.

HELLO! The same typewriter, but it is now Sivvy talking. I have been very wicked in not writing you, but am going to do so now. Ted & I had a fine drive down here monday, the hills all purple and smoky hazed and the air still as the inside of an iceberg. Just the change of scenery has been good for me: I have, alas, over 70 term papers to correct this weekend, plus class preparation, so will soon be blear-eyed again. But only 3 weeks till Christmas. Then the long winter stretch. We've been having "visitors" in class this last 3 weeks, & I did very nightmarishly in one class for two women professors, much better for the 2 men. I have heard unofficially that I will probably be asked back for next year and would have "good chances of promotion", but have chosen to get out while the gettings good. I see too well the security and prestige of academic life, but it is Death to writing. Vacations, as I'm finding out, are an illusion, & you must spend summers preparing new courses, etc. Writing is obviously my Vocation, which I am finding out the hard way, but Ted & I are fermenting good plans for this June 1st, hoping to rent a little apartment on the slummy side of Beacon Hill, which we love & work, me part time, Ted full time, at unresponsible, unhomeworked jobs (for money, bread & experience with unacademic people) & write for a solid year, then try for a grant to Italy on the basis of a year's manuscripts. Such a vision keeps me going. Had a fine time recording at Steven Fassett's studios on Beacon Hill[2] where all the poets record for Harvard, listened to his rare recording of Joyce, V. Woolf, etc. & were awed by autographed photos of old opera stars all around the walls & the incredible equipment which cut a record from the tape made of Ted's half hour reading in 5 minutes. A luxury dinner in JackSSweeney's apartment on Beacon St.[3] overlooking the lights of Boston, very posh, & met W. S. Merwin, & his red-haired

1 – SP's letter follows three paragraphs by ASP, which have not been transcribed.

2 – The Fassett Recording Studio was located at the home of Stephen and Agatha Fassett at 24 Chestnut Street, Boston. Stephen B. Fassett (1915–80); married to Hungarian pianist Agatha Illes Fassett (1911–90); head of the Fassett Recording Studio, where SP and TH recorded their poetry for the Woodberry Poetry Room at Harvard University, 1957–9.

3 – John Lincoln ('Jack') Sweeney (1906–86); professor of English, Harvard University; sixth curator of the Woodberry Poetry Room at Harvard University; married to Celtic literature scholar Maire Sweeney (1904–87); lived at 51 Beacon Street, Boston.

British wife,[1] he the most lucrative & machiavellianly-successful of young (30) American poets, rather unpleasant in many ways, but having plays produced in London & knowing all the producers, poets etc. of London & America by nicknames such as "Cal"(Caligula) for Robert Lowell,[2] etc. Ted & I devoured literary gossip & saw the same couple for lunch the next day in their rickety heavenly slummy Beacon hill apt[3] with a tar roof overlooking a panoramic view of the Charles River. I love that part of town & can't wait to find a place there, become unacademic, anonymous, & Write. Neither Ted nor I can be tame campus poets, unfortunately, but perhaps fortunately. We need varied, unintellectualized life around us & not this continual responsibility to improve courses, accept administrative work, etc. So our life will be hard, but we hope, rewarding in our deepest selves. Writing first, jobs fitting around it. We hope to see a lot of you this next year, while in B.

Hoping you can follow this! Had a fine morning at Lamont Library yesterday, with Jack Sweeney setting out a good stack of poets' recordings, a whole conference room to ourselves & me in on a special permission (it's ridiculous they don't allow women, isn't it?) Then the spaghetti lunch at Beacon Hill which confirmed our hunch that we'd look for a place there & walk the city into our sinews next year. O God, how I look forward to it: Boston's edible, not like NYC. Cambridge near, for plays, poetry, books, etc., but not oppressive & surrounding us with Phds as prodigal as pastel potted orchids. Drove to Dot's this noon for a marvelous dinner at which we toasted you & missed you much. A huge mammoth 20 pound turkey, nuts, cranberry jellies, creamed onions, squash & mince pies, wines, anchovies, do I make your mouth water? Ted never saw or ate such sumptuous foods. Grampy was dear, & loaned Ted a watch till Christmas as Ted's trying to set up a radio station for a couple of hours in Amherst for the Whmp[4] station manager: just a gamble at a part-time job which might make him feel better: he needs to see people & work some, as I do, but Northampton isn't a good place at all for the kind of queer offbeat interesting job he'd like, so we tried this, instead of selling in shoestores. If he can get sponsors, he will get a wage. Ted has, by the way, fractured

1–Dido Milroy Merwin (1912–90); married to American poet W. S. Merwin, separated in 1968 and divorced in 1978. Dido Merwin's maiden name was Diana Whalley.

2–American poet Robert Traill Spence Lowell, Jr (1917–77). In 1959, SP audited writing of poetry (English 306), Lowell's creative writing course at Boston University where he was lecturer in English.

3–The Merwins lived at 76 West Cedar Street, Boston.

4–WHMP is a Northampton, Mass., radio station.

his 5th metatarsal in his right foot to complicate matters---he did it by jumping out of an armchair while his foot was asleep!

It was almost 2 weeks before we figured his limp must be due to more than a twisted muscle & took him to be xrayed. So it is a fracture, & we had the bone set by the man who tended my fractured fibula, the guy who took the spur off Dimaggios ankle.[1] As soon as he gets the cast off he's going to take driving lessons, because he really feels the lack of knowing how to drive & I'll be glad to have him spell me on any trips we take. We honestly appreciate the use of your car, as we'd never be able to get groceries or me go home for lunch between classes if we didn't have the car. So blessings on your head. Next year, we figure we can walk everywhere, which is the blessing of city living as we simply won't be able to afford a car for milenniums. I want to finish my poetry book this summer, write a series of short stories & begin a novel, without anything such as a teaching job & preparation hanging over my head. So mother will teach me to use a dictating machine & I'll hire out at part-time jobs to give my life variety & contact with people, which every writer, or most, need, as a balance to complete solitude at the typewriter.

Mother, Ted & I had a really hysterical evening and dinner with Mrs. Prouty last night: she's obsessed with Ted, as she was with you, and really plays up to him, calling him handsome, trying to get him on Tv, etc. She has an "Ant Farm" which she watches constantly, & it's very strange & absorbing. Must close now.

Much love
Sivvy

TO *Aurelia Schober Plath*

Sunday 8 December 1957 — TLS with envelope, Indiana University

Sunday afternoon
December 8, 1957

Dearest mother . . .

This letter should by now greet you at Dotty's[2] and how happy I am to know you'll be out of the hospital today and on the road to recovery. It was wonderful getting your cheery letter and hearing about your rapid

1–Joseph Paul DiMaggio (1914–99); American baseball player for the New York Yankees.
2–The letter was sent care of the Benottis at their Weston, Mass., home.

improvement. Our family must really be pretty tough and resilient: you've been through so much hospital-treatment and are coming out better than ever! Ted is so happy to hear you're better too. We both are looking most forward to spending at least a week at home over Christmas vacation: probably driving down early Monday the 23rd and staying through till the next Monday: I'll have to choose books & outline my program for the 2nd semester so will want to be back here & have time to work steadily at the library.

Tell Dotty for me---I won't write a separate letter---how much I appreciated her kind and thoughtful notes about your progress: they really relieved me. Also, Ted & I loved the anniversary card and the bright cheerful napkins. Thanks again from both of us! We also were much amused at the little smiling face you drew on the card: it was so expressive!

I am sitting so cosily in my lovely black velvet toreador pants which I think are my favorite garment, my knee socks under them, and my little leopard slippers on, very warm & informal---I get weary of stockings, heels & chignon during the teaching week, so let my hair down literally & figuratively over the weekend.

This week has been in many ways one of the toughest for me: I worked on correcting my term papers starting last Saturday evening, all Sunday and Monday, from 7 am till midnight without a break: 700 pages to correct, 70 long paragraphs of comment to write, grades to make out. By the time I got through I was really exhausted, blear-eyed & doped. Tuesday I slowly pulled out of my fatigue & tried to arrange the 70 for a two-hour reading & discussion in all 3 classes: meaning separate preparation for each class & so I was behind all week with my work for class: coming home each night after a full day & having to get the next day's lesson prepared. Which I'll never do again. But the end of this story of drudgery is a happy one. I didn't miss a class & carried on till noon Saturday. My health has amazed me. I started with a sneezy mean cold driving up here on a week ago Saturday, really wet and impossible, but I took two of those amazing Coricidin tablets & my dear husband tucked me into bed for a day, feeding me hot milk and brandy and honey, which got rid of my cold & made it possible for me to do my correcting.

This Saturday, the minute I got through with my work, I rushed home, flew about cleaning up the house, did the weekend marketing and began cooking, for we'd invited four people over for Saturday night dinner:

the Bramwells (Joan & James),[1] a charming English couple, she the only woman on the English faculty besides me who's married, her husband the author of a successful book on a conscientious objector's experiences in the war which just came out this year; Sylvan Schendler,[2] a dark, plodding, rather pathetic fellow who is a great success in the English Dept. among the elder people & the students but who is divorced & seems rather alone, & Marie Boroff, a young woman Ted & I like who is also rather sad in her own way: she got one of Poetry Chicago's prizes ten years ago,[3] left off teaching at Smith to "write in NYC and have fun", and when that last failed, got her Phd. from Yale & is now teaching there half of the week, half of the week here. She seems very warm, kindly & lonely, in her early 30's I guess. She has admitted she doesn't have the talent to be a poet (she admires Ted's book very much) and wants to turn to critical writing.

Anyhow, I tossed off a sponge cake after the perfect recipe you sent me in England, made my little maple parfait with 6 egg yolks, maple syrup & 2 cups of heavy cream, frozen, mixed up a delicious spaghetti sauce, a French salad dressing, a salad of lettuce, romaine & chicory & scallions, garlic butter for French bread, and the clam-and-sour-cream dip I learned from Mrs. Graham[4] when Ted & I had cocktails with Dean Graham.[5] All this in the space of two hours. We served sherry & hot potato chips & this dip for beginning & then you should see how nice our round table looked, if a bit crowded, with my lovely West German linen cloth (pale nubbly yellow) from Esther & Paul,[6] my lovely pottery dishes & pewter & stainless steel gleaming by candlelight! Everybody talked & I slipped in & out with the dishes very easily. I've never made a meal for 6 before, just 4, and this was very successful I think.

1–British writer James Guy Bramwell (1911–95), who published under the pseudonym James Byrom. SP read Byrom's autobiography *The Unfinished Man* (London: Chatto & Windus, 1957).

2–Sylvan Schendler (1925–2002); assistant professor of English, Smith College, 1956–67; SP's colleague, 1957–8.

3–Marie Edith Borroff (1923–); associate professor of English, Smith College, 1948–60; SP's colleague, 1957–8. Boroff won the Fiske poetry prize issued by University of Chicago in 1943.

4–Elizabeth Ann McFadyen Graham (1907–97), married Edward Kidder Graham, Jr in 1935.

5–Edward Kidder Graham, Jr (1911–76); Dean of College of Liberal Arts, College of General Education and Graduate School, Boston University (1956–60), a resident of Wellesley, Mass., who lived around the corner from the Plaths at 7 Ingersoll Road.

6–Probably SP's cousin Esther Schober McCue (1912–80) and her husband Paul L. McCue (1908–85).

Ted & I went for a little midnight walk under the warm, wet blowy sky with a fuzzy blue moon overhead & then fell into bed as the clock struck twelve, utterly exhausted. We slept till noon this morning and woke feeling very refreshed. We cleared the mountains of dishes & glasses & the whole house in an hour by working together & had a nice little scrambled egg & onion lunch.

I've been giving myself the simple treat of doing odds & ends since then: I only have a few questions on 70 quizzes to correct which wont' take me more than an hour, & then two whole luxurious days to prepare the next two weeks work.

Remember that lovely Christmas card lyric on the little white, red & black card: "I heard a bird sing in the dark of December: we're nearer to spring than we were in September"?[1] Well, somehow, I've felt more philosophical this last week, in spite of my deep exhaustion: the year doesn't look quite endless. I also got a rather grim satisfaction that those 700 pages of papers[2] didn't floor me but that I got through them. Too, I am taking things which would earlier have floored me---occasional sassiness, poor preparation for class by some girls, difficult office hour conferences---more in my stride. I had a hard problem with a very nasty case of plagiarism in my last set of papers, so obvious as to be impossible as "a mistake", and had to send the girl to honor board. She is a very shifty character & wavering between a D plus and C minus, not preparing for class discussion, and unfortunately just the sort who'd do something like this. She claimed it was all a mistake, she just "didn't know how it happened," & I probably got much sicker over it then she did. But I sent her to honor board.

Although it is extremely painful for me not to write, knowing how even more painful it will be when I start to write in June, I've decided to make the best of a bad job & make them sorry to lose me. I have had several teachers say to me they've "heard" from students & visiting teachers (to my classes) that I'm a "brilliant teacher", so in spite of my obvious faults I can't be bad. One thing, I'm hardly ever dull, & since it's my first year, I think I'm doing about all I could ask of my ignorant self. I'm getting a little more realistic about it. If I can just get my preparation done a week ahead, instead of this last minute rush, I'll feel even more better.

Ted, at last, is writing wonderful poems again. He's gone through a dry spell & been unhappy with his bad luck about his leg, his missing

1–From the poem 'I Heard a Bird Sing' by Oliver Hereford. SP also quoted these lines in her journals on 29 January 1953. See entry 166, *Journals of Sylvia Plath*: 168.
2–'those ~~6~~ 700 pages of papers' appears in the original.

driving lessons, his not being able to get a job (there's no work there at all, really!) and his feeling of isolation. Now, after Thanksgiving vacation (which seemed to break the jinx of depression on us & get us rested & refreshed, thanks to your luxurious treatment) he's just turned out 6 beautiful poems, which give me at least a vicarious pleasure, & a delightful short fairy-story.[1]

I am so lucky to be married to Ted: we read poems aloud & discuss people & magic & everything, always interested and happy when not tired. If only we can get into our stride: our own writing life, then no weariness or worry will get at the deep part of us. I feel terribly vulnerable & "not-myself" when I'm not writing & know I can never combine teaching & writing, nor can Ted. So, only 6 more months!

Evidently I'm not alone in feeling exhausted about teaching! It seems to take much more out of the women than out of the men: probably the men get a certain physical satisfaction out of teaching the opposite sex. Some of the old-maid women teachers treat the girls like daughters. But they all get tired. Marie Boroff, who looks like a wreck, said she felt "great psychic exhaustion" with her two jobs, and that there was absolutely not energy left after a teaching day for creative work. Old Miss Williams,[2] another teacher, told me the same thing yesterday about her exhaustion after office hours. These people, however, can bear the tiredness because teaching is their Vocation, but it's not mine, even though I could be a good one if I had the scholarship & inclination to work with other writers' work & not produce my own. But it relieves me to think that even the seasoned ones have the same problems I do, doubts, etc.

Do look up, if you can, the Christmas book lists of this past week which have appeared in the Saturday Review[3] and the New York Times Book Section![4] Ted's book is listed in both under Poetry as one of the exceptional poetry books of the year! We are so pleased & happy about this! Only 250 to 300 books were listed out of over 10,000 and for his to be chosen in the poetry section, a slim section, is a wonderful honor, just what we'd hoped!

1–Probably Ted Hughes, 'Billy Hook and the Three Souvenirs'.

2–Edna Rees Williams (1899–1992); English professor, Smith College, 1930–64; SP's colleague, 1957–8. Williams co-directed freshman English (English 11) completed by SP, 1950–1.

3–'Yuletide Checklist', *Saturday Review* (7 December 1957): 39.

4–'A List of 250 Outstanding Books . . . A Christmas Guide', *New York Times Book Review* (1 December 1957): 73.

I must close now, so want to say how happy we'll be to see you in only two weeks! We are eating royally & are caught up on sleep. So don't you worry.

Much much love, love also to grampy, Dot & Joe, and Bobby & Nancy,[1]

love,
your own,
Sivvy

TO *Warren Plath*

Monday 16 December 1957[2] — ALS in greeting card (photocopy), Indiana University

<printed greeting>

Merry Christmas / and a / Happy New Year

<signed>

Love from Sivvy / & / Ted.

Dearest Warren . . .

I am just convalescing from a 101° fever & flu & trying to get enough head for making up 2 Dostoevsky classes this week before Christmas, so this will be a short note to be followed by a New Year's letter accounting for our holidays with mother at home – We hear wonderful things about your speeches in German & the appreciative 'knuckle-rapping'. Bravo. I am very wistful about German & want to revive my limited knowledge this summer day by day: I don't have much surplus energy now. Maybe when you're back you could help me with pronunciation! Ted's reviews continue to be excellent: the 'Book Review Digest'[3] this month gave his book 4 plusses & excerpts from 4 of the best: the "watch-Ted-Hughes-for-a-major-poet" kind. We are dreaming of living & writing in Boston next year & working for grants to Europe for the future, so we hope to see a lot of you from the time you get back. I am counting the days until June 1st – I understand "unofficially" they will want me to teach here next year, but I'll be writing, thank goodness.

xxx
sivvy

1 – SP's cousins Robert J. Benotti (1945–) and Nancy Benotti (1947–).
2 – Date supplied by Warren Plath.
3 – *Book Review Digest* (December 1957).

TO *E. Lucas Myers*

Wednesday 18 December 1957[1] ALS in greeting card with envelope,[2] Emory University

<printed greeting>
Merry Christmas
<signed>

from / sylvia

Dear Luke –

Very good to see your poems in Poetry this month.[3] The tessellated corn one has always been a favorite of mine. I am counting days till June 1st when I shall be free of this teaching & eye-socket searing over 70 papers every other week. Teaching is no job for a serious writer – uses the wrong kind of energy. We hope to set up shop on the slummy side of Beacon Hill next year. We both miss you. Will you ever come home?

Best of luck.
Sylvia

TO *Elinor Friedman Klein*

December 1957[4] ALS in greeting card, Smith College

<printed greeting>
SEASON'S GREETINGS.
<signed>

from Sylvia / & Ted.

Dear Elly . . .

It has come to this. I am sure you've moved 3 times since we last saw you, don't trust any of the 3 NY addresses I have for you & only have a vague Ouija board flash that you live in a laurel wreath. I am alive still, or at least much improved. I've had Aaron, Fisher, Dunn[5] & Hornbeak sit in

1 – Date supplied from postmark.
2 – Christmas card printed by Katydid cards.
3 – E. Lucas Myers, 'Journey in the Tessellated Corn' and 'Ballade of the Early Seas', *Poetry* 91 (December 1957): 181–4.
4 – Dated from internal evidence.
5 – Esther Cloudman Dunn (1891–1977); English professor, Smith College, 1922–60; SP's colleague, 1957–8. Dunn taught Shakespeare (English 36) completed by SP, 1954–5.

on my classes & in a gossipy way learn they think all is very lively & fine & I should be asked back in Feb. Only I'm not coming. I am looking to June 1st & my restored humanity with stoic but starved mien. Will creak into writing again & never stop – will even read what I want – which I don't have time to do now. Would love to hear from you – any chance of seeing you sometime from Dec. 31st–Jan 5th when we'll be back here from Wellesley?

Do write –
Love,
Sylvia

TO *Gerald & Joan Hughes*

December 1957[1]

ALS in greeting card,[2]
Indiana University

<printed greeting>
SEASON'S GREETINGS
<signed>

& much love / from Sylvia / & / Ted.

Dear Gerald & Joan . . .

Two stags leaving gold footprints & a gold sky full of snowflakes to say our "Merry Christmas" to you. My teaching turns to take up most of my time so far – keeping a week ahead of my 70 girls like a fox eluding the panting hounds & interviewing sobbing or angry or effusive ones, correcting avalanches of papers. Manage to cook a lot now, though, which I love – so Ted & I regale fellow-writers & teachers on wine or tea, casseroles & spaghetti sups, pineapple upside down cakes – my one main way of being creative, unless making up classes on DH Lawrence & Dostoevsky could be called remotely that. But come June 1st I'll be writing again at last, trying to finish my own first book of poems this summer & begin some stories. After a short dry spell, Ted is producing poems prolifically again & we hope to live & write in Boston next year, away from this grove of academe. Will write more during this vacation.

Love to you –
sylvia

1 – Date supplied from internal evidence.
2 – Christmas card produced by Carol Cards.

1958

TO *Warren Plath*

Monday 6 January 1958 — TLS (photocopy), Indiana University

Apartment 3 rear
337 Elm Street
Northampton, Mass.
January 6, 1958

Dearest Warren,

HAPPY NEW YEAR! Ted & I are so pleased with our lovely tablecloth which is gay and sunny with our pottery and stainless steel. Now that we've left Wellesley for 5 months, we won't be able to read your wonderful letters to mother unless she sends them on, so do talk to us on paper now & then and I'll try to reciprocate.

Our post-Christmas teaching is on me, and I have to slave today and tomorrow outlining discussion questions for 6 hours on Crime & Punishment, my present punishment for the crime of being out with pneumonia for the 3 past weeks. Most annoying, as I hadn't even had a cold all term, but I missed the last week of classes and all my vacation during which I had meant, as we all do, to catch up. I still have a good deal of battle-fatigue and a cough which keeps me awake, but hope to start teaching the day after tomorrow with fingers crossed that the sunny clear weather we've been having keeps up for two more weeks. Then it can blizzard during the exam period of two weeks while I try to outline my program for the 2nd semester & correct midyears snug in our little apartment, which I am really becoming quite fond of.

I just told our department chairman[1] this morning that I wasn't planning to come back next year---I waited until I heard they'd voted unanimously for my reappointment---and he was very sorry & surprised but I practically skipped out. I'm dying for June 1st & my apprenticeship to writing for a whole year. Now that it's 1958 it seems much nearer, as if I'll actually live to it, and I can enjoy my teaching much more seeing light ahead.

1–Charles Jarvis Hill.

Ted's life has picked up surprisingly, too. He has just gotten, in the New Year, his 3rd poem accepted by the New Yorker,[1] which will mean about $25 as it's a very short one, his first acceptance of a prose short story (8 pages) from Jack and Jill[2] which is a delightful fairy-tale for $50! We were amazed & joyous: it opened a really new market, a tough market, but means he has the encouragement to go on working on children's stories & books!

Also, after spending a total of about $45 on lessons, & license, Ted got his driver's license in Northampton today. Isn't that fine! I feel much relieved, as I can share driving with him & not take it all on my own shoulders, and he is very pleased.

We've earned, between us, since September 1st, over $700 on writing! Not bad, especially since I haven't written anything new or even tried. June 1st begins my all out effort! Even I am getting ideas for children's stories.[3] We are saving our writing money in a separate account & not touching it. Hope maybe to get a writing fellowship to help us to Italy the year after our Boston year, if we produce enough next year.

Ted also was offered out of the blue a part-time or full-time instructorship at the Univ. of Massachusetts in English this 2nd semester,[4] which would enable us to save money, as my salary's been barely enough to live on what with unexpected doctor's expenses. He's willing to take on full-time if he can get a small senior creative writing course, in addition to sophomore lit. & freshman comp., which would cut his paper-load. We're waiting to hear which it will be. I feel much better, & so does he, about saving something to collect bank interest, as he should be able to save his whole term's salary if we live spartanly. We look so forward to moving to Boston if we can find a good place & seeing much of you next year.

Love & write –
Sivvy

1–Ted Hughes, 'Shells', *New Yorker* (1 August 1959): 61.

2–Ted Hughes, 'Billy Hook and the Three Souvenirs', *Jack and Jill* (July 1958): 26–32. Illustrated by Joy Troth.

3–The idea for 'Changeabout in Mrs Cherry's Kitchen' appeared in SP's journals on 4 January 1958; *Journals of Sylvia Plath*: 304. Published as 'Mrs. Cherry's Kitchen' in Sylvia Plath, *Collected Children's Stories* (London: Faber & Faber, 2001).

4–In the 1958 spring semester, TH taught three courses in the English department at the University of Massachusetts, Amherst, which included 'Masterpieces of Western Literature', freshman English, and a creative writing class.

TO *Aurelia Schober Plath*

Monday 13 January 1958 TLS with envelope, Indiana University

Monday night
January 13, 1958

Dearest mother . . .

I suppose the two of us had rather rough weeks. I managed my full amount of classes and a faculty meeting last week, but it really took a lot of energy out of me, as I had no reserve of voltage to spare. Also, I had to prepare my work for the next day every night, so by the time Saturday came I was really beat. But we slept till noon on Sunday, which was a lovely icy blue day and went for a 5 mile walk which cheered us no end. I am still inclined to be rather depressed, a kind of backwash of convalescence, I guess, but should have a chance to rest up after this week while preparing for the 2nd semester before the exams come in.

Elly Friedman came over Saturday night with her latest boyfriend and I cooked a nice dinner for the four of us: white wine, clams & sour cream & potato chips for appetizer, roast beef, corn, mashed potatoes with onion, and salad, lemon meringue pie and coffee. I was pleased with myself, managing that after a full working week. Elly's Leonard[1] is a change from the usual mixed-up silly boys she's known before. Both Ted & I were delighted with him: he seems to be a handsome Jew, with no vanity, very strong and silent. He taught English at Michigan last year & is now writing & living with his parents. Ironically, Elly doesn't seem good enough for him: he is very intelligent and deep, but I suppose that is why they are attracted, she being so extroverted & actressy. We all saw a good movie[2] by Orson Welles, starring him, "Citizen Kane", with excellent photography, so it took my mind off weariness & my work.

I recently had a two hour and longer talk with one of my worst problem children, a girl who refused to talk in class & objected to being called on. She came in prepared to be very much on the defensive (she would whisper in class & make fun of other girls) but we got along immediately & I was very proud of my psychology & I think she left feeling excellently treated, although I told her several unpleasant things, such as that she had

1 – American fiction writer Leonard Michaels (1933–2003); B.A. 1953, New York University; Ph.D. 1967, University of Michigan; English professor, University of California (Davis and Berkeley), 1966–94; friend of Elinor Friedman Klein.

2 – *Citizen Kane* played at Sage Hall at 7:15 and 9:30 p.m. Admission was 50¢ and benefited the Smith College Relief Committee.

chosen to get an E in classwork, and that I'd like her to move into another section. Selfishly, I just wanted to get rid of her as she distracted the other girls, but I made a completely different point of it. We had also a good talk on religion & the course books, and I felt, ironically enough, that she was a kindred spirit of sorts. She wanted, ironically also, to stay in my class, but I managed to get around that, too. I do feel I am building up a pretty good relation with most of my students and am feeling some rather well-placed conceit as one of the more favored of the freshman English teachers. They are really good girls.

Did I tell you Ted has his driver's license. He passed with flying colors and is very elated about it. He hasn't heard whether he'll be teaching full or half time at the University. They really went all out to get him an 11 hour full-time program, with 2 soph lit. courses, one freshman english, and one small creative senior writing course, a very rare program for a beginner, but it will be very tough work. In a way, it will be just as good if he gets the half-time program & feels some freedom, but the pay we'll set aside for our projected year in Italy.

Do drop us a line when you can. Keep well & don't take on any extra work too soon!

P.S. Ted loves his bathrobe, which is a lesson to me never to jump too hastily to conclusions. I knew he'd enjoy it once he started wearing it & now he's always in it. Enclosed, the check for it. Do cash it right away, to help us keep accounts.

XXXXXX
sivvy

TO *Aurelia Schober Plath*

Monday 20 January 1958 — TLS with envelope, Indiana University

Monday
January 20

Dearest mother,

Thanks so much for letting us share this letter of Warren's. He does sound to be leading a rich, vital life. I'm enclosing his letters with your charge coins, the two heavy ones taped to a card.

My classes came to an end on Saturday, and I just woke up this noon with the sense of being knocked out cold for the weekend. I must have been really exhausted all this time, and rejoice at a week of no teaching and resting, even though I have to prepare rapidly for next semester.

Ted hasn't heard yet whether he'll be teaching half time or full time, we rather hope it's full time now, and his classes begin in ten days, so I hope we'll find out soon. One of his scheduled books is "Crime and Punishment", and I've just finished two weeks of lectures on it, so he can use my notes. Very convenient.

Friday night we went to dinner at the faculty club as the guests of a young, rather sad nice woman, who once left teaching at Smith to try to write for a year, but who came back. Then to a wonderful suspense movie by Hitchcock, "The Lady Vanishes",[1] which had me jumping at shadows behind doors for a few days. Saturday night we drove over to meet some people on the U. of Mass. faculty. Very different people. Somehow pathetic, broken, wistful, or just pedantic and cranky. At least Ted was relieved, & the prospect of work doesn't worry him now, as these people are hardly genii. But rather boring. Anyhow, he has some really good books to teach, & the recommendation will be very helpful in teaching jobs in Europe.

A week from today I have to give my midyear exam, & then correct 70 papers & make out midyear grades. But just not having to go out & teach is restful, and a pleasant change. Halfway through! And my whole attitude to teaching is changed. Simply knowing that I'm leaving in June has freed me to enjoy it & have a casual attitude which is evidently catching in a good way, as my 3 o'clock class in particular is more enjoyable, and I have a good feeling of general class sympathy, with the exception of course, of a few bored or stubborn ones. If I can just get ahead of myself in preparation things should ease up. But how I long to get at writing. To break into the pain of beginning again and get over the hump into something rich: my old life of poems and stories and articles, so once again I can look for the mails with some reason for eagerness.

Perhaps Monday March 31st and Tuesday April 1st Ted & I can come down to look at houses or apartments on Beacon Hill. We'd could move in on the 1st of June, I think. Or the 1st of July, if necessary. But I should think in June we'd find more people moving out. Have you heard of any rumors? We want to leave here on June 1st if we can. We want to know Boston like the back of our hand before we're through.

1–*The Lady Vanishes* was shown at Sage Hall at 7:30 and 9:30 p.m. Admission was 50¢ and was sponsored by the Community Service to benefit the Hampshire County Public Health Association from Christmas Seals.

Ted's had two more short poems accepted by the Sewanee Review as of today, which with their last acceptance of 2 makes a total of 4 to come out and "introduce" him to their readers.

Don't forget to drop us a line. Take care of yourself! Your winter commuting sounds ghastly, Can't Marion cook for a while? Ted is concerned too. They'd make you lecture on your deathbed there! Do write.

Much love,
Sivvy

TO *Edith & William Hughes*

Sunday 2 February 1958 TLS, Family owned

Sunday afternoon
February 2nd

Dear Ted's mother & dad . . .

You have no idea how we love getting your letters: every time they come we drop what we're doing and Ted sits down & reads them aloud to me. I like hearing about every little thing from the candy melting together in the candy jars at the little shop and what kind of weather is blowing over the moors---I loved our days up at the Beacon so much that I look on it as a real home & think of Ted's big desk waiting for us to write on it. So you can imagine how I like every word about it.

Ted has probably told you that he has a very good job for the next four months as Instructor of English at the University of Massachusetts in the next town, about 15 miles away. He came through his driving license test with flying colors and now drives my brother's solid little blue Plymouth car to work each day. He works from 8 am to 11 am on Tuesday, Thursday and Saturday, and from 3-4 pm on Monday, Wednesday & Friday, but is going to try to get those afternoon classes on the other days so he'll only have to drive over 3 days a week instead of 6. You can see how its a much easier schedule than his teaching boys at Cambridge. He has one course of freshmen, two of sophomores, & one creative writing class of seniors, which is very special for a first-year college teacher to get: all the members of the department who have been working there 10 years wish they had it. Ted just walked right in, with his book & good reviews, & they gave him this class, which sounds so interesting that I'd like one of that sort too: people who are really interested in writing are fun to teach.

It is very unusual for anyone without a Phd. (a doctor's degree) to get college-teaching jobs in America, but Ted's book is a strong recommendation. He could probably teach at either Amherst or Mount Holyoke: the first a boy's college, the latter a girl's college, much like Smith, if he wanted to next year, as they've both shown interest in him (they are 2 of the best colleges in America) but Ted wants not to teach but get some other kind of work (without homework or extra preparation) in Boston next year while I write for a change, and he'll have time to write too. Then, in the fall of 1959 we hope to come back to Europe for a year & look forward to visiting you then. This is a dream, but if we save what Ted earns this semester I think we can manage it. I hope to have a book written by the end of next year in Boston, so if I do, it will help.

My week and new semester begins tomorrow. I have been resting as much as possible, as the pneumonia left me really exhausted, not sick, but just very easily tired, so Ted has been taking very good care of me. I have taken on an extra little job in addition to my regular teaching which is going to an advanced course in American literature[1] which is taught by a world-famous critic,[2] and helping him correct most of his exams throughout the semester: I'll have to read all the books by Hawthorne, Melville[3] and Henry James, but they are good, so I should enjoy it and a few hundred extra dollars will be very welcome. I've just finished correcting my own 70 blue-booklets of midyear exams & am resting my eyes on the scenery outside our window: red tile rooftops and two big gray squirrels chasing each other from branch to branch of the tall bare elm trees.

Mother came up to visit our apartment for the first time this last weekend & stayed overnight with the lady downstairs. She thought it was a very fine place, with plenty of room, light and airy, and we are pleased with it too. We count on our fingers: 4 months more of work & then Boston, more writing and easier if less challenging, jobs for our bread & butter.

Ted has written two good short stories which we've sent out to a magazine: he can be a very good prose writer, too, I am sure of it, so I am suggesting subjects for him to write on about his own background in the moors which will be of great interest to the Americans and hope someday he may collect a book of Yorkshire tales. When we come back to visit you

1–Newton Arvin's English 321b, American Fiction 1830–1900. SP took this course in the second semester of the 1953–4 academic year.

2–Newton Arvin (1900–63), English professor, Smith College, 1922–60; SP's colleague, 1957–8.

3–American writer Herman Melville (1819–91).

we really must make up a whole notebook of all you know and all you remember.

Has Ted told you about the enormous snow sculptures made at the Winter Carnival at his University? He drove me over to see them yesterday and some were very impressive, several times taller than a man: one showed a drunkard leaning against a lamppost and looking at a huge pink elephant made out of snow (I have no idea how they colored it all) which reached up to the 2nd story of the building. Another showed two giants carving out a lacy snowflake, again, twice as high as human beings. There was a great prostrate dragon of snow with St. George standing by it, and a coach with six horses and Cinderella stepping out of it: very impressive: I wish you could have seen it.

Well, I must get back to work, so send much love to you both and will write soon . . .

love,
sylvia

TO *Edith & William Hughes*

Friday 7 February 1958[1] ALS, Emory University

Hello! You should see what a wonderful teacher Ted makes! He has got all his courses scheduled for Tuesday, Thursday & Saturday, so he only has to teach a 3-day week & doesn't have too much outside correcting & preparation to do. I am feeling much stronger & although still a bit washed-out on energy from the pneumonia I am finishing my first week of 2nd term this week with a much greater feeling of ease & enjoyment than I've ever had – I really am very fond of my 70 girls & will enjoy teaching them plays & poetry for the rest of the year. It is snowing now – great lacy flakes. We are going to a movie of Dickens' "Pickwick Papers" tonight.[2]

Love to you & birthday greetings for the 13th!

Sylvia

1 – Date supplied from internal evidence.

2 – *Pickwick Papers* showed in Sage Hall at 7:30 and 9:30 p.m. on 7 February 1958. Admission was 50¢ and benefited the Smith College Relief Committee. SP's journal entry for 8 February 1958 indicates she and TH saw *Pickwick Papers* with Smith College colleague Paul Roche.

TO *Olwyn Hughes*

Sunday 9 February 1958 TL (incomplete), British Library

<Typed on pink Smith College Memorandum paper with heading>

Date February 9 To OH From SH In re shoes, ships, sealing wax.

Dear Olwyn,

I am in the process of stealing, or rather stocking up on, tablet upon tablet of this pink official paper which Ted is enamoured of, before I leave the land of supply closets, blue exam booklets and comma splices this June. We both love getting your letters, which are serving as a kind of magnetic chain linking us to Europe where, as Ted & I remind each other, we intend to be the year after next, preferably in Rome or environs, preferably on luxurious grants, preferably not having to work for our pizza. We plan to write like fiends for a whole year until the papers mount and mount ceilingward & then apply for money to do the same thing in Rome. However, grants are a kind of in-group league: once you get one, you get another, and so on: no fair equitable distribution: this glassy blue-eyed descendent of Heine[1] Ted speaks of tried twice for a Guggenheim with glowing recommendations from ee cummings,[2] William Carlos Williams, Marianne Moore, et. al. and alas failed. But then, he is a lousy poet. Novels are much more promising, so I'm going to start working on mine after I pack away the last bluebook. Not writing this year has been the worst of it, & I feel much better now that I have shocked the whole English department by saying out-loud I am not coming back: this is without doubt the best college to teach at anywhere in America for several reasons: a three to four day week, relative freedom in course books, wonderful bright eager throngs of polished American maidenhood who answer questions & love hearing about the customs of native tribes and the philosophy of Locke[3] and symbolism in fairy tales, so it's all actually much fun, also 9 hours of teaching time, as opposed to the usual 12, & a lively young faculty. Ironically, now that I feel casual and masterful about the whole thing (after a hellish fall spent confronting ghosts of my old student selves in every cranny & coffee shop & teaching from lecture platforms my own professors taught from) one part of me feels sad to leave. I love the power of having 70 girls to teach, & get what

1–German poet Heinrich Heine (1797–1856).

2–Edward Estlin (E. E.) Cummings (1894–1962), often styled as e e cummings: American poet.

3–English philosopher John Locke (1632–1704).

is surely a dangerous enjoyment from shocking them into awareness, laughter & even tears, the occasion of the latter being a snowy Saturday spent evoking the bloody & cruel history of the Irish whiteboys, potato famines, mass hangings, etc. But it's only been since I decided officially to leave that I've enjoyed it: just as I'm sure the reason Ted is finding his teaching rather fun & a breeze (he's now got a 3 day a week program & very little preparation & correcting---really half a week off on a full salary) is because he knows he only has 12 more actual weeks of it. Both of us are, peculiarly enough, natural teachers. Which may come in handy when we get famous & are offered plummy salaries to give a couple of lectures a year at universities and write on our own the rest of the time, but which is at present dangerous to our own writing. Ted is already so advanced that his inner pressure is equal to the outer pressure of Great Works, but I feel that if I taught DH Lawrence stories for one more year, every time I sat down at the typewriter I'd begin "There was a woman who was beautiful, who started with all the advantages, yet she had no luck."[1] Oh, lost, lost.

Ted is writing some really fine things, recently. He's done two long & rich poems, very different, "Acrobats", all silver & dark and with that lovely dissolving of the abstract & philosophical idea into the forms of flesh and word sounds and rhythms. Also "Dick Straightup", which I think is also terrific, colored and bodied out---I can't stop reading it, and keep picking copies up off the floor: one of those apocalyptic characters, held to the earth in gianthood like Gulliver by the Lilliputian particulars. How does it feel to have a great and burgeoning poet for a brother? I have had such strange and luminous visions of his success & growth that I get the odd feeling now and then that this has all happened before, & will go on happening better and better. Ted put off trying prose until I told him how people would go wild with delight over the simplest of Mexborough & Heptonstall incidents, the way they love Dylan Thomas's tales of his Welsh boyhood, so Ted wrote two stories, short, which I think are fine: one called "Rats" about the little man who bit rats' heads for pints: a simple, understated story which gets terrific power from what isn't said---no hollering or pointing stances, just a vivid account built to a terrific dramatic pitch, and another "Grand Songs, Great Songs" which gets the hushed waxed polished straight stiffness of parlors & the atmosphere & aroma of pubs & again, tragedy under the surface texture of life. We've sent them off[2] & hope to hear from them soon: I'm sure

1–D. H. Lawrence, 'The Rocking-Horse Winner'.
2–TH to Edward Weeks (*Atlantic Monthly*), 21 January 1958; held by Yale University.

they'll be published somewhere. Also, he's probably mentioned the 8-page children's story "Billy Hook & the Three Souvenirs" which he got $50 for from The Children's mag in America, a very tight & select market. Success is so cumulative: to him who has to him shall be given, etc., and if a Name is built up, one can live on it. But we keep away from the circles of dilletanti & academic gents and ladies, like hermits much of the time, working & mountain climbing and eating great winey stews & endless crackly green salads with french dressing and all sorts of cheeses. Yea, privacy in America is possible: you can make very much your own life & actually live quite frugally, without tv or motor cars. Last week we spent an ice-blue sunshot Sunday climbing a freshly-snowed-on mountain,[1] alone: nobody in America climbs mountains in the winter if there aren't ski trails. We tracked rabbit and fox prints in the snow, breathing rarer and rarer air, picking up great hanging stalactite icicles and javelining them over snowcliffs, arriving finally in the full icey wind of the top, with a rickety white house, once perhaps a hotel, a broken down funicular railway, and a vast god's eye view of the ice-jammed Connecticut river, the Holyoke range of bare fir-bristling hills, and the distant glints of church steeples and haze of smoke spotting our far-off town. We are packing our heads full of heights & colored days. Our blue day fishing & browning last summer on the salt ocean, our walks in the queer pink light of the sunset moors, and the tinkling goat-footed mornings in Benidorm. Of all this, the world in our heads, we word-stitch and make fabrics.

Ted looks wonderful & already has 20 poems toward a second book, but I don't think he should be in a hurry to publish (critics love to compare second & third books unfavorably with the first) since he should be able to get every poem accepted by magazines before he goes between hard covers. I've gotten a kind of odd commission from a New York art magazine for a poem or poems about Art Work, part of a new series and very good price $50 to $75, so am going to live in the Art Libe[2] for the next few weeks & brood, maybe on Gauguin,[3] even DeChirico.[4] Strangely enough, I've been auditing a fine modern art course here[5] (there's a very good art department, real artists & a fine museum here)

<the rest of the letter is missing>

1–J. A. Skinner State Park in Hadley, Mass.

2–In the 1958, the Art Library was located in Hillyer Hall.

3–French artist Eugène Henri Paul Gauguin (1848–1903).

4–Italian artist Giorgio de Chirico (1888–1978).

5–Modern Art taught by Priscilla Paine Van der Poel (1907–94); art history professor, Smith College, 1934–72.. The course description reads: 'Contemporary art and its backgrounds

TO *Aurelia Schober Plath*

Sunday 16 February 1958 — TLS with envelope, Indiana University

Sunday night
February 16

Dearest mother,

Just a note in the middle of the blizzard which has been whirling outside all day to say how much we appreciated the lovely box of petit fours which arrived on Valentine's day with the little card. Ted, particularly, enjoys them and keeps nibbling away at them. We just finished a fried chicken dinner this noon, with creamed spinach and mushrooms, potato cakes, and frozen apricot bombe for dessert with coffee and those molasses crinkles Ted likes so well. So you see we eat like king & queen.

We were originally planning to come down this weekend to look at the Merwins' apartment in Boston which they have offered us to sublet, but we thought it over very carefully and decided against it. They are leaving at the end of March, so we'd have to pay almost 2 months' rent before moving in, and although it is a light airy top floor flat overlooking the Charles river, it is very dirty and $75 a month unfurnished which isn't much less than we're paying now, & on a main trafficy Beacon Hill street, West Cedar Street. So we thought we'd wait to look till April 1st for a quiet top floor flat, still airy & perhaps cleaner. Do you think this a good idea? Could you be investigating any in the meantime?

I do hope you're keeping well in this snowy & frigid windy weather. Have tea on coming home each afternoon. It works wonders.

Ted's teaching (3 days a week) continues to go well & the students obviously love him. He has written a few very good poems recently too.

By the way, could you cancel our dentist appointment for Friday March 21 (or take it yourself at 1:30) and make one for either Monday March 31 or Tuesday April 1st, preferably in the morning? Ted won't be free on the earlier date which we didn't know when we made the appointment.

I am finishing teaching James Joyce's Portrait of the Artist as a Young Man and this week beginning a 4 week course in tragic drama of important periods which I've introduced into the course myself, as a very miniature version of the course I took in tragedy at Cambridge last year: two plays

---

from Jacques Louis David and the French Revolution to the present. Open to sophomores by permission of the instructor. Open also in the second semester to students who have had a course in nineteenth-century art abroad' (49).

by Sophocles,[1] one each by Webster & Tourneur,[2] and 3 each by Ibsen and Strindberg.[3] Should be work, but fun. I guess this stretch until spring vacation, through sleet & snow, is the hardest.

Write soon & keep dry & rested.

Love,
Sivvy

TO *Warren Plath*

Sunday 16 February 1958 — TLS (photocopy), Indiana University

Sunday night
February 16,

Dearest Warren . . .

I have just finished correcting a set of papers and in the interim between tea and renewing my work of preparation for next week I thought I'd write you a note and enclose some of our duplicate clippings of reviews of Ted's book ranging from eulogy to venom. I may have quoted from some of these, but thought you'd like to see them: it keeps getting reviewed, not only in England and America, but in Ireland, Scotland and Australia.

I am getting much better at my teaching and actually got this whole last week prepared ahead of time so I only had to review my notes each night, a great improvement: we are finishing up Joyce's <u>Portrait of the Artist As A Young Man</u> and I must say that in teaching a book one learns it by heart, and gets a really amazing insight. However, this kind of organization and analysis is not the kind I'd use if I were reading the book in the light of my own writing: it is much too conscious and analytical. I have also gained great ease in the classroom & much more often enjoy myself thoroughly & feel I am a good & interesting if embryo teacher. But the work does leave me tired out, and my eyes tired from the eternal reading. So I look forward to a vacation: now is the hardest pull, the month through snow & sleet to spring vacation.

Since our Christmas ills, broken foot and pneumonia, Ted & I have kept well, knock on wood. Just now it is blizzarding and has been all

1–Greek dramatist Sophocles (*c.* 497–406/5 BCE). SP taught *Oedipus Rex* and *Antigone*.

2–SP taught *The Duchess of Malfi* by Webster and Tourneur and *The Revenger's Tragedy* by Middleton and Tourneur.

3–SP taught *Ghosts*, *Rosmersholm*, and *The Master Builder* by Ibsen; and *Miss Julie*, *A Dream Play*, and *Ghost Sonata* by Strindberg.

day in great windy swoops, and outside it is all whiteness swirling in the greenish cones of light from the streetlamps.

Ted is finding his teaching at the U. of Mass. much easier & rewarding than he thought it would be. He has only 3 days of classes: TThSat and 11 teaching hours: one freshman comp, 2 sophomore great books (Milton,[1] Moliere,[2] Goethe,[3] Dostoevsky, Eliot, etc.), and one small senior writing course which he enjoys and which, of course, his students love. He has been writing some good longer poems lately, one, "Dick Straightup", about a Yorkshire character, which I think you would enjoy.

I manage to give about one dinner a week to people on the faculty, three or four, and am becoming a pretty good cook, at least one of my mainline specialties. Did I tell you I've taken on an extra job as "reader" for Newton Arvin's course in Hawthorne, Melville & H. James? This means going to his classes (I took the course years ago) & marking about 50 of his exams a month for which I get paid. I am also going 3 hours a week to a wonderful course in Modern Art which is blessed to my eyes. I have received a letter from a New York magazine, Art News, offering me from $50 to $75 for a poem on a work of art, so I'm hoping to go to the Art Museum & meditate on Gauguin & Rousseau[4] and produce something this week---it's so tantalizing to have the outright assignment, I just hope I'm not all dried up.

I'm teaching plays till spring vacation: Sophocles, Webster & Tourneur, Ibsen & Strindberg, a capsule version of the tragic drama course I took at Cambridge & my own insertion into Eng 11. Should be fun.

We look so forward to seeing you this summer. Both Ted & I send much love. Write soon.

Love,
Sivvy

1–English poet John Milton (1608–74).
2–French playwright Jean-Baptiste Poquelin, known by his stage name Molière (1622–73).
3–German writer Johann Wolfgang von Goethe (1749–1832).
4–French painter Henri Rousseau (1844–1910).

TO *Jane Baltzell Kopp*

Tuesday 18 February 1958 TLS with envelope, Indiana University

<Typed on pink Smith College Memorandum paper; with heading>

Date February 18 To JB From SPH · In re Cabbages & Kings

Dear Jane . . .

The most convoluted and purple-fruited academic grapevine has it that you're now teaching at the University of New Mexico, which I gather isn't far from Texas and home country for you. I'd be most glad to hear from you & what shapes forms & colors life has taken since those last hot black-gowned days in the exam rooms opposite Trinity. Have you become a completely converted denizen in the academic groves? Every time I walk by Paradise Pond on these whipping windy blue days I feel the blade of irony enter in, being a rather antique and fallen angel on campus, so to speak. Irony with a capital I in class of course. What do you teach? Do you have time to breathe? To work on your own at whatever you want to work at?

After the first few week of confronting and laying all the unlaid ghosts of former selves, teaching on platforms where my teachers taught, etc., I feel at last come of age, enough, at least, to begin another kind of growing up. Amazing how our old 2000 years of Tragedy course resurrects: I am just about to embark on 4 weeks of drama, a sort of stew-pot of Greek, Jacobean & Ibsen & Strindberg picking up some of the central themes to unify the course, this all in Freshman English, 11, at present a pleasantly free course with 3 classes totalling about 70 very intelligent & eager girls who are fun & stimulating to work with.

Let this be a pink unofficial prelude (I am unable to resist the stocks of supply closet paper, hence write everything from letters to grocery lists to class notes on this) that The Powers That Be At Smith, and they be very powerful, should be writing you soon & are very interested. As far as I can see, which isn't too far, this is a wonderful place to teach, with many fine, brilliant & creative people---poets, artists, etc. It is with a double-self very regretful that I resigned, although there was this pressure, as in a high-grade aluminum cooker, for me to stay on. And on. But I don't want to live all my life, however paradisical it is here, at Smith & found I wasn't doing my own writing, but making up my courses & cooking & that was it. So I want to take off next year & write for a steady year or else I shall be senile & unable to type at all. Then, we hope to manage a year in Rome if we have produced enough literature to get some kind of grant.

Ted is wonderfully well, teaching full-time this semester (only 3 days a week) at the U. of Mass. where he does 2 great books courses, a freshman comp class & a senior creative writing class (much more versatile than my program) & does it easily as writing a poem, which he is also doing (being accepted by New Yorker at long last, 3 poems, & Sewanee Review & his book getting good reviews here, in England, Ireland, Scotland, and yes Australia where from the black bush anguished letters come begging for culture and more poems).

What's university life like in New Mexico? More casual, spacious? Or just what? What kind of faculty comrades do you have? And what is Stephen[1] (sp?) doing now.

For some reason I feel enormously fond of Cambridge, which blooms like a green Eden in my head continually and about which I long to write & remake legends. Was the graduation sumptuous? I feel much more partisan about Cambridge than I ever did about Smith: it seems one of those primitively mystic places, saturated with spirits of the past and whatever. All the gray sodden slovenly weather has vanished in my mind, leaving that delicate baby blue sky, and the ducks at the mill race and every detail bright and haunting as stained glass. How do you feel about it? Even though I remember much misery & weariness & confusion I still endow it with the light of gone, very gone youth, or whatever. Which is, I suppose, disastrous and maudlin.

Do you hear from Isabel? Margaret? My last word from Whitstead was from Jess,[2] who moved into our old flat and sold our mammoth outrageous couch for a net total of a shilling (we paid almost 10 pounds for it) at an auction & conscientiously wrote and asked me what to do about it. I recommended she stand herself & John to a glass of sherry, but they're probably teetotalers.

If you come East to home in RI or here to be interviewed, please let me know if you can come by for a visit. I'd love to see you again and meanwhile would very much like to hear about you, people, and whatever is going on, inside & out.

Do write.
All good wishes,
Sylvia Hughes

1–Shakespeare scholar Stephen Booth who was at the University of Cambridge as a Marshall scholar.

2–Jess Ivy Brown Bishop (1934–); from Durban, South Africa. B.A. 1954, University of Natal; 1956–8, English, Newnham College, Cambridge.

TO *Aurelia Schober Plath*

Sunday 2 March 1958 TLS, Indiana University

<Typed on pink Smith College Memorandum paper with heading>

Date <u>March 2, 1958</u> To <u>ASP</u> From <u>SPH</u> In re Cabbages & Kings.

Dearest mother:

Ted & I have spent a peaceful and lazy saturday evening (seeing an excellent art film on Goya[1] and a fine bull-fighting film, documentary[2]) and sunday. We cooperated at cleaning the house this morning like a dual whirlwind & both felt purged and rested for the remainder of the day, enjoying our ritual tea. We are living off a good lamb leg I bought this week, with lots of green salads, and did I tell you we bought an absolutely beautiful wine decanter which holds almost a quart, round, with a round bubble of a top, as a present for the anniversary of our meeting two years ago for only $5 (an Italian decanter made of blown glass at Murano, an island off Venice, which perhaps is an omen of our going to Italy the year after next!) We are immensely pleased with the decanter & delight to look at its beautiful lines on our table. Ted just got his poem "Crow Hill" which you & Marion have read accepted[3] in the "New Statesman and Nation." He is giving a brief reading of his poems this Tuesday night[4] at the University, along with three other English faculty university "poets" (who don't publish much). Ted has 23 poems toward a second volume of an intended 50 and 11 of these poems are already accepted for publication! Isn't that fine? I feel there is much greater strength, sonorous maturity and large scope in these poems than in most of the poems in his last book.

Now that I write "March" it seems close to real spring and liberation. I have had all sorts of suggestions & temptations to stay on here---teaching part-time, & it was even suggested to propose Ted for a position, but we both find the noise of route 9 & the closed-in community very tiresome & long to walk out into the little crook-streets of Boston and not onto a roaring highway, & to have the cultural advantages of Boston, too---museums, concerts, and libraries, with the pleasure of anonymity. I am itching to begin my novel and poems for my book, whose third and I hope

1–*The Glory of Goya* with music by Andrés Segovia; a film about Spanish painter Francisco Goya (1746–1828).

2–*Torero!* (1956), about the bullfighter Luis Procuna (1923–95).

3–See Janet Adam Smith to TH, 5 February 1958; held by Emory University. Ted Hughes, 'Crow Hill', *New Statesman* (15 March 1958): 352.

4–TH read his poems with colleagues David R. Clark (1920–2010), Robert G. Tucker (1921–82), and Leon Barron (1923–98) on Tuesday 4 March 1958 at 8:00 p.m. in the Student Union Norfolk Room. The event was sponsored by the Literary Society.

final title---"The Earthenware Head"---will be my last, and auspicious title, leading to publication: I project a year from this June which is the date of the competition I want to send it to.

I am really writing, as much as anything, to ask you to do some investigating for us via Dean Graham, or whoever is suitable. Would there be any possibility of Ted's getting a position as Instructor in English at BU next year?

He will have excellent qualifications: his MA from Cambridge he received this winter, excellent recommendations will be forthcoming from the University & he has varied experience with 3 different courses there. He likes the "unaffectedness" of the University students in contrast to the spoiled girls at Smith & finds what he calls the dowdiness of some of the University students refreshing. He teaches only 3 days, morning & afternoon of 2, and morning of the 3rd, and would like, if possible, a concentrated program, either all in the mornings, or on 3 days. Would there by anything at all available? He is, of course, publishing regularly.

We figured that teaching, IF he can get a good program at college-level, will be the best thing: vacations, free time during the week, and a full year's salary. Ted is very good at it, and enjoying it, and as I will be free I can take on the full load of household chores, which he has been halving with me this year, and even help him with his papers.

Could you find out if any place will be open at BU, and, if so, what kind of program would be possible. If anything is open, perhaps we could see about it at the end of March & the beginning of April when we come down.

I suppose Tufts might be another possibility, but BU would be ideal. The students, I suppose, would be a cut above the University, if anything.

Do let us know as soon as you can about this.

I hope you are keeping rested & well. I look forward to my vacation which begins in 2½ weeks & am crossing my fingers that my good health keeps up so I can work on that art poem as well as prepare my final 8 weeks of teaching. We are living economically & trying to get our budget down from its alarming previous average of $300 a month (so high partly because of doctor's & clothing bills) to $200, or, at least $250. Food, rent, and phone alone amount to about $200, with gas for the car. I'll welcome any budget-saving recipes you can send me. Made a batch of molasses crinkles this morning, which Ted likes.

Goodbye for now. Write soon,
Love,
Sivvy

TO *Gerald & Joan Hughes*

Tuesday 4 March 1958[1] TLS, Indiana University

<Typed on pink Smith College Memorandum paper with heading>

Date March 3, 1958 To Gerald and Joan From Sylvia
In re Cabbages and Kings.

Hello, you two. It seems months, years, even, since we've written you, & I hope you don't treat us as badly, but write back soon! I am about to walk a mile to the class in American Lit. which I'm "reading" for (this means correcting about 60 exams a month for the professor who is too august to do anything but lecture) and pick up a stack of blue books: my own teaching is going so well that I am doing this extra job for, obviously, extra money. I probably have told you that I am going to take this next year off to work full-time on a novel about an Americaine in Cambridge & on finishing a book of poems which I have about half done. I am having fun making up this month of my freshman course which I decided would be plays, and so the girls are having a very much condensed dramatic course drawn up from the year course I was examined on last June at Cambridge. I am rather amused thinking they are working on the same plays I was working on as a student last year: poetic justice and all that. I am also going three times a week to a lecture course with wonderful slides in Modern Art & loving it.

The lecturer in art, Mrs. Van der Poel, is very petite, dapper and exotico, who speaks about Picasso[2] as if he were a good friend, and he probably is, as she goes to Europe every years and owns her own African primitive masks and statues, her Picasso ceramics, her original Dufy,[3] etc. etc. I sit, letting the brightly colored Rousseaus, Gauguins, and Klees[4] sink into my head and make their own little weird worlds---whether of leafy jungles and moon-eyed tigers, or of Tahitian medecine-men & starched basque-bonneted ladies watching Jacob wrestle with his angel, or of little tipsy gilt spirits floating in a golden chaos, and ghosts like bundles of bedding waving adieu. Much fun & provocative. I keep wishing Ted could come to share it.

Ted, in case he is too modest to mention it, is writing wonderfully. Better than ever. He has 23 poems toward a second book (almost 24, as

1–Letter misdated by SP.
2–Spanish painter Pablo Picasso (1881–1973).
3–French painter Raoul Dufy (1877–1953).
4–Swiss–German artist Paul Klee (1879–1940).

he is working on a fine Wolf-head poem[1] now) and 11 of these are already published. Last minute bulletin! 13 already accepted – 2 bought today by Harpers![2] In a year from now, he should have about 50 & all of them as good or better, richer, stronger, than the best in "The Hawk In The Rain". I am very proud of him, & his development.

He also has picked up a full-time teaching job, 3 different courses & 11 hours altogether, & is doing a professional job at the University of Massachusetts. Tonight I'm going over with him while he gives a reading of some of his poems to students along with 3 other faculty members who "write", but don't really publish. I say "full-time", but Ted only teaches 3 days a week, Tuesday, Thursday & Saturday & gets full pay for half a year for teaching 14 weeks (in other words, he gets paid for a 12 week holiday in effect!) This kind of program is obviously much better for writing than any 5-day 9 to 5 job for him, especially with the long vacations, & it pays as well as a profession, which office jobs, or even editing jobs wouldn't do, so he's thinking of trying for a position in University teaching in Boston next year if he can get something as concentrated. If so, we will both spend the whole summer writing like mad.

Symbolically, last week, on the anniversary of the day we met (O fatal day) two years ago, we got a joint letter from Mademoiselle, a posh ladies literary magazine, accepting a poem from each of us.[3] Ted also has got a very fine lyric "Crow Hill" (has he sent it to you) accepted from "The New Statesman and Nation" the same week. I prophesy that he will be England's greatest poet in 10 years time: he is that now, of course, although everyone doesn't know it yet.

We have good fun: eat fresh steaks & roasts & salads & make a daily ritual of tea, which is somehow most sustaining & relaxing after a day's work.

Your house sounds amazing: how big is it, what colors is it inside? Did you design it: describe it to us as if we were walking in the front door with you. I wish you and the boys could take a vacation when we're in Italy which we hope to be in 1959-60, so we could all have a grand reunion at the Beacon. Is that impossible to dream about?

1–Ted Hughes, 'February'.

2–Added by SP in margin; probably Ted Hughes, 'Of Cats', *Harper's* (June 1958): 30; and 'Relic', *Harper's* (November 1958): 36.

3–Sylvia Plath, 'November Graveyard', *Mademoiselle* (November 1965): 134 and Ted Hughes, 'Pennines in April', which was printed with Sylvia Plath, 'The Times are Tidy', in Corrine Robins, 'Four Young Poets', *Mademoiselle* 48 (January 1959): 34–5, 85. The other two poets and poems featured were Howard Hart (1927–2002), 'When she is back', and Kathleen Fraser (1935–), 'Winter Beach'.

Must trudge out in the sludgy slushy march snow, which is all melting in great wet puddles, grimy, gritty, under a dirty-dishwater sky.

Write soon & tell us your news.

Much love to you both,
sylvia

TO *Aurelia Schober Plath*

Saturday 22 March 1958 TLS, Indiana University

<Typed on pink Smith College Memorandum paper with heading>

Date March 22, 1958 To Mother From Sivvy In re

Just a note to say that I have at last burst into a spell of writing. I was rather stunned Thursday morning, my first real day off after a week of correcting 70 papers, averaging midterm grades and writing a report on another senior thesis, but I had about seven or eight paintings and etchings I wanted to write on as poem-subjects and bang! After the first one, "Virgin in a Tree", after an early etching by Paul Klee,[1] I ripped into another, probably the biggest and best poem I've ever written, on a magnificent etching by Klee titled "Perseus, or the Triumph of Wit over Suffering."[2] A total of about 90 lines written in one day.

Friday went just as well: with a little lyric fantasy on a lovely painting by Klee on the Comic Opera The Seafarer,[3] a long and big one on his painting "The Departure of the Ghost"[4] and a little lyric on a cat with a bird-stigma between its eyebrows,[5] a really mammoth magic cat-head. These are easily the best poems I've written, and open up new material and a new voice. I've discovered my deepest source of inspiration which is art: the art of primitives like Henri Rousseau, Gauguin and Paul Klee and DeChirico. I have got out piles of wonderful books from the Art Library (suggested by this fine Modern Art Course I'm auditing each week) and am overflowing with ideas and inspirations, as if I've been bottling up a geiser for a year. Once I start writing, it comes and comes.

1–Sylvia Plath, 'Virgin in a Tree', inspired by Klee's 'Virgin in the Tree' (1903).
2–Sylvia Plath, 'Perseus: The Triumph of Wit Over Suffering', inspired by Klee's 'Perseus (Wit Has Triumphed over Grief)' (1904).
3–Sylvia Plath, 'Battle-Scene from the Comic Operatic Fantasy *The Seafarer*'.
4–Sylvia Plath, 'The Departure of the Ghost', later titled 'The Ghost's Leavetaking'.
5–Based on Paul Klee, *Cat and Bird* (1928); no copy of the poem survives.

I am enclosing two of the poems.[1] I am sending the two poems on the etchings to the sumptuous illustrated magazine "Art News" which asked me to write one or several poems for their series of poems on art. This assignment sent me off on a rich vein, and I hope they take both my poems & illustrate them, as I'd dearly love to possess copies of those two rare and generally unavailable etchings.

Today I had a reaction, feeling miserable and exhausted with my period, and drugging myself to a stupor with aspirin for lack of anything stronger. But after chicken broth I revive and am looking forward to writing another 90 lines tomorrow. If I can write, I don't care what happens. I feel like an idiot who has been obediently digging up pieces of coal in an immense mine and has just realized that there is no need to do this, but that one can fly all day and night on great wings in clear blue air through brightly colored magic and weird worlds. Even used the dregs of my inspiration to write about 6 of those Dole Pineapple Jingles! We could use a car, or 5, or $15000.

Hope you like these little poems.

Love,
Sivvy

40
"Battle-Scene from the Comic Operatic Fantasy The Seafarer"

(After Paul Klee)

It beguiles---
This little Odyssey
In pink and lavender
Over a surface of gently-
Graded turquoise tiles
That represent a sea
With chequered waves and gaily
Bear up the seafarer
Gaily, gaily
In his pink plume and armor.

1 – Sylvia Plath, 'Battle-Scene from the Comic Operatic Fantasy *The Seafarer*' and 'Departure of the Ghost' ['The Ghost's Leavetaking'], both typed on pink Smith College Memorandum paper with total line count in the top left corner and 'Sylvia Plath' signed at bottom right.

A fairy tale
Gondola of paper
Ferries the fishpond Sinbad
Who poises his pastel spear
Toward three pinky-purple
Monsters which uprear
Off the ocean-floor
With fanged and dreadful head.
Beware, beware
The whale, the shark, the squid.

But fins and scales
Of each scrolled sea-beast
Troll no slime, no weed.
They are polished for the joust,
They gleam like easter-eggshells,
Rose and amethyst.
Ahab, fulfill your boast:
Bring home each storied head.
One thrust, one thrust,
One thrust: and they are dead.

So fables go.
And so all children sing
Their bathtub battles deep,
Hazardous and long,
But oh, sage grownups know
Sea-dragon for sofa, fang
for pasteboard, and siren-song
For fever in a sleep.
Laughing, laughing
Of greybeards wakes us up.

Sylvia Plath

45

Departure of the Ghost

(After Paul Klee)

Enter the chilly noman's land of precisely
Five o'clock in the morning, the no-color void
Where the waking head rubbishes out the draggled lot
Of sulphurous dreamscapes and obscure lunar conundrums
Which seemed, when dreamed, to mean so profoundly much,

Gets ready to face the ready-made creation[1]
Of chairs and bureaus and sleep-twisted sheets.
This is the kingdom of the fading apparition,
The oracular ghost who dwindles on pin-legs
To a knot of laundry, with a classic bunch of sheets

Upraised, as a hand, emblematic of farewell.[2]
At this joint between two worlds and two entirely
Incompatible modes of time, the raw material
Of our meat-and-potato thoughts assumes the nimbus
Of ambrosial revelation. And so departs.

But as chair and bureau are the hieroglyphs
Of some godly utterance wakened heads ignore,
So these posed sheets, before they thin to nothing,
Speak in a sign language of a lost otherworld,
A world we lose by merely waking up

Into sanity: the common ghost's crowed out,
Worms riddling its tongue, or walks for Hamlet
All day on the printed page, or bodies itself
For dowagers in drafty castles at twelve,
Or inhabits the crystal of the sick man's eye---[3]

Trailing its telltale tatters only at the outermost
Fringe of mundane vision. But this ghost goes,

1 – '~~And~~ Gets ready to face the ready-made creation' appears in the original.

2 – 'Upraised, as a hand, ~~in~~ emblematic of farewell.' appears in the original.

3 – SP removed this stanza at Olwyn Hughes's suggestion. See SP to Olwyn Hughes, 27 October 1960.

Hand aloft, goodbye, goodbye, not down
Into the rocky gizzard of the earth,
But toward the point where our thick atmosphere

Diminishes, and god knows what is there:
A point of exclamation marks that sky
In ringing orange like a stellar carrot;
Its round period, displaced and green,
Suspends beside it the first point, the starting

Point of Eden, next the new moon's curve.
Go, ghost of our mother and father, ghost of us,
And ghost of our dreams' children, in those sheets
Which signify our origin and end,
To the cloud-cuckoo land of color wheels

And pristine alphabets and cows that moo
And moo as they jump over moons as new
As that crisp cusp toward which you voyage now.
Hail and farewell. Hello, goodbye. O keeper
Of the profane grail, the dreaming skull.

Sylvia Plath

TO *Peter Davison*

Tuesday 25 March 1958 TLS (photocopy), Yale University

<Typed on pink Smith College Memorandum paper with heading>

Date March 25th To Peter From Sylvia In re

this Sunday: Ted & I would both very much enjoy seeing you in Cambridge.[1] Would four or four-thirtyish in the afternoon be agreeable to you? We'll come then, if we don't hear different.

Both of us are looking forward to being in Boston this next year. In the last week of vacation I struck a good vein of poem-writing and am perishing to be at it in earnest and through with making up reasons for why people should like Gerard Manley Hopkins. Perhaps I shall just toss out critical weapons and read poetry aloud hour after hour and if they

1–See Peter Davison to SP, 20 March 1958; (photocopy) held by Yale University.

are still deaf, they're deaf. By this time next year I plan to have a poetry book ready (really my third, I've tossed a good two out in the past five years)[1] and at least a close-to-final version of a novel. Vacation this week has shown me how it will be: very unsocial, but fishing deep and reveling: it exhausts, but not like teaching or other people's work. Like my work, so that's all right.

Looking forward to Sunday. Our best to you.

sylvia

TO *Peter Davison*

Tuesday 22 April 1958

TLS (photocopy) on Department of English, Smith College letterhead, Yale University

Apartment 3 rear
337 Elm Street
Northampton, Mass.
April 22, 1958

Mr. Peter Davison
The Atlantic Monthly Press
8 Arlington Street
Boston 16, Mass.

Dear Peter,

After this delay I don't deserve to ask you to be so good as to whisk these under the august eye. But do use your good and acute eye on them. These are among my most recent poems,[2] so I am prejudiced in their favor, but also consider some of them the best I've done yet in the direction I want to go in.

Ted will send a group along shortly, as he is just finishing one he likes & would like to include. By the way, do you know if the editors have taken any action on the two stories he sent them, yes, eons ago? I believe they were titled "Grand Songs, Great Songs" &, I think, "Rats." We haven't heard a thing.

1–SP refers to *Circus in Three Rings*, submitted during her senior year at Smith, and *Two Lovers and a Beachcomber*, submitted as part of her Cambridge tripos. See journal entry for 18 February 1958, *The Journals of Sylvia Plath*: 332.

2–See Peter Davison to SP, 25 April 1958; (photocopy) held by Yale University. SP sent several poems; however, only 'The Disquieting Muses' and 'Snakecharmer' are named.

You were noble & heroic to forge through that demonish sleet (was it 11 days ago already?) and come to the reading.[1] Have you had anything as juicy as the Lana Turner-daughter murder[2] in your justicing?

We appreciate the books.[3] Ted snitched the Jung[4] first, I the novel: you were most thoughtful. I admire much in the novel, as far as I've gone: very fine vibrations, no? A sensitive net he casts. I am particularly interested in Rome as a setting & in the way it can be created: but I guess I am much more concerned with lights, colors & the painter's view of the world than the abstract philosopher's view, although I find myself with keen interest in the possibility of a certain creative morality, which is, I guess, in some eyes, dangerous amorality. But this is all going to work out in prose. I must now be quiet about it.

Do you think any of these poems are possibilities for the Atlantic? Does Editor Weeks think so? I would like very much to meet him some day, & so would Ted. Perhaps when we move to Boston?

Tea that day at your place was very good. Let us have any news: of you (& how is Nora?[5] have just finished her "Gift Horse")[6] the publishing world, & our writings,

Best wishes,
Sylvia

TO *Warren Plath*

Tuesday 22 April 1958 — ALS in greeting card[7] (photocopy), Indiana University

<printed greeting>

Salute! / Skoal! / cheerio! / prosit! / Here's how! / in any language . . . / here's a toast / to wish you / HAPPY BIRTHDAY!

1–TH gave a Morris Gray Poetry Fund reading at the Alumnae Room, Longfellow Hall at Radcliffe in Cambridge, Mass., on 11 April 1958, at 4:30 p.m.

2–On 5 April 1958, the movie star Lana Turner's daughter, Cheryl Crane, stabbed Turner's lover Johnny Stompanato to death. Reported in 'Killing of Lana's Gigolo Bares Violent Romance', *Boston Globe* (6 April 1958): 1, 37.

3–A note on the letter indicates that the books were *The Undiscovered Self* by Carl Jung and *Corruption* (1957) by British writer Nicholas Mosley (1923–).

4–Swiss psychiatrist Carl Jung (1875–1961).

5–American writer Nora Johnson (1933–2017).

6–Nora Johnson, 'The Gift Horse', *New Yorker* (19 April 1958): 37–44.

7–On Country Cousin birthday card.

<signed>

With lots of / love – / Sivvy / & / Ted

<inside a beer mug printed on the card SP has written: 'W.J.P. / April 27'>

April 22, 1958

Dearest Warren . . .

It seems a long time since my last writing, but I have been in a bit of a daze. A bad cold which sneezed & ran for a full week knocked me out before Ted's reading, but I taught in spite of it so I could give my classes free cuts of grace on April 11th. Imagine – we drove into a horizontal blizzard of sleet all the way to Harvard! In spite of the appalling weather, Ted had a loyal audience – among them many old troupers – Marty & Mike Plumer, Gordon – his eyes glowing with dollar signs, his mouth tongued with million-dollar deals relating to his new project – a Framingham Music Circus – Mrs. Cantor, dear Mrs. Prouty (who said in loud, clear tones: "Isn't Ted <u>wonder</u>ful?!"). He was – a very good hour of poems, old & new & talk in between. I met the young poet Philip Booth (who just received a Guggenheim) & we had a lovely dinner at Felicia's Café[1] near Hanover (?) Street with Jack Sweeney (whom we dearly love – he remembers your A's in some humanities course) & his lovely wierd Irish wife & (at last) Adrienne Cecile Rich & her husband[2] (she's the girl whose poetry I've followed from her first publication) The excitement tolled the end of my cold & I feel much better with the approaching spring – tulips, daffodils & magnolia now out in "our" park next-door. Were you joking about what Clem's girlfriend said about a new Faber anthology? I thought de la Mare[3] was dead. We take these things very seriously. Ted & I met a very strange & endearing poet of middle age – Lee Anderson[4] – who called & asked us to come to Springfield so he could make recordings of us both for the files of the Library of Congress.[5] He has a queer grey goatee, is

1–Felicia's Restaurant was located at 145a Richmond Street, Boston.

2–American poet Adrienne Cecile Rich (1929–2012) and Alfred Haskell Conrad (1924–70); associate professor of economics, Harvard University, 1954–66.

3–English poet Walter de la Mare (1873–1956). Warren Plath had presumably referred to Walter's son Richard, who was a director of Faber & Faber at this time.

4–American poet Lee Anderson (1896–1972). Anderson recorded SP reading her poems on 18 April 1958 in Springfield, Massachusetts, for the Archive of Recorded Poetry and Literature (Library of Congress).

5–Anderson recorded SP reading her poems on 18 April 1958 in Springfield, Mass., for the Archive of Recorded Poetry and Literature (Library of Congress). SP read 'Black Rook in Rainy Weather', 'The Earthenware Head' ['The Lady and the Earthenware Head'],

shy & kindly & has an 80 acre farm in Pennsylvania.[1] I drove Ted over & raced back for my 3' oclock, rushed back to the Springfield hotel, & we recorded. I was especially glad that Anderson, who'd never heard or read any of my poetry, was immensely impressed with the six or seven new poems I wrote this spring vacation. I do hope to have a poetry book finished sometime this fall!

An amusing & lucrative note – sent some old sentimental poems written at Smith to the Ladies' Home Journal – they promptly bought a sonnet[2] for $140. That's $10 a line! Very welcome. We love hearing about your adventures. Do try to look up Ted's beautiful blonde sister in Paris – she is golden-eyed, golden-haired & very delicate & tall as I am – looks about 18, although 28. She works for Nato – c/o the English Pool, Palais de Chaillot – Paris 16eme. Very worth your while – if you get this too late, try to make a side trip. DO write about England. Did you have a suit made? or see Cambridge?

Write soon –
love,
Sivvy

'Departure of the Ghost' ['The Ghost's Leavetaking'], 'The Disquieting Muses', 'Battle-Scene from the Comic Operatic Fantasy *The Seafarer*', 'On the Decline of Oracles', 'Poem for Paul Klee's "Perseus: The Triumph of Wit Over Suffering"', 'On the Difficulty of Conjuring Up a Dryad', 'November Graveyard', 'Sow', 'Spinster', 'On the Plethora of Dryads', and 'All the Dead Dears'. SP's poems have not been transcribed. TH read 'The Man Seeking Experience Enquires His Way of a Drop of Water', 'The Horses', 'Famous Poet', 'The Jaguar', 'The Dove Breeder', 'A Modest Proposal', 'Meeting', 'Wind', 'Roarers in a Ring', 'Things Present', 'Relic', 'To Paint a Water Lily', 'Dick Straightup', 'Crow Hill', 'The Acrobats', 'Witches', 'Bullfrog', and 'Thrushes'. Typescripts for all of SP's poems and the last nine of TH's poems held by Washington University (St Louis).

1–According to SP's address book, Anderson lived in Glen Rock, Pennsylvania.

2–Sylvia Plath, 'Second Winter', *Ladies' Home Journal* 75 (December 1958): 143; written on 8 March 1955.

TO *John Sweeney*

Sunday 27 April 1958 TLS, University College Dublin

Apartment 3 rear
337 Elm Street
Northampton, Mass.
April 27, 1958

Mr. John Sweeney
51 Beacon Street
Boston, Mass.

Dear Jack,

A small note to say how nice it was to see you again that evening with Adrienne at Holyoke,[1] a very good postscript to the lovely time, amid all that fury and mire of April 11th, at the aptly named Felicia's.

Our year has been much the finer for our knowing you and Maurya (I am never sure how to spell this & am sure there is an accent, and an e somewhere!)---and our meeting with the Merwins & the Conrads. We do look forward to the chance of seeing you once more before you set sail for Ireland.

I'm enclosing, as promised amid the turkey and rye-bread two weeks back, a few of the poems[2] I read for Lee Anderson.[3] Most of these---except "Black Rook . . ." and "The Earthenware Head"---were written quite recently, in the past month. I do hope you like some of them, parts of them. I am eager & more than eager to stop all other work, except sun-and-moon-gazing, while I work on finishing my book of poems which I hope to complete by next fall.

Our best to you and your wife,
Sincerely,
Sylvia Plath Hughes

1–SP refers to the Kathryn Irene Glascock Poetry Prize competition held at Mount Holyoke College on 18 April 1958. Contestants were Jan Burroway, Michael M. Fried, Jill Hoffman, Peter Livingston, Lynne S. Mayo, Peter Parsons, and Remington Rose. Judges that year were Rolfe Humphries, Adrienne Rich, and Jack Sweeney.

2–The poems have not been transcribed. The Woodberry Poetry Room, which Sweeney administered at this time, holds typescripts of the following SP poems: 'The Disquieting Muses', 'Poem for Paul Klee's "Perseus: The Triumph of Wit Over Suffering"' ['Perseus, or the Triumph of Wit over Suffering'], 'The Earthenware Head' ['The Lady and the Earthenware Head'], 'Departure of the Ghost' ['The Ghost's Leavetaking'], and 'On the Decline of Oracles'. 'Black Rook in Rainy Weather' does not appear to be part of the Woodberry's holdings.

3–See SP to Warren Plath, 22 April 1958.

TO *Lee Anderson*

Sunday 27 April 1958 TLS, Washington University (St Louis)

Apartment 3 rear
337 Elm Street
Northampton, Massachusetts
April 27, 1958

Lee Anderson
Glen Rock
Pennsylvania

Dear Lee,

I am enclosing copies, as promised, of the poems I read for your tapes two weeks ago: some carbons which I hope are legible, making up, I'm afraid, a rather vulgar motley of type-faces, or smudges.

One of the nicest things that happened to us this spring was our meeting you: as I said, after the student reading that night, we feel, perhaps a bit presumptuously, that we know you with that knowing which makes us think of you as a friend, not just an acquaintance.

We imagine you on the farm: 80 acres? and the great barn with the roof stove in by the snow. When we are able to travel, and travel for us means any arrow however short pointing away from Northampton, we shall appear on the edge of your acreage asking to see a cow, a field of wheat, and to hear you, and some of the recordings.

Meanwhile, our thanks for the pleasant surprise of that fair Friday ending an April week.

With all good wishes,
Sylvia Plath Hughes

TO *Edith & William Hughes*

Monday 28 April 1958 ALS, Family owned

April 28th

Hello there!

It is a rainy puddly Monday after a lovely clear sunny month. I just learned that my American literature professor isn't having class today, so I'm staying in bed cozily reading poems & Henry James – a novel called 'The Bostonians'[1] – very good & funny about the 'blue-stocking' women working for emancipation of women after the Civil War. Our house is cold – pleasantly reminiscent of England: Our landlady is most frugal & evidently turns off the heat for the year on the first warm day. Did you get the little 'petits fours' – or frosted tiny cakes we sent in the box? We want to be sure the grocer got the order right.

Ted has written some very good poems lately: he seems to be keeping up his gift in the midst of teaching – one about a pig, one about a cat & mouse, and one about the cat o'nine tails used in the British Navy.[2] He eats a lot of steak & salad & is in fine health. He has a very loyal & increasing following of admirers here in America – his children's story is coming out in Jack & Jill in July (and they are interested in more) so we'll be sure to send you a copy. In three weeks we'll celebrate our finishing teaching by a week's trip to New York City where we'll go to plays, art museums & up the Empire State Building & visit all the poets we can find. Then a whole summer of writing: what other job beside teaching pays for a 3-month summer vacation? I am hoping to finish a book of poems & start a novel by next fall.

We have borrowed the lovely green park[3] next door as our private garden for daily walks. It is made up of grassy stretches, pink flowering trees, a little wood of elms & a tall wood of pines, and a formal garden. The red, pink & yellow tulips are up, and daffodils, bluets, grape hyacinths & phlox. We found a pheasant lives in the wood, & the grass is covered in big red robins & the trees full of squirrels. I hope to have more publishing news soon.

Meanwhile – much love to you both –

Sylvia

1–Henry James, *The Bostonians* (New York: Modern Library, 1956). SP's annotated copy held by Emory University.

2–Ted Hughes, 'View of a Pig', 'Cat and Mouse', and 'Wilfred Owen's Photographs'.

3–Childs Park, Northampton, Mass.

TO *Oscar Williams*[1]

Tuesday 10 June 1958 TLS,[2] Indiana University

Apartment 3 rear
337 Elm Street
Northampton, Mass.
June 10, 1958

Dear Oscar . . .

We packed up & left New York days earlier than we planned and are now back in the green glooms of Northampton with the parkful of rabbits and mange-tailed squirrels and no sun in sight, all rain, but a peaceable Smith-girl-less Smith and stacks of folk and fairy tales from the library.

Before leaving the city we managed a day at the Bronx zoo regarding with special pleasure the gorillas, chimpanzees, polar bears and pig-headed turtles. Your garden in the air over the bay revolves in mind with all the bright light blue of the interior sky and the multicolored portraits and animals. A fine afternoon, and we are entrenched here among the good anthologies.

I hope you like the poems.[3] And we hope to see you again when we return. When does the new & Ted-ending anthology[4] come out?

With good wishes,
sylvia plath

1–American poet Oscar Williams (1900–64). Williams mailed a sound recording of *The Poems of Gene Derwood* (Spoken Arts, 1955) to TH in 1958; now held by Smith College. Williams lived at 35 Water Street, New York.

2–TH added a note at the bottom of the letter, which has not been transcribed. TH noted it was nice to meet Williams and apologized for missing a party they were invited to attend.

3–SP sent seven poems to Williams which have not been transcribed: 'Black Rook in Rainy Weather', 'Departure of the Ghost' ['The Ghost's Leavetaking'], 'Full Fathom Five', 'November Graveyard, Haworth' ['November Graveyard'], 'On the Difficulty of Conjuring Up a Dryad', 'Sculptor', and 'Sow'. SP inscribed 'Black Rook' on 4 June 1958: 'For Oscar Williams—for his sweet basil, his tugboats, the sun & him self—Sylvia Plath'. Williams regularly took photographs of his guests; there is one of SP alone, one of TH alone, and one of SP & TH. Typescripts and photographs held by Lilly Library.

4–*The Pocket Book of Modern Verse: English and American Poetry of the Last Hundred Years from Walt Whitman to Dylan Thomas* (New York: Pocket Books, 1958). TH's poems were: 'The Martyrdom of Bishop Farrar', 'The Hag', and 'The Thought-Fox'.

TO *Aurelia Schober Plath*

Tuesday 10 June 1958

TLS with envelope on Department of English, Smith College letterhead, Indiana University

June 10: Tuesday

Dearest mother . . .

A note to announce our return from a week in New York city: the details must wait till we arrive home Thursday, the 12th, and we will barter them with you for news of Bermuda. We were very tired, but managed an amazing lot of fun, meetings and walkings for miles in our 5 days. We just caught Ted's two publishers[1] before they sailed & had a posh pink-table-clothed dinner with them at the Biltmore.[2] Went to the tar-roofed top of a business building in Wall Street to the famous anthologist Oscar Williams' little crow's nest full of oil paintings & flowering plants made and grown by his dead poet-painter wife,[3] & mementoes of their dearest friend Dylan Thomas. A fine afternoon overlooking the bay & sniffing mint leaves, and we went to two parties with him afterwards to strange people he's published in his anthologies: one a rich 5th avenue party where we rode up in the elevator with Lionel & Diana Trilling:[4] the place was full of publishers, editors & Columbia professors. The novelist Ralph Ellison,[5] old Farrar[6] of Farrar, Strauss, Cudahy, the editor of the Hudson Review[7] & suchlike. Then a late & sumptuous bouffet at the home of Hy Sobiloff,[8] owner of Sloane's 5th Avenue Furniture store & very dull wealthy business people but a fine negro cook whose food & artistry in table arrangement of cakes & strawberries & melons & praised to her pleasure.

1–Charles Montgomery Monteith (1921–95), editor and director of Faber & Faber, 1953–73, vice-chairman, 1974–6, chairman, 1977–80; TH's editor; and Peter Francis du Sautoy (1912–95), director, Faber & Faber 1946–60, vice-chairman 1960–71, chairman 1971–7; member, Council, Publishers Association 1957–63, 1965–77, President 1967–9.

2–The New York Biltmore Hotel was at 335 Madison Avenue, New York.

3–American poet Gene Derwood (1909–54).

4–American literary critic and author Lionel Mordecai Trilling (1905–75); and American literary critic and author Diana Trilling (1905–96).

5–American novelist and literary critic Ralph Waldo Ellison (1914–94).

6–American editor, writer and publisher John Chipman Farrar (1896–1974); founder of Farrar & Rinehart, and Farrar, Straus and Giroux.

7–Probably George Frederick Morgan (1922–2004); poet, founder and editor of *The Hudson Review*.

8–American poet and entrepreneur Hyman Jordan Sobiloff (1912–70).

We spent a whole day at the Bronx zoo & happened by chance to sit on the train next to Clyde Beatty's brother[1] who works in a lion's cage there & is very happy & a charming person, telling us much about the animals. A beautiful zoo, with wide open spaces for most of the animals, not jail cells.

We took Patsy out to a little candle-lit cave in Greenwich Village for dinner to equate rent for the apartment she generously let us use[2] which of course saved us all living fees & made the trip possible. Then we went to a play by Garcia Lorca, "Blood Wedding."[3] I didn't tell anybody, but I thought you'd be amused at the coincidence that dogs my steps: coming down in the subway afterwards I almost ran into Dick Wertz,[4] Nancy Hunter's old flame, who was at Cambridge when I was and is marrying a Smith girl[5] from my class who is teaching with me this year. I was about to speak to him, as his back was turned to me, when talking to him I saw Richard Sassoon.[6] I kept quiet & passed by & probably only I of all the 5 people knew about it. Of all the people in NYC!

We walked miles, lunched with our editor friend at World Publishing Company & they are still interested in seeing my poetry book as it is early this fall. We strolled through Central Park, Harlem, Fifth Avenue & took Ted up to the top of the Empire State Building & had my fortune told by a summy subway gypsy whose card, ironically enough, showed a picture of a mailman & said I'd get a wonderful letter soon that would change my life for the better. We saw the Bowery bums & the Harlem negroes

1–Clyde Beatty (1903–65), a lion tamer and animal trainer. His brother, possibly Gail Tong.
2–Patricia O'Neil Pratson (1932–); B.A. 1954, English, Smith College; SP's friend from Wellesley. SP's address book, held at Smith College, gives her address as Apt. 22: The Spencer University, 523 W 121st St, NYC. The building name is 'The Spencer' and is in the Morningside Heights/Columbia University district.
3–Spanish poet and playwright Federico Garcia Lorca (1898–1936); his *Blood Wedding* (1932), was performed at the Actors' Playhouse at 100 Seventh Avenue South, New York.
4–Richard Wayne Wertz (1933–2002); B.A. 1955, Yale College; resident of Westminster College, Cambridge, 1955–6; M.Div. 1958, Yale Divinity School; Ph.D. 1967, Harvard University in history of American religion; roommate of Melvin Woody and Richard Sassoon at Yale College; dated SP, 1955–6; co-authored *Lying-In: A History of Childbirth in America*.
5–Sallie McFague (1933–), B.A. 1955, English, Smith College. An engagement announcement was printed in the *New York Times* on 2 February 1958; they did not marry.
6–Richard Laurence Sassoon (1934–2017); B.A. 1955, Yale College; attended the Sorbonne, 1955–6; dated SP, 1954–6. Sassoon was born in Paris, and raised in Tryon, North Carolina. There are very few letters from SP to Sassoon. SP biographer Andrew Wilson reports in his biography *Mad Girl's Love Song* (2013) that Sassoon told him 'Sylvia and I did correspond a lot and, long ago, visiting my parents' house, I looked in the attic in a trunk where I kept her letters and they were not there, which is a total mystery.' There are many letters from Sassoon to SP held by Lilly Library.

and the Fifth Avenue tycoons & best of all, Marianne Moore who was lovely at her home in Brooklyn[1] & admires Ted very much & served us strawberries, sesame seed biscuits & milk & talked a blue streak. Can we reserve tickets & take you to see her this Sunday?[2] Our last night after Marianne Moore was lovely too: two experimental Ionesco plays[3] & a good dinner in the Village.

We hope to come home for supper Thursday: my reading-recording is Friday afternoon[4] & we'll go to dinner with Jack Sweeney that night. Mrs. Prouty has asked us (Ted & me) for dinner Sunday noon, but I thought maybe you & grampy & Ted & me could have a special dinner Monday the 16th to celebrate our 2nd anniversary. How about it? And then we must return to Hamp & get to work. We also hope to look at Beacon Hill apartments while at home.

Much love,
Sivvy

<on page 1 of letter>

PS – Many thanks for the magazines–

TO *Warren Plath*

Wednesday 11 June 1958 TLS (photocopy), Indiana University

June 11, 1958

Dearest Warren . . .

It was fine to get your good letter. I am so happy you are coming home in only two months. Life here for the past month has been such a holocaust that I lost all sense of timing and have been a frightful letter writer as my work began to go round faster & faster like a merrygoround. Which, at

1–Marianne Moore lived in an apartment at 260 Cumberland Street, Brooklyn, New York.

2–Marianne Moore was the recipient of the Boston Arts Festival Poetry award and gave a reading in the Public Garden, Boston, on Sunday 15 June 1958. Moore's poem, 'A Festival', was written for the occasion.

3–Romanian playwright Eugène Ionesco (1909–94); his *The Bald Soprano* (*La Cantatrice Chauve*, 1950) and *Jack* (*Jacques ou la soumission*, 1955). The plays were performed at the Sullivan Street Playhouse, 181 Sullivan Street, New York.

4–SP recorded poems on Friday 13 June 1958, for the Woodberry Poetry Room, Lamont Library, at the Fassett Recording Studios. SP read 'Black Rook in Rainy Weather', 'Departure of the Ghost' ['The Ghost's Leavetaking'], 'Mad Maudlin' ['Maudlin'], 'Sow', 'November Graveyard, Haworth' ['November Graveyard'], 'Mussel-Hunter at Rock Harbor', 'On the Plethora of Dryads', 'The Moon was a Fat Woman Once' ['The Thin People'], 'The Disquieting Muses', 'Nocturne' ['Hardcastle Crags'], 'Child's Park Stones', 'Spinster', 'The

last, has stopped, & Ted and I are just beginning to recover, teaching over & done with for the present. I realize, as I start to write, how many letters I've written you in my head & how much I've missed you. There are so very few people in the world I really care about, & I guess you and Ted are the closest of all. Perhaps we can go for picnic & swim at the Cape to celebrate your return. I want so much, over the course of this next year, when I hope we'll be very close & you coming over to dinner often (we're going to look for a Boston apartment this weekend) and visiting us much, to hear, bit by bit, about your ideas and experiences in Europe and of your work at Harvard. You know I've always had a secret desire to go to Harvard, & the next best thing is your going. I have that horrid habit mothers get of being secretly determined all my sons will go to Harvard.

I finished teaching on May 22nd & felt honestly sorry to say goodbye to my girls. I was amused at my last day of classes to get applause in the exact volume of my own feelings toward every class: a spatter at 9, a thunderous ovation at 11 which saw me down two flights of stairs, and a medium burst at 3. Now that it is over, I can't believe I've taught 20 stories, 2 novels, 10 plays, and countless poems including the Waste Land. But I have. And I've done more than I thought or hoped for those first black weeks of teaching which upset me very much: I think I have chosen excellent works, won over my most difficult pupils & taught them a good deal. But on the whole, my colleagues have depressed me: it is disillusioning to find the people you admired as a student are weak and jealous and petty and vain as people, which many of them are. And the faculty gossip, especially among the men, over morning coffee, afternoon tea, and evening cocktails is very boring: all about the latest gossip, possible apointments, firings, grants, students, literary criticism: all secondary, it seems: an airtight secure community, with those on tenure getting pot-bellies. Writers especially are suspect if they don't place academic life first, & we have seen one or two of our writing acquaintances given very raw & nasty deals. Of course, we have been at an advantage, both having resigned in face of requests to stay. But it has been impossible for either of us to get any work done & we feel that if we drifted into this well-paid security we would curse ourselves in ten years time for what might have been.

I am sure, for example, that Ted has the makings of a great poet, and he already has some loyal supporters like Marianne Moore (whom we

---

Earthenware Head' ['The Lady and the Earthenware Head'], 'On the Difficulty on Conjuring Up a Dryad', and 'All the Dead Dears'.

visited at her Brooklyn flat this week in NYC) and TS Eliot, whom we hope to see when we go to England: Ted is better than any poet I can think of ten years his senior & I feel as a wife the best I can do is demand nothing but that we find workable schemes whereby we both can write & live lives which are dictated by inner needs for creative expansion & experience.

Of course there are very few people who can understand this. There is something suspect, especially in America, about people who don't have ten-year plans for a career or at least a regular job. We found this out when trying to establish credit at a local general store: we fitted, amusingly enough, into none of the form categories of "The Young American Couple": I had a job, Ted didn't; we owned no car, were buying no furniture on the installment plan, had no TV, had no charge accounts, came as if literally dropped from foreign parts. The poor secretary was very perplexed. Anyhow, I can talk to you freely about our plans, if not to mother: she worries so that the most we can do is put up an illusion of security: security to us is in ourselves, & no job, or even money, can give us what we have to develop: faith in our work, & hard hard work which is spartan in many ways. Ted is especially good for me because he doesn't demand Immediate Success & Publication, and is training me not to. We feel the next five years are as important to our writing as medical school is to a prospective surgeon. Ted says simply to produce, work, produce, read not novels or poems only, but books on folk lore, fiddler crabs & meteorites: this is what the imagination thrives on. The horror of the academic writer is that he lives on air & other peoples' second-hand accounts of other peoples' writing.

We have a friend named Stanley Sultan who has published several stories[1] & teaches writing here: he is very young & very academically inclined (wrote PhD. thesis on James Joyce)[2] and he showed us a story he'd just finished & obviously liked. It was written in the person of the wife of a Coney Island dwarf who had been killed as a kind of game by being forced to drink a six-pack of beer in a crowd who were angered at his trying to hinder a cat's killing a rat stuck in a drain-pipe. Well, the story seemed grey to us, & dull, but the point of view was good. What bothered us was the possibility of a cat killing a rat (rats being very strong,

1–SP was familiar with Sultan's short story 'The Fugue and the Fig Tree', which appeared in *The Best American Short Stories, 1953* (Boston: Houghton Mifflin, 1953). In *The Bell Jar*, SP's protagonist Esther Greenwood reads this story when recovering from ptomaine poisoning.

2–Stanley Sultan, 'The Art of Ulysses' (Ph.D. thesis), Yale University, 1955.

Ted having seen them kill cats & wound dogs seriously) by a few cuffs of the paw, and also the unlikelihood of a couple of young men being able to kill a dwarf by flooding his small stomach with six cans of beer on a main street in a crowd of people: simply to get down a sip of beer would be difficult enough, and all this wasn't described. But the reality of the story seemed very questionable. Anyway, this writer wasn't at all concerned with these problems, & surprised at our raising them: what mattered was: did we get the symbolism? the parallel between dwarf and rat? the rat stuck in the drainpipe and the round shape of beercans paralleling this. Well, you see what I mean: the writer is cut off from life & begins to think as he analyzes stories in class: very differently from the way a writer <u>feels</u> reality: which, according to many teachers, is too simple as such & needs symbols, irony, archetypal images & all that. Well, we will try to get along without such conscious & contrived machinery. We write, and wake up with symbols on our pages, but do not begin with them.

I had two ghastly weeks of correcting papers: 70 term papers of my own. 60 final exams in American Lit. course I correct for (which is very dull, as I know none of the students & have no reciprocal influence on them, but got $100 extra for this in the semester; yet realize I'd have been better off writing two poems for that price) & then all the senior exams in English which I learned the whole English faculty shares reading. My eyes got a queer stinging rash & I was glad to end it all on June 2nd.

Ted & I left for New York City immediately after my last papers & stayed with Patsy O'Neil & her roommate for 5 days which made our trip possible, as we had no rent extra & could cook food there. We lived, with the exception of a few meals, on frankfurts, hamburgs, bacon, eggs & coffee. I'm glad we went. It exorcised the academic year & we came back here to cool rainy green June weather renewed & ready to write. We saw much & walked prodigiously for our stay.

First off we met Charles Monteith & Peter Du Sautoy of Faber's and lunched with them in a plush pink room at the Biltmore just before they sailed. We liked them immensely & they promised to introduce us to "Tom" Eliot when we came to England next. We'd met du Sautoy at a cocktail party at an amazing modern house overlooking all the green mountains in Amherst & met many Amherst professors, plus Reuben Brower (sp?)[1] who I understand is master at Adams House & who was very nice. Then we went to the tip of Manhattan, by Wall Street overlooking the bay boats,

1–Cabot Professor of English and Master of Adams House, an undergraduate residential house of Harvard University, Reuben A. Brower (1908–75).

and climbed six flights in an office building to the little tar-rooftop eyrie of Oscar Williams, the wellknown poet & anthologist who is putting 3 of Ted's poems at the end of his revised Pocket Anthology of modern verse which begins with Whitman[1] and ends with Hughes.

Oscar Williams was a queer, birdlike little man, obviously very at-odds since his best friend Dylan Thomas & his beloved poet-painter wife Gene Derwood died in the same year. He lives in a tiny rooftop studio painted light blue, with a skylight, covered with oil paintings by his wife, bright colored animals & portraits, photographs of his dead loves, brick homemade bookcases full of poetry books, tables, floors and bathtub covered and full of unwashed glasses, and a fine little tar roof porch overlooking the gulls & boats and ringed with potted rosebushes & mint plants. He served us drambuie & we got along well. He then took us to two parties, one on 5th avenue at the home of a wealthy man whose poetry he published, where we went up in the same elevator with Lionel & Diana Trilling: and all afternoon had that odd feeling of recognizing famous faces from photographs: the negro writer Ralph Ellison, old Farrar, publisher, of Farrar, Straus & Cudahy; the editor of the Hudson Review & endless boring professors from Columbia. The next party was given by the owner of a famous furniture store on 5th Avenue, Hy Sobiloff, who also publishes poetry with Oscar & occasionally give 10 thousand dollars to buy permissions for new anthologies: very dull & wealthy stupid floordecorators & all Jewish businessmen named Goldstone: we ate well from a lavish bouffet & went home to Patsy's, very happy with our own lives.

We spent a whole day at the Bronx Zoo which was delightful: most of the animals were roaming in open places, none of the horrible prison-like cages at the Central Park Zoo where the lions can't turn around and the gorillas are morbidly depressed. Here we saw magnificent gorillas, four enchanting chimpanzees, four white playful polar bears, endless boa-constrictors (how I would like to see them fed!) pig-headed turtles, great raucous rainbow colored birds, and over all the queer scream of the free wandering peacocks who kept spreading admirable tails.

By coincidence on the train to the Zoo we asked a smiling young man next to us where to get off & he turned out to be Clyde Beatty's brother (the famous animal catcher & trainer) and was on his day off from work in the lion cage. He seemed one of the few people we'd met in NYC happy with his work.

1–American poet Walt Whitman (1819–92).

We wandered through Harlem (Ted first thought all NYC was made up of negroes), through Central Park, Greenwich Village where we took Patsy to dinner & the Lorca play "Blood Wedding" and later went to see two most entertaining experimental plays by Ionesco by a fine little troupe in an off-broadway theater seating about 150 people. We walked through throngs of Bowery bums, stared in shop windows, got my fortune told for 5¢ by a mechanical gypsy in the 8th avenue subway; my card had the picture of a mailman on it & said that soon I will get a wonderful letter which will change my life! How's that for hopeful? The lady with the glass eyes couldn't have come closer to my heart.

We also visited Babette Deutsch,[1] a small time poet & critic, who is married to the Russian scholar Avrahm Yarmolinsky[2]---she'd written in admiration of Ted's poems. And lunched with Dave Keightley, the friend of ours who was in the car accident & at the Holyoke hospital for several months. His publishing company editors, World Pub., are interested in seeing a ms. of my poetry book (now provisionally titled "Full Fathom Five") this fall. They've never published poetry before, but are interested in "genuine fresh talent" which I hope I have. I've been changing, I think much for the better, in my writing style: ironically, of the 35 or so poems I've published in my career, I've rejected about 20 of these from my book manuscript as too romantic, sentimental & frivolous & immature: my main difficulty has been overcoming a clever, too brittle & glossy feminine tone, & I am gradually getting to speak "straight out" and of real experience, not just in metaphorical conceits. I'll enclose a recent poem which I hope you may like.

I've two poems out in the June London Magazine, one in the obscure New Mexico Quarterly,[3] one in the British "Guiness" anthology of verse[4] published this May; Ted & I are each having a poem in the next annual British PEN anthology,[5] his "Thrushes", my "Sow", and each of us have 2 poems coming out in the annual Borestone anthology[6] in America: encouraging to be between hard covers, but not very lucrative as yet.

1–American poet and critic Babette Deutsch (1895–1982).

2–Author and translator Avrahm Yarmolinksy (1890–1975).

3–Sylvia Plath, 'On the Plethora of Dryads', *New Mexico Quarterly* 27 (Autumn 1957): 27.

4–Sylvia Plath, 'Spinster', *The Guinness Book of Poetry 1956/57* (London: Putnam, 1958): 88. SP's copy is held by Lilly Library.

5–Sylvia Plath, 'Sow', *New Poems* 1958 (London: Michael Joseph): 77–8; Ted Hughes, 'Thrushes', 53.

6–Sylvia Plath, 'Pursuit' and 'Epitaph for Fire and Flower', *Best Poems of 1957: Borestone Mountain Poetry Awards 1958* (Stanford, Calif.: Stanford University Press, 1958): 73–4; and Ted Hughes, 'Everyman's Odyssey', and 'The Thought-Fox', 43–4.

One thing which we haven't told mother for obvious reasons is that Ted applied for a Saxton writing fellowship for this year & we were sure of getting it for him as Marianne Moore et. al. volunteered to write & he had a magnificent project for a poetry book: it was the only fellowship, as a Briton, he was eligible for. Ironically, we learned this week, that the fellowship is run by trustees from Harper's and as he is published by them his project can't be considered on merit: if it had been so considered he obviously would have got a grant. So, with supreme & rather distressing irony, the very qualification of his worth, publishing a book, is his one flaw, rendering him ineligible. So I shall apply for the same grant (don't tell mother about this either) & Ted will apply for a Guggenheim for next year.

We have saved some money from our work this year & also earned about $1500 between us from writing (Ted's book has sold 1,700 copies in America and about 1,600 in England: supremely good for a poetry book, as is the $1000 he'll have earned out of it.) So this summer we will write "on salary" & hope for something to turn up in Boston: full-time jobs are obviously out, as our one wish is to write, & we don't want to live on our savings as they must take us to Europe for our projected year in Italy. We have considered the McDowell Writing Colony[1] as a last measure and also the possibility of living in someone's summer house rent-free in return for caretaking. But we would both like to live in Boston near the library, anonymous people, with no need for a car & very near publishers & editors and all Boston & Cambridge have to offer. God feeds the ravens. I hope you understand this better than mother does. When we are both wealthy & famous our work will justify our lives, but now our lives & faith must justify themselves. We live very simply and happily & walk each day in Our Park, which is nextdoor & which noone else frequents. There are several brown rabbits, two magnificent black frogs who swim like suave purple-bellied Martians & return our stares for hours, innumerable squirrels, bright yellow birds, red-headed woodpeckers and fruit trees and a garden which is mysteriously replanted as the flowers die: first tulips and daffodils then hyacinths: then one day we came back to find these gone and beds of geraniums and white petunias in their place. The little rose garden is just coming out, and about once a week we make off with a red or yellow rose.

We met the mad and very nice poet Robert Lowell (the only one 40ish whom we both admire, who comes from the Boston Lowells &

1–The MacDowell Colony is an artists' colony founded in 1907 in Peterborough, New Hampshire.

is periodically carted off as a manic depressive) when he came to give a reading at the U. of Mass.[1] He is quiet, soft-spoken, and we liked him very much. I drove him around Northampton looking for relics of his ancestors, and to the Historical Society & the graveyard. We hope to see him in Boston when we move down.

We've become good friends with Jack Sweeney who's head of the Lamont Poetry Library at Harvard & like him as much as anyone we've met here. I'm going to make a recording (did I tell you?) for the Lamont Library of my poems this Friday, so you can go up there & hear recordings of your sister & brother-in-law anytime![2]

Ted & I plan to celebrate our 2nd anniversary at home with mother this monday, june 16th. It seems impossible I've been married for two whole years, and much more impossible that I ever <u>wasn't</u> married to Ted! Oh we have rousing battles every so often in which I come out with sprained thumbs & Ted with missing earlobes, but we feel so perfectly at one with our work & reactions to life & people that we make our own world to work in which isn't dependent on anyone else's love or admiration, but self-contained: our best pleasure is writing at home, eating & talking & walking in woods to look for animals & birds. Money would be very helpful, but we have everything except this: and Ted's uncle is almost a millionaire (but very odd, with a mad daughter who will no doubt outlive us) and Mrs. Prouty who has adopted Ted ("he's so handsome: couldn't he get on Tv? etc.") occasionally sends us a hundred $ check for christmas or anniversary & we both feel genuinely fond of her, & see her as often as we can.

Well, I must close now, or I will be typing into tomorrow & next week. Here is a poem I made about the fiddler crabs we found at Rock Harbor when we went to get mussels last summer for fish bait. I hope you like it. If you find anything inaccurate about the crabs do tell me about it. Read it aloud – for the sounds of it.

1 – Robert Lowell read in the Old Chapel Auditorium on 6 May 1958 at 7:00 p.m.; the event was sponsored by the Literary Society.
2 – TH read 'Crow Hill', 'Acrobats', 'To Paint a Water Lily', 'Witches', 'Relic', 'Dick Straightup', 'Historian', 'Thrushes', 'Bullfrog', 'View of a Pig', and 'Of Cats'.

Mussel-Hunter at Rock Harbor

I came before the water-
colorists came to get the
good of the Cape light that scours
sand-grit to sided crystal
and buffs and sleeks the blunt hulls
of the three fishing smacks beached
on the bank of the river's

back-tracking tail. I'd come for
free fish-bait: the blue mussels
clumped like bulbs at the grass-root
margin of the tidal pools.
Dawn tide stood dead low. I smelt
mud-stench, shell guts, gulls' leavings;
heard a queer crusty scrabble

cease, and I neared the silenced
edge of a cratered pool-bed:
the mussels hung dull blue and
conspicuous, yet it seemed
a sly world's hinges had swung
shut against me. All held still.
Though I counted scant seconds,

enough ages lapsed to win
confidence of safe-conduct
in the wary otherworld
eyeing me. Grass put forth claws;
small mud-knobs, nudged from under,
displaced their domes as tiny
knights might doff their casques. The crabs

inched from their pigmy burrows
and from the trench-dug mud, all
camouflaged in mottled mail
of browns and greens. Each wore one
claw swollen to a shield large

as itself---no fiddler's arm
grown Gargantuan by trade

but grown grimly and grimly
borne for a use beyond my
guessing of it. Sibilant
mass-motived hordes, they sidled
out in a converging stream
toward the pool-mouth, perhaps to
meet the thin and sluggish thread

of sea retracing its tide-
way up the river-basin.
Or to avoid me. They moved
obliquely, with a dry-wet
sound, with a glittery wisp
and trickle. Could they feel mud
pleasurable under claws

as I could between bare toes?
That question ended it---I
stood shut out for once, for all,
puzzling the passage of their
absolutely alien
order as I might puzzle
at the clear tail of Halley's

comet coolly giving my
orbit the go-by, made known
by a family name it
knew nothing of. So the crabs
went about their business which
wasn't fiddling, and I filled
a big handkerchief with blue

mussels. From what the crabs saw,
if they could see, I was one
two-legged mussel-picker.
High on the airy thatching
of the dense grasses I found

the husk of a fiddler-crab,
intact, strangely strayed above

his world of mud---green color
and innards bleached and blown off
somewhere by much sun and wind:
there was no telling if he'd
died recluse or suicide
of headstrong Columbus crab.
The crab-face etched and set there

grimaced as skulls grimace: it
had an oriental look,
a samurai-deathmask done
on a tiger-tooth, less for
art's sake than god's. Far from sea---
where red-freckled crab-backs, claws
and whole crabs, dead, their soggy

bellies pallid and upturned,
perform their shambling waltzes
on the waves' dissolving turn
and return, losing themselves
bit by bit to their friendly
element---this relic saved
face to face the bald-faced sun.

****

This is written in what's known as "syllabic verse", measuring lines not by heavy & light stresses, but by the <u>number</u> of syllables, which here is 7: I find this form satisfactorily strict (a pattern varying the number of syllables in each line can be set up, as M. Moore does it) and yet it has a speaking illusion of freedom (which the measured stress doesn't have) as stresses vary freely. Don't follow my example: write soon! And I promise to answer.

Much love –
<u>Sivvy</u>

TO *Aurelia Schober Plath*

Wednesday 25 June 1958 TLS, Indiana University

<Typed on pink Smith College Memorandum paper with heading>

Date June 25 To You From Me In re odds & ends.

Remember, a year ago, we first set foot together on American soil? And the lovely party we had under the great awning in the back yard? Ted & I look back on our party with much pleasure.

Nothing of moment has happened since we came back. We've slept a lot, and I've been making banana bread of which we're very fond for tea. Both of us have written several good poems, but heard nothing about our work at the tardy Atlantic which has kept it for the usual half year: they ought to reorganize: no other magazine in the world keeps submissions so long.

We climbed to the peak of Mount Holyoke[1] & hoped to do it often, for there is a magnificent view, but I learned on reaching the top that there is a charge of 15 cents for each person who walks up: I can understand the parking fee, but got very angry that you couldn't even walk in a State park for nothing. Our park if full of mountain laurel now, very lovely. And the rose garden is in full bloom. I have written another poem about the latter[2] and about climbing the mountain.[3]

The thought of our apartment waiting in Boston is very consoling: we are really too isolated here & look forward to walking out in the streets & watching the odd faces, learning odd corners, going to the library, museums & foreign films.

Will write again soon –
Love
Sivvy

PS: We loved our 2nd anniversary dinner last week. And the stay at home was such a rest for us!

PS: One hour later: VERY GOOD NEWS: In the mail I just got my FIRST acceptance from the NEW YORKER![4] And not of a short little poem but of two very fat & amazingly long ones! "MUssel*Hunter At Rock

1–This incident became the basis for SP's short story 'Above the Oxbow'. The story describes J. A. Skinner State Park on Mount Holyoke.

2–Sylvia Plath, 'Fable of the Rhododendron Stealers', which is set in Childs Park, Northampton, Mass.

3–Sylvia Plath, 'Above the Oxbow'.

4–Howard Moss to SP, 24 June 1958; held by Smith College.

Harbor"[1] and "Nocturne",[2] the first 91 lines, the last, 45 lines! In our materialistic way, Ted & I figured, amid much jumping up and down, this should mean close to $350, or 3 full months of Boston rent! For two poems! They wrote a glowing letter, very generous for the New Yorker. It began:

"MUSSEL*HUNTER AT ROCK HARBOR seems to ma a marvelous poem, and I'm happy to say we're taking it for The New Yorker, as well as NOCTURNE, which we also think extremely fine."

How's that for a good beginning to a summer of work! You see what happens the minute one worships one's own god of vocation & doesn't slight it for grubbing under the illusion of duty to Everybody's-Way-Of-Life! This is well over 3 times as much money as I got for half a year of drudgery in that American lit course, correcting exams, and well over a month's salary for a week's work of pure joy. The Mussel Hunters may not come out till next summer, as they're very crowded with summer poems, but I should get the check in a few days. What a nice anniversary gift for our coming to America!

xxx

Sivvy

You see – the gypsy-fortuneteller with her card depicting the mailman was very right!

1–Sylvia Plath, 'Mussel Hunter at Rock Harbor', *New Yorker* (9 August 1958): 22.

2–Sylvia Plath, 'Night Walk', *New Yorker* (11 October 1958): 40; later titled 'Hardcastle Crags'. Correspondence about the title change from 'Nocturne' to 'Night Walk' for the periodical appearance is held in the *New Yorker* records, *c.* 1924–84 at the New York Public Library.

TO *Henry Rago*

Wednesday 25 June 1958 TLS, University of Chicago

Apartment 3 rear
337 Elm Street
Northampton, Mass.
June 25, 1958

Mr. Henry Rago
POETRY
60 West Walton Street
Chicago 10, Illinois

Dear Mr. Rago,

I'm sending along a group of recent poems[1]---the first poems after a year devoted almost completely to teaching. I hope you may like some of these well enough for publication in Poetry.

With all good wishes,
Sylvia Plath

TO *Olive Higgins Prouty*

Wednesday 25 June 1958 TLS on Department of English, Smith College letterhead, Indiana University

June 25, 1958

Dear Mrs. Prouty,

I'm writing a small note to say what a happy time Ted and I had with you last week! We count a visit with you one of our favorite treats when coming home and look forward to inviting you to mount the little elevator at 9 Willow Street in Boston, just off Louisberg Square, and come to sup with us in our small writer's corner over-looking the rooftops and the river!

Today is just a year's anniversary of our arrival in America, and I received some very good news: The New Yorker wrote me my first acceptance (after

1–The exact number of poems and the titles SP sent are unknown. It is likely SP sent 'A Lesson in Vengeance', 'The Death of Myth-Making', and 'On the Decline of Oracles', which were accepted by September 1958 and published in *Poetry* 94 (September 1959): 368–71.

10 years of rejections!) of two long poems---one, "Mussel-Hunter at Rock Harbor", the one I sent you and read last week; the other, "Nocturne", about a walk on the moor-tops in England. I am quite excited about these poems and the acceptance gives me great courage to go on working on my book of poems which I hope to complete in Boson this winter.

Ted is now working on a short story, "The Courting of Petty Quinnet", a Yorkshire tale, and we'll send along a copy of his fairytale in Jack and Jill as soon as it comes out next month: we hope you'll have a good time reading it.

Both of us are plunged in work, relieved by long walks in our park and up the neighboring mountains, which give us needed perspectives & far vistas after much close writing. We live, as you have said yourself, for finding the right words, the one word, right for its place. We'll write again soon.

Much love,
Sylvia Hughes

TO *Warren Plath*

Wednesday 25 June 1958 — TLS (photocopy), Indiana University

Wednesday: June 25th

Dearest Warren . . .

It is pleasant to think that in just about two months from today you will be home. Today marks the anniversary of Ted's & my landing in America, and I feel we have accomplished a great deal this year. The teaching has given us both confidence, a kind of intellectual discipline which, although it stopped us writing for the year, is bearing fruit now. We've just both been working on several poems which we think are quite an advance in our writing. We are extremely critical of each other, & won't let poems pass without questioning every work, rhythm & image: it is this, I think, this mutual creative & strict criticism, which most writers don't have who work alone. This way, the critics have less chance to point out weaknesses.

I got some very good news this morning: did I tell you in my last fat letter of about a week ago (I sent it airmail, have you got it yet?) about the fortune-telling card I got from the mechanical gypsy in the NYC subway that said soon I'd get a letter that changed my life? Well, maybe that's still to come, but this morning my FIRST acceptance by the New Yorker arrived!

If you can understand what this means, you'll see how pleased & encouraged I am. I've been sending poems to The New Yorker for 10 years & getting "please try us again" rejections. Well, this time it worked. And no tiny "filler" poems, either: they accepted two really long ones: "Mussel-Hunter At Rock Harbor" (didn't I send you a copy of that in the last letter? read it over & hear the gold jingling in the lines!) and "Nocturne", about a walk on the moor, the first poem 91 lines, the last 45! We quickly added up (the check's still to come) and figured I should get about $350 for the two, which is 3 months of Boston-apartment rent, or well over a month's teaching salary for about a week of work that was pure joy! This also gives me great courage for working on my poetry book this summer & will balance endless rejections. Instead of the usual New Yorker coolness I'd expect, Howard Moss, the poetry editor, opened his letter:

"MUSSEL-HUNTER AT ROCK HARBOR seems to me a marvelous poem, and I'm happy to say we're taking it for The New Yorker, as well as NOCTURNE, which we also think extremely fine."

Please don't think me a braggart to quote this, but I've been working really hard with hardly any recognition for over a year & is is delightful to think that some part of the world I love & have written about with hard work & words I love will be shared & appreciated by other people. The money also is pleasant, because It confirms what we've already decided: to live for our writing: if we can do so much (we've earned about $1,800 in writing since last June) on giving less than a month's total time to writing, what mightn't we do if we devoted a year, another & another to it? Anyway, we have saved enough from our salaries to pay for this year, even if I don't get the Saxton grant which I'm applying for, & then Ted will apply for a Guggenheim & marshal TS Eliot et. al. behind him. I'm hoping to spend a few hours a day this year studying & reading German, & perhaps you can loan me some of your books: can you bring home any Kafka[1] books in German? Id really appreciate that: also any other "literary" books you might get on your book-allowance. I'd like to read good works.

We just came from several days in Wellesley. We have an apartment in Boston on 9 Willow Street, Beacon Hill, & we love it & will move in September 1st. It has everything we planned to get except perhaps the two most practical things: low rent & a huge kitchen. The kitchen is pullman, pigmy facilities, against the living room wall, separated by a curtain, and

1 – German-speaking Bohemian writer Franz Kafka (1883–1924)

the $115 a month rent, although it includes the utilities, seems also to include the view, which is magnificent: a 3-way view, two bay-windows facing over the river. The bedroom & livingroom are very small, but the bay-window in each offers two "writing corners" which have a fine view of river, roof & treetops. It is luminously light, on the 6th floor, and seems to be quiet & in walking distance of all stores. It's just off Louisberg Square & we've signed up for a year. We hope you'll come often to visit & to dinner: I look so forward to seeing you often. I feel we should get to know each other again, we've been abroad so much! And Ted & I hope to manage a year in Italy & Germany before we begin a family. Will you be looking for an apartment in Boston or Cambridge?

It has been a cold, wet rainy June, with hardly a day of sun, so very nice for working. We climbed Mount Holyoke for the fine view over all the Pioneer Valley & river & were outraged to find that the State charges 15¢ per person to walk up: we'd been planning to hike up every other day. I don't know why I got so angry at this---I can see their charging a parking fee, but people who are energetic enough to sweat out the climb should get the state's views for their taxes.

Our park nextdoor is all mountain laurel now, & I've written a few poems about it---the stones[1] & the rose garden. I'm reading through Shakespeares plays & a Penguin book on the Aztecs, anthropology,[2] very absorbing. Ted & I plan to educate ourselves in history, art, literature, language & philosophy this year, to begin a kind of Renaissance self-education.

Mother seems in good health, and was still tan & elated from her trip to Bermuda when we were home. She really must have something like that to treat herself with every year. And from what she says, Grampy had a magnificent time too.

Have you found any interesting German girls? Mother mentioned you'd been dating a law-studentess. Do write soon.

Much love,
Sivvy

1–Sylvia Plath, 'Child's Park Stones'.

2–Possibly George Clapp Vaillant, *Aztecs of Mexico: Origin, Rise, and Fall of the Aztec Nation* (Baltimore: Penguin Books, 1950, reprinted 1955).

TO *Howard Moss*

Thursday 26 June 1958 TLS, New York Public Library

Apartment 3 rear
337 Elm Street
Northampton, Mass.
June 26, 1958

Dear Mr. Moss:

I am pleased that you like MUSSEL-HUNTER AT ROCK HARBOR and NOCTURNE.

I have made arrangements to have the book of poems I am completing this summer at the publisher's by fall. So although I am sure the book won't come out before Summer 1959, it may well come out then. Thus I would much appreciate it if you might manage to schedule MUSSEL-HUNTER this summer.

The last two lines of the poem are meant to be read ". . . this relic saved/face, to face the bald-faced sun." The idiom is "to save face" here. The crabs in "mottled mail of browns and greens" are the fiddler-crabs. The dead crabs in the sea may be considered to represent all Crabdom.

I am willing to change the title of NOCTURNE. Would NIGHT WALK be all right? I like the conciseness of that.

With all good wishes, I am
Sincerely yours,
Sylvia Plath

Mr. Howard Moss
THE NEW YORKER
25 West 43rd Street
New York 36, New York

TO *Olwyn Hughes*

Monday 30 June 1958 ALS, Washington University (St Louis)

Monday, June 30

Dear Olwyn –

Ted and I are just back from climbing Mount Holyoke – one of our peaks of exercise, taking a good hour to get up, under a green network of leaves, but the view worth it from the porch of a hundred-year-old hotel which housed Abraham Lincoln once, and Jenny Lind[1] who named the view 'The Paradise of America", although I suspect Jenny was over-ecstatic. She named our Smith frog-pool 'Paradise Pond.' From the top we can see north along the back of the broad winding Connecticut river, all the green patchwork of asparagus, strawberry & potato farms below. We're right in the middle of a great river-rich farming valley & so get vegetables & fruits fresh from the fields. I do like your sending those recipes of delectable things & will try this pepper & tomato & onion & sausage one soon. Try to get more such from the Hungarians – do any of them make a good borsch? Maybe Luke remembers the heavenly borsch the three of us had[2] at the restaurant with the bitchy old waitress whose daughter (probably chained to the stove) was a wonderful cook. Tell Luke for me to send ahead his favorite menus & I'll cook them if he promises to visit us. We'd both love to see him this August & will be here till the end of the month.

Ted thrives, & so do I, with no jobs. Both of us are meant to be wealthy & have convinced our Boston landlord[3] (dubious about our future rent-paying) that we are hourly having money pour in from magazines. As soon as I stopped work & started writing I sold my two longest poems to The New Yorker (my first acceptance from them) & we figure the check should total 3 months rent at least. This is very encouraging & especially so since I want to get a full first book of poems to the publishers this winter – I'm ditching old work at an amazing rate. Ted's second book is already magnificent – richness, depth, color & a mature force & volume. Slowly, slowly we hope to sell the poems. I know he is the great poet of our generation & feel that the most important thing is to somehow clear these next five years for a tough & continuous apprenticeship to writing – his children's story has just come out – delightfully & sprightly illustrations with it. We will try for grants, too. Our work should begin to speak for itself then. Our Boston apartment is minute, but aesthetically fine with its light, air, quiet & superb view. The city is a delight to walk in.

1–Swedish opera singer Johanna Maria (Jenny) Lind (1820–87).

2–According to SP's calendar, she, TH, and Luke Myers ate a 'depressing borscht & veal supper with Luke at bitter Franco Oriental' in Paris on 29 June 1956. SP drew a display of bottles and flowers; see *Journals of Sylvia Plath*: 571.

3–According to SP's address book, she and TH rented their apartment from Jacob Ham of Wm. C. Codman & Son of 30 Charles Street, Boston.

Do send on the Scorpio book. I'm extremely interested in seeing it. Ted & I both love getting your letters, especially long ones like the last, so do write soon again. Tell us more about deGaulle.

With love,
Sylvia

TO *Edith & William Hughes*

Tuesday 1 July 1958 — ALS with envelope, Family owned

Monday, – no Tuesday, July 1st

Dear Ted's mother & dad . . .

Suddenly, with July, the heat of sultry summer has jumped on us & we go about the house barefoot, in bathing suits, drinking iced drinks. Now that we're not teaching, we hardly know what day of the week it is, except that Sunday is the day the mailman doesn't come. We are eating well & coolly – chicken salads, cold roast beef, banana teabread, lots of fresh fruit & vegetables from the nearby farms.

Ted & I both thrive while working at writing & nothing else. The checks keep coming in. I just got £7: 7: – for my two poems in the June issue of The London magazine and expect, as Ted has probably said, a check over $300 for the two poems The New Yorker just accepted. I am very happy cooking, writing, reading (Ted has given me a lot of those little penguin books about animals, the origin of man, the Aztecs & so on) & going for walks. A woman in our park who seems to do part-time gardening as a charity showed us a nest of tiny baby rabbits under a green bush that grew flattened to the ground & we've discovered several bird's nests with babies in them. I am homesick for Wilfred's farm & look so forward to seeing all his animals when we come back to visit. I'd especially like to see some little ones born, as I never have.

Ted is writing some more good poems – he has a fine one about a great black bull[1] and a very brilliant one about the outlawing of the cat o'nine tails in the British navy. His story came out this month in Jack & Jill, the children's magazine & the best in the whole issue by far – it has some wonderful lively illustrations with it. I am hoping Ted will write more such stories.

Mother loves getting your letters & it pleases her so much to have you to write to. She would like to visit 'The Beacon' someday. I've told her so much about it.

1 – Ted Hughes, 'The Bull Moses'.

Our apartment in Boston is tiny – very little to clean – but has two wonderful window-views which will be ideal for us to write in. I hope to finish my book of poems this winter & Ted should finish his this next year. We have saved enough to live & write on this year, but I am trying for a grant & Ted will try for a Guggenheim for 1959 to see if we can keep our savings.

Yesterday we climbed Mount Holyoke again – that high tree-covered mountain overlooking the broad silvery Connecticut river & on the way up saw a strange little animal we'd glimpsed in the road while driving a few days ago. It was greyish-brown furred, with a short fat body, stumpy legs & tail & a sweet gentle mousish face. We got this one cornered for a good look – it just clattered its sharp yellow teeth in a scared way, & decided it was a groundhog (alias wood chuck). I wanted to pet it, but Ted said it would bite my arm off. So we let it lie.

Both of us are in excellent health & working well. Write soon –

Love to you both –
Sylvia

TO *Howard Moss*

Wednesday 2 July 1958 TLS, New York Public Library

Apartment 3 rear
337 Elm Street
Northampton, Mass.
July 2, 1958

Mr. Howard Moss
THE NEW YORKER
25 West 43rd Street
New York 36, New York

Dear Mr. Moss:

Here are the corrected proofs. I have checked and agreed on all your corrections (additions of commas and omissions of hyphens) except the problematic "backtrack" which I'd like to be one word,"backtracking", made from the verb "backtrack". Is that all right?

I also have inserted a comma after "save face" to eliminate what I don't consider a desirable ambiguity in the last two lines of "Mussel Hunter".

I also substituted the title "Night Walk" for "A Walk In The Night".

I do hope these corrections are satisfactory.

Sincerely yours,
Sylvia Plath

TO *Aurelia Schober Plath*

Saturday 5 July 1958 TLS, Indiana University

<Typed on pink Smith College Memorandum paper with heading>

Date July 5, 1958 To You From Me In re bits & pieces.

Dear mother,

It was lovely to have you call the other day, & I look forward to living in Boston where more frequent telephone chats won't be a luxury but a common occurrence.

The blessed fourth, very quiet here, brought cool air (from Canada?) and last night and today brought a drenching rain. The catalpas in the park are in full bloom, the water-lilies in the pond a radiant pink, as if incandescent, and great red & yellow toadstools of odd shapes sprung up under the pines. Ted & I discovered a baby-bird fallen out of its nest two days ago, apparently in its death-throes, on its back, with piteous shudderings. So we brought it home & made a facsimile nest for it out of soft rags & bits of paper. We tried gingerly to feed it bread soaked in milk & milk from an eyedropper, but it sneezed & didn't respond. Then by inspiration I got some fresh ground-hamburg & by that time it had gotten used to the nest and almost swallowed my finger with the meat: I feed it with my fingers which I guess it thinks are like it's mother's head. I am fond of the plucky little thing---the ouija-board says its a jay, because of its "pied-feathers", but I can't tell yet, its so tiny. I read recently that pigeons kept in tubes so that they can't use their wings fly when freed as well as ordinary pigeons, (this was an experiment to prove they fly by instinct, not just by teaching) so I hope my bird when freed will be able to take care of himself. Can you think of anything else suitable to feed it. I can't bring myself to feed it fresh-killed flies.

I am becoming more & more desirous of being an amateur naturalist. Do you remember if we have any little books on recognizing wild flowers, birds or animals in Northern America? I am reading some Penguin books about "Man & the Vertebrates"[1] and "The Personality of Animals"[2] & also the delightful book "The Sea Around Us"[3] by Rachel Carson; Ted's reading her "Under the Sea Wind"[4] which he says is also fine. Do read these if you haven't already: they're poetically written, but magnificently informative. I am going back to the ocean as my poetic heritage & hope to revisit all the places I remember in Winthrop[5] with Ted this summer: Johnson avenue, a certain meadow on it, our beach & grammy's. Even run down as it is, the town has the exciting appeal of my childhood & I am writing some good poems about it, I think. I'll enclose that poem "Night-Walk",[6] the other one the New Yorker accepted, which I think you've read: haven't got the check yet, because of that delay about Britishness, but should get it soon. The London Magazine envelope had 7 guineas in it---about $20 for my two poems in the June issue, quite pleasant. In two years of our marriage, writing only a total of a few weeks, Ted & I have made about $2,000 (not counting the New Yorker money which we are beginning our 3rd year with.

We did our Ouija board for the first time in America & it was magnificent fun: responsive, humorous & very helpful. It seems to have grown up & claims it is quite happy in America, that it likes "life in freedom", that it uses its freedom for "making poems", that poetry is made better by "practise". Thinking we might make use of it, we asked him (Pan, is his signature) for poem subjects (this is always the problem: a good poem needs a good "deep" subject). Pan told me to write about "Lorelei". When asked "Why the lorelei, he said they were my "own kin"![7] I was quite amazed. This had never occurred to me consciously as a subject & it seemed a good one: the Germanic legend background, the water-images, the death-wish, and so on. So the next day I began a poem about them,[8] & Pan was right, it is one of my favorites. What is that lovely song you used to play on the piano & sing to us about the Lorelei? I can't spell

1–Alfred Sherwood Romer, *Man and the Vertebrates* (Chicago: University of Chicago Press, 1941).
2–Harold Munro Fox, *The Personality of Animals* (New York: Penguin Books, 1947).
3–American marine biologist and author Rachel Carson (1907–64); her *The Sea Around Us* (New York: Oxford University Press, 1951).
4–Rachel Carson, *Under the Sea Wind* (New York: Simon & Schuster, 1941).
5–The Plaths lived at 92 Johnson Avenue, Winthrop, Mass., 1936–42.
6–The poem is no longer with the letter. However, a copy signed 'Sylvia Plath' in the top right hand corner, and likely the one SP sent, can be found in Poems, N–Z; held by Lilly Library.
7–SP added this sentence by hand in the margin.
8–Sylvia Plath, 'Lorelei'.

the German, but it begins "Ich weiss nicht was soll es bedeuten . . ."[1] or something to that effect. I hope Warren will be agreeable to exchanging a dinner at our place about once a week for an hour or two of German reading out loud. I am painfully beginning to review my German again by reading one by one the Grimm's fairytales in that handsome book you gave me (which I just love)[2] and making vocabulary lists from each tale, trying to review one grammar lesson a day. I suppose as one grows older one has a desire to learn all about one's roots, family & country. I feel extremely moved my memories of my German background, & Austrian, and also my ocean-childhood, which is probably the foundation of my consciousness.

Do go to the newstands when you shop & pick up a copy of the July Jack & Jill---you might get the Aldriches a copy. Ted's story "Billy Hook And The Three Souvenirs" is in this issue and, I think, charmingly illustrated.

The ouija-board also told Ted to write about "Otters",[3] so he is doing so, & the beginnings sound quite good. Pan claims his family god, "kolossus", tells him much of his information.

Ted & I took a drive in the country last week & saw a strange grey clumpish animal snuffing in the road; it waddled into the brush before we could tell what it was, rather like a grey raccoon or some badgerish rodent. Then we climbed Mount Holyoke again this Monday & saw a duplicate of the same animal just ahead of us. We ran & cornered it so we could look at it closely & the poor thing was petrified & clattered its long yellow teeth from the ferns, apparently its one defence (Ted said it would bite). It was a dear grey whiskered animal & we're convinced it was a groundhog (or woodchuck) as its stout waddly build, small round ears, clawed stumpy legs & rodent face look exactly like the dictionary picture of one. I wrote a little poem about it.[4] My book of poems is progressing quite well. I am rejecting every poem I am dubious about & making it a strong collection, I think. I have over 30 I am sure of & want to get 50 for the total. Did I tell you I've called it "Full Fathom Five". I do hope a publisher likes that title.

1–Heinrich Heine, 'Die Lorelei'. The first line is 'Ich weiß nicht was soll es bedeuten'.

2–*Märchen der Brüder Grimm: Mit 100 Bildern Nach Aquarellen* (Munich: Droemersche Verlagsanstalt, 1937); SP's copy held by Emory University. Contains Schoenhof's Foreign Book, Inc., Cambridge, Mass., bookseller label. With presentation inscription: 'Sylvia, für ein gutes Kind von ihrer liebende Mutter, 12/25/54'.

3–Probably Ted Hughes, 'An Otter'.

4–Sylvia Plath, 'Incommunicado'.

Well, that's all the news for now. Try to get to the Aldriches next week & call again. I get up about 7 each morning now as it's cooler & I must feed the little black bird.

Ted also sends love,
Sylvia

<on page 1 of letter>

PS: How much did the cleaning of our woolens come to?

TO *Warren Plath*

Wednesday 9 July 1958 TLS (photocopy), Indiana University

Wednesday, July 9, 1958

Dear Warren,

It was good to get your letter. Ted & I would like very much to meet you on August 24th, Sunday, at your ship.[1] Patsy has moved out of New York, so we won't have anyone to stay with & would have to drive down & back the same day. Perhaps you can advise us about where to look for parking places, what time you'll be coming in, what dock, ship, and whether it would be shorter to come to NYC from Northampton or Wellesley. We've never driven before down there.

Mother says youre going to Scandinavia: wonderful. When and where? Do the German girls compare with American? I am all for foreign relations: it is extremely pleasant to have extended my own affiliations & to feel I have also a permanent home in England, especially in such a beautiful moor-top place.

My New Yorker check came today for the two poems: even more than I expected at my most optimistic calculations: $377 ($239 for Mussel-Hunter and $138 for the other, Night Walk). Together with my sonnet for the LHJournal that makes a tidy sum of $517. For three poems, I feel this princely. In the last year, with royalties for Ted's book included, we have earned over $2,000, by writing alone. Of course, such windfalls as these are rare, but there is a pleasant steady piling up in our poetry account: we have a special bank-account set aside for writing so we can see at a glance how much we've earned: it is "magic money" & we feel we don't ever want to spend it. I am becoming extremely interested in money-managing,

1–Warren Plath arrived in New York, from Cuxhaven, Germany, on the MV *Italia* on 24 August 1958.

now that I have some to manage, & notice an amazingly radical change in me from my extravagant collegiate self. I've bought no new clothes since I've been married except some shoes & summer jerseys & feel most miserly: every small sum I think of in terms of a week's food, or a month's rent, & as we need to be frugal if we don't happen to get a grant this year, this niggard quality is all good to me.

I look around me in horror when I think of moving: heaven knows how we accumulated all those objects & weights which surround us and must be transported. Luckily our 6th floor apartment has a little elevator. We are scheduled to move out of here August 31st and into there Sept. 1st, but must make many trips. I haven't been out in the sun at all this summer---the first time in my life I'm not tan, but have been working hard at poems for my book: I've discarded all that I wrote before two years ago & am tempted to publish a book of juvenalia under a psuedonym as about 20 published poems have been ditched. I hope to get my poetry book together in early September or October & send it the round of publishers this winter. It should be a good collection. I feel I've got rid of most of my old rigidity & glassy glossiness & am well on the way to writing about the real world, its animals people & scenery.

Ted & I are recovering from a sad & traumatic experience. We picked up a baby bird that looked in its last death throes, fallen from a tree, & brought it home. We had it for a week, feeding it raw ground steak, worms, milk (probably a very bad diet) and got enormously fond of the plucky little thing which looked like a baby starling, with funny furry eyebrows. But when it ran, it fell, & looked to be badly injured. Its leg stiffened then (its pelvis must have been broken, or something) & it sickened, choking & pathetically chirping. We couldn't sleep or write for days, nursing it & hunting vainly for worms, identifying with it until it became gruesome. Finally, we figured it would be mercy to put it out of its misery, so we gassed it in a little box. It went to sleep very quietly. But it was a shattering experience. Such a plucky little bit of bird. I can't forget it.

I maybe mentioned this before, but I hope perhaps this year we can exchange dinner at our place for a bit of German reading aloud once every week or two: I am painstakingly beginning to review my grammar & working on translating my Grimm's fairytales but would be most grateful for work in reading & pronunciation. Would you be willing? I'd like anything you could get of Kafka's. I already have German-English editions of Rilke's Sonnets to Orpheus & Duino Elegies:[1] is there anything else of his? I know little about German writers, & would be grateful for your advice. As for memories of Europe, if you could without convenience pick up a good bottle of brandy or something equivalent, we'd love it. Ted & I don't drink cocktails but we do like a good after-dinner brandy. Or dinner wine. We are now drinking cold beer---I never used to like it but find it very refreshing.

Ted just sold 5 poems to The Spectator[2] in England: won't amount to more than $45, but good to get him read. Also, he's had a very nice admiring letter form the Buffalo NY University library[3] which has the best collection of poets' work-sheets & manuscripts in the world asking Ted to contribute some of his (for charity, but they got Auden, Thomas, etc. this way). Ted's second book is going to be magnificently better than the first. Already he has about 28 poem for it, 17 out of those already accepted for publication. He only needs about 15 more . . .

I have been slowly recovering from my long winter longeurs due to pneumonia and my flu in spring, plus a killing last two months of hard work. It is heavenly to think that just now, as I again feel stronger & rid of my pneumonia blues, I won't have to stop writing & start a new school year but can keep on with what I really want to do & for the first time apprentice myself to my trade.

Do keep me posted about news, new addresses. Ted sends love.

So do I –
xxx
Sivvy

1–Rainer Maria Rilke, *Sonnets to Orpheus* (London: Hogarth Press, 1949); SP's copy held by Smith College. The location of SP's copy of *Duino Elegies* is unknown.

2–Probably Ted Hughes, 'Crag Jack's Apostasy' and 'The Good Life', *The Spectator* 201 (4 July 1958): 19; 'The Retired Colonel', *The Spectator* 201 (22 August 1958): 260; 'Things Present', *The Spectator* 201 (3 October 1958): 454; and 'Pennines in April', *The Spectator* 201 (26 December 1958): 922.

3–David Louis Posner to TH; Posner (1938–85) was curator of the Poetry Collection. The Poetry Collection of the University Libraries, University at Buffalo, The State University of New York, holds TH's reply, undated.

TO *Aurelia Schober Plath*

Thursday 10 July 1958

TLS on Department of English, Smith College letterhead, Indiana University

Thursday: July 10

Dear mother,

I'm just enclosing a copy of the lease to our apartment before we sign it wondering if you'd mind looking it over & seeing if there are any hitches we mightn't have run across. It seems very grim to me, all the rights on the side of the agents: is it true that we'd have to repair plumbing & wiring if it was defective? I want to write them & make sure the refrigerator & stove are in good working order. Also they told us utilities were included in rent, but it seems by this that we should have to pay light & gas, another point we will write them about. Maybe you could just look this over & see if it's normal enough a lease, or suggest anything else we should write them about if you caught something.

I've told Warren we'll probably come pick him up in NYC if his ship doesn't come in at six in the morning. Maybe he'd be willing sometime to help us move some of our accumulated goods to Boston.

My <u>New Yorker</u> check came for the two poems: the handsome sum of $377. A good bit more than I expected. About 4½ months' food or over 3 months' Boston rent, however one looks at it. Ted just had 5 poems accepted in England by the <u>Spectator</u>: it won't mean more than about $45, but pleasant also: now 16 poems are accepted in the 2nd book already. The money in our exclusive poetry bank account has risen from 0 last Sept. to a plump $1,800 or $2,000 if we count Ted's British royalties. Ted has also been asked by an admiring curator of the Buffalo U. Poetry Collection for work sheets of his poems: no pay, but they have sheets from Auden, Thomas, etc. We climbed Mount Holyoke again today: strenuous but good exercise: a clear, cool sunny day.

Much love,

Sivvy

PS: I am delighted to hear about the Kokoschka:[1] I've admired the slides of his work very much this year in my modern art course: he is certainly fine.

Do look up Ted's Story in <u>Jack & Jill</u>.

S

1–Austrian artist and writer Oskar Kokoschka (1886–1980).

TO *Aurelia Schober Plath*

Saturday 19 July 1958 — TLS with envelope, Indiana University

Saturday, July 19

Dearest mother,

The fan arrived yesterday a few hours after your letter. A day, as you may imagine, of frosty cold air. Today also is cloudy and windy and not humid. Perhaps the fan will cow the summer into coolness. Ted immediately insisted that the room was stuffy, so we tried the fan this way and that, enjoying the breeze. It is quite wonderful and should annihilate any sluggishness due to heat here and in Boston. A welcome addition to our family: thank you so much. Only 2 screws and one bolt, or nut (hexagonal with a hole through the middle) came with it, and no directions. I have a feeling we should have more screws, though I don't know what for. Should we? I imagine it works best in the window, but we have it propped now on the floor, where it stands of its own accord, & we can tilt it anyway we want. Highly satisfactory.

Could you, through your Boston University discount place, get me two books for Ted's birthday? I wouldn't want you to get them unless you could get them at a discount & tell me how much they are, otherwise I can get them here at regular cost. They are "The Sea Around Us" by Rachel Carson (we've read it, but Ted would like to own it) and the book of poems "Lord Weary's Castle" by Robert Lowell,[1] c. about 1946, Harcourt Brace. This last is the most important. If you are able to get them, could you have them sent here to me? I'll write in them & birthday-wrap them.

Mail has been sparse & dull, for the most part. All the editors seem to be on vacation. Thank you specially for seeing about the apartment: this puts my mind much at ease. We seem to have collected an immense amount of luggage in our trips to and from home & maybe we can leave some things in our room at Wellesley: I'll have to educate myself into a miniscule kitchen after this elegant one.

I won't be able to call that woman, Mrs. Jacobs, from here before she goes, & would prefer not to use any more long-distance wire. Could you possible call her from Wellesley or BU & ask what she wants for the couch cover & the bedroom curtains? She bought the couch cover &

1–Robert Lowell, *Lord Weary's Castle* (New York: Harcourt, Brace, 1947); SP's copy, a birthday present from TH dated 27 October 1958; held by Smith College.

curtains from the girls who live there before her, & I hope she doesn't try to make any profit on them.

Your course of business machines sounds noble & time consuming. I hope it will indeed free you for this coming year & let you have extra-curricular activities.

I am finding it rather difficult to adjust to this sudden having-nothing-to-do. I realize that this is the first year of my life I haven't "gone to school" & thus haven't an imposed purpose to give direction to my days. My prose is quite painful & awkward to begin with, as my poetry is much more practised & advanced: I haven't written a proper story for several years & work each morning a few hours on exercises in description. I have always expected immediate success & am gradually inuring myself to slow progress & careful practise. I think I will need a part-time job in Boston to give my life a kind of external solidity and balance. I hope I can slowly & painstakingly develop writing as a part-time vocation, because I think I need a sense of purpose beyond cooking and cleaning house, and there is no other career I can feel really useful in and drawn toward that would combine with children. I feel the change to Boston will do me good, as the only people I run into here are left-over teachers from Smith. I will enjoy walking about the streets with Ted, observing people, feeling anonymous, & learning the highroads and back alleys. Also, I hope to renew & extend friendships: with Patsy, Marcia, the Lowells[1] etc. I miss having any girl-friends to talk to & exchange gossip & advice with. I guess already Im in that in-between state of emotionally moving, but not actually having moved yet.

Do write soon, or call.

Much love,
Sivvy

1–Robert Lowell and his wife, American writer Elizabeth Hardwick (1916–2007), divorced 1972. The Lowells lived at 239 Marlborough Street, Boston.

Sylvia Plath on the foredeck of the *Queen Elizabeth*, *c*. 25 June 1957.

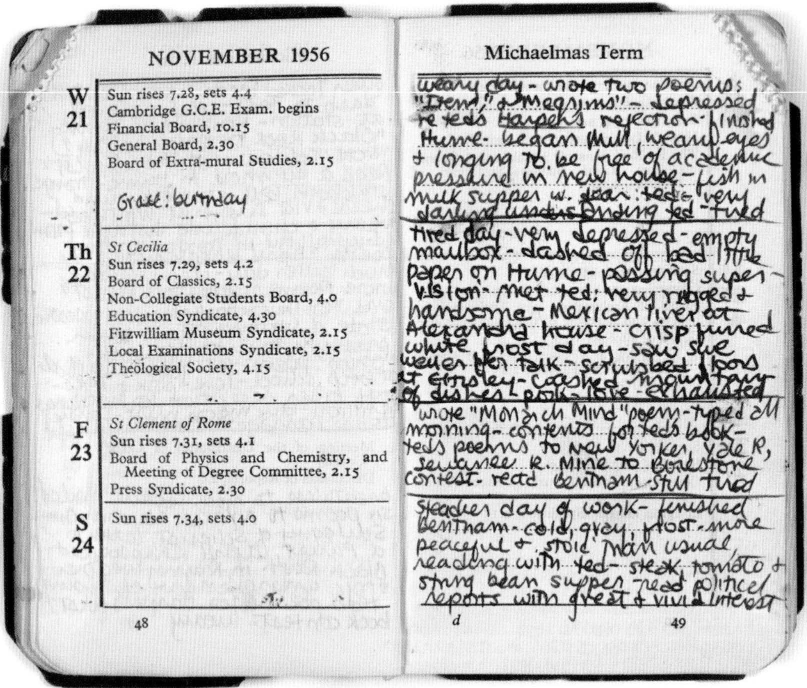

NOVEMBER 1956

W 21
Sun rises 7.28, sets 4.4
Cambridge G.C.E. Exam. begins
Financial Board, 10.15
General Board, 2.30
Board of Extra-mural Studies, 2.15
Grace: birthday

Th 22
St Cecilia
Sun rises 7.29, sets 4.2
Board of Classics, 2.15
Non-Collegiate Students Board, 4.0
Education Syndicate, 4.30
Fitzwilliam Museum Syndicate, 2.15
Local Examinations Syndicate, 2.15
Theological Society, 4.15

F 23
St Clement of Rome
Sun rises 7.31, sets 4.1
Board of Physics and Chemistry, and Meeting of Degree Committee, 2.15
Press Syndicate, 2.30

S 24
Sun rises 7.34, sets 4.0

48

Michaelmas Term

weary day - wrote two poems: "Item," & "Megrims" - depressed re ted's Harper's rejection - finished Hume - began Mill, weary eyes & longing to be free of academic pressure in new house - fish in milk supper w. dear ted - very darling understanding ted - tired

tired day - very depressed - empty mailbox - dashed off bad little paper on Hume - passing supervision - met ted; very rugged & handsome - Mexican liver at Alexandra house - crisp furred white frost day - saw Sue Weller for talk - scrubbed floors at Eltisley - washed mountains of dishes - pork - love - exhausted

wrote "Monarch Mind" poem - typed all morning - contents for ted's book - ted's poems to New Yorker, Yale R, Sewanee R. Mine to Borestone contest - read Bentham - still tired

steadier day of work - finished Bentham - cold, grey frost - more peaceful & stoic than usual, reading with ted - steak, tomato & string bean supper - read political reports with great & vivid interest

d 49

Sylvia Plath's pocket calendar, 21–24 November 1956.

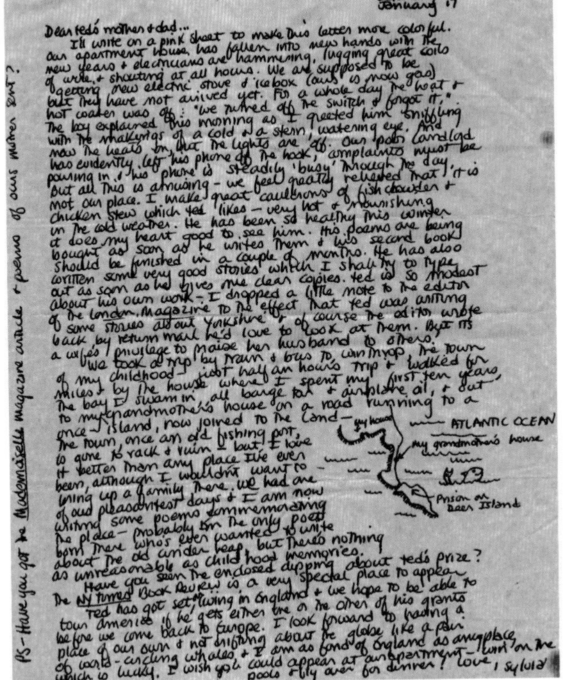

Saturday
January 17

Dear ted's mother & dad...
I'll write on a pink sheet to make this letter more colorful.
Our apartment house has fallen into new hands with the
new year & electricians are hammering, lugging great coils
of wire, & shouting at all hours. We are supposed to be
getting new electric stove & icebox (ours is now gas)
but they have not arrived yet. For a whole day the heat &
hot water was off: "We turned off the switch & forgot it,"
the boy explained this morning as I greeted him sniffling
with the makings of a cold & a stern, watering eye. And
now the heat's on, but the lights are off. Our poor landlord
has evidently left his phone off the hook; complaints must be
pouring in & his phone is steadily 'busy' through the day.
But all this is amusing - we feel greatly relieved that it is
not our place. I make great cauldrons of fish chowder &
chicken stew which ted likes - very hot & nourishing
in the cold weather. He has been so healthy this winter
it does my heart good to see him. His poems are being
bought as soon as he writes them & his second book
should be finished in a couple of months. He has also
written some very good stories which I shall try to type
out as soon as he gives me clear copies. ted is so modest
about his own work - I dropped a little note to the editor
of the London Magazine to the effect that ted was writing
some stories about Yorkshire & of course the editor wrote
back by return mail he'd love to look at them. But it's
a wife's privilege to praise her husband to others.
We took a trip by train & bus to Winthrop, the town
of my childhood - just half an hour's trip & walked for
miles by the house where I spent my first ten years,
the bay I swam in, all barge tar & airplane oil, & out
to my grandmother's house on a road running to a
once-island, now joined to the land -
The town, once an old fishing port,
is gone to rack & ruin - but I love
it better than any place I've ever
been, although I wouldn't want to
bring up a family there. We had one
of our pleasantest days & I am now
writing some poems commemorating
the place - probably I'm the only poet
born there who's ever wanted to write
about the old cinder heap, but there's nothing
as unreasonable as childhood memories.
Have you seen the enclosed clipping about ted's prize?
The NY Times Book Review is a very special place to appear.
Ted has got set living in England & we hope to be able to
tour America if he gets either one or the other of his grants
before we come back to Europe. I look forward to having a
place of our own & not drifting about the globe like a pair
of world-circling whales & I am as fond of England as any place,
which is lucky. I wish you could appear at our apartment - with on the
pools & fly over for dinner! Love, Sylvia

PS - Have you got the Mademoiselle magazine article & poems of ours mother sent?

Drawing of Winthrop, Massachusetts, from Sylvia Plath to Edith and William Hughes, 17 January 1959.

Glascock Poetry contestants and judges, *c.* 18 April 1959. Seated, from left: Marie Borroff, Prof. Joyce Horner, Moira Thompson '59, John Crowe Ransom. Standing: Jon Roush, Amherst '59, Sylvia Plath Hughes.

Items from the photograph album of Plath and Hughes's cross-country trip, *c.* 7–10 July 1959. Captioned on the album page by SP: 'Ready to start on our camping trip around America: July 1959'; 'Our Canada encampment: Rock Lake'; 'Feeding blueberries to a Canadian deer'.

Sylvia Plath at the Grand Canyon, *c.* 4–5 August 1959.

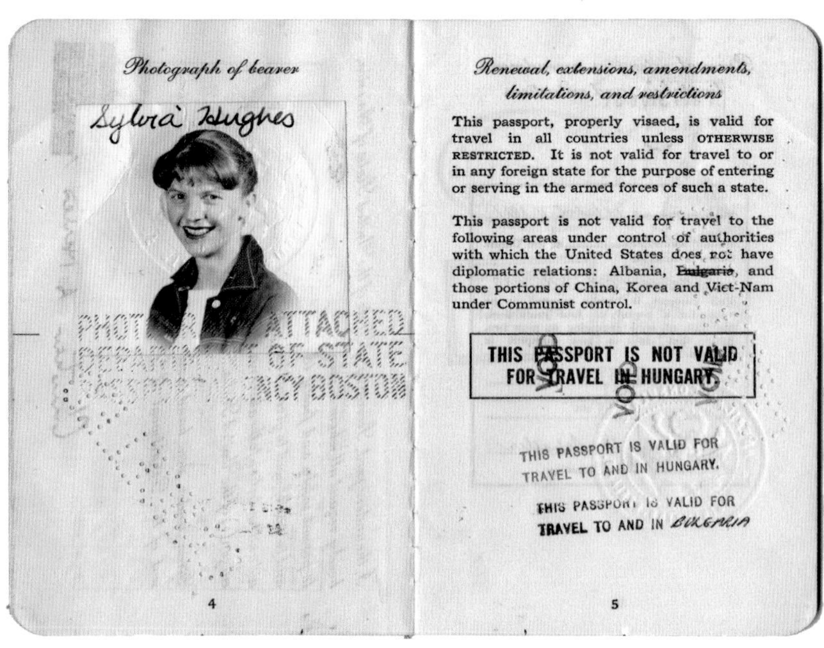

Photograph of bearer

Sylvia Hughes

4

Renewal, extensions, amendments, limitations, and restrictions

This passport, properly visaed, is valid for travel in all countries unless OTHERWISE RESTRICTED. It is not valid for travel to or in any foreign state for the purpose of entering or serving in the armed forces of such a state.

This passport is not valid for travel to the following areas under control of authorities with which the United States does not have diplomatic relations: Albania, ~~Bulgaria~~, and those portions of China, Korea and Viet-Nam under Communist control.

THIS PASSPORT IS NOT VALID FOR TRAVEL IN HUNGARY.

THIS PASSPORT IS VALID FOR TRAVEL TO AND IN HUNGARY.

THIS PASSPORT IS VALID FOR TRAVEL TO AND IN BULGARIA

5

Sylvia Plath passport photograph, *c.* September 1959.

Drawing of the dust jacket of *Lupercal*, from Sylvia Plath to Aurelia Plath, 16 January 1960.

Saturday, January 16th (2)

Dearest mother,

Ted & I arrived back at the Beacon last night after two gruelling weeks in London to find three good letters waiting from you: you have no idea how much mail from you means, especially now, when I most miss having you with us. The baby's Christmas package was waiting, too, with the three bright Carters nighties and the beautiful set of bootees, bonnet & sweater. I just wept with joy over the marvelous little teddy bear Warren sent, which brought back our family of teddy bears we had in Winthrop & all those wonderful stories you told us about them. I didn't write for so long because I was unbelievably tired and grumpy about our depressing search for an apartment in London & literally couldn't lift a pen. I really don't remember what I said in the letter I did write.

Now I am sitting in the big warm bathrobe Mrs. Hughes made me for Christmas with a crackling coal fire at my back, overlooking a sunny (for the first time in a month) landscape of dazzling snow-covered moortops and a raft of billowing clouds racing under a blue sky. Our first snow. I had a hot bath last night, my first in two weeks (Helga puts up with the lack of a bathroom in their London flat, and a public toilet 3 flights down in a dirty open cellar with a Germanic stoicism) & am just waiting till the water heats to wash my grubby hair. Now Olwyn is gone, the house is no longer overcrowded & very peaceful. No particular publishing news. I think Faber will use one or two of Ted's stories, we dont know which yet, in the anthology they're doing. I didn't send any in for I only had a couple of very American slangy ones & felt it better not to send them, especially as they are doing so much of Ted's work now, and are so polite it would embarrass them to reject anything. They sent on a copy of the papercover of Ted's book which amazed & delighted us: a triumph as covers go. The ground is a pale, almost neutral blue, some shades lighter than this paper, with black bold letters for Ted's name and outlined letters L (like that) which let the blue come through in all the other letters of the Lupercals except for bold red letters spelling the title out diagonally. It looks superb. I think Harper's will be using the same cover since they are just importing the book sometime in summer or fall & am glad. The book should come out here in late March or early spring & we'll send you a copy right away. It has a nice blurb on the front inner jacket & advertises Ted's last book on the back jacket flap with 3 very fine quoted statements from reviews.

After traveling endlessly on busses, subways & taxis, London having a terrifying area, and seeing ugly, dirty, too expensive furnished & unfurnished flats & getting more & more cold & tired, we ended up with two possibilities practically nextdoor to my doctor (an important consideration now, with my delivering the baby at home). One was an unbelievably big & beautiful furnished groundfloor flat overlooking a road and Primrose Hill (a green park across the street from Regents Park) from the big front room, and a charming garden & statues from the mammoth bedroom & glassedin kitchen & dining area, at 9 guineas ($27) a week, to be heated by electric fires (extra). We could have afforded this on the Guggenheim for a year & it would have been available right away, but the owner, who lived downstairs & was presently away doing

Drawing of the floorplan of the 3 Chalcot Square flat, from Sylvia Plath to Aurelia Plath, 24 January 1960.

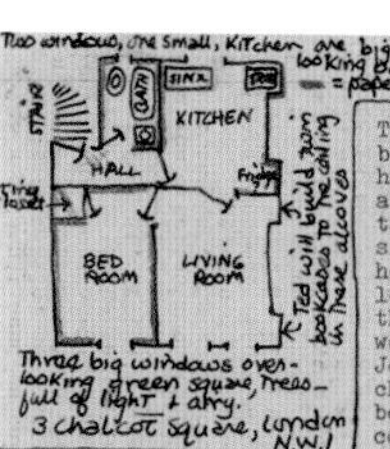

Sunday, January 24 (5)

Dearest mother,

Ted & I are back at the Beacon again on what should be, if all goes well, our last trip for a year. We have found the best way of getting up from London: a 4-hour express to Manchester, then a 1-hour train to Hebden Bridge, & the bus up to the moor-tops. I simply can't travel long distances on the busses here: they are unbelievably cramped & take twice as long as trains & stop at "tea-shops" where not even the tea is drinkable. I always make a picnic when we travel, take along a bottle of milk, a loaf of Jewish rye bread, sliced & buttered, cheese, fruit chocolate & occasionally hardboiled eggs. I have been eating well, as we buy our food in London to cook at Helga & Danny Huws' place where we stay, & Helga is a cook after my own heart: makes marvelous applesauce, a sort of yoghurt pudding with lemon juice & sugar, and once, at the start of our long, exhausting search when I was very downcast brought out a tin of "pepper-bread"(the nearest I can translate: her German sounded like pfeffer-brot), a spicy gingerbread with glazed almonds on it, & little crescent sand-tarts from a tin in her nursery cupboard. I must say all her Germanic-ness, her German talk to the adorable little baby girl Madelin & her rigorously clean housekeeping has sustained me through a very difficult period. I think I will give her a little wooden peppermill as a thank-you present & look forward to trying out Dot's carrot fruit-cake & my Christmas cookies next year: she will be a wonderful appreciat/or of them. Of course she puts up with a lot of things I could never countenance, such as no bathroom (only a toilet in the basement & no tub in the house) & no good heating & no good parks or gardens nearby, but the baby is spotless, in fine health.

I meant send the mail on here to the Beacon. After February 1st to 3 Chalcot Square, London N.W.1. I have drawn a little plan of the apartment. You can see it is small, but such a clean, new place (except for the 100 year-old floorboards) that the brightness makes up for it all. The tiny bathroom is newly put in, the walls scraped, the doors new & painted white, the woodwork white & the three windows in the front overlook a quiet green square instead of opposite housefronts; a rare blessing except in the Society Squares in the wealthy sections. As I say, we have ordered a marbled black linoleum (quite expensive: 12'4d. about $1.75 a square yard---how does that compare to home prices?) for bathroom, hall & kitchen, which are so small it won't amount to more than about $30. The landlord offered to paper the whole place, allowing a price of abt. $1.50 an 11 foot roll. We spent a morning at the hugest paper store in London Friday & for all the choice could find only about 3 papers we liked among the horrible, badly drawn assortment---even the very expensive ones suffered from a grim Victorian hangover. But those we picked we liked very much, especially the bedroom paper of roses on white. By having half the house papered & planning to paint livingroom & hall & two short walls in the kitchen ourselves (probably white as background to pictures) over a lining paper they will put up, we think the landlord will allow us the extra shillings per roll on the more expensive paper we chose. The kitchen paper is washable, & we'll go over the bathroom paper with one of the waterproofing preparations they have here. We'll paint the bedroom & livingroom floors a whited grey---or Ted will, for he'll do the heavy work. Our stove & bed are ordered to come February 1st, Monday. The papering & linoleum should be done by then. I am of course prepared for things to be held up or go wrong here & there, but hope for the best.

Edith Hughes, Ted Hughes, Sylvia Plath, and Frieda Hughes, 11 St George's Terrace, London, 5 June 1960. Captioned on verso by SP: 'Rebecca 2 months old. My skirt looks short here but it was just caught up. Taken near Ted's flat. There is a garden belonging to Merwin, a friend of Ted's, also a writer.'

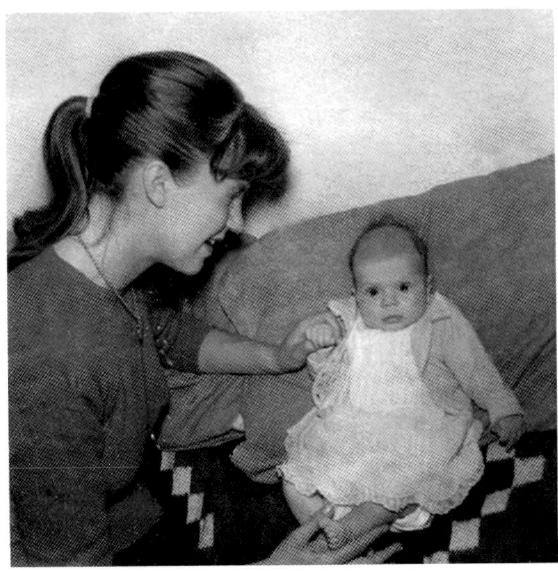

Sylvia Plath and Frieda, *c.* June 1960. Captioned on verso by SP: 'Frieda & me – she in her lacy white dress you sent – doesn't it look sweet on her?'

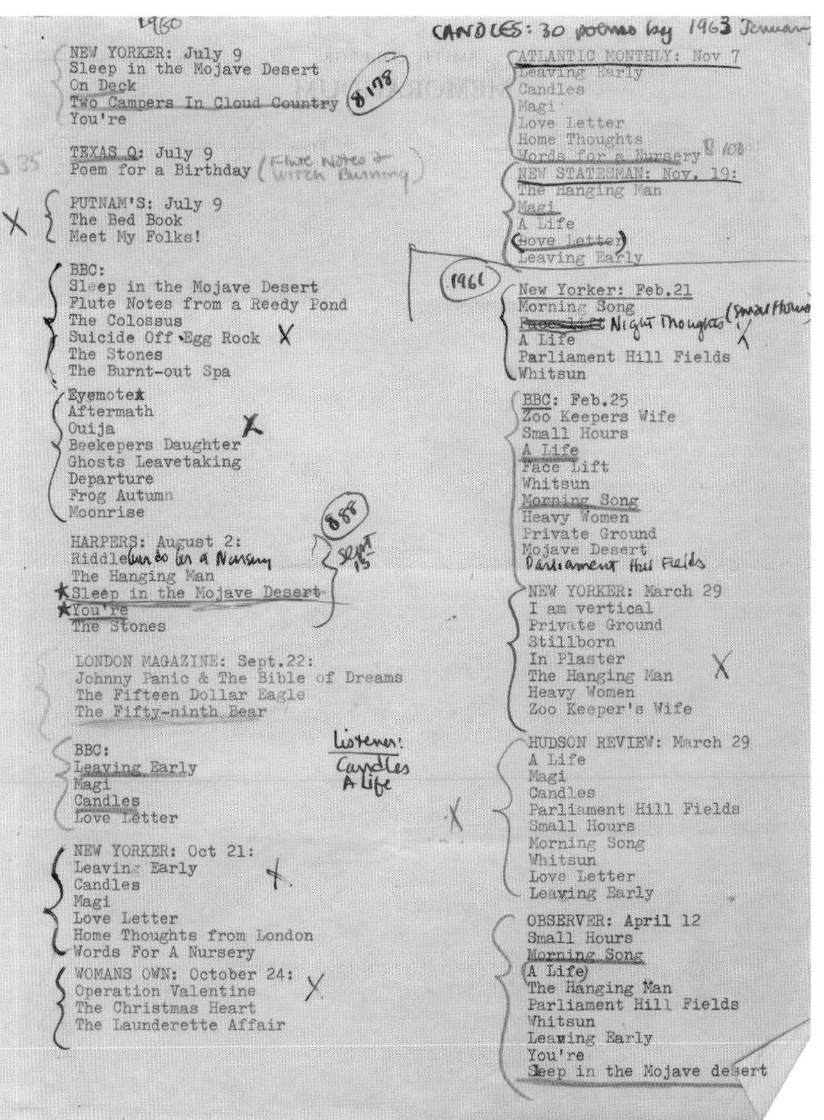

1960

CANDLES: 30 poems by 1963 January

NEW YORKER: July 9
Sleep in the Mojave Desert
On Deck
Two Campers In Cloud Country
You're

$178

TEXAS Q: July 9
Poem for a Birthday (Flute Notes & Witch Burning)

$35

PUTNAM'S: July 9
The Bed Book
Meet My Folks!

X

BBC:
Sleep in the Mojave Desert
Flute Notes from a Reedy Pond
The Colossus
Suicide Off Egg Rock X
The Stones
The Burnt-out Spa

Eyemote
Aftermath
Ouija
Beekepers Daughter
Ghosts Leavetaking
Departure
Frog Autumn
Moonrise

HARPERS: August 2:
Riddle Words for a Nursery
The Hanging Man
Sleep in the Mojave Desert
You're
The Stones

$88 Sept 15

LONDON MAGAZINE: Sept.22:
Johnny Panic & The Bible of Dreams
The Fifteen Dollar Eagle
The Fifty-ninth Bear

BBC:
Leaving Early
Magi
Candles
Love Letter

Listener: Candles A Life

NEW YORKER: Oct 21:
Leaving Early
Candles
Magi
Love Letter
Home Thoughts from London
Words For A Nursery

WOMANS OWN: October 24:
Operation Valentine
The Christmas Heart
The Launderette Affair

X

ATLANTIC MONTHLY: Nov 7
Leaving Early
Candles
Magi
Love Letter
Home Thoughts
Words for a Nursery $100

NEW STATESMAN: Nov. 19:
The Hanging Man
Magi
A Life
Love Letter
Leaving Early

1961

New Yorker: Feb.21
Morning Song
Face Lift Night Thoughts (Small Hours)
A Life
Parliament Hill Fields
Whitsun

BBC: Feb.25
Zoo Keepers Wife
Small Hours
A Life
Face Lift
Whitsun
Morning Song
Heavy Women
Private Ground
Mojave Desert
Parliament Hill Fields

NEW YORKER: March 29
I am vertical
Private Ground
Stillborn
In Plaster
The Hanging Man
Heavy Women
Zoo Keeper's Wife

X

HUDSON REVIEW: March 29
A Life
Magi
Candles
Parliament Hill Fields
Small Hours
Morning Song
Whitsun
Love Letter
Leaving Early

X

OBSERVER: April 12
Small Hours
Morning Song
A Life
The Hanging Man
Parliament Hill Fields
Whitsun
Leaving Early
You're
Sleep in the Mojave desert

Sylvia Plath's submissions list, 9 July 1960–12 April 1961.

Sylvia Plath atop Primrose Hill, *c.* 16 June 1960.

#35

Yorkshire: The Beacon
Saturday: August 27, 1960

Dear mother–

Ted & I have been up here in Yorkshire for a week, now & I am just beginning to feel that deep peaceful energy that comes from having completely unwound & caught up on months of hay fatigue. We have been simply eating, sleeping & taking long walks. I think you would love it up here – the unique combination of breathtaking scenery & invigorating air and no tourists. Ted's cousin Vicky drove us to Whitby, a British seaside resort, for a day & a night. We took the baby – who is a very good traveler. I always have to do a lot of thinking & preparing beforehand – bottles of orange juice, canned vegetables, diapers – but she is lulled by the motion of cars & trains. Whitby is a fishing port & resort – part of it "quaint" – incredibly steep cobbled streets, vistas of sea, bright painted herringboats, and the ruins of an abbey and old graveyard on one of the headlands with acres of bright pink-lavender heather in full bloom not a mile back – but there is something depressingly mucky about English sea resorts. Of course the weather is hardly ever sheer fair, so most people are in woolen suits & coats & tinted plastic raincoats. The sand is muddy & dirty. The working class is also dirty – candy papers, gum cigarette wrappers. My favorite beach in the world is Nauset & my heart aches for it. I don't know, there is something clean about New England sand, no matter how crowded. It poured the first day we were there & in spite of our waterproofs we got drenched, doggedly walking at the sea front & climbing the steep cobbled alleys. Thursday morning was fair, so we dried out our temper & shoes & ambled through the streets to various outlook points – buying Ted & me two identical fisherman's sweaters of white & black wool for about $6 apiece, and a brown sailcloth top for me & a shirt for Ted. Ted's uncle Walter, with his curious habits, had for some reason – probably secretly admiring Ted's sticking to his chosen way of life – stuffed about $150 into his pocket one night we were out at the local pub playing darts with him & Ted's dad, so we did not feel the strain of a holiday eating into our strict monthly budget.

Ted's mother has a lovely little garden up here – daisies, roses, poppies brightly surviving in the lee of a black stone wall. I prefer this landscape & air to the sea. If only we had a house to ourselves near none of Ted's relatives in a similar lonely spot we could get an immense deal done. As Ted says, most people's problem is lack of ideas, while his is that he has so many ideas & no really settled quiet place to write them. We're going to ask the lady in the attic above us if he can work there while she's at her job.

Drawing of sailcloth top, from Sylvia Plath to Aurelia Plath, 27 August 1960.

TO *Aurelia Schober Plath*

Friday 1 August 1958 — TLS with envelope, Indiana University

<Typed on pink Smith College Memorandum paper with heading>

Date August 1, 1958 To Mummy From Sivvy In re Odds & Ends

A beautiful day, our first back. Mail dull, on the whole, Editor Weeks still sitting out the half year on our manuscripts and not a word. I got a note this morning that Poetry (Chicago) are buying 3 of my poems: alas, they are 3 I have recently decided to leave out of my book, but I am not sorry to have them published for about $44---I added up the lines right away: two more weeks groceries. Ted has finally got the bank's notary public to sign his December royalties from Faber's, over $200 which he will leave in his British bank to welcome us when we return to England. It is so complicated, with all this dual tax business & exemptions. I have thought much, & wouldn't have Ted change his citizenship for the world. It is part of his identity, I feel, and will always be so.

I hope we didn't worry you about seeing Dr. Brownlee.[1] We simply wanted to get a total physical check-up (including the X-ray at the Deaconness) to see if I'd weathered pneumonia all right & wasn't anemic, as I'd been very tired & running a slight fever. I'm fine now, and all the tests show I'm in the best of health. Ironically, we didn't want to concern you, & probably you were more concerned hearing we went to the doctor from the busybody dentist.

I've thought very carefully about that Stenotype folder. I wouldn't want to learn just to get a job, as I don't want to be a conventional regular secretary. If I could be sure there would be a chance of getting in on part-time work, or even more, in the Boston courts, which interests me in itself, I would be interested in learning. But, as you can see, I want to have the jobs ahead of me to work for by learning, not to get through learning & "then see about work." I would also only be interested in learning how to Stenotype if I could learn very quickly & start work this winter so it would do me some good. Thus I'd be interested in hearing about the hours, practice time & span of learning needed for the daily course. Perhaps you could find out these things for me. I would enjoy having a practical skill that would take me into jobs "above average" or

1–Dr Robert Emery Brownlee (1911–2006). A resident of Wellesley, Brownlee was affiliated with the Newton-Wellesley Hospital in Newton, Mass., and the New England Deaconess Hospital in Boston.

"queer", not just business routine. My appearance & education should help me if I had the practical skill. But if I should get this Saxton grant for writing, I would have to give up the idea: I probably won't get the grant (which would pay for 10 months writing), & thus would like to have the facts about Stenotyping lined up. How heavy is the machine? Is the roll of tape expensive? I particularly want to know if I could get into court reporting. That's what I'd like to work for: would I need any other kind of experience? Would I be hired over people with shorthand? Could you investigate this? Those two main things: how long to learn the fastest way? Could I get into court reporting? and other jobs equivalently interesting?

We enjoyed our stay at home, & seeing Ruthie's adorable babies.[1] We both feel in the best of health and are looking so forward to the Cape in two weeks. We'll probably drive down the 18th or 19th at the latest.

Much love,
Sivvy

TO *Howard Moss*

Friday 1 August 1958 TLS, New York Public Library

Apartment 3 rear
337 Elm Street
Northampton, Mass.
August 1, 1958

Mr. Howard Moss
THE NEW YORKER
25 West 43rd Street
New York, New York

Dear Mr. Moss:

I received your letter[2] on my return from a brief vacation. I thought I'd just send along a note to say that I am satisfied with your suggestions for the three small changes in the poems.

Sincerely yours,
Sylvia Plath

1–According to SP's address book, Ruth and Arthur Geissler lived at 5 MacArthur Road, Natick, Mass.
2–Howard Moss to SP, 22 July 1958; held by New York Public Library.

P.S: After September 1st, my address will be:
Suite 61
9 Willow Street
Boston 8, Mass.

TO *Gerald & Joan Hughes*

c. Wednesday 13 August 1958[1] ALS,[2] Indiana University

I shall add a small note to this, although the reporter above has covered everything from philosophy to pike. It is 'early' – 10 am: Ted sits in a rocker, writing & munching pieces of buttered banana bread – he is appearing, it seems, in print every week in England – 2 poems in London Mag,[3] 2 in New Statesman,[4] 5 accepted by Spectator: his children's story in Jack & Jill was marvelously illustrated & only a few fingers of originality removed, not the whole thing butchered, as he'd have you believe. August has turned all at once crisp, blue, cool, what the Americans tenderly call "Million-dollar days", perhaps because the leaves rustle crisp & green as new bills. I think your house sounds wonderful. Did you design any or all of it? How's it furnished, etc? colors? Tell us all. We prepare to get some fishing tackle for our week at the Cape now. Ted's writing better & funnier short stories & I'm trying to persuade him to do a book of "Yorkshire Tales." Do write to us in much detail soon.

Love,
Sylvia

1–Date supplied from internal evidence.
2–SP added a note to a letter typed by TH, which has not been transcribed. TH included his poem 'Pennines in April' and alluded to 'Pike'.
3–Ted Hughes, 'Groom's Dream' ['A Dream of Horses'] and 'Constancy', *London Magazine* 5 (August 1958): 17–18.
4–Ted Hughes, 'Witches', *New Statesman* 56 (9 August 1958): 173. In Keith Sagar and Stephen Tabor, *Ted Hughes: A Bibliography, 1946–1980* (London: Mansell, 1983), no other poem appeared after 'Witches' until 'Of Cats', *New Statesman* 56 (25 October 1958): 564.

TO *Aurelia Schober Plath*

Wednesday 13 August 1958 TLS with envelope, Indiana University

<Typed on pink Smith College Memorandum paper with heading>

Date August 13: Wed. To Mummy From Sivvy In re Cape trip, etc.

Ted & I are chafing more & more to be off to the Cape: we plan now, if it's convenient with you, to move a load of belongings down to Wellesley Friday afternoon (thus we should be at home Friday evening, if for any reason you wanted to get in touch with us). Early in the morning Saturday, we'd like to leave for the Cape & should get there in time for lunch? Now would that be all right with you & Grampy? Where will you both sleep when we come? We don't want to make anybody uncomfortable.

Ted is dying to rent a little row or motor-boat & go fishing, so we are going to get some rods for his birthday present & hope to go again to the place in Chatham as often as possible. His birthday is the 17th, Sunday, & I'd like him to be on the beach & swimming then, not stifling in Northampton, or driving down. We are having our phone removed Friday afternoon, since we plan to come back only for a few days at the end of the month to pick up the remainder of our things.

The Christian Science Monitor bought my little 3-page descriptive article about the countryside around hidden acres,[1] the drawings of Mrs. Spaulding & her beach-plum barrel for $15, so I hope it comes out in time to show her. I want her to get ready to tell me about how she designs & builds those cottages, really practical details. The Sewanee Review has just accepted a poem of mine,[2] which should bring about $20 when it's published.

It's a hot, muggy day, no mail, and about to rain. We're reading Fabre's books about the life of a spider and the life of the scorpion:[3] fascinating and terrible.

Already I'm in that limbo between moves: half here, half there.

1–Sylvia Plath, 'Beach Plum Season on Cape Cod', *Christian Science Monitor* (14 August 1958): 17. The two drawings have the following captions: 'Picking over beach plums under the pines' and 'Potted plants and a wheelbarrow of beach plums'.

2–Sylvia Plath, 'Departure of the Ghost' ['The Ghost's Leavetaking'], published with 'Point Shirley', *Sewanee Review* 67 (Summer 1959): 446–8. See Monroe K. Spears to SP, 7 August 1958; held by Sewanee: The University of the South.

3–Jean-Henri Fabre, *The Life of the Spider* and *The Life of the Scorpion*, editions read unknown.

We are so grateful at the chance for a beach-week & look very forward to seeing you, Grampy & the Spauldings.

Until Saturday noon,
Much love,
Sivvy

TO *Elinor Friedman Klein*

Wednesday 3 September 1958 TLS, Smith College

Suite 61
9 Willow Street
Boston 8, Mass.
September 3, 1958

Dear Ellie . . .

Your letter arrived between several moves, irate landlady, crazy telephone company uproars, and the general untidy chaos of our move from Northampton to Boston. Now that we are here, in our miniscule & marvelously aesthetic two-room furnished flat, I don't know how I stood living in Northampton for a year. Nobody here has heard of Smith, or us, which is magnificent. I am sitting in my study-dining-room-living-room-kitchen at the bay window over-looking a superb view of Back Bay: a sizeable hunk of the Charles river, MIT, sailboats, the Hatch Shell,[1] And, to my Left, the Estimable John Hancock Building which flashes various weather signals in brilliant chromatics. I look over multitudinous chimney pots, tar roofs, tree tops. And can even see the ulmi americani of the Common from my desk. Oh yes, and the Hotel Statler.[2] You must come see. We even had a whole fire department howl up the hill to greet us at six yesterday morning, with black slickers and axes: smoke began blowing by me in the bed at dawn, and this seemed odd. I jumped up & saw people in the street staring at our windows from which the smoke floated. The hall was full of it & I was getting ready to brave the hideously rickety sixth floor fire escape which involved crawling out a high kitchen window, when the landlord's janitor said it was only rubbish caught in the incinerator shaft & he'd been dropping bricks on it to fix everything up.

1 – The Edward A. Hatch Memorial Shell is an outdoor concert venue on the Charles River Esplanade.
2 – Now the Boston Park Plaza Hotel, 50 Park Plaza at Arlington Street, Boston.

I want to hear more about your job. It sounds fascinating. We're planning to write here & maybe later in the year I'll take a part-time job to pay for groceries, but we are investing our time & going to work like fury for the first year of our lives at nothing but writing. Did I tell you I at last made the New Yorker? With two huge poems & a lovely letter & even lovelier check from Howard Moss. One poem, 91 lines, was in the Aug. 9th issue. Do look it up & say if you like. Ted's poems have just appeared in their first anthology: The pocket book of Modern Verse, ed. by Oscar Williams, the 1958 revised edition. The selections begin with Walt Whitman & end with Ted Hughes: 3 poems. I am very proud of this. We saw Oscar Williams while we were in NYC in June, & saw not the people we wanted to see most but left early, missing you & Alfred Kazin, after commuting hither & yon to see various literary ancients for Ted's application for a grant[1] this next year: Marianne Moore, Babette Deutsch etc. We thought we'd come again this fall, but have expended so much on this move that we are saying "next spring": so when can you come to Boston?

We are at present nursing two goldfish, some mouldy green Anacharis, pale green aquarium gravel and a shell which does the fish as a castle: do you know about where oxygen comes from? The fish have only 50 cubic inches of air surface which is half of the requirement for one fish & they keep hanging on the surface as if longing to come out and have tea in the sweet Bostonian air with us. Ted claims they are suffering, almost dying: we sprinkle anti-chlorine grains in the water, change the water daily. They haven't died yet, but are maturing under mysteriously adverse conditions, enriched by suffering. I have only a rudimentary & primitive tribal idea about oxygen: little specks, like invisible pepper.

Please write & tell us more about Mr. Crosby,[2] his wives, mistresses, & your celebrities. And try to come for dinner soon. Bring Leonard, he is so nice. What is he writing now? We promise an exquisite night view of the lit-up John Hancock building which is topped by a flashing red light, over a white light over the now-blue weather signal.

Love to you,

<u>sylvia</u>

1–TH asked American poets Babette Deutsch and Marianne Moore to recommend him for a grant from the John Simon Guggenheim Memorial Foundation; SP asked Moore to recommend her for the Eugene F. Saxton Memorial Fellowship.

2–John Crosby (1912–91) was the radio–television critic for the *New York Herald Tribune*, 1946–65; he also hosted the television show *The Seven Lively Arts* on CBS, 1957–8.

TO *Lynne Lawner*

Thursday 4 September 1958 — Printed from *Antaeus* 28, Winter 1978

Suite 61
9 Willow Street
Boston 8, Mass.
Wednesday, Thursday
September 4, 1958

Dear Lynne,

I have predictably lost your letter somewhere in our colossal & piecemeal move from Northampton via Wellesley, to Boston, where we are now ensconced in a miniscule & quite fine little furnished apartment at the above address on Beacon Hill. Two rooms, each with a big bay window overlooking rooftops, chimney pots, mosquito trees, and the blue of the Charles & the Harvard Bridge with elegant reflections at night & sailboats in the daytime. At my right, the pruned & plumed trees of Louisberg Square, at my left, the towering structure of the estimable John Hancock building which predicts the weather four hours ahead of time by means of colored lights. After Northampton, & the provincial rounds of professors at morning coffee, professors at tea, the same professors at cocktails and dinner and the Evening, and such, we are delighted with Boston. Having no car (a blessing on this hill) we tramp everywhere, to the docks to watch the deep sea crabs being unloaded, through little Italia on Hanover street, all pastry shops with gelati & spumoni and grocery stores carrying nothing in their windows but olive oil in monstrous cans & soap flakes, through the fabulous weekend open market on Blackstone Street which outdoes anything I've seen in England & Europe: cheaper than Paris: stalls of tomatoes, peppers, peaches, stacks of chickens & beefs, stalls undercutting each other, vociferous men tugging at one's arm: "I just cut those pork chops, just brought em up, you want juicy chops for da weekend?" "Razors, buy a razor." And so on. I renewed my childhood yesterday by riding on the swanboats with Ted. Boston is easily my favorite city in America. We plan to batten down & write here all year for the first time in our lives. We've saved enough from our teaching jobs so this is possible, if we only eat & pay rent. I have a very engaging dark-eyed dark-haired tall lean young Southern poet from Sewanee Tennessee here now, a friend of Ted's, who has published here & there in Poetry & the Partisan Review & who is teaching in Paris this year. I've told him about you & wish you would see him when you're in Paris. His name is E. (for Elvis!) Lucas Meyers, known as Luke, & his address in Paris is: 24 Rue Mouffetard, Paris V. Do look him up.

Tell me how you managed to switch your Fulbright to Florence & why. What happened in your winter & spring at Cambridge? How are KMP Burton, IV Morris tutor, et. al.? I wish you could come this way before you fly or sail over, to tell me about Cambridge at first hand. I'll make a final huge effort to find your address.

What's your novel about? What kind of style? I mean who are your mentors. I am ensconced between or among Henry James, Virginia Woolf (who palls, who never, I think, writes more than about tremulous party-dress emotions, except in the odd Mrs. Ramsey[1] – & who is, amazingly often awkward & lumbering in her descriptions) and DH Lawrence; Have you read his 3 volume collected short stories:[2] The Man Who Loved Islands etc.? Very fine, although many are, I think, pot-boilers. Where are you sending poems, where publishing: I believe I saw one in a NWWriting,[3] edited by Philip Booth. Can you send me some copies of recent poems? I am continually rejecting my old ones & am on my third "first book" which is completely different from the one I had gathered at the end of my senior year in college &, except for about 4 poems, completely different from the one I had gathered at the end of my Cambridge year. I keep having about 30 poems in it: as I write more, I reject more. At this rate, I'll publish when I'm 50. Tell me when your articles come out in Time & Tide. We hope, if we don't stay a 2nd year in Boston, to aim for Rome for a year after this. Have you met any British (or American) literati over there? Who did you know at Cambridge? I want to hear more about Cambridge. I really quite fell in love with it, probably because Ted happened to be there. I feel completely weaned from Smith: I had idealized the place because of my haloed position there the last two years & thought of it as Elysia. Now it seems like a never-never land where nobody has to do anything but drink coffee, read books & gossip: men gossipers are a million times worse than women, without anything of female solidity.

1–Protagonist in Virginia Woolf's *To the Lighthouse* (1927).

2–D. H. Lawrence, *Complete Short Stories* (London: Heinemann, 1955); SP's copy held by Smith College.

3–Lynne Lawner, 'If he stroke my cheek', *New World Writing: Tenth Mentor Selection* (New York: New American Library, 1956): 46.

What do you plan to do after the Fulbright? Go on to degrees? Work? Write? Hold salons? Do write soon.

Love,
Sylvia

TO *Peter Davison*

Sunday 7 September 1958 TLS (photocopy), Yale University

Suite 61
9 Willow Street
Boston 8, Massachusetts
Sunday, September 7,

Dear Peter,

I wonder if you are witnessing the same rainstorm at the moment. Our two bay-windows (one for Ted to write in, one for me) overlook rain-slicked rooftops, chimneypots, mosquito trees, a grey flat Charles river, and, I think, the Atlantic offices themselves, to the left, under the immense bulwark of John Hancock. Our flat is very small, two little rooms, but quiet, scenic and 6th floor airy: we are both delighted with it.

Could you come by for tea sometime after work this Thursday or Friday? Name your day and hour. We'll both be happy to see you. Our phone number is LAfayette 3-2843 & it should be working sometime early this week if they ever iron out the manifest, manifold confusions of lines, wires, missed appointments, & nonexistent repairmen. So give us a call & say when is best for you. We're right off Louisburg Square.

I have been working on a new group of poems this summer & was happy to get two long ones accepted by the New Yorker, my first after years of trying them. Ted has written some very fine poems lately & his second book is filling out: three of his first-book poems have just appeared in the revised Oscar Williams Pocket Book of Modern Verse & we are very pleased about this, his first anthology piece. Ted's written a half-hour verse dialogue (play practice) and a couple of good Yorkshire stories.[1] He has got out stacks of children's books from the Public Libe[2] & wants to work on children's stories intensely this year. His story in the July Jack & Jill came out delightfully illustrated.

1–Ted Hughes, 'Sunday' and 'The Rain Horse'.
2–Boston Public Library, located at Boylston and Dartmouth Streets, Boston.

Have you heard anything from Editor Weeks about the fate of our poems & Ted's stories? We are, as you may imagine, most eager to hear his verdict.

Our best to you,
Sylvia

TO *Edith & William Hughes*

before Thursday 18 September 1958[1] ALS, Family owned

<drawing of a scroll on which is written:
'September 18th / Happy Birthday / to you / From Sylvia'
decorated with flowers, candles, and a bird>

Dear Ted's mother & dad –

By now you have read about Ted's wonderful prize[2] – don't breathe a word of it till October 22nd, for it is to be kept strict secret till then! Isn't it wonderful: the honor & all the money. Ted & I are both extremely happy here in Boston – it is all quaint hilly streets, brick & stone cobbles – and our view is an inspiration. Our apartment is small but extremely attractive – it seems all windows! The livingroom walls are deep green, with gathered white curtains at the windows, a light whitey-grey sofa cover & a white-flowered dark green curtain shutting off the kitchen wall & covering the chairs. The bedroom – which has an even better view, has pale-blue walls & grey & white patterned curtains. Ted got two 6-foot planks very cheap & made himself a wonderful huge desk in the bay window overlooking the rooftops & River & sailboats. Now all you need to do is win the pools, hop in a plane and fly over to see us! We had Ted's friend Luke Meyers over for two nights & 3 days on his way back to Paris & had a lovely time walking about the city – having tea here, & raw quahogs (a kind of poor man's oyster) there. We should write a great deal this year with such pleasant surroundings & all the time in the world.

Love to you both –
Sylvia

<drawing of several different flowers in a row>

1 – Date supplied from internal evidence.

2 – 'The Thought-Fox', winner of the Guinness Poetry Award of £300, 1958. See T. L. Marks to TH, 1 September 1958; held by Emory University.

TO *Alice Norma Davis*[1]

Wednesday 24 September 1958 TLS, Smith College Archives

Suite 61
9 Willow Street
Boston 8, Massachusetts
September 24, 1958

Miss Alice Norma Davis
The Vocational Office
Smith College
Northampton, Massachusetts

Dear Miss Davis:

Two instructors from whom you may obtain references covering the courses I took at Newnham College are:

Miss. K. M. P. Burton		Mrs. Dorothea Krook
The Pightle		Lecturer in English
Newnham College	and	c/o Newnham College
Cambridge, England		Cambridge, England

Miss Burton was my Director of Studies, as well as my instructor in several courses, so she would be able to give you the fullest record of my work. Mrs. Krook was also my instructor for two years (for the Moralists paper), and I believe she has returned to her lecturing duties at the University after a year of absence. The head of the Fulbright Commission in London might also be of help in this regard. The address of the commission, when I left England, was:

The United States Educational Commission in the United Kingdom
71 South Audley Street, London W.1, England.

I'd like to expand a bit on my notes about vocational interests. In addition to jobs in downtown Boston, I can also consider jobs in the immediate vicinity of Harvard, as the subway service between Boston and Cambridge is excellent. I am not at all particular about the type of part time work I do, and am open to any suggestions you may offer.

While I am looking primarily for a part time job so that I can continue a writing project of my own this year, I would be happy to consider any full

1–Alice Norma Davis (1908–84); B.A. 1930, Smith College; director of the Vocational Office, Smith College, 1947–72. See Alice Norma Davis to SP, 23 September 1958; held by Smith College.

time job that involved newspaper, publishing, or editing work---anything, that is, of special interest in my field.

Sincerely,
Sylvia Hughes

TO *Dorothea Krook*

Thursday 25 September 1958 TLS, Central Zionist Archives

Suite 61
9 Willow Street
Boston 8, Massachusetts
U.S.A.
September 25, 1958

Dearest Doris,

I was so happy and proud to see your review of James in the London Magazine.[1] It made me most homesick for you, and your magnificent lectures, and the supervisions which, for me, were the major stimulus of my Cambridge experience. I do hope this letter finds you back at Cambridge and that you will forgive me for my long silence and write me a note soon, letting me know what you are doing, writing and thinking about. I have thought of you so frequently this past year of teaching at Smith that I imagine, I guess, that by some mystical intuition you may well be aware of this.

Last year I threw every moment of my time into teaching, and preparation for teaching. As an instructor of three classes in freshman English, each of which met three times a week, my job was to combine teaching of intelligent reading (stories, novels, plays and poems) with teaching of intelligent writing (including the details of source themes, sentence structure, the geography of the library, and so on). My students came from all over the United States with all varieties of preparation. Girls with bear-skin caps from public schools in the wilds of Minnesota (who confessed, with humble desire for improvement, to never reading a whole book) sat next to elegant blonde young ladies from the best New York City preparatory schools deep, at the moment, in Sartre,[2] or Finnegans Wake. With a few exceptions, most of my students were glisteningly eager

1–Dorothea Krook, untitled book review of *The House of Fiction* by Henry James, edited and introduced by Leon Edel (London: Rupert Hart-Davis, 1957), *London Magazine* 5 (July 1958): 68–70.
2–French philosopher and writer Jean-Paul Sartre (1905–80).

to work, think and talk. Our classes, inspected, at intervals, by professors in the department, were "discussion" classes. Instead of lecturing (I did continually, slip in five and ten minute lectures), I discussed. This means, usually, that the success of the class depends on a firm hand and, only too often, on the resources of a TV moderator. I felt a marked nostalgia for the inviolable voice of the lecturer in the upper class courses, and, often, the desire to take the girls on one at a time privately. Gradually, I became accustomed to preparing in rough question and answer outline the lecture I would have enjoyed giving, and getting the class to give me the half I left out, in a kind of cog-and-wheel cooperation. Since we are supposed to have everyone in the class speak at least once, and leave no "cold areas", students who haven't done their reading, or who are congenitally tongue-tied, are coaxed to speak up, even if what they say has little value. I am, by philosophy, I think, more dictatorial than is proper for an American. After I managed to work out a reasonably forceful discussion-maneuvering, I had an exciting time. Many of the girls will never need to take another English course; many of them would perhaps never read a poem again; I felt, now and then, like a missionary among the heathen. My texts were my salvation.

From a selected list, quite limited, of possibilities, I taught William James's "Varieties of Religious Experience", short stories by Hawthorne, Lawrence, James ("The Beast in the Jungle", "The Pupil") and Lawrence; "Crime and Punishment"; "Portrait of the Artist as a Young Man"; "Oedipus Rex", "Antigone", "The Duchess of Malfi", "Rosmersholm", "The Master Builder", "Miss Julie"; poems of Hopkins, Yeats, Eliot (especially enjoyed "The Wasteland")[1] and Auden and Thomas.[2] I had many doubts about the contemporary emphasis of the course, but as you probably know, this is where the Americans begin. All stems from Joyce, and works back, through Shakespeare, to the Greeks. I had my own two-month tragedy course, minuscule, and wished I could teach it for a year. All during the year the girls wrote papers. Every two weeks I read seventy papers, which nearly put my eyes out. I felt to be reading a massive, incurably botched, redundant novel-essay after a few months of

1–In addition to *The Waste Land*, SP taught 'The Love Song of J. Alfred Prufrock' and 'Journey of the Magi'.

2–SP taught 'As I Walked Out One Evening', 'Fish in the Unruffled Lakes', 'In Memory of W. B. Yeats', 'Law, Say the Gardeners is the Sun', 'Look, Stranger', and 'Musée des Beaux Arts' by Auden and 'After the Funeral (In Memory of Ann Jones)', 'Do Not Go Gentle into that Good Night', 'Fern Hill', 'The Hunchback in the Park', 'Over Sir John's Hill', and 'Twenty-Four Years' by Thomas.

this. Much time was spent in office hours, talking over various problems with the girls. A teacher is very much a part of the "campus life" here: Ted and I were invited to dinner with the girls at various houses at least once a week and only with effort did we keep it down to this. I found myself with a complex of double feelings at the close of the year.

One part of me rejoiced in the teaching, while wishing for less paper-work and more actual lecturing. I felt the need, too, for much more study, possibly specialization through work for a PhD., none of which was feasible at the time. The other part of me longed to be writing freely on my own: I found teaching inimical to working at poems and stories: my critical faculties kept slyly pointing out the immense gap between me and the haloed writers for whom I was priestess. Ted went through approximately the same experience. He had a job offered him at the University of Massachusetts (a state university, and, in a state of excellent large private colleges, not full of the best pupils: some were earnest, but near-illiterate. I was reminded a bit of your rugger players and the intricacies of Plato!) Ted, with his usual ease, taught three different courses ---freshman English (which in America usually means: how to write a clear sentence), a sophomore General Literature course which romped from Samson Agonistes[1] to Moliere, to Thoreau, with breath-taking agility; and an advance course in writing, which he enjoyed. He, too, stopped writing, during this period. We decided, although both warmly invited to teach the same courses this year, to rashly break our ties with the groves of academe (a lassooing of tall tree arises to mind at this melded metaphor), and to write for a year.

I found life, too, in Northampton, left much to be desired. Gossip among the entrenched and unentrenched faculty members, jealousies, coup d'états, promotions and student popularity ratings is unavoidable, as, I suppose, it is in every such semi-enclosed community. But in America, privacy is suspect; isolation, perilous. Coffee-houses, tea-hours, dinners and evenings bring one constantly in communion with one's colleague's. Pleasant enough, but oddly narrowing in some ways. And the more one advances, the more administrative duties stand in the way of the actual teaching (which is my favorite work): directing course plans, serving on the innumerable faculty committees, and so on.

1–John Milton, *Samson Agonistes* (1671).

So we are in Boston this year, the city I was born in.[1] We have a little two room apartment: I write in the livingroom-diningroom-kitchen (pullman, all in one wall, hostile to any elaborate housewifery, and that to the good) while Ted's study is in the bedroom, a desk of two fine sturdy planks in a window niche. We are on the cobbled, tilty summit (almost) of Beacon Hill, which, I fear, is deserted by the old Brahmins and inhabited by students and elderly telephone operators and young doctors and lawyers now. Each of us, in our sixth floor flat, has a magnificent bay window to work in, overlooking a panorama of orange tiled rooftops, chimneypots, and mosquito trees to the dull silver flat of the river and grandiloquent sunsets. We take long walks to the wharfs to watch the gulls, ships, and crab-merchants; read aloud, read silently---I am beginning the Notebooks of Henry James,[2] which I have never read, and finding surprising solace, encouragement, and challenge here. I find myself too, wishing furiously that the shade of James could somehow become aware of the intelligence, dedication, tact, and even love, which is devoted to his work today. Are you giving, still, your lectures on James? I remember these with the greatest pleasure, together with your lectures on the moralists and those on "Oedipus", Shakespeare and Ibsen. Rereading my notes,[3] I call up an image of the whole, your presence, your words balancing, tilting, with just the right emphasis, the precise revelation, in what I should like to call The Art of Lecturing. But I should like to have the original Platonic bed, and not a notetaker's smudged copy. What are the prospects for your books---on the moralists and on James? I look forward to their appearance most eagerly.

Ted's work is progressing admirably, and I feel in the presence of something particularly special---his dedication is complete, selfless and highly demanding. I am delighted that he enjoys Boston---he claims, everywhere, that the heavy stone buildings, the scraggly brick flats, the green park full of swans, remind him of England. His poems for his second book, which is about half-written, are far better, steadier, deeper, than anything in his first book. That, with its flaws in tone and maturity, which we see now, but did not, two years ago, has had, on the whole, an excellent critical reception in both England and America, and one of the poems in it has been chosen to receive the award for the best poem

1–SP was born in the Jennie M. Robinson Memorial Hospital, at Harrison Avenue and E Newton Street, Boston.

2–Henry James, *The Notebooks of Henry James* (New York: G. Braziller, 1955); SP's copy held by Emory University.

3–SP's notes held by Lilly Library.

published in Great Britain for the past year, a bolt out of the blue, which, in practical terms, will see us fed for ten months. Ted is now working on a verse play. He has applied for a Guggenheim grant, and T. S. Eliot and others are strongly behind him, but we won't hear about this till next spring, and his British citizenship may be against him. So we write and hope. If he received the grant, we would like to return to Europe for 1959-60, and spend some time in Cambridge. I would so much like to see you again, after the deep chagrin of having missed you this fall.[1] Did you have the opportunity to see Gary Haupt[2] at Yale on your visit here? I know he was a great admirer of yours and a fine student in his own right. How is he, and how is his career progressing?

I think also of dear Wendy Christie. I have not heard from her, but wish her well with much love. And your handsome, vital sister---I remember her with such pleasure. Is she studying at New Hall now? Please know that all this year your teaching, even the sense of your existence over the ocean, has been of the greatest help and encouragement. I would be so happy to have a note from you, but will understand if you are too much involved.

With warmest love,
Sylvia Hughes

TO *Elinor Friedman Klein*

Sunday 26 October 1958 TLS, Smith College

9 Willow Street
Boston 8, Mass.
October 26, 1958

Dear Ellie,

Come ahead Friday November 7th with your orchid leis and all and even Russ, yea him. Tell me what time you're coming. I got The Call when autumn began and wanted people wrought-up and around me, so I took a part-time job by going to an agency and demanding something with no responsibility or homework yet full of people. My first lead was what I am doing now, being a secretary for the Psychiatric Clinic at the Out-

1–Immigration records show Krook travelled in autumn 1957, not 1958. She departed England on the *Queen Mary* on 12 September 1957 bound for New York, and arrived back in Southampton on the Greek Line SS *New York* on 28 October 1957.

2–Garry Eugene Haupt (1933–79), American; B.A. 1955, Yale College; B.A. 1957, English, Pembroke College, Cambridge; dated SP in 1956.

Patient Dept. at the Mass General Hospital.[1] I belong to a city of welfare workers and feel pleasantly anonymous. I type fascinating records, meet troubled people who think they are going to give birth to puppies or that they have lived for three centuries or that they will go mad if they leave an ingredient out of a cake. People just like anybody on the subway or in the street: I meet them, and look them secretly up and down and secretly read their records which are delightfully particular. In and out of the office go 25-odd psychiatrists and students, from Norway, Persia, Iran, with weird accents, which I type up from an audograph.[2] I shall work at it until I have paid my week's salary to the agency and then maybe stop, for the part-time is almost full-time. Smith had asked me back for next year and offered even a writing course for me: for some reason, no doubt superficial as the two poems in the New Yorker, while others sweat for PhDs. I have nightmares about accepting, so must refuse. It's all so cosy there. I want to hear details about your famous and infamous work. What made Leonard go back to teaching after all his writing nobility? Is there some reason for him to want to earn money? Let us know what time you will come. Ted has just won first prize---did I tell you? I believe it was in last Thursday's Times[3]---over 3000 poems in England, with his poem "The Thought-Fox", in the Guinness competition. Have you seen Dave Keightley lately? How is the leg? Write & advise us.

Love,
Kitty & Levin[4]

1 – SP worked part-time as a secretary in the adult psychiatric clinic at Massachusetts General Hospital. See *Journals of Sylvia Plath*: Appendix 14 'Hospital Notes', 624–9.
2 – The audograph was used in dictation to record sound.
3 – 'News in Brief', *The Times* (23 October 1958): 6: 'POETRY AWARDS. – Mr. E. Hughes, of Boston, United States, who was born in Yorkshire, has won the first prize of £300 in the Arthur Guinness, Son and Company poetry awards, for his poem "The Thought-Fox".'
4 – Characters in Leo Tolstoy's *Anna Karenina* (1878).

TO *Esther*[1] *& Leonard Baskin*

Between Monday 17 November & Wednesday 10 December 1958[2] TLS, British Library

Suite 61
9 Willow Street
Boston 8, Massachusetts
The-night-before-

Dear Esther & Leonard,

It was quite wonderful to have your call. We felt you were in the room & wish you actually would be. We spent a good afternoon brooding in Mirski's showrooms.[3] The angel filled the air, and I feared for the ceiling and walls, he exerted such pressure. The feather-detail on the wings is magnificent. I had been wondering what the wings would do. He is an ikon to have in the head, and there he stands. I am particularly partial to the black-and-white "Death Among the Thistles",[4] am curiously deeply moved by it, those barbs and spurs and the bulbous deathlily-white head. "Tobias",[5] dog and fish, give our livingroom another room: I find myself going off into it.

I will work, Esther, on bullfrogs: I observed practically nothing else in Northampton and will dig up their gorier habits. Ted says you say they eat each other. I wish I could see this, but will do what I can with the slithering green (I saw some a purply-dark color too, I think) web-fingered monsters.

How is the blond Tobias? I miss him, he was such a good armful.

We are projecting a trip to Northampton so far in the spring, to maybe talk to a creative writing class, and will let you know when, because we would like to see you very much.

Love to you both, and Tobias
Sylvia

1–Esther Tane Baskin (1926–73); married to SP's colleague Leonard Baskin; mother of Tobias Isaac Baskin (1957–).

2–Date supplied from internal evidence.

3–Leonard Baskin's Sculptures Drawings Prints exhibition was held at Boris Mirski Gallery, 166 Newbury Street, Boston, 17 November–10 December 1958. Boris Mirski (1898–1974) was an art dealer and gallery owner.

4–Leonard Baskin, 'Death Among the Thistles', 1958.

5–Leonard Baskin, 'Tobias and the Angel', 1958. SP and TH's wood engraving, an artist's proof, of 'Tobias & the Angel' appeared at auction via Bonhams on 21 March 2018.

TO *Gerald & Joan Hughes*

c. mid-December 1958[1]

ALS in greeting card,[2]
Indiana University

<printed greeting>

Best Wishes for Merry Christmases / "Best of wishes for your Merry Christmases and your happy New Years, your long lives and your true prosperities. Worth twenty pound good if they are delivered as sent them. Remember? Here's a final prescription added, 'To be taken for life'." / Doctor Marigold's Prescriptions (1865)

We thrive. Ted has 4 poems accepted by Poetry (Chicago)[3] & is writing a book of humorous poems about relatives for children.[4] Merriest of Christmasses!

Love,
Sylvia & Ted

TO *Margaret Wendy Christie*

c. mid-December 1958[5]

ALS (copy) on verso of bookmark,
printed from *Cambridge Review*[6]

<Bookmark caption: PARADISE Detail of a painting by Giovanni di Paolo, Italian School of Sienna, Born 1402 or 1403; Died 1482 or after THE METROPOLITAN MUSEUM OF ART.>

Dearest Wendy –

Doris has the other half of Paradise. Are you here or in your new house – is it built? Ted & I, after both teaching English here last year, have retired to Beacon Hill, overlooking river and chimneypots, to write for a year – me finishing a first book of poems, Ted his second & a book of

1–Date supplied from internal evidence.
2–A short note added by TH has not been transcribed.
3–Ted Hughes, 'A Woman Unconscious', 'Cat and Mouse', 'To Paint a Water-Lily', and 'Lupercalia', *Poetry* 94 (August 1959): 296–300.
4–Ted Hughes, *Meet My Folks!* (London: Faber & Faber, 1961). Dedicated 'For Frieda Rebecca' and published on 7 April 1961 with illustrations by George Adamson. Rejected by Harper Publishers, Harcourt Brace, and the Atlantic Press in 1959.
5–Date supplied from internal evidence.
6–Published with a short memoir by Christie, 'Remembering Sylvia', *Cambridge Review* (7 February 1969): 253.

humorous poems for children. We think of you very often & would love to see you when we come back to England which we hope will be in a year or so. How are the lovely children? Ted joins me in sending love & warmest holiday wishes –

Sylvia Hughes –

TO *Olwyn Hughes*

c. mid-December 1958[1]

ALS on verso of bookmark, Washington University (St Louis)

<Bookmark caption: PARADISE Detail of a painting by Giovanni di Paolo, Italian School of Sienna, Born 1402 or 1403; Died 1482 or after THE METROPOLITAN MUSEUM OF ART.>

Dear Olwyn . . .

I've quit my amusing job at the City Hospital after two months & am battened down to writing. Weather here so frigid it hurts, Charles River Basin an evil-white-capped blue. Pitchblack at 5 pm. With the Parks lit up all red, green, yellow, full of live reindeer, black sheep, nativity scenes.[2] In one big shop there's a whole glassed-in window of motorized poodles baking Christmas cookies, in another a 3-window railroad train run by angels & white foxes: a blend of sublime & ridiculous. Do tell us which one of Luke's stories the Sewanee's taken[3] as we can't wring it out of him. And what was Thrushes in the Observer[4] for? We get dim rumors, but still haven't seen it ourselves. We miss you, wish we could summon you up like a genie out of smoke & incense – am beginning "Scorpion" – elegant & delightfully produced. Burn a candle for us.

With love –
Sylvia – Ted

1 – Date supplied from internal evidence.
2 – Cf. SP's poem 'A Winter's Tale'.
3 – Probably E. Lucas Myers, 'The Crest of Kelly-Haught', *Sewanee Review* 67 (Winter 1959): 63–86.
4 – Ted Hughes, 'Thrushes', *The Observer* (23 November 1958): 7. See Terence Kilmartin to TH, 13 November 1958; held by Emory University.

TO *John Lehmann*

Wednesday 24 December 1958 TLS, University of Texas at Austin

Suite 61
9 Willow Street
Boston 8, Massachusetts
USA
December 24, 1958

Mr. John Lehmann
THE LONDON MAGAZINE
36 Soho Square
London W.1, England

Dear Mr. Lehmann,

I was very happy to learn about your keeping my three poems[1] for the London Magazine. I wonder if you would be so good as to alter the French line in "Lorelei" to its English equivalent: "Drunkenness of the great depths".[2] This keeps the syllabic count, and I have had enough afterthoughts about the line to want it in English.

Ted and I are spending the year in a small flat-with-a-view on Beacon Hill in Boston, overlooking a vista of orange chimneypots which reminds me nostalgically of my view in Cambridge. We both worked teaching English at college and university last year and had too little time to write, so are writing hard this year. Ted is doing some stories about Yorkshire, very solid little worlds they are, and well into his second book of poems, and I am working on stories and poems also.

We are hoping very much to return to England in a year or so. Ted joins me in sending our warmest good wishes.

Sincerely,
Sylvia Plath

1–Sylvia Plath, 'Snakecharmer', 'Lorelei', and 'The Disquieting Muses', *London Magazine* 6 (March 1959): 33–6. See John Lehmann to SP, 10 December 1958; (photocopy) held by Smith College.

2–The line 'L'ivresse des grandes profondeurs' appears in stanza 11, line 2, of the publication of 'Lorelei' in *Audience* (Spring 1959): 33. Probably taken from Jacques Cousteau, *The Silent World* (New York: Harper & Row, 1953).

TO *Edith & William Hughes*

Tuesday 30 December 1958 ALS, Family owned

Tuesday – December 30

Dear Ted's mother & dad . . .

One more day of the old year – Ted has just finished making himself a remarkable wolf-mask for the New Year's Eve masquerade tomorrow night:[1] I found a marvelous peice of sealskin fur, black, in the attic rooms full of century-old dresses of her grandmothers & grandmothers-in-law where Agatha let me browse to my heart's content yesterday – with his two poems about wolves[2] in his second book and actually one line about "making wolf-masks mouths Clamped well on to the world".[3] I find the mask quite frightening – it has slit eyes which Ted has filled with yellow – very realistic, with room for his mouth to show so he can speak. With the real fur it is incredibly lifelike. <drawing of an arrow pointing at Ted Hughes's head and shoulders in wolf-mask> I am wearing an antique black dress & red cape for Red Riding Hood.

Ted has written two very funny children's stories & we are hoping Jack & Jill may like them. The weather here is quite clear – only one real snowstorm so far and that melted now.

Ted is reading the novel by the Russian nobel prize winner, Pasternak,[4] & I am in the middle of an autobiography of the French St. Theresa[5] – all the photos of her in the book are terribly touched up to make her look as if she has holy tears in her eyes and a sprouting halo –

The present book by John Press[6] arrived today & Ted is into it already – also the lovely flowered scarf & shaving soap from Hilda & Vicky – do say thanks to them for it – we'll write, too.

We love every letter we get from you – we can just imagine the Beacon & all the life & country surrounding it.

1–See also SP's journal entry for 31 December 1958; *Journals of Sylvia Plath*: 454.

2–Ted Hughes, 'February', and probably 'Lupercalia'.

3–Ted Hughes, 'February'.

4–Russian writer Boris Pasternak (1890–1960); his *Doctor Zhivago* (New York: Pantheon Books, 1958).

5–Probably *Autobiography of St. Thérèse of Lisieux* (New York: P. J. Kenedy, 1958). See *Journals of Sylvia Plath*: 589–94.

6–English writer John Press (1920–2007). Possibly John Press, *The Chequer'd Shade: Reflections on Obscurity in Poetry* (London: Oxford University Press, 1958). SP's copy held by Lilly Library.

I made a big pot of fish chowder today which Ted likes & eats bowls of – full of milk, onions, potatoes, fish stock & fish, very wholesome & convenient to dip out of the pot & warm up for the next few days.

Mother brought us a little bowl of three Christmas narcissus bulbs & the first one started to unfold its little white flowers today – dainty & star-shaped on top of a long green willowy stem.

Ted seems to have written all the news in his letter.

I just had three poems accepted by The London Magazine last week with a very nice letter from the editor – I don't suppose they'll be out for several months, but do keep a look-out for it. We'll let you know if we find out when they're appearing.

Keep well & have a happy new year –

with love,[1]
Sylvia

1 – SP refers to this letter in her journal: 'Ted read my signature on the letter to his parents as "woe" instead of love. He was right, it looked surprising: the left hand knows not what the right writes' (*Journals of Sylvia Plath*: 454).

1959

TO *Edith & William Hughes*

Saturday 17 January 1959 ALS with envelope, Family owned

Saturday
January 17

Dear Ted's mother & dad . . .

I'll write on a pink sheet[1] to make this letter more colorful. Our apartment house has fallen into new hands with the new years & electricians are hammering, lugging great coils of wire & shouting at all hours. We are supposed to be getting new electric stove & icebox (ours is now gas) but they have not arrived yet. For a whole day the heat & hot water was off: "We turned off the switch & forgot it," the boy explained this morning as I greeted him sniffling with the makings of a cold & a stern, watering eye. And now the heat's on, but the lights are off. Our poor landlord has evidently left his phone off the hook, complaints must be pouring in & his phone is steadily 'busy' through the day. But all this is amusing – we feel greatly relieved that it is not our place. I make great cauldrons of fish chowder & chicken stew which Ted likes – very hot & nourishing in the cold weather. He has been so healthy this winter it does my heart good to see him. His poems are being bought as soon as he writes them & his second book should be finished in a couple of months. He has also written some very good stories which I shall try to type out as soon as he gives me clear copies. Ted is so modest about his own work – I dropped a little note[2] to the editor of the London Magazine to the effect that Ted was writing some stories about Yorkshire & of course the editor wrote back by return mail[3] he'd love to look at them. But it's a wife's privilege to praise her husband to others!

<drawing of Winthrop, Massachusetts, with arrows pointing to 'My house', 'My grandmother's house' and 'Prison on Deer Island'. SP drew in waves and wrote 'ATLANTIC OCEAN'>

1–This letter probably corresponds to the letter dated '[Early 1959]' in Christopher Reid (ed.), *Letters of Ted Hughes* (London: Faber & Faber, 2007): 138–40.

2–See SP to John Lehmann, 24 December 1958.

3–See John Lehmann to SP, 30 December 1958; (photocopy) held by Smith College.

We took a trip by train & bus to Winthrop, the town of my childhood – just half an hour's trip & walked for miles – by the house where I spent my first ten years, the bay I swam in, all barge tar & airplane oil, & out to my grandmother's house on a road running to a once-island, now joined to the land – the town, once an old fishing port, is gone to rack & ruin – but I love it better than any place I've ever been, although I wouldn't want to bring up a family there. We had one of our pleasantest days & I am now writing some poems[1] commemorating the place – probably I'm the only poet born there who's ever wanted to write about the old cinder heap, but there's nothing as unreasonable as childhood memories.

Have you seen the enclosed clipping[2] about Ted's prize? The NY Times Book Review is a very special place to appear.

Ted has got set on living in England & we hope to be able to tour America if he gets either one or the other of his grants before we come back to Europe. I look forward to having a place of our own & not drifting about the globe like a pair of world-circling whales, & I am as fond of England as any place, which is lucky. I wish you could appear at our apartment – win on the pools & fly over for dinner!

Love,
Sylvia

PS – Have you got the Mademoiselle magazine article & poems of ours mother sent?

TO *Esther Baskin*

Saturday 17 January 1959[3] TLS, British Library

9 Willow Street
Boston 8, Massachusetts
Saturday[4]

Dear Esther,

This is a small note to say I was highly relieved to have your letter and spent a pleasant rainy yesterday at the Public Library reading about

1 – SP's 'Point Shirley' and 'Suicide Off Egg Rock'.

2 – The clipping is no longer with the letter. The only mention of TH in the *New York Times Book Review* at that time was in Lewis Nichols, 'In and Out of Books', *New York Times Book Review* (9 November 1958): BR8. The section 'Malt and Muse' discussed TH's Guinness Prize.

3 – Date supplied from internal evidence.

4 – Most likely 17 January 1959. See for reference, SP's *Journals* entry for 20 January 1959. See also SP's notes on frogs, undated; held by Lilly Library.

the Nightjar, Goatsucker, Churn-Owl, Evejar, Fern-Owl, Night-hawk, Puckeridge and Wheel-Bird. Our library is magnificent on birds and death on frogs; all you can learn about frogs here is which nerve twitches when you drop acid on their left nostril, no thank you. Also, I was in a mild state of paralysis between Ted's poem on Bullfrog (a jolly and humorous little NYorker piece) and Shakespeare. Between us all we will immortalize the animal kingdom: I lie in bed chanting Dog, Cat, Hog, Rat and on and on. I am enamoured of the Goatsucker and give me two weeks, one for the necks and ifrits, one for the poem.

We have The Seven Deadly Sins[1] and are delighted. I particularly love the brustly-pig-straddling Gluttoness and the old January on the breasted peacock. And Christ is magnificent. Ted, of course, has Lennie's proof of the wolf-skinned supplicant behind glass and salaams and prays under it. Did he tell you he made a wolf-mask? We had to go to a costume party New Year's eve and our Hungarian hostess let me raid her attic of Budapest ball gowns and Beacon Hill pomps. I came away with a red cape, for me, and a black mouldering sealskin scarf for Ted. You wolf, I said, and he went into the bedroom with scissors and thread and the fur, and came out with a long black snout and black pricking ears and the evil eye. It was a religious act, and the mask is awesomely comfortable to wear. One day it will stick, and his nails will grow.

He is drawing, at last, on Pikes. Many pikes. The best drawing he will send.

In Yorkshire there is a goose known as the Gabble-Ratchet.

Ted joins me in sending our best to you, Lennie and the gold Tobias,

sylvia

1–Anthony Hecht and Leonard Baskin, *The Seven Deadly Sins: Poems* (Northampton, Mass.: Gehenna Press, 1958). The engravings to which SP refers in the letter are 'Gluttony', 'Pride', 'Lust', and 'Avarice'.

TO *Esther Baskin*

Wednesday 21 January 1959 TLS, British Library

Suite 61
9 Willow Street
Boston 8, Massachusetts
Wednesday, January 21

Dear Esther,

I enclose the goatsucker poem, hoping some of it will please you. I've had a wonderful time working on it and it is, as you see, a sort of Goatsucker Sonnet, although the rhymes are half. All the details are borne out by the books, I think, and you probably know them: the Bird's also called the Puckbird, or Puckeridge after a disease it's supposed to give cows & weanling calves in England, so it's a double threat, in superstition, to cows as well as goats. And it's called the Devil-bird in Ceylon (evidently they call a lot of birds Devils there) and in Paraguay a Goatsucker-hunter, hunting by headlamp, says the bird's eye reflects light with a red shine, like a coal glowing, or an intense, deep ruby. I wish I could have got in the part about its perching lengthwise on a tree and looking like a warty knot, but there just wasn't place. Do feel free to not like it, or want this or that other than it is.

Did Ted or I tell you we are owners of a kitling? Granddaughter on one side of a cat belonging to Thomas Mann and, on the other, fruit of a pedigreed line of Mooncats and Honey Owls, Persian cats who move in a nimbus. Sappho, by name. The minute she walked into our apartment she went straight to a book of poems lying flat on the lowest bookshelf and possessed it. The book was a mere anthology, so Ted has substituted Eliot and Sappho approves.

Ted has drawn myriad pike and is sending his final iron-eyed head to you. With the block could he have wise advice? I can't wait to see the broadsheet.[1] Robert Lowell has seen the poem and has a good opinion of it, has sent it to IA Richards,[2] he says.

All Boston is blurred out today in a pale charcoal scrim of rain, sludge, slop, and no snow, only a wet, Old English bit by lamplight last evening, a little close white fur, and today everything in runnels and drips.

1–Leonard Baskin, *Pike: A Poem by Ted Hughes* (Northampton, MA: Gehenna Press Broadside (B6), 1959).

2–English literary critic Ivor Armstrong Richards (1893–1979) taught at Cambridge (1922–9, 1931–9) and Harvard (1939–63).

I am so eager to hear about the book.[1] You say it's about all done. Has Leonard finished the drawings? Do you know the Robert Graves[2] poem "Outlaws" which begins:

Owls---they whinny down the night;
Bats go zigzag by.
Ambushed in shadow beyond sight
The outlaws lie.

Old gods, tamed to silence, there
In the wet woods they lurk,
Greedy of human stuff to snare
In nets of murk.

Look up, else your eye will drown
In a moving sea of black;
Between the tree-tops, upside down,
Goes the sky-track.

Look up, else your feet will stray
Toward that dim ambuscade
Where spider-like they trap their prey
In webs of shade.

And on it goes. How pale are doves and lambs by comparison!

Our love to you, Leonard and Tobias

Sylvia

1–Esther Baskin, *Creatures of Darkness* (Little, Brown, 1962). Includes Ted Hughes, 'Esther's Tomcat'. SP's 'Goatsucker' was not selected.

2–English poet Robert Graves (1895–1985). Extract © Robert Graves (2000). Reprinted by kind permission of Carcanet Press Ltd.

Sylvia Plath
Suite 61
9 Willow Street
Boston 8, Mass.

The Goatsucker[1]

Old goatherds swear how all night long they hear
The warning whirr and burring of the bird
Who wakes with darkness and till dawn works hard
Vampiring dry of milk each great goat udder.
Moon full, moon dark, the chary dairy farmer
Dreams that his fattest cattle dwindle, fevered
By claw-cuts of the Goatsucker, alias Devil-bird,
Its eye, flashlit, a chip of ruby fire.

So fables say the Goatsucker moves, masked from men's sight
In an ebony air, on wings of witch cloth,
Well-named, ill-famed a knavish fly-by-night.
Yet it never milked any goat, nor dealt cow death:
It shadows only---cave-mouth bristle beset---
Cockchafers and the wan, green Luna moth.

1–There are several textual variations between this typed poem and its final appearance in SP's *Collected Poems* (London/New York: Faber & Faber/Harper & Row, 1981). In *CP*, the title was changed to 'Goatsucker'; line 11 ends with a comma; line 12 runs into line 13 without punctuation; line 13 begins with 'And'; and in line 14 'Luna' has a lower-case l, 'luna'.

TO *Elizabeth Ames*[1]

Wednesday 11 February 1959 TLS, New York Public Library

Suite 61
9 Willow Street
Boston 8, Massachusetts
February 11, 1959

Mrs. Elizabeth Ames
Executive Director of Yaddo
Saratoga Springs
New York

Dear Mrs. Ames:

My husband and I have just received your letter[2] about Yaddo and both of us would be extremely interested in applying for a visit there. We would appreciate it very much if you would be so good as to send us the necessary applications.

I notice from the brochure that the season at Yaddo runs from May to October, although most of the guests are said to come for May-June or July-August. Is there, then, a September-October period also? If there were, we would be most interested in the possibility for applying for this time of the season.

Sincerely yours,
Sylvia Plath

1–Elizabeth Ames (1885–1977); executive director of Yaddo, 1923–69.

2–Elizabeth Ames to SP, undated; held in Yaddo Records, 1870–1980, New York Public Library. From 9 September to 19 November 1959, SP and TH were guests at Yaddo, an artist's colony in Saratoga Springs, New York. SP was initially recommended to Ames by her creative writing professor Alfred Kazin on 3 February 1955.

TO *Lee Anderson*

Wednesday 18 February 1959 TLS, Washington University (St Louis)

Suite 61
9 Willow Street
Boston 8, Massachusetts
February 18, 1959

Dear Lee Anderson:

Thank you for your good letter. I am sending a manuscript---The Bull of Bendylaw And Other Poems---to the Yale Series competition this week. Your letter confirmed a wavering and subversive urge to do so.

Ted and I are living in a little two-room apartment at the above address with a sixth floor view of Back Bay, the Charles River Basin and gulls and sailboats. We would be delighted to see you here any time you chanced to come to Boston.

Ted is completing his second book and within five poems of the close. I am battling a sterner and less bucolic muse. We have a fine wild little cat, a tiger with a green stare.

Ted joins me in sending our best,
Sylvia Plath

TO *Elizabeth Ames*

Sunday 22 February 1959 TLS, New York Public Library

Suite 61
9 Willow Street
Boston 8, Massachusetts
February 22, 1959

Mrs. Elizabeth Ames
Executive Director of Yaddo
Saratoga Springs
New York

Dear Mrs. Ames:

Thank you for your letter[1] and the application blanks. We are enclosing the four sets of filled-in applications[2] together with clippings from our work.

I would like to note here that of the thirty-two or so published poems I have listed on my sheet over two-thirds were written while I was an undergraduate and do not form part of my projected book as, in one way or another, I do not consider them sufficiently mature work.

Sincerely yours,
Sylvia Plath

TO *Edith & William Hughes*

Thursday 26 February 1959 TLS with envelope, Family owned

Thursday
February 26, 1959

Dear Ted's mother & dad . . .

Snow has fallen here at last. We had a lovely teatime the other day, sitting high in our sixth floor eagle's lookout and the room bright with the white light of the falling snow, which fell down past us in large flakes to pile up on ground floor level where somebody else would have to worry about shoveling, and we could simply enjoy the landscape of peaked white rooftops and the white river behind the dark steeples and gables of the buildings. The air is clear crisp blue now and very invigorating.

1–Elizabeth Ames to SP, 13 February 1959; held by New York Public Library.
2–SP's and TH's applications held by New York Public Library.

Last night we went to the Blue Ship Tearoom[1] which is at the end of a perilously sagging wharf which looks about to cave in at any moment. The Tearoom is of old vintage, as my mother & father went there when they were courting, I believe, and on the third floor of the wharf with a fine view of the bay and ships and gulls. Inside it is very low ceilinged, all painted light blue with fishnets and Chinese crabs shells and lobstershells decorating the room, and gay blue tablecloths covered with a pattern of Moby Dick the white whale from Melville's book, and the fisherment hunting him down. We went to celebrate the third anniversary of our meeting at the party for the St. Botolph's Review, where I first saw Ted's poems. Ted had two delicious mountain trout after a fresh fruit cup, and I had a little fat duck, and we brought a bottle of French wine as the place didn't serve drinks, and enjoyed ourselves thoroughly. There was an oddly homespun quality about the evening as there were only about three other tables of diners beside ourselves (the place has just opened again after the owners spending the worst of the winter in Florida) and the waitress kept forgetting essential things like spoons which I would slip over and get when she'd gone out of the room, so as not to hurt her feelings. There was also a greyhaired pianist who evidently is installed there for life, who has been in France and plays Chopin, Debussy and Moonlight-Sonata Beethoven for the diners. Drunk with the idea of an audience (he seemed to be afraid we'd boo him and drive him out of the room with a pelting of T-bone steaks) he came in before every piece to ask us if "we'd like to hear the story behind it". One could hardly say no to the poor man, so he told us about the perfumes of the flowers of the French gardens that blew through this Nocturne, or the odd harp quaverings that inspired another. He even had a little contest, the reward being a rupee from someplace in India (worth, he said about thirty cents) for someone who could divide the distance to the moon by the distance around the world. I was so stunned at the simplicity of the question, and Ted was so chivalrous, that we didn't open our mouths, and a little lady from a country town a hundred miles away won the rupee.

I have been having fun braiding on a rug[2] which has light blue and red bands in it: I get the wool remnants from a Mill End shop out near mothers, cut the strips to the right size, and go to work. I have also been

1–The Blue Ship Tea Room, then on T Wharf. For her description of eating there, see 5 September 1958, *Journals of Sylvia Plath*: 418.

2–SP was at work on the rug from January 1959 through at least May. See SP's journals. SP picked up rag rug making in North Tawton; see Ted Hughes, 'The Rag Rug' in *Birthday Letters* (London: Faber & Faber, 1998).

learning to use the sewing machine at the house of Marcia Plumer,[1] a friend of mine from college, and am making my first simple pattern, a black and white print overblouse, very straight and not fitted, so the work is easy. You must smile at this, because you probably can sew blindfold & Walt's factory must make immensely complicated trousers and so on. Anyhow, I hope to finish the blouse this week and will draw the style of it.

Another book has come out with some of our poems in it---mine are old ones and much changed, or left out of the book I am working on. You might like to get a copy, I think it's 8/6. The title is POETRY FROM CAMBRIDGE, 1958, edited by Christopher Levenson and published by The Fortune Press, 15 Belgrave Road, London, S.W.1.[2] Ted has five poems in it (Thrushes, The Good Life, Historian, Dick Straightup, and Crow Hill) and I have four. Levenson, with his usual waywardness, has let several misprints get by in my things, as, on the contents page,[3] I am quoted as having gone to Brown University. and in the poem "Epitaph for Fire and Flower" on page 45 it should be "every weather-cock kiss hang (not hand) fire" in the fourth stanza, and "star's spent wick" (not wink) in the fifth.

Tell Vicky I think her nit-spotted Bug-gobbler is superb---very witty and sensitive with a colorful personality of its own, much better than the blue winged creature which I don't think a child would relate to, its so abstract. Also liked her drawing of her head and of you, very expressive lines. I have had a child's poem on a Goatsucker, in rough sonnet form, which I wrote for Esther Baskins book on Night Creatures (which Ted wrote "Tomcat" for) accepted by Hornbook, a monthly magazine that reviews children's books. On second thought, it wasn't the Goatsucker one, but one called The Bull of Bendylaw.[4] I sent the two, and willfully reversed them.

We are counting on you to win the Pools. One of the great rewards of living in England, in fact one of the great morale builders, must be the half-hopeful feeling one might just as well as not happen to win 75,000 Untaxable Pounds on the Pools & be set up for life. Keep making out

1–According to SP's address book, the Plumers lived at 26 Fairhaven Avenue, Concord, Mass.

2–Christopher Levenson, *Poetry from Cambridge* (London: Fortune Press, 1958); Sylvia Plath, 'All the Dead Dears', 'Black Rook in Rainy Weather', 'Miss Drake Proceeds to Supper', and 'Epitaph for Fire and Flower', 41–5; and Ted Hughes, 'Thrushes', 'The Good Life', 'The Historian', 'Dick Straightup', and 'Crow Hill', 25–8. Erroneously lists SP as having attended Brown University. Published twenty-two poets, among them David Wevill.

3–'on the ~~title~~ contents page' appears in the original.

4–Sylvia Plath, 'The Bull of Bendylaw', *Horn Book Magazine* (April 1959): 148.

those sheets. And when the great day comes, wire us, and we'll all set off for a trip round the world---you come pick us up here and we'll all sail on a luxury liner to Australia and from there to the Riviera and the Rhine and home again. Ted keeps telling me to realize all the odds against winning, and I probably do, but keep on dreaming.

We're just leaving now for a little walk in the snow.

Love to all,
Sylvia

TO *Lynne Lawner*

Wednesday 11 March 1959 — Printed from *Antaeus* 28, Winter 1978

March 11, 1959

Dear Lynne,

I am seizing a few moments after having typed my afternoon stint and while waiting for my very part-time boss[1] to come in and dictate me more letters to Poona etc. I work here in the shadowy stacks of Widener two or three afternoons a week: I should have shorthand, but by dint of furious made-up abbreviations, manage pretty well. Your Italian vignettes[2] are delightful, wonderfully colored and full of a special gilded light. Why don't you set a novel in Rome? The damnable thing is that Henry James has done it all, with his endowed and innocent Isabel Archer. The main interest about an American girl abroad is her slow mellowing into corruption, what else? I am envious. We dream of large sumptuous grants on which we will spend a year in Rome.

Ironically, I find that although I have always considered myself aware of the modern novel, my main awareness is of Henry James, Virginia Woolf and DH Lawrence. Formidable models and idols when confronting a blank page. So of late I have been cautiously ripping through a more recent vintage of work. Have you come across William Golding,[3] the British novelist? He has one terrifying and highly colored novel "Pincher Martin", or "The Two Deaths of Christopher Martin", the whole book being the blockishly real visions of a drowning man, who dreams in drowning of

1–Daniel Henry Holmes Ingalls (1916–99); assistant and associate professor, 1949–56, Wales Professor of Sanskrit and chairman of the department of Sanskrit and Indian studies, Harvard University, 1956–83; SP worked part-time for Ingalls, spring 1959.

2–See Lynne Lawner to SP, 7 December 1958 and 21 January 1959; held by Lilly Library.

3–English writer William Golding (1911–93).

his struggle to survive on a rock in the middle of the ocean. Hardly the sort of book to reassure a beginner at the trade, but magnificently original and strong. I have also finished the last of the Tolkien[1] trilogy, The Lord of the Rings, and have been immensely moved by it. I read the children's book, The Hobbit, which started off the cast of characters that moves, enlarges and immensifies in these books: I confess it moves me more than the Odyssey, or, for that matter, any epic I can think of at the moment. Let me know what you are reading, doing, thinking, writing. Please send me a poem, or any poem, you have done. The last I saw was Wedding Night of Nun, which was awarded the Borestone prize[2] in their book.

I am now back home. Ted is taking our small tiger cat with an impressive, if not evident, pedigree, to the vet's with Rosalind Wilson (one of Edmund Wilson's many offspring by his even more numerous wives)[3] and the cat (Sappho, of course)'s brothers & sisters, to be vaccinated against distemper. The kitten loves the typewriter and is now curled in my lap in a kind of literary hypnosis, watching the keys go up and down like dancing snakes. In her more energetic moods she tries to cuff them just before they hit the paper.

We have been having fun at the theater here. Got free tickets to a horrible play concocted by Faulkner,[4] about whom I have great reservations, for his one-time mistress Ruth Ford,[5] now wife of Zachary Scott,[6] I think, "Requiem for a Nun": except for one scene, a flashback, it is all non-theater, verbal rant about the novel "Sanctuary", from which Temple Drake emerges, twenty years later, even more of a bitch. The plot ambles about the central horror that her negro maid and babytender, a onetime whorehouse confidante, smothers Temple's baby in order to make Temple stay home from running off with the romeo brother of the guy she loved at the whorehouse (who got shot to death climbing up her drainpipe) and as a result is tried for murder & convicted. I never could quite accept the baby-smothering as a convincing gimmick to get Temple to stay home & be a good mother to her children (she only had one other).

1–English writer J. R. R. Tolkien (1892–1973).

2–Lynne Lawner, 'Wedding Night of a Nun', *Best Poems of 1955* (Stanford, CA.: Stanford University Press, 1957); won first prize for Undergraduate Poetry.

3–American writer and critic Edmund Wilson (1895–1972); daughter Rosalind Wilson (1923–2000) and son Reuel Wilson (1938–); Wilson's four wives were: Mary Blair, Margaret Canby, Mary McCarthy, and Elena Thornton.

4–William Faulkner, *Requiem for a Nun*, played at the Colonial Theater, 106 Boylston Street, Boston. The play ran for two weeks 12–24 January 1959.

5–American model and actress Ruth Ford (1911–2009).

6–American actor Zachary Scott (1914–65).

This was Theater Guild. This week we saw a new company, the Boston Repertory, do a very fine performance of "Six Characters in Search . . ." at the Wilbur.[1] Steve Aaron,[2] of Harvard, & some other Harvard guys are directing the company & it is wonderful to see good otherwise-unseeable modern plays, and old plays, performed by something more than an earnest undergraduate cast. Also saw at MIT a performance on DThomas' "Doctor & the Devils",[3] all about where med students get their cadavers from: written in movie scenes, so a lot of rushing about and reposing, but fun.

We have seen a little of Philip Booth, who is now trying to write at home on his Guggenheim with his wife and beautiful daughters[4] & sounding as if it were starvation pay. Also have seen a good bit of Robert Lowell whom I admire immensely as a poet, and his wife, who writes stories for the New Yorker. I have been auditing a poetry course he gives at BU with some bright young visiting poets, George Starbuck,[5] who is an editor at Houghton Mifflin, & has published everywhere, and Anne Sexton,[6] another mental hospital graduate, who Lowell thinks is marvelous. She is having about 300 lines coming out in the Hudson,[7] published in the Partisan,[8] New Yorker,[9] etc., without ever having gone to college. I like one of her long poems, about a very female subject: grandmother, mother, daughter, hag trilogy,[10] and some of her shorter ones. She has the marvelous enviable casualness of the person who is suddenly writing and never thought or dreamed of herself as a born writer: no inhibitions. Perhaps our best friends are these Fassetts around the corner: Agatha's

1–Luigi Pirandello, *Six Characters in Search of an Author*; opened on 3 March 1959, at the Wilbur Theatre, 246 Tremont Street, Boston.

2–Steven Arnold Aaron (1936–2012); B.A. 1957, Harvard University; founder and artistic director of Boston Repertory, 1958; assistant director at Loeb Drama Center, Harvard, 1959.

3–Dylan Thomas, *The Doctor and the Devil*, performed at the Little Theater, Massachusetts Institute of Technology, 20–31 January 1959.

4–Margaret Tillman Booth (*c.* 1924/5–); their daughters Carol, Margot, and Robin Booth.

5–American poet George Edwin Starbuck (1931–96); editor at Houghton Mifflin, 1958–61; married Janice King, 25 April 1955 (divorced); father of Margaret Mary, Stephen George, and John Edward by his first wife Janice King.

6–American poet Anne Harvey Sexton (1928–74).

7–Anne Sexton, 'The Double Image', 'You, Doctor Martin', and 'Elizabeth Gone', *Hudson Review* 12 (Spring 1959): 73–81.

8–Anne Sexton, 'Some Foreign Letters', *Partisan Review* 27 (Spring 1960): 272–5.

9–Anne Sexton, 'Sunbathers', *New Yorker* (13 June 1959): 93; and 'The Road Back', *New Yorker* (29 August 1959): 30.

10–Anne Sexton, 'The Double Image'.

book on Bartok's American Years[1] is magnificent. I have never heard her play the piano, but evidently she is accomplished as only a Hungarian can be; or something of the sort.

Please send me a page or more of Guiliani (in your translation).[2] How is your book coming.[3] You never told me about the way you got rid of your first grant (wasn't it a 2-year affair?) and onto the Fulbright. What happened to the Spectator (or was it another?) articles: did you publish there, and when? I really would love to read something of what you are doing.

How is your novel? I felt I had one, or the stuff of one; but encountered a huge block in trying to have the material take off from what actually did happen. I have been doing some poems this month, as always happens when spring nears, but they are grim, antipoetic (compared to the florid metaphorical things I had in Poetry, Chicago) & I hope, transitional.

The Lamont Poetry Prize is now the Thing to get, what Booth got. Dudley Fitts[4] is editing the Yale Series this year, a fall, I suppose, from Auden. But then, Auden never liked what I wrote. I hate the idea of trying to publish a book of poems without having got some sort of excuse for it which will get it reviewed. It is bad enough to go through the trauma of selecting and rejecting (I have done an immense amount of the latter, and have a ghost-book larger, and more-published than my present slim volume) without thinking nobody will even notice it: better scathing reviews than a dead silence. Or so I tell myself now. Actually, I think one stands a much better chance of having a book published in England, a book of poems – they have many companies, small, idiosyncratic (unlike Faber's & its classic list) and seem to publish vast amounts of unknowns: in America, an unknown without a reputable publisher is lost, lost. And most publishers are like the Atlantic Press (Little, Brown) & only publish one volume a year & that done by one who has already paid his way in novels or children's books. Enough.

What happened to your leg? It suddenly came onstage limping & not saying what was wrong. How, by the way, are the hospitals in Rome? Is there an "American" hospital? I don't know where, but I think I've heard of it.

1–Agatha Fassett, *The Naked Face of Genius: Béla Bartók's American Years* (Boston: Houghton Mifflin, 1958).

2–Lawner's friend; mentioned in 7 December 1958 letter as 'a lovely & very fine It. poet'.

3–Lynne Lawner, *Wedding Night of a Nun* (Boston: Little, Brown, 1964).

4–American poet Dudley Fitts (1903–68).

Have you by now invaded the Obscure Avenue[1] and seen the jeweled hand behind the trilingual annual yet? I understand her poetry editor (his face always altering in the altering lights) floats here and there picking up poems like lint, a huge bundle at his side, which he uses for obscure and unliterary purposes. Why don't you send them a bundle of stuff? I am deterred simply by trying to figure out return postage. Also I don't have anything long enough. I grind out little very minor poems. I had 3 of a longer sort in the latest, March I think, London magazine, which I wrote last Spring after a year's silence. I am leaving the rather florid over-metaphorical style that encrusted me in college. The "Feminine" (horrors) lavish coyness. The poems I have written in this last year are, if anything, "ugly". I have done many in syllabic verse which gives freedom of another sort & excited me for a good while, but they are pretty bare. The ones in the London magazine are the last of the lyric florid picture-poems.

It was spring yesterday, but now the snow is whitening around the three windows of my bay-desk. You say you have "Some truly strange poems". Please send me a couple. I may enclose something if only to lure you to do likewise. I read the gaga review on Vassar Miller,[2] thought her quoted poem boring and the ones in New Poets of England & America[3] not much better. May Swenson has a couple I like, one about V. Woolf,[4] among others. Except for M. Moore & Elizabeth Bishop what women are there to look to? A few eccentrics like Edith Sitwell,[5] Amy Lowell.[6] And the perennial Emily,[7] I suppose. Again, I say send me something. I shall send you mimeos of one or two I think and demand an exchange. Yes, I shall.

I have been having second thoughts about graduate school, such as "what fun to get a Phd". "What fun to have to learn German and relearn French and Latin." "How jolly to be a professional and have a big thesis

1–*Botteghe Oscure*, an Italian literary journal published 1948–60 and edited by Marguerite Caetani (1880–1963).

2–American poet Vassar Miller (1924–98). The review to which SP refers was likely for Vassar Miller, *Adam's Footprint* (New Orleans, La.: New Orleans Poetry Review Press, 1956).

3–Donald Hall, Robert Pack, and Louis Simpson (eds), *New Poets of England and America* (New York: Meridian Books, 1957); Millar's poems were 'Adam's Footprint', 'Apology', 'Autumnal Spring Song', 'Bout with Burning', 'Ceremony', 'Epithalamium', 'Love Song Out of Nothing', 'Paradox', and 'Reciprocity' (232–7).

4–American poet May Swenson (1913–89); her 'Frontispiece', *New Poets of England and America*, 300–1. Her other poems in the anthology are 'Question', 'The Key to Everything', and 'The Garden at St. John's' (301–4).

5–English poet and critic Edith Sitwell (1887–1964).

6–American poet Amy Lowell (1874–1925).

7–American poet Emily Dickinson (1830–86).

on something publishable." The horror comes when I think, OK, so I have this Phd, so where do I teach? I could only, I think, now consider a place in a city, like Columbia or Chicago or whatever big city it is they have in California, where my life could be as private as possible. Places, of course, where one has to be Diana Trilling to get a job. And the other places all exude for me the kind of stuffed intricate calm I experienced among the golden groves of Smith last year. I envision being fifty, haggard, stamping about, advancing to teach the Joyce Yeats Eliot course, and so? And the girls younger and more similar year by year. The little voyeuse in me, or whatever it is, says, oh, go live in England & no matter how poor you are, there will be France and Italy and Germany and Spain and Greece and you can study languages there, etc. etc. From this side of the Atlantic I again experience the weight of water between me and Europe that I am sure convinces some people Europe is a figment of a cracked brain.

Please tell me honestly what you think of these poems. Mad Maudlin is the earliest, written two winters ago, Green Rock, Winthrop Bay, written last spring, and Suicide off Egg Rock this spring (winter, rather). In the latter, I didn't choose the garbagey details to prove I wasn't going to blench, but wanted the energy of the waves and dog and child to be equally as terrifying to the man in despair. As you will see, I try for certain absolutely "plain" lines in it, pure statement, but of course the words twist in and try to color it up.

We don't know at present what next year will bring after September 1st when our lease here runs out. I have come to think we may start our first house in England, in the country outside London & expand from there: Ted is very homesick, and I am in many many ways more akin to the English temper than the American, but not in so many as to make me deny that I will feel a good bit in exile. Before we go, we would like to see New Orleans, Mexico, the canyon on the way to California, but that is also in question. An amusing note, I have been asked to be one of the judges of the Holyoke Glascock contest this year, along with John Crowe Ransom.[1] I don't know whether to laugh or be silent.

Tell me about you, your bothers as well as your pleasures. I feel an odd sisterly bond, partly because I feel, as I think and suspect you may, a dim doppelganger relationship with the few women I know who are very much physically & psychically akin to me. It would be great fun to see

1–American poet John Crowe Ransom (1888–1974). The third judge in 1959 was Marie Borroff.

you again, and if you would only stay in Rome another year maybe we would. At any rate, write me faster than I've written you and Send Poems.

With Love,
Sylvia

TO *Edith & William Hughes*

Tuesday 31 March 1959 TLS, Family owned

Tuesday
March 31, 1959

Dear Ted's mother & dad,

As I sit here at my high desk I look out into a grey hazy day, a suitable weather for the last of March, trying to be mild and warmish, but making me long only to limber my fingers around a cup of hot tea. It has been a raw, windy month, with a great load of snow dumped on us last week which is by now melted and gone.

I was very cross with the judges of the Maugham contest,[1] but after my first anger at the much-traveled Thom Gunn[2] I reflected that the judges probably figured Ted had enough with his 300 pound first prize this autumn & shouldn't be made fabulously wealthy with 500 pounds on top of it. I am sure he will win the prize with his next book which is almost done. His last five poems are the most colorful and exciting he has done yet. He will have 5 poems[3] coming out in a handsome magazine here, Audience, which has a lot of money behind it and prints drawings and photographs: Vicky would enjoy these. Do look up the last two London magazines, my poems are in the March, Ted's in the April issue;[4] I had 3 poems about the sea in this spring's Audience[5] & Ted will come out in the summer issue: isn't that nice: we always miss by a month in coming out together, but maybe the chivalrous editors think: Ladies first. I am enclosing a page[6] from the international newspaper I am publishing a few poems in a poem

1–Begun in 1947, the Somerset Maugham Award is an annual award, to be spent on foreign travel, given to the best writer(s) of a book in the previous year.
2–Anglo-American poet Thom Gunn (1929–2004).
3–Ted Hughes, 'Thrushes', 'The Bull Moses', 'The Voyage', 'Pike', and 'Nicholas Ferrer', *Audience* (Summer 1959): 55–61.
4–Ted Hughes, 'February', 'The Bull Moses', and 'The Voyage', *London Magazine* 6 (April 1959): 47–9.
5–Sylvia Plath, 'Lorelei', 'Full Fathom Five', and 'The Hermit at Outermost House', *Audience* 6 (Spring 1959): 33–6.
6–The enclosure is no longer with the letter.

I wrote about riding a runway horse[1] in Cambridge, England. I thought the article on the Yorkshire moors[2] might also interest you.

We had Easter dinner with my brother at mother's house Sunday, and it was a nice feast. My brother is relaxing more in his work at Harvard and going to work on a project translating scientific Russian this summer on the way to his PhD. Ted is accompanying me twice a week to Cambridge, via subway, where I work two afternoons in the Harvard library as secretary to the Head of the Sanskrit Department, which is fun: he is a poetic soul at heart & has given me two articles of his[3] on Sanskrit poetry of the Village and Field which Ted enjoyed. Ted is getting books from a Buddhist lady each week (it is almost impossible for a non-Harvard person to get at their great Library without paying large fees) and collecting fox stories which he will write up for a children's book.

Tonight we are going again to the Fassetts around the corner. They have just had their cat Scylla have another kitten & we will see it. But their cats are so inbred that they never litter like ordinary cats: they have two cats in great pain and one is always born dead, while the other has to be fed milk from the hand to live. Very sad.

This week, for some reason, things are at a standstill. Partly the season, I guess. We should have more news next week. Keep warm & keep working the pools.

With love,
Sylvia

1–Sylvia Plath, 'Whiteness I Remember', *Christian Science Monitor* (5 March 1959): 12. SP also published: 'Prologue to Spring', *Christian Science Monitor* (23 March 1959): 8, and 'Yadwigha, on a Red Couch, Among Lilies', *Christian Science Monitor* (26 March 1959): 8.

2–Probably Sylvia Plath, 'A Walk to Withens'.

3–One of these was probably Daniel Henry Holmes Ingalls, 'A Sanskrit Poetry of Village and Field: Yogeśvara and His Fellow Poets', *Journal of the American Oriental Society* 74 (July 1954): 119–31.

TO *Elizabeth Ames*

Wednesday 8 April 1959 TLS, New York Public Library

Suite 61
9 Willow Street
Boston 8, Massachusetts
April 8, 1959

Mrs. Elizabeth Ames
Executive Director
Yaddo
Saratoga Springs, New York

Dear Mrs. Ames:

We are both pleased and honored to receive your invitation[1] to arrive at Yaddo on September 9th and remain until November 9th.

We are happy to accept the invitation for the full period and look forward to spending those two months at Yaddo.

Sincerely yours,
Sylvia Plath & Ted Hughes

TO *Mary Stetson Clarke*[2]

Friday 10 April 1959 TLS, Smith College

Suite 61
9 Willow Street
Boston 8, Massachusetts
April 10, 1959

Dear Mary,

I was so happy to get your kind letter! Right now I am sitting at my desk overlooking the ruddy-brick rooftops of the Hill and the grey waters of Back Bay with the misty spring sky above it, which often puts me in such a rapt mood I am in danger of not getting to work, and spending hours staring at the white sails already visible on the water.

1–Elizabeth Ames to SP & TH, 3 April 1959; held by New York Public Library.

2–American writer Mary Stetson Clarke (1911–94); B.A. 1933, Boston University; ASP's former student at Melrose High School (1928–9) and close friend; purchased a book on learning shorthand for SP. Clarke later helped ASP prepare *Letters Home*.

You have been often in our thoughts. I am so glad that our visit with you and Susan[1] at Smith was a prelude to Susan's becoming a Smith Girl. It is a wonderful, wonderful place.

I have been having Ted dictate to me from the beginning lessons in the speedwriting book which was a godsend, and you so kind to be involved in the obtaining of it! It is just what I need, although my boss is understanding and dictates at the pace of a turtle.

We have both of us had an excellent and productive year in Boston, Ted just finishing a second book of poems, and me my first. Now I shall start looking about for a publisher, a much more difficult job for a poetry-writer than a novelist or a children's book writer, although we would like to do the latter very much, too. How magnificent your friend Betty George Speare[2] received the Newbury Medal: we saw a whole window of her books set out on Park Street & it looking charming.

After a brief trip to Smith and Holyoke this next week we shall be back in Boston till September 1st and wish you would give us a call any afternoon you are in town & drop by for tea threeish or fourish. We work from 7 to 12 in the morning very hard and then are delighted to indulge in recreation of another sort. We hope to spend two months at Yaddo, the writers' colony in Saratoga Springs, this fall as guests with nothing to do but write. It sounds like a dream just now.

Our best to you and the family,
Sylvia Hughes

1–Susan E. Clarke; matriculated with Smith College Class of 1963: B.A. 1964, Wheaton College; MBA 1972, Boston University.

2–American writer of children's books Elizabeth George Speare (1908–94). Speare won the 1959 Newbery Medal for *The Witch of Blackbird Pond* (1958) and the 1962 Newbery Medal for *The Bronze Bow* (1961).

TO *Monroe K. Spears*[1]

Friday 10 April 1959 — TLS, Sewanee: The University of the South

Suite 61
9 Willow Street
Boston 8, Massachusetts
April 10, 1959

Mr. Monroe K. Spears
Editor
THE SEWANEE REVIEW
The University of the South
Sewanee, Tennessee

Dear Mr. Spears:

I am happy to hear[2] that you are keeping "Point Shirley" for publication with "The Ghost's Leavetaking".

One or two minor changes I have made since in the poem I wonder if you would be so good as to alter on the copy you have: I should like "Revisited" dropped from the title so it reads simply "Point Shirley". Also I should like to leave out the word "dying" in the last line of the second stanza so it reads "Shark littered in the geranium bed." And then change the word "wring" in the first line of the last stanza to "get" ("I would get from these dry-papped stones").

I do hope these slight alterations will not be of any inconvenience.

Sincerely yours,
Sylvia Plath

1–Editor of *Sewanee Review* Monroe K. Spears (1916–98).
2–See Monroe K. Spears to SP, 7 April 1959; held by Sewanee: The University of the South.

TO *Ann Davidow-Goodman*[1]

Tuesday 14 April 1959 TLS with envelope, Smith College

Suite 61
9 Willow Street
Boston 8, Massachusetts
April 14, 1959

Dear Ann,

Sometimes I think I am a sleepwalker. I had your letter, with the wonderful happy-making cavorters on it around Christmas and started saving up things to tell you in a letter, and added this and that, and meanwhile the snows melted and with the green leaves coming out in Boston Public Gardens and white sails on the Charles River, which I can see from our window, realize with a pang that a quarter of a year has slipped by. Well, here is the letter and I hope you are not now living in Turkey or Poona or some other place.

What are you doing and what have you done these last five years? Persons, places, words. I look back with a kind of exhaustion at the voyagings and shifting of scenery and wonder where to begin. Much better would be seeing you in person. I have an aversion to reunions and wish very much you could manage a stop-over in Boston. We have, alas, no place to put anybody up in our two very small rooms – with a view, but you could get a room nearby & come for meals, swan-boat rides, and it would be such fun. We'll probably be here up till the end of August, and there is an arts festival, open-air exhibits etc., sometime in June for about a week. Couldn't you come for that, or any time?

As you can see, we have left Northampton. Ted was bothered by the extreme provincial nature of the town, seeing only one's colleagues for morning coffee, lunch, cocktails, dinner and the evening, and the gossip over students, who supply the main course of conversation, and the petty politicking for positions, promotions, etc. I was asked back, and also for this year to teach writing, which I would much less like to teach than freshman English (I managed to fit in Dostoevsky and Sophocles along with DH Lawrence and James Joyce). However, although I loved teaching, the great conflict was with writing. I wore my eyes out on 70 student

1–Children's book author and illustrator Ann Davidow-Goodman (1932–); daughter of Leonard and Claire Sondheim Davidow of Highland Park, Illinois; SP's friend. Ann Davidow withdrew from Smith College in January 1951 following her first semester; earned B.A. 1954, University of Chicago; married Leo Goodman 1960 (divorced 1976); married Russell Hayes 1983. Corresponded with SP, 1951–62.

themes every other week and had no energy for writing a thing. Ironically, I could have gone on teaching without a PhD because of my writing. But we made the break, both of us turning down teaching jobs to live on a shoestring for a year in Boston writing to see what we could do, and Ted has just finished his second book of poems and I my first, which I will start sending the rounds to publishers some time this summer. Unfortunately there is no money in the poetry books, although Ted's first book, being a prize-winner in America and a Book Society choice in England, sold more than many first novels. We have a steady trickle of little checks for magazine publications but not enough to bank on. So Ted is working on a play[1] and both of us plan to try our hand at children's books this spring. I hear from reputable sources that children's books are pleasantly lucrative, sell better and longer than most novels.

Which makes me wonder, have you tried illustrating children's books? Your drawings are so full of verve I should think you could make a wonderful thing of it. If I ever did get a book done would you think of doing pictures for it? What fun that would be. Please do write very concrete details about who you work for, and how and all else. O do come to Boston for a visit.

We have just been "invited" to an artists' colony in Saratoga Springs, New York, from September 9th to November 9th, a kind of great estate which feeds you and gives you a studio to finish creative work, no-talking to a soul from 9 to 4, and no organized activities, which lifts some of my suspicion of writers' colonies. And gardens, woods and bass-ponds. After that, Ted has just got word of a Guggenheim[2] grant which will keep us in Boston for six months and then take us to Rome for six months. Ted is so homesick for the moortops of Yorkshire that I think we may settle in England eventually.

All the more reason for you to come visit us before we go!

Please forgive my tardy letter and chalk it up to a horrible habit of procrastination. Do write, even just a note, as soon as you can, and please say you can come to Boston for a while!

Love,
Syl

PS It was very wholesome being reminded of my five-year-ago words about the New Yorker. It gave me a healthy perspective. Now you can

1–Ted Hughes, *The House of Taurus*, unpublished play.

2–TH received a $5,000 grant from the John Simon Guggenheim Memorial Foundation. See '45 Guggenheim Winners Here', *Boston Herald* (20 April 1959). Copy held in TH's scrapbook, Emory University.

record me as saying it is my lifelong ambition to get a story in the darn magazine!

sph

TO *Howard Moss*

Thursday 23 April 1959 TLS, New York Public Library

Suite 61
9 Willow Street
Boston 8, Massachusetts
April 23, 1959

Mr. Howard Moss
THE NEW YORKER
25 West 43rd Street
New York 36, New York

Dear Mr. Moss:

I am glad to hear[1] you are taking WATERCOLOR OF GRANCHESTER MEADOWS[2] and MAN IN BLACK[3] for The New Yorker and in agreement with your using the sub-title Cambridge, England under WATERCOLOR.

I am dubious about altering the last line of stanza 1 in WATERCOLOR. I mean "of good color" as an adverbial phrase parallel with "nimble-winged", the gist being "flits nimble-winged and colorful thickets". Is this grammatically possible and understandable? I am bothered by adding "is" after "and" because it alters my meaning and, I think, holds up the movement of the line, which I hope can be read "flits nimble-winged . . . and (flits) of good color". I very much hope it may be possible to do without adding "is".

With all good wishes,
Sincerely yours,
Sylvia Plath

1–Howard Moss to SP, 21 April 1959; held by New York Public Library.
2–Sylvia Plath, 'Water Color of Grantchester Meadows', *New Yorker* (28 May 1960): 30. SP's wishes regarding the suggestions made by Moss were respected and the poem read: 'Each thumb-sized bird / Flits nimble-winged in thickets, and of good color.'
3–Sylvia Plath, 'Man in Black', *New Yorker* (9 April 1960): 40.

TO *Alice Norma Davis*

Tuesday 28 April 1959 TLS, Smith College Archives

Suite 61
9 Willow Street
Boston 8, Massachusetts
April 28, 1959

Miss Alice Norma Davis
Director
The Vocational Office
Smith College
Northampton, Massachusetts

Dear Miss Davis:

Since your last letter of September 23rd I have had no word from you about jobs in Boston and Cambridge.

Now that summer is coming round I wonder whether any full-time or part-time jobs in Boston or Cambridge will be available, through your office, for the summer months. I should very much appreciate your letting me know roughly how much chance I stand of finding summer work[1] through the Vocational Office, if that is possible.

Sincerely yours,
Sylvia Plath Hughes, 1955

TO *Esther & Leonard Baskin*

Tuesday 28 April 1959 TLS, British Library

Suite 61
9 Willow Street
Boston 8, Massachusetts
April 28, 1959

Dear Esther & Leonard,

It was very good seeing you both, the Man With Owl,[2] and the lovely Tobias, and the Fire too, a week ago Friday.[3] We came back weary from

1–See Alice Norma Davis to SP, 29 April 1959; held by Smith College. Davis directed SP to Mary Albro (Smith College, 1936) director of the Radcliffe Appointment Bureau and their Seven College Directory of personnel officers who employed college-trained women.

2–Leonard Baskin, 'Seated Man With Owl' (sculpture, 1959).

3–TH lectured to two classes, English 11 (Freshman English) and English 220 (Practice in Various Forms of Writing) at Smith College on 16 April 1959.

our trip, mammoth stay-at-homes as we are, and are just now recovering, having slept 12 hours a night for the last week. It is so good to get back to work with no people no phonecalls no nothing.

What do you hear about the Night Animals. We are eager to get a copy of the book in our hands: tell the estimable Miss McLeod to get out her printed contracts and bind herself to something that will surpass Reid,[1] Shahn & Co. Ted is working on a children's book himself tentatively called Meet My Folks, poems about various mad relatives. Also a collection of Oriental fox stories (he thinks he may put a badger or two in as he likes them immensely, but I say just foxes, and then a whole book for badgers, they're fat enough). He is delighted with the prospect of four months more here ever since he discovered (last week) that an old red fox had made its abode under the Boston State House, tunnelling mysteriously about until unearthed by somebody from the Animal Rescue League.

Leonard, I want to ask you would you let me dedicate my poem "Sculptor" (which should be on that mimeographed sheet[2] we left with you) to you? It was written for you, but I felt you might not like the poem. I have not any poems dedicated to anyone, but would like to say: To Leonard Baskin under the title. Ted has given "Esther's Tomcat" to the world & this is what I would like to do with "Sculptor". I know parts of it are rank falsehood, for you claim to have no dreams, but let me know if you are willing, it would mean a very great deal. Rather like some lady from the Botteghe Oscure asking Michelange if she might dedicate a canzone to him, but then.

We will drive up again to see you before or after our two months at Yaddo.

Love to you both, & Tobias,
Sylvia & Ted

1–Scottish born poet and translator Alastair Reid (1926–2014).
2–This typescript of 'Sculptor' held in Hughes–Baskin Papers. Vol. iv: Add MS 83687, British Library.

TO *Emilie McLeod*

Saturday 2 May 1959 TLS (photocopy), Yale University

Suite 61
9 Willow Street
Boston 8, Massachusetts
May 2, 1959

Mrs. Emilie W. McLeod
Editor, Children's Books
THE ATLANTIC MONTHLY PRESS
8 Arlington Street
Boston 16, Massachusetts

Dear Mrs. McLeod,

I'm sending along The Bed Book.[1] I hope you may have as much fun reading it as I had writing it. I wrote verses about 10 beds in detail, as a kind of dialogue between Wide-Awake Will and Stay-Uppity Sue.[2] I think an illustrator would have a good time with it, and I tried to make it very pictorial, a few lines, or at most, a verse or so, for each possible picture.

At any rate, let me know what you think of it, and I'll be grateful for any criticism you may have---too many beds, too few, too what-ever-it-is. I'd be happy to do more work on it if you think it might help.

Ted is in the middle of "Meet My Folks", the book of rhymes about weird relatives, and doing research on Fox Tales of the Orient, which goes more slowly. He should have both of these done some time this summer.

With all good wishes,
Sincerely,
Sylvia Plath

1–In addition to the Atlantic Montly Press, SP submitted *The Bed Book* manuscript to the *Christian Science Monitor* (June 1959), Harcourt, Brace (23 September 1959), Macmillan & Company (27 October 1959), Wilcox & Follett (23 February 1960), William Heinemann (25 February 1960), Bodley Head Books for Children (1 March 1960), Macmillan (15 April 1960), World Publishing (20 May 1960), G. P. Putnam (9 July 1960). *The Bed Book* was published in 1976 with illustrations by Quentin Blake (London: Faber & Faber) and illustrations by Emily Arnold McCully (New York: Harper & Row).

2–The two characters in an early draft of SP's 'The Bed Book', later dropped.

TO *Edward Weeks*

Thursday 7 May 1959 TLS (photocopy), Yale University

Suite 61
9 Willow Street
Boston 8, Massachusetts
May 7, 1959

Mr. Edward Weeks
Editor
THE ATLANTIC MONTHLY
8 Arlington Street
Boston 16, Massachusetts

Dear Mr. Weeks:

I am enclosing a selection of recent poems,[1] set variously in Massachusetts, England and Spain, in hopes that you may like something among them enough for publication in the Atlantic. Perhaps "Alicante Lullaby" might be considered under Light Verse in the "Accent on Living."

With all good wishes, I am
Sincerely yours,
Sylvia Plath

1–A note on the letter indicates that Plath submitted eight poems including: 'Alicante Lullaby', 'The Eye-mote', 'Green Rock, Winthrop Bay', and 'The Other Two'.

TO *William Maxwell*[1]

Friday 22 May 1959 TLS, New York Public Library

Suite 61
9 Willow Street
Boston 8, Massachusetts
May 22, 1959

Mr. William Maxwell
THE NEW YORKER
25 West 43rd Street
New York 36, New York

Dear Mr. Maxwell:

I am sending along to you, at the suggestion of Alfred Kazin, two stories ---"Sweetie Pie And The Gutter Men" and "The Shadow"---in hopes that you may consider them for publication in The New Yorker.

Although I have had poems published in The New Yorker, I have not previously sent in any fiction. Other stories of mine have appeared in Seventeen and Mademoiselle.

With all good wishes, I am
Sincerely yours,
Sylvia Plath

TO *Edith & William Hughes*

Sunday 24 May 1959 TLS, Family owned

Sunday
May 24, 1959

Dear Ted's mother & dad,

Well, it is at last cool again, after a record heat spell which had Ted & me sitting sweltering in front of our fan drinking bottles of iced beer. It is a pleasant grey Sunday and very quiet and peaceful, and from where I sit I can see the green leaves of the Public Gardens across the roofs of the red brick buildings. We have just put $1,250 in the bank, the first quarter of Ted's Guggenheim money, and are feeling that pleasant sense of well-being which comes from knowing there is money coming in for the whole next year and nothing to worry about.

1–American editor and writer William Maxwell (1908–2000).

We had Herbert Hitchen[1] here yesterday, the Unitarian minister from Northampton, born in Yorkshire, who reminds us in many ways of Uncle Walt. He is full of stories and good humor and has done all sorts of things, farming, visiting the concentration camps on a relief mission after the war, and knows, or did know, all the poets in England & America and has an amazing collection of poetry & Irish books.[2] We are going to the annual New England Poetry Society "Golden Rose" meeting tomorrow as his guest at the Harvard Faculty Club---that is where Ted read the other week and was so enthusiastically received.

The prospect of driving to California and Mexico---if we can only get our apartment sublet for those two summer months---is making us work harder than ever. We have both finished books of verse-stories for children & are waiting to hear about them, both about finished a book of poems, and Ted is finishing his play, and I several stories which are better than any I have written yet. I have had a second article accepted[3] by the Christian Science Monitor, that international newspaper, called "A Walk To Withens" and it is about Ted & me going to Wuthering Heights. I'll send you a clipping when it comes out.

I am finishing up my part-time job as secretary to the Chairman of the Department of Sanskrit and Indian Studies at Harvard, very interesting work, as he is also the head of a wealthy family Hotel Spa in Virginia, and I write his lecture notes up about India, and letters to monks and Buddhists, and letters about ski lodges and snow-making machines. I just work two or three afternoons a week which is about right.

Did I tell you I am braiding a rug of strips of colored wool I get from Mill End Shops? It is very bright and cheerful & Ted likes it. He is fine, and I just got him a red & black wool sweater which looks wonderful on him.

Love to all,
Sylvia

1 – Rev. Herbert Hitchen (1894–1979); born in Norland, Yorkshire; pastor of the Unitarian Church of Northampton, Mass., 1958–66; collector of Irish literature.

2 – See Herbert Hitchen Irish Collection, 1908–70; held by Smith College.

3 – Sylvia Plath, 'A Walk to Withens', *Christian Science Monitor* (6 June 1959): 8. SP's first article, 'Kitchen of the Fig Tree', *Christian Science Monitor* (5 May 1959): 12.

TO *Gerald & Joan Hughes*

Sunday 24 May 1959   TLS, Indiana University

Sunday
May 24

Dear Gerald & Joan,

It was so good to hear from you. We are both very relieved that the jet airport will not take your house---the thought that they might made me curse every jet I heard breaking the sound barrier overhead 'Maybe that is one of Gerald & Joan's jets," thought I, "Blast them." We are thinking at present of getting a big house in the country outside London. As if we could afford it. But this Guggenheim money will pay our fares back to England and a year's writing, which will earn us heaven knows how much. Ideally, we'd like a house both in England & America, but we'll start with England---and enjoy staying close to Europe, as it seems as far as the moon from here.

We plan to take a camping trip this summer, borrowing my mother's car, to California and Mexico, through all the big national parks. I am very excited about this, and so is Ted, as we've never seen anything west of New York. Then we will go for September & October to this castle Artists' Colony in New York State where we have both been invited to spend two free months writing. I won't have to shop or cook, which will be a wonderful change, although I'll probably be dying for a homemade cheese cake or fish chowder after a week. We plan to write up all our summer experiences there, then sail for England sometime in the winter.

Ted & I have both finished writing books of verse for children & are hoping to sell them here. His is called "Meet My Folks", 8 very funny rhymes about a zany family. Mine is called "The Bed Book", about ten fantastic beds this little brother & sister dream up so going to bed would be interesting: they are terrible children and would stay up till midnight if their parents didn't give them opium or something. Ted's finishing his play, and I am finishing a couple of short stories. My ambition at this point is to get a story in the New Yorker. They have taken two more poems, so this year I have earned over $500 from them, for only 4 poems, which is rare pay. I've also got a second free-lance article accepted by The Christian Science Monitor, that international newspaper, and as they pay up to $50 an article, I hope to capitalize by writing our experiences up this summer.

Ted is thriving. He is handsomer than ever. I just got him a red & black-weave wool sweater which looks marvelous on him. And a couple of hopsacking neckties. If he has any faults they are not shutting the icebox (a kind of subconscious revenge on American appliances) and knotting his clothes up in unknottable balls and hurling them about the floor of the room every evening before retiring. Oh yes, and the occasional black Moods when he pretends the cat's ear is broken or that the air is full of Strontium 90. Other than these minor foibles he is extremely good-natured, thoughtful and almost normal. He eats well, too, although he complains that I am trying to kill him with protein diet (after he has come home from a friend's house this is, and eaten a 7 course dinner topped off by a layer cake saturated with brandy) and also that I hide things and secretly destroy them: i.e., mislaid papers, certain books, old coats, letters from the British tax authorities. I bear up as well as I am able.

I wish we could see you. If I ever get a Guggenheim we will come by packet boat to Australia for a visit. Couldn't you ever ever fly to England? For a visit? I hope we won't all be white-haired by the time we meet.

Do write us again soon. Send pictures of you & the children.

With love to all,
Sylvia

TO *Olwyn Hughes*

c. Monday 25 May 1959[1] TLS (incomplete), British Library

<first page not with letter>

2.

I have done four stories[2] this year which I am very pleased with, and am working on a fifth, and hope to get some response from them eventually as I send them around. I've been publishing a good bit in the Christian Science Monitor & they've accepted a second article from me about Withens, so I should get up to $50 for each article I do them, and plan to write a ream during our trip this summer. My big ambition at this point, besides, of course, getting a book published, is to have a story accepted by the New Yorker. They pay fabulously, and have much work, especially

1–Date supplied from internal evidence.

2–In a journal entry written one week later, SP rates her recent stories, in order, as 'Johnny Panic and the Bible of Dreams', 'The Fifteen Dollar Eagle', 'The Shadow', 'Sweetie Pie and the Gutter Men', 'Above the Oxbow', and 'This Earth Our Hospital' ['The Daughters of Blossom Street'].

the long biographical articles and articles by AJ Liebling,[1] which I admire immensely. Well, in 10 years of hard work at the trade, that may come. And suddenly my typewriter will turn to solid gold and the keys play the Eroica[2] or something equivalent.

In my teatimes I am braiding a rug of brightly colored wool remnants which I get from a Mill End Place and cut to size, and Ted is delighted with it. I find a great peace in working on it, as if all my worries and bothers flowed away in to the fabric and turned into bright-colored patterns, and Ted reads me Shakespeare while I work, so it is much fun.

I'm finishing my job as secretary to the head of the Department of Sanskrit and Indian Studies at Harvard, and I'll miss my boss---I only go 3 afternoons a week, so that is just enough to be fun, and I do his lecture notes up and letters to Buddhist monks and ad men and night watchmen and Governors of Virginia etc., as he is not only a teacher, professor, rather, an editor, writer, and father and speaker of Sanskrit, but the President of a Corporation and head of a fabulously wealthy Virginia Spa which is now making itself a ski-lodge and hiring a snow-maker to boot in the far south. The letters I do are much fun and I feel that, incognito, I have much insight into his family matters. He has an aunt who is a Lady in London, and earns, on the income tax forms I typed up for him, over $30,000 a year, and is always getting me to write the stock markets, selling hundreds of shares of National Can and buying Sheraton this or that. Well, enough. A rather special man for a professor.

<drawing of high cake pan>

Here is a heavenly sponge cake recipe which you should make in a high cake pan with a funnel in the center so the cake has a hole in the middle:

6 eggs (separate)
1½ cups sugar (sifted)
1⅓ cups cake flour
1½ teaspoons baking powder
¼ teaspoon salt
6 tablespoons water
½ teaspoon lemon extract
1 teaspoon vanilla

Directions for sponge cake: Beat yolks till lemon colored. Add sugar gradually. Add water & flavoring. Beat. Add flour gradually, beating.

1–American journalist A. J. (Abbott Joseph) Liebling (1904–63); married 1959–63 to American short-story writer and novelist Jean Stafford (1915–79).
2–Ludwig van Beethoven, *Symphony No. 3*.

Beat egg whites to froth; add baking powder and salt to frothy egg whites. Beat until very stiff. Fold gently, but thoroly into egg yolk mixture. Sprinkle granulated sugar lightly over top of cake before putting it in the oven.

Bake for one hour at 325°. Do not remove cake from pan till cake is cold.

Happy eating,
love
Sylvia

TO *Seymour Lawrence*[1]

Saturday 30 May 1959 TLS (photocopy), Yale University

Suite 61
9 Willow Street
Boston 8, Massachusetts
May 30, 1959

Mr. Seymour Lawrence
THE ATLANTIC MONTHLY
8 Arlington Street
Boston, Massachusetts

Dear Sam:

I am sending along two stories---THIS EARTH OUR HOSPITAL and ABOVE THE OXBOW---which I hope may interest you for possible publication in The Atlantic Monthly.

With the last manuscript I sent in, I waited over half a year for a No, and I wonder if I could get a faster verdict this time.

All good wishes to you and your wife,[2]

Sincerely,
Sylvia Plath

1–American editor and book publisher Seymour Lawrence (1927–94).

2–Merloyd Lawrence.

TO *Frederick Morgan*

Monday 1 June 1959 TLS, Princeton University

Suite 61
9 Willow Street
Boston 8, Massachusetts
June 1, 1959

Mr. Frederick Morgan
THE HUDSON REVIEW
65 East 55th Street
New York 22, New York

Dear Mr. Morgan:

I am happy to hear you are taking four of my poems[1] for THE HUDSON REVIEW, and particularly happy you have chosen the ones you did.

Here are some biographical notes: Born in Boston, 1932. B.A. from Smith College, 1955, and Cambridge University, 1957 (Fulbright Grant to England from 1955-1957). Instructor of English at Smith College, 1957-58. Secretary, Adult Psychiatric Clinic, Massachusetts General Hospital, 1958. Secretary to Chairman of Department of Sanskrit and Indian Studies at Harvard, 1959.

Poems of mine have appeared in Accent, The Antioch Review, The Atlantic Monthly, Audience, Harper's, The London Magazine, Mademoiselle, The Nation, The New Orleans Poetry Journal, The New Mexico Quarterly, The New Yorker, Poetry (Chicago) and The Spectator.[2] Other poems are scheduled to appear shortly in Arts in Society,[3] The Partisan Review,[4] The Sewanee Review.

After July 1st, my address will be: 26 Elmwood Road, Wellesley, Massachusetts.

Sincerely,
Sylvia Plath

1–Sylvia Plath, 'Ouija', 'Electra on Azalea Path', 'Suicide Off Egg Rock', and 'Moonrise', *Hudson Review* (Autumn 1960): 413–16.

2–Sylvia Plath, 'The Companionable Ills', *The Spectator* (30 January 1959): 163, and 'Main Street at Midnight' ['Owl'], *The Spectator* (13 February 1959): 227.

3–Sylvia Plath, 'Aftermath', 'The Goring', and 'Sculptor', *Arts in Society* 1 (Fall 1959): 66–7.

4–Sylvia Plath, 'I Want, I Want', *Partisan Review* 26 (Fall 1959): 558.

TO *Emilie McLeod*

Thursday 11 June 1959 TLS (photocopy), Yale University

Suite 61
9 Willow Street
Boston 8, Massachusetts
June 11, 1959

Mrs. Emilie W. McLeod
Editor of Children's Books
THE ATLANTIC MONTHLY PRESS
8 Arlington Street
Boston 16, Massachusetts

Dear Mrs. McLeod:

I was so happy to get your good letter[1] today. After a month away from Sue and Will I find them bothersome and your ideas for alteration stimulating and right. I have already begun revising along the lines you suggested, dropping the two children out, and the narrative line, and adding a verse or two for a loose (very loose) continuity.

It is exciting to see how much brisker and more fluid the book becomes by doing this. At this rate, I should have a revised version ready for you to look at next week. I hope you think the changes make for a better book. Ted wonders if there should be more beds, but I think you can judge from the Ten here, and those I mention at the beginning, whether you think the ms. stands as is.

I think what I may do is hold the ms. and give it to you when I see you. I've left a message today at your office for you to call me, and Ted and I would like so much to see you before you go to Palo Alto. The secretary said you come in Tuesdays and/or Wednesdays, and we'd be around any time after two Tuesday, & on Wednesday (Ted would be in all day, if you called). Other days are pretty free also, as we are working like fury on finishing our projects, hoping to start a camping trip to California and Mexico by about July 1st.

I may, if I get through to my satisfaction, send along the book to your office anyway at the beginning of the week and so perhaps it will be on your desk when you come in. In any case, do call during your day up here and let's try to get together.

Sincerely,
Sylvia Plath

1–Emilie McLeod to SP, 9 June 1959; (photocopy) held by Yale University.

TO *Ann Davidow-Goodman*

Friday 12 June 1959 TLS with envelope, Smith College

Suite 61
9 Willow Street
Boston 8, Massachusetts
June 12, 1959

Dear Ann,

It was wonderful to get your letter. I have withered to one of my silent centers where I feel very untalkative and so will simply say please come to Boston at the end of June. We are trying to sublet our place (as is everybody else in Boston) for July and August and if we are lucky enough to sell our view, height, light, air, peace and "Isn't-it-just-like-the-rooftops-of-Paris" aura we will be taking a camping trip to California and Mexico via National Parks and Pacific Ocean for those 8 weeks. But we'll be sure to be around upto the end of June. As I probably told you, our two rooms are so small we are constantly sitting on the cat, or I would ask you to stay here nights. But you would probably be happier in a Room of Your Own anyway nearby and we'd count on you here for meals, and I personally would count on talks on Public Garden Benches, etc. Funny, how little time we ever spent together, and yet how I feel you are one of Those Few People I really can talk to.

I wish you would bring samples of Let's Draw.[1] I'm amazed myself you don't rival Rosalind Welcher and her intellectual greeting cards, after that marvelous Christmas piece you sent.

I have finished my 9 page single- (I mean, double, but I am trying to pad it) spaced first book for Children, as I may have told you, about 10 fantastic and exotic beds. I think it would be highly amusing to have the first book I published (if ever) called the Bed Book, which this one is. Based on the fiction that children's beds, by nature of their age, are dull, merely for sleeping or resting, I rhyme, very simply, 200 two-beat lines about these queer beds. I have got the ms. back from the first place I sent it, a Press across the Public Garden[2] that produces only 4 children's books a year, so is a backwater of sorts, but also choosy, and the editor asked me to leave out the narrative frame & the brother & sister I had talking about the beds, so I've done this, and it seems better, and they

1–Ann H. Davidow, *Let's Draw Animals* (New York: Grosset & Dunlap, 1960).

2–The Atlantic Monthly Press, 8 Arlington Street, Boston; rejected by Emilie McLeod on 17 August 1959 on behalf of the Atlantic and Little, Brown.

asked to see it afterwards. The only trouble with this place is that their illustrators are generally completely without color and verve, to put it clearly, lousy. IF they accepted it (I'd actually, ideally, want a live place like Knopf or Macmillan or such) I'd try to beg them to line up Maurice Sendak[1] or Joseph Low[2] or Roger Duvoisin[3] or whichever one of the Will & Nicholas[4] duo does the drawings, but for a first book I suppose I would eat crow just to get it published. Only pictures mean so much for a children's book; make or break it.

I am currently quite gloomy about this poetry book of about 46 poems, 37 of them published (and all written since college, which means leaving out lots of published juvenalia). I just got word from the annual Yale Contest that I "missed by a whisper", and it so happened that a louse of a guy[5] I know personally, who writes very glib light verse with no stomach to them, won, and he lives around the corner & is an Editor at a good publishing house here, and I have that very annoying feeling which it is tempting to write off as sour grapes that my book was deeper, if more grim, and all those other feelings of thwart. I don't want to try a novel until I feel I am writing good salable short stories for the simple reason that the time, sweat and tears involved in a 300 page book which is rejected all round is too large to cope with while I have the book of Poems kicking about. Nothing stinks like a pile of unpublished writing, which remark I guess shows I still don't have pure motives (oh-it's-such-fun-I-just-can't-stop-who-cares-if-it's-published-or-read) about writing. It is more fun to me, than it was when I used it solely as a love-and admiration-getting mechanism (bless my psychiatrist). But I still want to see it finally ritualized in print.

Slowly, slowly, I write poems and they are about cadavers, suicides, Electra complexes, ouija boards, hermits, fat spinsters, thin spinsters, ghosts, old men of the sea, and, yes, fiddler crabs and mammoth pigs. They sell to magazines, I have broken in to the Partisan, the Hudson, the Sewanee Reviews this year and how nice. Only Poetry Books are a losing business: there are two annual award-and-publishing contests a year which assure the book reviews, purchase by book stores, notice. Other

1 – American illustrator and children's author Maurice Bernard Sendak (1928–2012).

2 – American illustrator Joseph Low (1911–2007).

3 – Swiss-born American illustrator and children's writer Roger Duvoisin (1900–80).

4 – Russian-born American artist Nicolas Mordvinoff (1911–73) and American author William Lipkind (1904–74) collaborated on children's picture books under the pseudonym Nicolas and Will.

5 – George Starbuck, *Bone Thoughts* (New Haven, Conn.: Yale University Press, 1960); Starbuck lived at 40 Grove Street, Boston.

than that, there is the list of publishers, most of whom publish one book a year to prove they are furthering the unlucrative arts, and that usually by somebody who has done novels, or sellers already for them. Tra-la. I must stop this. I have a Little List of places where I must send the damn thing. It is called "The Devil Of The Stairs".[1] The 6th title.

Please let me know when you are coming. The earlier in June the better. If youda stayed in Chicago Ida come to you this summa.

With best love,
Syl

PS: our phone number is LAfayette 3-2843 & Willow Street is the bar of an "H" between Mt. Vernon St. & Chestnut St., overlooking the oh-so-elegant Louisburg Square.

TO *John Lehmann*

Tuesday 16 June 1959 TLS, University of Texas at Austin

26 Elmwood Road
Wellesley, Massachusetts
June 16, 1959

Mr. John Lehmann
LONDON MAGAZINE
36 Soho Square
London W.1, England

Dear Mr. Lehmann:

I am enclosing a group of recent poems[2] in hopes you may like something among them enough for publication in THE LONDON MAGAZINE.

Ted and I are both working hard now on some stories and I think we may come up with something good enough to show you late this summer or in early fall. Ted's stories are set in Yorkshire, and I find them quite exciting---a new departure for him---and I am hoping to get him to give me some of his re-revisions final enough for me to type up.

1–This provisional title for SP's poetry collection is a quotation from T. S. Eliot's poem 'Ash-Wednesday'. SP submitted a book under this title to Knopf (8 June 1959), to the Viking Press (6 October 1959), and to Farrar, Straus & Cudahy (30 October 1959).

2–Two of the poems Plath submitted and had accepted were 'In Midas' Country' and 'The Thin People', *London Magazine* (October 1959): 11–13. SP and these poems mentioned in Anthony Curtis, 'Current Literary Periodicals', *Times Literary Supplement* (13 November 1959): 666.

With all good wishes from both of us,

Sincerely yours,
Sylvia Plath

P.S. We may be reached at the above address for the next half year or so.

TO Critical Quarterly

Friday 19 June 1959 — TLS, Private owner

26 Elmwood Road
Wellesley, Mass.
June 19, 1959

Proofs[1] corrected and enclosed.

Please note change of address to the above and send author's copies of the issue in which these poems appear together with the check to me at the above address.

Thank you.

Sincerely yours,
Sylvia Plath

TO *Ann Davidow-Goodman*

Thursday 25 June 1959 — TLS with envelope, Smith College

26 Elmwood Road
Wellesley, Mass.
June 25, 1959

Dear Ann,

By now you must be about to leave. We'd probably be here on the 29th, but in a state of chaos, and probably you better stick by your friend. We are plugging our children's books. I go see an editor at the Atlantic Press tomorrow, probably to get a rejection. Ever since an old jealous would-be-poet "friend" of mine, a very weak mixed-up male, got on their staff they've been rejecting my poems and publishing his (he publishes nowhere else)[2] and I am sure he would die if I ever turned out a publishable novel. Ted has got one rejection for <u>his</u> kids' book from his poetry publishers,

1–Probably proofs for TH's poems 'Hawk Roosting', 'Strawberry Hill', and 'November', which were published in *Critical Quarterly* (Summer 1959): 124–5.
2–Peter Davison, 'The Site of Last Night's Fire', *Atlantic Monthly* (June 1959): 50.

Harper's, which has a very lively children's department, but practically the same day T. S. Eliot wrote from the publishers he works for in England and said he liked it but felt it needed final polishing which he was suggesting on the ms, more exact rhymes & rhythms in some places. We are framing the letter. I never trust anybody until there is a signed contract.

Am just back from buying sleeping bags, camp stove etc. All we need is a tent and twenty bush natives to carry corn niblets and beer.

Write us at the above address (my safe home address) from England and make Ted homesick.

We will take a large raincheck on seeing you.

Love,
Syl

TO *Poetry Editor,* Accent

c. Monday 29 June 1959[1] TLS, University of Illinois, Urbana-Champaign

<Typed on pink Smith College Memorandum paper[2] with heading>

To Poetry Editor, ACCENT

I'm sending along a batch of recent poems[3] in hopes you may like something well enough for publication in ACCENT. My new address is: 26 Elmwood Road Wellesley, Massachusetts

With all good wishes,
Sylvia Plath

1–Date supplied: a reader's report form is dated 1 July 1959.
2–Paper roughly torn.
3–The reader's report indicates that *Accent* considered 'The Thin People', 'The Eye-mote', and 'Maudlin'; also present in the archive are typescripts for 'Green Rock, Winthrop Bay', and 'Landowners'.

TO *Aurelia Schober Plath*

Thursday 9 July 1959[1] ALS (postcard), Indiana University

Thursday
July 9th

1.

Dear mother –

Look at your map of the USA & Canada to the large green section of Algonquin Park in Ontario. I am writing this from a great rock facing the setting sun surrounded by nothing but soughing birches & pines overlooking Rock Lake one of the 'wildest' campsites here – 4 miles off a dirt road under the bend of Route 60. We arrived here about tea-time yesterday after crossing the St. Lawrence River & Customs & like it so much – we found a fine tent site <u>right</u> on the lake between two birches so the car is in the shade, rented a rowboat & last night rowed (the <u>only</u> people on the huge lake) under the stars & new moon on mirror-clear water. Our 1st night stop was in Whetstone Gulf in upstate New York between Boonville & Lowville on your map.[2] We fished all day today in perfectly deserted & lovely waters under great cliffs but caught nothing though we had many bites & lost lots of worms. Our camp-to-camp route involves much 10 hour driving so we are going to try spending a day or two after long stretches as we are doing now. The car is doing fine & we are thriving – hoping for more fishing & nature-trail walks tomorrow – then on to Sault Ste Marie & the long haul to Yellowstone

xx
Sivvy

1–Postmarked Sudbury, Ontario, Canada, 11 July 1959, 8 p.m.

2–SP and TH left Wellesley on 7 July 1959, stopping briefly in Northampton to see the Baskins before continuing on the first day of their trip.

TO *Warren Plath*

Thursday 9 July 1959[1] — ALS (picture postcard), Indiana University

<Picture postcard caption: MASSACHUSETTS TURNPIKE.>

Thursday – July 9

Dear Warren

Just wrote a USA-stamped card to mother & realized I can't mail it in Canada. We are camped on Rock Lake, right at water's edge with our own little beach; birch trees & rented rowboat – fished (caught nil, tho' the man right next door's wife caught 2 big lake trout) & had a fine time exploring our corner of this big lake – the park is <u>full</u> of lakes & very wild (Algonquin Park). We saw a baby raccoon where we stopped our 1st night in upstate New York. Picked wonderful wild blueberries at sunset over the lake. You & mother should try camping up here. Our equipment works fine – we have all we need of it.

With love,
sivvy

TO *Aurelia Schober Plath*

Saturday 11 July 1959[2] — ALS (picture postcard), Indiana University

<Picture postcard caption: A view from the highway in Algonquin Provincial Park: showing Lake of Two Rivers.>

Saturday

2

Dear Mother –

Ted & I are lunching in the sun in a meadow ten miles south of North Bay in Canada. Have had fine weather. Yesterday spent all day in our rowboat on Rock Lake under stone cliffs catching lots & lots of small lake perch – saved 11 of the largest & fried them for supper by the lakeside – desert being blueberries we picked on the high rock ledges. Today got up to the sound of loons at six – took a two mile 'nature trail' walk & fed lovely reddish deer from our hands with our leftover blueberries.

1–Postmarked Sudbury, Ontario, Canada, 11 July 1959.
2–Postmarked Sudbury, Ontario, Canada, 11 July 1959.

One stuck its head in the car window & licked Ted's face! We hope our pictures of this come out well – Now—on to Sault Ste Marie – follow us on your map! Will call Sunday

xxx
Sivvy

TO *Joseph & Dorothy Benotti*

Saturday 11 July 1959[1] ALS (picture postcard), Indiana University

<Picture postcard caption: Oxtongue Lake Bridge on Highway #60, near Algonquin Park, Ontario, Canada.>

Saturday: July 11

Dear Dotty & Joe . . .

We're driving west in Canada in the general direction of Yellowstone Park after two fine days tenting by Rock Lake at Algonquin Park – an unspoiled green wilderness where deer came down to the lake to drink & eat blueberries out of our hands. Spent 2 days rowing & fishing – caught enough small perch for a fish-fry supper. The weather & country are wonderful –

Love to all –
Sivvy & Ted

TO *Aurelia Schober Plath*

Sunday 12 July 1959 TLS with envelope, Indiana University

Near Sault Saint Marie, Michigan
Brimley State Park
July 12: Sunday

Dear mother,

It was so good to hear your voice today and get the news. I am especially happy to hear that my poem "The Thin People"---a long one---was accepted, and delighted about the acceptance from the Times Literary

1–Postmarked Sudbury, Ontario, Canada, 11 July 1959.

Supplement[1]---my first from there, and a very good paper. I also like the poems they chose. It has just begun to rain---our first rain while actually with our tent up, but we had a wonderful morning here, heating big pots of water & giving ourselves thorough sponge baths and I managed to get a hand laundry hung up on my line (clothesline stretching from our porch tent poles to a tree) and am now sitting snug in the shelter of the porch flap out in front of the tent, facing directly out to Whitefish Bay, not 50 yards from my seat on the comfortable picnic-table-bench combination supplied by the Park. Ted is inside the tent curled up on the airmattresses (actually the very most comfortable bed we have ever slept in!) reading and writing.

Already we feel we have been put to several tests and passed them all. Today I feel really rested and we are staying here tonight and Monday night in preparation for the long drives to Yellowstone which we hope to reach Friday or Saturday. We find it better to drive long stretches---yesterday's was the longest, I hope---about 400 miles from Algonquin Park up route 60 & 11 to North Bay and from there to Sault Ste. Marie, by ferry across the St. Mary River to Michigan's Sault St. Marie and out along dirt roads by the light of the moon to Brimley, which looks right across to Canada and the Bay which opens up into Lake Superior: I can't see the other shore! And it feels like the ocean. Freight boats passing through the Soo Locks (which we hope to visit tomorrow) hoo and whoo companionably out on the horizon line. We thought nothing could beat our setup at Algonquin Park, but this is even more scenic: it's so exciting to cook & do dishes right in the open with a wonderful view. Tonight I have promised Ted some Aunt Jemima pancakes and bacon, blueberry pancakes, with what we have left over in the way of berries from what the deer ate yesterday. Today seagulls cry directly overhead, resting on various tent poles. The camp was full last night when we drove in late---something we will never do again on a Saturday! so we found a rather makeshift spot down the road, and drove in at 9 to find lots of empty space, and maneuvered for what I feel like the best view among the 100 or so odd sites. It is really pouring now, and I am warm in my navy sweater & Ted's khaki jacket. I feel sorry for those people who are just trying to set up camp now. I had ample time to air out all our bedding and towels. We are as happy as we have ever been. We drive alternating 2 hour stretches at the beginning of

1–Alan Pryce-Jones to SP, 6 July 1959; held by Smith College. Sylvia Plath, 'Two Views of a Cadaver Room' and 'The Hermit at Outermost House', *Times Literary Supplement* (6 November 1959): 23, 29.

the day, and 1 hour stretches at the end, having tea, coffee, and snacks to break the intervals, and this is marvelously reviving. So far we have had three long drives: the one to Whetstone Gulf, New York (between Boonville and Lowville), then to Rock Lake, Algonquin Park, Canada, and then from there to Brimley, Michigan. We have roughly outlined a trip now from here to Iron River, Abercrombie (south of Fargo), and the Theodore Roosevelt Park to Yellowstone, all involving long drives, then to Salt Lake City with a stop between there and San Francisco. We plan to drive long laps, and then rest for a few whole days, wash, write, boat, fish, sun, swim and see sights, every 5 or 7 days or so. This is much better than driving 6 hours every day (and camping sites don't come up so often) and having only two hours everywhere. Yesterday we left our campsite in Canada at 8, having a lovely breakfast there, went on a 2-mile nature hike in the park, fed the deer, and really started driving about 10. We went through unbelievable stretches of country, unpeopled, green, with lakes and rivers everywhere. I am amazed at the terrible shoddiness of Canadian towns. They are literally <u>all</u> gas stations---a straight, flat pitted road down the center, with 10 to twenty gas stations, tar-paper shacks (I saw no real <u>houses</u> except in North Bay and Sault Ste. Marie, and those were ugly, if solid) and an amazing number of trailer camps. Ted and I counted 100 big aluminum trailers on the road in less than an hour. The only virtue of the place seems the country: the amazing three-dimensional skies with masses of sculptured cloud stretching away on all sides, mountains of conifers, fields of cows. And at every turn vistas of forest and water. The roads in a few places were under repair and a bit rough: the repaired ones were good: narrow but smooth, and often very straight, telephone poles diminishing toward the horizon. We felt the country was being invented before our eyes: a thin ribbon of gas stations and trailer camps and shacks flung up hastily in an immense and uncivilizable wilderness. I have never seen such masses of untouched land. An interesting thing was that everybody we spoke to in Algonquin Park had thick European accents: Germans, Dutch, Chinese too, all becoming "New Canadians". The country certainly does need men to develop it. Off the main ribbon of road all roads were dirt! I would like to drive up into eastern Canada someday: Quebec and Montreal must have a kind of culture of their own. The peculiar mindlessness of the Canadian scene impressed me: no books, no theaters, no libraries to be seen.

We crossed with our car on the little ferry operating between the two Sault Ste. Maries, at sunset, a spectacular view, and crossed the timebelt. Luckily for us we gained an hour: now we are on Central Time.

What amazes me most is our perfect satisfaction with all our equipment: for people who never camped, and so extensively, we have everything we need right to hand: our labeled foodboxes are like drawers. We can stop by a roadside in midafternoon and have tea and biscuits and cheese in ten minutes on our excellent stove, a real jewel. We change ice every day & all keeps cool in our refrigerator. Our tent is sturdy, Ted puts it up in ten minutes, and the raindrops just roll off it. As I said, our mattresses are like great featherbeds, and our sleeping bags wonderfully warm and light. For some reason, every time we pack the car we have more room, and it is like a house on wheels. Both of us are in excellent health, eating well (we treated ourselves to a steak dinner on completion of our long trek to Sault Saint Marie at a dimly lit diner). Except for a few insect bites around the ankles and neck we got when blueberrying (which stop itching immediately when we apply Caladryl) we are unscathed by chiggers, snakes or vampires. My first aid kit has everything we need, all in my small grey traveling case. The wash 'n dris are a blessing enroute.[1] Hot tea, a devilled egg and a face wash at 11 am or 4 pm can make one feel altogether freshened up. And the people who come to these camps are very quiet, keep to themselves, so even though there are tents to be seen in every direction, one is perfectly private. And the small children go to bed at sundown, so it is peaceful early.

Now we shall arrive in Yellowstone on either the 17th (Friday) or the 18th (Saturday) and I am going to see if we can pick up mail there. Tentatively we shall leave Wednesday morning July 22 for California and should be at Aunt Frieda's (also tentatively) about Saturday July 25th, or a day or two later, as we plan to spend some time in California, seeing San Francisco, camping on the coast, visiting friends in Los Angeles overnight, and Disneyland, before we go on to the Grand Canyon.

It has stopped raining & the sun is shining, all fresh and cool. California looks so lovely, with so many parks, I hardly can choose between them. Maybe we'll stay there and send the car back on it's own!

Aunt Frieda's address[2] is the one you better send all our mail to, we'll arrive there on the 25th or 26th as I said. Our next address will probably be Sewanee, Tennesee. Sundays I'll call about 6 or 7 in the evening.

1–Wash 'n Dri is a brand of moist, antiseptic lightly scented towelette.

2–Frieda Plath Heinrichs (1897–1970). Otto Plath's sister. She and her husband Walter J. Heinrichs (1887–1967) lived at 4579 Loma Vista Drive, La Cañada Flintridge, California.

Do make a chart of all poems accepted, etc. & send a carbon of it to Frieda as far as you've got it done in about 10 days.

Much love to you & Warren,
and thanks so much for your
wonderful help in getting off on
our trip,
Sivvy

TO *Aurelia Schober Plath*

Tuesday 14 July 1959[1] ALS (postcard), Indiana University

Tuesday: July 14th

Dear mother . . .

It is 5:30 pm & I am sitting in bright sun on a hayfield hilltop before our newly pitched tent looking through the branches of birch & appletrees into the glittering blue waters of Lake Superior which stretch to the horizon like a great sea. We decided to be adventurous & try asking for a tentsite at a farmhouse & chose the most beautiful we have seen – just north of Cornucopia, Wis. We got up at 4:30 am & left Brimley by 5 driving through farms & woods. We saw, at 7:40 am our first BEAR! standing up right at the roadside before a wooded area, ears pointed alertly, big & black – no park bear! It made our day. A deer bounded out at us a little later. We have fallen in love with Wisconsin – it is so uncommercialized – unlike Michigan – all bluegreen woods & lovely farms – We have driven all day and not left Lake Superior! Cornucopia is on a peninsula just above Rte 2 at Iron River & we took it as a side route hoping to be lucky & find just such a place as this, by the lake. We had the car oil changed yesterday & a new muffler installed. Do send any gas credit cards that you may get to Aunt Frieda's. Could you send a carbon of our publishing acceptances & rejections (with titles of poems rejected to the Central Post Office, (To Be Held: on it) at Yellowstone to reach there by July 22? Three more laps to Yellowstone!

xx
Siv

1–Postmarked Cornucopia, Wisconsin, 15 July 1959.

TO *Aurelia Schober Plath & Warren Plath*

Thursday 16 July 1959[1] ALS (picture postcard), Indiana University

<Picture postcard caption: K-5 LOOKOUT POINT, DEVIL'S ISLAND IN THE APOSTLE ISLAND GROUP LAKE SUPERIOR.>

Thursday: July 16 – en route through North Dakota: Fargo to Bismarck

Dear mother & Warren

With regrets we left our friendly family[2] at dawn in Cornucopia. I had spent a morning drawing boats[3] in the lovely harbor: our tent (we camped free for 2 nights) overlooked a point like this. We spent the afternoon fishing with Marcia, the Nozals 12-year old daughter – the family – including dog, cat, & ducklings – sat out in the apple orchard talking in the moonlight – Mr. Nozal, a commercial fisherman, is a wonderful storyteller – We ate blueberries, wild strawberries, perch I caught for supper – saw two red foxes on the road today. N. Dakota is amazingly flat, straight & yellow-green.

xxx
Sivvy

TO *Aurelia Schober Plath*

Friday 17 July 1959[4] ALS (picture postcard), Indiana University

<Picture postcard caption: Theodore Roosevelt National Memorial Park.>

Friday: July 17: Medora, North Dakota –

We camped overnight in a grove of trees in a minute town just west of Jamestown, N. Dakota & rose at dawn to drive under spectacular skies – half blue & clear & half black lit by sheet lightening – through marvelous endless prairies, rich with cows & unpeopled to this beautiful spot – the

1–Postmarked Jamestown, North Dakota, 16 July 1959.

2–Andrew Nozal (1902–94), his wife Helen Folezyk Nozal (1913–92) and their two children Richard Rory (1937–2003) and Marcia Nozal Baker (*c.* 1947–).

3–See Sylvia Plath, *Drawings* (New York: Harper Collins, 2013), 56.

4–Postmarked Medora, North Dakota, 18 July 1959.

'Badlands' literally lept at us out of the prairies – we have a tent site in a grove of cottonwoods looking over the Little Missouri River at a scene much like this one – have seen two antelope & a prairie dog – shall search for buffalo this pm. In fine health & spirits

xx
Sivvy

TO *Aurelia Schober Plath*

Saturday 18 July 1959[1] — ALS (picture postcard), Indiana University

<Picture postcard caption: Deer graze peacefully in their natural habitat.>

Custer, Montana – Saturday, 7/18

Dear mother:

I am writing this from a 'café' in a tiny town just an hour or so short of Billings – they served us a magnificent T-bone steak dinner for $2.50 & the lightest flakiest homemade boysenberry pie I have ever imagined. After a few mistakes, we are learning how to enter a strange town, sniff out its best piemaker & get a free campsite – tonight's will be on the grounds of the Congregational Church – 'they haven't got it grassed yet,' our waitress says. Saw wild deer like this grazing at dawn this morning & an eagle at Roosevelt Park. Ted typed his essay under the cottonwoods & we drove through Montanas yellow wheat & black earth fields stretching in alternate ebony & gold bands to the purple mesas on the horizon. Tomorrow: Yellowstone!

xxx
Sivvy

1–Postmarked Custer, Montana, 19 July 1959.

TO *Aurelia Schober Plath*

Monday 20 July 1959[1] ALS (postcard), Indiana University

YELLOWSTONE PARK: July 20

Dear mother –

It was good to hear your voice yesterday – We were weary from our long 2-stage drive from the N. Dakota badlands up here – Montana being the most beautiful state yet, cool, dry, sunny, with gold wheat fields, alternating with black plowed earth fields, stretching literally in wide bands to the horizon of purple mesas. We ate steak & delicious homemade boysenberry pie in Custer & slept in the churchyard! Now we are camped in a tentsite on Yellowstone Lake – lucky as ever – moved in after a trailer-family that left early this am. Slept late – we look right across at snowcapped mountains. Off the road 300 yards is Wilderness. A herd of antelope crossed our path at the entrance. We counted 19 bears & cubs & saw two big moose. Almost caught a big pink trout in the river rapids last night. Just finished cooking a good breakfast – grapefruit & honey, bacon & eggs & fried potatoes & coffee – in our cool sunny pine grove. Neither of us have seen such wonderful country anywhere in the world. Flowers everywhere, & animals & snow – Will call Monday night the 27th

xx
S.

TO *Aurelia Schober Plath & Warren Plath*

Friday 24 July 1959[2] ALS (picture postcard), Indiana University

<Picture postcard caption:
BLACK BEAR YELLOWSTONE NATIONAL PARK.>

On the road: after Kemmerer, Wyoming
Friday July 24

Dear mother & Warren –

A bear this size woke us by smashing the locked rear window of the car to smithereens at 3 am Wednesday & spent the night within a few feet of

1–Postmarked Yellowstone Park, Wyoming, 20 July 1959, 5.30 p.m.

2–Postmarked Salt Lake City, Utah, 25 July 1959.

us knocking cans open, devouring cookies & oranges. There is no way to escape bears as against-the-rules feeding makes them bold & they live on the trash cans. We wet the window hole with kerosene the next 2 nights & were left at peace – having thought cars bearproof. Fished from a rowboat in Yellowstone Lake for 2 days & caught our limit (6) of big lake trout each time & are still eating them. Saw all the wonderful geysers – left Yellowstone at dawn & hope to reach Salt Lake City today

xx
Sivvy

This card has a real bear print on it!

TO *Joseph, Dorothy, Robert, & Nancy Benotti & Frank Schober*

Friday 24 July 1959[1]

ALS (picture postcard),
Indiana University

<Picture postcard caption: THE TETON RANGE IN GRAND TETON NATIONAL PARK LIES BETWEEN JACKSON HOLE, WYOMING, AND PIERRES HOLE IN IDAHO – BOTH NEARLY AS FAMOUS IN FRONTIER TIMES, AS THE STARK GRAND TETON MOUNTAIN, WHICH RISES TO AN ELEVATION OF 13,766 FEET.>

En route to Salt Lake City –
Friday July 24

Dear Dotty & Joe & Bobby & Nancy & Grampy

We drove along past this lovely mountain range at dawn today – leaving Yellowstone after 5 exciting days camping on Yellowstone Lake, seeing the geysers & boiling pools & fighting off bears – we saw moose, elk, & 67 bears. Our ice chest is crammed full of bright pink fillets of 1½-2 lb. lake trout we caught in 2 days from our rented rowboat – Just drove over the state line into Utah. Can't wait to see California –

Love –
Sivvy & Ted

1 – Postmarked Salt Lake City, Utah, 25 July 1959.

TO *Aurelia Schober Plath*

Saturday 25 July 1959[1] ALS (picture postcard),[2]
Indiana University

<Picture postcard caption: POND LILLIES,
ISA LAKE YELLOWSTONE PARK.>

Salt Lake City – July 25

Dear Mother –

Here we are having an oil change – please send the ms. from Knopf[3] (not the Yale ms.[4] as it is different) after checking page order etc. to:

Editor,
HARCOURT BRACE & CO
750 Third Avenue
New York 17, New York

With a stamped, Self-addressed brown envelope enclosed, no letter – both big manila envelopes marked EDUCATIONAL MATTER each with a 9 cent stamp which is the right rate. Tell me the date you send it.

Love,
Sivvy

TO *Aurelia Schober Plath*

Sunday 26 July 1959[5] ALS (picture postcard),
Indiana University

<Picture postcard caption: L.D.S. TABERNACLE
SALT LAKE CITY, UTAH.>

Sunday 6:30 pm – Lake Tahoe California
July 26

Drove through arid Nevada gladly today from a night sleeping under the shooting stars among Sagebrush & grazing bulls. Cooked our last

1 – Postmarked Sacramento, California, 27 July 1959.
2 – TH added a note at the bottom of the letter about arriving at and swimming in Great Salt Lake. This has not been transcribed.
3 – Sylvia Plath, 'The Devil of the Stairs: Poems'.
4 – Sylvia Plath, 'The Bull of Bendylaw and Other Poems', book of poems submitted to the Yale Younger Series of Poets in February 1959.
5 – Postmarked Sacramento, California, 27 July 1959.

Yellowstone trout for lunch in the shade of the one roadside tree in all Nevada. Salt Lake desert at sunset spectacular! Heard the free noon organ concert in this Mormon Tabernacle & had great fun swimming in Salt Lake. Passed thru' Reno without knowing it – thought it was Sparks – awfully ugly place. Nevada our least favorite state. Detoured to a Camp on Lake Tahoe – to 'Frisco tomorrow –

Love,
Sivvy

TO *Aurelia Schober Plath & Warren Plath*

Tuesday 28 July 1959 TLS, Indiana University

Tuesday, July 28, 1959

Dear mother & Warren:

It was so good to hear your voices last night. We were on a nonstop combination of highway and toll bridges about the time I had planned to call, so that's why we were late. We had come on from Yellowstone, leaving early Friday morning. After the Bear Incident, that Tuesday night, we moved to a site a little higher up the camp, on a rise in the open sun, at a place where there were no garbage cans within 20 yards or so. We had been at the edge of the wood between the camp and Yellowstone lake and right at one of the very frequent garbage cans. The attitude towards bears at Yellowstone is a strange one. There are danger warnings everywhere about feeding bears---this is strictly prohibited by the rangers. Over 100 people are wounded by bears every summer. Yet all along the roads, bears are being fed by hand, coaxed to approach little Jimmy and stand up and smile so daddy can get the snapshot of the year, and so on. They do indeed look harmless and Teddyish, mooching along. Only to those who have encountered bears without bothering the bears does the great furry animal look ominous. We had left bears alone when we came back late from a drive around the Grand Loop seeing the geysers and pools to see the large shadow of a black bear almost up to its waist in the garbage can by our tent area. Although the garbage cans are like ours at home---in the ground and with metal lids---the bears are expert lid-flippers and make several visits along the can-circuit each night. The bear lumbered off through the camp at our headlights, and we cooked supper and went peacefully to bed, taking care to lock all our food up in the car and the trunk of the car and wash down the table and benches. At the blue moonlit hour of quarter of three I was wakened from a dream where the car blew to pieces with a great rending crash by an exactly (or at least very) similar crash and falling jangle. My immediate thought was that a bear had with one cuff demolished the car and was eating the engine out. I woke Ted and we lay for a few moments listening to the unique sounds of a bear rooting through our belongings. Grunts, snuffles, clattering can lids. We thought he might have somehow broken off the trunk door and got into our tinned supplies, divining food by a seventh sense. Then there was a bumpity rolling noise as the bear bowled a tin past our tent and I sat up quaking to peer out the tent screen. There in the blue wierd light of the moon not ten feet away a huge dark bear-shape hunched, guzzling at a tin. I found in the morning that it was the black-and-gilt figured cookie tin we took the date-nut bars in: it had been in the back seat of the car in my red bag, shut, full of ritz crackers and Hydrox cookies, and some postcards. The bear must have lifted out the bag after smashing the window, rolled the can about till the lid came off, undone the wax paper and eaten every last crumb. I found the postcards the next day, lying among the rubble, the top card of moose antlers turned down and face-up the card of a large bear with an actual bear paw-print on it. We lay there for what seemed years, wondering if the bear would eat us since it found our crackers so interesting. Just as we were relaxing and felt the dawn starting to lighten, we heard a heavy shuffling tread.

The bear, back from its rounds, had returned to the car. Ted stood up to look out the back window---it was all I could do to keep him from going out before to check on the damage---and reported that the bear was at the back of the car, halfway in the left rear window. It had discovered our oranges. From then until sunup we lay listening to the bear squeeze the oranges open and slurp up the juice---it was interrupted only by a car which drove by and scared it to run toward the front door of our tent. It tripped on the guy ropes anchoring our porch and for a moment the whole tent shook so we thought it had decided to come in. Then there was a long silence. Then more orange-squeezing. We got up rather shaken. The car window had been shattered down to the root, and wiry brown bear hairs stuck all along the edge of it. Amazingly, the story got around camp. An old regular came up to advise us that bears hated kerosene and to smear all our window frames with that. Another said bears hated red pepper. Well, we felt we had the daylight hours to build a fortress against our enemy who would indubitably return. So we moved some sites up, which cheered us. Then we packed everything of value and all food in the trunk. We reported the accident to the ranger, who recorded it, so it's there if the insurance people need it, and he was very noncommittal. I mentioned the incident to a woman up early in the lavatory, and she seemed very disquieted by my report of the broken window. It turned out she had just moved from West Thumb, another camp, where a woman had been killed by a bear Sunday, the night we came. The woman, hearing the bear at her food at night, had gone out with a flashlight to shoo it away and it turned on her and downed her with one vicious cuff. Naturally the story was hushed up by the rangers, but this woman who had been "sleeping under the stars" with her husband, felt concerned; especially since a bear growled them into flight when they hesitated about sharing their breakfast with it. Well, this story put proper concern into us too. By twilight we had the car kerosened, flung red pepper everywhere, sprayed Fly-Ded all about, drank ovaltine and took a tranquilizer each---which I had been saving for the Donner Pass, and went to bed at 9 pm to the usual shouts: "There it is", "Up there, a bear!" That night everybody banged the bear away with pans, for they run at noise; our story had got around. We slept the sleep of the blessed and the bear did not touch our kerosene-soaked poncho sealing the broken window. The next night the population of the camp had changed with movings in and out, and there was the old casualness, people photographing the bear, etc. We stayed an extra day, Thursday, and fished from a rowboat, catching our limit of 6 fine trout in 5 hours, throwing all the little ones away that we would have been excited about in Canada. This rested us fine, and we left Yellowstone Friday, driving through the beautiful Teton range, stopping to take a few pictures. We drove through rolling prairies and open ranges, and at about 5 the scenery suddenly changed (this amazes us---the queer immediate way each state asserts its own individuality) and was green and fertile, and we were in Utah. We crossed the Wasatch range, coasted downhill 10 straight miles, and Salt Lake City lay under us like a dream, all one story, green-lawned little homes. Unluckily for our repair of the window we arrived on Pioneer Day, a holiday, when Brigham Young first entered the valley. So we took a long winding road up one of the canyons, Big Cottonwood Canyon, and camped at the last site left at "Spruces". By then it was dark. Making sure from the ranger there were no bears about, ("Just some thieves") we rearranged our car in order again after our emergency crowding of the trunk. A white kitten walked across to us, with orange and black splotches, as if it owned us. So we fed it milk and tuna, and it stayed with us until we left. Evidently someone had lost it there. We have got to be experts on camp facilities. Prefer places with a view, near water, out in the open, with good lavatories. This place was rather dank and had not been cleaned out over the holidays. Yellowstone, in our loop at Fishing Bridge Camp Ground, right on the lake, was most sumptuous: mirrors, flush toilets, and hot water: all washed out every day. We reveled in this, washed clothes, etc., and did a load at the laundromat. Hope to do the same in San Francisco.

We slept late after our long drive from Yellowstone, treated ourselves to the best Kentucky fried chicken, rolls & honey, potatoes and gravy, I have ever eaten. Then drove out to the Salt Lake, a great molten silver body of water 14 miles from city limits, with a blue horizon line. Although it was a Saturday, very few people were at the two beach "resorts"---piers perched close together with fresh water showers and beer and hotdog stands. We walked over the ill-smelling grey-crusted salt flats into the water which rolled in, but never crested to a whitecap. The water tasted fantastically salt, and stung badly if splashed in the eyes. We started to swim, and burst out laughing. Our feet flew into the air, our heads bobbed up. We lay on the water, half in, half out, and dozed. Sat up comfortably as in an armchair, holding our knees. Then we showered, had a cold beer---it was very hot. And started on. We drove into the sunset---saw it set twice---over the luminous white barrens of the Great Salt Lake desert. Lightning slashed out of the purple clouds to our left. The sun set behind a red grid of clouds at the right. We passed over the border of Nevada, ate a steak, drove on an hour to a stop called "Oasis", a collection of gas tanks and a Cafe in the middle of nowhere. We got permission from the gas station attendant to sleep out on the prairies in back of his place, and woke once to see bulls grazing within feet of us. Up at dawn and on through the hottest barrenest scenery yet. We drank lots of water, got ice everywhere we could. Stopped just short of Lovelock by the roadside in the one tree we saw by the road in all Nevada. I cooked the last big orange fillets of our Yellowstone trout and had them with corn niblets, a tomato and lettuce salad and milk. This renewed us, and we drove through the brown, desolate slot-machine country, meeting our first real traffic since NYork at Reno, which we didn't know was Reno till we'd come into California. Another immediate change. Rivers, green-conifered hills, lushness and grandeur. We camped near Lake Tahoe---much too resorty for us, but clear and blue and very lovely in the more residential parts. Drove easily over the equivalent of the Donner Pass which I thus cleverly avoided, and stopped in the lovely palm-tree shaded Capitol Park of Sacramento in heat of 114 degrees to make tomato, ham & lettuce sandwiches which we ate with relish in the dark green shade. Then the fertile valley of golden hills opened up: vineyards, orchards. We stopped at a "Giant

Orange"[1] for fresh-squeezed orange juice on cracked ice. Drove on over a network of bridges to San Francisco, all white buildings glittering like an alabaster island surrounded by blue water. We drove 24 miles straight on, hot and weary, to what was listed in our camp ground guide as the nearest campground, Stinson Beach State Park. The road wound along a cliff in hairpin turns into the sunset for most most of those miles, with spectacular views of the Pacific, and only cows in sight. It turned out when we arrived at the "camp" that the Guide was "out-of-date", and the place had been converted to a parking lot. I was almost in tears, but Ted cheered me up, and we decided to try our luck in town. We had cold beer and wonderful fried chicken again, and the Cafe owner suggested we park behind his place and sleep on the beach down from the houses. Which we did, under the stars, and it was just wonderful. We entered the Park when it opened at 8 and took a lovely picnic table in a secluded grove where we had bacon and eggs and toast, and heated pots of water to wash in. We plan to stay here till sunset, sleep on the beach again, and go to San Francisco first thing tomorrow, get the window repaired, and see as much as we can of the city.

Then a beach camp half way to Los Angeles, then Aunt Frieda and our friends the Steins,[2] and then Grand Canyon. We'll probably get the AAA[3] to shortcircuit our trip, avoiding Mexico and using those days around here.

When we come home we look most forward to hot tubs and home baking. The bread across america is awful. We're going to try bakeries in San Francisco. I just don't understand when meat etc. is so good why there can't be more solid good bread on the market.

Well, we are fine, and both of us tanned, and having the experience of our lives. We hope to try some deep-sea fishing if we can here.

Love to you both, and Sappho –
Sivvy & Ted[4]

1–Founded in 1926, Giant Orange was a juice stand business with sites along many of California's highways.

2–Joan and Roger Breed Stein. Roger Breed Stein (1932–2010); graduate student at Harvard University, A.B. 1954, A.M. 1958, Ph.D. 1960; married to Joan Workman Stein (divorced 1976). According to SP's address book, the Steins' address was care of Mrs Carl Weiner, 1401 Stone Canyon Road, Los Angeles. Carl Weiner (1906–85) and Ruth Weiner (1906–2009).

3–American Automobile Association, founded in 1902.

4–TH added a note at the bottom of the letter, which has not been transcribed. TH noted that he and SP made a $10 bet on the number of bears, she guessing 93, he 71. They saw 67 bears. The 55th was the one which broke into their car. He also expresses pride at SP's

TO *Aurelia Schober Plath*

Sunday 2 August 1959 TLS, Indiana University

S unday
August 2

Dear mother . . .

It was good to talk to you this morning. We had a lovely big breakfast here at the hotel and have moved to a cool quiet room with its own bath for $11 for tonight to renew ourselves for the trip back. Mail up to August 17th should be sent c/o Meyers, Bairnwick, Sewanee, Tennessee, where Luke's mother[1] (about 11 children in that family---ballet dancers, writers, etc) has written to extend us a warm welcome: we also shall probably meet the editor[2] of the Sewanee review there, who has published poems by both of us. So we shall enjoy having them introduce us to the South.

PLEASE don't worry about my poetry book but send it off. I know about summer editors, but want to send it to as many places as I can. I also have gone over it very carefully and am not going to try to change it to fit some vague abstract criticism. If an editor wants to accept it and make a few changes then, all right. You need to develop a little of our callousness and brazenness to be a proper sender-out of mss. I have a good list of publishers and haven't begun to eat into it. The biggest places are often best because they can afford to publish a few new people each year.

Here are our checks. All to be sent by mail to the Boston 5 cent savings bank, with the deposit slip & bankbook & our 26 Elmwood address: Except Roland's check, to be deposited in our Wellesley Savings account. Ask for interest to be recorded, too, in both places (no, the Boston one doesn't come due till fall).

1-23	
210	$15
1-1	
210	200
5-20	
110	10.50

---

luck when fishing, his amaze at sleeping on the Pacific beach, and admits this was the best experience of his life.

1–Margaret Myers (1889–1970).

2–SP and TH met Monroe Spears and his wife Betty Greene Spears (1917–2009); see Monroe Spears to SP, 25 August 1959; copy held by Sewanee: The University of the South. In this letter he accepts SP's story 'The Fifteen Dollar Eagle'.

5-20
110 10.
1-8
210 13.75
85-465
614 44.
$293.25

To Boston Bank

Do save the Monitor clippings of my poems as they come out.[1]

Aunt Frieda had a wonderful cold chicken lunch, string beans, potato salad, tomato and lettuce salad, hot rolls, fresh pineapple, coffee cake and tea ready for us yesterday when we came. Both she and Uncle Walter are handsome, fun, and so young in spirit. They have a little green eden of a house, surrounded by pink and red and white oleander bushes, with two avocado trees loaded down with (alas) not yet ripe fruit, a peach tree, a guava tree, a persimmon tree, a fig tree and others.

Aunt Frieda has had some wonderful adventures, and is a great story teller. Ted gets on magnificently with Walter. We simply love them both. It is amazing how Frieda resembles daddy---the same clear piercing intelligent bright eyes and face shape. Ted & I plan to be home about the 28th or maybe even before, if we have no setbacks.

Love to you, Warren, and Sappho,
Sivvy

enc
The $18.07 bill for the window & 7 checks, all signed

Record of bear damage on file at Yellowstone (Fishing Bridge was our camp) – company can write them for it.

1–Sylvia Plath, 'Midsummer Mobile', *Christian Science Monitor* (1 July 1959): 8; 'Fiesta Melons', *Christian Science Monitor* (13 July 1959): 8; 'Song For a Summer's Day', *Christian Science Monitor* (18 August 1959): 8; and 'Southern Sunrise', *Christian Science Monitor* (26 August 1959): 8.

TO *Aurelia Schober Plath & Warren Plath*

Monday 3 August 1959[1] ALS (picture postcard), Indiana University

<Picture postcard caption: CABLE CAR TURNTABLE.>

August 3 – Monday – Leaving California

Dear mother & Warren –

We're driving in the cool of the afternoon out of Pasadena – more rested than ever yet from our luxurious 2 nights at a Pasadena Hotel – just wept to leave Aunt Frieda & Uncle Walter who are both so handsome – young-spirited. We love them both dearly. Frieda looks like a feminine version of Daddy. Tomorrow dawn – early – we'll cross the desert to Grand Canyon – then through Alberquerque & Dallas to New Orleans. Had car tuned up, lubricated, & 3rd oil change & it's running like velvet. Chevy man said it had been well cared for & in fine shape. Hope to be at Tennessee address by Aug. 15th –

xxx
Sivvy

TO *Edith & William Hughes*

Monday 3 August 1959[2] ALS (picture postcard), Family owned

<Picture postcard caption: Lombard Street, San Francisco, between Leavenworth and Hyde, popularly known as 'The Crookedest Street in the World'.>

August 3 – Monday

Dear Ted's mother & dad –

We're just leaving Los Angeles & had a wonderful stay with my Aunt Frieda & Uncle Walter (Frieda is my father's sister – I'd never seen any Plath relatives before her) eating lots of strange fruits – they have their own avocado, peach, guava & persimmon trees. We loved San Francisco – a beautiful pastel-colored city on 7 hills surrounded by blue Pacific. We rode the old-fashioned cable cars up the very steep hills, explored the

1–Postmarked Needles, California, 4 August 1959.
2–Postmarked Needles, California, 4 August 1959.

biggest Chinatown outside the Orient & ate at the fish pier – watched them unload huge salmon from the sailboats – On our way to the grand Canyon – Ted looks the best I've ever seen him!

Lots of love –
SYLVIA

TO *Aurelia Schober Plath & Warren Plath*

Thursday 6 August 1959[1] ALS (picture postcard), Indiana University

<Picture postcard caption: O. B. Chambers – Essex, California – Highway 66.>

Thursday – August 6 – en route thru Arizona

Greetings! I'm wearing with pleasure the trim, cool shorts & blouse you sent & Ted loves his shirt. This card commemorates the place just short of Needles where we sweltered among hordes of huge rubber-eating crickets. Ted has patched up all their holes, however. Grand Canyon was amazing – but we didn't work up energy enough to hike down & up. We're on our way to El Paso via Phoenix & Tuscon. Plan to park car there & walk across border for a visit of a few hours to Juarez – an easy & safe way of "seeing Mexico." Then on to New Orleans via the Carlsbad Caverns –

xxx
Sivvy

1 – Postmarked El Paso, Texas, 8 August 1959.

TO *Aurelia Schober Plath & Warren Plath*

Saturday 8 August 1959[1] ALS (picture postcard), Indiana University

<Picture postcard caption: Old Faithful Geyser, Yellowstone Park, Showing the great columns of water that rise well over one hundred feet in height during the hourly eruptions.>

August 8 – Saturday
en route to Carlsbad Caverns

We left El Paso after a morning exploring the tourist-trap streets of Juarez – bought nothing but two cold beers & left with no reluctance. Hope to arrive at Carlsbad in time to see the millions of bats leave their cave at dusk. Saw a wolf at the roadside in an Arizona wood. Have succumbed on occasion to $5 a night motels – after our tent blew in where we had camped among gigantic cactus outside Tuscon in a hot wind & electrical storm for example. We're in the best of health, & so is the car

xxx
SIVVY & TED

Should be home by Friday, August 21 (!) if we keep to present schedule

xxx
Sivvy

TO *Aurelia Schober Plath & Warren Plath*

Sunday 9 August 1959[2] ALS (picture postcard), Indiana University

<Picture postcard caption: King's Palace
Carlsbad Caverns National Park New Mexico.>

Sun. Aug. 9 – en route through Texas

Dear mother & Warren –

Ted & I had a fine afternoon in the cavern's yesterday – managed to see half of them in the afternoon & sat among the cactus gardens to watch the millions of bats pour out of Bat Cave at dusk – lucky timing – for it started to pour after they all were out & they all dove back in again –

1 – Postmarked Terrell, Texas, 11 August 1959.
2 – Postmarked Terrell, Texas, 11 August 1959.

a sight not usually seen till 4 am. Cooked steak, new potatoes & corn-niblets for supper. On our way through huge Texas to New Orleans

xxx
Sivvy & Ted[1]

TO *Elizabeth Ames*

Monday 24 August 1959 TLS, New York Public Library

26 Elmwood Road
Wellesley, Massachusetts
August 24, 1959

Mrs. Elizabeth Ames
Executive Director
Yaddo
Saratoga Springs
New York

Dear Mrs. Ames:

Thank you so much for your letter.[2] Ted and I have just returned home from a trip, or we would have answered you sooner.

At present, my brother plans to drive us to Yaddo, so we should arrive shortly after 1 the afternoon of September 9th. We will let you know if there is any change in these plans.

If it becomes possible to arrange an extension for us we should be able to stay on until at least Thanksgiving, and perhaps into December.

Our home address, by the way, is now the Wellesley address above.

We both look forward to meeting you this fall.

Sincerely,
Sylvia Plath

1–TH sent a postcard of Brulatour Courtyard in the French Quarter, New Orleans, to ASP from Sewanee, Tennessee. ASP annotated the postcard '1959, Aug. 14'. See *Letters of Ted Hughes*: 152.

2–Elizabeth Ames to SP and TH, 12 August 1959; held by New York Public Library.

TO *John Lehmann*

Tuesday 1 September 1959 TLS, University of Texas at Austin

26 Elmwood Road
Wellesley, Massachusetts
USA
September 1, 1959

Mr. John Lehmann
Editor
THE LONDON MAGAZINE
22 Charing Cross Road
London W.C.2, England

Dear Mr. Lehmann,

I am sending along to you a selection of stories---"The Wishing Box", "The Shadow" and "This Earth Our Hospital"---in hopes that you may find something among them which pleases you.

With all good wishes, I am
Sincerely yours,
Sylvia Plath

TO *Elizabeth Ames*

Saturday 5 September 1959 TLS, New York Public Library

26 Elmwood Road
Wellesley, Mass.
September 5, 1959

Mrs. Elizabeth Ames
Yaddo
Saratoga Springs
New York

Dear Mrs. Ames:

My husband and I will be unable to come to Yaddo by car as we had hoped. As our plans stand now, we shall take a Peter Pan (Trailways) bus from Boston in the morning of the 9th, to Albany, make a bus connection there to Saratoga Springs and arrive about 5 pm. We'll have dinner in town and arrive at Yaddo between 7:30 and 8 that evening.

With all good wishes,
Sincerely,
Sylvia Plath

TO *Aurelia Schober Plath & Warren Plath*

Thursday 10 September 1959 TLS, Indiana University

<Typed on pink Smith College Memorandum paper with heading>

Date September 10 To Warren & Mother From Me
In re Our arrival:

It is a beautiful clouded and cool morning, 9:30 to be exact. I am sitting in my "studio" on the third (top) floor of West House (where, on the first floor, we have our large bedroom, bathroom and closet, the combination about twice as big as our Boston apartment). The house is lovely, all nooks and angles, with several studios in it. The libraries and living rooms and music rooms are like those in a castle, all old plush, curios, leather bindings, oil paintings on the walls, dark woodwork, carvings on all the furniture. Very quiet and sumptuous. I am the only person on the top floor, and my study is low-ceilinged, painted white, with a cot, a rug, a huge heavy dark-wood table that I use as a typing and writing table with piles of room for papers and books. It has a skylight and four windows on the east side that open out onto a little porch looking over gables and into tall dense green pines. The only sound is the birds, and, at night, the distant dreamlike calling of the announcer at the Saratoga racetrack. I have never in my life felt so peaceful and as if I can read and think and write for about 7 hours a day.

Ted has a marvelous studio[1] out in the woods, a regular little house to himself, all glassed in and surrounded by pines, with a wood stove for the winter, a cot, and huge desk. I am so happy we can work apart, for that is what we've really needed. The food so far seems to be very good. Two cups of fine coffee for breakfast, a coffee roll, eggs done to order, toast, jam, orange juice, and a great dining room---we can eat any time from 8-9. Then we pick up box lunches, two little thermoses with milk and coffee, for lunch, so we won't be interrupted all day, and go off to work.

1 – TH's studio was called Outlook.

Usually in the summer there are about 30 people here, but now there are only about 10 or 12,[1] mostly artists and composers (who seem very nice) and a couple of poets[2] we have never heard of. A magazine room has all the reviews we like, and the British magazines. There seem to be lakes full of bass, a famous rose garden, and long wood-walks, all of which we look forward to exploring.

The trip yesterday was really gruelling. There was a two-hour wait at Springfield. In Albany there was no bus running at the hour we were told it would in Boston, the station was not air-conditioned, and full of flies and tropically hot, and the Montreal bus we were to take at 4:30 only allowed passengers from New York to board, so we were put on a non-airconditioned bus and dawdled through Albany in rush hour to Saratoga Springs where we sweltered for an hour and a half waiting until we could go to Yaddo at 7:30. Once there, we were shown about the grounds and the mansion, which will close at the end of the month, but which is a magnificent castlelike affair, red carpets, fountains, plants, gilding, heavy antiques and so on.

My typewriter is marvelous. I love it. Do forward all our mail immediately to us c/o Yaddo, Saratoga Springs, New York. We should have all sorts of things arriving---bank books, passports and so on.[3]

One thing: I would like some information about Austria, especially the Tyrol, for something I'm working on,[4] and would love it if you'd write me a descriptive letter about those places you visited: materials of the houses, furnishings, how old fashioned are they? sort of stove, any animals? colors and sorts of scenery, occupations, how children help with chores---little colored details like that---the clothes they wear and so on.

Do write us.

1–According to Yaddo's records, the guests at the time SP and TH were there included writer Charles G. Bell (1916–2010); composer Gordon Binkerd (1916–2003); composer Chou Wen-chung (1923–); painter Robert Fremont Conover (1920–98); painter Worden Day (1916–86); painter Arthur Deshaies (1920–2011); sculptor Lu Duble (1896–1970); painter Martin Janto (1918–93); painter Dwight Kirsch (1899–1981); writer Perrin Lowrey (1923–65); writer Sonia Raiziss (1906–94); painter Howard Sand Rogovin (1927–); painter Hyde Solomon (1911–82); writer May Swenson (1913–89); and composer Lester Trimble (1923–86).

2–Charles G. Bell and Sonia Raiziss.

3–SP's passport, issued in Boston on 8 September 1959, held by Emory University.

4–Sylvia Plath, 'The It-Doesn't-Matter Suit'. SP sent 'The It-Doesn't-Matter Suit' to Knopf on 18 September 1959; it was rejected by 4 October. The story was identified in the Plath collection at the Lilly Library *c.* 1995 and published by Faber (UK) and St Martin's Press (US) in 1996.

Love,
Sivvy

PS: In our room, you will find a large open cardboard box by my desk and the little window, on the floor. In it is a black covered thesis book which holds my poems. In either end of this, loose, there should be a copy of a poem about Boston called "A Winter's Tale" beginning "On Boston Common a red star".[1]

Could you please send it along?

xxx
s

TO *Aurelia Schober Plath & Warren Plath*

c. Friday 18 September 1959[2]   TLS, Indiana University

<Typed on pink Smith College Memorandum paper with heading>

Date Sept. 9 Friday, To Mother & Warren From Sivvy & Ted
In re odds and ends.

Dear Mother & Warren,

We're delighted you found the film. I felt quiet sad to think the parts of our trip we did want to remember---mostly animals and fish in various combination with ourselves---might be lost for good. I wonder if it would be too much for me to ask you to send along my overshoes (grammy's really---my pair has rips at the heel of each) as it is often very wet here, and that is the one thing I didn't have room for in my suitcase. Ted will buy some new ones here, as he needs them.

I am sitting up in my third floor study, with the rain falling with a pleasant tattoo on the rooftops I overlook, and on my skylight. We are excellently fed here. For breakfast, orange juice (canned), eggs to order, comb-honey, jam, toast, coffee rolls, excellent coffee, bacon on Sundays. Lunches get a bit tedious, as all sandwich lunches do (except our homemade sandwiches), but there are two sandwiches, one meat, one cheese of a sort, cookies or cake, fruit and two thermoses. Dinners are of a magnificent grandeur. Roast beef, broiled chicken, ham and sweet potatoes, roast lamb, and lots of vegetables from the estate garden, a mammoth salad---cucumbers, tomatoes, fine dressings---delicious breads,

1–See SP to Rachel MacKenzie, 20 September 1959.
2–Letter misdated by SP.

cornbread, biscuits, garlic bread etc.---and peach cobbler or chocolate souffle or something marvelous for dessert. And until the mansion closes we are eating there, all carved, heavy woods, diamond-paned windows overlooking green gardens and marble statuary, golden, deep rugs and antique velvet cushions, heavily gilt-framed paintings, statues everywhere. I love the elegance and peace of the whole mansion & shall miss it when it is shut.

Ted read some of his poems last night, and a departing novelist[1] read some chapters of a novel in progress---in our West House living room, which has an elegance of its own. All twelve Guests and the two hostesses[2] were there, and the reading went off very well. They invited us to stay till December 15th, but we think we should come home the day before Thanksgiving, so we'll have good time to be with you and to pack.

I wonder if our bankbook from the 5¢ Savings Bank has come yet? We had left it there with a British check that needed a few days to be collected, and really would like it, because we have over $70 floating around in odd checks to be deposited. By all means leave the passport there. I'm glad the ChScience check came---they should have their billing department notified of changes of address.

Please take it easy with teaching and have the doctor give you something so you can sleep.

Love to you, Warren & Sappho,
Sivvy

1–Probably Charles G. Bell, who departed on 18 September 1959.

2–Probably Elizabeth Ames and American poet Pauline Hanson (1910–2008); resident secretary of Yaddo, 1950–75; acting director, autumn 1959.

TO *Rachel MacKenzie*[1]

Sunday 20 September 1959 TLS, New York Public Library

Yaddo
Saratoga Springs
New York
September 20, 1959

Miss Rachel Mackenzie
THE NEW YORKER
25 West 43rd Street
New York 36, New York

Dear Miss Mackenzie,

Howard Moss suggested[2] that I revise a line in A WINTER'S TALE and resubmit it this fall. I have changed the line (stanza 3, line 3)[3] and am sending you the poem along with two others.[4]

Sincerely yours,
Sylvia Plath

TO *Aurelia Schober Plath*

Wednesday 23 September 1959 TLS with envelope, Indiana University

Yaddo
Saratoga Springs
New York
September 23, 1959

Dear mother,

Many thanks for your letter and for forwarding our mail, which has been arriving with pleasant frequency. We haven't got our Boston 5¢ Savings Bank Book yet and are concerned about it; has it come yet? If not, do send it on right away when it does.

Where are you taking your German review course? In Wellesley or Boston?

1–American writer and editor Rachel MacKenzie (1909–80).
2–Howard Moss to SP, 9 June 1959; held by New York Public Library.
3–The original line, stanza 3, line 3, read: 'Hair blonde as Marilyn's—', and was revised by SP to 'Haloes lustrous as Sirius—'. No draft of the original poem appears extant; however, Moss quotes the line in his letter of 9 June 1959 to SP, cited above.
4–Sylvia Plath, 'Magnolia Shoals' and 'Yaddo: The Grand Manor'; both poems rejected.

I haven't got the sponsor invitation yet.[1] Both Ted and I feel very strongly about this: we are in no position to be sponsors, to pay $20 for an event we won't even be able to hear, and we don't want our names on the list. Ted's relation to Eliot is poet-to-poet and publisher-to-author, and there would be nothing "politic" about paying to have our names on a list of sponsors. I don't remember any Mrs. Dunn,[2] and think there must be other people eager for the honor of sponsoring culture who have fat Wellesley purses and more desire to set themselves up as patrons. We can't even keep our membership in the Poetry Society,[3] a total of $15 a year, which is just too much for our budget. Both of us hope to meet Eliot in private in England, and appreciate your offer to reimburse us, but we just don't want to work that way. So if you want to sponsor him yourself, do, but leave us out of it. I don't feel it much of an honor to be asked for $20 in return for use of our names. It is ridiculous and pompous for us, who need to save everything we can, to set ourselves up in any such position, and anyone with sense should realize this. Well, enough of that. Eliot probably doesn't give a damn who is on the list: he is a fool if he does.

I have written a note to Marcia, and shall write to Mrs. Prouty, too. I read some of my poems here the other night, with a professor from the University of Chicago[4] who read from a novel-in-progress. Several people are leaving today, among them a very fine young Chinese composer we are very fond of, on his second Guggenheim this year. Women come here, I learned, who have families. They leave their children in camp or with relatives: a great rest for them. We get on well with the director and her secretary, and she wrote a little note that she hopes we come again before long for an even longer stay (they had invited us to stay till the 15th of December). So it is pleasant indeed to feel that this place will always be open to us. I imagine the MacDowell Colony will, too, since they sent us their application blanks, but this is obviously the finest of the three such institutions in America.[5] I particularly love the scenic beauty of the estate: the rose gardens, goldfish pools, marble statuary everywhere, wood walks, little lakes. Ted & I took out the estate rowboat in a very weedy little lake

1–Probably regarding T. S. Eliot's reading at the Boston University Theater, 29 October 1959. The event was sponsored by the Boston University Women's Guild.

2–Possibly Mary A. Dunn, president of the Boston University Women's Guild, 1961–3.

3–SP's Poetry Society of America membership card for 1959–60 appeared at auction via Bonhams on 21 March 2018.

4–Perrin Lowrey, who departed on 29 September 1959.

5–In addition to Yaddo and the MacDowell Colony, SP may have been referring to the Huntington Hartford Colony in Los Angeles, California. However, there were many additional artists' retreat colonies in the USA to which SP may be referring.

and caught a bass apiece Sunday, about3/4 of a pound each: not really too big, but enough for a lunch. Yet we threw them back. The food here is so fine we had no real need of fish to eat.

We had severe cold here, with frosts, but now it is warm enough to walk coatless again. We miss Sappho. We feed some of our milk to a white-pawed tiger cat here that jumped out at us from the woods, but no cat can compare to Sappho's delicacy and breeding.

Wish you might drive up here sometime to spend an afternoon with us.

With love to you and Warren,

Sivvy

TO *Aurelia Schober Plath & Warren Plath*

Wednesday 7 October 1959 TLS, Indiana University

<Typed on pink Smith College Memorandum paper with heading>

Date October 7 To Mother & Warren From Sivvy In re

Thanks for your good letter. What is Andrew Sinclair[1] doing in America, studying or writing? Is Clem going to get married soon to his girl,[2] and has she found a job? How nice that Shirley's[3] baby looks like Perry[4]--- I thought the first one looked too much like David.[5]

We really don't have any news---our life here is so secluded. We simply eat breakfast, go to our respective studios with a picnic lunch and write, read and study, then have tea, chat a bit, have dinner and read before bed. Once in a while we go into town, which is reminiscent of Northampton, as the girls' college Skidmore (a very dull looking place) is here. And the architecture is similar: that marvelously ugly red-brick and yellow-brick 1875 style.

Ted has finished his play[6]---a symbolic drama based on the Euripides play The Bacchae, only set in a modern industrial community under a

1–British novelist, historian and critic Andrew Sinclair (1935–).

2–Susan Marie Alliston (1937–69); married to Clement Henry Moore on 19 December 1959, at the Memorial Chapel, Harvard University. Warren Plath acted as usher. Alliston later dated TH.

3–Shirley Baldwin Norton (1931–95); married to SP's friend Perry Norton on 19 June 1954 (divorced 1978); mother of John Christopher, Steven Arthur, Heidi, and David Allan.

4–Charles Perry Norton (1932–), B.S. 1954, Yale College; M.D. 1957, Boston University School of Medicine; SP's friend from Wellesley. SP dated Perry Norton in high school and later dated his older brother Richard Norton.

5–David William Norton (1944–); youngest brother of Richard Norton.

6–Ted Hughes, *The House of Taurus*.

paternalistic ruler. I hope the Poets Theater will give it at least a reading. We have yet to type it.

I do rather miss Boston, and don't think I could ever settle for living far from a big city full of museums and theaters. Now Mrs. Ames, the elderly Mother of Yaddo, has left for Europe, there are only her poetess secretary Polly,[1] a very nice woman, two painters and a composer on a Guggenheim here. From what we hear, certain artists live on these colonies almost all year: spending four months in the winter at Yaddo, then moving on to the MacDowell colony. I could never do that myself: too much like living in a vacuum. But it is nice to know that practically any time we could invite ourselves back here. It might come in convenient some day. Ted loves it and is getting a lot of work done.

Do keep us posted on all the little neighborhood news and so on.

The bankbook, by the way, should arrive at home in about three weeks. I am glad I wrote the manager a letter: they had not sent the check to the British Revenue Service for collection yet! "A change in personnel" or some such. Got a nice letter from Mrs. Prouty in answer to mine, and look forward to a dinner with her sometime between Thanksgiving and our departure.

Lots of love to you both,
Sivvy

PS: congratulations to Warren on the reading of his paper. Where will the meeting be? Too bad it's not in California: then he could see Aunt Frieda.

TO *Edith & William Hughes*

c. Thursday 8 October 1959[2] ALS,[3] British Library

Greetings! I am spending a pleasant evening reading in our large white bedroom – everything's white-walls, beds, couches, lampshades, bureauscarves. It is like living in a great countryhouse, a fine library, fine grounds, fine cooking. Ted's getting a great amount of work done – I am deeply impressed by his play: I hope some Art Theaters will take it up – it should be exciting experimental drama. His proofs for the "Rain Horse" story[4] have come – a real masterpiece, not a word that could be altered, with a wonderful sense of the physical countryside – better

1 – Pauline Hanson.

2 – Date supplied from internal evidence.

3 – SP's letter is at the end of a letter begun by TH, which has not been transcribed.

4 – Ted Hughes, 'The Rain Horse', *Harper's* 220 (January 1960): 76–80.

than DH Lawrence's descriptive stories, I think. It's tentatively scheduled for December. Ted had his usual luck with his first prose piece – got into one of the best magazines. We went rowing on the mirror-clear lake this afternoon, all the gold leaves & white birches reflecting in the black surface. Ted caught two little bass which we threw back. I've been working on some short stories, have sold a few poems & drawings to the Christian Science Monitor,[1] which is handy money, and a longish "light" poem on Christmas in Boston to the New Yorker which pays very well. In two months, we'll be with you! Seems hardly possible –

Love,
Sylvia

TO *Aurelia Schober Plath & Warren Plath*

Tuesday 13 October 1959 — TLS with envelope, Indiana University

<Typed on pink Smith College Memorandum paper with heading>

Date Oct. 13 To Mummy & Warren From Sivvy In re

Greetings!

As usual our main news is that we are wellfed. Every dinner seems bound to outdo the last. Last night it was juicy ham, pineapple (baked), sweet potatoes, corn, spinach, salad, hot rolls, butter, and deep dish apple pie. That's just a sampling. After a week of solid steamy rain, we are at last having crisp, clear weather--the Green Mountains blue in the distance, the newly-fallen pine needles a resilient carpet underfoot.

TED's proofs for his Harper's story have come---very exciting, and it reads marvelously. It will have black-and-white drawings with it, I gather. Tentatively, it is scheduled for the December issue. We are very proud of

1–While at Yaddo, Plath sold two articles with drawings and four poems: 'Mosaics – An Afternoon of Discovery', *Christian Science Monitor* (12 October 1959): 15, with two drawings captioned: 'White plaster tenements on a cliff overlooking the fishing harbor at Benidorm, Spain' and 'A Spanish kitchen range with a petrol stove, oil bottles, milk can, and a stewpot'; 'Explorations Lead to Interesting Discoveries', *Christian Science Monitor* (19 October 1959): 17, with two drawings captioned: 'A colorful pattern of rounds and oblongs, knobs and wheels, legs and handles' and 'Each object has a line, a tint, a character of its own – the older and odder the better'; 'Yaddo: The Grand Manor', *Christian Science Monitor* (21 October 1959): 8; 'Magnolia Shoals', *Christian Science Monitor* (26 October 1959): 8; 'Dark Wood, Dark Water', *Christian Science Monitor* (17 December 1959): 12; and 'Memoirs of a Spinach-Picker', *Christian Science Monitor* (29 December 1959): 8.

it. It is a fine story. I hope I can hypnotize him to finish up one or two others.

The New Yorker at last bought the poem you sent me A WINTER'S TALE for their December 26th issue,[1] which is pleasant. There is a lot more competition for special seasonal occasions like that, and I wrote the poem as a light piece after that pleasant walk you and Warren and Ted and I took last Christmas time around Beacon Hill.

I also have had two little exercise poems accepted by the home forum page in the CSMonitor as well as two sets of two drawings (old ones) due to come out on the Family Features Page (they may have come out already) so keep on the lookout for them & clip them for me. A total of $46 from the paper this month: little things mount up.

Am very painstakingly studying German two hours a day: a few grammar lessons then translating a Goethe lyric or a page or two from the Kafka stories Warren brought me from Germany: listing all vocabulary and learning it. Hope to speed up after a few weeks at it.

Do write,
much love,
S.

TO *Aurelia Schober Plath*

Wednesday 21 October 1959 TLS, Indiana University

Wednesday morning, Oct. 21

Dear mother,

How nice to get your long newsy letters! I am so pleased to hear you sounding so well and happy. Just be careful and try to avoid colds this season. It is beautiful here now: very blue and frosty, all the pine cones fallen, and the new needles fresh and rosy underfoot. Ted & I are both in excellent health: I don't know when we've been so rested, getting about 9 hours a night.

Have you seen my two sets of drawings on the Youth Page of the Monitor these last Mondays---the 12th and the 19th? Do save them, because I would like copies of the drawings which came out well. The paragraphs were only written to glue them together and give them more likelihood of being printed. Have either my Yaddo or Magnolia Shoals poem come out on the Home Forum Page yet?

1–Rachel MacKenzie to SP, 6 October 1959; held by New York Public Library.

I envy you your German lessons. I am very proud you are taking them. I find going so slow when I do it all myself, and then do not have the stimulus of having to be catechized. I look forward to studying the records again when I am home. I can't speak at all, I am just trying to translate what I read. The records should help speaking. The box from Aunt Frieda was guavas. Weird. Evidently the California fires[1] are raging right behind her house.

I do hope Warren's rooming problem works out. It would be inconvenient for him to live at home all the time, but couldn't he come on weekends, since that's when the owners carouse? The people sound very unpleasant.

How is Sappho? I hope she gets over her wounds. Was it a squirrel that tore her mouth? Is she staying as small as ever?

Love,
Sivvy

TO *Aurelia Schober Plath*

Wednesday 28 October 1959 TLS, Indiana University

October 28: Wednesday

Dear mother,

It was so good to hear your voice yesterday. I loved the gaily decorated birthday telegram. It's so nice you have those few days around Thanksgiving off, it will be fun shopping and chatting together. I want Ted to feel he can work in Warren's room while I do most of the minutiae about packing.

No package yet! The notice for a package which I thought might be mine turned out to be an ms. for Ted from his friend Luke. Could you tell me what day and from where you sent the package, (was it to Mrs. Ted Hughes, or Sylvia Hughes?) or perhaps put a tracer on it? Was it registered? I am dying to see it & furious with the American mails.

How did the Gulf Oil bill-slips add up? I hope you could find the envelope.

I'd love to have your advice about something. We have the remainder of our ship-fare, $312, to pay, and I want to get the money from our Wellesley Savings Bank. Now I know I don't have a checking account there, but could I have them make out a withdrawal check from our acct.

1–A wildfire began on 13 October 1959, in the foothills north of Los Angeles including Altadena, Pasadena, and La Cañada.

to the United States Lines[1] for that amount, and endorse it? If so, could you send me my Wellesley bankbook and a withdrawal slip (which should also be in the letter file on my desk, if I remember rightly) so I could transact the withdrawal by mail? Don't they have postpaid envelopes, too, by which I could do this? I didn't think to bring that bankbook with me.

Today is a beautiful clear invigorating day after a week of steaminess and oppressive rain. Ted & I are so happy, and healthy---our life together seems to be the whole foundation of my being. Your birthday card & letter was wonderful. I do love to hear from Warren & treasure his rare letters. All this hard work now will give him an immense advantage in his professional life. I am so proud of that paper he has been asked to prepare.

I do hope you travel with the Nortons. They are so nice, especially Mildred, with her independent breeziness & adventurous soul. I am growing very pleased with the idea of living in England. The fastness & expense of America is just about 50 years ahead of me. I could be as fond of London as of any other city in the world---and plays, books and all these things are so much more within one's means. Travel, too. You must never take a ship again, but fly over to visit us.

Last night Polly, the very sweet woman from Brookline (a cousin of Wallace Fowlie)[2] who is assistant here, and who has had a book of her own poems published,[3] had two bottles of vin rose for dinner and a birthday cake with candles in honor of my day, which touched me very much.

I want Ted to take me on a trip around England, especially to Wales, and little fishing villages. When you come we should go on a jaunt of some sort, staying at old inns & taking country walks.

Do tell us about the Eliot evening!

Much love,
Sivvy

1–SP and TH sailed on the SS *United States* from Pier 86 in New York City, departing on 9 December and arriving at Southampton, via Le Havre, on 14 December 1959.
2–American writer and professor of literature Wallace Fowlie (1908–98).
3–Pauline Hanson, *The Forever Young: And Other Poems* (Denver: Alan Swallow, 1957).

TO *John Lehmann*

Thursday 12 November 1959 TLS, University of Texas at Austin

26 Elmwood Road
Wellesley, Massachusetts
U.S.A.
November 12, 1959

Mr. John Lehmann
Editor
THE LONDON MAGAZINE
22 Charing Cross Road
London W.C.2, England

Dear Mr. Lehmann,

I am pleased indeed to hear[1] you are taking my hospital story, particularly since I have come to agree with your opinions about the other two.[2] I also agree with you about the title of the story which now seems to me pompous and out-of-place. I would much prefer the title THE DAUGHTERS OF BLOSSOM STREET.[3] I feel this is simpler, more direct, and makes the point I want about the Secretaries being almost ritual, attendant figures in the euphemistic ceremonies softening the bare fact of death. I hope this title seems a better one.

Ted sent off two stories---THE RAIN HORSE and SUNDAY---a week or more ago by regular mail, I hope you have them by the time you receive this.

Both of us send our warmest good wishes.

Sincerely yours,
Sylvia Plath

1–John Lehmann to SP, 22 October 1959; (photocopy) held by Smith College.
2–In his letter, Lehmann writes, 'I think The Wishing Box very amusing and imaginative, but I wasn't convinced by the pay-off: the suicide not only seemed to me rather unconvincing but also somehow out of key' and 'I also thought there excellent things in The Shadow but again the pay-off, in my opinion, struck the wrong note'.
3–Sylvia Plath, 'The Daughters of Blossom Street', *London Magazine* 7 (May 1960): 34–8.

TO *Judith Reutlinger Anderson*[1]

Monday 23 November 1959 TLS, Private owner[2]

26 Elmwood Road
Wellesley, Massachusetts
November 23, 1959

Miss Reutlinger
601 Oak Street SE
Minneapolis, Minnesota

Dear Miss Reutlinger,

Thank you for your card.[3] "Lament" was published several years ago by the New Orleans Poetry Journal,[4] but I've lost track of both the date and number, and I think most libraries don't carry such very little magazines. I have a copy of the poem to hand, being in the throes of moving and clearing house, so here it is.

LAMENT

The sting of bees took away my father
Who walked in a swarming shroud of wings
And scorned the tick of the falling weather.

Lightning licked in a yellow lather
But missed the mark with snaking fangs:
The sting of bees took away my father.

Trouncing the sea like a raging bather
He rode the flood in a pride of prongs
And scorned the tick of the falling weather.

A scowl of sun struck down my mother,
Tolling her grave with golden gongs,
But the sting of bees took away my father.

1–Judith Margaret Reutlinger Anderson (1934–2008); B.A. 1956, English, Mount Holyoke College; Anderson conducted graduate work at the University of Minnesota, 1957–9.

2–Transcribed from images that accompanied its listing at two auction sales by Bonhams on 13 February and 22 June 2011. The letter sold through RR Auction, in October 2012 for $4,915.20.

3–The card has not been located.

4–Sylvia Plath, 'Lament', *New Orleans Poetry Journal* 1 (October 1955): 19.

He counted the guns of god a bother,
Laughed at the ambush of angels' tongues,
And scorned the tick of the falling weather.

O ransack the four winds and find another
Man who can mangle the grin of kings;
The sting of bees took away my father
Who scorned the tick of the falling weather.
****

No, I haven't published a volume of poems yet, but I hope to manage this in a year or so if fates and editors are willing.

All good wishes,
Sylvia Plath

TO *Rachel MacKenzie*

Saturday 28 November 1959 TLS, New York Public Library

26 Elmwood Road
Wellesley, Massachusetts
November 28, 1959

Miss Rachel MacKenzie
25 West 43rd Street
New York 36, New York

Dear Miss MacKenzie,

I'm happy to hear[1] you are taking THE NET MENDERS.[2]

Here are a few suggestions for placing the poem in the title or subtitle: THE SPANISH NET MENDERS, THE NET MENDERS OF BENIDORM, or THE NET MENDERS (Benidorm, Spain). Any of these would be fine with me, or any rearrangement of them.

With all good wishes.
Sincerely yours,
Sylvia Plath

1–Rachel MacKenzie to SP, 24 November 1959; held by New York Public Library.
2–Sylvia Plath, 'The Net Menders', *New Yorker* (20 August 1960): 36.

TO *Rachel MacKenzie*

Saturday 28 November 1959 TLS, New York Public Library

26 Elmwood Road
Wellesley, Mass.
November 28, 1959

Dear Miss MacKenzie,

I hope it won't lessen the chances of these poems[1] to follow so soon on the heels of the last.[2]

I did want you to have a look at them.

Sincerely,
Sylvia Plath

TO *Robie Macauley*[3]

Saturday 28 November 1959 TLS, Kenyon College

26 Elmwood Road
Wellesley, Massachusetts
November 28, 1959

Mr. Robie Macauley
THE KENYON REVIEW
Gambier, Ohio

Dear Mr. Macauley:

I am happy to hear you are taking "The Colossus" and "The Bee-Keeper's Daughter" for the Review.[4]

Here are a few notes. I graduated from Smith College, and from Cambridge University (where I spent 1955-57 on a Fulbright grant).

1–SP submitted: 'Flute Notes from a Reedy Pond' (section 5 of 'Poem for a Birthday'), 'Mushrooms', 'A Winter Ship', 'Two Views', and 'The Burnt Out Spa'. 'Two Views' is either 'Two Views of Withens', composed in 1957, or 'Two Views of a Cadaver Room' written earlier in 1959. It may be the former as Plath had had success with the *New Yorker* with her geographical poems (e.g. 'Watercolor of Grantchester Meadows' and 'The Net Menders'). According to SP's submissions list, she sent 'Two Views of Withens' to the *Atlantic Monthly* in January 1960. SP submitted 'Two Views of a Cadaver' to *The Nation* but did not record it on her submissions list.

2–SP sent 'The Sleepers', 'Polly's Tree', 'The Net Menders', 'Memoirs of a Spinach-Picker', and 'Dark Wood, Dark Water' on 3 November 1959.

3–Editor, novelist and critic Robie Macauley (1919–95).

4–Sylvia Plath, 'The Colossus' and 'The Beekeeper's Daughter', *Kenyon Review* (Autumn 1960): 595–6.

Poems of mine have appeared in The Atlantic Monthly, Harper's, The Hudson Review, The New Yorker, The Partisan Review, Poetry (Chicago), The Sewanee Review and elsewhere.

After December 9th my address will be:

c/o Hughes
The Beacon
Heptonstall Slack
Hebden Bridge, (near Halifax)
Yorkshire, England.

Sincerely,
Sylvia Plath

TO *Aurelia Schober Plath*

Sunday 13 December 1959

ALS with envelope on SS *United States* stationery, Indiana University

Sunday
December 13

Dear mother,

Ted & I are sitting at desks in the writing alcove after lunch. A grey whitecapped sea is washing past the window & the rope are all spread out on the main deck ready for the stop in Le Havre some time tonight. We're supposed to get to Southampton around 5 pm tomorrow & I hope all our baggage is there to greet us in good order – the baggage-man at New York told us our Hold baggage was luckily just one cubic foot under the limit, or we'd have had to pay the expensive excess space rates. We were amazed we had by chance come so close to our allotted total.

I have just finished reading Zivago,[1] which took me the whole trip & proved a good travel-book as it is all written in such short episodes you can break off anywhere. I was, on the whole, disappointed in it – never really felt involved with any of the characters which I think is a fatal flaw in a novel. The poetic descriptive sections about weather & seasons I thought very good.

My last night of sleep & good food at home cured my cold, it seems, & I have been well ever since. Ship-space is rather confined without the decks open – we've been out & walking around whenever possible, but except for one blue day the weather's been overcast – warmish, but wet.

1–Boris Pasternak, *Doctor Zhivago* (trans. Max Hayward and Manya Harari, 1958).

Our cabin[1] is comfortable enough – on a noisy deck, the same as the diningroom (which is convenient) which keeps it busy all day, & at night we are next to several roomsful of girls who dance & drink till 4 & 5 am & come home screaming & laughing up & down the halls: there's always a bunch of these. So we take naps after breakfast & lunch which pieces out our sleep. It seems we spend most of our time eating & sleeping. There seem very few Americans on the trip. The ship goes in to Bremerhaven, so there are lots of Germans, master-builders, evangelists (one who by mistake thought she had our room put a sign up in front of a bottle of gin & an ash tray installed by a man who also thought he had our room – reading: 'Bittè, rausch nicht und trink nicht' – 'These are deadly sins. Now she realizes her mistake, she continually greets us 'God Bless You' & 'Isn't Jesus wonderful?') Lots of very pretty children about, people spending Christmas in Europe with parents & relatives. Our tablemates are two nice young Danish farmers who have been on a farm-exchange program in California.[2]

The dramamine is a great help. I take about two pills a day, & feel no queasiness at all – I'm sure I would if I didn't have the pills, for the boat rolls & pitches very noticeably even when the sea isn't very rough & we are literally rolled from one side to another in bed. Ted is a wonderful comfort. He seems to need no dramamine at all & we walk out on deck whenever possible. Had one night of a fine moon & bright stars.

We're extremely eager to hear in detail of your interview last Wednesday and hope a letter is waiting for us at Ted's mother's house, where we should arrive Tuesday, or Wednesday at the latest if we're held up in London.

Do find out about forwarding our mail – I'm sure there must be some solution, for it would have to be forwarded even if we had no relatives to put on new stamps & I hope you can do it without charge.

The package for you (& Warren) from the Music Box[3] should arrive by December[4] 20th, or 21st the latest.

We are both in good health, eating wisely & modestly – lots of fresh & stewed fruit & milk. The food is so-so – Some things very good, too many steamed dishes which have waited too long on the counters. Last night, at the 'Gala Dinner' we had a nice rare steak, lobster newberg, dates & figs.

1 – SP and TH occupied tourist class cabin A-31.

2 – The SS *United States* manifest lists one passenger travelling on a Danish passport, Leif Hansen, a butler; and one passenger destined for Denmark, Carl H. Andresen, a restaurateur travelling on a US passport.

3 – The Music Box was a music shop then at 58 Central Street, Wellesley, Mass.

4 – 'arrive by ~~Sept~~ December' appears in the original.

Well, we are off to find some fresh air & will write again as soon as we get to Ted's parents house.

Love to you, Warren & Sappho –
Sivvy

TO *Joseph, Dorothy, Robert, & Nancy Benotti*

Sunday 13 December 1959[1] ALS in greeting card,[2]
Indiana University

<printed greeting>
Christmas Greetings / and Best Wishes / for a Happy / New Year
<signed>
with love to / all the Benottis / Sylvia & Ted

Dear Dotty & Joe & Bobby & Nancy –

We're writing this from the middle of the Atlantic, one day out of Southampton. Have spent most of our time eating & sleeping & me taking dramamine, as the ship rolls & pitches surprisingly although the seas don't look too rough. We had one lovely clear night with moon & bright stars, but it's been overcast since – warm enough to take brisk deck-walks.

Our evening with you was so happy & memorable – a real occasion, & we enjoyed every minute of it. We'll spend Christmas with Ted's parents in Yorkshire & then go apartment-hunting in London.

Love,
Sivvy

TO *Aurelia Schober Plath*

Thursday 17 December 1959 ALS in greeting card,[3]
Indiana University

<printed greeting>
Merry / Christmas / Happy / New Year
<signed>
with love / Sivvy & Ted

1 – Date supplied from internal evidence.
2 – Original De Rangel Creacion Fischgrund Christmas card.
3 – Panda Prints Christmas card designed by Rosalind Welcher.

Thursday
December 17,

Dearest mother –

How lovely it was to come here & find the letters waiting – so thoughtful of you to send them on. But please don't bother to send anything airmail except for your own letters & what may look like an important missive from the New Yorker – (I'm dying to see my NYorker poem[1] – does it look well?) You mustn't spend so much on stamps! See if you can forward sea-mail without adding anything.

Your Christmas package arrived the day after we came to the Beacon, looking very exciting – we'll save it for Christmas eve or morning – whenever the family has its Christmas. We stayed overnight with friends of Ted's in London – Danny Huws[2] (the one whose poems we've sold)[3] who is studying to be a curator of old Welsh & Celtic manuscripts, his very German wife Helga[4] & their exquisite 2 year-old daughter Magdelen.[5] The wife speaks German to the child & is, I think, very strict with her – the father speaks Celtic. Supposedly she will be trilingual. Myself, I think one other language is plenty. The child says 'Auf' & 'Mehr' but little else. She wears wonderful wooly smocks & amuses herself beautifully.

Both of us were exhausted when we got up here, having slept so little on the boat. Mercifully I was not at all seasick. We had tea at Ted's Uncle Walt's & he drove us up. We slept 12 hours the first night & a good long time last night. All our baggage & thinks have arrived & seem in good condition. It's been raining & blowing out, black sky all day. So we are sitting in great armchairs by roaring coal fires, very cosily. Olwyn, Ted's sister, is home from her theater job in Paris – her hair newly cut & curled looking handsome, chic, extremely nice. I like her a great deal.

Right after Christmas, before New Year's, we'll look for a comfortable apartment in London – in easy walking distance of one of the wonderful big London parks, quiet, sunny, with a good kitchen. And I'll get a doctor & hospital arranged for. I doubt if we'll go to Corsica at all. I had a feeling we wouldn't. Ted's as tired of traveling as I am.

1–Sylvia Plath, 'A Winter's Tale'.

2–Daniel Huws (1932–), British; B.A. 1955, Peterhouse, Cambridge; friend of Ted Hughes and contributor to *Saint Botolph's Review*. Huws lent Hughes his flat at 18 Rugby Street, London W.C.1, 1955–6.

3–Probably Daniel Huws, 'The Fox', *The Nation* (14 November 1959): 352–3; and 'The Holly' and 'The Survivors', *Sewanee Review* (Winter 1960): 93–4.

4–Helga Kobuszewski Huws (1931–).

5–Madeleine Huws (1958–).

I'm eager to set up our own place again. Ted's mother is <u>such</u> an awful cook – heavy indigestible pastries, steamed vegetables, overdone meat. I'll get my own kitchen shelf here & we'll shop for supplies tomorrow so I can make a few decent cookies & meatloaf & so on. How I miss your kitchen & our family tradition of wonderful food lovingly prepared! There's not even enough flour & sugar here for a cake! Everything very untidy, pots never quite clean, oven bubbling with old fat – a lot of bustle & nothing but burnt offerings. Olwyn – much more sophisticated & critical than even I – is a nice ally. We cook our own things. As soon as I'm in my own kitchen all will be serene, digestible & tidy again. Well, for a 10 day visit I can overlook such matters. The main thing is that the family is loving & closeknit.

I'm glad your talk with Kelly was positive in favoring your German. Hard work in it now will pay dividends in the end & I'm sure you'll love it & be glad for the intensive reviewing & study later. Do work on planning your summer in Germany in 1961! Let us know the latest developments. Have you talked with Peebles yet? Or that young man who has the friendly wife?

Keep your spirits up & get more of those pills you gave me for nights when sleep is extra important. Treat yourself well – have naps & relaxings, hot milk & honey & don't walk out in the rain. Don't forget to mail my Christmas cards. I'm mailing the rest from here.

Love,
Sivvy

TO *Rachel MacKenzie*

Friday 18 December 1959 TLS, New York Public Library

c/o Hughes
The Beacon
Heptonstall Slack
Hebden Bridge
Yorkshire, England
December 18, 1959

Miss Rachel MacKenzie
THE NEW YORKER
25 West 43rd Street
New York 36, New York

Dear Miss MacKenzie,

Here are the proofs of "The Net Menders". The suggestions for commas and hyphens are fine. I'd like "madonna" without a capital m, and would prefer "bride-lace" or "bridelace", to "bride's lace", if that is all right.

I'm sorry not to be able to be any help about Tomas Ortunio, one of the main back streets in Benidorm. At the time, someone suggested the street might be named after a local hero, but I don't have any Spanish histories handy and am quite curious to find out the origin of the street's name myself.

With all good wishes.
Sincerely yours,
Sylvia Plath

P.S. For the next half year or so I shall be living at the Yorkshire address above.

TO *Aurelia Schober Plath*

Saturday 26 December 1959 TLS (aerogramme), Indiana University

Saturday night
December 26, 1959

Dearest mother,

I am sitting, about to go to bed, in the little second parlor downstairs by a roaring coal fire with the rain swatting against the triple window in front of me, very comfortable, after a light supper of creamed turkey and mushrooms on toast I made. Olwyn is out for dinner; Ted's parents are dozing in the front parlor after admiring the lovely book on America you sent them (you couldn't have chosen better), and Ted upstairs in our bedroom at his desk, copying out the manuscript version of his first book which he hopes to sell to a man in London who is scouting for an American University out West.

It scarcely seems possible we have been here two weeks. I have spent most of my time eating and sleeping, and typing some things for Ted and the new manuscript of my poetry book (about 86 pages). It has rained and blown almost constantly (reread Ted's poem Wind, it's perfect), but we have gone out for brief walks. Now we are pretty much rested up and in very good health. Next Sunday, right after new year's, we go to London to stay a few days, as long as we need, to locate a good comfortable apartment within easy walking distance of a big park, shops, a laundromat, etc. in Central London. We look forward to the trip and hope to spend our evenings going to plays. We have had tea at each of Ted's relatives: an Aunt Hilda and an Uncle Walter (the wealthy one), and taught Ted's sister and Hilda's daughter Vicky (21, an art-teacher in grammar school, and very nice) how to play Tarock, and we play a great deal. I would like a refresher course with you experts, however, as I am sure there are many conventions we do not know---various ways to reveal yourself to your partner, etc. Anyway, your Tarock pack is in good use.

We loved your big package: opened it Christmas Eve. Ted looks handsome in his shirt, it fits perfectly. Oddly enough, I was just going to write you and ask you to get the pink version of that wonderful blue nightgown the day before! It is the warmest, lightest gown I have & the front opens far enough for me to nurse the baby in it. Imagine my surprise to open my package and find you had answered my thoughts! You also couldn't have gotten me anything more attractive and comfortable than those tights. I am wearing the black ones now. They look striking as stockings with my high heels, and of course go into my flat shoes and provide a much-needed warmth for my thighs, a real blessing. My wool knee socks didn't do this, and were too clumsy for any dressup occasion. Also, the elastic waist and pants' top fits me perfectly, even in my 6th month, and is a restful support on my legs. If you could possibly get me another black pair, just like these, I'd be most grateful. The red is lovely, for casual wear, but the black I can wear anywhere: it's amazing how smart they are with my red & black heels. The scarf for Olwyn was lovely, very chic. No other packages or letters have come: just the last bundle of letters in your airmail envelope: DONT send anything airmail, unless its a thin New Yorker letter, because it's outrageously expensive!

When Ted's two stories (The Caning & Miss Mambrett And The Wet Cellar) come back from the NYorker, let us know, & send them on to the Atlantic in the envelopes I've left you. When my big poetry ms. comes back from Farrar, Straus (they must have sent it by now) just keep it for scrap-paper:[1] I've typed up my large and new version of the book here.

So far, I've made fish soup, Dot's meatloaf, oatmeal cookies, apple kuchen, your bread stuffing (for the Xmas turkey which Ted & I cooked: a 7½ lb. turkey for $6! Isn't that an awful lot? Meat here is as expensive as at home, and cosmetics, too) . . . all of which makes me feel less homesick. Olwyn is very nice, a beautiful blond slim girl, my height & size, with yellow-green eyes and delicate graceful bone structure: looks 21, not 31. I get along with her much better now that she's really accepted me as Ted's wife & like her immensely. She has a long vacation from her job as sec./translator for a French theater agency in Paris, her most interesting job yet.

Dot's present to "Junior Hughes" was a pair of exquisite green bootees all laced with white ribbon. Ted & I wore our twin shirts on Xmas day; they are handsome. I'll write her tomorrow to thank her. Hope your record came, and that you like the pajamas, or get some you like in exchange! Do the gloves fit Warren? Ted's mother got him some good English gloves. I forgot your size-slips, yours & Warren's: do send them on. Olwyn gave me a marvelous pair of cinnamon-colored paris kid gloves which fit like a second skin: Vicky & Hilda gave me a perfume & talcum set; Ted's mom, two baby sweaters & two prs. of nylons; Ted's dad a 5 pound note. No tree, which I missed. But Ted & I will have a little one next year for our Nicholas/Katharine (do you like Katharine Frieda Hughes as a name?) DO WRITE. I miss you & Warren & Sappho immensely & look for letters.

Ted joins in sending love,
Sivvy

<on the return address side of letter>

PS: Weren't you the secretive one when we went running about looking for our big blue Turkish bath towel! Did you remember you had padded our presents with it?

1–This was SP's 'The Devil of the Stairs: Poems', which she submitted to Farrar, Straus on 30 October 1959.

TO *Joseph & Dorothy Benotti*

Sunday 27 December 1959 TLS (aerogramme), Indiana University

Sunday
December 27, 1959

Dear Dotty and Joe,

Ted & I are still up here in Yorkshire, and after New Year's this week will go down to London to look for an apartment there within easy walking distance of the city's big parks, shops and so on. Ever since we've come it's poured rain and been wildly windy: Ted's parents' house is on top of a hill and gets all the rough weather going. No snow for Christmas, just about a foot of water. I wonder if you had snow: we read about blizzards in America, but the papers didn't say just where.

We celebrated Christmas on the Eve, and were delighted with the beautiful presents. The warm slippers, Bobby and Nancy, are just the thing for this cold weather where there is no central heating (at least not in this house) and your breath stands out in white puffs when you're a few feet away from the fireplace. Ted & I wore the handsome twin shirts all Christmas Day: we made the turkey and stuffing, as Ted's mother's not a good cook: she boils everything, including steak, and her pastries which she makes without any recipe, would sink like a battleship. I've made your meatloaf, Dot, which everybody ate as if it were roast beef, and am eager to get to my own kitchen again, where I can try out the carrot-fruit cake, the lemon sponge cake and all. I do love to cook & just can't understand how anybody can be a bad cook when the recipes are so simple and easy to follow. Of course I try to make as much as I can, while I'm here, but it's a battle in a tiny, messy kitchen with no supplies. We remember with joy the superlative feast you made for us before we left, & I must say I come from a family of wonderful cooks, a tradition which I hope to keep up as soon as we find a place in London. Ted will finish the next half-year on his grant and then look for a job in London.

I just loved the baby's bootees! They are so delicate and pretty, really among the very "special" things I am getting together. I plan to get a doctor and hospital lined up in London the week after this, after investigating maternity plans on socialized medicine. Do call up mummy now & then & be optimistic and cheer her up---I know she'd love to be around when the baby's born, and want to help: and of course there's noone like your own mother. Mrs. Hughes is a very simple, but nervous woman, who can't imagine that hospitals in the city are better than drunken country doctors & it will be a relief to get away from her worrying. Luckily Ted will be free to help me through all this & is very strong, sensible and kind, a real support.

A hundred thanks again for the perfectly lovely presents (I've never seen shirts I like so much, just the right color & pattern for us) & Ted joins me in sending our best love to you all.

Affectionately,
Sylvia

1960

TO *Aurelia Schober Plath*

Sunday 10 January 1960 — ALS (aerogramme), Indiana University

Sunday
January 10

Dear Mother . . .

I have no idea when I last wrote you, but it was a long time back. Ted & I have been in London for just a week now and out of touch with everything in Yorkshire, including mail, so I don't know what's waiting for us there. The search for an apartment has been very tiring: London is so enormous in area, & very expensive by American standards.[1] We have limited our range by deciding against 'living out' in one of the depressing outer districts ½ hour away from the center, insisted on living near a big park, so I can enjoy wheeling the baby out. Furnished apartments are hard to get in town & to get a clean, cheerful one almost impossible. Dirty gloomy ones with kitchen, bath, bedroom & livingroom being about $21 a week & no heating or hot water. We saw one we'd have got like a shot on a newly decorated top floor in a charming (rare) street near Kensington Gardens with two bedrooms, a fridge, hot water for $24 a week but were appalled to find it had been taken half an hour before we could get there – the same with a basement flat near Regents' Park. All the other ones we've seen through agents & newspaper ads after endless bus & subway trips, are impossible. Now we are considering unfurnished flats & thanks to an industrious & influential British lady,[2] wife of a young American poet, will look at some tomorrow with hot water, central heating, a fridge – at about 10 minutes walk from Regents' Park & very good shops. We'd invest in a new double bed & get tables & chairs in second-hand shops slowly – a small start toward furnishing a home. But that's tomorrow. Junk & second hand shops here are good for sturdy furniture, china, etc.

1 – See TH to Stephen and Agatha Fassett, 14 May 1960, for more detail on the ship crossing, flat hunting, and the birth of Frieda Hughes; held by Houghton Library.
2 – Dido Merwin.

We started out living in a cold, cheerless room & breakfast place for $5 a day, but hunting for the other two meals was a bore & inconvenient so now we are much more comfortable & have moved into a spare room here at 18 Rugby Street with Helga & Daniel Huws & their 2-year old daughter Magdalene. Now we can easily cook our meals & that is very restful. Helga is a real German hausfrau – scrubs, polishes, so although they live in a condemned district her two floors are clean & colorful – her German cooking is delightful & makes me feel at home. We had a Sunday dinner of bratwurst & sauerkraut with juniper berries & a dessert of yoghurt & applesauce – she makes good Christmas cookies & had a wonderful tree – fat & green tablesize with flat stars of straw she made & yellow candles & hung with fruit & nuts. She talks German to the little girl all the time & disciplines her very strictly.

Thanks to Dido Merwin (the British woman) & her husband Bill I got an appointment with their doctor[1] yesterday – whom I liked immediately. He examined me, weighed me (I'm 145, only 10 pounds more than usual) & referred me to his partner who is an obstetrician[2] & I shall go to his prenatal clinic Thursday. The procedure here is radically different from America & I'm not sure but that I shall like it better. Hospital beds are spoken for at least eight months ahead of time & except in special cases all childbirth is 'natural', without anesthesia (because this is less expensive, I imagine) & the hospitals keep you 12 days. Midwives do most of the deliveries, or students. My doctor said at this date I could only be got in to hospital as an 'Emergency' patient – no bed, or ward or such – <u>or</u> I could be delivered at home by him or his partner, if I preferred them to a midwife, & be given care & advice by a trained nurse. After the first baby, most deliveries here are home deliveries. This sounded <u>much</u> the best thing to me & if one of these unfurnished flats comes through (they are just around the corner from his office) I shall be all set, & very glad to escape the crowded labor wards & hospital food, etc. Ted will cook & care for me, I shall get good sleep & not feel lonely & cut off as I would in a hospital. The best care here is under the System (my doctor treats wealthy people) & so the baby should be perfectly free – also reductions on milk & orange juice are given new mothers. If Ted had paid health insurance I'd even be paid about $30 for getting baby things by the state! So I hope we will get an apartment set up this week. I need a good bath

1–Dr John Woolnough Wigg (1904–71); lived at 114 Regent's Park Road, London N.W.1.
2–Dr Christopher Paton Hindley, B.A. 1951, M.B. B.Chir. 1954, Classics, Medicine, Trinity College, Cambridge.

& a good rest. We'll spend Mrs. Prouty's money on a bed for us, a crib & a pram etc.

The weather here has gotten very cold & bitter. No snow as yet. My coat & those tights you sent are a blessing. Looking for a place is worst when you've no real home-base to set out from. If you write me here this week I'm likely to get the letter soonest & look forward to hearing from you. I am dying to get a place of my own – clean & cheerful, however bare at first. Poor Ted has had a bad cold & both of us have been tired & gloomy from this running about – the worst season of the year, of course, to home-hunt. I shall make Dot's meat-loaf for us all tonight. Once we get a foothold in London, life will become much easier & pleasanter & I think I shall like it better than anywhere else, but I have gone through a very homesick & weary period. Mrs. Hughes has made me a marvelous wool bathrobe – warm as a coat, for Xmas.

Love to you & Warren.
S.

TO *Aurelia Schober Plath*

Saturday 16 January 1960 — TLS (aerogramme), Indiana University

Saturday, January 16th

Dearest mother,

Ted & I arrived back at the Beacon last night after two gruelling weeks in London to find three good letters waiting from you: you have no idea how much mail from you means, especially now, when I most miss having you with us. The baby's Christmas package was waiting, too, with the three bright Carters[1] nighties and the beautiful set of bootees, bonnet & sweater. I just wept with joy over the marvelous little teddy bear Warren sent, which brought back our family of teddy bears we had in Winthrop & all those wonderful stories you told us about them.[2] I didn't write for so long because I was unbelievably tired and grumpy about our depressing search for an apartment in London & literally couldn't lift a pen. I really don't remember what I said in the letter I did write.

Now I am sitting in the big warm bathrobe Mrs. Hughes made me for Christmas with a crackling coal fire at my back, overlooking a sunny (for the first time in a month) landscape of dazzling snow-covered moortops

1 – Carters is a brand of children's clothing.
2 – Cf. SP's 'The Disquieting Muses'.

and a raft of billowing clouds racing under a blue sky. Our first snow. I had a hot bath last night, my first in two weeks (Helga puts up with the lack of a bathroom in their London flat, and a public toilet 3 flights down in a dirty open cellar with a Germanic stoicism) & am just waiting till the water heats to wash my grubby hair. Now Olwyn is gone, the house is no longer overcrowded & very peaceful. No particular publishing news. I think Faber will use one or two of Ted's stories, we dont know which yet, in the anthology they're doing. I didn't send any in for I only had a couple of very American slangy ones & felt it better not to send them, especially as they are doing so much of Ted's work now, and are so polite it would embarrass them to reject anything. They sent on a copy of the papercover of Ted's book which amazed & delighted us: a triumph as covers go. <drawing of *Lupercal* cover> The ground is a pale, almost neutral blue, some shades lighter than this paper, with black bold letters for Ted's name and outlined letters <drawing of outlined letter 'L'> (like that) which let the blue come through in all the other letters of the Lupercals except for bold red letters spelling the title out diagonally. It looks superb. I think Harper's will be using the same cover since they are just importing the book sometime in summer or fall & am glad. The book should come out here in late March or early spring & we'll send you a copy right away. It has a nice blurb on the front inner jacket[1] & advertises Ted's last book on the back jacket flap with 3 very fine quoted statements from reviews.[2]

After traveling endlessly on busses, subways & taxis, London having a terrifying area, and seeing ugly, dirty, too expensive furnished & unfurnished flats & getting more & more cold & tired, we ended up with two possibilities practically nextdoor to my doctor (an important consideration now, with my delivering the baby at home). One was an unbelievably big & beautiful furnished groundfloor flat overlooking a road and Primrose Hill (a green park across the street from Regents Park) from the big front room, and a charming garden & statues from the mammoth bedroom & glassedin kitchen & dining area, at 9 guineas ($27) a week, to be heated by electric fires (extra). We could have afforded this on the Guggenheim for a year & it would have been available right away, but the owner, who lived downstairs & was presently away doing his decorating work in the Bahamas, had said No Children. We telegrammed

1–The proof, in blue wrappers, held by Lilly Library.

2–First and early editions of *Lupercal* exerpted quotes from A. Alvarez in *The Observer*, Robin Skelton in *Manchester Guardian*, Kenneth Young in the *Daily Telegraph*, Edwin Muir in the *New Statesman*, and unsigned reviews in the *Times Literary Supplement* and *Sunday Times*.

to see if a crib-size baby would be all right for a year, but there was & is as yet no answer. The other alternative (& a rare one) is a 3rd floor flat (unfurnished) in a 4 story (5, with basement) house in a quiet square overlooking a little green with benches & fence for mothers & children, in 5 minutes walking distance from Primrose Hill & beautiful Regents Park (with a zoo, swings, sandboxes, swans, flowers, etc.), a laundromat, shops, my doctors etc. The whole house is in the act of being all done over-over, painted, papered, a bathroom put in & would mean our starting in on buying our own things. The flat is really too small (a bedroom, livingroom & kitchen big enough for eating in, & minute bathroom) & lacks a study for Ted, but it is only 6 guineas ($18) a week (gas & electricity extra) on a 3-year lease which is sublettable or assignable. It won't be ready till Feb. 1st, another minor problem, & we'll need to buy a stove, little fridge & double bed & crib & two electric heaters (I've at last found a good model with a fan which circulates warm air) & lots of incidentals. Our marvelous friends the Merwins have tables, chairs & rugs to loan us until we pick up our own here & there in the excellent 2nd-hand shops in London. So we signed the lease this Friday[1] & hope now it goes through: at least we'll have our own things & can hang our own pictures etc. And an Ideal location, like living in a village yet minutes from the center of London. Getting a foot in is the hard part. We set aside the year's rent from the Guggenheim, have enough for 6 more months food & $650 to start with the major items of furniture. Write return mail what we should look for in a big double bed (what springs, mattress guarantee etc.). I'm going to see if London has diaper service. Will go down to London at end of next week to shop & get blood & urine test from doctor who I saw again this week. Why do they ask if any relative had diabetes? How hereditary is it?[2] We'll be here till Wednesday, then at 18 Rugby Street, London W.C.1. Forward mail here.

xxx
sivvy

1 – 'the lease ~~for~~ this Friday' appears in the original.
2 – SP's father, Otto Plath, died from complications with diabetes mellitus.

TO *Aurelia Schober Plath*

Saturday 16 January 1960 TLS in greeting card[1] with envelope, Indiana University

<printed greeting>

Let me be the ~~first~~ last / To wish you a / Merry Christmas!

Sat'day, January 16

Letter 2

Dear mother,

I've just been out for a brisk late afternoon walk in the sun to post an airletter to you, but this will probably also come at the same time as there is no collection till Sunday afternoon. I'm enclosing 3 checks made out for deposit to the 5¢ Savings Bank, totalling, I think about $113. I'm also enclosing an envelope which doesn't need stamping & a filled-out deposit slip. This should simplify things: just drop the envelope, with slip & checks in mail & they'll send the book back to you with a new envelope & slip. Could we leave the bank book with you (not the bank) to deposit checks from time to time? It wouldn't cost anything since you can bank by mail free in America. One thing: Do tell us the total every time the book comes back so we can see what we have: & keep track. I love seeing the account grow & we don't want to touch it. Bank interest here is a miserly 2% a year, not really worth it compared to the lush 3½% at the Boston 5¢ Bank. The only thing worth buying is National Savings Certificates which mature at 4% in a seven year period. Like Savings Bonds, only of course the percentage starts lower & goes up fast at the end of the period, so if you cash unmatured bonds you really don't get any more than you put in. The most you can buy is 750 pounds worth which matures to 1000 pounds in 7 years ($2,800). Don't you think it would be a good idea to buy as many of these as we can with our small poetry account here instead of leaving our poetry account in savings at only 2%? All dollar checks we'll simply plop into our Boston Savings account.

My maternity clothes are working out beautifully & are very warm. Although my London walking & trudging stairs tired me, I have been in surprisingly good health, probably because of the fresh air & exercise. I am taking your Vitamin C pills, 3 calcium pills & 3 iron pills a day. The iron pills my London doctor prescribed & they cost me 12¢, the token fee for filling a doctor's prescription under the Health System. I also get (or

1–Hallmark Contemporary Christmas card. SP edited the printed greeting herself to acknowledge its being sent just after the Christmas season.

should) a reduction in milk price & vitamins after I send in a certain form to the Ministry of Pensions, as an expectant mother. My doctor explained their system to me & it sounds very sensible. I will have the baby at home & I think this emotionally will be reassuring to me. As I probably said before hospitals here keep you 12 days, only 2 allow husbands to be around during labor etc., food is poor usually, sleep almost impossible with this hospital routine & only in abnormal cases do doctors deliver babies anyway. As soon as I tell the doctor my address next week, he will introduce me to the local midwife (a respected profession here) who will deliver the baby: he himself will stand by to give injections or analgesia if necessary. The midwife will come twice a day thereafter to help me bathe and care for the baby & instruct me about it. Ted's presence will be a great comfort & he will take wonderful care of me. I'll also probably go to a clinic for relaxing exercises & labor preparations as soon as we move in to our flat. I shall be relieved when the landlord's[1] signed copy of the lease arrives!

Delighted to hear you manage to get more tights. I am sure they are a main reason, along with vitamins & fresh air for me not getting a cold. We love to hear about Sappho: you paint such vivid pictures of her. I think we stuck the addressed envelopes to the Atlantic for the 2 NYorker stories in the bookcase in Warren's room (your room). I'd love to see some of those photos of grammy! I wrote Marion thanks before we left, in her Christmas card. So touched to hear Madeleine Sheets[2] wishing she might be my nurse; how I'd love to have her! I remember her wonderful combination of absolute efficiency & capability with her warmth and tenderness. Do tell her I love her for thinking of it.

Just drop the little enclosed card in the mail to the Academy of Poets, will you? They put an American stamp on it. And forward all our mail here to the Beacon. We won't be moving in to our flat (3 Chalcot Square, London N.W.1) until after February 1st anyway, or a few days later. We'll be at the 18 Rugby St. address this Wednesday night for a few days, to see my doctor, hunt for a bed, stove, etc. We hope too to have a phone without having to wait too long & if all goes well I should be able to talk to you right after the baby is born; or if I am voiceless, Ted will call right away. I can't imagine it being anything but a Nicholas. In the Drs. office I heard a mother say "I've brought Nicholas in" just by chance, & even

1–The landlord was Scott, Ford & Co., 38–40 Camden Road, London N.W.1.

2–Madeline Redmond Sheets (1905–2006). According to SP's address book, Sheets lived at 1 Weld Road, Stoneham, Mass. Sheets was a trained nurse.

Briget Bardot has given birth to a Nicholas.[1] Otherwise we'll have to get used to Katharine Frieda. From now on I hope to write at least once a week & more fully, of course, when we get settled. Maybe by the time you come in 1961 we'll have moved into a place big enough to put you up, but meanwhile, we'll just cross our fingers & look forward to that time

All our love to you & Warren,
xxx
Sivvy

PS: I don't think there's anything to add to the bank deposit slip enclosed in the envelope except the number of the bank book which I don't have.

I've been expecting a few bills which I can pay by what's left in my Wellesley Fells checking account which I hope to close soon & wonder if they've come yet. One from Dr. Brownlee (though he really did nothing for my ear), the Music Box & maybe another odd one or so. Do send them right on.

I've just washed my hair & tights & so feel much recovered. Mrs. Hughes made us some nice deep-fried haddock in batter for lunch. That is something she does well. The other thing is rice pudding, which as you may well imagine I let Ted devour. I have some steak & lettuce, which I shall soon wash & mix with some French dressing I made & eat a bowl of. Also oranges, which I squeeze for breakfast on an implement made to squeeze half a small lemon & hold just that much juice. I guess I am inclined to be more critical because I wish she were more like you . . . that I could learn things from her about cooking, babycare, etc. But I must really be a terror of a daughter-in-law, (Ted always brags of my cooking), typing away all day & measuring ingredients & eating meat rare & not falling into the rhythm of starches, sweets & tea which I am sure is the ruin of British teeth & health. So I shall concentrate on the good things she does: sewing, for example, & making excellent light fried foods; & gossip about Ted & London.[2] Once we get our own flat & the baby comes, we won't be visiting so much anyway, & when I do visit I'll feel more inclined to be sociable. When I'm critical I find it hard to hide it, as you know, & I've specially kept out of the kitchen today & eaten what she's made & praised it etc. She's really very warm & good-hearted & if anything, I think, inclined to be a bit frightened of me, so I'll try to relieve that.

Funny how critical one's inclined to be of one's own relatives: yet in comparison to one's inlaws how flawless & superior they seem!

1–French actress Brigitte Bardot (1934–); her son Nicolas-Jacques Charrier born on 11 January 1960.
2–'& gossip~~ing~~ about Ted & London' appears in the original.

I remember how angry I was with Frank & Dot for that underhand business with grampy's money; well, Ted's Uncle Walter really infuriates me on occasion, fat & entertaining & apparently fond enough of us as he is. Ted used him as a financial reference, or social reference, at the agents' in London & they wrote asking if Ted would be responsible in paying a 9 guinea a week rent (for that furnished place we wanted first). We heard this weekend that Walter had been scared by this letter, thought it was too much rent, Ted might run out of money "the year passes so fast", & he didn't know if he should write them. He also obviously feared he might be held responsible for Ted's not paying, a ridiculous thing for any business man to think. I was naturally outraged. Of course Ted will explain to him & get him to write something, but to think that that man has millions, or a million, earns $2,000 interest from stocks and shares every month or so & buys his mad daughter fur coats & diamond rings & highbred dogs, when Olwyn, Gerald & Ted & one other cousin are his other heirs, is so queer as to be unbelievable. Of course, it is a similar irony in our own family that Dotty & Joe have so much more money than we & couldn't have children of their own. Walter & his wife must secretly feel that the Hughes are intelligent & handsome & by definition deserve none of their help. Our lives could be quite different if Walter were enlightened. Houses in certain areas in London, like ours (once fancy private homes, then slums & boarding houses, now being done-over in a modern way) can be bought for very little now (4,000 pounds, for example) & gradually renovated (as ours is), many with back gardens, lived in, the top floors rented at high rents with as strict limits as one likes about tenants' quietness, & literally provide an income, as does the Merwins'. We'd love to do something like this: buy a house in London with a garden, modernize the 1st two floors, with studies, modern kitchen, play area, & also fix up the top two floors & rent them to quiet people. The demand for housing in London is constant & fantastic. $45 a week is moderate for a clean furnished flat with bathroom, kitchen, & about 3 other rooms. When the Merwins travel abroad, they rent their two floors to people who love cats (they have a marvelous Siamese), won't enter Bill's study, have no children, etc. And pay very high. The marvel about London houses is this back-garden in the better ones: you literally have flowers & trees in midcity, quiet, & all the advantages of city life. Ideally, we'd like a London house we could rent & get income from when away from it, & a little cottage by the sea, not the horrible compromise of a house in a dreary suburb. Commuting to London is lethal. In rush hours it takes about 2 hours to merely get across the city! Anyway, if we ever had any windfalls or won the pools, we'd look around for the right house. The thing to do is get it before it is done over. Dido Merwin did over hers from a bombed ruin & it is now a mansion. She bought it for 1,000 pounds just after the war. It is at the end of a deadend lane[1] facing directly onto Primrose Hill & their two top floors (they rent the bottom two) look out over endless miles of treetops. Bit by bit they have made it a mansion, using rents to improve it. She's a marvelous practical woman & I hope to learn all sorts of things from her. Our landlord, for example, makes a living buying up houses in rundown but pleasant areas, painting them & putting in bathrooms on every floor. From our house, for example, he must get over $100 a week. What one needs is the capital & the shrewdness & imagination. Dido's friends have almost all done this sort of thing. Investment in certain London real estate is a very solid thing, especially if you live in the place you buy & do a lot of the work, painting & finishing & so on. Well, enough of that. I would just love the chance of ending rent-paying & getting an income as well as a house of our own in London.

Do write soon & forward our letters.

xxx
Sivvy

TO *Brian Cox*[2]

Saturday 16 January 1960 TLS, University of Kansas

c/o Huws
18 Rugby Street
London W.C.1
January 16, 1960

Dear Mr. Cox,

I was pleased and honoured to hear[3] that "Medallion" has been chosen for one of the Critical Quarterly awards.[4] I should be very happy if you wish to consider the other poems[5] for publication in the magazine.

1–The Merwins' house was at 11 St George's Terrace, London N.W.1. TH and SP had use of a study in the house when the Merwins were abroad.

2–English poet and editor Brian Cox (1928–2008).

3–Brian Cox to SP, 13 January 1960; held by Smith College.

4–Sylvia Plath, 'Medallion', *Poetry 1960: An Appetiser* (*Critical Quarterly* Poetry Supplement 1, 1960): 20.

5–Along with 'Medallion', SP submitted 'The Beggars', 'Maudlin', 'The Burnt-out Spa', 'Blue Moles', and 'The Manor Garden' to the *Critical Quarterly* on 1 January 1960.

I wonder if you would be so good as to have my first name written out in full under the poem; if there's not time to do this before the poem goes to the printers I can always write it in on the corrected proof.

With all good wishes,
Sincerely yours,
Sylvia Plath

TO *Aurelia Schober Plath*

Tues.–Fri. 19–22 January 1960 TLS/ALS[1] (aerogramme), Indiana University

Tuesday, January 19

Dear mother,

It is about 3:30 in the afternoon. I am sitting in the parlor with the coal fire burning and a wet, sleety blizzard blowing outside against the windows, making the most of the dying light. The electricity mysteriously went off as I was about to heat some soup for lunch & heaven knows when it will come on again. Luckily I had just that moment finished baking a batch of oatmeal cookies to take down to London with us tomorrow. The stove here is electric (very poor for baking of any sort) & I'm glad not to have wasted my efforts. We have our lease cleared for the unfurnished flat in 3 Chalcot Square, London N.W.1 & will get a gas stove for that. We'll put what would have been our shipfare to America from the Guggenheim into a stove, a bed & mattress, &, I hope, into a small refrigerator. Unfurnished here means literally nothing: not even cupboards. We do have one small closet & will have to store most of our stuff for the time-being in our trunks until we get together a few bureaus. The main thing at this point though, is a pleasant location in London itself & nearness to my doctor. In a year, or a year and a half, we can move to a bigger place. Probably we won't be even barely settled in the apartment till the first week in February (our lease starts the 1st), so forward all mail here to the Beacon until February 1st. Would it be too much trouble to send on to us those 3 stories Mademoiselle rejected,[2] if they are not too dogeared to send out again? Send them by sea mail.

It has been a real treat to bathe & wash my hair & clothes & sit around in my warm bathrobe over french toast and coffee in the mornings after

1 – The first two paragraphs are typewritten, the remainder handwritten by SP.

2 – Ted Hughes, 'Sunday', 'Snow', and 'The Courting of Petty Quinnet', submitted to *Mademoiselle* on 5 October 1959.

the horrible two weeks in London. We'll be going down again tomorrow till the weekend for my doctor's appointment & to see if we can pick out a stove & bed to be installed & delivered by February 1st. Both of us look forward to having a place of our own & gradually accumulating pieces we like. Of course I have to wrestle with myself not to hanker after the things I left at home---the iron & board, the kitchen cupboard, china set, & most of all my beautiful mixing bowls which I preferred to leave than risk breaking. Objects do exert such a tyranny over one. There would have been so much I could borrow from home, too, if we'd been in America: the baby bureau and so on. Mrs. Hughes has given me two pure wool crib blankets, one pink & one blue, which are very nice, & I have just heard, o joy, that there is a diaper service in London (which I must investigate) which would be a godsend as I don't have a washmachine & will have enough to do without that. Drying space is the big problem here---no leaving things in the bathroom overnight, or down the cellar. When & if we buy a London house we will put in central heating & an American kitchen!

London: Friday January 22 – Arrived two days ago to find the lovely tights & mail waiting for us. Do forward Harper's letter[1] of acceptance of Mushrooms[2] – if they sent any. I need to see that kind of mail now. Could you put the two checks straight into our Boston 5¢ account along with the 3 checks I sent with the silly card last week. Your bed letter came in good time – we made what I hope will be a few good investments in these exhausting 3 days. Saw my doctor – the young one of the pair I've signed up with who I feel great trust in – I was tired & tearful from just the burden of all this walking about & decision making & he showed very kind & helpful understanding, prescribed a sedative & advised Ted to have me rest in Yorkshire a week (we go back tomorrow) & was immensely reassuring about the baby <text missing due to damage> & urine tests. I'll write in detail about the progress of our flat when I get back to Yorkshire. We got – after two days poking & prying & measuring – a lucky buy on a gas stove – a model with an electric timer going out of stock because a fancy new timer model with an electric light was coming in. We ferreted out the last one of the last model – no timer (it's supposed to be sent) but all the gas jets, oven, "grill" (broiler) just like the new expensive model, only a good $50 less. With installation fee it's £55. 16s

1–R. B. Silvers to SP, 8 January 1960; held by Smith College. *Harper's* rejected 'The Burnt-out Spa', 'The Manor Garden', and 'A Winter Ship'.

2–Sylvia Plath, 'Mushrooms', *Harper's* 221 (July 1960): 25.

(about $157) – four burners & very neat. Most stoves here are hideous – "grills" (a pan & rack – in even expensive stoves only about big enough for 3 pieces of toast!) at eye level in a kind of hood, tiny ovens etc. We've got a good big grill in the stove (above oven) & big enough oven. Tell me how American prices compare. Our bed we ordered.[1] 5 ft wide & 6' 6" long – the mattress has 1000 interlocking extra stout springs – we liked it much better than the Beautyrest we saw with 'pocketed springs'. The box spring below seems very firm. The bed ("divan") is low to the floor – no headboard or long legs – on 6 caster legs – looks very sturdy. We punched them & Ted lay down. If expense is a guarantee (there is a 10 year guarantee on the mattress – 5 more than most) this should be durable. We ordered a big size (costs more) at £59 ($165). Is that outrageous? These two are our main purchases – eating & sleeping being the center of one's existence, after all, & we will have them when the year's rent is gone. We also picked out a mottled black linoleum for bathroom, kitchen & hall floors (about $30) – the floorboards are awful – big, uneven, unfinished. We'll paint them French grey in livingroom & bedroom. Chose lovely rose paper for bedroom – white with exquisite pink roses – not cabbage, or bundles at abt $2.50. An 11 yard roll, a white ground with pleasant gay rose-red & green pattern of figures for two main opposing walls of the kitchen (a washable paper) at less than $2 a roll (the other 2 little opposing walls we'll paint white). Bathroom (minute) we have a black, brown & white print for – little cars, trains, birdcages wittily drawn & will waterproof it – I felt I could be daring there. Hall & living room we'll paint white ourselves & hang our pictures & put up bookcases. I'll send samples of the paper. The place always makes us very happy after each visit, no matter how tired & shop soiled we are & the location is near 2 charming parks & a marvelous shopping center.

xxxxx

Sivvy

PS[2] – So pleased about your prize – the first time I've ever know of anyone to win one of those things – good for Dot for spotting it! And I'm very touched at you putting it in the bank for the first grandchild. Either Nicholas * Farrar Hughes or Frieda Rebecca (to be probably called Rebecca – I'm bored by Katharine). Wouldn't you like a Becky? And the Frieda after Aunt Frieda? All sorts of signs point to a Nicholas – he's

1–SP and TH purchased their bed, bureaus, and baby crib from Bowman's Furniture Store, Camden Town. Later, SP furnished her 23 Fitzroy Road flat with Bowman's wares as well.
2–The postscript is written in the left margin of the first page.

patron saint of pawnbrokers & wolves (which does appeal to Ted). Don't forget to tell us how much our bank account total is at the 5¢ when you've put those last checks in. So I can keep a record here – I love to see it grow & we hope always to leave it there.

xxx

s

TO *Aurelia Schober Plath*

Sunday 24 January 1960 — TLS (aerogramme), Indiana University

<drawing of the layout of the flat at 3 Chalcot Square detailing 'Stair', 'HALL', 'BATH', 'Sink', 'Stove', 'KITCHEN', 'Fridge?', 'Tiny closet', 'BED ROOM', 'LIVING ROOM'.
SP has added red pencil lines indicating 'paper on walls'; with captions: 'Two windows, one small, kitchen are big, overlooking backyards'; 'Ted will build twin bookcases to the ceiling in these alcoves' (with arrows pointing to alcoves in livingroom); 'Three big windows overlooking green square, trees – full of light & airy'; and '3 Chalcot Square, London N.W.1'>

Sunday, January 24

Dearest mother,

Ted & I are back at the Beacon again on what should be, if all goes well, our last trip for a year. We have found the best way of getting up from London: a 4-hour express to Manchester, then a 1-hour train to Hebden Bridge, & the bus up to the moor-tops. I simply can't travel long distances on the busses here: they are unbelievably cramped & take twice as long as trains & stop at "tea-shops" where not even the tea is drinkable. I always make a picnic when we travel, take along a bottle of milk, a loaf of Jewish rye bread, sliced & buttered, cheese, fruit chocolate & occasionally hardboiled eggs. I have been eating well, as we buy our food in London to cook at Helga & Danny Huws' place where we stay, & Helga is a cook after my own heart: makes marvelous applesauce, a sort of yoghurt pudding with lemon juice & sugar, and once, at the start of our long, exhausting search when I was very downcast brought out a tin of "pepper-bread"(the nearest I can translate: her German sounded like pfeffer-brot), a spicy gingerbread with glazed almonds on it, & little crescent sand-tarts from a tin in her nursery cupboard. I must say all her Germanic-ness, her German talk to the adorable little baby girl Madelin & her rigorously clean housekeeping has sustained me through a very difficult period. I think I will give her a little wooden peppermill as a thank-you present & look forward to trying out Dot's carrot fruit-cake & my Christmas cookies next year: she will be a wonderful appreciator of them. Of course she puts up with a lot of things I could never countenance, such as no bathroom (only a toilet in the basement & no tub in the house) & no good heating & no good parks or gardens nearby, but the baby is spotless, in fine health.

I meant send the mail on here to the Beacon. After February 1st to 3 Chalcot Square, London N.W.1. I have drawn a little plan of the apartment. You can see it is small, but such a clean, new place (except for the 100 year-old floorboards) that the brightness makes up for it all. The tiny bathroom is newly put in, the walls scraped, the doors new & painted white, the woodwork white & the three windows in the front overlook a quiet green square instead of opposite housefronts: a rare blessing except in the Society Squares in the wealthy sections. As I say, we have ordered marbled black linoleum (quite expensive: 12'4d. about $1.75 a square yard---how does that compare to home prices?) for bathroom, hall & kitchen, which are so small it won't amount to more than $30. The landlord offered to paper the whole place, allowing a price of abt. $1.50 an 11 foot roll. We spent a morning at the hugest paper store in London Friday & for all the choice could find only about 3 papers we liked among the horrible, badly drawn assortment---even the very expensive ones suffered from a grim Victorian hangover. But those we picked we liked very much, especially the bedroom paper of roses on white. By having half the house papered & planning to paint livingroom & hall & two short walls in the kitchen ourselves (probably white as background to pictures) over a lining paper they will put up, we think the landlord will allow us the extra shilling per roll on the more expensive paper we chose. The kitchen paper is washable, & we'll go over the bathroom paper with one of the waterproofing preparations they have here. We'll paint the bedroom & livingroom floors a whited grey---or Ted will, for he'll do the heavy work. Our stove & bed are ordered to come February 1st, Monday. The papering & linoleum should be done by then. I am of course prepared for things to be held up or go wrong here & there, but hope for the best.

By the way, don't send us back the 3 stories of Ted's from Mlle, as I asked in my last letter unless it's too late. We wondered if we gave you the dregs of our checking account (abt. $25) after I've paid the few bills

I'm still waiting to get from it, if you'd send out a few stories to American places on our instructions? Or if this would be too much bother. It's only 9¢ to send out a heavy ms with no letter marked "Educational Matter" under the new law, & 9¢ for the enclosed stamped, returned-addressed envelope. Let us know if you'd be willing to do this. Have Ted's 2 stories come back from the NYorker yet? Or my 3 from the Atlantic? [1] Did you find the manila envelopes we made out for Ted's stories in the bookcase in your room? As I say, do send on any bills & any letters of acceptance or rejection. Ted's poem 'Tomcat'[2] came out in the Jan. 9th NYorker we hear. Did you get a copy forwarded from them? Or can you get one? Do cut out the Ladies' Home Journal article on babies[3] & send it on. There are only British women's magazines on the usual newsstands here & they are awful. Next Christmas you might think of a subscription to the LHJ for me, or the NY! I need a constant flow of Americana to enrich my blood!

Went to bed at 10 last night & slept 12 hours. Feel fine now. I try not to get out-of-temper with things up here: no eggs in on a Sunday, all the fry-pans filthy with old grease & rinds & stuck back in the oven. Mrs. H. never gets up till afternoon & I find myself in the position of being unable to eat most of her cooking: over-stewed meat in a leaden, burnt piecrust, canned apples in the same sort of crust, ugh! She just won't learn. I find myself particularly sensitive now & yearn for a little of your delicate tasty mothering, full fridge & marvelous snacks. Luckily we are only 1 mile from a magnificent open market & shopping center. Bought chicken livers (cat-food here) at less than 50¢ a lb & made myself a great panful with bacon in London. Will see my doctor the 1st week in Feb. when we move in & meet my midwife then & tell you all about it. Do write often to make up for your absence. Your letters are a tonic.

xxx
Sivvy

PS: Ted's revision of his children's book MEET MY FOLKS! has been definitely approved of by TSEliot & the Faber editors, & his 3 stories SNOW, SUNDAY & THE RAIN HORSE will appear along with those of

1–Sylvia Plath, 'A Prospect of Cornucopia', 'Johnny Panic and the Bible of Dreams', and 'The Fifty-Ninth Bear', submitted on 28 September 1959.

2–Ted Hughes, 'Tomcat', *New Yorker* (9 January 1960): 102; printed as 'Esther's Tomcat' in *Lupercal*.

3–The *Ladies' Home Journal* ran several articles on babies and children each month. Possibilites in this instance include Joan Younger, 'How America Lives: "Our Baby Was Born at Home"', *Ladies' Home Journal* (January 1960): 111–16; or Benjamin Spock, 'You Can Have Fun With Your Children', *Ladies' Home Journal* (February 1960): 77, 132–3.

5 other new authors in an anthology called INTRODUCTION[1] put out by Faber next fall (not any money in this to speak of, abt. $60 for the right to use the lot, but a good start!)

Do write more about your program for remedial reading: PLEASE say your giving up summer-session won't mean a change in your plans to come to England in '61!

What poems did Harper's reject?

TO *Aurelia Schober Plath*

Wednesday 27 January 1960 — TLS (aerogramme), Indiana University

3 Chalcot Square
London N.W.1
Wednesday, January 27th

Dearest mother,

Received your forwardings, being Ted's proof of The Rain Horse from the London Magazine, my proof from Harpers of "Mushrooms" & the other bits. Many thanks. The Harper's magazines * with Ted's story in haven't come yet: we're looking for them eagerly. Did you give a copy of the Magazine to Mrs. Prouty? I'm about to write her.[2] We're going down to London over the weekend to paint the floors & livingroom & hall walls of our little flat, although the bed & stove aren't ordered till Monday the 1st when we officially move in. The smallness of the flat has one advantage in that it will be easy & inexpensive to fix up very prettily. Do say what you think about what I told you of the bed & stove & how prices compare with American. We will wait until we are settled before looking for a refrigerator: I don't suppose I shall be able to get the American size. Most of them here are half that height, with very small freezer units. The most expensive of the models I've looked at is about $175. Is that outrageous? I really don't want to waste money getting these few main things second hand, as I am no judge of quality about machinery & will need a lot more experience before I become one. As I said, the Guggenheim will pay for these 3 big items, bed, stove & fridge, & keep us for a good six months, so Ted will have some time to make

1–*Introduction: Stories by New Writers* (London: Faber & Faber, 1960); featured A. O. Chater, Alan Coren, Ted Hughes, Jim Hunter, Jason McManus, and Julian Mitchell.
2–These last two sentences added by SP by hand in the margin.

up for the loss of these two tiring months traveling & flat-hunting to do some really concentrated writing. We hope to be able to rent a windowed storeroom during the day, or something equivalent, from the lady upstairs in the attic,[1] or, if not from her, nearby, for Ted to write in. And in a year, or a year & a half, locate a bigger place in the same area, which, as far as I'm concerned, is the pleasantest in London.

I made a mushroom omlette for breakfast & have been having a very pleasant & relaxing day, our trunks being packed & sent off to London at last. Ted has constructed a bird-feeding station & a clothesline wrapped with bacon rinds just outside the picture window, so against a backdrop of blue-misty green fields and blurred trees, I have been watching the marvelous little birds come: tiny robins, round, with a patch of warm orange like a bib; blue tits, smaller-than-sparrow-size versions of our jays; and the lovely multicolored chaffinches. I feel in very good health: quite recovered from my London stays, washed, shampooed, well-fed. I start the day with orange & grapefruit juice, drink lots of milk, eat brown bread, bananas. In a bit I shall make your nice apple crisp for dessert tonight, to have with steak & new potatoes. I am taking iron pills & every so often sleeping pills (not barbiturates) like those you gave me, for the baby kicks so much at night (it seems to wake up then) that it keeps me awake & then I'm always having to get up to the bathroom. So this way I can assure myself of a good night's sleep, which is really the foundation of my health: when I am as rested as I am now I feel I can cope with anything, while when I allow myself to get tired, I feel very homesick & blue. I really look forward to next week, settling in, and having sometime just to rock back & forth looking happily ahead to the baby! I have been rushing about so much I hardly notice being pregnant at all. I am an impressive size now, & got out the pretty red-quilted reversible top this week, the roomiest of the things we bought, which I had been saving, & feel quite new in it: a pleasant change. My only actual symptoms are a tendency to backache after standing, or typing (walking doesn't tire me: I manage two or three to five miles a day) & occasional heartburn which is evidently natural: I haven't much room for a stomach & have a very good appetite. Am looking forward to having the baby at home: I'd hate to be in a crowded hospital here for 12 (!) days, eating tasteless food. Ted will take wonderful care of me & is a fine cook in his own right. Can you get used to Frieda Rebecca as a girl's name? I think I'll write Aunt Frieda

1–Mary K. Morton. Morton and her attic living space inspired SP's poem 'Leaving Early', written on 25 September 1960.

about it, as I'm sure it would please her to know I want to name my first girl after her (even if this is a Nicholas Farrar, as I'm sure it will be). Isn't it wonderful to have a children's book ready to be dedicated to whoever it is!

The 3 stories Faber's will publish in their anthology next fall are: SNOW, SUNDAY & THE RAIN HORSE (the only ones Ted's sent them). Now, if you are willing, some notes for sending out stories (have the 2 NYorker stories come back yet?) Hold the Atlantic envelopes for the time-being & put SNOW, SUNDAY and THE CANING (wait to get this from the NewYorker) together with a manila envelope stamped with 9¢, marked "Educational Matter" & addressed to Ted c/o you, into a big manila envelope stamped with 9¢ & also marked "Educational Matter" & send the stories (in this order of arrangement: SNOW, THE CANING, SUNDAY) to: Miss Katherine Gauss Jackson,[1] HARPER'S, 49 East 33rd Street, New York 16, New York. When the stories have come back from there, from the NYorker also send SNOW, THE CANING, & MISS MAMBRETT & THE WET CELLAR to Editor Edward Weeks at the Atlantic in the envelopes we made out (they've seen SUNDAY already). Is that too complicated? We've made some changes in Petty Quinnett & need to retype it before sending out again. Let us know if these 2 moves are clear. Forward all mail to our new address now as we'll be working there from tomorrow on! We'll pick up any that's about to arrive here or at Rugby Street. Do write. Love to you & to Warren: how is he?

xxxxx

Sivvy

Did you get the 3 checks I sent? Has my monthly statement, with cancelled checks, come from my Weston Rd. checking acct. yet? I'd like to get that cleared up.

Since having the baby will cost me next to nothing, I plan to put Mrs. Prouty's $300 into things which will make life easy for me and the baby: a layette (rubber sheets, etc.), a crib big enough to last a few years, a carriage (any advice?) diaper service & so on. Don't tell her this, though – she'd be happier thinking I paid a doctor! Ted wears his lovely wool red & grey shirt all the time.

1–Book review and fiction editor at *Harper's*, Katherine Gauss Jackson (1904–75).

TO *Aurelia Schober Plath & Warren Plath*

Tuesday 2 February 1960 TLS, Indiana University

Tuesday
February 2nd, 1960

Dearest Mother, Warren & Sappho,

This is the first piece of mail to go out from our new residence. I am sitting typing at an old unpainted table loaned us by our friends the Merwins (who are loaning us chairs, a divan & china until we have leisure to find our own bargains), listening to hammers, clanking chisels, and the cries of children in the green square "Chalcot Square Gardens" the sign says below. These days will be given up to cleaning, painting & making shelves & shopping---the workmen are still with us, fixing the toilet cisterns & hot water taps (heated by a large gas tank on the wall in the kitchen) today. Yesterday they put the gas meters in, installed the stove, which is the most beautiful I have ever seen or worked on---four handsome burners which click to two positions "Full" or "Simmer", so there is no problem about low heat without the gas going out, my grill below, with a separate flame (I don't like floor-broilers, as there is too much kneeling or squatting to look at them---I just barely bend for this one) and then the roomy oven. This was a "reconditioned" model---used for a bit & completely made over. There isn't a sign of wear on it, and, as I said, it is 50 dollars (£20) less than the exact-same streamlined model new this year except for the timer. Mine runs by electricity & is made so you can set it & cook a meal while you're out all day. I wish you could see the stove! You will of course, in time. I loved putting out my beautiful pots and pans, Warren---I always think of you when I use them, which is often each day.

The bed came yesterday, too. Six feet six inches long & five feet wide ---most of my sheets don't tuck in at the side as the mattress is thick. We had a wonderful sleep on it last night, exhausted to the bone as we were from workmen arriving all day yesterday & all our trunks, suitcases & so on to be unpacked downstairs & carried up by armloads---the trunks are much too heavy to get up the narrow winding stair, especially as it is full of workmen's tools. Ted did all that lugging of all our books & clothes. We learned today that when we bought the bed the warehouse made a mistake & quoted us a price $30 less than it should have been, but we were allowed to have the bed for the price we paid (59 pounds--- the best, with two pillows amounting to about $170), which is nice. My pride and joy arrives Thursday: a beautiful refrigerator made by LEC, a

British firm that does airplanes etc. Most of the friges here are diminutive ---waist-high, with a table-surface top, about 3½ cubic feet capacity, a freezer just big enough for icecubes. Women here need a salestalk to buy one---most of them just use "cold-cupboards", the coldest windowsill or closet! At an expense of only about $30 more than the usual cupboard model, we are getting a marvel (abt.$200) with 6 cubic feet of space, a door inlaid with egg-racks, butter racks etc. and the biggest freezer I've seen yet here, going right across the top instead of at the side corner like our Willow Street freezer. It runs on electricity & is handsome. We looked at all sorts before choosing it, & think it a fine investment (do tell me your opinions on all this!)

The place looks like a railroad station now. Tiles will be put around the bathroom wall up to 4 feet & panels around the good-sized tub on Thursday. The livingroom is the catchall---floors unpainted, walls with liner-paper on ready for painting, full of all our cases, timber, etc. Ted will make bookcases for our two alcoves, get our books up (after painting the walls white) & then we'll paint the floor two coats of lino paint, pale grey, as in the bedroom, which makes the rooms look much bigger & very bright. I'm typing on a sample of our kitchen paper,[1] which is waterproof & very cheerful. The bathroom paper (I'm enclosing a dirty sample)[2] is the same design, only in neutral colors---it looks posh). We'll paint the bits of wall around the sink, window, ascot & stove in the kitchen white, & the opposite wall a rose matching the paper & continue the rose into the little hall (It's the same wall), & a little rose entry, plain. So no two patterned papers will adjoin---the livingroom plain white (brightened by our books, curtains & pictures) being the same backing as our kitchen & bedroom walls. We are having a marvelous time fixing the place up & don't mind investing energy in it, as we'll be here a good deal into our 3 year lease. I think $18 a week reasonable for such a lovely place, don't you? What I like best is the spanking newness of everything. All new fixtures, nobody's old stove to clean or toilet to scrub!

Here's more of our kitchen paper---as you can see, the pattern is a large one. Don't think of a washer. There's not a mite of space for it. By the time I have my second baby I expect we'll be in a place large enough for

1–The two-page letter is typed on the back of a continuous piece of the wallpaper, halved by SP. Among other objects, the pattern includes a birdcage, lamps, bicycles, car, hot air balloon, mailbox, and parking meter, in red, grey, black, and green on a white ground.

2–The bathroom wallpaper sample is no longer with the letter. The Lilly Library does have a sample of the bedroom wallpaper, labelled as such in SP's hand. The pattern's 'flat pink roses' feature in SP's 'Morning Song' (1961) and other creative works.

one. I will have diaper service, take the laundry twice a week (Ted can do this till I'm all rested up) to the laundromat around the corner & dry it on racks in the kitchen or bathtub overnight by having our electric fan-heater on, which only costs pennies a day. So don't worry about that. I do appreciate your offer, though! Oddly enough, in a country where washmachines are a luxury for most people, it's easier to get laundry done cheaply & conveniently because there is a demand for laundromats.

Our friends the Merwins are going to their farm in France[1] at the end of April & for the summer & are going to let Ted use Bill's study---the quietest place in London---and me use their garden while they're gone! Isn't that lovely. Dido said all we have to do in return (she always makes some little task, she says, so that people won't feel they're imposing) is keep their marvelous Siamese cat company (the girl who sublets the rest of the place from them feeds it) & mow the little lawn. They live five minutes away from us, so it will be heavenly. The widowed older woman who lives in the Russian-novel antique attic upstairs (she is an aged Bohemian, came here 20 years ago & is a French interpreter for the telephone company, surrounded by hyacinths & all sorts of flowering plants, grease & dirt, & dusty oil paintings & gin, very warm-hearted) says you can hear the lions & seals & foreign birds roaring & cawing in the distance from the Regent's Park Zoo when the windows are open in the summer! I just wish we could buy a house around here someday.

My prize is very simple & small: about $20 for a poem tied for first place[2] in a British critical magazine---poems were sent in from all over, but it made me cheered those dreary first weeks in London.

What we are happiest about is the wonderful news of Warren's exam results! I read your long letter aloud to Ted & shouted "Oh oh oh" out when I came to that section. He deserves it! A good reward for all that work. Ironically, a hard, grim time---as I think we all have felt in this last year---seems to make pleasant changes afterwards that much more appreciated. Do let him read this letter---I mean him to read them all & always imagine I am writing to both of you.

We are going to keep one big trunk here (I shall cover it & use it as a windowseat) to store our summer & winter clothes in. The others the ubiquitous Dido has offered to store in her big attic. She is a vibrant, fine woman in her late thirties (or older---she keeps herself very well) married

1–W. S. Merwin owned a farmhouse in Lacan de Loubressac, near Bretenoux, Lot, Midi-Pyrénées, France.

2–The other prize-winner was Alan Brownjohn, 'William Empson at Aldermaston', *Poetry 1960: An Appetiser* (*Critical Quarterly* Poetry Supplement 1, 1960): 21–2.

for the third time to this young American poet (he is about 32 or so). A fine thing for him: she has this wonderful London house---they live on the top two floors & the income from the lower two keep them. He has all his time for writing & is on his 5th book of poems, 2nd book of verse translations & does reviews. They bought an old farm in France for about $1,000 & live, as you may imagine, very pleasantly. He doesn't want children (is actually, I think, at heart quite cold & calculating) & lives for himself & his work, &, & guess, Dido too. I like them both very much, though. On second thought, Bill is very good too: he just came over in his old car bringing an enamel-top table for the kitchen & took us back for some good expresso coffee. I wouldn't have my doctor or this apartment, really, if it weren't for them: Dido told us about it---she actually went hunting for us.

The rest of the house is in chaos & will be for a week or more---the flat below us isn't finished, nor is the basement. And they are doing over the attic above us. By the time we are ready for peace & quiet, though, they will be done.

Did I tell you our kitchen, bathroom & little hall---all continuous, really, have been covered in marbled black linoleum? We bought it & the landlord's men fitted it & it looks beautiful & will clean marvelously. As soon as the traffic is over, I shall wax it.

We love hearing about Sappho's life & habits. Do forward all mail here now & write once a week. Things will have calmed down, I imagine, when I next write you & relative order been restored.

lots of love from us both,

Sivvy

Do say <u>Rebecca</u> & not Becky – not that I don't like Becky, but I much prefer the full names & will call the children the whole thing!

TO *Aurelia Schober Plath & Warren Plath*

Sun.–Mon. 7–8 February 1960 TL (aerogramme), Indiana University

<SP typed 'No. 1' on address side of letter>

Sunday evening
February 7, 1959 (60!)

Dearest mother & Warren,

Well, here I am, sitting at my little enamel table in the warm, cheerful kitchen, my Olivetti open before me, the timer (yours) ticking away, an apful kuchen in the oven & a chicken stew gently simmering on top of the stove. My stove is a delight---we've used the grill (I welcome the height of it, no kneeling), the oven (I made that tunafish loaf & some Scottish fancies last night---how do you keep the latter from sticking as they cool like barnacles to the cookie sheet, no matter how fast you scrape them off?) Today has been a much-needed day of rest, as both of us have been working enormously hard all week. We knew this would be the immediate difficulty of any unfurnished apartment---the large lump investment of money and energy, but this place responds so beautifully & we are so happy here we are glad, enormously so, that it is ours for three years (we can always sublease or assign it if we want, or need, to move out earlier). My constant joy is that you will be seeing the place when you come in 1961, mother.

The landlord was right in saying the opening date of the house should have probably been a week after February 1st, but we are so grateful to have a base, a home, that we don't mind the carry-on of repairs---workmen cheerfully whistling outside our windows at 7 am painting the plaster a lovely grey-white. Our bathroom will be tiled & the tub paneled tomorrow, & that should be the last they do in our apartment. They have still to do the stairs & main hall of the house & the basement flat is yet raw cement. We won't use the bathroom, except the toilet, till they've finished tomorrow, & I haven't cleaned the linoleum there or in the hall (big enough for a bureau or chest of drawers, very convenient) & won't till they're done. The kitchen is our center now---so new & gay with the bright paper on two walls. The outer wall we'll paint white & the inner opposite rose-vermillion to match the color in the paper I sent. Ted has made a marvelous open cupboard of 7 shelves in the kitchen alcove next the livingroom where I can store much of my gear & will make me the kind of long, narrow counter table I need between cupboard & stove, big enough for guests, later. My icebox came & is wonderful, very handsome & capacious, with its little trays of plastic pop-out icecubes, shelved door, etc. The British are still afraid of Big things---large economy sizes, and all the stoves & refrigerators we looked at, even the most expensive, had little mincey grilles & freezers: the one big enough for two pieces of toast, the other for a tray of icecubes & a box of frozen peas! Our freezer is marvelous, big enough to hold a roast, a brace of frozen boxes, a chicken etc, & our broiler is also fine & large. I am so pleased with our bed, stove & frige---I keep rubbing the latter over with a damp cloth just to see them sparkle.

Ted has made one fine set of bookshelves in the 7 foot alcove in the livingroom next to the windows & our books are up---the case is painted white, & he has just finished painting the livingroom walls white over the nice rough-textured liner paper, which looks wonderful---the room has a north-light overlooking the little green square of trees & pigeons & needs to be light. We are going to have a lovely engraving of Isis from one of Ted's astrology books blown up to cover one of the sidewall panels, a bright floorlength curtain that will pull at night over the whole two-windowed wall, & of course Ted's "Pike" & our Baskins. We'll do that floor last---a grey-white lino paint---the boards are so bad they'll need 3 coats, & then our Indian rug & my braided rug &, for the time being, some of the Merwins old furniture, until we can get some bargains at the multitudinous antique shops in London.

The bedrooms is like a bright arbor of roses We have ordered a five-drawer unpainted wood bureau (abt. 2½ ft. wide) at abt.$21, which we shall paint white. The little closet holds a surprising lot, & if it is necessary, we'll get a second bureau for the hall. We are beginning to get the 1st good sleeps we've had in 6 months---both of us don't sleep well when changing about all the time.

One great favor: could you possibly get & send me the biggest quilted bed pad going? Our bed is 5 feet wide by 6½ feet long, & noone here has heard of bedpads---they use blankets when they use anything! I'd love to get hold of one before the baby is born, as you may imagine, & would gladly pay you whatever it costs. Our ticking cover is so beautiful---pale blue with white figures, I don't want to risk spoiling it. Would that be too much to be of a bother? I'd rather have that than anything. (I'll continue this on another form.)

<on the return address side of letter>

Monday: february 8: Just got the Harper's today, forwarded from Yorkshire: so they took over a month. A manila envelope with my ms. of poems, rejected 5 poems & Ted's story SUNDAY also came: please say what magazine the latter is from so we can keep our records straight!

TO *Aurelia Schober Plath & Warren Plath*

Sun.–Mon. 7–8 February 1960 TLS (aerogramme), Indiana University

<SP typed 'No. 2' on address side of letter>

(continued)

As I say, the bedpad would be a wonderful convenience. I hate to waste a blanket where a launderable pad would do.

I do think I have Warren's skipants, but they are up in Yorkshire. I didn't really give a second look when I unpacked them, but I remember thinking they seemed peculiarly new! Shall I have them sent back? I'm awfully sorry to have walked off with them.

Today we slept till nine after going to bed well before ten, got up leisurely for a breakfast of oatmeal & raisins, applesauce & coffee. We make the oatmeal quite thin, not porridgey, & love it every morning with fruit. Fruit & vegetables here seem very cheap & good---a head of lettuce for 12 cents, a pound of chicken livers for 30 cents, two magnificent lamb chops for 30 cents---chicken is the one thing that seems expensive a dollar or two each, & they are just beginning to catch on to fattening them---most are scrawny, but ours seems quite tender. You see broiled-chicken shops everywhere. For lunch, Ted having painted on the livingroom wall <u>&</u> me having sat & rested in the kitchen, which gets the sun all day, I had a lamb chop, crispy potatoes with an onion chopped fine & cooked with them (my favorite way), an enormous salad of lettuce & chicory, cookies & milk. So you see I eat well. Pints of milk here are 2½ cups (aren't ours 2 cups?) and cost 8 cents a pint (we get ours delivered) and eggs, large, are about 50 cents a dozen. Do remind me of our American prices & compare them. Beds, it seems, are much more expensive here. But we got the best in the large shop & ordered one made to our specific size requirements, which added $30 to the price of the 4-foot wide one & the mattress is 8 inches thick & the most comfortable I've ever slept on. You'll have to take a nap on it when you come.

The Merwins offer of Bill's study for Ted from the end of April through the summer takes off all the strain of our being one room short when the baby comes, & they may (we hope) go to America next winter. Their house is only 5 minutes away.

This afternoon it was so pleasant---sunny all day, though fearfully cold (no snow at all here)---we went out for a two hour walk, across the street up Primrose Hill, which overlooks all London & is full of benches, groves of trees, across to Regents Park where I first lived (at Bedford College) when I came to London 5 years ago on my Fulbright. We skirted the wonderful zoo & peered at camels, llamas, Oriental deer & monkeys, all the children of London seemed out with their parents, then walked & walked over green grass to the islands of the bird sanctuary to see children throwing bread to the gorgeous ducks---all wierd colors, black swans, red-buff headed black & white striped, tufted greens & blues (Carolina ducks) & the common Bostonian mallard. There are boats here to take out under the little bridges in the summer, formal garden, fountains---all literally nextdoor to us. How I look forward to walking the baby out there---all the AA Milne[1] rhymes come to life! And "Ducks are a-dabbling".[2] What fun we shall have when you come.

Saw my young doctor for another checkup last Thursday. He seems immensely kind & capable. The baby had swum around headup since I saw him, so he moved him back into position again, head down (I didn't know this could be done) & said this was a common thing to happen in late pregnancy. I have to bring a urine sample for testing each time I come, & my blood-test showed I was type-O (Rh positive) & had a normal red-cell count for this time. I'll see him again in two weeks. My midwife, Sister Hannaway, should come to the house to see me sometime this week, & I will go to her relaxation classes in Bloomsbury Square as soon as I make arrangements with her. Now that the strain of looking for a place is over & the apartment responding so rapidly to our work, I feel happy as I've ever been in my life, both of us eagerly anticipating Nicholas-Rebecca, who has a book already waiting to be dedicated to him/her.

Your plans for work in remedial reading sound very rewarding & sensible, if also strenuous. Do go easy on loading yourself with extra work. Could you fit in at BU in that new capacity? I should think colleges or private schools would be better than public schools---at Smith, I know, a woman came a couple of times a week to give a sight & content-reading improvement course & her extra-curricular classes were eagerly attended. Do keep up the German & your eyes open for any foot or even toe-hold there. Both of us have our fingers crossed for you. Let us know all that develops.

Love to Warren & more congratulations on his wonderful midterm marks.

xxx
Sivvy

1–English auther A. A. Milne (1882–1956).

2–From Kenneth Grahame, *The Wind in the Willows* (1908); According to SP's diary, she finished reading this novel by 5 June 1944.

TO *Marcia B. Stern*

Monday 8 February 1960 TL (aerogramme), Smith College

<SP wrote 'No. 1' on address side of letter>

Monday afternoon
February 8, 1960

Dearest Marty . . .

Your good letter arrived in the midst of a very bleak month & cheered me no end. I decided to wait in answering until we had a London address, which I despaired of for many weeks, & now we have & I am in a much more optimistic frame of mind. Ted & I stayed up at his place in Yorkshire (pleasant enough, with its wild moortop views & great coal fires, but much too overcrowded to read a book in with Ted's sister at home from Paris & all manner of relatives dropping in, & the minute kitchen & generally messiness of Ted's mother who has a habit of leaving greasy frying pans unwashed in the oven, in cupboards etc. etc.) for 3 weeks & came to London just after New Year's to start what we were sure would be a pleasant, brief search for a furnished apartment near one of the big London parks---Regent's or Hyde---& to locate me a doctor & hospital. Well, we started out staying in a ghastly unheated $5 a night bed & breakfast rooming house, the cheapest available, & went to a few housing agencies who promptly told us there were no furnished flats near a Park in London for anything under $25 or more a week. London, as you know, is geographically enormous. We started on what was to be a dreary 2-week trek from one end to the other by tube, bus, foot, & every so desperate often, taxi, through rain & cold winds, eating bad minestrones in Soho when we could remember it, & seeing the most unbelievable places for even more unbelievable prices---an American poet over here, W. S. Merwin (he and his aging British wife have been very wonderful & helpful) agreed with me that the English are the most secretly dirty race on earth. And they are. Even the "new" furniture in the large department stores looks dirty & grim. Well, anyhow, we felt more & more weary, cold (very) & lugubrious. The one place we liked, prettily furnished, at the corner of Kensington gardens was signed up fifteen minutes before we saw it. The other---over-looking Primrose Hill & a garden with big windows & clean kitchen, had a decorator-owner on vacation in Nassau who wouldn't have any children. The unfurnished places demanded fantastic prices for "Fixtures & fittings" (nothing, really; perhaps a few light bulbs), hundreds of dollars---or "key money", a large bribe to landlord or agent to get in at all---and were usually cold, noisy, barnlike.

Our second pair of friends in London, barely acquaintances before this, the Merwins, took us in with wonderful encouragement. They fed us, warmed us, called up places, people & saw flats for us. Dido (Bill is her 3rd husband) is an amazingly vital fortyish woman full of verve, who bought a huge bombedout house after the blitz for under 3 thousand, slowly converted it, & now owns a place worth 60 thousand at the end of a dead-end terrace overlooking the green acres of Primrose Hill. She & Bill live on the rent from the artist who occupies the 2 basement floors. Anyhow, Dido dug up this place in Chalcot Square---a mere wet hole of plaster when we first saw it in mid-January, being done-over into flats from a tenement of Irish laborers in a rapidly up & coming section just one street behind Regents Park road, overlooking a little green square of trees & grass.

We felt unaccountably happy after visiting the place, just to smell fresh paint & see everything (except the floorboards which are 100 years old & all chewed up & which I have just finished giving a 3rd coat of lino paint in the bedroom) new---tub, sink, toilet. The thought of investing all the money & energy in bed, stove, refrigerator etc etc. gave us pause, also the Feb. 1st moving-in date which seemed very late on, with the baby due in late March. In the last 15-minutes of our ghastly 2 weeks we signed a 3-year assignable lease & crawled back to Yorkshire to lick our wounds. (We'd meanwhile moved in with the other couple we know who live in a condemned slum very cosily---a dear german girl, Helga, & her Welsh husband & their 2 year-old cherubic girl & felt a bit better---warmer at least). Our place is a room short of what we wanted, but the Merwins have offered Ted Bill's superlative study for the summer while they're at their farm in France, so he'll have a place to work, which makes me feel easy about that. We have a bedroom with one window looking over the square & the baby will sleep with us regardless of what Freud, Spock[1] et. al. have to say about the matter, a north-light livingroom (Ted's just finished painting the walls white over a pebbled liner-paper & put up twin huge bookcases in the little alcoves) with two big windows also overlooking the square---very like a Utrillo,[2] cream, grey & white plaster houses about 3 stories high opposite, full of birds & children. And a lovely sunny kitchen at the back, a tiny bathroom & small hall big enough for a bureau. We've invested in a great double bed a gas stove & a refrigerator & the Merwins

1–American pediatrician Dr Benjamin Spock (1903–98). SP's copy of his *Baby & Child Care* (London: Bodley Head, [1960]) held by Smith College.
2–French painter Maurice Utrillo (1883–1955).

have loaned us tables, chairs, china etc. out of their attic till we pick up some we like at 2nd hand shops.

(I'll continue this on another sheet! There's too much to say here!)

TO *Marcia B. Stern*

Monday 8 February 1960 TLS (aerogramme), Smith College

<SP wrote 'No. 2' on address side of letter>

Installment 2:
Monday: after tea

Hello again. You'll know the feeling I mean when I say I've been absolutely brainless simply from physical chores---for you must get days like that with the twins[1] where to read even a newspaper requires superhuman effort. Yesterday & today I have just begun to recover---we have been on the move for 6 months since leaving Boston last June & neither of us want to move for years, & then only to a larger, more permanent house. Just now the sun is setting---it's been marvelously clear for two straight days, very cold, no snow at all---over my view of chimney pots & bare treebranches, a lovely shade of rose & lilac. I am snug in the kitchen, the first room we did up---they put in (we bought) marbled black linoleum for the kitchen, bathroom & hall floors to cover the ghastly boards, be washable & keep out drafts---we're on the 3rd floor, by the way, only a rather sweet antique Bohemian lady-artist in the grubby attic above us, a rent-control tenant who can't be got rid of <u>&</u> who lives, apparently, on gin & pineapple juice among 20 years of dust & dozens of pots of multi-colored hyacinths.

Anyhow, here we are. Day by day things get better as I get the routines under control. At first we were too tired to cook or even sleep, the hot water took half a week to come on (heated by a big efficient gas Triton on the kitchen wall) & as I sit here the builders & landlords are coming in & out arguing about the peculiar stains & spots ("DAMP" is the word for it) that appear in the kitchen & bathroom outer walls. It is quite fun to see them going on---the suave blond landlord who promises to fix it all & really does, & is very shrewd with his builders, "Charlie, you're giving me the business, what's this, what's that," etc. Mornings at seven we're

1–Cary Plumer Frye and Douglas Plumer; twins born 16 December 1958 and adopted by Davenport (Mike) and Marcia Brown Plumer (later Stern).

wakened by the songs & whistles of the Irish boys on the scaffolding outside the windows, painting the house a delightful grey. "It'll be just like Chelsea," our landlord assures us. I think he's even pleased we're writers, something we've had to disguise elsewhere, for he does so want to produce an arty dwelling! Now that I'm resting I can be amused. Oh, in another week I shall feel human again. I may even read a book.

Please do write me at least once a month! I'd like to write about once every two weeks, just because things pile up so & I like to feel casual about talking back & forth. It means so much to me to have you to write to. I think what I'll miss most when the baby comes is you to drop in & any other relatives or friends to be about. Ted's won't stir out of Yorkshire. Dido Merwin also introduced me to her doctor (John Wigg, of all names) & his young assistant, very kind & attractive & capable, is my obstetrician. I am going to have the baby delivered at home---I'm too late to register at any hospital under the System & am taking this chance to have the baby perfectly free after paying to make sure of conceiving it! I shuddered at the word "midwife", but that's the way they do things here---a local midwife & her assistant covers a certain area. I hope to meet mine some time this week when she will come to the house & give me a list of things to have on hand – she brings the rest.

I'll go to her relaxation classes---it's all natural childbirth & Grantly Dick Read[1] over here. I'm sceptical, & was advised not to consider natural childbirth by my Md. in America, at least for the first, but they do give whiffs of gas & sedatives & my Dr. here has promised to stand by. Also, with Ted by my side I'm sure I shan't feel left & miserable as I would in a labor ward---I've never liked the idea of them, & in England they keep you in hospital 12 days! As is, Ted can cook what I like, be with the baby from the start, & the midwife will come each day to help care for it. Do tell me what you think about all this. In spirit I am all for home births with the father there. I just wish you were around to visit with afterwards. I've got all the lovely babythings you gave me waiting for the bureau coming this week, which I'll paint myself.

Neither Ted or I have written a line for so long we are slaving on the housework to get it done & some quiet hours free. His 2nd book, Lupercal, should come out here this spring & I'm not sure when Harper's will import it in America. We're excited because Faber is doing an anthology

1 – British obstetrician Grantly Dick-Read (1890–1959); SP's copy of his *Childbirth without Fear: The Principles and Practice of Natural Childbirth*, 3rd edition revised (London: William Heinemann Medical Books, 1959) held by Smith College.

of six short-story writers for next fall & are including 3 of Ted's stories--- one of them came out in Harper's this January, his first prose. Of course, nothing makes any money. We will try to stretch the Guggenheim out till Sept. 1st, a large order, but I get a pint of free milk a day & a free baby on the NatHealthService, so that helps. Do write soon, & I will too. Tell me all about the twins, I love hearing everything.

Best love to you & Mike & Cary & Douglas,

Syl

TO *Olwyn Hughes*

Monday 8 February 1960[1]

ALS[2] on pink Smith College Memorandum paper, Washington University (St Louis)

Dear Olwyn –

Only a note at the end of a Monday (the second) full of builders whistling & singing at our bedroom window on precarious scaffolding at 7 am, hammering & sawing & scattering curlycue shavings in the bathroom which as yet is useable only for the toilet & yet all grinding & groaning & promising completion this week – And for this we are grateful, happier as the place responds – painting the shocking chewed floorboards 3 times, the walls, the shelves (elegant) Ted is in the process of making & carrying, each of us, his one chair about as if we were enacting the immortal "Snow" (to appear next fall with two other masterpieces in prose in a Faber anthology by a wellknown . . . etcetera).

Your tip about the little Critical Quarterly contest acted upon, turned out well as Ted has said. In desperation the judges lumped the three prizes into one large one & split it between some other fellow & me – amounting, my share, to some interesting, uneven sum like £7. 7. 9d or some such.

I am in surprising good health for the ordeal of the last month – I don't think either of us has sustained such a prolonged period of crammed exhaustion & despair before – & physical cold, hunger & all the misères. By contrast – life seems heavenly here, better every day, & especially with the prospect of at least a 2-year stay in this place we're coaxing to shape with our bare hands. My one prayer is that the saws, nails & sawdust are out of the tub tomorrow, along with the workmen. One begins to feel

1 – Date supplied from internal evidence.
2 – SP's letter is at the end of a letter begun by TH, which has not been transcribed.

leprous after an interval. After this week, we hope to read, take up pens & perhaps feel as if we had brains, psyches, yea, even good genies.

Much love to you & do write soon –

Sylvia

TO *Aurelia Schober Plath & Warren Plath*

Thursday 11 February 1960 TLS (aerogramme), Indiana University

Thursday
February 11, 1960

Dearest mother & Warren,

A little middle-of-the-week letter to pass on some very pleasant news: picture (yesterday) your daughter/sister, resplendent in black wool suit, black cashmere coat, fawn kidskin gloves from Paris (Olwyn's Christmas present) & matching calfskin bag (from Italy), shining from her first bath in two weeks (having wangled the repairmen to get done at last with the bathroom cardboard tiling) and of enormous & impressive size, sailing into the notorious York Minster pub on Dean Street[1] in Soho, just off Shaftesbury Avenue about 12:15 & up to the bar to meet a pleasant half-American, half-Scots young editor[2] for the wellknown British publishers William Heinemann (publishers of Somerset Maugham,[3] Evelyn Waugh,[4] DH Lawrence, Erskine Caldwell[5] etc. etc.) & taking out a pen thereupon & signing on the counter the contract for her first book of poems, namely THE COLOSSUS.[6]

Which is to say, the first British publisher I sent my new collection of poems to (almost one-third written at Yaddo: 48 poems in all, after countless weedings & reweedings) wrote back[7] within the week accepting them! Amaze of amaze. I was so hardened to rejections that I waited till

1–The York Minster was at 49 Dean Street, London.

2–Publisher, poet, and translator James Michie (1927–2007) was SP's editor at William Heinemann and helped her prepare *The Bell Jar* for publication on 14 January 1963. Michie left Heinemann in 1962 to join Bodley Head.

3–English playwright and novelist W. Somerset Maugham (1874–1965).

4–English writer Evelyn Waugh (1903–66).

5–American writer Erskine Caldwell (1903–87).

6–Sylvia Plath, *The Colossus and Other Poems* (London: Heinemann, 1960). Published 31 October 1960.

7–James Michie to SP, 5 February 1960; held by Smith College. According to SP's submissions list, she sent the manuscript on 25 January 1960.

I actually signed the contract (with the usual 10% royalties, which, of course, will amount to nothing) before writing you. They do very few, very few poets at Heinemann & will do a nice book. It should come out late next fall, or at New Year's. It is dedicated to that paragon who has encouraged me through all my glooms about it, Ted. That means in our small family of soon-to-be three every member will have a book dedicated to him/her & written by some other member! Maybe the baby itself will inspire a children's book, or several!

THE COLOSSUS and Other Poems, by Sylvia Plath. For Ted. That is what the book is, named after the title of the 9th poem in it, one written at Yaddo.

Ted waited in a pub nextdoor for me to come in after seeing my editor (who now become my agents for America & will work on getting the book published there, if it doesn't get the Yale prize this year)[1] & we went to a pleasant, second-floor Soho Italian restaurant for veal & mushrooms to celebrate, having sat in the same restaurant in misery a month back, homeless & cold & very grim. Of course I shall write Mrs. Prouty of it.

I've just written, by the way, to our Weston Road checking account, closing it as the last check has come in & asking that a check for the remainder (just over $50) be made out to you & sent to you. Let me know that they do this. Could you pay the Music Box bill out of it & Dr. Brownlee's, if they come? And keep the rest to cover postage & perhaps the quilted bedpad. Will that be enough for all that? The Music Box is just for the little record & Brownlee for one office visit. We don't want to sully our 5 cent bank account with anything other than writing money. We also have, by the way, $1,037 in a savings account at the Newton Wellesley bank, which should be gaining interest---we have that book here. That is the account we will draw on if & when we need it: the 5 cent account is untouchable!

Our apartment is daily more comfortable & attractive. The livingroom is still without furniture of any sort with the crude floorboards unpainted ---we're saving that, those 3 coats, till last, for we have yet to paint a table, chair, chest of drawers. However, the two matching bookcases are up in the alcoves against a beautiful nubbly-textured white wall, the shelves white too, & brimming with our colored books. And Dido Merwin loaned us the curtains she had in Boston---a gay striped red & white which draws

1–SP submitted *The Colossus* to the Yale Series of Younger Poets on 25 January 1960. The Yale manuscript included 'Owl', 'The Beggars', and 'Ella Mason and Her Eleven Cats', which were not part of the Heinemann edition. SP slightly shifted the order of poems as well.

across the 2 windows in one bright swash at night to form one wall of the room. The bedroom needs only bureau & crib, & if we can pick one up, a rocking chair for me to nurse the baby in. The kitchen is still our center & the 2nd Pifco heater has come today---a neat mushroom shape & two are ample to warm the whole place & each about a penny a day to run. Made a banana bread, very good. My midwife is due to come visit today ---I missed her yesterday. My md. sent round a very bright, nice mother of 2 who lives around the corner & had my midwife for a home-delivery of her 2nd baby & is very enthusiastic about her: I'm going to tea with the girl (a former nurse) today. So you see how very extra-thoughtful my doctor (Christopher Hindly) is.

Much love to both of you, & the ineffable Sappho!

Your new authoress,
Sivvy

TO *Aurelia Schober Plath & Warren Plath*

Thursday 18 February 1960 — TLS (aerogramme), Indiana University

Thursday morning
February 18, 1960[1]

Dearest mother & Warren,

How good to get your two letters this morning & have you share my good news! It is wonderful how fast mail travels between Boston & London & makes you both feel so much closer. I am just about to go out for my every-other-week visit to my doctor, around the corner & to buy a few of the very few things on my list that my midwife gave me---the wonderful plastic pants came too, this morning, with Mrs. Spaulding's exquisite silver-white baby sweater set. I will write her today---how much that lovely set means to me: we must surely have the baby christened in a little ceremony now: I'm thinking of looking up the nearest Episcopal church & finding out about it.

My midwife came for the first time to the house on Friday: a surprisingly delicate, yet wiry Irishwoman of about forty with golden hair! A lovely lilting voice: she seemed both kind & warmhearted & extremely practical & capable: I trusted her right away. Sister Hannaway is her name. She had been practicing in this area for 15 years or so & assured me that the

1 – 'February 18, ~~1959~~ 60' appears in the original.

main difference between hospital care & home care was that home care was really private care, & couldn't be better. I look forward to receiving the bedpads---you must surely deduct them from the $50 the bank sends! I have a poncho here, which should double as a rubber sheet, a relic of our summer's camping. Most of the other things I have, too---bowls, pots for boiling etc. I have sheets for the baby's cot (which we have yet to buy) that Mrs. Hughes made me out of some old sheets she had, & two new blankets, pink & blue, wool, she gave me, very pretty. The main thing I need to decide about now is diapers (they are called nappies here). The diaper service costs about $1.20 a week for a 3-day a week delivery (the daily delivery is much more costly & seems unnecessary & a bother) of a total of 42 nappies, which averages about 6 a day. If I bought 4 dozen, I'd have a half dozen left over for emergencies. They also have a more expensive hire-service where they supply their own nappies---nappies are very dear here, it seems to me: over $4 for a dozen "muslin", & over $5 for a dozen "turkish"---I haven't seen either of these yet, so I haven't decided what to get. Or whether to pay extra & not buy more than a dozen myself but have the service nappies. Tell me what your advice is about this.

Just back from my doctor. I am in fine health & sleeping 9 hours a night, plus a rest in the afternoon. Things are, thank goodness, quieting down a bit, although the builders are still in the house, doing the basement, 2nd floor & attic apartments---only one other couple living here, on the ground floor, & the lady in the attic. How glad I am we are entrenched! They are about a month behind schedule, but by keeping after them, we are fine.

Dido Merwin found us a marvelous kitchen cabinet (looked hideous, dirty-cream-painted), an ideal size for our kitchen, narrow & long with 2-doors & 2 very capacious shelves a 2nd hand lady let us have for $2.80. Ted has had it in the little hall, stripping the 4 layers of paint & now we will sand the good base wood & as soon as that job's done, I'll wash & wax the sawdusty kitchen floor & we'll move it in. Then I can clean the hall of cartons & paint cans & relax. 4 light-wood sprightly kitchen chairs are due, made in Czechoslovakia & Ted is going to get me a tall stool so I can sit to do dishes & work at the counters. We're going to hard-wax the bedroom & livingroom floors tomorrow & polish with Dido's electric polisher to preserve the delicate light grey paint we've so laboriously put on. Some time later we'll paint the hall walls & 2 kitchen walls. Except for little conveniences like towel racks & lamps, we are very comfortable. The bed is a marvel---I've never slept so well in my life.

I'm eating ravenously: lamb chops yesterday, new potatoes, escarole & lettuce salad with cheese & hardboiled eggs chopped in it; my favorite salad is your carrot, raisin & nut salad which I have often. Ted got us a marvelous roast (rolled rib, no bones) this week for about $1.50---lasted us 3 dinners.

Tonight we're relaxing to the point of going to a movie, part of Ivan the Terrible,[1] with Dido & Bill. My book should come out sometime next autumn---I hope, in October, & be fat, with 50 poems in it. We love hearing about the gallivantings of Sappho, & her new rabbity escort. We saw little black kittens in a pet shop window & had to hurry past, because they only reminded us there was One Sappho & all others mere flashy copies.

Have Ted's 2 stories come back from the NYorkr (The Caning, Miss Mambrett) or my 3 from the Atlantic (Johnny Panic, The 59th Bear & Prospect of Cornucopia)? Let us know.

Love,
Sivvy

<on the return address side of letter>

PS: We're having $500 transferred from our Barclay's Bank here also a "just writing account" so the Boston account will be kept PURE![2] to the 5cent savings acct. in Boston because the acct. here is a $ acct. & not pounds, so be sure & ask them to record the large addition in our book & let us know what it is after expenses are deducted---should be over $500, or just!

Money should reach them in a week.

*Did you send Mrs. Prouty a copy of "The Rain Horse" in HARPER'S??

1–*Ivan the Terrible, Part 2*, released in Britain as *The Boyars' Plot*; was shown at the Academy Cinema, then at 161–7 Oxford Street, London.

2–SP circled 'Barclay's Bank here' and added 'also a "just writing account" so the Boston account will be kept PURE!' by hand.

TO *Lynne Lawner*

Thursday, 18 February 1960 Printed from *Antaeus* 28, Winter 1978

3 Chalcot Square
London N.W.1, England
Thursday: February 18, 1960

Dear Lynne,

On rereading your letter (which did reach me) I find a marked if unintentional irony in your "Coming? I'd never have believed it . . ." The last three months have been the most hectic & unsettled in our lives, with a Dickensianly grim & chilblain-ridden January hunt for a flat in central London near a big park (at which request the agents burst into hysterical laughter: no, we have no television connections). Our plans have markedly changed & Ted is finishing his grant in England (after our round-America-with-the-bears travels this summer & the suitcase-dwelling after Yaddo we are glad of it) mainly because we are desirous of settling & waiting for the arrival of the imminent Nicholas or Rebecca Hughes due at the end of March. I haven't even had time to fully take in the fact I'm pregnant & find it amazing that I'm to produce a child in 5 weeks. After traipsing all over the great areas of London & seeing filthy, cheerless, lightless, bathless places for $25 and up a week, & having the two places we liked snatched up minutes before we came, or barred because the fairy decorator owner couldn't abide children, Negros or dogs, our friends, the poet W. S. Merwin & his older, very energetic, very British, very thrice-married wife found us an unfurnished flat – one room too small, but right where the grass is greenest, on the north rim of Regent's Park. Last Sunday I paid a visit to the Park with Ted, to Bedford College (did you stay there?) & thus recalled the wide circle of my Fulbright arrival with my now-matronly return.

We've invested in a marvelous bed, stove & refrigerator, & the Merwin's have furnished us with tables & chairs out of their Victorian attic until we have time to browse about in the second-hand shops here. We've just finished an exhausting 3 weeks of floor painting (the boards are 100 years old, very chewed, full of nails & mouseholes, & imbibe 3 coats of paint), wall & table painting, scrubbing, waxing, sandpapering – except for the floors the place is new, renovated from a warren-brothel of Irish laborers into a posh little Chelsea-type house (our landlord's dream: he's actually pleased we're writers) on the slummy-elegant border of Regent's Park Road. We have 3 rooms & a bath overlooking a green square, trees, pigeons & seagulls & a Utrillo landscape (which in certain lights is very Italianate!) of yellow umber & white houses. In summer, they say, we can hear the lions roaring from the zoo across the Park. And we're two minutes from Charing Cross et. al. by bus or tube. Very light & airy on the 3rd floor. My aim is a London house eventually, in this very district, although a month ago I was cursing blue & black at everything Londonian.

Neither of us have written a thing for 2 months & are blue with the enforced nonwriting mess of dealing with Thingness. But now all is opening up & this weekend promises the end of our worst labors. Ted's second book of poems LUPERCAL (after the Roman festival) is due out here (at Faber) at the end of March along with the baby. His first children's book should come out here next winter, & 3 of his stories are to be in a Faber anthology next autumn. No money, of course, in any of this, but his writing is amazing – I've been especially excited about the prose (his first story "The Rain Horse" is in the Jan. Harper's).

My best news came last week: the British publishers William Heinemann have just accepted my first book of poems with what can only be called enthusiasm: I say "first", but of the 50 poems in it one-third were written this fall. Nothing is pre-Cambridge & over 50 have been weeded & let fall in spite of their claim of publication. It's been a long hard book in coming. To be called THE COLOSSUS after one of the father-worship poems in it. They say they'll look around for an American publisher, but I've had nothing but cold shoulders from them myself. After losing out in the Yale to old cold gold George Starbuck last year ("By a whisper") I got thoroughly grim & bloody-minded about it all. I think I shall be a very happy exile & have absolutely no desire to return to the land of milk & honey & spindryers.

PLEASE do write in answer: how are you doing so long in Rome??? What plans for return? Graduate work? Writing? Send some poems? Now we are really only a day apart by air – say something. About you, men, the Tiber, the color of things.

Love,
Sylvia

TO *Ruth Tiffany Barnhouse Beuscher*[1]

Thursday 18 February 1960 TLS (aerogramme), Smith College

3 Chalcot Square, London N.W.1
Thursday morning
February 18, 1960

Dear Dr. Beuscher,

I waited to write you until we had a London address & I a London doctor, which took a lot longer than we expected. After Christmas & New Year's in Yorkshire with Ted's parents, sister, assorted & continuous aunts, uncles & cousins, we came to a cold, bleak & utterly inhospitable London to look for (at first) a furnished apartment near one of the big parks & central to plays, shops, bookstores etc. We started out living in a grisly unheated bed & breakfast hotel which had the surprising advantage of being clean (very rare here) & applied at all the main agencies, starting what amounted to a 2-week trek by bus, tube, foot, & in occasional desperation, taxi, to the far-flung & dirty corners of the great city, finding flats, with 2 exceptions, dark, dank, full of coal dust & of expense that would have been laughable had the agents not kept straight faces. I felt miserable & ponderous in my 7th month, without anything resembling a nest to feather, & Ted felt equally badly & grim. We moved in with a German(she)-Welsh(he) couple & their 2-year old daughter in a condemned slum which was amazingly cosy in spite of no bathroom, where we could cook our meals, & the only other couple we knew in London, the American poet W. S. Merwin & his energetic, middle-aged, thrice-married British wife, began having us to heartening dinners, calling influential friends, agencies, etc. & ended up in introducing me to my (their) doctor, whom I like immediately, so we limited our search to the Regent's Park area. Against all our first resolves, we took on an unfurnished flat to be "ready" on Feb. 1st (no walls, no floors when we first saw it) & the Merwins promised to set us up in most necessary furnishings out of their capacious Victorian attic.

So here we are, 18 days after moving in, with the builders still cementing foundations, reinforcing the roof & whistling cheerfully. We are on the 3rd floor in a newly renovated house, airy, light, overlooking a green square with benches 'Chalcot Square Gardens', 2 minutes from my doctor's house & office, 2 minutes from Primrose Hill (which overlooks all flat-heeled London) & Regent's Park with its superb zoo (we can hear

1–SP's American psychiatrist Ruth Tiffany Barnhouse Beuscher (1923–99). SP was Dr Beuscher's patient at McLean Hospital in 1953–4, continued private therapy in person through 1959, and by letter into 1963.

the lions, they say, on hot summer nights), bird sanctuary, formal gardens ---play areas for children &, I feel, the ideal place for the baby. We have been painting floors, walls, making bookcases, stripping old painted cupboards & sandpapering chairs & are this weekend in sight of a halt. Have invested in a superb gas stove, refrigerator & enormous bed & are borrowing chairs, tables etc. from the Merwins attic until we can pick up things we like gradually at 2nd hand shops. My great wish now is a London house of our own, with its own garden. Its only a few minutes from here by subway or bus to Piccadilly, Charing Cross & Trafalgar Square. Now things are settling down, I can't think of anywhere else in the world I'd rather live & have no desire to return to America at all.

The obstetrician-half of my 2-doctor team is a young, kind & very good fellow (who trained at University College Hospital) who I am seeing free, on the System. As I am too late to register at a hospital, I am having the baby at home & very happy about it---I think hospital labor wards bothered me as much as anything, & I will have all the care here (analgesia, whiffs of gas & air etc.) I'd get in a hospital (immediate emergency squads if anything goes wrong) plus the privacy of my home, Ted's presence, & the continued care of my midwife---a wiry, golden-haired, tough & kindly Irish woman of 40 or so, who came to see me last week at home & assessed my cake tins for afterbirth receptacles etc. Over here it is all "natural" childbirth---making the mother do the work, with limited analgesia, in the ordinary cases, & breast-feeding for ages---I get, by the way, a half-price pint of milk (2½ cups here) a day on the System, plus no expense at all for the baby. I don't have any GrantlyDickRead illusions, but feel I have made the best arrangements for my own odd psychic setup---the doctor's promised to be there at the delivery in addition to the midwife & she'll come twice a day for 2 weeks to help me learn how the baby is bathed, nursed etc. Do let me know what you think about this!

Another nice thing: I just heard from the British publishers Wm. Heinemann (they do Somerset Maugham, Erskine Caldwell, DHLawrence etc.) an enthusiastic acceptance of my 1st book of poems (THE COLOSSUS), a third of which I wrote this fall: 50 poems in all. They'll be bringing it out next autumn & sending it about to publishers in America. So baby & 1st book are well on the way. I'd love to hear any last minute notes or words of wisdom---Nicholas or Rebecca is due March 27th. With Ted's 2nd book of poems LUPERCAL (Harper's will import copies later this year).

Love,
Sylvia

TO *W. Roger Smith*

Sunday 21 February 1960 TLS, Random House Group Archive & Library

3 Chalcot Square
London N.W.1
February 21, 1960

W. Roger Smith, Esq.
Assistant, Agreements and Rights Department
WILLIAM HEINEMANN LIMITED
15-16 Queen Street, Mayfair
London W.1

Dear Mr. Smith,

Here is a list of the poems in my book which have been published or accepted for publication in magazines and anthologies. In several cases the poems have not yet been printed; in others, they have appeared in more than one place. One or two have been printed, but I have not received copies, only cheques, so I don't know the exact date of publication. I'm not very sure what original copyright lines are and don't have a record of anything like that.

The Manor Garden:[1] CRITICAL QUARTERLY (to appear).
Two Views Of A Cadaver Room: TIMES LITERARY SUPPLEMENT (Nov. 6, 1959).
NATION[2] (appeared recently but I don't have the exact date).
THE GOLDEN YEAR[3] (1960. Anthology.)
Night Shift:[4] OBSERVER (appeared some time in 1959).
Sow: POETRY (Chicago) (July 1957).
NEW POEMS 1958 (Anthology.)
The Eye-mote:[5] CHELSEA REVIEW (to appear).

1–Sylvia Plath, 'The Manor Garden', *Critical Quarterly* 2 (Summer 1960): 155.
2–Sylvia Plath, 'Two Views of a Cadaver Room', *The Nation* (30 January 1960): 107.
3–Sylvia Plath, 'Two Views of a Cadaver Room', *The Golden Year* (New York: Fine Editions Press, 1960): 219–20.
4–Sylvia Plath, 'Poem', *The Observer* (14 June 1959): 22. Title changed to 'Night Shift'.
5–Sylvia Plath, 'The Eye-mote', *Chelsea Review* 7 (May 1960): 71.

Hardcastle Crags: NEW YORKER (October 11, 1958: appeared as "Night Walk").
THE GOLDEN YEAR[1] (1960).
LIGHT BLUE, DARK BLUE[2] (1960. Anthology.)
Faun: POETRY (Chicago) (January 1957: appeared as "Metamorphosis").
Departure: NATION (March 7, 1959).
The Colossus: KENYON REVIEW (to appear).
Lorelei: LONDON MAGAZINE (March 1959).
AUDIENCE (Spring 1959).
Point Shirley: SEWANEE REVIEW (Summer 1959).
The Bull Of Bendylaw: HORNBOOK (April 1959).
All The Dead Dears: GRECOURT REVIEW (November 1957).[3]
POETRY FROM CAMBRIDGE 1958 (Anthology.)
Aftermath: ARTS IN SOCIETY (Fall 1959).
The Thin People: LONDON MAGAZINE (October 1959).
Suicide Off Egg Rock: HUDSON REVIEW (to appear).
Mushrooms: HARPER'S (to appear).
I Want, I Want: PARTISAN REVIEW (Autumn 1959).
Watercolor Of Grantchester Meadows: NEW YORKER (to appear).
The Ghost's Leavetaking: SEWANEE REVIEW (Summer 1959: appeared as "Departure Of The Ghost")
Metaphors:[4] PARTISAN REVIEW (to appear, as "Metaphors For A Pregnant Woman").
Black Rook In Rainy Weather: ANTIOCH REVIEW (Summer 1957).
LONDON MAGAZINE (June 1958).
POETRY FROM CAMBRIDGE 1958.
Full Fathom Five: AUDIENCE (Spring 1959).
Blue Moles:[5] CRITICAL QUARTERLY (to appear).
Strumpet Song: POETRY (Chicago)(January 1957).
Ouija: HUDSON REVIEW (to appear).
Man In Black: NEW YORKER (to appear).
Snakecharmer: LONDON MAGAZINE (March 1959).

1–Sylvia Plath, 'Hardcastle Crags', *The Golden Year* (New York: Fine Editions Press, 1960): 220–1.
2–Sylvia Plath, 'Hardcastle Crags', *Light Blue, Dark Blue* (London: MacDonald, 1960): 166–7.
3–Sylvia Plath, 'All the Dead Dears', *Grecourt Review* (November 1957): 36–7.
4–Sylvia Plath, 'Metaphors', *Partisan Review* 27 (Summer 1960): 435.
5–Sylvia Plath, 'Blue Moles', *Critical Quarterly* 5 (Summer 1960): 156–7.

The Hermit At Outermost House: AUDIENCE (Spring 1959).
TIMES LITERARY SUPPLEMENT (Nov. 6, 1959).
The Disquieting Muses: LONDON MAGAZINE (March 1959).
GUINNESS BOOK OF POETRY: 3[1] (1960. Anthology).
Medallion: CRITICAL QUARTERLY Poetry Supplement (1960).
Two Sisters Of Persephone: POETRY (Chicago)(January 1957).
The Companionable Ills: SPECTATOR (January 30, 1959).
Moonrise: HUDSON REVIEW (to appear).
Spinster: LONDON MAGAZINE (June 1958).
SMITH ALUMNAE QUARTERLY[2] (February 1958).
GUINNESS BOOK OF POETRY (1958).[3]
Frog Autumn: NATION (January 24, 1959).
Mussel Hunter At Rock Harbor: NEW YORKER (August 9, 1958).
The Beekeeper's Daughter: KENYON REVIEW (to appear).
The Times are Tidy: MADEMOISELLE (January 1959).
Sculptor: GRECOURT REVIEW (May 1959).[4]
ARTS IN SOCIETY (Fall 1959).

That about does it, I think. Several other poems are out at magazines now and I haven't yet heard from them, but I will let you know if there are any more acceptances.

If it is necessary to publish a list of acknowledgements in the book itself, or credit lines, I should prefer the shortest possible form, leaving out the poem titles. Something like this:

Acknowledgements are due to the following periodicals where some of these poems have appeared: ANTIOCH REVIEW, ARTS IN SOCIETY, AUDIENCE, CHELSEA REVIEW, CRITICAL QUARTERLY, HARPER'S, HORNBOOK, HUDSON REVIEW, KENYON REVIEW, LONDON MAGAZINE, MADEMOISELLE, NATION, NEW YORKER, OBSERVER, PARTISAN REVIEW, POETRY (CHICAGO), SEWANEE REVIEW, SPECTATOR, TIMES LITERARY SUPPLEMENT. Anthologies: THE GUINNESS BOOK OF POETRY (Numbers 1 & 3), THE GOLDEN YEAR (1960), LIGHT BLUE, DARK BLUE (1960), NEW POEMS 1958, and POETRY FROM CAMBRIDGE 1958.

1–Sylvia Plath, 'The Disquieting Muses', *Guinness Book of Poetry 1958/59* (London: Putnam, 1960): 106–7.
2–Sylvia Plath, 'Spinster', *Smith Alumnae Quarterly* (June 1958): 71.
3–Sylvia Plath, 'Spinster', *Guinness Book of Poetry 1956/57* (London: Putnam, 1958): 88.
4–Sylvia Plath, 'Sculptor', *Grecourt Review* 2 (May 1959): 282.

Do let me know any other questions you may have.

Sincerely yours,
Sylvia Plath

TO *Brian Cox*

Monday 22 February 1960 TLS, University of Kansas

3 Chalcot Square[1]
London N.W.1
February 22, 1960

Mr. Charles B. Cox
THE CRITICAL QUARTERLY
The University
Hull

Dear Mr. Cox,

Just a note to thank you for my copy of Poetry 1960 and the cheque. I am happy to hear you will print "Blue Moles", "The Beggars" and "The Manor Garden".[2]

I have just heard from Wm. Heinemann that they are taking my first book of poems for publication; it should be out some time next autumn. I thought I'd let you know this, in case it might make a difference in which issue you wished to schedule the poems.

With all good wishes,
Sincerely yours,
Sylvia Plath

1–In an unidentified hand someone has written 'Ted Hughes's address' next to the return address.

2–Sylvia Plath, 'Blue Moles,' 'The Beggars', and 'The Manor Garden', *Critical Quarterly* 2 (Summer 1960): 155–7.

TO *Monroe K. Spears*

Monday 22 February 1960 TLS, Sewanee: The University of the South

3 Chalcot Square
London N.W.1, England
February 22, 1960

Mr. Monroe K. Spears
THE SEWANEE REVIEW
The University of the South
Sewanee, Tennessee
U.S.A.

Dear Monroe:

I'm sending along this sequence of seven poems[1] on the chance that you might consider publishing all, or part, of it in the SEWANEE. It is the final and most recent section of a first volume of poems Heinemann will be bringing out over here sometime next year.

Ted and I managed to extract a flat from a grim and grudging January London and are about through with the necessary scrubbing, painting & carpentering and looking forward to a spring of unbroken work. We're two minutes walk from Primrose Hill and a few minutes more from Regent's Park, a pleasant area.

Ted joins me in sending our best to you and Betty.

Sincerely yours,
Sylvia Plath

TO *Aurelia Schober Plath*

Thurs.–Fri. 25–26 February 1960 TLS (aerogramme), Indiana University

Thursday, February 25th

Dearest mother,

I have been having a pleasant day in bed, resting & reading. Ted & I are alternating, one day each a week, until we are fully recovered from the strain of the last months & the settling in. He had his Day Sunday: the one in bed orders what is desired for meals, reads, writes & sleeps. Now

1–SP's 'Poem for a Birthday'.

I am dressed and up and feeling much refreshed. Ted has made a beef stew which is simmering ready for our supper and we are going afterwards to the center of London to see Ibsen's "Rosmersholm",[1] something I have been looking forward to for a long time: my first Ibsen play seen staged. I find I am made much happier by tragedy, good tragedy, classic tragedy, in movies and on stage than by so-called "hilarious musicals and/or farces". We saw Brendan Behan's musical "The Hostage"[2] a while back & were both bored & depressed by what the audience lapped up as funny, very tawdry & puerile wit, no plot etc. Tragedy, on the other hand, really purifies & liberates me.

Last night Ted gave a reading of his poems at the Oxford Poetry Society.[3] We left after lunch by train, a one hour & 15 minutes trip. I had never been to Oxford at all, so we went a few hours early and though it was a cold, bleak inhospitable day, walked about the black, stone antique lanes and into the little green courts of one or two colleges. The architecture is immensely impressive: much more of it than at Cambridge, the eating places superb, and the atmosphere a really awesome cloistered one. The only trouble I saw was the terrible noisy roar of traffic, out-of-town traffic, on the main crossroads---so dense I hesitated to cross the street. None of the country & open sky spilling into everything as in Cambridge, but very much a big city. Yet once in a little crooked college court, the sounds of the modern world vanish by magic. I think both Ted & I would like to have gone to Oxford Too. We had a small tea while Ted ordered the list of his poems. His book LUPERCAL, officially out March 18th (I wonder if the baby will coincide!) came the day before, his six copies, very conveniently.[4] They've changed the blue of the cover to green, which put us off, & the red on the jacket & the purple on the cover are a bit of a clash to my morbidly sensitive eye, but looking at just the jacket, or, better still, the book without the jacket, it is a handsome affair. He gave a very fine reading, a few poems from his early work & the rest from LUPERCAL, to a middling-sized, enthusiastic & devotedly quiet audience, after we'd had wine & a superb Italian dinner with the members of the Inner Circle of the literary group there, including a very

1–Ibsen's *Rosmersholm* played at the Comedy Theatre on Panton Street.

2–Irish poet and writer Brendan Behan (1923–64); his *The Hostage* played at Wyndham's Theatre, on Charing Cross Road.

3–A flyer for the society announced that readings that term would be held in Jesus College at 8:15 p.m. In addition to TH, other readers that term were Donald Hall, Stephen Spender, and John Lehmann.

4–SP's presentation copy, signed and inscribed by TH, appeared at auction via Bonhams on 21 March 2018.

awkward, nice young American Jew from Princeton[1] who had been at the Glascock readings as a contestant the year I was at Smith (not my judging year). We took the train home right after & were in bed shortly after midnight.

The check for $50 should have reached you from my bank. Don't put a thing of it to the Nicholas/Rebecca account. Pay for the bed pads & some of the postage you've squandered on forwarding our mail. I'm curious to know what the pads cost: they should be a perfect fit. A bill from Brownlee may come, too. IF there is something left, we'd like a subscription to THE NATION (333 Sixth Avenue, New York) to keep up with American liberal politics.

Most of the story manuscripts we were looking for have come now, very battered & having taken about 8 weeks, I judge. The only ones I haven't heard from are my 3 Atlantic stories. It would help a lot, if you send any more over by sea, if you'd just look in, see what they are, & tell us by air mail what's coming: so we could go on sending things out. Do you remember sending an envelope back from the Atlantic?

My obliging editor at Heinemann said to tell him my birthday & he will try to get my publication date as close to that as possible! The gallantry of the British! My midwife came again yesterday with another health visitor: checked the bedroom, where I said I wanted to be delivered, took urine sample, blood pressure & felt the position of the baby & listened to its heart & pronounced me in excellent health.

Ted & I are sending off two copies of his book to you & Warren tomorrow. I am so proud of it. He is always mentioned here & there in articles now, coupled with Thom Gunn, a contemporary at Cambridge teaching in California, as "our best youngest poets" & will have his picture in a magazine THE QUEEN,[2] a sort of Harper's Bazaar here, as the only poet among 4 young writers: the photographer comes tomorrow. Next week we lunch Tuesday with Charles Monteith from Faber (TSEliot would be there if not in S. Africa, more's the pity) & the next day meet John Lehmann, British man-of-letters & editor of the London Magazine, which has been so hospitable to us. In two days N-R will be 8 months on & starting on the 9th. I am at last finding some leisure to read & Bill Merwin is supplying me with American history books. Hope to be writing

1–Probably Michael Fried (1939–), B.A. 1959, Princeton, who participated in the Glascock contest in April 1957 and April 1958.

2–Elizabeth Jane Howard, 'The New Young Writers', *The Queen* (March 1960): 141–2; photograph by John Hedgecoe; the other writers were Michael Campbell, Julian Fane, Keith Waterhouse, and Alan Sillitoe.

soon again, too. I feel much freer (and appreciated, by publishers at least) here to write than I ever did in America. I hope our mail-to-be-forwarded is lessening! We look forward now to living & writing in seclusion, & skimming the cream off London periodically. Eye-shopped at Liberty's the other day: oh, the teak furniture & copper, glass & steelware! So pacifying to see & feel beautiful things. Now we are "at home", London is a delight.

xxx
Sivvy

<on the return address side of letter>

PS Please do keep one copy of Light Blue, Dark Blue[1] – we were going to send you one anyway! How lovely of you to send diapers – tell me how much they are – I'm curious to compare prices – & take them out of the $50 too! If there's anything left of it by now! 'Rosmersholm' last night was excellent – we had sky-high balcony seats at 75¢ each & could hear every word clearly. KEEP RESTED: your program sounds Herculean & I don't want it to wear you down

xxx
Sivvy

TO *Aurelia Schober Plath*

Thursday 3 March 1960 TLS (aerogramme), Indiana University

Thursday evening
March 3rd

Dear mother,

I am sitting up writing this before turning into bed. This has been a very busy week: starting with the trip to Oxford a week ago we have been going about a good deal, paying official visits etc. as if trying to get as much as possible in well before the baby arrives. Ted's friend Luke Myers arrived on the weekend, and after one night with us, sleeping on the divan in the livingroom, went to stay with Danny & Helga Huws. I had all three of them over for dinner on Sunday night as a kind of housewarming---made Dot's veal scallopini, rice, salad & an orange cake. I really put my foot down about visitors now---I get tired easily & like the house to myself so I can cook, read, write, or rest when I please. I have really been strained

1 – In addition to publishing SP's 'Hardcastle Crags' and 'Epitaph for Fire and Flower', *Light Blue, Dark Blue* also published Ted Hughes, 'Macaw and Little Miss', 130–1.

living out of suitcases on shipboard, at Ted's crowded home & then in & out of boarding houses in London & with the Huws, so that I have no desire for people sleeping in my living room or causing me extra cooking or housework. Ted's sister is also coming to London this weekend, but she will stay with a girlfriend. I feel most like walking, reading & musing by myself now after three long months of enforced external, exerting & extrovert living.

Monday we went to a buffet with David & Barbara Ross[1] at which Luke, Danny & Helga & others were present---most of the crowd that published the one & only issue of the BOTOLPH'S REVIEW, where I first saw Ted's poems & at the celebration of which I first met him. David Ross, the editor, has a son (David is very young, 24, a stockbroker & diabetic: quiet & nice); Luke is to sail for New Orleans March 18th after his wife[2] who will have a baby in May (her mother, ominously called Big Cynthia,[3] has maneuvered him home, probably, I think, never to return: he is a very weak soul) & of course the Huws have their Madeleine & we are about to have our Nicholas/Rebecca. Amusing to see what paternal & familial fates have, 4 years later, fallen on such once confirmed bachelors! Tuesday we had lunch with two of Ted's editors from Fabers (after my relaxation classes at my Clinic) & dined sumptuously in a Soho Greek restaurant, blissfully ignoring prices---on chicken liver & salmon roe pate, a Moussaka concocted of cheese, aubergines, rice & chicken, Greek resinated wine, & a heavenly bowl of magnificent fresh fruit & cream for me---the men had shrove pancakes with rose-petal jam. They are working on getting an illustrator for Ted's children's book & we have our fingers crossed: they've written to our First choice & if he did it, it should sell marvelously. I won't breathe his name until we hear definitely: he may, of course, refuse to do it as he has no end of assignments. Wednesday evening we went for cocktails with John Lehmann, editor of the London magazine, who reminisced about his memories of Virginia Woolf et. al--- I met the popular British Oxford-graduate poetess Elizabeth Jennings,[4] a Catholic who reads for a London publishing house & lives in a convent while here, returning to her rooms in Oxford on weekends to write (she has

1–David Andrews Ross (1935–2012), British; B.A. 1956, history, Peterhouse, Cambridge; friend of TH and editor of *Saint Botolph's Review*; married Barbara R. Davies (1928–) in 1957.

2–Lucas Myers married Cynthia Sanborn Smith in Paris on 21 August 1959. Daniel Huws was best man. Lucas Myers sailed on Wednesday, 16 March 1960, on board the SS *Louise Lykes*. Cynthia Myers gave birth to Rosamond Myers on 1 May 1960.

3–Cynthia Sanborn Smith; shared the same name as her daughter.

4–English poet Elizabeth Jennings (1926–2001).

three volumes out---we got along very well. And a lawyer-poet-novelist, Roy Fuller[1] & lady novelist-reviewer, Christine Brooke-Rose.[2] I must get them all in my diary. Very pleasant time. Lehmann is publishing my "Daughters of Blossom Street" (changed from "This Earth Our Hospital") sometime this spring, May or so. I just got the proofs. He's also taken 2 more poems.[3] I went shopping on my own yesterday, too---took the bus just across the Hill at the Zoo & it dropped me right at Selfridge's,[4] that marvelous department store off Oxford Street---did you go there? I went straight to the baby department, sat in a chair, & was shown things & got my own first purchases (!)---practical things like rubber sheeting, Harrington towels & facecloths (used in the royal nurseries!), a couple of little undershirts, a receiving blanket & one "Present"---a beautiful white knit wool shawl-type blanket made in Scotland, very light & good for crib, carriage or just arm-bundle. Ted & I are going out to order a crib tomorrow & eagerly await the diapers you are so good to send: roughly when should they come? & do say how much they are---I'd like to compare. The cheapest pram I saw here is 15 pounds (and a handsome one): most run from 20 to 30 pounds (up to $90!) & are styled like royal carriages. A social-competing thing, really: the poorest mothers have the highest canopied prams---instead of cars. Babies are wheeled late: no cars again. We'll wait till the baby is here, & then probably settle for the $40 pram & count on it to last our 100 infants. After all, I have no other birth expense! Went to my doctor again to-day & he let me listen to the baby's heartbeat! I was so excited. He said the baby is in fine position; I like him much better than any doctor I had in America. All shots--whooping cough, scarlet fever, diptheria, polio, are given free & Health Visitors tell you when to get what. I won't go to a Clinic, but will have my doctor give them. I couldn't have kinder or better care. Happy to see our bank total: we can't wait to break the $5,000 mark! We hope to get our phone in next week, & will call you as soon as the baby is born to announce your Grandmotherhood. Having my book accepted here is very consoling at this time of change & anticipation. Ironically, two other British publishers (one the Oxford U. press) have asked to see a book since I signed my contract. I hope some American press will see fit to take it eventually!

xxx
Sivvy

1–English writer Roy Fuller (1912–91).

2–British writer and critic Christine Brooke-Rose (1923–2012).

3–Sylvia Plath, 'The Sleepers' and 'Full Fathom Five', *London Magazine* (June 1960): 11–13.

4–Selfridges is a department store chain with its flagship branch on Oxford Street, London.

TO *Aurelia Schober Plath*

Thursday 10 March 1960 TLS (aerogramme), Indiana University

Thursday
March 10

Dear mother,

I was very glad to get your letter today telling how you weathered the snowstorm. There were little accounts of it in the newspapers here,[1] and both of us were hoping you escaped being caught in it. That drive to and from BU must have been exhausting, but I am glad you got such good accomodations for the night. Here there has been not a whiff of snow all winter, and I am homesick for it: the last four months seem like a grey-brown drawnout November. Ted and I went for a walk on Primrose Hill this noon after lunch, and the air was mild and damply springlike, the sun almost warm, and green buds out on all the lilac bushes; the forsythia looks about to open.

We had a particularly tiring weekend, as Ted's sister came to London for three days---she stayed with a friend, thank goodness---and his friend Luke is here till the 18th staying with the Huws while his poor 7-month pregnant wife calls him long distance from New Orleans asking if she can fly over to have the baby in London. Ted is, if anything, too nice to his relatives and friends, and I got weary sitting for 8 hours at a stretch in our smokefilled rooms waiting for them to leave---impossible to nap or relax with so many people around. I feel very unlike entertaining anyone just now, simply "in-waiting", wanting to read, write in my diary, & nap. Luckily we have no more prospective visitors (knock on wood) & I have been able to lie down in the afternoons which rests me enough to sleep at night. The baby has been growing by leaps and bounds & the doctor said when I saw him today that it seemed to have very long legs, which accounts for the surprising occasional bumps & visible kicks which appear on my right side.

Tuesday I made a little informal supper for the Merwins---a chicken tetrazini, salad & lemon cake-pudding---that & cleaning house took me the whole afternoon. Then we went to see Marie Bell's famous French company[2] at the Savoy Theatre do Racine's Phedre in French. It was

1–*The Guardian* and *The Observer* ran several articles on a blizzard that affected Massachusetts and other US states in early March 1960.

2–French tragedian Marie Bell (1900–85); her company was called La Compagnie Marie Bell; played at the Savoy Theatre, Savoy Court, The Strand, London.

absolutely magnificent: my favorite Racine play. I didn't have time to reread the whole play before I saw it, but knew the plot well & understood enough of the marvelously spoken French to enjoy it thoroughly. I wanted to have the Merwins over at least once before the baby came, for they are going to France at the end of April & I may not want to cook dinner for anyone till after that. Ted's given them a copy of his book. which is officially out here next Friday, March 18th. We sent 2 copies off to you & Warren: do tell us in what condition they arrive: we had to leave one end open.

The Nation & Good Housekeeping came---did you specially want me to see the bank account story? [1] I saw you underlined it. All I can say is, it must have been an awful lot of money; and poor Morrie, for not enjoying it with his wife before he died! The sheets & bed pads came today, too: lovely! The pad just fits. We had to pay about $3 duty on it---was that because it was a gift over $10? I've never had to pay any duty before on anything you sent. I'll let you know when the diapers come. I have an odd feeling the baby may come any day now, although officially I have 17 days grace. We ordered a nice pale pink crib with safety lock-side & lead-free finish & a good crib mattress to come this Monday. I've got 2 nice pram blankets from Ted's aunt Hilda & from Luke's sister,[2] who lives in Surrey. And plenty of cot bedding. I am hoping that the dilatory workmen keep their promise to come tomorrow & fix the wallpaper the damp has spoiled on the outer kitchen & bathroom walls. Leakage from the attic windows, which theyve fixed. "Damp" disappears eventually, Ted says. And mend a broken windowcord & fix a few bedroom floorholes. The phoneman came today: the 3rd in a line: division of labor. Still the phone isn't working, for our other party has to be connected at the same time & they weren't home today. Our number, in case you have occasion to use it, is PRIMROSE 9132. Nice, what? It should be working by the time you get this, & about our first call should be to tell you when the baby comes. We're listed under Edward James Hughes. The phoneman was charming, a regular philosopher, who had been in America during the war, is a born Londoner & regaled us with accounts of his clients: Eleanor Farjeon (Fargeron?)[3] among them, a neighbor of ours, evidently.

1–Nancy Pope Mayorga, 'Money is Wonderful', *Good Housekeeping* 150 (February 1960): 66–7, 138, 140, 142.

2–Lady Rosamond Myers Thornton (1921–2017), who according to SP's address book lived at Thornwood, Littleworth Cross, Seale, near Farnham, Surrey. Married Sir Peter Eustace Thornton (1917–2013) in 1946.

3–Eleanor Farjeon (1881–1965) was an English author of children's books. Farjeon grew

Our books made him think us cultured, or writers, & he got off on the poets & playwrights & duchesses he has serviced. "Buckingham Palace is outside my route, unfortunately." I'm glad to hear Sappho is surviving the cat-covering weather. I'm thinking of investing in a vacuum-cleaner as sweeping these rugs is a poor substitute & raises a lot of dust, & when we at last get our own place, we'll have rugs, hopefully, of our own. Any advice on the subject? Do keep well, now, especially in this fickle winter-spring season! Ted joins me in sending love to you & Warren.

xxx
Sivvy

TO *Edith & William Hughes*

Friday 11 March 1960[1] ALS,[2] Private owner

Hello there. Until yesterday it's been raw, windy & bitter cold here, but our two Pifcos are ample to keep us warm. We went for a walk yesterday on Primrose Hill – it was mild & sunny & felt like spring. The lilac buds are green & the forsythia almost out. We got a nice letter from Hilda with the most beautiful pram blanket. I'll write her about it & send her our order for green cord. All the Captains & Kings have departed – for the time being at least – & Ted & I are trying to rest up from the last exhausting months so we have energy to slowly begin writing again. I just heard my book of poems should be out sometime next September, which is nice to look forward to. I am in good health, though I get tired easily – and need a nap every afternoon. We have been turning in early. Saw a wonderful French play – Phèdre by Racine – in French with a French troupe with the Merwins this week. We're looking forward to a peaceful spring of working, & the baby, who should be here by the 27th or so

Love to all –
Sylvia

PS – I think the pile of letters is in the top bureau drawer on the nightstand side –

---

up nearby in Adelaide Road but lived in Perrin's Walk, Hampstead, from the 1920s until her death.

1–Date supplied from internal evidence.

2–SP adds a note to a letter begun by TH, which has not been transcribed. In his contribution, TH asks for help finding an envelope of Guggenheim-related letters and an

TO *W. Roger Smith*

Friday 11 March 1960 — TLS, Random House Group Archive & Library

3 Chalcot Square
London N.W.1
March 11, 1960

W. Roger Smith, Esq.
WILLIAM HEINEMANN LTD.
15-16 Queen Street
Mayfair, London W.1

Dear Mr. Smith,

Thank you for your letter of March 8th. I very much appreciated your advice about copyright lines and shall certainly ask to have them printed with any poems of mine that may be accepted from now on.

Yes, I am an American citizen, although I expect to be resident in England from now on, as far as I know. I hope this doesn't cause you any inconvenience.

Sincerely yours,
Sylvia Plath

TO *Aurelia Schober Plath*

Thursday 17 March 1960 — TLS (aerogramme), Indiana University

Thursday
March 17

Dear mother,

It was good to get your letter today: I do look forward to them. Our phone is at last in, thanks to Ted going round to the other party on the line down the street & explaining our reasons for being eager to have the phone right away, so they kindly arranged to have one of them home from work about 4 to open the house, and I am very relieved the phonemen got the phones working: PRImrose 9132. So we will be able to call you.

American tax form. He notes that he is slowly getting back into writing after being away from it, discusses recent visits from his sister and Lucas Myers, and a get-together at Daniel Huws's with Matthew John Caldwell Hodgart (TH's director of studies during his first years at Pembroke College) and MacDonald Emslie (a fellow graduate of Pembroke College).

Officially the baby is due in 10 days, but right now I feel to have been waiting so long I can't imagine it ever coming. When I look at the pink crib (2'x4') I keep wondering what it will be like to see a breathing infant in it. This seems an enormous milestone to pass: three of us instead of two.

I've just come back from my weekly visit to the doctor & he says I'm in fine shape. Luke left at last on his tanker to New Orleans last night & I am relieved Ted can settle down to work. The Merwins---who visit us regularly, & Bill loans me books from his huge library: I'm starting to read French again: Ionesco, Sartre, Camus[1]---are planning to go to France at the end of April, which means the study will come free for Ted just as I'm recovered enough not to need his help substantially with cooking & housework, which is ideal. I think Bill may dedicate his book of translated Spanish ballads[2] to us: this moves us very much. Our whole very comfortable livingroom, down to the marvelous Victorian nursing chair, has been furnished out of their attic. Now slowly, out of second-hand shops, I hope we can start looking round for a few things of our own---china, chairs etc.

How much are good vacuum cleaners in America? I was shocked to get a glimpse of the prices here: up to $100. I feel I really must get one, as sweeping these carpets is a poor substitute & raises dust, & the area is rather sooty, like Boston, so once-a-week thorough scrubbing-down is a must. What sort of cleaner should I look for? And by the way, what size is that marvelous frying pan with the lid you have? I haven't been able to locate anything like it here yet & wonder how much yours cost. I really need one of those to take the place of my big electric frying pan. As far as I can see, everything you've sent has come except the diapers & I have faith they will come before the baby does. We are still after the builders to fix our fallen & damped wallpaper, broken windowcord & last floorholes, but they are irresponsible as mules, promise & no action. Yet we are so lucky to have this place, & the rent is low compared to anything so bright & new & in such a good district, that I don't mind the delay too much. We have yet to paint & fix up our little hall alcove. Hot water & heating---those two British bugaboos---are no problem. I can have a 9 lb. laundry done at the laundromat around the corner for about 45cents in the morning, hung up on my wooden rack in the tub, with one pifco on in the small bathroom, & completely dry by evening, which is convenient.

1–French philosopher and writer Albert Camus (1913–60).

2–W. S. Merwin, *Some Spanish Ballads* (London: Abelard-Schuman, 1961); the dedication in the book reads 'To Sylvia Plath and Ted Hughes'.

Ted's got me a sturdy plain wood 4-legged stool for my kitchenwork---a great saving of energy: no more long standing.

I am so happy you like your work with Dr. Noall[1] (Know-all, a formidable name for a Professor!) and am eager to hear all you can tell us about it. Wouldn't it be lovely if you too got assigned to lecture in England! Please do take special care of yourself in this precarious weather. The illusion of spring has receded here, & it is again grey, damp & wintry. Ted's book is officially out here tomorrow: do let us know when you get your copies. I am so proud of it. His story anthology should be out next fall, along with my book of poems, his children's book much later, in winter. Glad to hear of the tiny Partisan Review cheque[2] arriving & the note from the Yale Series. I wonder when & if my book will come out in America: it is a good, fat solid 50-poem book now & deserving of print there. I naturally would be very happy to be recognized in my own country!

Ted took me to the Regent's Park Zoo Monday afternoon & we had a wonderful time: saw the lions, tigers & birds of prey fed. One of the most undepressing zoos I've been to & a superb place for children: they have free pony rides in the summer & an enclosure of little common animals, rabbits, chicks, lambs, etc., for the children to pet. The reptile house is excellent: enormous anacondas, pythons & stone-age-looking white Chinese crocodiles. Great wierd rhinoceros, elephants, monkeys of all sorts. The most frightening specimen I think is the monkey-eating eagle which stares with mad blue eyes from under a feathery mop of hair past a fearsome bluish beak at a children's playground right in view of it, probably taking them for hairless monkeys. I do so wish we'd thought to go through Daddy's books before we left! If you found any Fabre books, or books with engravings & good illustrations, could you send a few on some day? Ted joins me in sending much love to you, Warren, & Sappho!

xxx

Sivvy

<on the return address side of letter>

PS – Have you ever tried this recipe for red cabbage? It's especially good with pork or sausages. Warren should like it: Sauté an onion or two, chopped fine, with a few strips of bacon, cubed. Add a cut-up red cabbage, shredded, which has been soaked in cold water, 2 tart cooking apples, sliced fine, a handful of raisins or sultanas & a cup of cider or red wine.

1–Dr Mabel Noall (1908–99).

2–See Joan Meyers to SP, 1 March 1960; held by Lilly Library.

Cover tightly & simmer for 2 hours, adding more cider or wine when[1] the first is absorbed – do try it!

TO *Aurelia Schober Plath*

Thursday 24 March 1960 — TLS (aerogramme), Indiana University

Thursday, March 24

Dearest mother,

It was so good to get your letter yesterday & hear how people are asking about the baby. It isn't due till the 27th (since it evidently isn't going to arrive early I wish it would come on that day to keep up family tradition!) and may of course be tardy. Another girl who goes to my doctor had hers two weeks late. So don't get too impatient. Of course, I am very impatient. This last month has seemed an eternity & I find it difficult to imagine this eager waiting will ever end. As I perhaps said, our phone PRIMROSE 9132 is working. The elusive little paperer has come & fixed our three delinquent walls & Ted has painted them. It only remains to paint one wall of the kitchen & the little hall a rose-vermilion, fix a windowcord, put up a kitchen shelf curtain . . . little things. Helga very sweetly hemmed two ceiling-to-floor length green corduroy drapes for the bedroom (which I cut & pinned) on her machine, so now the bedroom is pitchdark at night & the 4 o'clock dawn light doesn't wake me anymore. Of course the baby will soon take care of that! Anyhow, the dark forest-green looks handsome with the rose-wallpaper & white woodwork. We are delighting in our place more every day & Ted is back at work at his desk, much happier. He gets almost nervously sick when he hasn't written for a long time, & really needs careful handling. Once he has time & space to write, he is fine. That is the one thing I must always fight to give him: & these last 5 months have been a hard enough fight.

I was very sorry to hear about your laryngitis: ironically, your letter came just as I have lost <u>my</u> voice. This follows on the end of a very trying sinus-cold I came down with Saturday, after a Saturday dinner I gave for Helga & Danny Huws & their Madeline & Barbara & David Ross (she is an English teacher for foreigners & he the diabetic stockbroker) & their little Simon. I thought it might well be the last entertaining I do for some time, & both of those couples have been so kind, immeasurably, I wanted them. Simon's diaper came loose & he smeared a large mess over the floor

1 – 'cider or wine ~~if~~ when' appears in the original.

before indignant Madelin brought him to our notice, so Barbara popped him in our tub. Both children are beautiful, healthy & very amusing. Helga is due for a second in November & is very happy about it. My cold really knocked me out for two or three days, but Ted has been an angel, cooking, washing & waxing the kitchen floors, doing the last painting & getting me strong nosedrops & almost drowning me with honey & vinegar. As a result, my head is still stuffed, but I am no longer runny & twitchy & in excellent spirits. Glad to get the cold over with before the baby comes, even at the last minute. I only hope you haven't had a cold: loss of voice is usually the warning sign of too much fatigue. Take care of yourself! How I wish you & Warren could be miraculously transported over here to see the baby! I do so instinctively expect a Nicholas Farrar I hope I won't be too shocked at a Frieda Rebecca!

A picture & little writeup about Ted & his new book came out in THE QUEEN (a sort of posh ladies' magazine like VOGUE) along with 4 other young writers this week. He's written the BBC (at my suggestion, he is too modest to think of it himself) he is in London, & they have suggested 2 programs he might work up: one autobiographical & one an editing & reading of poems on animals---which would mean very good fees. Ironically, the editor of HARPER'S BAZAAR in America wrote Ted raving about "The Rain Horse" which she'd read in the London Magazine & offering $275 for it. Of course we'll have to say it's been done in America. But it's nice to have the story get such wide, enthusiastic notice.

My Irish midwife came yesterday, very cheering, pointed out all the baby's parts to me & its position. She too is a sinus-sufferer & so was hearteningly sympathetic. Your copy of the Ladies Home Journal arrived on the best possible day: Monday, when I was too miserable with my cold for anything but that. I read it from cover to cover & enjoyed it immensely. Perfect sickbed reading!

It is a fair, sunny day. Birds singing. Children playing in the square. But I am not going out at all now, lest I prolong my cold. Very cosy indoors. Felt well enough to make a banana bread, applesauce & chicken liver paté. Ted made a great vegetable soup. Saw both parts of Sergei Eisenstein's marvelous tour de force IVAN THE TERRIBLE[1] last week with the Merwins. A marvelous folklore library is just down the street

1 – Soviet film director Sergei Eisenstein (1898–1948), his *Ivan the Terrible, Part I & Part II*; played at the Academy Theatre.

from us.[1] I think I'd rather live in London that anywhere in the world: and get a seaside cottage in Cornwall someday too! This flat is the most delightful we've ever lived in. Ted's going to work on a libretto[2] for a modern young Chinese opera-composer we met at Yaddo. I hope that works out. Both of us send love to you & Warren

xxx
Sivvy

<on the return address side of letter>

*PS: Wonderful news via telegram just came for Ted – he's got the Somerset Maugham Award[3] for his book – about £400 – just over $1,000 – which has to be spent 'enlarging his worldview' in about 3 months abroad. We are envisioning the Greek islands next winter & all sorts of elegant sun-saturated schemes.

xxx
Sivvy

TO *Edith & William Hughes*

Friday 25 March 1960[4] ALS with envelope, Emory University

<on verso of envelope>

PS – Please send on any clippings you see reviewing Ted's book! We never see any papers here, it seems!

Love to all.
S.

1 – Possibly a reference to the Vaughn Williams Memorial Library of the English Folk Dance and Song Society, 2 Regent's Park Road, London.

2 – TH worked on a libretto based on the *Bardo Thodol* (*Tibetan Book of the Dead*).

3 – TH was awarded the Somerset Maugham Award in 1960 by the Society of Authors for *Hawk in the Rain*. The award is for foreign travel.

4 – Date supplied from postmark.

TO *Aurelia Schober Plath*

Sat.–Mon. 26–28 March 1960 TLS (aerogramme),[1]
Indiana University

Saturday noon: March 26

Dearest mother,

Well, all is quiet & uneventful. I somehow imagine I should be seeing large comets or lions in the street at this point, but can't believe the baby will ever come. I sort of expected it early---didn't we arrive early?---and really am set on the 27th, that mystical number for a date now, but this waiting feels ready to go on forever. The diapers came yesterday, no duty, & are neatly stacked under the crib. Only a few things---a bit of painting & hammering--remain to be done around the house. Except for supper at the Merwins Tuesday night I've stayed in for a week---annoying, especially as I have my enforced confinement coming any time---but I felt it would be best for my cold. My doctor came to the house after his calls Thursday & prescribed me some wonderful germ-killing spray. My nose still stuffs up, but this clears it immediately & for hours. I am up & about, had my first excellent night's sleep in a week last night. I keep imagining & looking for twinges; nichts. The only other large expenses we have ahead are a vacuum cleaner, which I may go to order Monday if it is sunny & nothing has occurred, and the pram. What a blessing to have no large doctor's bills to look askance at!

Your letter about Lupercal arrived today, & we're so pleased you like it & that the copies came intact. Ted is now in the middle of writing on a second play[2] & I am convinced it is only a matter of time before he does a stageable one. We got his official letter from the Secretary of the Somerset Maugham Trust today: he's got the 1960 award "on the strength of the literary quality and promise" of THE HAWK IN THE RAIN. This year the Award is £500! One hundred more than usual. About $1,400. We have to spend it within two years from now by spending "at least three months outside Great Britain and Ireland, with the object, not of having a holiday abroad, but of acquainting yourself with the manners and customs of foreign nations & thereby having an opportunity to increase your experience & knowledge for your future literary benefit." So we will take the three months in the sunny south (we've thought of France,

1–TH added a note at the bottom of the letter, which has not been transcribed. TH noted SP's efforts to see as many films as possible and SP's health being improved.

2–Ted Hughes, *The House of Aries*.

Italy, Greece) either next winter or the one after that. Ideally we'd rent a furnished villa on the Mediterranean, near a large & cosmopolitan enough city so I could register the baby with a doctor & have one of those foreign maid-babysitters so I could have at least 4-6 hours a day free to write too. The prospect of avoiding a dreary English winter & having enough to cover our rent here & a comfortable stay in Europe is very heartening to us both at this point. Of course I shall ask my doctor's advice about baby-care & plan to get all its injections over with before we go---they do them in the first years here. They ask Ted to write a thank-you note to Maugham in his French Riviera villa: how I would love to meet him! I am especially partial to the French Riviera because of the relative ease in language, but Rome & environs are a possibility---an immense English-speaking civilization there.

We hear the clear song of a certain thrush at dawn each morning. The square is full of children playing something like baseball with flat bats. The daily icecream truck jingles to a stop & the little ones all rush up. Oh, I am so impatient!

Monday noon: March 28. Well, I am about to go out shopping, round as ever. Since the baby did not take advantage of the significant 27th date I am sure it will wait till April Fool's Day, just to get into the main Plath Month.[1] Ted's bought me a marvelous huge covered French earthenware casserole & I cooked a whole pile of little tough pigeons in it (9cents each) & served them[2] with rice in which I stirred a delectable mixture of fried onions, garlic, raisins & blanched almond slices when it was cooked dry & fluffy. Marvelous. Ted took me to a good French movie "Les Enfants du Paradis"[3] last night---a period piece about the theater in 1840 France. I think we'll go to a movie a night now, there are such fine ones here---always 4 or 5 to choose from---or we'll perish of suspense.

Yesterday, lazing in bed & leafing through the Sunday Observer, I came on a marvelous review of LUPERCAL by A. Alvarez,[4] the intelligent reviewer (Oxford-Princeton, etc.) who had been approving, but with reservations, about the HAWK. A column & a half: excerpts: "There are no influences to side-track the critic, no hesitations to reassure him.

1–SP's father's birthday was 13 April; her mother's was 26 April; and her brother's was 27 April.
2–'served ~~it~~ them' appears in the original.
3–*Les Enfants du Paradis* (1945) played at the Academy Cinema.
4–English poet, novelist, essayist, and critic Alfred Alvarez (1929–); poetry editor of *The Observer*, 1956–66. A. Alvarez, 'An Outstanding Young Poet', *The Observer* (27 March 1960): 22.

Hughes has found his own voice, created his own artistic world & has emerged as a poet of the first importance . . . What Ted Hughes has done is to take a limited, personal theme and, by an act of immensely assured poetic skill, has broadened it until it seems to touch upon nearly everything that concerns us. This is not easy poetry to read, but it is new, profound & important." We cooed & beamed all day. At the movie everybody was reading the Observer & some were just at Ted's review! I turned a bit further: his picture, among the S. African massacres, news about the Maugham Award[1] & even a note about me "his tall, trim American wife . . . who is a New Yorker poet in her own right." We'll send you copies when we get some. Ted is being marvelously good & understanding. He's as impatient & eager as I, if that's possible. Well, keep calm for another week.

xxx
Sivvy

TO *Aurelia Schober Plath & Warren Plath*

Thurs.–Fri. 31 March–1 April 1960 TLS/ALS, Indiana University

Thursday evening: March 31

Dear mother & Warren . . .

I thought I'd enclose one of those Sunday clippings[2] about Ted's prize I wrote you about. It was good getting your letter today with the news about Lowell's National Book Award[3]---we love clippings about literary goings-on in America as we have really no other way of keeping in touch. I've read the Folk Medicine book[4] through & enjoyed it, although I think his emphasis on stopping drinking citrus juices is silly & his claims for honey & vinegar (that, for example, it will both reduce you & keep you from losing weight) are a bit extravagant. However, with the assurance it can't hurt us, we have our dark jar of mixture & spoon out doses daily.

Well, I guess I am going to have an April baby! I never did like the month of March---an exhausted, grubby end-of-the-year month---and

1–Pendennis, 'Ted 'n' Thom', *The Observer* (27 March 1960): 9; this article includes TH's picture.

2–Pendennis, 'Ted 'n' Thom', cited above. The clipping is with the letter.

3–Robert Lowell, *Life Studies* (New York: Farrar, Straus & Giroux, 1959), won the 1960 National Book Award.

4–D. C. Jarvis, *Folk Medicine: A Vermont Doctor's Guide to Good Health* (New York: Holt, Rinehart & Winston, 1958).

except for the magic date 27, really wasn't too eager to have a baby with a March birthday. Now April is another matter: spring in the very sound of it. Any day will be fine, after the first!

In her infinite wisdom,[1] the baby is waiting until my cold is all gone (I'm just at the last vestiges now, & feel close to my old self again), till the weather improves (it's been raw, sleety, utterly grey & nasty till today ---which is green, sunny & lambish), and till the very last touches are calmly put on the apartment. My midwife came yesterday & cheered us by laughingly predicting it would arrive at 2 am Sunday: I wish it would, because she is on duty this weekend, & if I had her (there is a shift of 3 midwives) I'd be overjoyed: we both are very fond of her. I saw my doctor today who examined me inside & out and said everything was ripe & ready for my having the baby in the next few days.

I am planning to wash & wax the kitchen floors tomorrow, wash my hair, etc. etc., so maybe the baby will be traditional & reward me by coming Saturday. I've finished sewing green corduroy curtains like those in the bedroom to cover my long & short sets of kitchen shelves, so now, when I have the pots & dishes put away, I can draw the curtains & the kitchen doesn't look "busy". We'll probably paint the hall tomorrow. And I'll go look at vacuums. As the doctor said, the baby can't get much bigger. He estimates about 8 pounds.

Ted & I took a lovely quiet walk this evening, under the thin new moon, over the magic landscape of Primrose Hill & Regent's Park: all blue & misty, the buds a kind of nimbus of green on the thorn trees, daffodils & blue squills out on the lawns & the silhouettes of wood pigeons roosting in the trees. A heavenly hour of peace & easy strolling, our first in weeks, what with my sinus cold & the atrocious weather.

I think, while I have the time & energy, I will write letters to people like Marty, Patsy, etc., & leave space to put a note about the baby & have Ted mail them when it comes. I want to have nothing to do after it comes, so am busying myself, cleaning house, etc. now. Waiting for Dot's meatloaf in the oven. Will make a big fish soup tomorrow.

Ted's been getting a flood of letters from all sorts of people about his award, a real stack of mail. Two requests to give readings (one in June, with me & someone else,[2] & one in December, which would pay

1–'In ~~his~~ her infinite wisdom' appears in the original.

2–Alan Brownjohn. See Dorothy Morland to Alan Brownjohn, 29 March 1960; held by Institute of Contemporary Arts London records (TGA 955), Tate Museum Archives, London. SP and TH were invited in separate letters also dated 29 March 1960. Karl Miller served as chair for the reading. In 1960, the Institute of Contemporary Arts was at 17–18 Dover Street, London.

about $35 for the hour), editors asking for poems, old friends stirred into writing, etc. I must type answers for him tomorrow, or they'll never get done.

Well, I'll put this aside for a day, in case I collect any more news.

PS[1]

April 1st: 1:15 pm: Well, just twelve hours ago I woke up groggy from two sleeping pills after one hour hardwon sleep & everything began. The miraculous rapidity of the delivery amazed even my seasoned doctor & midwife – which is why I had absolutely no anesthesia. The midwife – a capable little Indian woman I had visit me once before, came on her bicycle "to see how I was getting on" about 2 am & planned to see my contractions establish, leave & return after breakfast. In no time I was contracting violently with scarcely a second's rest – I thought the worst pains, just before the second stage of pushing began, were only the beginning & didn't see how I could last through 20 more hours of them, & suddenly, at 5, she said I was fully dilated & showed me the baby's head – a crack of it – in the mirror. She called the doctor, but he was at home & had no anesthesia handy & he came about 5:30 just in time to supervise the delivery. I looked on my stomach & saw Frieda Rebecca[2] white as flour with the cream that covers new babies, little funny dark squiggles of hair plastered over her head, with big dark blue eyes. At 5:45 exactly. The afterbirth came shortly after. Ted was there the whole time, holding my hand, rubbing my back & boiling kettles – a marvelous comfort. I couldn't take my eyes off the baby – the midwife sponged her beside the bed in my big pyrex mixing bowl & wrapped her up well, near a hot water bottle in the crib – she sucked at me a few minutes like a little expert & got a few drops of colostrum & then went to sleep. From where I sit propped up in bed I can see her, pink & healthy, sound asleep. We can't imagine now having favored a boy! Ted is delighted. He'd been hypnotizing me to have a short easy delivery – well, it wasn't "easy," but the shortness carried me through. I slept an hour or two after calling you – feel I could get up & walk about, but am of course, wobbly. The miracle is how after my sinus siege of two weeks & sleepless nights I should be lucky to have only 4½ hours labor – "A wonder child" the midwife said. Of course, of course! Ted brought me breakfast – I'd vomited up all that meatloaf at the start of labor – & a tuna salad, cheese & V-8 lunch which

1 – The postscript is handwritten by SP.
2 – Frieda Rebecca Hughes (1960–); daughter of SP and TH.

I've just finished with gusto. I feel light & thin as a feather. The baby is, as I said 7 lbs 4 oz, 21 inches long – and, alas, she has my nose! On her, though, it seems quite beautiful. Well, I have never been so happy in my life. The whole American rigmarole of hospitals, doctors' bills, cuts & stitches, anesthesia etc. seems a nightmare well left behind. The midwife came a second time at 11 am & will come again at tea time to wash me & care for the baby. I'll write soon again –

Love to "Grammy" & Uncle Warren from

Frieda Rebecca, Ted,
& your own Sivvy

TO *Marcia B. Stern*

Friday 1 April 1960 — TLS (aerogramme), Smith College

Friday afternoon: April 1st

Dearest Marty,

I am sitting up in bed typing on the Olivetti, eating yoghurt & maple syrup & staring amazedly still at pink, slumbering Frieda Rebecca Hughes who arrived at quarter of six this morning. She's lying in the crib a few feet away from the bed, dozing & snorkling as she has been since dawn, after a bath given her by the midwife in my biggest pyrex baking dish. Actually, the baby was officially predicted last Sunday the 27th, but I just grew bigger & bigger & nothing happened. I was wearing that very cool comfortable black & white checked blouse you gave me yesterday which turned out to be my last day of weighing 155 pounds. Saw the doctor & he predicted this weekend. Ted & I went for a long walk last twilight in Primrose Hill & Regents Park in a misty blue light under the new moon, all the buds out in a green haze, lambish weather after weeks of horrid raw grey sleety rain. I planned to wash & wax floors today, bake, sew, get the last things rounded up. Not to be.

I'd just got over two weeks of sinus cold which had left me exhausted & was aiming to write you a long letter, adding a note when the baby came. We'd expected nothing but a boy. Then at 1:15 this morning I woke after one hour's sleep, groggy from two sleeping pills which I've been taking since the baby's kicks keep me awake all night, to a rush of water & sudden contractions. Bang. At first I thought of going back to bed & calling the midwife at breakfast, but Ted called her & she (Sister Mardee, a little Indian woman whom I'd only seen once, part of the 3-woman shift) bicycled over to "see how I was getting on", planning to see me started in the first stage & come back at breakfast. I was tired, dopey, wanting to sleep & the pains getting closer & very severe. Thinking this would go on the proverbial 20 hours I felt I needed a shot of something, or gas. But she'd brought nothing, nor did my doctor when she called him at 5 am . . . because my rapidity was all unexpected. Ted was there, holding my hand, rubbing my back & the doctor arrived just in time to supervise the delivery after a total of 4½ hours violent absolutely natural labor. Evidently this sort of rapidity for a first baby is very rare. Except for the momentary despair at the worst part, which I thought was only the beginning, the experience was amazing. The intimacy, privacy, homeiness of it all seemed just what I needed: no tears, no stitches. The nightmare of labor wards, deep anesthesia, cuts, doctors bills etc. in American hospitals something I'm glad to be shut of. We have absolutely no expenses at all, & reduced milk & vitamin costs. As a result, in spite of little sleep & the tag ends of my old sinus, I am in fine spirits & dying to write you first off. My stomach is floppy & my muscles, but I am eager to be up, although the sister won't let me set foot on earth till tomorrow. I snuck in the livingroom to call mother when she'd left, though.

All other news seems pale beside this: Ted's book LUPERCAL is just out here, getting pretty good reviews & this Somerset Maugham award which will take us for 3 months to southern Europe either this winter or next. And my book of poems will come out this fall here---they're much kinder & open to poetry than in America, where loss of money is such a phobia.

Glug-glug says Rebecca, squidging up her face & trying to get milk out of her sheet corner. The midwife came again this noon to check on the baby & will come again this evening to bathe both of us. I am very impatient to be up and about . . . no hospital atmosphere to make me feel anything more than a rather miraculous & tumultuous night has occurred, but my typewriting is getting suspiciously boggled so I will sign off for now. PLEASE write soon & forgive my long silence. I'll write again when I am up & about.

Much much love to you, Mike Cary & Douglas

from Syl

<on the return address side of letter>

PS – I'd love to have any copies of BABYTALK[1] you could send. Frieda Rebecca's accomplishments to date are sleeping, sucking, holding people's

1 – Founded in 1935, *Babytalk* is the oldest baby magazine in the United States.

fingers, yelling bloody murder & looking generally like a rosebud in between!

XXX
S

TO *Olwyn Hughes*

Saturday 2 April 1960 ALS,[1] Emory University

Dearest Olwyn –

I am sitting up in bed surrounded by banks of iris, tulips & daffodils, messages of good will & your fine bottle of champagne on ice waiting to be broached with our first visitors & when I can manage a creditable amount. We loved getting your long letter & I was planning to write you at more length than this the night Frieda Rebecca descended on us. Except for my being exhausted from 2 weeks in bed with flu & sinus – the cloud I was coming under during your visit, I think – and my lugubrious interval of misinterpreting the worst contractions – between first & second stages – as only the beginning of a 20-hour anesthesia-less ordeal, I had a miraculous time, surprising both midwife & doctor, who had promised me gas, injections etc. to cover the worst. Frieda Rebecca forstalled them however & the rapidity of delivery made the violence & intensity worth it. The baby is oddly lovely – great blue-dark eyes & a furze of dark hair & legendary skin – Hughes hands &, alas, a Plath nose – but perhaps all babes have widish snubs. Apart from being wobbly on my feet & without apparent stomach muscles, I am in fine shape, learning to hold her & watching the midwife who comes twice a day to bathe her & daub me with various healing unguents. I got the little Indian midwife, not the blond golden-voiced Irish one I'd hope for, but we are both immensely fond of the Indian now we know her – she is immensely kind, capable & dotes on the baby. Ted's hypnosis, I am sure, made this unusual first labor possible – he was wonderful throughout & is getting expert at handling Rebecca (we're calling her that). I got up to talk to my mother & yours on the phone three hours after the baby came – hope you like your first niece –

Lots of Love,
Sylvia

1 – SP's letter is at the end of a letter begun by TH, which has not been transcribed.

TO *Ruth Tiffany Barnhouse Beuscher*

Saturday 2 April 1960 TLS (aerogramme), Smith College

Saturday: April 2

Dear Dr. Beuscher,

Ted & I are happy to announce the birth of Frieda Rebecca Hughes. She was born at 5:45 a.m. yesterday morning, April 1st, weighing 7 pounds 4 ounces, 21 inches long & covered with white cream like a floured pastry. I am now sitting up in bed typing letters after the morning visit of the midwife (it turned out to be the little Indian one of the triumvirate who delivered me & we have grown very fond of her) who bathes me & the baby, eating yoghurt & maple syrup & hardly able to take my eyes off the baby who has enormous blue eyes, a fluff of dark hair & seems to us extremely lovely: perfectly made.

Ironically, in spite of all my strict arrangements with doctor & midwife about plenty of pethidine[1] & gas etc. for my labor, I had the baby completely without analgesia of any sort . . . nothing but two bits of barley sugar the midwife happened to have in her pocket, & this due to the record speed of Rebecca's arrival. Ted had been hypnotizing me regularly with my daily bout of relaxing & napping to have "an easy quick delivery", which may have had something to do with it. It wasn't easy, but the whole thing lasted 4½ hours. I'd had a sinus cold for 2 weeks, not slept much & was rather run down; wakened at 1:15 a.m. Friday April 1st after a bare hour's sleep to feel the waters break. Contractions started immediately & were strong & regular every 5 minutes by the time the Indian midwife arrived on her bicycle at 2 a.m. without anesthesia or anything, just to see me "get established in the first stage of labor" & then return after breakfast. I felt unaccountably unwilling to have her leave: she rubbed my back, washed my face, tried to get me breathing deeply with the contractions, but I was groggy with a sleeping pill & very surprised I had no time to rest between contractions. By 5 I was fully dilated, no question of the midwife's leaving. She called my doctor, who had also thought to drop by after breakfast & he came just in time to supervise the delivery of the baby at 5:45. The cord was around its neck once "but loosely" & by following their directions of pushing & not pushing I wasn't torn at all, just nicked in the front, no stitches, nothing. The worst time for me psychologically was the series of consecutive intense contractions between the first & second stage which I thought were merely a sample of beginning contractions: I'd read about these 10 or 12 bad ones & if I'd recognised them, would have felt better.

1–Pethidine is a synthetic morphine-like opioid used for pain management.

As it was, I didn't see how I could stand 20 hours more of them. Almost immediately I wanted to push & the midwife let me go ahead. Then things were fine: I felt purposeful & controlled & able to sit up enough to see the baby's head-top in the mirror Ted held. We had expected nothing but a boy & both of us are so delighted with a girl we can't imagine now every having considered a boy as a possibility. The only really negative times were my vomiting a large dinner up as soon as the midwife came & those violent contractions, the worst, which I thought were a sample of early easy ones. The midwife thought at first I was exaggerating the intensity of them, but as soon as she examined me & saw where I was became nothing but praising & encouraging. I felt marvelous as soon as the baby lay on my stomach wiggling, had tea & slipped in to call mother as soon as doctor & midwife left. Ted was wonderful the whole time & delighted with his new daughter.

I am absolutely delighted with home delivery & wouldn't ever have a baby in hospital now. The nightmare vision of that delivery I saw at the Boston Lying-In - the mother too doped to know what was happening,[1] not seeing or holding the baby, cut open & stitched up as if birth were a surgical operation & sent off on a stretcher in the opposite direction from her child-is completely dissipated. No doctor's bills for us either. Every day I watch the midwife bathe the baby in my biggest pyrex dish & I let it suck every 4 hours & love having it right by me. She yelled for an hour off-and-on between 2 & 3 a.m. last night for the sheer joy of it & we were both very tired but she looked so amusing we sat up by candlelight & played with her a bit. So we nap in the day if she wakes us much. I don't know when I've been so happy. I am surrounded by flowers & telegrams & being tired, bloody & without apparent stomach muscles is just a stage to be grown out of, no real bother.

Other news seems pale beside this to both of us, but Ted's 2nd book LUPERCAL is out here as of March 18th, getting fine reviews, & he just received the Somerset Maugham award of over $1,000 for the "promise of his 1st book", the amount to be used for 3-months abroad in the next 2 years. So we'll be "forced" to find a villa on the Riviera this winter or next: utter bliss to think of a winter of sun & no sinus weather. My book of poems THE COLOSSUS is due out here early next fall & you'll receive one of the first copies. England is a marvelous country for babies & books & we are happy as we've never been anywhere else. Our dream is an eventual London house & garden. With his 2 awards & Guggenheim, Ted's won over $7,000 in the last 2 years: No doubt there'll be lean

1–See *Letters of Sylvia Plath*, Vol. 1, 416.

years in plenty ahead, but these fat ones are a great encouragement.

Lots of love to you & let me know when your next baby arrives[1] & who it is ~

Sylvia

TO *Aurelia Schober Plath*

Monday 4 April 1960

TLS (aerogramme),[2]
Indiana University

Monday noon: April 4th

Dearest mother,

Well, Rebecca is four days old, almost, and more beautiful than ever. It has been a lovely sunny morning outside & the trees look to be budding in the square. The baby is sleeping in the crib after being changed & bathed by the third midwife of the trio who work in my district, and I have taken my first bath which put me in very good spirits. I don't respond well to being bedded down & enjoyed getting up last night for a candlelight dinner with Ted: an unearthly veal casserole Dido Merwin brought over to heat up, which we made with some rice. I have a ravenous appetite, drink loads of milk & water, V-8 with gelatine to improve my nails, & orange juice. It is so wonderful not to be in a hospital, but bit by bit to slip back into my old routines as the midwife gives me the go-ahead & as I feel stronger. Just tidying up this or that while sitting on a stool or chair makes me feel pleasant. From now on the midwife will come only once a day, in the morning, to bathe & change the baby until the 8th day, when they will supervise my doing it. From then on, a Health Visitor will drop in now & then to check on any problems & advise me about injections, clinics etc. It is a process of gradual education, much better than being waited on hand & foot in the hospital & going home with a baby you've only seen once every four hours.

For the first week, these babies tend to cry & wake at night as they are bathed in the morning & therefore drowsy all day. Rebecca is no

1–Dr Beuscher had two children by her first husband, Francis Charles Edmonds Jr. (married 1941, divorced 1947 for extreme mental cruelty): Francis C. Edmonds III and Ruth T. Edmonds Naylor. She had five with her second husband, Dr William F. Beuscher (married 1950, divorced 1968): Robert Conrad, William David, Christopher Grey, Thomas Frederick, and John Franklin.

2–TH added a note at the bottom of the letter, which has not been transcribed. TH wrote with pride about Frieda's birth and on SP's general health and well-being.

exception, & yells herself into fine red fits any time from midnight to four! So I nap in the day to make up for lost sleep then & try to persuade Ted to do the same. You should see him rocking her & singing to her! She looks so tiny against his shoulder, her four little fingers just closing around one of his knuckles. Now, of course, she is sleeping like a top, rosy & pink-cheeked. Already she shows a funny independence & temper. When she wakes very hungry, instead of starting to nurse quietly she will cry, open her mouth & let go of the nipple, rage, wave her hands about, & then try with both hands to hold onto the breast & feed herself. Once she starts sucking, though, after a few minutes of this, she is steady & very efficient. I am on a 4-hour schedule (6, 10, 2, 6, 10, 2) of feeding her. When the midwife leaves me to take over at the end of the week I shall bathe her before her evening feed & she assures me that should help her to sleep before & after her 2 a.m. feeding. She is very small for her nighties & sweaters, so I shouldn't have to get anything for some time. First thing next week I shall get a pram & wheel her proudly around Regent's Park & Primrose Hill. I'm allowed to go out with her if it's nice on the 10th day, & I can't wait.

We have been surrounded by flowers (from the Merwins, Ted's parents, some friends of his) & messages of good will: telegrams from Marty & Frank, Louise, & grampy (Now GREAT-Grampy: I hope he's proud!)

We are dying to hear from you & Warren your reactions to all this. Everybody is most amazed by the rapidity of my labor, especially myself. I am sure one of the reasons I felt so well after the delivery & had no tears or anything is because I had no anesthesia & therefore was able to respond to all the directions of the doctor. And Rebecca, of course, looked lovely immediately, hasty lady that she was.

Things seem much calmer & more peaceful with the baby around than without. The Merwins are going to France for half a year at the end of this month, so Ted will have a study & utter peace by the time I have all my strength back & am coping with baby & household. Now I rely on his cooking, shopping, going to the laundromat etc. etc., & his help---so much better than a stranger's---will be invaluable in my quick return to normal activity.

I'll leave just a corner for him to say Hello. I trust you've informed the thousands of waiting relatives, friends & fellow-Americans of this Event. I'll be writing Dot, Frank, Aldriches, Cruikshanks etc. later this week when I've done more getting about.

Love to you, Warren & Sappho . . .
Sivvy

TO *Edith & William Hughes*

c. Monday–Thursday 4–7 April 1960[1] ALS, Emory University

10 pm

Hello there!

I am sitting up in bed writing surrounded by the lovely flowers you sent & getting ready to feed Frieda Rebecca before we turn in for the night. She is more adorable every hour, sleeps like an Angel, yells a bit in the early hours just for exercise & looks rather like a rosebud – very pink & delicately-made with perfectly formed little hands & feet: Ted is wonderful with her – a real help in these days while I am slowly getting back my strength, & an expert in wrapping her up & tucking her in after her feedings. I wouldn't be in a hospital for the world, it's so pleasant at home with all my things around me, the baby in the same room & Ted writing next door. I hope in two or three weeks or so to be more or less back to normal, but just now am very glad to have the midwife come each day to bathe me & the baby. Of course my two weeks of flu & sinus have something to do with my being wobbly. Luckily I got over that just before the baby came. It is so good to have her here at last after all this waiting.

We've been rejoicing here, too, about Ted's Somerset Maugham Prize – there's really nothing he could win now he hasn't won already! I am so proud of his book. It's beyond comparison.

Tell Hilda I just got the curtains sewn for the bedroom in the nick of time & the green cord looks beautiful – wonderful for protecting the baby from drafts – our windows are full of cracks & the cord is fine insulation.

You must come down later this spring when I am all recovered to admire the flat, Ted's masterful carpentering & the beautiful Rebecca.

Love to all,
Sylvia

TO *Aurelia Schober Plath*

Thursday 7 April 1960 TLS (aerogramme), Indiana University

Thursday: April 7

Dear mother,

Well, if I hadn't heard from you today I was seriously thinking of disowning my nearest kin! Ted said you'd probably be so busy informing

1–Date supplied from internal evidence.

half of America of this event that you'd not get around to writing me for at least a month. Anyhow, your letter was so cheering it made up for the days of waiting. I actually had a dream during my nap yesterday that Ted & I were waiting for you & Warren in the Wellesley kitchen. You both came in with huge armloads of groceries (this was before I read of your forgetting the groceries last weekend). "Well, what do you think of it!" we called out to you. Whereupon you handed us two letters, unstamped, that you had been about to send. I still haven't heard a word from Warren, so get him to write in person, even if it's only a little. The one infuriating thing about the general euphoria around here is that I have no relatives or friends of my own to admire the baby in person. Ted's people & friends are dear, the room is full of flowers, telegrams & cards & well wishes, but it isn't the same. Dido Merwin has been supplying us with delicacies off & on: blanquet de veau, trout in aspic, with eyes turned to pearls & lemon slices arrayed about, and when Ted went over to dessert & to meet Bill's publisher last night she gave him some beans in a pot & another stew to heat up. Such goodness is beyond thanks. Bill came over yesterday: my first visitor & the first to see the baby. He brought daffodils, a silver thimble for the baby & a pile of old New Yorkers for me, figuring with exact intuition I was ready for nothing more concentrated than first the jokes & cartoons, then the poems, then stories . . . short, amusing & something easy to pick up & put down.

The baby is sleeping sweetly after her 2 pm feeding, her little hands in the most delicate attitudes: her ballet-like gestures with her hands are one of the loveliest things about her. I have begun changing her diapers myself now & enjoy it immensely. She is very good & quiet & seems to like waving her legs about & being bare. Her navel cord dried up & fell off a few days ago & she has a perfectly lovely body. Last night she did her stint of crying before 10 pm which was very easy to take & she slept straight through till she woke me at three when I fed her, & slept again till 7. So I had my first good night's sleep for a week. When I bathe her at night she will probably sleep even more soundly. She seems to be taking our lead & waking a lot more in the daytime now. For the first few days, when she just had colostrum to suck, I fed her every 4 hours and then, as my milk started to come in, on demand about every 2 hours for a day & night so she'd get enough, & now she gets enough to last her exactly 4 hours after 20 minutes of energetic feeding. They put the baby to the breast at birth here, feed it nothing supplementary & the baby obligingly sleeps through the early days & its demand seems magically to produce the right amounts of milk. I never feed her from the bottle, but from the spoon, if I give her anything else, like water, & hope to wean her straight to the cup. My Indian midwife has been so encouraging & helpful about all this. I am going to make her Dot's carrot cake this weekend: she said she doesn't like bakery goods so I thought that would be a gift only I could give her & not something impersonal like candy or flowers. Dido Merwin came over this afternoon with one of her own christening presents: a little gold heart with 3 stones: they seem a pearl, turquoise & a pink stone. She does this out of love & loves only special certain people. She & Bill will be our godparents when the baby is christened, probably next winter when they come back from France: I'll make a feast & will investigate now about having the minster who married us do it in his church.[1]

No more words about hormones & growth-stopping please! I'm surprised at you. Tampering with nature! What an American thing to feel measuring people to ideal heights will make them happier or not interfere with other things. Whatever height Frieda Rebecca is, I shall encourage her to be proud of it. My own height, 5'9" which so depressed me once is now my delight: & I have a handsome tall living documentary of a husband to prove a tall girl need be nothing but fortunate in that line: once married, let other men be all short squat toads. Enough of that.

Helga, Danny & little Madeleine came this afternoon to bringing two sweet knit little German dresses for Rebecca when she's older. The baby sleeps with the light on, me typing, us talking. I've written Mrs. Prouty (havent heard from her for a long time: hope she's all right), Marcia, Aunt Frieda. Will spread out to others as I get more energy. I hope your myriad friends won't expect letters in answer to cards! Oh, also wrote Aunt Mildred her letter moved me so much & it so excited me they were thinking of retiring here: I wonder if they know how deeply fond of them I am. If they come, would you consider retiring to an English country house nearby? Warren will be the wealthy one of us two & be able to visit you in England, while we would only come to America on a paid-for reading tour or possible resident-poet year much later. I'm becoming more & more anglophile – watch out!

Love,
Sivvy

I'm going to have all my babies at home: I've loved every minute of this experience![2]

1–SP and TH were married by Reverend R. Mercer Wilson (b. 1887). Wilson lived at 13 Doughty Street, London; Dickens's house was number 48.

2–TH added a note on the return address side of the letter, which has not been transcribed. TH commented on Frieda's sounds, on SP's natural mothering instincts, and mentioned

TO *Gerald & Joan Hughes*

Thursday 7 April 1960[1] ALS,[2] Indiana University

Hello everybody! LUPERCAL preceded Frieda Rebecca by exactly two weeks but she arrived in a hurry to make up for it. Both productions have been well-received by the world at large & are, we hope, destined for brilliant futures. My first book of poems is coming out here next fall, & 3 of Ted's stories in a Faber anthology & his first children's book next winter, so we are thriving in London air & very happy with all things

xxx Love to all
Sylvia

TO *Peter Davison*

Wednesday 13 April 1960 TLS (photocopy), Yale University

3 Chalcot Square
London N.W.1, England
April 13, 1960

Dear Peter,

It was good to hear from you, and good to hear that you and Jane[3] will be spending the spring in Europe. One of the consolations of my in-the-main happy and probably permanent exile is that London is such a usual stopping place for American friends: a sort of ideal ambush.

We'd be happy to see you & Jane for dinner May 2nd---why don't you call beforehand and check with us. Our number is PRImrose 9132.

The bambino---Frieda Rebecca Hughes (to be called Rebecca)---arrived at the crack of dawn on April Fool's Day. I am now a strong advocate of the British Medical System, which gave me cold shivers when I first came over. I've had wonderful, exceptional doctor's care, home nursing for two weeks, cheap milk, vitamins & orange juice, and all free. A year ago if anyone had told me I'd have my first baby at home, delivered by a five-foot high Indian midwife without any anesthesia I would have called them mad. But as it happened, I wouldn't have it any other way.

---

a review of *Lupercal* in the *New Statesman*: Donald Hall, 'True and False Feeling', *New Statesman* (9 April 1960): 530.

1 – Date supplied from postmark.

2 – SP's letter is at the end of a letter begun by TH, which has not been transcribed.

3 – Jane Auchincloss Truslow (1932–81); B.A. 1955, English, Smith College; SP's housemate at Lawrence House. Truslow married SP's friend Peter Davison on 7 March 1959.

One small bit of business. I wonder if you could tell me roughly when those stories I sent in to the Atlantic early last fall were sent back. I haven't received them yet & feel they may have gone astray at one of my many forwarding addresses (there were 3: A Prospect of Cornucopia, The Fifty-Ninth Bear, and Johnny Panic and the Bible of Dreams).

Ted joins me in sending best wishes to you & Jane. We both look forward to seeing you two again.

Sincerely,
Sylvia Hughes

TO *Aurelia Schober Plath*

Friday 15 April 1960 TLS (aerogramme), Indiana University

Friday night: April 15

Dear mother,

It was good to get letters from you & Warren yesterday. I am sitting down for a few minutes over Ovaltine after Rebecca has been bathed, fed & bedded. I love to dress her in a fresh nightgown (the ones you sent: I have to roll up the cuffs, but they are ideal, easy to wash & dry) every night after her bath. She wears all the things you sent her: diapers, nighties, the rubber pants. I took a nap this afternoon & felt much renewed this evening, reading, typing a bit for Ted & so on. The baby still has her wakeful crying interval around her two o'clock feeding, although one night she slept through from an earlier feeding at one a.m. till I woke her just before 7. So we have been piecing together 2 & 3 hours of sleep these last two weeks which is tiring to people so addicted to 9 solid hours as we are. A nap in the afternoon though, & a hot bath on getting up in the morning, are marvelously renewing.

Rebecca's had a tub bath every day since she was born: first in my pyrex dish which wasn't really big enough. Then Ted got a little plastic dishpan which we use now. Her navel cord fell off in 4 or 5 days & I simply keep her navel cleared of the drop of blood which sometimes discharges with sterile cotton & the midwife says it will heal soon. I was officially discharged from the midwife's service yesterday, after 14 days of care. Our beloved Sister Mardi came after a week of alternation between the two other sisters, & I gave her one of the 3 carrot cakes I made which she very much appreciated, & hugged her. Today she dropped by with some free samples of "Gripe Water", a British remedy for hiccups & wind, & to say hello. At the end of one week the baby had gained back her birthweight & was again 7 lbs. 4 oz. At the end of this week she was almost 7 lbs. 12 oz. The midwife says I have enough milk for twins. Rebecca doesn't yell anymore once I pick her up, just gobbles away greedily. She is such a lovely baby I can't be away from her for long, but peek into the room to see how she looks. The midwife didn't slap her when she came: she just caught her breath, sneezed & there she was.[1]

I went out for my first little walks Saturday & Sunday in green & blue April weather, but felt terribly lonesome without a pram & the baby. Monday I went to town & found it takes 2 months to order a pram, so I bought the cheapest (!) one in the shop, just over $50. The rest were from about $70 to $100! I felt this was bought with Mrs. Prouty's money, which she wanted me to put into doctor's care (<u>Don't</u> tell her my home confinement was free!) It is a lovely pram, a white body & washable interior, black hood & weather apron. Very handsome & large. As I said, prams here take the place of cars. & I hope mine will hold a good many children. Of course it rained the day it was delivered & the day after. Ted & I first took the baby out yesterday, well bundled up, to Regent's Park. It was very cold but sunny, then, just as we got near home, it began to rain. But prams here are built for bad weather & wind & Rebecca slept warmly through it all. We took a few snapshots of us with the pram & one of Rebecca in the sunlight in the house. I shall look into flashbulbs. I wish I could get her in technicolor, her big dark blue eyes & pink cheeks.

Your work sounds so arduous. Have you had your spring vacation yet? Can you catch up then? We admire your courage & perserverance so much. I hope you sleep all right. My whole philosophy of life is dependent on getting enough sleep: without it, one gets completely demoralized. How is your work in remedial reading with Dr. Noall coming? Do tell us everything, your concerns and all.

These last two weeks, infact, the last month or so, have slipped by with my hardly noticing the dates & I am eager to begin writing & thinking again. The most difficult thing is the idea of leaving the baby with a sitter. We are invited to cocktails at Faber's next Thursday from 6-8 & shall presumably meet Eliot, yet I am so reluctant to leave the baby. I've heard of a good babyminding service that guarantees its people, all expertly trained in baby-care, 50 cents an hour, which the wife of an artist in the Merwin's house uses & shall try them. I do want to get about with Ted

1 – Cf. SP's 'Morning Song': 'The midwife slapped your footsoles, and your bald cry / Took its place among the elements' (*Collected Poems*: 156).

now & then but the 3-hour interval between her being fed & changed & starting again leaves time for little. I wish I could carry her like a papoose. I hate to think of her waking early as she sometimes does & some stranger just letting her cry. They don't believe in bottles here at all, nor do I & I wouldn't miss feeding her for the world. Well, I must get to bed now. Ted sends love. How is Warren's work coming? Will he get his scholarship next year?

xxx
Sivvy

TO *Aurelia Schober Plath*

Thursday 21 April 1960 — TLS/ALS (aerogramme), Indiana University

Thursday, April 21st

Dear mother,

I hope this letter gets to you by Saturday to say how much we look forward to your call on Sunday. I'm not sure exactly what the time difference is now, we've just a week ago changed to British Summer Time which gives us lovely long light evenings till about 8 pm. We lost an hour: I am always confused about what this does elsewhere.

The weather here has been beautiful, sunny & springy the last few days. I am sitting in our sun-flooded kitchen, waiting for a pan of hash to finish cooking, planning to feed Frieda Rebecca (we are oddly enough starting to call her Frieda!) at 2 & then go out to Regents Park for a walk & sit in the sun as I did yesterday. I always walk past the outer wall of the Zoo where I can see several animals---the mountain goats on their pinnacles, a lion through a hedge, a queer beautiful panda which is new & looks on fire: maple syrup color on top, marked with white, & darkening to black paws, lots of goats, kids, shetland ponies for the children to ride & pet, & a pen of marvelous black pot-bellied hogs, wart-hogs, I think, or something outlandish, with great black many-lined gorilla faces & remarkable brisk dancing piggy steps. Primrose Hill was brilliant green, covered with children: children rolling down in the sloping grass, kicking colored balls, taking their first steps. One woman even had her baby naked on its knees in the sun although the air was cold. I walked by the bird sanctuary to the boat basin where the water was crowded with skiffs & little sailboats & sat & read the proofs of Merwins fourth book of poems.[1] I am just getting over my tiredness from getting up at night. During the day the baby (known informally as The Pooker, or Pooker-Pie) wakes on the clock four-hourly & at night she shows reassuring signs of sleeping for 5 & even an occasional 6-hour interval. She eats like a little piglet.

3:15: I am now sitting on a bench, facing the sun in Regent's Park. They are mowing the lawns everywhere & the smell of cut grass, plants & warm earth is delicious. Nothing is so beautiful as England in April. I only wish you were here to walk out with me – by the time you come the baby herself should be toddling! I can't wait till she does laugh & communicate with us. She is so tiny still when she curls up she almost disappears. It is wonderful to feel hot in the sun again. Tonight I am employing the Babyminder Service[2] for the first time from 6 to 9ish (so we can go to Faber's for cocktails – hopefully to meet TS Eliot, we're not sure) & again tomorrow at the same time so we can go to dinner with Lee Anderson (he looks like a white-bearded civil war general, is a poet & has a farm in America – over here to record British Poets for Yale) in Soho. Tuesday we went to lunch with two ex-Cambridge people – a girl who works for the BBC[3] & is interested in Ted's writing a verse drama for them, & Karl Miller,[4] literary editor of The Spectator. Had very good onion soup & zabaglione – a dessert concocted of warm whipped eggs, sugar & wine – tastes heavenly, wish I could find out how to make it.

Last Sunday – another still warm sunny day, I had an immensely moving experience & attended the arrival of the Easter weekend marchers from the atomic bomb plant at Aldermaston to Trafalgar Square in London. Ted & Dido had left at noon to see Bill Merwin, who was with the over 10 thousand marchers come into Hyde Park & I left later with the baby to meet a poet-friend of Ted's, Peter Redgrove[5] & go to Trafalgar Square with him. He brought a carry-cot, which he is loaning us, & we carried the baby sleeping easily between us, installed the cot on the lawn of the National Gallery overlooking the fountains, pigeons & glittering white buildings. Our corner was uncrowded, a sort of nursery, mothers giving babies bottles on blankets & so on. I saw the first of the 7-mile-long

1–W. S. Merwin, *The Drunk in the Furnace* (New York: Macmillan; London: Rupert Hart-Davis, 1960).

2–Babyminders, then located, according to SP's address book, at 39 James Street, London W.1, and 88 George Street, W.1.

3–Possibly Sasha Moorsom (1931–93); Moorsom attended Cambridge; produced Ted Hughes, *The House of Aries*, BBC Third Programme (16 November 1960).

4–British editor and critic Karl Miller (1931–2014); editor of *New Statesman*.

5–British poet Peter Redgrove (1932–2003).

column appear – red & orange & green banners "Ban the Bomb" etc. shining & swaying slowly. Absolute silence. I found myself weeping to see the tan dusty marchers, knapsacks on their backs – Quakers & Catholics, Africans & whites, Algerians & French – 40 percent were London housewives. I felt proud that the baby's first real adventure should be as a protest against the insanity of world-annihilation – already a certain percentage of unborn children are doomed by fallout & noone knows the cumulative effects of what is already poisoning the air & sea. I hope, by the way, that neither you nor Warren will vote for Nixon.[1] His record is atrocious from his California campaign on – a Macchiavelli of the worst order. Could you find out if there is any way I can vote? I never have & feel badly to be deprived of however minute a participation in political affairs. What do you think of Kennedy?[2] The Sharpeville massacres[3] are causing a great stir of pity & indignation here. How long is it before you can expose a little baby to direct sunlight? We're dying to take snapshots of the baby. I've heard via cards, from Aunt Marion, Mrs. Railsback,[4] Dollie Beaton,[5] Mrs. Spaulding – thank them all for me. No word – at all from Dot & Joe, oddly enough. I'll try to write a note to them this next week. The days of this last three weeks have just flown by without my seeming to really accomplish anything except feeding the baby & us & writing a few letters. I really long for a house here near the Park & must learn from you how one sets about committing oneself to a house – I want lots of rooms so we can have more children – I would so like about four – I hate to be limited by money & space!

xxx
Sivvy

1–Richard Milhous Nixon (1913–94); 37th President of the United States. Nixon ran unsuccessfully against John F. Kennedy in the 1960 presidential election.
2–John Fitzgerald Kennedy (1917–63). Member of the United States House of Representatives from Massachusetts (1947–53); United States Senator from Massachusetts (1953–60) and 35th President of the United States (1961–3).
3–On 21 March 1960, sixty-nine protestors were killed at the police station in Sharpeville, South Africa.
4–Probably Barbara Varney Railsback (1915–2004), who with her husband Edward Neal Railsback (1916–2009) lived at 8 Ingersoll Road, Wellesley, Mass.
5–Probably Dollie Beaton (1902–68), who lived at 10 Ingersoll Road, Wellesley, Mass.

TO *Aurelia Schober Plath & Warren Plath*

Tuesday 26 April 1960 TLS (aerogramme), Indiana University

Tuesday morning
April 26, 1960

HAPPY BIRTHDAY " " " HAPPY BIRTHDAY " " " HAPPY BIRTHDAY " " "

Dear mother & Warren . . .

It was wonderful to hear your voices Sunday. Ted shouted "Many happy returns" into the phone, but I guess it was after you had been cut off. I am always sad at what little can be said on the phone . . . the main thing is hearing voices. You sounded so close. I had Rebecca in my arms all the time I was talking. How I wish you were here to admire her! To other people she must just be an ordinary baby, but I would love to have an admiring grandmother & uncle appreciate her unique and absolutely marvelous qualities! I shall send the snapshots, if any come out, as a belated birthday token. It is the morning of your birthday, mother, but I suppose you are still sleeping, as it is only 10 am here. And tomorrow, your day, Warren. And my half-day. I am so sorry if you had a long wait getting us Sunday. I have no calendar & both our watches need their straps repaired, so in the confusion of going out walking with Danny & Helga & Madeleine & serving them tea, & dropping over to say goodbye to Bill Merwin, who sets off by car for their farm in France ahead of Dido by a week, & their opening a bottle of champagne, I completely lost track of the day, time and all & was truly appalled to find it had got so late. I don't know how I can wait till next summer for the prospect of seeing you! Hearing your voice makes me feel your absence more: you feel so close it seems you should be able to drop right over.

The baby is staying awake much more, makes a really successful effort to hold her head up straight when we carry her on our shoulders, turns her face to a voice & seems to regard us with increasing intelligence. She seems also to be on the way to learning to sleep longer at night. I fed her a little later last night, about 11 pm instead of 10: she slept till after 5 am (which I counted as a 6 am feeding) & then till almost 10 am, so she actually skipped the night feeding as far as count goes. Her time of fretful crying is between 6 pm & 10 pm as Dr. Spock says is most common. Other than that she is a little angel. The two times I had two different baby-minders come last week reassured me immensely. They bring their own sandwiches (I leave out things for tea or coffee), knitting, & are very calm & expert, reporting on the baby's crying, gas bubbles etc. The last one I had works in the day at the Child Guidance Clinic under the London County Council & I enjoyed a little talk with her about her work while Ted & Lee Anderson had a glass of beer before we went out to a delicious dinner at The White Tower in Soho,[1] a Greek place. The charge after 6 is only 50 cents an hour & subway fare home (10 cents at most). By day, the charge is 60 cents. It seems very reasonable for such guaranteed expert service. I'm going to try a "relief bottle" for the baby one evening this week preparatory to our dinner at T. S. Eliot's May 4th, so I won't have to rush home then. Just us, the Stephen Spenders & the Eliots! The Faber cocktail party was great fun. The first time I had really dressed up for ages: everyone marveled I had had a baby just 3 weeks ago. I met a lively American girl[2] on a 2-year fellowship to Cambridge whose path crossed mine often in America: Faber's are doing her first novel, & I invited her & her Indian poet friend[3] to a spaghetti supper in early May. Met an old college-mate of Ted's now a TV producer of arty programs, drank champagne & felt very grand & proud of Ted.

Got a very nice letter from Edward Weeks at the Atlantic & have finally by doggedness broken through the Iron Curtain raised by Peter Davison's coming into power as Advisor on Poems & they accepted two[4]---the best of the sheaf I sent, gratifyingly enough, one of them the first in my book & written to the baby while I was at Yaddo: I'll get $75 for each, which is nice. Knew Peter was behind my rejections, oddly enough---he fancies himself as a poet, as you know---but felt once he thought he'd show-n off his power & glory he would find it difficult or pointless to keep rejecting my good things. & so it has come to pass.

We are caring for the Merwins garden in their absence & told to keep picking everything: roses, lilies etc. What a lovely chore: I am eager to get familiar with hollyhocks, peonies delphiniums and their seasons again. We'll water & fertilise the little lawn & Ted will mow it.

I am furious at BU's unheard of tactics! What cowardice, to omit the department from the catalogue without facing up to announcing it to you first! Are they just washing their hands of you thus mousily then? What are the prospects of your working into this remedial guidance then? Do

1–The White Tower, 1 Percy Street, London.

2–Janet Burroway (1936–); author of *Descend Again* (London: Faber & Faber, 1960). See *Memories of Whitstead* (10–13).

3–Zulfikar ('Zulfi') Ghose (1935–); Pakistani poet, novelist, and essayist.

4–Sylvia Plath, 'A Winter Ship', *The Atlantic* 206 (July 1960): 65; and 'The Manor Garden', *The Atlantic* 206 (September 1960): 52. With the two accepted poems, SP submitted 'The Sleepers', 'Polly's Tree', 'Blue Moles', 'In Midas Country', 'Two Views of Withens', and 'The Burnt-out Spa' on 25 January 1960.

keep us posted on all this. Ted joins in sending lots of love to you both. He's wonderfully good with the baby.

xxxxx
sivvy

TO *Aurelia Schober Plath*

Friday–Saturday 29–30 April 1960 TLS with envelope, Indiana University

Friday: April 29

Dear mother . . .

Well, here are the first snapshots of your granddaughter.[1] We hope you can get some idea of her from these muzzy pictures, although you really can't see how she looks with her eyes shut & her head bonneted. We'll investigate a flash-bulb. She looks so beautiful when she's awake & her head held up . . . no double chin then, but very slender & thin.

I'm enclosing two checks for deposit: the $19 one into the Boston 5cent savings account (shouldn't there be some interest by now? How much) and the little 4 dollar one into our Wellesley Account: I'm enclosing the book for the latter. There should be interest due there, too. Let us know what the totals come to.

Did Warren & I cry at all as babies? Frieda Rebecca no longer cries during the night, but from about 6 pm to 10 pm she yells bloody murder & won't be consoled by anything. Dr. Spock calls this very common "irritable crying" or periodic colic,[2] & she does have a hard time getting up her bubble after feedings, but I find it difficult to listen to her yell, really scream, without being able to do anything to make her feel better. She is very regular about her period of crying: the rest of the day she is placid & quiet as a clam.

Aunt Frieda sent me a lovely white lace bordered handmade smock for the baby. Very pretty & dainty. I shall write & thank her. I think it pleases her to have a namesake.

Tomorrow I am going with Dido to see Laurence Olivier[3] in Ionesco's play "Rhinoceros",[4] which I have luckily read in the original French:

1–The photographs are no longer with the letter.

2–Benjamin Spock, *Baby & Child Care*, 183.

3–English actor and director Sir Laurence Olivier, OM (1907–89).

4–Eugène Ionesco, *Rhinoceros* (1959); played at the Royal Court Theatre, 50–1 Sloane Square, London.

I suppose it will be translated, very modern & amusing. I look forward to the change.

Well, it is getting late. Ted should be home from an evening with Lee Anderson, the poet-recorder from Yale, soon & then I'll bathe & feed the baby & turn in. Ted has started working in Bill's study, & today I took the baby over in the carriage & mowed the little lawn, which we shall take care of all summer. The first iris are out, & the lilac beginning to open.

Lots of love to you, Warren & Sappho,

Sivvy

Saturday: April 30

PS: Just about to go off to laundromat. Got your good letter today: isn't it curious about Dot buying the Goodall's place[1] . . . you gave such a good impression of her funny reluctance to come out with the information as she answered your gradually involving questions. I wonder why they keep everything from you? It gives a very queer sense of their plotting this & that. And the ominous sense here of "If anything happens to Frank . . ." Can't he just clear out, take a year off? Sell his Philadelphia place & rest for a year at the Weston house? Crazy to wait until Fate steps ominously in & commands. I feel very badly about him.

A Lovely blue spring day. Very excited about the Olivier play, to see him on stage in the flesh, & in such a delightful play. About a whole village that turn into rhinoceroses except one last man.

Miss Warren immensely. I don't know how I can bear his not coming over with you. I have a very comfortable cot in the livingroom you could make up & sleep on. Presumably if our relations with the Merwins continue so amiably Ted can again have the study next summer & so he could go to the Office while you & I played about with the baby.

Oddly enough, Mrs. Pullings lovely spoon & fork arrived the morning as you mentioned it in your letter. Thank her warmly for me. I'll write a note soon.

Ted records his first BBC program[2]---a 20 minute reading & talk on various poets' poems about Creatures, including one of his own---next Thursday, for which he gets $75. They pay very nicely & he has one or two other program ideas on his mind.

Wish we could share this wonderful spring with you.

Lots of love,

1–Edwin Baker Goodall, Jr., a Wellesley physician, was the Benottis' neighbour and lived at 55 Silver Hill Road, Weston; he sold his house to the Benottis in October 1959.

2–Ted Hughes, *Themes:* 'Creatures', BBC Home Service (8 May 1960). TH read his 'Hawk Roosting'.

TO *Janet Burroway*

Tuesday 3 May 1960 TLS, Janet Burroway

3 Chalcot Square
N.W.1
May 3, 1960

Dear Janet,

Please do you & Zulfi come to dinner on Saturday about 7 pm. I'll do a very simple spaghetti as I said, or think I said.

Chalk Farm is the tube station nearest us, on the Northern line. Ask for Regents Park Road. You'll walk up over a railroad bridge, cross a Gloucester Road & keep straight on Regents Park Road till the next little street to your left[1] after Gloucester Road which will lead you soon into the Square. We're the grey house with white trimmings among other squalidia.

Looking forward to seeing you both then, (Our phone, by the way, is PRImrose 9132.).

sylvia

TO *Aurelia Schober Plath*

Thursday 5 May 1960 TLS, Indiana University

3 Chalcot Square
London N.W.1
Thursday, May 5: 2 pm

Dear mother . . .

How wonderful Sappho is going to have kittens. Oh, I wish we could somehow have one of them. You must describe each one in detail & note the day of their birth. We are very excited about this. So proud Warren has a scholarship next year.

I am about to take the baby out in the warm May weather to the Clinic[2] for weighing. My first visit there. A very nice Health Visitor dropped in yesterday, answered my little questions about this & that. Her name, ominously, is Mrs. M. A. Reckless! But she is pleasant & kindly. I really feel immensely well taken care of & looked after. The Health Center advises one about diet, weaning, weight . . . all really non-medical problems.

1–Berkley Road.

2–According to SP's address book, she took Frieda to the Linnet House Clinic on Charlbert Street, London N.8.

A really exquisite yellow sweater & darling yellow flowered sunsuit with plastic lining in the pants came today from dear Madeline Sheets: I'll write her. But they were just the sort of things I'd pick myself & should fit the baby later on.

This has been a full week. Ted's off this afternoon to record his BBC program on "Creatures" which will be broadcast Sunday. Also Sunday his book is to be reviewed over the BBC by the editor of the Times Literary Supplement.[1] I'm going to ask the lady upstairs if we can listen in on her radio.

Yesterday the proofs of my book THE COLOSSUS came in a paper binding. We are so excited. The book will look handsome. 88 pages long. The poems look so beautifully final. The printers-publishers page says: William Heinemann Ltd. London Melbourne Toronto Cape Town Auckland The Hague. © Sylvia Plath 1960 All rights reserved. And of course says For Ted on the dedication page. I can't get over it.

The Ionesco play I found wonderfully amusing. Olivier was magnificent as the stupid, human little clerk who remains a man while the village turns to a herd of rhinoceroi. Orson Welles directed the play,[2] & the chinless executioner of "Kind Hearts & Coronets"[3] was in it, a fine supporting cast. Dido & I enjoyed the whole thing immensely.

Had dinner at an excellent Indian restaurant with Peter & Jane Davison Monday, at the expense of the Atlantic. Peter is worse than ever. He was furious (although he tried to conceal this) that I'd sent my stories & poems directly To Edward Weeks & not through him. I figured he'd been behind the rejections of my things, as since he came on, not one of my pieces had been taken & he is very jealous, as he now considers himself a real poet. Evidently his job is furthered by "bringing writers in". But I was there before he came.

He also bragged about his work in the most puerile way. Said he read Ted's story in Harper's "the issue before the issue with a poem of mine[4] in it", and as we left them on the bus he yelled desperately after us: "Look for the Hudson Review, I have a long poem[5] coming out in it." Pity & shame compelled me from yelling back "I have four coming out in it." A very unpleasant person. They have a child due in autumn, which should prove his manhood to himself. But is so mean he defeats his own purpose

1–In 1960, the editor of the *Times Literary Supplement* was Arthur Crook (1912–2005).
2–'directed the ~~paly~~ play' appears in the original.
3–Miles Malleson (1888–1969), British actor, played the part of the hangman in the film. SP saw *Kind Hearts and Coronets* in Boston on 5 July 1952.
4–Peter Davison, 'To a Mad Friend', *Harper's* 220 (February 1960): 91.
5–Probably Peter Davison, 'Not Forgotten', *Hudson Review* 14 (Autumn 1961): 392–4.

as an editor. He can't bear to hear about our work, so of course we tell him nothing.

Last night at Eliot's was magnificent. By a miracle I got the baby bathed & fed, me bathed & dressed, Ted bathed & dressed & the babyminder instructed about the baby's relief bottle (she takes all 6 ounces beautifully: Ted tried her out on her first bottle while I was at the Olivier play, to see if it would work.) We took a taxi, as it was rush hour & the place a hard one to get to. A beautiful green May evening. Passed through streets I'd never seen: Little Venice, houses mirrored in a still green canal. Palace Gardens, streets of large pastel stucco houses with gardens & the street lined with pink & white flowering trees. We saw a For Sale sign & promised ourselves we'd make a symbolic effort to inquire about it. Oddly enough, the more we set our sights on, the more good fortune occurs. No harm in dreaming. I see a lawn full of babies & descendants of Sappho. And a bookcase full of books.

The Eliots live in a surprisingly drab brick building on the first floor.[1] A comfortable, lavish apartment. His Yorkshire wife Valerie[2] is handsome, blond & rosy. He was marvelous. Put us immediately at ease. We exchanged American travel experiences. Had sherry by the coal fire. I felt to be sitting next to a descended god: he has such a nimbus of greatness about him. His wife showed me his baby & little-boy pictures in their bedroom. His was handsome from the start. Wonderfully wry & humorous. Then the Spenders arrived, he handsome & white-haired, and she very reminiscent of Do Cruikshank: lean, vibrant, talkative, lovely. Her name is Natasha Litvin,[3] & she is a concert pianist. Talk was intimate gossip about Stravinsky, Auden, Virginia Woolf, D. H. Lawrence . . . I was fascinated. Floated in to dinner, sat between Eliot & Spender, rapturously & got along very well. Both of them, of course, were instrumental in Ted's getting his Guggenheim & his book printed.

If anyone else wants to write the baby's name on anything, do say her whole name Frieda Rebecca: that's the most sensible, as it gives her & us the option of what to call her. She takes marvelous notice of us now: gave Ted her first dazzling smile. Lifts her head up, looks round, & half turns over when I put her on her back to change her. She is so beautiful we can't get over admiring her. Everybody who sees her exclaims over her big blue eyes & long lashes. We're just madly in love with her.

1 – According to SP's address book, the Eliots lived at 3 Kensington Court Gardens, London W.8. The address is written by TH.

2 – Valerie Eliot (1926–2012); T. S. Eliot's second wife and widow.

3 – English pianist and author Natasha Spender (1919–2010).

Well, I must sign off & get out. Here are two more checks for the Boston 5 cents savings account. How much is it now, with the interest?

Much love to you, Warren, Sappho & embryos,

xxx
Sivvy

TO *Robie Macauley*

Thursday 5 May 1960 TLS, Kenyon College

3 Chalcot Square
London N.W.1, England
May 5, 1960

Mr. Robie Macauley, Editor
THE KENYON REVIEW
Gambier, Ohio
USA

Dear Mr. Macauley:

I thought I would write to let you know that my first volume of poems has been accepted for publication here in England some time late next fall or early winter, in case that might make a difference in the scheduling of the two poems ("The Beekeeper's Daughter" and "The Colossus") you have on hand.

Also, my address is now changed to the above London one.

With all good wishes,
Sincerely Yours,
Sylvia Plath

TO *Aurelia Schober Plath*

Wednesday 11 May 1960 TLS (aerogramme), Indiana University

Wednesday: May 11

Dear mother,

This week & next must be your very busiest. We are wishing you all the best luck on exams & hope you will make a special effort to keep in good health. The past week, with our going out for two dinners & my having two dinners (Saturday & Monday) has been so crowded I hardly remember when I last wrote you, but I think it was after the Eliot dinner. Now the 6 weeks are up since the baby's birth, we are just getting our heads above water. Ted is starting to work regularly over in Merwins study, which is a great relief for both of us. It is impossible for him to work in this little place with me cleaning & caring for the baby, & when he is out, I have the livingroom & desk to myself & can get my work done. After the Merwins come back in 6 months or so, we'll try to arrange Ted's getting or renting another room, perhaps even from the lady upstairs who goes to work daily. That would be most convenient. I find my first concern is that Ted has peace & quiet. I am happy then, & don't mind that my own taking up of writing comes a few weeks later. I feel now just to be myself again. Will probably have my post-natal checkup with the doctor tomorrow.

Frieda Rebecca has made wonderful strides this week. Her first dazzling smile was given to Ted, which delighted both of us. Now she often smiles. She still has her 6 pm to 10 pm colic, but we are calmer about it, although it is a strain. If I feed her about 11 pm she regularly sleeps through till 6 am without a peep, & no longer screams to eat on waking, but lies contentedly playing with her hands till I get up to change & feed her. She eats vigorously & fully, nonstop for half an hour, so fast she often gets hiccups & belches up a little milk. Did I say at 5 weeks she weighed 9 lbs. 4oz? She seems very healthy. I came in yesterday to find her facing a different side from the side I laid her down on, which startled me. She had lifted her head, gone onto her stomach & turned her face round. She kicked her blankets off, too. I don't know what I would do without Ted: he adores the baby & is continually marveling, hanging over her crib, on how beautiful she is. It is wonderful he is not the kind of father who ignore babies till they can talk. I have hung the little gold wood-shaving angel you sent us from Europe over the head of her crib.

Ted got a very touching letter from Somerset Maugham at his Riviera villa in answer to his thanks for the award. Maugham said he was "thrilled" at Ted's response: the award has been going on for many years, & Ted is only "the third person nice enough to write him"! He hopes to meet Ted when he comes to London in October. We were very excited & moved by this. As he says, he is an old man. How easy it is to underestimate the needs of the great to be appreciated! I rather hope Ted can strike up a relationship with him like mine with Mrs. Prouty.

Perhaps the happiest evening we've spent in ages was Monday night. I had Ann Davidow & her fiance Leo Goodman[1] for dinner. Remember Ann? She would have been my dearest friend at Smith if she hadn't left in the middle of freshman year. She & I took up where we left off 10 years ago. She graduated from the U. of Chicago & has had her first children's book (she's primarily an artist) accepted by Grosset & Dunlap: Let's Draw. I have so missed a good American girlfriend. Leo was a wonder: handsome, blond, blue-eyed & Jewish, on a Guggenheim at Cambridge, to be visiting professor at Columbia next year in mathematical statistics, very warm-hearted; that unique combination of the intellectual & loving-lovable Jew. He'd just been visiting his family in Israel & had fascinating & moving stories to tell. He was at Cambridge on a Fulbright in Ted's time, though they never met. Oddly enough, astrologically, Leo (his middle name means Lion in Hebrew too) is a Leo, as Ted is: a very powerful & successful sign, & Ann, with her birthday on October 26th is practically my Scorpio twin. We all got along marvelously & hope to see more of them before Ann returns to America.

By the way, when you quote Dr. Spock, quote his Index heads, not page or paragraph numbers as we must have different editions. Already my paperback copy is falling apart. Probably it will have disintegrated by her 1st birthday. At what age did I start Lalaing? FR is beginning to make odd little croaks & oofings, but no coo or laugh yet. And no singing. Ted joins me in sending our best love to you & Warren. When is Sappho due for her accouchement? I do hope she has as easy a time as I did. Luck & fortitude in your time of ordeal.

Lots of love,
Sivvy

1–Leo A. Goodman (1928–); B.A. 1948, Syracuse University; Ph.D. 1950, Princeton; professor of statistics and sociology, University of Chicago, 1950–86; professor of statistics and sociology, University of California at Berkeley, 1986–present. When Goodman met SP and TH, he was a visiting professor at Clare College, University of Cambridge, 1959–60. After his marriage to Ann Davidow on 28 August 1960, he was a visiting professor of mathematical statistics and sociology at Columbia University, 1960–1.

TO *Olwyn Hughes*

c. Monday 16 May 1960[1] ALS,[2] Emory University

Monday –

Dear Olwyn:

Ted's off to his study now, by 9 a.m. I mow the lawn & gather bundles of roses. Frieda Rebecca amazes & delights us more each day: she is now no longer wrapped blindly up in the bleak world of cries, hungers & air bubbles, but gives off dazzling, responsive smiles, recognizes us & seems pleased enough with what she sees, coos, is learning to laugh. I never thought any creature or event could set me bounding out of bed at 5 a.m., but her dawn-smiles are more than worth it.

Our life is as 'incognito' as we can make it & increasingly entertaining – an invitation to cocktails with Auden at Fabers (where I love to guzzle champagne) in the mail this morning. Dido Merwin took me to see Olivier in 'Rhinoceros' before she left for France – perfectly magnificent in spite of reviews[3] rating it below Pinter's 'Caretaker',[4] which Ted & I saw this week: my reaction to Pinter: how much better, profounder, Ted could do it. Also saw a superb Martian-set 'Antigone' at the ballet[5] – tragic, wordless – a ballet of black-cloaked women, a poison-green-clad Creon. London is meat & drink to me in spite of its dirt, & our corner a leafy bower.

Love –
Sylvia

1 – Date supplied from internal evidence.

2 – SP's letter is at the end of a letter begun by TH, which has not been transcribed. See *Letters of Ted Hughes*: 159–60.

3 – Probably J. W. Lambert, 'Sir Laurence to the Rescue', *Sunday Times* (1 May 1960): 25.

4 – English playwright and director Harold Pinter (1930–2008); his *The Caretaker;* performed at the Arts Theatre, London, until 28 May. Transferred to the Duchess Theatre, opening 30 May.

5 – *Antigone*, performed by the Royal Ballet, Royal Opera House, Covent Garden, London.

TO *Myron Lotz*[1]

Friday 20 May 1960 — TLS (aerogramme), Indiana University

3 Chalcot Square
London N.W.1
May 20, 1960

Dear Mike,

Just a brief note saying how good it was to hear from you & that Ted & I look forward to visiting with you again in June when you come to London.

Why don't you call us a day ahead & then come for spaghetti supper, if you can spare the time. If you can't, tea is fine. Our phone number is PRImrose 9132.

We're at present enjoying the proverbial English spring. Halcyon greens, flowers sprouting from people's ears, the barking of gay seals in the Zoo nextdoor. Just as I write this it starts to pour rain, & the temperature drops ominously.

All the best from both of us. Your trip sounds magnificent & we want to hear more. Ted's just got a Somerset Maugham award for his first book (the second came out over here this spring & is getting fine reviews) & it specifies 3 months travel abroad within the next two years, so we'll be forced out of our pleasant domesticity in London to a Riviera villa for a bit.

Until June,
sylvia

TO *Aurelia Schober Plath*

Saturday 21 May 1960 — TLS (aerogramme), Indiana University

Saturday morning: May 21

Dearest mother . . .

What an extravagant grammy you are! The darling two sets of pants & jackets came yesterday & I can't wait to put the baby in them. As luck would have it, we've been undergoing a week of raw, cold rainy weather

1–Myron Lotz (1932–99); B.S. 1954, Yale College; Henry Fellow, 1955–6, Oxford University; M.D. 1958, Yale University; intern at Massachusetts General Hospital, Boston, 1958–9; dated SP, 1952–4.

after a week of sun & blue skies, so I'll wait till it's a little warmer. They'll be ideal for summer. It's wonderful having a little girl---& such a pretty one: I'll have such fun dressing her up. Dear Aunt Elizabeth[1] sent an absolutely exquisite pale blue dress with a little white smock apron over it embroidered with rosebuds. Blue, at this point, is the baby's color, & I dress her almost always in that lovely blue sweater outfit you sent early on. Her eyes are so blue they send out sparks. I am crossing my fingers they won't change. She bears a very strong resemblance to Aunt Frieda in coloring & shape of her face, & I imagine her coloring is like daddy's was, too. She says Ga, & once, staring fascinated at Ted's picture as I changed her, a triumphant Da. But I suspect that was an accident. Do tell everybody she is Frieda Rebecca. So we can call her by which seems more natural when we address her by names other than The Pooker & Crumb-Bun Pie-face. We may well call her Frieda. How do you like the name Gwyneth for a girl? A Welsh name I discovered & think of as a possible name for a 2nd girl.

Do you know a Lola Walker[2] or a Lucy & David Webster?[3] We got a queer invitation to an At Home by the latter who said the former suggested they get in touch with us & are absolutely mystified. I thought these might be Britishers you met in America.

Ted made his second BBC program[4] this week, a recording of his story "The Rain Horse", a program which should bring in over $100 or so, with its rebroadcasting payment. Very nice. He has several projects going with them now---possibly a verse play, when he finishes it (he's doing another now), a poem & talk for high school students with other poets & critics, a long poem, etc. The BBC are the one organisation that pay excellently for poetry---$3 a minute for a reading, something like that. I got $70 for my story in the London magazine out this month, which I'll send on soon. My tattooist story[5] should be out in the autumn Sewanee Review. I am itching to get writing again & feel I shall do much better now I have a baby. Our life seems to have broadened & deepened wonderfully with her. Yesterday Faber sent on an envelope jammed with reviews of Ted's book: excellent without exception, all remarking how much better it is than his first, good though that was etc. I revel in such clippings. He works mornings &

1–Elizabeth Schober (1891–1971), who lived at 25 Primrose Street, Roslindale, Mass.

2–Possibly Lola Walker of 37 Longmeadow Road, Wellesley, Mass.

3–According to SP's address book, the Websters lived at 17 Spaniard's End, London N.W.3.

4–Ted Hughes, 'The Rain Horse', BBC Third Programme (29 July 1960). Recorded on 20 May 1960.

5–Sylvia Plath, 'The Fifteen Dollar Eagle', *Sewanee Review* 68 (Autumn 1960): 603–18. See Monroe Spears to SP, 5 May 1960; held by Sewanee: The University of the South. Spears rejected 'Poem for a Birthday'.

afternoons at Merwins study now & things are settling down. I am just crawling out from under the mountain of baby-notifications, thank-you letters & answers to Ted's voluminous correspondence since his book & Maugham prize: innumerable requests for him to give free poems, free talks, etc. He could waste all his time for nothing. As it is, we have to be very strict. We are giving a reading with another poet in a month, & Ted is reading for a group of medical students at a hospital here who want "contact with the outside world."

Ann Davidow & Leo Goodman drove us on a day's trip to Stonehenge a week ago, on Monday. It was an exquisite day & we passed through beautiful country, all the immense chestnut trees in bloom, golden laburnum, rhododendron banking the road like a bower. The baby was angelic: I fed her once in the car on the way & once sitting in a grassy ditch of buttercups the Druids thoughtfully provided just outside the circle of gigantic ominous upright stones. Ann brought a delectable picnic, cold rare roast beef, cheeses, cole slaw, etc. Leo is a friend of David Riesman's,[1] the sociologist, & was Riesman's candidate for head of the Sociology Dept. at Chicago in his mid-twenties. Imagine!

Could you, by the way, send that Library of Congress record[2] if it's still wrapped & not too much trouble? This week should be bringing the end to your jammed schedule & I hope you keep in good health & can begin to rest. What are you doing this summer?

Mike Lotz writes he is coming to London next month & will drop by to see us. Ironically, I seem to be likely to see more of friends here than in America. London is a perfect stopping-off place. It is heaven to have a 3-year lease here & not to think of moving, not for a good time. We've wasted so much time moving in the past years. I only wish our next move could be into our own house. But in order to take out a mortgage evidently one has to have a "regular job", & my main concern is that Ted doesn't have to take one. The more he writes the more he'll earn, but bank officials can't understand that sort of chanciness I guess. Damn his uncle anyway. He doesn't even draw a salary anymore for the taxes would be about 90%. & he even was scared to write a reference for Ted when we were about to rent a flat! I wish we could adopt Maugham as uncle. I want to read him all now – hope he survives till October!

xxx
Sivvy

1–American sociologist and educator David Riesman (1909–2002).
2–The Lee Anderson record made on 18 April 1958 in Springfield, Mass.; see SP to Lee Anderson and SP to Warren Plath, both 22 April 1958.

TO *Aurelia Schober Plath*

Monday 30 May 1960 — TLS (aerogramme),[1] Indiana University

Monday: May 30

Dear mother,

Congratulations to Sappho via you about her triplets! Ted & I were delighted with your descriptive letter about her successful confinement & only heartbroken we can't have one of the kittens if not the mother herself. Do keep us posted on their development. How superb the little black one must be!

I am at my livingroom typing table, and all I can see is one huge tree across the street & lots of sky . . . very green & pleasant. The wife of the successful artist who lives in the Merwins' lower flats introduced me to Queen Mary's Rose Garden[2] today in Regents Park: a little Eden, with a rock-garden island in the middle of a duck pool crammed with ducklings, the lush hybrid roses just beginning. She has a little boy under a year & is a pleasant girl. I hope you won't give our number or address to any more people we don't know, because it simply puts us in the position of refusing to go out (it's too expensive in time & money) & conspicuously not inviting anyone over because if we don't firmly put our feet down we will become simply a way-station for all sorts of travelers. The baby's feedings & keeping the house clean & cooking & taking care of Ted's voluminous mail plus my own have driven me so I care only for carving out hours where I can start on my own writing. We have mercilessly to cut out all but the most necessary engagements. After this month we are not going to give any poetry readings unless we are paid for them, for it is too expensive to hire sitters etc. & we want to see good plays & movies whenever we can. Already we have seen Peter & Jane Davison, the recorder Lee Anderson, Ann Davidow & Leo Goodman, & Myron Lotz is coming on their heels---all but Ann a distraction & expense. This may seem drastic to you, but even a modest fame brings flocks of letters, requests, schoolgirls asking for "the author's own analysis of the symbols in his stories" etc. ad nauseam. If Ted didn't have his study he'd

1–TH added a note at the bottom of the letter, which has not been transcribed. TH wrote about tracking Frieda's development in photographs and her appearances and sounds, on a forthcoming visit from his mother, and on SP's mothering.

2–See Sylvia Plath, 'Queen Mary's Rose Garden', *Collected Poems*: 290. SP's drafts of 'Queen Mary's Rose Garden' are on the verso of her later poem 'Wuthering Heights'; held by Lilly Library.

be distracted by the phone, the mail, & odd callers so he'd get no work done at all. And as his secretary and my own I have a personal reason for being strict. So please help us by not steering anyone our way.

The little suits you sent fit perfectly, are on the largish size even. So far she had grown out of nothing & still swims in her three nighties, cuffs rolled up, etc. I can't find anything like Carter's things here: only stupid cottons that have to be ironed, worn with slips under them. Do you suppose Carter's has some outlet over here? I wish I could find out. I can hardly keep from playing with the baby all the time, she is so responsive & smiley & pretty. She gets her first injection this Thursday, has her own little card, & will be finished with all by the time she is two. This is a triple threat: whooping cough, diptheria & tetanus. This week I may have energy enough to try her on water & orange juice. She seems to be growing fine on just milk, very satisfied. Ted's mother & Aunt Hilda are coming on a London tour this weekend & will drop in Saturday & Sunday: the first relatives to see the baby. I am so pleased they are coming.

I have at long last bought a vacuum: for approximately $50.[1] It is a new model of a Hoover (a good reliable make), a peculiar looking pink & white globe affair with an accordion-pleated extendable vacuum tube, several lengthening cylinders & spare nozzles for upholstery etc. I consider it a new toy: buzz round the house, from carpets to floors, sucking up everything in my path. Feel very happy with it, for previous to this my crude broom-sweeping merely raised & rearranged the accumulating dust & soot. I don't mind work if it's followed by results. I'll leave a space for Ted.

xxxxxxx
Sivvy

1–SP bought her vacuum for £18 from London Cooperative Society, 193 Camden High Street, N.W.1.

TO *Philip Booth*

Tuesday 31 May 1960 TLS (aerogramme), Dartmouth College

3 Chalcot Square
London N.W.1, England
May 31, 1960

Dear Philip,

It was wonderful to get your good if chiding letter. I see my mother has informed you well of our very serious little April Fool, who as I write this is just two months new and having her evening yowls. Nights she is divine, but from tea to bedtime she becomes wildly nihilistic & inconsolable. At dawn, she wakes me delicately with cooings tuned beyond Ted's powers of hearing and rewards my picking her up for nursing with dazzling & dimpled smiles. Oh, she is altogether lovely. Queer, we wanted nothing but a boy & now can't imagine ever having been such utter asses. Boys, ugh.

Good for "Spit".[1] And you didn't tell us where to look for it! Where? Ted's second book LUPERCAL is out over here and getting very good reviews indeed. His winning the Somerset Maugham travel award for his first book will take us sumptuously to Europe for a 3-month period some time in the next two years, when the baby is a bit sturdier, immuned to the world's diseases and so on. Just now it's wonderful to sit & sit & not move. After a ghastly January searching a filthy cold & expensive & ungodly far-flung London for some flat, some doctor, some something, the Merwins came to our rescue, introduced us to their very fine National Health doctors, loaned us attic furniture & scouted about for flats: that Dido! We are now comfortably at home in a defiantly white-painted (by Ted) livingroom surrounded by Ted's bookcases, Baskin's prints, overlooking a green-treed square with Utrillo orangey & cream plaster houses behind, around the corner from the Merwins & a small stone's throw from Primrose Hill, Regent's Park complete with Zoo, rose gardens, bird sanctuary (no shags)[2] & grassy acres. We also have a bedroom, kitchen-diningroom, bath & tiny hall on the 3rd floor of a newly converted house. Ted has the use of Bill Merwin's study while the Merwins are on their farm in France, & I the use of their garden, in return for flower-care, fertilizing & lawn-mowing, which I love. I am becoming an Anglophile, what with

1–Philip Booth, 'Spit', *Poetry* 99 (October 1961): 32.
2–Probably a reference to Philip Booth, 'Shag', *Poetry* 88 (July 1956): 240–1.

U-2's,[1] the boom of biological & chemical warfare plants in Maryland, the Chessman execution[2] & Dick Nixon to keep me beating my head for my homeland. How I wish I could have heard Roethke's poem on Nixon![3] Will it see print? Roethke is one of my most particularly favorite poets & I've never heard or met him. Wish he'd come here. We have our compensations. T. S. Eliot's new wife, very blond & wonderfully warm Yorkshire, invited us to dinner, which we had, intimately, with them & the Stephen Spenders. One of those holy evenings. Ted's been doing some programs for the BBC, a story of his own---the one published in Harper's last winter---and an anthology of people's animal poems, & we hope to see his first children's book, 8 amusing poems about odd relatives, out over here this winter. Both of us are thriving, doting parents.

Let us keep hearing from you! Ted joins me in sending love to you all –

Sylvia

TO *Alan Anderson*[4]

Saturday 11 June 1960 — TLS with envelope, Pierpont Morgan Library

3 Chalcot Square
London N.W.1
June 11, 1960

Dear Mr. Anderson,

I'm writing on my own behalf to say how delighted my husband and I were with the proofs of "A Winter Ship".[5] I'm sending back the one we like best, with the border round it. We thought we'd like the date, place and press in upright letters, as on the other proof, and my name deleted ---as I'll write that on the inside myself, with Christmas greeting too.

Would four dozen copies be too much of a burden for you?

1–An United States U-2 spy-plane was shot down over the Soviet Union on 1 May 1960.

2–Caryl Chessman, jailed for kidnapping, robbery, and rape, was executed on 2 May 1960, in California. His execution gave rise to a movement to ban capital punishment.

3–American poet Theodore Roethke (1908–63); probably his 'Political Song' ['Nixon Poem']; see Brett Miller, '*Chelsea* 8: Political Poetry at Midcentury', *Robert Duncan and Denise Levertov: The Poetry of Politics, the Politics of Poetry* (Stanford, Calif.: Stanford University Press, 2006).

4–British printer and publisher Alan Anderson (1922–); founder of the Tragara Press in 1954.

5–Sylvia Plath, *A Winter Ship* (Edinburgh: Tragara Press, 1960). Anderson estimates he printed about sixty copies. See TH to Alan Anderson, 19 May 1960; held by Morgan Library.

Thank you again for making such a lovely leaflet of the poem.

Sincerely yours,
Sylvia Plath

<on verso of envelope>

PS[1] – got a beautiful silver plate baby cup from Pat O'Neil. What's Betsy Powley's married name?[2] Got a letter from her about her baby

TO *Aurelia Schober Plath & Warren Plath*

Saturday 11 June 1960 TLS, Indiana University

Saturday: June 11

Dearest mother & Warren,

I'm sure I haven't written for ages. I've been going through a rather tired spell, & am just now catching up with rest again. It is now 10:30, my housework is done, & I look forward to a peaceful morning at home reading & writing, since it is a grey rainy day out. Ted's mother & aunt Hilda came down to London last weekend on a holiday tour via bus, very nice for me, since they stayed at a hotel & had most of their meals on the tour. They came over Saturday evening, and again Sunday afternoon---we went to sit in the Merwins garden---and stayed for dinner. Ted & I used their coming as a spur to finish up the house: I did a spring cleaning, scrubbing all the bookshelves & cupboards etc., and he painted the little hall and one wall of the kitchen a marvelous vermilion, which just picks out the vermilion in the kitchen wall paper & acts on me as a color-tonic. I can hardly stop looking at it, eating it up. I am so influenced by colors & textures. The red looks superb with the black-marbled linoleum, white woodwork & dark green cord curtains. All we need to do now is hang the last of our Baskins. A great admirer of Ted's, an artist[3] whom we haven't met, but who is an extremely amusing & vivid letter writer, is sending him an oil painting sometime next month. I hope it is good enough to hang. I'm very glad Ted attracts artist admirers, a much nicer crew than writers.

As I say, Ted's been getting all sorts of requests. One just came from a boy's school in Canterbury for a reading (with fee & accommodation)

1–SP intended this postscript to go to her mother in her letter of 11 June that follows but wrote it on the wrong envelope.

2–Betsy Powley Wallingford (1932–), SP's friend from Wellesley.

3–British artist and poet Graham Ackroyd (1920-). See TH to Graham Ackroyd, 5 May 1960. Printed in *Letters of Ted Hughes*: 161–2; original held with additional letters by University of Victoria, British Columbia.

next fall. I hope to go along with the Pooker to see that lovely town. Of course his animal poems are naturals for reading to young people. He wrote out a 10 page single-space sheaf of notes explaining his poems for Mrs. Prouty which I've typed up & sent off: she is so willing to try them out, we wanted to give her all the help necessary.[1]

You will probably get a letter from Ted's mother[2] about her visit. I could see the dear woman was trying to notice everything, what I wore & all, to tell you. The baby was very good on the whole. Tell Betty Aldrich I dressed her up in the dear little pink outfit with the blue embroidered Pooh, Piglet & Eyore on it for her first Sunday with relatives. We propped her up on a blue pillow which just matched her eyes, & with her little smiles she looked an angel. I'm feeding her a teacup full of cereal (instant Farex) twice a day now, & she wolfs it down, smacking, getting her hands in it, making humming noises. Today I'm going to try pureed carrots for lunch. Orange juice upsets her stomach yet, & causes her to spit up her last feed, even if I wait two hours to give it to her. When I try giving her cod liver oil she pretends she doesn't know what a spoon is for & deftly dribbles it all down her collar, so the doctor is prescribing another kind of drops, less fishy. I took her to the Clinic Thursday, at her 10 week mark, & she weighs 10 pounds 13 ounces. Her hair seems to be lightening in front, & her eyes are beautiful & blue as ever. We are mad about her.

I'm enclosing a check for $32 to add to our Boston writing account. Ted has just finished his second verse play: marvelously amusing & vivid, making his first one seem mere scratchwork in preparation. We'll try this with the BBC & the Poets Theater in Cambridge at home. They obviously want to do something by him there now his reputation's rocketed so, & were willing to do a reading of his first, & probably a performance if he rewrote it, but now we're withdrawing that, as he doesn't want it done, feels there's no poetry in it. This one is a marvelous thing. I was fascinated every minute. About a revolution's effect on the inhabitants of a mayor's farmhouse. He is also working---in his spare moments---on a novel about Yorkshire, which I am delighted about. Spurred, I think, by a review of a book on Yorkshire miners written by a young American journalist he was asked to try by the Nation.[3] I do hope they print it. He felt, of course, that he could do much better. And so he could.

1 – See Plath mss IV, which includes annotations by SP; held by Lilly Library.

2 – Edith Hughes to ASP, 11 June 1960; held by Lilly Library.

3 – Ted Hughes, 'England's Toughest Community', *The Nation* (2 July 1960): 14; a review of Clancy Sigal, *Weekend in Dinlock* (Boston: Houghton Mifflin, 1960).

Did I tell you we've seen the black & white line drawings for his children's book? Very fine & witty, for college people as well as children I feel. We'll get reams of copies & have fun giving them to the Aldriches & all our other friends: a real gift book. I can't wait to see the book itself. Ted got a very heartening notice from Fabers in the mail today: his book is selling so steadily & well (for poetry) that they are doing a second printing of it! So soon! We are delighted.

The marvelous box of baby-things arrived this morning. They are darling. I held them up in front of her & she gooed at them. I think you are dressing her for your arrival next summer! I find it hard to believe she will ever be big enough to fit them! Do by all means wash the things before you send them so they can go second hand. You have no idea how much it means to me to dress her in partly American clothes. I must find a good baby store over here, though.

My vacuum also has paper bags, a very odd semi-hemisphere shape, since the machine is round. I do hope they plan to keep them in stock for the next 20 years! By the way, I have been disturbed by finding a number of clothes moths flitting about. I only have our big trunk to store our woolens in: how can I guard against the moths & where do they come from? I think I will go to Dido Merwins dentist on Harley street. He is not National Health, but she says if you want to keep your teeth, you pay a dentist. We are so lucky to be able to profit by her wisdom. I'm keeping the house full of June roses from their garden.

How did the kittens invade your room? How adorable they must be. Congratulations to you & Warren on your exam results! What is Warren doing this summer? Ted's mother brought down a German flash camera they bought at a low price from the father of a boy who stole hundreds of dollars worth, no, <u>bought</u>, hundreds of dollars worth of goods after he ran away with his parents savings, & lived in great style in a hotel till his parents caught up with him. The camera was among his booty, & the poor father trying to get some money back. So we'll try to get a few good pictures now.

Love from us all,

Sivvy

<on page 1 of letter>

PS – I'm enclosing a proof of one of the poems[1] The <u>Atlantic</u> accepted & which an Edinburgh printer offered to set up in Christmas leaflets free of charge – another admirer of Ted's work.

1 – Sylvia Plath, 'A Winter Ship'. The proof is no longer with the letter.

TO *Aurelia Schober Plath*

Friday 24 June 1960 TLS, Indiana University

Friday: June 24

Dear mother,

These pictures,[1] taken when Frieda was 10 weeks old, the week Ted's mother came, give more of an idea of her. I love the one where she's looking up adoringly at Ted. The two larger snapshots were taken by Ann Davidow at Knole, & while the baby coyly stuck her hands in front of her face, I think they're good of Ted & myself. I'm sending these straight along to you & having another set made up from the negatives for us.

Last night Ted & I went to a cocktail party at Fabers given for WH Auden. I drank champagne with the appreciation of a housewife on an evening off from the smell of sour milk and diapers. During the course of the party Charles Monteith, one of the Faber board, beckoned me out into the hall. And there Ted stood, flanked by TS Eliot, WH Auden, Louis MacNiece on the one hand & Stephen Spender on the other, having his photograph taken.[2] "Three generations of Faber poets there," Charles observed. "Wonderful!" Of course I was immensely proud. Ted looked very at home among the great. Then we went to the Institute of Contemporary Arts & read our poems to an audience of about 25-30 young people with another poet (or, rather, non-poet, very dull).[3]

Thanks for the notes on moths. We love hearing about the progress of Sappho's babies: they seem to be having about the same care as ours! I'm sending along this little check by the way for deposit in our Wellesley account. Very grey here today; yesterday it poured, thundered & lightened. I am trying to arrange a little nap for myself in the afternoon. I get tired so easily. After a midnight curfew like last night, getting up at 6 am to feed Frieda (yes, we call her that now & it seems to suit her: we did really intend to name her after Aunt Frieda; she can take Rebecca if she goes through a romantic stage) I am exhausted by noon. I have kept up a schedule this week of going over to the study in the mornings, Ted giving Frieda her morning cereal which holds her till I come back. I am at the depressing painful stage of trying to start writing after a long spell of silence, but the mornings at the study are very peaceful to my soul & I am infinitely lucky we can work things out so I get a solid hunk of time off,

1–The photographs are no longer with the letter.

2–Mark Gerson (1921–) photographed the 'Faber Poets' at the party on 23 June 1960.

3–English poet and novelist Alan Brownjohn (1931–).

or, rather, time on, a day. Ted goes in the afternoons. He has written three or four very good poems toward a third book. Now he is out at a rare book dealers[1] who is going to sell the manuscripts of his two books to the University of Indiana, we hope, for a few hundred dollars. Of course they'll be worth more later, but he'll have other manuscripts then & we can do with the money now, skimping along as we are on the end of the Guggenheim which ended officially May 31st. Glad you liked the New Yorker poem. I should have another about women in a Spanish fishing village coming out this summer. Now I need to write some more I can sell to them. Ted is a marvel of understanding: helps me with dishes or a meal when he sees I'm especially tired & is strongly behind my having 3-4 hours of writing & study time a day. And he is wonderful with the baby, who dotes on him.

Well I shall sign off for now with love to you & Warren and Sappho and progeny.

Your own,
Sivvy

TO *Dido & W. S. Merwin*

Friday 24 June 1960 TLS,[2] Pierpont Morgan Library

Dear Bill and Dido,

It is a wet, ghoulishly grey evening, mucky-muggy, and all peaceful here, Frieda sleeping without murmer, very nice of her, and a big blanquette de veau conjuring up the two of you, your spirits at least, on the stove. Making your recipes, Dido, is a delectable rite in memory of you. Gradually we have got the baby so we can more or less not notice her, be surprised by her, so to speak, when we go into the bedroom. She's so funny, very droll and smiley with queer singsong noises she thinks is conversation, that we're entertained and wonder how we ever did without her. I've at last come out of my little treadmill of domesticity and now spend mornings in the study while Ted works at home, and he spends afternoon there. This is

1–Ifan Kyrle Fletcher, whose business, which he operated with his wife Constance, was located at 22 Buckingham Gate, London S.W.1. A note in SP's address book reads '(collecting mss., typescripts, corrected proofs)'. These papers comprise the Ted Hughes mss. at the Lilly Library.

2–TH added a note at the bottom of the letter, which has not been transcribed. TH commented on the ICA reading, mentioned that David Louis Posner was collecting manuscripts for the University of Buffalo, and the Faber party for Auden.

a very good arrangement for us both and it is absolute heaven for me to get away for 3 or 4 hours from the innumerable little umbilical cords tying me to icebox, phone, doorbell, baby and so on. Ted is relatively impervious.

Last night we went to the Faber party for Auden. I go mainly for the champagne, which I find more interesting than Auden, & consider it a duty to my thwarted sybarite soul to consume at least a bottle. We had a good time; I met McNeice, for whome I feel sort of amused and fond; he's a bit of a mess, but nice. Isn't Hedli Anderson[1] a superb splurge of colours? all flamey haired, green lidded, and encased in an expanse of vast flowery stuff. Spender there, very drunk; his wife drunker. Eliot amiable and ditto his blonde strawberry and cream wife. Afterwards we left for the ghastly ICA. Luckily we were well fortified with champagne, so managed to get through the evening in the angularly and marmoreally modern Dover Street rooms. An Alan Brownjohn, a nonpoet, read with us, short, fat-handed, dull, all the curses and a teacher too. Of the deaf. However, there was no yattering from the bar, which seemed closed. Wine and dry sandwiches were laid on for us. I am getting very commercial about reading for free, since it costs us a good deal for a baby-sitter. Money is the one argument.

The larkspur are magnificent, very hot blue-purple. I am especially fond of the little rose bushes at the back there, one with quite small pinky red blooms and another with hot orangey ones. All of sudden one day last week the central heating men vanished, an amazing feat. The day before I'd picked my way upstairs over pipes and an infinite array of queer dangerous bits of metal, the phone man was tinkering and I think somebody was there about plumbing. The next day not a stray nail and a shiny new boiler affair radiating potential efficiency from the closet. Popo has become madly affectionate after so crueely ignoring me last winter: every step of the stair he is plastered like a fur poultice against my ankles, saying whaat? whaat? Arnold Wesker's trilogy[2] is in the middle of playing here, so we'll try to see it. Do you know his things? Also Brecht's Galileo,[3] which I don't know at all. Soon, soon,

Love to you both from us all,
Love,
Sylvia

1 – English singer and actress Hedli Anderson (1907–90), second wife (1942–60) of Louis MacNeice.

2 – British dramatist Sir Arnold Wesker (1932–2016); his plays *Chicken Soup With Barley*, *Roots*, and *I'm Talking About Jerusalem* were being performed at the Royal Court Theatre.

3 – German poet and playwright Bertolt Brecht (1898–1956); his *The Life of Galileo* (1945), performed at the Mermaid Theatre, London, 16 June–1 October 1960.

TO *Ann Davidow-Goodman*

Wednesday 29 June 1960 TLS (aerogramme), Smith College

Wednesday afternoon: June 29

Dear Ann,

The pictures arrived, with your welcome letter, and they are splendid. I don't know whether it's your camera or the kindly spirit you took them in (a little of both I suspect), but we have never had any really good pictures of the two (now three) of us together, and these are It. We are delighted.

Strange, isn't it, that we had to hit upon London for our ten-year rendezvous. I felt all that time evaporate---a feat, when you consider what we must have crammed into that time on our separate courses. And it was wonderful to meet Leo. I can't tell you how he impressed us, so brilliant, kind, versatile & so very handsome, A match, a match. He dropped by briefly one afternoon a couple of days ago, extremely tan, or, rather, bronze, from horseriding he says. We extracted a promise that he return so we can all go to see Brecht's Galileo together when he comes to London for good.

I am gradually getting my nose above crib-level and going over to our study-on-loan after breakfast till lunch---as yet not the full four hours I plan to have, since I am pokey.[1] Ted feeds Frieda her cereal & milk from the bottle in mid-morning, angel that he is. Then he has the whole afternoon at the study. I am in that desert of trying to get back to work after over half a year silence, feeling very rusty & superficial, & wondering, as ever, if I shall ever do a good poem again. Ted says its a deal about trading a LET'S DRAW for a MEET MY FOLKS. We hope we see it in print this winter, in time for Christmas, but don't know just when. The artist evidently agreed to put in some Heath-Robinson[2] inventions for Uncle Dan,[3] but didn't dare put a fiercer head on the thistle. And he's leaving the American flags off the cover, I think.

We hired a babysitter from the agency last week for one of our rare jaunts to town together (a white-haired little ex-chicken-farmer came, who had lost several fingers with foul pest & called Frieda "the nipper") to meet W. H. Auden at a cocktail party at Ted's publishers. I always

1–SP wrote 'The Hanging Man' on 27 June 1960.

2–English cartoonist and illustrator William Heath Robinson (1872–1944), known for his drawings of complicated machines.

3–The sixth poem in TH's *Meet My Folks!*

hate meeting famous people at Affairs as I never can think of anything to say to them in that passing moment of introduction. But I do love the champagne Faber's serves & made a point to polish off the better part of a bottle. Ted had his picture taken with the other Faber Poets, Eliot, Auden, Spender & MacNiece, & it evidently came out in the Times,[1] which I haven't seen yet, but I was very proud of him. When one is so close to the red side of a checking account, there need to be compensations.

We miss you immensely. But hope at least to have a visit or two with Leo before he returns.

Love from us three,
Syl

TO *Aurelia Schober Plath*

Thursday 30 June 1960 — TLS (aerogramme), Indiana University

<SP wrote 'No. 1' on address side of letter>

June 30: Thursday pm

Dear mother,

I hope by now you have the little snapshots of Frieda Rebecca I sent. Surely we are not doting to think she is a pretty, lively baby. I took her this morning for her second series of triple-shots (whooping cough, diptheria & tetanus). She should be through all her shots by eight months. I feed her cereal in the morning now, a vegetable (carrots or peas) in the strained Heinz can (not jars, alas; she eats half a can at a time) for lunch, and cereal, or one of the strained-fruit & cereal combinations for supper. She has a wonderful humor. This week she triumphantly started sucking her thumb. Usually I let her suck on one of those rubber pacifiers (dummies, they are called here) & this satisfies her great urge to suck at this stage. I give her concentrated rose hip syrup (three times as much vitamin C as orange juice) in 4 ounces of water once a day between meals & she drinks it to the last drop. I'm also cautiously experimenting with concentrated orange juice greatly diluted in water, after her spitting upset the first time I gave it to her. She drinks some, but doesn't like it as much as the sweeter syrup.

Something odd happened to me today which both elated & depressed me. I was walking the baby about the neighborhood after her injection,

1–Philip Day, 'A Pride of Poets', *Sunday Times* (26 June 1960): 6.

the air too cold & windy to go far, and half-dreamily let my feet carry me down a road I'd never been down before. I came up another street I seldom if ever use a block away & saw a house being painted & papered with a Freehold for sale sign. Now Freehold houses (outright yours after buying) are rare in London: most have 99 year leases from an agency which keeps ownership, or, if they are freehold, have "part possession" which means they are let out, a couple of floors at least, to people under the old rent control laws which means they only pay a couple of dollars a week & don't have to move out. All seeming very odd to me, but I'm learning bit by bit. Of course houses are expensive here, as they are in any place where there is immense & continuous demand. But in our area, really quite slummy, there is great opportunity to get a house for less than it will be in even a few years, as it is just beginning to be fancied up. I was so excited about this house, 41 Fitzroy Road, the street where Yeats lived,[1] & one end of it showing the green of Primrose Hill, that I ran home with the carriage & called Ted up at his study. He came to have a look at it. I have been thinking ahead a good deal & this house had just the right number of rooms---built on the narrow plan of the houses here, at the end of a row joined together (very good, quiet on one side) & instead of backing onto another row, overlooking a charming Mews in back, only one floor high, so light floods in. A livingroom, diningroom & large light kitchen on the first floor overlooking a charming quiet little garden with one big tree, two big bedrooms & a bath on the second floor, two bedrooms on the third, & a marvelous big single-room study at the top. The basement, a self-contained flat, is let out, & the rent would be a sort of little income. All quiet, light & spanking clean, with only the floors to be done. Well, of course I had visions of a study for Ted in the attic there, a study for me, a bedroom for us, a nursery for the baby & a room for guests (you) now & the next baby (babies). Plus the dear garden to hang laundry in & put playpens in (It's a walled garden.) Such a house, behind the posh Regents Park road, yet part of an area not done-up as yet, on a corner, overlooking such a marvelous prospect, is just the Thing. I feel after our 3-year lease here (we could easily sublet this place) I simply don't want to move into rented rooms again. And Ted needs a study, & the baby will need a room. Thus a house is the only solution, & I'd rather pay off a mortgage than feel a landlord get everything. And we don't want a house to do up---we just aren't ready to give the time (or money) to that sort of chancey proposition. This place is priced at 9,250

1 – As a child, Yeats lived at 23 Fitzroy Road, *c.* 1867–72.

pounds (multiply by $2.80 for dollars). We called up the London County Council (after being advised by a house agent that they were better than banks or building societies as their rates of interest don't fluctuate). What they do is send a surveyor to value the property. They loan you 100% of their valuation (which may be less or more than the price) & I guess your payments to them are the mortgage & the difference between their valuation & the price a sort of down-payment, or what you have to pay outright to the owner's agents. Ted, of course, is much more hesitant than I to commit himself. I just don't want to touch that $5 thousand in our bank & am loth to jeopardize Ted's writing which he has just got going. One of us will probably have to take a job this fall in any case, as we are stretching the Guggenheim out till September 1st. Well, I am so tempted to somehow get hold of this place. London is the one place in Europe we could both easily get work & live cheaply in. I am thinking of work myself, if Ted would just feed the baby her noon meal, so he could write (I'll spill this over onto a second letter, with which I'll enclose a request to our Wellesley bank to draw out $1,000 & send it over) & earn us something. Have you, by the way, any ideas or suggestions. I do so miss somebody who has had experience in these matters to talk it all over with.

xxx
Sivvy

TO *Aurelia Schober Plath*

Thursday 30 June 1960 — TLS with envelope, Indiana University

<SP wrote 'No. 2' on the envelope>

June 30: Thursday

Dear mother,

Here's the second installment of my airletter, and the note asking to withdraw $1,000 from our Wellesley savings. Leave the odd $50 or $60 in to keep the account open & accumulate a few cents interest for Frieda someday.

Anyhow, somebody else will probably snap the house up. But we will have to think seriously of committing ourselves to a house in a year or two. To complicate matters, Ted (and this is a secret, don't let him or anyone know I've mentioned this) has signified a real desire to take a degree in zoology here in London, an external course at the University. Naturally this would be very difficult in any circumstances, especially if we were still just bleeding rent to landlords. But I do so wish I could see a way clear for him to do it. It would be a job he could give his heart to, & not the fancy literary white-collar work or English-teaching which would make him unhappy. Refer to this as the Plan if you write me about it, so he won't know I've said anything. It would be so wonderful to have a house you could come to next summer---to have plenty of room for once. Of course the isolated attic study (papered & very pleasant) & garden are the main attractions. Also the expandability of the place. The sad thing is that by the time one is amply ready to buy something, the place is gone. And we are only newly come to think of the responsibility of a house, having just weathered the new cares of a baby. As I say, the place has just been converted to a house from flats & newly done up, so all we'd have to do is get lino down in the kitchen & paint the floors (a big job, but we are expert at it now & could do only two floors first). Somehow talking about it makes it seem it might be real. But I feel as jealous about that $5 thousand as about a talisman. And I feel badly about paying about 5% interest or so on a mortgage. What interest did you pay?

Ted's picture, I gather, appeared along with Auden, Eliot, Spender & MacNeice in the last Sunday Times, though we haven't seen it. Can you look up a copy at BU library & see it there? Also, his book review about a half-novel on mining is out in the Nation of July 2nd. Maybe you'd like to pick up a copy on a newstand (it's an American weekly on newsprint paper) & read it.

Well, tell me what you think about all my ramblings.

Congratulate Warren on his exam results.

Blessings on the kittens.
Love,
Sivvy

<on verso of envelope>[1]

P.S. Ted's been offered <£160> (about $450) for his <manuscripts.>
PPS. Could you dig up our <damaged and missing text> of all America & send it? I thought we had it but we don't.

1–In the first postscript, the text appearing in < > is from *Letters Home*. It is possible that SP wrote 'mss.' rather than 'manuscripts'. In the second postscript, the editors conjecture SP may have asked for a map of America. Due to damage it is not possible to know the missing text.

TO *Alice Norma Davis*

Friday 9 July 1960 TLS, Smith College Archives

3 Chalcot Square
London N.W.1, England
July 9, 1960

Miss Davis, Director
Smith College Vocational Office
Smith College
Northampton, Massachusetts
U.S.A.

Dear Miss Davis:

I am at present living and looking for work in London, and have applied to the University of Cambridge Women's Appointments Board for help. The Director there asks me to have documentation about me (grades, job references and so on, I guess) sent to her, and I wonder if you would be so good as to send the necessary information on to her.

The papers should be addressed to:

Mrs. K. M. Baxter, M.A.[1]
University of Cambridge
Women's Appointments Board
6, Chaucer Road
Cambridge, England

If I can answer any questions or be of any help in this, do let me know.

Sincerely yours,
Sylvia Plath Hughes ('55)

TO *Aurelia Schober Plath*

Saturday 9 July 1960 TLS, Indiana University

Saturday: July 9

Dear mother,

It was good to get your letter with the nice reactions about Frieda's pictures. I hope the clipping I sent you of Ted enshrined between The Great amuses you too. He heard definitely this week that Indiana University is

1–Kathleen Mary Carver Baxter (1904–94), Secretary of the Women's Appointment Board and Fellow of Newnham College.

buying the manuscripts of his first two books for 160 pounds (or $450) which is good. Also, even better news came this week: the BBC Third Programme has accepted his second verse play "The House of Aries" for production this coming fall. Ted wrote the play in the three months after Frieda arrived, amazing when you consider the confusion & weariness of those early days. It is a marvelously funny, moving & serious play full of superb speakable poetry, about a revolution overtaking a sleepy little village. The scene is in the bedridden Mayor's house. It is relatively short, about 70 typewritten double-spaced pages & with a little cutting should take about an hour on the radio. We are really thrilled by this early commercial acceptance of his dramatic-verse. He has scrapped the first play "The House of Taurus" which really was only a rough rather unpoetic draft, or redraft, of a theme from the Bacchae with an antiquated social message. Interestingly enough, your letter about your dream of Ted's satire on Kruschev[1] arrived just before the BBC acceptance and one of the main characters in this play is the revolutionary Captain, a profoundly analyzed military figure. So you are prophetic. I hope his next play may see the stage! With this acceptance & encouragement, it is highly likely! The BBC has also asked to see some poems of mine for a program of New Poetry which is kind of them & I hope they take something. Ted has really done a good bit for them since we've come to London: an anthology of animal poems (which he wrote & read the explanations of), a talk with a critic about his poem "Otter" for the Home Service Schools program[2] (the poems analysed are modern, by Eliot, Yeats, Auden & Hughes!), a long poem about Frieda's arrival,[3] his "Rain Horse" story & now the play. If we were in America he couldn't take such advantage of his growing reputation. The Third Programme is a real blessing, & they pay wonderfully, about $3 a minute for poetry.

I'm enclosing a check from the Nation for $30 for Ted's bookreview for deposit in our Boston 5¢ savings account.

Frieda is better & better. A wonderful sense of humor & much amused by silly noises & outings. We left her over at Dido's with the woman living there now who lives rent-free in exchange for taking elegant care

1 – Soviet politician Nikita Khrushchev (1894–1971).
2 – Ted Hughes and A. Alvarez, *Talks for Sixth Forms*: 'Poetry and Performance IV – Ted Hughes', BBC Home Service (Schools) (10 February 1961).
3 – Ted Hughes, 'Lines to a Newborn Baby', *New Poetry*, BBC Third Programme (24 July 1960); pre-recorded on 14 July 1960. Not read by TH. Programme selected, introduced, and produced by Anthony Thwaite. The Programming-as-Broadcast sheet from the BBC lists the poem as containing 62 lines. In TH's *Collected Poems*, the poem is 32 lines.

of the Merwins Siamese cat & will occasionally babysit for us free. Leo Goodman, Ann Davidow's genius, drove us to see "Roots",[1] the middle part of a working-class trilogy by one of the very new young British play wrights. Very realistic, down to the eating of icecream & pouring potato water out of the potatoes. I kept thinking how much more amusing a play Ted could have done. Eliot has offered to read & discuss any plays in verse he does which is highly kind of him. My one aim is to keep Ted writing full-time. When I think how easily his uncle could help him until he gets making money I see red, but it is precisely one's aunts & rich uncles who won't help. The mad cousin barbara gets diamond rings & poodles, which she forgets she has in a day!

xxx
Sivvy

TO *George MacBeth*[2]

Saturday 9 July 1960 — TLS, BBC Written Archives Centre

3 Chalcot Square
London N.W.1
July 9, 1960

George MacBeth, Esq.
THE BRITISH BROADCASTING CORPORATION
Broadcasting House
London W.1

Dear George MacBeth,

I'm enclosing a group of unpublished poems[3] as I promised to do the other day when you called. I hope you find something you like.

With all good wishes,
Sincerely yours,
Sylvia Plath

1–Arnold Wesker, *Roots* (1958); played at the Royal Court Theatre.

2–Scottish poet, novelist, and BBC producer George MacBeth (1932–92).

3–According to SP's submissions list, she sent MacBeth 'Sleep in the Mojave Desert', 'Flute Notes from a Reedy Pond', 'The Colossus', 'Suicide Off Egg Rock', 'The Stones', 'The Burnt-out Spa', 'The Eye-mote', 'Aftermath', 'Ouija', 'The Beekeeper's Daughter', 'The Ghost's Leavetaking', 'Departure', 'Frog Autumn', and 'Moonrise'.

TO *Aurelia Schober Plath*

Tuesday 19 July 1960 TLS, Indiana University

Tuesday: July 19

Dear mother,

We received the $1,000 check in good order & have deposited it here. Thank you for sending it so soon. Both Ted & I are awestruck and immensely proud of your studies & the triple & quadruple life you seem to be leading. Housewife, teacher, student, mother, mistress of four cat-kittens (I do hope this number will diminish): I feel extremely lazy by comparison. I know how difficult it must be to be a novice among people who are already teachers. Don't let the jargon and references to things you haven't heard of bother you: every field seems to delight in this kind of mystifying doubletalk, and perhaps sociology and statistics are among the worst in this. It is common knowledge that much of the stuff is unreadable, pedantic & <u>bad</u> jargon English. Soon you will probably feel "in", after finding your way around in articles and reference books. I am skeptical of people whose God is testing, knowing how a cold, worry, or simply a lack of the right priming can make results go haywire. So keep several grains of salt handy, & your fine perspective!

I have the baby outofdoors downstairs in her carriage, where I can see her from the windows up here. It has been a ghastly July: rain <u>every</u> day, off and on, in great sudden gushes. The minute I rush down with Frieda in a "bright interval" a cold wind comes up with black clouds. It is raw and chilly all the time. I am very homesick for days that start out blue & clear & stay that way, and miss being tan, as I have always been in the summer. I am a horrid pale yellow. O England. I probably haven't written for a week as I have been suffering from a nasty boil on my lower lip: very very painful, and hideous, red, oozing blood & guck, so bad I didn't want to show my face in the street for fear of scaring children. I went twice a day to the doctor for penicillin injection & took penicillin pills, & just had to let it ooze. Now at last the swelling is gone, and the infection, although the new skin is crinkly & sore. The whole treatment cost me about 25 cents, the token fee for two boxes of penicillin shots! Thank god I live in a welfare state. Frieda continues with her monthly shots & my clinic visits for free advice. The lady doctor there is a handsome woman with <u>eight</u> children.

Ted got his nice check for $450 for his manuscripts this week, plus the information that the BBC will pay him $330 for his hour verse play, much more than we expected. Yes, they will do it with actors, sound effects, the lot. He is just finishing up the libretto for the opera of this modern Chinese composer we met at Yaddo, based on the Tibetan Book of the Dead, a difficult project. I received a lovely silver baby cup from Marion & Ruthie and a monogrammed set of silver (knife, fork, spoon) & inscribed aluminum baby cup (Rebecca . . . well, she'll learn her middle name that way) from grampy. I'll write thanks to both this week. Grace Berry[1] also sent a nice pajama set, which I've written her about. We both get so excited at gifts for the baby. By the way, I've received a note from Harrod's that Mildred Norton has asked them to find out what I'd like for a baby gift. Should I go over to the store & look around their baby dept? I'm rather at a loss as to how much she means the gift to be & don't want to be excessive. I'm thinking of looking for a folding playpen for Frieda. Her latest trick is holding her head up when lying on her stomach and looking all around. She squirms all over her crib & will yell for help when she gets a leg or an arm through the slats. Your Spock must be very different from mine (which is the revised, enlarged pocket edition): "Pacifier" begins section P in the index & he devotes 4 pages to praising it. Frieda won't look at hers anymore (it helped her over the colicky period very well) but settles on her thumb. Her eyes are still bright blue & she is in wonderful humor, laughing, enjoying being bounced on the bed, propped up sitting & talked to. She has a whole new range of voice noises.

I am writing Mrs. Prouty today, very sorry to hear she is so ill. Keep me posted on her progress, do. Tell Warren how pleased we are to hear his paper is done: tell him to sit out in the American sun for me. Are you going to vote for Kennedy? I'll disown you if you vote for Nixon.

Last night Ted & I had Leo Goodman for supper again, & he took us to a fine performance of Brecht's "Galileo" at the new Mermaid theater overlooking the Thames, all about Galileo's selling out to the church, recanting his views to live in physical comfort. We parked the baby with our sometime free-sitter, the woman living at the Merwins. Do let us know if you see any reviews of Ted's book in America.

Ted joins me in sending best love,
Sivvy

1 – According to SP's address book, Grace Berry (Mrs Courtice H. Berry) of 45 Brookline Drive, West Hartford, Connecticut.

TO *Alan Anderson*

Saturday 23 July 1960 TLS, Pierpont Morgan Library

3 Chalcot Square
London N.W.1
July 23, 1960

Dear Alan Anderson,

The pamphlets are absolutely beautiful. Ted and I are delighted with them, and especially with the handsome way you make up your covered booklets.[1]

It must be an immense satisfaction to have a library of such finely printed work. The mood---form and color---of the jacket designs are perfectly suited to the atmosphere of poem and story, I think.

Once again, thank you for your kindness and generosity in printing the winter ship.

Sincerely,
Sylvia Hughes

TO *Aurelia Schober Plath*

Tuesday 2 August 1960 TLS (aerogramme),
Indiana University

Tuesday: August 2

Dear mother,

I was just about to set off with the pram to the cleaners and grocery stores around the corner when a cloudburst arrived, so I've come back to wait till the sky clears and thought I'd improve the hour by writing a letter to you. I'm glad Mrs. Prouty is keeping in close touch with you. I'm sure your notes and such mean much to her. We're planning to write again soon and send her reproductions of a few of the baby snaps we sent you when we have more made up. Right now Frieda is dressed in a pale yellow dress bordered with white lace & matching yellow pants all ruffled with lace (a gift from Marcia, outgrown by her Cary: she sent me a bunch of dresses via a friend of hers last week for which I'm very grateful), lying on her stomach on a quilt on the livingroom floor, staring up at me with her

1–Alan Anderson printed two special copies of *A Winter Ship* on pale grey Ingres paper, bound in Cockerell marbled wrappers. He gave one to SP and kept the other. SP's inscribed copy to Anderson reads, 'for Alan Anderson / with thanks and / warmest good wishes ~ / Sylvia Plath'; held by Morgan Library.

big blue eyes. She holds her head up all the time now when on her stomach & loves to ride this way in her carriage, like a figurehead, looking at the leaves and people. Just this week she's become interested in the rattles (I have two) and reaches for them with intent concentration, grabs, waves them, and sucks them. She is also grabbing at faces, particularly intrigued by noses. We hope to borrow a pen from a friend of Ted's. I wish you could see her now. She is such a responsive merry little baby.

I think I got a lovely solution to Aunt Mildred's gift ticket at Harrod's. I really wanted one of those little hot water plates I remember we had as children. The baby has three cups---two silver (from Ruthie & Patsy) & one aluminum (from grampy) and two sets of silver, the baby set from Mrs. Pulling & the bigger one from grampy, so I did want a plate. Luckily Harrod's baby department (which is very fancy & expensive, with adorable imported clothes) was having a display of imported French hot water plates & I fell in love with them & got one with "La Ronde" painted on it and a little ring of children dancing among flowers & trees on the white china ground. The hole you pour the hot water in is stoppered by a white china rabbit. It only costs 15shillings 9pence (about $2.25) so I feel I've got just what I want & need at reasonable cost.

Helga Huws' German mother is visiting them: speaking not a word of English, very nice. She'll probably come again next summer so you could have conversations with her. She is minding the two babies tonight while the four of us go to see the Lunts[1] in Durrenmatt's play "The Visit".[2] Ted is doing two radio broadcast recordings today & tomorrow: one a conversation with a critic about his poem "The Otter" for a school service, the other a reading of a poem & a speech from his play[3] for a New Poems broadcast. Since moving in here this February we've earning well over a thousand dollars for our British writing account, which is nice. The BBC is very helpful.

You sound to be working much too hard if you have to refuse dinner engagements! I am so furious at BU, their whole mechanical behavior over abolishing your department. Just what did that charming gentleman you were interviewed by have to say about future work for you? Will there be an opening at BU for work in teaching reading? They damn well owe it to you. Is the German, even part-time, utterly out? You should be

1–Alfred Lunt (1892–1977) and his wife Lynn Fontanne (1887–1983), actors.
2–Swiss author and dramatist Friedrich Dürrenmatt (1921–90); his *The Visit* (1956); performed at the Royalty Theatre, Portugal Street, London.
3–Ted Hughes, 'Thistles' and 'The Captain's Speech' from *The House of Aries*, BBC Third Programme (21 August 1960).

having a summer off after this year of teaching & I am grieved you are working twice as hard. What are the prospects of a job in this work: is it all remedial? Please keep us informed about this. Wouldn't it be at all possible to teach shorthand & typing at another school in Boston? Surely they must need medical shorthand teachers locally. Well, enough about that. I think BU has behaved abominably.

Sunday we actually were out-of-doors for a whole day, seeing Leo Goodman off for America, lying on top of Primrose Hill in the sun. Ted actually got a sunburn & I the merest shade of brown. We had the baby naked on a blanket in the sun for a very brief while & she loved it. I only wish we would get a spell of such weather so I could let her play about naked on the grass. Next year it would be so nice if Ted & I would go away for a week to Wales or Cornwall and you could live here with Frieda. Of course she may not want to be left, but we could try a day first & see how she does. I look so forward to having you come over & enjoy her. I have discovered a delightful couple who run an art gallery in Camden Town,[1] a rare thing in this district, & spent all Saturday morning talking to them & going through the husband's drawings & paintings. I want to buy a miniature of a witch, a lovely thing, for Ted's birthday: only $3. If only I had a fortune I'd subsidize artists by buying their paintings. Well, into a raincoat & off to the shops. Love to you & Warren.

Take care.
Sivvy

1–Harry Gordon (*c.* 1920–2009) and Norah Gordon. The Gordons operated Parkway Gallery, then at 58 Parkway, London N.W.1.

TO *Robert Hemenway*[1]

Sunday 7 August 1960 TLS, New York Public Library

3 Chalcot Square
London N.W.1, England
August 7, 1960

Mr. Robert Hemenway
THE NEW YORKER
25 West 43rd Street
New York, N.Y.
USA

Dear Mr. Hemenway:

Thank you for your letter.[2] I am glad you like ON DECK and TWO CAMPERS IN CLOUD COUNTRY.

I think that the three changes you suggest are needed to clarify the poems and hope the following suggestions may meet with your approval.

In ON DECK I do want the transition to be from players of ship's games to players with the emotions. Shuffleboard certainly does suggest daytime games. Would "The bingo players" be all right with you here? Bingo is an evening game, and I meant "players" to have the slightly wider connotation of "people who habitually play" or "people who are fresh from playing". This phrase could thus include people out for an airing between games, or after games.

In TWO CAMPERS I agree with you about lichens; they would indeed probably grow on such rocks (although not on the precise rocks I remember). I would like to change the wording to read "These rocks offer no purchase to herbage or people," ---widening the reference to all vegetation.

In TWO CAMPERS, seventh stanza, "In a month we'll forget what plates and forks are for," is perhaps a little too strong. I'd prefer "In a month we'll wonder what . . ." which implies plates and forks are still there, but that they seem a bit fancy and superfluous as one descends more and more often to using fingers-easier, quicker, less washing up.

Let me know if you think these changes are helpful, or if you have any more questions. I wonder, by the way, how I should go about obtaining copyright for WATER COLOR OF GRANTCHESTER MEADOWS

1–Editor for *The New Yorker*, Robert Hemenway.
2–Robert Hemenway to SP, 29 July 1960; held by Smith College.

which appeared in one of your spring issues---I've had a request from an anthology for it.[1]

Sincerely,
Sylvia Plath

TO *Aurelia Schober Plath*

Tues.–Wed. 16–17 August 1960 TLS (aerogramme), Indiana University

Tuesday: August 16

Dear mother,

I have a feeling I haven't written for ages so probably haven't. Ted is off for the afternoon with his friend Danny Huws to look for some sturdy wooden chairs for us in the antique & junk dealers in Portobello Road and Frieda is woo-wooing in bed after her lunch feed preparatory to dropping off for her afternoon nap. Nothing much is new here. I have been getting little surprises ready for Teds birthday tomorrow---a Fortnum & Mason[2] chicken pie, expensive, but which he loves, a bottle of white wine, a photograph album in which I've pasted all our good pictures & written notes under them to encourage us to take more, a jar of maple syrup, and an original (!) painting in bright colors & ink of a sort of Aztec king done by the owner of our local art gallery & I feel marked down for me by his wife out of kindness, this last being the main item. If it's nice I hope to go on a picnic with him & Frieda in Hampstead Heath or just Primrose Hill, even though I have a dentist appointment early in the morning. I thought I would go to the Merwin's dentist in Harley street,[3] even though he is private & not a health system dentist & see if I like him. I am very suspicious of Health Service dentists, although probably if I got a good one I would be as well off as with my doctor-panel. But I am a bit unwilling to risk it. Friday I think we'll pack off to Yorkshire. Ted is a bit homesick for the moors & I think both of us would benefit by a change. With luck & an express train, the trip should only take half a day.

1–Probably Sylvia Plath, 'The Manor Garden' and 'Water Color of Grantchester Meadows', *Best Poems of 1960: Borestone Mountain Poetry Awards 1961* (Palo Alto, Calif.: Pacific Books, 1962): 102–3.

2–Fortnum & Mason is a department store best known for its food products, at 181 Piccadilly, London.

3–Probably James Mansie, who had his consulting room at 112a Harley Street, London, according to SP's address book.

We'll come down again next Wednesday, in time for Frieda's vaccination Thursday.

Your lovely package arrived this morning, and the card of the marvellous sad sack, which I'm saving tomorrow to put on top of Ted's gifts. Perfect timing. The socks are just handsome. I also loved Frieda's jersey & T-shirt. The little undershirts I tried on, and they are just what I need---very roomy, something for her to grow into. She is popping the seams of her first ones. Thanks so much. Mrs. Churchill[1] by the way sent the most adorable red & white checked gingham dress with hand smocking. I'll write & thank her, but you might mention it if you see her. Also please do tell Dot thanks for the cup! I had a suspicion it wasn't all from grampy. The knife, by the way, had the initials engraved on the wrong side, not that it matters. Do I need to write her a separate letter? I've written her before & haven't had a word from her since the baby came. Why don't you thank her for me.

We had lunch with one of the editors of the Texas Quarterly[2] last Saturday at his rented rooms, with several other people. He is a professor & charming, odd man. In addition to taking $100 worth of poems from the two of us,[3] he is buying one of Ted's stories (he's taking back two to decide which) for $100 also. He asked us to bring Frieda, and she was very good, sleeping the whole time. That evening a friend of Ted's sister, a young Hungarian poet & playwrite,[4] took us to dinner at a good Hungarian restaurant. I went off on my own last night to save the price of a babysitter & saw Lawrence Olivier in the movie of "The Entertainer".[5] An amazing part for him, very much the un-hero.

So glad you saw Mrs. Prouty. We are very concerned about her. Do stay overnight with her if you suspicion she might like it: the rich are so often merely left alone with their servants, oddly enough. I sense Maugham is also lonesome.

Warren was so good to write us on the day of Ted's book publication.

1–Helen M. (Saunders) Churchill (b. 1904), wife of Wilmer Holton Churchill (1903–89), a Wellesley neighbour, who lived at 30 Crown Ridge Road, according to SP's address book.
2–Probably Thomas Mabry Cranfill (1913–95), who according to SP's address book was living at 89 Albion Gate, London.
3–Sylvia Plath, 'Flute Notes from a Reedy Pond', *Texas Quarterly* 3 (Winter 1960): 120; Ted Hughes, 'The Caning' and 'Lines to a Newborn Baby', *Texas Quarterly* 3 (Winter 1960): 27–37 and 214; Sylvia Plath, 'Witch Burning', *Texas Quarterly* 4 (Autumn 1961): 84; Ted Hughes, 'Miss Mambrett and the Wet Cellar', 'The Captain's Speech', and 'The Gibbons', *Texas Quarterly* 4 (Autumn 1961): 46–55 and 146–7.
4–János Csokits (1928–2011). Csokits later worked with TH on a translation of the poet János Pilinszky.
5–*The Entertainer* (1960) was shown at the Odeon Marble Arch, Edgware Road, London.

Odd how he describes his dates by height! I have a kind of running graph in my mind of their heights and nothing else. Tell him to send us an autographed copy of his anthology with the essay in it. I'd be very proud to have it. As you were reading your World War II book about Colditz I was finishing Allan Morehead's Gallipoli:[1] absolutely fascinating & terrifying. One senses the awful stupidity of generals (all these were safe on islands & boats & utterly out of communication with the soldiers) & the criminal negligence of politicians in this greatest fiasco of the first world war. Ted's father fought at Gallipoli & a diary in his breast pocket stopped a bullet, so I felt incalculably lucky as I read of the mammoth, pointless slaughters that he survived & fathered the one husband I could imagine. I am trying to have a rigid housework schedule---laundry & market Monday, iron Tuesday, etc. to counteract the otherwise helterskelter days. When one only has one's inclination to consult, it is too easy to procrastinate. I am managing a fair amount of time for reading---just finished translating a play by Sartre---Le Diable et Le Bon Dieu[2]---but have had little energy for writing in anything but my diary, and a few light poems,[3] two of which I think the New Yorker will take. My ms. of poems should come back to you from the Yale contest, which I didn't win this year: the editor likes witty light verse & I guess mine's too serious for him. Keep the ms. & use it for scrap.[4] I do feel sorry no publisher in America seems to want my book, for I am sure it is better than most first books, but I am glad it will come out here. We have been having a few dry sunny days at last after a ghastly cold rainy summer, & I do hope we can get out in Yorkshire. The baby has hardly been out of sweaters all summer. She is getting very clever at holding on to things & still keeps her bright blue eyes, is growing a furze of light brownish second hair. She reminds me very much of shots of Warren when he was a baby. We should soon have more photos to send on.

Love to all,
Sivvy

PS: I'll be glad to hear your gruelling summer's over & you're at the Cape![5]

1–Australian writer Alan Moorehead (1910–83); his *Gallipoli* (London: New English Library, 1963); SP's copy held by Emory University.

2–Jean-Paul Sartre, *Le Diable et le Bon Dieu* (1951).

3–SP's recent poems were 'Sleep in the Mojave Desert' (5 July), and 'Two Campers in Cloud Country' and 'On Deck' (before 9 July 1960).

4–Yale rejected *The Colossus* on 2 August 1960; manuscript and rejection notice held by Lilly Library.

5–TH added a note on the return address side of the letter, which has not been transcribed. TH wrote about a visit to Hampstead Heath for a picnic and his gratitude for his birthday socks. He commented that Frieda was sleeping and SP drinking tea.

TO *Aurelia Schober Plath*

Saturday 27 August 1960

ALS with envelope,
Indiana University

Yorkshire: The Beacon
Saturday: August 27

Dear mother –

Ted & I have been up here in Yorkshire for a week, now & I am just beginning to feel that deep peaceful energy that comes from having completely unwound & caught up on months of half-fatigue. We have been simply eating, sleeping & taking long walks. I think you would love it up here – the unique combination of breathtaking scenery & invigorating air and no tourists. Ted's cousin Vicky drove us to Whitby, a British seaside resort, for a day & a night. We took the baby – who is a very good traveler. I always have to do a lot of thinking & preparing beforehand – bottles of orange juice, canned vegetables, diapers – but she is lulled by the motion of cars & trains. Whitby is a fishing port & resort – part of it "quaint" – incredibly steep cobbled streets, vistas of sea, bright painted herringboats, and the ruins of an abbey and old graveyard on one of the headlands with acres of bright pink-lavender heather in full bloom not a mile back – but there is something depressingly mucky about English sea resorts. Of course the weather is hardly ever sheer fair, so most people are in woolen suits & coats & tinted plastic raincoats. The sand is muddy & dirty. The working class is also dirty – candy papers, gum cigarette wrappers. My favorite beach in the world is Nauset & my heart aches for it. I don't know, there is something clean about New England sand, no matter how crowded. It poured the first day we were there & in spite of our waterproofs we got drenched, doggedly walking at the sea front & climbing the steep cobbled alleys. Thursday morning was fair, so we dried out our tempers & shoes & ambled through the streets to various outlook points – buying Ted & me two identical fisherman's sweaters of white & black wool for about $6 apiece, and a brown sailcloth top for me & a shirt for Ted. <drawing of sailcloth top> Ted's uncle Walter, with his curious habits, had for some reason – probably secretly admiring Ted's sticking to his chosen way of life – stuffed about $150 into his pocket one night we were out at the local pub, playing darts with him & Ted's dad, so we did not feel the strain of a holiday eating into our strict monthly budget.

Ted's mother has a lovely little garden up here – daisies, roses, poppies brightly surviving in the lee of a black stone wall. I prefer this landscape & air to the sea. If only we had a house to ourselves near none of Ted's relatives in a similar lonely spot we could get an immense deal done. As Ted says, most people's problem is lack of ideas, while his is that he has so many ideas & no really settled quiet place to write them. We're going to ask the lady in the attic above us if he can work there while she's at her job.

While up here we heard Ted read two poems on the BBC – one a speech from his play & the other called 'Thistles'. We've written Mrs. Prouty & sent her a copy of 'Thistles' & some (2) photos of Frieda & Ted & me from this batch I'm sending you.[1] What do you think of her? She loves playing with her toes & laughs every time I show her her face in the mirror.

I am also enclosing a check from the New Yorker for deposit in our Boston account for $178 – for two bagatelles,[2] light verse, not poems – I managed to write while going to the Merwin's study. I really hunger for a study of my own out of hearing of the nursery where I could be alone with my thoughts for a few hours a day. I really believe I could do some good stories if I had a stretch of time without distractions.

I made a meatloaf for supper last night, but have been letting Ted's mother do most of the cooking. I feel she hardly does anything but gossip & drink tea the year round & If I use her kitchen I feel to want to scrub it from top to bottom, so I've taken a vacation of sorts. She has been good about washing the baby's things – which I usually take to a laundromat at home. But I resolved before I came up that I would not do twice as much work as I do at home, which is what I did over Christmas – cooking for everyone, simply because no one bothered. I use disposable diapers for the baby while we're away, which are very convenient, if not as absorbent as the cloth ones.

I hope you have been having a good Cape vacation & resting from your arduous summer. Tell us about this new place you've gone. The baby is still wearing Mrs. Spaulding's exquisite sweater & bonnet & bootees – the handsomest things she has.

Lots of love to you & Warren. How is Sappho? What did you do with her while you were away?

xxx
Sivvy

1–The photographs are no longer with the letter.

2–Sylvia Plath, 'On Deck' *New Yorker* (22 July 1961): 32, and 'Two Campers in Cloud Country', *New Yorker* (3 August 1963): 28–9. Plath submitted the poems on 9 July 1960, along with 'Sleep in the Mojave Desert' and 'You're'.

TO *Aurelia Schober Plath*

Wednesday 31 August 1960 — TLS with envelope, Indiana University

Wednesday: August 31

Dear mother,

Ted & I are back in London, having come down on the train yesterday, and are immensely refreshed after our 10 days in Yorkshire. We only had one day without rain, but in our waterproof slickers and Wellington boots managed frequent good walks through Hardcastle Crags and up around the neighboring farms, admiring new calves and kittens and breathing the absolutely pure clear air. When you come over next summer, you must take a room around the corner at Sutcliffe's,[1] an excellent inn with good cooking & reasonable rates, and Ted & I and the baby will stay at his place. It would do us all a world of benefit. Both of us feel to have deeply rested & gotten a valuable perspective on our lives here. All the frustrations of habit fell away & we made several long-range plans. One of the things we enjoyed most was the freedom to walk out between the baby's feeds together, while Ted's mother babysat. It would be so marvelous to have you babysit for a few evenings or afternoons with Frieda next summer while we went out together. She is so good. She was an angel all the while we traveled. I am still nursing her and she is getting so eager to hold bottles & cups that I'm thinking of trying her with a sip of milk from the cup now at each meal. The diaper service is a wonderful help. I couldn't do without it. I found the 6 nappies a day just enough & now I only change her 5 times, I use the extra one as a bib. Ted's Uncle Walt & Aunt Alice gave her a lovely coverall towelling bib & sweater & bootees while up there. She discovered the coal fire, which fascinated her, and pleased everybody. If your are thinking of anything for Frieda, rather than a sleeper I'd love some more of those wonderful Carter's nighties you sent & which she is still wearing. She fills them now & I think they were 6 month size, so maybe the year size would be the next thing. Those rubber pants you got, in large size now, would also be convenient. Only please don't be extravagant. Anything blue, anything blue. Or white. She is a knockout in those colors. We are thinking of having her christened this fall when the Merwins come back (they are her godparents & Mrs. Spaulding's outfit & Aunt Frieda's dress should fit her then) if we can get

1 – Sutcliffe's Inn, then in Colden, approximately two miles from the Hughes family home.

the minister who married us to do it. I'm enclosing 2 copies of snapshots[1] I sent to Mrs. Prouty of the same vintage as the last bunch I sent you.

Ted has asked the kindly bohemian Mrs. Morton, who works as French translator at the telephone exchange, if he can use her room upstairs to write in while she's out. She was agreeable & he is up there now. We'll leave her a bottle of sherry every now <u>&</u> then as a thanks token. Much better than the Merwins. No obligations, & he just has to pop down when I call, for lunch. A lifesaver. He says its much more quiet & peaceful without all the distracting books & giddy hairdresser sublessees at Merwins. She leaves at 7:30 & is back at 5:30, so he has a good day. I wish you could see the mail he gets! Italian translators asking the British Council to speak to him, American editors over here hoping to meet him, magazines & newspapers panting for his poems & stories. He has already sold his 5 or 6 new poems several times over. He wants to work on a 3-act play now. He read his speech from his BBC play wonderfully over the radio & I can't wait to hear it produced there this fall. There is a fantastic market for plays in London---all youngish authors.

All he needs is one really good successful play, & we would have a good start. Our wish now is to get a car, a beachwagony affair, tour Cornwall & Devon, & buy a spreading country house with some land & settle down to write & raise a family. Once he has a successful play produced we could do this. And then buy a Hampstead-London house overlooking the Heath if we ever got really wealthy. I'm sure we could do a great deal in the peace of the country & a London house is simply out of our reach now---we'd ideally like to buy outright, or as nearly so as possible, to cut rent & rates. Well, since being in London, we've made the equivalent of $1,250 in pounds, which is nice, not counting what we sent you in dollars, which we pretend doesn't exist.

I am so relieved to hear you are through with that blasted summer school and that your classes are full up for this year. Is that even without the degree offered? FOR HEAVEN'S SAKE don't take any afternoon classes, but go home at 2 pm!!! Both Ted & I are vehement about this. It probably secretly makes you feel you are doing <u>some</u>thing to run yourself ragged every minute. Are you still in the dark about the fate of the secretarial department? Will they stop it at the end of the year? You said they didn't list it in the 61 catalogue, didn't you. Well, surely you can ask pointblank what's up as you can't really plan anything till you know. I've never heard

1–The photographs are with the letter: SP holds Frieda in front of their Isis reproduction; TH, seated, holds Frieda Hughes.

of such disgusting behavior on the part of administration anywhere else. How would it affect your pension if the department folded? Do say if it's definite they're ending it! By all means don't "lash yourself" another year at this remedial reading work! You have 2 fulltime jobs as it is. You have tenure. BU has no right to demand you knock yourself out at your time of life at this crazy double teaching-study program.

And don't think you should take courses to show them you're "game" for anything. You have your health and wellbeing to consider & nobody, no matter what age or health, could survive for long on your all-grind, no pleasures schedule. For your own sake & ours promise not to saddle yourself with any courses this year (unless German). Couldn't you find out if you could get a medical secretarial class at any of the other Boston schools? It is hardly a subject that isn't in demand. Why should you jump horses in midstream? I wish you'd spend half as much time in your afternoons playing with women's magazine stories, with feeling. Get a plot, imagine it in several scenes, with a character changing through events & finding something out about life & resolving problems. I'll edit anything you do for what it's worth. I bet if you pretended this was the way you had to earn some money, you'd turn out two or three things in the year. Why don't you try? Marion isn't around. You wouldn't be exhausted after a long day. Start with the things you know, your friend's stories, & pare them objectively to have a beginning, middle & end. Not just to copy the long span of life. You could do it. And I bet once you started, you'd have fun. You might start with someone resembling yourself, only with young children or something, whose job is threatened, & work it out via another character. Call it THE QUESTION MARK. What do you think?

By the way, how did our total get to be $5253.57 with the $3.60 Partisan check.[1] I had $5219.97 down plus $32 (Ted's partisan check)[2] written beside it: I don't know if that meant the $5219 included it, or should have it added. In either case, I cant see how it adds to $5253. Did you mean $5223.57? or $5255.57? Let me know, & what it makes with the $178 I sent last week, so I can keep my records straight.

Much love,
Sivvy

PS- Ted likes his socks very much.

1–Sylvia Plath, 'Metaphors for a Pregnant Woman' ['Metaphors'], *Partisan Review* 27 (Summer 1960): 435.
2–Ted Hughes, 'Hawk Roosting', *Partisan Review* 27 (Spring 1960): 271–2.

TO *Aurelia Schober Plath*

Tuesday 13 September 1960 TLS (aerogramme), Indiana University

Tuesday morning: September 13

Dear mother,

By now you must be back home. I hope the Cape gave you good weather. Tell us about it and make us homesick. Did Warren's girlfriend come down, and what is she like? September has brought us some extremely pleasant crisp sunny weather, and I have been able to get Frieda out in a sunsuit on a blanket on Primrose Hill, which she enjoys, kicking, laughing, and looking about. She is marvelous now, 15 pounds 1½ ounces on her 5th month birthday, healthily chubby and very bouncy. Her eyes are big and blue with striking long black lashes, and she has a head covered with light brown silky second hair. She is very curious, and when I have her out on her stomach in the carriage in the morning sun, which luckily strikes our little granite yard, she spends a long time head up, peering at the passersby and smiling at them so old ladies stop and coo at her. Ted & I are idiotically admiring of her. I put her on a different schedule this month which is working very well: I nurse her when she wakes up and let her play till we have breakfast when she gets her cereal. Then she has lunch of vegetable, fruit and grated cheese at 12:30, orange juice in midafternoon, & supper about 5:30. Gone are the 10 and 2 day feeds which so broke up my time. I just wish you could see her: she would steal your heart away, she is so sunny and full of chuckles at the little games we play with her.

Have you got to see Mrs. Prouty? It would be nice if you could do something for her like staying overnight when her servants are away: she has done so immeasurably much for us. I suppose your school has started. For heaven's sake promise not to ruin your good schedule by hurling yourself into more courses!!! And tell me just how your job stands, and pension & all. We are concerned about these things & want to know. I have a poem about the baby in this month's Atlantic and Ted has a wonderful review of his book by Stanley Kunitz[1] in the book section of this month's Harpers. Also, his picture & two poems[2] were in the September 9 issue of the special number of the Times Literary Supplement on the British

1–American poet Stanley Kunitz (1905–2006); his 'The New Books', *Harper's* (September 1960): 96–103.

2–Ted Hughes, 'Thistles' and 'A Fable', *Times Literary Supplement* (9 September 1960): xli and lxx. TH's picture appeared in 'Signs of an All Too Correct Compassion', *Times Literary Supplement* (9 September 1960): xiii.

Imagination, which it might amuse you to look up in the library. He has 3 or 4 speaking engagements at colleges and schools around London this fall for about $35 a time.

We are now thinking seriously about looking for a house on the seacoast in Cornwall---not a summer cottage, which most people want down there, but a sizable house with grounds. The rents are much much lower and one really gets something: I read of a charming place on the sea with a couple of acres, stream, orchard, just the thing, for about 4 thousand pounds. 4 or 5 thousand pounds could buy something very fine outright, I think. We'll wait till Ted finishes a full-length play & sees if he can get it staged, then get, hopefully, a station wagon, then a Cornwall House. If he is ever financially very successful, as he may well be, we would like to get a Hampstead house, right on the heath, an area which is full of exquisite houses and gardens, all expensive, but the sort of thing a playwright could afford. Anyway, tell us when you think you would be coming over here next summer & how long you could stay. We are cudgelling our brains to think of the best time to take our 3 months in Europe & probably will try this next March, April & May. Then we would have some money left over we hope, to live on the summer you came. If Ted could just get a play written & staged we could retire to the country & he could really work. He works 5 days a week in the lady's livingroom upstairs, a very quiet place, but dependent on her kindness, & he needs a study, so do I, and a yard for the children to play in. Well, these are all hopeful projects.

We went to two plays this last week, the remainin parts of the Wesker trilogy[1] which covers about 20 years (often in one play) about a Communist, or Socialist Jewish family: the ideology isn't at all moving, but the human situations are. The boy hugs his mother with the words "Well, the Labor government's in!" & it isn't the words, but the hug that matters. Ted's radio play is so queer & interesting that I'm dying to see this next one, which came to him in a dream. We left the baby with a girl at Merwins' & wangled a pass to the Picasso exhibit[2] again (we'd had to go separately before) Sunday morning when it was only open to a few people with passes, not the 6 thousand-a-day & had it all to ourselves. Met our friend & professor at Harvard, Jack Sweeney, who recorded us for the Lamont Library & he is due any minute for a visit to see the baby & we'll lunch with him tomorrow. Hope you got the new photos & my

1–British dramatist Sir Arnold Wesker (1932–2016); his *I'm Talking About Jerusalem* and *Chicken Soup With Barley*; performed on alternating nights at the Royal Court Theatre, London, England.

2–An exhibition of Picasso's work at the Tate Gallery, London, 6 July–18 September 1960.

New Yorker check. Do let me know the exact amt. in that bank! Wasn't it only 7 thousand you paid for our lovely Wellesley house?[1] How I wish you had a country place near here. I envy my neighbors who have English country grandmothers & are always exchanging visits!

Ted & your beautiful granddaughter join in sending much love –

Sivvy

<on the return address side of letter>

If there's any bank interest – do say how much – I think it shouldn't come till later this fall. Is it still 3¾%?

PS – Got your good letter from the Cape today – the $178 check arrived with the pictures didn't it? The new place you lived at sounds superb. How I long for Nauset beach! Perhaps Ted will get a lectureship in a few years to finance our going over.

xxx
Sivvy

TO *Aurelia Schober Plath*

Friday 16 September 1960 TLS, Indiana University

Friday: Sept. 16

Dear mother . . .

I hope you weathered the hurricane safely.[2] It sounded a powerful one from the papers. I am enclosing the real check this time, I hope. Yes, I had forgotten to add Ted's $30 Nation check which makes our totals agree: $5431.57. (including this chk.) I figure the interest should be $180ish. I'm also enclosing some ghastly snaps Mike Lotz took of us as you have a viewer.[3] He was sitting down in a chair & so got the baby from under her fat chin & she was fussy as due to be fed. Private viewing for you.

I have one or two little nagging details I wonder if you could help me with. One is: the rubber automatic air vent flew out of my pressure cooker & is evidently too tired to work. Could you order me one: PART NUMBER 1509 (75 cents) of MODEL 704 (4-Qt.) cooker from National Presto Industries, Inc., Eau Claire Wisconsin? Order one sent to me, I mean. They ask part & model number & the cost, & as I no longer have

1–The deed of sale for 26 Elmwood Road, Wellesley, dated 24 October 1942, lists a mortgage balance of $5,904.10.

2–Hurricane Donna, which made landfall on 12 September 1960 and affected the east coast of the United States from Florida to Maine.

3–The photographs are no longer with the letter.

a $ checking account I can't send them the money. Also, I'm enclosing my Smith due sheet for the same reason. If there's any cash left from that bit I made over to you in my Wellesley Fells account, could you send the enclosed form off? Otherwise, throw it out.

The cold weather, rain and so on is on us again & I don't suppose it will let up for six months. I am so glad the Cape did rest you up. You still haven't answered my questions about what is the official position of your department, job & pension with BU. Please do let us know about this in detail & what those louts are telling you they'll do with you, or to help you!

Have you seen anything of Mrs. Prouty since you've been back? I hope Warren has a pleasanter year this year. What is his Cambridge address & is he still living there? I hope he finds a girl he falls in love with, not just a girl who fills in the application blank of good-cook, good-looking-in-a-bathing-suit, tall etc. He should feel the one he marries is the only one not just one of many who would also do. Waiting for the right wonderful person is so much more important than getting the outer comforts of marriage at an early age. I feel I know what I'm talking about because I can't imagine being able to remotely stand any one else in the world but Ted. There he is, after him a huge gulf, and then the rest of the little people.

Let us know roughly when & how long we can expect you for next summer. I'd like to start looking forward to it now.

We had Leo Goodman, the young handsome statistician from Chicago here to dinner last night: he'd flown back from NYC for a few days and since we last saw him had married Ann Davidow which delighted us all. He is a rare person & so is she, our favorite couple along with the Baskins.

Frieda is better and better. Singing and holding a little glass of milk and sipping from it now---very clumsily, but making good tries: <u>I</u> hold the glass & guide it really, but she pretends to be doing it. The rest of the time I nurse her & am so glad to have avoided the ridiculous bother of sterilizing bottles & measuring formula which I only did once or twice early on when I went out to the theater. I am beginning to use the study (really the lady's little livingroom) upstairs 5 mornings a week. Hope I can get something done: very pleasant there.

Love to all
xxx
Sivvy

TO *Aurelia Schober Plath*

Friday 23 September 1960 — TLS with envelope, Indiana University

Friday: Sept. 23

Dear mother,

Hello. I hope your first weeks of teaching haven't been too strenuous and that you're coming right home after your last afternoon class! I'm enclosing these enlargements[1] of our favorite pictures out of the lot we sent you, thinking you might like them & want to send the little ones to some friends. Aunt Frieda & Mrs. Prouty already have copies of one or two of these, but I've sent them to noone else. I wonder, by the way, if you could look up the yellow-paper-backed copy of my speedwriting book (it should be in my bookcase or drawers or closet, near the surface of piles of magazines or something) & send it on to me. I'm also enclosing a check for two light poems from Harper's for $88[2] for deposit in our account.

Last night Ted & I went to John Lehmann's fashionable house[3] overlooking a green crescent in Kensington for drinks (it happened to be champagne, we were lucky). He's editor of the London Magazine, where we both publish a good deal, and is very odd and nice. I met my young publisher there and Ted the writer PH Newby[4] on the BBC who had accepted his play. The little balcony was open & the evening pleasant. Ted's play is being broadcast twice late this fall here, & his translation of 100 lines or so of the Odyssey[5] too as part of a series done by about a dozen different people. He found a word for word literal translation & made poetry of it. He's also been asked to be one of 3 editors of an annual anthology of poems[6] that carries a fee of about $70 which is nice.

I have just enrolled today at the Berlitz school[7] here for lessons in beginning Italian, as Ted I think would most like to go to Italy for his Maugham award & I definitely want to be able to speak and read Italian

1–The photographs are no longer with the letter.

2–Sylvia Plath, 'You're' *Harper's* 222 (June 1961): 40; and 'Sleep in the Mojave Desert', *Harper's* 224 (February 1962): 36. See R. B. Silvers to SP, 12 September 1960; held by Smith College.

3–John Lehmann, 31 Egerton Crescent, London S.W.3.

4–English novelist and broadcasting administrator P. H. (Percy Howard) Newby (1918–97).

5–Ted Hughes, 'Part 6, "The Storm" (Book V)', BBC Third Programme (10 November 1960).

6–Patricia Beer, Ted Hughes, and Vernon Scannell (eds.), *New Poems, 1962: A PEN Anthology of Contemporary Poetry* (London: Hutchinson, 1962).

7–In 1960, the Berlitz School of Languages was at 321 Oxford Street, London W.1.

to profit by this. The fee is 3 pounds for 15 hour lessons (small group lessons), about $8.50, which I think reasonable, & if I get on well & like their methods, I might try classes in German or French---they meet 2 nights a week usually. I have a unique opportunity to "try out" languages on the continent & want to take advantage of it. My first lesson is next week. I am also investigating the extension courses at London University which I am too late to register for this year, but which I would like to get into next year.

Frieda is thriving and at a very easy stage now. Don't get any rubber pants, if you haven't yet, as I've found a good place to get them here. I'm having great pleasure looking at baby things: got a little blue duck today that floats in the bath. When I hold Warren's teddy up to her and growl she bursts out laughing. Marcia Plumer's friend, newly married to an Englishman & now named Marcia Momtchiloff,[1] came for tea today bringing a nice snowsuit from Marcia---big, but Frieda will grow into it. She also offered to loan me her portable featherweight Singer sewing machine if I got some easy patterns & material to make Frieda dresses, which I'd like to learn to do with an eye toward getting a machine myself some day, and to help me learn to use it, which is lovely. Got a bright cheerful letter from Dot which means a lot to me. Glad to hear Bobby's on the football team & Nancy doing so well. I hear my girl, so I'm off to give her her supper & bath.

Love to you, Warren & Sappho.

xxxxxx

Sivvy

PS: Could you send me your measurements & Warren's for blouses, shirts, shoes, gloves – the lot – in case I ever come on anything nice?

1 – Marcia Van de Carr Momtchiloff (1930–); B.A. 1951, University of Rochester; married John W. Wideman, 7 September 1955; married Constantine N. Momtchiloff, 2 August 1960. There are two British addresses listed in SP's address book: 7 Ellesmere Court, Ellesmere Road, Weybridge, and Tangleways, Sheets Heath, Brookwood, Surrey.

TO *Aurelia Schober Plath*

Wednesday 28 September 1960 — TLS with envelope, Indiana University

Wednesday
September 28

Dear mother,

It was so nice to receive a letter from you today on the heels of your last, that I thought I'd drop you a note on the heels of my last & take the chance of enclosing this $50 check for two of Ted's poems from Mademoiselle[1] for deposit in our Boston account. What months do they do interest, by the way? I'm dying to see how much it is! Ted went off at 9:30 this morning to get the train to a Teachers College in Sussex where he is giving an hour talk and reading for $36. He has several odds & ends of projects to finish up now---the Oddyssey poem-translation for the BBC, revisions on his play-script which is scheduled for two broadcasts in late November & early December. Do you know anyone whose radio can get the BBC? It would be so nice for you to hear it. In Yorkshire we sat round at tea with all the relatives, tuned in and heard Ted reading two of his poems, one of them a speech from the play, which was lovely. He is also grunting over an article on the Arnold Wesker trilogy[2] of plays which we enjoyed seeing here this summer for the Nation. He was originally going to refuse to do the article, but I felt it was because he out of his great modesty felt he didn't know enough about the American theatre of the 30's & Clifford Odets'[3] plays (also about Jews & Communists), so I very slowly persuaded him to take a day or two to read Odets at the British Museum & that his own instinctive reactions were better than most garbled criticisms I had read. I also bought Penguin paperback editions of the 2 plays in print. Usually I let his judgment be the final arbiter on such matters, but here I felt he'd be glad he'd done an article which is right up his alley: Wesker is just my age & his play "Roots", the middle of the trilogy, is about Norfolk farmers & full of good things: it's coming to America this year, so see it if it comes to Boston. Although the Nation pays very little, both of us admire the magazine very much, & what it tries to do (Ted only got $30 for his book-review), and if the book editor likes what Ted does it will mean a couple of assignments a year and the

1–Ted Hughes, 'Thistles' and 'A Fable', *Mademoiselle* (March 1961): 204, 206.
2–Ted Hughes, 'Arnold Wesker: "A Sort of Socialism"', *The Nation* 191 (19 November 1960): 402–4.
3–American playwright and director Clifford Odets (1906–63).

odd extra $100. Ted is slaving on these bits now to clear the decks for his own play The Calm[1] which sounds marvelously exciting, very fully realized. One success could buy us a house: it's a gamble & takes faith, but Ted has every reason to feel he can do it. When Charles Monteith at Faber had lunch with Ted & Thom Gunn last week, he said "Tom Eliot is delighted with the drawings & poems in MEET MY FOLKS!" I can't wait to see the book: it is scheduled for Spring 1961, about in time for Frieda's first birthday. Did I tell you we went for drinks at John Lehmann's posh Kensington house (he's editor of the London Magazine) where both our publishers were, & the BBC man who'd accepted Ted's play & arranged for him to read his "Rain Horse" story, a writer I admire very much. We had lots of champagne on the balcony overlooking the green square. London is inexhaustible. Although I'd very much like to have a house in Cornwall I would have to have some arrangement whereby we'd be in London half a year and there half a year. Or 9 months & 3 months. Oh well. I am much more a city-dweller than Ted. September has brought crisp blue American weather: I have had Frieda out in her pram almost all day each day for the last week. She loves being in the little cement area out front because she can put her head up and watch all the people go past: she's very curious about everything.

I have grammy's warm fur carriage rug over her & she is down there now. You are an angel to get all those Carters things for her. She has plenty of summer clothes for next year when she's a year old, but very little except sweaters for this winter. I think I'll go out next week & get some red flannel & see if I can make up a couple of zippered sleeping sacks (I have one of Marcia's which is wonderful: the warmth of a flannel nightie but just an oblong bag so if she kicks her covers off, which she always does, she will be warm enough anyway. This isn't a heavy bag. Perhaps this other Marcia will show me how to cut a pattern from it & make a couple on her machine.

This weekend Ted & I are taking Frieda to the country house of some friends of ours: a Scots mathematician & his little American wife whom he stole from Radcliffe before she graduated. They are extremely nice & have just bought this house: will pick us up here Friday night & take us back Monday morning, as he starts teaching then. I look forward to this: they have lots of land.

Had my first Italian lesson at Berlitz last night. Very interesting. All verbal: he didn't speak a word of English (although he knows English,

1–Ted Hughes, *The Calm* (unpublished play).

I think). Just 5 of us in the class (they can go up to 15): all girls. One a very good one---has been in Italy & understands Italian & knows French & German & works for a wool export firm in the City. The others are little very young office-type girls, very cute, but already having trouble. We will get a Berlitz book, but not yet. We spent the whole time learning vocabulary of things in the room, masculine & feminine endings, negative & positive word order: a very good method I think, repeating things after the young, expressive teacher & learning by repetition. So much simpler than English or German! I want to work on my own in the little self-teaching Italian book I have so as to get the very most from my lessons. Tentatively we plan on going to Italy from March-May, to avoid the tourist rush. I'm going to ask my doctors about precautions for Frieda. She's marvelous now: her cheeks are getting pink from being out. I took her to the Scotchman's Zoo (the free outer walk in Regents Park where you can see some of the animals) & enticed a camel to bend over her carriage by feeding it grass. She was amazed & stared & stared. Every time I give her Warren's teddy & growl she laughs & pummels it. I bought her a little blue celluloid duck for the tub & she spends her whole bath trying to grab it & the minute she catches it making little squealing noises of delight. Ted & I are overjoyed with her. Ted's friend Luke sent her a really tiny silver baby cup (with Rebecca on it!) and flowers on the handle & she has been playing with this all morning. What fun we'll have when you come over! Be sure you bring a really waterproof raincoat and good overshoes so we can walk out no matter what! As soon as you can, let us know your dates. What kind of a place would you like to stay here? Bed & breakfast? How cheap? We could be looking around.

When I get really proficient in Italian (I'll take another course after this right up to the time we go abroad) I want to start conversational German & spend our next vacation in Austria---perhaps visiting that Inn you spoke of. My ambition now is to get 3 European languages really well. A unique chance, living so close to Europe. I've always wanted to be able to speak & read several languages, & with the reasonableness of these Berlitz courses I can. I would LOVE a subscription to the New Yorker. Ironically, I dreamed of getting one last night before your letter came. Well, best love to you Warren & dear Sappho.

xxx

Sivvy

<on verso of envelope>

PS – The pressure-cooker 'thingumbobs' arrived in good order today with the elegant blue pants – many thanks!

TO *Gerald & Joan Hughes*

Wednesday 28 September 1960[1] ALS, Indiana University

Dear Gerald, Joan & offspring . . .

Ted had already sealed up your letter in his secretive way but I made him open it again to let me gossip for a bit. How do you like our chico? Isn't Ted satanic over her? The lady blessing me & Frieda (who doesn't give a damn) is our Isis – we had an artist friend blow her up to lifesize from an astrology book. Down the side to the left are her other names: Isis, Minerva, Venus, Juno etc. She's one of the baby's godmothers. I don't think we've ever been as happy as in the last six months. The baby is so funny – singing, making faces, cuffing her teddy bear, giggling at our oafish attempts to amuse her. I put her on 3 meals a day at 5 months, so feel to have acres of time now that the 6 · 10 · 2 · 6 · 10 schedule is over. She eats like a pig, taking after her ma. Her eyes are an astounding blue, which neither of us gave her: she gets it from her two grandfathers. Already little boys hang about her carriage acting up for a smile. Every time I leave her to go inside a shop I find somebody or other kootchy-kooing over her when I come out – she looks at everybody & is very curious.

This afternoon I took her on one of my favorite walks in Regents Park by the 'Scotchman's Zoo' – where you can see a lot of animals without having to pay to go in. I attracted a large white camel from the zoo-goers at the opposite side of the outdoor cage by making sly squeaking noises & got the camel bending over Frieda's carriage eating grass from my hand. She was amazed & amused. I think she thought it was Ted in an overcoat.

Don't believe a word Ted says about his one-hour play! His usual black aftermath of self criticism just because he is working on a new – longer & better one. The play is super – you can't read it without picturing it happening. Full of brilliant, colorful <u>speaka</u>ble poetry: not the kind you have to stand stock still & orate. Some of the scenes are killingly funny. All the characters from the fat bedridden mayor with his oyster-farm (in a barrel) to his bawdy wife & her local bedfellows are packed with life – none of the usual stereotypes. It's terrific. Forget what he says.

We popped out for a couple of hours to a literary cocktail party in posh Kensington – at John Lehmann's, editor of <u>The London Magazine</u>. He's a regular publisher of our stuff. So we cultivate him. Both my publisher & Ted's publisher were there. And the writer PH Newby from the BBC who accepted his play. Lehmann was serving champagne – popping the corks & fizzing the stuff on his balcony over potted geraniums – and I managed

1 – Date supplied from internal evidence.

with my usual sleight-of-hand to enjoy a good bit of it. I could live & breathe champagne & only in a blue moon can indulge this instinct. Why don't you four blow yourself to a two week's jet flight vacation over here? Sell a couple of cars or something? Frieda says 'Ga!' which means she sends love.

So do I –
Sylvia

TO *Lynne Lawner*

Friday 30 September 1960 — Printed from *Antaeus* 28, Winter 1978

Friday: September 30, 1960

Dear Lynne . . .

I have just read your long letter of last winter over and like Van Winkle only realize that more time has passed than I thought possible. I miss you; I hope you are still in Rome. I asked a lady of buxom perfumed proportions who dropped by and drank tea with an astounding amount of sugar if you were still in the Via Flaminia and she, Maria Luisa Spaziani[1] or something like that, said yes. An immense cowlike and cabbagey calm settled on me during the last months of my pregnancy and this half year of nursing Frieda Rebecca. I am just slowly surfacing. The whole experience of birth and baby seem much deeper, much closer to the bone, than love and marriage. Have one, it's incredible. I think being mountainous-pregnant was my favorite feeling & I wish I could prolong it, it's so odd, being bony & thin, to become a pear. Ted hypnotized me to have an easy delivery, & the little Indian midwife who bicycled miles after our call at 1 am on the morning of (yes) April Fool's Day was amazed to find the baby almost in her lap by the time she arrived. At sunup precisely, 5:45 am, Frieda Rebecca sneezed & began life. I was immensely moved & heartened by the whole experience, which I had deeply feared, having seen a ghastly delivery in a charity ward in Boston at a very impressionable age as a freshman in college. You just can't get most women to talk honestly about labor. Ironically, after reading & being disgusted with Grantly Dick Read, who at one point says "Childbirth isn't physical!"[2] and goes ga-ga

1–Italian poet Maria Luisa Spaziani (1924–2014).

2–In the chapter of *Childbirth without Fear* entitled 'Philosophy of Childbirth', Dick-Read writes, 'Childbirth is not a physical function' (11). In SP's copy, she has underlined this sentence and added an exclamation mark in the left margin.

over the spiritual Nobility etc. of it all, and says you're only in pain if you're nervous, I, being as nervous as possible, had exactly 4½ hours of labor, without any anesthesia (except a barley sugar the midwife had in her pocket). A notoriously easy time for a first baby. All very violent, rapid, rather than the long-drawn-out horrors a German friend of mine describes. After a couple of really impressive contractions the whole stage of getting the baby out is really painless & terrifically exciting. Ted was there, & I in my little rosepapered bedroom, and the Indian midwife a mystical deliveress. The doctor (who was a Classical scholar at King's a few years before me) came in just in time to see the delivery. No time for the midwife to bike home for gas or anything. I was glad not to have it, for the minute they left I got up & put in a long-distance call home to my nerve-wracked mother. The baby had her first bath in a big pyrex baking dish & never left my side. All the impressive flashing of anesthetics, surgical instruments, masks etc. that goes on in American hospitals was absent & there was a primitive homeliness about everything that I heartily recommend to anybody with my peculiar set of nerves. Frieda is my answer to the H-bomb. I never gave a damn about babies till I had her; now I still don't give a damn about other people's, but regard her as a strange private miracle. All the stereotypes about smelly nappies, spoiled squalls etc. are so far fiction. She sleeps, eats, plays with a little silver cup & fur bear & sings and coos & is now gawping up at me with enormous blue eyes (which derive from her two grandfathers) from the floor of her playpen. This probably bores you. But I thought you might be curious, as I was before venturing into the holy state of Motherhood.

I dogged the shops in Charing Cross as soon as they let me out to walk, but could find no Botteghe's at all. Could you possibly loan me yours? I'd mail it back almost immediately. I am dying to read your stuff[1] in it. Ted & I are seriously thinking of taking his 3-month travel grant in Italy from March 1 to the end of May. Do you know of any villas, furnished (with cheap winter rates!) & empty then? Or of any small seacoast towns where we might find one? Please, please. If you are still in Rome I might persuade Ted to make that a base for going out to find a place. Let me know, ask your influential Moravias, etc. It would be so terrific to see you. I would just like a selfish few days where I could do nothing but accompany you about Rome & leave Ted to mind the baby, which he would be glad to

1–Lynne Lawner, 'Where are the Wings?', 'Fix Me a Batch . . .', 'His Lament', 'Purgatory', and 'Proof', *Botteghe Oscure* 25 (1960): 216–31. 'Proof' is prose, the other contributions are poems.

do. I suppose you'll write you'll be at Columbia then or something equally frustrating. Did you know Janet Burroway at Cambridge? She cut the Ideal Swath: acted in the Marlowe society, got a first novel out by Faber's, a First in Engl., a play-writing grant to Yale. A Professionale. What do you know of her? I find her cold & very clever, but feel – whether wrongly or not – that you & I are emotional sisters on the other side of the moon. I have an enormous white English pram with black hood & canopies & fittings & am soaking myself in Christopher Robinism in Regents Park. Ted is a hibernant. We occasionally see John Lehmann, had dinner at TS Eliot's, but that's it. He's got a one-hour poetic play scheduled for the BBC late this autumn. I would love you to share some of your Italianate wisdom with me. How did you learn the language? I'm starting with Berlitz here so I can converse with a doctor about any ailment Frieda may contract, but how did you get so conversation was 2nd nature? Did it take long? Please don't make me wait a year to find out & excuse my writer's coma on grounds of cowish amnesia.

Much love . . .
Sylvia

Please stay in Italy till March!

TO *Aurelia Schober Plath*

Saturday 8 October 1960 — TLS (aerogramme), Indiana University

Saturday morning
October 8, 1960

Dearest mother . . .

Well, ironically just about the time I received your letter announcing Warren had a cold, Ted & I have been down with the most miserable colds. Last week I started with a sore throat and aches in my bones, but managed to resist the nose part till yesterday, when it started to rain while I was out and I sat on a drafty bus. So my eyes and nose have been streaming and everything aching. Ted is just getting over a bad cold, and the dear little baby has a version of a cold---just a light occasional cough, sneeze & wettish nose at present. She seems happy enough, except that she woke me in the night for comforting & a little nurse. Now she is singing and playing with her spoons in her crib.

I am still miserable, but feel I have endured the worst. Ironically once you get the wet trickly itchy stage nothing seems to help or stop it. Even my strong nosedrops only give a second's relief. Enter winter. I am enjoying my Italian lessons every Tuesday and Thursday evening very much. We have a class of about 8 now, and by repeating and repeating phrases and questions---(never a cerebral definition or English question, but the expressive teacher makes us understand what he is saying in Italian by his gestures & acting out) one gets to <u>feel</u> what is right and wrong by hearing it. I hope to go on with these lessons.

Ted is going to buy a cheap radio this week. His story the "Rain Horse" is going to be broadcast over the BBC again next week[1] (I missed the first broadcast of him reading it), and his translation of a section of the Odyssey in a series of 12 translations by various people, and in November & December his play, which I have just finished typing up in final revised form. So I don't want to miss any of these. And the Third Programme has a lot I want to listen to---plays in French, etc.

I have a new & exciting hobby. You will laugh. Yesterday (my last day on my feet) I went downtown and bought three 2-yard lengths of material---one bright red Viyella (at $1.50 a yard), one bright blue linen, and one soft Wedgwood blue flannel with stylized white little flowers on it (both at about 50 cents a yard). I also got a dress pattern & nightgown pattern (Simplicity). Yesterday I completely cut out and basted (as much as possible without a machine) the little nightgown (in a one-year size.) It is exquisite. If I had a machine, I could have finished it then & there, but Marcia Plumer's friend, Marcia Momtchiloff, promised to bring over her portable sewing machine next week & leave it with me a bit, teaching me about hard bits like buttonholes & back openings which I'm not quite sure how to follow. I pinned the nightgown together to see what it would be like & it's a little fairytale thing. I plan to cut the blue linen for a long-sleeved dress today & have things all ready to machine-stitch when Marcia comes, with the few questions that need answering. Then I'll allow myself the luxury of the red Viyella. I'm making these in year sizes, so she'll not just spit all over them, but have something really pretty. I had priced some nightgowns in ghastly peach & baby blue colors at about $4 & now can have just what I want for her for about $1 a nighty & from $1 to $3 a best dress---and originals! I plan to use the nighty pattern over several times in different colors & patterns. My next purchase I'll save up for is a sewing machine!, I don't know when anything has given me as much pleasure as putting together the flannel nightie for Frieda---the pieces are so little they are very quickly done. If I practise a lot now, I'll probably be able to

1 –'The Rain Horse' was re-broadcast on Friday 14 October 1960, at 8 p.m.

make most of her clothes when she goes to school. The London stores are full of marvellous fabrics & I look forward to expanding my knowledge of them. Ted & I agreed that when we're wealthy, we will buy a loom, a kiln & a book-press and go into handcrafts (where the materials are expensive) & teach our children these things. We feel they are the most satisfying things in the world to do. I am awfully proud of making clothes for little Frieda.

Is your Puerto Rican girl a part of practice-teaching for your reading skills course? I am so glad you had that nice evening with your friends. I felt so badly when you said you had to refuse dinner engagements last summer!

By the way, the Poets Theater in Cambridge write that they are planning to "do" Ted's play this month.[1] We don't know whether this means just to give it a reading or to produce it & we have airmailed them the revised version. Could you---in the guise of an interested person only---call up or get a copy of their season's program (they have a box office number) & find if it's going to be produced & if so go to it & report to us? We want a secret incognito eye to see what havoc they wreak on it since we're not there to check.

Love from us all, & keep away from germs!

Sivvy

I have also bought[2] a few yards of matching continental embroidered tapes to sew on skirt border, collars & cuffs – much more handsome than any figured material.

TO *Ann Davidow-Goodman*

Sunday 9 October 1960 TLS (aerogramme), Smith College

3 Chalcot Square
London N.W.1, England
Sunday: October 9th

Dear Ann . . .

It is all I can do not to begin "Dear Mrs. Goodman" simply because I am so happy about your news. I picture you bringing Leo breakfast on your balcony with a view & leading an enviable gallery-theatre-and-

1 – The Poets Theatre, then at 24 Palmer Street, Cambridge, Mass., gave a staged reading of TH's *The House of Aries*, 2–4 December 1960.
2 – Added by SP by hand in the margin of the first page of letter.

vintage-movie saturated New Yorker existence.[1] Ted & I are very very full of rejoicing at two such good people taking upon them the mystic symbols (etc. etc.) of matrimony. I want a whole ream of your inimitable letterwriting about it all. Leo described so finely the garden ceremony, your toasting, which sounded admirable, and other little particulars at our last supper with him. I have no excuse for not writing sooner ("We must write Ann & Leo", Ted keeps saying, which means I must) except the rather somnambulistic sense that time doesn't matter between us. And all of us have been laid flat by bad colds, including Frieda who sniffled and sang while we sniffled and groaned---she seeming to accept her red nose as a perfectly normal part of the fallen state of humanity. Now we have had a long Sunday sit over griddlecakes and maple syrup and bacon and the Observer and Ted is closeted writing a long fantastic story and Frieda playing with her toy spoons and teddy bear and singing and cooing in her pleasant way, and I am just luxuriating in being able to breathe again.

Leo says your book is "sold out", and an impressive number of copies at that: how about sending us one as an advance trade for Ted's, which will be out in Spring 1961 just in time for Frieda's first birthday? Autographed, of course! I have been dying to see it for so long I will surely perish if not revived by the actual vision. Winter is here, the long wet grey half-year, and the leaves afflicted with jaundice and raining down from the trees. I am enjoying two nights a week at the Berlitz school learning Italian since Ted seems adamant about not spending his travel grant in France. I'm having so much fun saying "The teacher comes from the door and pushes the chair and puts the chalk in the box" in flawless Italian that I may even start another language after I can associate a few more elevated ideas in this one. I've also gone against a deep-seated hatred of anything to do with thread or thimble and blown myself to a few nightgown & dress patterns & bright bolts of cloth & rolls of continental embroidered tapes, and on the promise of a loan of a sewing machine & elementary instructions from a friend, have cut & basted some little storybook clothes for the baby. This is something of a miracle to me---I never liked dolls or such arrant housewifery, & the instinct has taken over in spite of twenty-seven (almost 28, alas) years of resistance.

I hope you both think of returning to Europe soon on another of Leo's superb grants which seem to give him such a magnificent tan, surpassed only by the really gilded Leo-look conferred upon him by marriage.

1 – According to SP's address book, the Goodmans lived at 7 West 96th Street, New York.

Are you working on that idea for a ?was it? Pelican book you showed up watercolor sketches for? Tell me what you are doing, thinking and planning. Also what New York is like. I have always wanted to live there for a year or more and do all the hundred things one can never do on a flying visit.

Except for a couple of auto collisions, housebreakings, deaths and babies, the jangle of rival icecream wagons and the regular noise of glass breaking outside, our square is peaceful and idyllic. I'm awfully fond of this patchy district now and can't really imagine living anywhere else. Although we are considering a cottage in Cornwall as seriously as two people can who have not yet put by a fortune. I'm making Ted scout for a little radio as in the next month or two he is having a story, his hour play & a translation from the Odyssey on the BBC & is notoriously casual about hearing them. I love tuning in and hearing his voice come out. Simple-minded pleasures.

My typing is getting worse, a sure sign of relapse: my coordination always goes off during these sinus-colds, along with my taste, sense of smell, vision & equilibrium. Ted each day says "If you <u>really</u> want to cure yourself . . .": each day the cure is different: no food (he specializes in this cure!) & orange juice & lukewarm water. Or honey & vinegar (I found a dead fly in his potion of this today). Or lots of brandy. I have been following this one. Ted joins me in sending much love to the two of you.

Sylvia

TO *Aurelia Schober Plath*

Thursday 13 October 1960 TLS, Indiana University

Thursday: October 13

Dear mother,

Well, the god of Britannia has sent us two consecutive days of October's bright blue weather. Unfortunately I haven't been able to have the baby out as she is still snuffly-nosed and I want her to be completely better before I expose her to the cold air. Did I ever tell you her surprising passion for ice cream? A couple of weeks ago on a Sunday Ted & I walked out to a pleasant Regents Park open-air coffee house and got some vanilla icecream. As a joke I held it up to the baby's mouth and she started to eat it, mooshing it over her face, but really liking it. She is very good in the day with her cold, but fussy at night, waking us up a couple of times or so.

I am almost all better, with the little cough in the morning and left-over lassitude I always have after a cold, but in good spirits. Ted is using the Merwin's study this month till Bill comes home while our lady upstairs makes up her mind if she'll let him use her place while she's out. She has portly gentlemen come up with her on occasion & a leaning toward untidiness which I think she would prefer to have kept private. If she says no, we'll advertise around the square: I'm sure some working person would be glad to have a little money for use of their room while they're out. I had a rather nondescript story accepted by the London Magazine today, called "The Fifty-ninth Bear"[1]---a fictionalized account of our bear episode last summer. It will mean between $50 to $75. I also should have poems out in the Kenyon Review & Hudson Review (although the latter may not be out till winter) & a story in the autumn Sewanee Review. Look them up among the BU periodicals & tell me if they're there. I'm curious. * I'm enclosing the check for $25 from the Kenyon for deposit in our Boston account, plus a little check made out to you to very partially go toward the Smith dues & pressure cooker plugs. Also a couple of snapshots[2] of the baby taken by Marcia Momtchiloff, not very good as they make her look much fatter than she is, but quite recent.

*Also inserting a $140 check from Sewanee Review which just arrived.

Dr. Gulbrandsen sent us an awfully sweet letter with some poems he'd written. Not poems, really, but little essays. I miss him. Do tell him so. And say on our return to America for a visit we will see him first off to have the ravages of English dentists repaired! We'll write him when we get a moment. Also a sweet birthday card from Aunt Frieda. I'm going to have that set of snaps I sent you last made up for her: evidently she and Walter as selling their cosy little home. She sounds happy about the move to a big trailer.[3]

Do secretly check up on Ted's play at the Poets Theater. They may be only going to give it a reading. But if it is going to be performed this month, find out at which theater and for how long.

Marcia is coming this Friday---I'm going to make some Vienna tarts in appreciation---with her portable sewing machine, so I can sew up the nightie & dress I have cut out & learn the few snaggy things like collars &

1–Sylvia Plath, 'The Fifth-Ninth Bear', *London Magazine* 8 (February 1961): 11–20. See Alan Ross to SP, 12 October 1960; held by Smith College.

2–The photographs are no longer with the letter. However, Momtchiloff shared a photograph she took of SP and Frieda with the editors, which is reproduced in this volume.

3–According to SP's address book, the Heinrichs moved to 130 Thor Road, 1844 Haster Street, Anaheim, California.

bias binding at the back opening. I am going soon to compare Singers & Pfaff machines (a German make) for price & performance---after I learn how to work Marcia's & treat myself to a table model when I have written & sold a story or two. Ted just bought the inside of a very expensive radio (no box) for under $30 & will make a wood box for it. I got lots of French & German stations on it last night & was very excited---could understand almost all the French & some of the German. Hope to hear his 'Rain Horse' story this week.

xxx
Sivvy

PS: would Warren like to be godfather to Frieda? Ted's already asked Olwyn as godmother & she needs a scientific godparent!

TO *George MacBeth*

Wednesday 19 October 1960 TLS, BBC Written Archives Centre

3 Chalcot Square
London N.W.1
October 19, 1960

Dear George,

You are the soul of patience. I am just sending along these four most recent ones[1] which I like better than the ones I last sent you, although you alas may not. Then I shall give you a rest.

Sincerely yours,
Sylvia Plath

George MacBeth
Producer: Talks Department
The British Broadcasting Corporation
Broadcasting House, London W.1

PS: I shall send along a couple of stories to Owen Leeming[2] in a few days.

1–SP submitted 'Leaving Early', 'Magi', 'Candles', and 'Love Letter'. Sylvia Plath, 'Candles' and 'Leaving Early', *The Poet's Voice* (20 November 1960); recorded, 26 October 1960. Sylvia Plath, 'Candles', *The Listener* (17 November 1960): 877.

2–New Zealand-born writer and radio broadcaster Owen Leeming (1930–).

TO *Aurelia Schober Plath*

Thursday 20 October 1960[1] TLS with envelope, Indiana University

Thursday: October 21

Dear mother,

Many thanks for sending the license on to me with the check. You must have all sorts of expenses because of us, & I hesitate to add one more by wondering if you could send me a sheet of 4¢ stamps some time, as we need them for the return-mail envelopes we send with mss. to America. I'll see that as soon as I get a check not sacredly dedicated to our writing account (such as from critical or ladies magazine extracurriculars) that you receive it made out to you & your Hughes expense account! I'm enclosing a $75 check for my four poems in this autumn Hudson Review for deposit in our account, which much be slowly creeping up toward the $6 thousand mark now. I'm dying to know what the interest is! Do tell us as soon as you know. You're an angel to do this bankclerk work for us.

Very mucky weather here. All of us are over our colds, Frieda clear-nosed & merry & no longer waking us up during the night. She is so adorable I hug her & kiss her a hundred time a day. How did you make those little chocolate blancmanges we used to turn upside down on a plate & dig holes in? I am going to try out some milk & egg custards & things for her. She has a fine, unfinicky appetite & seems to like chilled puddings ---I made her a maple cream (according to Rombauer) which she enjoyed. Her voice range is extending & she seems to be talking to herself now, with a great variety of sounds, daas and laas and maas.

My Italian lessons go well, although the office girls simply don't look at their books & forget during the week what they learned in the last lesson. Now we are in changing verb endings (I-you) they are floored, confused, stumped. The Berlitz books have no word of English in them & no grammar explanations, just the questions & answers we learn in class. I am supplementing by listening to a series of 40 Italian lessons over the BBC[2] & have sent for the booklet of lessons that goes with the series. Ted is writing an absolutely marvelous story set in London called "Sparrow Desert", chock-full of description, about a man following a strange girl.

1–Letter misdated by SP.

2–'Italian for Beginners' aired on Mondays at 7:10 p.m. and Fridays at 6:40 p.m. on the BBC Third Programme.

I think it is the best thing he's done & am dying to send it out, as although it is quite long, it should sell like a hotcake. Have you found out anything about his play at the Poets' Theatre?

Do vote for Kennedy! I am disappointed in much of the way he carries on his campaign and absolutely against his program for increased armament expenses, but in his criticism of America, instead of the deaf imbecilic "God's in his Heaven here" attitude of Eisenhower & Nixon, he seems to me well-meaning. And more realistic.

So Sappho is a mouser! She should visit us & she would have a feast. After the six mice we caught & liberated in the most sumptuous gardens we could find around here we have been less troubled.

Had a nice dinner with Danny & Helga Huws last night---she served stuffed red & green peppers & rice & a marvelous apple strudel. We always feast each other. She's expecting a second baby in a month. I finished sewing the details on my first nightie for Frieda & it's exquisite. I can't wait till that girl leaves her sewing machine with me. I did it with no trouble at all.

Love to you & Warren & Sappho . . .

Sivvy

TO *Owen Leeming*

Friday 21 October 1960 TLS, BBC Written Archives Centre

3 Chalcot Square
London N.W.1
October 21, 1960

Owen Leeming, Esq.
THE BRITISH BROADCASTING CORPORATION
Broadcasting House
London W.1

Dear Owen Leeming,

George MacBeth suggested I send along some stories to you, so I'm enclosing these three---THE FIFTEEN DOLLAR EAGLE, JOHNNY PANIC AND THE BIBLE OF DREAMS, and THE FIFITY-NINTH BEAR. The last story has just been accepted by the London Magazine, but I don't imagine they will get around to printing it for a long time.

The first two stories are written in a very slangy and colloquial idiom, with the dialogues in the first meant to be read in a kind of musical or poetically rhythmical interchange. I don't know what your subject taboos are, but have a suspicion they may include much of JOHNNY PANIC, a sort of mental hospital monologue ending up with the religious communion of shock treatment. I'd be very happy to have your criticism of these.

Yours sincerely,
Sylvia Plath

TO *Aurelia Schober Plath*

Wednesday 26 October 1960 — TLS (aerogramme), Indiana University

Wednesday, October 26

Dear mother,

Well, I sent off a heavy packet of two books---one for you and one for Warren---by surface mail yesterday. I would have sent them by air, but the price, even bookrate, was prohibitive as the books are fat and weigh a good deal. I am touched that my publisher got them out in my birthday week after I told him how superstitious I was. I hope the two printing errors[1] toward the end don't upset you as much as they did me! I've marked the corrections in your books and am appalled that after several proofreadings I was guilty of letting them get through, but Ted has reassured me about them & you do too. I am delighted with the color of the cover---the rich green oblong, white jacket & black and white lettering, and the way the green cover inside matches, with the gold letters. It is a nice fat book which takes up 3/4 of an inch on the shelf and I think they did a handsome job of it. Of course it isn't officially out here yet, but it should be in a week or so. I've ordered some more copies to send to friends & mailed one to Mrs. Prouty when I mailed yours, and will send to Marcia Plumer, Mr. Crockett etc. when I get the next lot---an expensive business, for after the first free 6 we have to pay a percentage of the price, but it's one of the few times one can be generous in an original way.[2]

1–'Mussel Hunter at Rock Harbor' ('air thatching' for 'airy thatching') and 'Sculptor' ('soldier repose' for 'solider repose') contain the typographical errors. See SP to Judith Jones, 5 April 1961.

2–SP wrote a cheque to Heinemann for £5 for her books on 27 October 1960. Signed copies were sent to or given to the following: Aurelia Schober Plath, Warren Plath, Ted Hughes, Olive Higgins Prouty, Charles Monteith, Ruth Beuscher, Wilbury Crockett, and Theodore Roethke (each now held privately); William and Edith Hughes (sold via Christie's auction in 1998 for $11,500); Olwyn Hughes (held by Washington University, St Louis); the Merwins

I had a card from Mrs. Cantor saying she would call between planes this afternoon, but will have to let Ted be my message bearer, as I am scheduled to go to the British Broadcasting Company to record two of my new poems (post-book) which they finally accepted after rejecting two groups[1] from my book. I am very pleased about this. One poem is a monologue from the point of view of a man about the flowers in the lady's room upstairs (where we aren't working any more---her visitors are something she wants to keep secret. Luckily for us, Ted has started working in the windowless box of our little hall which has just room for a chair and bureau and is doing wonderfully there---unlike me, he is better off without windows.) The other poem is about candles & reminiscences of grammy & grampy in Austria spoken while nursing Frieda by candlelight at 2 am. I'm very fond it.

Last night Ted & I went to dinner at Stephen Spender's house with an artist, the poet Louis MacNiece & one of his girlfriends, the novelist, ageing, with violet-white hair, Rosamond Lehmann[2] (one of the wellknown Lehmann family---her brother John being editor of the London Magazine & her sister Beatrix[3] being an actress.) Their conversation is fascinating ---all about Virginia (Woolf), what Hugh (Gaitskell) said to Stephen in Piccadilly that morning, why Wystan (WH Auden) likes this book or that, how Lloyd George[4] broke Spender's father's heart, and suchlike. Rosamond Lehmann's childhood was spent among such house-visitors as Browning, Schumann, or at least among memories of their visits---that whole old world surrounding them like a vision.

I received the lovely package with Frieda's things & the thoughtful pressure-cooker rim inclusion. Dot's pink sweater is lovely, & I'll write her about it,[5] as well as Mrs. Spaulding.

Frieda looks very well in pink, yellow & white, as well as blue. Mrs. S's sweater is lovely, only I do wish it were another color! The pajamas are wonderful. I put her in a pair of them, and although they are big, they are perfectly fine for her to start wearing now in this chilly weather. The builtin

---

(held by Morgan Library); Mike and Marcia Plumer (held by Smith College); Máire and Jack Sweeney (University College, Dublin); and Lucas Myers (offered for sale in 2017).

1–In addition to the poems SP submitted to MacBeth on 9 July 1960, she sent: 'The Eye-mote', 'Aftermath', 'Ouija', 'The Beekeeper's Daughter', 'The Ghost's Leavetaking', 'Departure', 'Frog Autumn', and 'Moonrise'; undated on her submissions list.

2–English novelist Rosamond Lehmann (1901–90).

3–English actress Beatrix Lehmann (1903–79).

4–Welsh Liberal politican David Lloyd George (1863–1945), British prime minister 1916–22.

5–See SP to Joseph and Dorothy Benotti and Frank Schober, 19 November 1960.

feet are good, too, as she always kicks off her booties. She's marvelous, better than ever, going Lalala and dadada to her bear, whom she loves to pummel and dance about over her head. She is just beginning to creep, a sort of combined on-all-fours rock with squirms and pushes. She loves books of all sorts. Ted taught her to beat on them like a drum and he does it three times & she does it three times and bursts out laughing. I think she will very soon enjoy cloth books. If I want to keep her quiet a minute while I change her I give her an envelope or card and she is immediately engrossed---of course she always ends up trying to eat it!

Ted & I are thinking of dividing up our trip abroad by 6 weeks in Italy & six weeks in Austria (which would be about Mayish if we do go this year). Where would you recommend? What's that Inn like you spoke of my relatives having? Of course we would pay! What parts are most beautiful in Innsbruck? What time do the Alpine flowers bloom? Do tell us if there is anything you'd recommend!

Ted's income from the BBC this year has been as good as a salary ---we've about $1,600 in the bank here from our English writing & he has an exciting prospect of doing broadcasts for school children which would go all over England with no paper-correcting or the personal drag of actual classroom teaching, which I hope he takes up. Love to you and Warrie from Ted, Frieda & me. Our names for our next 3 children by the way, are Megan (for a girl, nickname Meg) Nicholas & Jacob. How do you like them?

xxx
Sivvy

TO *Olwyn Hughes*

Thursday 27 October 1960[1] ALS,[2] British Library

Dear Olwyn –

I'll just add a note. I've been having a lovely birthday week to console me for catapulting so swiftly towards thirty. Woke this morning surrounded by lumpish brown packages each with a rhyme attached, a candle burning in the middle of a german coffeecake, Frieda sitting up, helped by Ted, on the bed holding the morning's mail & a bar of chocolate. We're immensely happy just now – not a fleeting thing but a sense of slowly getting toward

1 – Date supplied from internal evidence.
2 – SP's letter is at the end of a letter begun by TH, which has not been transcribed.

what we want & knowing what we want. Ted's hall study is a life saver, reproducing womb-like isolation, darkness & regular infusions of tea. I'm very excited about this story he is doing, 'Sparrow Desert' & I think he 'gets' London better than any other words about it I've read, masters it & serves it up. We're happy with my fat book in spite of 2 typographical errors we let slip which appalled me at first. You'll have an inscribed copy the minute I get the extras I ordered – in a few days, I hope. You have a fingerprint in the book – that verse you suggested I omit from 'The Ghost's Leavetaking' being junked to the poem's advantage, I think. I'm more tolerant of Spender than Ted – or corrupt enough to be amused by him & a bit fond of him – I very much like & admire his wife Natasha – a handsome & keen creature. We're looking forward already to Xmas & seeing you.

Love,
Sylvia

P.S. I think Janos'[1] play superb & he a very dear fellow. Frieda says La la la & agrees

xx

TO *Aurelia Schober Plath*

Friday 28 October 1960 TLS, Indiana University

October 28, 1960

Dear mother . . .

I think this birthday has been the best of all. I woke yesterday morning to find myself lying surrounded by interesting knobbly brown parcels, a german coffeecake with a candle lit in the middle of it, and Frieda sitting at my side, supported by Ted, holding the morning's mail and a bar of my favorite German chocolate. Ted really knocked himself out: I have a new badly needed pair of red plush slippers lined with white fuzzy wool, <u>two</u> pairs of plastic overshoes, one for heels, as Ted wanted me to have something easily carried about for this showery London weather, a Fortnum & Mason chicken pie (our standby for special occasions), a bottle of pink champagne, the Tolkien Trilogy <u>Lord of the Rings</u>[2] (the adult version & extension of my beloved <u>Hobbit</u>)---this for Frieda & me,

1–János Csokits.

2–SP's copy of the Tolkien trilogy, inscribed by TH, appeared at auction via Bonhams on 21 March 2018.

and three wonderful slabs of strange cheeses for us to test. A gooey ripe brie, a superbly mouldy blue stilton & a fat round Wensleydale in a cloth sack all its own. I loved the cards & letters from you & Warren. I consider the load of pajamas for Frieda my present from you---I'd so much rather get something for her. Betty A's suggestion of wearing pj's in the day is something I'm already doing---she's draft-tight then.

Frieda had her second polio shot this week & my kind doctor said he'd fit me up with a medical kit & advice when we go to Europe. I am happier living in London than anywhere else in the world, particularly in this corner, and we have our eye on Chalcot Crescent, a quiet attractive & utterly unique street around the corner from us for a house. We are both so pleased even with our too-small flat that a house in this neighborhood would be wonderful. We are using our winter-season passes to the Zoo to good advantage. The owls look at Frieda and she looks at them. I think she would love cloth books. She crawls all the way down to the bottom of her crib to pat Little Boy Blue's face (he is painted at the foot), while smiling & cooing, and adores playing with the labels sewn on her blankets.

I do wish Betty hadn't said she was a friend of the family at the Poets Theatre. We wanted to find out about this in <u>absolute</u> secrecy, which you could have done by simply asking for their fall program. The whole point was to have them not know we were inquiring about it or telling anyone. Well, better let the affair drop now. We made out the last little $4 check to you because we don't like to feel our requests are slowly bleeding you for money & it is very helpful for you to do small things for us which keep us from the pother of getting international money orders, etc. Thus we're enclosing another check (we don't want to pollute our writing account with things not from writing) made out to you to cover Ted's application for a renewal of his reentry permit. Could you enclose the permit, a check for $10 made out to the Immigration Office (it says exactly the words for this on the back of the permit) and the witnessed application in an envelope & get it to the address in Boston (or whatever---Ted has the blank at the moment so I don't know exactly) by the Nov. 4th date? Sorry to trouble you about this. And thanks so much for the big sheet of 4¢ stamps.

Ignore this – we're sending the forms to Germany, as the Consul told Ted to[1]

Keep the check for past & future expenses

1–This sentence and the next added in the margin by SP.

My main desire now is to get a sewing machine. I have set myself the task of getting it by some commercial means---not just by literary poems and stories. Well, I should have $50 for my reading & recording 2 new poems at the BBC and possibly the same amount for recording poems for the Lamont library, so maybe will put that toward it. I hate the new plastic-looking singer models & will try to get a second-hand, electric run table-model (one you put on a table) of the old black gilt-trimmed variety which I like. When that money comes in. They have lots of good second-hand machines here.

Tuesday night we are going to the annual Guinness Awards champagne party (the award Ted got while in America) which should be fun. Hope you get my book in good order. Tell me what you think of it.

Lots of love to you & Warren,
Sivvy

TO *Aurelia Schober Plath*

Sunday 6 November 1960 — TLS with envelope, Indiana University

3 Chalcot Square
London N.W.1
October (excuse me,
November 6: Sunday)

Dear Mother,

I'm enclosing two of the latest shots of the Pooker, alias Bunzo Bun.[1] She is patiently playing with the old toys---rattles, teething ring, plastic spoons---but eager for new things, especially anything with pictures on it. For treats she has her little Bunzo Bear, who she knocks about and hugs, and her silver cup and a cowrie shell. She sings now, a little high voice and funny look, and talks and answers us by making Brr noises. I found out that the girl on the first floor, expecting a baby any day now, had borrowed a sewing machine, so took advantage of her generosity and nipped down a few afternoons this week to sew my second venture for Frieda---a brilliant blue linen dress with a trimming of continental embroidery on the hem and waist (I made this up, taking my clue from Helga, who also uses these tapes---they ensure an absolutely original dress) of pink and yellow flowers on the same blue ground. It is very

1–The photographs are no longer with the letter.

handsome and styled like this: <drawing of a child's dress> I went to look at Simplicity patterns yesterday and drooled at a whole series of "Tyrol" outfits---black bodices, full bright-colored skirts and white blouses. Most of course were for 2, 3 & 4 year-olds. I have my eye on a nice pattern for the 2 yards of red Viyella I bought. I hope I can get a good 2nd hand singer for about $90. The new ones (horrible looking) cost over $300! I hate the modern design & like the old black models with gold filigree painted on them---like grammy's. It's amazing how hard it is to get really nice solid-color children's dresses unless you get expensive imported ones for $10 to $15.

I gather you are going to the reading of Ted's play. Do let us know what you think of it and just how they do it. He is now working on the rewriting of the libretto of the Tibetan Book of the Dead for that Chinese composer. He is very encouraged about it and really mastering it now. I think we'll go up to Yorkshire over the weekend, as he has been asked to be present at a literary luncheon in Leeds about northern writers which will be put on television, with John Betjemann's[1] program. I hope he gets his face into the screen! Then he has a lecture at the University of Hull. We both feel to need a weekend holiday.

Last week we went to the annual Guinness awards at the famous Goldsmith's Hall[2] in the City---drank lots of champagne, heard who got the money this year (Ted got the $850 first prize two years ago) and the poets read their poems. Quite pleasant and amusing. Had Helga and Danny over for a big dinner last night. I made a delicious cream of mushroom soup out of Rombauer, pork, parsley carrots, rice pilaf and a delectable pudding out of Italian chestnuts cooked in milk and brandy, sieved and topped with whipped cream and grated german chocolate. Helga's 2nd baby is due this month, so I wanted them for a little feast beforehand. Thanks very much for the chocolate blancmange recipe. Had a lovely dinner the other night with a young couple[3] around the corner in Chalcot Crescent---where we'd love to live if only a house came up, quiet, pretty, with nice professional families---and neighbors of theirs, a lively older couple[4] on the BBC. I am immensely fond of this neighborhood!

1–Poet Laureate John Betjeman (1906–84); his series *John Betjeman as the Book Man*. The Yorkshire episode aired on 20 November 1960.

2–Goldsmith's Hall is located at Foster Lane and Gresham Street, London. The winners were Thomas Blackburn, David Wright, Louise MacNeice, and R. S. Thomas.

3–Probably Catherine Frankfort and Johannes B. Frankfort, who lived at 18 Chalcot Crescent.

4–Possibly John Sherwood (1913–   ) and Joan M. Sherwood, who lived at 2 Chalcot Crescent.

Love to all
xxx
Sivvy

PS – Got a Press ticket from Stephen Spender for the last day of the Lady Chatterley trials[1] at the Old Bailey – very exciting – especially with the surprising verdict of 'not guilty' so Penguin books can publish the unexpurgated edition – a heartening advance for DH Lawrence's writings!

TO Atlantic Monthly

Monday 7 November 1960[2] TLS,[3] Yale University

Four poems and two versifications,[4] the latter (Words for a Nursery and Home Thoughts from London) meant to be submitted to Accent on Living.

sp

TO *Ruth Tiffany Barnhouse Beuscher*

Monday 7 November 1960 TLS, Smith College

3 Chalcot Square
London N.W.1
November 7, 1960

Dear Dr. Beuscher,

I'm enclosing a picture of our Frieda,[5] together with her pet Bear, whom she likes to hug, pummel and sing to. She is the most exciting thing that's happened to us---very bouncy, healthy, full of chuckles and a lovely responsive sense of humor. She has conversations with us---going

1–SP attended the second day of the obscenity trial for *Lady Chatterley's Lover*, held on 27 October 1960 at the Old Bailey in London. Witnesses for the defense included Graham Goulden Hough, Dame Helen Louise Gardner, Joan Bennett, Dame Rebecca West, John A. T. Robinson (bishop of Woolwich), Vivian de Sola Pinto, Rev. Alfred Stephan Hopkinson, and Richard Hoggart. See SP's notes in *Journals of Sylvia Plath*: 595–9.
2–Date supplied.
3–Letter typewritten on piece of scrap paper; possibly an envelope.
4–The poems Plath submitted were: 'Leaving Early', 'Candles', 'Magi', 'Love Letter', 'Home Thoughts from London', and 'Words for a Nursery'. SP's submissions list records that the poems were sent on 7 November 1960. The only extant typescript of 'Home Thoughts from London' is on the verso of her later poem 'Wuthering Heights'; held by Lilly Library.
5–The photograph is no longer with the letter.

variously Brrr or Dadada or simply opening her mouth and singing Ahhh when we sing to her. Both Ted and I are converted to little girls and have names for at least a couple more, in addition to our list of boy's names. I've found myself surprisingly fascinated by Singer sewing machines---one of those formerly unnoticed objects---and by sniffing out one or two in the homes of friends, have made Frieda a nightgown and a smashing bright blue linen dress bordered with those handsome continental embroidered tapes and have material and ideas for a whole wardrobe. It's almost impossible to get handsome solid-color clothes for little girls, or good patterned clothes, unless you buy expensive imported things---all the year-old gift dresses waiting in Frieda's drawer are white nylon or orlon or such with candy-pink or baby-blue smocking. Ted's promised me money for a 2nd-hand Singer from his radio play so I hope to be sewing in earnest by Christmas. I love the chance to do original dresses for very low prices & look forward to dressing Frieda's dolls & extending my range.

I've sent along to you by snailpace sea-post, a copy of my book of poems THE COLOSSUS---many of which, especially the father ones, I wrote while seeing you that year we lived in Boston.[1] I'm very pleased with the way they produced it, and hope someday it may come out in America, although the firms my publisher has sent it to have proved adamant so far. I haven't written much at all this last year---mainly a few light things for the New Yorker & Harper's & two poems I'm reading over the BBC, but I now feel to be emerging from my cowlike six months of amaze over Frieda and able to abstract myself enough to write half a day. I'm still nursing her, which pleases me very much: it's been one of the happiest experiences of my life. I didn't know what I was missing, really, in not having children, & now only look forward to buying a house big enough to hold as many as we want, with enough rooms so I can shout to Ted in his study from the nursery or kitchen and he be far off and in such peace he can't hear. He now valiantly works in our windowless hall which is womblike and utterly without distraction, and gets an immense amount done, which makes me happy---he likes the comfort of working at home, being slipped cups of tea and so on. This week he is going to Leeds to be on John Betjemann's program---a literary luncheon stressing northern writers. I hope he gets his face on the screen! To Ted's mother, appearing on television with that best-selling nonpoet Betjemann would

1–See journal 12 December 1958–15 November 1959 in *The Journals of Sylvia Plath* (2000).

be the height of Ted's career. Oh, I'll also stick in a copy of a clipping[1] that I'm proud of, taken at a Faber party---Ted where he should be. TS Eliot is quite fond of him & we had a wonderful dinner at his place last spring, which I may have mentioned to you. I honestly felt in the presence of a holy being. (The bit in the article about the baby is a quote from me, by the way.)[2]

Ted & I are very tentatively thinking of going to Corsica this spring to spend his travel grant, if I don't get an interesting enough part-time job beforehand & if the baby is in good health. Do you have any practical advice about travel or living abroad with a one-year-old? Most of my friends groan when I suggest it & say babies are into everything & very difficult & transitional at that stage. We could, of course, wait half a year, but ideally would like to go this spring, partly because we need to draw the money & partly because it's such a nice time of year. My doctor says "don't trust Italian doctors" and promises to fit me up with a medical kit. I am most moved and admiring of the medical treatment Frieda & I have been getting for free over here and particularly in favor of socialized medicine for old people---the doctors I've been to are also very much in favor of it. It's ideal for Ted & I not to have a looming bill for each baby we want---I'm sure we'll have more here than we would have in America!

Both of us are enjoying London a great deal; we've winter-season tickets to the zoo and go at least once a week. Frieda and the owls eye each other in amaze; I do think she outstares them. Ted's just done a story set mainly in the zoo which we hope to sell in America. I wangled a press pass from Stephen Spender the other night to the last day of the Lady Chatterley trials at the Old Bailey. I was delighted to be there, only sorry I'd missed the days of famous witnesses---stayed from about 10:30 to 3, when the surprising verdict of "not guilty" came from the unpromising prosperous middleclass looking jury after a very biased, sneering summing up by the judge[3] who tried to influence the jury against the "egghead" witnesses. The court (the famous Number One) was small and jammed. I had lunch in a lovely little dark Fleet Street pub with a girl reporter and an American free-lance journalist, listened to the cases of arson, rape, etc. sandwiched in before the jury returned, and enjoyed my day-out immensely. Ted is

1–The clipping is no longer with the letter.

2–Philip Day's 'A Pride of Poets' (cited earlier) reads, in part, 'Waiters with trays edge through the talkative throng. "What, off to New York tomorrow?" "Give America my love-hate." . . . "My dear, I'm *so* pleased your husband won the award. When are you going abroad to celebrate it?" "Well, not till the baby can appreciate Europe a bit better."' (6).

3–Irish-born barrister and High Court judge Sir Laurence Byrne (1896–1965).

an angel about my excursions, feeds Frieda lunch and so on. The main thing we miss is going out together as much as we used to. We do have babysitters, but not as often as we'd like. However, we're together so much that it's probably a good thing for us to explore London separately.

I've been taking lessons in conversational Italian two nights a week at the Berlitz school here in preparation for our trip and hope to really develop my reading knowledge of Italian, French and German, while practising speaking in trips to the continent. I've always wanted to be able to read these languages and now have a good chance, living so near to the countries in question.

You'll be getting a copy of Ted's MEET MY FOLKS! sometime this spring---it should be out around Frieda's first birthday, and probably one or more of your boys will be of an age to be amused by it. Do tell me about your fifth---boy or girl, name and so on. Does your housekeeper, by the way, do all the things like laundry, dishes, cooking and so on? Looking ahead into the far future when we may have managed a house, I would probably want someone at least to take over for 4-5 hours in the morning do chores & mind babies. I find I don't need a full day---only the first half and a quiet evening---to feel I am leading my own mental & creative life. Then I am absolutely unfazed by domesticalia.

Best love to you,
sylvia

TO *Owen Leeming*

Friday 18 November 1960 TLS,[4] BBC Written Archives Centre

3 Chalcot Square
London N.W.1
November 18, 1960

Dear Owen,

Thanks for your letter. I think it would probably be most helpful for me to come in and talk when I have another batch of stories to dig into.

4–TH added a note at the bottom of the letter, which has not been transcribed. TH commented that although he had sent off the story that SP mentions to a magazine he thought Leeming might be interested in seeing it as well.

Meanwhile, I'm taking the opportunity of enclosing a story[1] Ted wanted you to see.

Sincerely,
Sylvia Plath

TO *Aurelia Schober Plath & Warren Plath*

Saturday 19 November 1960 TLS (aerogramme), Indiana University

Saturday, November 19

Dear mother & Warren,

I feel I haven't written you for ages, which is probably true. Frieda has been teething---she has her lower front right tooth through and the one next to it coming in, and cries off and on all night---great miserable yowls impossible to ignore, and the one thing that seems to comfort her is nursing. Luckily I am still nursing her, it would be ghastly to have to make up bottles. She drinks very well from a tiny cup she has when I hold it for her. I got a sort of soothing syrup from the doctor & tried children's asprin in orange juice, but nothing seems to stop her 2 or 3 am crying bout. I'll probably see the doctor again this week. I only hope she isn't like this with every tooth. During the day she seems to find comfort in chewing on ovaltine rusks---at least this stops her crying. She is creeping all about now, banging on an overturned cake tin like a drum, and when we say "Kiss your mummy", she puts her little face to my cheek and goes "Mmmmm". This is the sweetest thing she does. I am amazed that she seems to understand what we say.

Don't worry about the pajamas fitting her: they have tons of room yet. She'll be growing into them for half a year yet, and they are wonderfully convenient, as I keep her in them and a sweater in the daytime. I've just written to Dotty today about the pink sweater thanking her. I don't know if I said in my last letter that my book costs about $2.15 (15 shillings) here, very reasonable compared to American prices, and my publisher is Wm. Heinemann, 15-16 Queen Street, London W.1. Since I got no prize or any American publisher, they haven't bothered to advertise it, so I probably won't make a penny on it unless I get some award later to call it to the public's attention---the 10 extra copies I ordered more than cancelled out my tiny pre-publication sale. Well, it's a nice gift book. I'm glad your

1–Probably Ted Hughes, 'The Harvesting'.

copies arrived safely. My publisher thought the acknowledgements were superfluous---only one or two magazines require them, and usually they are put in as a kind of courtesy to the magazines and bolstering of the writer's ego. I'm glad they didn't---my list was so long it would have looked ostentatious. Both of us are getting more retiring about blazoning biographies & publication-notices everywhere. Ted didn't go to the TV dinner after all. His radio play was broadcast Wednesday night with two star actors[1] from West End plays now on in London in the leading roles (from "The Caretaker" and "Passage to India" respectively), and in addition to being reviewed in the next day's Times,[2] the panel of Sunday critics[3] on the radio will review it, & it's been reviewed already over the radio Thursday on a program called Comment.[4] Ted hates such a feeling that the critics are almost ready to snatch his work out of his hand, and I can sympathize with him. He has finished with his scheduled talks, lectures and commissions at last and is now free to work on his three-act play and I shall see he is kept clear of all distractions. His broadcast translation of a passage from the Odyssey was very well reviewed in the Sunday papers,[5] and I am going to hear myself read two poems over the radio Sunday night, so it has been a full week.

I hate to bother you about this again, but could you look around once more for that yellow paperbound Speedwriting book or beg, borrow or steal another copy & airmail it to me? I have or might have a chance at quite an amusing job later this year if I brushed up my speedwriting which stood me in excellent stead with that exacting head of Harvard's Sanskrit Department. It may be in my bookcase, drawers, closet or even down in the basement in a pile of notebooks. Could you pretend some reason for getting a copy as you did before? I never will need shorthand as this would cover all my needs. I'm dying to get hold of it.

I sprained my foot last week running for a bus in the dark on a wet night---at first I thought it was broken but the xray showed it wasn't. It swelled alarmingly, but is ok now. My doctor (a very handsome psychiatrist also on my panel whom I hadn't met before) told me of a house that will be coming up for sale in The Crescent, right around the

1–The readers for *House of Aries* included Diana Olsson, Peter Woodthorpe (*The Caretaker* by Harold Pinter), and Norman Wooland (*A Passage to India*; E. M. Forster's novel adapted for the stage by Santha Rama Rau).
2–'A Dramatic Poem About Violence', *The Times* (17 November 1960): 16.
3–Reviewed by Cyril Ray, *The Critics*, BBC Talks Department (20 November 1960).
4–Reviewed by Karl Miller, *Comment*, BBC Talks Department (17 November 1960).
5–Paul Ferris, 'Radio Notes', *The Observer* (13 November 1961): 30.

corner, a charming street unlike anything around here with Primrose Hill visible at the end of it. It costs, I gather, about 7 thousand pounds & the lady may have already promised it to someone, but I'm going over to see her this week I think as part of my program of investigating everything that comes up in this district. We will really need a house of our own after our lease is up here & I'd like more room for Frieda and more babies! It seems impossible to manage at this point, but who knows what Ted will have written in a year's time. We are thinking of postponing our months in Corsica till a year from this spring, when Frieda is talking and walking.

Much love to you both from the three of us,

Sivvy

TO *Joseph & Dorothy Benotti & Frank Schober*

Saturday 19 November 1960 TLS (aerogramme), Indiana University

3 Chalcot Square
London N.W.1, England
November 19, 1960

Dear Dotty, Joe & Grampy,

It was so good to get your newsy letter. I love hearing about your doings and Bobby and Nancy, and only wish I had a private jet service so I could get over to see you all for the Christmas holidays! The adorable pink sweater arrived for Frieda, Dotty, and she looks wonderful in it---a very becoming color. A sweater is the most-needed thing for a baby in this climate with no central heating. We loved the little cup, too, and Frieda is drinking from it, with help and me holding it. (I don't think there were two cards in the packet, for I looked through---maybe they forgot. Anyhow, a thousand thanks for the cup. Don't worry about the Rebecca on it: everybody who put names on anything put Rebecca and it was our fault because we didn't know till she was born that she would be called Frieda!)

Frieda is teething now and very upset by it: she cries off and on in the night and Ted and I are getting a bit haggard. During the day she is an angel, with a big appetite and funny little games. She creeps all round her pen, bangs on an over-turned cake tin like a drum, and when we say "Kiss your mummy" she puts her face to my cheek and goes "Mmmmmmm" with a little smack. She is a doll.

Ted had his hour-long play on this week and it will be broadcast again in December. I went to the final rehearsal last Sunday and was very excited. They had two "name" actors who are currently in West End productions (the stars, no less) read two of the main rolls. Anything he does now is jumped on and noticed: this play is being reviewed over the radio Sunday by the weekly panel of critics and has already been reviewed in another program called Comment. Ted had a Greek translation on the radio this week too which was favorably reviewed in the papers, & I'm reading two poems on a program Sunday night. It's lots of fun to tune in and hear people doing our stuff! Now Ted's working on a three-act play. Maybe someday you'll be able to go see his plays on Broadway! Anyhow, he loves his work.

We hear Grampy had a super-gorgeous pre-birthday dinner in Concord. Wish we could have been there.

Much love to all,
Sylvia

TO *Aurelia Schober Plath*

Friday 25 November 1960 TLS, Indiana University

3 Chalcot Square
London N.W.1
November 25, 1960

Dear mother . . .

First of all, tell Warren how proud Ted & I are that he passed his Orals! From our permanent vacation over here he sounds to be performing Herculean labors. How much chance is there that he might come to London for that conference---can he apply for it? We would be overwhelmed with joy if he could come. He would be knocked silly by little Frieda. She has two small scallop-edged teeth in the bottom front of her mouth now and is just the sweetest tempered funny thing---she stood up yesterday! We were aghast, as she doesn't sit up by herself yet. She saw the colored beads on her playpen, pulled herself up on her knees to reach them by tugging on the bars, and then onto her feet. Of course she didn't know what to do then, and Ted caught her in time. I hope she'll leave that trick alone for a while yet. I've had her vaccinated the second time this week and hope it takes, as it's a bore to keep her out of the tub. She loves her baths now and kicks so hard water flies all over me and the room. She eats rusks by hand now and I can always quiet her with one of those. One of her favorite pastimes is banging at her reflection in a shiny pie tin with her hand or any noisy object she can get hold of. She is crammed full of giggles, singing, talking and sweet expressions.

I'm enclosing another cheque for our Boston account from the New Yorker for a poem of Ted's.[1]

Mrs. Prouty sent me a cheque for $150 to celebrate the publication of my book, the dear thing. I won't earn another thing on that, so we're putting it toward current expenses. Ted has the best story he's done yet, about a fat man shooting rabbits at harvest-time[2] accepted by the BBC today, which will mean a nice sum---he'll read it, and then it will probably be played twice, once in Christmas week. It's a dazzling story. I'm going to send it to magazines in America now.

I caught a nasty cold somehow yesterday and am nursing it today. We have tickets to Chin-Chin,[3] a play translated from the French, tonight, so I'm hoping that will help me forget my sniffles.

Dido has leant (loaned) me an old hand-wind Singer out of her attic, so I'll be able to defer that expense for a while. I wrote Dot, by the way, this last week, and Mrs. Spaulding (the 2nd time) and Mrs. Churchill long ago. They're crazy to ask you to be chairman of the church fair. What about all the wealthy madams who sit about having their fingers manicured during the day?

Helga Huws had a baby this week, her 2nd daughter, Lucy Teresa. I visited her at the hospital and saw the little thing in her nursery---made me want another <u>really</u> small one immediately. I would so like a permanent spacious place where I could have as many children as I wanted!

Let us know how Ted's play sounds.

Lots of love,
Sivvy

1–Howard Moss to TH, 22 November 1960; held by New York Public Library; for Ted Hughes, 'Still Life', *New Yorker* (15 July 1961): 24.

2–Ted Hughes, 'The Harvesting', BBC Third Programme (17 December 1960); re-broadcast (24 January 1961).

3–François Billetdoux, *Tchin-Tchin* (1959); performed under the title *Chin-Chin* from 3 November 1960 to 25 March 1961 at Wyndham's Theatre, 32 Charing Cross Road, London.

TO *Aurelia Schober Plath*

Monday 28 November 1960 TLS (aerogramme), Indiana University

Monday night
November 28

Dearest mother,

I'm sitting here in the late evening, curtains drawn, the little Pifco warming the room cheerily, in my bathrobe, on one of Ted's rare nights out. He has driven to Coventry with Dido Merwin and John Whiting,[1] a playwright, to see Bill Merwin's play at the repertory theatre there, The Golden West, or gilded west.[2] Bill is in America, collecting thousands on lectures & readings. Ted left about 3 and won't be home till 3 or 4 am as its a long drive, so I've had one of my rare, rare times to myself. I realize how crowded we are here when I am alone for a bit, enjoying every minute of it, feeling inclined to do little secret things I like. My cold vanished as quickly as it came without the usual drag, so I'm in pretty good spirits, and the baby didn't catch it. Her vaccination (2nd) looks to be taking well, a big bubble blister, and I'm relieved. We went to dinner last night with the sister of Ted's friend Lucas Meyers (we met the sister, a charming 35ish Southerner with a brilliant English professor husband and a darling little boy after 11 years waiting for a baby) who's here with her husband on a grant,[3] so slept late this morning. I then spent the morning of this invigorating clear blue ideal London day in the estate agents office learning about mortgages, rent controlled tenants, and other details I determined to educate myself about. And collected their list of houses for sale around here. Then went downtown to Piccadilly, under the superb avenue of trumpeting angels on Regent Street (beautifully illuminated at night) to the exhibit of paintings by a Corsican woman[4] I admire in a posh gallery where I amused myself by boldly inquiring the prices of the ones that I liked---all, of course from between 1 to 3 thousand $. Then dashed home in time for Ted to leave. A busy afternoon at the laundromat, shopping, listening to my radio-Italian lesson (a course of 40 the BBC is broadcasting), bathed & fed the baby, & gathered my courage

1–English actor and dramatist John Robert Whiting (1917–63)

2–W. S. Merwin, *The Gilded West*, performed at Belgrade Theatre, Coventry.

3–Marie Elizabeth Jeffreys Myers (1925–) and Calhoun Winton (1927–); married 30 June 1948 in Sewanee, Tennessee. Their son, Jeffreys Winton (1959–).

4–Argentinian surrealist painter Leonor Fini (1907–96); exhibition at the Kaplan Gallery, 6 Duke Street, London, 2 November–3 December 1960.

to take my letter of introduction from one of the dearest doctors on my panel of 5 (the one who came to see about my sprained ankle) and headed around the corner to 4 Chalcot Crescent, just 2 houses & a road away from Primrose Hill, an open sunny quiet street unlike anything else in this district of slum or opulence---modest adorable houses. Dr. Horder[1] had told me---when I impulsively asked him to produce a miracle & put us on to one of these rare sought-after houses in the Crescent, about this house of Mrs. Waley's[2] (sister-in-law to the Chinese translator, Arthur Waley)[3] which she plans to sell in about a year from this January (an ideal time for a move for us!!!) As I said, the dr. told me it would be about 7 thousand pounds, very reasonable for a Park location house you have nothing to do to. Mrs. Waley was at her country house,[4] but a Mrs. Hankin[5] who lived there showed me in. It was love at first sight. My experience of house-viewing and assessing in the past months (I was teething so to speak) has taught me what I want. This was it. A gem. Four floors, about 2 rooms on each floor. The top floor is rented out to two girls & we could rent it for a nice little income until our family grew big enough to use 8 rooms. The basement has a large front room (generally used as kitchen-nursery in the other posh houses around) with big windows, a sturdy kitchen in back overlooking a little cement area roomy enough for baby-carriage & sandbox, and steps up to a charming tiny garden with bay tree, cherry tree & a grape vine Mrs. Hankin makes jam from. The first (ground) floor has a large room made from two small ones, built-in bookcases---the sort you could make a living-room-study or living-room-dinette, beautifully proportioned. A little 2nd kitchen on the landing which could be a sewing room. Then: Two divine bedrooms, the front one with French windows and a balcony from which we could see the moon over Primrose Hill, then (she said) two more bedrooms upstairs. There seemed several toilets & one comfortable bathroom. She knew my name, that Ted had a Somerset Maugham award & seemed congenial, giving me the name & address of Mrs. Waley's country home, so I could ask for "first refusal" & saw me off into the night with "meanwhile, dream your dreams". Oh mother for the first time I saw us living in a house perfectly suited to our needs!

1–Dr John P. Horder (1919–2012). Horder lived at 98 Regent's Park Road, London.
2–Margaret Hendella Waley (1896–1988) and her husband Hubert David Waley (1892–1967) lived at 4 Chalcot Crescent according to the *1960 London Electoral Register*.
3–English orientalist Arthur David Waley (1889–1966).
4–In SP's address book, there is an address for Mrs Waley, which is Beachy Ride, Great Cheverell, near Devizes, Wiltshire.
5–According to the *1960 London Electoral Register*, Agnes M. Hankin was a resident of 4 Chalcot Crescent with the Waleys.

I do so want at least four children & am head over heels in love with London. We have well over 7 thousand $ saved now, & with furious work & luck might manage enough in a year's time to make about between a half & third downpayment. A 3 thous. pound 20-year mortgage would only amount to under $500 rent a year or so, if I calculate right, less rent than we pay now for our cram-jammed place! What do you think of this? As Ted lets me go ahead, I have to do all the learning myself. The house is attractively enough decorated & painted so we'd have to do nothing for a start & could gradually add bits of furniture. I feel cool-headed about this & its location is not-yet-discovered---except by a few people. Ive already met two families of our would-be neighbours & love them: a street of youngish, quiet, family-centred professional people: BBC, psychiatrist, artist etc. I am working very hard now on something I never really attacked right: women's magazine stories. Very rusty and awkward on my first, I got into the swing & am half through my second with a plot for a 3rd Ted & I worked out together called "House of My Heart". I also have a fine lively agent[1] (who wrote me about a story of mine in the London Magazine) whom I've met & who is affiliated with one of the best NYC agencies & so after I get my earliest acceptances in the many women's weeklies here, they'll send any stuff good enough to the SatEvePost, etc. For the first time I feel I know where I'm going---a couple of American sales could make the house a reality! Do write me about your thoughts on this house – a year just gives us time to gather forces & $$$.

xxx

S.

<on page 1 of letter>

PS – The front rooms on each floor of the house are central heated!

Frieda is fine – more fun every day. I'm just wild about her & after seeing Helga's 2nd daughter, dying to have space for another <u>really</u> little one!

<on the address side of letter>

PS Where's my <u>New Yorker</u>??? No sign of it yet!

1 – Probably Jennifer Hassell, who worked for A. M. Heath & Co., 35 Dover Street, London.

TO *Olwyn Hughes*

Monday 28 November 1960[1] ALS,[2] British Library

Dear Olwyn –

Ted only left me the barest fringe. Saw a superb exhibit today of the paintings of the fabulous Léonor Fini who divides her time between Corsica & Paris – Do you know her work? She's a polyglot herself, given to wearing animal masks about the house & has – among some bad stuff – jewel-like misty otherworldish damsels & cadavers with a wierd, terrifying beauty, like necrological mannequins – I'd like to pay a pilgrimage to her Corsican monastery – reachable only by donkey. We're suffering late autumn exhausture & blues & eager for the cowlike peace of Yorks. at Christmas.

xxx
Sylvia

TO *Aurelia Schober Plath & Warren Plath*

Wednesday 14 December 1960[3] TLS in greeting card,[4] Indiana University

<printed greeting>
Greetings / for / Christmas / and / the New Year

Dear mother & Warren . . .

I am writing this on the eve of our departure to Yorkshire: both of us are dying to go, recharge our batteries, and come back ready for intense work by New Year's Day, brimful of energy to carry out our projected ideas. I am writing in a litter of BBC contracts, Christmas cards and Frieda's winter clothes, having just read a poem for a book-review of my book over the radio[5] (which will be broadcast next week, a day after Ted's story, "The Harvesting"). All in all, his play brought in about $600 from its two radio performances, which was worth it. Don't take his elaborate metaphysical

1–Date supplied from internal evidence.
2–SP's letter is at the end of a letter begun by TH, which has not been transcribed.
3–Date supplied from postmark.
4–Christmas card printed by Greenslade & Co. (Reading).
5–Edward Lucie-Smith, *New Poetry*, BBC Third Programme (18 December 1960); included in the programme were 'A Winter Ship' and seven lines from 'The Colossus'. The BBC booking form states that rehearsal and pre-recording took place on 13 December 1960.

explanations too seriously and don't show them to anyone.[1] He is so critical of the play---which I think reads perfectly as a symbolic invasion of private lives and dreams by mechanical war-law and inhumanity such as is behind the germ-warfare laboratory in Maryland---that he feels a need to invent elaborate disguises as a smokescreen for it. Both of us have emerged with heads above water after a deeply demanding year and are eager to plunge into our "new" lives of writing and private forays on London's wonders.

I must confess I opened your marvelous parcel which arrived yesterday so I could sort out what things to take to Yorkshire. I hope you'll forgive my practicality, but we have an immense deal to lug up there. I am stunned and delighted with Frieda's things! Ours of course---shirt, tights, slip & the good books, are fine, but you should see Ted: "Let's open Frieda's now!" We're both happiest with things for her. She loves her Raggedy Ann, Warren. Laughs at it and fingers the button eyes. And loves the squeaky chicken: she holds it up to me for me to make the noise by pressing it, and bangs it on the floor herself to make the peeps. The rag books are a godsend: I shall ration these myself. And the pajamas roomy (very---should last months). I'm mad for the slacks---especially the ones with pointed toes & pompons! Dot sent 10$ which arrived safely (I told her so on the envelope of her Xmas card) & I bought a handsome pale blue wool sleeping bag with it which converts to a bathrobe when they outgrow the bag bottom---I'll use this as a winter coat and pram suit. I bought her a bright red peaked pixie cap & she looks like Infant Christmas in it.

I hope your presents arrive in time. They are separate---the big box is for you, mother, the smaller for Warren. I felt your thing was just you, mummy, color, style, texture, everything. Hope it fits. I couldn't resist it. And Warren's I felt were him. Hope you are in agreement. I sent Dotty & Joe the merest trifle---two candles made in the shape of Italian chianti bottles with labels and all---an odd, if inexpensive thing. I spend a lot on Xmas cards, stamps etc. & yet did want to remember them. Do you think that will be OK? I've sent lots of cards and in many enclosed my poem about a "Winter Ship" off T-Wharf which I hope won't be too heavy going for anyone---its mainly descriptive.

1–See TH to ASP and Warren Plath, [early December 1960], printed in *Letters of Ted Hughes*: 170–7.

We got a long, marvelous letter from Mrs. Prouty & have sent her off a card with letters & poems[1] from each of us. I am so pleased her reaction to my book has been so enthusiastic. I only hope I get a woman's story or two published in time for her to see them, as I think that would please her most of all. We are going to take the money she sent us ($300 in all) for Frieda & my book & buy livingroom furniture with it next month to replace all Dido Merwin's stuff. Our relation with her & Bill whom we have large reservations about, has been made false by our living off her second-hand things: she & he feel they can walk in on us any time, expect us (especially Ted) to come over for dinner as domestic "lions", and both of us feel the need to free ourselves from this uncomfortable dependency. We've let Mrs. Prouty have an idea of what we plan to do, thinking she'll approve: it will mean getting on our own feet here without feeling like Exhibit A. Ted's work is so good he doesn't need "contacts" of any sort. The next step, of course, is a house. I am very excited that children seem to be an impetus to my writing, and it is only the lack of space that stands in my way. As soon as I start selling women's magazine stories I could afford a half-day babysitter or something equivalent to do the drudge-work. I think Ted & I will probably decide to appear on a radio program called "Two of a Kind"[2]---an interview series with husbands & wives who have the same profession. Keep after that speedwriting book. All sorts of queer parttime jobs crop up here.

Oh, how I'm longing for the deep dreamless sleeps of Yorkshire! We're both so tense we need to unwind for weeks. We'll be back here by New year's day. I've got my first two New Yorker's already & revel in them. It's like getting a fresh present from you every week! Much Much love to you and a thousand Christmas wishes

Your own,
Sivvy

1–SP sent 'Candles' to Olive Higgins Prouty with the following inscription: 'for Mrs. Prouty / with love – / Sylvia / December 10, 1960'; held by Lilly Library. The location of the card and letter is unknown.

2–Sylvia Plath and Ted Hughes, 'Two of a Kind: Poets in Partnership', BBC Home Service (31 January 1961); re-broadcast 19 March 1961. The series aired from 25 August 1959 to 27 October 1964.

TO *Ann Davidow-Goodman & Leo Goodman*

c. Saturday 17 December 1960[1] TLS/ALS in greeting card,[2] Smith College

<printed greeting>
Christmas Greetings
<signed>
from / Sylvia, Ted & Frieda

Hello you two . . .

Excuse our long, inexcusable and groggy silence. We have the two fine books, yours, Ann, I think a sure rival to Sir Lear.[3] We look forward to nurturing Frieda to an age where she will lisp the rhymes & point in delight to the matching animals. We have been involved in a round of time & energy consuming small potatoes and are resolved to live like hermits,(if not saints, Leo) from now on & work work work. As if to challenge this resolve Ted got a wicked telegram from ABC television[4] this morning (heaven knows how they knew where he was) asking him to appear as poet-of-the-year. He refused, in spite of his mother's wailing wall scene. So much for that.

Frieda has been miraculously transformed into a standing wonder. Her eyes are much larger and bluer and stop even more people in the street. She never cries out of petulance or anger, only for tooth-cutting (she has two scalloped beauties the better to gnaw us with on her lower jaw) or other rare aches, and greets us two grim atheists every morning with angelic smiles and pink cheeks and winsome games of tongue-clicking, pie-tin beating and standing-laughing, to sweeten our natures. She never bothered with sitting, just rose one day by hauling herself up on her cribrail and stood, very proud of herself. Would you two, by the way, consider being her godparents-in-absentia, since you were such in spirit and presence this summer? Ted & I can't think of any luckier combination of stars, talents and felicities to be Frieda's symbolic guardians! Wishing you two golden ones well,

much love,
Sylvia[5]

1 – Date supplied from internal evidence.

2 – Christmas card depicting three kings bearing gifts; designed by Sheila Parry for Libertys.

3 – English author and illustrator Edward Lear (1812–88).

4 – A former British television company, which operated in northern England.

5 – TH added a note on the left inside page of the greeting card, which has not been transcribed. TH wrote about the illustration of the three kings depicted on the front of the

TO *Philip Booth*

c. Saturday 17 December 1960[1] ALS in greeting card,[2] Dartmouth College

<printed greeting>
Happy Christmas
<signed>
from Sylvia, Ted & Frieda

PS. A note from the moors of Yorkshire where we are staying till New Years to recuperate from London – it is cold as a well in January & the air like solid clear glass we can walk through miraculously. Frieda thrives. She has suddenly decided to stand up. Her eyes are huge blue saucers. She is an angel to confound us atheists with the gifts of her humour and rosebud cheeks. You must understand this wonder three times over –

S.[3]

TO *Wilbury Crockett*

c. Saturday 17 December 1960[4] ALS in greeting card, Private owner[5]

<printed greeting>
WITH BEST WISHES FOR / CHRISTMAS AND THE NEW YEAR
<signed>
from / Sylvia, Ted & Frieda Hughes

Dear Mr. Crockett,

I was delighted to have your good letter and to know THE COLOSSUS is safe in your discriminating hands. Most especially Ted & I were joyous

---

card and made a reference to SP's current pregnancy. TH commented on Ann's book *Let's Draw*, and wishes them well in 1961. He ends on a string of adulatory adjectives regarding Frieda.

1–Date supplied from internal evidence.

2–Christmas card depicting two shepherds and five sheep; designed by Sheila Parry for Libertys.

3–TH added a note on the back of the card, which has not been transcribed. TH composed a story about the scene depicted on the card.

4–Date supplied from internal evidence.

5–Sold at auction with a signed/inscribed copy of Sylvia Plath, *The Colossus and Other Poems* (London: Heinemann, 1960) by Sotheby's on 14 July 2009.

to hear of your award and year in New York! We have always longed for the 'excuse' or 'gift' of a year in that superb city, and it is fine to hear how admirably you & the family take to the rich life.

We are extremely happy in our small northern niche in London where Regents' Park, Primrose Hill & the Zoo are our backyard, so to speak, & long for a house in an adjoining street. We glut ourselves on the cheap play tickets, foreign films, galleries and all the best fare, while living like Anonymous creatures, Ted studiously avoiding the requests for public appearances that find their way to us. We had a wonderful dinner with T. S. Eliot (who is an editor at Ted's publishing house), his charming Yorkshire wife & Mr & Mrs. Stephen Spender at the Eliots' home here. I was thrilled. Eliot has suggested revisions for Ted's children's book of light verse which Faber is publishing this spring & we treasure the ms. with his notes on it. A warm welcome awaits you here anytime you pass through London again!

Fondest Christmas wishes to you, Mrs. C. & Debbie & Steve!

Sylvia

PS. Frieda Rebecca Hughes arrived on April first 1960 – at home, delivered by a little Indian midwife & is the sun of our life – we both dote on her!

TO *Aurelia Schober Plath & Warren Plath*

Saturday 24 December 1960 | TLS (aerogramme), Indiana University

Saturday
December 24, 1960

Dear mother (!) & Warren . . .

Happy Christmas Eve. Ted & I have been up here in Yorkshire for a week now & I am writing in the calm before the crowded 3-day holiday. The sun has burned through the mists and grey sheep are grazing on the field in front of my window. We've managed to borrow a crib, pen & tiny carriage for Frieda & she is more enchanting every day. I've had a tiresome cold for the last week & Frieda has woken us at 3 am every morning with her two new top teeth which are cutting their way through, so I am still a bit haggard, but in good spirits. Ted looks ten years younger. His decision to refuse speaking engagements & cumbersome commissions has relieved both of us---he refused a request to appear on TV as "poet of the year", much to his mother's disappointment, but I understand very well how public life appalls him. He is upstairs now working on his full-length play.

I hope you enjoyed that Sunday Observer review about my book[1] (I was glad we weren't in London, for I know Dido Merwin was dying for A. Alvarez---the bright young critic who's married DH Lawrence's grand-daughter by Frieda[2] & her first husband[3]---to review Bill Merwin's book & it would be difficult to toss off such a review where my book got first place, most space & best notices.) I was very encouraged by it. We enjoyed listening to Ted's story Saturday & my book reviewed Sunday along with Pasternak,[4] EE Cummings,[5] Betjemann[6] & others[7] & I reading one of the poems. I hope I can persuade the BBC to accept a program about young American woman poets which I am drawing up, now that they seem willing enough to record my odd accent. I've had a very heartening letter from my young agent who liked my second woman's magazine story[8] very much & has sent it out. I probably won't hear about either of these first two for weeks, but am beginning a longer more ambitious one today about a girl who falls in love with a beautiful old house & manages finally to possess it: a kind of parable for my loving this house with a bay tree in Chalcot Crescent. I'll have a story in the LHJournal or SatEvePost yet. Ted & I wrote out the plot for a romance set up here on the moors[9] & we have two more coming up---a suspense story about an art gallery (I'll do research on forgeries, lost old masters & quiz our artist gallery-owner friends on this) & one about a lady astrologer for which Ted is going to work out horoscopes. The wonderful thing about these stories is that I can do them by perspiration, not inspiration---so I can work on them while Frieda is playing in the room & so on. My agent wants me to come in & talk to her again---she knows all the editors & magazines & her practical knowhow is extremely helpful. As soon as I am good enough,

1–A. Alvarez, 'The Poet and the Poetess', *The Obsever* (18 December 1960): 21.

2–Ursula Barr, married in 1956; divorced in 1961.

3–Frieda Lawrence's first husband was British philologist Ernest Weekley (1865–1954); married in 1899, divorced 1914.

4–Boris Pasternak and Michael Harari, *Poems 1955–1959* (London: Collins and Harvill Press, 1960).

5–E. E. Cummings, *Selected Poems, 1923–1958* (London: Faber & Faber, 1960).

6–John Betjeman, *Summoned by Bells* (London: John Murray, 1960).

7–Brian Higgins, *The Only Need* (London: Abelard-Schuman, 1960); D. J. Enright, *Some Men are Brothers* (London: Chatto & Windus, 1960).

8–Probably Sylvia Plath, 'The Lucky Stone', published as 'The Perfect Place'. See SP to ASP, 26–9 September 1961. SP set the story in Whitby, England, which she visited in August 1960.

9–Probably Sylvia Plath, 'A Winter's Tale'; held by Smith College.

she'll send my things to their New York counterpart. I'm heartened she thinks my first two real attempts are good enough to send around here.

Ted & I have had some wonderful moor walks, 10 mile or so hikes, & the air here is superb. Do plan to stay in England at least a month this summer. Ideally, we'd like you & Frieda to get acquainted by your staying near us & having lunch & suppers with us, then maybe we could go off to Ireland or France for 5 days or a week while you lived at our place with Frieda (I trust this wouldn't be a chore!) & then later we could all go up to Yorkshire for a week where you could stay at a nearby inn with excellent food. If you allowed yourself at least a month, we could take everything in a leisurely way. I wish I could leave Frieda even for a day with Mrs. Hughes, but she is so unwatchful I wouldn't feel easy. Yesterday for example I went to take a nap & when I came down Frieda had eaten most of a chocolate ornament covered in tinfoil which fell from the tree while Mrs. H. just looked on—"she did seem busy in the corner". Luckily the bits of tinfoil didn't seem to bother her, but I could imagine her eating bits of broken glass with Mrs. H having the same reaction! It's really too bad she isn't a good cook, or knitter or something beside a tireless & repetitive talker. When you come up you must rival her with memories of us as children! I wish I had some of my own relatives to admire Frieda. Is there any chance of Warren coming to that conference in London?

Do make a final search for that bright yellow paper-back speedwriting book! It must be at home. I think we left some boxes of books in the cellar & in the attic (my first thought was my bookcase, the closets, the bureaus). I am so frustrated without it, as in a few days I could get my speed back & apply for one of these part-time jobs as secretary to a woman journalist or architect or such that come up on occasion. Couldn't you invent some pretext to get the book from the school as a teacher? By the way, Marion said you'd a job offer in your new field. What was it? I just feel if I walked into the house I could put my hand on the speedwriting book! In future years, if you want an easy solution for presents to us, you might send on piece by piece my favorite children's books---that big orange "Cuckoo Clock"[1] for one, & my beloved Red books. We never did get "Mary Poppins"[2] did we? I'd love her books too. Hope your packages arrived all right.

xxx
Sivvy

1–Mrs Molesworth, *The Cuckoo Clock* (1877).
2–P. L. Travers, *Mary Poppins*; first published in 1934.

<in left margin of page 1 of letter>

PS – Frieda says "Mum-mum" & can sit down as well as stand up with ease, as well as bend down to pick up a rusk with one hand while standing & holding on to something with the other. Hope you liked the colored pictures.

1961

TO *Aurelia Schober Plath*

Sunday 1 January 1961 | TLS with envelope, Indiana University

3 Chalcot Square
London N.W.1
January 1, 1961

Dearest mother,

How good it was to have your happy letter. You sound in wonderful spirits and I hope you keep them and your health through the longish winter drag till springtime. Ted and I came back from Yorkshire Saturday & had the misfortune to be on a train whose steam-pipe was broken so it was absolutely unheated & freezing cold all the long trip down & we could do nothing about it. Luckily I could bundle the baby in her carrycot (which she has just about outgrown) under two blankets & she wore the lovely pale blue blanket-snowsuit I got her with Dot's money. Nevertheless, I came down with the worst case of flue I've had yet, and the baby caught a cold, so after my week-long cold in Yorkshire plus the baby waking us for hours every night cutting her two top teeth, I have been pretty oppressed. I hope that we can reserve you a nice room at Sutcliffe's, a fine old-farm house Inn about 15 minutes walk from the Hughes, and stay up in Yorkshire for one week out of your (I hope) at least 6-week stay. Then you could take long moor-walks with us, I could take you to Haworth and so on. I don't think we will plan to spend Christmas in Yorkshire again. In the first place, winter is an awful time to travel with babies---colds simply spoil everything, and then the Hughes house is too small to take us all. In addition, Olwyn made such a painful scene this year that I can never stay under the same roof with her again. She has never hidden her resentment of me, & her relation to Ted is really quite pathological---I think they slept in the same bed till she was 9 years old & probably this is one of the reasons she never married. In any case, she has never spoken to me, asked me one personal question or done anything but ignore me & make it plain she has come to see Ted. Naturally, this hurt me very much, but I never crossed her, because I knew Ted was fond of her. Evidently one of the things she finds hardest to take is that I have opinions & ideas which Ted respects---she has been used to dominating him in their childhood---and this Christmas my book happened to have a surprising spate of rave reviews (I'll send you some)---over the radio, in the Sunday papers & so on. Olwyn seemed to have some chip on her shoulder & all at once, when I asked her to please stop criticizing Ted & me, which she had been doing since she arrived, she turned on me with an hysterical outburst of fury, in front of her mother & Ted accusing me of being a "nasty bitch", eating too much Christmas dinner, acting as if their house was my home, daring to say I didn't like a particular poet she liked (she has no qualms about criticizing poets I!like) & what seemed worst to her, not putting her up at our place last spring when I was expecting Frieda at any moment. Well, we all sat astounded as this kept on and on---full of venom she had been storing up since I married Ted. I tried to explain I wouldn't want my own mother living with me in such cramped quarters when having a baby---I think she dimly wanted it to be her baby---but she kept on saying how she was the daughter of the house & I wasn't & actually calling me by my maiden name "Miss" . . . which I think shows how horrified she was at Ted's marriage.

It was so apparent that she resented my <u>existence</u> as Ted's wife---the fact that I had thoughts, a career, a child & had been treated lovingly like a daughter by dear Edith and as one of the family by the aunts and uncles---that this break can never be mended. The insult and venom she let loose---while saying, imagine, that <u>I</u> was intolerant, selfish, inhospitable, immature & I don't know what else---is something that can never be mended, at least not until she gets married herself. Luckily Ted is mature enough & loves me enough to see what an impossible situation this is and agrees that someone who sees me only as a nasty bitch shouldn't be Frieda's godmother and won't be. Nevertheless, I am rather heartsick about the whole mess, especially at the sorrow all this caused poor Edith, whom I am very fond of. We'll just plan to stay in Yorkshire in summer instead of winter, because I refuse to be ousted from my "family abroad" through Olwyn's furies. Evidently she said such awful things to Gerald's Australian wife when she was staying with them, that poor Joan packed her bags and headed to the train station in tears. So I feel it's not just me, but the image of a rival in Olwyn's warped mind that makes her try to annihilate her brother's wives---and of course her relation to Ted is a rather obvious Freudian one, and quite horrifying.

Well, Frieda luckily is too young to absorb such things & I'm determined she'll never be in a situation to do so again. I am, as you may imagine, delighted to be back in our little flat & to feel the world come back in proportion. I'm eagerly awaiting word about my two ladies' magazine stories (which my agent, at least, is delighted with) and working on a longer third. I've also been asked to edit an American supplement of modern poetry[1] by a critical magazine here and to allow two poems from The Colossus to be published in a British anthology of modern British poetry[2] because I "live in England, am married to an Englishman, & the editor admires my work". All of which is very nice, & probably my good reviews will bring more such little offers my way. In spite of the oppressions, illnesses & nagging bills of the last six weeks I am happy as I have ever been, & Ted and I are finding continuous & amazing joy in our little Frieda who is, we are forced to admit, getting prettier every day. She has four teeth now, stands & sits down vigorously, walks round her pen holding on to the side rail & bangs her little chicken to make it squeak. Ted's aunt Hilda & cousin Vicky (a young art teacher) gave her a big brother to little Bunzo Bear and a pair of red rompers & a marvelous brightly painted abacus. She has a nice little family of animals & dolls & we are dying for her to get to the stage of coloring books. Dido sent a collection of children's poems by Robert Graves[3] (a friend of hers) to start her book collection.

I do hope you can manage to stay here at least six weeks. When you make reservations definite, do let us know. I wish you could stay past July 31 by a few days, as Ted is giving the speech at his old Yorkshire school at graduation[4] & it would be convenient to be up there then, but even if you couldn't stay on, we would. I thought I'd tell you that what we hope ---in addition to having you ensconced in a room near here---is that you & Frieda get along so well that we could go to the Merwins wonderful farm in France for a week's holiday (children are taboo there!) while you live here & care for Frieda. Would that be too much for you? There are

1–Sylvia Plath, *American Poetry Now* (Hull: University of Hull, 1961); a supplement of the *Critical Quarterly*.
2–Sylvia Plath, 'Frog Autumn' and 'Metaphors', in Kenneth Allott (ed.), *Penguin Book of Contemporary Verse 1918–60*, 2nd edition (Harmondsworth: Penguin Books, 1962): 388–90. In his introduction Allott writes, 'and I have claimed Sylvia Plath as English because she is married to an English poet and settled in this country, although she was born in Boston and the main literary influence on her work is John Crowe Ransom' (16). SP's copy held by Lilly Library.
3–Probably Robert Graves, *The Penny Fiddle: Poems for Children* (London: Cassell, 1960).
4–TH spoke at Mexborough Grammar School on 18 July 1961. An article, 'Hawthornden Prize Winner at Mexborough Speech Day', ran in the *South Yorkshire Times* on 22 July 1961. SP and TH arrived half an hour late due to car troubles, and the article printed a photograph of SP and TH with two students. SP assisted in handing out awards.

all the stores you could want two-minutes around the corner & you'd be comfy in our flat with fridge, stove etc. Then we would also like to plan a few days in Cornwall by some sea-beach, probably with you and Frieda. Maybe we could all rent a cottage for a week. Ted wants to look round for possible houses there. That is about all we've planned---we can work out details when you come. I'd like to do a bit of touring London with you while Ted babysits, as I've seen so little of it!

We are planning an absolutely unsocial, quiet hardworking winter here now. I have been bothered lately by what my doctor calls a "grumbling appendix"---occasional periods of sharpish pain which then go away, but my appendix is extremely tender to touch. I am thinking seriously of asking him to let me have it out at some convenient (if that's ever convenient!) time this spring, as I have nightmares about going to Europe on our Maugham grant, getting a rupture and either dying for lack of hospital or being cut up by amateurs, infected, ad infinitum. Don't you think it would be advisable to have it out now? I feel I'm living with a time-bomb as it is. Have you any idea how long one is hospitalized, how painful it is, etc? Naturally one is reluctant to get oneself in for an operation like that if one isn't forced to it, but I don't want to worry about rupture in Europe, or during pregnancy. Encourage me, & I'll have it out with my doctor. I'd wait, of course, till Frieda was fully weaned & I was in good health.

I'm glad you're going on with your reading course now that you're so far with it. What's the position about the life of your department now at BU? It must be nice to think that you can get good-paying part-time work in Wellesley after you're retired. <u>What</u> was that job Marion said you were offered? Tell Betty Aldrich how much her marvelous family photo meant to us. That's my favorite sort of Christmas card. Keep well & much love to you & dear Warren . . .

xxx

Sivvy

<on verso of envelope>

PS – The date of Ted's Yorkshire speech is July <u>18th</u> so that would make our stay there earlier.

TO *Brian Cox*

Sunday 1 January 1961[1] TLS, University of Kansas

3 Chalcot Square
London N.W.1
January 1, 1960

Dear Brian,

Thanks very much for your good letter. I think the supplement of recent American verse is a highly exciting idea and should be delighted to edit it. I already have an embryo list of poems by young poets I know or know of who are too new to be at all familiar here, and of new poems by better-known poets . . . probably the hardest thing will be putting a tight lid on this and keeping the number from growing too great!

Could you give me some idea of a deadline? I want to look through some books that will probably be hard to get hold of over here, and it may take some time to locate them.

All good New Year wishes to you and the CQ,

Sylvia Plath

TO *Ruth Tiffany Barnhouse Beuscher*

Wednesday 4 January 1961[2] TLS, Smith College

3 Chalcot Square
London N.W.1
January 4, 1960

Dear Dr. Beuscher,

I wonder if I could write you about an old and ugly problem that reared its head with renewed vengeance this last week---namely Ted's sister. I'd appreciate it immensely if you could drop me a few helpful and commonsensical words on the subject as you did four years ago when she was endeavouring to send a sequence of her female Hungarian friends to live with us.

We all went up to Yorkshire for Christmas: Ted, me, the baby & Olwyn fresh from Paris dressed completely in black with her hair dyed bright red. She has always had a cold, and what I call for lack of a better word "sophisticated" control of her emotions in relation to me: treating me

1–Letter misdated by SP.
2–Letter misdated by SP.

with a definite, yet civil dismissal, rather like an obtuse piece of furniture that somehow got in her way. She never talks to me, but through me, around me and to Ted, and never in all the years I've know her has she asked me a personal question or made a comment on anything involving me. I felt, and foolishly it now seems, that she would grow to accept Ted's marriage and forgive me for being a person with marked opinions, feelings and "presence", but this Christmas some small spark touched off the powderkeg & she made obvious to Ted & his mother what I've known all along: that her resentment is a pure and sweeping and peculiarly desperate hatred. Curiously I was very relieved: her total & patronizing snubbing of me was not pleasant (she always calls me "little", although I'm a good inch taller than she is). You remember "little" was also a favorite word of mine! – diminishing to innocence & harmlessness emotions I deeply feared![1] Anyway, we had been living in the same small house for a week and I felt that the "surface" between us was better than usual, but on the last day of our stay---Ted's and mine---the outburst came. Olwyn had been nagging at us for being too critical of people ever since she came up & finally I asked her to lay off & said she was as critical as the two of us put together. This is the first time I actually confronted her in the open & the transformation was astounding. She started to fume and shriek and the stream of words ran more or less "youre a nasty bitch, a nasty selfish bitch, Miss Plath" (she calls me by my maiden name as if by that she could unmarry me) "you act as if our house were your palace, I watched you eat Christmas dinner & you certainly stuffed yourself, you think you can get away with everything, you're trying to come between Ted & me, you bully me and my mother and Ted. I'm the daughter in this house. You criticized a book I bought last year (this being a nice enough poet whose poems neither Ted nor I like), you criticized a friend of mine (this being a dull Dutchman Ted & I found dry & boring) you're a bitch, an immature woman, inhospitable, intolerant . . ." and on and on. Earlier on, on returning from shopping with Ted, she said to me with one of her inimitable smiles "All the people on the bus thought Ted had a new red-headed wife." And Ted's mother did say blandly that the two of them slept in the same bed till Olwyn was 9 and Ted 7. So she does have a five year lead on me.

I said very little & Ted & his mother sat stunned. The main thing she seemed to resent was my existence as Ted's wife, not just me. She of course criticizes poets and people with a vengeance, but my disagreeing with

1 – This sentence added by SP in the left margin.

her she couldn't take, nor my own writing, either. It so happened that at Christmas my book had a whole spate of very good, even rave, reviews in Punch,[1] the weeklies, the Sunday papers & over the radio---with Ted reading a story on the radio one day, & me reading a poem in a review on the next & maybe this public recognition of me as Ted's wife & a poet in my own right also irked Olwyn.

The oddest thing is that the main crux of her fury stemmed from a visit she paid us last spring, just as I was expecting to go in to labor any day. She came to London for a weekend (I had visions of a sisterly interest in my feelings, confinement etc. etc. & projected my desire for a comforting woman relative onto her) & instead of coming alone, brought two friends ---one of them a total stranger. They sat round & smoked & Olwyn talked to Ted about astrology. I served them all lunch; they stayed on, obviously expecting me to serve them all dinner. I suggested we go out for fish & chips. Olwyn, it turned out, wanted to live with us---in our two rooms ("you had plenty of room" she cried last week). I tried to explain that I wouldn't want my own mother sleeping on the couch in the livingroom when I went into labor at home & at that point didn't feel like waiting on houseguests, worried as I was about the hereditary possibility of having a mental defective like Ted's two cousins. I have an odd feeling she wanted my baby to be her baby. Ted asked her to be godmother & I didn't object, when the baby was born, although both of us agreed after this Christmas blowup that it was silly to have a godmother & spiritual guide for Frieda who honestly thought her mother was nothing more than a nasty bitch.

As you may imagine my old Wicked Witch trauma came into action again. All the bright right answers about my also being a daughter in the house, if only by law, and the suggestion that Olwyn marry and have a few babies before she lecture me about the meaning of womanhood---said themselves later in my head. She acted like a jealous mistress, down to the red-dyed hair---as if by treating me like dirt & Ted like Prince Charming, we must fall apart by sheer disparity. She also said I'd driven her from her own house, she'd never come home from Christmas again, now wouldn't I be happy etc. The morning we left---neither Ted or I having slept & his mother having cried all night---she threw her arms around me, smiled, said "I'm sorry" & ran back to bed. I don't quite know what she was sorry for: surely not for hurting me, or for saying the truth, but perhaps for showing herself in the open before Ted.

That evening, as Ted & his mother just sat round (much as they do when Ted's idiot cousin comes for tea, greeting everything from her new

1–Peter Dickinson, 'Some poets', *Punch* (7 December 1960): 829.

diamond ring to her yowling "Shut up, damn you" or "I'm going to put my head in the gas oven" with smiling nods & "Now, now, Barbara".) I put the baby to bed and went for a long walk in the full moon over the moors, utterly sick. What upset me most was that neither Ted nor his mother <u>said</u> anything. I simply said "Go on, Olwyn, tell me all of it." Ted appeared with his nice sane art-teacher cousin in a car as I was nearing Scotland. He had evidently hit his sister & told her off after I'd gone. Later, he said what we'd just witnessed was a pathological case & that we'd better steer clear of Olwyn till she got married. Luckily I remembered your wise advice that the woman who shouts her head off most seems in the wrong regardless of who's right & I was glad I hadn't retorted to Olwyn in kind.

My question is: now what do I do? I honestly don't feel I can "forgive & forget" & go back to that fake relation of entertaining Olwyn while she talks to Ted through me & lets me wait on them both. I think that next Christmas we'll stay here at home: I don't want to live cramped under the same roof up there with Olwyn again, nor do I want her to get one-up on me by staying away and having all the relatives blame me for it, nor do I want to run into the round of double-flu the three of us came down with coming & going. I hope we can visit Yorkshire with mother this summer & continue our pleasant & happy relation with Ted's parents & aunts uncles & cousins at nicer times of the year. Yet we are between Paris & Yorkshire & I half-expect Olwyn to turn up here & start more trouble. The thing I <u>dont</u> want is what I think she dimly wants: that by my refusing to see her I drive her & Ted to having clandestine meetings, where I would then obviously appear a mean, domineering figure. I think that if she wants to come here or for Ted to come there that the baby & I should go along, although my presence is intolerable to her. Yet as long as Ted thinks we should steer clear of her I'm perfectly happy. Luckily <u>he</u> isn't in doubt about who he's married to, although he's deeply hurt by the whole situation. Do you agree I should just shut up about it, never refer to it or try to underline Olwyn's hatred---since I deeply feel Ted is with me and for me? What attitude should I take when we meet again? Generous, I suppose.

Earlier, I would have been seriously threatened by all this. As it is, I feel sickened enough, but somehow quite steady. My role as Ted's wife, Frieda's mother, a writer, <u>me</u>---is beginning to flower into what I always dreamed of. I think Olwyn would "take" me if I were, like most of Ted's previous girlfriends a "mealymouthed little princess" (which is what she called them, scornfully). I may have gone through just this goody-goody stage with my series of pseudo-mothers---Mrs. Prouty, Mary Ellen Chase, Mrs. Cantor ad inf, but I am not prepared to regress & efface myself with Olwyn. She has a queer way of trying to judge and bully our marriage: "You're unhappily married, why don't you buy a house in the country, London is so ugly . . ." and so on. If I felt worried by this, I would be worried about being worried. We want a town house, a Cornwall seaside house, a car & piles of children & books & have saved about $8 thousand simply out of our writing in the past five years toward these dreams & feel in the next five years we may nearly approximate them. This is our business, & the lord knows our life together since Frieda's arrival has been full of fun & happiness . . . as if she, by her droll, adorable otherness opened a whole new world for the two of us. She's like a sort of living mutually-created poem who will, of herself, find a shape, a rhythm & who seems to thrive on the love and games and words we share with her. I think at last that I may break into the women's magazines over here with stories---I have a very encouraging agent (my ultimate aim is the good old LHJ and SatEvePost) and that this four-hour-a-day stint I put in is utterly consistent with being a good mother: I have a career which is fun & which I respect myself for having & which is a home-career: I'm always on hand for crises, meal-making and child-care and flexible enough to dovetail these with my own work. I also think my whole mind is more lively and inquiring and interested in other mothers and other people because of my new direction (as distinct from the slice-of-life arty story I used to try to do). And the LHJ seems a lot healthier to me than the I-remember-when-I-was-a-child-in-Westchester-county/Bangok/Tibet etc. that one finds in the estimable <u>New Yorker</u>.

Anyhow, my first American ladies' magazine story will be dedicated to you: it was you started me reading the LHJ. Please excuse the single-spaced rant & write if you've a minute.

Love,
Sylvia Hughes

PS. One small footnote that made me feel I wasn't quite alone in Olwyn's black book. Ted told me that she was "even worse" (god save her) to her <u>other</u> sister-in-law, a bouncing, blond extrovert Australian who married her other brother (older by eight years). Evidently she so dug in to this poor girl during her first visit to England & her husband's family that Joan packed her bags in tears & Ted just rescued her from the railway station as she headed back to Australia. As Ted said, "if she did that to Joan, not caring much about Gerald & never writing him, you can imagine how much more she resents you." I certainly can. She writes Ted a voluminous, loving, intimate letter once a week and goes desperate if he doesn't reply in kind. I remember your saying when I spoke of their childhood intimacy that this sort of thing never ends or undoes itself. I'm willing to accept this, as I would not be if Ted seemed more ambivalent in his emotional ties. But what about the future? I can quite imagine Olwyn marrying a man she hates, or committing some other symbolic suicide --- her outbreak in Yorkshire was a form of self-mutilation: I forced her into her ugly temper, her exile from her own house & so on.

Anyhow, enough of that. I would appreciate a straightforward word from you. I feel I've come a long way since the last bout with Olwyn, but have a long way to go yet before I become the wise wife I'd like to grow into.

You should see Frieda: four teeth, two top & bottom, she stands & walks round her crib and pen holding on, plays with her tub-duck, squeaky rag chicks & bears & has a huge appetite. People still stop in the street to exclaim over her big blue eyes which is heartening as I think she is doomed to straight-as-a-stick brown hair like Ted & me. She shows a marked liking for books---even if her interest is mainly crumpling the crackly pages.

S.

TO *Aurelia Schober Plath*

Tuesday 10 January 1961 — TLS (aerogramme), Indiana University

Tuesday, January 10

Dearest mother,

Your lovely New Years letters have arrived and meant a very great deal to me. I'm so glad you like the blouse. I just had vision of you in it & it was the only one of its kind & color in the store so I felt fortunate at finding something I thought would suit you so well. I hope Warrie forgives the unimaginativeness of Ties as a gift & likes the color & patterns which I felt would look distinguished on him. I got his dear letter the other day. You are a genius to locate a Speedwriting book! I don't know what ever could have happened to the one I had! In any case, I'll guard these with my life---they will probably come in handy more than once. I'm really an awful correspondent this Christmas, I've felt so blue with these repeated sinus colds. I just got over a two-week bout at Christmas to come down on an unheated train & got laid up worse than ever & am just now feeling slightly better after 10 days of misery when to cook a meal seemed a superhuman effort. In addition, the sickenly unpleasant scene Olwyn staged at Yorkshire bothered me more than I can tell & the thought that she's up there poisoning her mother against me is very sad---Mrs. Hughes wrote us a tart letter very unlike her---something to the effect that we should ex<u>pect</u> to get flu when traveling on a Saturday in holiday season etc. etc. Naturally she would take Olwyns side right or wrong, but the Olwyn has always bossed that house shamefully & as Ted says, her outburst derived from an idiotic jealousy. I hope we can go to Yorkshire this summer for a week together because I am reluctant to give up my pleasant relation with Ted's aunts, uncles & art-teacher cousin, but I shall see to it that our Christmasses are spent <u>at home</u> where my children imbibe Christmas spirit and not the venom that I had to suffer this year. I can always say that holiday travel brings on flu, which it does & have a pleasant time here. Do encourage me, I feel the lack of some relative or friend to bolster my morale. I am going to have an interview with a surgeon on Friday the 13th (I hope the verdict is more auspicious than the day) about my appendix & I suppose my job is to convince him it should come out before I go to Europe. I hope you second me in this, as I find it a bit hard to more or less volunteer for an operation of any sort that isn't an emergency necessity.

Dido Merwin has been angelic, encouraging me to have my appendix out (saying she wouldn't let me visit them in France if I had it in because of the dangers of sepsis, no-anesthesia, peritonitis and on and on if one gets a rupture in the country) & telling me how easy it was for her. We had her for dinner the other night---made Dot's veal scallopini---do tell her how I think of her while making her recipes & try to pry a few more from her. Made her carrot cake for Christmas. Dido brought the first four volumes of Beatrix Potter's classic Peter Rabbit series[1] which are enchanting & plans gradually to give Frieda the whole set. She's an ideal godmother---full of wise advice about Frieda's education here and so on. Bill, now in America on a lecture tour, has managed to get Ted & me two reviews to do on the <u>Nation</u>.[2] They are really the nicest people we know here.

So glad you got the Manchester Guardian review[3] (how glad I am I left the Ella Mason poem out of my book!) & do by all means send Mrs.

1–*The Tale of Peter Rabbit* (1902), *The Tale of Squirrel Nutkin* (1903), *The Tailor of Gloucester* (1903), and *The Tale of Benjamin Bunny* (1904).

2–It does not appear these reviews were either written or printed.

3–Bernard Bergonzi, 'The Ransom Note', *The Guardian* (25 November 1960): 9. Smith College holds two clippings of Bergonzi's review; one from the above cited appearance and another from the *Guardian Weekly* (1 December 1960): 11.

Prouty a copy. That's what I had hoped to do if I got more than my own copy, which I have.

Frieda has settled back into her usual easy schedule now that we're back & she is sleeping in the livingroom. Her cold has left her---luckily hers are pretty light---and she looks the picture of health & prettiness. I think I'll probably wean her completely to the cup this month, as if I have my appendix out I shall have to do so. She drinks very nicely from the cup now, a little silver cup, although she is tempted to knock it away and be done with it every now and then. I can't wait till you see her. I am proud to say she is very good and unspoiled. She is used to company---having us around---but plays by herself all the day and only cries when she is hungry or tired or teething. I want her to be a self-sufficient creature who can read or color or play with toys while I work nearby. Of course at mealtimes, rising & bedding we dandle her and sing to her and make little games, but none of this holding her on the lap all day as Mrs. Hughes did which was nearly the ruin of her. Could you come over mid-Junish rather than early June? If we <u>do</u> go to Europe after my possible operation that would give us the clear 3 months we're supposed to spend. The other alternative is that I might get a job but that is dubious just now. In any case, we are looking forward to seeing you!

Had a very sweet British poet, Thom Gunn, who is teaching at Berkeley for lunch yesterday, passing through London on <u>his</u> Maugham award.[1] I wish he lived near us, he is a rare, unaffected & kind young chap. Next week Ted & I are recording a radio program of 20 minutes interview called Two of a Kind----about our both being poets, & Ted's doing a program for the Carribean services. Now he's typing out two children's programs[2]---one about writing a novel (which he tried successfully with his Cambridge schoolboys) & the other a personal reminiscence about how catching animals turned into writing poems. He & Frieda are my two angels – I don't know how I ever managed without them.

xxx to you, Warrie & Sappho –
Sivvy

1–Thom Gunn won the Somerset Maugham Award in 1959, the year before TH.

2–Probably 'Writing a Novel – Beginning', *Listening and Writing*, BBC Home Service (Schools), (20 October 1961); and 'Capturing Animals', *Listening and Writing*, BBC Home Service (Schools), (6 October 1961).

TO *Aurelia Schober Plath*

Friday 27 January 1961 — TLS (aerogramme), Indiana University

Saturday (no, Friday)
January 27, 1961

Dearest mother,

Well, your letters have kept coming & coming & increasing my morale immensely through a rather glum period & now that I am recovered enough to write letters I realise how long a silence I've plunged into. Do forgive me. I've embarked, with Ted's help, on a drastic program to pull my health up from the low mid-winter slump of cold after cold, & am eating big breakfasts (oatmeal, griddles & bacon etc., with lots of citrus juice), tender steaks, salads & drinking the cream from the tops of our bottles with iron & vitamin pills. We try to be in bed by 10 & are not going out socially at all. I feel immensely homesick when you talk of white snow! All we've had here since October is grey rain. One day we got up in muggy greyness & it got blacker & blacker till by 10 am I had to put all the light on. Bless your snow for a change, there's nothing drearier than a wet grey gritty winter! I've hardly been able to get Frieda out at all. I've got her down to one 6 am nursing a day & this week hope to tail that off so she's drinking wholly from her cup. She is cutting a new tooth & very fretful, poor baby. When we let her creep without her pen, she laughs & whizzes over the rug. Her standing is a bit of a problem for she does it all the time in her crib---sometimes I have to lay her down about 10 times in a row when she is ready for a nap, she puts her finger in her mouth for a minute, breathes quietly, & then, even if I hide & don't go out of the room, she giggles (thinking she's given me time to leave) & whoops, she's standing up & walking round her crib.

I'm <u>so</u> looking forward to next summer. <u>Could</u> you possibly alter your flight time to cover August 20th? (You better sit down, now, perhaps!) The reason I'm asking is that I discovered today your 2nd grandchild is due about then & I'd be overjoyed to have you there to meet Nicholas/Megan when he or she arrives! Ted & I are very pleased at the news & have our fingers crossed that this Mrs. Waley in Chalcot Crescent will decide to sell her house (she doesn't know yet whether she'll sell or rent it). It is <u>the</u> place we'd like to move---right around the corńer, & it needs no other fixing up than settling in. Of course, it would solve our space problem beautifully, but I don't want to push her. So we'll just wait & hope a place near here turns up by New Year's next year. The way things look now, I will probably have my appendix out some time in February (my doctor advised an early date as I'm pregnant & says there's absolutely no danger), rest all March, & head to Southern Europe for April, May & the larger part of June on the Maugham grant. Then here for a leisurely July with you (a week in France for us, perhaps), savoring Frieda & being together. I wish the 4 of us could manage a trip to the Scilly Isles which we hear are beautiful, but that would probably mean reservations way in advance. Do tell me you'll try to stay & see the new baby!!!

I've taken on a temporary part-time job which is lots of fun to keep me from brooding about my hospital sojourn which I don't look at all forward to! If you know anyone who's had an appendix out, do reassure me. I have a mortal fear of being cut open or having anesthesia. I don't know how I can stand being away from the baby 2 weeks---that will be the hardest thing of all, she is prettier & more adorable every day.

Anyhow, my job is from 1-5:30 & involves copy-editing & page layout for the big spring issue of The Bookseller,[1] a trade organ which comes out weekly but has 2 big bi-annual issues full of ads & bibliography of all coming books in England + 150 pages editorial sections (fiction, biography, children's etc.) with 400 or so pictures. I've been rewriting picture captions & a lot of publicity dept. biography material from all the various publishers & the editor was pleased enough to let me lay out the whole children's section of pictures & galley proofs (18 pages)---where I had the fun of pasting the notice of Ted's children's book in a prominent position! I'll be through in about 2 weeks---the office is lovely, with a red Turkish carpet on the 3rd floor overlooking a pleasant square & I'm having fun learning about printing & editing. Also, the money helps us over this bare time between grants. We pretend our writing money isn't there & never touch it, as it is House Money. Don't you think a downpayment of 3 thousand pounds on a 7 thousand pound house would be respectable? A 20-year mortgage at 5% would mean only about $560 + interest to pay a year, just about what we're paying now for our flat! Does that sound reasonable to you? Salaries are so low here (the average shorthand-typist gets $28 a week!---top-executive sec. abt. $40) that Ted could easily earn by writing full-time in a quiet study what he could slaving in some 9-5 job. The BBC has accepted his children's program[2] material & wants

1–SP worked part-time for *The Bookseller*, 13 Bedford Square, London W.C.1. The spring issue was published on 11 February 1961; TH's *Meet My Folks!* is mentioned on page 427.
2–Possibly Ted Hughes, 'The Gentle Art', *The World of Books*, Home Service (25 February 1961). Between 1961 and 1964, TH's children's programmes were broadcast by the BBC Home Service and published as *Poetry in the Making: A Handbook for Writing and Teaching* (London: Faber & Faber, 1967).

more. Of course, all he needs is one really successful play! Oh, how I look forward to your coming! My heart lifts now that the year swings toward it---we'll get you a comfortable room & breakfast place in easy walking distance when we know your exact dates & plan some lovely times. What fun if we could all have a week together by the sea in Cornwall or the Scilly Isles! Do tell me you're happy about our coming baby! We already love it. A big hug for you & Warren . . .

xxx
Sivvy

<on the return address side of letter>

PS: Got a lovely New England Calendar & adorable book for Frieda from dear Aunt Marion: do thank her & say I'll write when I've recovered a speck more; & lovely letters from Aunt Dot & Aunt Mildred which meant an immense deal. I really am very hungry for my relations! How they would love Frieda! A nice letter too from Mrs. Prouty & a dear one from Marty Plumer to whom I sent 2 handsome hand-knit sweaters for her twins---she's sent so much to Frieda!

xxx
s.

TO *Eleanor Ross Taylor*[1]

Friday 27 January 1961[2] — ALS with envelope, Vanderbilt University

3 Chalcot Square
NW1
Friday

Dear Mrs. Taylor,

I'm sorry to be letting you know so late, but I discovered at the office today that it's my Saturday to work, so we won't be able to come round[3] tomorrow night as we had hoped since Ted will have to stay home & care for the baby till I get through.

I do hope we'll be seeing you both again though, in the near future.

With best wishes,
Sylvia Hughes

1–American poet Eleanor Ross Taylor (1920–2011); married to American author Peter Taylor (1917–94).
2–Date supplied from postmark.
3–SP addressed the letter to 25 Kensington Gate, London.

TO *Aurelia Schober Plath*

Thursday 2 February 1961 TLS (aerogramme), Indiana University

Thursday: February 2

Dear mother,

Thanks a thousand times for your good newsy letters & the yellow shorthand (excuse: speedwriting) book which arrived this week. I'm most grateful. I'm so happy to hear of your lunches, dinners, symphonies & ballets with your good friends. I only hope you make a special effort to take things easy this next crowded semester so you will be well-rested when you come to see us. Already I am thinking of all the pleasant little things we will find to do.

I went to see my doctor this morning & he predicts August 17th for the baby's arrival, Ted's birthday. How I wish you could switch to a flight to cover that date! It would be such fun having you come to see one baby & go away having seen two. We had one or two clear blue days this week & Ted sent me up to Hampstead Heath one morning where I walked round over an hour through woodland & by open hilly meadows---a nice place for picnics & the baby's rambling in good weather. I felt much renewed, & my concentrated diet & vitamin-taking is already having its effect.

My afternoon job is very pleasant & I have done about 60 pages of layout now, which I enjoy very much---balancing the pictures & photographs & jacket designs on double-page spreads, ordering the publishers according to importance & pasting the galleys into place. I get to do all the little rush jobs of typing as my speed is the marvel of the office where the few others hunt-and-peck & I sound like a steam engine in contrast. My afternoons out have helped Ted really plow into his play & I think this one will probably be really stageable. He's full of ideas & in wonderful form. We heard our 20 minute broadcast "Poets in Partnership" this Tuesday morning, where an acquaintance of ours on the BBC asked us questions & we ended by reading a poem each[1]---quite amusing. Ted has had his children's broadcasts accepted & they want him to do more.

1–SP read 'Mushrooms'; TH read 'Pike'. Both poems and the interview released on *The Spoken Word: Sylvia Plath* (London: British Library Publishing, 2010). The BBC Written Archives Centre holds an initial transcription of the recording, which has a brief introduction by Leeming, many lines of conversation cut from the final broadcast, and TH reading 'Bullfrog'. It is unclear how the decision was made, or who made it, to read 'Pike' instead of 'Bullfrog'.

Patsy ONeil Pratson writes she has a little boy, Lincoln Frederick, born January 24th, & I am so pleased. We have as names the old Nicholas Farrar & the new Megan Emily (I like Meg as a nickname, don't you? Anyway, get used to it. The Emily is a feminizing of daddy's Emil & also for E. Dickinson and E. Bronte[1]). I plan to make several brightly colored maternity smock tops with continental embroidery tapes on them for my "Italian summer wardrobe". That simplifies everything. Now I've got to find some sort of bathing or sunsuit, for I want to swim this spring! If we take the travel grant in April, May & June, it should support us into the fall. Did I ask you before, by the way, to glance at the electric frypan recipe book (in the frypan down cellar?) & copy out the recipe for pineapple upside down cake (including the separate recipe for batter?) I'd like to try that in my pan here as it was always one of my spectacular deserts.

Ted & I went to a little party last night to meet the American poet I admire next to Robert Lowell---Ted (for Theodore) Roethke. I've always wanted to meet him, as I find he is my Influence. Ted gave me his collection "Words for the Wind" this Xmas[2] & it's marvelous. Look it up in the library---I think you would like the greenhouse poems at the front very much.

He's a big, blond, Swedish looking man, much younger seeming than his 52, with a brassy, superficially goodlooking ex-student wife[3] about as nice as nails. Ted & I got on well with him & hope to see him again.

I should probably go into hospital at the end of this month. My doctor says it's the best time---after my first 3 months pregnancy---& perfectly safe. Dido Merwin gave us a great shock, returning from a "week in the country" to whip off her scarf & show us a bandaged head & no more jowls---she had a face-lift in secret & came to encourage me about the new anesthesias & cutting etc., since she's about as morbid as I about them. We were sorry she did it in a way & wonder what Bill's reaction will be---he's in America earning $$$ on a reading tour. She's slimmed drastically & of course the plumpness just hung in wrinkles & she said she didn't want people thinking Bill had married his mother (she's 40ish & he 32, only he looks under 20). I have a very moral attitude that one should earn good wrinkles & face up to them & I'm sure catty women will find more nasty things to say ("She's scared to lose him, had her face

1–English novelist and poet Emily Brontë (1818–48).

2–Theodore Roethke, *Words for the Wind* (Garden City, N.Y.: Doubleday, 1958). SP's copy, inscribed by TH for Christmas 1960 and later by Roethke, appeared at auction via Bonhams on 21 March 2018.

3–Beatrice O'Connell Roethke (*c.* 1926–); married 1953.

lifted" etc.) than they have already. Well, we love them both dearly & couldn't have nicer godparents for Frieda. I look so forward to our visit to their farm & vineyard in France which your visit will make possible for us! I'm looking most forward to Italy & practicing my Italian! If only that lady around the corner would sell us her house we'd be really well settled! I'm in much better spirits with the promise of spring & summer & your coming. You will be mad for Frieda: she's the prettiest little girl I've ever seen & sweet as can be. I want a house big enough for at least four! Roethke said any time Ted wants to teach at Washington State to give him a nod – so in a few years we'll no doubt make another American year! Lots of love to you & dear Warren.

xxx
Sivvy

TO *Anne Sexton*

Sunday 5 February 1961

TLS (aerogramme),
University of Texas at Austin

3 Chalcot Square
London N.W.1, England
Sunday: February 5th

Dear Anne,

Your card, forwarded by my mother, arrived while the beginnings of a letter to you still stuck in my typewriter, the occasion being my reading & re-reading of To Bedlam,[1] with its fine red, purple & black on white & the beautiful words of Lowell[2] which put you up there along with Pasternak. It was terrific having my favorites back again together with the newer ones you were doing when I left ("Elegy in the Classroom"[3] among them!).

We thrive so in London we'll probably stay forever & my children will no doubt talk back to me with clipped Oxford accents till I knock their jaws into proper shape for the old broad A. Our first is a marvelous blue-eyed comic named Frieda & has convinced both of us we want to found a dynasty.

1–Anne Sexton, *To Bedlam and Part Way Back*, (Boston: Houghton Mifflin, 1960).

2–Robert Lowell, from the front jacket: 'Swift lyrical openness ... an almost Russian abundance and accuracy. Her poems stick in my mind. I don't see how they can fail to make the great stir they deserve.'

3–Anne Sexton, 'Elegy in the Classroom', the penultimate poem in part 1 of *To Bedlam and Part Way Back*.

I'd love to hear news of you, your poems, local literary gossip (especially about the House of Lowell) & suchlike. Please tell Maxine[1] I much admired her featured Fräulein poem[2] in the recent New Yorker---I think its about my favorite of hers, partly, perhaps, because I'm devoted to the horrors of Struwelpeter.[3]

I'm delighted to have your reactions to my book[4] which has been received with great hospitality by reviewers over here & only hope someday I can find an American publisher who agrees with you! We've met, in passing, Stephen Spender, Louis MacNeice, Auden, Thom Gunn etc. & this week Roethke whom (as you can no doubt see by my book) I admire immensely. Our big surprise was dinner with Mr. & Mrs. T. S. Eliot at their house, together with the Spenders which was aweinspiring. Valerie Eliot is a Yorkshire girl & very fine.

Please sit down one day between the poem & the stewpot & write a newsy letter.

Love,
Sylvia

TO *Aurelia Schober Plath*

Monday 6 February 1961 — TLS (aerogramme), Indiana University

Monday: February 6

Dearest mother,

I feel awful to write you now after I must have set you to trying to change your plans & probably telling Warren & your friends about our expecting another baby, because I lost the little baby this morning & feel really terrible about it. The lady doctor on my panel came about 9 after Ted called in & will come again tomorrow so I am in the best of hands, although I am extremely unhappy about the whole thing.

I looked so forward to sharing a new little baby with you & felt that some good fate had made this one to coincide with your visit. I am as sorry about disappointing you as anything else, for I'm sure you were thinking of the birth as joyously as I was. The doctor said one in four

1–American poet Maxine Kumin, (1925–2014).

2–Maxine Kumin, 'Fraulein Reads Instructive Rhymes', *New Yorker* (14 January 1961): 30.

3–Heinrich Hoffman, *Struwelpeter* (1845), a popular German children's book.

4–Sexton's copy of *The Colossus* (Heinemann, uncorrected proof) held by the Ransom Center, University of Texas at Austin. Also inscribed by George Starbuck.

babies miscarry & that most of these have no explanation, so I hope to be in the middle of another pregnancy when you come anyway. Luckily I have little Frieda in all her beauty to console me by laughing and singing "Lalala" or I don't know what I'd do. I'm staying in bed & Ted is taking wonderful care of me. He is the most blessed kind person in the world & we are thinking of postponing our Italian trip till next fall as Frieda will be walking & well on by then, & perhaps giving ourselves a two-week holiday in the Scilly Isles this April---if we get some of the money that Ted's applied for from the Royal Literary Fund which is supposed to aid "distressed authors" with family difficulties.

All weekend while I was in the shadow of this he gave me poems to type & generally distracted me, & I couldn't wish for a better nurse & comfort. I have, as you may imagine, an immense sympathy for Dotty now & as I grow older feel very desirous of keeping in touch with my near kin. When you come this summer we shall have lovely times with Frieda & I hope I'll be safely on with another Nicholas-Megan. I've been commissioned to write a poem for the summer festival of poetry[1] here which is an honor as only about a dozen are invited to contribute,[2] so I'll try to plunge into work, too, now, as it is a good cure for brooding. Do keep in touch with Mrs. Prouty---I wouldn't mind your mentioning this to her in a casual way---it would probably be better for her to hear of it from you rather than me. I always make it a point to sound cheerful & wanting for nothing when I write her. Do write & cheer me up.

Lots of love,
Sivvy

1–Sylvia Plath, 'Tulips', *Poetry at the Mermaid*, held at the Mermaid Theatre, London, 16–23 July 1961; SP read 'Tulips' to an audience on 17 July 1961.

2–The eleven other contributors were Thomas Blackburn, 'En Route'; Austin Clarke, 'Forget Me Not'; Michael Hamburger, 'Anachronisms'; Ted Hughes, 'My Uncle's Wound'; Patrick Kavanagh, 'The Gambler: A Ballet with Words'; Norman MacCaig, 'Snow in Princes Street'; Richard Murphy, 'The Progress of a Painter'; William Plomer, 'Reading in the Garden'; Hal Summers, 'Songs from a Revue'; R. S. Thomas, 'Not So'; and Laurence Whistler, 'The Nine-Day City'.

TO *Aurelia Schober Plath*

Thurs.–Fri. 9–10 February 1961 TLS (aerogramme), Indiana University

3 Chalcot Square
London N.W.1, England
Thursday, February 9th

Dearest mother,

I do hope the sad news in my last letter didn't cast you down too much. I forsaw how you'd enjoy sharing the good news with all our friends and relatives and only hope it hasn't been too hard to contradict our optimistic plans. I hadn't told anyone over here, thank goodness, so I don't have to suffer people commiserating with me which I couldn't stand just now. As the doctor said, it will probably just mean having a baby in late autumn instead of late summer. All I can say is that you better start saving for another trip another summer & I'll make sure I can produce a new baby for you then! Ted & I think seven is a nice magical number & both of us feel our true vocation is being father & mother to a large brood. Megan isn't pronounced Mee-gan, but the way, but Meg-un, with a short "e." Forget about King Lear!

We have had a sprinkling of clear invigorating blue days this week & I've had Frieda out in the park while I sat on a bench & read my weeks <u>New Yorker</u> (you have no idea what pleasure the weekly arrival of this magazine gives me!) and let the sun shine on her sleeping face. I'm running a hot tub now & preparing to spend the best of the day out in the park again with her. I'm feeling pretty well back to normal now & my daily routine with Frieda & Ted keeps me from being too blue. Ted's been extravagant & got us tickets to "The Duchess of Malfi",[1] Webster's wonderful play, starring Dame Peggy Ashcroft[2] tomorrow night, so we're looking forward to that. He's an angel & has made breakfast for me all week & done the washing up & heavy work & so on. He is writing magnificently on his full-length play & it is the best thing he's done. Probably good enough to get a <u>full</u> production at the Poets' Theatre &, we hope, to be staged somewhere here. If all goes well, he should finish it in a month or so. He's also writing a lot of very lively amusing colorful poems. And has ideas for stories (he wants to get out a volume) & another

1–John Webster, *The Duchess of Malfi,* performed at the Aldwych Theatre, 49 Aldwych, London.
2–English actress Dame Edith Margaret Emily Ashcroft (1907–91).

children's book. I feel so proud, coming on reviews of him here & there, "Ted Hughes, the well-known Poet" and so on. We have just heard from Yale that they are going to produce a full record of Ted reading his poems in their new series, with his picture on the jacket & so on---they've only got about 20 poets on their list so far, so this is very nice. Get your friends to buy copies when it comes out!

If you haven't already gone to the bother of changing your plane flight, do keep the earlier date as the weather will no doubt be best then & since we won't go to Italy till fall now, we'll be here to greet you. I feel easier taking Frieda later in the year, as she'll be toddling & eating pretty much what we eat by then, & it would be a pity to miss the English spring, which is the only really <u>sure</u> good weather of the year. She looks adorable in those dress-panty outfits you sent & I look forward to her wearing them this spring in the sun---she's a chubby little girl-butterfly in them, such a darling.

Friday: The marvelous Santa Claus package arrived this morning! I wish you could see what a merry time we had with it---Ted had to show Frieda the marvelous teething necklace right away & I was amazed by your clairvoyance---I was hoping to go out next week & get Frieda some deep blue tights to go with the dress I made her as Helga is having a birthday party for her 3-year-old next Saturday! Imagine my surprise & joy when I saw just what I'd wanted in your packet! And the smock-top with blue embroidery is adorable. I love the blue sweater & extravagant snowsuit: I imagine that will be ample for her next winter. <u>And</u> the Mary Poppins books which <u>I</u> plan to take to hospital with me for light reading when I go! You are an angel!

We hope to see the poet Theodore Roethke again this week. He teaches at the University of Washington (Seattle, I think) & mentioned that Ted should let him know if he wants a job there for a year. We hope to take a return-year in America some time within the next 5 years & finance it by Ted teaching on the West Coast at Berkeley (where his friend & co-English poet Thom Gunn teaches) or Washington, & perhaps summer-school for 6-weeks in New England---a friend just asked if he'd take $1,000 for doing 6 weeks at Worcester at Clark University[1]---I'm sure when the time comes something will work out. In any case, I am looking immensely forward to seeing you this summer. Thanks for all the speedwriting books. When the children are in school I'd like to work into an editing job & an easy

1–Possibly SP's former colleague Stanley Sultan, who joined the English faculty at Clark University in 1959.

way to start is by being part-secretary. I tried on the blue tights & white smock last night to see if they'd fit for Helga's birthday tea this weekend & they're perfect! We'll try to get some color pictures of her soon. I had her weighed at the clinic this week & she's 19 pounds 1 ounce. She's more cuddly every day. Ted joins me in sending you lots of love. Is there really a chance of Warren's coming to England this fall?[1] I'd like to make sure of being here if there is!

Love,
Sivvy

TO *Aurelia Schober Plath*

Sunday 26 February 1961 TLS (aerogramme), Indiana University

Sunday: February 26

Dear mother,

By the time you get this letter, I shall probably have had my appendix out & be well on the road to recovery. I got my "invitation" to come to hospital this afternoon, so I imagine I shall be operated on sometime tomorrow. It's the 27th, so I hope it's a lucky day for me. I've had this hanging over my head for almost two months now, & shall be very glad to get rid of it!

I've got all the house in order, supplies in for Ted, and yesterday baked a banana bread, tollhouse cookies, & today am making apricot tarts & griddle batter, so he shall have something to go on with. By the way, whenever you do send a packet, do you suppose you could pop in a package or so of chocolate bits? I can't get them here, & tollhouse cookies are our very favorite. The ones I made this weekend, I made with bits brought back by a friend of Marcia Plumer's, from her Christmas visit in America.

I dressed Frieda in her blue tights & white top for the Huws birthday party for Madeleine & she looked wonderful. The blue sweater is especially beautiful on her, & I love the needlecord overalls with the feet in (which I also can't get here) which come out of the washmachine daisy-fresh. Sweaters & things-with-feet are what I appreciate most in

1–Warren Plath presented a paper entitled 'Automatic Sentence Diagraming' at the International Conference on Machine Translation of Languages and Applied Language Analysis in Teddington, 5–8 September 1961.

this climate! Her favorite toy now is that little world-shaped round rattle with the cat-face on it. I shall miss her immensely these next two weeks, but am somewhat consoled, because Ted is an expert at taking care of her, and full of loving attentions, songs and games. Any mail you send here, he'll bring into hospital; my address there is Ward 1, St. Pancras Hospital, 4 St. Pancras Way, London N.W.1. It's only about a 15 or 20 minute walk away & less by bus, so Ted will be able to visit me in the meagre evening hours.

As if to cheer me up, I got an airmail special-delivery letter from the Atlantic, accepting a 50-line poem I did as an exercise called "Words for a Nursery",[1] spoken in the person of a right hand, with 5 syllables to a line, 5 stanzas, & 10 lines to a stanza. Very fingery. I imagine that will bring in about $75. I have started writing poems again[2] & hope I can keep right on through my hospital period. I'm bringing a notebook in with me as you (& Ted) suggested, to occupy myself by taking down impressions.

Ted has just heard that 4 of his 8 poems will be published, with illustrations, on the Children's Page of the Sunday Times[3] in mid-March, for about $120. The book is due out at the end of March, just in time for Frieda's first birthday, and this should help the sales a great deal, I think. The Times photographer came round to the house to take pictures of Ted last week. He will be really cloistered for the next two weeks with plenty of time to write, so we hope he'll get through with his play, called The Calm (it's a sort of dark opposite to Shakespeare's Tempest.)

I probably told you about Ted & I doing a recorded interview for a BBC radio program called Two of a Kind a couple of weeks ago. It was about 20 minutes long & ended with each of us reading a poem. Well, they broadcast part of it again on the Sunday following on the weekly-roundup program & evidently it was used as a "model" for the Talks producers, for they decided to give it a full rebroadcast after that on the weekend, & add five minutes more or so, which doubles the $75 fee. We got some funny letters, among them one[4] offering us a big house &

1–See Phoebe Adams to SP, 17 February 1961; (photocopy) held by Yale University. Sylvia Plath, 'Words for a Nursery', *Atlantic Monthly* 208 (August 1961): 66.
2–SP had written, recently, 'Parliament Hill Fields' (11 February); 'Whitsun', 'Zoo Keeper's Wife', and 'Face Lift' (14 February); 'Morning Song' (19 February); 'Barren Woman' (21 February); and 'Heavy Women' (26 February).
3–'A Poet Jokes About His Folks', *Sunday Times* (26 March 1961): Magazine 37. Only three poems were published: Ted Hughes, 'My Sister Jane', 'My Grandpa', and 'My Brother Bert'.
4–Possibly from Elizabeth Sigmund. Elizabeth Sigmund (1928–2017) and David Compton (1930–); lived at the time at Tythecott Mill, Tythecott, Buckland Brewer, Devon; married in 1952 and divorced *c.* 1967; three children: Margaret (1951–), Hester (1954–), and James (1959–); Elizabeth married William Sigmund in 1973.

garden (I'm not quite clear under just what circumstances) since I had said our dream was to have a place big enough so we could yell from one end to the other without hearing each other.[1]

Dido Merwin is flying by jet tomorrow to rejoin Bill in America where he's been getting rich by giving a tour of readings. She treated us to two plays this week---"The Devils",[2] a dramatizing of Huxley's "The Devils of Loudon"[3] by a modern English dramatist John Whiting, a friend of Dido's Ted has met, and then Middleton's "The Changeling",[4] a fantastic & marvelous resurrection of the Restoration play with Goya sets & costumes. We've also been slipping up the subway line once a week for the series of 12 Ingmar Bergman[5] films in Hampstead,[6] so I've been beguiling the time. I do love London. I had a gallery-going spree & went to five in one afternoon.

Well, I've just finished baking the half-moons & am off to hospital with my kit-bag.

Lots of love,
Sivvy

PS: No duty to pay on the package. The vitamins are much appreciated---I cant have too many!

TO *Aurelia Schober Plath*

Wednesday 1 March 1961 ALS, Indiana University

Wednesday: March 1

Dear mother,

I am writing this to you propped up in my hospital bed less than 24 hours after my operation – which I had Tuesday about 11 am, instead of Monday as I thought. I must have really been secretly worried about my appendix a good deal of the time, as now that it is gone I feel nothing but immense relief & pleasant prospects ahead. The worst part was coming in Sunday night & finding I had to wait a day longer than I thought – being

1–In response to Leeming's query of 'How – how much room have you got to live in?' SP said, 'We're dreaming of a house where I can shout to Ted from one end to the other and he won't be able to hear me, but I don't know how far away that is.'
2–John Whiting, *The Devils*, performed at the Aldwych Theatre, London.
3–English writer Aldous Huxley (1894–1963); his *The Devils of Loudun* (1952).
4–English Jacobean playwrights Thomas Middleton (*c.* 1580–1627) and William Rowley (*c.* 1585–1626); their *The Changeling*, performed at the Royal Court Theatre.
5–Swedish film director and producer Ingmar Bergman (1918–2007).
6–Everyman Cinema, 5 Holly Bush Vale, Hampstead, London.

'under observation' Sunday night & Monday. The progress they've made (since I had my tonsils out) in anesthetics is wonderful. I had an injection in my ward bed which dried up all my saliva & so on & made me pleasantly drowsy. A very handsome young lady anesthetist introduced herself to me & said I'd see her later. She gave me an arm-shot in the anteroom which blacked me out completely. I drowsed pleasantly the rest of the day after they'd given me a shot of pain killer & was ready to see dear Ted when he came during visiting hours in the evening bearing a jar of freshly-squeezed orange juice, a pint of milk & a big bunch of hothouse grapes – none of which they've let me touch yet. I had a slight attack of nausea in the evening & promptly threw up a mug of ovaltine I persuaded them to give me. The food is pretty awful, but Ted brought me two huge rare steak sandwiches (we've discovered a marvelous tender & flavorful cut with no bone or fat which I think corresponds to the tenderloin of a T-bone steak) & a tin of tollhouse cookies – which I'll eat later on.

He is an absolute angel. To see him come in at visiting hours, about twice as tall as all the little stumpy people with his handsome kind smiling face is the most beautiful sight in the world to me. He is finishing his play & taking admirable care of little Frieda.

I am enclosing a check for $100 for deposit in our Boston account – On my first night – Monday – here Ted was able to bring me an exciting air letter from The New Yorker[1] offering me one of their coveted 'first reading' contracts for the next year! This means I have to let them have the first reading of all my poems & only send poems elsewhere if they reject them. I had to laugh, as I send all my poems there first anyway. I get $100 (enclosed) for simply signing the agreement, 25% more per poem accepted plus what they call a "cost-of-living" bonus on work accepted amounting to about 35% more per year, plus a higher base rate of pay for any work they consider of exceptional value. The contracts are renewable each year at their discretion. How's that! As you may imagine, I've been reading & re-reading the letter which came at the most opportunely cheering moment.

I am in a modern wing of this hospital – all freshly painted pink walls, pink & green flowered bed curtains & brand-new lavatories – full of light & air – an immense improvement over that grim ward at Newton-

1–Howard Moss to SP, 24 February 1961; held by Smith College. The first-reading contract was signed by vice-president R. Hawley Truax. W. S. Merwin had written to the *New Yorker* asking if they could do anything to help out SP and TH by offering one of them a first reading contract; see W. S. Merwin to Howard Moss, 19 February 1961; held by New York Public Library.

Wellesley where Ted & I visited you! The nurses are all young, pretty & cheerful – no old crochety hags or anything. I am in a big ward, divided by a glass & wood partition with about 17 beds on my side. The women at my end are young & cheerful. One has a T-B knee three had bunion operations – a couple are in plaster casts. I'm really as serious a case as any of them – a great relief to me, for I dreaded a ward of re<u>all</u>y sick people lying about & groaning all the time.

Later: now Teddy has come so I shall sign off.

With much love to you & Warrie –
Sylvia

TO *Aurelia Schober Plath*

Monday 6 March 1961 — ALS with envelope, Indiana University

Monday, March 6

Dear mother,

I am writing propped up in my hospital bed, 6 days now after my operation. My stitches are 'pulling' & itching, but the nurses say that's a sign I'm healed & they want to come out. I'm hoping I may get rid of them today. Actually, I feel I've been having an amusing holiday! I haven't been free of the baby one day for a whole year & I must say I have secretly enjoyed having meals in bed, backrubs & nothing to do but read (I've discovered Agatha Christie[1] – <u>just</u> the thing for hospital reading – I am a whodunit fan now), gossip & look at my table of flowers sent by Ted's parents, Ted, Helga Huws & Charles Monteith, Ted's Editor at Faber's. Of course <u>before</u> my operation I was too tense to enjoy much & for two days after I felt pretty shaky since they starve you for about 40 hours before & after, but I was walking around the ward on my 3rd day & gossiping with everyone. The British have an amazing 'stiff upper-lipness' – they don't fuss or complain or whine – except in a joking way & even women in toe to shoulder casts discuss family, newspaper topics & so on with amazing resoluteness. I've been filling my notebook with impressions & character studies.[2] Now I am mobile I make a daily journey round the 28 bed ward stopping & gossiping – this is much appreciated by the bedridden women (most of them are) who regard me as a sort of

1 – English crime novelist Agatha Christie (1890–1976).
2 – See 'The Inmate' in 'Appendix 10', *Journals of Sylvia Plath*: 599–608.

ward newspaper & I learn a great deal. They are all dying to talk about themselves & their medical involvements. The nurses are very young, fresh & sweet as can be, the Sister (head-nurse) lenient, wise & humorous & all the other women & girls wonderfully full of kindness & cheer. The ward is modern, freshly-painted pink-peach, with pink & green flowered curtains round the beds, good reading lights & overlooks, on my side a pleasant park with antique gravestones – so aesthetically I feel happy – your ward at Newton-Wellesley was the grimmest I've ever seen! And my stay at Cambridge hospital little better.[1] The food is pretty flat & dull, but each day Ted brings me a jar of fresh orange juice, a pint of creamy milk & a steak sandwich or salad so I'm coming along fine. I feel better than I have since the baby was born & immensely relieved to get rid of this troublesome appendix which has probably been poisoning me for some time.

The ward doctor said I'm fine inside – perfectly healthy in every way, so that's a relief. I've been on a strong diet of iron & vitamin pills & haven't had a cold since that ghastly Christmas interval. Saturday & Sunday visiting hours are from 2-3:30 instead of at night, so I persuaded the Sister to let me meet Ted & Frieda out in the park both days. It was utter heaven – I hadn't seen the baby for 5 days & missed her a lot, so I hugged her & fed her her bottle of juice. Luckily both days were balmy & sunny as summer, all the crocusses & daffodils out. I felt immensely lucky & happy to be sunning on the 4th & 5th days after my op, feeling fine except for itching stitches. Ted has been an angel. I sense he is eager for me to come home & little remarks like 'I seem to be eating a lot of bread' & 'Doesn't the Pooker make a lot of dirty pots' tell me he is wearying of the domestic routine. Poor dear, I'd like to know how many men would take over as willingly & lovingly as he has! Plus bringing me little treats every night.

Fortunately there seem to be only two 'serious' cases now – although one youngish woman did die while I was too drugged to notice much of it – a brain operation who still is in a coma after half a week with tubes in her nose & a skull-sock on her head & an old lady run over by a car with both legs broken who keeps shouting 'Police, policeman, get me out of here' & calling the nurses 'devils who are trying to murder her' & knocking the medicine out of their hands. Her moans 'O how I suffer' are very theatrical & as she is shrewd all day, picking up the least whisper, & as they give drugs for pain, I think most of this is an act for attention. I find all of us are more entertained than annoyed by this as our days are

1–See *Letters of Sylvia Plath*, Vol. 1, 1095.

otherwise routine & she adds a good bit of color with her curses & swears & the sudden crashes as she flings glasses of medicine about.

Anyhow, I shall be glad as anything to get out – the Sister just came back & said she never took stitches out till the 7th or 8th day so I'll have to wait some more & am getting very impatient. I hope, if all goes well, to be home by Friday, March 10th.

Lots of love,
Sivvy
(your appendix-less daughter)

TO *Edith Hughes*

Monday 6 March 1961 — ALS, Family owned

Ward 1
St. Pancras Hospital
4 St. Pancras Way
NW1
Monday, March 6

Dear Edith,

Well, this is the 6th day after my operation & I am feeling much better than I have for the last 3 months. Your beautiful spring bouquet came last week and your nice newsy letter which cheered me up immensely. As Ted probably told you, I had to go into hospital a week ago Sunday two days before my operation & was so nervous waiting I hardly ate a thing. The nurse's here are wonderful – very kind & efficient – and I am in a big ward of about 28 women divided in two parts by a partition. It has just been painted, with little green & pink flowered curtains up round each bed & is light & airy, so very cheerful – not old & grim like the ward I was in at Cambridge when they thought I had appendicitis before. I was drugged all Tuesday so felt no pain & Wednesday & Thursday felt a bit sore & pale – they starve you for 40 hours or so before & after appendicitis so your intestines will be empty – but after that perked right up. Ted saw me every night & I looked forward to his visit all day. Now I am waiting for my stitches to come out, which I hope will happen in the next few days as I want to get home. The other women & girls here are wonderful – full of good spirit & fun – there are only two really sick ones. One had a brain operation & is unconscious all the time with tubes up her nose & looks quite gruesome & the other is an old lady who was run over & both her legs broken. She yells a lot – it sounds like playacting but may not be – calls "Police, help, police, get me out of here!" & calls the nurses devils who are trying to murder her & knocks all the medicines out of their hands & won't take them. I must say it is entertaining as little else happens, though I hope she isn't really in pain – they're so good about giving drugs I don't think she is.

It has been like spring here the last days & Saturday & Sunday afternoon during visiting hours I got permission to sit out in the sun with Ted & little Frieda – he pushed her down in the baby carriage – & we sat in the pretty park in back of the hospital. I hadn't seen Frieda for five days & missed her so much I couldn't stop hugging her. Ted is so sweet & thoughtful & brings me milk & orange juice each day which we dont get here.

Love to all,
Sylvia

PS. Hope Vicky is recovered now.

TO *Dido & W. S. Merwin*

Tuesday 7 March 1961 ALS, Pierpont Morgan Library

Tuesday, March 7th

Dearest Bill & Dido,

I have your good fat blue air letter to hand here, my writing board propped on my stitches (which are still In) & so much to tell you of – bits & pieces – I hope the paper holds out. You are both Angels & your benevolent influence (in the classic astrological sense) floats around you, behind you & over even the great green Atlantic. I'll get my 'op' story over first. I took the bus to Camden High Street in the rain Sunday night – hours late for my appointed arrival as I spent the day baking breads, pastries & all sorts to last Ted the week & also just plain didn't want to go. I took out the map the St. Pancras Hospital (Branch of UCH[1] in NW1) sent me, hefted my cases & started in the wet Sunday blankness of C-Town in what seemed to me the right direction. Half an hour later I was ingeniously lost in the backstreets – the only people in sight rushed toward me with what I thought odd haste. They asked piteously where they were. By this time I wanted a policeman, an ambulance, any damn thing. My 2-weeks hospital-reading felt like a bricklayers kit. Finally, in some obscure dank quarter, I found a 'sweet old lady' & asked her 'Where is St. Pancras Hospital'. She took one look at me, called her husband who

1 – University College Hospital.

was pottering under his car & they insisted on driving me there. I sat in the back among oil cans & promptly started bawling. The old lady obviously hoped I was an unwed mother, but was consoled when I told her I was to be cut open. I had managed to get several miles away from the hospital & it was a long drive. My sister coolly informed me I would not be operated on till 'some time Tuesday – probably late afternoon'. When my jaw dropped & hung she asked wonderingly what I'd expected. I did, by dint of much self-expression, manage to be done Tuesday morning & sat like a deep-frozen rabbit all Monday while they extracted blood, nostril-germs & samples of everything I had to give . . . never saw the doctor whose name hung over my bed & two housemen – one a 'Registrar' – which sounded ominously like a highup office boy 'did me'. I'm done up with Black Silk. The funny thing is, I'm having more fun here than I have in months. You were absolutely right about the anesthesia, Dido – just my thing. I went out Plonk. A handsome lady anesthetist came in & told me just what she'd do ahead of time – and after it they gave me heavenly pain-killing injections which caused me to 'float' over my inert body feeling immensely powerful & invulnerable. Let me tell you though that Monday night, the worst because of waiting, the blessèd New Yorker form came through. O Bill you don't know how it sustained me & you are an angel to have nudged the Mossy stone into action. As I blacked out I thought of it with great joy & it was signed soon after, under the influence of morphia, but genuinely. I am in a sunny airy modern ward of about 28 beds – yes, there's a diabetic with a leg off – a superb antique Jewess from Hackney – but no one complains, whines or acts ill. I thought it was a ladies tea party when I first came in. I know more about England from this visit than I've learned in 5 years – there's the lot here & I am one of the few walking patients & so have become ward newspaper & the repository of superb anecdotes & life-stories.

My diary is brimming with notes – we've got an old crone who hits doctors with her purse & calls for the police out her window – she broke 2 legs in a car accident & hurls her medicine jars about & seems to have colorful DTs – very theatrical. A doll from RADA[1] with suspected appendicitis who lives in Welling Garden City[2] – one of those synthetic Suburbias & after pressing confessed she was born in Yorkshire. Several magnificent Camden-Town originals with bunions – one Daisy, opposite

1 – Royal Academy of Dramatic Art (London).

2 – SP likely meant Welwyn Garden City, a town in Hertfordshire, approximately twenty miles north of London.

me, a born marvel 'I got to break wind dont I'. A suicidal Scorpio secretary who didn't have enough bobs for the gas meter – she's my pet. A real Country lady with paddocks in South Devon in plaster up to her neck who reads 'Horse & Hound' & is visited by hideous chinless nieces – just like your superb poem[1] about people with fancy family ancestors, Bill. Ted comes rushing in each day during visiting hours – loaded with creamy milk, fresh squeezed orange juice, V-8 & steak sandwiches – dying to hear the latest tales. I'm having my first real rest for a year & piling up a huge book of anecdotes, quotes & notes. My side hurt like hell but I am so goddam cheerful that when I say 'God, the codeine!' In a noble whisper, I get it without a murmur. I eat all the food & ask for the scrapings of the pot (they're very niggardly) which has permanently alienated the Country lady. The night your letter arrived, Dido, I had just refused a monstrous Rice Pudding. The sister thought I was suffering a relapse. Ted is incredible . . . he works & manages Frieda & brings me stuff. My 4th & 5th day I wangled a full afternoon in the dear green antique Park in back of the hospital full of Jane Grundy & William Godwin[2] & other relicts with Ted & Frieda – he pushed her down in the pram as babies aren't allowed in ward. She beamed & punced my nose. I think my stitches may come out today – if so, I'm home Thursday. My mother writes her dates for flight are set: June 18 to Aug 4 – so you name 10 days in July. I dream of you both & your farm like some plummy Eden we all deserve very much. Bill – get well! Dido'll see to it.

LOVE – SYLVIA

TO *Aurelia Schober Plath*

Friday 17 March 1961 — TLS (aerogramme), Indiana University

Friday: March 17

Dear mother,

A thousand apologies for this great gap between my letters. I have been so heartened by yours, & say with great pleasure "in three months from tomorrow" you will arrive over & over. I have been in a kind of grisly coma these last 10 days & fit for little but vegetating. As you know, I had

1–Possibly Merwin's poem 'John Otto', *The New Yorker* (29 March 1958): 30; this begins: 'John Otto of Brunswick, ancestor . . .'
2–Memorials are placed in the St Pancras garden such as for Jane Grundy (1784–1854) and the philosopher William Godwin (1756–1836).

my appendix out on Tuesday the 28th, then my stitches came out Tuesday the 7th (the worst bit of all---I hated the niggling twinges of each of the 9, plus the pulling off of a large plaster bandage much more than the actual operation experience) & I was let go home Wednesday the 8th, with strict orders not to do any lifting or heavy work for 2 weeks but to behave "like a lady" or I'd feel as if run over by a small bus etc. etc. Well, ironically, I enjoyed my hospital experience immensely, especially my springlike afternoons in the hospital park & garden every day from my 4th post-op day on as the weather was mild & sunny. The most difficult part has been this home convalescing. Poor Ted insists he likes doing all the baby-lifting & laundry-bring & so on, but he's been at it over a month now since my miscarriage & I do think it bothers me more than him. I'm a model convalescent if I'm waited on by anonymous people whose job it is, but very bad at sitting loosehanded about our own small rooms. I also found it awfully depressing to rise on a sunny day & think: now I'll bake some tea-bread, wash my hair, write some letters, & then feel unlike lifting a finger. And poor Frieda decided to teethe some more the minute I got back, so we've been sleeping in fits & starts. I must say that the last 6 months I have felt slapped down each time I lifted my head up & don't know what I'd have done if Ted hadn't been more than saintly & the baby adorable & charming. I write you about this now it's over & not in the midst of it. Luckily, for all my misfortunes, I have a surprising resilience & today, 2½ weeks after my op feel very close to a self I haven't been for sometime & full of hope. The weather is amazing: real June days. I've been up on the Hill each day with Frieda out on the grass on a blanket lying in the clear sun & tomorrow start going over to the Merwins study in the morning again. I hope to be able to use these 3 months, until you come writing. Well, I have sat round "like a lady" & this Tuesday go back for a checkup. After my appointment at the main hospital with the surgeon whose name was over my bed, I saw no more of him & was "done" by his deputies in the annexe hospital who checked up on me. I didn't care: I was admirably treated & the nurses & other patients were sweethearts & my 3-inch herringbone very neat.

One thing this experience has pressed on me is our very definite need for a house by 1962. Then Ted could work off in a study while I had temporary help do house-drudging during baby-confinements & any illness that comes up & not feel guilty at using Ted's noble kindness. A house & a car. We have everything else & that's all we need to make the fullest life possible for both of us. We are seriously thinking of getting a car before we go on the Maugham thing in September---a station-wagon ---so we would travel easily with Frieda with none of the ghastly trouble of luggage train schedules & meals out---take it to Europe with us, you see. Then we could ferret out little fishing villages & so on & do a bit of looking around. If Ted had free scope for his writing, he'd earn much more than we could here at any job.

Actually, the most wonderful thing you could do for us would be to live here with Frieda for 2 weeks while we had our first real vacation in France with the Merwins (who don't allow children!) We have also a chance at staying with a philanthropist friend of theirs in South Spain afterwards & if you & Frieda got on well & it wasn't a strain on you, we'd love to go there for a week. This would enable me to have a 2½ week worriless lie in the sun which I need above all. We have all the conveniences here: a 3-day a week diaper service to the door, shops literally around the corner ---a fine butcher etc., the park across the street & cheap baby sitters I'll introduce you to so you can shop downtown & go to what plays you like. I thought we'd plan to go off 10 days to 2 weeks after you came to give us time together & you to get used to your lovely grandchild. She's getting amazingly pretty. Our doctor is also around the corner.

I so appreciated your $10: Ted got me, on my orders, a stack of DH Lawrence---novels & stories & travelbooks, which I've been reading: the only diet I felt like. I'll use the remains to buy a fine art-book when I take my 1st trip downtown. I was most touched by your taking up knitting, having wistfully said often that neither of F's grandmothers knit. I'd rather have handknit sweaters than anything & welcome the Wedgewood blue one. I'll take her measurements when she wakes up. I'd love to have it to keep admiringly till she grows to fit it. Dot sent me a sweet letter & recipe for which thank her & explain my slowness in answering. Her letters mean a great deal to me. Is there still a possibility of Warren coming over this fall???

XXX to you both,
Sivvy

FRIEDA:

Underarm-waist: 5 inches
Underarm-wrist: 7 inches
Shoulder: wrist: 8 inches
} The best I could do as she was very wiggly[1]

1 – SP bracketed the three measurements by hand and added this sentence.

Ted's Times poems will be out Sunday March 26th – a week later than we thought.
PS: I loved your get-well cards!

TO *Aurelia Schober Plath*

Monday 27 March 1961 TLS with envelope, Indiana University

3 Chalcot Square
London N.W.1
Monday: March 27

Dearest mother,

It is a chill blue March day: our summer warmth has left us for a while, and I enjoy the long light we have since the time changed this week ---it's so gloomy to have it dark at teatime! We are coming along very well. I am resting and resting---whenever I feel overtired I take the next day off, so to speak, & sit about reading & relaxing, even though I do often feel very lazy!

Ted's children's poems came out in the Time's yesterday (3 of them) & I'm enclosing a clipping.[1] We are delighted at the advance publicity for his book which should be out within a month. He also had a letter from Lord David Cecil[2] saying he'd been awarded the Hawthornden Prize for Lupercal for 1960---it's a very prestigeful fiction and/or poetry award here---gold medal and, I think, 100 pounds---Dom Moraes[3] the young Indian poet got it some years ago, & the young writer Alan Sillitoe[4] whose first novel was made into a movie. The presentation is around the end of May, so it should get into the papers about then & is a very good way to keep up his book sales. We figured he's earned about $1,500 from the BBC alone this year, which we hope to keep up---he's had the outline of another hour-drama accepted and they seem eager to take anything he does.

1–The clipping is no longer with the letter.
2–British biographer and academic David Cecil (1902–86). The Hawthornden Prize is awarded for 'imaginative literature' to a writer under the age of forty-one.
3–Dom Moraes, *A Beginning* (London: Parton Press, 1957) won the Hawthornden Prize in 1958.
4–English writer Alan Sillitoe (1928–2010); his *The Loneliness of the Long Distance Runner* (London: W. H. Allen, 1959) won the Hawthornden Prize in 1959; his *Saturday Night and Sunday Morning* (London: W. H. Allen, 1958) was made into a film in 1960.

You gorgeous sweater arrived! It is the most divine shade of blue---not that "baby-blue", but the exact color of her eyes. I'm sure she'll be into it in a year or so. I am more pleased about your knitting for her than anything. In England "a sweater a day keeps the doctor away"---she's always wearing sweaters. She has a 5th bottom right tooth out & more showing. She is a little girl suddenly and amazingly wild & pretty-looking. She stands up barely leaning back on her pen with no hands, flies round the outer rail hand over hand. I dreamed she started toddling last night, but I just let her do what she wants when she feels like it. The thing that fascinates her most is paper: she doesn't tear books, but when I give her a New Yorker after I've read it, she sits down in such a comical way with it on her lap, opens it, holds it up as if reading & crows with surprise & delight over each new page, pointing to the faces or emblems & hitting them. She imitates our faces now, claps her hands & is really enjoying her bear and raggedy Ann as other beings to pummel and talk to. We are very happy, looking forward to getting a small station wagon hopefully before you come. Then we can really take advantage of our life: going on country & Cornwall trips when other people have to work, avoiding traffic & holidayers & being portable with babies. We want to take the wagon when we go to Europe on the Maugham which we are seriously thinking of postponing until next spring---the latest time possible. Ted brought me a little bouquet of yellow primroses yesterday with a handsome edition of the Oxford Book of Wild Flowers[1]---the remains of that kind $10 you sent. He is the sweetest most thoughtful person in the world. I have had a rather glum winter & he has tirelessly stood by & cheered me up in every conceivable way.

A sweet note & yellow pajama set came from Do Cruikshank & some picture books from Aunt Marion. I'll write them within the week. Could you tell me: the names of the Cruickshank children, the names of the Aldrich children (from Duane down), & the names of Ruthie Freeman's children in order from the oldest to youngest?

I'm enclosing two checks for deposit in our account. I think there's also April interest isn't there? Did you get the 2nd $100 check I sent you---both the New Yorker $100 and the Atlantic Monthly $100?

I'm delighted to hear Warren is so well. Oh I hope he can come over this fall! I hope this Easter brings a real rest for you. For heaven's sake don't

1–S. Ary and M. Gregory, *The Oxford Book of Wild Flowers* (Oxford: Oxford University Press, 1960). SP's copy, signed and inscribed by TH, appeared at auction via Bonhams on 21 March 2018.

knock yourself out & come over exhausted! I'm sure the plane flight will be restful & brief compared to the ship. You must let us know where in London to meet you. I'll start looking around for a bed & breakfast place.

Well, I'll say goodbye for now. I had my checkup at the hospital last week & I am pronounced fine. They said my appendix showed "adhesions" which meant it was inflamed inside. It's wonderful to be rid of it, to know there's only one appendix & I'm quit of it & the worry about it for the rest of my life.

Keep well & rested!

Lots of love,
Sivvy

TO *Marion Freeman*

Tuesday 28 March 1961 — TLS (aerogramme), Smith College

3 Chalcot Square
London N.W.1, England
March 28, 1961

Dear Aunt Marion,

I have been writing you a letter in my mind for months, but what with my rather hectic life lately I've had to put off most of the things I wanted to do, and am just now getting round to saying how lovely the "Pat the Bunny" book[1] and New England calendar were at Christmas, and what fun the picture books that came this week! I'm sending mother some color photos of Frieda for her birthday (don't tell her!) and you'll see one there of Frieda pointing to her face in the mirror of the Bunny book which she loves. She takes after us---she's mad for books, and turns the pages & laughs at the pictures in an adorable grownup little way. She is such fun now---she seems to have turned into a little girl overnight & looks so cute in her little dresses.

I am feeling immensely better after having had my appendix out a few weeks ago, about a month to be exact. I looked forward to a grim time after a glimpse of a British hospital ward the last time I was here, but the hospital I was in had a new surgical wing painted pink with flowered bed curtains & cheerful washrooms & absolutely darling young nurses, and overlooked a green park where I was allowed to sit out with Frieda and

1–Dorothy Kunhardt, *Pat the Bunny* (1940).

Ted every afternoon from my 4th post-op day on. In addition, the 28 bed ward was full of interesting people, young and old, so I had quite a sociable time as I was one of the few people who could walk around, and I felt actually sorry to go home.

Ted's children's book had a few poems printed in the London Sunday Times this week as a preview & will be coming out this month---funny jingles about odd relatives called "Meet My Folks!" Ruthy will be getting a copy for her brood about then. How I'm looking forward to seeing mummy this summer. I'm already counting the days!

Much love to all,
Sivvy

TO *Philip & Margaret Booth*

Wednesday 29 March 1961 TLS (aerogramme),[1]
Dartmouth College

3 Chalcot Square
London N.W.1, England
March 29, 1961

Dear Philip & Margaret,

Hearty apologies for the great silences over here. We have all sorts of excuses, mainly a manic-depressive winter full of flu, miasmas, near bankruptcy, nights full of teething yowls from our changeling, topped off by my grateful departure from my very nasty tempered appendix several weeks ago. Why is it when things go bad, they always get worse? Ted has admirable explanations for all the megrims by way of planetary influences and starry malevolences. At any rate, we've had an early English spring & a resurge of health, hope & pound-notes, so are feeling much better. And I am again back to my American plateau of fearsome health (knock on wood, please.)

As a kindred insomniac, Philip, I very much liked your poem.[2] Ted is only one-third editor of this book into which a few Americans sometimes

1–TH added a note at the bottom of the letter, which has not been transcribed. TH thanked Booth for a poem and commented on his editorial role and the kind of poetry he was reading for the PEN anthology. He wrote about SP's recent progression in her poetry, likely, he concluded, as a result of her recent illness and appendectomy.

2–A number of poems in Booth's second collection, *The Islanders* (New York: Viking Press, 1961), are on the theme of insomnia. See specifically 'The Total Calm' (pp. 31–2), 'If It Comes (33–4), 'Night Notes on an Old Dream' (35), and 'The Owl' (36–7).

sneak, so he's sent the poems off on the rounds to the others & they will fight together about what's what later this spring. I've appreciated immensely your helpfulness about my book & did have a letter from the North Carolina press (a very nice one) about simultaneously with a drunken note[1] from my charming young British publisher in New York saying that somebody there might well want the book if I changed one or two slight things. So I'm crossing my fingers that when he comes back to London to roost, he'll have a definite contract. If so, I'll let you know when & where it'll come out & you can do me the kind favor of writing an enormously long review interspersed with exhortations to run out & buy the book immediately written between the lines in invisible onion juice. I am particularly sorry the Boston publishers (you know who) won't take it, as every damn poem in it's been published in some fine magazine by some fine upstanding responsible American editor. I am obviously not fashionable.

We hear great burbles of success from Boston---Adrienne with a 3rd book[2] & Amy Lowell Grant[3] on top of the Guggenheim[4] (I hope she'll manage to see us over here), Maxine Kumin with a baker's dozen of children's books,[5] Starb. & Sext. best-sellers. O heaven. I understand Cal's interned again (via Dido Merwin's news). If my book does get published by a reputable place in America, Philip, I wonder if you would be so good as to be a reference for me for a Guggenheim? I don't suppose I have much chance for one in England, but they do odd things & I'd give anything for Nanny-money so I could get a half-a-day's solid peace to work each day. And you, as a previous winner,[6] I could touch for luck.

I'll leave an inch or two for Ted.

Love to you 5,
Sylvia

1–James Michie to SP, undated (*c.* March 1961), telling SP that Alfred A. Knopf wanted to publish *The Colossus* if she left out one poem 'that they think is too Roethkesque'; held by Smith College.

2–Adrienne Rich, *Snapshots of a Daughter-in-Law: Poems, 1954–1962* (New York: Harper & Row, 1963).

3–Adrienne Rich was the recipient of the 1961–2 Amy Lowell Poetry Traveling Scholarship Fund which enables a US-born poet to spend one year outside North America in any country they feel will enhance their work.

4–Adrienne Rich was awarded a Guggenheim in 1959, her second (the first was in 1952). Rich's husband Arthur Conrad was also a 1959 recipient (for economics).

5–Maxine Kumin published five children's books in 1961–2.

6–Booth was awarded the Guggenheim in 1958.

TO *Dorothy Schober Benotti*

Wednesday 29 March 1961 TLS (aerogramme), Smith College

3 Chalcot Square
London N.W.1, England
March 29, 1961

Dear Dotty,

It's been wonderful having your good letters, and I'm just getting round to answering as I have been very lazy (doctor's orders!) this last month & put everything off. It's just a month now since I had my appendix out, & I'm feeling better than I have since before Frieda was born---all my old energy coming back. Hospital (on the National Health Service---for free) was actually fun. I was in a 28-bed ward, partitioned in half, in a newly painted wing, pink walls, flowered bed curtains & modern bathrooms, with sweet young nurses. I had the best of care & since I was one of the few cases allowed up immediately I had great fun walking round visiting with everyone & heard several interesting life stories. Of course having Ted standing by meant everything. He got a local babysitter & didn't miss one day of visiting hours: each time he came he brought a glass bottle of freshly squeezed orange juice, a pint of cream & a big steak sandwich. From my 4th post-op day on I was allowed to sit out in the green park behind the hospital in the afternoons (which were luckily like spring ---balmy & sunny---the whole time) with Ted & Frieda: he'd wheel her several miles in her carriage to get there as babies aren't allowed to visit in hospital and I would have been miserable if I hadn't seen her at all. I had my 9 stitches out 8 days after my op (the worst part, I thought!) & was home on the 9th day. I found it depressing for a week or two having to let Ted do all the lifting of the baby & laundry & so on, because I kept wanting to take charge, but he wouldn't let me do a thing & as a result I'm very fit now. All the women in the hospital thought it was amazing he would take care of a baby so willingly & well & so do I! It makes up a bit for not having any of my own relatives around to cheer me up. Ted dotes on Frieda & is wonderful with her.

Oh, she's so cute now. She's been fussy with 2 new teeth, making a total of 6, but she's suddenly become a little girl---her hair's just long enough & I dress her in little dresses which she immediately gets dirty. She loves to play with magazines & opens them like a book, pointing at the pictures & laughing. Ted's children's book "Meet My Folks!" is coming out in time for her first birthday & is dedicated to her.[1] We'll be sending along a copy to you when we get our orders---I think it'll amuse you---8 funny poems & drawings about silly fictitious relatives.

I love hearing all your news about Nancy & Bobby. I made the orange tea bread yesterday & it was terrific, so moist & fruity---don't forget a recipe each time you write. You make such good things!

Lots of love to all,
Sylvia

TO *Alan Ross*[2]

Sunday 2 April 1961 — TLS (postcard), University of Texas at Austin

3 Chalcot Square
London N.W.1
April 2, 1961

Dear Alan Ross,

Thanks very much for your note, but I'm afraid Ted and I won't be able to make the publication day[3] this week. All good wishes to you and the magazine in any case.

Sylvia Hughes

TO *Aurelia Schober Plath*

Wednesday 5 April 1961 — TLS with envelope, Indiana University

3 Chalcot Square
London N.W.1
Wednesday, April! 5[4]

Dear mother,

Thanks a thousand times for the enchanting blue-smocked Polly Flinders[5] dress for Frieda! I dressed her up in it today with the matching

1–SP's and FH's presentation copy, signed and inscribed by TH, appeared at auction via Bonhams on 21 March 2018.

2–British poet and editor Alan Ross (1922–2001); Ross was editor of *London Magazine* from 1961 until his death.

3–Possibly for Ted Hughes, 'The Harvesting', *London Magazine* 1 (April 1961): 41–7.

4–'Wednesday, ~~March~~ April! 5' appears in the original.

5–Polly Flinders was a brand of children's clothing.

light blue tights Dotty sent (together with a beautiful blue corduroy & romper set!) and a new pink coat her great Aunt Hilda in Yorkshire sent & took her out for her first day at the playground. They have little cage swings for babies so they can't fall out & you should have seen Frieda! She looked marvelous, her blue eyes matching her little blue outfit, & she hung on & laughed & laughed as I pushed her back and forth & she was fascinated by all the other children & the dogs. You'll have a wonderful time with her---it's like playing with a live sweet-tempered adorable doll.

I have so many people to thank for things! Tell Dotty I'm delighted with the rompers & blouse & especially the gorgeous tights (which I can't get here). Do Cruikshank sent a lovely yellow pajama set, Ted's mother a pink sweater handknit by a traveling nun (!) & red cotton rompers & an easter egg & Hilda the pink coat & an easter egg & Marty Plumer a homemade light blue denim dress that looked wonderfully Martyish. Luckily Ted's book comes out this month, so we're blowing ourself to a great stack of copies[1] and sending them to all these good people we've been wanting so much to do something for. We may not have much money, but we'll always have plenty of books!

I'm enclosing Ted's half-yearly royalty check from Harpers for deposit ---$168. I'm puzzled about your statement of our account: there's $125.85 more in it than I thought should be in it. Now this queer figure looks like interest, but you wrote me in March, so the April interest couldn't have been added yet, could it? My last figures are from October, when $97.14 interest made the total up to $5,907.21. Then the total of $266 I sent this month makes $6,173.21. When and what is the $125.85???

We've been very hectically busy lately---a spate of seeing people, poets paying Ted pilgrimages, movies, plays, teas. Tomorrow we do a joint broadcast over the BBC for America (it's called "The London Echo")[2] ---reading poems & talking about our childhoods. It's supposed to come out over a lot of networks in America. Next week Ted goes on the BBC television for about 7 minutes talking about his children's book--- probably they'll flash a drawing on the screen while he reads the poem to go with it. I'm glad he'll do this as I think it may magnify the book sales considerably & the reason he consented is because it's not a "literary pose". He wouldn't go on TV as a poet of the year before, & I guess it's

1–According to SP's chequebook, they ordered eighteen copies on 14 April 1961, fifteen copies on 13 June 1961, and an additional six on 25 August 1961.

2–The BBC Written Archives Centre has a contract for this programme dated 4 April 1961; SP and TH were to be paid 10 guineas for the appearance; SP's name has been crossed out in pencil. No known recording is extant.

a good sign. I've asked to come along & see it as we don't have a set, so it should be fun.

Best of all, he's just been commissioned by Peter Hall[1] (Director of the Royal Shakespeare Theatre & husband of Leslie Caron[2]) for a play for their London company. This is an incredible stroke of luck, as only very wellknown playwrites have been commissioned so far & it means the play Ted is working on will have the best reading & if it's good enough to produce, the best cast & production it could have.

We are thrilled by this---we have yet to hear just how much money it is---because it means that Ted's plays will go straight to the best director in England for a reading & even if this one isn't accepted (we have to keep telling ourselves this, to calm down, because we think it's a superb play---we'll be sending to the Poets' Theatre as well, so you may have a chance to see it too!) the next ones no doubt will be. Oh you wait, we'll be wealthy yet.

Frieda's birthday was lovely. We sang to her on getting up in the morning & let her play in bed with us. Then we presented her officially with her books (Ted's among them), her picture (by our neighborhood artist whose exhibit we're going to next week), a lovely blue fairytale landscape with Japanese lantern-like plants, her clothes (quite a mound), and five great balloons---one a big green one with zoo animals printed all over it and a long cylindrical orange one with a face and blue ears. The balloons scared her to death at first & I was sorry I got them, but the next day she woke up & rushed over to them & batted them around fearlessly. When they broke because she insisted on biting them she didn't even exclaim & she's still playing with the two that are left. I'd made a little cupcake with a pink candle which we lit and give her at teatime & she ate most of it sitting up in her little party dress. She is still playing with your birthday card. Tear them up, the idea! She loves paper cards above all (the rag books count no longer)---crows with delight at the pictures, points to the faces, opens them, pretends to read them and really has a fine time. She is mad for books---probably because we read all the time.

Thanks so much for the $5. You mustn't go on lavishing things on me!! I'll wait till I think: oh, I wish I could have that, or do this, & then take it out & get it or do it.

1–English theatre and film director Peter Hall (1930–2017).

2–French film actress Leslie Caron (1931–); divorced 1965.

Ted requests that if you ever send any more packages in addition to the hundred you've just sent, could you please add a few Crest toothpastes. I believe they have fluoride in them or something.

Well, I'm off to bed,

Lots of love,
Sivvy

TO *Judith Jones*[1]

Wednesday 5 April 1961 — TLS (aerogramme), University of Texas at Austin

3 Chalcot Square
London N.W.1, England
April 5, 1961

Mrs. Judith B. Jones, Editor
ALFRED A. KNOPF INC.
501 Madison Avenue
New York 22, New York
USA

Dear Mrs. Jones:

I am delighted to have your letter[2] and to know that Knopf is interested in bringing out THE COLOSSUS.

I am very much in agreement with you about the greater part of "Poem for a Birthday". It is the only poem in the book written under the undiluted influence of Roethke, and I now feel it is too obviously influenced. There are, however, two sections of the poem I wonder if you would reconsider and perhaps be willing to publish on their own---"Flute Notes From a Reedy Pond" and "The Stones". These poems were written separately and much later than the other five in the sequence and have been published as separate poems in America where the others have not.[3] I think, particularly in "The Stones", that the verse form and cadence is like nothing in Roethke. "Flute Notes" I feel is also stable and quite formal and a poem on its own, but I am most concerned about the chance

1–American editor and writer Judith Jones (1924–2017).

2–Judith Jones to SP, 29 March 1961; held by Smith College.

3–SP's 'The Stones' was not published in the US until it appeared in Knopf's edition of *The Colossus* (1962); the two poems from the sequence that were published were 'Flute Notes From a Reedy Pond' and 'Witch Burning'.

of ending the book with "The Stones". The whole experience of being broken and mended, together with the ending "Love is the uniform of my bald nurse" etc., seems to me the way I would like to end the book. I'd be delighted to unburden myself of the other five.[1] Do let me know what you think of this.

I admire Stanley Kunitz[2] and his work immensely and am particularly glad to have his opinion on my book. Here are the poems I would be willing to cut out: POINT SHIRLEY, METAPHORS, MAUDLIN, OUIJA and TWO SISTERS OF PERSEPHONE. If you would consider keeping "Flute Notes" and "The Stones" at the end as two separate poems, that would make a total of 40 poems in the book (instead of 50) which seems to me a good and reasonable number.

There are also two misprints in the book[3] I'd like to correct: In "Mussel Hunter at Rock Harbor" on p. 73, verse 3 line 4 on the page, it should be "airy thatching" (not air thatching) and in the last line of "Sculptor" on p. 79 it should be "solider repose" (not soldier!)

I'm eager to hear what you think of these suggestions. As for the rest, I couldn't be more in agreement with you and Mr. Kunitz.

Sincerely yours,
Sylvia Plath

TO *Theodore Roethke*

Thursday 13 April 1961 TLS, University of Washington

3 Chalcot Square
London N.W.1, England
April 13, 1961

Dear TR---

Here is the book[4] you were meant to have while you were here. I hope you won't hate me for the last sequence of 7 poems which show me so far under your influence as to be flat out. I'm negotiating with Knopf (bless

1–Sylvia Plath, *The Colossus & Other Poems* (New York: Alfred A. Knopf, 1962); published on 14 May 1962; excluded the following poems printed in the Heinemann edition: 'Metaphors', 'Black Rook in Rainy Weather', 'Maudlin', 'Ouija', 'Two Sisters of Persephone', 'Who', 'Dark House', 'Maenad', 'The Beast', and 'Witch Burning'.

2–Jones wrote to SP, 'Stanley Kunitz, who read the collection, suggested to me that he thought it could be cut down considerably.'

3–See SP to ASP, 26 October 1960.

4–SP included a copy of the Heinemann edition of *The Colossus* with the inscription: 'For Theodore Roethke with much love and immense admiration, Sylvia Plath, April 13, 1961'.

them) now for an American edition of the book and they've made me promise to leave the Birthday sequence out since they think I'm too in love with your work as it is. But I couldn't wait for the American edition, I wanted you to have this.

It was wonderful seeing you in London though for not long enough & Ted & I hope we may manage a year teaching on the West Coast somewhere within the next couple of years & hope we can see a lot more of you.

If you think any of these are any good or that I should be allowed to write any more would you be a reference for the Guggenheim I'm applying for this year? I'd rather have you than anybody so I ask you first. Please don't forget to ask your publishers to send on I AM SAID THE LAMB.[1]

With love,
Sylvia

PS- I'm enclosing 'Tulips' written after my latest bout in hospital.

SP

For Theodore Roethke from Sylvia

Sylvia Plath
3 Chalcot Square
London N.W.1, England

Tulips

The tulips are too excitable, it is winter here,
Look how white everything is, how quiet, how snowed-in.
I am learning peacefulness, lying by myself quietly
As the light lies on these white walls, this bed, these hands.
I am nobody; I have nothing to do with explosions.
I have given my name and my day-clothes up to the nurses
And my history to the anesthetist and my body to surgeons.

They have propped my head between the pillow and the sheet-cuff
Like an eye between two white lids that will not shut,
Stupid pupil, it has to take everything in.
The nurses pass and pass, they are no trouble,
They pass the way gulls pass inland in their white caps,
Doing things with their hands, one just the same as another,
So it is impossible to tell how many there are.

1–Theodore Roethke, *I Am Said the Lamb* (Garden City, NY: Doubleday, 1961).

My body is a pebble to them, they tend it as water
Tends to the pebbles it must run over, smoothing them gently.
They bring me numbness in their bright needles, they bring me
 sleep.
Now I have lost myself I am sick of baggage---
My patent leather overnight case like a black pillbox,
My husband and child smiling out of the family photo;
Their smiles catch onto my skin, little smiling hooks.

I have let things slip, a thirty-year-old cargo boat
Stubbornly hanging on to my name and address.
They have swabbed me clear of my loving associations.
Scared and bare on the green plastic-pillowed trolley
I watched my teaset, my bureau of linen, my books
Sink out of sight and the water went over my head.
I am a nun now, I have never been so pure.

I didn't want any flowers, I only wanted
To lie with my hands turned up and be utterly empty.
How free it is, you have no idea how free---
The peacefulness is so big it dazes you,
And it asks nothing, a name tag, a few trinkets.
It is what the dead close on, finally; I imagine them
Shutting their mouths on it, like a Communion tablet.

The tulips are too red in the first place, they hurt me.
Even through the gift paper I could hear them breathe
Lightly, through their white swaddlings, like an awful baby.
Their redness talks to my wound, it corresponds.
They are subtle: they seem to float, though they weigh me down,
Upsetting me with their sudden tongues and their color,
A dozen red lead sinkers round my neck.

Nobody watched me before, now I am watched.
The tulips turn to me, and the window behind me
Where once a day the light slowly widens and slowly thins,
And I see myself, flat, ridiculous, a cut-paper shadow
Between the eye of the sun and the eyes of the tulips,
And I have no face, I have wanted to efface myself.
The vivid tulips eat my oxygen.

Before they came the air was calm enough,
Coming and going, breath by breath, without any fuss.
Then the tulips filled it up like a loud noise.
Now the air snags and eddies round them the way a river
Snags and eddies round a sunken rust-red engine.
They concentrate my attention, that was happy
Playing and resting without committing itself.

The walls, also, seem to be warming themselves.
The tulips should be behind bars, like dangerous animals;
They are opening like the mouth of some great African cat,
And I am aware of my heart: it opens and closes
Its bowl of red blooms out of sheer love of me.
The water I taste is warm and salt, like the sea,
And comes from a country far away as health.

TO *Aurelia Schober Plath*

Friday 14 April 1961 — TLS (aerogramme), Indiana University

3 Chalcot Square
London N.W.1, England
April 14, 1961

Dear mother,

Your absolutely beautiful <u>second</u> sweater arrived this week & I tried it right on Frieda and it fits wonderfully and roomily over her little dresses and looks marvelous! I can't tell you how pleased I am with it. I love the style with the deep bottom turn-up at the waist and she looks a tiny schoolgirl in it! The other sweater you sent is a real party sweater with all the openwork at the top but I think this sort is even handsomer in its way for everyday wear. The nun-knit one isn't a patch on these---the style is like an old man's button-down vest, but of course I don't say so!

It has been real April weather---showery and moist. I have been working like mad in Merwins study every morning and find if I just have five hours to write from 8-1 I can do all my housework and business during the rest of the day with a serene mind. I hope to heaven we'll have found a place here by next New Year! It's amazing the change that's coming over this neighborhood. It's been a real slum and the lovely houses let go terribly, rented out as rooms for laborers. Now piles of young professional couples our age are moving in, doing the houses over into family residences & planning to settle in with their children near the good state-supported free schools (which even teach Greek in some places!) and parks. I have asked Ted to go off and find out about mortgages this week because I have an awful feeling that nobody will give a free-lance writer a mortgage although our income equals that of most of the people around us in regular jobs. It would be awful to have a good house come up & then find we couldn't get any mortgage. A couple of our friends who have bought houses have bought them outright, but as most of them cost about 7 thousand pounds now we'd only have about a third to put down. I'm going to ask Ted to try and ask his uncle for a thousand pound loan when we finally do have a house to buy. But I'm skeptical. It's sad to know in five years we'll have the money but by then it will be too late. We really need one in the next year. I'm full of this because two houses are coming up for auction[1] this week in the neighborhood (I could never bring myself to bid for a house!) & I'm going along for the fun of it with a new Oxford-graduate neighbor[2] of mine whose husband is a financial-page journalist, both lovely, with a darling little girl. I am happier in this neighborhood than I have ever been anywhere in my life and the thought of ever having to move away from my marvelous midwives, doctors, friends, butcher & baker and parks and plays and all I enjoy so much is unbearable. I'd like to live here the rest of my life. Of course as soon as we got a house settled we could negotiate for a teaching year in America as we'd have a place to leave all our stuff here and could easily rent it for a year. I know I'm boring about this, but it's the main big step ahead and somehow it seems the one problem: we have all the rest: love, work we love & that supports us, a wonderful baby etc. etc.

Aunt Frieda sent a darling light blue dress made in the Phillipines this week. She and Walter have moved to a trailer camp which they seem wonderfully enthusiastic about. I've got a pass to Ted's TV show which will be broadcast live this Wednesday & I'm fascinated to see it. Thanks a million for the research into our deposits. Wish I could think what the $71 was. Ted's being featured in the Observer this week,[3] a livelier rival to

1–Per Lorna Secker-Walker, the houses were 8 and 9 Chalcot Square, London N.W.1.

2–Lorna (Lea) Secker-Walker (1933–), her husband David Secker-Walker (1932–2014) who worked as deputy City editor for the *Sunday Telegraph*, and their daughter Joanna (1959–). The Secker-Walkers lived at 5 Chalcot Square.

3–Ted Hughes, 'Last Lines', 'Sugar Loaf', 'Gog', 'Wino', 'Flanders, 1960', and 'Toll of Air Raids', *The Observer* (16 April 1961): 31. Includes a brief article about Hughes entitled 'In the Picture'.

the Times (Sunday papers), with 6 poems and a little article by our friend and critic A. Alvarez. We'll send clippings.

We're mailing off a whole load of Meet My Folks today to friends and neighbors in America by sea mail, Aldriches, Cruikshanks (do they have a c in Cruick???), Ruthie Geissler etc. We have our eye on a small station wagon that seats 5 & has two back doors that open for loading luggage and a back seat that folds forward to make lots of room for babies' beds and so on. We could buy it outright with the money we've saved in our account here writing in the last year & probably will. Hardly anybody garages cars. There's no snow & acres of parking room in front of these houses in our end. Ted is dying for a car (!) because he wants to go off to Cornwall & the country & I think it wise to get it now though it means a big dent in our savings. It will cost about $1,876 new & we've decided to get a new one as neither of us knows a thing about cars & we mistrust all 2nd-hand dealers & have no wise car-machine-minded people who could test a 2nd hand one. Ted's radioplay was broadcast a 3rd time this week bringing his earnings on it up to over $900 this year.[1] He's almost finished this huge 5-act play[2] called 'The Calm'. You'll be getting photos of Frieda in good time. "Isn't April coming soon?" Her birthday picture isn't of her but a painting of a magical blue landscape an artist friend did & we gave her for her birthday. What's with Warren & Margaret?[3] Are they getting married? I hope she's not too dull, I get no real picture of her at all. Hope I have some good literary news for you soon.

A millions XXXs
<drawing of station-wagon>
Sivvy

<on page 1 of letter>

PS – Have you ever thought of knitting any booties? Or are they too hard? I'd dearly love some to go with these sweaters! F's foot is just about 4 inches long from toe to heel

xx
s

1–*House of Aries*, BBC Third Programme (8 April 1961).

2–'this huge 5-act ~~one~~ play' appears in the original.

3–Margaret Wetzel Plath (1938–92); B.A. 1960, Colby College; M.A. 1961, Radcliffe College. Married Warren Plath, 2 June 1962.

TO *Aurelia Schober Plath*

Saturday 22 April 1961[1] TLS in greeting card[2] with envelope, Indiana University

<printed greeting>
With Happy Birthday *Greetings and Best Wishes / from*
<signed>
from Sivvy & Ted & Frieda start here→

Dear mother,

Here are your Birthday pictures.[3] I hope you like them. Frieda's much prettier than the colored ones show (taken at 10 months) because she has more hair, as you can see in the one with the two of us together. She is a marvelous child & I'm sure in no time you & she will be very close. She is so outgoing & after the first few minutes of getting used to someone very friendly. I take her up on Primrose Hill every fine afternoon & she crawls in the grass, laughing and waving at babies and dogs and standing up, holding on to her pram. I have such fun with her, I'm just dying for a house and room for lots of babies.

I am working fiendishly at the Merwins study 7 mornings a week, as they are coming home at the end of May and I've a lot I want to finish before then. I have found that the whole clue to my happiness is to have 4 to 5 hours perfectly free & uninterrupted to write in first thing in the morning---no phones, doorbells or baby. Then I come home in a wonderful temper and dispatch all the household jobs in no time. Thank goodness the Merwins are going to France shortly after they come home, so I hope to have the study till next fall. When we do get a house, I'll get a morning nanny I think. I find I enjoy all the little niggly jobs like ironing & floor scrubbing when I've had my Morning.

Business: I'm enclosing $200 of checks to deposit. What does that make, with the April interest??? I hope when we come to withdraw most of this to pay for a house you won't feel too lonely! We hope to get our station wagon in a month or so, we've put down a deposit, and Ted is taking driving lessons preparatory to getting a British license. They are much stricter here, & I'll want lessons as well before I venture on the other side of the road. It will be a small black wagon with light wood frame,

1 – Date supplied from postmark.
2 – Jarrold & Sons, for Cathay Arts, birthday card. 'Happy Birthday' added by SP.
3 – The photographs are no longer with the letter.

red upholstery & goes 40+ miles to the gallon which I gather is rather wonderful. I'm enclosing a little picture[1] of it. This will mean ease in all of us going to Yorkshire---we'll probably go for a week from July 17th on (after we've come back from Europe) as Ted is going to be guest speaker the next day at his old school and has to read at a poetry festival here in London that day. Roughly, this is what we plan: 10 days to 2 weeks together in London with you on your arrival, our leaving for France the last few days in June, 28th or so, & returning about 2½ weeks in time to leave with you & Frieda for Yorkshire the 17th, then back to London, with maybe a jaunt to Cornwall or Devon before you go. I'm trying to get the bulk of my writing done before you come, but even if I work in the mornings we'll have the whole rest of the day together & you could take Frieda to the park in the mornings, or see things you wanted to see in London. Less than two months! I am looking so forward to showing you everything & having you see your beautiful granddaughter!

I got a pass to the rehearsal and production of "Wednesday Magazine",[2] the hour-long TV show Ted appeared on last week. It was fascinating---a big barn of a studio full of lights & little groups of participants---a famous pianist & her collection of elephants & a grand piano in one corner, an actor & actress in bathrobe & slippers at breakfast in another, Romeo & Juliet going on in Arabic on a balcony in another & a street lamp & pushcart full of artificial fruit with a lavender seller in another & Ted & his interviewer & a huge blown-up drawing of the Owler out of his book in another. The cameras wheeled from one group to another & snippets of movies filled in the intervals. I watched the TV monitor screen at the same time as the real studio. First they did a run through, then criticized it, then broadcast "live". Ted looked marvelous, so handsome & sweet, & read his Owler poem while the camera moved from his face to the big drawing. I was very proud. I do hope it sells some copies of his children's book! The minute we got home another TV man called up wanting to do a feature program of him reading poems in Yorkshire, but Ted says this is his first & last TV program. He'll get another avalanche of publicity on May 31st when he's presented with the Hawthornden prize, so wants to keep as quiet as possible. I'm enclosing the poems & article[3] on him that came out in last Sunday's Observer---the Times' rival & a far livelier paper. It is so marvelous having married Ted with no

1–The photograph is no longer with the letter.

2–Ted Hughes, 'My Grandpa', *Wednesday Magazine*, directed by Richard Francis, BBC Television, 19 April 1961.

3–The poems and article, cited in SP to ASP, 14 April 1961, are no longer with the letter.

money & nothing in print & then having all my best intuitions prove true! Our life together is happier than I ever believed possible and the only momentary snags are material ones---our lack of a house is the one thing we want to change. I want Ted to have a study where he doesn't have to move his papers or be bothered when there are visitors, and where I can have an upstairs room in peace in the morning while someone minds the children in the basement nursery. Then, too, we'll be able to plan a year in America, because we'll have a place to leave our furniture and books and gear. Anyhow, the station wagon will make this summer and our Maugham trip to Europe a joy instead of a burden. It is so easy traveling in a car with a baby when you can feed them when they want, or have them nap on an improvised bed. Ted & I will bring a portable camp stove to Europe too, so we'll be able to see a lot more than we would if we were carless & stuck in some one town.

I feel so fine now this appendix worry is over and Frieda is safely a year old, I want to consolidate my health and work in the coming year. We have good friends here, most of them our age, and as Ted says, in positions of power, and the older people we know are influential and benevolent, so I feel very much at home. The BBC really supports us. Our income from them in the past year has bought us our car.

Do keep in good health, now, mummy, & have a Happy Happy Birthday!

Lots of love,
Sivvy

PS – Did you & Warren get your Birthday Present Books?

TO *Warren Plath*

Saturday 22 April 1961[1] TLS in greeting card[2] (photocopy), Indiana University

Dear Warren . . .

With great effort I have figured you must be 26. I say with great effort because I always figure your age from mine and I am having increasing difficulty in remembering mine. I get vague reports of you from mother. I half expect to hear from her that you are married & have ten children one of these days. Who is this Margaret? Give me a picture of her. Verbal or actual. All I can conjure up is somebody sitting in a rocker and singing "Mein ruh' ist hin. . ."[3]

I hope these pictures,[4] which I scrupulously divided between you & mother and which mother will probably appropriate, give you some idea of your neice & godchild (niece?) She is much better looking than the colored ones, as they put a funny yellow cast on them---the transparencies I have of those are better. You will notice Little Bunzo Bear and Raggedy Ann in her animal & people family. She loves them.

When will you know if you can come to the conference in England this fall? I'm dying to see you. Somehow I feel we say nothing by letter & I do wish you could visit us. We're getting a little station wagon---we've put down the deposit & hope it arrives well before mother comes, so we'll be more mobile now. It makes traveling with Frieda seem possible & we'll probably take it to Europe with us.

Please write now & then,

Lots of love,
Sivvy

1–Date supplied from internal evidence.

2–KG birthday card.

3–Franz Schubert, *Gretchen am Spinnrade* (1814); based on text from Goethe's *Faust*.

4–The photographs are no longer with the letter.

TO *Elizabeth Kray*[1]

Wednesday 26 April 1961 — TLS (aerogramme), Academy of American Poets

3 Chalcot Square
London N.W.1, England
April 26, 1961

Miss Elizabeth Kray
THE POETRY CENTER
YM and YWHA
Lexington Ave. & 92nd Street
New York 28, New York
USA

Dear Miss Kray:

I was happy to have your letter and your kind invitation to read on the Poetry Center "Introductions" series.[2]

I'm not planning to come to the United States next year, but do hope to make a return visit a year or so after that, so I'll let you know in advance when I eventually plan to come, and perhaps we can arrange for a reading then.

Ted joins me in sending best wishes,

Sincerely yours,
Sylvia Plath

1–Elizabeth D. Kray (1916–87); head of the Poetry Center at the YM-YWHA in New York, 1954–62.

2–Kray wrote to Peter Davison on 13 April 1961 asking if he expected SP to be in the US in 1962. Davison replied on 17 April passing on their address. Copies of letters held by Yale University.

TO *John Lehmann*

Wednesday 26 April 1961 TLS, University of Texas at Austin

3 Chalcot Square
London N.W.1, England
April 26, 1961

John Lehmann, Esq.
31 Egerton Crescent
London S.W.3

Dear John,

I'm applying for a Eugene F. Saxton fellowship (an American grant for youngish creative writers) in order to complete a novel I'm working on,[1] and I wonder if you would be willing for me to list you as a literary reference.

You've been so encouraging about my short story ventures I thought you would be a good person to ask, and I'd be honored to have your name on my list.

With warmest good wishes,
Sincerely,
Sylvia Plath

TO *Leonard Baskin*

Wednesday 26 April 1961 TLS (aerogramme), British Library

3 Chalcot Square
London N.W.1, England
April 26, 1961

Dear Leonard,

Ted and I await your arrival---at any time of the day or night and for one meal or a dozen---with great joy.

Our phone number, not listed in the book, is PRImrose 9132.

Best love to you, Esther and Tobias, from the three of us.

Sylvia

1–Sylvia Plath, *The Bell Jar* (London: Heinemann, 1963). Published on 14 January 1963 under the pseudonym Victoria Lucas.

TO *Ann Davidow-Goodman & Leo Goodman*

Thursday 27 April 1961 TLS with envelope, Smith College

3 Chalcot Square
London N.W.1, England
April 27, 1961

Dear Ann and Leo,

It was lovely to have your letter and Frieda is very pleased to have two such goldenly constellated godparents. You made yourselves godparents, whether you knew it or not, by your heavenly solicitude last spring. Now that the green and sunny season is come round again it underlines our missing you. Our only consolation is that Leo will probably be flown to England periodically to jack up their statistical flat tires, and you, Ann, will fly with him.

How marvelous the job offers sound. I wish, selfishly, that you would settle in New York which is so near visiting distance from Boston, but if you insist on going back to Chicago we shall just have to track you out there when we finally get round to coming back for a year's stay, which we hope to do soon after we manage to locate and buy a house in the immediate neighbourhood. We are treating ourselves to a small versatile Morris station wagon this spring which is supposed to do over 40 miles to the gallon and have space for innumerable babies.

A copy of Meet My Folks! is on its way to you. It came out just in time for Frieda's birthday and some came out in the Sunday Times and I had fun last week watching Ted appear on a "live" TV show called Wednesday Magazine, a very mixed bag of People about Town including a famous lady pianist with a collection of toy elephants, a lavendar-seller and an old-iron collector who remembered the antique cries, an actor and actress from a variety skit, Romeo and Juliet in Arabic, a film clip of spring lambs, and Ted, reading the Grandpa's an Owler poem in front of a huge blowup of the drawing. He looked beauteous but won't do it again.

My mother is flying over in mid-June and we are working like blacks to finish things before she comes so we can take a vacation at W. S. Merwin's farm in mid-France for two weeks while she lives here with Frieda---which will be my first real vacation for too long. Ted is finishing a long five-act play and I am over one-third through a novel about a college girl building up for and going through a nervous breakdown. I have been wanting to do this for ten years but had a terrible block about Writing a Novel, Then, suddenly, in beginning negotiations with a New York publisher for an American edition of my poems, the dykes broke and I stayed awake all night seized by fearsome excitement, saw how it should be done, started the next day & go every morning to my borrowed study as to an office & belt out more of it. I'll have to publish it under a psuedonym, if I ever get it accepted, because it's so chock full of real people I'd be sued to death and all my mother's friends wouldn't speak to her because they are all taken off. Anyhow, I have never been so excited about anything. It's probably godawful, but it's so funny, and yet serious, it makes me laugh.

Frieda had a fine first birthday. I'm enclosing a picture[1] of her getting acquainted with one of the family of balloons. Our bedroom, by the way, blooms under the Chinese bauble chandelier which is wonderful fun. Frieda is mad for it, and I set it twirling while feeding and changing her under it and she's quiet as a mouse.

Lots of love from the three of us –
Syl

TO *Aurelia Schober Plath*

Monday 1 May 1961 — TLS (aerogramme), Indiana University

3 Chalcot Square
London N.W.1, England
MAY DAY

DEAR MOTHER,

GOOD NEWS GOOD NEWS GOOD NEWS!

I hoped it would come by your birthday, but here it is on Mayday instead.

ALFRED KNOPF will publish THE COLOSSUS in AMERICA! This is no doubt what Mrs. Prouty's garbled account was about. They wrote me an optimistic letter about a month ago---and I guess I shouldn't have mentioned it to her until it was definite, so I decided not to jinx my luck and to keep quiet until I heard definitely, which I did today.[2]

Knopf wanted me to revise the book---leave out about 10 poems, especially those in the last sequence. Well, by a miracle of intuition I guessed (unintentionally) the exact 10 <u>they</u> would have left out, they wanted me to choose independently. I am delighted. I can correct my

1 – The photograph is with the letter.
2 – Judith Jones to SP, 28 April 1961; held by Smith College.

typing mistakes and leave out the poems that have been criticized to good purpose here, making a total of 40 instead of 50 in the book---40 being the usual length for volumes.

After all my fiddlings and discouragements from the little publishers it is an immense joy to have what I consider THE publisher accept my book for America with such enthusiasm. They "sincerely doubt a better first volume will be published this year".[1]

Now you will be able to have a really "perfect" book to buy at Hathaway House, see reviewed etc. etc. It is like having a second book come out---this one the Ideal. Ever since their first letter came I had a night of inspiration and then started writing 7 mornings a week at the Merwins study and have done better things than ever before, so it is obvious that this American acceptance is a great tonic.

I don't know just when it will appear over there, but I'll keep you posted.

LOTS OF LOVE,
Sivvy

TO *Judith Jones*

Tuesday 2 May 1961

TLS (aerogramme),
University of Texas at Austin

3 Chalcot Square
London N.W.1, England
May 2, 1961

Mrs. Judith B. Jones, Editor
ALFRED A. KNOPF Inc.
501 Madison Avenue
New York 22, New York
USA

Dear Mrs. Jones:

I am delighted to have your letter and to know that "Flute Notes" and "The Stones" may end my book. I am also pleased that our opinions seem to coincide so closely.

1 – SP slightly misquotes Jones's letter which reads 'I have also checked to see if the collection would not be eligible for the Lamont Poetry Award because I sincerely doubt that they are going to find a better first volume this year.' Because it had been published in Britain *The Colossus* was not eligible.

Since last writing you, I have been having second thoughts about "Point Shirley", and think your idea of leaving it in is a good one.[1] It is a much more recent poem than the other two you mention and, I think, a more vivid and better one. Of those, I should be glad to leave out "Black Rook in Rainy Weather". I choose to leave out this, rather than "The Ghost's Leavetaking", partly because the reaction to the Ghost over here has been pretty favorable, notably in Roy Fuller's review in the London Magazine.[2] Then, with "Black Rook" (and "Metaphors"), left out, the ghost is sandwiched between two very concrete descriptive poems---"Grantchester Meadows" and "A Winter Ship", which make a better contrast I think, than the two we are going to omit.

I am happy that my book has had a trial run in England, as it has made me much more objective about the poems and will result, I think, in a much stronger and shorter book in America. I'm sorry, of course, about missing out on the Lamont[3] as a result.

I look forward to hearing about publication plans.

Sincerely,
Sylvia Plath

TO *A. E. Dyson*[4]

Wednesday 3 May 1961 TLS, University of Kansas

3 Chalcot Square
London N.W.1
May 3, 1961

Dear Tony,

A note in haste with a few recent poems.[5] I only have these on hand as I'm head over ears in the middle of a long prose thing and not doing

1–On 'Point Shirley', Jones wrote, 'I like those that seem to come out of your New England past and it strikes me as a very well-made poem with many lines of startling vigor and sharp observation leading up to a beautifully cadenced ending.'

2–Roy Fuller, *London Magazine* (March 1961): 69–70; Fuller wrote: 'The language of this poetry is unusual but not eccentric, with a great gift for the right epithet, the metaphoric noun. The following examples come from an excellent poem called "The Ghost's Leavetaking" . . .' (70).

3–The Lamont Poetry Selection was given for a poet's first published book by the Academy of American Poets.

4–British literary critic and lecturer A. E. (Anthony E.) Dyson (1928–2002).

5–Sylvia Plath, 'I Am Vertical' and 'Private Ground', *Critical Quarterly* 3 (Summer 1961): 140–1. Plath also submitted 'Heavy Women', 'Whitsun', 'Small Hours' ['Barren Woman'],

anything else right now. I hope something among them seems okay to you.

I'm enclosing the Larkin[1] poem Brian sent. I was disappointed in it at first. Then I felt much as Brian did, & started to like it. I think it does what it does well, though what it is doing is not very large. I guess, in the end, I am just not sure about it.

I hope to have the anthology poems typed up by the end of the month. I still have a couple of fringe poems I am hunting down. For blurb, why don't you say something to the effect that this sampling will include poems by lively American poets of all persuasions (from Beat Corso[2] to Wilbur the Elegant),[3] stressing young poets and new books (this includes Stafford,[4] who is an old poet, but just has an exciting first book out & needs to be known.) About 18 poets, and over 20 poems.

The memory of that corn-on-the-cob floats in my head like a celestial relic.

All the best,
Sylvia

PS: My mother will be here in July for her first visit, so Ted & I will be spending all our time showing her round and don't dare to make any other commitments!

TO *Aurelia Schober Plath*

Monday 8 May 1961

TLS with envelope,
Indiana University

Monday: May 8

Dear mother,

Glad to hear the details of our rising bank account and that your are as pleased about Knopf as we are. It's as good as getting two books for one.

'Parliament Hill Fields', 'The Hanging Man', 'In Plaster', 'Stillborn', 'Leaving Early', and 'Zoo Keeper's Wife'.

1–English poet Philip Larkin (1922–85). The poem is no longer with the the letter but may have been Larkin's 'Naturally the Foundation will Bear Your Expenses'.

2–American beat poet Gregory Corso (1930–2001); Corso was not included in the anthology.

3–Richard Wilbur, 'Potato', *American Poetry Now* (1961): 9.

4–American poet William Stafford (1914–93); his *West of Your City* (Los Gatos, Calif.: Talisman Press, 1960); his 'In the Oregon Country', 'The Well Rising', and 'A Survey', *American Poetry Now* (1961): 6–7.

Ted's just had his story "Snow" accepted in America by Harper's Bazaar,[1] the very fancy fashion magazine, so we should have another check to round out our 7th thousand to send pretty soon.

We are both working very hard---Ted is typing his 5 act play and has got over the 100 page mark, and I've finished my commissioned poem for the summer poetry festival at the Mermaid Theatre and everybody seems very pleased with it.

I am going to a first night at the opera[2] at Covent Garden tonight with the Secretary of the Arts Council, Eric White[3]---a distinguished white-haired gentleman who has taken an interest in us. His wife[4] is going to be out of town so he invited either one of us & Ted let me go. Last week he and his wife treated us to a box at the Covent Garden performance of Rigoletto[5] which delighted us---I'm very fond of opera but know nothing about it and have hardly heard any of it, a situation which I hope to remedy.

We've engaged you a room at a modest but, I think, comfortable place called the Clive Hall Hotel.[6] The rooms are small, but clean and freshly painted---it's the nearest place we could find, as ours is a very residential district, a very nice 10 minutes walk away over Primrose Hill. Bed and a substantial breakfast is about $3.15 a night. I hope that's all right. We plan to have you share lunch & supper with us.

I'm having Ted make out the other little check to you as well---could you send off $5 with the enclosed Alumnae Association blank? The $100 is Mrs. Prouty's check for 10 copies of "Meet My Folks"---we're to keep the leftovers! Deposit this in our Wellesley account, will you? That's our gift and miscellaneous account. There's still about $50 in it, isn't there? I know just what supper you're going to have on your arrival§

xxx
Sivvy

1–Ted Hughes, 'Snow', *Harper's Bazaar* (October 1961): 183, 216–17, 221.
2–Probably the Welsh Opera Company in Giuseppe Verdi's *La Battaglia di Legnano*; the first night was 8 May 1961 at the Sadler's Wells Theatre, Rosebery Avenue, London E.C.1.
3–British musicologist and composer Eric Walter White (1905–85). White was Secretary of the Arts Council of Great Britain.
4–Edith Dorothy 'Dodo' White (1909–77); married 15 December 1939.
5–Verdi, *Rigoletto*, performed at the Royal Opera House, Covent Garden, on 22, 26, 29 April, and 1 May 1961.
6–Clive Hall Hotel, 27 Fellows Road, London N.W.3.

TO *Charles Osborne*[1]

Tuesday 16 May 1961 TLS, University of Texas at Austin

3 Chalcot Square
London N.W.1
May 16, 1961

Dear C. O.

Our baby unearthed this shortly after your departure. I trust it belongs and will come in handy.

It was much fun having you here,

sph

TO *Aurelia Schober Plath*

Sunday 28 May 1961 TLS (aerogramme), Indiana University

Sunday May 28th

Dearest mother,

I haven't written for about a hundred years, due to a very huge pile of jobs & harassments. Thank you so much for the lovely booties which fit perfectly & which Frieda has been wearing daily. We loved the packet with all the good things. I have bought a featherweight pushchair (folding in one easy motion to go in the car) with a hood & weather cover so your trips to the park with Frieda will be easy & pleasant. I think Dido Merwin may let you have her room during your stay, which would be ever so much better than the rather shabby hotel (I got the best I could nearest to us). You'd have a fine view of Primrose Hill, a kitchen to cook breakfast in and be 2 minutes from us---there is also a very pleasant Australian professional woman living in another room, caring for the cat. I do hope this works out---it would save you a good bit of money & energy!

Leonard Baskin, the American artist & Smith professor, has been in London for 10 days, after opening a big show of his in Rotterdam[2] which will tour Europe for a year. Ted has a proverb "Guests and fish stink on

1–Australian writer and critic Charles Osborne (1927–); assistant editor of *London Magazine*, 1958–66.

2–Sponsored by the International Council of the Museum of Modern Art, the Baskin exhibition opened at the Boymans/van Beuningen Museum, Rotterdam, Netherlands, 7 May–2 July 1961. It then travelled to Berlin (Amerika-Haus, 16 September–15 October 1961) and Paris (Centre Culturel Américain, 13 November–15 December).

the third day" which began to apply after a while. At first I was touched that Leonard came to us---it happened that no one knew him here, & he is very famous & has crowds of followers in America. Well, he more or less invited himself to stay with us---a ghastly arrangement as each night we had to move Frieda into the kitchen, & Leonard stays up late & sleeps late, which would be fine if we had a house, but difficult with the baby & in such close quarters. Also, he does not eat fish, eggs, milk, cheese, vegetables, salad, salt, pepper, onions or liquor of any sort & I got a bit fed up trying to think of what to feed him. At least Ted went to a few museums with him & on a trip to Oxford & Cambridge (our car had just come, & Leonard used Ted like a chauffeur) but about all I saw of him was dirty dishes, unmade beds and piles of dirty shirts and socks which he left for me to do. Of course neither of us wrote for 10 days & felt exhausted by the end. We began to feel used, and now face a mountain of piled up commissions & assignments. So that's why I haven't written.

Dido & Bill are back from America for 10 days before going to France. Then we will have 10 days respite. We want to have all our jobs done by the time you come so we can really vacation and enjoy every minute with you. I must say I will be enormously grateful for 2 weeks free of babytending. I don't feel to have had a holiday since I've been in England, and the thought of driving & gourmandizing in France with Ted, & getting tan & rested, is what keeps me going just now. The car is very snug & the back seat folds down & gives lots of storage space. Ted drives beautifully (he took 4 lessons) & has a British license. I don't drive it yet, as I want lessons & a license first---driving on the left is against my instinct!

I hate to ask anything of you at this busy date, but I wonder if you'd look in the Hathaway Bookshop or BU Library for a book of poems by May Swenson (not May Sarton---another poetess![1]) and copy out 2 or 3 poems---the first one (I think there may be 2 books[2]) is a poem about a bruised fingernail[3] & I think it comes first in the book, the next "AT Breakfast" about an egg, ending "Ate a sun germ---good."[4] And one called "By Morning" about snow falling. I am making a little anthology of American poems and just can't get hold of her book here.[5]

1–American poet May Sarton (1912–95).

2–May Swenson, *Another Animal* (New York: Scribner, 1954) and *A Cage of Spines* (New York: Rinehart, 1958).

3–May Swenson, 'Almanac', *A Cage of Spines* (New York: Rinehart, 1958): 9.

4–Swenson's 'At Breakfast' ends 'a seamless miracle / Ate a sun-germ / Good.' ASP sent typescripts to SP, which are held by Smith College.

5–May Swenson was not included in SP's *American Poetry Now*.

I know you're pressed for weight in your case but do you think you could wrap up those five black-and-white cups and saucers of my best teaset upstairs in your clothes (as I did to bring them over) and bring them? It would mean more to me than anything---they cost a lot & I have nothing nice for tea-serving & wouldnt dare to have them crated. I'm not bothered about the big pot or the pitcher & sugarbowl, just the cups and saucers.

Three weeks! What time will you be arriving? I already know what I'll have for supper---something quite simple but very good. You will adore Frieda. She can stand up by herself now without pulling herself up, in the middle of the floor, and is so pretty and funny. I'm glad you're seeing her at this age, because she is so responsive & will get to know you specially, unlike a new baby, who just lies about.

Ted's just finished typing his play---about 115 pages, and I'm working on a 20 minute radio program of my poems[1]---I feel we really deserve a rest and a change. I hope the weather is better when you come. May has been the coldest nastiest month of the year yet.

Lots of love to you and Warren,
From Sivvy

TO *Aurelia Schober Plath & Warren Plath*

Tuesday 6 June 1961 — TLS (aerogramme), Indiana University

Tuesday, June 6th

Dear mother and Warren,

You have no idea how happy your wonderful letter made us! I have been hoping and hoping Warren would come, and now my wish is granted! We shall sample good restaurants in Soho and there should be some good plays on then. Should I reserve a room with a double bed for Warren? Most single beds are so short, and a double would give him room to stretch out.

Is it Monday morning the 19th you are coming, mother? I had thought it was Sunday the 18th, but of course that is probably the day you leave.

1–Sylvia Plath, 'The Living Poet', BBC Third Programme (8 July 1961); recorded on 5 June 1961. SP read poems with American-born actor and author Marvin Kane (1929–2012): 'The Disquieting Muses' (SP), 'Sleep in the Mojave Desert' (Kane), 'Suicide Off Egg Rock' (Kane), 'Spinster' (SP), 'Parliament Hill Fields' (SP), 'You're' (Kane), 'Magi' (Kane), 'Medallion' (Kane), and 'The Stones' (SP).

You should see a lovely sunrise. I believe there is routine transportation from the Airport into London. Maybe you could call us from the airport as soon as you get in, let us know where and when you'll be arriving in London, and we could meet you in the car. I think you'll be a lot more comfortable at the Merwins. It is so near, and Dido's room is so lovely, and Molly,[1] the little Australian hairdresser is at work all day. I'll be working in the study over there in the morning and Ted in the afternoon, probably, and then there won't be a mile trek everytime you want to rest or get something. The Merwins get an indefinable something out of knowing us (Ted being a British lion in Dido's eyes) and we have got over feeling we can't repay them in kind, especially as it gives them a certain odd pleasure to see us living on things out of their attic.

One important thing, before I forget: could you airmail my American driver's license to me immediately???[2] I believe I did get it renewed and you kept it over there. I'm having my driving test here next week and need the license to turn in. I have very little hope of passing the test, as driving with a left-hand floor gear with 4 gears, and on the left of the road, and with all sorts of military forms to turning the steering wheel and signalling with both hand and light I find very difficult. I am having a few lessons, though. At least Ted passed his test, so we are mobile. The car is small, but roadworthy, and should make our Maugham trip to Europe with the baby a pleasure instead of a laden march. Frieda loves riding in her baby car seat in the back and is securely strapped in.

Ted went to receive his 100 pounds Hawthornden award last Wednesday, the speech given by the poet C. Day Lewis,[3] who is charming. Yesterday morning I spent at the BBC recording a 25 minute program of my poems and commentary, with an American boy reader[4] for some of them, for my "Living Poet" program in July. There is a Living Poet every month, and I am on a list of Americans among Robert Lowell, Stanley Kunitz and Theodore Roethke, which I find quite an honour.[5] We'll miss the program as we'll be in France, but you must listen and tell us how it is. Got $60 for the morning's work, and will be paid for the poems

1–Molly Raybould, identified in a letter from ASP to Warren Plath, 30 July 1961; held by Lilly Library.

2–SP's driving licence and other identification and membership cards appeared at auction via Bonhams on 21 March 2018.

3–British poet C. (Cecil) Day Lewis (1904–72).

4–Marvin Kane.

5–Americans featured in 'The Living Poet' series, with broadcast dates, were: Richard Wilbur (1 January 1961); Theodore Roethke (8 February 1961); Robert Lowell (5 March 1961); Randall Jarrell (10 April 1961); and Stanley Kunitz (12 May 1961).

separately. We've taken on the Merwins accountant[1] to figure our income tax as it is absolutely hopeless to do it ourselves, with all the conflicting American and UK laws. I think he'll be well worth a fee in peace of mind to us. UK tax, unfortunately, is much worse than American!

The one thing I long for now is a house! As soon as our income tax for this year in the UK is cleared we will see how much of a mortgage the St. Pancras Council would give us and try to line a place up by winter here. As Ted says, he could treble his income as soon as he has a study where he could keep his papers and not be interrupted, and I also could afford a morning babyminder and am interested in working on a novel. Then, too, you and Warren could count on a guest room---if you have that, then everybody can lead their own lives and there is no overcrowding. Oh, it would be so nice if you could plan 6 weeks over here every summer! If you just had to save up for the round-trip fare and we had a guest room, you'd have next to no other expenses, and then Ted and I could take an annual two-week holiday in the middle of your stay while you got re-acquainted with your grandchildren. I feel I haven't had a proper holiday for 4 or 5 years! Our summer in Northampton was depressing, and our tour around America magnificent but the pace tiring, and since the baby's come I haven't had a day off! The thought of going off alone with Ted for 2 weeks is just heaven. We have reservations for June 30th to July 14th, and plan to take a little 5 or 6 day trip alone in France before going to the Merwins. I think you will be very comfortable here with the baby---I have a 3-day a week diaper service, a laundromat around the corner, and all shops, and she is so pretty and funny you will just adore her. Yesterday she took down a saucer from the kitchen shelf & put it on the floor. Then she took down a cup & put it on the saucer. Then she picked up the cup & pretended to sip, & put it back in the saucer & burst out laughing in pleasure at herself. This must come after a year of watching us drink tea!

Lots of love to you both,

Sivvy

1 – According to SP's address book, probably E. J. Edwards of Pawley & Maylon, Chartered Accountants, 42 Welbeck Street, London W.1.

TO *Brian Cox*

Saturday 17 June 1961 TLS, University of Kansas

3 Chalcot Square
London N.W.1
June 17, 1961

Dear Brian,

Many thanks for your letter. Here are the proofs.[1] I shall have the whole anthology to you within a week, and have just received books or poems from the last few poets I've been waiting for. I sent a small blurb to Tony Dyson[2] at the Other Place,[3] saying simply that this Small Anthology of American Poets includes a selection of youngish or new (this covers the few old poets who are new, with first books) American poets ranging from Gregory Corso to Richard Wilbur (i.e., encompassing the Beats and the Elegant Academicians). Over 15 poets. Over 20 poems.

Sincerely,
Sylvia Plath

1–The proofs, probably for 'I Am Vertical' and 'Private Ground', are no longer with the letter.

2–See SP to A. E. Dyson, 3 May 1961; held by University of Kansas.

3–Refers to Dyson's employer, Bangor University, Wales, where he was an assistant lecturer in English literature.

TO *Howard Moss*

Saturday 17 June 1961 TLS (aerogramme), New York Public Library

3 Chalcot Square
London N.W.1, England
June 17, 1961

Mr. Howard Moss
THE NEW YORKER
25 West 43rd Street
New York, New York
U.S.A.

Dear Mr. Moss,

I am very happy you like TULIPS.[1] I am giving a small reading of poems here in London next month and have promised to include TULIPS among them. I wondered if it would be all right with you to have TULIPS mimeographed on the program sheet.[2]

With all good wishes,
Sincerely,
Sylvia Plath

1–Probably Howard Moss to SP, 14 June 1961; copy held by New York Public Library. Moss rejected 'Insomniac' and 'Widow', which according to SP's submissions list she sent on 29 May 1961. Sylvia Plath, 'Tulips', *The New Yorker* (7 April 1962): 40.

2–Sylvia Plath, 'Tulips', *Poetry at the Mermaid* (London, 1961): 53–4. SP read 'Tulips' to an audience on 17 July 1961. The reading was recorded by the British Library. Introducing the poem, Plath said: 'The poem I'm going to read tonight is called "Tulips" and it was occasioned quite simply by receiving a bouquet of red, spectacular tulips while convalescing in hospital.'

TO *Brian Cox*

Sunday 25 June 1961 TLS, University of Kansas

3 Chalcot Square
London N.W.1,
June 25, 1961

Dear Brian,

Here is the little anthology.[1] I've put under the name of each poet (arranged alphabetically) the publisher and book title, or magazine, where I found the poem.[2] On second thought I've left out any poems of my own as my own reaction to anthologists who take anthologies as opportunities for publishing their own poems is not a very kind one.[3]

Let me know what you think of this, what outrages or pleases you.

All good wishes,
Sylvia (Plath) <signed>
Sylvia Plath

TO *Warren Plath*

Tuesday 27 June 1961[4] ALS (photocopy), Indiana University

Dear Warren –

Mother is at the moment bathing Frieda, I halfway through making a strawberry chiffon pie & Ted typing a letter to T. S. Eliot. Its taken

1–The typescript SP submitted included: 'The Stoic: For Laura von Courten' by Edgar Bowers; 'A Dreamed Realization' by Gregory Corso; 'The Way' by Robert Creeley; 'The Brown Studio' by Barbara Guest; '"More Light! More Light!"' by Anthony Hecht; 'Love Fast' by Sandra Hochman; 'An Armada of Thirty Whales' by Daniel G. Hoffman; 'Another Year Come', 'The Native', and 'Pedigrees' by W. S. Merwin; 'Fools Encountered' by E. Lucas Myers; 'Concerning the Painting "Afternoon in Infinity" by Attilio Salemme' by Hyam Plutzik; 'The Evil Eye', 'Living in Sin', and 'Moving in Winter' by Adrienne Rich; 'Kind Sir: These Words' and 'Some Foreign Letters' by Anne Sexton; 'Carentan O Carentan' and 'The Dream House' by Louis Simpson; 'The Marsh' and 'Operation' by W. D. Snodgrass; 'In the Oregon Country', 'A Survey', and 'The Well Rising' by William Stafford; 'Ab Ovo' by George Starbuck; 'Almanac' by May Swenson; 'Potato' by Richard Wilbur; 'A Late Afternoon in Western Minnesota' by James Wright. Typescript held by University of Manchester. The anthology ultimately had several different poems. Excluded were those by Corso, Hochman, and 'Carentan O Carentan' by Louis Simpson. Included were 'I Only Am Escaped Alone to Tell Thee' and 'The Vacuum' by Howard Nemerov, and 'The Five-Day Rain' by Denise Levertov.
2–'where I found ~~it~~ the poem' appears in the original.
3–SP's working papers for *American Poetry Now* are scattered. One document has 'Moi (Magi)' which shows that 'Magi' may have been the poem she considered.
4–Date supplied from postmark by Warren Plath.

mother about a week to recover from that sleepless night & the usual strain of getting used to a new place, but her being just about across the street in the Merwin's grand bedroom (free too) with a corner to cook her own breakfast, & us being settled here, & the lovely Park, she is thriving, Frieda is at her best – so pretty & loving – she & mother get on wonderfully, so I shall feel relatively easy leaving them. I've got in a large store of food, so they should have fun. I am dying for a holiday not having been free of the baby or cooking for well over a year & no respite since our American tour. We are overjoyed at your coming & shall go off to Italy with Frieda after you depart. We're both doing a reading of our commissioned poems for the poetry festival at the Mermaid Theatre on July 17th – then all up to Yorkshire for a week where we have mother a lovely room reserved at a nearby farm Inn. We took her to see "Ondine"[1] with Leslie Caron (the play) the other night – just her thing, all magic & fairytale. We miss you & can't wait till you come. Write mother at this address.

Love,
Sivvy

TO *Aurelia Schober Plath*

Thursday 29 June 1961[2] ALS (picture postcard),[3] Indiana University

<Picture postcard caption: ROUEN (Seine-Maritime) Le Gros Horloge (1389); postmarked Rouen, Seine Maritime, France, 29 June 1961.>

Thursday –

Dear mother:

We are sitting under an umbrella waiting for our café au lait in Rouen, a wonderful antique town with an open market just beyond this beautiful clock bridge where we have bought a lunch of milk, bread, cheese & fruit for a picnic. A heavenly boat trip over yesterday[4] – calm, bright sun. We stopped for a French lunch in a sleepy town & drove to a superb beach,[5]

1–Jean Giraudoux, *Ondine*, performed by the Royal Shakespeare Company at the Aldwych Theatre, 49 Aldwych, London.

2–Date supplied from postmark.

3–Postcard numbered 1 in unknown hand, possibly by SP.

4–SP's passport indicates she and TH sailed from Dover to Boulogne.

5–Probably the beach at Berck-sur-Mer, which became the subject of SP's poem 'Berck-Plage'.

swam, collected shells for Frieda & sunned. Drove on to Rouen through green wheat fields We find no tourists – only holidaying French people, which is very fine. Now on to Mont. St. Michel. Twenty kisses to our little angel.

Love
Sivvy & Ted

TO *Aurelia Schober Plath*

Sunday 2 July 1961 — ALS (picture postcard),[1] Indiana University

<Picture postcard caption: LE MONT SAINT-MICHEL (Manche) Ensemble Sud par Grande Marée; postmark illegible.>

Sunday: July 2

Dear mother . . .

We are sitting in a little "crêperie" in Douarnenez, a lovely fishing port in Finisterre[2] waiting for our crepes – a lacey thin pancake served with butter or jam or honey & cider to drink, for our Sunday supper. We have been swimming in clear Atlantic water, eating mussels, cockles, lobster & giant crayfish – 5 course dinners for less than $3 for the 2 of us. We have spent today – our first cloudy one – exploring two rocky points at the very west of Brittany. Have bought two little presents for Freda. If for any reason you need to, use our doctor's – you can use them free as a guest.

We hope to be at Merwins Wednesday – I'm dying to hear how our angel is.

Lots of love to you both –
xxx
– S.

Don't forget to hear my BBC program this weekend – (Saturday 9:30 pm I think)

1 – Postcard numbered 2 in unknown hand, possibly by SP.
2 – Situated at the Pointe du Raz; see SP's poem 'Finisterre', written 29 September 1961.

TO *Aurelia Schober Plath*

Thursday 6 July 1961 TLS with envelope, Indiana University

Thursday: July 6

Dear mother,

I am delighted by your 2 good letters so full of Frieda. I loved hearing every word about her: already she seems like a different child, she is growing so fast, and while I am having a wonderfully restful time I miss her immensely. The Merwins farm is idyllic, with a superb view, plum trees country milk, butter & eggs, a billion stars overhead, cow bells tinkling all night softly, and Dido is the world's best cook. They made the whole place over from a pile of bramble-covered stone and it is full of antique furniture salvaged from peasants barns, stripped of varnish & waxed to a satin finish. Ted is so rested it does my heart good. I am tan at last from sunbathing on the geranium-lined terrace and relieved for a time to be completely free of mail, phone calls and London. Today we are going to a local market fair. Dido's cooking is better than any we've had yet.

I am glad to hear you are taking in a play. Do ask the red-haired Doris Bartlett[1] at the Express (or is it United?) dairies just opposite the foot of St. George's Terrace to babysit next Thursday afternoon or any evening after 7 if you want to got shopping downtown Thursday. I hope you aren't having too strenuous a time with Frieda, who sounds ten times livelier now that she's walking. Do take it easy. How & where are you sleeping? Yorkshire should be a nice rest for you. I am so renewed I am dying to take care of Frieda again. We'll be home in time for supper Friday the 14th, I imagine, and plan to leave for Yorkshire very early the following Tuesday for a good week. Then after we come back to London Ted & I may go to Devon for a day or so to look at houses. I would so like to have a place lined up before we go to Italy this fall. I'm very glad my nice neighbors have been so good. Katherine Frankfort's little boys[2] are very sweet especially the youngest & Lorna Secker-Walker's little Joanna a doll. Frieda enjoyed her 2nd birthday party very much. I've got a lovely deep blue wool sleeved Blue Riding Hood cape & hood

1 – Doris Bartlett was employed by United Diaries at 126 Regent's Park Road, as well as by Babyminders, the service SP and TH used for babysitting. Bartlett lived nearby at 27 King Henry's Road.

2 – Justin Frankfort and Thomas Frankfort.

with white embroidery for her in Quimper[1] which should be wonderfully handsome for a winter coat.[2]

See you in a week. Keep us posted.

Rest yourselves!

Love,
Sivvy

TO *Aurelia Schober Plath*

Monday 10 July 1961 — ALS (picture postcard), Indiana University

<Picture postcard caption: Montignac-sur-Vézère (Dordogne). Grotte de Lascaux; postmarked Saint-Céré, France, 12 July 1961.>

Monday – July 10

Dear mother . . .

We saw these small vivid caves yesterday with the prehistoric paintings. Your good letter came about Frieda's new teeth. I dote on every word about her & now am so brown & fat & rested (thanks to Dido's celestial cooking – she won't let me wash a dish) I am ready & eager to come home. Dido & a Spanish duchess friend[3] of hers are brewing up a banquet for a famous French tapestry-maker – Jean Lurçat[4] – who is coming tonight. Only 4 days till we're home! Haven't felt so fine for 5 years. I bought 2 cheap French cotton smocks for her (Frieda) at the fair & a handsome dress for me (needs the hem let down) at a fancy shop for only $5.50.

XXX-XXX to you & F.
Sivvy

1–Quimper, Brittany, south of Douarnenez.
2–Frieda's blue French coat appeared at auction via Bonhams on 21 March 2018.
3–Margot Pitt-Rivers.
4–Jean Lurçat (1892–1966).

TO *Dido Merwin*

c. Sunday 30 July 1961[1] ALS,[2] Pierpont Morgan Library

Dear Dido –

A small, practical PS to send along measurements for that sepia sweater (I liked the style of Ben's[3] & a generous collar). I imagine I take a rough size 38, but here are the exact inches:

armpit – bottom: 14 inches
back-neck – bottom: 20½ inches
bust: 35 inches
shoulder – wrist: 22½ inches

Let me know if the estimable lady needs any other details. We'll send a cheque as soon as you let us know what she charges.[4] I look forward to getting Jeanna's remnant to patch my hem ere I get too fat for all such fripperies. Dr. Wallace[5] is a dear – he's referring me to Dr. Battle.[6] We are returned from a glorious week of bilberrying & moorwalking in Yorkshire & planning to surfeit mother with Stonehenge & the Tower of London[7] before her flight home on Friday. Having her so close at hand has been a great relief & Molly has filled a gap I'm afraid I'm no good at – a sort of chatty solicitous companion – for which I'm grateful. Your cooking floats before – or rather behind – me in the guise of celestial platters & sweet dreams.

Love to you & Bill –
Sylvia

1–Date supplied from internal evidence.
2–SP's letter is at the end of a letter begun by TH, which has not been transcribed.
3–American publisher and writer Ben Sonnenberg (1936–2010).
4–SP sent a cheque to W. S. Merwin on 20 October 1961.
5–According to SP's address book, Dr H. J. Wallace consulted at 80 Harley Street, London.
6–According to SP's address book, Dr Battle consulted at 61 Wimpole Street, London.
7–In a letter to Warren Plath, ASP indicated the visit to the Tower of London was planned for Monday, 31 July 1961.

TO *Aurelia Schober Plath*

Monday 7 August 1961[1] TLS (aerogramme), Indiana University

Tuesday: August 7

Dear mother,

Well, London doesn't seem the same with you departed. I hope the trip back wasn't too tiring. Did Warren meet you on time? Both Ted and I thought you looked very athletic and healthy when you left. We have been sleeping and resting, Ted taking Frieda out in the mornings and me taking her in the afternoons. Today there was a great wind, which blew down a lot of branches, and she loved it. She is learning to walk along with one now, and covers an amazing distance. I ran into that Crystal (is that her first name? Or last) and Gilbert today who spoke to Frieda very fondly and said they were sorry to have missed you the Friday you left---evidently they had hoped to see you in the park. Is she German? She seems very nice. What is her whole name?

The day after you left we had a letter that Sir Arundell[2] agreed on the price of 3,600 pounds for the house, so we have sent in our 10% deposit. I guess that's just about the equivalent of $10,000. I am a bit overcome by the notion of moving everything, but our possessions will seem very small compared to the house itself. We will have to furnish one room at a time. I am a bit homesick for London, as I always am before leaving a place, but welcome the space and country peace for the next few years. Ted is in seventh heaven. We have been working, alternating my mornings and his afternoons, at the Merwins study and this works out beautifully, as neither of us wants to work the whole day at a desk.

Your presence is everywhere, and your good influence, too. I am taking about 5 vitamins a day, a long walk with F. every afternoon, and feeding her chopped meat and potato. She says Baw-pee for bottle and listens so carefully when you tell her a new word. I have made her another nightie out of the white-figured red flannel, just like her blue one, which looks adorable on her, and gotten some red Viyella (at just over $3) for a maternity blouse for me, and a pattern for a red Viyella dress for her, plus a Simplicity sewing book, from which I hope to learn how to make button holes and so on. Now I think I will look for an old Singer.

1–Letter misdated by SP.

2–British diplomat Sir Robert Duncan Harris Arundell (1904–89), son of Constantine Harris Arundell (1863–1945) and Katharine Juliana Harris Arundell (1866–1957), who lived at Court Green, North Tawton, Devon.

If you have the College Taxi people crate my beloved china set & send it to us at Court Green, North Tawton, Devon, we'll be endlessly grateful & probably there to receive it, as we hope to be moved by August 31. Also, would it be possible for[1] Warren to bring our sleeping bags rolled up with a strap round them? We think we may have a double bed given us and if he could bring the two bags he would have bedding & could stay with us. They would probably be very light. But awkward.

I bought Frieda a sturdy pair of red laced size 5 shoes today, as you instructed: they are still very big for her, but she likes playing with them.

I have taken the film of Frieda in to be developed & hope to have the snaps to you in a week. I also bought my first present for Nicholas-Megan at Selfridge's---a handsome blue handknit Spanish-made baby sweater, for about $3, which I think quite reasonable. I had given one like it to Helga Huws for her 2nd baby and have long coveted one. I am sure all the London shops will have branches in Exeter, but am laying in a few niceties.

By the way, the paper nappies you bought are <u>much</u> superior to the ones I remembered using, & we'll take that kind to Italy. I am wearing the lovely Viyella blouse which Ted likes immensely and which I rate tie-favorite to my own red and green one. I feel like a new person in it. The color is just perfect.

I will be so happy to get to the house and start fixing it up. It is basically such a beautiful place, and now you will have a lovely country house to visit next summer! I look forward to sampling our apples, making sauce (Has grammy any recipes for applesauce?) and anticipating our bank of spring daffodils. I think both of us will produce lots of work. Italy is of course something I just won't think of until it comes, but we hope to save half of the money of the grant and certainly can use it! To get to us Warren should find out the express (I think it leaves 11ish in the morning) from London that passes through North Tawton (the station) & write or telegram us the time & day of his arrival so we can be at the station to pick us up. We'll probably have a new phone number from what's in now, so he might ask Information for the Hughes of Court Green if he wants to call. We look so forward to seeing him! We miss you immensely & count on seeing you next summer---thanks so much for making our trips & house-finding a possibility.

Lots of love,
Sivvy

1–'would it be ~~im~~possible for' appears in the original.

TO *Aurelia Schober Plath*

Sunday 13 August 1961 TLS, Indiana University

3 Chalcot Square
London N.W.1
Sunday: August 13

Dear mother,

A thousand thanks for the $5,880 check which arrived this week, and for your own $1,400 loan (no need to put gift on this, as loans are untaxable). I'm enclosing a check for $275 to be deposited in our 5 cent savings account to relieve the large gap there a trifle. I'd tell as few people as possible about the house till we're actually in it (these typing eccentricities are caused by Frieda's begging "Up!" and being taken in my lap to type for a minute). The owner agreed to have the whole dwellinghouse treated & guaranteed for woodworm as a condition of our buying it, & hasn't done more than the roof, so unless he gets through with the whole thing we won't consider it. I'm pretty sure he'll end up by carrying it out, though.

Ted & I are seriously thinking of giving up the Somerset Maugham award, unless of course they'll give us another 2-year extension. The prospect of cramming in a trip to Europe after a move to a house which will need a lot of attention and before a 2nd baby just doesn't seem worth 500 pounds, even though we were hoping to save half of it. Both of us feel we could get enough writing done if we had a relatively peaceful fall to make up for not taking the grant & feel an immense pressure lifted not to have to go abroad. We've had enough of moving around to last for years.

I'm enclosing[1] the best shots of the baby in the last roll. There are some more on a roll we haven't finished yet & we'll send the best of those on too when it's been developed.

Could Warren stick a big thick heavy comb in his luggage for me? I haven't found anything strong enough to withstand my hair here. Ted & I had our babysitter Doris in Thursday afternoon and had a lovely time at the National Portrait Gallery and the British Museum, and only wished we'd started to take an afternoon off together every week to explore London---it's so much more fun than going alone. I'm busy giving a couple of dinners for people we want to see before we go off.

1 – The photographs are no longer with the letter.

We put an add in the paper[1] for our flat (with a $280 fee for "fixtures & fittings" to cover the cost of our decorating, lino, shelves & solicitor's fees & to deter an avalanche of people---the custom here) & had 8 responses & 2 couples who arrived & decided they wanted it at the same time. Very awkward, especially as Ted & I liked one couple, the boy a young Canadian poet, the girl a German-Russian whom we identified with,[2] as they were too slow & polite to speak up & officially the other chill busybody man got it by sitting down & immediately writing out a check. We felt so badly we tore up his check that night & told him we were staying & then dug out the other couple & said they could have it. So I hope our Court Green move goes through. The couple are coming to supper this week.

I was so glad to hear you arrived home safely in spite of the delay. And your words to the Canadian woman were vicariously most satisfying! The sort of thing one seldom has the presence of mind to say & wishes one had said too late. Congratulations!

Keep your fingers crossed for us about Court Green!

Love to you & Warren,
Sivvy

TO *Gerald & Joan Hughes*

Saturday 19 August 1961 — TLS (aerogramme), Indiana University

Saturday: August 19th

Dear Gerald, Joan, Etc.,

You see what I am driven to. Separate letter paper. Leave me a space, I beg, letter after letter, but Ted slyly finishes the last inch on the quiet, mails his opus, and makes me out a silent, taciturn post, which I am not. Not in the least.

I liked the painting very much, Gerald. My great extravagance, bottled up with all the little ones that don't have a chance to show in our present circumstances, would be to go around to the galleries buying the paintings I like, art being my alternate love to writing. As it is, I just go to the

1–The advertisement read: 'PRIMROSE HILL Unfurn. 2 rms. k. & b 6 gns. p.w. F. & F £100. 17 mth lse., renewable. PRI 9132 after 6 p.m.', *London Evening Standard* (10 August 1961): 10.

2–Canadian poet and translator David Wevill (1935–) and his wife Assia Wevill (1927–69), who was employed in the advertising industry and was a translator.

galleries. The friend Ted showed the painting to is fantastic, our age, but set & peculiar in his ways, and a regular art critic noted for his own finds. His latest is an original of a Van Dyck[1] he picked up as a "copy". He showed us his collection of drawings by reasonably famous Italians the night we went to ask about your piece.

We are wild about the Devon place. I don't know how much Ted told you about it in his letter, did he say we're buying it from a Sir Robert Arundell? He almost didn't go see it, because for some reason he is prejudiced against titles, & we only saw it for fun because of its having a thatch which we had resolved not to touch. Of course it was enchanting, made us fall in love with it---it's white, with a black base-border & this bird-haunted-straw top. We are going to be camping out for a year or so, because we have almost no furniture or carpets, and a long list of repairs such as having up the floors in the two front rooms downstairs and getting them cemented (the wooden joists are resting on the earth "as is usual for such old places"), and then replastering all the rooms when we redecorate them, and so on. We have been plagued by dreams of woodworm & deathwatch beetles, as we said we'd only buy the place if Sir Robert had a woodworm company treat it & guarantee it for 20 years, which he is, if a bit draggingly, doing.

I shall miss London in lots of ways, but hope I can get a lot of writing done free from entertaining and people-seeing, and that both of us can earn a house here by the time schooling matters for the children of which we are due another in January, much to our joy---then we can winter in town & spend all the nice weather in the country. Of course we'll probably be broke till 50 attending to our thatch, but I have grand dreams. Anyhow, I am trying to finish a first novel before we move & will make an effort to get it published to see if I can scare up some carpet money.

Frieda is a blue-eyed, brown-haired doll, very funny and full of jokes, and loving, kisses her toys & jabberwocks at them, kisses our manuscripts & us and everything. Says "ba" for ball & cookie and appee (apple) and bawpee (bottle) and UP UP UP. She is our great toy & keeps us in charming tempers. Ted is wonderfully happy about this place: it is his one big dream & I am so glad it's coming so beautifully true. Six bedrooms! Frieda gave him a bunch of seed packets for his birthday. We'll be good gardeners. Keep writing.

Much love to all,
Sylvia

1–Flemish Baroque artist Anthony Van Dyck (1599–1641).

TO *Eric Walter White*

Tuesday 22 August 1961 ALS, British Library

3 Chalcot Square
London N.W.1
August 22, 1961

Dear Eric,

I am happy to enclose the work sheets of Insomniac[1] & happy to hear from the Cheltenham Festival Organiser[2] that sleeplessness has its own very pleasant reward.

Sincerely,
Sylvia Plath

Eric White, Esq.
THE ARTS COUNCIL OF GREAT BRITAIN
4 St. James's Square
London SW1

TO *John Sweeney*

Tuesday 22 August 1961 ALS with envelope, Harvard University

3 Chalcot Square
London NW 1
August 22, 1961

Dear Jack,

Here are the work-sheets of "Tulips" which I have specially saved for you out of my weekly holocaust of draft sheets. Ted & I loved that wonderful, wonderful dinner with you after the Festival.[3] Frieda has appropriated Ted's Indian.

1–Sylvia Plath, 'Insomniac', winner of the 1961 Guinness Poetry Award and first prize at the 1961 Cheltenham Festival of Art and Literature. SP's award was £75; the ceremony was held at Goldsmith's Hall, London, on 31 October 1961. The judges for the competition were Elizabeth Jennings, Laurie Lee, and Anthony Thwaite. Second and third prizes were awarded to Herbert Lomas for 'The Fear' and Alastair W. Thomson for 'Date Palms'. A typescript of SP's poem, which was submitted under the pseudonym 'Saratoga Smith' and received a grading of B++ by the judges, is held by the Victoria and Albert Museum Archives.
2–G. A. M. Wilkinson.
3–SP read 'Tulips' at the Poetry at the Mermaid Festival. On 27 July 1961 Sweeney wrote to Stephen Fassett, 'And it was for me very moving to hear and see Sylvia – the only woman on the stage that evening and the only American on the stage! She read with great grace and

We have plunged & bought an antique thatched house, barn, stables, orchard, vegetable garden on 2½ acres of walled land in Devon & will move in by September 1st. It is lovely to see Ted's main dream come true – the River Taw is thick with fish.

Our new address:

Court Green –[1]
North Tawton
Devon

Love from us three to you and Mairé,

Sylvia →[2]

TO *Brian Cox*

Thursday 24 August 1961 TLS, University of Kansas

3 Chalcot Square
London N.W.1
August 24, 1961

Dear Brian,

Here is the new order. I like it much better & I hope you do. I am enclosing several extra poems. I mean some of these to be put in definitely, not as extras. The four "extras"[3] which can be left out or in as space permits I have enclosed in parentheses on the Contents sheet. (A Late Afternoon in Western Minnesota, Almanac, The Five-day Rain, Love Fast,).[4]

The dinner was lovely & I delighted in my annual corn-on-the-cob. If all goes well, we move August 31st to Court Green, North Tawton, Devon. Let me know if you have any questions.

Best wishes,
Sylvia Plath

---

clarity and command and the poem she read is a humdinger . . . And Sylvia has promised to lend the Poetry Room the worksheets of the poems she read'; letter held by Houghton Library. Sweeney displayed 'Tulips' in the Woodberry Poetry Room October–December 1961. The worksheets for 'Tulips' are held by Houghton Library.

1–An addendum to their address, by TH, has not been transcribed.

2–TH added twelve lines of verse (two stanzas of six lines each) on the back page of the letter, which have not been transcribed. Ted Hughes, 'To F. R. at Six Months' (Section I), *Collected Poems of Ted Hughes* (London: Faber & Faber, 2003): 97.

3–'the ~~five~~ "extras"' appears in the original.

4–'Love Fast, ~~Song in the Studio of Paul Klee~~)' appears in the original. Paul Carroll, 'Song in the Studio of Paul Klee', *The Nation* (4 March 1961): 192.

TO *Aurelia Schober Plath & Warren Plath*

Friday 25 August 1961 TLS (aerogramme), Indiana University

August 25, 1961

Dear mother & Warren,

It was lovely to get your letters---especially yours, Warren, telling us about probably coming to Devon on the 9th of September! Drop us a note when you get to London letting us know the hotel you are definitely staying at with its street address, & we'll write & tell you our phone number so you can let us know what time your train will get in and so on. If all goes as planned, we should be moving into Court Green on Thursday, August 31st. The owner is having the whole house treated and guaranteed for woodworm as he had promised, & this is written into the contract, which we shall sign this weekend. We shall still no doubt be in a pretty primitive state by the time you come with no rugs or curtains or extras---our furniture will barely fill 2 of our 8-odd rooms, but we hope to add to it bit by bit through country auctions and so on. And a surplus of empty rooms will be heavenly for a while. I am so glad you'll have a chance to see the place so soon, though, Warren, & can carry firsthand tales of it back to mother, who we hope will be seeing it next summer in a more advanced state.

Thanks for all your multitudinous transactions, mother. How much was the china sending & wrapping??? I'll settle with you on that from our Wellesley account if you'll let me know. I have put aside the money for Ted's sweater & grampy's wonderful gift with which I shall, regardless of all other expenses, buy myself a rug. Naturally this immense deposit and all the expenses of moving out and in and fixing up will require us to camp out more or less for the first year. But we hope to recoup our funds soon on writing. Ted's children's broadcasts on the BBC have been very enthusiastically received and he has an open ticket there to do as much as he wants, plus an invitation to do occasional editing on the Children's Page of the Sunday Times (whose Childrens Editor he lunched with and liked very much), and several other editing jobs, not to mention his wanting to finish a story collection which Faber's is eagerly awaiting. I have never seen him so happy. Both of us feel a wonderful deep-breathing sense of joy at the peaceful secluded life opening up for us, and delighted that our children will have such a wonderful place to live and play in. That check you deposited, by the way, was for Ted's story Snow, which was accepted by Harper's Bazaar. Isn't that nice!

Do tell Betty & Do I'll be dropping them a line as soon as we're settled mother, for I want to send them belated thanks for the box of clothes on Betty's part, & the yellow pajama set on Do's. Right now it seems a miracle that we shall ever get packed and moved. I have dozens of lists of this and that to do and pack. It will be heavenly not to have to move our stuff for indefinite years!

Frieda is wonderfully good-humored. Her teething seems to have let up. She says "I-see" for Isis & points to the picture, sniffs at all pictures of flowers, however tiny, added "cook-ee" to "ap-pee" to mean food of all kinds & feeds and talks to her dolls and bears in a funny squeaky voice.

I had a very nice letter[1] from Alfred Knopf (my lady editor there) saying my book of poems (40 poems, a much more concise, tight book) is due out in Spring 1962. I feel very excited filling out the Knopf Author's forms, after all these years of wishing I could get a book published by them!

My next letter should be written from Court Green! I can't wait to see what it feels like to live there. I shall investigate about a Bendix, mother, as soon as may be, as it would be absolute heaven to get one before the new baby comes. It is really the only make I'm interested in. What a dream it would be to have one. I'm really sick of lugging great loads to the laundromat each week--usually two a week now, for some reason.

We've been having farewell dinners with our closest friends here. We know a few quite marvelous couples---a Portuguese poet and exile & his wonderful vital wife[2] & Alan Sillitoe, the young & famous author of the novel Saturday Night and Sunday Morning (made into a movie) and his American wife,[3] and of course our nice neighbors. Fortunately we are on the holiday route to Cornwall, so stand a chance of seeing them about once a year. I shall look forward to the solitude.

I am going out tomorrow to look for a 2nd hand sewing machine like the one I've borrowed from Dido. It is wonderful, paradoxically, not to have the strain of going to Italy on top of us any more. The money we hoped to save out of it just wasn't worth it to us. Now we will be able to write all fall in peace, before the new baby arrives, and get a lot done.

1–Judith Jones to SP, 22 August 1961; held by University of Texas at Austin.

2–Portuguese writer, scholar, and political activist Helder Macedo (1935–) and his wife, literary translator and teacher Suzette Macedo (1931–). The Macedos lived at 24 Fitzjohn's Avenue, London N.W.3.

3–American poet Ruth Fainlight (1931–). The Sillitoes met SP and TH at the Hawthornden Prize ceremony on 31 May 1961 and lived at 24 Pembridge Crescent, London W.11.

We'll probably set you to minding Frieda in the mornings, Warren! I imagine baby sitters will be harder to get in the country.

Lots of love from us 3,
Sivvy

TO *Frank Schober*

Friday 25 August 1961 — TLS (aerogramme), Indiana University

3 Chalcot Square
London N.W.1, England
August 25, 1961

Dear Grampy,

Ted and I were overwhelmed and delighted by your wonderful gift of $100! I have put it aside to buy a nice red rug for our livingroom after we move into our new house. We are so happy to have a place of our own at last, with land and a garden and an orchard and plenty of room for your great-granddaughter to run around in. Ted & I hope to get a lot more writing done this way as each of us will have a quiet study.

Already we are planning on planting beans and peas and tomatoes and spinach and lettuce and asparagus and corn and heaven knows what else next autumn. Probably we shall turn from writers into market gardeners! Or apple growers---we've lots of fine apple trees. I do wish you could magically fly over and see our place. We are delighted with it.

Thanks again for your generous and thoughtful housewarming gift, and lots of love to you from Ted, Frieda and myself,

With love,
Sylvia

TO *Aurelia Schober Plath*

Monday 4 September 1961 — TLS (aerogramme), Indiana University

Monday: September 4

Dear mother,

Well, I am writing this from my big back kitchen (not really a kitchen, for I cook & wash up in a small room across the hall) at Court Green, surrounded by my copper saucepan and copper whatdoyoucall it (that

Frank gave me) and Dutch teaset that you brought, all displayed in the various lovely nooks and crannies. A large coal stove warms this room and keeps all the water piping hot (although we can switch on hot water independently of it in the electric immersion heater upstairs), and at last I have all the room I could want, and a perfect place for everything. My pewter looks beautiful in the parlor, where Ted is building bookshelves.

We moved without mishap on Thursday, our furniture just fitting in the small movers van (the move cost just under $100), and had a fine hot sunny blue day for it. Ever since a fog has shrouded us in, just as well, for we have been unpacking, scrubbing, painting and working hard indoors. The house surprised us---everything seemed so much better than we had remembered it: new discoveries on every side. The Arundells had left it clean-swept and shining. The woodworm people were just finishing work, so there is the fading aroma of their disinfectants. The place is like a person: it responds to the slightest touch & looks wonderful immediately. I have a nice round dining table we are "storing" for the couple who have moved into our London flat, and we eat on this in the big back room with light green linoleum, cream wood paneling to shoulder height, & the pink-washed walls that go throughout the house which I love---there's lots of space for Frieda to run about & play & spill things----really the heart-room of the house, with the toasty coal stove Ted keeps burning. Across the back hall---finely cobbled stone, one of the best touches---is my compact work kitchen: my gas stove (I had gas brought up to the house for this), loads of shelves & a low ancient sink which I am going to have changed to a modern unit immediately. Off this small room is a cool whitewashed larder where I have my fridge & hope to have my Bendix. The only self-service Launderette is 20 miles away in Exeter, so I searched round for a Bendix shop Saturday & plan to go in this week & order a machine. I will have to have a plumber install my new sink unit & run pipes into the larder, but we need a plumber anyway to fix the toilet upstairs. That is really the only major work that needs doing now. I am dying for a Bendix!

I was lucky in that Katherine Frankfurt let me have a double bed & mattress, an old greenish rug (which came out very nicely after I had it cleaned), two wood chairs & a marble-topped wine cabinet for the negligible price of moving them from her mother's house to ours, as none of the other relatives wanted them, so Warren will have a place to sleep on when he comes. I look forward to hearing from him, & from you too! He will be our first guest & we really long for someone to confirm our affection for our wonderful home.

We have been so busy indoors that we've hardly had time to do more than survey our grounds (the main crop of which is stinging nettles at present, and, of course, apples). I went out with Frieda & got a big basket of windfalls for applesauce, enough blackberries for two breakfast bowls, and about five pounds of fine potatoes from a hill of them someone had forgotten to dig up. I have the place full of flowers---great peachy-colored gladiolas, hot red & orange & yellow zinnias. The front flower gardens are weedy, but full of petunias & zinnias & a couple of good rosebushes. My whole spirit has expanded immensely---I don't have that crowded, harassed feeling I've had in all the small places I've lived in before. Frieda adores it here. The house has only one shallow step to get down from the back court into the back hall, and another shallow step into the front garden, so she can run in and out easily with no danger of falls, & loves tramping through the big rooms. She needs two naps a day again, she gets so tired with all this exercise.

What is so heavenly here is the utter peace. Very nice tradespeople, a retired couple from London[1] at the end of our drive who brought a tray of tea the day we moved in & curious & amiable natives. Our phone number, by the way, is North Tawton 370. I am going to a pre-natal clinic at the doctors[2] up the street to get myself on his panel. This is a wonderful place to have babies in. My main concern is <u>rugs</u> (after plumbing & Bendix) and curtains & pillows. We can't wait for you to see it. Wish you could come in the spring---we have piles of lilac (which I hadn't noticed before), daffodils, laburnum, cherry, apple, honeysuckle---and must be legendarily charming then. Ted has a superb attic study under the thatched eaves. I have chosen the best front bedroom for my own. Bought a lovely old reconditioned Singer sewing machine for $33.60 before leaving London – hand-wind.

xxx
Sivvy

1–Percy Key (1894–1962) and Rose Emma Key (1900–72), who lived at Number 4 Court Green Cottage, the nearest to the house.

2–SP's doctor in North Tawton was Hugh Basil G. Webb (1926–2006), who lived at Mistlemead with his wife, Joan M. Cairns Webb, and two daughters, Holly and Claire. His surgery was just down the lane from Court Green, off Market Street.

TO *Charles Osborne*

Monday 4 September 1961 TLS, University of Texas at Austin

Court Green
North Tawton
Devonshire
September 4, 1961

Dear Charles,

Please forgive me for RSVPing a week after the event, or nearly, but September 1st also marked our moving day to this antique thatched farmhouse in Devon and all correspondence got shelved in the process.

We are here, as far as we know and hope, forever, surviving on our own apples and potatoes left over from the previous owner.

Ted joins me in sending best wishes for the LM, Australian stories, and you too.

Sincerely,
Sylvia Plath

TO *Howard Moss*

Monday 11 September 1961 TLS (aerogramme), New York Public Library

Court Green
North Tawton
Devonshire, England
September 11, 1961

Dear Mr. Moss,

Thanks very much for your letter[1] about The Rival.

I think the poem is most easily explained as a contrast between two women: the speaker, who is a rather ordinary wife and mother, and her "rival"---the woman who is everything she is not---who obsesses her. This woman terrifies the speaker and dominates her thoughts, seeming almost superhuman ("Spiteful as a woman, but not so nervous . . .") and, in the third section, grows impressive and omnipresent as a sort of goddess.

1–Howard Moss to SP, 29 August 1961; held by New York Public Library. In the letter Moss suggests revisions to 'The Rival' and rejects SP's 'Face Lift' and 'Stars Over the Dordogne'. Moss later rejected 'The Rival' in a letter dated 26 September 1961; held by New York Public Library.

This other woman seems to find a vicarious satisfaction in battening on the speaker's life---enjoying her baby, for instance. "You sat in the next room . . ." is past tense as it refers to her presence at the baby's birth.

In the third section the speaker tries to lose the image of her rival in the impersonal spaces of the sky and the sea, but finds it impossible to do so. She even fancies what it would be like if the other woman were dead and buried, but realizes the woman would still be present to her and that she must accept her as she is.

If you think it would help clarify and simplify the poem to omit the second section, I think this might be a possibility. Also, if you feel another title would be better I'd be glad to have any suggestions.

With all good wishes,
Sincerely,
Sylvia Plath

Mr. Howard Moss
The New Yorker
25 West 43rd Street
New York 36, New York
USA

TO *Ruth Fainlight*

Monday 11 September 1961 TLS, Ruth Fainlight

Court Green
North Tawton
Devonshire
Monday: September 11

Dear Ruth,

By now you must be out of Woolavington Wing[1] and safely back in Pembridge Crescent. I hope your stitches were easy and that they used the most decorative of embroidery threads. They sewed my side up with black silk after taking away my appendix last winter, which I thought too somber.

The days have flown over our heads in an aroma of death-watch-beetle-killer and drying paint. At last we are emerging, and taking in our estate of stinging nettle. Ted has made bookshelves, I have whitened bureaus and a kitchen cupboard we found here for a desk, and except for the

1 – Woolavington Wing, then part of the Middlesex Hospital, Mortimer Street, London W.1.

barren expanse of floorboards and bare windows, we are settled. I shall scour the sales for 2nd hand Orientals.

We have apple pie, applesauce, apfel kuchen, and will have every Apple Thing in the Joy of Cooking before the fall is out. Also lots of big blackberries. Somebody left a hill of potatoes which pleased me immensely: I never saw one forked up before & it gave me a great primitive satisfaction: We Shall Survive. Ted digs all morning and plans immense vegetable plots in his dreams. We each have a study: Ted has 3 or 4 in case he wants a change.

Alan's wonderful book[1] is my bedtime reading. Ted keeps pinching it. He thinks it is Alan's best, & so do I. Ted will tell you himself how he admires it; he doesn't usually read novels, but I can't stop him on this. It is a huge book, in a profound sense. I love the incredible, vivid wealth of detail.

I may possibly be coming to London Tuesday October 31st for the Guinness Poetry Party. I'm not sure, but if so, would it be convenient for me to descend on you overnight? I am very reluctant to go without Ted, but somebody has to mind Frieda and I don't think anyone local would stay overnight here and do all the bother with her. I long to go to London, even for a movie or for a play, but am notoriously bad at going to things myself, spoiling for company. Anyhow, let me know if that day would be okay, and I'll let you know if I'm able to come later on.

Ted & I felt the best part of our latter days in London were seeing you two. You must come down for a weekend some time in the late, grim heart of autumn. We miss you very much.

Love to you both from us three,
Sylvia

1–Alan Sillitoe, *Key to the Door* (London: W. H. Allen, 1961); SP's copy held by Emory University bearing the inscription 'To Sylvia and Ted, for their new house! Love, Alan & Ruth'.

TO *Aurelia Schober Plath*

Friday 15 September 1961 TLS (aerogramme), Indiana University

Friday night: September 15

Dear mother,

It seems strange to think that Warren will reach you before this letter does, though both depart on the same day.[1] We saw him off at the little North Tawton station this morning at 11:30 after a breakfast of orange juice, fried egg & crispy potatoes & apple cake, and the house seemed very lonesome without him. He has been really a wonderful part of the family---sanding an immense elm plank[2] which will make me my first real capacious writing table, discovering a set of wooden blocks in the cottage attic and cleaning them up for Frieda, chopping wood, mowing the lawn, and in general making himself useful.

We've had a lot of fun while he was here---explored the Exeter cathedral, took a picnic to Tinagel (very commercial) and found a high cowfield nearby overlooking the sea to eat it in, drove to an auction at which we bought a little (4x6) Indian rug for Frieda's room, and ate out at our local inn, the Burton Hall Arms[3] (a roast beef dinner for just over $1 a person) which gave me a welcome change from cooking. I hope Warren didn't starve while he was here, although our meals in the evening are always late, as I have to make them after the babys supper & bath, I tried to feed him along the vast lines to which he is accustomed!

Your check for the Bendix came, mother, and thanks a million times. I have found a Bendix place (after a long search) in Exeter, and the man has come & written out what the plumber should put in. I have a nice cold white larder room off the small cooking-kitchen where I plan to put it, along with the icebox. I don't mind at all not having a drier as I don't like bone-dry clothes and can hang my 9-lb. load overnight in front of the coal stove & iron them the next day. I hope to have a new sink unit (my present one is about 2 feet high) and my Bendix in a month or so. Then life will be very easy. My best news is that the pleasant robust woman[4] who has cleaned Court Green for 11 years is going to come to

1–Warren Plath wrote to his mother on 10 September 1961 and drew plans of the house and grounds at Court Green; held by Lilly Library.

2–This writing table is held by Smith College.

3–Burton Hall was originally built in Norway; it was dismantled in 1872 and brought to Bouchiers Hill, North Tawton.

4–Charwoman Nancy Norah Willcocks Axworthy (1918–81); married to Walter Axworthy (1915–87), who was a carpenter, bellringer at the church, head of the North Tawton fire

me for 3 hours each on Tuesdays & Thursdays to wash my lineoleums, vacuum, dust & iron (my least favorite chore) at guess what, 2/6 an hour! (That's what Lady Arundell[1] paid her!). That means just over a dollar for a 3-hour morning's work. She seems a nice, vigorous woman, with a husband and grown daughter, and she starts work next week.

How many ounces are there in an American tomato soup can you use for tomato soup cake? I didn't think to question, but our cans seem to be bigger than yours, as my cake was a bit "wet". Thanks for the pound cake recipe. I'll use it soon. I love new recipes. We went blackberrying with Warren[2] & got about 13 cups full. Devon is one big blackberry hedge now.

Frieda adores her singing doll. It's moving scared her at first, but now she puts it down to watch it move & cuffs it fearlessly & laughs. She trails her wooden beads around, both strings, like two tails, and can put the thread in, but hasn't yet got the knack of pulling it through the bead, although she works hard at it. Her red sweater is our very favorite. It looks gorgeous with her red plaid wool pants you got. Her latest feat is picking the black blackberries: you should have seen her doing this from Ted's shoulders as he picked below her!

After a Saturday-Sunday visit from a very sweet young Portuguese couple we knew in London this week, things should quiet down. Ted has the most wonderful attic study, very warm under the peak of the thatch and over the hot water boiler. He looks happier and better every day. I never have known such satisfaction just seeing him revel in this place and leading at last exactly the life he wants. I adore my own study, and after I get my great plank table, paint the woodwork white, get a rug & maybe an upholstered armchair, it will be heavenly.

The 3rd package of our china set came before Warren left, the only one with anything broken. I noticed it was insured & wondered if we could claim anything on it---one dinner plate & two bowls were broken, due to packing, I think. The top & bottom were thickly padded, but the two packages inside not padded from each other, so the 8 dinner plates must have acted as a battering ram on the 2 bowls. Also, we only got 6 bowls in all (I think we had glued one broken one which didn't come), 7 small butter plates & 7 dessert plates. Is that what you sent? Let us know if

---

brigade, and teacher of woodworking at the local school; two children: Terence L. (1939–) and Maureen (1941–); lived at 39 Fore Street, North Tawton, Devon.

1–Lady Joan Ingles Arundell (1904–84).

2–See SP's 'Blackberrying'. In 'The Beach' (*Birthday Letters*), TH identifies the location as Hartland, Devon.

we should do anything about the broken stuff. I've kept the insurance number. In any case, it's wonderful to have the china with us, especially the glass decanter and the lovely teapot Warren so kindly brought. Now we hope to pick up a few nice bits of furniture at the multitudinous sales (auctions at houses) around here. They are great fun to go to.

Oh, saw my doctor---a young Perry Nortonish type whose surgery is 3 houses up across the street(!) and his marvelous midwife-nurse[1] whom I liked immediately. I look forward to my home delivery here now, these 2 people being very important in my life---I couldn't be better pleased with them. I just love it here, & look so forward to you coming over and enjoying it with us next summer.

Much love from us 3,
Sivvy

TO *Jennifer Hassell*

Saturday 16 September 1961 TLS (fragment),[2] Smith College

Court Green
North Tawton
Devonshire
September 16, 1961

Miss Jennifer Hassell
A. M. HEATH & CO. LTD.
35 Dover Street
London W.1

Dear Miss Hassell,

I'm sending along the manuscript of THE BEDBOOK, verse for a children's picture book, and my husband's book for children MEET MY FOLKS! in case you think they're worth passing on to your office mate[3] in charge of Children's Books on the chance of selling my ms. in either or both England and America, and my husband's book in America. His book has been rejected over there by the Atlantic Monthly Press, Harper's and

1–Winifred Mary Hope Davies (1908–81).

2–On the verso of this letter draft is a handwritten list of American periodicals and SP's poems published therein, likely for the Acknowledgements in the Knopf edition of *The Colossus*.

3–SP lists the literary agents Mark Hamilton and Susan Balfour in addition to Jennifer Hassell under A. M. Heath & Company in her address book.

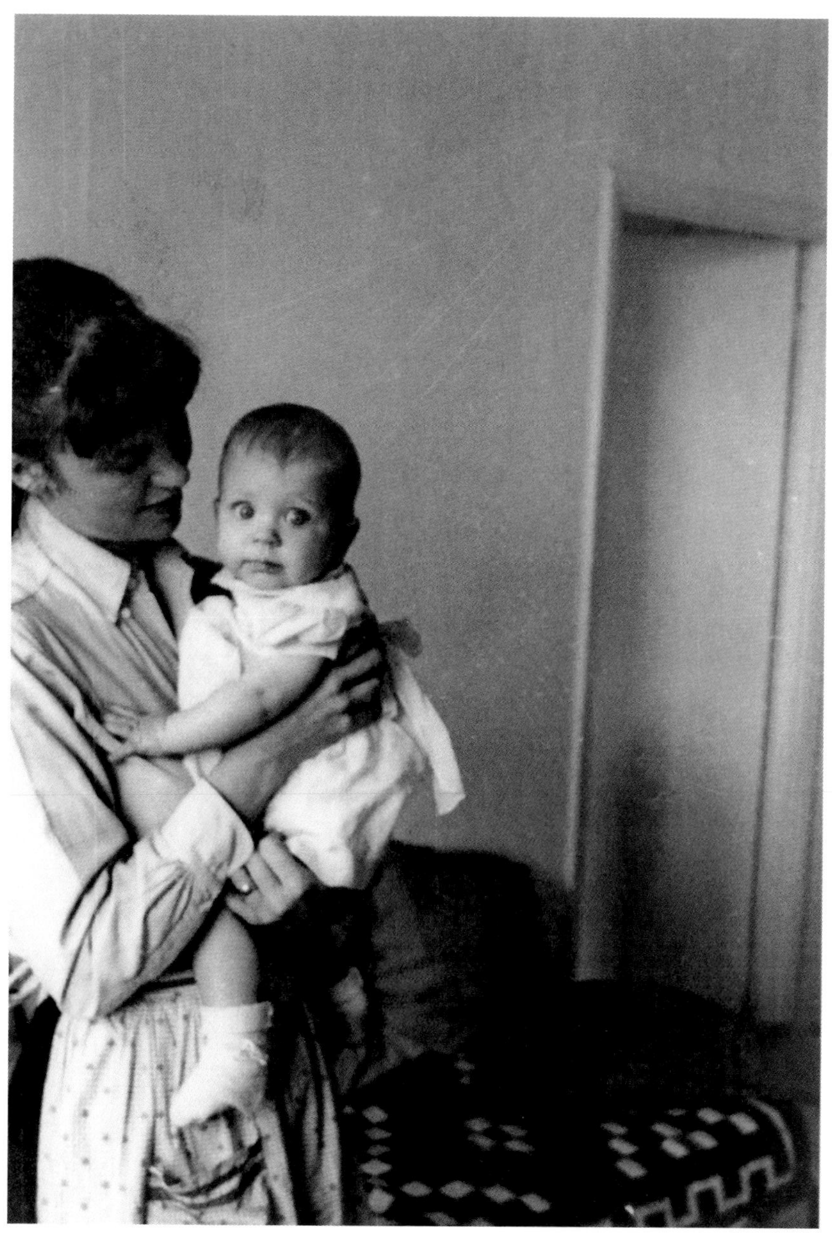

Sylvia Plath and Frieda Hughes in 3 Chalcot Square,
c. 23 September 1960.

surprising verdict of 'not guilty' so Penguin books can publish the unexpurgated edition – a heartening advance – for D.H. Lawrence's writings!

PS – Got a press ticket from Stephen Spender for the last day of the Lady Chatterley trials at the Old Bailey – very exciting – especially with the

3 Chalcot Square
London N.W.1

October (excuse me, November 6: Sunday) 1960

#46

Dear Mother,

I'm enclosing two of the latest shots of the Pooker, alias Bunzo Bun. She is patiently playing with the old toys---rattles, teething ring, plastic spoons---but eager for new things, especially anything with pictures on it. For treats she has her little Bunzo Bear, who she knocks about and hugs, and her silver cup and a cowrie shell. She sings now, a little high voice and funny look, and talks and answers us by making Brr noises. I found out that the girl on the first floor, expecting a baby any day now, had borrowed a sewing machine, so took advantage of her generosity and nipped down a few afternoons this week to sew my second venture for Frieda---a brilliant blue linen dress with a trimming of continental embroidery on the hem and waist (I made this up, taking my clue from Helga, who also uses these tapes---they ensure an absolutely original dress) of pink and yellow flowers on the same blue ground. It is very handsome and styled like this:

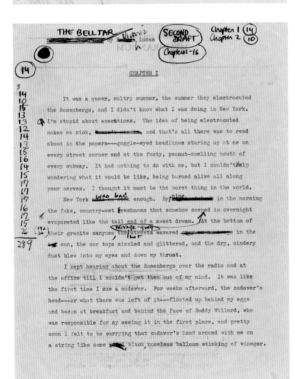

I went to look at Simplicity patterns yesterday and drooled at a whole series of "Tyrol" outfits---black bodices, full bright-colored skirts and white blouses. Most of course were for 2,3 & 4 year-olds. I have my eye on a nice pattern for the 2 yards of red Viyella I bought. I hope I can get a good 2nd hand singer for about $90. The new ones (horrible looking) cost over $300! I hate the modern design & like the old black models with

Drawing of a child's dress, from Sylvia Plath to Aurelia Plath, 6 November 1960.

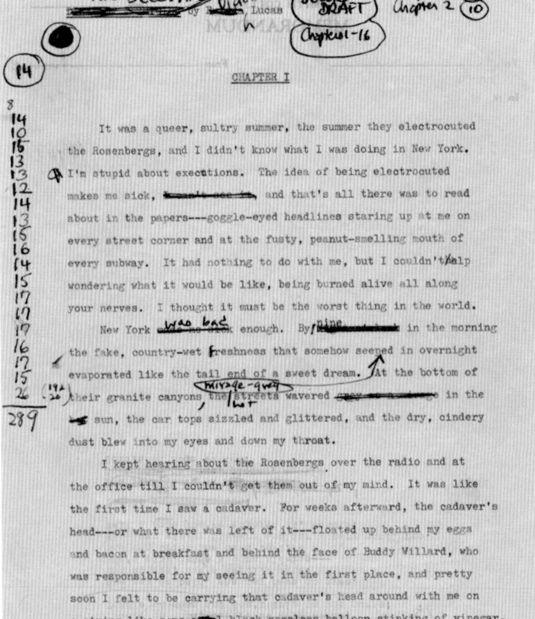

THE BELL JAR by Victoria Lucas

SECOND DRAFT

Chapter 1 (14)
Chapter 2 (10)

Chapters 1-16

CHAPTER I

It was a queer, sultry summer, the summer they electrocuted the Rosenbergs, and I didn't know what I was doing in New York. I'm stupid about executions. The idea of being electrocuted makes me sick, and that's all there was to read about in the papers---goggle-eyed headlines staring up at me on every street corner and at the fusty, peanut-smelling mouth of every subway. It had nothing to do with me, but I couldn't help wondering what it would be like, being burned alive all along your nerves. I thought it must be the worst thing in the world.

New York was bad enough. By nine in the morning the fake, country-wet freshness that somehow seeped in overnight evaporated like the tail end of a sweet dream. At the bottom of their granite canyons, the hot streets wavered mirage-grey in the sun, the car tops sizzled and glittered, and the dry, cindery dust blew into my eyes and down my throat.

I kept hearing about the Rosenbergs over the radio and at the office till I couldn't get them out of my mind. It was like the first time I saw a cadaver. For weeks afterward, the cadaver's head---or what there was left of it---floated up behind my eggs and bacon at breakfast and behind the face of Buddy Willard, who was responsible for my seeing it in the first place, and pretty soon I felt to be carrying that cadaver's head around with me on a string like some black, noseless balloon stinking of vinegar.

The Bell Jar, second draft of Chapter 1, *c.* April–July 1961.

Sylvia and Frieda, January 1961. Captioned on verso by SP: 'Frieda Rebecca age 9 months plus her mother & her teddy bear.'

Frieda's first birthday, 1 April 1961. Sent with letter to Ann Davidow-Goodman, 27 April 1961. Captioned on verso by SP: 'Frieda plus birthday cake & birthday balloon, April 1, 1961.'

Sylvia Plath, Frieda holding daffodils, and Nicholas, Court Green, Devon, late April 1962.

Ted Hughes, Sylvia Plath, Frieda Hughes, and Vicky Farrar, sitting on deck chairs, Court Green, Devon, Easter 1962.

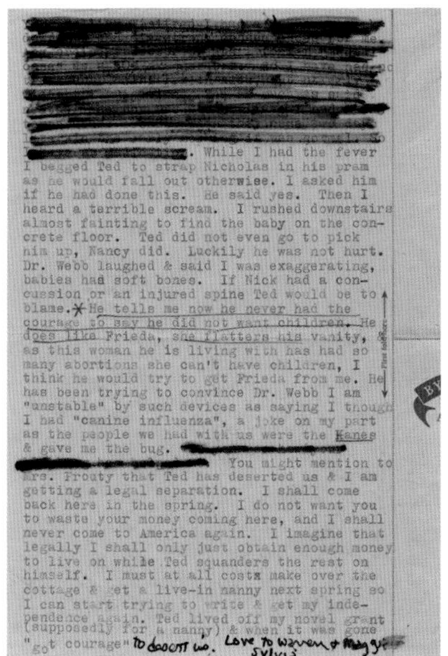

. While I had the fever I begged Ted to strap Nicholas in his pram as he would fall out otherwise. I asked him if he had done this. He said yes. Then I heard a terrible scream. I rushed downstairs almost fainting to find the baby on the concrete floor. Ted did not even go to pick him up, Nancy did. Luckily he was not hurt. Dr. Webb laughed & said I was exaggerating, babies had soft bones. If Nick had a concussion or an injured spine Ted would be to blame. * He tells me now he never had the courage to say he did not want children. He does like Frieda, she flatters his vanity, & as this woman he is living with has had so many abortions she can't have children, I think he would try to get Frieda from me. He has been trying to convince Dr. Webb I am "unstable" by such devices as saying I though I had "canine influenza", a joke on my part as the people we had with us were the Kanes & gave me the bug.

You might mention to Mrs. Prouty that Ted has deserted us & I am getting a legal separation. I shall come back here in the spring. I do not want you to waste your money coming here, and I shall never come to America again. I imagine that legally I shall only just obtain enough money to live on while Ted squanders the rest on himself. I must at all costs make over the cottage & get a live-in nanny next spring so I can start trying to write & get my independence again. Ted lived off my novel grant (supposedly for a nanny) & when it was gone "got courage" to desert us. Love to Warren & Maggie

Sylvia

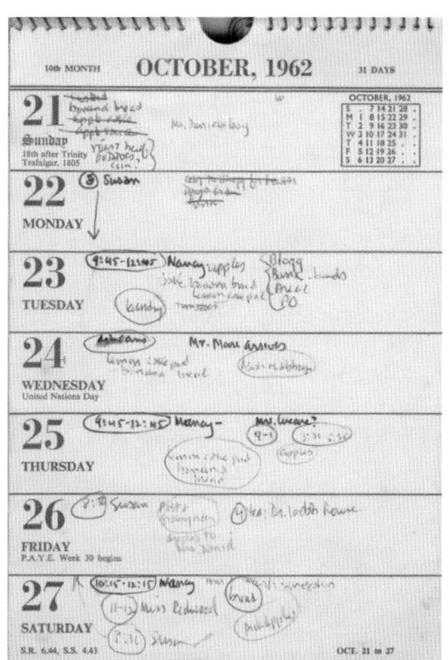

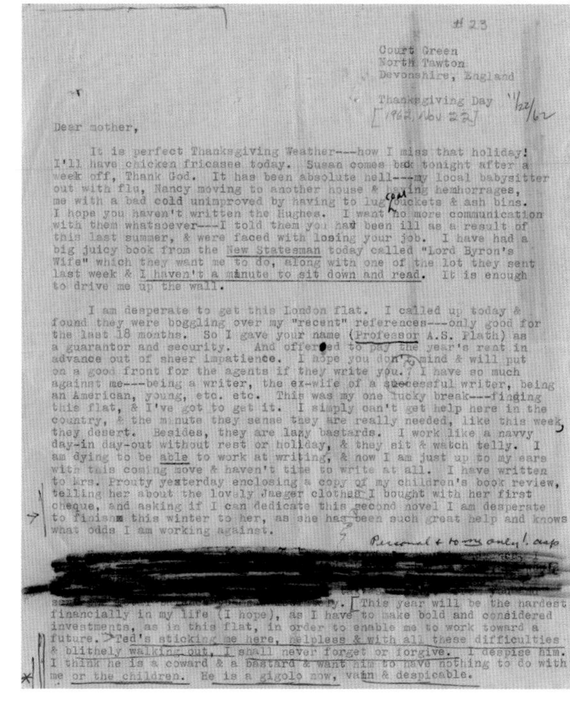

#23

Court Green
North Tawton
Devonshire, England

Thanksgiving Day 11/22/62
[1962, Nov 22]

Dear mother,

It is perfect Thanksgiving Weather---how I miss that holiday! I'll have chicken fricasse today. Susan comes back tonight after a week off, Thank God. It has been absolute hell---my local babysitter out with flu, Nancy moving to another house & having hemhorrages, me with a bad cold unimproved by having to lug coal buckets & ash bins. I hope you haven't written the Hughes. I want no more communication with them whatsoever---I told them you had been ill as a result of this last summer, & were faced with losing your job. I have had a big juicy book from the New Statesman today called "Lord Byron's Wife" which they want me to do, along with one of the lot they sent last week & I haven't a minute to sit down and read. It is enough to drive me up the wall.

I am desperate to get this London flat. I called up today & found they were boggling over my "recent" references---only good for the last 18 months. So I gave your name (Professor A.S. Plath) as a guarantor and security. And offered to pay the year's rent in advance out of sheer impatience. I hope you don't mind & will put on a good front for the agents if they write you. I have so much against me---being a writer, the ex-wife of a successful writer, being an American, young, etc. etc. This was my one lucky break---finding this flat, & I've got to get it. I simply can't get help here in the country, & the minute they sense they are really needed, like this week, they desert. Besides, they are lazy bastards. I work like a navvy day-in day-out without rest or holiday, & they sit & watch telly. I am dying to be able to work at writing, & now I am just up to my ears with this coming move & haven't time to write at all. I have written to Mrs. Prouty yesterday enclosing a copy of my children's book review, telling her about the lovely Jaeger clothes I bought with her first cheque, and asking if I can dedicate this second novel I am desperate to finish this winter to her, as she has been such great help and knows what odds I am working against.

Personal & to me only!

y. This year will be the hardest financially in my life (I hope), as I have to make bold and considered investments, as in this flat, in order to enable me to work toward a future. Ted's sticking me here, helpless & with all these difficulties & blithely walking out, I shall never forget or forgive. I despise him. I think he is a coward & a bastard & want him to have nothing to do with me or the children. He is a gigolo now, vain & despicable.

Above: Redactions and red biro annotations made by Aurelia Plath on page 2 of SP to ASP, 23 September 1962.

Top right: Sylvia Plath's Letts Royal Office Tablet Diary, 21–27 October 1962.

Right: Redactions and red biro annotations made by Aurelia Plath on page 1 of SP to ASP, 22 November 1962.

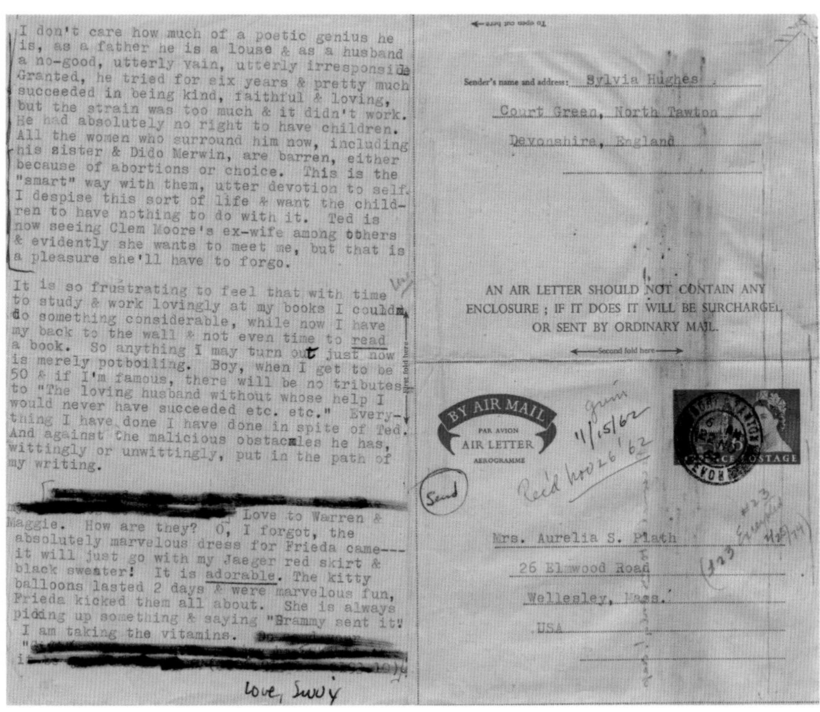

I don't care how much of a poetic genius he is, as a father he is a louse & as a husband a no-good, utterly vain, utterly irresponsible. Granted, he tried for six years & pretty much succeeded in being kind, faithful & loving, but the strain was too much & it didn't work. He had absolutely no right to have children. All the women who surround him now, including his sister & Dido Merwin, are barren, either because of abortions or choice. This is the "smart" way with them, utter devotion to self. I despise this sort of life & want the children to have nothing to do with it. Ted is now seeing Clem Moore's ex-wife among others & evidently she wants to meet me, but that is a pleasure she'll have to forgo.

It is so frustrating to feel that with time to study & work lovingly at my books I could do something considerable, while now I have my back to the wall & not even time to read a book. So anything I may turn out just now is merely potboiling. Boy, when I get to be 50 & if I'm famous, there will be no tributes to "The loving husband without whose help I would never have succeeded etc. etc." Everything I have done I have done in spite of Ted. And against the malicious obstacles he has, wittingly or unwittingly, put in the path of my writing.

Love to Warren & Maggie. How are they? O, I forgot, the absolutely marvelous dress for Frieda came--- it will just go with my Jaeger red skirt & black sweater! It is adorable. The kitty balloons lasted 2 days & were marvelous fun, Frieda kicked them all about. She is always picking up something & saying "Grammy sent it!" I am taking the vitamins.

Love, Sivvy

Sender's name and address: Sylvia Hughes

Court Green, North Tawton

Devonshire, England

AN AIR LETTER SHOULD NOT CONTAIN ANY ENCLOSURE ; IF IT DOES IT WILL BE SURCHARGED OR SENT BY ORDINARY MAIL.

BY AIR MAIL
PAR AVION
AIR LETTER
AEROGRAMME

11/15/62

Rec'd Nov 26 '62

Send

Mrs. Aurelia S. Plath

26 Elmwood Road

Wellesley, Mass.

USA

12th MONTH **DECEMBER, 1962** 31 DAYS

16 Sunday 3rd in Advent. Ember Week

17 MONDAY

18 TUESDAY Last Quarter

19 WEDNESDAY Ember Day

20 THURSDAY

21 FRIDAY S. Thomas. Ember Day. P.A.Y.E. Week 38 begins

22 SATURDAY Ember Day. Shortest Day S.R. 8.3, S.S. 3.54

DEC. 16 to 22

Above: Redactions and red biro annotations made by Aurelia Plath on page 2 of SP to ASP, 22 November 1962.

Top right: Sylvia Plath with Nicholas Hughes, Court Green.

Left: Sylvia Plath's Letts Royal Office Tablet Diary, 16–22 December 1962.

Right: Vandalism (removal of SP's signature) from SP to ASP, 4 February 1963.

23 Fitzroy Road
London N.W.1

February 4, 1963

Dear mother,

Thanks so much for your letters. I got a sweet letter from Dotty & a lovely hood & mittens for Nick from Warren & Margaret. I just haven't written anybody because I have been feeling a bit grim---the upheaval over, I am seeing the finality of it all, and being catapulted from the cowlike happiness of maternity into loneliness & grim problems is no fun. I got a sweet letter from the Nortons & an absolutely wonderful understanding one from Betty Aldrich. Marty Plumer is coming over at the end of March which should be cheering. (Mrs. Prouty has sent another check & dear letter.) I have absolutely no desire ever to return to America. Not now, anyway. I have my beautiful country house, the car, and London is the one city of the world I'd like to live in--- with its fine doctors, nice neighbors, parks & theaters & the BBC. There is nothing like the BBC in America---over there they do not publish my stuff as they do here, my poems & novel. I have done a commissioned article for Punch on my schooldays & have a chance for 3 weeks in May to be on the BBC Critics program at about $150 a week, a fantastic break I hope I can make good on. Each critic sees the same play, art show, book, radio broadcast each week & discusses it. I am hoping it will finish furnishing this place & I can go to Court Green right after. As Marty for a copy of the details of the two places & the rent & maybe you could circulate them among your professor friends, too.

I appreciate your desire to see Frieda, but if you can imagine the emotional upset she has been through in losing her father & moving, you will see what an incredible idea it is to take her away by jet to America! I am her one security & to uproot her would be thoughtless & cruel, however sweetly you treated her at the other end. I could never afford to live in America---I get the best of doctor's care here perfectly free & with children this is a great blessing. Also, Ted sees the children once a week & this makes him more responsible about our allowance. I have no desire ever to live in Wellesley, it always stifled me, & I think living with relatives is a very bad policy. I shall simply have to fight it out on my own over here. Maybe someday I can manage holidays in Europe with the children & so on. The children need me most right now & so I shall try to go on for the next few years writing mornings, being with them afternoons & seeing friends or studying & reading evenings.

My German au pair is food-fussy & boy-gaga but I am d[...] best to discipline here, she does give me some peace mor[...] free evenings, but I'll have to think up something new [...] as these girls don't want to be so long away from Lond[...] start seeing a woman doctor free on the National Hea[...] been referred by my very good local doctor which sh[...] weather this difficult time. Give my love to all.

Sylvia Plath to Ruth Beuscher, 4 February 1963, Page 1.

23 Fitzroy Road
London N.W.1

February 4, 1963

Dear Dr. Beuscher,

I write from London where I have found a flat & an au pair and can see ahead financially for about a year. I thought I'd get an unfurnished flat, furnish it by poems & loans, & rent it out summers to touristswhile I went back to Devon, to earn most of the rent for it & Ted says he'll try to pay us about $280 a month while I try to make up the rest by writing. I have finally read the Fromm & think that I have been guilty of what he calls 'Idolatrous love', that I lost myself in Ted instead of finding myself, and this was why deeply underneath the marvelous loving, the writing, the babies I feared his loss, his leaving me & depended on him more & more, making him both idol & father. There was enough identity left to me in Devon to make me feel immense relief at his departure & at the prospect of divorce---now I shall grow out of his shadow, I thought, I shall be *me*. While we were married we were never apart & all experience filtered through each other. On a grownup level, I don't think I could have endured a marriage of infidelities. I had a beautiful, virile, brilliant man & he still is, whatever immaturities there may be in his throwing over everything in such a violent way. He has said he is sorry for the lying, and shows concern that we get on on our own.

What appals me is the return of my madness, my paralysis, my fear & vision of the worst---cowardly withdrawal, a mental hospital, lobotomies. Perhaps this is accentuated by my seeing Ted once a week when he comes to see Frieda---seeing how happy & whole & independent he is now, how much more I admire him like this, & what good friends we could be if *I could manage to grow up too*. He is gaga over this ad-agency girl who has gone back to live with her 3rd husband to keep the passion hot, although she did live for 3 weeks with Ted & flew to Spain for a holiday with him. If I were simply jealous about *this* it would be okay. But I know Spain and lovemaking would do me no good now, not until I find myself again. I feel I need a ritual for survival from day to day until I begin to grow out of this death & found Fromm's recommendation for concentration, patience & faith gave me a kind of peace, but that I keep slipping into this pit of panic & deepfreeze, with my mother's horrible example of fearful anxiety & "unselfishness" on one side & the beauties of my two little children on the other. I am living on sleeping pills & nerve tonic & have managed a few commissions for a magazine & the BBC and poems very good but, I feel written on the edge of madness. The publicity of Ted's leaving is universal & I was taking it all with dignity & verve at first---people were buying poems & putting BBC work in my way, &Iam scared to death I shall just pull up the psychic shroud & give up. A poet, a writer, I am I think very narcissistic & the despair at being 30 & having let myself slide, studied nothing for years, having mastered no body of objective knowledge is on me like a cold, accusing wind. Just now it is torture to me to dress, plan meals, put one foot in front of the other. Ironically my novel about my first breakdown is getting rave reviews over here. I feel a simple act of will would make the world steady & solidify. No-one can save

Sylvia Plath to Ruth Beuscher, 4 February 1963, Page 2. The letter is postmarked 8 February and, unusually for Plath, ends mid-column on the page.

me but myself, but I need help & my doctor is referring me to a woman psychiatrist. Living on my wits, my writing---even partially, is very hard at this time, it is so subjective & dependent on objectivity. I am, for the first time since my marriage, relating to people without Ted, but my own lack of center, of mature identity, is a great torment. I am aware of a cowardice in myself, a wanting to give up. If I could study, read, enjoy people on my own Ted's leaving would be hard, but manageable. But there is this damned, self-induced freeze. I am suddenly in agony, desperate, thinking Yes, let him take over the house, the children, let me just die & be done with it. How can I get out of this ghastly defeatist cycle & grow up. I am only too aware that love and a husband are impossibles to me at this time, I am incapable of being myself & loving myself.

Now the babies are crying, I must take them out to tea.

With love,
Sylvia

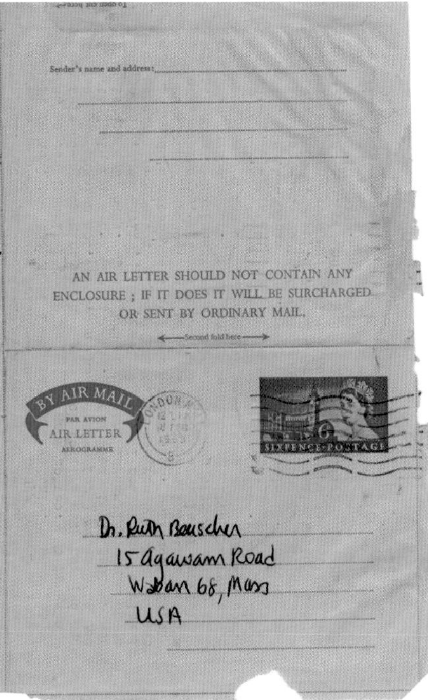

Athenaeum, but no <text missing> there has seen it. As for my ms., the l <text missing> it but w <text missing> as

TO *Aurelia Schober Plath & Warren Plath*

Tues.–Fri. 26–29 September 1961[1] TLS (aerogramme), Indiana University

Tuesday: September 27

Dearest mother & Warren,

How nice to get letters from the two of you this week. I am so glad the return plane flight went off well. The days have just flown since I last wrote, and we have established a very pleasant rhythm here. Right after breakfast I go up to my study to work at the marvelous six foot natural wood table (which you helped finish, Warren!) while Ted carpenters or gardens in the back, with Frieda. He gives her lunch & puts her to bed about noon, & I come down & make our lunch & by the time I am finished picking up the house & doing dishes Frieda is up and out front with me gardening or mending or whatever, and Ted is in his study. Thus both of us get half a day out-of-doors and half a day writing (which is all either of us wants!) and Frieda is out all the time.

I have amnesia about what I wrote in my last letter, mother. The red sweater is wonderfully roomy & should fit for a long while. It's our very favorite. Now I have so much space everything is much easier & I find myself washing Frieda's sweaters almost every day. She alternates those wonderful wool pants. She gets very dirty here, as when we garden, she must come out with her little pail and shovel & scoop up dirt all over herself. What's the smallest size USA dungarees??? I am going to make a bunch of little cotton smocks to go over her wool sweaters & pants which I can wash every night to save dirtying them too much. She is in her element here---plays more & more by herself in the giant playroom, running in and out; plays with my pots & pans. I got her a little bell-ringing imitation lawnmower to push today, as she loves to see me mow the lawn & she's overjoyed. She wears her sunhat you bought for Italy all the time & has loved that musical doll to such distraction it is a bit grey ---I simply can't get it away from her. Do you think washing it with warm soapsuds & a nail brush would hurt the musicbox? I mean not putting it in water, of course, but lightly washing the fur. She adores this doll also,

1–Letter misdated by SP; dates supplied from internal evidence.

I think, because it has a real mouth, which she is always trying to feed. You should see her cradling it and kissing it and putting it to bed in a piepan! She says: all gone, more milk, egg, eye, car, etc., still not a lot, but she understands very involved directions like Feed some apple to baby. It is amazing how easy she is to take care of here.

Did I say the check for the Bendix came, & a thousand thanks? My life will be much easier when it finally arrives. My cleaning woman is a blessing. She does the upstairs Tuesday & the downstairs Thursday, plus almost all the ironing. I don't know what I'd do without her! I look so forward to the "day-after" neatness of her floorscrubbing. I have just been to Exeter for the day, shopping for bits and pieces. Did you say you knew of a 2nd hand rug place in London? I don't know why this occurred to me, but I thought you might have said something about it. Rugs is the main thing now.

Friday: Wonderful clear blue weather. I have my front garden all weeded & trim & mowed. Could you find out what name the True Boston Magnolia has? We want to order a couple of bushes. Ted has planted winter lettuce & is digging a big strawberry bed: he has made my desk, a sewing table, a baby gate for the stair---is a natural carpenter! We are so happy. 72 apple trees! For Christmas do you think our American Santa might dig up some seeds for real American corn (I hear Country Gentleman is good---the Merwins have it in France) and Kentucky wonder beans, or some good thin green pole bean. Nothing like that here---only thick, broad beans & corn for pigs. So glad to get your new letter & hear the hurricane passed off safely for you.[1] Had a lovely letter from Peg Cantor, to whom I'll write today.[2] Had also a wonderful letter from Mrs. Prouty enclosing a check for $200! I had been feeling a bit blue because I just didn't feel I could go out and get a really fine rug or two (bedroom & living room are the two places I need them for most) with our mountain of moving-in expenses, including a bill of close to $300 from our lawyers for a multitude of fees. But now I can add her check to grampy's & get something really good. Ted has been driving 35 miles to the BBC station at Plymouth to record 4 small programs for the Woman's Hour.[3] I am immensely relieved there are recording stations here, for we shall start some income again. He is finishing

1–Probably Hurricane Esther, which affected New England in late September 1961.

2–See SP to Margaret Cantor, 30 September 1961.

3–Ted Hughes, 'Fire', *Woman's Hour*, BBC (25 September 1961); 'Air', *Woman's Hour*, BBC (2 October 1961); 'Earth', *Woman's Hour*, BBC (9 October 1961); and 'Water', *Woman's Hour*, BBC (16 October 1961).

a radio play for the 3rd programme,[1] & Vogue wants a children's poem[2] for $50, & there is the series of the Times Children's Pages,[3] so no lack of assignments. I am very encourage by selling my first woman's magazine story;[4] my 2nd hasn't sold yet, but the fiction editor of one of the two big women's weeklies here wants to see me & talk over their requirements on the strength of it. So I shall push this. I'll get into the Ladies' Home J yet! Yes, I will get a complimentary New Yorker subscription the minute mine expires. Frieda is in fine health, Ted taught her to feed herself. I have a potty chair which she plays with but how does one get her to pee in it???

Lots of love,

Sivvy

TO *Ruth Fainlight*

Friday 29 September 1961 TLS, Ruth Fainlight

Court Green
North Tawton
Devonshire
September 29, 1961

Dear Ruth,

I am desperate for apple recipes. Let me know the lot. Have you anything for Stinging Nettles? Surely they have some nutritive value!

I want to hear all about Alan's sitdown story.[5] The New Statesman and Observer are our only source of World News, and down here they sound curiously watered and otherworldly. After a month of hard labor ---carpentering, painting, weeding, mowing, and feeding my terrifying enormous brother who came for a week, we are at last writing something, me in the mornings, and Ted afternoons & eves. We take turns minding

1–Ted Hughes, *The Wound*.

2–Ted Hughes, 'Nessie', *Vogue* (December 1961): 165.

3–Ted Hughes, 'Mainly for Children' [Antoine de Saint-Exupéry, *The Little Prince*], *Sunday Times* (25 February 1962): 45; 'Mainly for Children' [Kenneth Grahame, *The Wind in the Willows*], *Sunday Times* (15 April 1962): 34; 'Mainly for Children' [H. G. Wells, *The War of the Worlds*], *Sunday Times* (24 June 1962): 29; 'Mainly for Children' [Henry Williamson, *Tarka the Otter*], *Sunday Times* (16 September 1962): 18; and 'Mainly for Children' [Apsley Cherry-Garrard, *The Worst Journey in the World*], *Sunday Times* (18 November 1962): 27.

4–Sylvia Plath, 'The Perfect Place', *My Weekly* 2498 (28 October 1961): 3–7, 31. SP's typescript (carbon), with original title 'The Lucky Stone', has annotation 'Sold £15. 15. 0 by Jennifer Hassell'; held by Smith College.

5–Alan Sillitoe was arrested with 1,300 other pacifists in an anti-nuclear sit-down demonstration at Trafalgar Square on 17–18 September 1961.

Frieda and hacking and pasting at the house. Do you know anything about good carpets? Right now I am morbid about acres of bare floorboarding full of dead death-watch beetles.

I should arrive at Waterloo at about 3:30 pm & come straight to you. Then leave just before 6 for the Guinness thing, then have supper with my publisher & come in early. I'll probably shop a bit the next morning & take an afternoon train home that day. I most miss good movies. I can barely stand to read the reviews of them, I get so movie-mad. It will be terrific seeing you both.

Love,
Sylvia

TO *Margaret Cantor*

Saturday 30 September 1961 TLS (aerogramme), Private owner

Court Green
North Tawton
Devonshire, England
September 30, 1961

Dear Peg,

It was wonderful to get your lovely letter here. It felt very natural to hear your voice, and I wanted to sit right down and say hello. I wonder if you know how much we think of you! Ted and I are always so eager to hear news of you through mother or Warren, and both of us look forward to catching up with you annually through your wonderful newsy Christmas letter. You are one of Ted's very favorite American families, and I think he enjoyed being at Kathy's wedding[1] as much as about anything we did on our visit.

Our home is a dream---white plaster under its peak of straw thatch. The thatch is a home for countless birds who come and sing and preen before slipping in their special crevices every night. All I can see from my study window is great trees, clouds and blue sky. We have had some fine blue September weather, crisp and clear, and I have been out weeding my front flower garden, while Ted digs up the large vegetable garden at the back to make room for a strawberry patch.

The house has a lovely feel to it---as if it had been full of warm fires, and flowers, and happy children. And indeed it was the boyhood home

1–Katherine Cantor married Scott William Miller, 13 June 1959, at the Cantors' home in Waban, Mass.

of Sir Robert Arundell, the Governor of the Bahamas,[1] who sold it to us. Frieda is in her element, toddling about and imitating all we do---spooning dirt over herself, which she thinks is digging the garden, and eating endless apples. After being so long cramped in two city rooms with no garden, it is heaven to lose ourselves on our green acres. I work in my study every morning, while Ted carpenters or gardens with Frieda at his side. Then he works in the afternoon and evening while I cook and sew and pick flowers. It is a lovely rhythm. I feel I learned so much from you in that beautiful summer in Chatham---the real joy of creative homemaking. I think back on that as the happiest summer of my teens---it just glows gold, the color of the Chatham sands.

Do know that we think of you very, very often! Ted joins me in sending best love to all,

Affectionately,
Sylvia

TO *Peter Davison*

Saturday 30 September 1961 TLS (photocopy), Yale University

Court Green
North Tawton
Devonshire, England
September 30, 1961

Dear Peter:

I am writing in answer to your good letter to Ted.[2] He was very pleased with the review, and is sending a copy on to Bill Merwin at his address in France.[3]

We also have just bought a house---in Devon, so the above address should be our permanent one for, we hope, a long, long time. It is a wonderful, ancient (how ancient nobody knows) old farmhouse, white, with a great peaked thatch, surrounded by its own 2½ acres, apple orchard, flower and vegetable garden, on the edge of a small, but surprisingly thriving town with bank, butchers, chemists, all the conveniences, and the bluegrey

1–Over time Arundell was governor of the Windward Islands, governor of Barbados, and acting governor-general of the West Indies.

2–Peter Davison to TH, 18 September 1961; (photocopy) held by Yale University.

3–Peter Davison, 'Self-Revelation in the New Poetry', *The Atlantic* (November 1961): 170–4. In addition to reviewing *Lupercal*, Davison also reviewed Merwin's *The Drunk in the Furnace*.

outlines of Dartmoor just to the South. With our 12 rooms we can at last think of putting people up, so you and Jane must think of staying with us on a return trip to England. We are only 4 hours from London by express train, so Ted can go on easily doing his freelancing for the BBC.

I am enclosing a group of poems by Ted[1] which we were going to send on just about the time your letter arrived, with Wodwo in for good measure, in case you would like to publish it in America.

We are delighted to hear about Angus (what a fine name!) and tell Jane she must send me a gossipy letter someday, all about the baby, and Smith news, and news of her own self. Frieda loves it here, after the cramping two-room no-garden London flat. She rushes in and out, spoons dirt over herself, which she thinks is gardening, and eats endless green apples from our orchard, which don't seem to affect her adversely.

All the best from us three to you three,

Sylvia Hughes

Mr. Peter Davison
Executive Editor
THE ATLANTIC MONTHLY
8 Arlington Street
Boston, Massachusetts
USA

TO *Aurelia Schober Plath*

Friday 6 October 1961 — TLS (aerogramme), Indiana University

Court Green
North Tawton
Devonshire, England
Friday: October 6

Dear mother,

It is just past ten, and I am sitting downstairs in the big kitchen this morning, with the Aga cooker (coal-burning) Ted stoked earlier warming the place cosily and Frieda running to and from her playroom with new toys to potter about with at my feet. Ted is off for most of the day to have the car checked, do the laundry and shop in Exeter & join the libraries there, so I have a day to catch up on baking and mending. It is lovely

1–The poems sent were: 'Sugar Loaf', 'Last Lines', 'Fishing at Dawn', 'The Rescue', 'Memory', and 'Wodwo'.

and cosy here now, and I have been working in my study till noon every morning. Ted and I are dreaming up plots for women's magazine stories and I have just finished the 3rd since we started this & my 1st here, and will be seeing the Fiction Editor of one of the women's magazines who is interested in me when I go to London at the end of the month to pick up my 75 pounds poetry prize at the Guinness party & see my publisher.

Ted had a day in London this Tuesday---leaving the house at 5:30 am, catching the 6:30 express from Exeter and getting in in time for a long day of recording at the BBC[1] from 10:30 to 4, with a posh lunch in Soho with the head of the Arts Council, for whom he will be co-judge[2] of the next two years' Poetry Book Society Selections (at about $150 a year). Ted is almost through with his new radio play, and we feel we are really beginning to produce things.

Had a lovely letter from Dotty this week, enclosing $25 as a housewarming gift. Wrote her thanks last night. Our bank manager informed us that Mrs. Prouty's check was dated 1962! I told him I simply couldn't write her & ask her to change it, so the bank is sending a note about it to her bank, & I guess they'll take care of it officially. Lucky for us she didn't date it 1970!

I am enjoying my handwind Singer sewing machine very much. It is just my speed, and I am making Frieda a series of gay cotton smocks to go over her woolens---I can wash the smocks much more easily. Yesterday I had the plumbers in from 9-5, fixing the indoor toilet up with a new cistern, installing a modern sink unit in the kitchen & laying the pipes for the Bendix, a lot of work as they had to go through a 3-foot stone wall from the kitchen into the larder where the machine will be, but amply worth it for me! Now all I have to do is pester the Bendix people to deliver it!

Nancy Axworthy, my cleaning lady, is more and more indispensable. She, of course, is more accustomed to the house than I as she has worked here 11 years. Her husband is a carpenter and evidently a town figure---one of the church bellringers, assistant head of the fire brigade, woodworking teacher at a night class, and so on. She is a sweet, fresh-faced healthy person & the midwife said that when the new baby comes she'd probably be happy to come for a few more hours a week & help with washing up and so on. I feel very lucky!

1–Possibly Ted Hughes, 'Capturing Animals', *Listening and Writing*, BBC Home Service (Schools), 6 October 1961; 'Writing a Novel – Beginning', *Listening and Writing*, BBC Home Service (Schools), 20 October 1961; and 'Writing a Novel – Going On', *Listening and Writing*, BBC Home Service (Schools), 25 November 1961.

2–TH and Anthony Thwaite were co-judges for the 1962 Poetry Book Society selections.

Did I tell you that Ted is having a selection of poems from his 2 books come out in a Faber paperback jointly[1] with selected poems by Thom Gunn, another Faber poet Ted's age?

We are being deluged by flower and fruit catalogues Ted has sent for, full of tantalizing colored pictures & descriptions. Do find out the official name of the Boston magnolias! I hope we can get their twin here. All of us are very healthy with our wholesome diet. I have 30 Vitamin A & D pills a month for 6¢ from the Welfare service, and Frieda has A & D drops which she takes every day, so don't worry about us in that respect. The one person I wish we could import is Dr. Gulbrandsen! My midwife has told me a good dentist in Exeter who does scrape teeth, but evidently only in London do they Xray, so I'll simply have to plan a trip there once or twice a year to an Xraying dentist, probably as a private patient.

Frieda responds more & more to her life here. She is delighted with her big playroom, the bay window of which I use for my sewing table, and Ted is going to build some shelves in an alcove for her toys, so she can have them all arranged in full view instead of jumbled together. She is incredibly neat---picks up every little crumb she drops & gives it to us & tries to sweep up anything spilt with a dust pan or sponge.

Do be sure and take it easy now you have all this statistics testing and make Warren and Margaret cook you meals on the weekend, instead of the other way round.

Lots of love from all of us,
Sivvy

TO *Ruth Fainlight*

Friday 6 October 1961 ALS, Ruth Fainlight

Court Green
North Tawton
Devonshire
Friday: October 6

Dear Ruth,

A small note to say you are an angel for the terrific apple recipes & how I hope you are all right. It's difficult & in a way impertinent to tell you

1–Thom Gunn and Ted Hughes, *Selected Poems* (London: Faber & Faber, 1962). SP's presentation copy, signed and dated by TH, appeared at auction via Bonhams on 21 March 2018.

how very much I am wishing things to go well for you, because noone can ever really identify deeply enough with someone else's special predicament to make the words 'I know how you feel'[1] carry their full weight. But our sad & confusing experience of losing a baby last winter has made me feel much closer to the difficulties & apprehensions of childbearing & much more profoundly involved with them. Please tell me if I am descending on you at a lousy time. Or let me know at any time if you'd rather be left in peace. I'd love to see you in any case & will come as planned unless you tell me best not. We are liking our place more & more. When you are able you & Alan must come for a bucolic country weekend & live on apples & fat cream.

Lots of love,
Sylvia

TO *Judith Jones*

Saturday 7 October 1961

TLS (aerogramme),
University of Texas at Austin

Court Green
North Tawton
Devonshire, England
October 7, 1961

Mrs. Judith B. Jones
ALFRED A. KNOPF
501 Madison Avenue
New York 22, New York
USA

Dear Mrs. Jones:

Thanks very much for your two letters of August 22nd and September 19th.[2] I've been up to my ears in moving our household from London to Devon (the above address should be permanent for a long while), or I would have answered them sooner.

1–Fainlight had experienced a miscarriage. This recalls the first stanza of 'Elm', the poem which SP would dedicate to Fainlight: 'I know the bottom, she says. I know it with my great tap root: / It is what you fear. / I do not fear it: I have been there' (*Collected Poems*: 192).
2–Judith Jones to SP, 22 August and 19 September 1961; held by University of Texas at Austin.

I have today sent off letters to the 17 or so American magazines in which my poems have appeared asking that the assignment of copyright be sent to you at Knopf. One or two of the magazines (Chelsea Review, Grecourt Review, Hornbook and Smith Alumnae Quarterly) are pretty small, so I don't know if they are copyrighted, but I wrote them, just in case.

I had called W. Roger Smith at Heinemann to find out if the British permissions extend to American publication, but he seemed to know less about copyrights than I did, which was very little help. I guess my call was the occasion of his letter to you.[1] He said he would "take care of everything", but there seems to be a good bit of fog in the London publishing offices.

I don't know your form for acknowledgment pages, but I'd like just to head the page Acknowledgments & list alphabetically the magazines that published the poems: ARTS IN SOCIETY, THE ATLANTIC MONTHLY, AUDIENCE, CHELSEA REVIEW, CRITICAL QUARTERLY, ENCOUNTER,[2] GRECOURT REVIEW, HARPERS, HORNBOOK, HUDSON REVIEW, KENYON REVIEW, LONDON MAGAZINE, MADEMOISELLE, NATION, NEW YORKER, OBSERVER, PARTISAN REVIEW, POETRY (CHICAGO), SEWANEE REVIEW, SPECTATOR, TEXAS QUARTERLY and TIMES LITERARY SUPPLEMENT. I would also like to thank Elizabeth Ames and the Trustees at Yaddo, where many of the poems were written.[3]

I'm delighted with the contents of the book as they now stand & so happy it has been pruned.

Sincerely,
Sylvia Plath

1–W. Roger Smith to Judith Jones, 4 September 1961; held by University of Texas at Austin.
2–Sylvia Plath, 'A Winter Ship', *Encounter* 15 (February 1961): 23; and 'The Colossus', *Encounter* 18 (April 1962): 56.
3–It is likely the poems and periodicals listed on the verso of the letter to Jennifer Hassell, 16 September 1961, correspond to this list.

TO *Copyright Department*, Hudson Review

Saturday 7 October 1961 — TLS (aerogramme), Princeton University

Court Green
North Tawton
Devonshire, England
October 7, 1961

Copyright Department
THE HUDSON REVIEW
439West Street
New York 14, New York
USA

Dear Sir:

Alfred A. Knopf, publishers of my forthcoming book of poems, have asked me to obtain the assignment of copyright for my poems Moonrise, Ouija and Suicide Off Egg Rock which appeared in THE HUDSON REVIEW.

I wonder if you would be so kind as to send the assignment of copyright to:

Mrs. Judith B. Jones
Alfred A. Knopf
501 Madison Avenue
New York 22, New York.

Yours sincerely,
Sylvia Plath

TO *Copyright Department,* Poetry

Saturday 7 October 1961 TLS (aerogramme), University of Chicago

Court Green
North Tawton
Devonshire, England
October 7, 1961

Copyright Department
POETRY
1018 North State Street
Chicago 10, Illinois
USA

Dear Sir:

Alfred A. Knopf, publishers of my forthcoming book of poems, have asked me to obtain the assignment of copyright for my poems Metamorphosis (now titled Faun), Sow and Strumpet Song, which appeared in POETRY.

I wonder if you would be so kind as to send the assignment of copyright to:

Mrs. Judith B. Jones
Alfred A. Knopf
501 Madison Avenue
New York 22, New York.

Thank you very much.

Sincerely yours,
Sylvia Plath

TO *Edith & William Hughes*

Monday 9 October 1961 TLS, Pierpont Morgan Library

Court Green
North Tawton, Devon.
Monday: October 9

Dear Edith & Willy,

I've been meaning to post a note every time Ted sends a letter, but he always gets them off too fast, so I'm writing one now on my own. We are wonderfully happy here. You would be so pleased if you could see Ted---

he has his big dream come true, and at a very early time in life, as you say, Edith. He has a wonderful cosy attic study under the thatch, very warm, just over the immersion heater in the bathroom, and I have a study facing out front, with a view of our two laburnum trees & the sweet church.[1]

Frieda is in seventh heaven. She runs round, singing and playing---none of the fussing she used to do in our crowded two-room flat. In the morning I write & Ted carpenters or gardens with Frieda to keep him company. Then in the afternoon I cook and sew (on my 2nd-hand hand-wind Singer I bought for 12 pounds in London) and weed the flower garden and play with Frieda while Ted writes, and he writes in the evenings, too. So both of us get plenty of exercise and all the time to write we want, and Frieda always has company. Next year we shall try to sell our apples & make some money on them. We are getting lots of flower & fruit catalogues & gardening books, so we shall learn all about them.

Ted has already been to London to do his BBC Children's Broadcasts, & I will go at the end of the month to pick up my 75 pound cheque for my poem at the Guinness Poetry Awards and also to see the fiction editor of WOMANS REALM,[2] you probably know it, the woman's weekly magazine like Woman's Own, who is interested in my short stories & wants to tell me what they want at their magazine.

I have a nice midwife & young doctor here, and we are looking forward to the new baby shortly after New Years. The woolly sheets are <u>wonderful</u>, Edith! They will keep us cosy through the winter. We keep the Aga going & it warms the house & heats the water nicely. The clean rags are so convenient. I always welcome them, as in a house as big as this with so much to fix up one is always wanting rags. I do have the recipe for tomato chutney you sent & shall make up a big lot now I've got apples in plenty.

After we get our first moving-in expenses sorted out, I shall spend some of my prize money and poem money on carpets, which will make a nice change from the bare boards. If I can get these Woman's magazine stories going, a couple a month, I should be able to furnish the house beautifully in time!

Very best love to you both,
Sylvia

1–St Peter's Church, Essington, North Tawton.
2–Probably Antoinette Rose, listed in SP's address book, who was an editor at *Woman's Realm*, then at 189 High Holborn, London.

TO *W. Roger Smith*

Wednesday 11 October 1961 TLS, Random House Group Archive & Library

Court Green
North Tawton
Devon.
October 11, 1961

Roger Smith, Esq.
WILLIAM HEINEMANN LTD.
15/16 Queen Street
London W.1

Dear Mr. Smith,

Thanks very much for your letter of October 10th. I'm glad to hear "Medallion" will be included in THE LONDON BRIDGE BOOK OF VERSE.[1]

My birth date is October 27, 1932. Guard it well, because after I have reached the ripe age of 30, I shall never mention it again.

All good wishes,
Yours sincerely,
Sylvia Plath

TO *Aurelia Schober Plath*

Friday 13 October 1961 TLS, Indiana University

Court Green
North Tawton
Devonshire
Friday: October 13

Dear mother,

Enclosed is a small check for deposit to our Boston 5¢ Savings. We are resting that account a bit & depositing $ checks here until we get over the hump of our first year with all the big initial expenses. But this check is too small to have the exchange discount deducted! I have saved about $500, half gifts, half my own literary earnings this fall, for rugs,

1–Sylvia Plath, 'Medallion', *The London Bridge Book of Verse* (London: Heinemann, 1962): 88–90.

but will wait a month or so & look around while we pile up a bit more money for food & drink. I plan a bright red rug for my study (where no children will come, so it won't need a pattern to hide dirt!), a forest green one to go under the small flowered Indian one we bought at auction for Frieda's room, and a light pink & green & white floral for our bedroom. The red oriental for the livingroom is something worth waiting-for; and, eventually, red stair & hall carpets.

The Bendix has arrived! Huge and beautiful. Now I await the men to install it---everything is done separately here! The plumbers did a lovely job & my new kitchen sink unit is very handsome. I have been painting shelves Ted built in the playroom alcove for Frieda's toys and sewing things. The second blue crisp fall day after lots of rain---very invigorating. Our apples are delicious, better than any I've tasted.

Delighted to hear you've ordered dungarees! The package for Frieda arrived this week & it was the best yet---the tights are just wonderful, and the gorgeous-colored snap-in corduroy suit! She looks like a pixie in the red coat, and the pajamas are very very roomy & bunny-soft. Thank you a billion times! F. is impossible about training. She won't sit on her seat for 2 seconds & has the habit of having her movement during her nap, or very irregularly. I've sat & I've sat & I've sat like Horton the Elephant,[1] but still have to get her to go once. Then I'm sure she'd catch on. Oh well, there's no rush.

Frieda's Christmas doll sounds heavenly. I'll get Ted to make a wooden cradle for our Christmas present & I'll paint it.

I've decided the best way to grow into the community here is to go to our local Anglican church, & maybe belong to its monthly mother's group.[2] I wrote the rector[3]---a Protestant Irishman with very broad background (Chicago, Africa) about this & he came & said he'd go through the creed & order of service with me, but that I'd be welcome (I'm afraid I could never stomach the trinity & all that!) to come in the spirit of my own Unitarian beliefs. I like the idea of Frieda going to Sunday school nextdoor---the church is "low" (like our Episcopal, I guess), & has a champion crew of 8 bellringers who delight us every Sunday. My cleaning

1–A reference to Dr Seuss's *Horton Hatches the Egg* (1940).

2–SP's attendance at the mother's groups inspired her story 'Mothers'; typescript held by Smith College. Posthumously published as 'The Mothers' Union', *McCall's* (October 1972): 81, 126, 128, 130, 142.

3–The rector of St Peter's Church at this time was Reverend William Lane (d. 1973).

woman's husband is one of them. I'm having Mrs. Hamilton[1] the wife of the dead coffee plantation owner & local power, to tea today. She is old, booming, half-deaf, with a dachshund named Pixie. I'm having Ted come to help me out! He's just finished the radio play he's been working on, & I've a couple of good poems.[2]

Lots of love,
Sivvy

TO *Brian Cox*

Tuesday 17 October 1961 TLS, University of Kansas

Court Green
North Tawton
Devonshire
October 17, 1961

Dear Brian,

Thanks very much for your letter. I do hope you sell more copies of American Poetry Now! I'm glad most places are being reasonable about permission charges.

Ted suggests you send copies of your letters to Howard Nemerov,[3] c/o The Department of English, Bennington College, Bennington, Vermont, and to Louis Simpson,[4] c/o Thom Gunn, 975 Filbert Street, San Francisco, California. These may be more direct routes than via publishers. Adrienne Rich is traveling about Europe on a Guggenheim this year, so probably that's why you haven't heard from her. We are dropping a note to Merwin at his French address about the two poems.[5] I don't know a thing in the world about Gregory Corso, unfortunately. I hope O.U.P works out the copyright formula all right.

I'd be grateful if you could leave out all the poems not on my definite list.

1–Sybil Merton Hamilton (d. 1963), widow of Francis Monteith Hamilton (d. 1935). According to SP's journals, Mrs Hamilton lived at 'Crispens', 5 Market Street, North Tawton.

2–According to SP's *Collected Poems*, she had recently written 'Wuthering Heights' (September 1961); 'Blackberrying' (23 September 1961); and 'Finisterre' and 'The Surgeon at 2 a.m.' (29 September 1961).

3–American poet Howard Nemerov (1920–91).

4–Jamaican-American poet Louis Simpson (1923–2012).

5–See TH to Dido and W. S. Merwin, *c.* 20 October 1961; held by Morgan Library.

Ted & I would like very much to make it to Bangor.[1] Tony's flat sounds heavenly. Ideally, my mother might be here to care of our hopefully by then 2 infants, and if so, there should be no complications.

I'll include some brief introductory notes.

Best wishes,
Sylvia

PS: How about saying simply:

AMERICAN POETRY NOW is a selection of poems by new and/or youngish American poets for the most part unknown in England. I'll let the vigor and variety of these poems speak for themselves.

I'm also including a new poem by Simpson I wish you could fit in.[2] (It seems to me "American" in a particularly fine sense.) But I suppose you're all set up.

S.

TO *Aurelia Schober Plath*

Sunday 22 October 1961 — TLS (aerogramme), Indiana University

Sunday: October 22

Dear mother,

Well, the connections are connected, the gorgeous white machine works! I spent all Wednesday morning with the Bendix demonstrator, doing a sample wash (mine!) and he testing all the parts. My wash looked millions of times whiter than my usual wash, partly I think because I always cram those commercial Bendixes too full, not wanting to make the lengthy trip to Exeter more than once a week, so the clothes never had a chance to shake out and swish about. I am delighted with the machine, and look forward to starting my Birthday week with a bright white Monday wash. I'll probably wash twice a week, or twice every other week now, so things don't pile up. I got the man to recommend good commercial suds & am thinking of buying a 56 pound bag they sell which Bendix launderettes use. You can imagine what a lot off my mind (and back) this Bendix is!

1–SP and TH travelled to Bangor University in Wales on 26 July 1962 to participate in a joint reading for the *Critical Quarterly* on 28 July 1962.

2–The poem is no longer with the letter. Possibly 'My Father in the Night Commanding No' from *New Yorker* (21 October 1961): 56 or 'A Farm in Minnesota', *New Yorker* (9 September 1961): 121. TH mentioned 'My Father in the Night Commanding No' in the letter to the Merwins cited above.

I have no worries about managing the new baby now & will probably be able to have Nancy a couple of hours extra then to do all the ironing of nappies. Thank you endlessly for this.

I have delayed my usual Friday letter because I, too, have been feeling tired this last week or so, although I have nowhere the reason you have! Ted is so good. I lie down for an hour after our lunch, now, before Frieda gets up from her nap, and he insists I do so every day. Then I can face the busywork of the afternoon. It seems impossible one can get tired doing something one loves to do, but I suppose writing is strenuous, and I should consider my mornings at my desk as work, rather than play. We do go to bed in good time---lights out by 10 or 10:30, and Frieda generally lets us sleep till 8ish. I guess the baby is getting perceptibly heavy now, too, and I am grateful for Ted's nightly hypnotizing which put me straight to sleep.

Frieda is sweeter and more winsome than ever. She gets the best of each of us, I think---neither of us having to mind her when we want to write, but while we're doing things she can watch and participate in. I went out to see the two of them in the garden this morning, and Ted was planting strawberries and Frieda was following him with her little shovel, religiously imitating his every gesture, looking like an elf in that wonderful cotton red coat and hood you sent. I'm awfully glad you got size 3 dungarees. I'll be able to pad her with sweaters and so on through the winter and not fear her muddying herself.

So glad you liked "Snow". I haven't seen HARPERS BAZAAR yet. Hope they send us a copy. Actually, I think you're closest to Ted's meaning ---it's not a philosopicial equation so much as just the *feeling* of being lost and struggling against terrific unknowns and odds, something most people feel at one time or another. I find it the most compelling of Ted's stories because it *fits* one's own experience so beautifully. It's incredible how moving it is, with just one character, the snow & the chair, but I feel it has a deep psychic insight into the soul's battles.

If you happen to think of it, or *ever*, get a holiday or minute, could you pack me off a *Ladies' Home Journal* or two? I get homesick for it (no other, Mcall's or Womans Day will do!) It has a special Americanness which I feel to need to dip into, now I'm in exile, and especially as I'm writing for women's magazines a small way now. I shall have fulfilled a very longtime ambition if a story of mine ever makes the LHJ.

Later: A wild, blowy night, with gusts of rain. Went to my first Anglican service with the lively retired London couple down the lane. It's a sweet little church, and I found the service so strange. I suppose it would be very familiar to you, like a sort of watered Catholic service. The choir &

congregation singing is amazingly strong and good for the small number of people there, and I do like hymn-singing. I think I will probably go to Evensong off and on and then send Frieda to Sundayschool. I'm sure as she starts thinking for herself she will drift away from the church but I know how incredibly powerful the words of that little Christian prayer "God is my help in every need" which you taught us has been at odd moments of my life, so think it will do her good to feel part of this spiritual community: so she'll have known it. I must say I think I am a pagan-Unitarian at best! The songs and psalms and responses and prayers are fine, but the sermon! How a bad or a good sermon can determine one's reaction! I suppose there aren't many Bill Rices in the world. Our little Irish rector is very simple. When he talks of sinfulness, I have to laugh. It's a pity there aren't more fiery intellectuals in the ministry. It seems to draw meek, safe, platitudinous souls who I am sure would not face the lions in the Roman arena at any cost. And in these more elaborate services what a lot of kneeling standing and sitting there is! Like a class in bible calisthentics.///I'll send off a statement for breakage. DO tell me what DATE your statistics courses are DONE. I want to look forward to it & count the days!

XXXXX
Sivvy

TO *Marion Freeman*

Thursday 26 October 1961 TLS (aerogramme), Smith College

Court Green
North Tawton
Devonshire, England
October 26, 1961

Dear Aunt Marion,

A thousand thanks for the lovely birthday hankie and the housewarming cheque! With the latter I shall buy one of the small brightly gleaming pieces of copper or brass I see so often at country auctions and hanker after. Its lustre will remind me of your kind thoughts.

Ted and I are so happy with our new home. It is just exactly right for us, one of those mystical appearances which makes one believe in destiny. Our thatch is full of robins and wagtails and birds which wake us in the morning chirping, and I love looking out and seeing no houses, just the church spire and our own grassy acres, trees and flowers. We have fine shops just around the corner, so I have all the advantages of real country (sheep baas and cow moos!) with civilization, too. It will be a place to visit when you come to England! I am just dying for mother to see it, after our cramped flat last summer, which she managed with such angelic fortitude.

Best of all, we have all the time for writing we want---me in the morning, when I'm fresh, without time yet to get muddled with grocery lists & cooking recipes, & Ted in the afternoon & evening when he works best. He is finishing a radio play & I just had my first little story come out in a women's magazine over here---a very amateurish thing, maybe someday I'll get one in the Ladies' Home Journal, a much more advanced and professional magazine than any of the women's weeklies over here. I get homesick for it now & then!

Frieda is blooming with all the fresh air and room. She runs round from front garden to back fearlessly, carrying whichever of her toys is her current favorite in a little basket.

Had a darling letter & photo from Ruthie. Thank her for me & give my love to all the Geisslers & to Dave. And keep a good bit for yourself!

Lots of love from us 3,
Sylvia

TO *Ruth Fainlight*

Thursday 26 October 1961[1] TLS, Ruth Fainlight

Court Green
North Tawton
Devon.
Thursday

Dear Ruth,

A small note to ask if I could possibly cadge a 2nd night with you---Wednesday. I'm treating myself to a ticket to the Royal Court[2] that night on the grim principle that you never know which fling is your last. At least I don't know when I shall be seeing the beloved crapulous face of my dear London again, so I am trying to cram all that is possible into my brief

1–Date supplied from internal evidence.

2–Edward Albee, *The American Dream* (1961) and *The Death of Bessie Smith* (1959), performed on Wednesday 1 November 1961, at the Royal Court Theatre.

time. Be sure & tell me if you are planning parties or resting I'll louse up. Don't bother to answer, you can say what is what when I come.

Love to both,
Sylvia

TO *Aurelia Schober Plath*

Thurs.–Mon. 26–30 October 1961 TLS, Indiana University

Court Green
North Tawton, Devon.
October 26, 1961

Dear mother,

I'm enclosing a statement to the postoffice about the broken dishes. I think I'd almost rather have you deposit what money you collect in our Wellesley account, as we really aren't pressed for a set of 8. All 44 pieces were there. I'm also enclosing a $5 check from dear Aunt Marion for deposit in the Wellesley account. I'm depositing this one here on 2nd thought. I've written to thank her, and to Mrs. Pulling for the lovely pink blanket (babies') she sent.

I can't understand our Boston bank total. You say with the little $12 check it is $1,788.44, but I only have two deposits recorded after we withdrew our housemoney, making the low of $1,231.31---Ted's $275 for his story, and this $12.31, making $1,518.44. What's this extra $260?[1] I can't think of any writing money I've sent since August.

Ted has written a lovely poem about the Loch Ness Monster for Vogue (a children's poem) over here, the British edition, & has got a pile of children's books on animals coming from the New Statesman for him to review. They are sending me a pile of bright children's picture books to review as well (since I modestly said that was my level at present) ---all free & to keep. I am quite pleased, because I think I can judge the art work pretty well, & am delighted to tuck these away to bring out later for Frieda, about $15 worth. We got our copy of Harper's Bazaar today. Isn't it amazing, Robert Lowell,[2] Marianne Moore[3] & Ted in the middle of all those fancy corsets! Lucky for us they have piles of money.

1–'extra $260?~~??~~' appears in the original.

2–François Villon (trans. Robert Lowell), 'The Great Testament', *Harper's Bazaar* (October 1961): 154–5.

3–Marianne Moore, 'My Crow Pluto, the True Plato', *Harper's Bazaar* (October 1961): 184–5.

The "sophisticated" audience thus has fashion, plus cocktail party gossip talk---"name writers", usually only a 2-page spread you'll notice, so it doesn't strain the brain. The editors are generally very brainy women & the fashion blurbs written by Phi Beta Kappa English majors. Poor things.

Later: October 30, Monday.

I am sitting in our "parlor" at the very sweet little bureau-type desk Ted bought at an auction last week for $15. It's rather like yours, with 3 drawers & a slant top that opens out to write on & pigeonholes for letters. I love it. It frees our desks of business and personal letters. We were awfully lucky---it was sold at noonish in the daylong auction amid bricabrac that went for a dollar or two. Another desk like it but much uglier, went for $50 later in the day among big items bringing about $100 when there were lots more people.

I go to London tomorrow to collect my 75 pound prize and see the Woman's Mag editor and leave my manuscripts with the bookdealer who bought Ted's on the chance they might sell them. I am going to the theatre Wednesday on your birthday money, & shall have a nice meal beforehand: I thought you'd be pleased at my spending it that way. I look forward to the treat, as I don't imagine I'll have another chance at a fling till you come next summer.

Had a lovely birthday---Ted got me a lot of fancy cans of octopus & caviar at a delicatessen, two poetry books[1] & a Parker pen & a big wicker basket for my laundry. I wish you could see Frieda in her red jacket-hood: she looks so comically like that little red kewpie doll she carries round. The pale blue snowsuit jacket is her "best"---I am always with her when she wears it & it is gorgeous on her, very roomy. It will be lovely all this cold season. We've got about 50 childrens books to review in all now, a real gift, because we can't review more than 10 apiece . . . everything from "The Cat in the Hat Comes Back"[2] to the story of Elsa the Lioness & her cubs.[3] A good $50-$60 worth. My acquisitive soul rejoices.

Well I hope the Strontium 90 level doesn't go up too high in milk---I've been very gloomy about the bomb news; of course the Americans have contributed to the poisonous level. The fallout shelter craze in America

1–SP was given two books by R. S. Thomas, *Tares* (1961) and *Song at the Year's Turning* (1960) with gift inscription by TH. Both appeared at auction via Bonhams on 21 March 2018.

2–Ted Hughes, 'A Few Sweet Words', *New Statesman* (10 November 1961): 704–5; reviews of Dr Seuss, *The Cat in the Hat Comes Back*; Lydia Pender, *Barnaby and the Horses*; Lilli Koenig, *Timba*; Lilli Koenig, *Gringolo*; and George Selden, *The Cricket in Times Square*.

3–Joy Adamson, *Living Free* (London: Collins and Harvill, 1961); Ted Hughes, 'According to Elsa', *New Statesman* (10 November 1961): 712.

sounds mad.[1] Well, I would rather be in Devon where I am in the country than anywhere else just now. Keep well!

xxx
Sivvy

TO *Helga Huws*

Monday 30 October 1961 TLS, Helga and Daniel Huws

Court Green
North Tawton, Devon.
October 30: Monday

Dear Helga,

It was wonderful to have your big, newsy letter, & it made me very homesick for you all. We have been at Court Green since September 1st, and are settling down quite happily. I find the space, the quiet, the fresh air, and the obvious joy of Ted & Frieda make up for most of my cherished London vices---sour cream & cream cheese among them---and except for occasional bouts of despair at our acres of bare boards (we haven't been able to afford any rugs yet, what with our downpayment, rates, mortgage, repairs, moving expenses & all the lot of big bothers involved in buying a house) am in good spirits.

Of all the places we saw in Devon while my mother was in London minding Frieda this is the only one we could have lived in---the others were hideous, laughable (compared to their descriptions in the agents' circulars---an "ornamental swan pond", for example, proving to be a kind of open cesspit that had obviously been used for drowning children) and much more expensive. We fell in love with Court Green---It was, of course, the only place with a thatch & we had solemnly sworn No Thatches (fear of fire, expense, rain, predatory birds, etc.). It is a very very ancient farmhouse (so old there is no knowing how old, with an old burial mound[2] on the property) with castle-thick walls in the original back part & about 10 rooms, yet very compact & not at all rambling, feeling almost small (except when I look at the floor-space). Downstairs there are two front rooms, one very long, which is Frieda's playroom &

1 – *The Guardian* and *The Observer*, among other newspapers, reported daily on radioactive fallout and its effects. See for example, 'Fall-Out Shelter Hazard', *The Guardian* (30 October 1961): 9.

2 – According to the Devon Historic Environment Record, the castle motte on the property is thirty-five metres in diameter, two metres high, and probably dates to the twelfth century.

my sewingroom (I hope to be able to put down lionoleum someday) and a small room with a tiny fireplace we use as our library, with our books & a little oak desk we bought at an auction. Then a hall between leading to a cobbled (!) hall in back between the big kitchen with an Aga that we use for a diningroom, and a little cooking kitchen across the hall I use for cooking, washing up, and a sort of cold larder beyond where I have my fridge & vegetables. Upstairs there are four large bedrooms & one small (for Frieda), one of which is my study, & then a lovely little peaked attic up some stairs under the thatch which is where Ted works. We have a U-shape of outbuildings around a cobbled courtyard---a big thatched barn, stables (!), and a thatched cottage which someday we would like to make into a guest house for mothers-in-law and such people. But those are all 10-year plans. The house is white, with a black trim & this primeval peaked thatch. We have just over two acres of land, mostly stinging nettle, but Ted is digging up the big vegetable garden & we'll hope to live on them---he's already put in strawberries, and we have about 70 apple trees, eaters & cookers---though sadly the crop this year is very poor everywhere & we are almost through ours. And blackberries everywhere in season. I have a tiny front lawn carved out of the wilderness---a laburnum tree, lilacs & a few rose bushes. We adjoin the town church, Anglican, with its own 8 famous bellringers. I've started to go to it, as it is a lovely church & in spite of my heathen nature, I'd like to start Frieda et. al. off in Sunday school. Sadly, the vicar is a little dull simple man. We are pretty much surrounded by our own land & Ted is planning impenetrable screens of evergreens to shield us from the few chimney tops we can see.

Luckily I don't require the intimacy of other people to keep me happy ---our family circle is very tight and pretty self-sufficient, because although these Devon villagers are friendly (they greet you in the street and so on) they are all inter-related in intricate ways, and we are quite outlandish. All sorts of curious enquiries as to what we (or Ted) do, and if we plan to stay and so on. There's a nice lively retired couple next-door in a little cottage---pub-keepers from London, and a great booming wife of a dead tea-plantation owner in India at the bottom of the lane, and a very pretty (but dumb) mother of 3 little girls also named Sylvia[1] whom the vicar sent "to be my friend", but no soul-mates. We actually bought the place from

1–Sylvia J. (West) Crawford (1935–); mother of Beverly A. (1956–), Rebecca J. (1959–), and Paula J. (1961–); married to Maurice Gordon Crawford (1932–2006); lived at 25 North Street, North Tawton.

a Sir Robert Arundell (he had been made a Sir, not born one), it was his boyhood home, and so we are in a way lords of the manor, although it is a very ancient manor, with plaster crumbling ominously behind the wallpaper which obviously holds it on, and a billion birds living in our thatch, and nettles overall. But it has all sorts of curious advantages---water, electricity and gas, 2 minutes from 2 banks, 3 grocery stores, 3 butchers (one quite good), a fine chemist & one mile from a railway stop that is 4 hours express from Waterloo---it seems odd, that we should be embedded in such deep country, with cows and sheep heard all the time (Frieda points out the window and goes "Baaa" when she wakes each day), yet not utterly isolated. It is an ugly town, but I am quite perversely fond of it.

I even have a cleaning woman---a robust blond Devon mother in her 40s named Nancy Axworthy who 2 mornings a week, for 2/6 an hour (that's what Lady Arundell paid her!) does all my floors & scrubbing & cleaning & even some ironing when she has time. She is wonderful & has taken care of the place for 11 years, so is more at home than I.

Frieda has blossomed here---her learning to walk really drove us out of London. Now she trots round after Ted in the morning when he's gardening, and after me in the afternoon when I'm baking and sewing (I got an old 2nd hand handwind Singer before leaving London, rickety, but I love it), copying everything we do & in general being good-tempered. I have trouble feeding her for the first time---she must have instinctively picked up my dislike of eggs & cereal because she wants all meat and cheese and potatoes, for breakfast and supper as well, and she is a terrifying perfectionist, getting very upset when she can't fit <u>all</u> her blocks in one small basket, or pick up <u>all</u> her Russian doll parts at once. And she is still in nappies: how did you train Madeline? Frieda will sit on her little plastic pot, but has absolutely no idea she's to pee in it. She has only a few words yet and it's impossible to communicate this very strange notion to her. I was hoping she'd be miraculously trained by the time January 11th & this new baby arrives. Hoho.

You <u>must</u> come visit us. It would be a drive through lovely country ---couldn't Danny drive you all down some weekend? We're 22 miles beyond Exeter, 7 miles from Okehampton. We were given a double bed before we left out of someone's mother's stuff, and if you came before January I could have a cot for Madeline, or even after---the baby could sleep in our carrycot. We have so much room & it's a good place for the children to play. Do say you could come for a weekend! I'd really love having you around again---it would be such fun. You haven't let us have <u>your</u> new address. Ted will probably put in a note to Danny.

Lots of love,
Sylvia

Much later – he's so lazy I'm sending this off without!

TO *Aurelia Schober Plath*

Sunday 5 November 1961 TLS (aerogramme), Indiana University

Sunday: November 5

Dear mother,

It was lovely to come home from London and have your nice letter waiting. We have been having some fine, crisp blue weather, and my day in London was fair, which is all one could ask. The train trip was very pleasant---I had lunch going up & going down, which I enjoyed immensely, about $1.60 for soup, fish, meat & vegetables, dessert or cheese & biscuits, with beautiful countryside to watch sliding by---only 4 hours in all, a seeming miracle. I stayed 2 nights with our friends, the Sillitoes. The first night I went to the Guinness party & was, to my surprise, called on to read my poem with the regular Guinness winners which included Robert Graves in the fabulous Goldsmith's hall in the City, although my prize was for another & much smaller little contest. And I picked up my 75 pound check. Then had a little supper with my publisher, & home. The next day was all business---I typed my children's book review[1] at the Sillitoe's, saw the very nice & encouraging women's magazine editor, had lunch with another pregnant lady poet I met at the Guinness party, dropped some manuscripts at an agents in hopes of selling them at an American university, and had a bit of tea before the two plays by the young American author Edward Albee.[2] London is very tiring when one doesn't have a place of one's own, and the getting about a Herculean task; I found myself criticizing the soot & the horrid suburbs & the exhaust

1–Sylvia Plath, 'General Jodpur's Conversion', *New Statesman* (10 November 1961): 696, 698; review of Janet Charters, *The General*; Jacqueline Ayer, *A Wish for Little Sister*; Gaby Baldner, *Joba and the Wild Boar*; Ludwig Bemelmans, *Madeline and the Gypsies*; Elizabeth Rose, *Charlie on the Run*; Joan E. Cass, *The Cat Thief*; Roger Duvoisin, *A for the Ark*; Françoise, *The Things I Like*; M. Sasek, *This is Venice*; and Elizabeth Poston, *The Children's Song Book*.

2–American playwright Edward Albee (1928–2016).

and dying to get home to clear air and my own acres and two darlings. Ted & Frieda met me at the station, Thursday afternoon, my train exactly on time. None of us had been able to eat or sleep very well apart, and now we are all thriving again.

I have marked down your finishing date on my calendar and look so forward to hearing you are safely and healthfully through your courses! The next five months are grim ones---I always feel sorry to have the Summertime change, with the dark evenings closing in in midafternoon, and will try to lay in some physical comforts this month---the best insurance against gloominess for me. It's incredible to think that carpets can create a state of mind, but I am so suggestible to colors and textures that I'm sure a red carpet would keep me forever optimistic. This month, too, should see the end of the worst bills and some income from what we've been working on. I'll send you a copy of our children's book reviews when they come out---I just got a lovely songbook[1] worth over $4 which I look forward to using when we can manage to buy a piano---all the lovely ones "I had a little nut tree", carols, rounds and game songs "Looby Loo" & "Lavenders Blue". I think I've had more pleasure from these brightly-colored free review books than anything just lately. What I particularly like is judging the color and design---something I think I can give a real feeling of.

I am just now at the stage I was when we moved into our London flat, but a lot more comfortable & with a lot less to do, although I feel very ponderous & look immensely forward to my after-lunch lie-down. Frieda too seems suddenly to have increased in weight, but I have no way of telling how much she weighs now.

Ted has just finished typing his new radio play for the BBC---a poetic drama for voices (not acting) about the delusions of a soldier with a wound, very fine. Now he is working on 6 selections from children's books for the Times, each of which will have an introduction. We have really done a great deal since we have come, these last two months. I have to keep myself from asking that everything be done at once---the whole house, for example, needs replastering, as much of the plaster is dry & crumbly behind the paper, but except for one or two spots, we should be all right for several years yet. And I'll be going to Exeter in the next week or 10 days to price rugs & buy curtain material.

I'm amazed to hear you've done a sweater for the January baby---I just don't see how you manage! It sounds divine. Dressed Frieda in that

1–Elizabeth Poston, *The Children's Song Book* (London: Bodley Head, 1961).

sea-greenblue corduroy zipper suit you sent for tea with a young, pretty mother of 3 girls (one Rebecca)---she named Sylvia, oddly enough. She came over with her new baby & 2 year-old Rebecca whom Frieda bullied loudly & fearlessly, reducing her to tears by trying to snatch her cookies & teddy. Both of them made fearful wails & roars.

Went to the Anglican chapel evensong again tonight---it's a peaceful little well on Sunday evenings, & I do love the organ, the bellringing & hymn-singing, & muse on the stained-glass windows during the awful sermons. The three windows, lit up on Sunday evenings, look so pretty from our house, through the silhouettes of the trees. Youll have a <u>real</u> rest & holiday when you visit us this time---sitting out on our lilac-sheltered lawn in a deck chair with the babies playing, <u>no</u> steps nor traffic nor anything but country noises. .

Lots of love to you & Warren
xxx
Sivvy

TO *Howard Moss*

Wednesday 8 November 1961 — TLS (aerogramme), New York Public Library

Court Green, North Tawton
Devonshire, England
November 8, 1961

Mr. Howard Moss
THE NEW YORKER
25 West 43rd Street
New York 36, New York
USA

Dear Mr. Moss:

Thank you very much for your letter of October 27th.[1] I'm glad to hear you're taking BLACKBERRYING[2] for the New Yorker.

I think I have a way out of "face" and "faces".

1–Howard Moss to SP, 27 October 1961; held by New York Public Library. Moss rejected 'Wuthering Heights', 'Finisterre', and 'The Surgeon at 2 a.m.'

2–Sylvia Plath, 'Blackberrying', *New Yorker* (15 September 1962): 48.

How about:

"To the hills' northern face, and the face is orange rock
That looks out on nothing . . ."[1]

I like this much better myself, with the minor change in line 7 as well, and hope you think it clarifies the stanza.

With all good wishes,
Yours sincerely,
Sylvia Plath

TO *Alan Ross*

Thursday 9 November 1961 TLS, University of Texas at Austin

Court Green
North Tawton
Devonshire
November 9, 1961

Dear Alan Ross,

Just a note to say that Ted and I both hope to be able to manage to do something for the Poetry number.

All good wishes from both of us,
Sincerely,
Sylvia Plath

Alan Ross, Esq.
THE LONDON MAGAZINE
Doric House
22 Charing Cross Road
London W.C.2

1–In stanza three, lines 6–7 originally read, 'To the hills' northern face, and their faces are orange rock. / They look out on nothing, nothing but a great space . . .'; held by Lilly Library.

TO *Aurelia Schober Plath*

Thursday 9 November 1961 TLS (aerogramme), Indiana University

Court Green, North Tawton
Devonshire, England
November 9: Thursday

Dear mother,

I hardly know where to begin. Your good bonus letter came today, and all sorts of nice things have been happening. Ted woke up this morning and said "I dreamed you had won a $25 prize for your story about Johnny Panic". Well I went downstairs and found out I had won a Saxton grant for $2,000![1] I have been waiting for over half a year to hear from them, and as both Ted & I have been rejected by them (Ted because he was published by Harper's, & they give the grant) and I because I applied for poetry & they don't like to give money for poetry---I had no hope. Well I applied for a grant for prose this time, & got the amount I asked for (I had it figured so I wouldn't have to work & could have a nanny & household help, etc.). They pay in quarterly installments, as parts of a project are completed, so I should get my first lot in a week or two! It is an absolute lifesaver. I hadn't wanted to spend my gift money on carpets right away, because I didn't know how our expenses & income would work out for the rest of the year, & now, within the next month, I hope to have my study, our bedroom & Frieda's & the stairs all carpeted, & possibly the livingroom. Amusingly enough, two carpet samples I'd ordered---turkey red for my study & forest green for Frieda's room---came today! We are members of "Better Buying"[2] now, an organization that you can buy all the good makes of cars, machines, carpets etc. from with a 15% discount if you pay cash in 7 days after delivery. So I am going to get the best of carpets! Naturally I wish I'd known about Better Buying before, but better late than never. All the guarantees operate as usual.

Life in town has been more & more fun. They had a Hunt Meet in the square yesterday: all the local foxhunters, in red jackets, brass buttons & velvet caps drinking whisky on horseback, all sorts of fascinating faces, & a pack of spotted, sulphurous dogs---a toot of a horn & they galloped

1–Ruth Hill to SP, 6 November 1961; held by Smith College. SP's award was for $2,080 and was paid $520 quarterly. Smith College holds two typescripts of SP's quarterly progress reports from 1 May 1962 (chapters 9–12 of *The Bell Jar*) and 1 August 1962 (chapters 13–16).

2–Better Buying Service, 56 Grosvenor Street, London W.1.

off. We took Frieda to watch & she loved it. Oddly moving, in spite of our sympathy for foxes. We went for a long walk with Frieda first thing in the morning it was so lovely---the hedgerows a tapestry of oak leaves, holly, fern, blackberry leaves all intertwined, the green hills dotted with sheep and cows, and the pink plaster farms very antique. Frieda is a great walker, as you know.

Then, today, we had an auction to end auctions in our own town. A 17th century house with a pretty front but ghastly situation down by the river at the town-bottom was auctioned, with all the stuff in it. Warren would have enjoyed this! Ted & I & Frieda went to the "viewing" in the morning & marked down all the stuff we wanted. Then Ted spent the afternoon down there bidding. What we got was just fantastic! It wasn't the sort of auction to attract dealers (no silver, copper, antiques etc.), so Ted walked away with everything we wanted for next to nothing. 12 cents for a table we'll paint over, under a dollar for a lovely china "biscuit barrel" with pink cherries and green leaves on it and a wicker handle which I'd have paid piles for, I think it's quite fine, about 60 cents for a big handsome <u>comfortable</u> upholstered chair with arms & a high scrolled back (the <u>only</u> chair that rest my rear & back, all the rest of ours are hard wood) which I'll have re-upholstered in black corduroy for my study; an old sewing box, mirrors; a dresser for the guest room for $1. The only "expensive" things were a pile of garden tools Ted got for about $10. We had a wonderful night admiring our stuff & planning to paint this and polish that. The big chair, another nice wood chair for my typing at my desk & the cherry pot and little antique mirror I'm going to reupholster in red are my joys.

Tell Warren the <u>New Yorker</u> just bought a poem of mine I wrote here called "Blackberrying", about the day we all went blackberrying together down the lane that sloped to the sea and got such a lot. I don't know when they'll print "Tulips"---probably in the season! I'll send for a copy of my awful first ladies' mag story---very stiff & amateurish. It came out my birthday week; I got a very sweet fan letter for it in which the woman, also a writer, took me for an expert on Canada & Whitby, this sailing port I visited for a day. Very flattering!

Frieda is better & better. She says "hole" (a sophisticated notion Ted taught her) and "nana" for Banana & is picking up words eagerly now. I've met a very pretty mother here---no soul mate, but awfully nice. Her name is Sylvia Crawford & she has 3 little girls, the middle one, 2½ years, named Rebecca. Isn't that odd? Thanks for the bank statement. I <u>thought</u> we weren't so rich! Dont buy a Britannica, however nice. I really don't think one uses them that much, & good schools should have them in stock. I'll send you clippings of our children's book reviews---the editor is very very pleased. & so are we, with all the lovely books.

xxx
Sivvy

PS – That fox book sounded handsome.

TO *Brian Cox*

Tuesday 14 November 1961 TLS, University of Kansas

Court Green
North Tawton
Devonshire
November 14, 1961

Dear Brian,

Thanks for the proofs.[1] I'm glad the permissions are coming in---I do hope Nemerov's come, because he is a pivot of the selection, I think. And I do hope that sales continue to rise!

I wasn't sure if you wanted the proofs back. Let me know. Here are the corrections I've made:[2]

Barbara Guest:[3] The Brown Studio:
Lower case t in line 6.
Lower case w in 7th line from end.
Comma, not period, after 'phantom', 3rd line from end.
Lower case t in 2nd line from end.
Anthony Hecht:[4] "More Light! More Light!"
Capital A in 4th stanza, 4th line.
W. S. Merwin: The Native:
"So that one beast" (not "best"), stanza 5, line 6.
Anne Sexton: Some Foreign Letters:
"I read how your" (not "you"), stanza 4, line8.

1 – The corrected proofs for *American Poetry Now* held by Smith College.

2 – A comparison of the letter to the printed pamphlet shows that not all of SP's corrections were made.

3 – American poet Barbara Guest (1920–2006).

4 – American poet Anthony Hecht (1923–2004).

That's all I could find. Oh dear, I wish Hecht hadn't changed his line--- & shall probably wish the same about Adrienne's changes. But that's their godly privilege.[1]

All best wishes,
Sylvia

TO *James Michie*

Tuesday 14 November 1961 TL (carbon), Smith College

Court Green
North Tawton, Devon.
November 14, 1961

Dear James,

No, I've not forgotten about the libel issue. In fact, I've thought about little else. I've gone through the book with great care and have prepared a list of links of fiction to fact, and a list of minor corrections which should alter most specific factual references.[2]

Of course you're right about the name of author and heroine needing to be different. I've decided to call the heroine Esther Greenwood, so all references to her and her family should be altered accordingly (pp. 22, 33, 41, 53, 59, 60, 61, 72, 77, 79, 127, 128, 145, 157, 188, 189, 195, 197, 203, 205, 212, 216, 221, 225, 229, 230, 232, 233, 237, 244, 250, 253, 257, 258, 261, 264).[3]

The whole first half of the book is based on the Mademoiselle College Board Program for Guest Editors. I have changed the number of girls from 20 to 12, and the girls (Doreen, Betsy, Hilda et. al.) are all fictitious. I honestly don't see that I say anything nasty or defamatory about the magazine (unnamed in the book). The ptomaine poisoning incident takes place at another magazine, fictitious, called Ladies' Day, a made-up name. The editor Jay Cee (there are dozens of editors on this magazine) is fictitious & the only unfavorable thing about her is that Doreen calls her "ugly as sin". Surely no present editor who is not

1–In '"More Light! More Light!"' Hecht modified the original line, 'Thousands sifting down through the crisp air' to 'Ghosts from the ovens, sifting through crisp air'. There were no changes to the Rich poems.

2–The list is held by Smith College.

3–Page numbers correspond to a later typescript draft, held by Smith College. SP missed a couple of page numbers, thus when the proof of *The Bell Jar* was prepared the original protagonist's name, 'Miss Lucas', appeared on pp. 187–8. These were corrected before the first edition was printed in late 1962.

beautiful could sue me for this? The opportunities for suing authors as mentioned under libel in my writer's handbooks seem infinite. For example, I am aware of no "Doctor Gordon" practising as a psychiatrist on Commonwealth Avenue in Boston, but how is one ever to find out if there is a Doctor Gordon, as the name is common? Presumably any old Doctor Gordon could sue me for saying he gave a bad shock treatment. Do reassure me on this point!

Next, the "big eastern women's college" the girl attends is based on Smith, but could be any of half a dozen---Holyoke, Vassar, Bennington, etc. I don't think I say anything defamatory about the college anyway.

Doctor Gordon (p. 137 and following) is fictitious. Mr. Manzi (p. 36) is fictitious. Irwin (p. 244) is fictitious. These are the only people I can think about who I say unflattering things about. My mother is based on my mother, but what do I say to defame her? She is a dutiful, hard-working woman whose beastly daughter is ungrateful to her. Even if she were a "suing" mother, which she is of course not, I don't see what she could sue here. If there is anything, let me know.

Buddy Willard is based on a real boy---but I think I have made him indistinguishable from all the blond, blue-eyed boys who have ever gone to Yale. There are millions, and hundreds who become doctors. And who have affairs with people.

The Deer Island Prison[1] (pp. 161-2) is a real place by its real name. I think I am very nice about it.

The "city hospital" in Boston could be one of several. I don't think I defame it anyway. The private hospital in the counter (p. 202 and following) is based on the mental hospital in Robert Lowell's Life Studies ("This is the way day breaks at Bowditch at McLean's),[2] but as I don't name it and as there are lots of other hospitals like it sprinkled over Massachusetts, I think it is unidentifiable. All I say about it is laudatory anyhow.

Jane (I'm changing her name to Joan) is fictitious, and so is her suicide ---I mean it isn't based on a real one. The women at the hospital are all fictitious.

1–Deer Island Prison (*c.* 1880–1991) was located on the southernmost tip of Winthrop. The island is now a waste water treatment plant.

2–Robert Lowell, 'Waking in the Blue', *Life Studies* (New York: Farrar, Straus & Giroux, 1959). SP attempted suicide on 24 August 1953, was treated at several local hospitals, and spent most of her time at McLean Hospital, Belmont, Mass. For letters written during this period, see *Letters of Sylvia Plath*, Vol. 1, 649–72.

Oh yes, the Amazon hotel in New York (p. 4) is based on a hotel called the Barbizon.[1] But aren't I nice about it?

I do hope there are no grave grounds for libel in any of this. There are so few people or institutions that I can be said to "defame" in any way, and the few I criticize I certainly don't think are recognizable. Do tell me what the lawyer says. I don't want to get paranoid & think I can't ever say anything nasty and foul about Mrs. Gleek, for fear thousands of Mrs. Gleeks I don't know and never knew will rise up and drive me and my babes into the woods.

Here are the minor corrections I want to make:

p. 33: Omit "literary" in "literary editor".

pp. 41 & 82: Change "Vee Ell" to "Ee Gee, the famous editor".

p. 42: Omit "dried-up".

pp. 54 & 82: Change "Plato" to "Socrates".

pp. 62, 63; 212 & f: Change "Jane" to "Joan" throughout.

p. 90: Change "Latin and mathematics teacher" to "private school teacher".

p. 66: Omit "Harvard" from "Harvard Medical School".

p. 94: Change "important history lecture" to "important economics lecture".

p. 125: Change "Radcliffe" to "Barnard", and "Harvard" to "Columbia".

p. 124: Change "Virginia" to "Elaine", "eight" to "six", "Victoria" to "Esther".

p. 130: Change "Virginia" to "Elaine".

pp. 146, 149, 150: Change "Carling" to "Walton".

p. 161: Change "Point Shirley" to "The Point".

p. 191: Change "the city hospital" to "a city hospital".

p. 226: Change "when there was another Jane in the room" to "when she knew what my name was perfectly well".

One last, & for me very important point: after much waiting I have at last received this American grant for the novel, which will come in 4 installments, the last, I imagine, arriving about next August. Thus it is imperative that nobody knows I've done this till then---I'll let you know when the last installment arrives. I'll have to acknowledge the grant on the book jacket, too. This will give me time to write in peace & eat complete meals, a blessing all round, so I rely on you to maintain a large Hush round the book.

Best wishes,

1–The Barbizon Hotel for Women was at Lexington Avenue and E 63rd Street, New York.

TO *Ruth Fainlight*

Tuesday 14 November 1961 TLS, Ruth Fainlight

Court Green
North Tawton, Devon.
November 14: Tuesday

Dear Ruth,

It is with some shock I see two weeks have scuttered past. I don't know what I would have done without you and Alan & those lovely tea-mashings in London. That beautiful bang-out night on the double-dose of Soneril[1] (sp?) sent me back to Ted in fine form. As a result of my money collecting sojourn I am going to Exeter this week to survey acres and acres of carpets. I sold some of the ton of mss. I brought to the Curly Fletchers & so feel justified for lugging round all that scrap.[2]

We now have a wood fire in the livingroom every night and got our One upholstered smashing Victorian chair (in shabby genteel black horsehair)[3] for 5 bob at an auction in town. So I sit in comfort for the first time in months, padded all about. Life here is very pleasant in spite of absolutely black weather & huge winds. Had a hunt meet the other day in the Square: sulphur-yellow spotted hounds, red jackets, brass buttons, lecherous-faced whipholders drinking whisky neat on horseback. A toot, & they galloped off. The fox was nowhere.

I can't get Meima Bacha (sp?)[4] out of my head. I am in my 2nd year of persuading Ted to get a radio that says something beside Bockle bockle bockle.[5] Both of us send love. We are counting on you coming to us at least by spring. Daffodil-time.

xxx
Sylvia

1–SP may be referring to the barbiturate Soneryl, which was used to treat insomnia.

2–These papers form 'Plath mss' at the Lilly Library.

3–SP's Victorian chair appeared at auction via Bonhams on 21 March 2018.

4–Meima Bucha is a person Fainlight knew when growing up. Ruth Fainlight, 'Meima Bucha: A Childhood Memory', *Woman's Hour*, BBC Light Programme (28 November 1961). See also Ruth Fainlight, 'Meima-Bucha', *Canadian Jewish Review* (28 March 1952): 8; and Ruth Fainlight, 'Meima-Bucha', *Daylife and Nightlife: Stories* (London: Deutsch, 1971).

5–SP uses the phrase 'bockle bockle bockle' at the end of Chapter 11 of *The Bell Jar*.

TO *Aurelia Schober Plath*

Monday 20 November 1961 TLS with envelope, Indiana University

Monday: November 20

Dear mother,

Very nice to get your letter today. Bitter weather has set in, and I am going to London from Exeter on a day-return ticket some day this week to order carpets at that place where I can get a 15% discount on the best makes of carpet. I have already examined carpets at an Exeter store & the red one for my study, the red for the stair & the green for Frieda's room should present no problem---I'll get fine quality all-wool. I know plain colors show every spot, but in my study I'll be in slippers & no one else enters it, and in Frieda's room the rug will be covered by a little flowered one which will take the wear. The bedroom I'll try to get a nice floral one. The livingroom is the problem. We may just wait till you come in summer & go to London together looking for a place that sells 2nd hand Orientals---first hand ones are of course out of reach & I do want something special---figured, of course, and darkish & quite fine. We have an old rug in here to see us through the winter. I do hope I can get the ones I order in by Christmas---it is so bare & cold with just the boards. We are ordering 2 more Pifcos---those little electric heaters, to plant about various strategic rooms.

I am enclosing a New Yorker check for deposit in our Boston bank ---for my poem on that day we went blackberrying with Warren. I can afford to add a bit to our American account now I have this grant---the first installment, $520, came this week. Don't worry about my taking on anything with the Saxton. Just between the two of us (and don't tell anyone) I figured nothing was so sure to stop me writing as a grant to do a specific project that had to be turned in at the end, with quarterly progress reports---so I finished a batch of stuff[1] this last year, tied it up in 4 parcels, & have it ready to report on bit by bit as required. Thus I don't need to write a word, if I don't feel like it. Of course the grant is supposed to help you <u>do</u> writing, not for writing you've done, but I will do what I can and feel like, while my conscience is perfectly free in knowing my assignments are done. Guggenheims, such as Ted had, are much easier ---they ask for no reports or work once you get it, you're perfectly free. Anyhow, I'd never have applied for a Saxton unless I'd gotten something

1–Sylvia Plath, *The Bell Jar*.

ready---I don't believe in getting money for something you haven't done yet, it's too nervewracking.

Those Stanford-Binet tests[1] sound very energy-consuming. How many more do you have to do? I hope you sit down to a cup of hot tea afterwards.

It is time for Frieda's supper & tub. She is getting more & more sweet-tempered now thank goodness---she went through an awfully fussy I-want period. Ted has just finished another children's broadcast for the radio and this winds up the load of pressing assignments he's had over his head for the last half year---now he is perfectly free for his own work again. I'm enclosing the reviews[2] we did for the New Statesman, hoping they'll amuse you, especially as you mentioned the first of the Elsa books. A nice bookish Christmas package from you arrived today, by the way, which I'm saving to put under our tree. I'm afraid our giving this year will be pretty much limited to cards---and, hopefully, snapshots. Since we're not going up to Yorkshire either, of course, with the baby so near, we won't be doing more than cards with them, either.

Did I tell you I got 100 pounds (or $280) for about 130 pages of poetry manuscript of mine from a bookseller in London who is buying stuff for the University of Indiana? They'd already bought about £160 worth of Ted's stuff, & he got £80 from some other dealer, so we've made a good bit off our scrap paper. Needless to say this comes in very handy just now.

Take care of yourself these grim, dark days. Love to you & Warren.

xxx
Sivvy

TO *Olwyn Hughes*

Monday 20 November 1961[3] ALS, British Library

Dear Olwyn –

It was very good to hear from you & to have the lovely book of Billetdoux[4] – just what both of us need. I've been sitting in front of the wood fire Ted builds each evening & cutting the pages of "Va Donc"[5] which I've just begun: fascinating & queerly delicate & weird. We

1 – Stanford-Binet is an intelligence test.
2 – The reviews are still with the letter.
3 – Date supplied from internal evidence.
4 – François Billetdoux, *Théâtre* (Paris: La Table Ronde, 1961).
5 – François Billetdoux, 'Va Donc Chez Törpe' (1961).

thought 'Tchin-Tchin'[1] superb in London & I wish we could see this too when it comes on. You have no idea what a treat something like this is to us immured among cows & sheep & the amiable stump-warts, as I call the local women – (our lane in particular has odd deformities – an ancient hunchbacked lady named Elise,[2] apparently born without parents of either sex, a wildly blind man[3] & so on – but all very nice.)

Our move is a great & pleasant shock to both of us – it happened so fast & seemed such a gigantic thing, sinking our lives & savings into a place chosen from a two-day tour, but our instincts, which we operated on, stood us in good stead, & the place has all sorts of odd, wry, endearing advantages which emerge bit by bit. Ted has a wonderful study under the thatch – peaked, insulated by straw (which itself is crammed with birds) & up its own steep stair. I have one on the second floor overlooking the front yard & local church & graveyard which suits me beautifully. None of the old stowing of manuscripts under the carpet when the cooking pots came out. Frieda loves it & trots around boldly pointing to birds & mimicking sheep & dogs. She is very odd looking, with great blue clear eyes & feathery straight brown hair (like Ted & me), & a sort of lit expression. She's incredibly loving & trusting – rushing up to strangers in the street & grabbing their hands & running along with them, chasing cats with little kissing noises & so on, & out-of-the-blue coming over to hug one or the other of us.

I can't imagine living anywhere else now, nor can Ted. He's got through a pile of commissions that have been chasing him for the last half year & divides his time between gardening & carpentering & writing & looks years younger, very vigorous & happy, this being just what he wanted. Our unique combination of seclusion on our 2½ acres, & 5 minutes distance from surprisingly good village shops; and antiquity in the house itself, but with hot water & gas & so on – is ideal for us. We are still very primitive inside – both of us being a bit morbid about our acres of bare floorboards stained & redolent with death-watch beetle killer. But now I at last have this American writing grant (for a novel) which comes in 4 installments & will provide carpet money & a lot of needed repairs – we have a sort of 5-year plan of these. But spring should see us with carpets, new house foundations, an acre of daffodils, apple trees in bloom & all the rural delights. We are both working wonderfully well & seem

1–See SP to ASP, 25 November 1960.
2–Elsie Taylor lived at a Court Green cottage on Market Street. See Sylvia Plath, 'Mystic'.
3–Frank Harold Watkins (1884–1964); married to Leila Watkins (*c.* 1884–1965), lived in the first of the Court Green cottages.

to have – at last – all the time in the world to do so – plus planning tons of strawberries & a great vegetable garden for next year. Winter is the real test – already it is bone cold & we have ordered more Pifcos. I hope to get carpets in to stop some of the most howling drafts. Have you read Marguerite Duras?[1] Is she good? Or any of those in her group we keep hearing about over here?

Love from us all,
Sylvia

TO *Gerald & Joan Hughes*

Wednesday 6 December 1961[2] ALS in greeting card,[3]
Indiana University

<printed greeting>
With best wishes for Christmas and the New Year
<signed>
with love from / Sylvia, Ted, & Frieda

Court Green
North Tawton, Devon

Dear Gerald, Joan et al.

We are undergoing genuine Christmas weather – yesterday, driving back from Plymouth where Ted did a BBC Broadcast[4] & we shopped for a rug to cover some of our acres of as yet bare boards (he ended up buying a 2' × 4' Chinese goatskin on top of an Indian rug – guess whose side of the bed it will be on!) The first snow flew down at us & it was awe-inspiring driving back over the dark reaches of Dartmoor. Hail this morning – then everything clear again. I miss my crisp white 6 foot American blizzards – we used to have such fun sledging & building igloos. I suppose I'll be telling Frieda about "the old days in the old country" where everything was just slightly legendary.

We are gradually getting Court Green into shape – a house this old needs one five-year plan, then another. Ted is now painting the ghastly

1–French writer and film director Marguerite Duras (1914–96). Duras is associated with the *Nouveau Roman* group. Duras, along with group members Alain Robbe-Grillet and Nathalie Sarraute, were featured in David Stuart Hull, 'Russian Film Direction . . . and the French in Moscow', *The Guardian* (10 August 1961): 4.

2–Date supplied from internal evidence.

3–Christmas card designed by J. F. Wilkes for the Gordon Fraser Gallery.

4–Ted Hughes, 'Writing in Britain Today', BBC Overseas Service (5 December 1961); see Kay Fuller to TH, 30 November 1961; held by BBC Written Archives Centre.

floorboards upstairs which were driving us both to feel like ill-kept horses in a barn, & we hope to have carpets in by Christmas to keep out the drafts. Next spring the floors of the front downstairs should come up & the woods-joists on wet-earth foundations be changed for concrete to keep us from sinking any further into the ground. The wallpaper should hold the plaster up for a few years & the billion birds hold the thatch on for as long out of sheer self-interest – they live under it, too. I love it here, & so does Ted. He looks wonderful, very happy & is able to be relatively unbothered by his famousness which hounded him in London. I've an American grant to finish a novel, so we shall weather the first year of giant bills & tax inspectors all right. Loved the pictures of you. Do write – you too, Joan.

xxx
Sylvia

TO *Ann Davidow-Goodman & Leo Goodman*

c. Thursday 7 December 1961[1] ALS in greeting card,[2] Smith College

<printed greeting>
With best wishes for Christmas and the New Year
<signed>
from Sylvia, Ted & Frieda

Court Green
North Tawton
Devonshire

Dear Ann & Leo –

It seems ages & years since our wonderful summer with you & we miss you very much. We have, in one swoop, left London & bought a wonderful ancient country house, white, with a peaked thatch & its own cobbled court surrounded on 3 sides by thatched barn & stables (empty as yet, Ann!). The oldest walls of Court Green, originally a farm, are 3 feet thick & we have a historic fortress-mound under a giant elm on our property of 2 ½ acres, plus 70 apple trees. We have a spare bedroom & a thatched cottage (very dilapidated – which we hope to fix up) & are only 4 hours from London by express train. Please come back to England & visit us.

1–Date supplied from internal evidence.
2–Christmas card designed by Sheila Parry for Libertys.

We live in the midst of a thriving & friendly Devon town, our house being more or less the 'manor house' the boyhood home of one Sir Robert Arundell, who sold it to us. We all three adore it. Frieda moos & baas & peeps back at cows, sheep & birds. We are again painting ancient floorboards & going to country auctions to buy odd bits for our 10 or so rooms. To my surprise, I miss cosmopolitan life very little. Devonshire people are curious, but very warm & friendly.

Please do write & tell us how you both are, what doing & all.

All the best Devonian & Cornish beaches are within an hour's drive. Come for a little holiday.

Much love from us 3 –
Sylvia

TO *Marcia B. Stern*

c. Thursday 7 December 1961[1] TLS, Smith College

Court Green
North Tawton, Devon.

Dear Marty,

It was terrific having your letter and all the good news. Oddly enough, just as you wrote about your new sink I was having my sink ripped out & a new one installed: my old sink being 2½ feet high, set on two columns of rotten bricks & a kind of antique upchuck speckled color, with perpetually damp drainingboards & a drain up which enormous slugs with black horns climbed overnight to greet me first thing in the morning. I still have scars on my wall which Ted plastered after about a month & someday now will try to match the elusive shade of pale green paint, which graces our kitchen walls. The house itself though is just wonderful. I am quite used to its peaked thatch & love the millions of birds who live in it, even the blue tits who drink the cream off our milk. I don't know just how much I told you about the place, which is right in the middle of the quite ugly, grey cementish town of North Tawton (now seeming beautiful & sweet to me). When all the foliage is out, you can't see any houses, nothing but the 12th century Anglican church facing the house across an acre of green field. Now, though, with the leaves gone, we are surrounded by neighbours which comforts me on dark nights, as some of the desolate country places we saw gave me the creeps. And I like being

1 – Date supplied from internal evidence.

two minutes walk from the shops & chemist & PO. Spring at our place is, from all accounts, idyllic, with 70 apple trees in bloom, laburnum, lilac & a field full of daffodils, but right now we are battening down for the full blast of wet English winter. Up to now we have been living on the bare, dirtyish floorboards which the British seem to specialize in, but we have just budgeted after the first staggering pile of solicitors & surveyors fees, downpayment, plumber, electrician, mover, back income tax ad inf. & have ordered carpets for the upstairs bedrooms, hall, stair and front room, which I hope may arrive by Christmas. I have been stitching curtains & snake-shaped draftstoppers on my handwind singer, & Ted is painting the floorboards, after much procrastination.

The people of the town are obviously very curious about us (and how we live), but extremely friendly & nice: everybody says Good morning to everybody in the street. We have all those small things which I depend on: a good baker, a good butcher, a good chemist. I have a robust red-cheeked woman named Nancy Axworthy come in for 2 mornings a week to clean for a total of just over $2: a lifesaver, because the house is huge. If you knew how we were counting on your coming to visit us when you come to England, you would buy your tickets right now! How soon do you think you can come? At last we have lots of room. Upstairs we have our bedroom, a small one for F, & my study facing front, & the bathroom, guestroom & an other room we won't use till we refloor it probably, over the back. Plus Ted's attic study up a flight of stairs. I hope someday we can make our thatched cottage into a guest cottage. But that will be after our 5 year plan of repairs, which continues this spring with laying a cement foundation in place of the wooden joists on bare earth in the front of the house, & laying lino in the children's playroom & hall over that. Once that's done, I shall feel we can rest a bit. And someday we'll have to have the whole interior repapered and re-plastered, as the plaster is crumbling behind the paper in places. But not for a bit.

I find I miss London very little. My thoughts of having an eventual city house there have faded, & on my one or two visits back I was oppressed by the dirty air & crowds & got quite homesick. We are surrounded by high green pastures full of cows & sheep, which Frieda loves, & Dartmoor is just 15 minutes away. I hope we find some nice beaches this summer, as we're under an hour from all the Cornish & Devon ones. I think the twins would have wonderful fun here---loads of space to run round, and the 4 hour express to & from London is just a mile down the road. What I miss most is (I don't quite know how to put it) "college-educated" mothers. I got to know several nice, bright girls in London whom I miss, but there is nobody like that round here---I've met one very pretty local girl (named Sylvia, queerly enough) with 3 daughters whom I like, but it's all baby talk. I find myself liking baby talk, but I miss the other things---notions, ideas, I don't know what. Luckily Ted keeps me from getting too cowlike.

How I envy you, the Fair Housing Practices Committee & the Unitarian church! This seems to me so valuable and practical, such a satisfying way of putting abstract principles into groundroots action! I think our little local church very lovely---it has 8 bellringers & some fine stained-glass windows, but I must say the Anglican religion seems terribly numb & cold & grim to me. I started going to Evensong on Sundays as a purely community thing, having asked the Rector (a rather stupid little Irishman who knew Jomo Kenyatta[1] in Africa, but is terribly dull & full of platitudes) to tell me about the service. The singing & chanted responses of the first half are fine & in an aesthetic way I can respond to them, but the sermons! All the awful emphasis on our weakness & sinfulness & being able to do nothing but through Christ etc. I am perfectly prepared to see in one's innate laziness & faults an analogy to an original flaw, but the Trinity seems to me a man's notion, substituting the holy ghost where the mother should be in the family circle, almost a burlesque. And I guess I am simply what the minister called one Sunday "an educated pagan" (after seeing our books, I'm sure, which apparently terrified him). But I do want Frieda to have the experience of Sunday School, & the Anglican church is the church in the community, so I may keep up the unsatisfactory practice of going, although I disagree with almost everything. I'm sure if there were simply an intelligent minister it would be better. Tell me your thoughts on this. Weren't you at one time an Episcopalian? I know I always envied my mother's having been brought up in the Catholic church as a child because she had a rich & definite faith to break away from, & I think that it's better to have a child start this way, than be the only one who doesn't go to church at an age when religious and philosophical arguments mean nothing to them, & he only feels curious and outcast.

In theory, we divide our days, so I work in my study in the morning & Ted carpenters, gardens, does odd jobs & minds Frieda. Then I take over & cook & sew & have Frieda with me in the afternoon while Ted writes. Then we spend the evenings by a crackling wood fire reading or listening to music or whatever. But I feel to do very little work. A couple

1–Jomo Kenyatta (1894–1978); leader of Kenya, 1964–78, and a member of the Kikuyu, Kenya's largest ethnic group.

of poems I like a year looks like a lot when they come out, but in fact are points of satisfaction separated by large vacancies. I've done a woman's magazine story which came out here & have hopes of someday turning something out good enough for the Ladies Home Journal---this a kind of journeywork I'd like because it would be a good source of income. As it is, we have been very lucky piecing together a pleasant living from odd jobs---reviews, radio broadcasts, poems and so on. It is a relief not to have money flowing out in rent, never to return. I shall be happy when we have paid back our borrowings from our parents & our relatively modest mortgage & have only upkeep and running expenses to worry about. It isn't accurate to say we live on writing, as we've been lucky with writing grants & prizes which have seen us over financial humps that the weekly trickle of earnings wouldn't cover, but now we have space, we have all the time we need to work & none of the old worries about where we shall be next year.

We are also expecting a 2nd infant this next month, as Peter D. has probably told you (I am amazed at how he heard of it, but Ted mentioned it to some Cambridge person in London & woof! it flew). The reason I haven't made announcements etc. is because we lost our second baby 4 months along last year (it was supposed to be born on Ted's birthday in August), & I had started to tell family & relatives, & felt so depressed at telling them we'd lost it that I thought I'd wait this time till the event was safely upon us. The doctors gave no reason for a miscarriage, but as I had my appendix out 3 weeks later, it might have been that, or not. Anyway, I am crossing my fingers that this one will be fine, although once you lose a baby, or know about anyone else who had one born with this or that wrong, you feel what a precarious miracle the whole process is. Frieda is at last spouting words after everybody telling me they talked at 8 months etc. I just can't get worried about walking & talking ages---after all, you do both the rest of your life, & simply let her grow as she feels like it. Now she babbles about doddies & pawbooks & dark (she runs & points & says "dark" as soon as the sun sets, because one morning we took her out when it was dark & tried to explain it to her). She is lots of fun & very dear. Still with bright blue eyes unlike either of us. Do write soon.

Lots of love from us all,
Syl

TO *Aurelia Schober Plath*

Thursday 7 December 1961 TLS with envelope, Indiana University

Court Green
North Tawton, Devon.
Thursday: December 7

Dear mother,

It is a marvelous, crisp, clear December morning, and I am sitting in the front room with Ted & Frieda overlooking our acre of grasses which are white with frost. After a week of black, wet sunless weather, everything seems suddenly bright & Christmassy. I am trying to get off the bulk of my American Xmas cards by ordinary mail today so I will be a bit saving.

The reason I haven't written for so long is probably quite silly, but I got so awfully depressed two weeks ago by reading two issues of the Nation---Juggernaut, the Warfare State,[1] about the terrifying marriage of big business- and the military in America, and the forces of the John Birch Society etc., and another about the repulsive shelter craze[2] for fallout, all very factual & documented & true, that I simply couldn't sleep for nights & with all the warlike talk in the papers such as Kennedy saying Kruschev would "have no place to hide", & the armed forces manuals indoctrinating soldiers about the "inevitable" war with our "implacable foe", I began to wonder if there was any point in trying to bring up children in such a mad self-destructive world. The sad thing is that the power for destruction is real and universal, and the profession of generals who on retirement become Board Heads of the missile plants they have been feeding orders. I am also horrified at the U.S. selling missiles (without warheads) to Germany, awarding former German officers medals---as the reporter for the liberal Frankfurt paper says, coming back to America from his native Germany it is as if he hadn't been away. Well, I got so discouraged about all this that I didn't feel like writing anybody anything. Ted has been very comforting & so has Frieda. One of the most distressing features about all this is the public announcements of Americans arming against each other---the citizens of Nevada announcing they will turn out bombed & ill people from Los Angeles into the desert (all this official), & ministers & priests preaching that it is all right to shoot neighbors who try to come into

1–Fred J. Cook, 'Juggernaut: The Warfare State', *The Nation* (28 October 1961): 299–307.
2–Roger Hagan, 'When the Holocaust Comes', *The Nation* (4 November 1961): 341; and John Kay Adams, 'The Reluctant Moles', *The Nation* (4 November 1961): 341–8.

one's bomb shelters. Thank goodness there is none of this idiotic shelter business in England: I just wish England had the sense to be neutral, for it is quite obvious that she would be "obliterated" in any nuclear war & for this reason I am very much behind the nuclear disarmers here. Anyway, I think it appalling that the shelter system in America should be allowed to fall into the hands of the advertisers---the more money you spend the likelier you are to survive, etc., when 59% of taxes go for military spending already. I think the boyscouts & the American Legion & the rest of those ghastly anti-communist organizations should be forced to sit every Sunday before the movies of the victims of Hiroshima, & the generals each to live with a victim, like the human conscience which is so lacking to them. Well, I am over the worst of my furore about all this. Each day seems doubly precious to me, because I am so happy here, with my lovely home & dear Ted & Frieda. I just wish all the destructive people could be sent to the moon.

Well, I didn't want to write anything until I felt in better spirits. We have started painting the floors upstairs, preparatory to ordering our rugs, & it makes an immense difference in our morale. Living on dirtyish bare boards in very cold weather is grim. Now Ted has laid down a white undercoat in every upstairs room but one (which we won't use till we refloor it) & is bordering the edges that will show with pale grey lino paint, as in our London flat. Everything as a result looks airy, light and spanking clean. I have looked & looked at carpets, in Exeter, London & Plymouth, & feel now that our choice is right & sensible. We ordered a lovely all-wool Indian carpet for our bedroom (10'7" x 9'3") with an off-white, rose & green border & center medallion, at just under $150, about half price of the carpet, also Indian, but larger & fancier, that I saw in London.

I am also ordering this week the rugs I saw in London---a super red one for my study, a matching red, but cheaper because shorter-piled, for the stair & hall carpet, forest green for Frieda's room, & a handsome figured rug for the livingroom (all-wool Wilton---the rest are all-wool too), with a rich red background & green & white figured border & center medallion, all these with matching underfelts (I saw foam-rubber underlays but didn't like it---I'm sure damp would crumble it). I hope these get to us by Christmas: the whole lot, 4 rugs & the staircarpet & underfelts should amount to about $750 which I don't think too bad, as $325 of that is gifts from grampy, Mrs. Prouty & Dot & I've the rest easily with the sale of my poetry mss. for $280 & my Guinness poetry prize, both bolts out of the blue, as it were. I feel we have made a good investment. Next spring we hope to have saved enough to have cement foundations laid under the front half of the house & black & white squared linoleum on top of that in the playroom & hall. Then we shall rest a bit.

I have been sewing curtains for Frieda's closet & odd windows here & there & have ordered enough for red corduroy drapes for our front room French windows & short curtains for the window over the windowseat, plus 3 cushions, covered in matching red cord for the windowseat, which shall do us as a sofa---there really isn't room enough for anything like that in the front room anyway.

Piles of packages have come---the wonderful one with the nighties I liked so much for Frieda when she was little, the handsome plaid pants with the warm red lining, the wonderful cord things which will be ideal for her "gardening" this spring. Thank you, thank you, thank you. Then today came a big Xmas parcel from you with the two Ladies Home J's which I fell upon with joy and rejoicing---that magazine has so much Americana I love it. Look forward to a good read by the wood fire tonight, & to trying the luscious recipes. Recipes in English women's magazines are for things like Lard & Stale Bread Pie, garnished with Cold Pigs Feet, or Left-Over Pot Roast in Aspic.

A huge packet from Dotty also arrived. I'm enclosing a card for her,[1] if you want to put it in with anything of yours. I feel so thwarted not to be giving out <u>any</u>thing but cards after last Christmas, especially as I just love buying presents for people, but we have felt we need to really pinch this year to weather the piles of bills for plumbers, electricians, extra heaters, coal, land tax, house tax, solicitors, surveyors, movers and all the mountaining things. As if to sanction our move, we have been <u>very</u> lucky in earning money this fall---my Saxton, in 4 installments is ample to live on; the enclosed cheque is part of the <u>Atlantic Monthly</u> fee of $125 for two of Ted poems[2] they just accepted (the rest will follow on our filling out tax exemption forms). Now we can afford to let our American cheques build up that account again. Each September 1st we plan to pay you & Ted's parents back each $280 of your loan which has been such a help in saving us tons of mortgage interest. I am very pleased we will be able to meet our heap of largish expenses---nearly 2 years of English income tax which our blessed London accountant is figuring out, & back dues for Nat. Health over $2 a week which we want to catch up with now.

1 – The card is no longer with the letter.

2 – Ted Hughes, 'The Rescue', *Atlantic Monthly* 209 (March 1962): 65; and Ted Hughes, 'Sugar Loaf', *Atlantic Monthly* 209 (May 1962): 69. See Peter Davison to TH and SP, 4 December 1961; held by Yale University.

Our Indian carpet came & our bedroom is just beautiful with it. Ted got a lovely Chinese goat-skin rug to fill the odd empty space, long black and grey silky hairs, and that makes it very special. We ordered the remaining rugs from London today & hope they come before the baby does.

You have no idea how forward we are looking to your visit this summer! You should have a real vacation this time. Sitting out in deck chairs with your 2 grandchildren & exploring the Cornwall beaches. By the time you come the house should be in very nice shape, and all the foliage at its best. We have 2 more Pifcos, making 4, now. The cold is bitter. Even my midwife said it was too Spartan for a new baby & to warm things up. The halls are hopeless, of course, but the Pifcos do a wonderful job in closed off rooms. The cold seems to keep us healthy---none of us has been taken with a cold yet (knock on wood)---we look fat as bears with all our sweaters, but I find this nippy air very bracing & so does Frieda. Her fat cheeks bloom, even though her breath comes out in white puffs. Much healthier than the overheating we had in America. I am only sorry you have had such bad luck of getting sick over Thanksgiving & having relapses. How are you now? Aren't you through in 6 weeks with all your remedial reading program? I will be so relieved when you get done with it.

We had a lovely time laughing over the take-off issue of Mademoiselle. And now I am embedded with the Journals, especially delighted with the apple-recipe issue.[1] I love all the bits of gossip & clippings you send. So glad to hear Sonia Thorguson[2] is married, she's such a lovely girl. I wonder if Ruth Geisel[3] will ever get married?

I hope Warren is having a peaceful and pleasant year & isn't too overworked. I feel dreadfully lazy myself. I really write terribly little---I was like this, I remember, before Frieda came: quite cowlike & interested suddenly in soppy women's magazines & cooking & sewing. Then a month or so afterwards I did some of my best poems.

I rely on your letters---you are wonderful to keep them so frequent in spite of your load of work & being sick.

All of us send love,
Sivvy

1–Carol Truax, 'The Apples You Couldn't Resist', *Ladies' Home Journal* (October 1961): 88, 90.

2–Karin Sonja Thorgerson Galmarino (*c.* 1930–); 1948, Wellesley High School; lived at 381 Weston Road, Wellesley; married Alberto R. Galmarino (1928–2004), *c.* September 1961.

3–Ruth Geisel (1932–); friend of SP; attended Wellesley High School and Dana Hall School; B.A. 1953, English, Wellesley College; lived at 5 Durant Road, Wellesley, Mass.

TO *Brian Cox*

Tuesday 12 December 1961 TLS, University of Kansas

Court Green
North Tawton
Devon.
December 12, 1961

Dear Brian,

I was delighted with American Poetry Now---thought the cover[1] handsome, and the setup of the poems worked out very well indeed. I do hope it continues to sell.

We see nothing but the Observer & The New Statesman---the rest is cows and sheep. Could you give me a notion of what the Times Lit. Sup.[2] said? I'd like so much to know what poets people like & what poets people miss etc.

We are stuffing our cracks against the winter blasts and readying for three months in which we should have nothing to do but write and dream of strawberries & cream, so hope to have some produce of poems by spring.

All best wishes,
Sylvia Plath

1–The cover of *American Poetry Now* was designed by T. E. Burrill.

2–[G. S. Fraser], 'American Poetry', *Times Literary Supplement* (8 December 1961): 881; Fraser reviewed the pamphlet favourably.

TO *Judith Jones*

Tuesday 12 December 1961 TLS (aerogramme), University of Texas at Austin

Court Green
North Tawton
Devonshire, England
December 12, 1961

Mrs. Judith B. Jones
ALFRED A. KNOPF INC.
501 Madison Avenue
New York 22, New York
USA

Dear Mrs. Jones,

Thanks very much for your good letter of November 22nd.[1] I'm delighted about the Saxton Fellowship too, as it comes at a specially providential time and enables me to go on writing to schedule in spite of the obligations of our recently acquired pre-Domesday farmhouse and orchard and the prospect of a second infant around New Year's. If all goes according to plan, as I think it will, the novel should be finished by early next fall and I imagine Heinemann will send a copy along to you---they seem to be in touch with some other editor at Knopf in any case.[2]

I'm glad all the assignments of copyright are coming in. Milton Greenstein,[3] the New Yorker man, wanted to be very sure his magazine is properly acknowledged, and this is the form he gave me for acknowledging the New Yorker in my book:

The poems Hardcastle Crags, Man In Black, Mussel Hunter At Rock Harbor, and Watercolor Of Grantchester Meadows, appeared originally in The New Yorker.[4]

I must sound an awful curmudgeon about photographs, but I am so buried in the country now that all I see is babies and cows and sheep, no photographers near, and my husband and I are so unphoto-conscious we don't even have a camera. I know from my Smith and Mademoiselle days that the publicity photo is a great necessity, and have piles from

1–Judith Jones to SP, 22 November 1961; held by University of Texas at Austin.

2–Heinemann was in touch with William A. Koshland.

3–A lawyer and former vice president and assistant secretary of the *New Yorker*, Milton Greenstein (*c.* 1912–91).

4–Milton Greenstein to SP, 17 October 1961; held by University of Texas at Austin.

that ancient era, but hope the public can get by without anything until I again return to civilisation. I don't know when this will be. The YMHA have asked me[1] to do a reading, & I do love giving readings & did a lot in London and over the BBC, and certainly would do so if I ever made a return visit to America.

Do let me know how the book is getting on. When is it due out?

With warmest good wishes,
Sylvia Plath

TO *Aurelia Schober Plath & Warren Plath*

Friday 15 December 1961[2] — ALS in greeting card[3] with envelope, Indiana University

<printed greeting>
With best wishes for Christmas and the New Year
<signed>
with love from / Sivvy, Ted & Frieda <drawing of a star>

Thursday, December 15

Dear mother & Warren . . .

It seems impossible that it is only ten days to Christmas – I have been so immersed in household fixing & thinking of the arrival of the new baby that I've done little but get off a few cards. I mailed almost everybody's (your neighbors) sea-mail a week ago – let me know if they arrive in time! Frieda is playing at my feet with a spool of thread – she loves looking at pictures now & can say "owl" & "doddie" & "cow" & point them out. She is very sweet & good lately & a fine walker. We have been taking her out a lot on some of the pleasant roads near here & have found some lovely spots nearby on Dartmoor where we can picnic next summer when you come, mother. We look so forward to your coming & seeing us in such lovely surroundings. I hope the enclosed photographs[4] give you some idea of the handsome lines of Court Green.

Did I tell you our Indian carpet (off white & rose) & goatskin came for the bedroom? They make it feel like a place of luxury now. We have

1 – See SP to Elizabeth Kray, 26 April 1961.
2 – Letter misdated by SP.
3 – Christmas card designed by J. F. Wilkes for the Gordon Fraser Gallery, Bedford, England.
4 – The photographs are no longer with the letter.

ordered the other rugs from London & I hope they come before the new baby. They certainly do make the house feel warmer. Frieda loves rolling on the bedroom rug.

The bank manager's wife[1] – a very lively & entertaining Irishwoman – paid a "call" on us this afternoon & regaled us with all sorts of stories. I look forward to getting to know her better – evidently one couple of tenants here (before) the last shiftless lot – a fertilizer salesman who plowed up our tennis court) were a Belgian & a Cornishwoman from South America who did gorgeous handweaving they sold to Harrods & Fortnum & Mason & wealthy locals.

I can't tell you how much we like it here. The town itself is fascinating – a solid body of interrelated locals (very curious), then all these odd peripheral people – Londoners, ex-Cockneys, Irish. I look forward to getting to know them slowly. The bank manager's wife, the doctor & his family & the redoubtable Nurse who doesn't miss an addition on every house visit. The bank manager's wife has a daughter of 15[2] at school in Oxford & says there are no children her age here at all. But I should be much luckier. Every time I visit the doctor's surgery I see a raft of new babies. Most of them very attractive little things.

I have been grandiose & ordered a turkey for our Xmas dinner. I love turkey & shall enjoy living off it cold. Is a 10 lb. turkey a good size? It is about as small as they come. And I shall stuff it with that nice stuffing you use, mother. We have a little evergreen tree waiting to be brought in which I shall hang with some German spice cookies in tinfoil I got & Woolworth's balls & a few birds which reminded me of our lovely peacocks.

It will be our first Christmas on our own as heads of a family, & I want to keep all our old traditions alive. I wish I had a Springerle pin! We ate a batch of apricot half-moons last night – how I love them. Do explain to Dot if you can that we are being Spartan about gifts this Christmas. I hope by next year we can be as generous as our wishes! In spite of our fabulous bills, back taxes & Nat. Health, we are doing surprisingly well. My NYorker contract for poems was renewed[3] for

1–Marjorie Pearson Tyrer (1912–89); married to George Dugdall Tyrer (1906–75), who was the manager of the National Provincial Bank at the corner of North Street and Market Street, North Tawton.

2–Nicola Tyrer (1946–). Tyrer was enrolled at the Headington School, Oxford.

3–Howard Moss to SP, 8 December 1961; held by New York Public Library.

another year, & I've been asked to be one of the 3 judges for the Guinness contest I won this year.[1] Ted & Frieda send lots of love & so do I.

xxx
Sivvy

TO *Aurelia Schober Plath & Warren Plath*

Monday 18 December 1961 TLS in greeting card[2] with envelope, Indiana University

<printed greeting>
Merry Christmas – Happy New Year
<signed>
with love / Sivvy, Ted & Frieda

Monday: December 18

Dear mother & Warren,

I hope these color shots[3] of Frieda arrive in time for Christmas, but if not they should make a bright postscript to it. I think they really do our blue-eyed angel justice for a change. That gnarled branch to the right of our door is an antique honeysuckle. Don't you think we have a nice place? I'm also enclosing 2 checks for deposit in the Boston 5cent Bank. The New Yorker accepted 2 more of my poems this week,[4] along with renewing my year's contract. Very encouraging. My publisher sent me Memoirs & Correspondence of Frieda Lawrence[5] for Christmas. Isn't that dear of them. We are very happy, healthy, and frosty just now. I drove to Exeter today for a bit of shopping[6] in a lovely white frost---all the cows and sheep were pink against the white slopes of the hills. The electrician came today & put our power plugs in 4 rooms, so we can have the Pifcos all about and keep snug. I have at last got my red corduroy for livingroom curtains & windowseat; Ted's finished the last of the floorpainting. We've got such lovely piles of presents from everyone---both of us are more excited at

1 – SP was a judge for the prize along with George Hartley and John Press.
2 – Christmas card designed by J. F. Wilkes for the Gordon Fraser Gallery, Bedford, England.
3 – The photographs are no longer with the letter.
4 – Sylvia Plath, 'The Moon and the Yew Tree' and 'Mirror Talk' ['Mirror'], *New Yorker* (3 August 1963): 29. Howard Moss to SP, 12 December 1961; held by New York Public Library.
5 – Frieda Lawrence, *The Memoirs and Correspondence* (London: Heinemann, 1961); SP's copy held by Emory University.
6 – SP wrote cheques to Waltons for red corduroy, Tanis Brothers for a sweater for TH, Canor Brothers for a bathrobe, and Colsons for a blanket.

something for Frieda than anything for ourselves. Ted will make a wood cradle for her doll which I'll paint this week, & I'll make Dot's carrot cakes, which are such nice holiday fare.

Do explain to Dotty that we are just sending Christmas wishes & love this year, since the house is eating up just about everything else. Next Christmas should be quite settled. Our big present to ourselves is that we are paying off our £600 mortgage this Christmas. Isn't that wonderful! It is because the Maugham people didn't take back the grant when we told them we couldn't use it in the 2 year period given, but let us keep it. So we will save all that interest. I hope you have recovered from your bad cold, mummy. Do write that you are better. I hope you don't overdo this Christmas. Give our best love to Dotty & Joe. Dotty's letters mean a lot to me & I feel more & more close to her.

Love from us all,
Sivvy

TO *Howard Moss*

Monday 18 December 1961 — TLS (aerogramme), New York Public Library

Court Green
North Tawton
Devonshire, England
December 18, 1961

Mr. Howard Moss
THE NEW YORKER
25 West 43rd Street
New York 36, New York
USA

Dear Mr. Moss,

I'm very glad to hear you are taking THE MOON AND THE YEW TREE and MIRROR TALK. By all means change the title of MIRROR TALK to MIRROR.[1] I think that's much better. I consider myself, with

1–Howard Moss to SP, 12 December 1961; held by New York Public Library; Moss requested the title change because of a preference against poems with the word 'Talk' in the title, a Rodgers and Hammerstein song entitled 'Happy Talk' being the reason. SP had also submitted 'Last Words' and 'The Babysitters', which were rejected.

few exceptions, a rather numb hand at titles, and am usually most grateful for any alternative suggestions.

Thanks so much for the clippings. Buried as we are among Devon hedges and livestock, we don't get a chance to keep up on these at all.

All good wishes,
Sylvia Plath

TO *Aurelia Schober Plath*

Friday 29 December 1961 — TLS (aerogramme), Indiana University

<SP wrote '1' on address side of letter>

Friday: December 29

Dear mother,

I am sitting in our livingroom by a crackling wood fire, our mantel still gay with red candles and about 50 Christmas cards, our fat little tree with its silver birds and tinsel and spicecake hearts still up, and the new red corduroy curtains I have just finished drawn, making the room bright and cheerful, like the inside of a Valentine. I had 3 cushions made of foam rubber for our windowseat and covered in the same red cord (much too ambitious a job for me) and this weekend hope to finish the pleated red underfringe from cushions to floor. The stair carpets have come---a rich red, and Ted is laying them. It is a heavenly difference in feel and illusion of warmth. We have thick underfelts to go under the carpets, hair felts, so I'm sure that keeps some cold out. We just await the livingroom carpet & the one for my study & F's bedroom. The midwife suggested I get a thermometer to see the temperature of the new baby's room. I was amazed. The general level of the house---in halls & unheated rooms, is about 40° (38° in our bedroom in the morning!). An electric heater gets it feeling very hot at 50-55°. Now I am positively sweltering in the livingroom at 60°. It all depends on what one gets used to. We have all been (knock on wood) in excellent health---not one cold yet, and I do think this change from central heating, with the constant sharp contrasts of cold & hot, outside and in, is responsible for our healthy winter so far. Frieda blooms like a rose. I hope you have the colored pictures by now. Isn't she a little darling?

Our Christmas was the happiest and fullest I have ever known. It is the first one we "made ourselves", from start to finish. We trimmed the tree and set out our amazing stacks of gifts (from everybody, it seems) on

Christmas Eve. Then Christmas day we started the 3 of us off with our daily ration of soup-plates of hot oatmeal (something you & grammy taught me), then led Frieda into the livingroom, which she had not seen in its decorated state. I wish you could have seen her face. She went right up to the tree and touched a silver ball. Then she saw her Baby (the marvelous one you sent) & made the funniest little gesture, put her arm behind her head and said "Oh" and rushed to pick it up. We had, for our gift to her, made a lovely cradle for it. In the wonderful Woman's Days Aunt Marion sent (you must tell her about our using them, I'll write too, later) we found the perfect pattern for a wood cradle.[1] Warren's package arrived just in time---suspecting their toolishness, Ted opened his early, utterly delighted, & made the cradle. I painted it white and then put hearts & flowers & birds on it in red, green, blue & yellow enamel. Then I made a red cord bedspread. That baby really looked handsome. And the ponytailed baby, & the teensy one in the carriage (which Frieda loves & persists calling a car) completed her delight. She carries them all round with her, has to sit them in her highchair. Her first words on waking are "Babies, babies". To save myself the endless work of getting all 3 babies into her arms all the time, I thought I'd put one away for a bit till she got used to them, but she looked all round, saying "More babies, more babies" in the most plaintive voice, so I relented & got them all out again.

Then we carefully & slowly unwrapped all our presents. Really, mummy, you outdid yourself! Your pink sweater set is heavenly. (Do you expect a girl?) And the lovely blouse in my favorite colors of blue & green will hearten me immensely as soon as I get out of these shredding maternity clothes---I've been wearing the same sweater all winter! I just love the nighties---they came as my other simply fell from my back: I had washed it & worn it every week for over 2 years! I think Frieda's skirt is about my favorite---the red one. She looks such a treat in it, with her tights. Tights are a godsend. I don't know how we'd get through the winter without them! Oh, I think you'll go bankrupt if you get any more grandchildren! And Dotty's package was full of lovely things. She has wonderful taste---I adore the blouse she got me. And the sweaters for Frieda, just as she had outgrown all but your red one were providential. The Fox book[2] Ted had to read immediately. He said it was the most beautiful children's book he had seen---and it means so much to me, being set in New England! His

1–See SP to Marion Freeman, 31 January 1962.

2–Possibly Peter Spier, *The Fox Went Out on a Chilly Evening* (New York: Doubleday, 1961).

very favorite presents were the Fox book & Warren's tools, which he hasn't put down since he got them. He's been fitting in the staircarpet clips with them today & says they're marvelous & "very American"---meaning streamlined.

I was so glad to hear about your feast at Dot's & that you are accepting invitations! I spent the rest of Christmas making my 1st simply beautiful golden-brown turkey with your bread dressing, creamed brussels sprouts & chestnuts, swede (like squash, orange), giblet gravy & apple pies with our last & preciously saved own apples. We all 3 had a fine feast in the midafternoon, with little Frieda spooning up everything. Then a quiet evening by the fire counting all our hundreds of blessings & beaming. I look so forward to our doing this every year. Our house is a perfect "Christmas" house.

xxx
Sivvy

Oh yes! Three cheers for the Ladies' Home Journal! I'll love it.

TO *Aurelia Schober Plath*

Friday 29 December 1961 — TLS (aerogramme), Indiana University

<SP wrote '2' on address side of letter>

2nd installment

Dear mother . . .

There's so much to say I just couldn't fit it in to my last letter. That was our Christmas. Ted's mother & father went to dinners at their relatives, too (Olwyn stayed in Paris translating a play for her play agency---we've both "written" to each other,[1] a step, so the gap is bridged as I wanted it to be by this Christmas)---Aunt Hilda's & then Uncle Walter's. Ted called them afterwards & they seemed to have had a simply wonderful time. I think all of us descending on them was a great expense and strain, & this time they were treated & feasted. So we'll go on like this & pay our visits in the summer when there is no competition on the roads & the weather is good & everybody doesn't just exchange colds. I want to establish a Christmas tradition in my own home now. I hope by next Christmas, when the playroom is livable, we may have a little piano on which I can play carols. I made 3 of Dot's delicious carrot cakes this year (plan to give one

1–See SP to Olwyn Hughes, 20 November 1961.

to my midwife when she's done her job with the baby---she's a wonderful woman, bakes her own bread). Now I have discovered I have none of the recipes for the Christmas cookies you put on your Christmas plate. I'd like all. Especially the sand tarts you cut in shapes & decorate & the chocolate flat ones you decorate with almonds. Our neighbors have been so sweet. We got cards from our Nancy Axworthy (who brought Frieda a little plastic doll in a shower bath that really squirts water! We gave her a bottle of very excellent port---the holiday drink here: she was giving dinner for 9 & her only daughter had a 21st birthday, much celebrated here) & 4 or 5 of our nearest neighbors. An old couple at the bottom of the lane brought a bouquet for me of giant chrysanthemums, & Rose Key, our nearest neighbor, a woman with 3 daughters in London & a spry lovely retired husband, made up a little box of candy for Frieda which I let Ted devour. Our house is full of nuts, tangerines, pears, figs and dates. Oh, we had a lovely time. Everybody is so warm & friendly to us.

One amusing thing: our redoubtable Nurse-midwife who was obviously measuring us sternly (as artists and outlanders) suddenly capitulated with surprising warmth. Her son[1] had come home from his very good school in North London & asked if she knew a Ted Hughes. A friend of his, it seems, was a "fan" of Ted's & had written Ted & the answer came back with a North Tawton postmark. This really Established us in the good lady's eyes. I'm sure we're the questionmark of the community: now Ted is "placed" as a rather famous Britisher. My doctor is very nice & good. I've started taking sleeping pills for my arms have been a bother---all pins & needles & often so painful I can't lay them anywhere at all: evidently a normal symptom of some pregnancies & common locally---but these pills really put me to sleep at night, for which I'm most grateful. Otherwise I'm just fine.

All through this I've not said anything about Warren's engagement. How wonderful! I wish he and Maggie would visit us after they're married. They could stay at the local Inn we dined at if they found our place too noisy with babies, as they well might! Do send a glossy of her Bachrach picture.[2] I'm sure we'll love her & hope Warren is as happy as she must be.

What fun for you to have all the very most traditional trappings for one of your 2 children (diamonds, Bachrach &, I imagine, a very formal wedding)---especially the son (should save you the wear and tear!) Wish

1–Kenneth Garnett Neville-Davies (1943–).
2–Bachrach photography, 647 Boylston Street, Boston.

so much I could attend. Do you think it will be this June? You must give me some notion of what they'd like for a present. Did I tell you, by the way, that Ted's Uncle Walter gave us £100 as a Christmas present? (He's evidently been doing this for brother Gerald a long time who has a Jaguar & other cars). Seems we only needed to show we didn't need it (I'm so glad we never asked him for a loan!) and he is so impressed by our house photographs & purchase that he'll probably favor us with a visit this spring! Edith sent us a lovely pink double blanket for our bed & two blue ones for the babies. I've also bought the handsomest & lightest & warmest pink blanket in the world for our bed (we're putting the 2 flimsy ones on the guest bed---fine for summer). Santa gave Ted a Jaeger sweater---fawn, cardigan, very posh & handsome to replace his tattered ones, & me a feathery warm rose mohair robe with big collar to solace me in my pre- & post confinement. All very necessary for survival, but very nice. I loved your encouraging letter & article---I'd come to the same lookout myself. We've had two days of storybook weather. The merest dust of snow on everything, china-blue skies, rosy hilltops. New lambs in the fields. Its the second coldest winter this century the farmers say. Took Frieda for little trots on Dartmoor & our local heights this week. She said "no" for snow. Can finish the Hi-diddle-diddle rhyme on a picture card with "poon" & thinks everything with fuzz is a "doddie"---her favorite animal. You should see her baby her babies---feed them her biscuits, hold up a clock to their ear so they can hear it tick, cover them up. They couldn't come at a better time---to get her used to the baby idea. She is so loving---I'm sure she gets it from us! Ted is an angel – so thoughtful.

xxx
Sivvy

1962

TO *Aurelia Schober Plath*

Friday 12 January 1962 TLS (aerogramme), Indiana University

Court Green, North Tawton
Devonshire, England
January 12, 1962

Dear mother,

Well, Nicholas-Megan was officially due yesterday, and no sign. So this baby will probably delay a few days like Frieda, and keep us all in suspense. I've so enjoyed your long, newsy letters! I've felt lazier and lazier and more & more cowlike. The doctor's sleeping pills are very good---we've been sleeping about 10 hours a night, and Frieda just plays quietly however late we get up. I've given up all pretence of working in my study these last weeks, I am simply too ponderous! As far as I can tell by these weird English weights (in Stones) I weigh almost 170! With my clothes on, of course, and that accounts for a lot---layer after layer of sweaters & tights. As it is, I go to bed after lunch, for being up on my feet 4 hours is like a day's work in the fields, and sleep about 2 hours then. Ted helps me with Frieda---lifting her in and out of bed & highchair and dressing her ---she's so funny, like a little worm, & delights in toddling off as I sit with her clothes, too weighty to chase after her. "Bye-bye", she says gravely, waving & shutting the door of the bathroom closet, or popping behind the curtains of the closet in her bedroom. Then she giggles & peeps out. Her "Baby" & "Ahh-hee" (a white elephant from Olwyn) go everywhere with her, also the darling pony-tailed Baby you sent in the bath---Frieda is always combing her hair with a tiny brush. She insists they be fed, too, & shares her snacks with them. She is so pretty and loving, we just adore her. I hope this next baby is anywhere near as nice. Did Mrs. Magandantz[1] have any doctor's explanation as to why one's arms go all prickly & bloated-feeling? There seems to be no remedy for it. Right now I feel

1–Melitta Hey Magendantz (1906–86); married to Dr Heinz Magendantz (1899–1972); residents of Newton, Mass.

I am typing through a field of sandy needles, and I am always dropping things or running my finger through with pins when trying to sew---very inconvenient, but I persist.

All our rugs have come. The livingroom is lovely now, with my red cord curtains & red cord windowseat, and the all-wool Wilton, basically red, but with the usual border and center medallion and patterned all over with off-white, green and black leaves and flowers, so it should not show wear easily. We need it for company and evenings. Children are taboo. I'm sitting in it now with Ted, very cosy & bright.

Everyone around is so amiable. The shopkeepers inquire after me, & it seems all North Tawton is awaiting the baby! I like the bank manager's wife (where we went for a cocktail party the Saturday before New Year's) very much---she is about 50, but seems of-an-age to me, a spry, witty-tongued Irishwoman with a daughter of 15 at prep school. Her husband has had 2 heart-attacks & obviously lives under the shadow of this, but is very perky and pleasant. I have also met the Doctor's Wife (at the party) & liked her a lot; she is my age, with 2 daughters. I hope she invites me over some time. I expect slowly we shall edge in to the Best Society---very amusing.

Ted & his poet-twin here, Thom Gunn (who actually lives & teaches in Berkeley) are bringing out an anthology by half-a-dozen American poets[1] for Faber. Faber are also bringing out a paperback edition of their own selected poems. My little shilling anthology of American poets I edited for the Critical Quarterly here has got very good reviews & seems to be selling well. Each day I bake something to hide away for Ted & Frieda when I'm recovering from the new baby. I have a box of sand tarts cut in shapes with cherries & almonds (F. calls them "moon-cookies"), a box of tollhouse cookies & a fruitcake. Tomorrow I'll try an apple pie with the very last of our apples.

I hope Warren takes all I write you for himself too. I love hearing about Aunt Maggie. We'd so like to see them here. Don't worry about money, for them! Ted & I had <u>nothing</u> when we got married, & no prospects. And in 5 years all our most far-fetched dreams have come true. We look so forward to your visit this summer! It does my heart good to hear you have knitting in your hands again (and not just from my own greedy motives!) and that you are seeing friends. You must do more & more of this---you

1–Thom Gunn and Ted Hughes (eds), *Five American Poets* (London: Faber & Faber, 1963); featured Edgar Bowers, Howard Nemerov, Hyam Plutzik, Louis Simpson, and William Stafford.

owe it to yourself. I hope you will find life here easy & relaxing: I am having the baby in the guestroom, where you'll be, & we have fixed it up quite comfortably, although the old rug is shabby. We've painted the floor & I've made curtains. You must bring a bathingsuit, too! I hope we can go to some nice beaches together. Of course Frieda will remember you! Deep down, if not obviously. You'll have more lovely times together. Do tell me Betsy Powley's address & I'll write her. I'll write Dot[1] & everybody as soon as the baby comes.

Lots of love,
Sivvy

TO *Aurelia Schober Plath*

Thurs.–Sat. 18–20 January 1962 TLS (aerogramme), Indiana University

January 18, 1962
5 p.m.

Dear mother,

By now I hope you have received the telegram Ted sent this morning with the good news of the arrival of our first son Nicholas Farrar Hughes[2] (I almost wrote Nicholas-Megan!) last night at 5 minutes to midnight, making another 17th date in our family, after Ted's August 17th. I am sitting up in bed, feeling fine and refreshed after an afternoon's nap, Nicholas in a carrycot at my side getting pinker and pinker. He looked very swarthy to me when he arrived, like a wrinkled, cross old boxer, and still is a Farrar type, although Ted suggests his head-shape resembles Daddy's. Now he has turned quite pink and translucent, though. All during the delivery I felt it would be a boy---my notions that he was a much bigger & heavier baby proved true, and no illusion---he weighed in at 9 pounds 11 ounces, compared to Frieda's ladylike 7 pounds 4 oz., and I had a lot more work with him than with her. Woke at 4 a.m. the morning of the 17th with niggly contractions that came & went all day while I did as much cooking as I could, till 5 p.m., just after Frieda went to bed, when they started to get very strong. I had a visit from both midwife & doctor during the day ---both very kindly and encouraging. Then at 8:30, when the contractions were established at every 5 minutes, Ted called the midwife. She brought

1–See SP to Dorothy Benotti, 31 January 1962.
2–Nicholas Farrar Hughes (1962–2009), son of SP and TH, was born on 17 January 1962.

a cylinder of gas & air & she sat on one side of the bed & Ted on the other, gossiping pleasantly together all 3, while I breathed in my mask whenever I had a strong contraction & joined in the conversation. I had used up the cylinder & was just beginning to push down when the baby stuck & the membrane didn't break. Then at 5 to 12, as the doctor was on his way over, this great bluish glistening boy shot out onto the bed in a tidal wave of water that drenched all 4 of us to the skin, howling lustily. It was an amazing sight. I immediately sat up & felt wonderful---no tears, nothing. It is heavenly to be in my own house---I'm in the guest room which is ideal. Beautiful clear dawn & full moon tonight in our huge elm. Everybody in North Tawton turned to stare at Ted when he came into town---Rose Key, our cottage neighbor, brought a little knitted suit & the banker's wife sent a card & towel. I gave the midwife my traditional carrot cake. She is a wonderful woman. You should see her with Frieda ---(we showed Frieda the baby this morning & she was terribly excited)--- the midwife has Frieda come in and "help" as she fixes the baby, advising me to share the tasks, even if it takes longer. I didn't even know Frieda could understand, but she did everything the midwife said---held the safety pins, kissed the baby, helped wrap him up & then sat & held him all by herself! She was just bursting with pride. Having the baby at home is so restful. Nancy came today & did the downstairs & will be glad to come extra time for ironing or washing up. Ted spent the afternoon with the BBC producer[1] of his new radio play[2]---or poem for voices, who came down from London to see him about details. Coincidentally, this man's birthday was yesterday, too. Now everything is quiet and peaceful & Ted is heating the vichysoisse & apple pie I made to tide us over.

Later: Saturday, January 20th. I have today marked as a red letter day because your exams will be over, & all that extra work for your courses. I'm sure I've been as concerned for you about this as you've been about me & the baby! Hope all went well, & that you have a lovely dinner at Dot's. Loved the newsclipping of Margaret.[3] I look so forward to an amiable sister-in-law! <u>She</u> certainly has nothing to fear from me! I only wish I could share in the fun & plans for the wedding. Would you think me crazy to ask you a favor? Could you possibly get me 2 size 34C Maidenform white cotton bras & 2 pairs of white size 6 six briefs

1–English radio producer and bookseller, Douglas Cleverdon (1903–87).

2–Ted Hughes, *The Wound*, BBC Third Programme (1 February 1962).

3–Probably 'Miss Wetzel, Warren Plath Are Engaged', *The Townsman* (Wellesley), (11 January 1962): 3.

(elasticized not open round the leg rim) at Filene's[1] & airmail them? Would it be stupidly expensive if you just wrapped them in paper? I have no underwear, everything has just fallen to shreds & no notion of when I'll feel like driving for a day in Exeter to shop again, & I know just what American things fit me. If this is too extravagant, don't bother. I'm slightly dazed & have no notion of common sense at the moment. Everyone is very sweet in town & Rose Key will bring us Sunday dinner in a covered dish. Isn't that thoughtful.

After both Ted's & my first shock at having a boy, we think he is marvelous. He did look grim & cross at first, his head all dented where he had caught high up & had to really push to get out, but overnight his head & features altered. Already I can sense a very different temperament from Frieda's---where she was & is almost hysterically impatient, he is calm & steady, with big dark eyes & a ruddy complexion. Very restful & dear.

Well, Ted's going to post befor the weekend so I'll say goodbye for now. Do write me lots of newsy letters now you are more free.

Lots of love,
Sivvy

TO *Aurelia Schober Plath*

Wed.–Sat. 24–27 January 1962 — TLS (aerogramme), Indiana University

Wednesday: Jan. 24

Dear mother,

Well, Nicholas is a week old, and I have spent my first whole day up. Things have calmed down considerably, and by next week I think we will be placidly back to schedule. I've had a rather tiring week as the first night the baby was born I couldn't sleep for the excitement, & the nights after that the baby cried all night (I suppose this is the one advantage of a hospital or home nurse!), but now he is settling down to more of a schedule & the doctor gave me a couple of relaxing pills to get me to sleep till I get rested up again. It is wonderful having all this room. While the baby was up nights, I slept with him in the guest room so Ted could have an unbroken night in our room & be ready to cope with Frieda & the cooking & washing up the next day. Now I am back to cooking again, sitting on my stool. I will go on having my nap every afternoon & sitting

1–Filene's was a department store chain with its flagship branch in Boston.

in my study in the morning. This morning I took a hot bath first thing, put on proper clothes & felt very fresh. I simply wore through the seams of all the underwear & maternity skirts & tights I wore in the last months & looked like a great patchy monster at the end. It is heavenly to have a whole wardrobe to choose from again.

Your red sweater arrived just in time for me to christen it today. It is wonderful! Ted & I just gaped at it. The cuffs and yoke neck are so becoming & the color a tonic after my funereal maternity blacks. I shall probably wear this sweater out before you come! It is ideal for nursing because it is a cardigan & I have no cardigans, so I can wear it over all my button-down-the-front blouses, & it is so deliciously warm! Did it take you ages? I'd like to order another some day. In dusty rose or wedgewood blue. The self-covered buttons are very handsome. I'm so relieved you're done with your courses. Was the exam Saturday very hard? Will you have time now for more visiting with people & friends?

My favorite midwife, who delivered the baby, was only with us for one day alas. Her 80 year old father who lives in a neighboring town, was very ill with pneumonia so she took a "holiday" to nurse him. The 2nd midwife was Irish & had been a "society" midwife at one point ---even worked with Grantly Dick-Read, the natural childbirth man, for a while. She's been pleasant, but not with the immense moral force and calm of Mrs. Davies---I was so lucky to have her! I have all sorts of little neighborly attentions---the bankers wife brought oranges yesterday & a custard today. The bank manager himself dropped in to collect her---poor man has had 2 heart attacks already, very sweet person. I do enjoy Marjorie Tyrer, his wife. She seems to be a bit of a lone wolf---she is Irish, with a very funny, sharp tongue, full of gossip & evidently not loved much in the town, & I am a good listener. She has a pretty daughter of 15 at private school in Oxford. They found Ted's picture in Vogue[1] in a dentist's office, & a poem of mine in this week's Sunday Observer,[2] so we are more or less discovered, & have a kind of pleasant status. Rose Key brought a lovely roast beef dinner for us all Sunday. I think we're incredibly lucky to have fallen in a place that isn't all "locals"---these are all "foreigners", like us. But the local people are awfully nice too. I'll make up plates of Xmas cookies next year as my kind of hospitality, after your custom.

1–Probably in John Wain, 'The Popular Art of Poetry', *Vogue* (July 1961): 72–3, which featured individual photographs of TH (taken by David Bailey), William Empson, Thomas Kinsella, and Louis MacNeice.
2–Sylvia Plath, 'The Rival', *The Observer* (21 January 1962): 31.

One bit of practical advice I'd like to ask. Ted wrote a life insurance broker firm after an ad in the paper. We know nothing about rates or kinds of insurance, but this sounded very good to us. What do you think of it? "£6,500 immediate family protection, which includes a with-profits endowment estimated to produce £2,500 payable to you at age 65 with an annuity alternative of £280 at an annual premium of £47.3.11. Assuming incoming tax allowance at the standard rate, this works out at 15/5 (just over $2) a week." This is the sort of policy we would like, with choice of a lump sum or annual "pension" at the end, as of course our job is not pensionable. Multiply by 3 or $2.80 for a rough or specific American translation. Of course we'd need a lot of savings as well, by that time! Let me know what you think.

Saturday: Interrupted by a nasty bout with milk fever, a temperature of over 103 for 2 nights, much worse than that I had with Frieda.[1] I'd have sweated myself back to normal by morning when the nurse came, very annoying. They are shocked if you take your own temp here. Finally the doctor came across with some shots of penicillin---I'm sure if I'd had them immediately I'd not have got so burnt out, but this is not London. Now at last I am cool again, if a bit spent. Believe me, I shed some tears for our "grammy". Ted's been a saint, minding Frieda all day, making me mushrooms on toast, fresh green salads & chicken broth. I hope when you come we can give him a 6 week holiday from any babycare. He needs it---and we both need a few day excursions off on our own, fishing or boating. Margaret's exquisite sweater set arrived. I think its the sweetest I've seen. If Warren makes her anywhere near as happy as Ted has made me, she will be the 2nd happiest girl in the world.

xxx
Sivvy

1–This bout of milk fever inspired SP's abandoned poem with alternative titles 'Fever', 'Fever in Winter', and 'Fever 103'; held by Smith College.

TO *Mary Louise Vincent Black*[1]

Tuesday 30 January 1962 TLS (aerogramme), Collection of Sarah Funke Butler

Court Green
North Tawton
Devonshire, England
January 30, 1962

Miss Mary Louise Vincent
Assistant to the Director, Meridian Books
119 West 57 Street
New York 19, New York
USA

Dear Miss Vincent,

Thank you very much for your letter of January 25th. I am forwarding it, as you suggested, to Heinemann, who I think probably control "Black Rook in Rainy Weather"---I can't think who else would control it---and asking them to write you about it.

Here are the items you asked for meanwhile:

1. Date and place of birth: October 27, 1932 in Boston, Massachusetts.
2. Occupation: Housewife & mother of two small children.
3. Titles of books and names of magazines where published:

THE COLOSSUS (Poems), Knopf, 1962.

The Atlantic Monthly, Harper's, Mademoiselle, The New Yorker, The Hudson Review, The Kenyon Review, The Partisan Review, The Sewanee Review, The Nation, The London Magazine, Encounter, The Observer, The Spectator, The Times Literary Supplement, etc.

Sincerely yours,
Sylvia Plath

1–Mary Louise Vincent Back (1926–2006); a secretary for Meridian in the early 1960s who later worked for Duke University Press.

TO *Aurelia Schober Plath*

Wednesday 31 January 1962 — TLS with envelope, Indiana University

Court Green
North Tawton
Devonshire, England
January 31, 1962

Dearest mother,

Enclosed is the precious negative of Frieda in her red nightie in the black chair for you to have made up for as many of your friends as want them. I wonder if you have it made up large for yourself, if you'd have a big one made for us too. I am already getting so much to miss the lovely little stages Frieda goes through and wish I could simply keep her little toddling baby-self as well as the growing girl. She seems enormous to me now that I have Nicholas. Let us have the negative if you will, when you're done with it.

The two enclosed checks are part of this incredible yearly contract I have with the New Yorker, not for any special poem. The smaller is the "cost of living adjustment" for the last quarter, & the larger the adjustment of the cost of living adjustment for the whole year (for which I've already had some checks). I think this must be some marvelous scheme on their part to avoid income tax. If I get all this for the few odd poems I send, I imagine the fiction writers must be able to buy penthouses! I just hope I can get back to writing poems soon again.

I now feel fully recovered from my milk fever. The penicillin did it. I still take long naps in the afternoon. Had my first night's sleep last night unaided by pills---Nicholas still wakes an extra time besides his 2 o'clock feed, but is working from a 3 to a 4 hour schedule slowly.

After 2 years suffering from that radio that was no radio, utterly unable to get the Third Program here or in London, we treated ourselves to a gorgeous radio. Like all good things, it turned out to come from North Tawton. Just as in desperation Ted was going to Exeter to buy one, George Tyrer, the bank manager came over & told us about this wonderful electrician here, who called & said he had two fine VHF radios. He brought them over, & it was a treat to hear music pouring out of them without a touch of static. We chose the best model which just gets the 3 British stations, not all these foreign stations, which I'd never listen to really. He installed it & rigged up a huge permanent ariel on the roof. The cabinet is handsome, small, of mat-finished walnut, no great garish chrome or knobs. We listened to a new translation of the Agamemnon by Aeschylus last night,[1] almost in tears of joy. It came clear and resonant. Now I will be able to hear all sorts of music & plays & language lessons. The real reason for my hurry was that Ted's next play "The Wound" has its first broadcast tomorrow night & after my heartache at hearing his last through impossible static & interference, I wanted to enjoy this one. He is brimming with ideas for plays, books, etc. And getting interesting books to review from his friend at the New Statesman---one on the 6 great snakes of the world,[2] for instance.

Please give me some notion of what Maggie & Warren would like for a wedding present. I'd like to set aside about $50 for them. I'm only afraid my taste isn't traditional enough for them & would love your guidance. Could I get something here in Exeter they'd like in the way of silver, or send you a check & have you get something? I'd like it to be something really special.

I have got awfully homesick for you since the last baby---and for the Cape & deep snow & such American things. Can't wait for your visit.

Love to all,

Sivvy

PS: Thank you so much for the bras & pants which came today! A lifesaver. Nicholas looks darling in your pink sweaters. Have written Margaret about her lovely white sweater-set. Do you think you could teach me to knit this summer.

<on page 1 of letter>

PS: My book should be coming out from Knopf on April 23rd in time for your birthday. And I should have 6 poems in a paperback anthology[3] there in May by Meridian Books – NEW POETS OF ENGLAND & AND AMERICA: 2nd selection. Ted's in it too.

1–'The Oresteian Trilogy of Aeschylus: Agamemnon', BBC Third Programme, 30 January 1962, 8:55 p.m.

2–Probably Clifford H. Pope, *The Giant Snakes* (London: Routledge & Kegan Paul, 1962); TH's copy held by Emory University.

3–Sylvia Plath, 'The Colossus', 'Snakecharmer', 'Black Rook in Rainy Weather', 'Mushrooms', 'Blue Moles', and 'The Ghost's Leavetaking', Donald Hall (ed.), *New Poets of England and America: Second Selection* (Cleveland: Meridian Books, 1962): 328–34. Ted Hughes, 'The Thought-Fox', 'Roarers in a Ring', 'A Dream of Horses', 'Hawk Roosting', 'The Retired Colonel', 'An Otter', 'November', 'Thrushes', 'Pike', and 'Pibroch', *New Poets of England and America*, 76–86.

TO *Dorothy Benotti*

Wednesday 31 January 1962 TLS (aerogramme), Indiana University

Court Green, North Tawton
Devonshire, England
January 31, 1962

Dear Dotty,

I've been meaning to write you for ages, but after Christmas I thought 'I'll just wait till the baby comes', and then the last two weeks have just flown, midwives in and out, the usual sleepless nights until the baby settles down to a feeding schedule, with Ted minding Frieda and cooking meals till I was up and about again. Now at last things have settled down and I begin to feel my old self. We were overwhelmed with your wonderful Christmas package, Dotty! You've got the knack of picking out just what I would myself---I love my dark blouse, so refreshing to have something new & special after months of the same old maternity clothes! And the sweaters for Frieda were just the thing---we all go around buttoned up into sweaters till spring here. And Ted is wearing his lovely socks, & baby Nicholas enjoying his towel and the other very convenient things. We had such a nice Christmas, although it was our first alone---we felt we wanted to start our own little traditions. I made a 10 pound turkey, my first, and it came out fine. And your carrot cake, which has become a part of our holidays. We had a little evergreen which we decorated, partly with cookies, which Frieda could pick off and eat. Her big moment was discovering the baby doll mother sent, and a white elephant from Ted's sister. She still won't be parted from either---they go with her everywhere. Ted had made her a cradle out of wood which I painted white & enameled with hearts & flowers, so now she can "play baby" with me.

Mother sounded to have such a wonderful time with you all at Christmas. Her letter about it just glowed. I am so relieved she is done with all that awful course work. Now maybe she will relax, and knit, and visit more. We look so forward to having her with us---she will find it a vacation, I think, not like London, sitting out in our garden in a deck chair with her grandchildren, discovering the local beaches with us, and picnicking on Dartmoor. I adore our house. We do have a job keeping it warm---a big coal stove heats the large kitchen-diningroom, where I dry all my clothes. Small electric fan heaters heat the rooms we use most. We have wood fires in the livingroom in the evenings, very cheery. Everybody says our place is gorgeous when the daffodils and cherry and apple trees are in bloom. I can't wait. It will be so nice to get the children out of doors & out of heavy woolens. I miss the snow---we never have any here, just grey rain which gets boring after 6 months of it.

I was very lucky to have the head midwife of the 3 covering our district deliver Nicholas before she went on a 2 week "holiday" to nurse her very sick old father of 80. She was wonderful, very comforting. I had a cylinder of gas-and-air to breathe when I wanted it, & in between she & Ted & I gossiped happily about the local people & affairs. The neighbors have been so sweet---I hardly know many of them, & they brought flowers, a knitted suit for the baby, fruit, & one woman made a roast beef dinner for us the Sunday after Nicholas was born. I felt so touched by all this kindness, especially as we're so new here.

I have a very vigorous red-cheeked country-woman come in 2 or 3 mornings a week to do the heavy cleaning---one morning she does the bedrooms & bathroom & stair, vacuuming, changing beds, washing the tub & floor etc. The other day she washes my acres of kitchen floor & does the rest of the downstairs. Now the baby is here, I have her in an hour or two extra to help with the mountains of ironing. My Bendix is a real blessing now. She only costs about 35 cents an hour! Even as it is, I have my hands full, with cooking & two little babies---I don't know what I would do without her.

How much fun your New Year's party sounds! You are all so lucky to have such a big, close-knit family. That's what I miss most about being in England---not having the reunions with all my relatives and friends every year. Thank goodness mother is able to get over; I hope Warren gets a job or position that enables him to come over, too. We are dying to see Margaret. I'm so glad you like her. She certainly does sound devoted and a fine girl for Warren. I do hope we get the chance to meet her!

Frieda seems so big to me, now I have the little baby. She is very heavy to lift. I find myself missing already all the little cute stages she has outgrown and looking forward to them in little Nicholas---I can't believe Nancy and Bob have grown up so fast. I remember Bob as a darling little dark-eyed baby in diapers.

Well, give my love to the family. Every time I write you, Ted starts remembering those wonderful barbecues in your back yard and the horse & buggy rides. Maybe someday we'll fill our own stable with a pony!

Lots of love to all,
Sylvia

TO *James Michie*

Wednesday 31 January 1962 TLS, Random House Group Archive & Library

Court Green
North Tawton
Devon.
January 31, 1962

Dear James,

I wonder if you'd be so good as to pass the enclosed letter on to your person in charge of permissions.

Meridian Books want to print my poem "Black Rook in Rainy Weather" (not in the Knopf edition) in an anthology and want to know if you control permissions rights and, if so, what is your fee and what credit should be used.

They sound in rather a hurry about this, and as I imagine Heinemann does control the permission rights to the poems in my book, I'm passing their letter on as they request.

All good wishes,
Sylvia

TO *Marion Freeman*

Wednesday 31 January 1962 ALS (aerogramme), Smith College

Court Green
North Tawton
Devonshire, England
January 31, 1962

Dear Aunt Marion,

Happy New Year to you! I hope this letter finds you well on the mend from pneumonia, which mother says got you into hospital. Do take care and don't do too much even though you feel lots better---I learned this when I had pneumonia while teaching at Smith.

By now you have probably heard about the birth of Nicholas Farrar Hughes on January 17th. I had him at home, delivered by a local midwife, and he's just a darling. I think it is wonderful that Ruthie manages 4. Right now, a new baby, and Frieda at the age where she can just reach another stage of shelves and tables, I feel to have my hands full. Do tell

Ruthie how I loved the pictures of her family---they are such handsome children, every one so bright and pretty. We did like the cute boy & girl pictures she sent---they will decorate the babies room.

I want to say thank you so much for the lovely engagement calendar---I so enjoy keeping my days recorded with pictures to remind me of America. I wish it were possible to fly back for visits with the speed of thought! You have no idea what a hit the Woman's Days made here! There simply are no magazines like this in England. They came just as Ted & I were puzzling how to make a cradle for Frieda's christmas present. On the off chance I opened to the How-To section, and sure enough, there was a pattern for a lovely wood cradle, which Ted proceeded to cut out. I got ideas from the wonderful colored section on quilting patterns & enameled the cradle with hearts and flowers.[1] So you are indirectly responsible for what we think, and Frieda thinks, is a very nice cradle!

I am so relieved mother is through her courses, and hope she finds time now for relaxing and visiting and knitting. We are dying to have her come over here this summer. I get really homesick for her---it must be so nice to be able to drop in on your children and grandchildren whenever you feel like it.

Ted joins me in sending best wishes for your health. Pass on my love to Ruthie.

Lots of love,
Sylvia

1–The design for the cradle and SP's template for decorating it and other furniture was from *Woman's Day* (November 1961): 39, 44, and 105. The cradle, along with a wooden chair, trestle table, and waste-paper basket, are held by Smith College.

TO *Olive Clifford Eaton*[1]

Thursday 1 February 1962 TLS (aerogramme), Indiana University

Court Green
North Tawton
Devonshire, England
Thursday: February 1st

Dear Mrs. Eaton,

Mother tells me you are responsible for making the absolutely beautiful blue blanket with the pink embroidery and the handsome potholders which we received in our wonderful Christmas package from America. I did want to tell you how much I am enjoying both of these things. Our new baby, a boy---Nicholas Farrar Hughes---was born on January 17th, at home, delivered by the local midwife, and is now sleeping cosily upstairs wrapped in the blue blanket. I'm so glad to have "something blue" for him. And the potholders came just as I was about to throw away an old pair of pot-holding gloves that were all worn out, so fitted in beautifully and cheered up my country kitchen.

Mother says the delicious carrot cake recipe I got from Aunt Dot came originally from your files, through grammy. I like the cake so much I make it as a Christmas cake, and gave the midwife one after she had delivered the baby.

The weather here is very grim and English---grey and rainy, none of the white American snow I love so much. But Ted has found our first snowdrops and primroses, so we look forward to spring not too far off, when our acre of daffodils and our 70 apple trees and several cherry trees will be in bloom---a lovely sight we have not yet seen, we are so new to the house.

I hope this letter finds you well. Ted joins me in sending best wishes and in admiring the lovely blanket and potholders.

A very happy New Year,
Sylvia Plath Hughes

1–Olive Clifford Eaton (1887–1981); a friend of the Schobers and the Plaths.

TO *Judith Jones*

Friday 2 February 1962 — TLS (aerogramme), University of Texas at Austin

Court Green
North Tawton
Devonshire, England
February 2, 1962

Mrs. Judith B. Jones
ALFRED A. KNOPF INC.
501 Madison Avenue
New York 22, New York
USA

Dear Mrs. Jones,

Thanks very much for your letter,[1] and for the proofs of THE COLOSSUS[2] which arrived today. There are just three minor corrections I have to make.

1. In "A Note About the Author" it should say that I taught at Smith <u>after</u> the Fulbright to Cambridge (not before).

2. In "A Winter Ship" (p. 44) the first line should read "At this wharf there are no grand landings to speak of." (instead of "no grand lands").

3. In "Man in Black" the two lines beginning "Snuff-colored sand cliffs . . ." should be lined up with the rest of the lines and not set to the left.

I thought the proofs looked very fine. Our daughter Frieda, by the way, was joined by our first son Nicholas two weeks ago. Now all is peaceful again, I am back at my novel.

With best wishes,
Sincerely,
Sylvia Plath

1–Judith B. Jones to SP, 11 January 1962; held by University of Texas at Austin.
2–The proofs are held by Smith College.

TO *Aurelia Schober Plath*

Wednesday 7 February 1962 TLS (aerogramme), Indiana University

February 7: Wednesday

Dear mother,

Thank you so much for sending the bras & briefs---you got just what I wanted, & I suppose it seems silly to ask for you to go downtown for me as it were, on another continent, but you have no idea how much it meant---I won't be able to shop for weeks yet, when the baby is on a more fixed schedule, and small things still loom very large. I get so impatient with myself, chafing to do a hundred things that have piled up, and barely managing one or two. Nicholas is very good during the night at last, waking like clockwork at 2 a.m. and 6 am with no crying in between. If he cries, it is in the afternoon or evening. Tell Warren to get a big house with a soundproof bedroom before he has a baby---I'm sure the night waking & crying would knock him out. I am lucky and have got in the rhythm of just dropping right back to sleep after I feed him, but I look very forward to when I can sleep 8 hours in a row. I don't know what I would do without Nancy---she is coming about two hours a week extra now to help with my mountains of ironing. I have fallen newly in love with my Bendix. Right now I am doing about 3 full loads a week, what with all the sheets, towels and an astounding assembly line of nappies from Nicholas. We use disposable ones for Frieda, otherwise things just wouldn't go round. It is heavenly to lie down upstairs and come down and find the kitchen floors washed, or to bake a cake and go upstairs and find all the rugs clean. Even so, I find my hands full. Did you have any household help when we were little? I seem to remember a succession of Annies and young women with red fingernails, I suppose when I am caught up on sleep everything will get done faster. I have a lot to catch up on, like clothes to be mended & cleaned & Frieda's woolens keep me doing a daily handwash. Perhaps at the end of the month I shall be back in my study again. Ted is still taking the brunt of Frieda---she needs watching every minute. Her favorite trick is peeling our poor wallpaper off the wall, there are so many cracks she can get her fingernails in, and then running and pointing & saying "Bah Poo" in outraged tones, as if somebody else has done it. She has, all since I was down & out with the baby, discovered how to throw things down the toilet, tear up minute bits of paper or cotton & sprinkle them over the red hall carpet, uproot bulbs from flower pots, draw on the walls with coal, and today discovered a cache of candy wellmeaning people had given me for her over a longish period, which I was saving to distribute among visiting children, and had half-sucked most of it & stuck it all over her and in her own little hiding places before Ted found her out. Now that the baby is getting toward a 4 rather than a 3 hour schedule I should be freer to keep an eye on her. I am still delighted with my forsight at getting all the quarterly assignments for my grant done & packaged ahead. I do hope to get back to writing soon, though. I am taking all those bottles of pills you sent, and wonder if it isn't the combination of them, especially the Vitamin C, which has kept me without a cold so far this winter (knock on wood). Oh, how I look forward to your visit! How I envy girls whose mothers can just drop in on them. I long to have a day or two on jaunts with just Ted---we can hardly see each other over the mountains of diapers & demands of babies. Nicholas is so cute---he weighed over 10 lbs. 2 oz.---had gained back his birthweight & more.

Ted's play was beautifully produced & he is so full of ideas for others. He is also reviewing animal books fairly regularly for the <u>New Statesman</u> & going on with his broadcasts for children which have been very enthusiastically received. I am so longing for spring. I miss the American snow, which at least makes a new clean exciting season out of winter, instead of this 6 months cooping-up of damp & rain & blackness we get here. Like the 6 months Persephone had to spend with Pluto. I get such pleasure hearing what lovely surprises your friends are planning with you. You deserve every bit of it & more, & it makes my spirit much lighter to think of you having outings instead of that deadly double-grind---that really depressed me. Do tell Dotty how much it means to me to keep in touch with her. She writes such nice newsy letters now. I do miss not having relatives to share my children with. Or my closest friends. You & Warren will just have to come over here often enough to keep me from getting too homesick, & get to know the babies as they grow up. Oh, the wonderful springerle pin & nut grinder (it <u>is</u> a nut grinder isnt it?) arrived today. I will try it out on a batch of springerle first thing. I find baking all my home recipes is very cheering---made Dotty's 6-egg sponge this week, banana bread & lemon cake pudding. My regret is that I've found nowhere in all England that sells refined molasses! Just crude black---and my favorite cookies & breads are made with molasses. By the way, could I ask you to slip a tube of cocoabutter into your next packet? Resolved to try England, we asked the chemist for cocoabutter. He said it didn't seem to come commercially, but he'd get some. The result: a packet of infinitesimal splinters. Ted & I melted it in the oven, & got a cake of the stuff, but with[1] a ghastly rancid smell. My first Ladies' Home Journal came & I read it from cover to cover. Have written Mrs. Eaton, Dotty, Mrs. Freeman, Margaret & Mrs. Prouty. Everybody over there is so good to us, & you the most. Do keep telling me all about the wedding plans. How I'd adore to come.

xxx
Sivvy

TO *Aurelia Schober Plath*

Tuesday 13 February 1962 TLS with envelope, Indiana University

Tuesday: February 13

Dear mother,

This letter has hung around so long I am just enclosing it[2] in this one or it will never get off. I don't know where the time has gone! I seem to need to sleep all the time, so drop back after feeding Nicholas at 6 and don't get up till after 9, then the day is a whirlwind of baths, laundry, meals feedings & bang it is time for bed. Both Ted & I seem to need twice as much sleep as normal people, and are unable to function efficiently if we have a bad night. I wish I liked black coffee---it might wake me up, but I am living on bowls of eggnog and hot milk and ovaltine for beverages.

Nicholas is absolutely darling. He seems so far advanced as a baby---I keep him on his stomach as I did Frieda, for she did pushups & developed her muscles early this way & I saw a 7 month baby who had lain on his back absolutely helpless when put on his stomach. Now Nicholas lifts his head and turns it from side to side when lying down. He has great very dark blue eyes which focus and follow your face or the light, unlike Frieda, whose eyes crossed alarmingly for a long time. He has a real little boy look, & his fuzz of brown babyhair looks like a crewcut. His eyebrows are strange---a quite black curved line over each eye, very handsome. I imagine he will have a rather dark handsome craggy face, although now he is soft as a peach. You'll enjoy seeing him still at a real baby stage when you come. I have washed both your pink sweater & Margaret's & they both came out beautifully. I don't know whether it is the wool or whether I am just a better washer. I did rub Frieda's at the

1 – 'the stuff, ~~with~~ but with' appears in the original.

2 – The previous aerogramme letter from SP to ASP, 7 February 1962, was not postmarked.

wrists & elbows a little---she gets so black even in a day, with food snacks & coal & all the muck of our farmy place it seemed impossible to get out the dirt just by squeezing. But now I squeeze.

The darling valentine for Frieda arrived---it seemed just made for her, and she has been carrying her handkerchief around in her pocket, she is especially delighted because there is an elephant on it. She is always running into me & lifting a finger & saying "O, baby cry" (without the r) or "Shh, beddie-bye". Of course the baby usually isn't crying at all. She is going through a very pretty amusing stage now---she will point to the patch she tore off her wallpaper & cluck her tongue and I say[1] "Who did that" and she shakes her head chidingly and says "Bah Poo" (bad girl), and I say "Who's the bad girl" & she points to herself and says "ME" and burst into uproarious laughter. She is such a sunshiney thing. I can't wait till she gets interested in reading. She looks at magazines & pictures a lot, picking out with great pride the mummies and daddies and bawpees and cars and shoes and spoons and things she can recognize. She is unerring---and knows the tiny bird on the New Yorker masthead is an "Ow".

I was fascinated to hear about Dick Norton's[2] starting a practise---how perfectly Dickensian! I would love to know details about David. Why does he find his parents difficult??? How is it Perry didn't save any money? O I love hearing all these bits of personal detail about the people I used to know. New people are never as interesting as the ones one grew up with. Local news in North Tawton---the rector is being moved down from his hill house to the empty lot directly opposite us---they are knocking down the wall across the way much to our sorrow & Ted is going to invest in a screen of trees. A man fell from his window in the town square last night (this Nancy told me in answer to my query if anything more blew down in the town in the high wind) & the wall was theatrically splashed with blood when I went to market---he was 80, & evidently suffered only head injury & shock. The bank manager & his wife dropped over this afternoon after half a week in London. Rose Key's old husband Percy is in hospital for a fortnight checkup---he has been losing weight & feeling depressed. I came on her in tears today & will have her for a hot dinner this week.

1–'and ~~say~~ I say' appears in the original.

2–Richard Allen Norton (1929–); B.A. 1951, Yale, resident of Jonathan Edwards College; M.D. 1957, Harvard University; dated SP, 1951–3. There are very few letters from SP to Norton as they were not retained. There are many letters from Norton to SP held by Lilly Library. Married Joanne Colburn (1932–) on 9 June 1956, at the Wellesley Hills Unitarian Church, Wellesley.

I hope it is not cancer or anything awful. She's awfully sweet, with 3 daughters in London. Took Nicholas for his first visit to the redoubtable Mrs. Hamilton, the midwifes aunt, a fine old woman.

We have gorgeous big double snowdrops in bloom, a scattering of primroses & countless daffodil sprouts. When the apple trees bloom I am just going to take Frieda & Nicholas & lie in the orchard all day![1]

Much love to all –
Sivvy

TO *Aurelia Schober Plath*

Saturday 24 February 1962 — TLS (aerogramme), Indiana University

Saturday: February 24

Dear mother,

The bitter cold of winter has descended upon us again, after a longish lull. Next fall I think we will invest in even two more little Pifco electric heaters---they are wonderfully satisfactory, and we really need one in each room: it's a bore to lug them from room to room, and I am getting expert in snapping them on half an hour or so before I want to use a room, so it is cosy. I keep one on in the baby's room all day, and we are sleeping there till the cold lets up as it is the warmest room in the house. We are looking so forward to spring. Snowdrops are blooming all over our place in shady nooks, and our first daffodil of all the multitudes of plants sprung up bloomed this week---we keep puffing out to look at it and admire it. Ted has planted several nut, plum, pear and peach trees he ordered this week, and yesterday Frieda and I went out for a brisk hour to pull up the dead annual shoots in the garden & I look so forward to sowing the brightly colored seed packets of seeds I've bought & seeing what comes up. I find being outdoors gardening an immense relaxation & hope we have some successes with our fruit, vegetables & flowers.

I am feeling in fine shape again---having made a much more rapid recovery than when I had Frieda. Partly because Nicholas is so little trouble. He only cries when he is hungry and loves being sat up and talked to---he smiled a few times at me this week and is so sweet, a little sweet-smelling peach. I feel I really <u>enjoy</u> him---none of the harrassment & worry of Frieda's colic and my inexperience. I love playing with him.

1–This paragraph typed in the margin of the first page of the letter.

I also am rested enough to find energy to play with Frieda in the 2nd half of the day, and concentrate my attention on her then. She is very squirmy & active, will hardly sit quiet a minute. We are teaching her to build blocks and she is getting more & more interested in picture books. Luckily when I am busiest with the baby---bathing & nursing him, Ted is downstairs with her, so her life is really very little changed, although she would cuff him if she could & gets fussy & babyish if Ted is away in the morning & she has to watch me tend to him. But this is perfectly natural. She is very radiant now---I dressed her in that very handsome openwork blue sweater you knit some time ago and her pale blue cord pants & she looked like a forget-me-not.

All the older people here seem ill---George Tyrer, the bank manager had a mild heart attack again this week, preventing him & his wife & daughter from coming to dinner with us,[1] and Percy Key had some part of his lung taken out at a Chest Hospital, for what his wife still doesn't know---TB or cancer, I wonder. It is amazing the way simple people accept medicine as a kind of miracle they never question. Ted's radio play was repeated[2] this week, very nice, as it doubles the money for it, making a total of about $730 for the 2 performances. A selection of his poems is being translated into Swedish[3] & published there, & 2 selections are coming out in various paperback anthologies here.

I am immensely grateful for the BBC Third Program & have sent for 2 booklets for 2 language courses that begin this week, one in German & one in French.[4] They have exercises & pronunciation & I find them excellent. Oh, I have thought of a lovely wedding present for Warren & Margaret if they would like it---how about the most beautiful blanket in the world? A Moderna Sorrento blanket. They come in exquisite single shades, or in double shades (rose & deep rose, or pale yellow & daffodil, or light green & deep green etc.) one color on each side, and are the lightest, warmest fluffiest handsomest things I've ever seen, guaranteed for 10 years, moth proofed etc. I got a pale rose/carnation one for our double bed & am mad about it (about $35 for this 100 x 100 inch one) and they are made, interestingly enough, in the town of Ted's birth---

1-According to SP's Letts Royal Office Diary Tablet for 1962, the Tyrers had been scheduled for dinner on Sunday, 25 February.

2-Ted Hughes, *The Wound*, BBC Third Programme (17 February 1962).

3-Ted Hughes, 'Kvinna Utan Medvetande' ['A Woman Unconscious'], 'Tankeräven' ['The Thought-Fox'], 'Wodwo' ['Wodwo'], *Rondo* 1: 4 (1961): 14–16.

4-According to SP's Letts Royal Office Diary Tablet for 1962, she began listening to 'Keep Up Your French' on 1 March and 'Keep Up Your German' on 5 March.

Mytholmroyd, Yorkshire. I'll get a list of colors, & if they would like one maybe they could pick a shade & tell me the best size, & whether 2 singles or a double. Do you think that is a good idea?

I hope they aren't piling extra duties on you in college in revenge. From now till April 1st is the most treacherous season, so take care. We have all 3 been in fine health (knock on wood) miraculously all winter, much due, I think, to those ascorbic acid Vitamin C pills you sent which I take every day, & to our bowl of orange juice every morning. We like our Court Green more & more & more. I am dying to get it all fixed up as we want. It will take years of course, especially the grounds. Do thank Aunt Marion for me for the check for the baby & the Woman's Days. And I'll write Dotty soon with Frieda's size. I am looking so forward to your coming. I have Nancy a 3rd morning a week now for 2 hours of ironing, so I am free of most drudgery except that of cooking & washing up & babytending, all of which I more or less enjoy – so we should be free to sit & the garden & play with the babies most of the time.

Love to all
xxx
Sivvy

TO *Aurelia Schober Plath*

Sunday 4 March 1962 — TLS (aerogramme), Indiana University

Sunday: March 4

Dear mother,

Honestly, you are a marvel of intuition! We have been having our worst cold spell yet here, and I was huddled over the fire with Ted, looking so blue he like Sir Walter Raleigh[1] took off the Jaeger sweater I gave him for Christmas and put it round my shoulders. Then the doorbell rang. It was the mailman with your latest package. I opened it, and there in the middle of the lovely babyclothes was The Jacket! Surely you never told me it was coming---it was a complete surprise. I put it on right away and gave Ted back his sweater. It is <u>ideal</u> for everything. First, it is beautifully warm, with that furry lining. Next, it is stylish, so I don't feel like an old bundle of oddly assorted knitting. I can wear it in the house and be both warm and neat looking. In spring and fall I can wear it outside as well. I just

1 – English gentleman, writer, and explorer Sir Walter Raleigh (1552–1618).

love the color and cut. It fits perfectly. It is the nicest thing you could have thought of to see me through the rest of the winter and years to come! I have just got fed up of winter. We are going to see about weatherstripping our outside doors which have rather large gaps around the edges letting in the cold air and wind, and also are investigating builders for putting in the cement foundation under our front two rooms, which can then have lino put down, and we will be sealed and cheered against the onslaught of next winter. We did have a lovely snow a few days ago---my first snow in England. For a few hours every twig was all thick with white and you couldn't see a thing beyond our land, but then the sun came out and by noon the whole vision had melted.

I received a lovely blue corduroy romper-and-jersey set from Aunt Elizabeth, whom I shall thank.[1] I loved the baby things for Nicholas you sent---they will be so nice when he is crawling in the sun on a blanket this summer. I am managing to get about two and a bit more hours in my study in the mornings and hope to make it four when I can face getting up at six, which I hope will be as soon as Nicholas stops waking for a night feeding. The day seems to just fly by after noon, though, and I am lucky if I get a fraction of the baking or letterwriting or reading or studying done that I want to. When the good weather comes it should be a lot easier. The winter is a grubby time with little children, indoor washing, and no snow to play in. In six more weeks the time will change, and we'll have the lovely long days again.

I so enjoyed hearing about Margaret's wedding dress. It sounds gorgeous. I do wish I could share in all the plans---it would be fun to be so close to a formal wedding. How nice that is what Warren wants, too. Let me know what you and they think about a blanket as a present and I'll get a list or sampling of colors in Exeter---I hope I'll be ready to go there in a week or two. Ted has found a good dentist, recommended by our midwife, and I'll start going as soon as Ted's finished his own series of sessions.

I have got sent some autobiographies and biographies from the New Statesman for review (where my review of children's books appeared) and am enjoying the book on Josephine,[2] Napoleon's wife, very much. I expect another batch of books this week, from which I'll choose some,

1–See SP to Elizabeth Schober, 23 March 1962.

2–Hubert Cole, *Josephine* (London: Heinemann, 1962); reviewed with Peter de Polnay, *A Queen of Spain* (London: Hollis & Carter, 1962) in Sylvia Plath, 'Pair of Queens', *New Statesman* (27 April 1962): 602–3. Joséphine de Beauharnais (1763–1814); first wife of Napoleon Bonaparte (1769–1821).

and will try to do a review so they'll ask me again. It's fun getting all the free books.

Frieda is getting better and better at imitating what we say, and talks to herself ceaselessly over her picture books in her own brand of prattle. "Oh boy-baby. Bear gone. Moo-cow" and so on. She says "snow" and pronounces the Ws" very carefully. She was very amused by the snow---we took her for little walks in her boots. Oh, a letter came from the London toy store saying you've given us 5 pounds credit (a thousand thanks), no toy catalogue though. Honestly, you must go slow, mother! You have been so generous with things for Frieda and Nicholas I am concerned about your budgeting!

I am hoping the next installments of my grant in May and August carry us over the first year's hump of major expense for furnishings and repairs; it couldn't have come at a better time. I am getting very excited about the possibilities of our garden, and hope we can conquer our nightly enemies, the snails. By the way, if you know anybody who has ever kept a couple of chickens for eggs, let us know hints about it. I know Dot & Joe keep theirs in battery. Well, we are thinking of simply getting half a dozen & letting them run around loose in an enclosure. I'd adore to have our own fresh eggs!

You would so enjoy Frieda now. She is a good walker and full of tricks to make us laugh. She is always stuffing things in her pockets, nails, nuts, keys, and has mastered the art of saying "Please" (without the l) and the possessive---"Mummy's poppy" (pocket), "Daddy's keys" and "Baby's bath". I am beginning work on something amusing which I hope turns into a book (novel), but may be just happy piddling. I find long things much easier on my nature than poems---not so intensely demanding or depressing if not brought off. Luckily the English will publish almost anything in the way of a novel, so I have hope. It's almost April! Take care.

Lots of love,
Sivvy

TO *Ruth Fainlight*

Sunday 4 March 1962 TLS, Ruth Fainlight

Court Green
North Tawton
Devon.
March 4, 1962

Dear Ruth,

I've been writing to you in my head for weeks but as a result of post-baby lethargy have been absolutely mum. We have a boy baby (his sex a great surprise to us both) named Nicholas Farrar Hughes, born on January 17th at 5 minutes to midnight. I am appalled to see how long ago that is, but my pregnancy cowishness seems to last for some time after I have got back to my pleasant old skimpy-stomached self. Nicholas was a very different experience from Frieda, who arrived bang-bang in under 5 hours with no dawdling. I confidently expected to be in danger of dropping Nicholas in the garden or something. But he took a whole day nagging, in which I sat on a stool & baked great amounts of stuff for us to live on for days afterwards. Then the pains got serious the minute Frieda was in bed & we called the midwife who brought her gas & air. This was great fun---we sat, Ted on one side of the bed, & the midwife, who is a very noble and fine woman, on the other, & I retired behind my mask at intervals & felt very sociable and delighted with the conversation all about the town, our house, its history, past tenants, etc. I was beginning to push, very pleased with my control, when the gas gave out & the baby stuck. There we were. What they call "nature's anesthesia" kept me from more than a dumb crossness at the delay, but the midwife (not given to alarm) said "I nearly thought we had an emergency" after it was over. The baby flew into the room in a wall of water, very blue, cross and male. I thought I must be torn to bits, but not a scratch. He weighed 9 pounds 11 ounces, compared to Frieda's ladylike 7 pounds 4 ounces---details which never interested me before my own immediate experience of them. His head had evidently stuck & he looked fearfully low-browed and tough until his skull-plates shaped up. Ted & I had been expecting a girl---thinking, I suppose, that Frieda would be less jealous of a girl, and both having got so fond of her we couldn't recapture our original desire for a son. It took us overnight to come round. Then a rather wicked 10 days of Ted cooking & minding Frieda & me coping with a succession of strange midwives (mine was on "holiday" tending a father of 80 with pneumonia) and nightly milk fevers with a temperature of over 103 which left me bang, in a sweat, just before the doctor arrived every morning & which nobody but myself believed. Great consternation at me taking my own temperature. All this passed as a dream. Now it seems preposterous & rather funny.

I am so eager to hear your news. Please be better than me & drop one little note about your baby---sex, name, date, poundage, oh you know. Or get Alan to do. We are both hoping you won't give up the idea of visiting us this spring . . . only 4 hours from Waterloo by carrycot. Do come. We are a baby-farm with every convenience. I am very happy with Court Green, my study, the babies, but mad for someone to talk to & woefully self-pitying about our just discovering you & Alan & then moving off. The women here are much worse than the men, who at least have their work. It's like a cattery. I never knew what "provincial" meant before. Ted joins in sending love. Please say you may come – Mayish?

Lots of love & good luck. Do write me – it's so good to get your letters.

Sylvia

TO *Aurelia Schober Plath*

Monday 12 March 1962 — TLS with envelope, Indiana University

Court Green
North Tawton
Devonshire, England
Monday, March 12

Dear mother,

It was so nice to get your letter saying Margaret & Warren would like a blanket. I'm going to Exeter to the dentist this week so I shall see about ordering the two-tone rose one and having it sent. I was so touched to think I shall pass on your lovely Bavarian china---that's the set with the dark-green background to the border, isn't it? One feels a girl is the one to appreciate the domestic things, for she is the one who uses them---I know I shall reserve my treasures for Frieda. I am getting very sentimental about family things. For instance, someday I hope to be well-off enough to send for grammy's desk. I'd like it to be Frieda's little desk. I have such happy memories of it, and could never find anything with such associations---it's close to priceless.

I look very forward to shopping around Exeter with you---I know very little about it, my visits were so soon curtailed. I think the idea of tweed skirts and matching sweaters a handsome one. I'm sure we'll find something. I hope Dotty's got my letter with Frieda's measurements & thanking her for the lovely package. I'm astounded at all the people you say are sending packages!! I look so forward to your visit this summer I can hardly sit still. It is a red-letter occasion for me because for the first time I shall be sharing my house. Which you were so instrumental in enabling us to find last summer, & to buy! I just adore the place. I picked our very first bouquet of daffodils yesterday & put them in a glass & brought them up to Ted's study with his tea.

I'm sure you'll find us very rough, still---although we are wonderfully civilized compared to when Warren was here. We have arranged to have the playroom & hall floors filled in with cement & bitumen & lino tiles put down---something I hope's got over with within a month, this being the last "big" immediate thing. The playroom (where I am typing) is a fun room. I look forward to filling it with handpainted furniture, chests for toys & the like---I want to paint them white, with a design of hearts & flowers, have an old piano and so on. A real rumpus room. Now it's just bare boards & deck chairs & a welter of Frieda's toys.

Frieda is christening the wonderful dungaree set you sent today---digging all morning in the garden with Ted. She is beautiful. She has just struck the most perfect stage, pink cheeks, clear blue eyes and her feathery brown hair. She is picking up words very fast now, and phrases---too cold, too hot, a bit hot, boobarb for rhubarb, open nut, daddy's screw, more tea, and so on. She's so funny. We're arranging to have the children baptized on Sunday afternoon, March 25th, by the way. Although I honestly dislike, or rather, scorn the rector. I told you about his ghastly H-bomb sermon, didn't I, where he said this was the happy prospect of the Second Coming & how lucky we Christians were compared to the stupid pacifists & humanists & "educated pagans" who feared being incinerated etc. etc. I've not been to church since. I felt it was a sin to support such insanity even by my presence. But I think I shall let the children go to Sunday School. Marcia Plumer sent me a copy of a wonderful sermon by her local Unitarian minister which made me weep, on fallout shelters. I'd really be a church-goer if I was back in Wellesley or America---the Unitarian church is my church. How I miss it!!! There is just no choice here. It's this church or nothing. If only there were no sermon, I could justify going to the ceremony with my own reservations. Oh well.

As I say, we are still rough---very creaky floors, leaky faucets, peeling paper & plaster & so on. But the house has a real, generous, warm soul to it. And responds so beautifully to any care we take. I so enjoy sitting here, watching the sun set behind the church. I think I will go just wild when our trees start blooming---there are fat buds on the lilac. I think the most exciting thing to me is owning flowers and trees!

Nicholas is immensely strong. He holds his head up for ages, like a Sphinx, looking round---the result of my keeping him on his stomach. I think his eyes may be hazel, like Ted's---they are a deep slateblue now. I love him so dearly. I think having babies is really the happiest experience of my life. I would just like to go on and on.

I'm enclosing a check for some poems in the March issue of Poetry Chicago[1] for deposit in our account. Wasn't Ted's Atlantic poem nice!

I am enjoying my slender foothold in my study in the morning again. It makes all the difference in my day. I still get tired by teatime, and have spells of impatience for not doing all I want in the way of study and reading. But my mornings are as peaceful as churchgoing---the red plush rug and all, and the feeling that nothing else but writing and thinking is done there, no sleeping, eating or mundane stuff.

I have the queerest feeling of having been reborn with Frieda---it's as if my real rich happy life only started just about then. I suppose it's a case of knowing what one wants. I never really knew before. I hope I shall always be a "young" mother, like you. I think working or having any sort of career keeps one young longer. I feel I'm just beginning at writing, too. Doing prose is much easier on me, the concentration spreads out over a large area & doesn't stand or fall on one day's work, like a poem.

Ted has just made another stand for integrity & privacy by refusing to do a TV program on the Poet in the Process of Composing a Poem from Start to Finish. Did I tell you he's being translated into Swedish? The Swedish language looks wonderful, with the craggy character of German & none of the pedantry. A drawing of Ted, from a photograph, was in the copy of the Swedish magazine that came. Frieda came running in with it, pointing to the drawing and saying "Daddy, Daddy". Then she pointed to the line that hung in midair at the back of his neck and said "Oh, broken."

I hope you are going on being very careful about driving in all that snow. There were pictures in our paper yesterday about the wreckage on Fire Island, New York.[2] Did you weather that storm all right?

1–Sylvia Plath, 'Stars Over the Dordogne', 'Widow', 'Face Lift', 'Heavy Women', and 'Love Letter', *Poetry* (March 1962): 346–51.
2–'After the storm . . .' *The Observer* (11 March 1961): 1.

Is there any chance of our getting any American corn seed with directions, do you think? Ted is starting to plant things & we are loaded with seed packets & fertilizer, and Slug Death.

Well, I must get supper for my family. Lots of love from us all,

Sivvy

TO *Paul & Clarissa Roche*

Monday 12 March 1962 TLS, Smith College

Court Green
North Tawton, Devon.
March 12, 1962

Dear Paul & Clarissa . . .

It was wonderful to hear from you. Perhaps (I hope for you) you are by now in Greece. The thought of going alone (or going anywhere alone) must be heaven. What sort of a friend do you have who would look after three children??? I wish we could find one like that. But my own ties to the babies, nursing and so on, are so strong, I don't think I could stop---we dream of a few months in a place like Corsica, but would have to take babies with, which puts dreams off.

Isn't there any chance of you two coming down overnight or something? I am particularly desperate that Clarissa does not disappear back to America without my seeing her!! We do have an extra double bed & would so love to see you. Our house is 1 mile from the North Tawton station, which is an easy 4 hours by direct express from Waterloo. How about a flying visit??? We are so stuck, with this new infant, and very broke with piles of necessary house repairs, plus investment in what Ted hopes will be a sort of lucrative garden, but hopeful as I am, I am oppressed by the large nocturnal armies of invisible slugs which devour everything local. We are armed with lethal pellets of SLUGIT and SLUGDEATH. Wish us success.

The all-to-brief heaven of our moving in last fall to halcyon weather and our own (very small) apple harvest was neutralized by this awful winter. I thought I was bearing up fine, ho-hoing when the midwife told me that a temperature of 38 was really too chill for a new baby and so on in the bedroom. We all lasted the winter with no colds or illness, then I was diagnosed in the last week to have Chilblains. I had though I'd merely been victim to a horde of migrant fleas or floating stinging nettle pollen, but the word Chilblains undid me. It suggested that all the time I was thinking myself nobly above the cold, the cold was meanly nipping my ankles & leering. I got very grim. Especially as our electric bill rocketed to almost 25 pounds for 3 months and I was still cold. But then a day of sheer sun last week had me & the babies out in the garden, me weeding our antique cobbles with love & pruning roses, and if only the weather would relent, I would be ecstatic, bucolic and so on. Our acre of daffodils is brightly beginning to show. The sparrows hold on our thatch with their communal spirit. Do come and say hello to us. At least write. I am nearly done with a quite grossly amateur novel the small grant for which is enabling us to live with less desperation than usual this year, and to do repairs we could never manage on our uncertain dribbles from poems, reviews etc.

How lovely it would be to see you! Do give us hopes. Ted joins in sending love,

Sylvia

TO *Elizabeth Schober*

Friday 23 March 1962 — TLS (aerogramme), Indiana University

Court Green
North Tawton
Devonshire, England
March 23, 1962

Dear Aunt Elizabeth,

I have been meaning to write for ages to thank you for the darling blue corduroy baby suit you sent for Nicholas, but ever since the baby's arrival in January I have done hardly anything, it seems, but take care of the children. It has been very, very cold here, and our primitive heating by electric fires a bit too primitive to keep all the cold out, but miraculously the babies seem to thrive anyway, and have had no colds all winter, nor have we.

Ted is busy planning a large vegetable garden, and I took advantage of the first warm sunny day in about half a year last week to put the babies out and weed our antique cobbles in the front and prune some rose bushes. We have a lot of work ahead of us, with our 2½ acres, but I adore gardening (although I am just a raw beginner) and it is so easy to work at it with the babies nearby.

Frieda has turned into a wonderfully pretty little girl, amazing both Ted & me---we hardly feel to deserve her. She is very lively and excitable, with big blue eyes. Nicholas is quite different. Even at 2 months, he seems much more peaceful, quiet and dark. It is hard to tell what color his eyes will be---they are a dark slate-blue now. Ted thinks they will be hazel, like his. That would be very nice.

We have a lot of dreams about fixing the place up---getting the old tennis court into shape, growing luxury items like asparagus, strawberries & mushrooms, plus all sorts of flowers, but just now I will be delighted if we manage to produce a few onions!

You are an angel to think so generously of us. You have such exquisite taste. I am looking forward someday to another baby girl who will inherit the lovely blue party dress you sent Frieda when she was little. This blue cord suit will be perfect for Nicholas---blue is really our family color!

Lots of love,
Sylvia

TO *Marvin Kane*

Friday 23 March 1962 TLS, Indiana University

Court Green
North Tawton
Devon.
March 23, 1962

Dear Marvin,

Many thanks for your good letter. We are really rooting ourselves in Devon, having bought an ancient thatched farmhouse complete with cobbled courtyard, thatched barn & cottage, stables & 2½ acres including 70 apple trees & millions of daffodils. Both of us are rather stunned---we did it, or rather, discovered the place, in one fell swoop last summer, goaded to it by the prospects of a second infant, now two months old, and the morbid leakage of rent. We were, without quite knowing it, very lucky ---this "ugly ancient decayed market town" (as the guidebooks have it) has all the practical things which I as a loyal American housewife demand ---butchers, grocers, banks, & a good chemists & fine midwife. People are surprisingly friendly & the country peace is very good for writing.

Both of us, out of the blue, have become very excited about the possibilities of our land---and Ted is laying out an ambitious vegetable garden. Eventually I hope to try my hand at raising the bits of Americana I most miss---Country Gentlemen corn, Kentucky wonder beans, pumpkins---the lot. As we are plagued by large, insatiable & invisible nocturnal slugs, we may not have all the luck we need. But we are armed with pellets of SLUGDEATH and SLUGIT. Wish us success!

The program[1] sounds an exciting one. I hope it is destined to be broadcast in England & not just on the overseas services, so we can hear it. I'd love to be on it. The only problem, as you can guess, is that I never get up to London, with this baby, even for a day (I miss London a lot more than Ted does!) Is there any possibility of the BBC (or somebody) loaning you a tape recorder? In any case, we'd very much enjoy seeing both you & your wife Kathy[2] down here. It is right on the way to Cornwall, hardly a detour at all. If you let us know the day, let's plan on you having lunch or supper with us.

North Tawton is between Exeter & Okehampton, just to the north of the A30, & about 7 miles before Okehampton. Our phone number, by the way, is NORTH TAWTON 370. If the operators claim there is no North Tawton just tell them to connect up through Okehampton, which is big enough to be known, & which knows of our existence.

Do let us know if you can stop by. The weather should be gentler & our place showing a few signs of the idyll we hope it will 10 years hence be! And try to wangle a tape-recorder. Won't the BBC consider you as a traveling correspondent?

All good wishes,
Sylvia

TO *Aurelia Schober Plath*

Tuesday 27 March 1962

TLS with envelope,
Indiana University

Court Green
North Tawton
Devon.
Tuesday: March 27, 1962

Dearest mother,

So nice to get your happy springy letter! I have been suffering from the March megrims---we seem to have had nothing but a horrid raw damp

1–Marvin Kane, 'What Made You Stay?', *A World of Sound*, BBC Home Service (7 September 1962); a series about Americans who decided to live in Britain; Kane interviewed SP on 10 April and 20 August 1962.

2–Kathleen Mary (Kindley) Kane (1928–97); married in London in 1952; the Kanes lived at 9 Holland Park, London W.11.

east wind (which blows around our antique back door & straight through the house) for the last month. March is the worst month when it is mean, it seems one has used up all one's resistance to winter, & is left vulnerable. Just when I was most dismal we had one glorious sunny day when I had the babies out & and ate out & gardened from sunrise till sunset. We all got little sunburns & felt wonderful. Then the cold & grey closed in again. I am becoming a devout gardener---knowing nothing about it. It is so soothing & kindly to work in the earth, pruning, digging, cutting grass. Ted is doing wonders with the back which will be our vegetable garden, digging & fertilizing it. I hope we have some luck, though I expect this year we'll be mostly learning. Do make Frieda a "corn-bag". We eventually hope to get our little greenhouse working, too. I have so many ideas for flowers: I love the outdoor exercise. Frieda has a little imitation lawnmower with a bell & she follows me around with mine, which she calls "Mummy's Oodle-Ooo", after noise it makes. She says "daffdee" for our daffodils, which are coming out in their heavenly startling way, like stars. I am going to be practical and sell bunches of a dozen a week via the local greengrocers who have offered to buy any of our surplus flowers and vegetables. Eventually we'd like the garden to pay for itself.

I think your chance to buy Margaret's Syward's car shouldn't be missed: when you want & need to buy a new car again, you'll be uneasy if you don't have one you can rely on, & this is that sort. So I am refunding with great thanks your loan which helped us get the house so you can get the car for your birthday. I am so glad we are in a position to do this. I love the idea of not being indebted in any way. That seems a marvelous thing to me at our age! I'm enclosing a letter to the bank so they can make you out a check from our account. Now you won't need to think of cashing in any securities. Please do buy the car right away.

I am sitting in our "red room", the babies in bed, and Ted in London for the day doing a BBC broadcast[1] on his children's poems; I'm enjoying some Haydn[2] piano sonatas over the BBC --- you can almost listen to good music continually on one or the other of the two good stations. I long for a 2nd hand piano! That is the next thing we'll save for, after the playroom floors are done: the man should do them (or start to) any

1–Probably Ted Hughes, 'Meet My Folks!' *Listening and Writing* BBC Home Service (Schools), 30 March 1962. TH also met Anthony Thwaite and Eric Walter White for lunch to discuss the Poetry Book Society Summer Choice selection. See correspondence held by Victoria and Albert Museum Archives.

2–Austrian composer Joseph Haydn (1732–1809). The Haydn sonatas were broadcast on the Third Programme at 8 p.m.

day now. It will be an upheaval for about 10 days, but very much worth it! I am so grateful for my Saxton grant---modest as it is, it has enabled us to buy rugs & make the most needed alterations in the house. I have a great yearning to practise piano again---when we get the piano I'll ask for some of my old music! I have such a nice children's songbook from my reviewing I long to play the songs to Frieda.

My poems should be in the March issue of Poetry. I got the dearest handsomest little cocoa or rather café-au-lait colored corduroy suit for Nicholas from the Aldriches & the sweetest long letter from Do Cruickshank saying a parcel was on the way---shall write them both soon.

The christening Sunday went very well. I had said I wanted it in midafternoon when the rector had some other babies saved up. Originally Margery Tyrer was going with us, but she came down with bad bronchitis, so I asked Rose Key instead. Margery had loaned me the sweetest christening dress which her 15-year-old daughter Nicola was christened & which is made of Limerick lace from her grandmother's wedding-gown. Of course you could hardly see this under all the sweaters & blankets & bonnet I swaddled Nicholas in against the cold, but I liked the idea of it. Frieda looked a doll in the little blue French coat & white & blue embroidered pinafore we got to match it last summer. She carried her minute "dodie", a little plastic dog Ted got her, which I am sure made her behave. Both children were angelic, & someone else's baby, bless it, squalled through the service. So they are christened.

The Exeter dentist[1] seems very good---the nicest thing I can say is that he reminds me of Dr. Gulbrandsen. I get free care for a year on the National Health after a baby; Ted's course of treatment---several weekly appointments, was only the token pound ($2.80), so I have at last got a good dentist without having to pay steep private prices. He is very attractive & genial with two children under 10, so I hope he lives a long time & stays in the district! He has very good ideas about children---I felt him out about this, & he said to bring Frieda along when I come next time for a few rides in the chair so she'll get used to him & the office before she ever needs any work done. And he also seems to believe in saving, not pulling, teeth & regular half-year checkups, so I am very relieved with him.

I ordered the two-tone rose blanket at the store in Exeter---they have to order it from the Yorkshire factory because it is a specially large size, so

1–Probably D. A. Reaney, 8 Elm Grove Road, Exeter, whose name and address appear in SP's address book.

they'll let me know when it's sent off to Margaret. I do hope they like it! I want to know when it arrives safely!

I think that when the good weather comes I shan't set foot in the house! I really haven't had a proper summer since I've been in England; in London summer doesn't count. After I've soaked up six months outdoors I may be more eager to spend the winter six writing & studying & turning pale. I am thinking of learning to ride horseback at one of the local riding schools about here---I anticipate Frieda & Nicholas learning to ride, or wanting to, and would like to be practically grounded myself. But this is as yet a notion. I mean straight riding---no jumping or hopping or skipping. Life begins at 30!

Keep me posted on all the wedding plans. Is there any chance of Warren & Maggie ever getting over here???

Lots of love to all,
Sivvy

PS: Do you have grammy's recipe for bread? Does it kill yeast to mix it with a too-hot liquid? I've been trying to make my own bread, but for some reason it won't rise---I use dried yeast & think I may have scalded it. The loaves are flat & dark & primitive but taste good & Ted loves them. However, I'd like to make a proper loaf!

xxx
s.

TO *Ruth Tiffany Barnhouse Beuscher*

Tuesday 27 March 1962 — TLS (aerogramme), Smith College

Court Green, North Tawton
Devonshire, England
March 27, 1962

Dear Dr. Beuscher,

It was wonderful to get your letter. I've thought of you so often & am so glad you are still there to talk to! We, too, have moved since I last wrote, & bought a house.[1] I am still overwhelmed & very proud---it is not only big, it is huge, rooms we haven't even used yet, plus two studies, a dusky attic one up a flight of stairs all to itself for Ted under the thatch

1 – According to SP's address book, Dr Beuscher moved from 776 Webster Street, Needham, Mass. to 15 Agawam Road, Waban, Mass.

(we have a thatch) & a big light sunny one on the 2nd floor for me with a lush red carpet & six foot elm plank table Ted sanded to velvet for me. Our finding Court Green was a fantastic stroke of luck. We almost went mad, or were mad, last summer when mother came over---in our narrow 2 rooms 2 steep flights up in London, with Frieda having learned to walk & bouncing from wall to wall & another baby due & rent flowing out morbidly with no returns. So we left mother with Frieda & took a weekend off to drive to Devon (Ted's always wanted to live there; I'd never seen it) to find a house. In two days. We had a list we'd weeded out & our first night was hysterical---funny, but unhopeful. The places were something out of Charles Adams---a dying Great Dane met us at one door (the houses of our size are invariably ancient decayed rectories) & there were no lights, except via an engine loud as souls in Hades, the "ornamental lily pond" a sort of baby-trap sump & one of the "two capacious garages" was a pile of rotted boards. At the other house, hung on a cliff over the sea with nothing to do but fall off the porch into it, a desperate woman kept pouring us more & more tea & telling us what a fearsome place it was (but very nice when sunny); one place, uninhabited, had so many palpable spooks (the "oak paneling" in the diningroom peeled off like paper) Ted & I banged into each other in a panic to get out. The modern places (1930ish) were worst, mean, cramped, hideous British-respectable. Then we found Court Green. We had laughed about it, because it had a thatch (something we resolved never to touch) & was owned by a Sir, but it knocked us over. Very cheap, too, compared to the rest of the awful lot, because no-one wanted it---too big for a retired couple, too far from Exeter, the nearest main city, for commuting. It is white, with a storybook peaked thatch riddled with birds, an ancient cobbled courtyard surrounded on 3 sides by a thatched cottage, thatched barn (our garage) stables etc, with 2½ acres, one of solid daffodils just now leaping to life, 70 apple trees, a large vegetable garden which we hope eventually to make pay for itself, laburnum, lilacs, cherry trees, all of which we've not seen in bloom & are dying for. We had them treat the place for woodworm (which it had) before buying it, with the aid of loans from both our parents. It even has an overgrown tennis court I hope to be rich enough to reclaim when the children are old enough. I have never felt the power of <u>land</u> before. I love owning bulbs & trees & all the happiness of my 17th summer on a farm[1] comes back when I dig & prune & potter, very amateur. The town (we are in the middle of it, though when leaves

1–Lookout Farm, South Natick, Mass. SP worked there in the summer of 1950.

are out it can't be seen---our house is the Manor!) is described as an "ugly decayed market town" but it looks beautiful to me: a good young doctor, a fine midwife, chemist, banks, butchers & all sorts of odd colonials & kind, open locals whose Devon accent sounds indistinguishable to me from American. The winter has been grim---we heat by coal, & mushroom shaped electric fires in every room, & I got what I thought was a Dickensian disease---chilblains. Sir Robert was born here, his ancestors all rectors (he is a Made Sir, Governor (ex) of the Bahamas, I think). We love it. 4 hours from London by express, so we later hope to makes stays there. Nicholas Farrar Hughes was born January 17th, at home, a day-long labor, with the midwife coming in the evening to hold my hand on one side & Ted on the other, all 3 of us gossiping happily about the town, previous tenants of our house, etc. I had lost the baby that was supposed to be born on Ted's birthday this summer[1] at 4 months, which would have been more traumatic than it was if I hadn't had Frieda to console & reassure me. No apparent reason to miscarry, but I had my appendix out 3 weeks after, so tend to relate the two. Nicholas is very different from Frieda---who is lively, hectic, & a comic. He is dark, quiet, smily & very much a Hughes. I love him & nursing him & have never got such fun out of anything as my babies. We have names for at least 2 more. I have a very nice ruddy Devon woman in 3 mornings a week (she's cared for the house 11 years) to do all the work I hate---ironing, floor-scrubbing. She likes it & costs about 35¢ an hour. So I can spend my time doing what I like best---gardening, cooking (I am trying to do my own bread, but it won't rise & is like a primitive black loaf, but Ted loves it) & playing with the babies. I write in my study mornings, which is all I need to make me feel professional & creative. I have actually done my first novel (after 10 years of wishful thinking): wrote it in under 2 months & it will come out here next year under a pseudonym, because I want to feel free to play around before I do something I really think seriously competent. Could I dedicate it to R. B.?[2] It is a serio-comic (if that's possible) book about my New York summer at <u>Mademoiselle</u> & breakdown, fictionalized, but not so much that doing it & coming back to life is due so much to you that you are the only person I could dedicate it to. It is an immense relief to me

1–SP meant the previous summer. See SP to ASP, 6 February 1961.

2–In a letter to SP of 17 September, Dr Beuscher writes 'I would love to have the dedication to RB. I have often thought, if I "cure" no one else in my whole career, you are enough.' Letter held by Smith College.

to feel I can write you every so often; it heartens me no end to feel you are there, whether I talk to you or not.

Very much love,
Sylvia

TO *Ann Davidow-Goodman & Leo Goodman*

Wednesday 28 March 1962 TLS, Smith College

Court Green
North Tawton
Devonshire, England
March 28, 1962

Dear Ann & Leo,

The lovely big card & costumed children arrived to our present & Frieda's future delight. Here is my favorite-yet picture[1] of your goddaughter (I don't think I've sent you a color one of her have I?) She is sitting in the only upholstered chair in our house---an auction triumph we got for 75¢. The nightgown is one of my primitive sewing efforts. See, her eyes are still blue. The villagers can't seem to get over them.

We have been enduring the winter. Bit by bit making room by room habitable. With coal, wood & electric fires: still a freezing temperature in the drafty halls. Horrible weather: grey tombstone skies, sleet, a mean wind set perpetually in the east. Every nice day or sunny hour we rush for hoes, spades, pruning shears & attack the garden, Ted preparing the large vegetable beds at the back & me among the roses at the front. We are very excited, gardening being such a miraculous and pacifiying pastime. Hope eventually to have all our own vegetable needs & a surplus for the local greengrocer. We dream of a few laying hens, hives, mushrooms. But if we bring a vegetable edible to the pot through the barrage of bugs the books say await each green sprout, I shall be utterly satisfied. I am to the end of my patience with the weather. The doctor's diagnosing what I thought were stinging nettle bites as Chilblains almost demoralized me. I thought I'd been vanquishing our 38° interior temperature with noble spirit, then to learn the cold had been so secretly and nastily getting at me---well!

Nicholas Farrar Hughes arrived on January 17th. I had him at home with our admirable local midwife who breeds Pekinese puppies in her spare time. A fine lady. She sat on one side of the bed & Ted on the other,

1–The photograph is no longer with the letter.

all 3 of us gossiping about the locals, with the cold dark night outside. Very cosy & nice. Nicholas is a true Hughes---craggy, dark, quiet & smiley, unlike the lively & almost hysterically active Frieda. I am emerging slowly from the inarticulate cow-state I go into before & after each baby & getting morning hours in my study again, slowly flexing my fingers and telling myself life begins at 30.

You sound very happy & wise to be back in Chicago. The bits you wrote about sit-ins[1] was fascinating & surprising, Ann. I'd always though the U. of Chicago was the most progressive of places racially. Has anything else happened? Do you really have a shelter craze over there---it sounds very grim in the papers: reverends saying it's ethical to shoot your neighbors at the shelter door & so on. Say it's not so grim.

When are you going to take another European holiday, or sabbatical??? We'd so love to see you over here. Only 4 hours from express by Waterloo we are---so you see it's easy. But I imagine Leo would prefer to cruise up in his own Daimler. Ted joins me in sending much, much love and telling you to come visit us soon.

Keep writing!

Love,
Sylvia

TO *Marion Freeman*

Wednesday 28 March 1962 — ALS (aerogramme), Smith College

Court Green
North Tawton
Devonshire, England
March 28, 1962

Dear Aunt Marion,

I don't think I ever wrote to thank you for the lovely card and baby gift you sent---I have been mum as a cow these last two months & hardly written a word. We have been having terribly, typically English weather: dark, cold and wet. Both of us seize every nice day or hour to work out in the garden. We are very amateur, but very enthusiastic, and hope eventually to supply all our own vegetables plus a surplus for the local green grocer. But this first summer I expect we will be mostly learning

1–In early 1962, the University of Chicago experienced sit-ins by the Congress of Racial Equality (CORE) to oppose segregated off-campus residential areas.

from our mistakes. They say it is the coldest March since 1909 and I believe it!

The children are so much fun. Frieda is putting together little sentences and can say "daff-dee" for daffodil, and our daffodils are about the only sign of spring. We have an acre of them & I can see the early ones now, blowing & yellow as stars in the grey rain. Very cheering.

Nicholas is a very good baby, only crying when he is hungry, & smiley and patient. Frieda is at a really pretty stage and a good companion when I am baking or gardening, playing happily & imitating everything I do.

I hope you have got well over the pneumonia mother said you had---I learned from my own experience with it that the drugs make you feel so fine you want to be to work in a minute, when you really need to take it easy for a bit longer. I feel if the spring just sets in, and I can get the babies out in the sun, everything will be wonderful. Ted just came back from a day in London last night to do some children's broadcasts for the BBC educational radio programs. They like his work, & it gets to a lot more children than regular teaching plus being no strain: no discipline or any such problems.

We are looking very forward to seeing mother over here this summer. It should be a real vacation for her this time, just sitting in the garden & playing with the two babies. I have a local woman in to clean 3 mornings a week, or I don't know how I'd cope with our big house, grounds, two babies & my work & Ted's secretarial work. Life is very busy & lots of fun. I so enjoy the Woman's Days. They make me quite homesick, with all the lovely American recipes & how-to-do things!

Pass on my love to Ruthie & her brood.

Lots of love,
Sivvy

TO *Helga Huws*

Thursday 29 March 1962[1]

TLS with envelope,
Helga and Daniel Huws

Dear Helga,

The green sheet is me. Somehow these bilious colored lettersheets of Ted's multiply rather than diminish. I have mentally written you half a dozen letters since Christmas, but am only just now surfacing from the

1–Date supplied from postmark.

cowlike stupor I seem to enjoy immediately before and after a baby. I am delighted with our Nicholas; Ted is cooler. I think he secretly desires a harem of adoring daughters. Nicholas is very much a Hughes: oddly like photographs of Ted's brother Gerald, dark, quiet, smily. Our house is so big now that he doesn't live with us, or on us, as Frieda did in London, so he perhaps seems thereby more of a stranger & relatively no trouble. Frieda would tear him to bits if she could get her hands on him; she'll say "ear" and try to pull it off like an anatomy student. I had a lot longer & harder labor with Nicholas---he took all day & just emerged five minutes before midnight. Luckily I had said I wanted gas & air, so was very sociable & chatted with Ted & the midwife with none of the blind mindless gripes, but the gas & air ran out just as the baby stuck when the pushing part began. My old luck. His head stuck & the midwife afterwards said she thought it would be an emergency, but I was too dumb to worry. The doctor was called, but minutes before he came, Nicholas flew into the room in a wall of water which soaked everyone present, blue, frowning, with a low dark brow. Ted & I were stunned at his being a boy: it took us twenty-four hours to adjust. Luckily his low brow was only a temporary phenomenon, a result of his fight to get out, & the skullplates shaped up very nicely overnight. He is angelic, no colic, no tantrums, as with Frieda. 9 pounds 11 ounces at birth. Or have I told you? I am so blank I'm not sure if I've written about him really, or just in my head.

We love the song books. We are waiting any day for a builder to rip up our damp wood floors, lay a cement & bitumen foundation & lino tiles in the playroom & hall, so there will be a washable rugless passage from front to back of the downstairs, childproof. Then I shall agitate for a second hand piano. The song book has all my own childhood favorites & I long to play to Frieda.

I wish we could see you. This winter is very grim. I feel cheated of all my summers since we came to England---London summers don't, somehow, count. And now we are chafing at rain & sleet & a fixed east wind which slices malevolently all round our ancient back door straight back through the house. I got very morbid when the doctor told me I had CHILBLAINS. Have you ever had them? I thought they were a Dickensian disease & had been so proud I was stoic against the cold, that I was utterly demoralized not so much by the stingy itchy sores themselves but by the idea the cold had secretly got at me when I thought I was winning out. When will you have your kitchen & bathroom wing built on? It sounds marvelous. I think we will become devout gardeners if we can ever bring a vegetable or flower through all the plagues and blights the books say awaits them.

Then we think of hens, hives, mushrooms. In the one or two nice days I've been happily scratching myself up in ignorant pruning of rosebushes & brambles. No leaf in sight. Only daffodils, startling & foolhardy in this graveyard weather.

No real friends here, only nice neighbors, a pleasantly gossipy if catty Irish banker's wife; we must look awfully queer to the locals. Do write. About you, the children, anything.

Love,
Sylvia

TO *R. B. Silvers*[1]

Sunday 1 April 1962

TLS (aerogramme),
Library of Congress

Court Green
North Tawton
Devonshire, England
April 1, 1962

Mr. R. B. Silvers, Editor
HARPER'S MAGAZINE
49 East 33rd Street
New York 16, New York
USA

Dear Mr. Silvers,

Thanks very much for your letter.[2] I'm happy to hear you like Leaving Early and Private Ground.[3] I am having a first book of poems come out in America this spring, but these poems are both too recent to be in it, and probably won't get between hard covers for years.

With all good wishes,
Yours sincerely,
Sylvia Plath

1–Editor and co-founder or the *New York Review of Books* Robert B. Silvers (1929–2017).

2–R. B. Silvers to SP, 27 March 1962; held by Library of Congress. Silvers rejected 'The Babysitters', 'Wuthering Heights', 'Magi', 'A Life', 'Candles', and 'Small Hours' ['Barren Woman'].

3–Sylvia Plath, 'Private Ground', *Harper's* (August 1962): 55; Sylvia Plath, 'Leaving Early', *Harper's* (December 1962): 82.

TO *George MacBeth*

Wednesday 4 April 1962 TLS, BBC Written Archives Centre

Court Green
North Tawton
Devon.
April 4, 1962

Dear George,

I am sending along this batch of recent, unpublished poems[1] for your perusal.

Did you see the excerpt from the report of the police commissioner in a recent Time magazine?[2] I particularly enjoy "Afterlife". "Mother Superior" and "Ash"[3] make my hair stand on end: I think they are fine.

All good wishes from Ted and myself. We are very grim in this blustery lead extension of March & up to our ears in unset onion sets & unseeded seed potatoes.

Sincerely,
Sylvia Plath

George MacBeth, Esq.
Talks Department
THE BBC
Broadcasting House
London W.1

TO *Marvin Kane*

Saturday 7 April 1962 TLS, Indiana University

Court Green
North Tawton
Devon.
April 7, 1962

Dear Marvin,

It was so good to have your letter and hear you are coming down this week. I have duly booked you a double room for Tuesday night at our

1–According to SP's submissions list, she sent 'Blackberrying', 'The Surgeon at 2 a.m.', 'Mirror', 'The Moon and the Yew Tree', 'The Babysitters', 'Little Fugue', 'An Appearance', and 'Crossing the Water'.
2–MacBeth's poem 'Report to The Director' quoted in *Time* 79 (9 March 1962): 92–5.
3–Poems by George MacBeth.

local North Tawton manor, the Burton Hall Arms, about 5 minutes from us. It manages to squeak in the AA[1] book so shouldn't be too fearsome.

I shall meet you at the station Tuesday at 2:49. Look for somebody covered with straw and red mud. The weather has been so horrid I only hope something better turns up by the time you do. Gale winds have carried off our lettuces & large spiders are appearing everywhere, most frequently in my coffee cup, before breakfast.

We are looking so forward to seeing you!

Till Tuesday, then
Sylvia

TO *Aurelia Schober Plath*

Sunday 8 April 1962 TLS (aerogramme), Indiana University

Sunday: April 8

Dear mother,

Honestly, the reason I have been so slow in writing is that I have said to myself: I will write tomorrow, then it is sure to be a sunny day & how cheerful I will be. Believe it or not, we havent seen the sun for three weeks. I realize now I must have geared myself to last till April 1st, when I thought spring must by the law of averages appear. Well, it has just gone on with black days, rain, howling gusts from the north and east without relief. I've only had the children out one day, three weeks ago. I am simply fed up with winter. At least it is supposed to have been the coldest March in over 70 years. We are also having our floors done---all last week & all this next, workmen are hacking about. They have cemented the playroom & this week will cement the floors in the downstairs hall. I just learned that it will take two weeks for the cement to dry properly before the lino can be put down. So by your birthday, I expect things will be settled. I have been painting odd bits of grubby wood furniture---a table, a chair---white, with designs, very primitive, of hearts & flowers, which cheers me up & should look gay in the playroom.

We have been heartened immensely by all the marvelous packages which arrived this past week from you & Dot. It is better than Christmas. I don't know how you do it!! I am resplendent in my new blue sweater & black jerkin (which will be marvelous in spring over all my smashing

1–Automobile Association, founded in 1905.

blouses), and Frieda hasn't taken off the little red knitted hat bandeau since she got it. She has been riding her Gee-gee rocker, which I got her for her birthday from you & she loves it. She is just big enough to manage it, so it will last her for ages. We have had a pleasant birthday with her ---last Sunday. Taught her to say "Birt-dee" & "Me two". She blew out her candles & was delighted by colored soapbubbles we blew. We gave her a set of wooden American alphabet blocks. She got piles of cards & carried them all about. Loved the little cow-jumped-over-the-moon card. Honestly, how did you find time to do all that knitting! I think F's dark blue sweater with the silver buttons is the nicest style yet on her; I love the collar. And the slippers! One small suggestion---I wouldn't send toothpaste with clothes, the tube always squashes; luckily it congeals & doesn't get over anything, but it's a bit of a risk.

The store in Exeter informed me they have sent off the rose blanket to Margaret's address in New York. Do let me know when it arrives and if it is in perfect condition---I've had it insured. Hope they like it. I am so sorry to miss their wedding. Imagine, Ted has the chance to go to anywhere in the world for 10 days at the expense of the Alitalia jet lines. It sounds very queer, but one of their public relations men is a poet & offered the trip to Eliot & Auden who I think declined & Ted was next on the list. We have a great aversion to flying separately, if at all, & I think Ted is so involved in his garden that he won't go after all. I know where I would go---straight to Egypt & sun all week under a pyramid.

We have been very grieved by the news that George Tyrer, the bank manager, was retired after his last heart attack. They move to the outskirts of London in 5 weeks. I feel very sorry for myself, as Marjorie has been my best & only friend here so far & I liked her pretty 16 year old daughter Nicola who was at school in Oxford. They have sold us some beautiful things which just complete our livingroom---a brass coal scuttle like an embossed helmet, a round brass engraved table & an antique Elizabethan dropleaf table which goes perfectly under the French window in no space at all & opens out generously for writing on.

Now that the weather is going to be supposedly more springlike we shall have some friends down from London, so I shall have some company. A young American boy & his wife are coming Tuesday, he to do a BBC interview with me for a series on why Americans stay in England. It better be sunny by the time he comes, or I won't have so many reasons! I am glad to hear you have had your moles off: I did see a doctor about mine, but he said they were healthy. He gave me the address of a very fine London surgeon so I can have them off when I want---the one on my chin I'll be gladdest to get rid of. Maybe I'll treat myself to it the summer after this, when I can leave the babies for a few days. I look so forward to you coming! I have just got winter-tired these last days---don't want to see another dish or cook another meal. My poetry book is officially due out May 14th.[1] It is very handsome, as I think you'll think when you see it--no errors in this one. Knopf seem very enthusiastic about it. Ted's children's programs are so wonderfully received he has a running request for as many as he can provide. Frieda is prettier every day. I was so distressed to hear little Pell is diabetic.[2] However did they find that out? I am enjoying my Bendix so much! I don't know how I ever did without it. It is so nice to hear it rumbling & think it is doing all my work for me. I washed Frieda's blue snowsuit in it & it came out lovely.

Well, I hope by the time I write again I may have all my seeds planted & be out with my babies. Our daffodils & jonquils are wonderful: I've picked about 300 these last 2 weeks & they're only beginning. Once a week I pick for <frie>nds & myself, & once a week to sell at the <market.>[3]

Lots of love to you & Warren.
Sivvy

TO *Aurelia Schober Plath*

Monday 16 April 1962 — TLS (aerogramme), Indiana University

Court Green
North Tawton
Monday: April 16

Dearest mother,

I am sitting at the lovely oval dropleaf oak table we bought from the Tyrers, looking out hopefully over my acre of shivering daffodils & the lilac buds on this black, frigid day as if it would make spring come in earnest. It is colder than Scotland, colder than for 70 years, which is little consolation. Even the local people are very gloomy. I am in the red room, our most cherished & comfortable spot, which is completed beautifully by the handsome brass coal scuttle & brass round table, so its all dark reds, dark polished woods & gleaming brass, with these beautiful French

1–Judith Jones to SP, 3 April 1962; held by University of Texas as Austin.
2–Pell Cruickshank.
3–The last sentence of this letter is damaged. The text appearing in < > is supplied by the editors based on the remaining evidence.

windows looking over the front garden. I have just put both babies in bed ---an energetic two-hours work: Nicholas now eats a bowl of runny cereal every night with beams and chuckles. He is so handsome. I put Frieda in her blue sweater with the silver buttons & she spent the afternoon on her Geegee rocker, also giving her bears & babies rides. I am now awaiting Ted's return from a day-trip in London where he is making a BBC broadcast, a recording[1] & seeing Leonard Baskins show of engravings for which he has been asked to write the foreword,[2] an honor we think. I have a nice big Irish stew ready, with cheese dumplings, which he likes. We still have our bare concrete floors, & I am agitating to have them tiled before Easter---Ted's mother & father & Aunt Hilda & Vicky were planning to drive down for the weekend. But probably or maybe they can't be done till next week, in which case we shall ask them to delay a week, as it is very grim with just concrete & we don't want them to see the house at anything but its best, since they'll have that memory of it for a year.

I loved your big fat letter. Honestly mother, you should know me well enough & that I know you well enough not to think you connected the loan with the car! We had previously gone over our finances & discovered with joy that we thought we could pay <u>both</u> our parents loans back within a year from our purchase of the house, so I was only delighted to hear you had something as nice to buy as that car which you <u>must</u> buy at $800. We would have sent the authorization anyway & independently. We have been so grateful at the help you & Ted's parents have given us which enabled us to get away without paying any interest to speak of, & as soon as you both have your checks, it will mean we own the house, so you may imagine how eager we are to be on our own completely. We love the place so much our mutual nightmares have been about being forced for some reason to give up Court Green. Now we have the floors done, we shall rest with repairs for a year or so. Several rooms need replastering & repapering, but aside from this the place is in solid good shape. I am so excited about your coming. You will adore Frieda: she is just lovely. Very excitable however: she bursts into tears if you raise your voice & I look forward to her having playmates when the good weather starts, so she'll get used to not being the only one. Nicholas is a darling, full of little responsive smiles & a talky coo. I never dreamed it was possible to get such joy out of babies. I do think mine are special. We had a young American

1–Ted Hughes, 'The Poetry of Keith Douglas', BBC Third Programme (31 May 1962).

2–Ted Hughes, 'Introduction', *Leonard Baskin: Woodcuts and Engravings* (London: R. W. S. Galleries, 1962): 3. The exhibition was held at R. W. S. Galleries, 26 Conduit Street, London, 1–26 May 1962.

I know, & his British wife, down last week, he to do an interview with me for the BBC on why I stayed here, & they brought an acquaintance with two of the most ghastly children I've ever seen---two girls of 5 & 6. They had no inner life, no notion of obedience, & descended shrieking on Frieda's toys, running up & down through the house with mucky boots & jabbering. Their mother was a tearful, ineffectual character. They almost knocked us out. I felt I could kick them. They kept sneaking up to peer in the rooms & at the baby though they'd been told repeatedly not to. How I believe in firm loving discipline! But they were Australians, not English. Now we are planning to have several couples we like down in the next month. Honestly, I wish you knew how much I miss Warren & Margaret! I already love Maggie sight unseen from what I've heard of her, & think of what lovely times we could all have together. I have such lovely children & such a lovely home now, I only long to share them with loving relatives! That is the hardest thing about being over here ---not having my own admiring relatives to appreciate my babies! Got a sweet letter from Mr. Crockett today---evidently inspired by my New Yorker poem (which I haven't yet seen, the magazines are late) about the appendectomy. How sad about Steve's retreat home. I must say I thought it odd he hadn't applied anywhere in advance! As for the baby pictures of Nicholas, I quote a similar authority: ISN'T APRIL COMING SOON? The 26thish part. Be patient! There is also a little package of something you've seen already, but not in its present handsome form, which may arrive a bit later. So glad you liked the poems in <u>Poetry</u>. I don't feel they're my best, but it's nice to get the "exercises" published, too. The "News from home"[1] is of course your letters, which I look forward to above all. I was so distressed to hear about the Ladies Home Journal![2] I do hope they survive---I've always had an ambition to get a story in there! How I wish you could see us now with all the daffodils. I pick about 600 a week for market & friends & notice no diminishing. They are so heavenly. We even had an antiquarian come to visit our Ancient Mound last Sunday! If only this blasted cold black weather would clear up, I would feel like a new person. You must send pictures & a word by word account of Warren's wedding. Tell me when the blanket gets to Margaret

xxx
Sivvy

1–Sylvia Plath, 'Stars from the Dordogne': 'I shut my eyes / And drink the small night chill like news of home' (*Collected Poems*: 166).
2–On 25 March 1962, the *Ladies' Home Journal* announced it was changing from monthly production to ten issues a year.

TO *Leonard Baskin*

Monday 16 April 1962 TLS (aerogramme), British Library

Court Green
North Tawton
Devonshire, England
April 16, 1962

Dear Leonard,

I am sitting at our mammoth recently-acquired heavy oak reputedly-Elizabethan table overlooking our acre of shivering daffodils under the churchyard wall on this black & frigid day & thinking very hard of you & Esther. Ted is in London for the day, seeing your show at the Hon Erskine's[1] so he may do something as nearly worthy as possible. Both of us were thrilled at your thinking of Ted to do the introduction. I am newly involved with our new Nicholas Farrar, a wintry Capricorn, which Ted says serves him right for studying astrology & casting aspersions. O Leonard I have so many times thought of writing & written in thought: it incredible what wounds & damages a few silly hours can do. I can only say, not in explanation or apology, but simply in fact, that when you came Ted & I were as near to desperate as possible, only he shows such things less & is of a more open & unfrantic nature. Anyhow, I was very much worried at being in the middle of a first novel & living in that tiny hole with no place or time to finish it & having to forgo the art galleries & green breathing space & time to write which is my life blood & makes it possible for me to be domestic & motherly, which latter is my nature only some of the time, & only when I have the other consolations & reprieves. As Ted has told you, almost immediately after, we made a radical break with our frenzies & sunk everything into Court Green.[2] An ancient, loving, amiable white farmhouse with 70 apple trees, miraculous daffodils of which I pick 500 a week with no sign of diminishment, and enough land to, we hope, eventually support us on vegetables when we learn enough, and flowers for the spirit. I have a study all my own, where I retire mornings; Ted has a study under the thatch, very dark & secret.

1–Honourable Robert Erskine (1930–); Erskine is listed in SP's address book at St George's Gallery, 7 Cork Street, London. See also Neville Wallis, 'Straight from the Wood', *The Observer* (4 November 1962): 29, which refers to 'the American Leonard Baskin (whose brooding figures are stored in Robert Erskine's portfolios at St George's Gallery in Cork Street)'.

2–See TH to Leonard Baskin, [August 1961], published in *Letters of Ted Hughes*: 186–7; original held by British Library.

There is ample room. We are, at last, in a place which does not cramp & confine us & bleed nonreturning rent monies, and are expanding with the blessedness of it. Our one wish is that you visit us when you come over for the show & enjoy a slice of the Devon spring & erase those sour memories which grieve us both. We are very lucky, this year, that I have a relatively small Saxton grant to finish the novel which enables us not to worry about the rather awesome expenses in this first year of making the house livable & babyproof. I had put your name as a character reference for this ages ago, & if you could possibly have been this after last summer I can only think you had more faith in my fearsome nature than I had myself. Frieda has responded miraculously to our space & greenness; she is very luminous & blue-eyed, with a language all her own & a very tremulous quick spirit. Nicholas is dark, Farrarlike, like Ted, quiet & smiley & utterly lovable. We are only 4 hours by express from Waterloo & could meet you at the North Tawton station whenever you could come. Do say you will, & when. I would mean an immense lot to both of us. Please let us know of Esther, to whom much, much love, and of Tobias, whom I imagine as a great blond & leonine giant.

I shall leave some space for Ted, when he returns.

With love,
Sylvia

TO *Ruth Fainlight & Alan Sillitoe*

Monday 16 April 1962 TLS, Ruth Fainlight

Court Green
North Tawton
Devon.
April 16, 1962

Dear Ruth & Alan,

We are so <u>so</u> delighted to hear about the arrival of David![1] Baby boys are wonderful beings & he and Nicholas should be able to coo & gurgle at each other companionably when you come down. We're glad to hear you have a car (that must mean you passed the stiff & military British tests, Alan!) because it is so easy to travel with a little baby when you have a car. Just sit yourselves on the A30, will you!

1–David Sillitoe (1962–).

The weather here is horrid. Black, with Siberian east winds. Our daffodils are out in force, shivering wildly, & very wonderful among the taciturn black twigs. I pick over 600 a week for market & friends & twice as many pop open right away. Do let us know when you think you can come. We would so love to see the three of you & could give you a quiet place to work, Alan, if you felt like it. We are lousy with studies!

How I loved Ruth's poem in Encounter![1] It is a real White Goddess poem,[2] and a voice on its weird fearsome own. I think it is a rare thing. O please do say you can come, & when. May should be a beautiful month, simply because this blasted April glowering can't hold out that long.

Ted joins me in sending love & healthful wishes to all 3,

Sylvia

TO *Aurelia Schober Plath*

Saturday 21 April 1962[3] — TLS in greeting card[4] with envelope, Indiana University

<printed greeting>

Happy Birthday / If it comes true – / This wish for you, / There'll always be a share / Of each good thing / That life can bring / For you – and some to spare. / Best Wishes / and Many Happy Returns / of your Birthday

<signed>

with love / from / Sivvy & Ted & / Frieda & Nicholas

Dear mother:

These pictures[5] do not, of course, do Nicholas justice, but we think they are very nice. I wish you could be spirited here now. Our daffodils are in full bloom and they are the most beautiful flowers in the world---big hothouse blooms, the starry jonquil sort, some with vivid orange centers, some with white petals & yellow trumpets. They are massed in circles and swatches from our front gate to the house side; there is a big patch in the vegetable garden, but my favorites are those strewn on the hill at the back under the apple trees. Ted and I picked 40 dozen in a beautiful pink

1–Ruth Fainlight, 'The Sapphic Moon', *Encounter* 18 (February 1962): 77.
2–A reference to Robert Graves, *The White Goddess: A Historical Grammar of Poetic Myth* (London: Faber & Faber, 1948).
3–Date supplied from postmark.
4–J. Arthur Dixon birthday card.
5–The photographs are no longer with the letter.

twilight yesterday for market today, & you simply couldn't tell where we'd picked them. The birds were singing, and a big yellow moon was coming up in our great elm tree. It is like a fairytale here. More beautiful than the Cambridge backs. If I have any luck with planting, I should have heavenly cut flowers all summer. I pick daffodils for anyone who comes at a shilling a dozen & love it. As Ted says, you really get acquainted with the plants, picking them. We'll try to get some color pictures this week. It is still raining, but lovely silvery rains. I wish I could send you a cartload of these daffodils for your birthday, knowing how you love them! We are so pleased, the New Statesman must have liked our children's book reviews last fall, for they have asked us to do the same for the spring supplement. As they only review children's books twice a year, we get stacks---and I am about to pick up my lot of pictures books at the post office. Did you see "Tulips" in the April 7 New Yorker? It was fascinating to also see the odd & revealing lyric by W. S. Merwin[1]---we think he must be parting from poor Dido, whose facelift was a last, desperate measure. We are immensely happy in North Tawton. In five years it should be a bower of flowers.

Lots of love,
Sivvy, Ted, Frieda & Nicholas

TO *Warren Plath*

Saturday 21 April 1962[2]

ALS in greeting card[3] (photocopy), Indiana University

Dear Warren –

We think so often of you & Maggie & only hope you will let us know you will soon come to visit us. I hope you get your great carnation blanket soon. Take it easy & send us pictures of the wedding.

xxx
Ted, Sivvy
Freda & Nicholas

1 – W. S. Merwin, 'As By Water', *New Yorker* (7 April 1962): 47.
2 – Date supplied from internal evidence.
3 – On Hallmark Contemporary birthday card.

TO *Aurelia Schober Plath*

Wednesday 25 April 1962 TLS (aerogramme), Indiana University

Wednesday: April 25

Dearest mother,

How I wish you could see us now! I am sitting out in a deck chair in shorts in heavenly hot sun, smelling the pungent box bushes at our door & the freshly mown & plowed tennis court, Baby Nick (as Frieda & therefore we now call him) asleep among the daisies in his pram, Frieda so excited she can hardly nap, and Ted out back beaming among the few strawberry plants that survived the late frosts. On Easter Sunday the world relented & spring arrived. Our daffodils are in full bloom. We picked about 1000 this week and I look out over a literal sea of several thousand more. I keep finding new treasures: little yellow & pink primroses & grape hyacinths opening in a grassy tangle by the lilac hedge, the spikes of lily of the valley poking through a heap of dead brambles. I think I would like nothing better than to grow flowers & vegetables. I have such spring fever I can hardly think straight. I am dying for you to come & to see it all through your eyes. I got your room all fixed up & cleaned yesterday. Two months seems such a long way away!

Hilda & Vicky stayed with us over Easter. We were very surprised they did not bring Ted's parents, but hope Uncle Walter may bring them later. Evidently the long winter, arthritis & the prospect of the day's trip put Edith off. I am so glad you aren't a stayathome like that! Hilda & Vicky pitched right in with dishes & cleaning, so were no extra work. They are both very lively & nice. But then we made the mistake of letting a young Swedish lady journalist[1] invite herself the day they left---I had found out the time of the last train back to London that day so we would not be stuck with her, but she was after the personal, & hinted around about staying. At the same point the Tyrers called & wanted to know if they could "read in our garden". We were very glad to have the excuse of company. The Tyrers are really, on the eve of their departure, becoming impossible---pushing their very silly, snobby 16 year old daughter on us to the point of suggesting we have her come & stay with us (!) all because, I think, they have seen Ted & me in the Sunday papers lately.[2] They have really been

1–Swedish writer and translator Siv Arb (1931–2015).

2–TH was featured with a photograph and mention in Philip Toynbee, 'From Virgil to Kingsley Amis', *The Observer* (22 April 1962): 20.

"friends" out of a necessity, not out of any kindred spirit (Marjorie & Nicola are so malicious about everybody & everything here I can't help wondering what they say about <u>us</u> the minute our backs are turned). As Ted said, it is so beautiful here we have to be careful people don't use us as a public promenade. We moved here for privacy, and are just learning the lessons of having possessions. I am so glad you are coming for I can simply say we have you with us all summer. We are also getting used to having people fit in with our schedules. I work in the morning & let guests get their own breakfasts when they wake up, so I don't hang around all morning waiting. Then I come down for lunch, & Ted goes up & works in the afternoon. I think you will find us very peaceful. You can sit out in the garden all morning, with Frieda & Nicholas, reading or knitting or sunning. The house is so big there is really no crowding. Do bring any recipes, or advice for preserving things you can---I'm hope to learn to bottle all our garden surplus, like our famous rhubarb. Also any advice & figures about life insurance: I do want Ted to take out a policy this summer & we know nothing about it. O it is so heavenly here I can hardly speak. Little Frieda is always picking daffodils & arranging them in bowls of water. "Pick daffdees" & "Out with Baby Nick oodleoo (lawnmower) she says.

My book should be out in America May 14th. Do send any clippings of reviews, however bad. How I would love Mrs. Prouty to come. We have a very fine pompous hotel in town on the hill she could stay overnight at. Do tell her! I got Do's wonderful package the day before Easter. I'll write to thank her today. She is a positive darling. I am delighted with everything in it. You must help me hem & shorten <u>my</u> winter skirts! I look so out of date with them down to my shins! Nancy's mother-in-law died of a heart attack last week & the funeral is today. I sent an armload of daffodils via the little hunchback friend of Nancy's who lives at the bottom of our lane. How I've missed her this last week! I am glad if the old woman had to go she went quickly, as I simply couldn't do without Nancy now. A 10-room house, acres of garden, writing & two babies is work enough for three people! Did I tell you the <u>New Statesman</u> must have liked our children's reviews last fall, for they have asked us both again this spring, They only review twice a year, so I have the half-year's accumulation of children's picture books---27, free! I just love doing this. And Ted has as many again of animal books. He has just finished another children's broadcast. He is the star writer for the children's programs (educational) now, & gets loads of fanmail. You must be full of plans for Warren's wedding. How soon could they think of coming? I wish <u>some</u>body could come around

Easter next year to admire the daffodils. Of course, early September is lovely, with apple pie every day for breakfast! I think I was meant to be a gardener. I wouldn't leave this place for a billion dollars. It is a miracle we found it, & you were instrumental in minding Frieda & freeing us at that time. When I met that Swedish girl at the station, how I wished it was you! The train ride is through such beautiful countryside. Frieda loves her Geegee rocker. "Getup pony" she says.

Lots & lots of love,
Sivvy

TO *Alan Sillitoe*

Saturday 28 April 1962 TLS, Ruth Fainlight

Court Green
North Tawton
Devon.
Saturday: April 28

Dear Alan,

It was wonderful to get your letter and hear you are coming. May 2nd couldn't be better---you should just catch the last marvel of our daffodils which have been astounding us since Easter. I pick about 40 dozen a week for market, but it doesn't show.

We'll have supper waiting[1] for you any time you arrive. Our phone number is North Tawton 370 in case you need it. The only things I suggest you bring from London are the Royal Court and the Hampstead Everyman.

Ted joins me in sending love to all,
Sylvia

1 – According to SP's Letts Royal Office Diary Tablet for 1962, she planned to serve spaghetti and lemon meringue pie.

TO *Marvin & Kathy Kane*

Monday 30 April 1962 TLS, Indiana University

Court Green
North Tawton
Devon.
The Eve of Mayday

Dear, dear, dear Marvin & Kathy!

No no we are not dead, nor furious at air motes nor any such thing. Only exhausted. It is the sudden spring weather which has been with us since Easter Sunday, and our mad attempt to plant in one sweet week all we should have been planting since Christmas. We have been rendered absolutely inarticulate, a sort of laborer's dopiness takes us immediately after eating uspper (you see) and we fall like great stones into bed to wake like mutes at dawn & stagger out with minute black particles which we stick into the soil. I have literally put my nose to the earth every day for the last week & am at last rewarded by a multitude of infinitesimal green shoots which I do not think are dandelions. Ted has pairs of leaves he thinks may be radishes, and little spikes of shrunken onions. We are very hopeful.

How we loved seeing you! It is incredible how we immediately feel fond & possessive of you as if we had known you years. The Cornwall trip sounds mean---Horrid. Ted says everybody down there has their eye on the summer trade, ergo money. Come in early September, he says, when the tourists are gone & the long winter stretches. We know, just recently, of a couple[1] with a cottage near Bideford for 25s. a week. With no electricity, of course, but a garden. Come in early September & visit us again, but bringing just pure sweet sugar Kanes, no Roses![2]

I am so so glad about the BBC program. I felt very nervous that you would ask to extend it on the basis of those tapes & kept wishing I was a negro ballet artist[3] or something really interesting, but I had fun jabbering & I hope you can cut it into something that is fun. I am sure you will.

1–Elizabeth Sigmund and David Compton.

2–Possibly John A. and Sarah A. Rose, who were neighbours of the Kanes at 6 Holland Park, London W.11. 'Roses' is also a well-known brand of the Cadbury confectionery company.

3–A possible reference to Pearl Primus, whom SP saw at Smith College on 7 February 1951; see *Letters of Sylvia Plath*, Vol. 1, 277. Alternatively, a possible reference to another participant in the interview series, jazz singer and entertainer Adelaide Hall; the others were advertising representative Dick Danners; newsman Arthur Radin and his wife Angelica Mason; and actor and song writer James Dyrenforth.

We had Ted's aunt & cousin descend on us over Easter, but they are the mucking-in-with-the-dishes sort, so not much trouble. It is these long days that are so disastrous. You think you have an evening, so work in the garden till sunset & bango, time for bed, the mind lying silent like a big cabbage.

I am really looking forward to my mother coming in June! I am so scatty from my char deserting me for two weeks (her mother-in-law died) and ironing & such mountaining, floors growing lichens, & Frieda discovering worms which she calls "Oos" & drops in my coffee at dull moments that I would welcome a soul, even a maternal one, who would like to cook a meal, bath a baby & dry a dish.

Ted joins me in sending love. Write us. We love your letters. & will both write again when we have recovered somewhat from this back-breaking & mouth-shutting land reclaim.

With love to both,
Sylvia

TO *Aurelia Schober Plath*

Friday 4 May 1962 TLS, Indiana University

Court Green
Friday, May 4, 1962

Dear mother,

These cards[1] (I mean photographs---Frieda calls them cards) are meant for a late birthday surprise. We took them Easter Sunday, the first day of real spring. I think you can see some of the reasons I am so happy. This is just the very smallest corner of our daffodils. Frieda is an expert at picking handsome bouquets---you simply mention the word daffodil and she is off. You will love the children. Nicholas smiles & laughs & is wonderfully responsive to attentions & kind words. Frieda thirsts for knowledge & laps up every word you tell her. We understand her, but strangers don't.

I am enclosing a little card for Dotty's birthday book. I've got a nice big birthday card I'm sending her separately. I am glad you remind me of these things. I was touched to hear Mrs. Prouty would like to see us. I shall write & beg her to come. It is only 4 hours by train. There is a nice big Inn five minutes away which serves bed & breakfast & dinner & is

1 – The photographs are no longer with the letter.

manorial, if she would rather stay there than overnight with us. I do wish she would consider it.

Got a dear sweet letter from Margaret which I will answer very soon. I have been dashing round so madly with spring planting, mowing, babies & letters & projects & reviews that I seem to fly. Blessed Nancy is back, after burying her mother-in-law last week & I am so grateful. It was awful without her. Now it is spring, it is just heaven here. I never dreamed it was possible to be so happy.

I am also enclosing two checks to deposit. Did you get the two checks in your birthday letter to deposit? Or was it one check? Anyway, the last two I sent were one for my poems from Harper's & one of about $12 for Ted from Harper's[1] (mine was about $136). I enclose two Texas checks now, any way, totaling $135. The New Yorker just accepted a short poem[2] about the old man Percy Key walking on our hill among the narcissi & the poetry editor wrote "I have heard nothing but the most extravagant praise of TULIPS. Everyone I know thought it extraordinary. So do I."[3] This sort of thing is immensely warming & encouraging.

We have the Sillitoes here now---Alan, his American writer-wife Ruth & their month-old son David. They are marvelous guests---Ruth helps cook, Alan washes up, they take walks on their own & our life proceeds as usual. I don't feel a drudge because they chip in & I work in my study as usual in the mornings. I don't know if I mentioned how I appreciate the Bendix each time I use it! It makes washing just no chore at all.

Our daffodils are waning, but our cherry trees are coming into bloom---better than Washington! Bright red leaves, and fluffy round pink blossom. It is like a little garden of Eden. I hope Do & Betty Aldrich both got my notes of thanks for their presents. Betty's little-boy suit is just darling, & Do's package was crammed with kind & wonderful things, everyone just right.

Lots of love to everybody.

XXX
Sivvy

1–Possibly Ted Hughes, 'Her Husband', *Harper's* 223 (December 1961): 28.

2–Sylvia Plath, 'Among the Narcissi', *New Yorker* (3 August 1963): 29.

3–Howard Moss to SP, 18 April 1962; held by New York Public Library; Moss rejected 'Crossing the Water', 'An Appearance', and 'Little Fugue'.

TO *Judith Jones*

Friday Saturday 5 May 1962 — TLS (aerogramme), University of Texas at Austin

Court Green
North Tawton
Devonshire, England
May 5, 1962

Mrs. Judith B. Jones
ALFRED A. KNOPF
501 Madison Avenue
New York 22, New York
USA

Dear Mrs. Jones:

I am appalled to see a month has passed since I got your letter[1] & THE COLOSSUS. All I can say is that the sudden arrival of our very very late English spring had Ted & me almost flattened (quite pleasantly) by our first ambitious spring planting (optimistically intended to supply us with vegetables for the rest of the year) and we are only now surfacing from our mute weeks of sticking little black specks into the earth and scattering Slugdeath and Slugit to annihilate that vast subterranean population of night-eaters.

I am perfectly delighted with THE COLOSSUS. I think the production is wonderful, love the colors of the cover & jacket & the splendid size of the print (Ted & I have a horror of tiny print). To my mind it is the "final" first book. The English one being a trial run. I am so happy with what you have done with it. A long, long time ago when I had my first story published in Mademoiselle, Alfred Knopf wrote[2] & said he hoped Knopf could publish a book of mine someday, & I have always wished to have a book right for Knopf & am so delighted with this one.

I'd be immensely grateful if you'd send on any or all clippings, as I never see such things here, & thrive on criticism of all sorts, especially the adverse sort. I find it very helpful & stimulating to get fresh slants.

1 – Judith Jones to SP, 3 April 1962; held by University of Texas as Austin.
2 – See Harold Strauss to SP, 26 June 1952; held by Lilly Library. The letter expressed interest in publishing a novel. See *Letters of Sylvia Plath*, Vol. 1, 463.

Do give my regards to Marybeth Weston[1] & say I'd be happy to send her any information she needs if she does an article.

It is like a little Eden here now, with our thousands of daffodils, narcissi, six very pink fluffy cherry trees and 70 apple trees about to break into bloom. Gardening is a wonderfully pacifying alternate to writing, which is also going beautifully, Nicholas being an extremely agreeable individual.

All good wishes,
Sylvia Plath

TO *Gerald & Joan Hughes*

Wednesday 9 May 1962[2] ALS,[3] Indiana University

Dear Gerald & Joan & everybody –

I am sitting in my plushy little study overlooking a corner of our beautiful fluffy pink cherry blossom & eating one (or more likely two) of Ted's trout. It is wonderful: I open one eye about 4:30 a.m. & see this shadowy figure rise up & vanish. Then when I wake up in earnest & go down to make breakfast at 8 there is Ted beaming over a plate of bright gleaming red-spotted trout. I can't wait till my mother comes this summer so I can have the babies safely with her & go off with Ted to fish. I adore fishing & have a sort of perpetual beginner's luck because I guess I am always a nitwit beginner. We both just finished reviewing some children's books[4] for the New Statesman. It is such fun – they only review children's stuff twice a year so we get a great accumulation of stuff (which we can keep or sell). Ted gets animal books & I get picture books. I get so excited to see all these brightly-colored stacks of free books. I pretend Frieda can understand them, but of course she can't yet. It is really me I await them for. I must have a child mind. Nicholas is gorgeous. Very well-behaved &

1–Marybeth Little Weston; former college board editor at *Mademoiselle* during SP's guest editorship (as Marybeth Little) and former gardening editor of *House & Garden* magazine. Weston was interested in writing a piece on SP and TH for *Horizon* magazine.

2–Date supplied from internal evidence.

3–SP's letter is at the end of a letter begun by TH, which has not been transcribed. For TH's portion, see *Letters of Ted Hughes*: 198.

4–Sylvia Plath, 'Oblongs', *New Statesman* (18 May 1962): 724; review of Peter Hughes, *The Emperor's Oblong Pancake*; Tomi Ungerer, *The Three Robbers*; Wanda Gág, *The Funny Thing*; Benjamin Spock, *Dr Spock Talks with Mothers*; Elizabeth and Gerald Rose, *The Big River*; Joan Cass and William Stobbs, *The Cat Show*. Ted Hughes, 'Dr. Seuss', *New Statesman* (18 May 1962): 726; review of Dr Seuss, *One Fish Two Fish Red Fish Blue Fish*; Eilís Dillon, *The Cat's Opera*; Gavin Maxwell, *The Otter's Tale*; Marcelle Vérité, *Animals of the Forest*; Eric Roberts, *Oddities of Animal Life*.

full of smiles & dark, handsome & Farrar-looking – everybody says he looks like you Gerald, when you were an infant. He is certainly a Hughes & a relief I must say it is to see his calm little face after one of Frieda's passions. She is beautiful but of a rapid, hysterical temperament. We are thrilled at the possibility of your coming over & as near as Wales. We hardly dare talk of it, but walk with crossed fingers.

Love to all,
Sylvia.

TO *Ruth Fainlight*

Saturday 12 May 1962 TLS, Ruth Fainlight

Court Green
North Tawton
Saturday: May 12

Dear Ruth,

Thanks very much for your letter. It was heavenly having you and Alan and David here, and like a vacation for me. Ted who usually claims I am killing him by offering him a potato now daily urges me to make scalloped potatoes just like yours because that is the way he loves them best. I have sent off for the Brer Rabbit bottles[1] & await their arrival armed with all my molasses recipes.

Could I dedicate my elm tree poem[2] to Ruth Fainlight? (Or would you prefer your maternal & wifely self, Ruth Sillitoe? I had thought of the poet-self first). I'd like to very much. I feel very involved & admiring of your imagery.

We ate our first miniscule radish this week, in a ceremony, with butter. If Ted is as eager to pull our stuff up as with this, we shall be living like midgets on infantine vegetables. You must make your coming down a ritual too, like the Rites of Spring.

Lots of love from all of us,
Sylvia

1 – Brer Rabbit is a brand name of sugarcane molasses, a favourite ingredient of SP's.
2 – Sylvia Plath, 'Elm', written on 19 April 1962.

TO *Aurelia Schober Plath*

Monday 14 May 1962 — TLS with envelope, Indiana University

Enc: 2 checks for $27 & $45

Court Green
Monday: May 14

Dear mother,

I hope by now you have received the color photos & have some idea of our lovely daffodils that have now vanished. We earned about $17 or so by selling them, very small in amount, but we are proud of it because it makes it seem as if the place is "earning." If we have a good apple harvest we should earn some more. The cherry petals are just beginning to blow down like pink snow, & the laburnum & lilac are just opening a few buds, and a few apple trees are blooming in the orchard. There are bluebells everywhere, a lovely thundery purple, and a few beautiful "pheasant's eye" white narcissi are opening on the back hill, alone among the daffodils in being delicately scented, with a short, bright yellow trumpet ringed with red. I prowl about the place daily for little bouquets of this and that.

Did Dotty get her birthday card all right? My book officially comes out in America today. Do clip & send any reviews you see, however bad. Criticism encourages me as much as praise.

I know you have drastic luggage restrictions, but I thought I would mention a few items we would love to have, in case Warren & Margaret might bring something too sometime. We would adore our victrola, as we now have room & money for any needed transformer. Also, would it be at all feasible to take apart our fishing rods (especially my little spry one) & wrap them in paper & send or carry them?[1] Maybe they could be sent.

I would also love a little bottle of aniseed flavoring for springerle which I can't find anywhere here. I have luckily, courtesy of Ruth Sillitoe, found a London store which will send on Brer Rabbit molasses & mazola is everywhere, so I am set pleasantly on these things. We have a nice young Canadian poet & his very attractive, intelligent wife coming down for this weekend---they're the ones who took over our lease for the London flat. Then Ted's parents will probably be driven down by his Uncle Walter for the next weekend. I shall be glad to get them over. I honestly think Edith is terribly lazy---she stays in bed till noon & has nothing to do but

1–SP's and TH's fishing rods appeared at auction via Bonhams on 21 March 2018.

worry about her arthritic knee & eats such a stupid diet---all starches & sweets. And of course she's no help at all with babies (they exhaust her) or cooking or anything. Well, she has a good heart, I guess. I'm just glad I have the mother I have!

Nicholas has for some reason been crying at night, so I am rather weary. I think, my firm resistance to the long hard winter has hit me now that it is nicer & I can relax. I just don't want to do a thing, or rather, I want to, but don't feel like it---I have had mending stacked up for months & am tired of my own cooking with no energy to try any of the exotic recipes I get in my beloved Journal. O pooh. We have huge amounts of wonderful legendary rhubarb which we inherited. Have you any canning advice? Maybe you will supervise some of my canning this summer. We have a fine dark "winecellar" which asks to be crammed with bright glass jars full of good things.[1] How did you & grammy can? When did you sterilze the stuff? My cookbook is very confusing about this. Did I tell you the lino was down by Easter & is ideal? Has Maggie got the blanket yet? How big is their new bed? Will it fit?

xxx to all, Love,
Sivvy

<on verso of envelope>

PS: Did you get any refund for my broken pottery? The British postmaster checked up in person here ages ago.

1–Cf. SP's 'Wintering', *Collected Poems*, 217–19.

TO *Howard Moss*

Monday 21 May 1962 TLS, New York Public Library

Court Green
North Tawton
Devonshire, England
May 21, 1962

Mr. Howard Moss
THE NEW YORKER
25 West 43rd Street
New York 36, New York
USA

Dear Mr. Moss:

Just to be on the safe side, I am enclosing THREE WOMEN, a poem for three voices which the B.B.C. Third Programme is producing, in case you think any of the lyrics, perhaps towards the end of it, might be suitable for publication on their own. I am also sending along three[1] other new poems with it.

I was very happy indeed to hear that people liked TULIPS.

Sincerely,
Sylvia Plath

TO *Aurelia Schober Plath*

Thursday 7 June 1962 TLS (aerogramme), Indiana University

Court Green
Thursday, June 7

Dear mother,

Forgive me, forgive me for what must seem a huge silence. The days slide by so fast here that we seem to be living out of Time in a kind of country eternity. I have reached, I think, the last of my "guests" with 6 days of Ted's mother, father & Uncle Walt. That is partly why I have been so quiet. They were the end of a long string, and the only people who really were no strain but a great help were the wonderful Sillitoes &

1 – 'along ~~two~~ three' appears in the original. The three poems SP sent with 'Three Women' were 'Elm', 'The Rabbit Catcher', and 'Event'.

their month-old baby. But that's partly because Ruth is a poetess herself & Alan a writer like Ted---pitching in & not needing to be formally "entertained". Ted's mother stayed with us & the men stayed up at the Burton Hall hotel much to my relief. I made a few big meals for everyone & we ate at least half of our dinners out. Mrs. Hughes is very sweet & did a whole pile of darning on Ted's socks (!) which I have no patience for. As she sends him these big wool things, she is an expert at doing it, & I felt it was a good way for her to feel useful with no real strain. They went on car-jaunts with Walt & were immensely impressed & proud of our place. I am glad they, like you, have had a part in helping us get it.

This is the fourth day in a row of absolutely halcyon blue clear hot weather. I took off from my study the last 3 days & had a little Lookout Farm. I weeded all our onions & spinach & lettuce, out in the garden from sunrise to sunset, immensely happy, with Frieda digging in a little space "helping" & Nicholas in the pram sunbathing. This is the richest & happiest time of my life. The babies are so beautiful. Yesterday afternoon went to the local playground[1] with Sylvia Crawford, a very lovely-looking dark-haired girl twin in age to Warren, with 3 little girls, one named Rebecca just a little older than Frieda. The playground is set high up with a lovely view of Dartmoor. Just now the two laburnum trees are in full bloom & sit right in front of my study window. Isn't it odd that I've written about Golden Rain Trees in my book[2] & now have six---2 out front & on at the side of my study & the rest about! I am praying some apple bloom hangs on till you come! We are enjoying our own lettuce & radishes. Two weeks from today you come! I can't wait to see the place through your eyes. Work inside the house has come to a standstill with the demands of the big gardens, so I hope you'll overlook minor cracks & peelings!

I hope when you come to really work mornings every day in my study ---I look so forward to your playing with Frieda. She'll love you. She's at such a wonderful teachable stage now. I'd like to get into a long work which I've been unable to do with all the spring interruptions of other people. O it is so beautiful here. Bring Bermuda shorts for wear about the garden---we're pretty private. Of course no one wears them in town! And one warm outfit. Thanks a million for the molasses! I've made mountains

1–The local playground is off Barton Street, North Tawton.
2–Sylvia Plath, 'The Beekeeper's Daughter', *The Colossus*: 'The Golden Rain Tree drips its powder down', (London: Heinemann, 1960): 75; (New York: Knopf, 1962): 73.

of gingerbread. I'm learning to do gros point tapestry[1] for cushion & seat covers. Wonderfully calming.[2]

I hope Warren & Margaret got our little telegram of good wishes which I sent to the New York address. Ted found we had one word extra & put in Frieda. I was very cross when I found he hadn't put Nicholas as well, but tell them we meant to. I felt very very sorry for myself at not being at the wedding & look forward to a full account from you in the next day or so. Even to the last minute I considered squandering our savings & flying over by jet! Tell me all about it!

We've been doing quite well although we don't seem to be working. I've had a long poem (about 378 lines!) for 3 voices accepted by the BBC Third[3] (three women in a maternity ward, inspired by a Bergman film)[4] which will be produced by the same man who does Ted's plays & who'll be down here[5] to discuss production with me! Ted did a beautiful program[6] on a marvelous young British poet, Keith Douglas,[7] killed in the last war, saying how shocking it was no book of his was in print. In the next mail he got grateful letters & inscribed books from the poet's 75 year-old impoverished mother[8] & a suggestion from a publisher that Ted write the forward to a new edition of the book! Both of us mourn this poet immensely & feel he would have been like a lovely big brother to us. His death is really a terrible blow & we are trying to resurrect his image & poems in this way. I have been asked to do a short talk for a program

1–Assia Wevill sent SP the materials and instructions for the tapestry. See Assia Wevill to SP, 22 May 1962; held by British Library. Wevill indicates that SP was interested in *The Sunday Times Rose Bouquet*, printed in 'Mainly for Women', *Sunday Times Magazine* (17 January 1960): 19; the tapestry was designed by Anita Skjold. SP started but did not finish the tapestry. After SP's death, Elizabeth Sigmund found and completed the tapestry; however, over the years it eventually 'crumbled and disintegrated into nothing'. See Elizabeth Sigmund and Gail Crowther, *Sylvia Plath in Devon: A Year's Turning* (Stroud: Fonthill Media, 2014): 70.

2–At the bottom of the first page of the letter, SP wrote '(I didn't know this was here!)'. She is referring to an abandoned letter by TH which begins 'Court Green, North Tawton, Devon. // Dear Bill, Th'.

3–Sylvia Plath, 'Three Women: A Poem for Three Voices', BBC Third Programme (19 August 1962); re-broadcast 13 September 1962.

4–Ingmar Bergman, *Brink of Life* (1958); also known as *So Close to Life*. *So Close to Life* played at the Academy Cinema, London, beginning 24 February 1961.

5–According to SP's Letts Royal Office Diary Tablet for 1962, she met Douglas Cleverdon for lunch in London on 3 July 1962.

6–Ted Hughes, 'Keith Douglas', BBC Third Programme (31 May 1962).

7–English poet Keith Douglas (1920–44); Douglas was killed in action during the invasion of Normandy.

8–Marie Josephine Castellain Douglas (b. 1887).

called "The World of Books"[1] & Ted's children's programs are classics ---he gets fan letters from all over the place. His radio play "The Wound" will be broadcast a third time[2] this summer, which means another blessed $300 out of the blue. We are trying to save a bit now while I still have one more installment of my grant. Perhaps in a couple of years we'll do a poetry reading tour in America & earn a great pot. They pay one to two hundred a night!

Love to All the Plaths,
Sivvy

<on the return address side of letter>

PS. Got the wedding letter today. Sounds heavenly!

S

TO *Marvin & Kathy Kane*

Saturday 9 June 1962 TLS, Indiana University

Court Green
Saturday: June 9

Dear, dear Marvin & Kathy . . .

Please interpret our silences as Spinach. Honestly, they are as innocuous! We are living here in a kind of country Eternity where time has no meaning. I measure it by the length of shadows, & the spinach-silence is a real thing. I shut my eyes and see spinach. Ted, I have discovered, is a wonderful planter but does not see weeds. I see weeds. We are thus an ideal couple. The past weeks, especially with the good weather (after a huge flood of Ted's relatives, among whom one uncle counts for three in size & appetite), I have been out in the garden from morning till night digging & hacking the huge weeds from square after square of vegetables. By evening, when I have all my pleasant hobbies lined up before me--- photos to paste in album, friendly letters, gros point of gross roses etc. etc.---I am so stupid-cow-tired I just put it all off & fall into bed. Hence the silence. Please please understand our brutish ways. We are too simple to have undertones.

1–Sylvia Plath, 'Sylvia Plath Speaks on a Poet's View of Novel Writing', BBC Home Service (7 July 1962); re-broadcast 13 July 1962; recorded 26 June 1962. Published as 'The Novelist and the Poet', *The Listener* (7 July 1977): 26; and as 'A Comparison', *Johnny Panic and the Bible of Dreams* (London: Faber & Faber, 1977): 62–4. See Phillippa Pearce to SP, 30 May 1962; held by BBC Written Archives Centre.

2–Ted Hughes, *The Wound*, BBC Third Programme (14 July 1962).

I really love doing the vegetable garden much more than flowers, though I do love picking & arranging flowers. Anyhow, after I saw Ted through the worst of the immediate weeding I went out front hopefully to look at my labeled flower beds. To my surprise, where I had planted neat little rows of seeds, there was nothing to be seen but a complete carpet of one particular kind of plant. I could not understand it. I felt very badly. I had planted nothing so universally. It seemed, O God, to be a Weed. On looking very close, I did spy one or two rather feeble other things. They may be the plants. Or of course they may be a rather weaker kind of weed. I wish you were here, Kathy! We could sit & talk & do a lovely Zennish plucking in rhythm of the minute ubiquitous weeds (symbolising the foul world of minutes or something). Now I have to do it all alone. It should take about a year.

We loved you in THE DAY THE MONEY STOPPED,[1] Marvin. Ted & I kept poking each other: That's Marvin. You did a terrific job. That's what I call Drama. I only pray you get the grant. Ted will do all he can, but feels a bit shy of his own power as he applied and didn't get it. But then he had nothing like the professional experience & works you have.

Suddenly we have an antique beehive, given us free by one of the many local beekeepers. O you would have laughed. We went to the North Tawton beekeepers demonstration this week. The rector was there, & the midwife. All donned those funny screen hats. Then we went out & stood while one Charlie Pollard[2] made 3 hives out of one & Ted & I stood like dummies trying not to get stung, feeling agonizing sting-like itches as billions of bees zinged against our veils. Now we have this old hive which Ted will scrub & I paint white & green with maybe a few pink roses on to hearten the bees. When you see us this fall we may well have home-made honey to offer you with apples. Provided the Queen doesn't scorn our ignorance & Swarm.

Please keep us posted on all your BBC things, Marvin, & things with you in them. We love hearing them. Much love to you both, & forgive our farmhandish manners. We are lousy correspondents & keep a kind of inner monologue going in our heads which we count as sort of phantom letters!

Love,
Sylvia

1–Marvin Kane, *The Day the Money Stopped* (adaptation of Brendan Gill's 1957 novel), BBC Home Service (28 May 1962); a note of the performance is in SP's Letts Royal Office Diary Tablet for 1962.

2–Charles William M. Pollard (1908–95), a Devon beekeeper who lived in Mill Lane, North Tawton, and at 'Lauriston', Prospect Hill, Okehampton.

TO *Gerald & Joan Hughes*

Sunday 10 June 1962 — ALS[1] (aerogramme), Indiana University

June 10: A week of hot blue days has arrived & I can hardly uncrook my back. Ted is a marvellous planter but does not see weeds. I see weeds. I have been happily browning in the dirt of our lovely vegetable garden uprooting gigantic nettles, dock, dandelions etc. etc. from pathetic thread-thin leeks, spinach, lettuce & so on. The babies are very brown & juicy. Six laburnum trees drip gold everywhere: my favorite tree. We still manage to work hard turning out BBC stuff. I've just had a long dramatic poem accepted which is three women thinking to themselves in a maternity ward. One has a son & lives in the country, one has a little illegitimate daughter & one has a miscarriage – all very emotional, but fun to do & a sort of wage that is nice. After a long string of spring guests, my blessed mother is coming now for 6 weeks to babysit, help & generally free us for a few jaunts. We are both getting piles of exercise, impossible in the city, & working & wrestling with our land. Our latest acquisition is an old bee-hive we are cleaning & painting in hopes of supplying our own daffodil-apple blossom honey. We keep discovering odd gems of people buried here – tea today with a retired Major[2] & C.I.D[3] man from British Guiana.

Love to all,
Sylvia

1–SP's letter is at the end of a letter begun by TH, which has not been transcribed.
2–Major Stanhope Mince Billyeald (1893–1968) and his wife Bertha (Manly) Billyeald (1900–68), who lived at 'Eve Leary', Eggesford Road, Winkleigh. SP and TH met them at a meeting of the Devon Beekeepers.
3–Criminal Investigation Department.

TO *Alfred Young Fisher*

Monday 11 June 1962 TLS, University of North Carolina, Chapel Hill

Court Green
North Tawton
Devonshire, England
June 11, 1962

Dear Alfred,

After all these years, finally, a Book. I hope you will like some of it. I got to remembering those fine afternoons in my senior year at Smith under your office gable. The book is your due. Those afternoons are at the deep root of it.

We are committed to the country---only in England could two poets & a line of infants enjoy such worrilessness as we do on our ancient smallholding---thatch, acres of apple trees, daffodils, laburnum, owls, bees. We write in shifts, balancing babies in between, & the great vegetable garden on which we live. I do a lot for the BBC, am on a 2nd book of poems, much freer than this, & have had a first novel accepted over here. It is wonderful to discover one's destiny.

I have a crazy favor to ask. Ignore it if it seems unusually crazy. I got so used, at Smith, to scribbling poems on the back of those big pink Smith College Memorandum sheets I have a fetish for them. Do you think I could send a check to someone & buy about a dozen of those pink pads???[1] My Muse is mad for them!

Seven year's-worth of gratitude for helping to make these poems possible.

Affectionately,
Sylvia

1–Letter accompanied by a half-sheet of pink Smith College Memorandum paper and a signed and inscribed copy of *The Colossus* (Knopf): 'For Alfred Young Fisher – / my not-forgotten maestro, / a second circus – / Sylvia Plath / Court Green / North Tawton / Devonshire / June 7, 1962'.

TO *Aurelia Schober Plath*

Friday 15 June 1962 TLS (aerogramme), Indiana University

Court Green
Friday: June 15

Dear mother,

Well, this is the last letter I will be writing before you come! I hope you get it before you go: I don't even know when you're leaving home! I have been working so hard physically out in the garden that I am inarticulate and ready for bed by evening, hence my long silences. I don't know when I've been so happy or felt so well. These last few days I have been weeding our strawberry patch & setting the runners, just as I did on Lookout Farm, and at night I shut my eyes & see the beautiful little plants with the starry flowers & beginning berries. I love this outdoor work and feel I am really getting in condition. The amount of weeding this place needs is phenomenal. I have completely neglected my flowerbeds at the front for the pressing needs of the vegetables. How huge the back garden seems from weed-level! And now Ted is spreading his planting onto the plowed tennis court. I get such pride in eating our produce! The strawberries are very few---I figure if all ripen we (you too!) should have a saucer of about 20 each! But next year I should have trebled our plant supply from my set runners. We had the first cuttings of spinach tonight---absolutely delectable. And rhubarb & radishes. Every day we walk out together and take in the progress of our rows.

Today, guess what, we became bee-keepers! We went to the local meeting last week (attended by the rector, the midwife & assorted bee-keeping people from neighboring villages) to watch a Mr. Pollard make three hives out of one (by transferring his queen cells) under the supervision of the official Government bee-man. We all wore masks & it was thrilling. It is expensive to start bee-keeping (over $50 outlay), but Mr. Pollard let us have an old hive for nothing, which we painted white & green, & today he brought over the swarm of docile Italian hybrid bees we ordered and installed them. We placed the hive in a sheltered out-of-the-way spot in the orchard---the bees were furious from being in a box. Ted had only put a handkerchief over his head where the hat should go in the bee-mask & the bees crawled into his hair & he flew off with half-a-dozen stings. I didn't get stung at all, & when I went back to the hive later, I was delighted to see bees entering with pollen sacs full & leaving with them empty---at least I think that's what they were doing.[1] I feel very ignorant, but shall try to read up & learn all I can. If we're lucky, we'll have our own honey too! Lots of people are really big keepers in town, with a dozen to 20 hives, so we shall not be short of advice. When we have our first honey, I think we shall get half a dozen hens.

Luckily I have lots & lots of work to do like painting furniture & weeding, because I am so excited about your coming I can't sit still! I wish now you had seen the house in its raw state so you would see how much we have done! Of course there is still an immense deal to do, and my eyes are full of five-year-plans.

Got an absolutely enchanting letter from Warren in Bermuda on an anniversary card---the first I've ever got from him full of vivid color & discriptions of things---Margaret must be a real tonic for him! You must tell me their address when you come & I'll write a long over due letter. I can't wait to see the two of them here---Warren will really appreciate all the improvements since his time!

We went to tea in a neighboring town with a marvelously doughty woman we met at the bee-meeting. Her husband is a Major, a retired C.I.D. inspector from British Guiana, and her amazing 89-year-old father[2] a retired police inspector too. She has 12 hives, a huge hennery & vegetable garden & a giant grapevine filling her greenhouse. Showed me all her albums---of her shooting jaguars & making a locomotive & railway in the wilderness. We're going to tea this week to see the estate of a friend of the midwife's whose husband is in TV.[3]

Frieda & Nicholas are getting brown & are so wonderful I can't believe it. They are such happy healthy babies, I adore every minute of them. Ted & I are arranging a day in London about a week after you come to do a broadcast[4] see an art exhibit & maybe a foreign movie. It's exciting as a safari to Africa to me to think of a day away!

Did I tell you I've just had a long (378 line) dramatic poem for 3 voices accepted for the BBC THird Program---three women in a maternity ward,

1–Cf. SP's bee poems, particularly 'The Bee Meeting', 'The Arrival of the Bee Box', and 'Stings'.

2–George T. Manly (*c.* 1873–1962).

3–Terence C. Macnamara (*c.* 1903–78) and his wife Kathleen Jones Macnamara (1901–87); lived at Cadbury House, near Thorverton, Devon. According to SP's Letts Royal Office Diary Tablet for 1962, they visited Mrs Macnamara on 13 and 20 June.

4–Ted Hughes, 'Creatures of the Air', *Listening and Writing*, BBC Home Service (Schools), 29 June 1962; recorded 26 June 1962. SP and TH saw the film *Last Year at Marienbad* which played at the International Film Theatre, 90–2 Westbourne Grove, London. See TH to David and Assia Wevill, *c.* 27 June 1962 (incomplete draft); held by University of Victoria.

each soliloquizing in poems. When you come I really must sit in my study in the mornings! Six weeks seems such a short time. I realize how terribly much I have missed you (and Warren too!) now that the time draws close to see you again.

Lots of love, & a smooth trip!

Fond wishes from us all,
Sivvy

TO *Philippa Pearce*[1]

Friday 15 June 1962 TLS, BBC Written Archives Centre

Court Green
North Tawton
Devon.
June 15, 1962

Miss Philippa Pearce
Producer – The World of Books
THE BBC
Broadcasting House
London W.1

Dear Miss Pearce,

I am enclosing a copy of my talk.[2] As you can see, it is a comparison of some few aspects of the poem and the novel from a poet's point-of-view. I hope it is all right, and the right length.

It appears that I shall now be able to be in London on Tuesday morning, June 26th. Would it be at all possible for me to record with you some time that morning? My train gets into Waterloo by 10:30 a.m. Perhaps you could let me know by telephone whether I should plan on recording then.

With all good wishes,
Sincerely,
Sylvia Plath

1–Philippa Pearce (1920–2006); producer at the BBC and author of children's books.
2–The enclosure is no longer with the letter.

TO *Olwyn Hughes*

c. Monday 18 June 1962[1] ALS, Washington University (St Louis)

Dear Olwyn –

I am enclosing a picture[2] of Nicholas Farrar Hughes on his christening day (March 25) in a gown of antique Limerick lace borrowed from the Bank Manger's wife & cut from her grandmaw's wedding dress. I hope it is not filched by French censors, plastiquéd, or seized as a representation of Salon in disguise. Nicholas is marvellous – calm, dark, wise, full of trills at the back of the throat & a Buddha-look I find infinitely endearing. Frieda a weird tornado with large angel-inhuman pale-blue orbs; refers to self as "Fee-fah" & pees on the floor so she can demand a mop although I have painted her potty seat with pink daises to beguile her into it. I just feel to be lifting a nose & a finger from the last 3 years cow-push of carrying, bearing, nursing & nappy-squeezing. My study is my poultice, my balm, my absinthe. I've just done a very long dramatic poem for 3 voices (3 women in a maternity ward, miscarriages, illegitimacies & such, after Bergman) which Douglas Cleverdon, Ted's producer, will produce. Very excited about the chance to do longer stuff. We're having our first day in London together next week – our train fares (fantastically high now) paid by the B.B.C., each of us to do a program, Ted for the Children's School hour on air – birds & me a guest spot on "The World of Books." We are lucky to have such bread & butter stuff & it is a diversion – as money bleeds away so fast here – the house just devours it: everything from slug killer to thatch insurance to fire extinguishers, & as we still owe over £400 we are working like mad. How I sympathize with your electric bill! Ours is over £25 a quarter & I somehow never count on it & am always floored. The sinus business sounds ghastly. Sinus has always been my own worst illness & the only relief I ever got was with a cocaine spray which worked wonders & lifted the manic depression I usually got. Then it got so bad I had it operated on, or rather drained, with a local, day after day for a summer & it has never been so bad. You don't want France or England with that, you want Arizona.

I agree with you about "My Sad Captains".[3] I'm getting very fond of Gunn & you named some of my favorites. It's partly, I think, because I've

1–Date supplied from internal evidence.

2–The photograph is no longer with the letter.

3–Thom Gunn, *My Sad Captains and Other Poems* (London: Faber & Faber, 1961).

since met & very much liked him. In the same way I'm very sympathetic to Alvarez's poems, some of them, because I like him & know something about how his wife's knocked him about & gone off.

I am working like a black now weeding, mowing, & scything. And painting a great lot of ugly wood furniture in black gloss or white gloss with hearts & flowers all over it to make "sets" for this room or that. My mother arrives this week for the summer, a heavenly blessing, a sort of free mother's help, babysitter & part-time cook all of which I am desperate for with this William Morris[1] making & designing of things, babies & incipient books. We are slowly being absorbed – tea-partied by ret'd. Majors & active midwives.

Get well fast.

Love from us 4,
Sylvia

TO *George MacBeth*

Tuesday 19 June 1962 TLS, BBC Written Archives Centre

Court Green
North Tawton
Devon.
June 19, 1962

Dear George,

I am delighted you are taking "The Surgeon at 2 a.m."[2] and would be very happy to read a Carolyn Kizer.[3] Could you get her poem to me before I come up? I'd like to brood on it.

I wonder if I could come up the week after the one ending Friday June 29th and record some morning of just about any day? I have a very crammed day at the BBC Tuesday 26th and can't really manage to arrange the infinite complications of babysitters, wipers & minders twice in the same week. The earliest train from here gets into Waterloo about

1–A reference to English textile designer, writer, and social theorist William Morris (1834–96).

2–Sylvia Plath, 'The Surgeon at 2 a.m.', *The Poet's Voice*, BBC Third Programme (24 August 1962); recorded 10 August 1962. Also, Ted Hughes, 'The Road to Easington' and 'Out', *The Poet's Voice*, BBC Third Programme (24 August 1962); recorded 10 August 1962. See George MacBeth to SP, 14 June 1962; held by BBC Written Archives Centre.

3–American poet Caroyln Kizer (1925–2014). SP read Carolyn Kizer, 'The Great Blue Heron', *The Weird Ones*, BBC Third Programme (4 November 1962); probably recorded 9 August 1962.

10:30 a.m., so I could be at your place about 10:45-11:00. Let me know if that next week would be all right with you, & if so, what morning.

Sincerely,
Sylvia
(Sylvia Plath)

George MacBeth, Esq.
Producer, Talks Department
The BBC
London W.1

TO *Aurelia Schober Plath*

Thursday 21 June 1962[1] ALS,[2] Indiana University

for mother
~ welcome to Court Green ~

from Sivvy & Ted

<enclosed with a Liberty of London scarf>

TO *Marvin & Kathy Kane*

c. Friday 22 June 1962 ALS,[3] Indiana University[4]

Dear, dear Marvin & Kathy –

If you think we are trying to plan your lives for you, you are right. This Kathleen Macnamara is a minute, fiery white-haired woman with black eyes, two pekinese, a cat, a rose garden, a gardener, the most gorgeous old re-made 19-room rectory in the heart of green stillness. Of course you may not want to save money all <u>this</u> much – but the arrangement sounded so oddly <u>like</u> you – a 3rd floor sanctum under the eaves up an antique stair – 2 big rooms & a central boxroom (twin beds & bedding there), a small boxroom & possible study. Mrs. Macnamara is delighted at the idea Marvin would just write – she simply wants a woman to "do what she would do" – cook (in a fabulous red-brick-floored kitchen with aga, also a second modern stove), keep the 19 rooms in order & help entertain.

1–Date supplied from internal evidence.
2–Note written on wrapping paper from the Gordon Fraser Gallery, Fitzroy Yard, off Fitzroy Road, London.
3–SP's letter is at the end of a letter begun by TH, which has not been transcribed.
4–Date supplied from internal evidence.

A big, wandering house where you would need maps to find each other. This would amount to free room & board & a wage for Kathy's services around the house. If you dug in for say a year & wanted a change, you'd be in the heart of cottage country, have saved all your takings & be able to pick your spot. Of course Kathy may be horrified at us putting her to work about at a house, but I remember, I think, she said she liked this sort of thing. If you did get on with this Kathleen it should be marvelous fun. I thought neither of you drove – izzat so? The big town[1] is about 10 miles away. We'd visit you often. We're mad for the place. In case all this is around the bend, just say so, & we & Mrs. M. will keep on keeping our eyes out for cottages. We thought the plays[2] were terrific, Marvin! I never heard Ted belly laugh so. We don't get anything but the Observer so please copy out the Times review verbatim for us.[3]

Our phone number is North Tawton 370 in case you want to question or confirm anything in a a hurry. Rest assured that we will keep looking for cottages if you can't stand the notion of this business. As Ted says – if you're interested the husband Terence could interview you in London. He works for ITV I think & is due to retire in a couple of years – goes down on weekends to Devon.

My mother is here now for the summer. She couldn't open the train door (who could, those diabolical things) in time & jumped off the moving train with all her belongings. At that moment we all arrived. I felt of course that it was all my fault for not arriving in time to see her knocking on the window to be let out! A bad night (Is the ankle broken? Sprained? Strained?) smoothed out. The swelling went down. All is calm. Now I shall try to manipulate mornings of writing & become an articulate beast again.

Let us know what you think –

Lots of love
Sylvia

1 – Exeter.
2 – Possibly 'The Ducks and the Drakes', *The Impostors*, BBC Home Service (29 May 1962) and 'The Man Who Sold the Eiffel Tower', BBC Home Service (12 June 1962).
3 – Possibly Peter Wilsher, 'Heart of the Matter', *Sunday Times* (3 June 1962): 48.

TO *Marvin & Kathy Kane*

Saturday 30 June 1962 TLS, Indiana University

Court Green
Saturday: June 30

Dear Marvin & Kathy,

I enclose the clipping[1] (aren't I scrupulous?) which is very fine & right. Could you give us some very practical idea about what sort of place you would like---I mean, this Macnamara woman has news of a semi-detatched cottage in the beautiful country near her place with a garden, but, I gather, unfurnished & you would need a car to get to the shops. S O what are you prepared to do? It seems there is electricity there, but you would have to get it connected up or something. There is also another place we are following up, through friends. Do you require anything? I mean, like shops. And furniture. And for roughly how long are you prepared to stick it out? If we know a few details like these we can probably be of more use. At least we can make encouraging gestures after these two places.

My mother is a blessing. We are writing again, both of us, and she gets on beautifully with the babies, minds them, bakes cookies. O it is lovely. We are writing a few poems.[2] And manage a mad morning at the BBC (working for train fare & a flight back so I can feed the baby) once in a great while.

Love to both & let us know,
Sylvia

TO *Clarissa Roche*

Wednesday 11 July 1962 TLS, Smith College

Court Green
Wednesday: July 11

Dear Clarissa,

Pardon my long silence, but my mother has arrived out of the blue to stay with us till mid-August, and things are hectic as you may imagine. I think you would probably not want to invest in our local Inn (but let us know if you would), and wonder if you could postpone your babysitter till after mother has left? Then the spare room would be free again, and the visit possible at our house.

1–The clipping is no longer with the letter.
2–SP, 'Berck-Plage' (30 June 1962).

We have been consumed by this long drought, lifting anxiously the lolling heads of our otherworldly plants and begging them to hang on. Cars with loudspeakers have announced it is an offense to water the garden by hose from the tap. You have to cart it out in buckets and pretend it is your used bath-water. I get homesick for you just writing to you. If you could afford the hotel now you could have all the meals here so it wouldn't be too bad, and I'm sure you'd get on with mother. If this is not feasible, how about some time in August?

Ted too sends love,
Sylvia

TO *Ruth Tiffany Barnhouse Beuscher*

Wednesday 11 July 1962 TLS, Smith College

Court Green
North Tawton
Devon.
July 11, 1962

Dear Dr. Beuscher,

I honestly hope you feel you can answer this letter by return, as I am suddenly, after all that happy stuff I wrote you some while ago, at sea, and a word from you I could carry around with me would sustain me like the Bible sustains others. I didn't say in my last letter how ghastly that sounded to have gone through, about your father.[1] It sounded so close in its way to my own trouble that I was astounded. I still credit you, I think, with some vestige of supernatural powers which can transcend the factual lumps of experience and make them harmless, or at least, not seriously or permanently wounding. What I wanted to say, without knowing quite how, is that I am very very sorry.

What I need some good wise word on is the situation between Ted & me.[2] As you can tell from my last letter, I thought I had at last stepped into the life that would be the growing-pot for us both---the alternation of outdoor work in the garden & fishing for Ted, with each of us writing more and better than ever in our separate studies, and the two beautiful babies and nothing to worry about but fallout, I felt Life Begins at 30.

1–Dr Beuscher's father, Dr Donald Grey Barnhouse (1895–1960) was a Christian preacher, pastor, and writer. He died on 5 November 1960 following an operation for a brain tumour.
2–TH and Assia Wevill had begun an affair which was discovered by SP on 9 July 1962.

Then everything went queer. Ted began to leap up in the morning & intercept the mail. He began to talk, utterly unlike him, of how he could write & direct film scripts, how he was going to win the Nobel Prize, how he had been asleep all the time we were married, recoiling, as the French say, so he could jump the better. How he wanted to experience everybody & everything, there was a monster in him, a dictator. Und so weiter. He would come out with these things after spurts of lovemaking as in our honeymoon days, asking me like a technician, did I like this, did I like that. Then round on me for holding hands & being jealous of other women.

I just felt sick, as if I were the practise board for somebody else. I get these semi-clairvoyant states, which I suppose are just diabolic intuition. I picked up the phone & a nasty man's voice asked if Ted could take a call from London.[1] Ted always wants me to find out who it is, so I asked, & the man said he was sorry, the person didn't want to say. I felt thick with my own dumbness & called Ted. It was a woman, saying "Can I see you?" He said she didn't say her name & he had no idea who it was. I was pretty sure who it was. A girl who works in an ad agency in London, very sophisticated, and who, with her second poet-husband,[2] took over the lease on our London flat. We'd had them down for a weekend, and I'd walked in on them (Ted & she) Tête-a-tête in the kitchen & Ted had shot me a look of pure hate. She smiled & stared at me curiously the rest of the weekend. She is very destructive---had so many abortions when she was young she only miscarries now, wants to die before she gets old, tried to kill her first husband with a knife when he married another woman, after she herself had deceived him; now she thinks her second husband is 'Past his best, poor thing'. Calls her first husband on the phone (getting a man to ask for him, to get round the wife) and meets him for lunch. She kept calling a while, for no apparent reason, seeming almost speechless when she got me. Then, it seems reasonable to believe, she repeated her usual trick to get through to Ted. And when I got up to his study, to clean up as I do, empty envelopes in her hand were lying round, dated during all the time he'd been leaping up for mail. Ted said "No," she couldn't see him, over the phone. But I was standing there, stunned. Then the next day, after a night of no sleep & horrid talk (me asking him for god's sake to say who it was so it would stop being Everybody), he took the train to

1 – Cf. SP's 'Words heard, by accident, over the phone' written on the same day as the letter.
2 – Assia Wevill's husbands were: John Steel (married 1947; divorced 1949); Richard Lipsey (married 1952; divorced 1959); and David Wevill (married 1960–9, until Assia Wevill's death).

London for a "holiday." He assured me, in a flash of his old self, that me & the children were what he really loved & would come back to & he was not going to London to lie about & had not touched another woman since we were married. I have discontinued the phone, for I can't stand waiting, every minute, to hear that girl breathing at the end of it, my voice at her fingertips, my life & happiness on her plate.

I suppose this all sounds very naive to you. It is, after all, what seems to happen to everybody. Only I am not, as Ted says, blasé enough. I care to a frenzy. I could never satisfy myself by "getting even" with other men: other men mean nothing to me---they are repulsive. This is one thing I want you to see: Ted is so fantastically unique---beautiful, physically wonderful, brilliant, loving, eager for me to do my own work, without (as I thought) a lie or deceit in his body. It is the <u>lying</u> that kills me. I can face nasty truths, unpleasant facts. I am sure a possessive wife would have driven most men mad before this. But I just don't have the ability to care nothing about other women chasing Ted. He is very famous over here, and a real catch. Women are always writing him, drooling about his poems etc., begging him to tell them about his life, etc. As you may imagine, movie stars have nothing on a handsome male poet. He seemed to want to flee all big publicity---TV & so on, & was furious when I let any cameramen into the house. But now it is different: I have been a jinx, a chain.

Well, if he would tell me the truth about the letters & phonecalls & his flying off, I would be in some way purged. But now it balloons up before me like a great fantasy which I sense, but cannot limit to reality. I am not generous. His being with another woman, especially a woman who spites me & is dying to stop my creative work, like this one, makes me retch. I cannot sleep. I cannot eat. It is because I feel I can never trust him again, and have been perhaps a fool to be so happy and trusting in the past.

If I could carry on normally, I might be more rational. But I keep having to run off to cry and be dry-sick as each image of that girl assaults me, and her pleasure at hearing me nonplussed on the phone, of taking my life and joy. I can't imagine a life without Ted. But I am not like other wives who tolerate all---marriage to me is a kind of sanctity, faithfulness in every part, and I will not ever be able to love or make love again in happiness, with this looming in front of me. It is his wanting to <u>deceive</u> me that is so like this girl & unlike him.

What can I do? I would never in my life think of divorce, because I married till death and am his wife till death. He can have tarty women & bastards, but only one wife and her children. And that's me. I am simply not cool & sophisticated. My marriage is the center of my being, I have given everything to it without reserve. Worst, my writing is killed by this mess. I write, not in compensation, out of sorrow, but from an overflow, a surplus, of joy, & my ability to criticize my work & do it well is my objectivity, which stems from happiness, not sorrow. The day after Ted left, I got the proofs of my first novel.[1] It saved the day for me: I roared and roared, it was so funny and good. But then there is the big empty bed & I am like a desperado, & take the baby in with me. Then all night it is visions of that woman with Ted, her delight. I imagine idiocies---her coming to live here, me breaking her nose & knocking her teeth out. I think if she killed, or tried to knife, her first husband, she would quite like to kill me. And she is so outwardly sophisticated, so mocking. I have never learned the art & never will. I break up in pieces, cry, rave.[2] I am proud. I will not be made a fool of. Let me learn the true things, not be diddled & betrayed. I think I am not good in the part of wronged wife. A wronged wife is at such a disadvantage because she feels so right, and this is my desperation. I hate the thing in Ted that can jeopardize and ruin everything like this and expect to have a wife-secretary-mother-dishwasher-housekeeper waiting to take him back, refreshed. Until the next letter, the next come on. I have nothing to refresh me. I am left here, with the evidence of the phonecall, the evidence of the oddly coincidental departure, the evidence of my each sense. I can never forget or forgive this. I suppose people would tell me I am lucky---he seems to want us as homebase still. Well, I can't be any sort of sweet homebase for stuff that makes me gag. I feel ugly and a fool, when I have so long felt beautiful & capable of being a wonderful happy mother and wife and writing novels for fun & money. I am just sick. What can I do?

To make things worse---or better---my mother is here for six weeks. She has taken over some of the meals & babyminding & freed us both to do our work & go off on day-jaunts. I was so happy. I get on pretty well with mother now, because I keep off the great controversies, and she is a real help & I make her feel this. But you can imagine how images repeat themselves---here I am, alone with my mother & the children! I am so numb I am only glad she looks after Frieda, because I am hollow as a zombie inside & without motion. My milk has soured or something, because the baby has been having diarrhea day and night since this bloody phonecall.

1 – SP's revised proof with autograph corrections and first Heinemann edition, both inscribed with her name and address, appeared at auction via Bonhams on 21 March 2018.
2 – C.f. SP's 'Elm': 'Now I break up in pieces that fly about like clubs.'

I have a feeling, when I try to look at what is I am sure my unique predicament (unique because I am unable to swallow this behavior as if it never was, unable to accept clean breaks, like divorce, because I am in spirit and body married forever to this one person, unable to forget), that people or you or anybody would say---let him go, let him get It out of his system. Well, what about my system? How do I get this other It out? This jealous retch, this body that comes, laughing, between my body & his body.[1] If he would only say who & what it was. Then It would have limits. But this intangible, invisible, infinitely possible thing is killing me. How can I live without him? I mean, if I could write & garden & be happy with my babies, I could survive. But I am so sick & sleepless & jumpy all is a mess. I suppose it might be good if mother could go---she has just over 3 more weeks. I tell her nothing: 'Ted is on a holiday in London, to do some radio programs.' She is good, doesn't pry, makes herself scarce. She said the other day "I am so glad to see you so happy," Well, that was the death knell. I have been trying to start a 2nd novel & said laughingly to Ted: Now if I can just keep happy & peaceful for 6 weeks I can do it. Later he flew at me "Why should I limit myself by your happiness or unhappiness?"

Well, that's it. I feel you, having been once divorced and being a psychiatrist, not an Anglican rector, will feel I am a dog-in-the-manger about divorce (which has not, by the way, really entered our talk, except that Ted says it would be a good thing if his older brother,[2] whom he idolized, should get divorced---a stand-in for his own wish?). I simply would never do it. I honestly do believe I am wedded to Ted till death. Other men seem ants compared to him. I am physically attracted to no-one else. All the complexities of my soul & mind are involved inextricably with him. And I do feel I lead an independent life---I work, write, have my own art & reputation, my babies. Yet this is dirt in my mouth if I can't trust and love him.

O I would be so grateful if you would sit down and send me some word. I can talk to no-one about this---mother, of course, least of all. She does not even know I have written a novel. She is in almost utter bliss. Please, please, do write me. I have got nothing but the bloody empty envelopes secreted by Ted in stupid places, and would like some word of my own. What can I do about the bloody lying? his refusal to come out & say: this is the way it is---I have seen so-and-so, it is she, not everybody, and you

1 – Cf. SP's poem 'The Other': 'Sulfurous adulteries grieve in a dream. / Cold glass, how you insert yourself / Between myself and myself.' (2 July 1962).
2 – 'a good thing ~~for~~ his brother' appears in the original.

can bloody-well lump it. That would be salutary as a slap in the face. And then, how can I be, if he comes back? When I am full of hate, resentment, a wish to kill this bloody girl to whom my misery is just sauce. And how can I stop being miserable? I hate myself like this. I do need word!

Please write, right away, if you can.

With love,
Sylvia

TO *Marvin & Kathy Kane*

Sunday 15 July 1962 TLS, Indiana University

Court Green
North Tawton
Devon.
July 15, 1962

Dear, dear Marvin & Kathie,

It was great to get your letter. We have been up in a heaval with my mother here (she stays way into August) as with no matter what good will & fortitude mater's turn to witches after a certain amount of days if left in the sun. And I have a ghastly suspicion I have broken my toe. Which I shall see about tomorrow.

Our whole search for cottages ended up in only the two we said---both without bits & pieces or electricity (could you use a battery wireless?). Anyhow, we keep reading the ads. The cottage of the dead man's[1] next to us is up for sale furnished for 2,500 pounds (ha!!) any takers?

I am excited about being on a program all to myself Marvin, you are very good. Will it mean money? We are very broke now having sunk all into the house repairs & payment. Ted told me he had sent back "We're just not practical"[2] before I read it, but that was not true as I found it this week in the midst of huge angst & dolor & laughed like crazy. If it could make me laugh then, in the grave of a great deal, it is genuine grand comedy. The grant people sound hopeful. I think the poetry-popular-anthology reading is a great idea and much fun and would love to do it some time latish fall when I've weaned Nicholas which should be about then.

1–Percy Key died on 25 June 1962 and was buried on the 29th in the cemetery off Exeter Street, North Tawton.

2–Marvin Kane, *We're Just Not Practical*, a play about a couple working as housekeepers in a boardinghouse and their bad luck.

Ted says he will drive up definitely to move you down or what if you want. Wish me mother-fortitude!! And a not badly broken toe.

Love,
Sylvia

TO *Ruth Tiffany Barnhouse Beuscher*

Friday 20 July 1962 TLS, Smith College

Court Green
North Tawton
Devonshire, England
Friday: July 20

Dear, dear Dr. Beuscher,

First of all, please charge me some money. I feel a fraud and a heel to be cadging time and advice out of you for nothing. If I were in America, I would be asking you for a few sessions for which I'd want to pay, and right now, a few airletters back and forth could do me a powerful lot of good. You are a professional woman whose services I would greatly appreciate, and as a professional woman, I can pay for them what anyone else would. No need for cut rates or student's fees. My last New Yorker poem earned me $270,[1] so I can afford the luxury of a good psychiatrist which is you. Let me know what would be best. Maybe a letter from me & an answer from you we could count as a session. Bill me, huh? Right now, I need some good talk to carry me on.

I wrote you in the middle of my agony-week, when I hadn't come to the climax of it & been freed to see what I had to see, & so was half begging you to reassure me that at least my old dream-idyll was a right one even if it worked out wrong. The virginity, as it were, of our marriage ended Friday the 13th (O we are very superstitious in our house) & I went to a friend's[2] with the baby leaving mother here with Frieda & went through the whole bloody thing minute by minute, surrounded by 4 cats (one of which produced 3 kittens), a dog, and many hens and pigs. At first I thought, why couldn't Ted just go away & find freedom this way? Why did he have to fuck this woman in this nasty way, almost killing me & her husband & Frieda etc. by the upset of the shock. Then, after I had got over the nausea, got the doctor to knock me out for 8 hours after a week

1–SP's 'Tulips'.
2–SP visited the Comptons.

of no eating or sleeping, I thought: Thank God. I am free of so much. And this was probably the most economical way to do it, although at the time of my misery I thought it the cruellest.

I think you could do me some more good now, because I think I am willing to see a lot more than I could or would when I last saw you. I remember you almost made me hysterical when you asked me, or suggested, that Ted might want to go off on his own. This was heresy to me then, the Worst. How could a true-love ever ever want to leave his truly-beloved for one second? We would experience Everything together. I began to worry about the purity & strength of my love when I found myself thinking: Why doesn't the bastard leave the house & let me put my hair up & dust & sing. I think obviously both of us must have been pretty weird to live as we have done for so long. Of course I suppose any husband of mine would have a large flow of my feeling for my father to complicate our relationship. And Ted has as I think you will admit, a rather large dose of mother-sister worship in him. And hate of course.

I was always having nightmares about Ted dying or being in accidents & for this reason could hardly bear to let him out of my sight. For fear he would desert me forever, like my father, if I didn't watch him closely enough. And he must have had enough desire for womb-comfort to stick it out. Well, we are 30. We grow up slowly, but, it appears, with a bang.

Anyhow, Ted came back. It occurred to me almost immediately that he felt a lot worse than I did. Not sorry-worse. He just wasn't purged, because he hadn't had my particular wild agony. And the bloody girl wasn't very sensual. She complained a lot about her abortions & what a bad hostess I was, going off on my own to my study etc. etc. Well you bet I went off. All she wanted was for me to sit on the bed while they fucked. No thanks. Yes, she is the Sister. This occurred to me on the train down from London where I did a job yesterday.[1] She is the barren & frigid symbol of sex. (I honestly think Ted's sister may be a virgin. She is beautiful, smart, but absolutely uncreative & cold.) When I was at my lowest, thinking grimly: What has this Weavy Asshole (her name is actually Assia Wevill) got that I haven't, I thought: she can't make a baby (and really isn't so sorry), can't make a book or a poem, just ads about bad bakery bread, wants to die before she gets old & loses her beauty, and is <u>bored</u>. Bored, bored, bored.

1 – SP, George Hartley, G. Arthur Wilkinson, and Eric Walter White met at White's office, 4 St James's Square, London, on 19 July 1962 to finalise the contest winners. Due to illness John Press was unable to attend. Second and third prizes were awarded to Harold Massingham for 'Graveside' and Marion Lineaweaver for 'The Sound of My Habitation'. Judges were paid 20 guineas for their work.

With herself & her life. She literally moved into our London flat (after we left!). She came down here & wanted to move into my life. Well, the old girl has done me a big favor. The funny thing is, I don't think she must really enjoy sex, except in her head. One of her many odd gimmicks is that she calls up her old first husband and goes ga-ga because "It sounds as if we were in bed together." That is another difference between us. Believe me, I would have the bloody man in bed. I am that shameless. I hate mental titillations that don't come off in reality.

One thing about sex. I hate comfortable rituals. I like all sorts of positions at a lot of odd times of day, & really feel terrific and made new from every cell when I am done. I actually wondered at one point if Ted was sick. Well, of course, how can one keep up that intensity & variety every day & night for over 6 years. A biological & psychological impossibility I would think. And I have my pride. I mean, I was not schooled with love for 2 years by my French lover for nothing. I have in me a good tart, as distinct from a bad tart: I feel all I feel, which is a lot, & which I think men like to feel they can do, and I do not need to pretend I feel, or to feel only in my head. Well I want this tart to have a good life again. I'm damned if I am going to be a Wife-mother every minute of the day. And as I am a pretty faithful type, and have no desire left for malice or revenge on Ted, to "get back at him", I'd just as soon make love with Ted. But coming from a distance, from a space, a mutual independence.

Ironically, this great shock purged me of a lot of old fears. It was very like the old shock treatments I used to fear so: it broke a tight circuit wide open, a destructive circuit, a deadening circuit, & let in a lot of pain, air and real elation. I feel very elated. The little conventional girl-wife wanted Ted to come back & say: My God, how could I hurt you so, it will never happen again. But I knew I really couldn't stand him to say that, & he didn't. He told me the truth about the femme fatale, which freed my knowledge to sit about in the light of day, like an object, to be coped with, not hid like some hairy monster. And I didn't die. I thought my capacity for conventional joy & trust & love was killed, but it wasn't. It is all back. And I don't think I'm a suicidal type any more, because I was really fascinated to see how, in the midst of genuine agony, it would all turn out & kept going. I really did believe it was the Worst Thing that could happen, Ted being Unfaithful; or next worst to his dying. Now I am actually grateful it happened, I feel new.

As I say, I have no desire for other men. Ted is one in a million. Sex is so involved with me in my admiration for male intelligence, power and beauty that he is simply the only man I lust for. I know men feel differently about sex, but I thought they too were capable of deep and faithful love. It is not very much consolation to me that Ted really deeply & faithfully loves me, while he follows any woman with bright hair, or an essay on Shakespeare in her pocket, or an ability for flamenco dancing. If he thinks they're real, and they think they're real, what good does my thinking they're unreal do? They're real enough to hurt me, and make me lose my pride and my joy in my mind and body and potential talents. The thought of Ted making physical love to them, registering them under my name in hotels, letting all the people we know see this, hurts and nauseates me horribly. I feel if he really loved me he would see how this hurt damages my whole being, makes it barren, & deprives me of joy in lovemaking with him.

All the stupid little things I did with love---baking bread, making pies, painting furniture, planting flowers, sewing baby things---seem silly and empty to me without faith in Ted's love. And the children who so delighted me are like little miasmas, crying for daddy. Of course mother's being here through all this hasn't helped. She officially knows nothing---I don't talk to her about it---but she has seen everything. I think in one way she hates me for having deprived *her* of her vicarious dream-idyll, and in one way she is viciously glad: "I *knew* men were like that," I feel her thinking. "Horrid selfish bastards, just like my husband. And Sylvia thought hers was an exception!" It has been humiliating for me to have her here through this, gloating over my weaning the baby, wailing "O you looked so happy and *beau*tiful when I came . . ." implying I am now a tired old hag. I had been getting on quite well with her before, but this has put a ghastly strain on our pleasant if distant relationship.

One or two practical questions: shall I refuse to tell our friends and relatives about this? I really have no desire to complain to anyone & I hate people maunching over my business. And shall I ever let Ted's sister come down here? I honestly *don't* want to feel her gloating, offering to provide Ted with nice Paris models & scolding me for being a dog-in-the-manger. Ted is free, why can't he go see her on his own? Or would it be wiser to have her come, try to deflect her vileness (she is dying for Ted's brother to get divorced---the Other Women in her family are intolerable to her) and weather a visit.

Ted has stopped doing any man's work about the place. Should I take on the weeding, mowing, hoeing and go on figuring the income tax, paying the bills (he defiantly misads & botches the checkbook), without a murmur? He once said he hated me asking him to do jobs (I mean *heavy* work, not lady-work) around the house; I stopped; he doesn't do any.

I love this place and get on well with the people in the town, thank god. It is my first home. But I am ready to pack off on trips in a flash, anything. Do you have any advice about these other women. And how to maintain my own woman-morale from day to day. And toughen myself!

Love to you,
Sylvia

PS: I'd feel awfully relieved if you'd see fit to agree to a few paid airletter sessions! And can I dedicate my novel to R. B. or would this be unethical or a bother? It may not be High Art, but it is good & funny.

TO *A. Alvarez*

Saturday 21 July 1962 TLS, Smith College

Court Green
North Tawton
Devon.
July 21, 1962

Dear Al,

Let me know what you think of the 3 poems I sent.[1] I am, as you will gather, a bit of a clairvoyant. But that has nothing to do with poetical quality. I know "Elm" is too long & fat for the Observer but thought it might amuse you in one way or some other. And maybe the other two, though not so gigantesque, are too late, or you don't like. Or both. I like your opinions. I don't mean, agree. But like. And I am tough enough, so don't be ginger.

I'd be grateful to have a whole No, or whatever, soon, because I need to flog round what I've got. Money money. You know. Please don't be "nice".

Love,
Sylvia

1–According to SP's submissions list, she sent 'Event', 'The Rabbit Catcher', and 'Elm' to *The Observer* on 30 June 1962 and at a later unspecified date, 'Crossing the Water', 'An Appearance', and 'Little Fugue'. Sylvia Plath, 'Crossing the Water', *The Observer* (23 September 1962): 25; 'Event', *The Observer* (16 December 1962): 21; 'The Rabbit Catcher', *The Observer* (7 February 1965): 26.

TO *Richard Murphy*[1]

Saturday 21 July 1962 TLS, University of Tulsa

Court Green
North Tawton
Devonshire, England
Saturday: July 21

Dear Richard,

I don't know how fast the cogs of officialdom work, but I could not deny myself the pleasure of letting you know right away that "Years Later", the Epilogue of the "Cleggan Disaster" has won first prize in the Cheltenham contest. I suppose you have already heard, or will soon hear this from Mr. Wilkinson, the chairman of the festival. The Epilogue, because we felt that touched heights perhaps greater than in the earlier part.

I now have a question to ask you. Is there any chance of Ted & me coming to Bofin[2] around the last week in August or first week in September? I don't know how long you run your boat, or what your terms are, but for me at least, I desperately need a boat and the sea and no squalling babies. We are now trying to negotiate a family to come & mind Frieda (2 years) and Nicholas (6 months), and I should know Monday if and exactly when they can come. If they won't, then I shall have simply to hire someone. But if you could let me know right away if any week in late August or early (first week) September would connect us with you & your blessed boat, it would be so nice.

It would also be lovely to see you again.[3] The center of my whole early life was ocean and boats, and because of this, your poems have been of especial interest to me, and I think you would be a very lovely person for us to visit just now. Is there any kind old soul on the island who would feed & bed us & would it be possible to bring the car there, or would we have to leave it on the mainland? I hope, while in Ireland, we may also collide with Jack & Maire Sweeney, of whom we are very fond. And maybe Dublin. I have never been before.

Do tell me I am not being an awful bother. And please do say we may come on your boat. I have always desired, above many things, a friend with a boat. Ted sends his best, and hopes you will take us on.

1–Irish poet Richard Murphy (1927–2018).

2–The island of Inishbofin, which lies seven miles off the coast of Ireland. Murphy operated the *Ave Maria*, a Galway hooker, from the fishing village of Cleggan, where he lived.

3–SP met Richard Murphy on two occasions in 1961. The first at the Poetry at the Mermaid Festival on 17 July, and then later at the Guinness Poetry Awards on 31 October.

Again, congratulations, & warmest good wishes.

Sylvia Plath

P.S. Eric White said something about Faber & Eliot having accepted your poems.[1] I am so very glad. It is so deserved!

TO *Ruth Tiffany Barnhouse Beuscher*

Monday 30 July 1962 TLS, Smith College

Court Green
North Tawton
Devonshire, England
Monday: July 30th

Dear Dr. Beuscher,

I do hope you will agree to a few paid letter-sessions. I have even been wildly thinking of saving my money to fly to America for some person-to-person sessions with you, if that were possible, but I have to do a few more novels to manage that, I think. This seems a violent change-point in my life, & I feel to need to work toward as much insight as possible to change with it & weather it in a creative way, not withdraw from it. I feel I could ruin everything now by persisting in blindness & ignorance.

I have been at a nadir, very grim, since my last letter to you. What I would like to do is isolate and purge the father-feelings from my relation with Ted. I see I've been a fool to indulge in these---I've been frantic if Ted came home later than he said, for fear he might be in an accident; I've not wanted to stay alone overnight in the country, because the darks of Dartmoor scared me; I've let him buy the meat (my father always brought home our groceries from work) & had Frieda play with him mornings while he worked in the garden & I wrote. We had reasoned that this last arrangement was "economical"---freed me for writing at my peak period to earn money & Ted had to do the chores around the place anyhow, so why not let Frieda play along. He's always loved her & loved teaching her things. Well, I see my fear of accident & dark as repetitions of fears for the life of my father: they are gone from me. I shall do all the shopping & baby-minding (I am now just about successful enough to hire a local babyminder for 4 hours a morning) as these have turned from casual jobs into symbols of whose sex is what. What other practical things can I do?

1–Richard Murphy, *Sailing to an Island* (London: Faber & Faber, 1963).

And what, above all, does Ted think I am? His mother? A womb? What can I do to stop him seeing me as a puritannical warden? He says he doesn't want any more children & wants to make over our cottage & hire a live-in nanny to free me (fine by me!); when Nicholas came, he said he felt the baby was a usurper. I don't think he'd have felt this if it had been a girl---so does that make Ted my baby as well as me his? Ye Gods. I would like a couple more children---later, when I have this live-in nanny so I can take off.

Anyhow, Ted is on the rampage---writing letters and even radio broadcasts about the advantages of destruction, breaking one's life into bits every ten years, and damn the pieces. His favorite poem of his own is pure ego-Fascist, about a hawk "I kill where I please because it is all mine."[1] I realise now he considered I might kill myself over this (as did the wife of someone we know well), and what he did was worth it to him. I have always admired him for this inner pride and energy---most people just haven't got the power in them. But I would like to break my life, & go ahead with him, not be relegated to the homefront: the suffering & pitied but very repugnant mother-wife.

The real crux to me now is what to do about the Other Woman business. Maybe a lot of my nausea & shortness of breath & sleeplessness is due to my second loss of a second father. Okay. I want to get rid of those little-girl desires & fears. But some of it is that I am horribly hurt in my morale as a wife. Ted had one girl after another till he met me. And I had enough inner pride in myself as a woman not to fear other attractive woman---I liked them as friends myself. Now Ted is looking everybody over. And with him, it's not flirting, it's bed. We went for a ghastly poetry reading together to Wales this week.[2] I had just weaned the baby in a hurry, my milk was going anyway, & I didn't want to take the baby along. Well there was a very lovely 18 year old blonde secretary, just married. Ted eyed her, immediately made a date to read in her hometown and asked me what I thought of her, why didn't she quite come off? Well he always criticizes a woman he's after. To put me off. What am I to do? Ted says he hadn't been infatuated with anybody for 6 years since me, till this ad-agency girl. Am I to cheer him off onto one infatuation after another now? I have too much pride to say: O please God, it kills me to think of all these other women knowing you and your body and laughing at me, doing the dishes & wiping noses in Devon. My other impulse is to say: O fuck off, grab

1–TH, 'Hawk Roosting'.
2–See SP to Brian Cox, 17 October 1961.

them all. What seems civilised & sophisticated to the people we move among seems stupid and boring and selfish to me. Am I an idiot to think that there is some purpose in being bodily faithful to the person you love? In riding through infatuations without always indulging yourself, if you know it hurts someone? I mean, my pleasure in lovemaking is spoiled by thinking: is he comparing my hair to this one, my shape to that one, my talents to the other?

I am sick of being suspicious. I would rather know the truth about everything, than merely suspect it. And be told by all the other people who love to pass on nasty news---and when you're famous as Ted is over here, they are legion. How can I have any self-respect? I hate the idea of living here in the country with the children & having Ted go off & sleep with various women & come back exhausted & refreshed to write, be fed etc. It humiliates me. I simply can't laugh and blow smoke-rings. He hates me to be tearful, but my god, the prospect of this makes me cry. I don't ask for "conventional" safety, but how can I make our relationship "fundamentally safe", as you suggest it can be? When I think he wants to follow every infatuation into bed, shall I just let him? This is what freedom, it seems, means to him. And just about all. He is handsome & fantastically virile & attractive. I am not beautiful. When I am happy, I can glow & burn, but what have I in this to make me happy? I bear his name; I have born his children. He loves me in a way. Shall I just sit around waiting till some girl agitates him to get a divorce? I mean, I want to write, travel, etc. etc., but it is pretty hollow to me when my relation to my husband is such a lousy one. How can I have the guts to cheer him on to new women, wait & wait, wondering how long it will last, and then welcome him home, no tears, no bitchery, no nothing. How can I make these women unnecessary to him? And keep up my own sense of seductiveness and womanly power? I don't want to be sorrowful or bitter, men hate that, but what can I do in face of these prospects?

What I need now is the guts not to be lugubrious or accusing when I am tired, or my morale is low. I want Ted to understand I am not a doll-wife who can be lied to & kept happy. I want the dignity of facing facts, & facing them before all my friends & relatives. There are a few things I do think important. I'm not French enough to enjoy entertaining people who sleep with my husband, & having the little bitches criticize my hostessery into the bargain. I'd like honestly to know roughly where Ted is, so I could get in touch with him at a GPO or something in case of emergency. If he is fucking about with someone, I'd rather know it straight out, than get suspicions, intimations, anonymous phonecalls & letters. Do you think I am still asking too much? I mean, I do think I am prepared to do an awful lot. I am a good cook, I mow the lawn, am getting to be a good gardener, I weed, afford a cleaner, earn half our income (this I feel is an advantage to both of us, for it frees Ted from a dull job to support us, & gives us travel money), make out the income tax, am a feeling & imaginative lay, & probably can write quite funny & good books.

What I see now I could not have stood, what would to me have been the real worst, was for Ted to come & say: I want this girl for my wife & to bear my children. But of course, he felt his problem was womb-engulfment & did not want a wife or children at all. I at one point told him: I am saving you from ever getting mucked up with a wife & children again: you can have tarts & bastards, but if any other woman gets refrigerators & nappies in her eyes, you can say you have a really good old wife at home who is saving you to be free & not get stuck in the wallow of domesticity again. And he does genuinely love us. He says now he dimly thought this would either kill me or make me, and I think it might make me. And him too.

What I also need is wisdom for him. He takes a lot of understanding. He is, I am sure, a genius. A really great writer, a handsome and great man. I have been so hurt this week I feel like upchucking at the thought of his laying about with other women just this minute. But I would like to be able to cope with this again, if it came up. If he needed to test his freedom, to test me. And believe me, women are dying to get their hands on him. And on me, too. I honestly don't ever, by cowardice, boringness, accusation, limitedness, ever want to give Ted the chance to think he should trade us in for a better family model. I am sure there will be other pressure points, as he proves & proves his freedom to himself, & I would like to feel I could write to you for a talk at those times, & be billed, as for interviews.

What I am not is a Penelope type.[1] I have come to this country town because Ted said it was his dream---apples, fishing, peace, clean air, etc. etc. I had wanted to stay in London, because I liked all the social life, movies, art exhibits & rush. Well now I love it here, & this is the first home I've had, very beautiful, & with some fine people in the neighborhood. It is a good base. But I am damned if I want to sit here like a cow, milked by babies. I love my children, but want my own life. I want to write books, see people & travel. I want, eventually, to make over our separate cottage

1 – A reference to Homer, *The Odyssey*. Penelope was the wife of Odysseus who, while she had suitors, remained faithful to her husband in his absences.

& hire a nanny. So I've got to work hard. I refuse the role of passive, suffering wife. I think your advice about not having any more children for years a good one. I <u>think</u> I'd like a couple more someday, but only when I've got a nanny to free me.

I am, by the way, not fat!! I have the gift God gives some skinny women, namely that having babies & nursing them have given me a better figure than I ever hoped for, & my waist is the same (with all this lugging of fertiliser pots, mowing lawns & weeding huge vegetable patches) & I can wear clothes with good style. My nose, I fear, is unalterable, but otherwise I might become vain & insufferable, so the good lord has seen fit, in his wisdom, to load me with it. My hair (I remember you once said: Either very short or very long, no shillyshally pageboys) is very long.[1] I sometimes walk about in it like a shawl, & have a good enough coronet effect which few women can attain, with braids in a kind of pillbox.

I would like some time to have you discuss what you suggest about being in my own womb & having babies & my "prehistoric cave". I get a terrific sensual pleasure in being pregnant & nursing. But I must say, I get a terrific sensual pleasure in being light & slender & fucking as well.

Can you think of any other discontents of Ted's I might forsee? I think he will need to prove conclusively & perhaps several times (<u>soon</u>), then maybe less often, that he is "free". He says this means travel, not tarts, but I feel naturally now the two go together. What I don't want to be is an unfucked wife. I get bitter then, & cross. And I feel wasted. And I don't just mean the token American what-is-it twice a week, front to front, "thank you darling" either. It might simplify things if I could desire other men, but I need to admire them too, & find them attractive, & there are very few of these, & I'm not likely to meet them in cow country.

Practically, Ted needs a job of some sort that takes him away quite regularly. I think this might be managed with speaking engagements: he gets enough requests, & could thus travel throughout England, spacing them one or two a week. But I honestly don't feel like sticking through the bloody country winter with no husband to come home & share experiences for weeks on indefinite weeks. I like to go on long holidays too.

Can you suggest a gracious procedure when you see some little (whoops, not little, big!) tart is after your husband at a party, or dinner or something? Do you leave them to it? Engage a hotel room? Smile & vanish? Smile

1–Possibly a reference to SP's 20 March 1959 journal entry: 'A desire to get my hair cut attractively instead of this mousy pony tail. Will no doubt go out and get a pageboy cut as of old' (*Journals*, 475).

& stand by? What I don't want to be is stern & disapproving or teary. But I am only human. I have to feel I have some ground-rights. So far, I have only said I don't want the bitches to sit around the house expecting me to cook them nice dinners. But I don't find joy in the general sexual exchanges one finds in our world. I mean, Ted is unique to me. I would like to be unique to him. And wise. Yes, wiser than he is in some ways. By the time I am 50 I want to be very experienced & have purple hair & be very wise & have interesting children & piles of money.

Can you weed through this & tell me where you think I am fooling myself, near truth, downright stupid. What can I legitimately ask of Ted? And he of me? A funny footnote: all through this Ted's been writing a radio play fittingly called "Difficulties of a Bridegroom". It was accepted on the condition that he re-write the reality frame of the bridegroom's encounter with a dream femme fatale so the audience would know what was real & what wasnt. A nice parable illustrating your point about the reality of this woman.

Thanks a million times for the letter. Do answer this. & bill me for the lot.

Love,
Sylvia Hughes

P.S. All day I have been planting out my seedlings from their greenhouse "growing pots" into open ground. "Hardening them off" is the horticultural expression.

TO *Marvin & Kathy Kane*

Friday 10 August 1962[1] TLS, Indiana University

Court Green
North Tawton
Devon.
Friday: August?

Dear, dear Marvin & Kathy---

It is all set. Ted will pick you up at your place around about noon on Monday, deposit your boxes where you will and bring you back for a late dinner with us Monday night. We are both very happy about the prospect of you coming.

1 – Date supplied from internal evidence.

I came back[1] with marvelous train companions---an absolutely stunning blond pure Cockney girl and completely unspoiled working at Butlin's holiday camp[2] (Ooo it's a brothel) who told me all about everything including her love for her boss (He's only 25 years older 'n' me) and left me all her pork sandwiches at her stop, then a very swish English mother whose husband is a biologist and who descanted to me on the rareness of happy marriages (hers being one, she says, roundly thumping on wood).

There is a woman it seems eager to come 5 mornings a week to mind the babies, so I should be initiating her Monday I hope, and starting to write mornings again.[3] I just heard from my sometimes patroness that she is alighting in London this Wednesday[4] night midway between a trip from America to Russia & wants to see Ted & me for dinner that night in London. So maybe you can babysit for us that night??? She is very impulsive (with a huge lineage of great-grandchildren, alas) and I feel this is a very important meeting. I hope to sort of mention in a casual way my dreams of scrimping & making over the cottage.

Thank you thank you thank you for an absolutely saving day. I felt terrific coming back, renewed in every cell & slept the sleep of the deserving, sans pills. So you see what a fine influence you both are!

Much love,
Sylvia

1–SP travelled to London the day before, 9 August 1962, probably to record at the BBC; see note in SP to George MacBeth, 19 June 1962.
2–A chain of holiday camps in the United Kingdom.
3–According to SP's Letts Royal Office Diary Tablet for 1962, this was Mrs Bires, who began working at Court Green from 9 a.m. to 1 p.m. on 20 August 1962.
4–On 15 August 1962, SP and TH stayed at the Connaught Hotel, Carlos Place, Mayfair, London, as guests of Olive Higgins Prouty, and saw Agatha Christie's *The Mousetrap* at the Ambassadors Theatre, West Street, London.

TO *George MacBeth*

Wednesday 15 August 1962 TLS, BBC Written Archives Centre

Court Green
North Tawton
Devon.
August 15, 1962

Dear George,

I think the Penguin book of Sick verse[1] is an inspired idea, and am delighted to hear you are doing it. I've been meaning to send off these two recent poems[2] to you for consideration for the BBC, and I thought I'd enclose them now, In case they strike you as being darker than my other darks, sicker than the old sicks.

Very best wishes.
Sincerely,
Sylvia Plath

George MacBeth, Esq.
44 Sheen Road
Richmond
Surrey

TO *Aurelia Schober Plath*

Friday 17 August 1962 TLS, Indiana University

Court Green
North Tawton
Devon.
August 17, 1962

Dear mother,

I am enclosing these pictures[3] for you, which I think came out very well. I took them to London on Wednesday to show Mrs. Prouty. I will have a couple made up and send them to Marcia Plumer. We did go to London, had cocktails, dinner & saw Agatha Christie's "Mousetrap", a play which has run for 10 years. She put us up at her hotel, the Connaught, and it is the loveliest hotel I've ever stayed in---very intimate, clean, yet antique-

1–George MacBeth (ed.), *The Penguin Book of Sick Verse* (Harmondsworth: Penguin, 1963); includes Sylvia Plath, 'The Surgeon at 2 a.m.' and 'In Plaster', 14–16; 20–2.

2–SP sent 'Berck-Plage' and 'The Other'.

3–The photographs are no longer with the letter.

feeling. No great impersonal grandeur. We had hot baths & breakfast in bed. It was wonderful to see Mrs. Prouty again, and that nice Claire,[1] her rather dowdier sister-in-law companion. It is so sad---did you hear, Mrs. Prouty's nasty cook (whom I never liked) deserted her to work in a bank, her maid had a heart attack & her gardener, or is it chauffeur, is demanding more money when she thinks he already gets too much. None of her children[2] want anything from the house. I can't bear to think of her selling it. Evidently she undertook this strenuous trip to escape those painful worries. She was beautifully keen, although Claire says she suffers from aphasia, and forgets terribly. She asked Ted & me about our work with her usual insight. She means an immense deal to me. I hope you drop over to see her now and then. Her loneliness must be appalling.

Winifred has at last found me a nice shy woman with two children in school to come work for me 4 hours a morning 5 mornings a week. It would have been impossible for Nancy to mind babies & clean too, I should have seen that, but at least she will feel I thought of her first. Both Nancy & this woman are on holiday this week, so you can imagine what a mess the house is & how little peace I have.

But Monday I shall train the new woman, and Tuesday Nancy is back, so help is in sight. At least I should be able to count on them. A business arrangement, with money paid, is the only thing I can count on. I am very eager to get the cottage started this winter & try to finish it by next summer. Then get a full-time nanny.

We now have with us a young American writer who was evicted from his London flat, and his wife. They are fantastically neurotic, she has dozens of illnesses, all untreatable because she has decided she is allergic to any medicine that might help---for instance, she has ulcers, she says, yet can't swallow, she says, milk. And migraine, but is allergic to codeine. And she is a fanatic about food. I just take all this calmly. They are living in the guest room---I said we would take them in rent-free for a month or 6 weeks until they got rested enough to look for another flat, if they would help pay for the food and help with the children. They took over the day we were in London and it nearly killed them. They have said they will stay while we go to Ireland, which would be wonderful, as the children get on beautifully with them, but I have grave doubts as to their staying power. I shall ask them to tell me now, so I can hire a nurse if necessary. I simply must go to Ireland and sail for a week. Mrs. Prouty

1–Claire (Kane) Prouty, sister-in-law of Olive Higgins Prouty.
2–Olive Higgins Prouty's children were Richard, Olivia, and Jane.

is scheduled to come to dinner here September 9, Sunday, & we hope to leave the next day.

It was very kind of you & Warren & Margaret to remember Ted's birthday. I have seen the doctor's wife, whom I very much like, about riding lessons & she is going to ask the woman next week & we may take them together. She is going to get a pony, & someday I would like a pony for Frieda.

Lots of love to all,
Sivvy

PS: Thanks for F's pretty pants. I'm enclosing a wellmeaning letter[1] from dear dumb Edith.

TO *Richard Murphy*

Friday 17 August 1962 TLS, University of Tulsa

Court Green
North Tawton
Devon.
Friday: August 17

Dear Richard,

Your latest telegram arrived yesterday when we were away for the day in London and we have no phone, so I am writing. As things now stand, I am reasonably sure we can leave Devon on Monday, September 10. I don't know how long it will take to get to you, but when we do we could stay about a week. Do you have life preservers! I don't want you writing another prize-winning poem about our eyeballs boiling in the sea![2]

Could you drop us a note with some advice about the best way to get to your place from wherever the boat to Ireland lands? We will be without a car & travel by train or bus or mule or whatever is most expeditious. Do let us know what to do about getting to your island! I don't know when I've looked so forward to anything. I am sick of the bloody British sea with its toffee wrappers & trippers in pink plastic macs bobbing in the shallows, and caravans piled one on top of the other like enamel coffins.

Fond regards,
Sylvia

1–The letter is no longer with SP's letter.

2–There are several references to eyes in Murphy's poem 'The Cleggan Disaster' but here Plath likely refers to the line 'His eyes, scalded by the scurf of salt' (*Sailing to an Island*, 27).

TO *Anne Sexton*

Tuesday 21 August 1962 TLS (aerogramme), University of Texas at Austin

Court Green
North Tawton
Devonshire, England
August 21, 1962

Dear Anne,

I was absolutely stunned and delighted with the new book.[1] It is superbly masterful, womanly in the greatest sense, and so blessedly unliterary. One of the rare original things in this world one comes upon. I had just said the day before "One book I will buy is Anne Sexton's next," & there it was, in the morning mail the next day. I have these small clairvoyances. But I don't have to be clairvoyant to see the Pulitzer and National Book Award and the rest in your lap for it.

I think "The Black Art" comes in my top favorite dozen, with Northeaster Letter,[2] Flight, the Letter Crossing Long Island Sound,[3] Water, Woman with Girdle, Old, For God While Sleeping, Lament. Hell, they are all terrific.

Tell me what it is like to be a Lady Poet Laureate. How was the Radcliffe Grant,[4] did it really free you from the drudge of housework? And who is He? of the letters & Flight? Tell me how things are with you, with Maxine and George. Who do you see, know, now? I am bedded in the country with Frieda and a very fine 6 months son Nicholas, keeping bees and raising potatoes and doing broadcasts off and on for the BBC. I would love one of your newsy letters to stick on the wall.

Let me know when & where I can see the new stuff you must have done since the book. I loved the flies in their foul caves poem,[5] but see no magazines except the New Yorker, which is a free copy. More power to you, although you seem to need nothing---it is all there.

Love,
Sylvia

1–Anne Sexton, *All My Pretty Ones* (Boston: Houghton Mifflin, 1962). SP's copy held by Smith College.
2–Anne Sexton, 'Letter Written During a January Northeaster'.
3–Anne Sexton, 'Letter Written on a Ferry While Crossing Long Island Sound'.
4–In June 1961, Sexton was awarded a $3,000 grant by the Radcliffe Institute for Independent Study.
5–Anne Sexton, 'The Sun', *New Yorker* (12 May 1962): 44.

TO *Aurelia Schober Plath*

Monday 27 August 1962 TLS (aerogramme), Indiana University

Monday: August 27

Dear mother,

Thank you very much for your letter, and the sweet little bunny cards for Frieda. She plays with the pop-beads all the time and the other day came into the room with her red sweater and said "Gammy make noo." We have a young couple living with us now, the Kanes, he an American writer of plays & depressive, & she a big-boned kind Irish orphan and manic. After the usual jerks of a living-in relationship, we seem to have settled down. In return for free board & room Kathy helps me with the babies & cooks one meal a day. So I hope to have my "mornings" as long as they care to stay, and that they will at least stay through my hoped-for Ireland trip about September 10, to 20. Mrs. Prouty is scheduled to come for dinner Sunday the 9th, so hope she can make it. I am thinking seriously of closing the house up for the winter and taking the babies to winter in Spain. I have just recovered from a bad bout of flu, which the babies caught too, and my weight has dropped after this worrisome summer, and I do not think it wise to try to undergo another English winter just now. If plans work out, I should drive down in mid-November, get a villa and stay till early March. I do not know what I would have done without Kathy Kane to mind the babies while I was sick; they were evicted from their London flat and our mutual needs seem to coincide.

We have removed 3 combs from the beehive and used Winifred's honey extractor & should have about 10 bottles. It is delectable stuff. The weather here has been ghastly---nothing but rain. Today is sunny & blowy & I hope it keeps up, for I have my first riding lesson this afternoon,[1] and after Ireland hope to share them with Joan Webb, the doctor's pretty and very nice wife who has taken them for a year.

I hope you will not be too surprised or shocked when I say I am going to try to get a legal separation from Ted. I do not believe in divorce and would never think of this, but I simply cannot go on living the degraded and agonized life I have been living, which has stopped my writing and just about ruined my sleep and my health. I thought I would take almost anything to give the children an illusion of home life, but I feel a father

1 – SP took riding lessons with Miss P. B. Redwood at Lower Corscombe Farm, Corscombe Lane, near Okehampton.

who is a liar and an adulterer and utterly selfish and irresponsible is worse than the absence of a father, and I cannot spend the best years of my life waiting week after week for the chance returns of someone like this. What is saddest is that Ted has it in him to be kind and true and loving but has just chosen not to be. He spends most of each week in London, spending our joing savings on himself & his pleasures, and I feel I need a legal settlement so I can count on so much a week for groceries and bills and the freedom to build up the happy pleasant life I feel it in myself to make, and would but for him make. I have written Edith telling her I deeply love her & Willy & Walter & Hilda & Vicky, & told her the truth of Ted's desertion during your stay & his utter faithlessness & irresponsibility. I just could not receive any more of her sweet dumb letters asking about the garden and saying what a fine, happy, restful time you must have had. I have too much at stake and am too rich a person to live as a martyr to such stupidity and heartlessness. I want a clean break, so I can breathe and laugh and enjoy myself again.

The woman Winifred got for me came one morning, then sent her husband to say it was too hard work. Well, I have Kathy for the time being and really couldn't afford anyone now. The kindest & most helpful thing you could do is send some warm article of clothing for Frieda at Xmas. I have plenty for Nicholas. And a big bottle of Vitamin C tablets for me if you would! I can't afford another cold like this one. I do hope Warren & dear Maggie will plan to come in spring, & that I can have Marty & Mike Plumer as well. I try to see the Comptons weekly & have met some nice couples with children there. I would, by the way, appreciate it if you would tell no-one but perhaps Margaret and Warren of this, and perhaps better not even them. It is a private matter and I do not want people who would never see me anyway to know of it. So do keep it to yourself!

I am actually doing some writing now Kathy is here,[1] so there is hope. And I feel if I can spend the winter in the sun in Spain I may regain the weight & health I have lost this last 6 months. I meant you to have such a lovely stay, I can never say how sorry I am you did not have the lovely reveling and rest I meant you to have. I am glad to hear that grampy is better off in the home and think that decision was the best & only one. Tell Dotty to go on writing me, she means a very great deal to me. I love you all very very much and am in need of nothing, and am desirous

1 – SP may be referring to her unfinished novel *The Interminable Loaf*, later titled *Doubletake* and then *Double Exposure*. TH calls the novel *Double Exposure* in his introduction to SP's *Johnny Panic and the Bible of Dreams*. On 10 August, in SP's Letts Royal Office Diary Tablet for 1962, she wrote 'Start Int. Loaf!!!'

of nothing but staying in this friendly town & my beautiful home with my dear children. I am getting estimates about re-doing the cottage so I someday can install a nanny & lead a freer life.

Lots of love,
Sivvy

TO *Howard Moss*

Friday 31 August 1962

TLS (aerogramme),
New York Public Library

Court Green
North Tawton
Devonshire, England
August 31, 1962

Mr. Howard Moss
THE NEW YORKER
25 West 43rd Street
New York 36, New York
U.S.A.

Dear Mr. Moss:

I'm sending along ELM again, with some new poems.[1] I thought your comments[2] perfectly good and well taken.

There is absolutely no relation of the poem's meaning to the girl I dedicated it to---she is simply someone I like who liked it, and when I print it in a book, I'll dedicate it to her then. No need to in magazine printing.

The poem, without the dedication, I hope explains itself. The "she says" is the elm. The whole poem is the elm talking & might be in quotes. The elm is talking to the woman who contemplates her---they are intimately related in mood, and the various moods, I think, of anguish, are explored in the poem. Let me know if this makes any difference. I realize it is a rather wild & desperate piece. But, I hope: clear, clear.

All good wishes.
Sincerely,
Sylvia Plath

1–This submission included: 'Berck-Plage', 'The Other', 'Words heard, by accident, over the phone', 'Poppies in July', and 'Burning the Letters'.
2–See Howard Moss to SP, 27 June 1962; held by Smith College.

TO *Eric Walter & Edith White*

Monday 3 September 1962[1] ALS,[2] McMaster University

P.S. Dear Eric & Dodo –

I am just through a week of influenza & about as strong as a dead codfish, but hope to be well enough in two weeks or so to really recover on Richard Murphy's boat. Poetic justice I think. I am desolate not to see you & the Sweeneys, I had so been looking forward to the dinner! The Nolans[3] are a great consolation – visionary cartography. Love to you both & Jack & Mairé when they come.

Sylvia

TO *Ruth Tiffany Barnhouse Beuscher*

Tuesday 4 September 1962 TLS (aerogramme), Smith College

Court Green
North Tawton
Devonshire, England
September 4, 1962

Dear Doctor Beuscher,

I'd be awfully grateful just to have a postcard from you saying you think any paid letter sessions between us are impractical or unhelpful or whatever, but something final. Believe me, that would be a relief. It is the feeling of writing into a void that never answers, or may at any moment answer, that is difficult. I'd rather just have you say "shut up" than feel my words dangling in space.

I thought for a time I would just give Ted his head, and could laugh at the lot of it and be my own woman. Any kind of caution or limit makes him murderous. But what he does is go each week to London, spend lots of money on himself, then come home (why does he come home?) and lay into us: this is a Prision, I am an Institution,[4] the children should

1–Date supplied from internal evidence.

2–SP's letter is at the end of a letter begun by TH, which has not been transcribed. TH expressed disappointment that they could not travel to London to see the Whites and the Sweeneys due to SP's flu and 103-degree temperature. He commented on some Sydney Nolan prints and arranged to visit London to meet a co-judge (Ian Fletcher) for the 1963 Poetry Book Society selections.

3–Australian painter and printmaker Sydney Nolan (1917–92).

4–Probably a reference to Marianne Moore's poem 'Marriage': 'This institution, / perhaps one should say enterprise' (*Collected Poems*, 69).

never have been born. He may need a flogging post but I'm damned if I'm going to be it. I started having blackouts last week & made the mistake of asking him to put off his weekly spree a day and help me, as I also had two sick guests. He said I was blackmailing him with my health, so I quickly drove him to the train. When he came back I had galloping influenza, chills & fever of 103 nonstop for 3 days, a real experience, very British, which my doctor assured me there was no medical aid for. Why he had nursed families of 9 all with influenza, and they just lay about and died for a week until one of them could crawl up & brew tea. I see now I can't convince Ted I can change or have changed. His lies are incredible & continuous---daily I find out his accounts of meeting people in London, dining, etc. are all made up. I think this may be because he unconsciously so resents my possessing any part of his life he cant bear to tell about even small things truly because I thus possess the knowledge of them. But I am so weak with this bloody influenza, and the prospect of being forbidden ever to go to a play, party, dinner, movie or anything with him is so mean, I think the only thing that may dent into his head I do not honestly want to eat him is for me to get a legal separation. The idea of no husband, 2 babies, a 15 room house & 2½ acres is a grim one, but I am no martyr & I want my health back & am sick of being called a possessive institution, e.g. an old womb. I have an awful lot to distract me, and a legal separation may just set Ted whirling into this wonderful wonderful world where there are only tarts and no wives and only abortions and no babies and only hotels and no homes. Well bless him. Your last letter was a big help, but I think Ted is trying to drive me by his behavior week by week to separate, he hasn't quite got the guts to do it all by himself, so I shall have to get a lawyer & help him.

The whole influenza business made me furious. I got it from these bloody guests who were to help me with the babies in exchange for room & board, & of course it looked like blackmail. I begged the doctor to get me a home-help so Ted could go off freely, but instead he sonorously talked to him of manly responsibilities, the old red flag to the old bull. Now I am having Ted try & get a nanny down from London for a week or two. Then I shall try to get this cottage on our property made livable & try to get a full-time nanny. Then I shall write novels, learn to ride a horse, which I am just doing, and try to do more stuff for the radio & take a day a week in London for plays, movies, art shows & shopping. That's half a year away, but it keeps me going. And I am a hell of a success with poppies, nasturtiums & sunflowers. I've got an absolute octopus of nasturtiums crawling across the court. And bees. I've just bottled 12 jars of my own honey: Next year it should be a hundred. Then maybe I'll go into business.

I wish to hell I could have a few talks with you. Nobody else is any good to me, I'm sick of preamble. That's why I thought if I paid for a couple of letters I might start going ahead instead of in circles. But please just say it won't work or you've a full schedule or something. I would be glad of that definiteness.

With love,
Sylvia

TO *Judith Jones*

Wednesday 5 September 1962 — TLS (aerogramme), University of Texas at Austin

Court Green
North Tawton
Devonshire, England
September 5, 1962

Mrs. Judith B. Jones
ALFRED A. KNOPF
501 Madison Avenue
New York 22, New York
U.S.A.

Dear Mrs. Jones,

Thank you for your letter[1] and all the contents. I am glad that you sent on the Marianne Moore letter,[2] I do like to see everything. I am sorry Miss Moore eschews the dark side of life to the extent that she feels neither good nor enjoyable poetry can be made out of it. She also, as I know, eschews the sexual side of life, and made my husband take out every poem in his first book with a sexual reference before she would put her name to endorse it. But she is a scrupulous letter writer, so bless her for that! I'd love to have a list of the poets you sent my book to, just to know who has seen it. A very full and favorable review appeared in the Sewanee Review

1–Judith Jones to SP, 30 August 1962; held by University of Texas at Austin.

2–Marianne Moore to Judith B. Jones, 7 April 1962; held by University of Texas at Austin. See also Marianne Moore to SP, 14 July 1958; held by Smith College.

this spring,[1] some time about then, but as it was of the English edition I suppose you wouldn't have seen it.

The novel is as good as done. Heinemann will be publishing it over here. I'll get on to them to send you a copy in a few weeks when it's ready. I hope a few things in it will make you laugh.

Thanks very much for your kind concern.

Yours sincerely,
Sylvia Plath

TO *Marvin & Kathy Kane*

Wednesday 5 September 1962[2] ALS, Indiana University

Court Green
North Tawton
Devon.
Wednesday

Dear Marvin & Kathy,

Thank you for the lovely card. It must be heaven there.[3] Since you left I have had terrible influenza, fevers of over 103° & killing chills & have been able to swallow nothing but water, so am very weak, hence the shortness of this, I can hardly write. I am forwarding 2 letters separately.

Have you any idea where Frieda's dolly pram is? Did she leave it at the playground? We can't find it any where & she is desolate.

Good news, we have got a nanny to come while we are in Ireland so you need not worry about breaking your holiday. We would have had no rest worrying about your health & didn't want to spoil your good time.

Love,
Sylvia

1–E. Lucas Myers, 'The Tranquilized Fifties', *Sewanee Review* 70 (Spring 1962): 212–20.

2–Date supplied from internal evidence.

3–The Kanes were in Cornwall. SP's address book indicates they were likely at 'Felpham', Headlands Road, Carbis Bay. By the time SP visited the Kanes on 13 October, they had moved to a house called 'Quaintways' in Hicks Court, The Digey, St Ives.

TO *Elizabeth Sigmund*

Saturday 8 September 1962 TLS, Indiana University

Court Green
North Tawton
Saturday: Sept. 8

Dear Elizabeth,

Forgive me for not writing sooner. Since I saw you last,[1] I have had a ghastly week of influenza, nonstop fevers of over 103° alternating with killing chills and unable to swallow anything but water. I have never really been ill before, the time I had double pneumonia was nothing to this, and now I have lost a great deal of weight and am so stupidly weak I can do nothing. I have been wanting and wanting to write a note, but just fall back in bed after the smallest task. Now I am still very wobbly, but better.

After eating us out of house and home for over two weeks, and losing Frieda's brand new doll's pram our "guests", who were to help with the children, left for a holiday in Cornwall. Luckily we were able to get an expensive but reliable nanny from an agency in London in the nick of time, so are planning to leave for a week in Ireland next Tuesday. It is now a health trip for me. I see now that no matter how awful anything is, if you have health, you are still blessed.

When I come back I shall bring over a load of potatoes and onions. I long to see you. Frieda talks so often of "Baby James" and has begged me to get her a "lil tiny piano" like the one she saw at your house.

Please send on my copy of David's book.[2] I'm dying to read it, it looks just the thing to cheer me up, all about murder.

Love to all,
Sylvia

1–According to SP's Letts Royal Office Diary Tablet for 1962, she saw the Comptons on Wednesday, 29 August 1962 at 3 p.m. A note indicates she gave them 'potatoes, onions etc.'
2–David Compton (as Guy Compton), *Too Many Murderers* (London: John Long, 1962).

TO *Richard Murphy*

Saturday 8 September 1962 ALS, University of Tulsa

Court Green
North Tawton
Devonshire, England
September 8

Dear Richard,

Thank you so much for your good letter. We have got a nanny for the babies so can leave here with easy heart. We plan to take the train to Holyhead Tuesday night, cross to Dublin by night, say hello to Jack Sweeney & come by rail to Galway Wednesday eveningish.[1] Shall call as soon as we arrive. We would love to stay in your cottage.[2] I don't know when I have looked so forward to anything.

Warmest good wishes,
Sylvia

TO *Ruth Fainlight*

Saturday 8 September 1962 TLS, Ruth Fainlight

Court Green
North Tawton
Devonshire, England
Saturday: September 8

Dearest Ruth,

I have been wanting so long to write you and now I have your new good letter. The reason I haven't written is because I've had a ghastly summer ending in a bout of influenza which just about did for me---I never had it before, nonstop fevers of over 103° alternating with killing chills and too weak to drink anything but water. The doctor told me something I didn't know which is that there is nothing modern medicine can do to relieve or combat flu, but he is a bastard & maybe that is not true. Anyhow, I have lost a great deal of weight & am worried about my bloody lungs, as I had double pneumonia not too long ago. And I am weak as a dead cod. I wake, thinking, now I will jump up, feed Nicholas, bath & change him, feed Frieda, do a laundry, figure the income tax and whee, one bout of

1–In the margin, an unidentified hand has written '(Sept 12)' in pencil.
2–The Old Forge, Cleggan.

coughs and I am back on the pillow the color of a French bean with the sweats, the shakes, crap to it all. I hate sickness & being sick & this has been a great blow to me.

One good thing is that I think Ted will set us up for 3 months in Spain this winter, way down south around where Ben is.[1] For December, January & February presumably. He still has officially to take the Maugham grant, so this is an excuse to do it, plus the fact that I don't think I could stand an English winter just yet. Now I beg you to give me any practical hints you can think of to make it easier traveling by car with kids. What route did you take, where stay, did you reserve ahead, etc. etc. Ted never will make a plan till the day ahead, but I would like to know what I can expect. Are there Paddipads[2] in Spain. Strained babyfoods? Is there a God? Where is Franco?[3] You are such a practical one, Ruth, and Alan too. Maybe you can tell me some things to expect & plan for.

Of course it is much easier with a nursing baby. Nicholas has, since I've been ill, been on bottles, although I hope to have weaned him to a cup by the time we leave. I suppose we should have a Primus[4] to boil milk & water. And make Farex[5] & heat tins. Maybe I can train him to crap out the window. He is gorgeous now. Big dark eyes, hair that looks as if it wants to curl & get light, and bouncey, creepy, fascinated by grass, which he eats madly if he can lay a finger on it. I adore him. Ted never touches him, nor has since he was born. Very curious. I would love to get Nick & David together now, like we did that time on the bed. They could probably Greek wrestle. Maybe we can meet, if we come to Spain in December. I hope to get a babyminder there. It is almost impossible here. I am going to fix the cottage so it is livable & try next spring to hire a nanny. Have a 2nd novel I'm dying to write and no time. Which I suppose is better than lots of time & no novel. I miss you so much, all 3. It was such fun having you here. Please say we can come visit,[6] or you come, when we are in Spain. And please write. I enclose a battered copy of your Elm poem, Ruth.

Love to all,
Sylvia

1–According to SP's address book, Ben Sonnenberg was in Málaga, Spain.
2–Paddi Pads was one of the first brands of disposable nappies.
3–Spanish military leader and dictator Francisco Franco (1897–1975).
4–A brand of camping stove.
5–A brand of baby and infant foods.
6–The Sillitoes were in Tangier, Morocco.

Sylvia Plath
Court Green
North Tawton, Devon.

Elm

(for Ruth Fainlight)

I know the bottom, she says. I know it with my great tap root:
It is what you fear.
I do not fear it: I have been there.

Is it the sea you hear in me,
Its dissatisfactions?
Or the voice of nothing, that was your madness?

Love is a shadow.
How you lie and cry after it!
Listen: these are its hooves: it has gone off, like a horse.

All night I shall gallop thus, impetuously,
Till your head is a stone, your pillow a little turf,
Echoing, echoing.

Or shall I bring you the sound of poisons?
This is the rain now, this big hush.
And this is the fruit of it: tin-white, like arsenic.

I have suffered the atrocity of sunsets.
Scorched to the root
My red filaments burn and stand, a hand of wires.

Now I break up in pieces that fly about like clubs.
A wind of such violence
Will tolerate no bystanding: I must shriek.

The moon, also, is merciless: she would drag me
Cruelly, being barren.
Her radiance scathes me. Or perhaps I have caught her.

I let her go. I let her go
Diminished and flat, as after radical surgery.
How your bad dreams possess and endow me!

I am inhabited by a cry.
Nightly it flaps out
Looking, with its hooks, for something to love.

I am terrified by this dark thing
That sleeps in me;
All day I feel its soft, feathery turnings, its malignity.

Clouds pass and disperse.
Are those the faces of love, those pale irretrievables?
Is it for such I agitate my heart?

I am incapable of more knowledge.
What is this, this face
So murderous in its strangle of branches? ---

Its snaky acids hiss.
It petrifies the will. These are the isolate, slow faults
That kill, that kill, that kill.

TO *Kathy Kane*

Friday 21 September 1962 TLS, Indiana University

Court Green
North Tawton
Devon.
Friday, September 21

Dear Kathy,

It was so cheering to have your letter when I came back. Actually the nanny had forwarded it to Ireland, so I had to wait till today for it to be forwarded back, and when I asked who the letter she had forwarded was from, in case it was urgent, she said it was from somebody in London. So you see you are safe, she & everybody thinks you are there.

I found the little pram, many thanks. The nanny[1] was wonderful, the children were thriving when I came home & everything spick and span. I am trying to get her back for another week now, as I have to go to London to see a solicitor.[2] I will wait till I see you to say anything, but the end has come. It is like amputating a gangrenous limb---horrible, but one feels it is the only thing to do to survive.[3]

I am very interested in the poetry tour. Would there be room for me & the babies to pay you a short visit? There is no question of Ted coming. Do you have a phone I could call you at? Or could you write & say. Perhaps Monday October 1st? I should have the business done by then I hope. Do write anyway.

Love to both,
Sylvia

TO *Richard Murphy*

Friday 21 September 1962 TLS, University of Tulsa

Court Green
North Tawton
Devonshire, England
September 21

Dear Richard,

I am enclosing my unused ticket from Galway to Dublin, good for three months, in hopes that you or Seamus or Owen[4] may find it of use. I cannot thank you enough for your hospitality & the wonderful wonderful food of Mrs. Coyne.[5] The boats & the sea were like a great cure for me.

May I say two things? My health depends on leaving England & going to Ireland, & the health of the children. I am very reluctant to think that the help you gave with one hand you would want to take away with the

1–Sheena Cartwright; lived in Totnes, South Devon.
2–According to SP's Letts Royal Office Diary Tablet for 1962 and address book, on 25 September she met Charles Mazillius of Harris, Chetham & Co., 23 Bentinck Street, London W.1.
3–In August 1940 SP's father Otto Plath stubbed his toe and because of his untreated diabetes developed gangrene in his left leg. It was amputated above the knee on 12 October.
4–Probably Mary Coyne's sons Seamus Coyne and Owen Coyne.
5–Mary Anne Coyne (*c.* 1896–2002), Richard Murphy's housekeeper; lived in Knockbrack, Cleggan.

other. I am in great need of a woman like Kitty Marriott[1] & if there is one thing my 30th year has brought it is understanding of what I am, and a sense of strength and independence to face what I have to. It may be difficult to believe, but I have not and never will have a desire to see or speak to you or anyone else. I have wintered in a lighthouse & that sort of life is balm to my soul. I do not expect you to understand this, or anything else, how could you, you know nothing of me. I do not want to think you were hypocritical when showing me the cottages, but it is difficult to think otherwise. Please let me think better of you than this.

Secondly, I was appalled to realize you did not understand we were joking when talking about my writing New Yorker poems about Connemara. I would not do that even if I were able, and as you know I have not written a poem for over a year & cannot write poems anyway when I am writing prose. So there is no question of your literary territory being invaded. My novel is set in Devon, and it is this I hope to finish at Glasthule.

I feel very sorry to have to retract my invitation to visit us at Court Green as it would have given me great pleasure to have you see it---I think you have a feeling for land, and this is very beautiful land & I imagine I feel about it the way you do about your hookers---proud of it, and of what I have made of it and hope to make of it, and eager to feel it is appreciated, not hated. But Ted will not be here, as I had thought when I asked you, and when he is not here I can see no-one. My town is as small & watchful as yours & a little cripple hunchback with a high black boot lives at the bottom of my lane & all day & all night watches who comes & goes. This is really very funny. There is nothing for the poor woman to see. So I am very sensible of your concerns. I shall try to bring a nanny with me in December & then maybe get someone to live in & help with the children, & you shall see neither hide nor hair of anybody. Other people only get in the way of my babies & my work & I am as dedicated to both as a nurse-nun. Please have the kindness, the largeness, to say you will not wish me ill nor keep me from what I clearly and calmly see as the one fate open. I would like to think your understanding could vault the barrier it was stuck at when I left.

Sincerely,
Sylvia

1 – Kitty Marriott, a local woman from whom SP intended to rent a cottage called 'Glasthule' in Moyard.

TO *Ruth Tiffany Barnhouse Beuscher*

Saturday 22 September 1962 TLS, Smith College

September 22, 1962

Dear Dr. Beuscher,

Your letter[1] came today, at a most needed moment, and I feel the way I used to after our talks---cleared, altered and renewed. I am really asking your help as a woman, the wisest woman emotionally and intellectually, that I know. You are not my mother, but you have been the midwife to my spirit. There are breaking points and growing points; I had my last great bout ten years ago when I met you, and now that I am in the middle of another, in soul-labor and soul-pain as it were, I turn to you again, because you are the one person I know who will not advise me to numb or degrade or give up or diminish myself. If I could write you once a week for the next few weeks, & get a short answer, practical, a paragraph---your paragraphs are worth a ton of TNT---it would be the greatest and best thing in my life just now. My life at present is made up of amiable bank managers accountants, insurance salesmen, solicitors and the local doctor. The midwife is sensible and kind but totally without imagination or much intelligence. I value my life, what it can be in all its yet unworked veins of creativity and variety, so much that I would spend my savings in America to come over by jet on the chance of having an hour a day for a week talking to you, but if you were able to manage a paragraph or so, I think this would not be necessary. I want to be able to initiate my new life, my separate life, as soon as possible, and for this a live-in nanny is essential, and I had probably better save what I've got left for this. We lived off my $2,000 nanny-grant-to-write-a-novel all this year: as soon as the last payment stopped, Ted "got courage" and left me. So, no 2nd novel, yet, no nanny, no money. And no Ted.

The end---the end for me at least---just blew up this week. I have been very stupid, a bloody fool, but it only comes from my thinking Ted could grow, and grow up, not down, and my wanting to give us a new and better and wider start. I was prepared for almost anything---his having the odd affair, traveling, drinking (I mean getting drunk)---if we could be straight, good friends, share all the intellectual life that has been meat and drink to me, for he is a genius, a great man, a great writer. I was ready for this, to settle for something much different and freer than what I had

1 – See Ruth Beuscher to SP, 17 September 1962; held by Smith College. Dr Beuscher rejected the idea of SP paying for their correspondence, calling the idea 'irrelevant'.

thought marriage was, or what I wanted it to be. I changed. I have a rich inner life myself, much I want to learn & do, and this blessed gift made me feel capable of quite another life than the life I had felt at heart I really wanted. Even our professional marriage---the utterly creative and healthy crictical exchange of ideas and publication projects and completed work ---meant enough to me to try to save it. But Ted, his attitudes and actions, have made even this impossible, and I am appalled. I am bloody, raw, nerves hanging out all over the place, because I have had six stormy but wonderful years, bringing both of us, from nothing, books, fame, money, lovely babies, wonderful loving, but I see now that the man I loved as father and husband is just dead. (Father means father to the children, but it is a slip, too; he fathered me through barren places & setbacks). I realize, stunned, that I do not like him. Although he is handsome, I can hardly look at him, I see such ugliness---I suppose it is not there for other people, he is a charmer, it is there in our relationship.

After the first blowup, when mother was here---and I think Ted secretly meant her to be here; when he wants to torment me, knowing my horror and fear of her life & the role she lived as a woman, he tells me I am going to be just like her---Ted came home and said it didn't work, the affair was kaput. I believed this. He said he would be straight, now that I wouldn't be tearful or try to stop him from anything---he only wanted to go up to London on drinking bouts with a few friends. He went up half the week every week. The minute he came home he would lay into me with fury---I looked tired, tense, cross, couldn't he even have a drink, what sort of a wife had he married etc. I was dumbfounded---his fury seemed all out of proportion with what he said he'd been doing, & I was quite happy, if understandably apprehensive, getting on at home. Then I found out by accident that this little story & that about what he'd been doing weren't true. Mrs. Prouty treated us to a night & a day at the fanciest hotel in London & I never had such good loving, felt it was the consecration of our new life. He went to have a bath & I next saw him coming in fully dressed with a funny pleased smile. He had called some friends to have a drink. Fine, said I, I'd love a drink. No, I was to go home on the next train. He didn't come back for a couple of days and even then I thought he was doing what he said, I was trying so hard to believe he knew what straightness and reality meant to me. Now, of course, I see this saying the affair was over was just an elaborate hoax, & his furies equal to what he was really doing.

I had the flu, as I said, was terribly weakened by this & lost of a lot of weight suddenly. We had an invitation to go to Ireland to a poet's house in the wilds of Connemara (I'd just given him a £75 poetry prize, so this was gratitude) & sail on the old Galway hookers he'd salvaged & ran in summer as fancy tourist fishing yachts. I got a flossy nanny for the babies. All I wanted was my health back---I had been on a liquid diet for weeks. Well it was wonderful in this way---an Irish woman cooked, got me to eat 2 eggs & half a loaf of her brown bread & her cows' milk & hand churned butter for breakfast, the sea gave me my appetite back, and I love fishing. Ted lasted four days. He left while I was in bed one morning saying he was going grouse shooting with a friend.[1] I haven't seen him since. He left me with all the baggage to carry back, and I got a telegram when I got home, addressed from London, to keep the nanny, he might be back in a week or two. I had let the nanny go by the time I got the telegram & made him dinner, & she had another job when I called her. Then I had all the fun of reading the real meaning into what I found so emotionally upsetting week after week after week. Ted is very faithful. He stopped sleeping with me. He kept groaning this other woman's name in the night. I see now it is she he was being faithful to, but I was in agony, not know what was wrong. He did tell me that when we were courting the women with whom he boarded crawled over him all night but he refused them: I thought this was only a historical statement, but now I see this is how he is & why he has stopped sleeping with me. And the one or two times he did turn to me it was degrading, like going to the toilet, he made so sure I felt nothing, and was tossed aside after like a piece of dog sausage. Well I am neither my mother nor a masochist; I would sooner be a nun than this kind of fouled scratch rug. Ted is so stupid. He honestly is sure I would rather have this than nothing. He doesn't see how I can get on without him.

I have got someone to take care of the children and am going to London this Tuesday to see a very kind-sounding solicitor recommended to me by my accountant in order to get a legal separation. Ted seems to need to come home every week to make my life miserable, kick me about & assure himself that he has a ghastly limiting wife, just like his friends do, three of whom have left their wives this year. He hates Nicholas. When I had the flu I told him to be sure Nick was strapped in his pram as otherwise he would fall out, was he strapped? Yes, Ted said. Later I heard a terrible scream. The baby had fallen out onto the concrete floor, Ted had never

1–TH went to the house of Irish painter Barrie Cookie (1931–2014) at Ballagh, Quin, County Clare. Cooke was married to Harriet Pearl (Leviter) Cooke (1936–90), and had two children Liadin (1958–) and Julia Alison. TH left Ireland, met Assia Wevill, and travelled to Spain until the end of September.

strapped him in, and did not even go to pick him up, the cleaning lady did that. He was unhurt. See, said Ted. He could have had concussion or broken his spine. He has never touched him since he was born, says he is ugly and a usurper. He is a handsome vigorous child. Ted beat me up physically a couple of days before my miscarriage: the baby I lost was due to be born on his birthday. I thought this an aberration, & felt I had given him some cause, I had torn some of his papers in half, so they could be taped together, not lost, in a fury that he made me a couple of hours late to work at one of the several jobs I've had to eke out our income when things got tight---he was to mind Frieda. But now I feel the role of father terrifies him. He tells me now it was weakness that made him unable to tell me he did not want children, and that his joyous planning with me of the names of our next two was out of cowardice as well. Well bloody hell, I've got twenty years to take the responsibility of this cowardice. I love the children, but they do make my plans for a life on my own quite difficult, now they are so small & need such tending. He has never bought them clothes, my mother has sent these, but now I hear she has lost her job, the department is closed, so he'll just have to pay up.

Money is a great problem. We were doing fine, the house paid up, a car, starting to save a bit---now he is spending over $100 a week of our joint savings on his London life. He has never paid a bill---always misads & louses up the checkbook at the times I've asked him to take that over, so I'll have to make it right---and has no idea of yearly rates, taxes, bills. I have the financial year always pretty well in hand, & know when to say we should work hard. He means well---says all he wants is to live his own life & send us 2/3 of what he earns. But unfortunately the kind of women he chooses do not mean well. I even think someday he might try to take Frieda from me. She flatters his vanity. "Kiss daddy", he says when he comes home, making no move toward her. That is as far as fatherhood goes; she is very wild & lively and pretty. The woman I guess he's now living with spent all her time here taking pictures of Frieda & buying her presents. I trust noone now. I dearly love Ted's mother & father & aunt & cousin & uncle---but God help me when Olwyn his sister takes over. Ted has even told the doctor I thought I had "canine influenza" to "show I was unstable"; this was a joke on my part; our guests were called the Kanes & I got the germ from them. But I am upset about this---I honestly think they might try to make my life such a hell I would turn over Frieda as a sort of hostage to my sanity. I am so bloody sane. I am not disaster-proof after my years with you, but I am proof against all those deadly defences

---retreat, freezing, madness, despair---that a fearful soul puts up when refusing to face pain & come through it. I am not mad; just fighting mad.

One good thing about Ireland, I found a fine woman, one of the old horse-and-whiskey-neat set, with a gorgeous cottage & views she would let me for the winter. She has a Connemara pony, her own TT tested cows (which I'd like to learn to milk) & butter churn & could show me all the wild walks & would welcome the children. I got on there so well, I think I will rent Court Green, if I can, for the three worst winter months & go to Ireland, coming back in spring with the daffodils & kinder weather. The children would love this, I would be safe from Ted, & get the first months of separation underway in a fresh setting. I can't stand the feeling here now of my being left, passive. I need to act. To leave the place myself. When I come back it would be to something else, and I would have had time to fatten and blow myself clear with sea winds & wild walks. This is where my present instinct to salvation leads.

The worst thing is, as you say, psychologically, the fear and danger of being like my mother.[1] Even while she was here she began it: "Now you see how it is, why I never married again, self-sacrifice is the thing for your two little darlings etc. etc." till it made me puke. From the outside, our situation is disconcertingly similar---two women "left" by their men with two small children, a boy & a girl & no money. Inside, I feel, it is very different. I want it to be. Mother has suggested I live with her, as she lived with her mother. I never could or would, & right now I never want to see her again. She was always a child while my grandmother was alive---cooked for, fed, her babies minded while she had a job. I hated this. Her notion of self-sacrifice is deadly---the lethal deluge of frustrated love which will lay down its life if it can live through the loved one, on the loved one, like a hideous parasite. Lucky for me, I love my writing, love horse-riding, which I'm learning, love bee-keeping and in general can expand the area of my real interests so that I think my children will have a whole mother who indeed loves them, with vigor and warmth, but has never "laid down her life" for them. Do you think I am getting to the right place here? Psychologically the children & my relation to them as a husband-less woman is my greatest worry. I don't want Frieda to hate me as I hated my mother, nor Nicholas to live with me or about me as my brother lives about my mother, even though he is just married. I remember asking my mother why, if she discovered so early on she did not love my

1 – Dr Beuscher wrote, 'The psychiatric pitfall that I see is your succumbing to the unconscious temptation to repeat your mother's role – i.e., martyr at the hands of the brutal male.'

father, that her marriage was an agony, she did not leave him. She looked blank. Then she said half-heartedly that it was the depression[1] & she couldnt have gotten a job. Well. No thanks.

It is Ted's plunge into infantilism that stuns me most. From a steady driver he has added 20 miles to his average speed, suicidal in our narrow lanes, and police summons for violations filter in week by week. He's hated smoking as a habit, never smoked: now he is a chain smoker; I guess she smokes. I can stand a lot of things---if he were kind or wise or mature I would laugh at these things, but they are part of a syndrome. He has no idea of what he is losing in me; this hurts most of all. He is desperate to freeze me into a doggy sobby stereotype that he can with justice knock about. My sense of myself, my inner dignity and creative heart won't have it. It is the uncertainty, the transition, the hard choices that tear at me now. I think when I am free of him my own sweet life will come back to me, bare and sad in a lot of places, but my own, and sweet enough. Do write. If only a paragraph. It is my great consolation just now, to speak & be heard, and spoken to.

With love,
Sylvia

TO *Aurelia Schober Plath*

Sunday 23 September 1962 — TLS (aerogramme), Indiana University[2]

Sunday: September 23

Dear mother,

Thank you for your letter. I was appalled to hear your department is closing. Is not the university obliged to fit you in elsewhere? I had thought you said that. What happens to your pension, and what year is your job officially ended. Please tell me all about this as you may imagine I am very concerned.

The children are fine. Nicholas has cut his first tooth and is the most energetic and bouncy child imaginable. He crawls all over the playroom, playing with Friedas blocks, much to her consternation. "Put in pen, put in pram," she tells me to do with him, and gathers all the toys he seems

1–A reference to the Great Depression (1929–39).

2–When ASP sold SP's papers to Indiana in 1977, this letter and the one from SP to ASP of 22 November 1962 were placed under seal.

to like in a little heap out of his reach. We all went to the playground yesterday afternoon & only that little blond boy Stephen[1] was there, the one I guess who attended Frieda at the birthday party. He showed off gallantly, climbing up the slide backwards & doing tricks on the swings, but unfortunately fell off & cracked his head on the concrete, so I had to rush over & comfort him, he was crying so hard. The nanny I had was wonderful, a whiz. She brought a little dog & Frieda still talks of "Miss Cartwright & the liddle doggie". I came back unexpectedly a day before I said, and found everything in applepie order, the children fresh-washed & happy in bed---the true test.

Had a nice letter from Dotty. Will write her soon. Just now I am up to my neck in bank managers, insurance brokers, accountants and solicitors. I had a wonderful 4 days in Ireland, treated to oysters & Guinness & brown bread in Dublin by Jack & Maire Sweeney of the Lamont Library at Harvard, then 2 eggs, homemade butter & warm milk from the cows every breakfast in wild Connemara, about 50 miles from Galway. Ted was there, but had no part in my happiness, which was compounded of the sailing, the fishing, the sea and the kind people & wonderful cooking of an Irish woman from whom I bought a beautiful handknit sweater for $10 which would be $50 in America. I also was very lucky in finding a woman after my own heart, one of the sturdy independent horse-and-whisky set, with a beautiful cottage (turf fires---the most comfortable & savory fire imaginable), her own TT-tested cows & butter churn which she will rent to me for December through February, and show me all the sea walks. Spain is out of the question. Ted has spent all our savings to the tune of $100 a week & hasn't worked for 4 months. I think this Irish woman & I speak the same language---she will live nextdoor in a cottage of hers, she loves children, and I have no desire to be in a country, alone, where I do not even speak the language. I will try to rent Court Green for these months. I would go mad alone here, I want to be where no possessions remind me of the past & by the sea, which is for me the great healer. Ted deserted me again in Ireland, saying he was going grouse-shooting for the day with a friend. I believed him, as he had said he would tell me the truth, however difficult. He left me to come home alone with all the heavy baggage & when I returned I found a telegram from London saying he might be back in a week or two. I realized every week the elaborate tissue of lies he had invented while I thought I was leading a real true life. I go Tuesday to a London solicitor to get a legal separation.

1–Possibly Stephen C. Drake (1958–); lived at Essington Park, North Tawton.

Your telling Winifred I had a nervous breakdown has had disastrous consequences for me. Any ordinary doctor treats a former "mental case" as a 50% exaggerater. So I have had no treatment. Winifred is nice, but utterly without imagination. She so much as said neither she nor Dr. Webb believe I had a 103 temperature because when they came two days later in the early morning it was normal. So I have no medication.[1] While I had the fever I begged Ted to strap Nicholas in his pram as he would fall out otherwise. I asked him if he had done this. He said yes. Then I heard a terrible scream. I rushed downstairs almost fainting to find the baby on the concrete floor. Ted did not even go to pick him up, Nancy did. Luckily he was not hurt. Dr. Webb laughed & said I was exaggerating, babies had soft bones. If Nick had a concussion or an injured spine Ted would be to blame. He tells me now he never had the courage to say he did not want children. He does like Frieda, she flatters his vanity, & as this woman he is living with has had so many abortions she can't have children, I think he would try to get Frieda from me. He has been trying to convince Dr. Webb I am "unstable" by such devices as saying I thought I had "canine influenza", a joke on my part as the people we had with us were the Kanes & gave me the bug. So you see how your blabbing has helped me.[2] You might mention to Mrs. Prouty that Ted has deserted us & I am getting a legal separation. I shall come back here in the spring. I do not want you to waste your money coming here, and I shall never come to America again. I imagine that legally I shall only just obtain enough money to live on while Ted squanders the rest on himself. I must at all costs make over the cottage & get a live-in nanny next spring so I can start trying to write & get my independence again. Ted lived off my novel grant (supposedly for a nanny) & when it was gone "got courage" to desert us.

Love to Warren & Maggie
Sylvia

1–'Your telling Winifred . . . So I have no medication': these sentences redacted by ASP in black felt tip pen. Over time the ink has faded and the text below is readable with the assistance of Photoshop. Similar measures were taken to restore additional redactions in several letters through 22 November 1962.

2–This sentence redacted by ASP.

TO *Aurelia Schober Plath*

Monday 24 September 1962 TLS (aerogramme), Indiana University

Court Green
North Tawton
Devonshire, England
Monday: September 24

Dear mother,

I feel I owe you a happier letter than my last ones. Now that I have come to my decision to get a legal separation, and have an appointment with an immensely kind-sounding lawyer in London tomorrow (recommended to me by my equally kind accountant) I begin to see that life is not over for me. It is the uncertainty, week after week, that has been such a torture. And of course the desire to hang on to the last, to see if something, anything could be salvaged. I am just as glad the final blows have been delivered. Ted's lying to me about Nick & having him strapped in the pram & letting him fall on the concrete, deserting me in Ireland & other foul stuff I won't go into, and spending, I now find on checking our bank statements, checks he never entered in the book in addition to the large sums listed,[1] plus his insistence on coming home about once a week & making life utter hell & destroying my work, plus living off my novel grant till it was too late for me to do the cottage over & get a nanny with it, have just finished everything. He is not only infantile, but dangerously destructive, and I feel both the children & I need protection from him, for now & forever. The woman I gather he is with---I have no notion of where in London he is or when he will come home---has done charming things like attacking her first husband with a knife and slashing up the inside of his car & so on, and I think Ted's desire to "show the doctor I was unstable" by telling him I thought I had canine influenza (!) is prompted by her---they would one day I think like to get Frieda. Well, I shall get the law on my side.

It is a beautiful day here---clear and blue. I got this nanny back for today & tomorrow, she is a whiz, and I see what a heaven my life could be if I had a good live-in nanny. I am eating my first warm meal since I've come back---having an <u>impersonal</u> person in the house is a great help. I went up to Winifred's[2] for 3 hours the night I realized Ted wasn't coming back,

1 – Smith College holds SP's and TH's cheque books. TH withdrew £87 in cash from 21 July to 23 August.

2 – Winifred Davies's house was 'Longmeadow', off Exeter Road, North Tawton.

and she was a great help. She more or less confirmed my decision. And since I have made it, miraculously my own life, my wholeness, has been seeping back. I will try to rent Court Green for the winter & go to Ireland ---this is a dream of mine---to purge myself of this awful experience by the wild beauty I found there, & the children would thrive. Quite practically, I have no money to go farther. I have put all my earnings this summer in a separate account, the checking account is at zero, and there is £300 I have taken from our joint savings just about the last of them! as Ted said at one point I could, as some recompense for my lost nanny-grant, to build over the cottage. This is a must. Also getting TV for a nanny. I can't have one live in this house---or I could have no guests, & I do want to entertain what friends and relatives I have as often as I can. I dream of Warren & Maggie! I would love to go on a skiing holiday in the Tyrol with them someday. I just read about it in the paper.[1] And then if I do a novel or 2 I might apply for a Guggenheim to go to Rome---with nanny & children. Right now I have no money---but if I get the cottage done this winter while I'm away, I might sink all my savings in a nanny for a year. My writing should be able to get her the next year, and so on. If I hit it lucky, I might even be able to take a London flat & send the children to the fine free schools there & enjoy the London people (I would starve intellectually here), renting Court Green for the winter, & come down on holidays & in the spring, for the long summer holiday. I feel when the children are school-age I want to be able to afford this. Some lucky break---like writing a couple of New Yorker stories in Ireland, or a play for the BBC (I've got lots of fan mail[2] for the half hour interview I did on why I stayed in England---many advising me about special brands of corn to grow!)---could make this life a reality. But first the cottage, then the nanny. I'll have to do this out of my own small pocket, as I imagine Ted will only have to pay for the children. It is incredible what resources & hope I find now I see I have got to get Ted legally out of my life. I have to pay the price for his "cowardice" in not telling me he didn't want children etc. Oddly, though I loved him, what I saw he could be, I don't like him now at all. I despise wantonness & destructiveness. He has chosen to be like this, and he has no notion of what he is losing in me & the children. Well he is a bloody fool. Took Frieda to the playground again today. She is talking wonderfully, says names. I'm getting her two kittens from Mrs.

1–Probably an article on 'Austria' featured in the Modern Living Travel section of *The Observer* (23 September 1962): 35.

2–John Powell to SP, 17 September 1962; held by BBC Written Archives Centre. Powell, a producer for the BBC, sent SP listeners' letters.

Macnamara next week & trying to go somewhere, on some visit, every afternoon with them, to keep very busy.

Lots of love to you, Warren & Maggie,

Sylvia

TO *Aurelia Schober Plath*

Wednesday 26 September 1962 TLS with envelope, Indiana University

Court Green
Wednesday, Sept. 26

Dear mother,

I went up to London to the solicitor yesterday. A very harrowing but necessary experience. No knowing where Ted is, except in London, I got a numb utterly dumb letter from him with no address. I think he is possessed. The solicitor said he was worthless & to get clear. They are trying to trace him. I hope he will have sense enough to settle out of court & agree to an allowance, but I think whoever it is is driving him to spend everything may well prevent this. He is utterly gutless. Lies, lies, lies.

The laws, of course, are awful---a wife is allowed 1/3 of her husband's income, & if he doesn't pay up, the suing is long & costly, if a wife earns anything, her income is included in his & she ends up paying for everything. The humiliation of being penniless & begging money from deaf ears is too much. I shall just have to invest everything with courage in the cottage & the nanny for a year, a nanny, & write like mad. Try to get clear. I'm sure the American laws aren't like this. I hope Ted will have the decency to give us a fixed allowance & settle out of court. Together we earned about $7,000 this year, a fine salary, I earning one third. Now it is all gone. I am furious. I threw everything of mine into our life without question, all my earnings, & now he is well-off, with great potential earning power, I shall be penalized for earning, or if I don't earn, have to beg. Well I choose the former. I am enclosing an authorization for you to draw $500 from our Boston account. Put it in your bank. Then write me a check for that amount so I can say it is a gift. I'm sick of trying to explain our savings on income tax. The solicitor told me to draw out everything I could from our joint accounts to pay bills. Ted has left me no alternative. He owes me my novel grant back. He can pay me what my nanny got---£10 a week plus board and room.

I have written Edith I am getting a legal separation & will take it to court if necessary, although I have less to gain, if he proves obstinate. He is a vampire on my life, killing and destroying all. We had all the world on tap, were even well off, now this insanity on his part will cost us everything.

Thank God the solicitor said I could take the children to Ireland. I am hoping to let this place, but must go even if I can't. I despise Ted & the kind of creature he has made himself, & let him be made into. He had it in him to be the finest & kindest & best father & husband alive, & now thinks all feeling is sentimental & womanish.

Do mention if you can to Mrs. Prouty the situation. It is difficult, I feel, & not my place, for I want nothing from her, but I would like her to know the truth, that I am deserted, he wants no children, nor any marriage bonds & has left me incommunicado with a pile of police & library fines to pay, & a mountain of bills. I am sorry to be so worrying at this time when your own concerns are so pressing, but I must get control of my life, the little I have left.

With love,
Sivvy

<on verso of envelope>

PS: The playroom rug finally came. It i <damaged> Makes all the difference between a mausol<eum and a> warm cosy sittingroom. Nick's eyes are a beautiful clear brown. He sits up all by himself. I am having tea in the playroom now with the children & Frieda is industriously moving all her toys out of Nick's reach. She is great company now---spanks me & says "Naughty mummy". Winifred has found me a woman for 3 mornings a week,[1] 3 hours each, 9 hours in all. Better than nothing. Came today & said she'd come tomorrow. Very pretty & dear to the children. The nanny a marvel, 30 but looks 18. But so used to royalty!---suggested she come to Ireland with us, for the trip. If she can't come I'll get another.

Love,
s.

1–According to SP's Letts Royal Office Diary Tablet for 1962, this was a Mrs Weare.

TO *Aurelia Schober Plath*

Saturday 29 September 1962 TL (incomplete), Indiana University

Court Green
North Tawton
Devonshire
September 29, 1962

Dearest mother,

It is going on 6:30 in the morning & I am warm in my study, Pifco going, with my first cup of morning coffee. Winifred, for all her lack of imagination, is full of good sense & I love her for it. She is very busy, so after my on 3 hour evening session with her when deciding what to do, I only will see her briefly, for social occasions & practical questions. It was she who suggested that when I wake up early & am unable to sleep I come in and work on my novel before the babies get up & go to bed shortly after they do. Well, of course just now my emotions are such that "working on my novel" is so difficult as to be almost impossible, but I actually did do 3 pages yesterday, & hope to work into it, first numbly, then with feeling. It is the evenings here, after the children are in bed, that are the worst, so I might as well get rid of them by going to bed. I feel pretty good in the morning, & my days are, thank goodness busy. I find that by eating my meals with Frieda in the kitchen it is easier to eat something, & every day I religiously make tea in the nursery at 4, try to invite someone or take them to see some one, so each day I have a time with other people who know nothing, or at least who are darling, like the Comptons.

I do have to take sleeping pills, but they are, just now, a necessary evil, and enable me to sleep deeply & then do some writing & feel energetic during the day if I drink lots of coffee right on waking, so I shall go on taking them as long as I have to.

Ted has, quite simply, deserted us. I have not seen him for almost two weeks, since Ireland, and he has given me no London address. It is difficult to manage the telegrams, the police summonses for his traffic offenses & refusals to answer them & the questions of Nancy, the bank manager & all, but I think most, or some of them realise what has happened & I just hold my head high. It is horribly humiliating to be deserted, especially in such a foul way, with no income, nothing, but now I have faced it I feel much better. I am not hiding it from myself. I have written about this to Edith. I earnestly love her & the relatives up there & feel for them like a 2nd family. I only hope they will let me visit them with the children when this has blown over. Ted is just not going to deprive me of them, and I think they honestly love the babies very much. Edith is dear & sweet & this must upset her terribly.

The solicitor says I am within my legal rights & certainly to draw all money out of our joint accounts & put them in accounts of my own since my husband has deserted me & left me with nothing else to pay for food & bills. So do send me that $500 "gift" and another $500 at Christmas, if I need it. I have to make an outlay for the cottage this winter, & get a nanny in spring. Having the nanny here from the agency made me realize what heaven it would be. & I don't break down with someone else around,

<The rest of the letter is not present.
In *Letters Home*, the letter ends here with a closing 'Love, Sivvy'.>

TO *Kathy Kane*

Saturday 29 September 1962 TLS, Indiana University

Court Green
North Tawton
Devonshire
Saturday: Sept. 29

Dearest Kathy,

Your letter was so sweet & cheering. I have been just about stunned & distracted. Quite simply, Ted has deserted us---I don't mean gone on holiday, I mean just deserted. He left me in Ireland and I haven't seen him since---two weeks now, and have just discovered that everything he told me about his doings in London was elaborate lies & he had been drawing out our small savings without listing them in the checkbook at the rate of £50 a week & then looking blank and saying he had spent it on a few cigarettes. I can't tell you the terrible sadistic footnotes, they are too involved and elaborate and poetic. Of course it is this other woman, but it is also all his old drinking friends & new friends. Just now I do not see how we are going on, because of the money.

I went up to see a London solicitor on Tuesday & he is trying to trace Ted, who has left no address, to see if he will settle on a yearly sum out of court. He is berserk. He used up all my novel grant, then got courage to say he was through the marriage & never had courage to tell me he didn't want children. I struggled all the lean years, now he is earning well, bang. Frieda lies on the floor all day & sucks her thumb & looks miserable.

I would have loved staying in London, but for Ted's saying he hated it---there I could have friends, a job, babyminders. I am going potty with noone to talk to. I am going to try to rent the house in Ireland, where I found my health, if not my happiness, and try to heal by the wild sea there. It is very difficult to try to make a start of any sort with no job, no money & two infants. I don't know whether I said Ted almost killed Nicholas while I had flu---I kept asking if he had him strapped in to the pram & he lied & said yes, then I heard a terrible scream & came down. He had not strapped him in, & the baby had fallen onto the concrete. Ted didn't even bother to pick him up. He could have broken his head or hurt his little spine. Every day I try to go to tea with someone. The evenings are hell. I can't sleep without pills. Well, if I can just live through this fall, & try to get my novel done somehow, then go to Ireland for the worst three months & come back with the daffodils, maybe the spring & summer will bring new life & new plans.

Was there any reply about the readings, Marvin? Even as late as next year I'd love to do it---maybe Kathy could mind the babes the afternoons we're off---I could drive us. I just need something to think about. I would love to come down this next Friday[1] for the weekend but will wait to see what my solicitor says in the mail this next week---I've got to get Ted cleared up & some money in first. How do you get down by car? O, I'll find out. I love you both. Do write, even if just a note. Frieda keeps saying "See Kathy & Marwin soon."

Lots of love,
Sylvia

TO *Olive Higgins Prouty*

Saturday 29 September 1962 — TLS (aerogramme), Indiana University

Court Green
North Tawton
Devonshire, England
September 29, 1962

Dear Mrs. Prouty,

Thank you for your dear, dear letter. I am so glad you enjoyed your dinner & visit here---it meant the world for me to have you, for reasons

1 – 'this next ~~Thursday or~~ Friday' appears in the original.

I was unable to say at the time. I remembered the lovely dinners you used to have at your place and tried to have clear soup & roast as you had, hoping it would remind you of home. I so much needed someone else to see all the beauty of the place, and what it had been made and could be.

Nicholas loves his little soft man toy with the lovely sweater & pants, and Frieda adores her little "tiny dollies". I am sitting now at tea in the playroom where we had lunch, watching the grey skies of autumn. I was out this morning trying to harvest some of our enormous crop of apples.

I do have some sad news. I did not want to tell you while you were here, and the worst had not yet come, but it is so on my mind I thought I would let you know, rather than pretend. Ted has deserted us. He lived all year off my novel grant, which was to have bought me a full-time nanny, and then he "got courage" to tell me he wanted no more of marriage, and had not had the courage to tell me he never wanted children. Of course there is another woman, who has had so many abortions she can't have children & is beautiful and barren and hates all I have created here. Ted left me in Ireland and I have not seen him since nor do I know his address. I found he had drawn out all our savings, too, so I am having to take legal proceedings. I saw a good lawyer in London this week who is trying to trace Ted. I hope he will settle a yearly allowance on us out of court, but he has been so cruel & hurtful to me and the babies that I think I may have to go to court to get an allowance for them. He says all the kindness and sweetness I loved & married him for was mere sentimentality & he is through with living for anything but himself. I feel I am mourning a dead man, the most wonderful person I knew, and it is some stranger who has taken his name.

I suppose suffering is the source of understanding, and perhaps one day I shall be a better novelist because of this. It is the children I find hardest to face---I thought I was giving them the best father in the world. I write at my novel now from about 5 a.m. when my sleeping pill wears off, till they wake up, and hope to finish it by mid-winter. It is funny, I think. At least I hope so.

I write you, too, because I know you have had great sorrows in your life, and I have often thought that if I could be as intuitive and wise as you are when I am your age that I would be very proud. You listen to everything, and feel into people---all that time we spoke of unfaithful men that evening at the Connaught for instance it was as if you intuitively grasped what our situation was. That was the happiest night of my life for months, and I guess I will remember it as the last happy night with Ted, now happiness, the word, has ceased to have meaning for me.

I will stay in England, because I love it here. This winter I hope to rent the house for 3 months & go to a cottage I found in Ireland with the babies where I could take long walks by the wild sea, milk cows, churn butter & live by savory turf fires---I adored Ireland, it gave me back my health after the flu, if not my happiness. Then in spring I shall return here & try to write my way back to a flat in London in the fall & winter, so the children can go to good free schools, saving this place for the holidays & the summer. You can imagine what memories every handmade curtain and hand-painted table have for me now! The hard thing is realising that Ted has gone for good. I loved the man I have lived with 6 happy years with all my heart, but there is <u>noth</u>ing of this left, there is only a cruel & indifferent stranger. Luckily Dr. Beuscher & my stay at McLean's gave me the strength to face pain & difficulty. It will take time to mend, & more time to begin to feel there is any other life possible for me, but I am resolute and shall work hard. I am so glad you have seen the dream I have made---as far as it got. Do write me. I live for letters & value you as a kind of second, literary mother.

With much love,
Sylvia

TO *Ruth Tiffany Barnhouse Beuscher*

Saturday 29 September 1962 TLS (aerogramme), Smith College

Saturday night: Sept. 29

Dear Dr. Beuscher,

I am sorry to write so much, but it is my one hope, I think I am dying. I am just desperate. Ted has deserted me, I have not seen him for 2 weeks, he is living in London without address. Tonight, utterly mad with this solitude, rain and wind hammering my hundred windows, I climbed to his study out of sheer homesickness to read his writing, lacking letters, and found them---sheafs of passionate love poems to this woman, this one woman to whom he has been growing more & more faithful, describing their orgasms, her ivory body, her smell, her beauty, saying in a world of beauties he married a hag, talking about "now I have hacked the octopus off my ring finger." Many are fine poems.[1] Absolute impassioned love

1 – Two poems have been identified as likely having been written to Assia Wevill. TH's 'Only your ivory body' (first line) and 'Sunlight', which are uncollected, unpublished poems in both manuscript and typescript drafts. 'Sunlight' is dated 'North Tawton – October 1962'. Held in the Ted Hughes papers, Emory.

poems---and I am just dying. I could stand tarts. She is so beautiful, and I feel so haggish & my hair a mess & my nose huge & my brain brainwashed & God knows how I shall keep together. He has spent all the money, left me with nothing. I have almost the equal of my novel grant in our small savings, and the bit I've earned since then---nothing else. The solicitor has told me to draw out the money from our savings (joint) since he's left me with nothing. I am just frantic.

If I had someone living with me, I would not break down & talk to myself, cry, or just stare for hours. But I have no-one---no friends, no relatives. I feel like begging my well-offish aunt to come---just till I rent the house for the winter, if I do, and go to Ireland. I hope the Ireland idea is a good one---it is all I can think of, I just can't cope with a foreign language & can't drive the babes to Spain all myself. I shall try to hire a nanny to make the Ireland trip. And there is no money, just my savings, but I feel I've got to invest in some move. I've got to keep the house, which is in both our names, for later, for when I'm human. It is our one security & such a fine place, it would fetch nothing, no-one but us would have liked it. By sleeping pills I sleep a few hours. I force an egg down with Frieda. I have a woman help 3 mornings a week & try as many days as I can to flog myself out to tea with my few neighbors & the babies. Then the terrible evenings settle in. The shock of this has almost killed my heart. I still love Ted, the <u>old</u> Ted, with everything in me & the knowledge that I am ugly and hateful to him now kills me. He has kept this affair a rabid secret, although seeing my intuitions. Once I asked if he wanted a divorce and he said no, just a separation, he might never see me for 50 years but might write once a week. I am drowning, just gasping for air. I have written Mrs. Prouty whom we entertained here about it, but the laws here horrify me---a woman is only allowed 1/3 her husband's income, if I have the house it would be next to nothing, then if he doesn't pay it is a long & costly suit to get it. If I earn anything I am penalized by having it counted as part of his income & in effect pay my own way! I think Ted will not now settle out of court, as I'd hope---for even to run the place (cheaper than living in a one-room flat in London) & eat, nothing for me, would cost £800---he made twice that this year. And will make more & more & I have nothing.

What kills me is that I would like so much to be <u>friends</u> with him, now I see all else is impossible. I mean my God my life with him has been a daily creation, new ideas, new thoughts, our mutual stimulation. Now he is active & passionately in love out in the world & I am stuck with two infants & not a soul, mother has lost her job, I have <u>no-one</u>. The part about keeping my personal one-ness a real help.[1] I must. But my god I can't see to <u>thinking</u> straight. I'd ideally like to earn my way to a flat in London in fall, winter & spring & rent this place, then come here in summer. <u>How</u> can I tell the babies their father has left them. How do you put it? Death is so simple. Where shall I say daddy is? I had my life set as I wished---beautifully and happily domestic, with lots of intellectual stimulus & my part-time writing. I have no desire to teach, be a secretary ---and god knows how I can write. I feel Ted hates us. Wants to kill us to be free to spend all his money on her, and English laws are so mean, I have no hope of even subsistence if I go to court. And small hope of earning my way out of it as I would like. I feel so trapped. Every view is blocked by a huge vision of their bodies entwined in passion across it, him writing immortal poems to her. And all the people of our circle are with them, for them. I have no friends left except maybe the Alan Sillitoes who are in Morocco for the year. How and where, O God do I begin? I can't face the notion that he may want me to divorce him to marry her. I keep your letters like the Bible. How should I marshal my small money? For a nanny for a year, O God, for what. And how to stop my agony for his loved body and the thousand assaults each day of small things, memories from each cup, where we bought it, how he still loved me then, then when it was not too late. Frieda just lies wrapped in a blanket all day sucking her thumb. What can I do? I'm getting some kittens. I love you & need you.

Sylvia

PS:[2] Bless you for your advice about a divorce which arrived this morning – just in time as Ted arrives too, for the last time.[3] There is a dignity & rightness to it. I was clinging to dead associations. I do not want people to think I am a dog-in-the-manger – "poor man, she won't let him marry." I do know he's a lousy husband & father – to me at least. And I may, at 50, find a better. I am writing from 5-8 a.m. daily.[4] An immense tonic. Before the babies wake.

P.S. Much better. The divorce like a clean knife. I am ripe for it now. Thank you, thank you.

1–In her 17 September letter to SP, Dr Beuscher wrote, 'First, middle and last, do not give up your personal one-ness. Do not imagine that your whole being hangs on this one man . . .'
2–The postscript is written in the left margin of the first page.
3–Dr Beuscher writes, 'If you really mean it about separation and not liking him, I would advise going whole hog and getting a divorce.' See Ruth Beuscher to SP, 26 September 1962; held by Smith College.
4–SP wrote 'For a Fatherless Son' (26 September 1962).

TO *Richard Murphy*

Sunday 7 October 1962 TLS, University of Tulsa

Court Green
North Tawton
Devonshire, England
Sunday: October 7

Dear Richard,

The review[1] was lovely, it was fine to see it there in the middle of everything, and so spacious. Only Ted says they were jackdaws.[2] As far as I'm concerned every black bird is a rook. It was like a brilliant enamel, your account of the place, & made me homesick for it, the first pure clear place I have been for some time.

Please let me know you got my note & if the ticket was any use. I shall be coming to Moyard with Ted's aunt as a companion & hope to get an Irish girl to live in & accompany me back, if I have the luck of the Irish. I shall try for a good Catholic, and maybe she can convert me, only I suppose I am damned already. Do they never forgive divorcées? I am getting a divorce, and you are right, it is freeing. I am writing for the first time in years,[3] a real self, long smothered. I get up at 4 a.m. when I wake, & it is black, & write till the babes wake. It is like writing in a train tunnel, or God's intestine. Please make me happy & say you do not grudge me Moyard. I shall be well & eternally chaperoned & only the cows shall see me. It would hurt me terribly to think of you with clenched teeth in Cleggan.

And tell me about Cheltenham.

Regards,
Sylvia

1–Richard Murphy, 'The Empty Tower at Ballylee', *The Observer* (7 October 1962): 29; a review of several books published in 1962 including W. B. Yeats, *Explorations*; J. M. Synge, *Collected Works: Poems*; and Stanislaus Joyce, *The Dublin Diary of Stanislaus Joyce*.

2–In his review, Murphy mentions his recent drive 'to the poet's Tower at Ballylee with some friends . . . We found the square fortress towering over the ford of a trout-stream. Rooks flopped from the vacant windows . . .' (29).

3–In the week prior to this letter, SP had written: 'A Birthday Present' (30 September); 'The Detective' (1 October); 'The Courage of Shutting-Up' (2 October); 'The Bee Meeting' (3 October); 'The Arrival of the Bee Box' (4 October); 'Stings' (6 October); and 'The Swarm' (7 October).

TO *Aurelia Schober Plath*

Tuesday 9 October 1962 — TLS with envelope, Indiana University

Court Green
North Tawton
Devon.
October 9, 1962

Dear mother,

I don't know where to begin. I just can't take the $50. I don't need it. I want to be sure you drew the $500 from my savings. For God's sake, give me the feeling you are tamping down, taking care of yourself. Just sold a long New Yorker poem.[1] I'll get by. Ted has agreed to give us £1,000 a year maintenance. This will just take care of rates, heat, light, food, with £200 for the children's clothing & upkeep expenses. I want nothing for me. I'll pay the upkeep & gas & taxes on the car, Ted's life insurance, which is made out to me, & will be a kind of pension, if he doesn't die, and for nannies. Right now I get up a couple of hours before the babies & write. I've got to. I want no loans, no mercies. If Mrs. Prouty feels like any concrete help, fine. She can afford it, you can't.

What I am afraid of is that when Ted's working class family & sister get hold of him they will tell him £1,000 is enough for me to go to Paris on. I have made out accounts, & it is a scrape. They take no account of the kid's growing up, of us being three growing adults. I pray he will sign the maintenance before they get him to Jew us. The courts would give me nothing. They are bastards in England.

The reaction of Ted's friends & relatives will be---she's got everything, house, car, pay her nothing! The Yorkshire-Jew miserliness will try to screw me yet. I'm sitting here till the end of November when I go to Ireland. Every one in town knows, suspects. I had to call the police after a storm because I thought someone had broken in---a window was smashed. Ted was gone, & this husband actually did try to get him with a knife & I was scared he might come down here & do us in if Ted wasn't found. But that's over. Ted is in love, humming, packing, leaving this week. He'll live with the woman, I think marry her, though he won't admit it. To hell. Every time he wants to hurt me, or pay me back for having to pay maintenance, he can just not pay, or hurt through the children.

1–Howard Moss to SP, 26 September 1962; held by Smith College. Sylvia Plath, 'The Elm Speaks' ['Elm'], *New Yorker* (3 August 1963): 28.

I am getting a divorce. It is the only thing. He wants absolute freedom, and I could not live out a life legally married to someone I now hate and despise. Ted is glad for a divorce, but I have to go to court, which I dread. The foulness I have lived, his wanting to kill all I have lived for six years by saying he was just waiting for a chance to get out, that he was bored & stifled by me, a hag in a world of beautiful women just waiting for him, is only part of it. I am sure there will be a lot of publicity. I'll just have to take it; my one worry is that Dotty, being Catholic, will turn from me because of the divorce. Can she seethat I want to be free from his hate & grudge against me, that there is no honor or future for me, chained to him? If I am divorced, he can never be unfaithful to me again, I can start a new life. It is the hardest 30th birthday present I could envision. I am fighting on all fronts, I have to stand my ground.

I should say right away America is out for me. I want to make my life in England. If I start running now I will never stop. I shall hear of Ted all my life, of his success, his genius, his woman, his women. I must make a life as fast as I can, all my own. He has been brutal, cruel, bastardly, cowardly and the flesh has dropped from my bones. But I am stubborn. I am a fighter. Money is my only way to fight myself into a new life. I know pretty much what I want.

I have got to get a woman here for the next two months, which will be the worst. My old nanny is with the Astors, but I've written the agency for another. I hope Ted's aunt Hilda will come down then, when she's trained a secretary to take her place, and make the trip to Ireland with me. I shall try to get an Irish girl there to live in & come back, have her live in the guest room till the cottage is ready. Ted has put my life two years back. A year here hand-hemming my own grave, then a year to get out. I want to have a flat in London, where the cultural life is I am starved for, and use this place as a country-house for holidays & the long summer. Frieda & Nick need the stimulus of the fine free London schools, and the country in between. America is out. Also, as you can see, I haven't the strength to see you for some time. The horror of what you saw & what I saw you see last summer is between us & I cannot face you again until I have a new life, it would be too great a strain. I would give heaven & earth to have a visit from Aunt Dot, or Warren & Margaret. Can the latter come in spring.

The shock to me is an enormity. Ted has lied to the end, and only on the last days has he had the courage to tell me what I believed was a delusion. I was very stupid, very happy. I found Ted has been building a secret London life all this summer[1]---a flat, a separate bank account, this woman, who I am sure will now leave her second husband & marry Ted. He gave me no time, no inkling, to make any plans of my own. As you may imagine, the court case is for me to appear in, not him. A necessary evil.

Please tell no one but the relatives of this divorce till it is final. I want it very much. I have to want it. I want Ted utterly out of my life. I have been so shamed and degraded it has almost killed me, and the agony I have had to get the truth is the last I will ever go through. He has been both mean and utterly brutal. He is very pleased with himself and whenever he wants to be very very pleased sort of hums & says "I think £1,000 is too much. You can economize, eat less roasts, etc., etc." He goes Thursday. He doesn't care about things. I have to behave carefully, so his relatives won't turn on me. I think the divorce case may do this. I have got to have it for myself, my honor, my life. But he may pretend he doesn't want it, just doesn't want to live as father & husband & would pay for us out of court, the "gentleman" he has been. He is capable of anything, when after what he wants, and he says for a long time he has not wanted us.

Dot's letter a great consolation. Reassure me she'll accept the divorce & not stop her kindness for that. I have <u>no-one</u>. He has stuck me down here as into a sack, I fight for air & freedom & the <u>culture</u> & libraries of a city.

Got Frieda a red duffle coat, a blue wool bathrobe & two wool dresses in Exeter yesterday. The first clothes Ted has bought her. I am dying to go to Ireland. I need three months away to recover. Everybody in town leering and peering. In spring I'll have strength to cope with the rest, the return, holding my head up. I can't sleep without pills & my health has been bad, after the flu. I've had shock after shock, as Ted has fed me the truth, with leer after leer. I told him that was all I wanted of him, the truth at last, not to hear it bit by bit from others. He couldn't even manage that. The husband chased him with a knife, then tried to commit suicide, etc. etc. No one will ever believe the Ted I know. I am sure now he is "absolutely free" he will be charming. He chose to live with this woman in the same street as the church in which we were married. Oh well, enough.

Do you suppose Warren & Margaret could go with me on a holiday to Austria & Germany next spring or summer? This may sound insane, but I have <u>nothing</u>, nothing to look forward to. It would be something. I would love them. And what a rest, to be among relatives. I never want to return to America, except maybe in the far future, for a Cape Cod visit.

1 – 'all this ~~time~~ summer' appears in the original.

I hate teaching, hate jobs. All I want to do is write at home. And be with my kids, and see movies, plays, exhibits, meet people, make a new life.

I've got to do something for my morale. Ireland is the first thing. Tell me what Prouty says. Ted's in his heaven, the world's is oyster. He's avenging himself for six year's of faithfulness – "sentimentality."

Love,
Sivvy

PS: Do you suppose either Warren or Aunt Dot could fly over to be with me for a few days when I have to face the court? I don't know whether it will be this autumn (I doubt, alas) or next spring, but I will need protection. I look to Warren so now, that I have no man, no adviser. He was so good and sweet here. Ted is desperate for money to go off with this woman & as he has earned nothing all summer, tried by fantastic nastiness to wrench from me the last two installments of my novel grant I kept by me when I realized he was going to desert us, by saying if I had the money I could live on it, no nanny. I hope when he gets off with her he will not be so nasty. He laughs at me, insults me, says my luck is over, etc. He goes tomorrow.

Everything is breaking---my dinner set cracking in half, the health inspector says the cottage should be demolished, there is no hope for it, so I shall have to do over the long room instead. Even my beloved bees set upon me today when I numbly knocked aside their sugar feeder & I am all over stings. Ted just gloats. Perhaps when he is gone the air will clear. I long for Warren & Margaret. I must get to London next fall. I must face the hardest thing---Ted's probable second marriage & his fame & meeting him & his triumphant model with her exotic looks & news of them everywhere. When I have done that, I will know I am not running when I move. The humiliation of having to wait on my husband's whim to get money to keep the house & children going is my most difficult shame just now. Please tell Warren to write & say he & Maggie will come in spring. In Ireland I feel I may find my soul, & in London next fall, my brain, & maybe in heaven what was my heart.

Love,
Sivvy

<at top of page 5 of letter, above paragraph beginning
'Got Frieda a red duffle coat . . .'>

P.S. What exactly is the 5¢ Savings Acct total now?

<on verso of envelope>

PS: Please send a sheet of 4¢ stamps & a glass measuring cup – mine broke!

TO *Ruth Tiffany Barnhouse Beuscher*

Tuesday 9 October 1962 TLS (aerogramme), Smith College

Court Green
North Tawton
Devonshire, England
October 9, 1962

Dear Dr. Beuscher,

I am a bore, but things are resolving. I see and see and see. Ted is home this week, packing for good. He would have left me with all the lies, but bit by bit, the truth has come out. Or what he thinks is the truth. He has been building up a secret life in London all summer---flat, separate bank account, this woman, another woman. He's lied to the end. He is mad for this woman, afraid to tell me so I won't go through with the divorce (I think). I guess her 2nd husband will either divorce her or commit suicide. I found he went after Ted with a knife at Waterloo Station & tried to commit suicide after.[1] Ted says he has been a hypocrite for at least the last 3 years of our marriage, I have been eating not real bread, but a delusion of love. He has nothing but shattering things to say of me, seems to want to kill me, as he kills all he does not want. He has "agreed" to pay £1,000 maintenance for the house-running & children a year. This is scrape pay, and I tried to show him, by accounts, there was nothing for me in it. Now he is utterly loveless for me & us, and triumphant in going, this week, to this woman, to take her off, I guess, to marry her, to tour Europe, he is turning into a terror, a miser, a Yorkshire Jew, as he says. I'm not to have sherry, to have roast beef, I'm to smoke the last quarter inch of my cigarette---"they're expensive". £1,000, he taunts me, seems too much. I have accounts to show it is heat, food, light, children's clothes & repair bills. I am an unpaid nanny. But from his new mind he is leaving me the house, the car, why more? And of course the law here would be merciless, I would get nothing, 1/3 of his income when & if he chose to pay it, less if he left the house, which is in both our names. The minute he wants to show his power---and I feel this terrible hate, the desire to torture me of my last sense, as if to revenge himself for 6 years kindness & faithfulness ("sentimentality" he says) & for my having children, now a burden---he starts on the money, pretending he mightn't want to earn much. He can sell a poem manuscript at $100 a throw, has radio plays in Germany, children's books, he is on the brink of great

1 – According to Assia Wevill's biographer this was on Friday 13 July 1962.

wealth & this year alone earned £1,500 by hardly lifting a finger. He told me I could tell the children they were to "live like the people". Ergo, the meanest of the mean English working class. Which he comes from. It is this working class Yorkshire mind he is trying to kill us from. How can I ever get free? My writing is my one hope, and that income is so small. And with these colossal worries & responsibilities & no-one, no friend or relative, to advise or help as things come up, I have got to have a working ethic. I can't face suing for lack of support now, I have nothing to go on with, no reserves of cash. The humiliation of being dependent for my children's support on a man I hate & despise is a torture. I want nothing for myself, but he switches on & off like an electrode. I face the worst (for me): he will live with this woman, marry her, they will have a wonderful life---wealthy, no children, travel, people, affairs, & every time they are bored, screw us by forgetting the money. Bloody hell. In three months I've got the full picture – the near worst. I long for the divorce, for my independence, like clear water. I have two months to go on here, then Ireland for Dec-Feb, which I hope will blow me clear. I am, in my good minutes, excited about my new life. I want to fight back to a London flat by next fall, keep this place for summers. Perhaps when his first kicking, killing passion is past, & he is free, & with this woman, Ted may be not such a bastard. Our marriage had to go, okay. But she makes the going foul. I am dying for new people, new places, a bloody holiday. In a year I hope to have enough guts to face them, they deliriously happy, wealthy, popular at whatever party or place I meet them at, in myself, my dignity, which is there, though Ted laughs, scoffs, kills. She is all that is desirable, ergo I am a hag, a fool. I want no more of him. I have to be nice, can't afford the luxury of a fury even. Be good little doggy & you shall have a penny. It is the last degradation. Right now I hate men. I am stunned, bitter. I want to go back to London, read, see plays, exhibits, build back the mind this country has dulled, & the babes. Sex is easily dispensed with, I see. My dream is to fight for my writing so I can get into New Yorker stories, something, big money. Then keep him paying for the kids forever, sue if I have to, but not have to grovel for the kids as I would if I had no resource to go on with while having a court case. I have to stay here in England, to keep a grip, & to not run---Ted is everywhere in the literary world, like T. S. Eliot. He has junked me at the foulest time in the foulest way, living a lie & letting me live a happy one, till he got guts, i.e. passion, to break hotel sinks, burn curtains & go off without paying (as he did their first night) & say "ta, ta, tough about the kids, but you did want them, didn't you." I have the consolation of being no doubt the only woman who will know the early years of a charming genius. On my skin. Like a Belsen label. Do write.

Love,
Sylvia

TO *Howard Moss*

Wednesday 10 October 1962 TLS (draft), Smith College

Court Green
North Tawton
Devonshire, England
October 10, 1962

Mr. Howard Moss
THE NEW YORKER
25 West 43rd Street
New York, New York
U.S.A.

Dear Mr. Moss,

I am delighted to hear that you are taking ELM for THE NEW YORKER. I am happier to have you take this than about any of the other poems you have taken---I thought it might be a bit too wild and bloody, but I'm glad it's not.

I think "Soliloquy of the Elm" would be my alternate to "The Elm Speaks", but I think I like your title better. Yes, I think I do.

I am sending the latest batch.[1] I'm sorry about the length of "Bees", but it would go on, and I'll send it just for the record.

Sincerely,
Sylvia Plath

1–SP submitted: 'A Birthday Present', 'The Detective', 'The Courage of Quietness' ['The Courage of Shutting-Up'], 'A Secret', 'For a Fatherless Son', and 'Bees' (a sequence comprising 'The Bee Meeting', 'The Arrival of the Bee Box', 'Stings', 'The Swarm', and 'Wintering').

TO *Howard Moss*

Wednesday 10 October 1962 TLS (aerogramme), New York Public Library

Court Green
North Tawton
Devonshire, England
October 10, 1962

Mr. Howard Moss
THE NEW YORKER
25 West 43rd Street
New York, New York
U.S.A.

Dear Mr. Moss,

I am delighted to hear[1] that you are taking ELM for The New Yorker. I'm happier about your taking this than about any of the other poems of mine you've taken---I was afraid it might be a bit too wild and bloody, but I'm glad it's not.

I think SOLILOQUY OF THE ELM would be my alternate to THE ELM SPEAKS, but I think I like your title better. Yes, I think I do.

I am sending the latest batch. I'm sorry about the length of BEES, but it would go on, and I'll send it just for the record.

I wonder if I could ask you a practical favor. Could you send the stuff back airmail? I'm sticking on as many stamps as I can, but I never know the return air rates, and as I'm a bit hard up I want to get these round as fast as possible. I'd be happy to have you dock my check for it.

With warmest good wishes,
Sincerely,
Sylvia Plath

1–Howard Moss to SP, 26 September 1962; held by Smith College.

TO *Aurelia Schober Plath*

Friday 12 October 1962 TLS (aerogramme), Indiana University

Court Green
North Tawton
Devonshire, England
Friday, October 12

Dear mother,

Your fat nice letter received with many thanks. Do tear my last one up. It was written at what was probably my all-time low and I have an incredible change of spirit, I am joyous---happier than I have been for ages. Ted left yesterday, after a ghastly week, with all his stuff, clothes, books, papers. Instead of returning home to blueness & gloom, as I expected, I found myself singing, washing Frieda's hair, rubbishing out junk, delighted. At last everything was definite, no more waiting, worrying, trying to decipher lies. It is over. My life can begin. Ted did see some money was in the bank & in his present state of mind is willing to pledge £1,000 for our support a year. He is going off, I gather, to live with this woman. When our divorce is final I am quite sure he will marry her, and have the distinction of being her 4th (!) husband. I don't envy either of them. He has behaved like a bastard, a boor, a crook, & what has hurt most is his cowardice---evidently for years he has wanted to leave us & deceived us about his feelings, although this is the first (and last) time he has hurt us in any way. If only he had told the truth at the start, six months ago, for this summer, the flu, my weight loss, have really set me back. But I am full of fantastic energy, now it is released from the problem of him. I have a great appetite---when I came home from driving him to the station I ate a great plate of potatoes & lamb chops, my first good meal in months.

Got a darling letter from Warren today. It means more than I can say. Part of my hardship is being stuck down here in limbo with no real old friends or relatives. Saw Winifred today, & she says she'll write you[1] how fine I am now he's gone. This week is a bit of a drag. I have ordered a nice new nanny from this agency in London, & they say she'll arrive next week sometime. I hope. So glad you & Warren are behind me in the nanny line. If I didn't write I'd go mad with boredom. I never wanted to live in the country full-time & don't intend to. I'll keep this place as a summer house

1 – That autumn, Winifred Davies wrote to ASP on 22 September, 25 October, 3 November, and 5 December 1962; held by Lilly Library.

& try to rent in winter & get in a London flat by next fall. I am dying for London---the plays, art shows, people with brains, & the free lance jobs. Frieda & Nich can go to good London schools & have a heavenly country house & all the beaches for summer. I must have a nanny full-time. Now the cottage is out, I am having the long room made over, new floors & will furnish as a bed-sitter with TV. Guests can stay in the pink room & up in Ted's attic. I hope to keep this (very expensive) nanny until Ted's aunt Hilda comes, as she hopes to, at the end of November, to accompany me to Ireland. I like Hilda, she is spry, & was left to bring up Vicky alone, & is on my side. I must keep them on my side (never say I'm happy---as soon as they think I want the divorce, not Ted, their Yorkshire-Jew quality will say not to pay me a penny as I have the house. I've to be very careful. Ted does want the divorce, thank goodness, so shouldn't be difficult). Ireland in my darling cottage from Dec. 1–Feb. 28. I should recover on the milk from TTtested cows (hope to learn to milk them myself), homechurned butter & homemade bread. And sea!

Every morning, when my sleeping pill wears off I am up about 5, in my study with coffee, writing like mad---have managed a poem a day before breakfast![1] All book poems. Terrific stuff, as if domesticity had choked me. As soon as the nanny comes & I know I've got a stretch of guaranteed time, I'll finish the novel. I have 40 children's picture books at my side to review, for the leftish weekly I've done them for before.--- "Horton Hatches the Egg" among them! So send no children's books. I've mountains. Nick has two teeth, stands, sits, is an angel. Ted cut F's hair short & it looks marvellous, no mess, no straggle. She has 2 kittens from Mrs. Macnamara, Tiger-Pieker and Skunky-Bunks, the first a tiger, the second black & white. She adores them, croons "Rock a bye baby, when the bough breaks" at them. They're very good for her now.

Did you see my poem "Blackberries" in the Sept. 15 New Yorker? Wrote that when Warren was here last year. Mrs. Prouty, bless her, came through with $300, so I am all right for nannies for a bit. Hope, when free, to write myself out of this hole. Do have Warren & Maggie let me know as soon as they know when they're coming next spring. I would give the world if they'd take (I mean go with) me to Austria & Germany. I should have earned enough by then to deserve a holiday & leave the kids with their then (I hope) full-time nanny. I need a bloody holiday. Ireland is heaven, utterly unspoiled, emerald sea washing in fingers among green

1–Since writing to Murphy on 7 Ocotber, SP had completed: 'Wintering' (9 October); 'A Secret' (10 October); 'The Applicant' (11 October); and 'Daddy' (12 October).

fields, white sand, wild coast, cows, friendly people, honey-tasting whisky, peat (turf) fires that smell like spiced bread---thank God I found it. Just in time. I go riding tomorrow, love it. Shall send F & N to church in London, not here! I miss brains, hate this cow life, am dying to surround myself with intelligent good people. Shall have a salon in London. I am a famous poetess here---mentioned this week in The Listener[1] as one of the half-dozen women who will last – including Marianne Moore & the Brontes!

xxx
Sivvy

<in left margin of page 1 of letter>

PS: Forget about the court case – I'll manage that fine alone. Every experience is grist for a novelist.

<on page 1 of letter>

My solicitor is Mr. Charles Mazillius
Harris, Chetham & Co. Solicitors
23 Bentinck Street, London W.1

My bank: The National Provincial
The Square, North Tawton, Devon.

Am having a phone put in again, not listed, so I can call out & have friends call in.[2] Look forward to it.

1–Elizabeth Jennings, 'Mrs Browning. By Alethea Hayter', *The Listener* (13 September 1962): 400. Jennings writes, 'Memorable English or American women poets can be numbered on less than two hands; one thinks of Emily Brontë, Emily Dickinson, Marianne Moore, Edith Sitwell's early work, Anne Ridler, Kathleen Raine, Elizabeth Bishop, Sylvia Plath, and scarcely anyone else.'

2–On 9 July, upon intercepting a telephone call from Assia Wevill to TH, SP had ripped the telephone line out of the wall.

TO *Howard Moss*

Friday 12 October 1962 — TLS, New York Public Library

Court Green
North Tawton
Devonshire, England
October 12, 1962

Dear Mr. Moss,

I'd be grateful if you'd consider this[1] with the last lot I sent and send it back with them.

Yours sincerely,
Sylvia Plath

TO *Warren & Margaret Plath*

Friday 12 October 1962 — TLS (aerogramme, photocopy), Indiana University

Court Green
North Tawton
Devonshire England
Friday: October 12

Dearest Warren & Maggie,

Your lovely letter arrived today & cheered me immensely. How often I have thought of you both! I have been through the most incredible hell for six months, influenza, the lot, and amazingly enough, now that Ted has finally packed his bags & left for good (yesterday), I feel wonderful. As I told mother in the letter I am writing today, I am so relieved to have broken through all the endless lies and to have something <u>definite</u>, that the release in my energy is enormous. Ted is, I see, just reverting to type. The good, kind, domestic person he has been these six years was a terrible strain on him & I believe he has made this experience so awful & hurtful as a kind of revenge on me for having "reformed" him. I never thought I would ever in my life consider a divorce, but am now looking forward to it. I want in no way, not even legally, to be associated with the life Ted will now live. The one thing I retain is love for & admiration of his writing, I know he is a genius, and for a genius there are no bonds & no bounds.

1 – Most likely 'The Applicant' and 'Daddy', which Plath handwrote on her submissions list with the batch sent on 10 October 1962.

I feel I did discover him, worked to free him for writing for six years, & now suddenly on the brink of enormous riches (his manuscripts of one poem now fetch at least $100!) it is hurtful to be ditched and left to live on crumbs while he squires models & fashion plates etc. etc. But thank God I have my own work. If I did not have that I do not know what I would do. I have a considerable reputation over here, and am writing from dawn to when the babes wake, a poem a day, and they are terrific. Have just sold another fat one to the New Yorker. Did you see "Blackberrying" in the Sept. 15th NY, Warren? I wrote that about the time we went when you were here.

So glad you are behind me on the nanny, Warren. I am & have been an intelligent woman, & this year of country life has been, for me, a cultural death. No plays, films, art shows, books, people! All for Ted's "dream", & now I am stuck. But not for long. I plan to go to Ireland to a lovely cottage by the sea for Dec-Feb to recover my health & my heart, then return here for spring & summer, see you & Maggie I hope & pray, my good friends the Alan Sillitoes, now alas in Tangier for a year, & Marty & Mike Plumer if they come. The loneliness here now is appalling. Then I shall fight for a London flat by next fall. Frieda & Nick can go to the good free London schools & have a lovely summer place here. I shall try to rent this in winter. I shall be able to do free-lance broadcasting, reviewing, & have a circle of intellectual friends in London. I loved living there & never wanted to leave. You can imagine how ironic it is to me that Ted is now living there, after he said it was "death" to him, & enjoying all the social & cultural life he has deprived me of. I am making the long room over & hope to be able to support a full-time nanny on my writing. I will try to finish my novel & a second book of poems by Christmas. I think I'll be a pretty good novelist, very funny---my stuff makes me laugh & laugh, & if I can laugh now it must be hellishly funny stuff.

I wish you would both consider going on a holiday to Germany & Austria when you come. You should know some lovely places in the Tyrol & I would love to go with you! I just dread ever going on a holiday alone. I could leave the babies with the nanny for a couple of weeks, & you could begin & end your stay here. I would be very cheerful & entertaining by then, I promise you. Just now I am a bit of a wreck, bones literally sticking out all over & great black shadows under my eyes from sleeping pills, a smoker's hack (I actually took up smoking the past month out of desperation---my solicitor started it by offering me a cigarette & I practically burned off all my eyebrows, I was so upset & forgot it was lit! But now I've stopped.) I do hope Dotty isn't going to snub me because of the divorce, although I know Catholics think it's a sin. Her support has been marvelous for me. I hope you can tactfully convey to mother, Warren, that we should not meet for at least a year or a year & a half, when I am happy in my new London life. After this summer, I just could not bear to see her, it would be too painful & recall too much. So you & dear Maggie, whom I already love, come instead. Tell me you'll consider taking (I mean escorting! I'll have money!) me to Austria with you, even if you don't, so I'll have that to look forward to. I've had nothing to look forward to for so long! The half year ahead seems like a lifetime, & the half behind an endless hell. Your letters are like glühwein to me. I must really learn German. I want above all to speak it. Do write me again. So proud of your Chicago speech, Warren! I want both you & Maggie henceforth to consider yourselves godparents to both Frieda & Nick. Lord knows, they need as many as they can have, & the best!

Lots of love to you both,
Sivvy

PS: We have two kittens – Tiger-Pieker & Skunky-Bunks.

TO *Aurelia Schober Plath*

Tuesday 16 October 1962 — TLS (aerogramme), Indiana University

Court Green: Tuesday October 16

Dear mother,

I am writing with my old fever of 101° alternating with chills back. Two things: I must have someone with me for the next 2 months to mind the babies while I get my health back & try to write. I have got to get to Ireland by December 1st. Write nothing to any of the Hughes. I stupidly told Edith in a letter this morning that Ted had finally deserted & you would appreciate a word[1] that they care for me & the babies, although Ted does not. This noon I got, from Hilda, the "Family position". The materialistic, appalling Yorkshire-Jew skinflint: "Forget Ted, count myself lucky to have a house, car, two babies & the ability to earn my whole living at home instead of having to go out & work for a boss!" When they hear that Ted has pledged, or was going to, £1,000 for heat, light, food & the children's clothes---my rock-bottom expenses, I fear they will try to torture me to death. I have been advised to have nothing to do

1–See Edith Hughes to ASP, 17 October 1962; held by Lilly Library.

or say to Ted's relatives till the custody of the children is decided & the divorce final. Nothing will matter to them. Words will only make them turn their full fury on me. They have utterly no imagination, no notion of our standard of living. I see clearly Ted will as soon as he goes home this fall, utterly justify to them his actions by saying he will "support us". £1,000 is fantastic to them, insanity. Olwyn will return. I have got to get to Ireland. I need Dotty, or Margaret---just for 6 weeks, two months, to protect me. Ted & his woman (he will have the distinction of being her 4th husband, thank god I think she is barren) have already wistfully started wondering why I didn't commit suicide, since I did before! Ted has said how convenient it would be if I were dead, then he could sell the house & take the children whom He likes. It is me he does not like. I need help very much just now. Home is impossible. I can go nowhere with the children, & I am ill, & it would be psychologically the worst thing to see you now or to go home. I have free doctor's care here, cheap help possible though not now available, and a home I love & will want to return to in summer to get ready to leap to London. To make a new life. I am a writer. I hate teaching. I am a genius of a writer, I have it in me. I am up at 5 writing the best poems of my life, they will make my name.[1] I could finish the novel in six weeks of daylong work. I have a gift of an inspiration for another. Got a $100 "Birthday present" from Dotty today. $300 from Mrs. Prouty. Thank God. Very bad luck with nanny agency, a bitch of a woman is coming tomorrow[2] from them, doesn't want to cook, do any breakfast or tea, wondered if there was a butler. £10 a week. If I had time to get a good nanny, possibly an Irish girl to come home with me, I could get on with my life. Ted is dead to me, I feel only a lust to study, write, get my brain back & practice my craft. I have, if you want to know, already had my 1st novel finished & accepted--- it is a secret, & I am on my 2nd. My 3rd – the idea – came this week. After Ted left with all his clothes & things I piled the children & 2 cats in the car & drove to stay with a horrid couple I know in St. Ives Cornwall ---the most heavenly gold sands by emerald sea. Discovered Cornwall, exhausted but happy, my first independent act! I have no desire but to

1–Since writing to ASP on 12 October, SP had completed 'Eavesdropper' (15 October) and 'Medusa' (16 October). SP submitted 'Eavesdropper' with seven other poems to *Poetry* on 23 November. Accepted in Henry Rago to SP, 27 December 1962; letter held by Smith College. Sylvia Plath, 'Fever 103', 'Purdah', and 'Eavesdropper, *Poetry* (August 1963): 292–8. SP made revisions to 'Eavesdropper' on 31 December 1962; however, as Ted Hughes noted, 'No final copy was made' (*Collected Poems*, p. 294).

2–According to SP's Letts Royal Office Diary Tablet for 1962, the nanny appears to have been a Miss Hutchins. SP wrote 'Miss Hutchins' on 17 October.

build a new life. Must start here. When I have my 2nd book of poems done, my 3rd novel, & the children are of age, I may well try a year of creative writing lecturing in America & a Cape summer. But not just now. I must not go back to the womb or retreat. I must make steps out, like Cornwall, like Ireland.

Please share this letter with Dotty & Mrs. Prouty. I am all right. I know I sound insane, but could either Dot or Margaret spare me 6 weeks. I can get no good nanny sight unseen, I could pay board & room easily & travel expenses & Irish fares. I am as bereft now as ever. I am terrified of the Hughes family. Now is their most "sympathetic time"---wait till they hear about the money! I must have someone I love who is of course not you, to protect me, for I fear they will by more torture try to get me to the wall. When Ted left I felt a peace and joy I have not known for a year at bottom half a year on the surface. He has squelched me, I need no literary help from him. I am going to make my own way. Next fall I must get to London, & the children to London schools. Know my only problems now are practical: money health back, a good young girl or nanny willing to muck in & cook which I could afford once I got writing. The strain of facing suing Ted for support, with the cruel laws here, is something I need to put off just now. Could Margaret fly over, get a new job when she comes back? Or Dot? My flu with my weight loss & the daily assault of practical nastiness---this nanny sounds as if she will leave in a day or so & the fees are fantastic for over here---has made me need immediate help. I'm getting an unlisted phone put in as soon as possible so I can call out, you shall have the number. The babes are beautiful, though Frieda has regressed, the pussies help. I cannot come home. I need someone to cover my getting to Ireland. I can't rely on any nanny at this short notice ---I just can't interview them. Do let me know what you all think. The life in Ireland is very healthful, the place a dream, the sea a blessing. I must get out of England. No word to the Hughes, no answer if Edith writes. I cannot see Hilda---it would be insanity. I am happy, full of plans but do need help for the next 2 months. I am fighting now against hard odds & alone.

xxx
Sivvy

<on the return address side of letter>

Please have a family powow & answer this as soon as possible!

Lots of love.
S.

Be "careful" on telegrams!

TO *Aurelia Schober Plath*

Tuesday 16 October 1962 | TLS (aerogramme), Indiana University

<SP wrote '2' on address side of letter>

Court Green
October 16, 1962

Dear mother,

Mention has been made of my coming home for Christmas---which alas this year is impossible from every angle, psychological, health, babies, money. I gathered from Dot's letter you might all chip in to do this. Do you suppose instead there is any possibility of your chipping in and sending me Maggie? By next spring I should have my health back, the prospect of visits from friends like the Sillitoes & Marty & Mike, good weather. Could she come now instead of then? I already love her, she would be such fun and love the babies. We could go to Ireland together & get me settled in & she could fly home from Dublin well before Christmas. Do I sound mad? Taking or wanting to take Warren's new wife? Just for a few weeks! How I need a free sister! We could go on jaunts, eat together, I have all the cleaning done & someone who'll mind the babies 9 hours a week.

I need someone from home. A defender. I am terrified of what will happen when Ted goes home this fall & they find out I need & expect some financial support. They are inhuman Jewy working-class bastards. There is no hope or help in them. I must have nothing ever to do with them. You see what I am up against from Hilda's letter! I have a fever now, so I am a bit delirious. I live on sleeping pills, work from 4 a.m. to 8 a.m. On the next few months depend my future and my health. I must get to Ireland, away from the Hughes malice. Ted almost killed me the 10 days he was home for not giving him the last installment of my novel grant "for a nanny" which we lived off all year to help his writing. If he had any honor, any soul, he would have told me he was planning to desert us & for God's sake to take my novel grant & use it for a nanny. I hate & despise him so I can hardly speak.

I dread the nanny who is coming tonight, she sounded such a bitch over the phone, so snotty, wanting a "cook" etc. I simply can't afford these high fees & a bad lazy nanny. It's the worst thing for the children, these changes. If only Maggie could come for six weeks, then I could get settled in Ireland & look around for an Irish girl! I would have a blood ally. I fully expect Ted's family will put me through the gruelling tedium of having to sue for any support at all, & then the courts will only allow a pittance & penalize me for anything I earn! Do see if Maggie & Warren could make this great & temporary sacrifice. I am fine in mind & spirit, but wasted & ill in flesh.

I love you all,
Sivvy

TO *Aurelia Schober Plath*

Thursday 18 October 1962 TLS (aerogramme), Indiana University

Court Green: Thursday
October 18

Dear mother,

Do ignore my last letters! I honestly must have been delirious to think I could uproot other people's lives to poultice my own. It was the bloody fever that just finished me. I went to the doctor---no medication, of course---then to bed at 8 p.m. Yesterday I was much better. The Health Visitor came to see Nicholas & gaped at me: My, Mrs. Hughes, you've lost weight! I told her I was up at 4 a.m. every morning, writing till the babies woke & she looked concerned. I guess my predicament is an astounding one, a deserted wife knocked out by flu with 2 babies & a full-time job! Anyhow, Winifred, bless her, came round last night with some hopeful news---a young 22-year-old nurse[1] nearby would "love" to live in till mid-December, visit home one day a week etc. I could propose the Irish trip after she'd settled in, she thought she'd be game. She'd want to be home for Xmas & have to go back to London as staff nurse in January, but it's this limbo through to Ireland I've got to settle. Evidently they'll invite me round to tea to discuss business---about 5 guineas a week ($15) plus board & room should be okay, Winifred thinks. Half of the fee for the bastardly nanny who arrived last night. She's an old snobby snoop & I can't wait to get rid of her. It's cost $10 just to hire her through this fancy agency which in desperation I've had to use---I just don't have time to shop around. Nancy commiserated with me this morning on her, the young nanny was so nice. I shall work this one so hard for the next few days she'll be glad to go, & I'll tell her I've a "permanent" nanny who wants to cook, which

1–Susan A. O'Neill-Roe (1940–). O'Neill-Roe worked for the Great Ormond Street Hospital, London.

she doesn't. Hilda, Ted's aunt, wrote today about coming down soon, so I shall sweetly & tactfully tell her I've been ordered to have a live-in nurse by my doctor (close to true) since I've been flattened by influenza. That will put the wind up them, & keep them away, with no hurt feelings. So this is the position. Get Maggie & Warren to promise a visit & trip with me next spring.

The weather has been heavenly. Fog mornings, but clear sunny blue days after. I have a bad cough & shall get my lungs Xrayed as soon as I can, & my teeth seen to. Up at 5 a.m. today. I am writing very good poems.[1] The BBC has just accepted a very long[2] one which I'll go up to record. I have no feeling for Ted, except that he is an absolute bastard. No word from him. He promised to see my lawyer, agree to a yearly fee, provide a witness for the divorce (I think he'll marry this woman & be her 4th husband) & he can't even write to say if or whether he's done it. I am myself, proud, and full of plans. Got a darling letter from Clem today, very fond of him, like a second brother, and his mother. Shall write his father & hope to see him in London,[3] just for human contact & advice, as I plan to be recording up there around then. As soon as I get this young nanny I shall junk this old hag. Ted's nasty walkout---he coolly told me it was not living in London he hated, but living with me! too bad he didn't tell me then!---has given me no time. I need time to breathe, sun, recover my flesh. I have enough ideas & subjects to last me a year or more! Must get a permanent girl or nanny after this young nurse whose father writes children's books & whose mother[4] is the secretary of the local Bee-Keepers club. She sounds nice. Everybody here very good to me, as if they knew or guessed my problem.

If Ted doesn't agree to a decent maintenance of £1,000 a year, which he can earn by snapping his fingers (he's offered a semester lecture post in

1–Since writing to ASP on 16 October, SP had completed 'The Jailor' (17 October) and 'Lesbos' (18 October).

2–See George MacBeth to SP, 16 October 1962; held by BBC Written Archives Centre. 'Berck-Plage', *The Poet's Voice*, BBC Third Programme (17 November 1962); recorded on 29 October 1962.

3–A note in SP's address book indicates Leonard Moore was at the Hotel Meurice, Bury Street, London S.W.1, 24–31 October 1962.

4–Alan C. Jenkins (1912–96) and Nancy Letitia Whitaker Jenkins (née Bovill) (1916–2012). Nancy Jenkins had Susan while married to Richard O'Neill-Roe. The Jenkinses lived at 'Pear Trees', Belstone, near where SP took her horse-riding lessons. Alan Jenkins gave SP a signed and inscribed copy of his *White Horse and Black Bulls* (London: Blackie, 1960) which appeared at auction via Bonhams on 21 March 2018.

America for £2,000, plus a reading tour & has 2 more books[1] taken etc.) I'll simply sue him & his family will rue the day of their skinflintery. Even if I only get a court-decreed pittance I shall do it. This bitch of Ted's is barren from all her abortions & has been offered an ad agency job at £3,000 a year, a fortune here, so he can bloody well afford us. He'll just have to learn he can't kill what he's through with, namely me & the babies. I shall live on here, & eventually in London, happy in my own life & career & babies. As Mrs. Prouty says, he must be kept aware of his responsibilities. I think he half-hopes they can drive me to America, to be supported by my family or something! Well, I love it here, even in the midst of this. I see it is imperative to have a faithful girl or woman living in with me so I can go off for a job or a visit at the drop of a hat & write full-time. Then I can enjoy the babies. It is lucky I don't have to work out.

I just haven't had energy to write to Warren again, or Mrs. Prouty or Dot. I hope you share my news with them & say I'll write as soon as things simmer down. Now the nanny is here, I hope to get into my waiting novel. I shall write Clem, too. It is the voices of friends that I miss, in my little mausoleum in the country. Ted made sure I was utterly cut off from culture, plays, libraries, people, work, resources & my writing stopped & my grant gone before he got "courage" to kick me & the children over with a hate & venom & sadism I shall never forget & shall commemorate in my next novel. As if hating me for making him "nice" & "good". I am fine. Just need a settled nanny & to rest & write & letters. I love & live for letters.

xxx
Sivvy

1–Possibly Ted Hughes, *How the Whale Became* (London: Faber & Faber, 1963) and *The Earth-Owl and Other Moon-People* (London: Faber & Faber, 1963). A third book was published the following year: Ted Hughes, *Nessie and the Mannerless Monster* (London: Faber & Faber, 1964).

TO *George MacBeth*

Thursday 18 October 1962 TLS, BBC Written Archives Centre

Court Green
North Tawton
Devonshire
October 18, 1962

George MacBeth, Esq.
The British Broadcasting Corp.
Broadcasting House
London W.1

Dear George,

I am very happy to hear you are taking "Berck-Plage" for "The Poets Voice". I sort of had you in mind when I wrote it and did hope you might like it. Monday 29th October would be fine for me to record it. Could you make it some time in the morning? My train gets into Waterloo well before 10.30, so I could make it to the BBC by 10.45, I should think.

Let me know if this is okay. Looking forward to seeing you,

Yours sincerely,
Sylvia Plath

<written at top of letter>

P.S. Ted's story "Snow" appeared in Harper's Bazaar in America & in the Faber edition of short stories by 6 young writers brought out some time back.[1]

1–SP was probably replying to something in George MacBeth to SP, 14 June 1962; held by BBC Written Archives Centre.

TO *Olive Higgins Prouty*

Thursday 18 October 1962 TLS (aerogramme), Indiana University

Court Green
North Tawton
Devonshire, England
Thursday: October 18

Dear Mrs. Prouty,

Thank you a thousand times for your dear, intuitive letter and the wonderfully helpful check. What I have lived through these past three months seems like a dark dream from which I have only the desire to disassociate myself. Ted left us for good a week ago, taking all his things. He has evidently been secretly planning to desert us all along, withdrawing money from our joint account unknown to me, getting a London flat and mailing address, and leaving us with no access to him at all, and no explanation. I guess he thought we could just live here on potatoes and apples. His desertion, without a word, a week after I almost died from influenza, decided me on a divorce. On his return to get his things, after my solicitor's agents unearthed him from London, he was furious I had not committed suicide---evidently he and his new flame had discussed this, in view of my old nervous breakdown. If I were dead, he said, he could sell the house, which we jointly own, and take Frieda---he never has loved or touched little Nicholas---as this woman has had so many abortions she can't have children. Needless to say, my six years of absolute love and trust have been killed completely in three months. The poor 3rd husband of this woman, also a poet and a friend and a great admirer of Ted's, tried to kill himself when he knew what Ted had done, but Ted only laughed.

I suppose it is something to have been the first wife of a genius. Ted is now on the brink of wealth, and wants us to have nothing. His family is behind him---the meanest, most materialistic of the English working class. I think I shall probably have to sue him to get any support of the children at all, but that is something I shall face later. Right now my one concern is to write and write and get back my lost weight and my health. My midwife has a temporary nurse up her sleeve who might live in with me for the next 6 weeks. I hope to winter in Ireland in a lovely cottage I found there, with the babies, free from the terrible memories and emptiness of this place, and to return in spring with the daffodils. Then I shall try to get a permanent live-in nanny, or an Irish girl, so I can write and go on day jobs to broadcast on the radio in London. For the time being, without help, I get up at 4 a.m. when my sleeping pill wears off and write till 8 a.m. when the babies wake, my only "free" time, and I am writing the best poems of my life. As soon as I get a live-in nanny I shall finish my novel. My dream is to get back to a London flat by next fall and use this place only as a summer house---the schools in Devon are terrible & the complete lack of cultural life---libraries, museums, theaters, films, intelligent people---is a sort of mental torture to me, a vacuum. It is ironic that Ted should have pretended that this was his dream, to get me to leave the London I loved, and then desert me to live in London himself before a year was out, but I feel I have a deeper sense of human nature now than ever in my life, and that out of grief a great strength and understanding is coming. I should be a compassionate novelist!

I feel happy and resolute now I am decided on a divorce---I have no wish to be the wife, even in name, of a person like Ted, who cannot just leave what he does not want, but wants to kill it. Like a true genius, he will live only for himself and his pleasures, and I wish him joy. I can even laugh when I think of him being the 4th husband of this woman. They are both so handsome & faithless they should be a perfect match. I am eager to begin my new life and impatient with all the legal and business tangles I have to solve. I want only to write, and feel that the children, having only one parent, need me at home most of the time, although Ted's family would have me put them in an orphanage & work as a waitress rather than get any support from Ted, for in their eyes his fame is all, he can do no wrong.

I have just sold a long poem about our Elm tree to the New Yorker for $156, very encouraging. Since my contract with them, they buy a good many of my poems. I also am scheduled to record a long one for the BBC this month. Miraculously, and like some gift, my writing has leapt ahead and not deserted me in this hour of need. I have devotion to it---what else but my babies could get me up at 4 in the morning! I have, too, great joy in my work. I hope to have a second book of poems ready soon, and a second novel written by the end of the winter if I am lucky in finding a suitable woman or girl to help with the children and cooking. Do reassure mother about my state of mind. It is only my rather wasted physique that needs building up, & that is simple enough, given my optimism and happy spirit. I go horseback riding---learning---each week & it is a great pleasure. Do write. I love your letters.

Warmest love to you & Taupe,
Sylvia

TO *Warren Plath*

Thursday 18 October 1962 TLS (aerogramme, photocopy), Indiana University

Court Green
North Tawton
Devonshire, England
Thursday: October 18

Dear Warren,

Your welcome letter arrived today, together with a very sweet and moving letter from Clem. I am writing him in the same mail as this. I certainly want to see his father. As it happens, the BBC have just taken a long gruesome poem of mine, so I can go up to record it during his stay, expenses paid, & a good local temporary nanny is imminent, thanks to the efforts of blessed Winifred Davies, our midwife. I have a horror now (don't tell mother) whom I shall fire tomorrow---she is a snobby snoopy old bitch & has upset my faithful cleaner Nancy & the babies & me & is terribly expensive. I got her from the same agency as my young dream-nanny who came while I was in Ireland & have resolved never to get someone sight unseen again. Ted's fantastic thoughtlessness, almost diabolic---he keeps saying he can't understand why I don't kill myself, it would be so convenient, & has certainly tried to make life hell enough ---has set me back a year or two in my own life. I know just what I need, what I want, what I must work for. Please convince mother of this. She identifies much too much with me, & you must help her see how starting my own life in the most difficult place---here, not running, is the only sane thing to do. I love England, love Court Green for summers, want to live in London in fall & winter so the children can go to the fine free schools & I can have the free lance jobs & cultural variety & stimulus which is food for my year-long culture-starved soul.

I fear I wrote two worrying letters to mother this week when I was desperate at hearing the "Hughes position", which is that I am bloody lucky to have a house & car & to be able to "earn my own living" (I can just about earn the "extras"---a nanny, Ted's high life insurance & the car insurance & gas), & of course not to expect a penny from Ted. This cheery letter came just as I had a recurrence of my old flu fever & chills & weakness, and I was terrified that as soon as they hear from Ted he has said he would pledge £1,000 a year (a fortune to them, although he can now earn twice & thrice that at the turn of a finger) to cover our very basic running expenses---taxes, heat, light, food, clothes for the children (nothing for me)---that they would descend, the charming Olwyn in advance, & literally try to do me in. The most sordid thing is Ted's playing on my nervous breakdown, & telling me how convenient it would be if I were dead. I think he actually counted on my committing suicide. The poor husband---the 3rd---of this charming woman, did try to commit suicide, because he honestly loved & admired Ted, was a minor poet too, & to Ted this was only sauce. Do try to convince mother I am cured. I am only in danger physically, mentally I am sound, fine & writing the best ever, free from the long cow-sludge of domesticity from 4 a.m. to 8 a.m. each day. I did not tell mother that I almost died from influenza, that is why I begged to see Maggie. I thought a loving humane sister-in-law whom I already love dearly, would protect me from further assaults while I got back my weight, my health. But now I am better & if this local nanny comes through & covers my trip to Ireland I should be safe, for a while.

I shall certainly see Clem's father. I am in a very difficult position as Ted can earn large & indefinite amounts & not report half of them---thousands of $ for ms. sales alone. Legally I am only entitled to 1/3 of his income, less if I have the house, & if I earn anything, I am penalized, for then it becomes 1/3 of our combined incomes. If he doesn't pay, I have the long tedium of suing. He is, I now see, fully indulging the bastard & killer in him & his fantastic hatred & sadism toward me & Nick is probably the result of resentment at having led 6 years of good, kind faithful behavior. He evidently meant to secretly, suddenly & completely desert us without money or access to him, or support, thinking, it now appears, that we could live here on potatoes & apples. I want a clean, quick divorce. He says he will dock any legal expenses from the money he pledged us! I think when his family masses behind him, I shall have to face yearly suing. I am a writer & that is all I want to do. Over here I can earn quite a bit from the radio, live on little, get free medical care, & have had my 1st novel accepted (this is a secret, it is a pot-boiler & no-one must read it!) & am ready to finish a 2nd the minute I get a live-in nanny. I plan to have the "long" room done over this winter (the cottage has been ordered demolished by the health inspector!) as a bed-sitter with TV & invest in a "permanent nanny" when I return from Ireland in March. I must have someone live in, or otherwise I don't eat & can go nowhere. By next fall I hope to have earned & written my way to a flat in London where my starved mind can thrive & grow. My God, Warren, imagine yourself on an endless potato farm forever deprived of your computers, friends, relatives & only potato people in sight. I am an intellectual at heart---this will be a fine summer house for the children, but the schools are awful, they must go to school in London. Do reassure mother. I hope my new nanny will want to manage Ireland.

xxx

sivvy

<on page 1 of letter>

PS: Please try to keep writing me too! I live on letters & have no other source of contact with relatives & friends just now! Even a paragraph from you is a great tonic!

TO *Clarissa Roche*

Friday 19 October 1962 TLS, Smith College

Court Green
North Tawton
Devonshire
October 19: Friday

Dearest Clarissa,

You have no idea how much your sweet letter meant to me, which came today. I congratulate you on the new baby, and if she takes after the others & you she will be a blond lucky goddess. I'm so glad you heard the baby-borning program[1]---I'd never been in a maternity ward except to see someone's else's baby born, but a stay in hospital after I had my appendix out gave me the atmosphere.

What I say next may come as a bit of a shock. Since I last wrote you I am having to divorce Ted. He has, in effect, deserted me and the children, saying he never had courage to tell me he didn't want them until we had two. I loved London life & did not want to leave---coming to the country was his idea, his "dream", as he said. I guess he thought we could live on potatoes & apples. The fact that he left the week after I almost died of influenza last month, & that his family does not want him to support us in any way, is just one step, I guess, in the path of poetic genius. Needless to say, I would just adore to see you & Paul. I am at present totally without access to friend or relative and have been stupidly ill, lost a lot of weight & am running a flickery 103° fever, getting up each morning at 4 a.m. to write, my one quiet time.

My one main problem is to find a loyal live-in girl who can baby mind & cook breakfasts & teas while I write. I am having to get rid of a ghastly snoopy scabby senile agency nanny tomorrow who has almost scared the

1 – Sylvia Plath, 'Three Women'.

babes out their wits in 2 days, but hope next week to have the help by day of a pretty nurse for the six weeks before she goes up to London to be a staff nurse there. I have a double bedroom that will be free when she goes on a holiday for a week in mid-November. Could you come then? There's a carry-cot here for the babe, a Bendix for nappies & a huge welcome for you both.

Perhaps you can imagine what it's like for a sociable city intellectual like me, dying to write, read, see places, plays, people etc. to be stuck among cows, cow people, without an adult to speak to; and now that Ted is earning fabulous sums, without baby shoe money. I am hoping to go for a rest-cure to Ireland with the babes by the sea near Galway to get back my flesh & try to finish a novel in December through early March. Do you know anyone who would like to rent a big beautiful farmhouse with Wilton carpets, 2 double bedrooms, a babies room, a huge sunny playroom, a Bendix, fridge, all shops in 2 minutes, garden, seclusion, 4 hours from Waterloo by the town station at a low rent for 3 winter months? Or starting next fall? Next fall, I hope to write my way back to a London flat & keep this place for summers, but that is as yet a dream. My dream. But that's the dream I want to live in. As soon as I know the nurse's holiday week I'll let you know, but please do write & say you'll try to come then, mid-November. I love you both dearly & would be heartbroken to miss you!

Sylvia

TO *Aurelia Schober Plath*

Sunday 21 October 1962 — TLS (aerogramme), Indiana University

Sunday: October 21

Dear mother,

Will you please, for goodness sake, stop bothering poor Winifred Davies! You have absolutely no right or reason to do this, and it is an endless embarrassment to me. She is busier than either you or I, and is helping me as much as she can and knows and sees my situation much better than you do. It was incredibly foolish of you to send her a telegram ---she came over this afternoon and said you sent her some wire to tell me to "keep the nanny" & "the salary would be paid from over there" etc.[1]

1 – See back of SP to ASP, 16 October 1962, #2; held by Lilly Library. ASP drafted telegram text: 'Please see Sylvia now and get woman for her. Salary paid here. Writing.'

Will you kindly leave her out of it? Why didn't you wire me? And to imply that money is available from over in America is the worst thing you could do---it completely falsifies my hard-up predicament, everybody thinks Americans are rich and my problems are magnified. I can't see how you could be so silly! Just like telling them I had a nervous breakdown when I have a fantastic job to get this stupid doctor to admit I have a fever even when he takes it on his office thermometer. This is one of the reasons I find your presence so difficult. These absolutely scatty things! My business in this town is my business, & for goodness sake learn to keep your mouth shut about it. Winifred knows the nanny I had was atrocious---an old bitch, the children were shrieking in terror the whole time she was here, & I had to take over poor Nicholas completely, she yelled at him so, & even my serene Nancy was almost hysterical after the woman was at her for a morning. I sent her back Saturday morning, after my fever went up to 103° again. You have no idea what you are saying when you blithely talk about "hiring nannies." No nanny wants to live out here in the middle of nowhere, without Tv* or amusement. And I shall never again hire a woman without an interview. It is ridiculous. Winifred has got me a young nurse to come in days for about the next six weeks. I should be able to calm down & do some work & sit & think. I have got to get a flat in London by next fall, or I shall go stir crazy.

*I shall rent a set next spring when I get the room made over.

I cannot understand Ted's insanity & irresponsibility, sticking me down here, in an unsellable, unrentable huge house with grounds needing a full-time gardener, no nannies available, no culture, no people, nothing, then congratulating himself on deserting us with "a house and car". It is as if, out of revenge for my brain & creative power, he wanted to stick me where I would have no chance to use it. I think now my creating babies & a novel frightened him---for he wants barren women like his sister & this woman, who can write nothing, only adore his stuff. I love Court Green & will find it a wonderful summer retreat. I am even enjoying my rather frustrating (culturally & humanly) exile now. I am doing a poem a morning, great things,[1] and as soon as the nurse settles, shall try to draft this terrific second novel that I'm dying to do. Don't talk to me about the world needing cheerful stuff! What the person out of Belsen---physical or

1–Since writing to ASP on 18 October, SP had completed: 'Stopped Dead' (19 October); 'Fever 103°' (20 October); and 'Amnesiac' and 'Lyonnesse' (21 October). 'Amnesiac' originally included two numbered sections. SP ultimately kept the second part and discarded the first, which was posthumously titled 'Lyonnesse'. See SP to Howard Moss, 15 November 1962.

psychological---wants is nobody saying the birdies still go tweet-tweet but the full knowledge that somebody else has been there & knows the worst, just what it is like. It is much more help for me, for example, to know that people are divorced & go through hell, that to hear about happy marriages. Let the Ladies' Home Journal blither about those.

Please do understand that while I am very very grateful indeed for financial help from people who have money, like Mrs. Prouty & Dot, & while I should be glad for the odd Birthday & Xmas present from you, I want no monthly dole, especially not from you. You can help me best by saving your money for your own retirement. I am just furious at Ted, putting me in this intolerable position. If I had lots of money, I'd just buy my way out. I know just what I want & want to do. I made a roast beef potato & corn dinner, with apple cake today, had the bank manager's[1] handsome 14 year-old son & a schoolfriend in---they'd had Ted's poems in class. They were charming. I dearly love the people I know in town, but they are no life. I am itching for museums, language study, intellectual & artistic friends. I am well-liked here, in spite of my weirdness, I think, though of course everybody eventually comes round to "Where is Mr. Hughes." I hate Ted with a passion. Years of my life wasted while he knew, even in London, what he was going to do! I am appalled. If only I could earn enough to buy myself into a London flat! I have so much writing in me, the children are a kind of torture when on my neck all day. If I get a good girl, a good nanny, permanent, I can have my own life too. I adore the babies & am glad to have them, even though now they make my life fantastically difficult. If I can just financially get through this year, I should have time to get a good nanny, & even a London flat. The worst difficulty is that Ted is at the peak of his fame & all his friends are the one's who employ me. But I can manage that too. Had a lovely afternoon out with the children, mowing the lawn, Frieda playing with the cats & a stick & Nick laughing wildly at them all. He is a sunshine; Frieda gets awfully whiney, but that is because of the big changes. Let me know roughly when & for how long Warren & Maggie can come next spring, so I can start planning a rota of guests!

Love to all,
Sylvia

1–According to SP's Letts Royal Office Diary Tablet for 1962, the new bank manager was a Mr Daniels.

TO *Ruth Tiffany Barnhouse Beuscher*

Sunday 21 October 1962 TLS, Smith College

Court Green
North Tawton
Devonshire, England
October 21, 1962

Dear Dr. Beuscher,

Since I last wrote you, everything has blown up, blown apart, and settled in new and startling places. I wrote you in a state of crisis---when Ted's poems told me what he hadn't the guts to tell me and had lied blue to keep me from knowing, that he was madly in love with another woman & will probably become her 4th husband. What has astounded me is my reaction to his departure---for good, last week, and to my decision to get a divorce as fast as I can. I felt the most fantastic exhilaration & relief. I understand now what you meant about being in my own womb, my own primal cave. I was so far gone in I was cow-dumb. In the last 3 years I have produced & nursed for 10 & 6 months respectively, two children, had a miscarriage, and been so intrigued & delighted by my bodily processes & infants I have been out for the count. Also, my relation to Ted was in many, many ways, gravely regressed, more & more I was calling on him to be a father & hating myself for it. After I drove him to the station with his things, I returned to the empty house expecting to be morbid and huge with gloom. I was ecstatic. My life, my sense of identity, seemed to be flying back to me from all quarters, buried hidden places. I knew what I wanted to do, pretty much who I was, where I wanted to go, who I wanted see, even <u>just how</u>, when I get to a good London haircutter, I wanted to do my weird hair. I was my own woman.

My sex confidence suffered a hard blow---it is not easy to face a gossipy professional world in which my husband's best friends are my employers and know they all know I have been deserted and for whom and under what conditions. But I go up to record a long poem for the BBC next week & will start announcing the divorce. I am happy about it, very very happy & this will come through. I have enough energy to manage fallout, escaped Dartmoor convicts,[1] etc. for a lifetime. All during my 6 years of marriage I wondered what to write <u>about</u>, my poems seemed to me like

1–SP may be referring to articles printed in *The Guardian* on 11 October 1961 and 4 May 1962 about escaped convicts.

fantastical stuffed birds under bell jars.[1] Now I get up at 4 a.m. every morning when my sleeping pill wears off & write like fury till 8, stuffing the babes with rusks & juice. I am doing a poem a day, all marvelous, free, full songs. Every thing I read about, hear, see, experience or have experienced is on tap, like a wonderful drink. I can use everything. I think my marriage, though it had much good, was a pretty sick one.

Ted has reverted to pretty much what he was when I met him---"the greatest seducer in Cambridge",[2] only now it is "the world", he wants to be an "international catalyst". Even in love with this barren ad agency writer who commands a huge salary & puts it all on her back, he picks up Finns in coffee bars & takes them to hotels---he & this Assia are such a perfect match I laugh in my guts when I think of them married. They look exactly alike: the same color, shape, everything. She is his twin sister, & like his sister, barren, uncreative, a real vamp. All sophistication. They smoke (Ted, a nonsmoker, has been desperately practising) & drop names of the opposite sex, to titillate each other. They will be elaborately unfaithful to each other, very rich, & have no children, I presume, if her 2 abortions & 4 miscarriages can let me have this satisfaction.

I suppose it will be hell for me to meet them together at my first party or literary affair. But I will. Oddly, I think some day she & I may be friends, not friends, but speaking. Ted says she has got my book out of the library, adores my work, etc. etc., & although both of them behaved like bitch & bastard in this, she at least had the guts to tell her husband at the end how serious things were. Ted had planned to simply desert me, without address, without money & without explanation. His stay here before the final departure almost killed me. I have never felt such hate. He told me openly he wished me dead, it would be convenient, he could sell the house, take all the money & Frieda, told me I was brainless, hideous, had all sorts of flaws in making love he had never told me, and even two years ago he had not wanted to live with me. I was aghast at this last---why then, stick me in Devon (his "dream") in a huge house with grounds needing a full-time gardener, away from all culture, movies, plays, art shows, museums, libraries, brainy & smart people, with two babies, then desert and cut off the money! Why in God's name should the killing of me be so elaborate, and the torture so prolonged! It will be at least a year

1–In an early draft of her recently completed poem 'The Jailor', SP wrote similar imagery: 'That being free / ~~Of the bell jar in which I am the dead white heron~~ / Of the bell jar in which I turn & burn / An airless heron'. See also SP's 'Queen Mary's Rose Garden'.

2–SP was told 'He is the biggest seducer in Cambridge.' See *Journals of Sylvia Plath*, 213.

before I can muster a flat in London---I love living there, all the good free schools & the best doctors are there, and the people, the events I want. He told me in London it was death to him, got me down here hand-hemming curtains & painting furniture for a year hoping to see him radiant with what he wanted, & he seemed to be, then pouf! Two years of hypocrisy, just waiting for the right bed to fall in? I can't believe it. It just seems insane to me.

Ted is on the brink of real wealth. His mss. sell for $100 a poem, just the handwriting. He is at the peak of fame. I was scrimping 6 years for this, balancing check books, dying for first nights, trips, dresses & a nanny. His family wants him to give us nothing. He has left me no address, I have no word, & no sign he means to live up to his pledge of £1,000 a year. I hope time may mellow him toward the children, but I doubt it. His ethic is that of the hawk in one of his most famous poems, being taught to all British schoolchildren: I kill where I please, it is all mine. He was furious I didn't commit suicide, he said he was sure I would!

Just tell me where all this hate comes from? He says he thinks I am "dangerous" toward him now. Well, I should think so!

I see, too, that domesticity was a fake cloak for me. My trouble is that I can do an awful lot of stuff well. I can give a floor a beautiful scrub, cook a fine pie, deliver a baby with ease, and stitch up a nightgown. I also love hanging out a clean laundry in the apple orchard. But I hate doing housework all, or much of the time. I have been running a 103 fever out of sheer mad excitement with my own writing. I am ravenous for study, experience, travel. I love learning how to manage things---I have kept bees this year, my own hive, & am very proud of my bottled honey, & my stings. I am learning to ride horseback & the riding mistress is delighted, I am a natural. My mind is dying of starvation here. And I am tied by nothing but money. And the sense my husband wants to kill me by cutting it off altogether, so I am hogtied & can't work. It's enough to make any woman sail to Lesbos![1]

What I don't want is a nice, safe, dull, sweet reliable husband to take Ted's place. He has to marry again---who'll cook? And what a showpiece for looks he's got! But me. My independence, my self, is so dear to me I shall never bind it to anyone again. Most men who are domestic are dull ---I hate routine jobs, and most men who are creative or scientific miracles are bastards. I don't mind knowing a bastard, or having an affair with a

1–SP completed her poem 'Lesbos' three days prior to writing this letter.

bastard, I just don't want to be married to a bastard. I suppose it sounds as if I think all men are bastards, I don't, but the interesting ones I would rather have as either friends, lovers or both, than husbands. Faithfulness, the ethic of faithfulness, is essentially boring. I see that. Ted made much better love while he was having these other affairs, & the tart in me appreciated this. But I also just haven't the time to be married to a philanderer. That bores me too. There is so much else besides sex. I want my career, my children, and a free supple life. I hate this growing-pot as much as Ted did.

I guess I haven't really been "cured". I seem to have acted, in a different key, my mother's relation with my father---and my joy in "getting rid" of Ted is a dangerous one. I don't think I could bear living forever with one man, or even for long with one. I like being alone too much, being my own boss. I am not attracted to women physically, although I do admire beauty---I say that is the novelist in me & maybe it is. By brains and variety & I hope a slowly learned subtlety, I have to make up for the looks I haven't got, but I am so happy, everything intrigues me, I have become a verb, instead of an adjective. It is as if this divorce were the key to free all my repressed energy, which is fierce from six years of boiling in a vacuum. I still am very interested in other men, or rather, after 6 years of having only one man attract me as much as Ted---what I wouldn't give to see him now!---I am again interested in other men, but few men are both beautiful physically, tremendous lovers & creative geniuses as Ted is. I can't even imagine anybody ever making me feel passionate enough to have an affair, after him. And I am so bloody proud & particular. Well anyway, if I can only crawl back to a niche in London I should have enough men friends & enjoy dinners, plays, the peripherals.

One thing this has intensified is my dislike of my mother. She has identified so completely with me or what she thinks is me, which is really herself, that she can't eat, sleep etc. What I see now I despise about my mother is her cravenness. Her wincing fear, her martyr's smile. Never has she taken a bold move, she has always stuck quietly in one place, hoping noone would notice. Her letters to me are full of "one can't afford one enemy", "the world needs happy writing". Basta! If I couldn't afford an enemy, I couldn't afford to live, & what the person from Belsen wants to hear is that someone else has been there, and knows the worst, too, that he is not a freak, not alone. Not that the birdies still go tweet-tweet.

When I get a good nanny my life will be possible. When I get back to London, & maybe some money, it will be heaven. I love you for listening.

Each of your letters is so rich, they last like parables. Shall get the Fromm book.[1]

With love,
Sylvia

TO *Ruth Fainlight*

Monday 22 October 1962 TLS, Ruth Fainlight

Court Green
North Tawton
Devonshire, England
October 22, 1962

Dearest Ruth,

I have been meaning for so long to answer your lovely, long fat letter. My riding mistress (I am learning to ride!) has been spinning me the most marvelous tales of her wartime life in Algeria & North Africa so that, with your description of your heaven, I would give my good thumbs, or whatever, to fly to you this winter, even for a week. If I should have a stroke of luck, meaning selling a very long poem or something, would you consider it mad---just me?

The Elm poem has had a kindly fate. The New Yorker just took it. I thought it astoundingly bloody & morbid for them, but they took it, only they made me leave off the dedication---for them---because they said it looked as if you & I had a secret & they didn't want their readers to feel left out! So I shall have to postpone our secret to my 2nd book, in which your name will be blazed. It is your poem.

My next news may make you sit down. I am getting a divorce from Ted. I write you in confidence, and as a sister-mother-muse-friend. I know you & Alan must have all sorts of wonderful and famous friends, but to me you are the dearest couple I knew in England. You can imagine, Ruth, after our talk about less-famous, or even infamous wives of famous husbands, how I automatically assume that all "our" friends will now of course be just Ted's friends. I hope that with us it is not so. I am very happy about the divorce, it is as if life were being restored to me. The details, however, are very unsavoury.

1–In her 26 September letter to SP, Dr Beuscher suggested SP acquire a copy of Erich Fromm's *The Art of Loving* (London: Allen & Unwin, 1960). SP's copy, with a Foyle's sticker on front pastedown and dated 9 November 1962 in her hand, held by Emory.

A week after I almost died of influenza this summer Ted took the opportunity of telling me he had never had the courage to say he didn't want children, that the house in the country (his "dream", for which he got me to leave the life in London I loved) was a sort of hoax, and bye-bye. His family wrote how lucky I was to be able to earn my whole (!) living at home instead of having to put the children in an orphanage & go out to work for a boss. Ted told me I could economize by not drinking sherry, smoking, eating expensive meat & that the children could learn to "live like the people". I guess you and Alan know what *that* is like. And also just how much the odd poem brings in. I guess this is just one step in the path of poetic genius, but being temporarily stuck in deep country with a running fever of 103°, two babies, no help, and the threat of no money---and none of the cultural life, movies, plays, art shows, museums, libraries, *people* which I so loved in London, & Ted in London, spending his very considerable income on himself, is enough to drive me up the wall. It will be probably a year before I can work myself & the babes back to a London flat where I can get a live-in nanny (so I *can* work!), none want to live here in cow land, and right now, after this year of hand-hemming curtains for Ted's dream house & producing a son he never bothered to tell me he would promptly desert, a year seems one long, unending limbo.

Well, so much for this mother in me. The writer is delighted. I am up at 4 a.m. every morning when my sleeping pill wears off, madly writing a poem a day before breakfast and the babies wake. I am engaging a local nurse, home from London hospital, for about six weeks, after two agency "nannies" came & went, to help me in the day so I can *try* to finish the second novel. There is not enough money, of course, for me to move very far. I have provisionally let a cottage on the wild sea of Galway in Ireland where I am thinking of wintering with the babies. I'd have to milk cows, draw well water, burn & cook on the lovely peaty turves, but I think I might get back my health. I have to have a chest Xray, with these fevers & rather shocking loss of weight. I feel you & Alan will be able to imagine pretty much what sort of a life it is. In London, I could have a nanny, free lance work, writing time, good free schools, & all the people & events I could wish. You can imagine how I feel about Ted watching us invest everything in this place, he writing glowing letters about it, and then quite coolly saying plenty of children get along without fathers and are poor etc. and walking out for good.

If you know anyone among your friends who might like to rent this very comfortable place for three months this winter *or*, more important, for half a year or more starting next fall, do let me know. Maybe when you are back in London yourselves you could keep an eye out for me for a furnished London flat in your area that would hold me, the babes & a nanny or au pair girl. I know flats are fantastically hard to get, & from outside London an impossibility, but I must get back. Maybe you will have a friend who wants to sub-let. Anyway, do promise to come for a visit, all of you, and lovely David, who will probably be having wrestling matches with Nick, who is a real bruiser now, as soon as you can on your return next spring. I shall probably return with the daffodils & stay the summer, when the great cold & emptiness of my beautiful Malmaison is not so noticeable.

Psychologically, Ruth, I am fascinated by the polarities of muse-poet and mother-housewife. When I was "happy" domestically I felt a gag down my throat. Now that my domestic life, until I get a permanent live-in girl, is chaos, I am living like a spartan, writing through huge fevers & producing free stuff I had locked in me for years. I feel astounded & very lucky. I kept telling myself I was the sort that could only write when peaceful at heart, but that is not so, the muse has come to live, now Ted is gone, and my God! what a sweeter companion.

Please do write. My one communication with the outer world at the moment is by mail, and your letters so dear. Tell me what you are thinking, doing, looking at. What is Alan writing? When will you come home, and will it be to the London flat? I am dying to see you, & if any of the financial grimness of my life lets up before you return, would so love to fly out for a short visit. But that, I guess, is just a dream right now.

Love to you, Alan & David,
Sylvia

TO *Aurelia Schober Plath*

Tuesday 23 October 1962 — TLS (aerogramme), Indiana University

Court Green
Tuesday: October 23

Dear mother,

Please forgive my grumpy sick letters of last week. The return of my fever, the hideous nanny from whom I expected help, and my awareness of the "Hughes position" combined to make me feel the nadir had been reached. Now everything is, by comparison, almost miraculous. I hardly dare breathe. Winifred found me the prettiest, sweetest local children's nurse, age 22, who lives in the most gorgeous house at Belstone, just overlooking Dartmoor, who is coming in days until she goes back in December to be staff nurse at a famous children's hospital in central London. She has been here two days, from 8:30-6, and the difference in my life is a wonder. I think she will go to Ireland & see me settled in. With her it would be a lark. I see now just what I need---not a professional nanny (who are snotty & expensive) but an adventurous young cheerful girl (to whom my life & travel would be fun) to take complete care of the children, eat with me, at midday---an "au pair" girl, as they say here. "One of the family". I shall try to get an Irish one when I am in Ireland, then maybe a foreign one (preferably German so she can teach me the language!) if I get back to London next fall. This girl is the daughter of the local secretary of the Bee Keeper's Society, a lovely woman with a gorgeous home, and her step-father is a writer of children's books! How's that for luck! I love Susan O'Neill-Roe, she is a dear with the children. I come down & cook us a big hot lunch and we & Frieda eat together in the playroom. Then I lie down for an hour's nap. I make a pot of tea in midafternoon & chat over a cup. O it is ideal. And Nancy does the cleaning. I am so happy & doing so much work, just in these two days,[1] I can hardly believe it. My study is the warmest, brightest room in the house. After Susan goes in the evening, I come up with a tray of supper & work again, surrounded by books, photos, cartoons & poems pinned to the wall.

I have put my house deeds in our local bank, under my name, with Ted's life insurance policy & the fire insurance policy. The bank managers beautiful 14-year old son, a friend & the b-m's little daughter came Sunday to see Ted's works, helped me translate a Latin children's book I had on Ferdinand the Bull,[2] to review, and utterly delighted me over apple cake & milk. I am having a heater put in the car, & shall now start all my arrangements for the formidable trip to Galway through the AA.

Susan is coming up overnight while I go to London for a few days next week---to record a poem for the BBC, to see Mr. Moore I hope (I've written him), and, hopefully, the head of the British Arts Council who has just put an exciting job in my way. There is to be another big Poetry Festival[3] in London this July at the Royal Court Theater (a big famous

1–According to SP's Letts Royal Office Diary Tablet for 1962, SP took care of a number of errands which may explain the two-day break in writing poems.

2–Probably Munro Leaf, *Ferdinandus Taurus* (London: Hamish Hamilton, 1962).

3–Festival of Poetry, Royal Court Theatre, 15–20 July 1963. The American Poetry night was held on 16 July 1963; presented by Eric Mottram, with assistance from John Hollander and

adventurous theatre) for a week. I've been asked to organise, present and take part in the American night! It means I'd have to be an actress-hostess of sorts. A fantastic challenge---me, on the professional stage, in London. But I think I shall undertake it. By next spring I should have managed to come up with a live-in girl, & this Arts Council man I think will help throw a few jobs my way when he knows my predicament & sees I am willing to tackle everything. Don't you think I should do it?

O the package came today, too! How wonderful. I am mad for Nick's fuzzy red pants. And the blue sweater set! Thank Dot a billion times. And the pastels, both sorts. O mother, I shall find time to use them too. I must be one of the most creative people in the world. I must keep a live-in girl so I can get myself back to the live, lively, always learning & developing person I was! I want to study, learn history, politics, languages, travel. I want to be the most loving & fascinating mother in the world. London, a flat, is my aim, and I shall, in spite of all the obstacles that rear, have that, and Frieda & Nick shall have the intelligences of the day as their visitors, and I the Salon that I will deserve. I am glad this happened and happened now. I shall be a rich active woman, not a servant-shadow as I have been. I am so glad to have SHIP OF FOOLS.[1] I have been dying to read it. I shall bring it for wild, wet nights in Ireland.

Now do write Winifred and thank her a thousand times for obtaining this girl for me at the most difficult & necessary period of my life! I feel this London trip will do me a power of good---I shall cram in every film & play I can! To think that bastard Ted has been secretly doing this all summer & spending everything, & me stuck home, scrimping! It just makes me boil. I should love to use your birthday check on a Chagford dress.[2] I want some of those hair-grips---copper, or wood, a curved oval, with a kind of pike through it, for the back of my hair, & to get the front cut in a professional fringe, so the front looks short & fashionable & I can have a crown of braid or chignon at the back. I shall have to take all my hems up. Almost all my clothes are 10 years old! Just wait till I hit London. Ted may be a genius, but I'm an intelligence. He's not going to stop that. I've taken my first lot of the vitamins---a thousand thanks.

Love to Dot, Warren & Maggie too
sivvy.

Jonathan Williams. Poets included Robert Lowell, Muriel Rukeyser, and Ronald Johnson; Guy Kingsley Poynter read from *Paterson* by William Carlos Williams.

1–Katherine Anne Porter, *Ship of Fools* (Boston: Little, Brown, 1962).

2–Possibly a reference to the market town of Chagford in Devon.

TO *Eric Walter White*

Tuesday 23 October 1962 TLS, University of Texas at Austin

Court Green
North Tawton
Devonshire
October 23, 1962

Dear Eric,

I am writing you in the same post that I am writing Patric Dickinson[1] to say how interested I am in the American evening at the Royal Court this July and proposing to see him to discuss the organizing, which I am on the fence about, but certainly interested in.

What I wonder, Eric, is if you and dear Dodo could possibly put me up on the night of Monday, October 29th. I know you mentioned you might do this when the Sweeneys were here, which is why I ask. I'm recording a long poem at the BBC Monday, and having to stay over on business, and just have no place to sleep. Please do say if you have guests, or children in residence! I'd probably try to take in a movie or a play, as I am starved for these things, after a year of enforced exile from my beloved city, and would just sleep quietly if you had the odd corner.

In any case, I would dearly love to see you & Dodo again. I may have to stay till Wednesday. I have no phone, though I'm having one put in, but a letter reaching me by Saturday should do it. I'll be in London by Monday at 10:30 am & recording till noon.

Fondest regards to you both.
Sylvia

1–According to SP's address book, she met British poet Patric Dickinson (1914–94) at the Savile Club, 69 Brook Street, London W.1.

TO *Michael Carey*[1]

Tuesday 23 October 1962 TLS, Assumption College

Court Green
North Tawton
Devonshire
October 23, 1962

Dear Reverend Carey,

Please do forgive me for not answering your letter sooner, but I have been laid low by influenza on my small farm with two very small children, so my correspondence has suffered as a result.

I should be very happy to have a look at your poems. The one thing I <u>can't</u> promise is to tell you whether or not to go on writing! If you enjoy it, do it, and fine! "Success" or publishing should be no guide as to whether you should write or not, your own feelings must tell you that. I shall certainly tell you frankly what I think is good and less good in your work. But do go on drinking with the gods and goddesses at Pieria in any case!

And if you ever care for lesser fare, in the form of a cup of tea, while in England, do feel welcome at the above address (half an hour from Exeter by train) until December at least, after which date I shall be trying to finish a novel in the wilds of Western Ireland.

Yours sincerely,
Sylvia Plath

TO *Aurelia Schober Plath*

Thursday 25 October 1962 TLS (aerogramme), Indiana University

Thursday: October 25

Dear mother,

Thank you for your last letter. This time I shall accept the much-traveled $50 as a birthday present! I shall buy a dress, have my "fringe" cut & get a copper hair thong instead of my elastic![2] I shall try & do this in London next week, so you can imagine me having fun. I have a lovely 2 days planned---recording at the BBC in the morning Monday, an afternoon

1–Father Michael Carey (1928–2007); 1951, Assumption College, Worcester, Mass. Carey was studying at Oxford and wrote to SP asking if she could critique his poems.
2–'hair thong (for) instead of my elastic' appears in the original.

reading all my new poems to the famous critic & Observer (big Sunday paper) poetry editor,[1] probably an evening party at a Literary Society to celebrate an anthology I'm in[2] & of which Ted was one of the 3 editors. I have to get used to seeing him---and whoever is with him---at literary affairs, so may as well start now. The next morning, a meeting about the Royal Court Theatre American Poetry Night next summer, then lunch & a recording[3] for the Harvard Poetry Library, then home. Susan O'Neill-Roe will be staying over those nights, the children love her. Since she has come, my life has been a joy.

For goodness sake, stop being so frightened of everything, Mother! Almost every other word in your letter is "frightened"! One thing I want my children to have is a bold sense of adventure, not the fear of trying something new. I have a beautifully furnished, cosy cottage in Ireland, near the sea, but very secluded, & the woman is a friend of the poet we visited this summer. Too, I have a young couple with 2 children within driving distance, he a painter & she a lovely American. So I shall be as well off as here. The winter couldn't be any worse than here, & if I chained myself to my Bendix I would never see the world. So do forget all your nervous worries. I hope to get an Irish girl to help me days over there, and, if I like one, to take her back with me. Susan will make the trip over with me, so that will be fun. So do stop dreading everything. I am having a wonderful time. You better get some sleeping pills if you're up at 2 a.m. Now Susan comes, I get up at 7. I eat an egg for breakfast every day, or bacon & bread, a big hot meal at lunch, and nourishing soup & sandwich at night. Probably a lot more than you do!

My health, with this young girl here, is rapidly returning. I have no cough at all, and no fever. I hope, when I am in London next fall, to get a German "au pair" girl from an agency recommended by that sweet Catherine Frankfort---do you remember her? I had a letter from her today, telling me about her German au pair girls, and she asked to be remembered to you, she says she remembers you so vividly. I look very forward to trying, through various friends, to get a London furnished flat next fall & taking up old friends & making new. I could get all sorts of free

1–SP went to Al Alvarez's flat at 74A Fellows Road, London N.W.3.

2–SP attended the English PEN party. Sylvia Plath, 'Candles' and 'You're', *New Poems 1962: A PEN Anthology of Contemporary Poetry* (London: Hutchinson, 1962): 95–7.

3–SP had lunch with Peter Orr (1931–2001) of the British Council, recorded fifteen poems and gave an interview for a series titled *The Poet Speaks*; SP read 'The Rabbit Catcher', 'Ariel', 'Poppies in October', 'The Applicant', 'Lady Lazarus', 'A Secret', 'Cut', 'Stopped Dead', 'Nick and the Candlestick', 'Medusa', 'Purdah', 'A Birthday Present', 'Amnesiac', 'Daddy', and 'Fever 103°'.

lance jobs if I lived in London during the school year & vacationed here in summer. I have quite a reputation over here, my whole professional life is here. The nice local woman I had in 9 hours a week before Susan, comes now on Susan's day off---very convenient.[1] On my birthday, if it's nice, I'll be at my horseback riding lesson---I'm "rising to the trot" very well now, tell Dotty & Nancy, they'll know what I mean! My riding mistress thinks I'm very good.

Forget about the novel & tell no-one of it. It's a pot-boiler & just practice.

I am immensely moved by Warren & Maggie being willing to uproot themselves to help, and so glad this won't in any way be necessary! They are just darling, & I hope they'll come for a holiday next spring. Do let me know as soon as possible when & how long I can plan on it!

Now stop trying to get me to write about "decent courageous people" ---read the Ladies Home Journal for those! It's too bad my poems frighten you---but you've always been afraid of reading or seeing the world's hardest things---like Hiroshima, the Inquisition or Belsen. I believe in going through & facing the worst, not hiding from it. That is why I am going to London this week, partly, to face all the people we know & tell them happily & squarely I am divorcing Ted, so they won't picture me as a poor, deceived country wife. I am not going to steer clear of these professional acquaintances just because they know I am deserted, or because I may meet Ted with someone else. I am now so glad to get rid of him I shall just laugh.

Mr. Moore wired that he is leaving London before I come, but my life is working out so well, & my solicitor is helpful, so I really don't need him now. I look forward to the directions of the Taroc pack. Frieda wore the new little plaid skirt today with a red sweater & red tights---she looked adorable! She loves her crayon book & scribbles in it happily. "Grammy send crayons," she says.

Now don't you all feel helpless any more. I am helped very much by letters, the birthday checks. If Ted gives me £1,000 I shall manage very well, with just an "au pair", the car & his insurance to pay. And my holidays. The insurance, if I pay, will come to me at the end, like a pension, so I think it's wise, if high. About 25 thousand $ I think at the end of 30 years counting the interest! & 15 thousand $ if Ted dies before this.

Love to all,
Sivvy

1–According to SP's Letts Royal Office Diary Tablet for 1962, this was Mrs Weare. She worked on Thursdays.

TO *Clarissa Roche*

Thursday 25 October 1962 TLS, Smith College

Court Green
North Tawton
Devonshire
October 25, 1962

Dearest Clarissa,

Your sweet letter arrived today, & this is just a note to say things are calming down here, with a temporary darling children's nurse coming in days to help with the babes, & life has been heaven since she started coming. She'll be with me through my trip to Western Ireland in early December, where I am wintering with the children. She is going on holiday from November 15-20, so could you & Paul come for a couple of days in about then? Looking forward to your company is a great treat. I am in fine spirits, if understandably furious to be left in the lurch with the little babes just after I almost died of flu. I think you're quite right about ego, Clarissa. Ever since I wrote my novel for example (which Ted never read) Ted has been running down the novel as a form---something "he would never bother to write". It seems so stupid to me, because he is undeniably a poetic genius. I am delighted to hear about Paul's novel![1] Furious criticism is just the thing to make it sell. Please bring a copy! And of the poems![2] And any Sappho[3] you've got in trans. I must read her---a fellow lady poet! You are an angel, Clarissa, just write & say when you can come! We're (North Tawton Station*) 4 hours from Waterloo & I'll meet you in the car at our station.

Love to all,
Sylvia

*It's half an hour beyond Exeter.

1–Paul Roche, *Vessel of Dishonor* (New York: Sheed & Ward, 1962).
2–Probably Paul Roche, *The Rank Obstinacy of Things: A Selection of Poems* (New York: Sheed & Ward, 1962).
3–Greek poet Sappho (*c.* 630–580 BCE); lived on the island of Lesbos.

TO *Olive Higgins Prouty*

Thursday 25 October 1962 TLS (aerogramme), Indiana University

Court Green
North Tawton
Devonshire, England
October 25, 1962

Dear, dear Mrs. Prouty!

How I appreciate your great kindness and concern! And your letters, they are best of all. I only hope mother did not worry you too much. I was at what I truly believe was a nadir when I wrote her---with a fever, a terrible agency nanny, an old snoopy grumbly woman who scared the children into screaming fits by her crossness & whom I had to dismiss almost immediately, and then the news that Ted's family is all behind him & considers me & the babies a bother! Since I wrote, my blessed local midwife has found me the dearest local girl, a 22-year-old children's nurse, who is coming in from 8:30 a.m to 6 p.m. daytimes and taking complete charge of the children, who love her, and going to Ireland with us before she returns to be staff nurse at a famous children's hospital in London in mid-December. This is a godsend to me, I have been working hard & happily since her coming, cooking a big, hearty dinner at noon which she & little Frieda & I eat in the playroom . . . you remember, where we ate when you were here.

I do so appreciate your generous offer to take care of her salary, but she is only $15 a week, and I can easily manage that from my latest New Yorker poem. If Ted gives us the £1,000 a year he promised, my own earnings should take good care of the rest. I am going to London for two days this next week to do some work, while this young nurse stays overnight with the babies. I have some very exciting projects, I'll tell you what they are.

Monday morning I am recording a long poem for the BBC (they will pay my expenses going & coming). That afternoon A. Alvarez, the top poetry critic in England and poetry editor for the Observer (the big Sunday paper here, twin to the Times) will hear me read all my new poems aloud at his home! He is a great opinion-maker & says I am the first woman poet he has taken seriously since Emily Dickinson! That evening I shall go to a literary party to celebrate a poetry anthology I am in, & which Ted was one of the 3 editors of. He will probably be there, and with someone else, but I must get used to meeting him at these literary gatherings & braving it out, or I shall lose all sorts of professional opportunities. Luckily my love for him has been completely killed by his actions this last year, so it will only be hard "socially", not emotionally. Tuesday I shall meet an official on the British Arts Council who has invited me to organize & produce an American Poetry Night next summer at the Royal Court Theatre, one of the biggest theatres in London. I would have to be "produced" like a professional actress, but think I should take up the challenge. Then I make a recording of poems for the Harvard Lamont Library. Then Home!

I shall let you know as soon as my phone is in! I would love to hear the voices of my dear ones & feel a bit closer a bit faster than on these air letter forms! I see now I need not a nanny---they are very snobby & status-seeking here, always after Majors & Royalty---but a "mother's help", a cheerful, intelligent girl who isn't above doing dishes & who will be like a lively younger sister for me. I am feeling so much better since this young nurse has been coming---eating with appetite, managing all the mountains of business letters, organizing my coming London trip. My cough and fever are quite gone. I feel, with health, I can face anything, and am in excellent spirits. This nurse is so capable & sweet!

My study has become a haven, a real sanctuary for me! I have late poppies, bright red, & blue-purple cornflowers on my desk now, & plan to make curtains of a kind of rich red-purply stained glass pattern to match the rug. Here is my hearth, my life, my real self. I have never been so happy anywhere in my life as writing at my huge desk in the blue dawns, all to myself, secret and quiet.[1] I know you will understand this ---this quiet center at the middle of the storm. If I have this, the rest of my life will settle into pleasant lines. Now I have 40 children's picture books to review! I shall forge my writing out of these difficult experiences---to have known the bottom, whether mental or emotional is a great trial, but also a great gift. That is why I feel that when writing to you, I am writing to a sort of literary godmother, a person who will really, deeply understand. I know you will feel as proud of my independence as I am. Do keep writing! I love your letters.

With love,
Sylvia

1–Since writing to ASP on 21 October, SP had completed: 'Cut' and 'By Candlelight' (24 October); and 'The Tour' (25 October).

TO *Warren & Margaret Plath*

Thursday 25 October 1962 TLS (aerogramme, photocopy), Indiana University

Court Green
North Tawton
Devonshire, England
October 25: Thursday

Dearest Warren & Maggie,

Just a short letter to say how immensely grateful I was to feel you both so thoroughly behind me that you would consider uprooting your lives for our sake! Thank goodness it won't in any way be advisable or necessary! My main setback was having this awful shock---of Ted's desertion---come the week after my influenza with no time or energy to do all I had to do to keep going on a day-to-day basis, let alone cope with the endless practical ruins that ass left behind him. Ever since the 22-year-old children's nurse Susan O'Neill-Roe has been coming days from 8:30 to 6, my life has been heaven. I get up about 7 a.m., have an egg for breakfast, then go up and work, coming down at noon to make a big hot meal for Susan, Frieda & me, which we eat sitting in the cheery playroom. Then work, after an hour's rest, a cup of tea with Susan, and before I know it the babies are in bed & I feel wonderful. I see now what I need is known as an "au pair" girl over here, they are very cheap---and a London friend of mine recommends Germans as, she says, they are usually plain, fat (thus on a diet!) and studious, thus in a their rooms a lot! I want to apply for one so I can also speak, or practise, German with her. Nannies are out. They are snob-status-seekers of the worst sort here, very expensive, & won't touch "domestic" work, i.e. dishes etc. My trouble, of course, is living in the country. I'm sure summer in the country might appeal, but young girls want London, education etc. So do I! I would like an educated girl ---they charge so little because they want to be "one of the family", & my life should be exciting enough, if I could get a furnished flat for the school year in London, to keep such a girl happy. So at least I know what I want (I didn't, before) and at what agency I can get it! I would never hire a girl without a careful extensive interview. This last sight-unseen nanny was the end, my Lord, of almost all of us, including my faithful Nancy Axworthy! And the one before her, good as she was, found the post "unsuitable" because of no cook, butler, TV etc. etc. & went from me to the Astors, so you can imagine what sort of a house she wanted!

This coming two-day London trip has set me up like a tonic. I've not had a treat to myself for over a year! As I've written mother today, I'm recording for the BBC Monday & Harvard Lamont Library Tuesday, have an interview about this American Poetry Night at a London theatre next summer, which I'm considering organising & presenting---a terrific challenge, I'd have to be "produced" like an actress, but I don't think I should let such chances slip, & then the critic of the Observer is giving me an afternoon at his home to hear me read all my new poems! He is the opinion-maker in poetry over here, A. Alvarez, & says I'm the first woman poet he's taken seriously since Emily Dickinson! Needless to say, I'm delighted.

Now can you possibly get mother to stop worrying so much? Her letters are full of worries, & to hear she can't sleep after 2 a.m. etc. etc. is no help to me, only an additional worry. I do think I have adjusted to very unpleasant circumstances very fast, considering I was ten down with flu, & am now very busy, but fine, knowing just where I want to go. I have a gorgeous plush house hired in Ireland, much cosier, smaller & easier to manage than this, sheltered, with a lovely woman, the owner, in a cottage next door & willing to babysit & help shop etc. She is a long acquaintance of this poet we sailed with. And also a couple with 2 babies within driving distance whom I like very much, the wife an American, the husband a successful painter & friend of Jack Sweeney, who took us out for oysters & Guinness in Dublin. Mother is so anxious about new steps she is always after me to stay put & be safe. It is very important for me to make new discoveries now, & I am very stable & practical & cautious & thoroughly investigated this house & surroundings before hiring it. I need to get away from here for a change, after the hell of this summer, and am lucky to have such a delightful place fall into my lap. As I said to mother, winter can't at the North Pole be worse than here! Do let me know roughly when & for how long you both can come next spring. I'd so love to leave the babies with a girl, if I've got one, & go to Austria or somewhere with you. I've not had a holiday on my own for two years, & as you may imagine, after these events, the court trial ahead heaven knows when, & Ted able to be sticky or "forget" about money whenever he feels like it, I shall need a holiday on my own, preferably with two lovely people like you! I adore you both, have the gorgeous wedding picture on my desk where I can see it as I work. Do write.

Lots of love,
Sivvy

<on page 1 of letter>

PS: Hope my letters to you at "Bauks" Street arrived! It sounded like a sort of odd squawky place to live! Is Banks right?[1]

TO *Eric Walter White*

Friday 26 October 1962 TLS, University of Texas at Austin

Court Green
North Tawton
Devonshire
October 26, 1962

Dear Eric,

You and Dodo are perfectly wonderful to take me on Monday night. I am so eager and excited about coming up to my beloved London after my more or less enforced purdah in the West Country, and very much intrigued by your new move.[2] I love Islington, and I think it must be heaven to live there. I know I would greatly wish to live there.

I am jamming all sorts of literary business into Monday and Tuesday, so should not be bothering you till probably early Monday evening. I will call you Monday afternoon to make sure all is well. I'm hoping to do a BBC recording, a recording for the Harvard Library at Albion House,[3] and to see Patric Dickinson.

All my best to you and Dodo, and I'll be ringing you Monday afternoon.

With much gratitude,
Sylvia

1–According to SP's address book, Warren and Margaret Plath lived at 35 Banks Street, Cambridge, Mass.

2–The Whites lived at 21 Alwyne Road, London N.1. Another address, in TH's hand, appears in SP's address book: 55 Cholmley Gardens, London N.W.6, but it is unclear when this was added.

3–Albion House, 55 New Oxford Street, London W.C.1A.

TO *Olive Higgins Prouty*

Friday 2 November 1962 TLS (aerogramme), Indiana University

Court Green
North Tawton
Devonshire, England
November 2, 1962

Dear Mrs. Prouty,

Thank you for your wonderful letter which arrived today. Your letters are a wonderful life-line. My phone is in: the number is NORTH TAWTON 447. I faced the most difficult time this week in London---did my recordings, then went to a literary party and faced everybody, all the malicious questions, the gloating nastiness that is part of the gossip world. Everybody is delighted at what Ted has done---he is so famous, and all I can do is face the spotlight with dignity, not hide. I felt it was best to get it over with at once---as many people as I could. Being the wife of the most famous poet in England is not easy, but I felt I did best to see the lot of people at once. I simply say I am very happy about the divorce because it frees me for a life of writing in peace. They are disappointed, because they expect me to be full of revenge & frustration. Slowly, I hope, the furore will die away. You are absolutely right about the need for me to strike London now. Ireland was an evasion. I am now in the process of trying to get a furnished flat in London big enough for me, the babies & and au pair girl for the winter months. After this dear nurse goes, I shall not be able to get live-in help here, so I must go to London for this. I go up again this week to flat-hunt. I don't care how awkward it is, as long as I have a girl to mind the babes so I can just sit and meditate, & write.[1] In spring, I would like to return to my beautiful home---with an au pair girl---for the summer. What I hope to do this winter is get an unfurnished London flat on a long lease for next year, one I really like, in Hampstead. As a London home so the children can go to the fine free schools there (the schools here are awful), saving Court Green for holidays & summers. I would slowly furnish the London flat out of 2nd hand things, then let it at high weekly rates for the summer. There is no trouble renting a furnished flat out in London. I hope to work on writing all this winter so I can amass a sum

1–Since writing to Olive Higgins Prouty on 25 October, SP had completed: 'Ariel' and 'Poppies in Ocotber' (27 October); 'Nick and the Candlestick' and 'Purdah' (29 October); and 'Lady Lazarus' (23–9 October).

to buy the lease---they do things on leases a lot here, long leases, not just buying outright. You are a guardian angel to send a check for a mother's help. I have such difficult things to face this year it will be my salvation to just sit at my desk in peace, gathering the force of my soul, beginning all anew, all over.

I must have Nicholas' eye operated on some time,[1] it is a bit skew, or crossed, they tell me, so want to be in London for this too. I alşo badly cut my thumb and the country doctor here, fool that he is, botched it, so the top is dead, did not mend, & it is septic, so I have an appointment with my old London doctors next week, to see if I will need anything drastic like cutting or plastic surgery. This young nurse I love with all my heart. She knows everything, & has stood by me like an angel, & will move to London with me, instead of Ireland if I can get a flat, till early December.

I am so delighted with this nurse: I went to a movie with her & her nice mother last night, a foreign movie, as their guest. I realized I had not seen a movie or a play (except for that lovely night with you) for over a year! How wise you are to talk about postponing the Ireland trip! I shall only go now as a last resort, if I can't find a London flat. It seems there is a kind of telepathy between us, for I had just decided that I must have the courage to return to London <u>now</u>, when it is most difficult, or I will find it harder & harder, & be more & more outside the literary business circle. If I face a return now, I can face anything. And nothing could be harder, so it must, of necessity, get easier.

The <u>Observer</u> critic thought my poems were marvellous & took two on the spot.[2] I feel I am writing in the blitz, bombs exploding all round. I have seen the man about the American Poetry night at the Theatre in London & will do it. I don't care how hard it is, I shall do it. I am very excited. I want to shirk <u>nothing</u>. To flee <u>nothing</u>. I have bad times, of course, when I feel grim, but have all sorts of ways to cheer myself. Don't tell mother, but I smoke now. It is a great relief, very comforting. I was up till 3 a.m. last night doing a book review of the Diary of Opal Whiteley,[3] an

1–According to SP's Letts Royal Office Diary Tablet for 1962, she took Nicholas to the Okehampton Eye Clinic on 20 November.

2–Sylvia Plath, 'Poppies in October', *The Observer* (6 October 1963): 24; and Sylvia Plath, 'The Horse' ['Ariel'], *The Observer* (3 November 1963): 24.

3–Sylvia Plath, 'Oregonian Original', *New Statesman* (9 November 1962): 660; reviews of four books: E. S. Bradburne, *Opal Whiteley*; Evan Hunter [Ed McBain], *The Wonderful Button*; Leo Lionni, *Little Blue and Little Yellow*; and Elizabeth Rose and Gerald Rose, *Punch and Judy Carry On*; five other books were briefly recommended: Tomi Ungerer, *The Mellops Go Flying*; H. E. Bates, *Achilles the Donkey*; Dr Seuss, *Horton Hatches the Egg*; Gaby Baldner, *The Penguins of Penguin Town*; and Reinhard Herrman, *The Creation*.

Oregon child of the backwoods, written at 6 & published in the Atlantic Monthly in 1920 as "The Journal of an Understanding Heart"[1]---do you remember it? She had a crude, cruel mother & claimed to be descended from French royalty. A beautiful book, all about her animals & country life. I'll send you a copy of the review when it comes out---it's like being back at Smith, working for deadlines! I need hard work & love it. I love you too. Writing & my babies are my life, & you understand both with the heart of a kindred spirit.

With much love,
Sylvia

TO *Aurelia Schober Plath*

Wednesday 7 November 1962 TLS (aerogramme), Indiana University

London: November 7

Dear mother,

I am writing from London, so happy I can hardly speak. I think I have found a place. I had resigned myself to paying high sums for a furnished place for the winter while I looked for an unfurnished one with a longish lease that I could then furnish & let for fabulous rates in spring & summer while I was at Court Green. By an absolute fluke I walked by the street & the house (with Primrose Hill at the end) where I've always wanted to live. The house had builders in & a sign "Flats to Let"; I flew upstairs---Just right (unfurnished), on 2 floors with 3 bedrooms upstairs, & lounge, kitchen & bath downstairs and a balcony garden! Flew to the agents---hundreds of people ahead of me, I thought, as always. It seems I have a chance! And guess what, it is W. B. Yeats' house. With a blue plaque[2] over the door saying he lived there! And in the district of my old doctors, & in the street I would want to buy a house if I ever had a smash-hit novel. I am now waiting for the tedious approval of the owner & for my references to go through. Ted is behind me in this, he took me round looking at places. Now he sees he has nothing to fear from me---no scenes or vengefulness ---he is more human. His life is nothing to me & I am now staying with

1–Opal Whiteley, 'The Story of Opal: The Journal of an Understanding Heart', *Atlantic Monthly* (March 1920): 289–98. American nature writer and diarist Opal Whiteley (1897–1992).

2–Installed in 1957, the plaque at 23 Fitzroy Road reads 'William / Butler / YEATS / 1865–1939 / Irish poet / and dramatist / lived here'.

a wonderful Portuguese couple, the girl a best friend of Ted's girl friend, & they see how I am, full of interest in my own life, & are amazed, as everyone is, at my complete lack of jealousy or sorrow. I amaze myself. It is my work that does it, my sense of myself as a writer,[1] which Mrs. Prouty above all understands. My hours of solitude in my study are my most precious, those, & the hours I spend with my darling babies. I am, I think, & will be when I get this London flat (I hope) arranged, the happiest of women. Now I am free from Ted everybody loves me---I mean everyone I deal with. I am so happy & full of fun & ideas & love. I shall be a marvelous mother & regret nothing. I have two beautiful children & the chance, after this hard, tight year, of a fine career---schools & London in winter, Court Green, daffodils, horse-riding & the beautiful beaches for the children in summer. Pray for this flat coming thru. I would try to get a 5 year lease. Then in 5 years I hope to be rich enough to buy a house in London, rent flats at the bottom & live at the top, rent my furnished part in summers---so easy here it is a sure income. I have real business sense. I am just short of capital right now. I would be right round the corner from Catherine Frankfort etc., whom I'm so fond of, on the Hill, by the Zoo---minutes from BBC! And in the house of a famous poet, so my work should be blessed. Even if I don't get this place I should be able to get one like it near it sooner or later. It's about time my native luck returned! And I have, on the advice of Catherine Frankfort, applied for an au pair girl, preferably German. They get only £2 (about 5 dollars) a week plus board & room, & are students, wanting to be part of the family. They would mind the babies mornings & study at classes afternoons & babysit nights, with one day off! Just what I want---for I want to devote myself to the babies afternoons myself, take them to teas & visits & walks. Mrs. Prouty called me. I was thrilled. I am dedicating my 2nd book of poems (almost done) to Frieda & Nicholas in England. Maybe I'll dedicate it to her in America, if it gets taken there.

I have found a fabulous hairdresser in a town next to North Tawton[2] ---Doctor Webb's wife, of whom I'm very fond, told me of them. I had my fringe cut just before I came up to London in the most fashionable style ---high on top, curling down round the ears---and kept my long coronet in back. It looks fabulous and the cut, shampoo & set was only a dollar-fifty. From the front I look to have short hair, & from the back, a coronet. I am

1 – Since writing to Olive Higgins Prouty on 2 November, SP had completed: 'The Couriers' (4 November); 'Getting There', 'The Night Dances', and 'Gulliver' (6 November).
2 – Winkleigh.

going to get some fancy combs & clips for the back & do away with the elastic. Ted didn't even recognize me at the train station! My morale is so much improved---I did it on your cheque. Men stare at me in the street now, I look very weird & fashionable. Now I shall get an Xmas dress for myself with the rest of the money. I hope to be able to move up here before Xmas. I shall get toys for Frieda & Nick with your money, at Hamleys. When I appear at the Royal Court this summer I shall be a knockout. My haircut gives me such new confidence, truck drivers whistle & so on, it's amazing. I am so happy back in London, and when I came to my beloved Primrose Hill, with the golden leaves, I was full of such joy. That is my other home, the place I am happiest in the world beside my beloved Court Green. If I get the lease now, I should be able to write for 5 years & save up to buy a house there, & then the children would have the best of both worlds. Living apart from Ted is wonderful---I am no longer in his shadow, & it is heaven to be liked for myself alone, knowing what I want. I may even borrow a table for my flat from Ted's girl---I could be gracious to her now, & kindly. She has only her high-paid ad agency job, her vanity & no chance of children & everybody wants to be a writer, like me. I may be poor in bank funds, but I am so much richer in every other way I envy them nothing. My babies & my writing are my life & let them have affairs & parties, poof! What a bore. Love to Warren & Maggie.

Wish me luck.
Sivvy

TO *W. S. Merwin*

Thursday 8 November 1962 TLS, Pierpont Morgan Library

Court Green
November 8, 1962

Dear Bill,

Your letter[1] was waiting for me tonight when I got back from London from flat-hunting & thank you so for writing. I will talk to you straight out as I always did. I want simply to say that I have loved both you & Dido dearly, with immense fondness & sensibility for our close relation in London. When I came to this August, after almost dying of influenza &

1–The Pierpont Morgan Library holds a typescript carbon letter from W. S. Merwin to SP, 5 November 1962. Merwin's is a response to a letter from SP written *c.* 31 October–1 November. The location of this letter is unknown. We can infer that SP asked Merwin to participate in the American Poetry night at the Festival of Poetry, Royal Court Theatre.

being left with a high fever, no help, the 2 babies in the country to which I'd come because Ted said it was his life, & faced the practical problems, which were many, my first thought was to turn to friends who might give me a cup of coffee & some practical advice. I'd heard Frieda was a latent schizophrenic, after her shock at Ted's disappearance & she had upsetting fits, & also the baby needed to see an eye specialist. My one thought was to get back to London where I could get free-lance jobs, good medical care & a flat. I was fantastically relieved when Ted wrote Dido was in London, for I have always admired & loved her, & my first act, after a long seige of illness & on getting to London, was to call her & ask to talk to her, because I had some worries about the babies. I called her as Frieda's godmother & as a woman I thought would meet me, independently, in my new independence. I don't know if you can imagine how I felt when I realized Dido was home & refused to speak to me. I was simply stunned. Ted has since told me that Dido is no friend of mine & to forget her. My one thought was---was it an illusion, an hypocrisy, all that love & friendship I thought was for me as well as Ted?

I wrote you after this, in something of horror, wanting to think that perhaps my real admiration for you & your work & just the good times we all had in London were real, that just because Dido would not speak to or see me when I was desperate for a talk from someone wise & whom I'd loved, it didn't mean you too would simply pack your tent & walk off. Naturally you can't see from where you are, but there are no <u>sides</u> to be taken. All our mutual friends, the best ones, I have re-established happy relations with for I loved them & they really loved me & I have nothing to say but that I wish Ted well & have loved him so that as long as he is happy & writing it is all I wish. What has been very sad & very hard is to feel that you & Dido alone have turned your backs & evidently feel it impossible to be friends independently. I took you so seriously as godparents for Frieda, & to be refused Dido's voice when I was desperate to get to London & have her seen by a good child psychiatrist is something I still can hardly believe.[1] I now believe it, & accept it. What I cannot do is understand it. It did seem incredibly inhuman & hurtful to me. I also feel awful to think that you & Dido are of such a oneness that I must accept her act as yours, too. You ask if you could do anything to help.[2] The one great good thing you could do is confirm that there was a reality in

1–'can~~not~~ believe' appears in the original.

2–In his letter Merwin writes, 'if there's some way I can help please tell me what it is' and 'Let me know if I can do something to help.'

our friendship & that it might independently continue. You are the only friends that our divorce has cost me, & the hardest for me to lose. Having felt so keenly, last week in London, the loss of Dido, I wanted some sign I might not have lost you. Naturally I wouldn't think you'd hide anything from each other! I just thought you might not be the same.

As soon as I get back to London, a flat, & can start writing myself to a mother's help & seeing friends, my life will be what I want. Domesticity always bored me, & I will simply buy myself a foreign girl, as Dido once advised, to free me for what I want to do, which is write. All I want is my own life---not to be anybody's wife, but to be free to travel, move, work, be without check. I thought you of all people would understand this. I can't imagine you thinking I'd want you to alter your fondness & respect for Ted when what he's done hasn't altered mine! I think he is a genius & the best living poet & I wish him joy. Just at the moment I've a lot of practical bothers, but who wouldn't---they are slowly melting, & I may have a very lucky break about London at any moment. The stereotype of two divorced people being in two camps, & everybody having to take sides, just doesn't work here. Ted is getting me writing jobs, I am delighted to be free of the need to crop my life to his will or that of any man, & now a London flat looms as possible after my year of intellectual purdah here in Devon, I am intensely happy.

The one mar on my happiness is my very keen sense that you & Dido, alone of all our dearest friends, have taken sides, & such extreme sides, & apparently such irrevocable ones. It just makes me feel I was an idiot to think either of you ever cared for me or my work at all. I meant to give you a poem like a loaf of bread---I don't have anything else I can give. Ted has told me to give Dido up. Must I give you up too? Ted told me, as the friend of mine he still is, to expect nothing from her. OK. Was I wrong in thinking you were real as well? Please just say straight out. The worst is better said than left silent.

Sylvia

Please send copies of the poems when you've got them. My poetic judgment is still pure!

TO *Eric Walter White*

Wednesday 14 November 1962 TLS, University of Texas at Austin

Court Green
North Tawton
Devonshire
November 14, 1962

Dear Eric,

Thanks so much for forwarding the letter.[1] You and Dodo were angels to put me up, hot bath and all. I am working very hard to have a place in London in the New Year, which would be sixth heaven in itself, and, if I get the marvelous place I've applied for, seventh heaven at the least. It was lovely, seeing you both so beautifully installed in your new place.

Yes, I'll be in Devon, till I have the London address I've always wanted. I look very forward to planning the American Poetry night for next July, and hope I'll have the pleasure of seeing you both again when I'm living in my blessed London once more.

Warmest regards,
Sylvia Plath

TO *Howard Moss*

Thursday 15 November 1962 TLS (aerogramme), New York Public Library

Court Green
North Tawton
Devonshire, England
November 15, 1962

Dear Mr. Moss,

Thanks very much for your letter.[2] I'm sending back the second section of AMNESIAC as you suggest. It really is quite independent from the first

1–See Eric Walter White to SP, 6 November 1962; held by McMaster University. The letter came to SP care of the Poetry Book Society. It is possible the letter was in regard to SP being asked to be one of three judges of the Guinness Poetry competition, which was announced the day after SP's death in 'Cheltenham Festival of Literature', *Financial Times* (12 February 1963): 22. The other two judges were Jon Silkin and Edward Lucie-Smith. SP was not replaced with a third judge. See SP to ASP, 21 December 1962.

2–Howard Moss to SP, 7 November 1962; held by Smith College. Moss rejected 'Poppies in October', 'Ariel', and 'Purdah'.

section, I think---being about the amnesiac, where the first part[1] is simply about the town forgotten, the Lyonnesse.

Yours sincerely,
Sylvia Plath

Mr. Howard Moss
THE NEW YORKER
25 West 43rd Street
New York 36, New York
U.S.A.

P.S. Now I've typed it I like it much <u>better</u> without the first half! Thank you.

sp

TO *Peter Davison*

Friday 16 November 1962 TLS, Yale University

Court Green
North Tawton
Devonshire, England
November 16, 1962

Mr. Peter Davison
THE ATLANTIC MONTHLY
8 Arlington Street
Boston 16, Mass.
USA

Dear Peter,

I'm sending on this rather alarming wad of new stuff[2] and eager to have your opinion about it. As I'm rather hard up at the moment, I'd be awfully grateful if you could get a rapid hearing for these!

Best of love to you, Jane and Angus (Is it Angus?).

Sincerely,
Sylvia Plath

1–Sylvia Plath, 'Lyonnesse'. See also note on 'Amnesiac' and 'Lyonnesse' with SP to ASP, 21 October 1962, above.

2–SP sent: 'Fever 103°', 'Nick and the Candlestick', 'Purdah', 'A Birthday Present', 'The Jailor', 'The Detective', 'The Courage of Quietness' ['The Courage of Shutting-Up'], 'Lesbos', 'Eavesdropper', and the five bee poems.

TO *Aurelia Schober Plath*

Monday 19 November 1962 TLS (aerogramme), Indiana University

Court Green
Monday: November 19

Dear mother,

Thanks so for your good letter. I haven't written sooner because I have been fantastically busy. My correspondence alone would keep a full-time secretary going---I've had letters from physiotherapists asking for a copy of a poem about living in a Plaster Cast to read to her patients and just now a fan letter from an Australian gynecologist who heard from a "colleague in London" about my maternity ward poem for 3 voices on the BBC & wanted a copy as he'd done a lifelong study in miscarriages.[1] I am thrilled. The medical profession has always intrigued me most of all, & the hospital & doctors & nurses are central in all my work. I'm hoping to get my dear Susan O'Neill-Roe to take me into her Children's Hospital when we're both in London. Just now is "one of those weeks"---Susan has a week off in London, my local babysitter is out with flu, Nancy is moving from one house to one nextdoor & all 3 of us have colds. In spite of it, I am happier than ever before in my life. I realize now that all my married life I have sacrificed everything to Ted & his work, putting his work first, going to get part-time jobs, with great faith in his future wealth & fame. I never even got a new dress or went to a hairdresser! Now he goes out with fashion models. Well, I have finished a 2nd book of poems in this last month, 30 new poems,[2] & the minute I get a mother's help in London I will do novel after novel. Even in the greatest worry & adversity, I find I have simply neglected all my own talent, & thank God I have discovered it in time to make something of it! I took Mrs. Prouty's first check, as she said to, & went to the Jaeger shop in Exeter. It is <u>my</u> shop. I got an absolutely gorgeous camel suit (out of Vogue) & matching camel sweater, a black sweater, black & heavenly blue tweed skirt, duck-green cardigan, red wool skirt & in St. Ives got a big pewter bracelet, pewter hair clasp,

1–See SP to Douglas Cleverdon, 19 November 1962.

2–Since writing to Olive Higgins Prouty on 2 November, SP had completed: 'Thalidomide' (8 November); 'Letter in November' (11 November); 'Death & Co.' (14 November); 'Years' and 'The Fearful' (16 November); and 'Mary's Song' (19 November). 'Death & Co.' was the last poem SP wrote which was to be included in *Ariel*, her second volume of poetry.

pewter earrings & blue enameled necklace.[1] All my clothes dated from Smith and were yards too long & bored me to death. I am going to get a new black leather bag & gloves & shoes & just take my new things to London. I feel like a new woman in them, and go each week to have my hair shampooed & set in neighboring Winkleigh for under $1! My new independence delights me. I have learned, from Nancy, how to keep the big coal stove going in the kitchen, & it is heaven, heats all the water, dries all the clothes immediately & is like the heart of the house---even Ted couldn't keep it going overnight, & I can keep it going for a week. I love Court Green & am going to see that gradually my dream of it comes true.

Am going to dinner with Winifred Wednesday & bringing the Taroc cards as she is having friends. Had Clarissa Roche, the American wife of a British poet teaching at Smith when I was, for the weekend with her newborn, 4th baby. Went Saturday for lunch with Susan's parents at their gorgeous home in Belstone with Frieda and met Mark Bonham-Carter,[2] the handsome Liberal candidate down here (married to an American) & also director of a London publishing house. Liked him immensely. Frieda, I wish you could have seen her! In a new blue wool dress I got. Absolutely marvelous manners, sat up & ate all through the long dinner like an angel. Very polite. I love going out with her. Already she is saying "Go to London. See Zoo. See lions and baby owls." She will love it there.

I am in an agony of suspense about the flat. I was first on the list of applicants! Already I have met an offer for £50 more a year, now they have sent out for my "references", in other words, to solicitor, banker, accountant, to see if I can afford it. I had the uncanny feeling I had got in touch with Yeats' spirit (He was a sort of medium himself) when I went to his tower in Ireland---I opened a book of his plays in front of Susan as a joke for a "Message" & read "Get wine & food to give you strength & courage & I will get the house ready."[3] Isn't that fantastic? I would have to get a stove, new furnishings. Then I could rent it out by the week at fantastic rates in the summer when I was at Court Green and almost cover

1–According to SP's Letts Royal Office Diary Tablet for 1962, she visited St Ives on 13 November.

2–English publisher and politician Mark Bonham Carter (1922–94); married Leslie Nast in 1955.

3–W. B. Yeats, *The Unicorn from the Stars*: *Collected Plays of W. B. Yeats* (New York: Macmillan, 1953); SP's copy held by Smith College with the passage underlined, starred, and annotated: 'Nov. 13, 1962 The prophecy – True?' Yeats's text reads: 'Go, then, get food and drink, whatever is wanted to give you strength and courage. Gather your people together here, bring them all in. We have a great thing to do, I have to begin—I want to tell it to the whole world. Bring them in, bring them in, I will make the house ready' (347).

the year's rent! I am a real businesswoman, & if I only had capital would make a bid for the house from the owner, rent the bottom (bsement) flat, keep 3 floors for myself & rent those furnished for the half year I wasn't there. Then I would have an income! It is so frustrating not to be able to do this! I will die if my references say I'm too poor! Living in Yeats House would be an incredibly moving thing for me. I didn't tell you of my thumb[1]---it's now healed---because Dr. Webb made an assy botch of it, it is now deformed, because he did not put a proper bandage on it or even a tape to hold the top in place, nor look at it for 10 days, just left the black smelly bottom part of the bandage & put a clean outside on. I went back to my darling Regent Street[2] doctor who fixed it properly, as much as he could & saved the top, although the side is gone. They say one of Nick's eyes is slightly crossed (!) so I'm seeing an eye specialist this week. And my dentist. Am riding twice a week now. Have some fascinating historical biographies from the N. Statesman to review; am sending the almost full-page children's book review to Mrs. Prouty. Got $50 from Dot. Bless her. Will write her.

Love to all,
Sivvy

TO *Douglas Cleverdon*

Monday 19 November 1962 TLS, BBC Written Archives Centre

Court Green
North Tawton
Devonshire
November 19, 1962

Dear Douglas,

I wonder if you could have a copy of the script of "Three Women" sent to an Australian gynecologist who is very interested in it. His name & address are:

W. J. Rawlings FRCOG[3]
12 Collins Street
Melbourne, Australia.

1–See Winifred Davies to ASP, 3 November 1962; held by Lilly Library.

2–SP probably meant Regent's Park Road.

3–William Joseph Rawlings (1903–70), a Fellow of the Royal College of Obstetricians and Gynaecologists.

I also wonder if you could send me about half a dozen mimeographed copies, as I've had several requests for it.

So sorry to have missed you & Nest[1] the night I was in London, but I was flat out after travelling from 5 a.m. I hope, with luck, to be installed with the babies in London in the New Year, finishing a second novel and free lancing, & would so enjoy seeing you & Nest again then. Love to Nest and that marvelous pre-Raphaelite boy[2] whose name I always forget.

Sincerely,
Sylvia Plath

TO *Stevie Smith*[3]

Monday 19 November 1962 TLS, University of Tulsa

Court Green
North Tawton
Devonshire
Monday: November 19

Dear Stevie Smith,

I have been having a lovely time this week listening to some recordings of you reading your poems for the British Council,[4] and Peter Orr has been kind enough to give me your address.[5] I better say straight out that I am an addict of your poetry, a desperate Smith-addict. I have wanted for ages to get hold of "A Novel on Yellow Paper"[6] (I am jealous of that title, it is beautiful, I've just finished my first, on pink,[7] but that's no help to the title I fear) and rooted as I have been in Devon for the last year beekeeping and apple growing I never see a book or bookseller. Could you tell me where I could write to get a copy?

Also, I am hoping, by a work of magic, to get myself and the babies to a flat in London by the New Year and would be very grateful in advance

1–Nest Cleverdon (1920–2003), Douglas Cleverdon's wife.

2–Probably Francis Cleverdon (1960–).

3–British poet and novelist Stevie Smith (1902–71); see Stevie Smith to SP, 22 November 1962; held by Smith College.

4–Recorded 12 June 1961.

5–Stevie Smith, 1 Avondale Road, Palmers Green, London N.13.

6–Stevie Smith, *A Novel on Yellow Paper* (London: Jonathan Cape, 1936). TH gave SP a copy of Stevie Smith, *Not Waving But Drowning* (London: Andre Deutsch, 1958) for Christmas 1960, which appeared at auction via Bonhams on 21 March 2018.

7–SP drafted much of *The Bell Jar* on pink Smith College Memorandum paper.

to hear if you might be able to come to tea or coffee when I manage to move---to cheer me on a bit. I've wanted to meet you for a long time.

Sincerely,
Sylvia Plath

TO *W. Roger Smith*

Monday 19 November 1962 TLS, Random House Group Archive & Library

Court Green
North Tawton
Devonshire
November 19, 1962

Roger Smith, Esq.
Agreements & Rights Department
William Heinemann Ltd.
15-16 Queen Street
London W.1

Dear Mr. Smith,

Thanks very much for your letter of November 5th. I'm glad to hear they want "Mushrooms"[1] for a spoken recording, and certainly grant permission. I must say 2 guineas seems a tiny sum. How about 5 guineas? Or am I just sounding like an American capitalist. Maybe you could sound them out about it. I'd rather have 2 gns. than nothing, but would rather have 5 than 2. See what you can do and let me know.

Best wishes.
Sincerely,
Sylvia Plath

1–Sylvia Plath, 'Mushrooms' and 'Morning Song', John Wain (ed.), *Anthology of Modern Poetry* (London: Hutchinson, 1963): 68–70, 91. See A. Tarcy, Sound News Productions, to Heinemann, 1 November 1962; W. Roger Smith to SP, 5 November 1962; and Smith to Tarcy, 21 November 1962; held by Random House Group Archive & Library. 'Mushrooms' does not appear to have been used in the sound recording.

TO *Leonie Cohn*[1]

Tuesday 20 November 1962 TLS, BBC Written Archives Centre

Court Green
North Tawton
Devonshire
November 20, 1962

Miss Leonie Cohn
The BBC
Broadcasting House
London W.1

Dear Miss Cohn,

My husband has written telling me that you would like a few sentences of outline for the programme "Landscape on Childhood".[2] I enclose[3] a paragraph. I'd be grateful to hear from you[4] direct what sort of emphasis you precisely want, as my husband has given me only the most general of notions.

Yours sincerely,
Sylvia Plath

TO *Olive Higgins Prouty*

Tuesday 20 November 1962 TLS, Indiana University

Court Green
North Tawton
Devonshire England
Tuesday: November 20

Dear Mrs. Prouty,

I have been meaning to write you as soon as my state of almost unbearable excitement and suspense is over, but as it still continues, I decided I couldn't keep quiet any longer. What has happened is that by a kind of magic fate I saw <u>the</u> flat (unfurnished) in London and am now

1–BBC producer Leonie Cohn (*c.* 1917–2009).

2–Sylvia Plath, 'Landscape of Childhood'. Posthumously titled 'Ocean 1212-W'; read by June Tobin for *Writers on Themselves*, BBC Home Service (19 August 1963); printed in *The Listener* (29 August 1963): 312–13.

3–The enclosure is no longer with the letter.

4–See Sheila Grant to SP, 30 November 1962; held by BBC Written Archives Centre.

waiting to see if the client approves of my references. Let me tell you a little of the background. When I was in Ireland in August[1] after my long seige of flu, I went to visit the tower of the famous Irish poet W. B. Yeats. What I found there was a magic, untouched spot, no sign of people, only a poem on the walls, wild rhubarb, an apple orchard gone wild and a soft grey donkey with kind eyes. Although at that time I felt dead and ill in body, I felt my soul respond to that peace and felt somehow in tune with Yeats who must have loved it. Then, when I was last in London, rather depressed with all the ugly furnished hideously expensive flats Ted had taken me to look at, I felt compelled to walk down my dear streets by Primrose Hill and Regents Park where I'd had Frieda. I felt compelled to walk down Fitzroy Road, and there to my amaze was Yeats' old house (with a blue plaque "Yeats Lived Here") with builders in and a signboard up "Flats to Let". I was astounded---I'd walked by that house time and again and wished it were for let or for sale. I flew to the agents. By an absolute miracle (in London where people are cutting each others throats for flats) I was first on the list to apply! It is a very complicated process ---they write your banker, accountant & solicitor & ask if you can meet payments etc. then you get your solicitor to draw up a lease. I am in agony. It is just what I want, right round the corner from my old panel of wonderful doctors & the park & minutes by bus from the BBC. My dream is selling a novel to the movies and eventually buying the house from the present owner. I am applying for a 5 year lease, the longest I can get.

The strange part is that when I came back to Devon I said laughingly to my young nurse "I will shut my eyes and open my book of Yeats poetic plays & get a message from him." I did this, and the words I put my finger on were "Get wine and food to give you strength and courage and I will get the house ready." I was amazed. I knew Yeats was a sort of medium and believed in spirits, and although I am very sceptical, I certainly think it would be symbolic for me to live in the house of a great poet I love, which happens to be on the street I would love to live on most in London! But probably the owner won't approve of writers! If I could get it I would try to be in by Christmas.

I am a very good businesswoman, and what I would plan to do with this unfurnished flat on 2 floors---3 bedrooms upstairs, a large lounge-dining room, kitchen & bath downstairs---would be slowly furnish it,

1–SP visited Ireland in September, not August. She repeated this mistake in several subsequent letters.

poem by poem, in beautiful taste from second hand shops, living on straw mats & pillows in the meantime, then rent it at very high rates by the week in the spring and summer which would cover a large part of what I pay for it unfurnished. The weekly rents for furnished flats in London is astronomical, and I could make this quite economical by letting it out when I want to be at Court Green with the babies in spring and summer, when London is flooded with tourists. Eventually I hope to write a novel that will sell, really sell (I have novels in me, one after the other, just crying to be written) and buy a house in this road and furnish it---3 floors for myself, a mother's help & the children (there are only about 2 rooms to a floor), a garden, & a basement flat let out. When I went to Court Green I would have no trouble letting my flat, and my rent income should cover my expenses. I am amazed at my practicality & business sense. Having to handle this large place, taxes, insurance, repairs, has made my hard-headed streak define itself. Now winter has come, I lug great buckets of coal and keep the Rayburn stove going in the kitchen day and night. I am very proud of being able to run it (Ted never could), my cleaning woman taught me how, and it keeps the water boiling hot, dries the wet clothes overnight and is really "the heart of the house." I also carry dustbins, mow lawns and next spring will try to learn to dig so I can have some garden. I would like to live in London for the school year, so the children can go to the good free schools (the schools in Devon are awful), so I can have a mother's help & write (no mother's help wants to live in the country) and fill myself with art exhibits, interesting people, books and cultural life. The utter lack of cultural life of any sort this last year and a half has been a great trial to me. When I was back in London I literally wept to see paintings, I had missed them so. I was so happy there, and faced all the people including Ted and now have nothing to fear, only work to look forward to.

I must tell you that I took your advice and went shopping with part of that first check you sent! I looked in my wardrobe & was astounded. In the 7 years of my marriage I have never bought a new dress or had a hairdo! All my clothes dated from Smith and were too long and o so familiar. I had always thought I would never cost Ted anything, so he could write & not have a job, and now he is going out with fashion models after telling me he thought clothes were superficial! Well, I got the front of my hair cut & set and kept the long coronet of braid at the back. Then I bought a gorgeous camel-colored suit at Jaeger's, with a matching sweater, and a pewter hairclasp and bracelet, and a black sweater & blue-and-black tweed skirt and new shoes & I felt like a new woman. When

I met Ted at the train in London he didn't even recognize me. I am going to leave all my old Smith clothes in Devon & just take these new ones to London. I want my life to begin over from the skin out.

I am enclosing a copy of my review[1] of children's books which came out last week in the New Statesman, as I thought you might enjoy it, especially the part about the Opal Whitely book, which fascinated me. My children's reviews are beginning to "take"---Faber & Faber quoted one in an advertisement[2] & I opened one book to find a former review of mine of an earlier one in the series on the back jacket.[3] Needless to say I love doing children's picture books as the art & production interest me most & I have piles of free review copies for the children. They liked my review at the New Statesman & have just sent me 5 historical biographies from which I am to choose one to review. If I were living in London I'd simply see these editors, tell them what I'd like to try, and get lots more work. I would also have no trouble getting a mother's help as they all want to live in London.

I hadn't told mother about my cut thumb as I thought it would worry her, but I guess the midwife wrote her. My country doctor made a shocking botch of it---he didn't even affix the cut top with a tape or stitch and when the time came to look at it a few days later just left the dirty black bandage & put something clean on top. As a result, in 10 days, I had a deformed & very stinky thumb---my nurse thought it might be septic. So I went back to my dear London doctor who bandaged it properly & saved most of the top, although the side has a bad scar. He said it could have healed perfectly if it had been taken care of properly in time. So you can imagine how eager I am to get back to my old doctors! This one is a fool and is spoiled by only having ignorant country folk as patients who never question him. I am all right now, thank goodness, although for a while I thought I might lose my thumb.

I saw the producer of the poetry week at the Royal Court Theatre & am definitely doing the American Night in July. I am very excited about this.

The children are blooming, although we all have had colds this week---my nurse's week off. They tell me Nick has a slightly crossed eye, which I,

1–The clipping is now held by Lilly Library. SP drew stars by the title and her name; Prouty added pencil annotations.

2–SP's review of Elizabeth & Gerald Rose, *The Big River*, quoted in *The Observer* (17 June 1962): 27; '"A clear, poetic account of a river's genesis and progress to the sea, with superb illustrations"—Sylvia Plath, *New Statesman*'.

3–SP's review of Wanda Gág, *The Funny Thing*, quoted on rear jacket flap of Wanda Gág, *The ABC Bunny* (London: Faber & Faber, 1962): '"An excellent read-aloud adventure for very young children . . . all the finality of a good fable." *New Statesman*'.

doting mother that I am, never noticed. So I'll have it seen to by a specialist when I get to London. I bless the welfare services in medicine time & again. I took Frieda to lunch with the parents of my nurse & the Liberal party candidate Mark Bonham Carter (son of Lady Violet Bonham Carter)[1] and a director of Collins publishing house. He was charming, and Frieda ate with the grownups & behaved enchantingly. I am very proud of her. She keeps saying "Go to London and see the zoo!"

I hope to really get into my second novel this winter & finish it as soon as I get to London & can count on a mother's help. It is to be called "Doubletake", meaning that the second look you take at something reveals a deeper, double meaning. This is what was <u>going</u> to be the "Interminable Loaf"---it is semi-autobiographical about a wife whose husband turns out to be a deserter and philanderer although she had thought he was wonderful & perfect. I would like very much, if the book is good enough, to dedicate this novel to you. It seems appropriate that this be "your" novel, since you know against what odds I am writing it and what the subject means to me. I hope to finish it in the New year. Do let me know if you'd let me dedicate it to you. Of course I'd want you to approve of it first!

With love,
Sylvia

TO *Ruth Fainlight*

Tuesday 20 November 1962 TLS (aerogramme), Ruth Fainlight

Court Green
North Tawton
Devonshire
Tuesday: November 20

Dear Ruth,

Thank you so for the wonderful long letter & the poem. I think <u>Mist</u>[2] has a beautiful pace to it, the way it rises & crests, I most especially like "Layered like receding planes of a Japanese print" & "Mind's heedless gliding to the final sea./The trees were more than noble vegetables/More

1–British politician and diarist Violet Bonham Carter, Baroness Asquith of Yarnbury, DBE (1887–1969).

2–Ruth Fainlight, 'Mist', *Cages* (London: Macmillan, 1966): 8.

than convenient gallows."[1] It is lovely. I have been up to my neck in pragmatics. You can imagine how easy it is hunting for a flat in London from down here! By great luck my midwife cornered a lovely 22-year-old on holiday at home from the Great Ormond Street Children's Hospital where she is a nurse and she is with me till mid-December. Just now she's got a week off, my local babysitter is sick & my char is moving from one house to another & all 3 of us have colds, plus me with 5 historical biogs to weed out for the New Statesman, so basta! I did manage two visits to London in the last month, with the young nurse living in, & was astounded at my reaction. I almost wept to see paintings, I could not stop talking with people---I have been literally culture-less, movie-less etc. for well over a year, and totally incommunicado with intelligent adults since Ted left, now 4 months ago. My one drive is to a flat in London, and if my fantastic experience comes true I shall think I am a medium.

What happened was, I went to Yeats' tower in Ireland in August, near dead from flu & the prospect of bringing the children up alone on next to nothing, & felt there that although I was dead in body, my soul began to wake. It was very weird, feeling this timelessness of the untouched place, its beauty, the immanence of Yeats. Then, in London, utterly desolate with unsuccessful flat-hunting, I felt compelled to walk down Fitzroy Road---remember, where you were considering a house---where I'd always wanted to live. There were builders in Yeats' house & a sign out Flats to Let. I flew to the agent & by a miracle was first to apply for the unfurnished maisonette. But I am still waiting for my bloody references to be approved---I'm sure they'll say I don't have a steady income, being a writer, etc. etc. Anyhow, I came back to Devon & jokingly said to my nurse "I'll open Yeats' plays & get a message from him." I shut my eyes & pointed, then read from "The Unicorn from the Stars": "Get wine & food to give you strength & courage & I will get the house ready." I was scared to death, but very excited. I felt oddly in touch with the old boy, who believed in spirits too. If he is really serious, he'll inspire me to do a novel & sell it to the movies & then I shall buy the bloody house from the owner. I covet it beyond belief, with that blue plaque! O hell, the client won't like writers. Wish me luck, though. I would have to furnish it with straw mats & pillows & live on squid stew, but I actually cried in London I was so happy to be seeing people, talking, eating out, and went to movie after movie. The country is fine for holidays, but Ted's getting

1 – By the time it was published in *Cages*, Fainlight had changed 'Mind's heedless gliding to the final sea' to 'That heedless gliding by one firm act of art'.

me here where I can't get help so I can write & making it so hard for me to get where I can write & be human has been hard to take. If I do a good enough novel can I dedicate it to you & Alan? David too. My life seems to be spent furnishing a new place every year! I pray, if this Yeats flat comes through, to be in by the New Year & return here with the daffodils & clement weather (& go back to it next fall.)

Which brings me to my invitation---you must come down to Devon with David while Alan is in Russia & I wish he could come too. I think I will want to return here then---for my bees & my riding & my flowers. But God knows I am so starved for London I can hardly sit still. I have, alas, no money to move farther, & it is impossible to travel in the car now with Nick able to waltz about, for I can't drive & tend to both children. I will apply for a mother's help, foreign, the minute I hit London, so I can write full-time. I hope to furnish an unfurnished flat for the school-year in London, then rent it by the week, furnished, at fabulous prices in spring & summer. If only I could write a selling novel & get capital I'd get a house. In Fitzroy Road. Hoho. Once I get to London, a mother's help, & day after day to write, my life will be utter heaven.

I miss you & Alan & David very much. Agreeing where to live is a real problem. My being stuck here is a result of following Ted's cry that London was killing him, and of course I now carry coal & ashbuckets & shovels of muck like a navvy. But I get a terrific pride out of keeping the huge old Rayburn going (my char gave me lessons), it is the heart of the house, dries everything overnight, keeps the water boiling hot. I am learning to rise to the trot & it is heaven riding under the tors of Dartmoor. To keep this as a holiday place & establish myself in London while the children are at school is my dream. I'm hoping to make over the wreck of a room Alan used as study into a bed sitter so I can entertain more in spring & summer. Dartmoor convicts[1] keep escaping on these black nights & I keep an apple parer ready & the door bolted. Do write again when you get this & let me know your plans. Let's spend April as neighbors, whether in London or here---it would be fun with you here & wonderful for the babies.

Love to all,
Sylvia

1–HM Prison Dartmoor is near Princetown, Devon, approximately twenty-three miles from North Tawton. Two men escaped the prison on 14 November 1962, and were captured the day before this letter was written.

TO *Michael Carey*

Wednesday 21 November 1962 TLS, Assumption College

I send the book under separate cover.

Court Green
North Tawton
Devonshire
Wednesday: November 21

Dear Fr. Michael,

Do forgive me for being so long in writing, but I have been juggling two infants, 70 apple trees, syrup-eating bees and all sorts of negotiations which may get me a flat in London for the winter---hopefully the house of W. B. Yeats, plaque and all. Now for being frank. First let me say I love your pseudonym, Michael of the Six Dreams. How many languages do you know? Your epigraphs come from several.

I see two poets in you. The first is what I would call lyrical-traditional, a bit too much given to whimsy and the fey. The second, the much more interesting one, to my mind, is the one who produces meticulously-observed phrases like "wrapped in a mouse-colored twilight", "geraniums drenched in blood", "corrugated sands", "relax their boa's hold", "petroleum frenzy", "black macadam altars" and passages in The Shetlands like

Day and night the ocean speaks
And rage in his breath.
Eternal: the wedlock of wave to seacrag.

These are phrases and lines of the 20th century---they have a power and vitality you must develop. How much poetry do you read, and by read I mean study. Read Thomas Wyatt[1] for lyrics, but tense & special ones. Read, of course, Gerard Manley Hopkins. I think you have learned much from the Anglo-Saxons, that your May Morning poem has lots of exciting things in it & shows a real development. Beware, for Heaven's sake, the fey, the pretty, the "cute"---you know what I mean---the "butterscotch curls & marshmallow ears". This is fun, but only fun. It is "verse", entertainment. I think you should let the world blow in more roughly. Read Eliot, Pound[2] (you do dedicate a poem to him), study the assonances & consonances in Emily Dickinson (beloved of me) for a subtlety far beyond exact rhyme. And sweep out the archaicisms---"Tis", "Opes",

1–English politician and poet Thomas Wyatt (1503–42).
2–American poet and critic Ezra Pound (1885–1972).

"Alway". Modern poetry has blown these out. Do read Hopkins. Have you read his notebooks? I believe Penguin has a paper edition.[1] Rhymes, exact rhymes, and especially feminine rhymes tend to "jingle" too much. Try more free things like Fragment XXXVIII[2] which I love. Speak straight out. You should give yourself exercises in roughness, not lyrical neatness. Say blue, instead of sapphire, red instead of crimson. Forget witches and elves for a bit.

I am myself, ironically, an atheist. And like a certain sort of atheist, my poems are God-obsessed, priest-obsessed. Full of Marys, Christs and nuns. Theology & philosophy fascinate me, and my next book will have a long bit about a priest in a cassock. Did you ever live in Boston? That is my birth-city. I think I will send you a poem of my own, very rough, but about the Christ-ness in all martyrs, and written by a mother of a son.

Warmest good wishes,
Sylvia Plath

PS: What does Fr. stand for? Frère? Friar? Do say God bless. I need it, God Knows!

Mary's Song

The Sunday lamb cracks in its fat,
The fat
Sacrifices its opacity---

A window, holy gold.
The fire makes it precious,
The same fire

Melting the tallow heretics,
Ousting the Jews.
Their thick palls float

1 – Probably *Poems and Prose of Gerard Manley Hopkins* (Harmondsworth: Penguin Books, 1953). TH's copy held by Emory University.

2 – SP might be referring to poem 38 'To what serves Mortal Beauty?' in *Poems and Prose of Gerard Manley Hopkins*, cited above. According to editor W. H. Gardner's note, poem 38 includes 'common rhythm highly stressed' (232). SP quotes the first lines of poem 7 'God's Grandeur' and poem 36 'The Leaden Echo and the Golden Echo' by Hopkins in her *Journals* (24 January 1953: 164).

Over the cicatrix of Poland, burnt-out
Germany.
They do not die.

Grey birds obsess my heart,
Mouth-ash, ash of eye.
They settle. On the high

Precipice
That emptied one man into space
The ovens glowed like heaven, incandescent.

It is a heart,
This holocaust I walk in,
O golden child the world will kill and eat.

TO *Aurelia Schober Plath*

Thursday 22 November 1962 TLS (aerogramme), Indiana University[1]

Court Green
North Tawton
Devonshire, England
Thanksgiving Day

Dear mother,

It is perfect Thanksgiving Weather---how I miss that holiday! I'll have chicken fricasee today. Susan comes back tonight after a week off, Thank God. It has been absolute hell---my local babysitter out with flu, Nancy moving to another house & having hemhorrages, me with a bad cold unimproved by having to lug coal buckets & ash bins. I hope you haven't written the Hughes. I want no more communication with them whatsoever---I told them you had been ill as a result of this last summer, & were faced with losing your job. I have had a big juicy book from the New Statesman today called "Lord Byron's Wife" which they want me to

1–When ASP sold SP's papers to Indiana in 1977, this letter and the one to ASP of 23 September 1962 were placed under seal.

do,[1] along with one of the lot they sent last week & I haven't a minute to sit down and read. It is enough to drive me up the wall.

I am desperate to get this flat. I called up today & found they were boggling over my "recent" references---only good for the last 18 months. So I gave your name (Professor A. S. Plath) as a guarantor and security. And offered to pay the year's rent in advance out of sheer impatience. I hope you don't mind & will put on a good front for the agents if they write you. I have so much against me---being a writer, the ex-wife of a successful writer, being an American, young, etc. etc. This was my one lucky break---finding this flat, & I've got to get it. I simply can't get help here in the country, & the minute they sense they are really needed, like this week, they desert. Besides, they are lazy bastards. I work like a navvy day-in day-out without rest or holiday, & they sit & watch telly. I am dying to be able to work at writing, & now I am just up to my ears with this coming move & haven't time to write at all. I have written Mrs. Prouty yesterday enclosing a copy of my children's book review, telling her about the lovely Jaeger clothes I bought with her first cheque, and asking if I may dedicate this second novel I am desperate to finish this winter to her, as she has been such a great help and knows what I am working against.

Now f<or business?>. If I am to pay the year's rent in advance, I must <. . . m/an>y American banks and <move/some?> here, so would you please close both the 5 cent account and the Wellesley account & <illegible text> check which I can list on tax as a "gift" from you and send the total balance to me immediately.[2] This year will be the hardest financially in my life (I hope), as I have to make bold and considered investments, as in this flat, in order to enable me to work toward a future. Ted's sticking me here, helpless & with all these difficulties & blithely walking out, I shall never forget or forgive. I despise him. I think he is a coward & a bastard & want him to have nothing to do with me or the children. He is a gigolo now, vain & despicable.

1–Sylvia Plath, 'Suffering Angel', *New Statesman* (7 December 1962): 828–9; review of Malcolm Elwin, *Lord Byron's Wife* (London: Macdonald, 1962).

2–'Now . . . to me immediately': These sentences, comprising four and a half lines in the original letter, were redacted by ASP in black ink either at the time the letters were being prepared for *Letters Home* or during the sale to the Lilly Library in 1977. ASP added a note in pen: 'Personal & to me only! asp'. It has been possible to transcribe some of the redaction because of fading ink, as well as using UV light on the original and through manipulation of a scan of the letter in Photoshop. Some text remains obscured. According to the London Wills and Probates records, at the time of her death, SP had £2,147 4*s.* 2*d.* in her bank account. Issued to TH on 22 May 1963.

I don't care how much of a poetic genius he is, as a father he is a louse & as a husband a no-good, utterly vain, utterly irresponsible. Granted, he tried for six years & pretty much succeeded in being kind, faithful & loving, but the strain was too much & it didn't work. He had absolutely no right to have children. All the women who surround him now, including his sister & Dido Merwin, are barren, either because of abortions or choice. This is the "smart" way with them, utter devotion to self. I despise this sort of life & want the children to have nothing to do with it. Ted is now seeing Clem Moore's ex-wife[1] among others & evidently she wants to meet me, but that is a pleasure she'll have to forgo.

It is so frustrating to feel that with time to study & work lovingly at my books I could do something considerable, while now I have my back to the wall & not even time to read a book. So anything I may turn out just now is merely potboiling. Boy, when I get to be 50 & if I'm famous, there will be no tributes to "The loving husband without whose help I would never have succeeded etc. etc." Everything I have done I have done in spite of Ted. And against the malicious obstacles he has, wittingly or unwittingly, put in the path of my writing.

I'll send some authorizations to close my accounts at the banks.[2] Love to Warren & Maggie. How are they? O, I forgot, the absolutely marvelous dress for Frieda came---it will just go with my Jaeger red skirt & black sweater! It is adorable. The kitty balloons lasted 2 days & were marvelous fun, Frieda kicked them all about. She is always picking up something & saying "Grammy sent it." I am taking the vitamins. Do send your "Gift" cheque as soon as may be. Shouldn't it be just about $900 ($706.95 plus $193.10).[3]

Love,
Sivvy

1–British poet Susan Alliston Moore. Moore worked as a secretary for Faber & Faber; see Susan Moore to SP, 4 February 1963; held by Smith College.
2–This sentence redacted by ASP.
3–This sentence redacted by ASP.

TO *Clarissa Roche*

c. Wednesday 28 November 1962[1] TLS, Smith College

Court Green
North Tawton
Devonshire
cWednesday

Dearest Clarissa,

It was heavenly having you & the babe to cheer me in the midst of that howling weather. Frieda still says "See little baby on toot toot". The hedgehog sounds a dear. After rattling my American mother & offering madly to pay a year's rent in advance, I seem to have the owner's 'approval' & hope to get my solicitor to drum through the bloody contract so I can have a London Christmas. Keep up those pagan prayers!

Lots of love to all,
Sylvia

Will call Paul Wednesday, though that's the day I probably go home!

TO *Aurelia Schober Plath*

Thursday 29 November 1962 TLS (aerogramme), Indiana University

Court Green
Thursday: November 29

Dear mother,

I was so glad to have your letter saying you got my last letter. I think I will get the flat & hope to move in about December 17. They are at the "draft contract" stage: it is all so slow & Dickensian. The owner's solicitor sends a draft to my solicitor, who checks with me, then back to the other, then back to mine! They were sticky, the estate agents, about my "recent" references & lack of a steady job. So I offered you as "guarantor" (don't worry, I shan't need you!) & stressed your long job with BU. If they write, sign yourself Professor! I also offered to pay a year's rent in advance. The chance at this place (I'll take a 5 year lease) is fantastic. It is like a weird dream come true. My dream is to sell a novel to the movies & bribe the owner to sell me the house; I want that house. I am sending back your Lombard Bank book; I shall have no need for it, & no need to use it as

1–Date supplied from internal evidence.

security for the flat. You can imagine how silly it is to have something like that around which Ted might see if he comes to visit the children, etc. And for goodness sake don't say "unless you are safe & reasonably happy, I can't live anyway"! One's life should never depend on another's in that way. Why do you identify so with me? That sort of statement only makes one chary of confiding any difficulties in you whatsoever, as I am sure you will see if you think of it.

My thumb is fine now. I shall have Nick's eye seen to in London when I am back with my panel of blessed, excellent doctors. I can't wait. I have been culture-starved so long, utterly alone, that these last weeks are a torture of impatience. Winifred has been wonderful. I had her & Garnett over for a very special dinner last night, Sue here as well.[1] Everybody had a lovely time---my chicken with orange, honey & wine sauce, rice, corn, fried bananas, apple cake, date-nut bars & coffee. I had Susan's parents over for dinner Saturday night, & a nice Irishman & his wife & 3 children for tea Sunday.[2] When I get safely into this flat I shall be the happiest person in the world. I shall apply immediately for a live-in mother's help & get cracking on my novel---I hope to finish it by the date of that contest you sent information of, even if I don't win, which I won't, it will be an incentive. This experience I think will prove all for the best---I have grown up amazingly. Did I say I was taking out the policy on Ted's life because if I pay, I get about 10 thousand pounds at the end of 30 years if he lives. I'll need a pension of some sort, & this is the only way I can think of doing it. It is a "with profits" policy. 5 thousand pounds on his death only, but about twice that, with accrued interest if it matures. Winifred advised me to see a local truck man about moving, very nice, & he will take all my stuff up on the Day for under $50! I am only taking the babies' stuff & will furnish slowly so I can rent it at high rates, furnished, in the summers. Stunned to get a check for about $700 from Aunt Dot today. I will write her. I just burst into tears at her sweet letter, I was so moved, by that & the story of the check. Shall put it to the flat rent. This year is of course the hardest, but once I am in London falls & winters, working, I expect to be self-sufficient. Frieda & Nick are crawling happily about the study as I write. They are so cute together.

1–According to SP's Letts Royal Office Diary Tablet for 1962, SP hosted the dinner on 27 November.

2–Frederick Gilbert Foster (1920–2000), his wife Marian Robley Foster (1932–) and their three children: Aidan (1957–); Gerald (1958–); and Bride (1961–). At the time Marian Foster was pregnant with her fourth child, Rona (1963–). According to SP's address book, the Fosters lived at Park View, North Tawton.

I was amused to find out both Susan & her mother were going to my hairdresser on Sue's afternoon off! Well, imitation is sincerest flattery. I am up to London again this week to arrange a stove, straw mats, phone etc. for the flat & see a man for lunch[1] about a reading at an Arts Centre in Stevenage---the man I am working with for the Royal Court Theatre Night put him onto me. Once I get started, I should be able to get lots of speaking engagements. It will be lovely to have both Susan & Garnett in London & coming to tea! Susan's boyfriend,[2] a free-lance journalist, lives right round the corner from me & Garnett's police beat[3] is within five minutes! I am so fond of both.

My solicitor is gathering the evidence necessary for a Divorce Petition. I think there should be no trouble, as Ted is very cooperative. I hope to go to a local seamstress in London & get her to take up all my old skirts etc. I have sent Mrs. Prouty a copy of my big children's book review & asked her to show it you (I am sure you will understand my sending it her first!) I am very smug at a review of the most fascinating book I've just done! LORD BYRON'S WIFE! I am very lucky to get it, it costs $6.50, a fortune here, & all the big papers have already given it full-page treatment.[4] I've been asked to do it for the New Statesman by a friend of ours who is literary editor[5] & who knew I'd love to get my hands on it! Incredibly, the portrait of Augusta, Byron's sister, is the dead spit of Olwyn! Only she sounds immensely nicer & had lots of children. Shall send this to Mrs. Prouty too. Thought it a good way to please. Have asked if I can dedicate my 2nd novel to her---the one I hope to finish this winter. Hope she agrees. Don't worry about my paying bills. I pay them immediately, always have.

Love to all,
Sylvia

1–Probably John Somerville of Bedwell Community Association, Stevenage, who is listed in SP's address book.

2–Corin Hughes-Stanton (1933–). Hughes-Stanton lived at 2 Willes Road, off Prince of Wales Road, London N.W.5.

3–According to SP's address book, Neville-Davies lived at 40 Beak Street, London W.1.

4–Reviews appeared in *The Guardian* on 23 November and *The Observer* on 25 November.

5–Karl Miller; see SP to Karl Miller, 29 November 1962 (draft).

TO *Harriet Cooke*

Thursday 29 November 1962 TLS, Private owner

Court Green
North Tawton
Devonshire
November 29

Dear Harriet,

Your letters are so dear & I was looking so forward to seeing you & Barrie & the babes that I am cast down to say I shan't be able to come after all. I loved Connemara above any place I've ever been, but luck, rather fantastic luck, will get me to a London flat before Christmas, I hope. I have to go anyhow to see an eye specialist about Nick's slightly skew eye (which I don't think is skew but the midwife insists), & have been alone in this desolate place with the babes for almost 4 months now, so am mad for the sight of humans who can read, talk, movies, plays, galleries & all the things Ted's "notion" of country life has kept me from. Ironically he got me down here, saying London was killing him, then packed off after I had flu. I guess he didn't mention to Barrie I'm divorcing him for desertion & all the rest of it. My coming to Devon on Ted's account has stopped my writing because no-one will come to be mother's help in this desolation & the locals are all too lazy to work! So of force I must live in London to get a mother's help so I can finish my second novel---a pot-boiler, I fear, due to my need for dough. I pray I can manage a holiday in Ireland (West) next fall again. I loved it so there I never want to go anywhere else!

The story of this flat around the corner from where we used to live is very odd. I visited Yeats tower at Ballylea[1] when in Ireland this August & felt weirdly at peace. Then, utterly desperate & despairing of a flat, I was stalking my old haunts in London & happened to pass by Yeats' house in Fitzroy Road, which I'd often looked at longingly. There were builders in & a signboard out. By some miracle, London being London, I was first to apply for the maisonette & am now at draft contract stage. When I got home I said jokingly to my nurse "I'll open a book of Yeats' plays & get a message from him about the flat." When I opened my eyes I was pointing to the words "Get food & wine to give you strength & courage & I will get the house ready." How's that. I am starting to read my Tarot cards in earnest now.

1–Thoor Ballylee Castle, Ballylee, Gort, County Galway.

Do keep in touch with me---I so long to see you again, I remember you so vividly from that brief visit. The hero of my present novel is a painter, so I'd like to see some of Barrie's stuff. Can I see it anywhere in London? Now I have the prospect of living where I want to, I am very happy about the divorce, freed from some very nasty people & the sort of women who live from abortion to abortion & facelift to facelift---not my sort at all. I am just dying to get to London & a mother's help so I can finish my next novel & 2nd book of poems! Ted & I are friends as much as can be at times like this, so do you go on writing me as well! I'll let you know my address when this (bless it!) contract is safely through & you both, & babes have a standing invitation for tea! Or squid stew! My 'economy' meal.

Love,
Sylvia

TO *Karl Miller*

Thursday 29 November 1962 TLS (draft),[1] Smith College

Court Green
North Tawton
Devonshire
November 29, 1962

Karl Miller, Esq.
NEW STATESMAN
Great Turnstile
London WC 1

Dear Karl,

I found LORD BYRON'S WIFE far and away the finest of that bunch you sent, so stole the 300 words or so you allotted one of the others for Annabella for it as well.[2]

1–SP's second draft of 'Kindness' (1 February 1963) was later typed on the verso of this draft letter to Miller. An annotated typescript of SP's long review of the British edition of Malcolm Elwin's biography of Lady Byron (Anne Isabella Milbanke Byron) is held by Smith College.

2–'I found LORD BYRON'S WIFE far and away the ~~most important~~ of that ~~lot~~ you sent, so stole the 300 words or so you ~~said I could take for~~ one of the others & ~~added them to this~~ as well. ~~I hope that is okay~~.' appears in the original.

After Christmas I should be living at 23 Fitzroy Road, N.W.1---Yeats' house no less, plaque and all.

Yours sincerely,
Sylvia Plath

TO *Michael Carey*

Thursday 29 November 1962 TLS, Assumption College

Court Green
North Tawton
Devonshire
November 29, 1962

Dear Fr. Michael,

The blessing was lovely & I do feel better for it. I know why you had the 'horrible sinking feeling' that you called me Edith---Edith is the name of my mother-in-law. How odd of you.

I didn't mean dissect by study, which is the process you describe as study. I meant learn by heart. The same thing happened to me with Milton; I hate him too, although by myself I did not. It was a horrid dull studious teacher did it![1]

I would answer the autobiographical questions if I knew what you meant by what. Dear Father Michael, I meant above. I like it better written out, why not, it is a fine word.

Sincerely,
Sylvia

Now what is "A. A."? Please could you bless Yeats' house as well! I think it is coming through, & Lord knows I need it!

1–During her third year (1952–3) at Smith College, SP completed English 39b (Milton) taught by Eleanor Terry Lincoln.

TO *Aurelia Schober Plath*

Friday 14 December 1962 — TLS (aerogramme), Indiana University

Friday: December 14

Dear mother,

Well, here I am! Safely in Yeats' house! I can just about allow myself time for a cup of tea & a bit of letter writing after the immensity of the move---closing up Court Green & opening this place. And I can truly say I have never been so happy in my life. I just sit thinking Whew! I have done it, and beaming---shall I write a poem, shall I paint a floor, shall I hug a baby? Everything is such fun, such an adventure, & if I feel this way <u>now</u>, with everything bare & to be painted & curtains to be made etc., what will I feel when I get the flat as I dream it to be! Blessed Susan stayed with me through the move up & a day after,[1] so I could make innumerable dashes into town ordering & buying the most necessary things. Now I have to fix the place up so I can get babyminders in off & on & then a mother's help to live in. We had a lovely drive up---a clear, crisp blue day. I had spent the week before in London in the terrible & fascinating smog---so thick you couldn't see a hand ahead, which lasted the whole time I was up signing the lease & arranging innumerable details.[2] I arrived here to find no gas stove in & no electricity connected! As I dashed out, Susan nobly holding the babies in the car, to drive to the gas board, I left my keys in the open flat & the door blew shut! Well, it was a comedy of errors. The obliging gas boys climbed on the roof & jimmied a window & installed the stove, the Devon mover did it all by candlelight (which I had foresight to bring!) & by getting laryngitis I persuaded the electricity people to connect us up---the agents hadn't sent them the right keys. The minute this was over, everything went swimmingly. I was dumbfounded at the people who remembered me---you too. The laundromat couple rushed up, they had been in Boston since we last met, they wanted to be remembered to you. The people at the little dairy-grocery shook hands & remembered me by <u>name</u>, & the <u>nappy</u> service man I called up remembered me & welcomed me back! Well, it was like coming home to a small loving village. I haven't had a second to see Catherine Frankfort or Lorna Secker-Walker yet, both

1–SP moved to 23 Fitzroy Road on Monday 10 December.

2–According to SP's Letts Royal Office Diary Tablet for 1962, she may have travelled to London on 3 December. On 4 December she had a meeting regarding the Stevenage reading and had lunch in Leicester Square. Dense smog covered large parts of England during the week of 3 December 1962.

of whom have had new babies,[1] I've been so busy on my own with Frieda & Nick I can only work evenings at the house & writing. So the next five years of my life look heavenly---school terms in London, summer in Devon. I only pray I earn enough by then to offer the widow who owns this place so much she'll sell it me! I feel Yeats' spirit blessing me. Imagine, a Roman Catholic priest at Oxford, also a poet, is writing me & blessing me too! He is an American teacher-priest who likes my poems & sent me his for criticism. I thought this would please Dot!

The first letter through my door was from my publishers.[2] I spent last night writing a long broadcast[3] of all my new poems to submit to an interested man at the BBC[4] & have a commission to do a program on the influence of my childhood landscape---the sea. Oslo, Norway, radio[5] wants to translate & do my "Three Women" program set in the maternity ward & A. Alvarez the best poetry critic here thinks my second book, which I've just finished, should win the Pulitzer Prize. Of course it won't, but it's encouraging to have somebody so brilliant think so. As soon as I get my mother's help---I hope early in Jan., I'll finish my 2nd novel. I am writing these 'potboilers' under a pseudonym!

Please for God's sake don't waste another minute worrying about me. Now I've got rid of Ted, to whom I've dedicated such time & energy & for such reward, I feel my life & career can really begin. He's taken with him the harem of barren bitches who bore me only envy & now everyone I know is good & loving. I took F & N to the Zoo Wednesday & had a heavenly time. N slept, but Frieda was thrilled. Then I took them to the Primrose Hill playground Thurs. & had fun on the swings etc. They are so happy & laughing, we have such fun. F. does her puzzle in 5 seconds, reads books with me & loves coloring. I'm going to make their bedroom ---the biggest, a playroom too. I brought the Geegee horse & the favorite toys. My bedroom will be my study---it faces the rising sun, as does the

1–Nicholas Frankfort (1962–) and Sebastian Secker-Walker (1962–).
2–Probably Elizabeth Anderson (Heinemann) to SP, 10 December 1962; held by Smith College; regarding sending *The Bell Jar* to Elizabeth Lawrence at Harper & Row in New York. SP also received a letter from David Machin (Heinemann), 12 December 1962; held by Smith College. Sent to Court Green, Machin enclosed an advance copy of *The Bell Jar*.
3–This broadcast never took place, but SP included the following poems: 'The Applicant', 'Fog Sheep' ['Sheep in Fog'], 'Lady Lazarus', 'Ariel', 'Death & Co.', 'Nick and the Candlestick', 'Letter in November', 'Daddy', 'Fever 103°', 'The Bee Meeting', 'The Arrival of the Bee Box', and 'Wintering'; a complete script held by British Library; an incomplete script held by Smith College.
4–See Douglas Cleverdon to SP, 11 December 1962; held by Smith College.
5–See SP to R. G. Walford, 14 December 1962; held by BBC Written Archives Centre.

kitchen. Viewed the full moon from my little 'balcony' in sheer joy. It is so light here. The only real job is painting the floors---I've ordered rugs & mats. I adore planning the furnishing. You were very wise about a double bed---I'll get one.[1] I have a single on loan from Portuguese friends. The cats are being fed by friends in Devon.[2] I strung all my own onions & brought them, a bag of potatoes & my own apples. And a big bouquet of my own beautiful green & white holly with red berries is in my newly polished pewter set. I am so happy I just skip round. Please tell darling Dotty her blessed 'investment' is enabling me to furnish the flat straight out instead of poem by poem, as I'd thought. I had to pay a year's rent in advance to get it, so was immensely grateful. You won't be needed as a reference. I had the darlingest young solicitor at my firm do the lease business for me---we were exchanging advice about kinds of paint at the end. Everybody--Frank, Dot, Mrs. P. says you worry if I don't write. For goodness sake, remember no news is good news & my work is so constant I barely have a second to fry a steak. Don't make me worry about you.

Lots & lots of love to all, your happy

Sivvy

<on the return address side of letter>

Have told Mrs. P. I would like to dedicate my 2nd novel to her. She wanted to be sure I was dedicating something to you, so I said I was dedicating my 3rd book of poems[3] to you---I'm dedicating the 2nd one I've just finished to Frieda & Nick, as many poems in it are to them, & I'm sure you approve! Don't want Mrs. P. to feel I'm 'expecting' anything, though!

TO *Dorothy Benotti*

Friday 14 December 1962 — TLS (aerogramme), Indiana University

Friday: December 14

Dear Dotty,

It was so wonderful to hear your voice over the phone, sounding just as if you were next door! I was so excited about getting the flat---everybody says it was a miracle, including my solicitor---and here I am, in my favorite

1–See ASP to SP, 4 December 1962; held by Smith College.

2–See SP to Gilbert and Marian Foster, 15 December 1962.

3–Since writing to ASP on 19 November, SP had completed: 'Winter Trees' (26 November); 'Brasilia' and 'Childless Woman' (1 December); and wrote the first version of 'Sheep in Fog'

house in my favorite neighborhood, happy as a clam! The children are thrilled, too. Frieda has been dying to go to the Zoo, two minutes away, & I took her & Nick Wednesday---she was fascinated by the owls that "had bottoms just like Frieda", the lions, the new baby elephant & the penguins swimming round. She is such fun, such company, & Nick is the sturdiest handsomest little boy imagineable, he just laughs & chuckles all the time. They are so good. I put them into the same cot in the morning & all I hear is laughs, till I've got breakfast. I am dying to take them round to all my old friends here, all of whom have had new babies. It is like a village---so many shop people remembered me & welcomed me back! It is heaven to be surrounded by people & to know as soon as I get my phone I'll have all sorts of friends dropping round & be able to go out. Imagine, I've not seen a movie for 2 years! I am just starved for fun & chat. The country is lovely in spring & summer, but my work & dearest friends are in London. Already I have two BBC broadcasts to do & a poetry reading & then this big American poetry night to produce at one of the most famous theatres here this spring, a real great job. I am delighted you think I have an English accent, Dotty. Everybody over here thinks I come from the Deep South, they think my American accent is so broad!

I am now in the little limbo between mother's helps. My dear nurse saw me through to a day after my move, & then went on deserved holiday before she starts work as an operating theatre nurse at a children's hospital near here this January, & as her boyfriend lives very near me, I hope to see a lot of her---I love her like a younger sister for what she's been through with me. I was in London all through the smog making the final arrangements for a gas stove,[1] electricity to be connected, a phone (which takes ages here) & signing the lease. It was incredible, thick white for 5 days, you couldn't see your hand before your face & you can imagine what it was to get round! All the busses were stopped at one point. But I did it. And then I came home & in four days did all the packing & closing up of Court Green---you can imagine what that involved! I spent a day stringing all my onions & brought a load up with a load of my own potatoes, apples, honey & holly. I am very proud of my gardening & hope to plant a lot of stuff next spring down there too & keep my bees going. I got off the leading rein on my horse just before I left & have had some heavenly rides under the moors. I hope Frieda & Nick learn to ride very

---

(2 December; revised 28 January 1963). 'Years', 'The Fearful', and 'Mary's Song' may have been considered as the start of SP's third poetry collection.

1–Smith College holds SP's chequebook stub indicating she paid £16. 5. 0 for the cooker on 12 December 1962.

young. I seem to get on with the horse I must say, & my riding mistress is very pleased. You can imagine what a relief riding has been through all this trouble & having to take on all a man's responsibilities as well as a woman's. Well, <after I g>et this lovely flat all fixed up---and your 'investment', b<less it, is> making that possible right away---I shall know what I'm <doing for the> next 5 years & can maybe take a little rest! Right no<w I hardly have> time for a cup of tea, I have so many irons in the fire![1]

I got your dear letter today & went out & bought steak & lamb chops. Now I've finally got here after half a year of being stuck & not knowing if I ever could manage it, I am so happy I am ravenous & eat like a horse. I hope to get off sleeping pills as soon as I get through the first week or so fixing this place up, I must say they have kept me going, otherwise I'd have been awake all night, & one is just no good without sleep. I wish you'd talk mother out of worrying! Hard work never killed anybody, & I think hardship can be a good thing. It has certainly taught me to be self-reliant, & I'm a lot happier because of it! What in heaven's name has mother to worry about! I am fine & happy & so are the babies. It only adds to my worries to think she is worrying. Do try to set her right, Dotty. And say no news is good news. If she had any idea how hard I work, taking care of the babies, writing billions of business letters, doing writing jobs etc. she would understand I can't be writing letters every second much as I'd like to. Now I'm settling in I shall write once a week. I am with the babies all the time & they are angels. It is good this blew up while they are so little, for while Frieda sometimes mentions daddy, Nick has never known him, & I am so happy with my new life it is contagious. The kind of people I know are good & honest & love me & the children, I am glad to get rid of the rest. I hope by the New Year to have got this place pretty well furnished & cosy & get a mother's help to live in by then. And then I should be able to really get on with my career---it is lucky I can write at home, because then I don't miss any of the babies' antics. I just adore them. The navy-hooded sweat shirt sounds marvelous! I must say there is nothing like American clothes. Everybody here envies my American babies clothes. You have no notion how much your cheery letters mean! My nurse has taken some color shots of me & the babes I hope will come out – I'll send them on as soon as they do.

Love to all –
Sivvy

1–A portion of this letter is torn away. The text appearing in < > is from *Letters Home*.

TO *R. G. Walford*[1]

Friday 14 December 1962 TLS, BBC Written Archives Centre

23 Fitzroy Road
London N.W.1
December 14, 1962

R. G. Walford, Esq.
The BBC
Broadcasting House
London W.1

Dear Mr Walford,

I should be glad to have you send the Norsk Rikskringkasting, Oslo, a copy of my script THREE WOMEN. You have my general permission to send my works abroad on the above conditions without further reference to me.

Yours sincerely,
Sylvia Plath

TO *Frieda Plath Heinrichs*

c. mid-December 1962[2] ALS in greeting card,[3] Private Owner

<printed greeting>
SEASON'S GREETINGS / MEILLEURS VOEUX / FELIZ AÑO NUEVO
<Signed>
Lots & lots of love / from Sylvia, / Frieda & Nicholas

Have just moved into a lovely London flat for the winter.
Letter later!

S.

1–Head of BBC copyright.
2–Date supplied from internal evidence.
3–Christmas card of 'The Messenger . . . from a painting contributed to UNICEF, the United Nations Children's Fund, by Arnold Blanch of the United States of America.'

TO *Douglas Cleverdon*

Saturday 15 December 1962 TLS, BBC Written Archives Centre

23 Fitzroy Road
London N.W.1
December 15, 1962

Dear Douglas,

Thanks so much for the copies of "Three Women".* It was lovely to have a letter from you[1] waiting in my new flat---did Ted tell you it is Yeats' house, plaque and all, & that I've been dying to live here ever since I saw it three years ago? A fantastic series of luckinesses saw me into it, including my getting a "message" from Willy himself. The babies adore it, especially the immediate Zoo.

I've written up a broadcast of a selection of my new poems, with commentary, which I enclose. I do hope you like them. They are so new, none have yet been printed, although THE LONDON MAGAZINE has accepted 'The Applicant'[2] and the OBSERVER has accepted 'Ariel'.

We will be camping out a bit till I get my ancient Yeatsy floors painted & a mother's help lured to live in <u>and</u> a phone, all of which I hope to accomplish by the New Year. Very warmest good wishes for now & Christmas too to you and Nest.

Sincerely,
Sylvia
(Sylvia Plath)

Douglas Cleverdon, Esq.
Features
The BBC
Broadcasting House
London W.1

*Could you have the BBC send a copy to that Australian gynecologist whose address I sent you? Thanks very much.

1–Douglas Cleverdon to SP, 12 December 1962; held by Smith College.

2–Sylvia Plath, 'Stopped Dead' and 'The Applicant', *London Magazine* 2 (January 1963): 14–16. See Alan Ross to SP, 2 November 1962; held by Smith College.

TO *Gilbert & Marian Foster*

Saturday 15 December 1962 TLS, Private owner

23 Fitzroy Road
London N.W.1
December 15, 1962

Dear Gilbert & Marion,

Well, I am here safely in Yeats' place at last, surrounded by acres of floors which I shall slowly & I am afraid lazily start to paint. Our moving in was a comedy of errors---I arrived to find no gas stove, no electricity connected up & as I ran out to see the gas people leaving the keys in the open flat, the door blew shut. Luckily the gas boys were experts at jimmying windows & we moved in by candlelight: Very Dickensian.

I hope by now Bennett[1] has come round for the key to let out the water in the cistern & the pipes (and brought the key back!) so I'll have no worry of water freezing or pipes bursting.

Do get the potato sack out of the hall closet, use all the onions & the apples. I took the babies to the Zoo the other day, it's right across the street, & Frieda was thrilled by the owls & lions & a new baby elephant. Nick just slept. I hope the enclosed cheque[2] will see Skunky-Bunks & Tiger-Pieker through some Topcat & Christmas milk & that they are not too much trouble. If one or both are female, Gilbert, could you have her or the Shee fixed by the vet? Let me know & I'll pay the bill, so I won't return to thousands of kits.

Happy Christmas to you all, & many thanks for everything!

Sylvia

1–James Bennett, a local builder.

2–SP sent the Fosters a cheque for £15. Marian Foster recalls that they did not cash the cheque as they felt SP's generous offer to help themselves to her store of onions, potatoes, and apples was more than fair compensation for taking care of the cats.

TO *Mary Coyne*

Saturday 15 December 1962 TLS, University of Tulsa

23 Fitzroy Road
London N.W.1
December 15, 1962

Dear Mrs. Coyne,

I have had to move to London for the winter to have my little boy's eye seen to by a specialist & operated on, so I would be very grateful if you would send on my sweater & the little girl's sweater suit to me at the above London address, if you have not already sent them to Court Green. If you have already sent them there, they will be forwarded to me.

Do tell Mr. Murphy I am living in Yeats' house in London---with the blue plaque and all. It will amuse him, as Yeats' was a famous Irish poet & I am very lucky to be living in his house, it is a real inspiration to my writing.

Best wishes for the Christmas season,

Sincerely,
Sylvia Hughes

TO *Olive Higgins Prouty*

Saturday 15 December 1962 TLS, Indiana University

23 Fitzroy Road
London N.W.1
December 15, 1962

Dear Mrs. Prouty,

The miracle has happened. I am writing from Yeats' house in Fitzroy Road & I don't think I have ever been so happy in my life. Even the young solicitor of my firm who got the lease through so I could move in Monday says it is a miracle of will power & persistence. All during that thick smog which stuffed every crack of London with white cotton wool I was up here, pushing through the 5-year lease, arranging about gas & electricity & a thousand other things. Moving in was a comedy of errors ---I arrived with the babies & my nurse to find no electricity connected, no gas stove, & as I rushed out to see the stove people I left the keys in the open flat & the door blew shut! Well the gas stove boys forced a window & loaned me a candle & my nice Devon mover did all the moving in by candlelight, so it was very Dickensian. After that, everything went swimmingly. My nurse stayed just a day before going on holiday so I could make numberless safaris to town ordering what was needed. Now I am alone with the babies until I get floors painted & the room fixed up so I can lure in a mother's help. I just sit beaming, looking at my bare boards, I am so happy. The children are happy, too. They are singing in their little cots like birds, & laughing.

The windows are low enough for them to see out, & even Nick is fascinated by the goings on in the street---the dogs, cats & passing pony carts. It is heaven for me to be among people. To be anonymous, in myself. Last night I wrote out the script of a long broadcast of my new poems for a BBC producer who is very interested in them, & I also have a commission to do a program called "Landscape on Childhood", about how my childhood environment influenced me. The Norway radio wants to translate the program of mine about 3 women in a maternity ward & the critic A. Alvarez, the best here, says he thinks my second book of poems which I have just finished should win a Pulitzer prize! Of course it won't, but it's nice he thinks so. As soon as I get my mother's help, which I hope will be early in the new year, I shall finish my second novel. I shall rent the flat out furnished in summer to, I hope, Americans, & make back much of what I have invested in it. I spent a Sunday stringing my onions & brought them up with a load of my Court Green potatoes, apples, honey & beautiful holly. I am very proud of my garden produce & hope to keep it going summers. Having to close up that big house & open this flat has given me an immense pleasure in businesslike dealings, I feel to have grown up a great deal in the process.

I enclose my review of LORD BYRON'S WIFE, which appeared in the New Statesman[1] & which I thought would amuse you---so much is relevant, even Ted's attachment to his sister who never wanted him to marry & who is, alas, nowhere near as nice as Augusta! It is a big book here & I was lucky to get to review it, it was one of the lead reviews. Do pass it on to mother when you see her!

Now to answer your last good letter[2] & the questions about Ted. I was appalled to hear from my solicitor about what the courts allow a woman here. One-third of her husband's income at most, less if she keeps the house, and if she works it is one-third of their combined incomes, so if I earn 1,000 $ & Ted earns 2 thousand, he need pay nothing! I am penalized for earning. Also, as he is a writer & his income is only what

1–The clipping, with pencil annotations by Prouty, is held by Lilly Library.
2–Probably Olive Higgins Prouty to SP, 27 November 1962; held by Smith College.

he makes it & he can conceal much of it, from odd sources which do not report income, I am 'lucky' to have him agree to a thousand pounds a year, which is I think much more than a court would allow. Whatever his income, I need a constant & regular sum, for my bills are constant. Now he is well-off he wants to keep it all to himself & has actually told me to buy my clothes in the British equivalent of Filene's basement, while his married girlfriend spends on herself alone twice what he allows me for myself & the children a week. Well, I have my lovely Jaeger clothes & I feel like a new woman in them. As soon as I get my mother's help & the flat fixed, I shall have lots of jobs. This woman, who is still dangling her 3rd husband, has brutalized Ted beyond belief---taught him it is "clever" & "sophisticated" to lie & deceive people and so on. Ted can always revenge himself on us for existing by simply refusing to work or to pay us, & then it would take ages to go through court to get anything, as my lawyer says, so I would be silly to put pressure on Ted, it just makes him more beastly. If he gives me the £1,000 I shall work hard to make up the rest myself & be glad to be rid of him. I shall, if the chance arises, see what Ted thinks about making Court Green & the car over in my name. But I have to go gently.

How understanding you are about my needing time! I sometimes think that if I ever get enough time I may write something really worth while! As it is, by writing from 4 am to 8 am I have finished my second book of poems. The New Yorker has just renewed[1] my yearly 'first reading' contract & accepted a lyric called 'Amnesiac'[2] about a man who forgets his wife & children & lives in the river of Lethe. Guess who! I am dedicating this book of poems to Frieda & Nicholas & shall dedicate the 3rd book of poems which I have already begun to my mother. That is why I asked if you would let me dedicate my 2nd novel DOUBLETAKE to you---if you thought it good enough, for I thought mother would like a book of poems best & you as a novelist would like the novel best!

I took both babies to the Zoo this week---Nick slept, but Frieda was absolutely fascinated by the lions and owls, the new baby elephant and the penguins swimming in their "bath". It is such fun to take Frieda about, she remembers & notices everything, it is like have a fresh expanded consciousness. The thing she was most impressed about was that the monkeys "couldn't get out". I thought that a very advanced notion for a

1–See Howard Moss to SP, 7 December 1962; held by New York Public Library.
2–Howard Moss to SP, 30 November 1962; held by New York Public Library. Sylvia Plath, 'Amnesiac', *New Yorker* (3 August 1963): 29.

girl of 2½! Do try to persuade my mother, if you can, that she has nothing to worry about. I have been so crushingly busy with this move I've hardly had time for a cup of tea & now I am settled I shall write every week, but it only adds to my worries to hear she is worried. I am very happy & delighted to be back in my element in London. Hard work never hurt anybody & I think these new responsibilities have made me grow up a lot & certainly given me very rich material for writing!

Best love to you,
Sylvia

TO *Douglas Cleverdon*

Sunday 16 December 1962 TLS, BBC Written Archives Centre

23 Fitzroy Road
London N.W.1
December 16, 1962

Dear Douglas,

Just a little note to say, in case Ted's forgotten to call you about it, that I've used your name as a reference for applying for a priority phone, as I can't get one for months otherwise & need it rather fiercely for my free-lancing. All I guess they'll want, if they contact you, is confirmation that I need a phone right away for journalistic work & that I do & have done programs for the BBC.

I hope this isn't too much of a bother! Very many thanks anyhow.

Sincerely,
(Sylvia Plath)

Douglas Cleverdon, Esq.
Features, The BBC
Broadcasting House
London W.1

TO *Michael Carey*

Sunday 16 December 1962 TLS, Assumption College

23 Fitzroy Road
London N.W.1
Sunday: December 16

Dear Father Michael,

The various blessings have triumphed & the babies & I installed over the Yeats plaque. We moved in by candlelight, as the Electricity Board hadn't bothered to connect it, in spite of my smog-muffled arrangements the previous week, so it was very Dickensian. We will be camping out more or less until I get several acres of ancient floorboards painted by hand, rather a trial as I would, in the evenings, much rather write poems. Do drop by for the cup of tea I couldn't give you in North Tawton anytime you happen to be up around Primrose Hill. It's my very favorite district in London, for when I was reading English on a Fulbright at Cambridge I was first installed in the middle of Regents' Park to be 'initiated'. And we spend a great deal of time at the Zoo!

My answer to the 'what' question is the Troll King's answer out of Peer Gynt---'Myself'.[1] Very much so, thank God. Now you will surely think I am unredeemable, but do go on blessing me nonetheless!

All best Christmas wishes,
Sylvia Plath

TO *Aurelia Schober Plath*

Friday 21 December 1962[2] TLS with envelope in greeting card,[3] Indiana University

Dear mother,

I do hope these pictures[4] convince you of the health & happiness of us three! Susan took them, & for Xmas blew up 4 big ones for me. Frieda & I are having a December picnic in St. Ives, Cornwall![5] I have never

1–Henrik Ibsen, *Peer Gynt* (1867). SP read *Peer Gynt* in November 1955. See SP to ASP, 21 November 1955 (*Letters of Sylvia Plath*, Vol. 1, 1013).

2–Date supplied from postmark.

3–Written on an Arnold Blanch UNICEF Christmas card.

4–The photographs are no longer with the letter.

5–According to SP's Letts Royal Office Diary Tablet for 1962, she visited St Ives on 13 November 1962; there is no evidence to support a visit in December.

been so happy in my life. By some miracle everybody has delivered & done everything for me before Xmas---their usual "after Xmas" excuses melting miraculously away: I have fresh white walls in the lounge, pine bookcases, rush matting which looks very fine with my straw Hong Kong chairs & the little glasstopped table, also straw & black iron,[1] in which I can put flowerpots & currently have a lilac hyacinth. I have found the most fantastic store---Dickens & Jones,[2] which knocks Harrods out the window. I spent the rest of Mrs. P's clothes money & feel & look like a million---got a Florence-Italy blue & white velvet overblouse, a deep brown velvet Italian shirt, black fake-fur toreador pants, a straight black velvet skirt & metallic blue-and-black French top. One or two other outfits made me drool, notably some Irish weave shirts--I love everything Irish, as you may imagine! But I stopped at a Viennese black leather jerkin! I haven't had a new wardrobe for over 7 years & it's done wonders for my morale. You should see me nipping round London in the car! I'm a real Londoner at heart, I love Fitzroy Road & this house above all. A lovely tea with Catherine Frankfort, her husband & 3 boys yesterday. Their new baby is named Nicholas. Got a lovely Scots woman babysitter from the Baby Agency while I went shopping, she had my dinner warm when I returned, & got in my old Doris, who loves the children, so I could see a marvelous new Ingmar Bergman movie[3] that night. Will have Xmas dinner with this lovely Portuguese couple who've been putting me up on my London visits & who've loaned me a bed. Just had two long bee poems accepted by the Atlantic,[4] & have been asked to judge the Cheltenham poetry contest again this year. I am in 7th heaven. Now I am out of Ted's shadow everybody tells me their life story & warms up to me & the babies right away. Life is such fun.

Katherine is finding out about a little nursery school[5] round the corner where I might send Frieda mornings. The weather has been blue &

1–The glass-topped table appeared at auction via Bonhams on 21 March 2018.

2–Dickins & Jones, Regent Street, London.

3–SP saw Ingmar Bergman, *Through a Glass Darkly*, at the Cameo-Polytechnic Cinema, 307 Regent Street, on 20 December 1962.

4–Sylvia Plath, 'The Arrival of the Bee Box' and 'Wintering', *Atlantic Monthly* 211 (April 1963): 70–1. See Peter Davison to SP, 20 November 1962; held by Smith College. See also *Atlantic Monthly* to SP, 4 December 1962; held by Yale University.

5–According to SP's Letts Royal Office Diary Tablet for 1962, this was Dibby's on Regent's Park Road. Most likely in a block of houses called Regent's Park Gardens on Regent's Park Road that were demolished in 1963. Lorna Secker-Walker recalls that, over the course of several years, Dibby's had various addresses in Primrose Hill, including a location on Primrose Hill Road which was also demolished in the 1960s. Nicholas Frankfort recalls attending Dibby's on Princess Street.

springlike & I out every day with the babies. Still have the babies floors to paint, the au pair's floors, the hall floors & 3 unpainted wood bureaus. Blue is my new color, royal, midnight (not aqua!). Ted never liked blue, & I am a really blue-period person now. With lilac & apple green accents. If you ever want to make another hit, send some more kitty balloons! I read a picture book with Frieda every night. My bedroom has yellow,& white wallpaper, straw mat, black floor borders & gold lampshade---bee colors, & the sun rises over an 18th century engraving London each day. I'd like to live in this flat forever. Mrs. P. sent me $100 for Xmas. Sent her the Byron review---do ask to see it.

Lots of love to you, Warren & Maggie,

Sivvy

PS: Tell everyone of my move, hence no cards this year. I've not had a second.

TO *Aurelia Schober Plath*

Wednesday 26 December 1962 TLS (aerogramme), Indiana University

23 Fitzroy Road
London N.W.1
Wednesday: December 26

Dear mother,

I wish you could see me sitting here in my gorgeous front room. Even though the day is grey & white with frost the rooms white walls flood it with light & there is a very strong oriental feeling to it with the Hongkong cane chairs, rush mats & Tokyo & Arabic glasses in lovely clear colors. I do hope you explain my move prevented me from thinking of sending any American Christmas cards this year. I did rush off about 2 dozen over here & hope you will be mollified by some color photos which I am waiting to get from Susan. I am wild for the exquisite Japanese hair ornament Warren & Maggie sent, am wearing it now at the end of a long braid, it just goes with my decor. Dear Dotty sent a $20 bill & I shall treat myself to a green velvet set of Oriental toreador pants & top at that marvelous Dickens & Jones shop in Regent Street right after this Boxing Day holiday. It is amazing how much my new hairdo & new clothes have done for my rather shattered morale. I had a lovely tea with the Frankforts, with the two beautiful blond Secker-Walker children & their parents (they lived two houses down from our Chalcot Square place)

& with Susan's Kentish Town journalist who invited a charming architect & his wife & their little girl, just Nick's age, & some others. Garnett, Winifred's son, dropped by & is coming for dinner Sunday. I plan to throw myself into painting the rest of the upstairs floors & 3 whitewood bureaus this week so I can give myself the treat of applying for an au pair first thing in the new year. I have been resting a bit the last few days. We went for Christmas dinner with a very nice Portuguese couple in Hampstead---they made a goose which they lit with cognac & gave Frieda a tiny toy piano that plays simple songs & Nick a rubber rabbit. I thought the outfits for Nick & Frieda Warren & Maggie sent just lovely, do thank them for me. I have been so preoccupied I have barely had time to cook. Catherine has told me of a little nursery school just round the corner which takes children from 9:30 to 12:30 & I shall try Frieda at it next week. She seems to blossom on outside experiences with other children & I think she needs this. Marty Plumer sent me a marvelous apron & the babies 'Make Way for the Ducklings'.[1] I've not written her or anyone, but shall do as soon as I get my au pair & work started. I am hoping the BBC accepts my 20 minute program of new poetry---the producer thinks they are wonderful, but the Board still has to approve.[2] Then I have the commission for a program on my childhood landscape, or in my case, sea scape. Did I say Mrs. P. sent $100? And bless you for your $50. I have double expenses just now---the closing expenses at North Tawton & the rather large opening ones here, but once I am settled here it will be 5 years blessed security & peace & <u>no more floor painting</u>! Which is a lot to look forward to & in which time I should have produced a lot of work. How lucky I am to have two beautiful babies & work! Both of them have colds, which makes them fussy, but I keep them warmly dressed & they take long naps. Did Maggie knit that gorgeous blue sweater for Frieda? Their color pictures are lovely---Frieda has claimed them. She says of every sweater "Grammy made that."

Frieda loves the little mouse that came in Warren's parcel. She came in holding a rusk in her hands just as the mouse is holding the corn & said 'Like mouse.' She is unique in seeing resemblances to things. Just now I held her up to see a fine snow falling & she said 'Like Tomten book',[3] which is about a little Scandinavian dwarf on a farm in the snow. I took the very favorite picture books to london & we 'read" one each day. I am

1–Robert McCloskey, *Make Way for Ducklings* (1941).

2–See Douglas Cleverdon to SP, 20 December 1962; held by Smith College.

3–Astrid Lindgren and Harald Wiberg, *The Tomten* (London: Constable, 1962); adapted from a poem by Viktor Rydberg.

enjoying just sitting about with the children & making tea & breathing a little. I don't feel to have had a holiday for years! Nick is wonderfully happy & strong. I do notice now that his left eye is slightly turned in, although for the longest time I just couldn't see it, so I am going to my local doctors this week to ask what they think about it.[1]

Well, I hope to drop over to the Frankforts a bit later this evening for a "Boxing Day" supper with them & his mother.[2] Ted is spending the Christmas up in Yorkshire, & I naturally do get a bit homesick for relatives & was grateful to have Christmas dinner out with these friends. Frieda did very much enjoy opening presents, but is much too young to grasp more than that "Santa brought it for Frieda." She is very encouraging about my painting floors, getting up & praising me in her little treble each day 'Good mummy, paint floors all clean for Frieda." She is such a joy to take out & I like having her play with the very charming children in the neighborhood.

It is now snowing very prettily, crisp & dry, like an engraving out of Dickens.

Lots of love to all,
Sylvia

TO *Daniel & Helga Huws*

Wednesday 26 December 1962 TLS, Helga and Daniel Huws

23 Fitzroy Road
London N.W.1
Boxing Day

Dear Danny & Helga,

You have no idea how your two good letters cheered me, & how Frieda loves the little toy village you sent---she keeps pointing to the church & then to a church steeple she can see in the distance & saying "Go in there some day soon." I hope it simply means she may be very spiritually inclined!

By a very wierd combination of luck & hard work I am sitting in an unfurnished flat in Yeats' house (plaque & all!) in Fitzroy Road around the corner from our old place, the babies playing with snuffly Xmas colds, &

1–According to SP's Letts Royal Office Diary Tablet for 1962, she saw Dr Horder on 28 December to discuss 'Nick's eye', 'Sleeping pills', and 'weight'.

2–Art historian Henriette Antonia Groenewegen-Frankfort (1896–1982).

a fine white snow falling on the 18th-century-engraving houses opposite. I have a 5 year lease. It happened like a miracle, Danny, shortly after I saw you---I had been looking at fantastically expensive furnished places & in utter despair decided to walk my dear, old haunts round Primrose Hill. A board advertising flats to let in Yeats' house---which I'd always looked at longingly---was out. I flew in a taxi to the agents & was first to apply for the maisonette on the first & top floor---3 beds, lounge, kit & bath. When I got back to Court Green I told my nurse I'd get a "message" from Yeats, shut my eyes & opened to the quote "Get wine & food to give you strength & courage & I will get the house ready." And you can imagine how hard it was, with my utter lack of references & a steady job! In the end I had to bluster about being an American & offer the year's rent in advance, going quietly into debt for that amount on the side. In the next week I hope to paint the rest of the floors upstairs & lure in an au pair so I can write mornings & try to earn some money. It is the luckiest thing that has happened in a bad very bad year. Oddly enough, out of the blue, all sorts of people have decided I need praying for, or that they want to pray for me---from a Roman Catholic priest-poet at Oxford to an Evangelist from Sweet Home, Oregon, who saw a picture of me at 19 in some magazine or other & has since been sending me Guitar records of spirituals! I just accept the prayers with thanks.

I am so relieved to get out of North Tawton I just sit back & breathe heavily---it seemed so impossible for the last half year, left alone there as I was without help with the babies after I almost died of flu this summer. It was only this darling young nurse home on vacation from a London children's hospital who worked for me about 6 weeks & made me eat etc. who enabled me to come up & scout out a place. I am going to the doctor this week to see if he can help me get off these sleeping pills I've been taking every night & am now addicted to. I think I'll keep on smoking a little while longer, I'm actually alas beginning to like it! You can imagine how the small town gossip went---I actually had to stop going to some shops to escape the leering questions about where my husband was, wasn't it lonely all alone in such a big house, etc. The fouler gossip was that I wasn't married anyway as I got mail under my maiden name!

I am so happy to be back among Frieda's old playmates---most mothers have babies Nick's age now, as she is slowly coming out of the awful regression she went into after Ted's desertion---she was always his little pet. I try to take her out to tea with other children almost every afternoon & hope to start her at a little nursery school here next week, if she likes it. She keeps saying in a delighted treble "Look at all these people." You ask about divorce, Helga---Ted wants one, & since marriage gave him no sense of obligation to the babies it will make no difference what he has. It was inconceivable to me at one point & very hard to come to, as I never believed in it myself, but it is better to be free of him. Your letter moved me very much, Danny---it helped me a lot to hear your feelings of Ted, & I think you are right about him. His guilt alas makes him very hard & cross & hurtful, and you can imagine the public humiliations one has to face, being in the same work & Ted being so famous. But I think he will come round about once a week & take the children to the Zoo. Probably you know the woman he is with is on her third husband & has had so many abortions she can't have children. She is part of this set of barren women, which includes Dido Merwin, that I am so glad to get rid of. I guess I am just not like that. I had a terrible experience calling Dido Merwin as Frieda's godmother when I was in London---as Frieda had been diagnosed as a latent schizophrenic as a result of this, & she was the only person I thought could advise me about doctors & a flat. She knew I was calling on her as a godmother, but because she was so glad she at last had Ted living at her place[1] she made it clear she was home but refused to speak to me.

Both Ted & I have agreed to write off the Merwins as Frieda's godparents & wonder if you would be her godparents instead. I take this as a very serious thing, & it almost killed me for Frieda's sake, to think of the heartlessness & hypocrisy behind Mrs. Merwin's refusal to answer when she knew I was worried about the babies going into hospital. But then, she has always disliked children & devoted her life to herself. I find now that this breakup has occurred I am free of many such people who courted Ted for his fame, & of course it has hurt me deeply that he has more or less sold out to them. But now I am here the desperate mother in me, which is so saddened at losing the children a father, can see Ted as a great poet & wish him his own brand of happiness & that he write well. It is also hard to have undergone, all summer, his new practise in lying which this woman has taught him, as she has enjoyed lying & being faithless to all 3 of her husbands & came into my house & wanted all I had & took it. Ted has always seemed so straight to me, brutal if he wanted, but not lying, so that I can hardly believe he thinks it sophisticated & grownup & crafty. But I guess I'm just simple-minded.

It is heaven to have people to talk to after 6 months of solitary confinement in the country. I hope to rent this place furnished by the week

1–TH lived for a period at Dido Merwin's mother's flat at 17 Montagu Square, London W.1.

to wealthy Americans or something in the summer & return summers to Court Green. Please say you will all come for a visit with me next summer! I miss you very much & would give anything if you would drop by if & whenever you are in London. I have, as you may imagine, more or less ignored Christmas this year, but send my dearest love to you both & the beautiful babies! Do write.

Love,
Sylvia

TO *Ruth Fainlight*

Wednesday 26 December 1962 TLS (aerogramme), Ruth Fainlight

23 Fitzroy Road
London N.W.1
Boxing Day

Dear Ruth,

Your good letter about your flat was waiting for me the night I got back to Court Green after signing the 5 year lease for Yeats' place in the brain-stopping smog, & I am sure it helped me get it. I am now sitting in the first floor lounge with the snuffly babies, who both have Xmas colds, watching a beautiful frosty snow fall on the 18th-century-engraving housefronts opposite & thanking God & Yeats & whoever that I got out of the Devon pig fields before the real cold set in. How I look forward to your return at the end of February! It is my plan to return to Court Green in spring, Aprilish, for the summer & try to let out this place by the week furnished at fabulous rents to American tourists to recoup on the debt I got in by offering sanguinely to pay the year's rent in advance---my last card in overcoming objections to my lack of references, steady job etc. Please plan on coming back to Devon with me! It would be such fun to open the place up in spring there with you, and after my experience alone there this fall & winter, with all the villagers coyly asking where my husband was & wasn't it lonely living all alone in such a big house, etc., with Dartmoor convicts escaping[1] etc., I want lots of company & lots of babies around when I get back! I adore Fitzroy Road & would like by hook or crook to

1–After SP's last letter to Fainlight on 20 November 1962, and her move to London on 10 December, two additional prisoners escaped from HM Prison Dartmoor on 21 December 1962.

write such an obscene or merely good novel that I made some money & could tempt the widow who owns this very house. The Yeats "aura" is very calm & benevolent---everybody looked mesmerized & delivered all my straw mats & Hong Kong furniture before Xmas. I am slowly getting the floors painted, & hope to make one final push & get the upstairs ones & 3 whitewood bureaus done before New Years. Then <u>five guaranteed years</u> of no more floor painting! I've done it every year it seems, usually 7 months pregnant, now not so, & what a relief it will be to stop. I have been out round Regents Park & Primrose Hill each day with the babies, drinking in the old scenery which I love so, & taking the babes to tea with the very charming children who live round & are Frieda's old playmates ---Frieda has regressed terribly after Ted's departure, she was his little pet, & I became very worried, as she had shrieking tantrums and so on & it was difficult not to be furious, as she was obviously trying me, but then she was also so obviously miserable. Now I am going to send her to a little nursery school mornings around the corner, as seeing other children seems to do her a lot of good & bring her out of herself.

I hope to get the au pair's room ready by the New Year & lure in one then so I can try to finish my 2nd novel. My first comes out next month under a psuedonym & I've finished a 2nd book of poems which I'll slowly sell one by one & then try to get printed. Do hurry back & then maybe I can persuade you to go to some movies & plays with me & to get Nick & David wrestling again. Christmas was a bit of a large gap & I very glad to get rid of it & eager to get an au pair & to work, which does all sorts of salutary things for one!

Love to all & very eager for your return!

Sylvia

1963

TO *Aurelia Schober Plath*

Wednesday 2 January 1963 TLS (aerogramme), Indiana University

23 Fitzroy Road
London N.W.1, England
January 2, 1963

Dear mother,

I am so glad you got the pictures safely. I got a nice letter from Marty & am so glad she & Mike plan to come briefly <u>alone</u> early this spring. For goodness sake do tell people I am separated from Ted &, if you feel like it, divorcing him! It is odd to get cards from people like the Aldriches to us <u>both</u>, there's no point in you keeping up any pretence. I see they're expecting a <u>9th</u> baby! Do congratulate Betty for me & send my love. The babies & I have just got over very nasty Xmas colds & are now fine. Probably you have heard we've had fantastic snow here---my first in all my years in England. I heard Devon was completely cut off by 20 foot drifts & they were dropping bread & milk by helicopter![1] Well, I just got out in time! The English, being very English, have of course no snow plows, because this only happens once every five years, or ten. So the streets are great mills of sludge which freezes & melts & freezes. One could cheerfully use a dog sled, & I wish I had a sled for Frieda for they are sledding on Primrose Hill, it looks so pretty! I am trying her at the little nursery school around the corner where Catherine Frankfort sends her boys, 3 hours a morning 5 days a week for just over $4. They drink cocoa & play. Some mornings she is more tearful than others, but she does need to be free of mummy for some time, & I need desperately to have time to work---I put Nick down for a nap which he's ready for by then, having been up & playing & shaking his cot since 6! I have a BBC assignment to do 'live' next Thursday night, reviewing a book of American poems on a

1–For example, see 'More blizzards on the Way', *The Guardian* (2 January 1963): 1.

weekly New Comment program,[1] so my being back is already getting round. It takes months to get a phone here, but once I get all these things done I'll be set for 5 years & one can do a lot in that time! Garnett came for a dinner & a lunch & did help paint the border of one floor in the children's room, which I will make into their playroom when the mother's help comes---the rug for that has come & it is now very cosy up there. I have to finish the floors in the mother's help's room & in the upstairs & downstairs halls, give 3 bureaus 2 coats of paint each, & then I should be able to take a rest---except for sewing some curtains! The car is really snowed up. I don't want to use it until some of this Arctic is thawed.

The wonderful package from Dot & you came the day after Boxing Day which is the holiday the day after Christmas. Much better then! I was astounded at all the toys & beautiful clothes! Nick loves the baby doll which he seems to think is another of his own sort, & chews the little mouse Warren sent as a cat would! All I had to pay was about 60 cents for the package being forwarded from North Tawton. Margaret's package arrived before Xmas & the sweater was lovely---is the hood for Frieda or me! It is very large, I think it must be me! I am so glad Grampy could spend Christmas Day with you, and do give my love to Frank & Louise ---I believe I wrote them thanking them for their $25 cheque but thank them again for me anyway.

It is such a relief to be back with my wonderful and understanding Doctor Horder. He has given me a very good tonic to help me eat more, is checking my weight---I lost about 20 pounds this summer---& has sent me to have a chest xray after hearing of my 103° fevers,[2] so I am in the best of hands. He will tend to the business of Nick's eye as soon has he has got me straightened out. You talk about 'the problems at BU'. What are they? What is your position there and what will it be in the future? Tell me. I want to know these.things. Also, could you give me some idea when Warren & Maggie are coming over? I probably won't go to Court Green till about Mayday this year, as I have had such a fore-shortened stay in London & part of it taken up by much manual labor.

1–Sylvia Plath, review of *Contemporary American Poetry* edited by Donald Hall; *New Comment*, BBC Third Programme (10 January 1963). SP's copy of *Contemporary American Poetry* is held by University of North Carolina at Chapel Hill and includes her autograph and address in black ink on the half-title page with her underlinings and markings throughout the text. A date of '10–1–62' is written in pencil in a different hand above Plath's name. The writer of this date may have mistakenly written '62' rather than '63'.

2–According to SP's Letts Royal Office Diary Tablet for 1962, SP went to University College Hospital for a chest x-ray on 1 January 1963.

Now here is something you could help me on---ask the Nortons etc. I want to send a blurb to the big universities advertising this maisonette to let from roughly May--Sept at about $75 a week and Court Green from Oct---April at about $35 a week (plus some care-taking) for people on sabbatical leave who have families (better no families in London, or only grown children!). I thought this would be a good way of making my rent as having to pay this year in advance has been a large whack. Also, people like places arranged ahead of time, & this is ideal for Parks, the West End, Universities, etc., while Court Green, very convenient to London, would be fine for a professor's family & he finishing a book. I'll make up a blurb & send you it, if you think you could post it at BU and maybe Warren at Harvard. I would take lets for years ahead, too, as I plan to stay here for the school year & be in Devon for the summers. See if the Nortons have any advice! Or customers! Do pass on love to Warren & Maggie & Dot & Joe.

xxx
Sivvy

TO *Marcia B. Stern*

Wednesday 2 January 1963 TLS (aerogramme), Smith College

23 Fitzroy Road
London N.W.1
January 2, 1963

Dearest Marty,

I have been wanting & wanting & <u>wanting</u> to write you & have been so snowed by circumstance, outrageous fortune[1] & the lot that I haven't had time to <u>sit</u> much less send one Xmas card this year! What has happened has been that Ted's suddenly decided he doesn't want any children, home, responsibility etc. & left me with the lot, after I almost died of flu this summer at Court Green. So I was alone on the small farm, too weak to even hold the baby & utterly incommunicado for some time. Then my wonderful Devon midwife got a lovely 22-year-old children's nurse who was on holiday to come work as a mother's help for 7 weeks (<u>no</u> au pair or mother's help from any agency would come or stay with

1–A reference to Hamlet's famous speech in Act III, Scene I of *Hamlet*. Underlined in SP's copy of *The Complete Plays and Poems of William Shakespeare* (Boston: Houghton Mifflin, 1942); held by Smith College.

me, as it's deep country with no TV etc. etc. & fine in spring & summer but primeval in fall & winter). I flogged myself up to London every other week, doing odd jobs on the BBC etc. & facing all the uproar that occurs when somebody as famous as Ted starts acting scandalous---especially hard as in our work we meet all the same people. At first I had thought of burying myself & the babies in Western Ireland for the winter---where I had discovered a wonderful town on the sea with an Irish poet sailing the old Galway Hookers & cooking on turf, drinking John Jameson whisky & bog water & milking cows, to avoid the inevitable small town gossip in Devon & just get the hell away from it all. But then a small miracle happened---I'd been to Yeats' tower at Ballylea while in Ireland & thought it the most beautiful & peaceful place in the world; then, walking desolately round my beloved Primrose Hill in London & brooding on the hopelessness of ever finding a flat single-handed, furnished ones being outrageously priced & unfurnished just beyond my strength, I passed Yeats' house, with its blue plaque "Yeats lived here" which I'd often passed & longed to live in. A signboard was up---flats to let. I flew to the agent. By a miracle you can only know if you've ever tried to flat-hunt in London, I was first to apply, & got rid of all the stickiness about my not having a job, references etc. by saying poo I was an American & would they like the year's rent in advance, & going quietly into debt on the side. Well, I am here on a 5-year lease & it is utter heaven. I have to be in London to get a live-in mother's help, which I desperately need, jobs on the BBC & reviewing etc. & good free schooling for the children. I shall try to rent this place furnished to well-heeled Americans for about 5 months in the summer---they go at about $75 a week, and try to rent my gorgeous country house with Bendix et. al. in fall & winter, at much less. Maybe you could give me some advice about this---I thought I'd send blurbs to Smith, Harvard, etc., for it's ideal for sabbatical year people, finishing books or with families. This flat is on two floors on a road off Primrose Hill, the Zoo & Regents Park (with playgrounds, etc.) with 3 bedrooms, a big handsome lounge, kitchen (where I eat at a counter on bar-stools) & even has a little balcony I hope to sit out on with you in spring! And Its Yeats' house, which right now means a lot to me. I guess you can imagine what it's like coping with two infants, free lance jobs, painting & decorating acres of floors & haunting sales for curtaining etc. Toute seule!

I am, thank God, on the panel of my old, free, wonderful doctors, who have been sending me for chest xrays (I lost 20 lbs. this summer, which I can ill afford & had these 103° fevers) & giving me tonics to make me eat, pills to sleep etc. The last 6 months have been a unique hell, but that's finished & I am fine now. Very glad to be rid of all the bitches & bastards that dog social lions. Oddly enough, all the phonies came loose with Ted & everybody I know now is normal & nice. I think your idea of coming alone with Mike is wonderful---I have bęen so utterly flattened by having to be a businesswoman, farmer---harvesting 70 apple trees, stringing all my onions, digging & scrubbing all my potatoes, extracting & bottling my honey etc.---mother, writer & all-round desperado that I'd give anything for a brief week in which somebody, some dear friends, went places, ate, talked, with just me. How I understand & sympathize with your visit to your father! I feel like a very efficient tool or weapon, used & in demand from moment to moment by the babes. And Ted's clearing off after 6 years of utter scrimp with all the money, living on brandy & not a worry in the world, as soon as real fame & money pour in, is enough to cure anyone of self-sacrifice. His manuscripts sell for over $100 for a couple of handwritten pages. Since he's never paid a bill or figured inc. tax or mowed the lawn etc. he's no notion of what it takes & if I'm lucky we'll get about $2,800 a year. I'm in the process of a divorce suit now & will be very glad when that's finished---I somehow never imagined myself as the sort! I hope to be finished with painting floors & sewing curtains etc. in a week & then lure in one of these foreign students to mind the babes mornings so I can write. Nights are no good, I'm so flat by then that all I can cope with is music & brandy & water! I am thrilled you'll come in March or early April. Then we can go to plays, on park walks etc. here. I'd love you to see Court Green too, but am not sure when I'll get back – around Mayday. Do write!

Love,

Syl

<on page 1 of letter>

PS: A thousand thanks for the lovely Xmas parcel! I have read & read the Duck Book to F & worn the apron (veddy English & very me!) every minute since I got it---instead of the ghastly old rags I'd been wrapping round!

TO *Olive Higgins Prouty*

Wednesday 2 January 1963 TLS (aerogramme), Indiana University

23 Fitzroy Road
London N.W.1, England
January 2, 1963

Dear Mrs. Prouty,

At last I find myself with a moment to sit down with a cup of coffee & wish you a Happy New Year and thank you for the lovely Christmas card, which reminded me so of my beloved Boston Common under snow, and the generous enclosure! I am absolutely in love with my flat & quite amazed when I look round after having been here only a little over 3 weeks, to see what I have done single-handed! I have painted all the floors (2 coats!) except the halls & stair & laid down rush matting---very cheap & beautifully Oriental looking. My colors in the lounge are midnight blue, apple green & lilac, a refreshing change from my scheme at Court Green & I have some little handblown Arabic glasses I love, to carry it out, & plan to get bit by bit second hand pieces of pleasing lines & lacquer them in black & handpaint designs on some. I am trying Frieda at a little nursery school for 3 hours in the morning, which will give me a bit of time to work until I finish sewing all the curtains for the mother's help room, paint her bureau & go to the agency to find a good one! Then I should really be able to work. What I hope to do is rent this charming place out furnished by the week from about May 1 through September to visiting Americans---I shall send notices to the various universities, as it is ideal for a sabbatical year, & rent my lovely Court Green in fall & winter at much less if I can find someone! I do hope I can thus make a business proposition out of it!

Already I find my being in London is getting round---I have a job on the BBC this next week to broadcast "live" my opinions on an Anthology of American poetry on a weekly New Comment program so have to study these next evenings instead of painting bureaus! If I am lucky in getting a mother's help I should be able to finish my novel this winter and try my hand at a few short stories. The BBC is considering a 20 minute broadcast of my new poems with comment & explanation & I do hope they take it. I have also to do this program about the influence of my childhood landscape which I look very forward to. I am enjoying living off my own potatoes, hand-strung onions, apples & honey & the doctor's wife's strawberry jam! The midwife's son who is a policeman in London stopped by for dinner this week & to help me paint one floor.

We have had the first real snowfall I've seen in all my years in England! The street looks like a frosty 18th century engraving. Of course the English, being English, have no snowplows, so to get from shop to shop one climbs mountains of sludge. The children & I have all had flu over Christmas, it has been very cold, but I am back with my old, wonderful doctors, & he is giving me tonic to help me eat more & gain back the 20 lbs. I lost this summer & sending me for chest xrays, so I am in fine hands & glad to be away from the Devon doctor who improperly bandaged my badly cut thumb last month so it went septic & was unnecessarily deformed! Luckily this London doctor helped save the top, though I did lose the side. It is so beautiful here, & I so love living in Yeats' house. Do write soon! Did I say I had two long bee-keeping poems taken by the Atlantic Monthly?

Love,
Sylvia

TO *George MacBeth*

c. Fri.–Tues. 4–8 January 1963[1] TLS, BBC Written Archives Centre

23 Fitzroy Road
London N.W.1

Dear George,

Sorry this is late, but I've been down with the flu & so have the children. If there's any ghastly message or changes or such maybe you could call Ted & he could get a message to me before Thursday night when I'll see you at the BBC at 7. I won't be getting a phone for a couple of weeks yet & the md's put me pretty much incommunicado.

Best wishes,
Sylvia

1–Date supplied from internal evidence.

TO *Charles Osborne*

Wednesday 9 January 1963 TLS, University of Texas at Austin

23 Fitzroy Road
London N.W.1
January 9, 1963

Dear Charles,

Here is the cheque back, with some more poems.[1] I am at present writing by candlelight with cold fingers, a sinister return to Dickensian conditions thanks to the Electricity Board, from Yeats' house off Primrose Hill where I've just moved into a flat with the two babies. If you are not a childphobe & ever happen to be in the district, I'd be happy to have you drop round for a cup of coffee or tea.

All good wishes,
Sylvia Plath

PS 'Berck-Plage' has been read on the 3rd Programme but not published

TO *Gilbert & Marian Foster*

Wednesday 9 January 1963 TLS, Private owner

23 Fitzroy Road
London N.W.1
January 9: Wednesday

Dear Gilbert & Marion,

Happy New Year to you. I am just crawling to consciousness after 10 days of influenza which the babies had too, all of us flat out with a day-nurse through this ghastly weather. I hope you are all right & that Court Green has not collapsed under a great weight of snow.

Nurse D. tells me the town opinion is that I should give Nancy the opportunity to 'look after' the place since she's done it for 11 years etc.

1 – According to SP's submissions list, she sent 'An Appearance', 'The Bee Meeting', 'Years', 'The Fearful', 'Mary's Song', 'Stings', 'Letter in November', 'The Couriers', 'The Night Dances', 'Gulliver', 'Cut', and 'Berck-Plage' on 17 January 1963. She annotated the list on 25 January indicating that nine poems were accepted. See Charles Osborne, undated (*c.* 24 January 1963); held by Smith College. Sylvia Plath, 'The Bee Meeting', 'Stings', 'Cut', 'Letter in November', 'The Couriers', 'Mary's Song', and 'Years', *London Magazine* 3 (April 1963): 24–32; 'Berck-Plage', *London Magazine* (June 1963): 26–31. Although SP underlined 'An Appearance' on her submission list – her usual practice in recording acceptances – it was not published in the *London Magazine*.

& so since I do want her back very much as house-help next spring I'm writing in the same mail to her to say if she feels strong enough (she had been ill), would she get the key from you, keep an eye on it & take over the feeding of the cats. I rely on Nurse D. to keep me informed of the general cess-drift of town furies. Did I tell you there's a big potato 'pie' in the back garden, to the right as you enter the gate at the end of the court? You are welcome to this, & if they are not rotted (Ted packed it), could you sometime send me up a bag? I've got plenty of apples & onions but we've been living on potatoes. Let me know if Nancy takes up her option to do the cats---if she does maybe you could give her the remnants of that cheque, if any? How are they? And you & our Friend & Rector! Do write.[1]

Fondest good wishes,
Sylvia

TO *Paul & Clarissa Roche*

c. Wednesday 9 January 1963[2]   TLS, Smith College

23 Fitzroy Road
London NW1
Wednesday

Dear, dear Paul & Clarissa,

I am writing you from bed where the doctor has put me to say how wonderful it was to see you & the beautiful children that day.[3] I shall never forget the dear tea you left me with – I really thought I was dying & began having blackouts that night while the two babies later ran scalding fevers. My very wise and kind doctor got me a private day-nurse for 10 days or I don't know what I would have done. Your wonderful perceptive letter about the novel[4] –you are the first to read it – came at a most needed moment & I think you see just what I meant it to be. One day when there is a good enough one it shall be dedicated to you both. I am slowly getting able to breathe & see & hope a darling little 18 year old 'au pair'

1–A note on the letter indicates a response was sent on Friday 11 January 1963.

2–Date supplied from internal evidence.

3–According to SP's Letts Royal Office Diary Tablet for 1962, the Roches visited on Thursday 3 January 1963 at 1 o'clock.

4–According to an unpublished work by Clarissa Roche, Plath lent her the proofs of *The Bell Jar* to read with a promise to send a signed volume when she received her author's copies.

I interviewed while more or less in a coma may move in at the end of next week, if she wasn't too frightened by the hospital atmosphere!

Much love to all,
Sylvia

TO *Aurelia Schober Plath*

Wednesday 16 January 1963 — TLS (aerogramme), Indiana University

23 Fitzroy Road
London N.W.1, England
Wednesday: January 16

Dear mother,

Thanks very much for your letter & the cheque. I am slowly pulling out of the flu, but the weakness & tiredness following it makes me cross. I had a day nurse for a week when I was worst & the children had high fevers (little Frieda got a ghastly rash which turned out to be an allergy to penicillin which she can't have) but then she got a cold & went home, just as well, for she used up that $50 cheque, they are very expensive! The children are themselves again, thank goodness. I took Frieda to nursery school again yesterday & she seemed to really enjoy it, the mistress said she was much more at home. Catherine Frankfort has been so sweet, coming round with her boys & doing some shopping for me. The weather has been filthy, with all the heaped snow freezing so the roads are narrow ruts & I have been very gloomy with the long wait for a phone which I hope to get by the end of the month after 2 months wait! which makes one feel cut off, and the lack as yet of an "au pair". I did interview a very nice German girl of 18 from Berlin whom I wanted & engaged, but her employer is making difficulties for her leaving & I hope to goodness I hear this week that she is coming. Then I should feel cheered to cook a bit more---I've been so weak I've just wanted boiled eggs & chicken broth. I did get out for a small BBC job the other night, very pleasant, reviewing a book of American poetry & entertained with drinks & sandwiches, & I have a commission for a funny article[1] which I just haven't had time or energy to think of. I still need to sew the bedroom curtains, have some

1–SP probably completed '"America! America!"' by *c.* 21–2 January 1963; see Bernard Hollowood to SP, 23 January 1963, accepting the piece; held by Smith College. Sylvia Plath, '"America! America!"', *Punch* 244 (3 April 1963): 482–4.

made for the big front room windows & get a stair carpet & oddments ---it is so hard to get out to shop with the babies, but I've decided to use the agency babyminders who are very good though expensive for a few nights out this week---a very sweet couple have invited me to dinner tomorrow & me & the babies to dinner Sunday & I think I may go to a play with this Portuguese girl. I just haven't felt to have any identity under the steamroller of decisions & responsibilities of this last half year, with the babies a constant demand. Once I have an au pair, the flat finished--- after all, it is furnishing for at least 5 years done, and should always be my "London furniture", so it is an investment---and a phone & routine I should be better I think. Ted comes about once a week to see Frieda & sometimes is nice & sometimes awful. It is very hard for me to think of him living in an expensive flat,[1] being wined & dined, taking his girlfriend to Spain without a care in the world when I have worked so hard all these years & looked so forward to what I saw was to be our good fortune. But I get strength from hearing about other people having similar problems & hope I can earn enough by writing to pay about half the expenses. It is the starting from scratch that is so hard---this first year. And then if I keep thinking, if only I could have some windfall, like doing a really successful novel & buy this house, this ghastly vision of rent bleeding away year after year would vanish, I could almost be self-supporting with rent from the other two flats---that is my dream. How I would like to be self-supporting on my writing! But I need time.

I guess I just need somebody to cheer me up by saying I've done all right so far. Ironically there have been electric strikes & every so often all the lights & heaters go out for hours, children freeze, dinners are stopped, there are mad rushes for candles. Sue & her sweet boyfriend Corin took me out to a movie the other night, & I realized what I have missed most, apart from peace to write, is company---doing things with other people. Thank goodness I got out of Devon in time, I would have been buried for ever under this record 20 foot snowfall with no way to dig myself out. Nancy is feeding the cats, I sent her a $15 check. I hope to be able to rent this place furnished from about Mayday through September & go to Court Green then. I was very lucky in calling the Home Help Service[2] which sends out cleaners to sick or old people & got a wonderful vigorous

1–According to SP's address book, TH had a flat at 110 Cleveland Street, London W.1.
2–London County Council, Home Help Department, St Pancras Town Hall (now Camden Town Hall), Euston Road, London N.W.1.

woman, named Mrs. Vigors (!)[1] who works at about twice Nancy's pace & had the place gleaming in about 2 hours. I got a terrific lift from it & hope I can persuade her to come to me on her own Saturdays after I no longer qualify as a person in need. It is very hard to get good cleaners here & she has two young girls & is very good with the babies.

Do give my best love to Dot & Joe and Warren & Margaret & I hope to write in a week or so saying I have got this au pair---she left some of her stuff & seemed a very nice cheerful girl whom the children liked.

Love to all,
Sivvy

TO *Leonie Cohn*

Tuesday 22 January 1963 TLS, BBC Written Archives Centre

23 Fitzroy Road
London N.W.1
January 22, 1963

Miss Leonie Cohn
Talks Department
THE BRITISH BROADCASTING CORP.
Broadcasting House
London W.1

Dear Miss Cohn,

Thanks very much for your extremely helpful letter of January 17th.[2] It does give me a much clearer idea of what you want and I think 20 minutes would be fine, with incidents. I have been slowed up a bit by a move from the country to London and nursing my two infants through the flu, but hope to have the script to you in a week or two.

Yours sincerely,
Sylvia Plath

1–Possibly Mrs Catherine Vigors (1933–99), 31 Cathcart Street, London N.W.5; SP's address book lists 'Mrs. C. Vigors, Kentish Town'.
2–Leonie Cohn to SP, 17 January 1963; held by BBC Written Archives Centre.

TO *Olive Higgins Prouty*

Tuesday 22 January 1963 TLS (aerogramme), Indiana University

January 22, 1963

Dear Mrs. Prouty,

How good to get your letters! They are like soul letters to me. I have not answered sooner for since Christmas the babies and I have been very ill with high fevers & flu and had to have a day nurse. And as you have no doubt heard, the weather has been fierce. It is a miracle I got out of Devon in time---it is buried under mountains of snow. In London they have no snow-removal equipment, so one climbs treacherous mountains to shop, & it is months before they let you have a phone. I am still waiting. My doctor here---my old doctor---has been a source of great help to me (I am still on sleeping pills & tonics to help me eat), but I do occasionally miss that wonderful Doctor Ruth Beuscher I had at McLean's who I feel could help me so much now. She did write me a letter or two, very helpful, but it's not the same as those hours of talk. I have, miraculously, an 18-year-old German girl I am trying to train, living in as of this week.[1] In return for food, a room & about $5 a week she will take care of the children for 6 mornings and babysit an occasional evening. I have not been alone with myself for over two months, when I had my dear young nurse in Devon, and this has been the keenest torture, this lack of a centre, a quietness, to brood in and grow from. I suppose, to the writer, it is like communing with God.

I am hoping now to get back into shape with this article for the BBC on my childhood landscape---the literal seascape, with incidents and perhaps a story or two, then the novel I have not dared to touch, as you say, until I saw ahead I could sit to it <u>every</u> morning and fear no interruption. You were so wise to advise me to wait till I could have some more hours <u>daily</u> without break.

I think when my health comes back a bit more strongly, I shall paint the remaining floors and bureaus and fight spartanly with words all morning, being wholly a mother in the afternoon with my two darlings, taking them to tea and the park. Frieda makes me so sad. Ted comes once a week to see her, she hangs on him dotingly, then cries "Daddy come soon" for the rest of the week, waking in the night, tearful and obsessed with him.

1–The au pair was hired from the Anglo Continental Bureau, then at 148 Walton Street, London S.W.3. SP sent a cheque for £5. 6. 0 on 22 January 1963.

It is like a kind of mirror, utterly innocent, to my own sense of loss. Ted is, for the time, allowing me $280 a month which pays for food, gas, light and taxes in Devon, but not the rent or furnishings for the flat. I spent all I had to put down on the year's rent in advance, which I had to do to get it, & hope to get it furnished nicely enough to rent it this summer when I go back to Devon. How often I feel the need of business advice, now I have all this on my shoulders! I was just feeling, after 6 years of spartan work & living, that our lives were moving into a wider phase of ease, Ted was getting so successful & I loved my mornings at my desk, which helped, my home, my babies. Now this awful woman who is still deceiving her 3rd husband & has abortion instead of babies is dangling him, it is all very public & I face this, and he lives in an expensive flat in Soho, showers everything on her, takes her on flights to Spanish holidays & so on. I think my salvation will be to plunge into my work---I simply can't afford to think whether is is any good or <u>will be</u> good—that is a luxury. I must just write.

The rent is my one worry---five years of rent would be a deposit on the house, and at the end of 5 years I will have nothing. So I dream of writing a novel that could earn me the right to go down to Surrey & make the owner an offer for the house---I could just about live off the income from the bottom two flats & would not have this awful sense of hurling blood-money into an abyss. The schools in London are good, the jobs are here, the mother's helps are here: Devon is blessed in the summers and holidays and wonderful for the children. I must just resolutely write mornings for the next years, through cyclones, water freezeups, children's illnesses & the <u>aloneness</u>. Having been so deeply and spiritually and physically happy with my dear, beautiful husband makes this harder than if I had never known love at all. Now he is famous, beautiful, the whole world wants him and now has him. He has changed so that the old life is impossible---I could never live under the same roof with him again, but I hope for the children's sake that each week he visits I can be brave and merry, without sorrow or accusation, and forge my life anew. My Xrays, thank goodness, are clear. I hardly glimpse my young children's nurse at all, now she is back at work, but went to a movie with her last week. Ted has---together with the dear, kind man you & I both saw & knew---some of the inhumanity of the true genius that must kill to get what it wants. Now he has utter freedom, to live, adored & the center of gossiping women who collect social lions, to have affairs, holidays. It is hard, his casting off me and the children at this moment and after all these years of love & work, but I desperately want to make an inner strength in myself, an independence that can face bringing up the children alone & in face of great uncertainties. Do write me again! Your letters are like balm, you understand the writer in me, & that is where I must live.

With love,
Sylvia

TO *Leonie Cohn*

Monday 28 January 1963 TLS, BBC Written Archives Centre

23 Fitzroy Road
London N.W.1
January 28, 1963

Miss Leonie Cohn
Talks Department
THE BBC
Broadcasting House
London W.1

Dear Miss Cohn,

Here, as I promised, is the script for my talk on the landscape of childhood. I hope it is the proper size; do let me know[1] if you think it is all right.

Yours sincerely,
Sylvia Plath

1–See Sheila Grant to SP, 31 January 1963; held by BBC Written Archives Centre; and Leonie Cohn to SP, 8 February 1963; held by BBC Written Archives Centre and Smith College. The letter at Smith College, which is the one received by SP, includes a handwritten postscript lacking from that held by BBC Written Archives Centre.

TO *Aurelia Schober Plath*

Monday 4 February 1963 TLS[1] (aerogramme), Indiana University

23 Fitzroy Road
London N.W.1
February 4, 1963

Dear mother,

Thanks so much for your letters. I got a sweet letter from Dotty & a lovely hood & mittens for Nick from Warren & Margaret. I just haven't written anybody because I have been feeling a bit grim---the upheaval over, I am seeing the finality of it all, and being catapulted from the cowlike happiness of maternity into loneliness & grim problems is no fun. I got a sweet letter from the Nortons[2] & an absolutely wonderful understanding one from Betty Aldrich. Marty Plumer is coming over at the end of March which should be cheering. Mrs. Prouty has sent another check & dear letter.[3] I have absolutely no desire ever to return to America. Not now, anyway. I have my beautiful country house, the car, and London is the one city of the world I'd like to live in---with its fine doctors, nice neighbors, parks & theaters & the BBC. There is nothing like the BBC in America---over there they do not publish my stuff as they do here, my poems & novel. I have done a commissioned article for Punch on my schooldays & have a chance for 3 weeks in May to be on the BBC Critics program[4] at about $150 a week, a fantastic break I hope I can make good on. Each critic sees the same play, art show, book, radio broadcast each week & discusses it. I am hoping it will finish furnishing this place & I can go to Court Green right after. As Marty for a copy of the details of the two places & the rent & maybe you could circulate them among your professor friends, too.

1–The bottom-right corner of this one-page letter has been torn off. The text appearing in < > in the last paragraph is from *Letters Home*. When the letter was transcribed *c.* 1974 it was intact, and at some point between then and 2013, when the letter was transcribed for this book, it was intentionally damaged, removing SP's signature.

2–The letter does not apparently survive. Probably prompted from the 19 January 1963 letter from Patricia Ehle Goodall (1929–2009) to the Nortons excerpted in *Letters Home*. SP hosted Goodall and her husband John Latimer Goodall (1929–2010) and their daughter Susan Goodall that day. SP went to dinner at the Goodalls' residence at 189 Sussex Gardens, London W.2, on Friday 8 February 1963. Goodall was a cousin of Perry Norton's first wife Shirley Baldwin Norton.

3–Olive Higgins Prouty to SP, 25 January 1963; held by Smith College.

4–See Philip French to SP, 21 January and 1 February 1963; held by BBC Written Archives Centre.

I appreciate your desire to see Frieda, but if you can imagine the emotional upset she has been through in losing her father & moving, you will see what an incredible idea it is to take her away by jet to America! I am her one security & to uproot her would be thoughtless & cruel, however sweetly you treated her at the other end. I could never afford to live in America---I get the best of doctor's care here perfectly free & with children this is a great blessing. Also, Ted sees the children once a week & this makes him more responsible about our allowance. I have no desire ever to live in Wellesley, it always stifled me, & I think living with relatives is a very bad policy. I shall simply have to fight it out on my own over here. Maybe someday I can manage holidays in Europe with the children & so on. The children need me most right now & so I shall try to go on for the next few years writing mornings, being with them afternoons & seeing friends or studying & reading evenings.

My German au pair is food-fussy & boy-gaga, but I am d<oing my> best to discipline her, she does give me some peace mor<nings & a few> free evenings, but I'll have to think up something new <for the country> as these girls don't want to be so long away from Lond<on. I am going to> start seeing a woman doctor free on the National Hea<lth, to whom I've> been referred by my very good local doctor which sh<ould help me> weather this difficult time. Give my love to all.

<Sivvy>

TO *Marcia B. Stern*

Monday 4 February 1963 TLS (aerogramme), Smith College

23 Fitzroy Road
London N.W.1
February 4, 1963

Dearest marty,

Your letter was like a shot of brandy or a shot in the arm, I'm not sure which, but wonderful. You are so blessedly understanding about everything, flu included. Everything has blown & bubbled & warped & split---accentuated by the light & heat suddenly going off for hours at unannounced intervals, frozen pipes, people getting drinking water in buckets & such stuff---that I am in a limbo between the old world & the very uncertain & rather grim new.[1] The best news of all is you & Mike

1 – Cf. Sylvia Plath, 'Snow Blitz'.

coming. It is the nicest thing I've had to look forward to for an age---being cut off from my dearest friends & relatives has been very hard, but how wonderful that you will come! I long to have somebody really play with & love the babies---it is still a fantastic shock to me that they are so beautiful & dear & will have, in effect, no father. Ted comes once a week like a kind of a apocalyptic Santa Claus & when I'm in the country I guess half years & years will go by without him seeing them at all. Otherwise, he lives just for himself without a care in the world in a Soho flat, flying to Spain on holiday & so on & universally adored. You have no notion how famous he is over here now. I fought my way back to London as fast as I could because I wanted to face all the publicity & get it over with, as everybody I work for free-lance also employs Ted, & I have to start making a life of my own, having been catapulted out of the cow-like bliss of nursing Nick & maternity. Thank God it is a wellfare state & I can get free doctoring. How I wish you could see my beautiful country house. Maybe somehow, if no one is renting it this spring, we could all drive down.

Do stay closer than Kensington! I've heard friends recommend the Ivanhoe Hotel, Bloomsbury Street WC1 as very pleasant & central, & it's right on the bus route here. How about that?

Your being my agent for the house & flat would be the most wonderful thing you could do, Marty. I was getting very depressed about the responsibility of this, America seemed so far away. This year, the London flat would be available from about May 20th (earlier next year) into October. Here's info: 2 floor maisonette in Yeats' house with 3 bedrooms, kitchen-dinette, bath, lounge & balcony just off Primrose Hill, Regents Park & the Zoo & minutes by tube & bus from the West End. Electric heaters, furnished, hot water electrically heated. Fridge. $60 per week plus light, phone, heat, gas. (Do you think this is okay for price---it's a high class district). Minutes from launderette & all shops.

COURT GREEN: $30 a week, plus expenses of fuel, phone etc. Beautiful big thatched Devon country house with 2½ acres of garden & flowering trees: October to April (exact dates to be arranged). Three beds, study, bath, kitchen, dining kitchen, big sunny lino-tiled playroom, living room, Bendix, big fridge, Wilton carpets, electric immersion hot water heater, choice of wood, coal or electric fires. 4 hours express to Waterloo. English country town 20 mile from Exeter.

It would be wonderful if anybody wanted to work a whole year's exchange, but a long let of either place would be wonderful, too. I should think the Yeats place would appeal to English professors on sabbatical!

I would love to go out to supper with you both & to a few movies or plays. I have been very lax about cooking & eating while alone in Devon & the problem of getting somebody to live in & help with the babes mornings so I can write & to be company for me & free me a few evenings is a big one. I now have a rather boycrazy & food-fussy german au pair whom I have to lecture to about maternal responsibility---it is pretty easy to get these in London, but none of them will go to the country for 5 months as far as I can see & it is there I most need someone. I am turning over the possibility of an older mother's help-housekeeper sort of person, although I do find young girls more cheering.

How I do look forward to seeing you both & how very much I do need a spring tonic! I am dying to see what you think of my little Frieda & Nick.

Lots of love,
Syl.

TO *Michael Carey*

Monday 4 February 1963 TLS,[1] Assumption College

23 Fitzroy Road
London N.W.1
February 4, 1963

Dear Father Michael,

Please don't worry about critiques or harshness,[2] I enjoy both. I've been silenced by everybody's having flu & fevers & am just now creeping enough out of my post-flu coma to start to cope with sewing curtains & writing dawn poems,[3] and minding babies.

I don't think any good poet wishes to be obscure. I certainly don't; I write, at the present, in blood, or at least with it. Any difficulty arises from compression, or the jaggedness of images thrusting up from one psychic ground root.

1–Written in the bottom left corner, presumably in Carey's hand, is: 'She died Feb. 11, 1963 R.I.P.'

2–See Michael Carey to SP, 28 January 1963; held by Smith College.

3–Since writing to Dorothy Benotti on 14 December, SP had revised 'Sheep in Fog' and completed 'The Munich Mannequins', 'Totem', and 'Child' (28 January); 'Paralytic' and 'Gigolo' (29 January); 'Mystic', 'Kindness', and 'Words' (1 February); and 'Contusion' (4 February). SP wrote 'Edge' and 'Balloons' the following day (5 February). In addition to '"America! America!"', by 28 January SP had also completed two prose works: 'Landscape of Childhood' ['Ocean 1212-W'] and 'Snow Blitz'.

How about Yeats for the lyrical?

All best wishes,
Sylvia

TO *Ruth Tiffany Barnhouse Beuscher*

Monday 4 February 1963[1] TLS (aerogramme), Smith College

23 Fitzroy Road
London N.W.1
February 4, 1963

Dear Dr. Beuscher,

I write from London where I have found a flat & an au pair and can see ahead financially for about a year. I thought I'd get an unfurnished flat, furnish it by poems & loans, & rent it out summers to tourists while I went back to Devon, to earn most of the rent for it & Ted says he'll try to pay us about $280 a month while I try to make up the rest by writing. I have finally read the Fromm & think that I have been guilty of what he calls 'Idolatrous love',[2] that I lost myself in Ted instead of finding myself, and this was why deeply underneath the marvelous loving, the writing, the babies I feared his loss, his leaving me & depended on him more & more, making him both idol & father. There was enough identity left to me in Devon to make me feel immense relief at his departure & at the prospect of divorce---now I shall grow out of his shadow, I thought, I shall be me. While we were married we were never apart & all experience filtered through each other. On a grownup level, I don't think I could have endured a marriage of infidelities. I had a beautiful, virile, brilliant man & he still is, whatever immaturities there may be in his throwing over everything in such a violent way. He has said he is sorry for the lying, and shows concern that we get on on our own.

What appals me is the return of my madness, my paralysis, my fear & vision of the worst---cowardly withdrawal, a mental hospital, lobotomies. Perhaps this is accentuated by my seeing Ted once a week when he comes to see Frieda---seeing how happy & whole & independent he is now, how

1–The sender's name and address is left blank on this aerogramme and the postmark reads: 'LONDON N.W.1 / 12[45] PM / 8 FEB / 1963'.

2–Fromm writes on 'idolatrous love' in *The Art of Loving*, 99–100. On idolatrous love, which SP underlined and starred in her copy, Fromm states: 'If a person has not reached the level where he has a sense of identity, of I-ness . . . he deprives himself of all sense of strength, loses himself in the loved one instead of finding himself' (99).

much more I admire him like this, & what good friends we could be if I could manage to grow up too. He is gaga over this ad-agency girl who has gone back to live with her 3rd husband to keep the passion hot, although she did live for 3 weeks with Ted & flew to Spain for a holiday with him. If I were simply jealous about this it would be okay. But I know Spain and lovemaking would do me no good now, not until I find myself again. I feel I need a ritual for survival from day to day until I begin to grow out of this death & found Fromm's recommendation for concentration, patience & faith gave me a kind of peace,[1] but that I keep slipping into this pit of panic & deepfreeze, with my mother's horrible example of fearful anxiety & "unselfishness" on one side & the beauties of my two little children on the other. I am living on sleeping pills & nerve tonic & have managed a few commissions for a magazine & the BBC and poems very good but, I feel written on the edge of madness. The publicity of Ted's leaving is universal & I was taking it all with dignity & verve at first---people were buying poems & putting BBC work in my way, & I am scared to death I shall just pull up the psychic shroud & give up. A poet, a writer, I am I think very narcissistic & the despair at being 30 & having let myself slide, studied nothing for years, having mastered no body of objective knowledge is on me like a cold, accusing wind. Just now it is torture to me to dress, plan meals, put one foot in front of the other. Ironically my novel about my first breakdown is getting rave reviews over here.[2] I feel a simple act of will would make the world steady & solidify. No-one can save me but myself, but I need help & my doctor is referring me to a woman psychiatrist. Living on my wits, my writing---even partially, is very hard at this time, it is so subjective & dependent on objectivity. I am, for the first time since my marriage, relating to people without Ted, but my own lack of center, of mature identity, is a great torment. I am aware of a cowardice in myself, a wanting to give up. If I could study, read, enjoy people on my own Ted's leaving would be hard, but manageable. But there is this damned, self-induced freeze. I am suddenly in agony, desperate, thinking Yes, let him take over the house, the children, let me just die & be done with it. How can I get out of this ghastly defeatist cycle

1–See Fromm, *The Art of Loving*, chapter IV, 'The Practice of Love', 107–33.

2–Since publication on 14 January 1963, reviews of *The Bell Jar* appeared in *Glasgow Herald* (17 January), *Oxford Mail* (17 January), *Time & Tide* (17–23 January and 31 January), *Evening Times* (Glasgow, 18 January), *Express & Star* (19 January), *The Times* (24 January), *New Statesman* (25 January), *Times Literary Supplement* (25 January), *Scotsman* (26 January), *Sphere* (26 January), *Sunday Telegraph* (27 January), *The Observer* (27 January), *Birmingham Post* (29 January), *The Listener* (31 January), and *The Guardian* (1 February). It is not clear which reviews SP saw.

& grow up. I am only too aware that love and a husband are impossibles to me at this time, I am incapable of being myself & loving myself.

Now the babies are crying, I must take them out to tea.

With love,
Sylvia

INDEX

ABOUT THE AUTHOR AND EDITORS

SYLVIA PLATH (1932–1963) was born in Boston, Massachusetts, and studied at Smith College. In 1955 she went to Cambridge University on a Fulbright Scholarship, where she met and later married Ted Hughes. She published one collection of poems in her lifetime, *The Colossus and Other Poems* (1960), and a novel, *The Bell Jar* (1963). Her volume *Ariel* (1965) secured her reputation, and *The Collected Poems* (1981), which contains poetry written from 1956 until her death, was awarded the Pulitzer Prize for Poetry.

Archivist PETER K. STEINBERG has published more than a dozen articles on Sylvia Plath. He wrote the introduction to *The Spoken Word: Sylvia Plath* (2010) and is the coauthor of a book of essays, *These Ghostly Archives: The Unearthing of Sylvia Plath* (2017). He maintains the oldest continuously updated website for Plath, *A celebration, this is* (www.sylviaplath.info), as well as the *Sylvia Plath Info Blog* (http://sylviaplathinfo.blogspot.com).

KAREN V. KUKIL curates the Virginia Woolf and Sylvia Plath collections at Smith College in Northampton, Massachusetts. She also teaches in the Archives Concentration Program and is the editor of *The Journals of Sylvia Plath, 1950–1962* (2000). Her exhibitions include *"No Other Appetite": Sylvia Plath, Ted Hughes, and the Blood Jet of Poetry* (Grolier Club, New York, 2005) and *One Life: Sylvia Plath* (National Portrait Gallery, Washington, DC, 2017).